A History of
Jewish-Muslim Relations

From the Origins
to the Present Day

A History of Jewish-Muslim Relations

From the Origins to the Present Day

Edited by Abdelwahab Meddeb and Benjamin Stora

Translated by Jane Marie Todd and Michael B. Smith

This book was prepared with the assistance of the French Ministry of Culture
—Centre National du Livre (CNL).

Avec le soutien du

Centre national du livre

Princeton University Press
Princeton and Oxford

Published in France under the title *Histoire des relations entre juifs et musulmans des origines à nos jours,* © 2013 Éditions Albin Michel

English translation © 2013 by Princeton University Press

Requests for permission to reproduce material from this work should be sent to Permissions, Princeton University Press

Published by Princeton University Press, 41 William Street, Princeton, NJ 08540

In the United Kingdom: Princeton University Press, 6 Oxford Street, Woodstock, Oxfordshire OX20 1TW

press.princeton.edu

All Rights Reserved

Brief passages quoted from cited works published in French or other languages have been translated from the French by the translators

ISBN 978-0-691-15127-4

Library of Congress Control Number: 2013937928

British Library Cataloging-in-Publication Data is available

Printed in China

1 3 5 7 9 10 8 6 4 2

Contents

Part Four: Transversalities
Edited by Abdelwahab Meddeb and Sylvie Anne Goldberg

A general bibliography, index of people and place names, full table of contents, and acknowledgments are placed at the end of the book.

Foreword

This book came into being in response to a threefold need: scholarly, political, and pedagogical.

In the first place, we noticed a gap in international historiography. Although many studies have been published in various countries on the fate of the Jewish communities in one Islamic context or another, far fewer attempts have been made to provide a comprehensive view of the history of the Jews in the Islamic world. The most recent and most remarkable of these is an enormous enterprise, published in six volumes by Brill in 2010, the *Encyclopedia of Jews in the Islamic World*. But there was still no major survey that placed the story of the relationship between Jews and Muslims within a global history where Christendom, and then more generally, Europe and the West, was constantly interfering. Above all, no book had focused on that *relationship* or explored the thousand and one modalities of mutual influence that it covered.

Such a scholarly orientation also has a political dimension, which we will not deny. Our conviction is that only by tracing the historical *longue durée* with the methods of the human sciences and by means of an interdisciplinary approach can we shed light on the vicissitudes of the present and counter the generally negative representations of the Other.

The *History of Jewish-Muslim Relations* is therefore the "biography" of a living and complex relationship, which we have chosen to present within a pedagogical perspective. In that aim, this book aspires to be as accessible as possible to the non-academic reader. It consists of four parts, easily identifiable by their dominant color: three chronological sections (medieval period, modern period, contemporary period), followed by a long section called "Transversalities," which provides syntheses of the religious, philosophical, artistic, and sociological themes. The incessant interference between synchrony and diachrony is thereby neutralized, as much as was possible in this extraordinarily rich history.

We wanted this book to be intelligible when read from beginning to end but also when consulted at random. Two modules of short texts are intercalated among the long, comprehensive articles: the "Nota bene," against a colored background, provide portraits or focus on one particular subject or another; the "Counterpoints," indicated by quotation marks, present excerpts from historical texts. Many cross-references and text boxes defining vocabulary, as well as two indexes at the end of the volume, allow readers to move around in the book by following developments around a word, an individual, or a theme.

The decision to create a richly illustrated book belonged to the same threefold necessity. In the first place, it fulfilled the scholarly need: reproductions in the margins of the articles have the value of historical evidence. To meet the political need, a collection of documents and works presents the full range of relations between Jews and Muslims, from the most extreme antagonism to the remarkable parallels, to the most advanced artistic cooperation. As for the pedagogical need, how better to train the eye to read the present than by running through the images—negative or positive—that enriched the past?

Also of note, this publication has had an international dimension from the start. Conceived and edited in France, the book is appearing simultaneously in English, courtesy of the prestigious Princeton University Press. Beyond the importance of this translation, which will be able to reach other audiences (and, in particular, readers in dozens of the countries dealing with the problems under discussion), this decision highlights a peculiarity of the book. It is well known that the Anglo-American mode of writing history differs appreciably from that of continental Europe, and each mode has influenced, to a greater or lesser extent, the historiography of the countries in question here. In the case at hand, the choices of the editors and of the scholarly board allowed a subtle mix of styles and methodologies, thus enhancing the collective nature of this publishing venture.

This book, then, aspires to be a beginning as much as a definitive work, a foundation for future research and, let us hope, a catalyst for future dialogue.

Jean Mouttapa and Anne-Sophie Jouanneau
Éditions Albin Michel, Paris

Editorial Committee

Abdelwahab Meddeb (editor)

He has taught comparative literature at the Université Paris Ouest-Nanterre–La Défense and has been a visiting professor at Yale University, the University of Geneva, and the Free University of Berlin. He is the author, notably, of *Talismano* (Christian Bourgois, 1979); *Tombeau d'Ibn Arabi* (Fata Morgana, 1987); *La maladie de l'Islam* (Seuil, 2002); *L'exil occidental* (Albin Michel, 2005); and *Pari de civilisation* (Seuil, 2009). As director of the review *Dédale*, he devoted a double issue to Jerusalem, *Multiple Jérusalem* 3–4 (1996). He produces the radio program *Cultures d'Islam* on France-Culture.

Benjamin Stora (editor)

Professor at the Université Paris-8 and at the Institut National des Langues et Civilisations Orientales (INALCO), he has been a visiting professor at New York University and at the Free University of Berlin. A specialist in the history of the Maghreb, he has published, notably, *La gangrène et l'oubli: Mémoire de la guerre d'Algérie* (1991) and *Imaginaires de guerre: Algérie-Vietnam* (1998), both published by La Découverte; *Algérie-Maroc: Histoires parallèles* (Maisonneuve et Larose, 2003); and *Les trois exils des Juifs d'Algérie* (2006) and *Voyages en post-colonies: Viêt-nam Algérie Maroc* (2012), both published by Stock.

Mohammad Ali Amir-Moezzi

Director of Studies at the École Pratique des Hautes Études (EPHE-Sorbonne) and a specialist in the history of Qur'anic exegesis and classical Islamic theology, he is the author of *The Divine Guide in Early Shi'ism: The Sources of Esotericism in Islam* (State University of New York Press, 1994); *La religion discrète: Croyances et pratiques spirituelles dans l'Islam Shi'ite* (Vrin, 2006); and *Le Coran silencieux et le Coran parlant: Sources scriptuaires de l'islam entre histoire et ferveur* (CNRS Éditions, 2011), among others. He also edited *Dictionnaire du Coran* (Robert Laffont, 2006).

Jean Baumgarten

Research Director at the National Center for Scientific Research (CNRS), he has taught at École des Hautes Études en Sciences Sociales (EHESS) in Paris. His work focuses on early Yiddish literature and the cultural history of the Ashkenazi world. He has published, most notably, *Naissance du hassidisme* (Albin Michel, 2006) and

Le peuple des livres: Les lectures populaires dans la société ashkénaze, XVIe–XVIIIe siècle (Albin Michel, 2010).

Denis Charbit

A lecturer in political science at the Open University of Israel, he is the author of *Sionismes: Textes fondamentaux* (Albin Michel, 1998); *Qu'est-ce que le Sionisme?* (Albin Michel, 2007); and *Les intellectuels Français face à Israël* (Éditions de l'Éclat, 2009).

Mark R. Cohen

Mark R. Cohen is Khedouri A. Zilkha Professor of Jewish Civilization in the Near East at Princeton University. His publications include *Under Crescent and Cross: The Jews in the Middle Ages* (Princeton University Press, 1994; revised edition 2008) and *The Voice of the Poor in the Middle Ages: An Anthology of Documents from the Cairo Geniza* (Princeton University Press, 2005).

Jocelyne Dakhlia

Director of Studies at the École des Hautes Études en Sciences Sociales (EHESS) in Paris and a specialist in the historical anthropology of the Maghreb and Islam in the Mediterranean, she is the author of *Divan des rois* (Aubier, 1998); *Trames de langues: Usages et métissages linquistiques au Maghreb* (Maisonneuve et Larose, 2004); *Islamicités* (PUF, 2005); *L'Empire des passions* (Aubier, 2005); *Lingua Franca* (Actes Sud, 2008); and *Les Musulmans dans l'histoire de l'Europe*, vol. I: *Une intégration invisible* (Albin Michel, 2011).

Gad Freudenthal

Director of Research Emeritus at CNRS and professor at the University of Geneva, he is the author of *Aristotle's Theory of Material Substance* (Oxford University Press, 1999) and *Science in the Medieval Hebrew and Arabic Traditions* (Ashgate Publishing, 2005). He also has edited several books, including *Studies on Gersonides: A Fourteenth-Century Jewish Philosopher-Scientist* (Brill, 1992); *Studies on Steinschneider* (with Reimund Leicht) (Brill, 2011); and *Science in Medieval Jewish Cultures* (Cambridge University Press, 2012). He is the editor of the journal *Aleph: Historical Studies in Science and Judaism,* founded in 2001.

Sylvie Anne Goldberg

Director of Studies at the École des Hautes Études en Sciences Sociales (EHESS) in Paris (Centre for Jewish Studies at the Centre for Historical Research), researcher at the Centre Marc-Bloch (Berlin), and a visiting professor at the Hebrew University of Jerusalem (Israel) and the University of Pennsylvania, she is the author of numerous books on the history of Judaism, including *La Clepsydre I: Essai sur la pluralité des temps dans le Judaïsme* (Albin Michel, 2000) and *La Clepsydre II: Temps de Jérusalem, temps de Babylone* (Albin Michel, 2004). She also edited the French edition of the *Dictionnaire encyclopédique du Judaïsme* (Robert Laffont—Éditions du Cerf, 1996).

Mohammed Kenbib

A historian and professor at University Mohammed-V in Rabat (Morocco), he is the author of numerous books and articles, including his dissertation, published as *Juifs et Musulmans au Maroc, 1859–1948* (1994); *Les protégés* (1996); and *Temps present et fonctions de l'historien* (2009), all published by University Mohammed-V in Rabat. He also contributed to the *Encyclopedia of Jews in the Islamic World* (Brill, 2010). He has been a visiting professor at the University Paris-I (Panthéon-Sorbonne), the University of Oxford, and a number of American universities.

Elias Sanbar

Elias Sanbar, a historian and writer, has taught at the University of Paris 7 (Jussieu) and at Princeton University. From 1981 to 2006 he was the editor in chief of the *Revue d'études palestiniennes*, which he founded at Éditions de Minuit, and is also the translator of the poetry of Mahmoud Darwish. He has been Ambassador and Permanent Observer of Palestine to UNESCO since January 2006. His many works include *Le bien des absents* (Actes Sud, 2001); *Figures du Palestinien: Identité des origines, identité de devenir* (Gallimard, 2004); and *Dictionnaire amoureux de la Palestine* (Plon, 2010).

Gilles Veinstein (1945—2013)

Former chair of Turkish and Ottoman history at the Collège de France and director of studies at the École des Hautes Études en Sciences Sociales (EHESS) in Paris, he was editor of *Le Paradis des infidèles de Mehmed Efendi* (Maspero-La Découverte, 1981); co-editor of *Histoire des hommes de Dieu dans l'Islam et le Christianisme* (Flammarion, 2003); author of *Le sérail ébranlé: Essai sur les morts, dépositions et avènements des sultans Ottomans, XIVe–XIXe siècles* (Fayard, 2003) ; and co-author, with John Toland and Henry Laurens, of *Europe in the Islamic World: A History* (Princeton University Press, 2013).

Introduction
Abdelwahab Meddeb, Benjamin Stora

Parallel Memories

" I grew up in a traditional religious household in the section of Tunis near al-Zaytuna Mosque, a hive of Qur'anic activity. My grandfather and my father, ulema and *mudarri*, promulgated their doctrinal authority from their pulpit at the Great Mosque, built in the mid-ninth century. Its *mihrab* was redone in the Hispano-Moorish style by an Andalusian architect expelled from Spain in 1609, along with the rest of the Moriscos. Like so many others, he found refuge and a new home in Tunis. My father's colleagues met at our home for seminars to study the hadith and the *tafsir*. From my father I learned the Qur'an, starting at age four or five. During the month of Ramadan, I went every evening to al-Zaytuna Mosque for the supererogatory prayers, the *tarawih*. There, for nearly an hour every night, part of the Qur'an was recited: the goal was to read the entire Book during the holy month.

Abdelwahab Meddeb has taught comparative literature at the Université Paris Ouest-Nanterre–La Défense and has been a visiting professor at Yale University, the University of Geneva, and the Free University of Berlin. He is the author, notably, of *Talismano* (Christian Bourgois, 1979); *Tombeau d'Ibn Arabi* (Fata Morgana, 1987); *La maladie de l'Islam* (Seuil, 2002); *L'exil occidental* (Albin Michel, 2005); and *Pari de civilisation* (Seuil, 2009). As director of the review *Dédale*, he devoted a double issue to Jerusalem, *Multiple Jérusalem* 3–4 (1996). He produces the radio program *Cultures d'Islam* on France-Culture.

I mention all these details to convey the idea that my ear, my body, my senses, and my mind were permeated with the scansions of the Qur'an, the modulation of the prayers and scriptures. In summer we lived at the seaside resort of La Marsa. I would go past the synagogue located behind the town hall, near the market in Marsa-Résidence, where many Jews lived. The murmur of Jewish prayers sent shivers through me. That recitation, barely chanted, heads swaying to its rhythm, reminded me of the Qur'anic readings I heard at home or at al-Zaytuna Mosque. Such proximity, such similarity, confused me: I wondered where identity and difference lay. Was this the same prayer in a different language? These Jews, whom I saw on a daily basis, bore within themselves what made them similar to me and also what made them different. It was that difference in resemblance that confused me.

In the early 1960s, having reached adolescence, I rediscovered the same proximity, the same resemblance, when I saw Jews walking along the avenues downtown. They were so close, and at the same time they embodied the ideal of modernity and of Europe. By virtue of their urban presence, I perceived them as Tunisians who had completed their modernization/Westernization. They became an object of fascination for me and a figure of identification, possessing what Jacques Derrida would call an "unfaithful faithfulness": unfaithful to that part of their tradition that made them unsuited for evolution and freedom, they were faithful to what in the same tradition resisted as a trace. Through them, I saw fulfilled the possibility of being in the world and of still perpetuating what resists and what remains of the origin. In short, I told myself that, whether one is a Jew or a Muslim, it is possible to be Tunisian and modern. Evolution was not mere betrayal. That is what the Jews' presence evoked for me in Tunis, where, moreover, they exemplified joie de vivre, hedonism, a positive diversity. Bringing with them the Mediterranean habitus, they drew Tunis northward and made it the sister city of Rome or Athens. They enacted the pleasures of days and nights spent on terraces, in cafés, in bars, in restaurants. After the Jews left, Tunis began to drift to the East and became the little sister of post-Nasserian Cairo.

What I also found formative, performative, and stimulating was the participation of brilliant Jewish intellectuals in the discussions that followed showings at the film library. It was through them that I discovered that cinema is one of the fine arts, a synthesis of the entire corpus of literary, pictorial, and musical works, lying somewhere between theater, opera, the novel, painting, philosophy, semiotics, history, and anthropology. Let me add to that the role played for my generation by the Jewish teachers we had at secondary school, then at university. They spoke to us as Tunisians who were agents of modernity. I am thinking especially of Marcel Maarek, a mathematics professor; of Jean-Pierre Darmon and Juliette Bessis, professors of history; and of so many others, including Boulakia, Naccache, Perez, Bellaïche, Slama, Valensi, and Sebag. We perceived them as teachers but also as peers, allies, elders, friends, who initiated us into critical thinking, into freedom, and helped us to mold ourselves through self-awareness."

Abdelwahab Meddeb

"

I was born in Constantine in the large Jewish quarter called the Charrah. In the twelve years I lived in that city, I have no memory of ever entering a European apartment. People always say it is difficult to gain entry to the homes of Muslims, that they form a closed society, but I remember things differently. The music and the prayers of the religious holidays, Mawlid or Ramadan, have stayed with me. The Jewish quarter overlapped with the Arab quarter, so that we knew the rhythm of their lives, and they the rhythm of ours. You heard prayers when you passed the mosques, and these prayers had the same resonance as those at synagogue. And yet, the Jews of Constantine felt French and had distanced themselves from the "natives," even if they tended to "go native" (*vivre à l'indigène*). "Going native" was in fact a time-honored expression. For the religious holidays, at Passover, my maternal grandparents adopted "native dress"; we ate on the floor, seated on ottomans, and they recited the Haggadah as their ancestors had done.

I was never surprised to see women in "native dress." My maternal grandmother herself dressed that way. She spoke only Arabic, and that was the language I used to communicate with her. And the Muslim woman who came to the house on Saturday to do the ironing and, as Shabbat required, to turn on the lights and light the stove, removed her veil as soon as she arrived. I spoke to her a great deal, in both French and Arabic. I also had fun with Smaïl and Sebti, the two Muslim employees in my father's semolina business. So we were close.

Benjamin Stora is a professor at the Université Paris-8 and at the Institut National des Langues et Civilisations Orientales (INALCO). He has been a visiting professor at New York University and at the Free University of Berlin. A specialist in the history of the Maghreb, he has published, notably, *La gangrène et l'oubli: Mémoire de la guerre d'Algérie* (1991) and *Imaginaires de guerre: Algérie-Vietnam* (1998), both published by La Découverte; *Algérie-Maroc: Histoires parallèles* (Maisonneuve et Larose, 2003); and *Les trois exils des Juifs d'Algérie* (2006) and *Voyages en post-colonies: Viêt-nam Algérie Maroc* (2012), both published by Stock.

Things went no further, however, even in Constantine, despite what some have said. To be sure, there was undoubtedly more permeability there than elsewhere, at least in the public space, between the Jewish and Muslim communities—some twenty thousand and some sixty thousand people, respectively, out of a population of a hundred thousand, where Europeans were in the minority. But in Constantine, as elsewhere, segregation between communities prevailed and, as is well known, later caused problems in that country. The Jews lived among themselves, with their own customs and beliefs; the Muslims and the Europeans did the same. There was not really any exchange in the private sphere. And Diderot public school, not far from Grand Street, where I lived in the heart of the Charrah, was not very integrated. In my class, I remember about five Muslim students to about twenty Jews and five or six Europeans. That attests to the legal, political, social, and economic inequalities in colonial Algeria in the 1950s.

In the end, what did we have in common, Jews and Muslims? Languages (Arabic and French), a temporality marked by a liturgical rhythm, musical affinities, culinary traditions, and also the market and the streets. The women, veiled all in black, whom I encountered there personified in my eyes a pious Islam attached to tradition. Around me I saw a Judeo-Muslim life. I even participated in it, speaking Arabic with my mother ("give me water," "go buy some bread," "go tell your father"), the language of everyday life. But I felt French. That was the important thing. To be and appear *like* the French. The desire to imitate and to assimilate was very strong, to the great dismay of the city's rabbis, who warned of the risks of the community's dissolution. Ultimately, it was through my different relationship to Arabness and to Islam that the feeling of belonging to France took root."

Benjamin Stora

Memories at work

We have chosen to evoke these parallel memories because they form the preamble for the historian's task: two lines of reconstituted memories illuminated by the present, as memories are. They might run along parallel paths, right next to each other, but would they ever meet? The practice of history, of deconstructing memorial representations, of rooting out nostalgia, can account for a complex, fluctuating reality based on these memories (and never without them). That practice can resituate differences and conflicts but also points of intersection and mutual influences. The lines are never clear or sharp, the parallels never strict. They sometimes veer off course, cross, and even blur.

This book, in which we conceal neither the dark days nor the joyous hours, has the humble ambition of making contemporary research available to readers in order to propose a synthesis of the memories on both sides. It will serve as a preamble. The intention is that it will be continued, that it will prompt exchanges and dialogue. Our wish is to give the researcher's laboratory the opportunity to contribute toward the citizen's common sense. Then each side will be in a position to make a final assessment of the contentious issues, reaching a compromise that will allow them to work toward a reconciliation (without necessarily obscuring what is irreconcilable). Our ambition is also to make available to the authorities in the countries concerned the pedagogical material that will allow them to bring the education systems closer together, to establish the learning fundamentals of mutual acknowledgment, long anticipated and still unrealized.

This material, secreted by human lives poised between peace and violence, makes possible the ethics of *substitution*. In reading this encyclopedic survey, every Jew will be able to put himself in the place of the Muslim, and every Muslim in the place of the Jew. Both sides will be able to suspend exclusivism, to reverse the conventional hierarchies, and to experience the dialectic of identity and difference as if from the inside.

In this book, we have not sought to present a Judeo-Muslim history that would be convergent from the start. But we have gathered together some of the most eminent specialists in the world to restore a *relationship* between Jews and Muslims as it took root over the course of their history. We were determined to escape the distortions that isolate both groups. We were therefore intent on crossing borders to break free of the constraints of communitarianism and nationalism, and to situate that relationship on the horizon of universal history, where it had its beginning. We have taken care to ensure that the focus remains on the state of knowledge, while avoiding the pitfalls and prejudices that sometimes get in the way of a scholarly appraisal of both Islam and Judaism.

We therefore cover the entire geographical space where that relationship found expression, following the historical phases it passed through. Do we need to point out that this relationship was at its most intense at the very moment when Islam came into being? We find in Medina, in the third decade of the seventh century, the matrix in which that relationship took shape, through attraction and repulsion, alliances and separations, similarities and dissimilarities, identity and difference, friendship and enmity, convergence and divergence, hospitality and hostility, receptiveness and rejection, recognition and refusal, confirmation and repudiation. Living in close proximity, each of the two communities constituted for the other the challenge of alterity, which could escalate into violence.

Do we need to reaffirm from the outset that Islam in its early days attempted to bring about a convergence with Judaism, before later distinguishing itself from that religion? Did not the Muslims first turn toward Jerusalem to pray? It was through the connection to Ishmael that the figure of Abraham was revived, reoriented toward Mecca, to give a scriptural foundation to the Arabian backdrop. And so reconstructed myth encountered history. That new Islamic assertiveness would turn violent in the Medinese context, where the battle against the Jews was fueled by two motives. The first was political: it belonged to the strategy of founding a new city,

> **" This history of the relationship between Jews and Muslims has until now been underestimated, as a result of the various Israeli-Palestinian conflicts. "**

which required ending the hegemony of the tribes. The second motive purported to be theological: it took the form of a Qur'anic restaging of the biblical scene that depicted the disobedient "children of Israel" incurring God's wrath.

This same structure would adapt to the vagaries of history, through the tension between religion and politics and the contribution to civilization. Over the course of centuries, this structure came to have a place in a region that ranged from Arabia to Andalusia and included Syria, Egypt, and the Maghreb. We follow its permutations from Baghdad to Delhi, taking a detour through Isfahan and Istanbul. We rediscover it in more recent times, active in diasporas across Europe and America.

This history of the *relationship* between Jews and Muslims has until now been underestimated, as a result of the various Israeli-Palestinian conflicts. It has occupied only a discreet place in the field of studies devoted to these two large communities, because it was considered almost nonexistent after the recent division between them. It is time to atone for that neglect by undertaking a polyphonous inscription of that relationship.

A shared life

This book is in the first place a *reunion*, a *restoration* of the ancient historical bonds established between Jews and Muslims for more than fourteen centuries, from the first appearance of the Qur'an to our own time—fourteen centuries of passions and oppressions, of sometimes tragic, sometimes auspicious relations. We give a detailed and systematic description, adhering to the current state of research, of the social and cultural historical processes at work in the two communities. Different aspects of the lives of these communities are evoked: the *dhimma*, the legal status granted to the Jews in Islamic countries; shared ways of life and different cultures in the Islamic world; community and religious structures; relations with other worlds, the Christian world in particular; and the economic activities of the different social groups. The various realms of daily life are also discussed within the particular register of reciprocal representations.

Readers will therefore span the history of the many countries where, for a long time, Muslims and Jews lived side by side, face-to-face, together or separate: three continents, east to west, north to south, from Morocco to Iran and India, from al-Andalus to Yemen, from Algeria to Egypt and Mesopotamia, from Asia Minor to the Balkans. They will discover the metamorphoses that the Muslims and Jews underwent, voluntarily or by force, from the building of the Muslim empires to the arrival of the European colonial powers; the problems in assimilating to the dominant culture; the upheavals in the modes of organization of the communities; their demographic growth; evolutions in professional activities; their cultural and political rise or decline. This book appeals to real history and does not remain obsessed with the myths that have influenced behaviors. As a result, representations of the other shift, and the dynamics of history is restored.

At a time when this relationship is faring poorly—very poorly—it is out of the question to dissimulate the religious conflicts and also those that arose within political and social history. We situate the following contributions at the center of that tragic scene. We have endeavored to make possible a disinterested, balanced, calm history, something that seemed impossible at first glance. But that history is not constituted solely of conflicts. It has also had its moments of *convivencia*: not only through what can rightly be called the "Andalusian myth" personified by Ibn Naghrela, Jewish poet and scholar, man of the pen and of the sword, the first vizier and the leader of the Muslim armies in the Zirid principality of Granada, but also in twelfth-century Abbasid Baghdad, where Benjamin of Tudela bore witness to the glory of his coreligionists, and in Ayyubid Cairo, where Maimonides brilliantly saw to the material and spiritual prosperity of his community. Maimonides's son even went so far as to adapt the Sufi system of Islamic mysticism to the faith of his fathers.

We could cite other examples of *convivencia*. Let us confine ourselves to Moshe ibn Ezra's ringing paean in the eleventh century to the Arabic language, which, according to him, contains an "innate" poetic energy (an energy that, in every other language, has to be acquired), and which contains, as well, a philosophical and scientific memory, the legacy of the nations that converged in Arabic through the phenomenon of translation. In short, the Jewish thinker tells us that Arabic is the vehicle of civilization. Let us add what the Muslims, in the voice of Ibn ʿArabi (twelfth to thirteenth centuries), say about the Jew. Taking the philological approach to the extreme, the great master of Sufism grants a spiritual dimension to etymology. He traces the word *yahūdi* (Jew) back to the verbal root *h.w.d.*, whose primary meaning is "to come to repentance, to return to one's duty," and whose secondary sense is "to speak softly." The Andalusian mystic thus confirms the Jew in his dual aspiration: to be both ethical and humble. Ibn 'Arabi even goes so far as to violate the fundamental rule of philology so as to reinforce his "spiritual" etymology, connecting the word "Jew" to a second verbal root: *h.d.y.* He thereby reveals the proximity of that word to the Qur'anic term *hudan*, "direction par excellence," which, within the horizon of Islamic scriptures, refers to nothing other than the Qur'an itself. Ibn 'Arabi seems to be suggesting that the Jew was already on the right path that the Muslim was being told to walk. It is as if he anticipated, by his own methods, the idea Hegel would later formulate in a completely different context: that Islam is simply the universalization of Judaism.

We shall not forget that some Jews shared the dark night of colonialism with their conquered Muslim compatriots. Nor shall we forget the part the Jews played in the modernization of their countries, whether by participating in the establishment of the press, theater, and even caricature as a form of political protest (here we are thinking of the Egyptian Jew Abu Naddara) or in the emergence of an awareness of the national patrimony. Consider, for example, that the restoration of the Islamic monuments of Cairo was conceived and overseen by Max Herz, a Hungarian Jewish architect and a naturalized Egyptian. Herz earned the title of pasha, which, let us note, honored merit apart from any privilege of wealth or bloodline.

In the age of reform, beginning in the mid-nineteenth century, Muslim elites—from Istanbul to Jerusalem and from Tunis to Cairo—sought to adopt the notion of enlightened citizenship, based on the principles of positive law. That weakened the edifice of the shari'a, religious law, by reorienting personal status toward equality, without distinction of gender, ethnicity, or religion. Within that context, the Jew Israël Wolfinson, alias Abu Dhu'ayb, who held the chair in Semitic languages at the Academy of Sciences in Cairo, brought out a monograph on Maimonides written in Arabic. In his *Musa Ibn Maymun, Hayatuhu wa Musannafatuhu* (*Life and Works of Maimonides*; Cairo, 1936), Abu Dhu'ayb spoke as a Jew to his Egyptian fellow citizens, Christian and Muslim. He demonstrated that the medieval Jewish author was of concern to them, in the first place because he wrote in Arabic and because he dealt with theological questions that could clarify some of their own dogmas, while at the same time informing them about their Jewish compatriots' faith. In short, Wolfinson's aim was to provide Jewish sustenance for the nascent consciousness about national heritage, which is plural and bears within it the diverse legacy of internal otherness.

In addition, we shall note the Muslims who defended Jews when they were being crushed by the Nazi machine. Muslim Arabs used their political sovereignty (however relative during the protectorate) to shield their Jewish subjects. Such was the case for Mohammed V in Morocco and also for Moncef Bey in Tunisia, though he maintained ambiguous relations with the German authorities. Other Muslims, ordinary citizens, unconditionally rescued Jews. We are thinking especially of the Tunisian Khaled Abdelwahab, who in early 1943 alerted a Jewish family under threat, helped them to flee Mahdia, and provided them with safe haven for four months on his isolated farm. Let us also mention the case of Albanian families who took in and supported without compensation Jewish families targeted by the Nazi laws in early 1944. They were honored by Yad Vashem with the title "Righteous among the Nations."

Separation

This history of relations between Jews and Muslims is being written at a time when these relations have reached a dead end. Whereas most Jews lived in Muslim empires in the Middle Ages, in the Ottoman Empire during the modern period, and, finally, in the Muslim countries that emerged from the European colonies after World War II, they left these regions en masse, in wave upon wave, in the 1950s and 1960s. Is the famous Crémieux Decree of September 1870 ultimately behind the Jews' mass departure for the West? We know that this decree, which granted French nationality to the Jews of Algeria but not to the Muslims, deeply divided Algerian society, pitting one group against the other. Its impact on the Muslim world as a whole is perceptible even now.

Separation may have come as a result of France's foreign intervention. But a little-known episode in the war of colonial conquest that the French army waged against Emir Abd al-Qadir in the 1830s gives a different, less simple view. Algerian Jews, wishing to shed their condition as *dhimmī* when the French arrived in Mascara, were slaughtered by Arab cavalrymen. But the Jews later returned to this city, which had become Emir Abd al-Qadir's capital. This attitude marks all the ambiguity of the relationship that had been established over long centuries between the Jewish and Muslim communities. The Jews truly had the desire for emancipation, for equality, but they also wished to remain attached to the traditional practices—religious, cultural, linguistic—of a life in common. This wavering on the part of the Jews of Mascara was symptomatic of their divided feelings toward the East and the West. We know that the passion for equality prevailed over the force of tradition and that, en masse, the Jews of Algeria would choose France after 1870, leaving behind their condition as "natives." Different questions would later affect both communities "from the inside," questions turned inward and no longer concerned solely with their interrelationship. In the early twentieth century, nationalism was everywhere the order of the day. For the Jews, the Zionist movement, which began in Central Europe, raised questions about the need for a Jewish state, the permanence of Jewish identity, assimilation, the relationship the Diaspora Jews would maintain with Palestine—and then with the State of Israel—and the role of religion in defining Jewish nationalism. For the Muslims, the anticolonial nationalism that developed after the foreign invasions prompted inquiries as well. Arab nationalism, which combined references to Islam, republicanism, and socialism, took root among the urban elites in the societies of the Maghreb and the Mashriq. This reclaiming of identities would lead to divisions. Not all the definitions of nationalism coming from the West were positive: the ideas of European totalitarianism (from the struggle against democracy to the single-party cult) would also win followers. Against the backdrop of an ancient anti-Judaism based on religion, the racial ideologies conveyed by Nazism would find an audience. Anti-Semitic theories of a "Jewish conspiracy" would persist and even thrive in ultra-nationalism and political Islamism.

At the same time, Muslim societies entered political modernity by wresting themselves from colonial rule. During the establishment of the new nation-states, priority was given to the economy, at the expense of minorities and the fate reserved for them. As this colonial history was coming to an end, most of the Jews from the Muslim countries gradually became integrated into Western culture, even *before* their departure. The old ghetto communities, the *mellahs*, the *hara*, were already being drawn to the West.

In most of the Eastern countries, various historical events would accelerate the separation between the Muslims and the Jews. In Greece during World War II, the extermination of the majority of Jews resulted in the disappearance of Jewish life. In Egypt, the Suez crisis of 1956 emptied the country of its Jews. In Morocco and Tunisia, the Six-Day War of 1967 was the decisive impetus for mass departure. In Algeria, the end of the colonial regime in 1962 led to the extinction of Jewish life. In general, three major events determined the separation of the two communities: World War II and the Shoah; the creation of the State of Israel in 1948 and the exodus of the Palestinians; and the consequences associated with conflicts with Israel, such as the Suez expedition and the Six-Day War. In other countries, such as Iran and Turkey, the Jewish communities have continued to exist, despite the departure of many of their members.

Returning histories: Identities

The trauma of the exodus has not gone away, however. The Eastern Jews, legally assimilated in the West, united around a set of secularized practices and religious traditions, have a strong sense of being a minority and a profound attachment to democratic principles. But they have never really forgotten the East. Nevertheless, a feeling of unease about, or even rejection of, Islam has spread since the Palestinian Intifadas of the 1990s and 2000s, and since the rapid expansion of Islam, which accompanied Khomeini's return to Iran in early 1979.

Muslim societies for their part, notwithstanding the persistence of anti-Semitic discourses, have seen a renewal of interest, quiet but real, in protecting the heritage of the Jewish communities. In that spirit, a voluminous book that inventories the synagogues of Tunisia has met with a favorable reception. One of the reasons for that new awareness is that the younger generations are anxious to identify the buried traces of their recent or distant history. In the last few years, academic research in the Arab and Muslim world (for example, the colloquium held in Essaouira, Morocco, in 2011) has occasioned a proliferation of studies, echoes of which can be found in this book. We wish in particular to pay tribute here to André Azoulay, adviser to the king of Morocco, who has encouraged the trend toward acknowledging the Jewish share in the configuration of national identities, not only in his own country but also elsewhere in the Maghreb and the Arab East.

This book proposes to span fourteen centuries of shared history and to call into question some of the cultural assumptions we take for granted, particularly concerning the irreducible opposition between the two worlds, Jewish and Muslim. In it readers will discover the cultural matrices within which Judeo-Muslim coexistence took shape, and how it abruptly fell apart. The introduction of the weight of history, the analysis of ancient experiments, the contributions that can be discerned in them, and the values inseparable from them, open on vistas that are still of great relevance today. These have to do with the place of religion in the definition of political ideologies, the status of minorities vis-à-vis all-powerful nation-states, and the persistent traces of vanished cultural universes.

> *This book proposes to span fourteen centuries of shared history and to call into question some of the cultural assumptions we take for granted, particularly concerning the irreducible opposition between the two worlds, Jewish and Muslim.*

The last part of the book, dealing with the theme of "transversalities," allows us to understand the place of the Other by surveying the points of convergence. At precise historical moments, the Other ceased, precisely, to be identified as *other* but was rather seen as participating in a common purpose. This is illustrated, for example, in the contacts between Jewish and Muslim scholars in the Middle Ages.

More broadly, this last section shows that the Jewish community under Islamic rule was one minority *among others*. It situates the relationship between Jews and Muslims not within a (potentially antagonistic) duality but rather within a diversity of communities. There are several ways of being Jewish, several ways of being Muslim, several ways of being a minority. Contemporary literature, in particular, has aptly illustrated this dynamic, especially in connection with "Arabness" (*arabité*), another component of identity that is examined and redefined here.

In this collection, not only religious affiliation but also cultural, political, and anthropological identities are considered. In the case of Islam, a pair of adjectives indicates that distinction: "Muslim" has to do with the religious aspect, "Islamic" with the political, cultural, or contextual. That distinction is respected as often as possible in this book. Unfortunately, that useful duality has no Jewish equivalent. On the religious question in the strict sense, we have sought to achieve a balance, so as not to simplify the complexity of influences. We have endeavored to resituate these two forms of monotheism in terms of the singularity of each religion and also in their proximity to each other. That proximity was manifest from the outset, inasmuch as Judaism and Islam are not only *religions of the Book* but also *religions of law*.

A global, not a local, history

In reality, this book is a global history: it does not confine itself to distant territories. On the contrary, its place is within the heart of a geographical center: the Mediterranean (expanding to the north, east, and south) and, to a lesser extent, the Silk Road, another major axis (with Iran in its trajectory). The relationship between Jews and Muslims has taken different forms everywhere (depending on whether these groups were a minority, subordinated to other powers, sovereign or in expansion, and

> *In reality, this book is a global history: it does not confine itself to distant territories. On the contrary, its place is within the heart of a geographical center.*

so on). The forms taken over the course of history tell us about the transformation of empires into nation-states, European ascendancy, the rise of nationalism and the totalitarian peril, the confrontation between the American and Soviet blocs, and globalization.

The religious dimension of their relationship appears in this book as a prism, casting its lights on the underlying political machinery. The status of a religious minority is always a valuable index by which to assess a society's operation. This becomes clear in looking at the parallel status of the Jews in the Latin and Islamic medieval worlds, and in the parallel status of minorities under Ottoman, and then colonial, rule. It is also evident in the persistence even today of Ottoman and medieval motifs in the Middle East. Israeli law, for example, inherited some of the Ottoman categories of the *millet*. In addition, Israeli democracy entails the de facto inequality of the Arab Palestinian minority, an inequality that varies depending on whether the person in question is a Christian or a Muslim Arab. It is surprising to note that the equality of citizens affirmed in Israel still retains the traces of an inequality attributable to the status of the *dhimmī*, which is, as it were, now reversed.

This global history indicates that the place of the Other in a society is emblematic of its foundations and also of the global balance of powers that is acting on that society. It tells us, finally, about the identity of each one of us.

Transcriptions

The publisher has chosen to adopt, whenever possible, a simplified transcription for Arabic and Hebrew that does not include diacritical marks (except in the chapter on languages, where they are necessary).

Arabic transcription table

ا	ā	ض	d	د	d	ل	l
ء	ʾ	ط	t	ذ	dh	م	m
ب	b	ظ	z	ر	r	ن	n
ت	t	ع	ʿ	ز	z	ه	h
ث	th	غ	gh	س	s	و	w
ج	j	ف	f	ش	sh	ي	y
ح	h	ق	q	ص	s		
خ	kh	ك	k				

Long vowels are transliterated with a macron (ā, ī, ū).

Hebrew transcription table

א	ʾ	ל	l	ז	z	צ	ts
ב	v	מ	m	ח	h	ק	k
ב	b	נ	n	ט	t	ר	r
ג\ג	g	ס	s	י	y	ש	sh
ד\ד	d	ע	ʿ	כ	kh	ש	s
ה	h	פ	f	כ	k	ת\ת	t
ו	v	פ	p				

The initial *aleph* is not included (for example, *adam* and not *'adam*), nor is the final *hei*, except when it has actual value as a consonant or when it is part of the standard English spelling (*Torah*, for example).

Part I

The Middle Ages

Prologue

The "Golden Age" of Jewish-Muslim Relations: Myth and Reality
Mark R. Cohen

In the nineteenth century there was nearly universal consensus that Jews in the Islamic Middle Ages—taking al-Andalus, or Muslim Spain, as the model—lived in a "Golden Age" of Jewish-Muslim harmony,[1] an interfaith utopia of tolerance and *convivencia*.[2] It was thought that Jews mingled freely and comfortably with Muslims, immersed in Arabic-Islamic culture, including the language, poetry, philosophy, science, medicine, and the study of Scripture—a society, furthermore, in which Jews could and many did ascend to the pinnacles of political power in Muslim government. This idealized picture went beyond Spain to encompass the entire Muslim world, from Baghdad to Cordova, and extended over the long centuries, bracketed by the Islamic conquests at one end and the era of Moses Maimonides (1138–1204) at the other.

> **Mark R. Cohen**
>
> Professor of Near Eastern Studies at Princeton University, he holds the Khedouri A. Zilka Professorship of Jewish Civilization in the Near East. His publications include *Under Crescent and Cross: The Jews in the Middle Ages* (Princeton University Press, 1994; revised edition 2008).

The idea stemmed in the first instance from disappointment felt by central European Jewish historians as Emancipation-era promises of political and cultural equality remained unfulfilled. They exploited the tolerance they ascribed to Islam to chastise their Christian neighbors for failing to rise to the standards set by non-Christian society hundreds of years earlier.[3]

The interfaith utopia was to a certain extent a myth; it ignored, or left unmentioned, the legal inferiority of the Jews and periodic outbursts of violence. Yet, when compared to the gloomier history of Jews in the medieval Ashkenazic world of Northern Europe and late medieval Spain, and the far more frequent and severe persecution in those regions, it contained a very large kernel of truth.

The image of the Golden Age remained dominant among scholars and in the general public throughout the nineteenth century, as Jews in Europe confronted a new, virulent strain of political anti-Semitism, reinforcing a much older feeling of alienation and persecution in Christian lands. It endured well into the twentieth century, as the flames of Jew hatred burned ever brighter in Europe, culminating in the Holocaust.

This scene, depicting a Jew and a Muslim, is often used to illustrate the golden age of interfaith relations in Al-Andalus. *El Libro de los Juegos*, commissioned by Alphonse X of Castile, thirteenth century. Madrid, Escurial Library, fol. 63 recto.

In the twentieth century, Muslims appropriated the Jewish myth of the interfaith utopia as a weapon against Zionism and the State of Israel. They expressed this both in political broadsides and in books and articles about Jews or about non-Muslims in general in the Middle Ages. The leitmotif of these writings is Islamic "tolerance" (Arabic *samāḥa* or *tasāmuḥ*), often contrasted with the persecutions of medieval Christian society. Characteristically, these writings soft-pedal the legal inferiority of the Jews and gloss over, or ignore, episodes of violence that call the harmony into question.[4]

The response on the Jewish side has been to turn the idea of the Golden Age utopia on its head.[5] Muhammad, the revisionists insist, was bent on extirpating the Jews from the very beginning. The Qur'an and other early Islamic sources are packed with anti-Jewish, even anti-Semitic, venom. And, rather than protecting the Jews, Islam persecuted them relentlessly, often as badly as medieval Christendom. This undisguised rejoinder to Arab/Muslim exploitation of the old Jewish depiction of interfaith harmony constitutes a "counter-myth of Islamic persecution." Adapting the famous coinage of historian Salon W. Baron, who labeled historiography about medieval Jews living under Christendom a "lachrymose conception of Jewish history,"[6] we may call this a "neo-lachrymose conception of Jewish-Arab history."[7] It has taken hold in many circles and has flourished in the soil of the ongoing Israeli-Palestinian conflict. The chief proponent of the "neo-lachrymose school," Bat Ye'or, pseudonym for Gisele Littman, has made famous the term "dhimmitude" to describe all the humiliating restrictions imposed by Islam on Jews and Christians in Muslim-Arab lands since the rise of Islam.[8]

The highly politicized debate, exacerbated by the worldwide fear of Islamism and by the Islamophobia following the attack by radical Muslims on the World Trade Center in New York on September 11, 2001, makes the questions that underlie this book all the more controversial, but, at the same time, all the more begging for dispassionate inquiry.

Jewish-Muslim relations: The comparative perspective

The most useful way to understand Jewish-Muslim relations in the Middle Ages is to compare the Muslim world with the Christian world of Northern Europe. The choice of Northern Europe is dictated by the fact that there relations between Jews and Christians, reasonably tolerable in the early Middle Ages, declined precipitously later on to become the worst in Europe, leading the way in persecuting and ultimately expelling the Jews from Christian society. By choosing this case to compare with the Islamic world, one is able to isolate the specific factors determining how Jews were treated by the majority of society. In this way, this comparative study also constructs a paradigm that can be used to explain Jewish-gentile relations in pre-modern times in general.

If Islam seems to have been more tolerant than Christendom, this is true only in a qualified sense. In the Middle Ages, tolerance, in the modern, liberal meaning of full equality, was not considered to be a virtue to be emulated. Monotheistic religions were by nature mutually *intolerant*. Adherents of the religion in power considered it their right and duty to treat the others as inferiors rejected by God, and, in extreme cases, to treat them harshly, even to encourage them (in some cases by force) to abandon their faith in favor of the faith of the rulers. Though the religious minorities (Jews living under Christian rule; Jews and Christians living under Muslim rule) were hardly happy with their second-class status and legal inferiority, let alone the occasional persecutions, for the most part they accepted their inequality and subordination with resignation. As long as they were allowed to live in security and practice their religion without interference—this was "toleration" in the medieval sense of the word—they were generally content. For them, as for their masters, the hierarchical relationship between chosen religion and rejected religion, between superior and inferior, between governing and governed, was part of the natural order of things. The subjugated people may have dreamed of a reversal of the hierarchy, in history or in the messianic era, but for the time being, generally speaking, they bore their fate with a certain amount of equanimity.

The paradigm

The paradigm that results from this comparative approach delineates five inter-related factors that explain why anti-Jewish violence was so much less prevalent in the Islamic world than in Northern Europe. Violence was related, in the first instance, to the primacy of religious exclusivity. Historically, religious exclusivity characterized both Islam and Christianity. But anti-Jewish violence was more pronounced in Christendom because innate religious antagonism, present from the first decades of Christianity, was combined with other erosive forces. The second component of the paradigm is legal status; namely, the evolution of a special law for the Jews and a system of baronial or monarchical possessory rights—though varied in character and uneven in its application in different times and places—that could be manipulated in an arbitrary manner. This law frequently clashed with its competitor, papal policy, and the Jews were frequently caught in the middle. The third element concerns the economic circumstances that excluded the Jews from the most respected walks of life.

Religious exclusivity, a special, arbitrary legal status, and economic marginalization interacted with another adverse factor, the fourth element of the paradigm: social exclusion, which steadily robbed the Jews of their rank in the hierarchical social order. Last, the gradual replacement of the ethnic pluralism of Germanic society of the early Middle Ages by a medieval type of "nationalism," paralleling the spread of Catholic religious exclusivity to the masses and the rise of the crusading spirit in the eleventh century, contributed to the enhancement of the Jew's "otherness" and to his eventual exclusion from most of western Christendom by the end of the fifteenth century. Before that, the Jews survived among Christians—were "tolerated" in a manner of speaking—in part because they performed useful economic services for Christian rulers, such as importing precious spices and other goods from the East and paying taxes from the proceeds of commerce and moneylending; and in part because of a doctrine of Saint Augustine that proclaimed that the Jews played an important role in Christian salvation history as a fossil religion: witnesses, by their abjugated state, to the triumph of Christianity, bearers of the Old Testament, and ultimately by their conversion to Christianity at the time of the Second Coming of Christ.

❭ See article by John Tolan, p. 145.

In the Islamic world, the erosive factors described above were less severe. Religious exclusivity was modulated by the multiplicity of non-Muslim religions, primarily Jewish, Christian, and Zoroastrian. The Qur'an itself, for all its harsh language referring to Christians and Jews, contains the nucleus of a kind of religious pluralism.[9] A Qur'anic verse, "there is no compulsion in religion" (Sura 2:256), was understood to mean that the non-Muslims were not to be forcibly converted. Moreover, as venerated "People of the Book" (*Ahl al-Kitab*), Jews and Christians were allowed to live securely in their autonomous communities and to develop: they were not fossils.

❭ See article by Mark R. Cohen, pp. 58-71.

Legally speaking, Jews shared with other non-Muslims the status of *dhimmīs*, or

▶ See
Counterpoint,
The Pact of
'Umar,
pp. 72-73.
"protected people." In return for security, freedom of religion, and communal autonomy, they were obligated by the Qur'an to pay an annual poll tax. They were also subject, in theory, to regulations prescribed in the so-called Pact of 'Umar and kindred documents, which imposed limitations on their conduct. New houses of worship were not to be built and old ones could not be repaired. They were to act humbly in the presence of Muslims. In their liturgical practice they had to honor the preeminence of Islam. They were further required to differentiate themselves from Muslims by their clothing and by eschewing symbols of honor. Other restrictions excluded them from positions of authority in Muslim government.

The Muslim pragmatism

De facto, however, these discriminatory regulations, most of them originating outside Islam, were largely honored in the breach, often with the tacit approval of Muslim rulers. The rules limiting the free practice of religion were frequently overridden in practice by the more pragmatic policy of the conquest treaties, which protected houses of worship and guaranteed freedom of religion. The discriminatory

> *These discriminatory regulations, most of them originating outside Islam, were largely honored in the breach, often with the tacit approval of Muslim rulers.*

restrictions were likely adopted by Christian converts to Islam serving in Muslim government who wished not to be confused with their former coreligionists.[10] Many of the rules of differentiation, it has recently been shown by the historian Milka Levy-Rubin, imitated discriminatory practices in Sasanian society aimed against the lowest class of Zoroastrian society.[11] Whether they originated in Byzantine or in Sasanian practice, however, many of these foreign practices conflicted with the pragmatic spirit of "live and let live" of early Islam and so could often be overlooked or ignored in the day-to-day realities of Muslim and non-Muslim coexistence.

This coexistence is particularly evident in economic life. Jews were not limited to a small range of pursuits isolated from the rest of the population in deplored professions like moneylending, as in Europe. They worked as craftsmen, pharmacists, and physicians; as craftsmen in textiles, in glassmaking, and in jewelry; as retailers in the marketplace specializing in a whole host of products, including foodstuffs; in long-distance commerce, as government functionaries; and in many other walks of life. In these endeavors, Muslims and Jews (and also Christians) manifested "loyalties of category," to use terminology coined by historian Roy Mottahedeh, that straddled the Muslim and non-Muslim divide and mitigated the discrimination inherent to the ever-present religious hierarchy.[12]

In the Islamic marketplace, there existed a substantial degree of interdenominational cooperation. Jews mixed freely with their Muslim counterparts, even forming partnerships, with a minimum of friction. Jews lent money to Muslims, but the reverse was also true. When, after about the twelfth century, Jewish economic circumstances declined, this was not a confessional phenomenon alone, but one that Jews shared with the Muslim majority, though as a minority group they naturally experienced greater hardship.

Speaking in social-anthropological terms—and this provides an important corrective to the view that Islam is fundamentally oppressive, if not persecutory—the rules of the Pact of 'Umar and other restrictions served as a means to create and preserve a "natural" hierarchy, in the sense that it characterizes most religious societies in premodern times. In the Islamic hierarchy, everyone had a rank, including non-Muslims, who occupied a low rank, to be sure, but a secure rank nonetheless. Jews occupied a permanent niche within the hierarchical social order of

> **"In the Islamic marketplace, there existed a substantial degree of interdenominational cooperation."**

Islam, and, though marginalized, they were not ostracized or expelled. The original and long-lasting ethnic and religious pluralism of Islamic society encouraged a certain tolerance of diversity. The diffusion of hostility among two and in many places three "infidel" religions helped mitigate the Jews' "otherness" and prevent the emergence of the irrational hatred we call anti-Semitism. As humiliating as the restrictions in the Pact of 'Umar were (when successfully enforced), Jews and other non-Muslim People of the Book seem to have grudgingly accepted them because they guaranteed their security, and because they, especially the religious leaders, wished to maintain a separate identity for their own communities.[13] In such an atmosphere, Jews—and not just the philosophers and the physicians among them—fraternized with Muslims on a regular basis with a minimum of hostility. This sociability constituted an essential ingredient in the cultural interchange between Jews and Arabs in the high Middle Ages.

For all these reasons, the Jews of Islam had substantial confidence in the *dhimma* system. If they kept a low profile and paid their annual poll tax, they could expect to be protected and to be free from economic discrimination—not to be forcefully converted to Islam, massacred, or expelled. To be sure, the system occasionally broke down. A ruler, goaded by pious Islamic clerics, might crack down on the *dhimmī*s for ignoring the regulations of the Pact of 'Umar. But serious persecutions were exceptional. The most infamous one occurred in the mid-twelfth century, when the fanatical Muslim Berber Almohads, the "Islamists" of their time, destroyed entire Jewish communities in North Africa and Spain, and forced thousands of Jews and Christians to accept Islam, even as they imposed their own stringent form of Islam upon impious Muslims. Also notorious, because of the rare preservation of detailed Islamic and Christian sources, was the destruction of houses of worship and forced conversions ordered by the "mad" caliph al-Hakim in Egypt and Palestine at the beginning of the eleventh century. Violent, too, was the assassination in 1066 of the

▶ See Nota bene, al-Hakim, pp. 106-107.

"haughty" Jewish vizier Joseph ibn Naghrela, successor of his more illustrious father as head of the Jewish community in the Muslim principality of Granada, Spain, and the subsequent "pogrom" against the Jewish quarter of the city, with great loss of life. The incident was apparently triggered by an Arabic poet who wrote a poem in which he called the Jews "apes and pigs," quoting a Qur'anic motif (e.g., Qur'an 5:60) and excoriating the Jews for violating the code of humility vis-à-vis Islam. Exceptional as it was in targeting the Jews per se, the sorry episode is regularly cited by proponents of the "neo-lachrymose conception of Jewish-Arab history" as a typical example of Islamic anti-Semitism.[14]

▶ See article by Mark R. Cohen, pp. 546-553.

During these rare episodes, Jews felt the impact of violence no less than the Ashkenazic Jews of Europe, but they did not preserve them as part of a collective memory of suffering the way their Ashkenazic brethren did. They recognized these as temporary lapses of the *dhimma* arrangement and trusted that forced conversions, a violation of Qur'anic law, would be reversed after the initial zealotry faded. Doubtless this is one factor among others that explains why Jews in Islamic lands under threat favored "superficial conversion" (like the Islamic *taqiyya* recommended for Muslims faced with persecution for heretical beliefs) over martyrdom, unlike their self-immolating Ashkenazic brethren, who had little hope of being officially allowed to return to Judaism after their baptism. In this respect the Jews of Islamic Spain and other places in the medieval Islamic world where occasional acts of intolerance threatened Jewish life anticipated the response of Jews in Christian Spain—the so-called Marranos—who converted to Catholicism rather than accept a martyr's death during and after the pogroms of 1391.[15]

Judeo-Arabic culture

▶ See article by Marina Rustow, pp. 75-98 and Part IV, p. 653 and following.

The paradigm summarized here helps explain not only Muslim-Jewish coexistence but also why Jews were so open to Arab-Islamic culture. Other contributions to this book will describe this is detail. Here I shall limit myself to a few general comparative observations.

For the Jews in the Middle East and Spain, Arabic was the key to an entirely new way of thinking. There, too, Jews abandoned Aramaic for the new language, but Arabic functioned both as the language of high culture *and* the common tongue of both Jews and Arabs in everyday exchange. It was at the same time linguistically akin to Aramaic and Hebrew, with morphological forms and cognates that facilitated transcribing Arabic into Hebrew letters and reading it—the form of Arabic we call Judeo-Arabic. Assimilating Arabic was even less of a "leap" for the indigenous Aramaic-speaking Jews of the Middle East than it was for Jewish immigrants to Europe making the transition from Aramaic to European vernaculars. Furthermore, Arabic, the language of the Islamic faith, like the faith itself, was less repugnant and less threatening to the Jews than the language and doctrine of the Christian Church.

By the tenth century, therefore, some two and a half centuries after the rise of Islam, Jews had made a total and largely effortless transition from Aramaic to Arabic and now used Arabic, not only in daily speech but for nearly everything they wrote. This prepared them to share lock, stock, and barrel in the high culture of Islamic society. Islam came into contact with the science, medicine, and philosophy of the Greco-Roman world centuries earlier than European Christendom. Translated early on into Arabic, these works gave rise to what the German scholar Adam Mez famously called "Die Renaissance des Islams."[16] Jews of the Fertile Crescent, the heartland of the Islamic Empire and the first center of the new Arabic science, medicine, and philosophy, had both access to and interest in the translated texts read by Muslim intellectuals. This facilitated the cultural *convivencia* of the Judeo-Arabic world, which began in the eastern Islamic domains and spread to the Muslim West. It led to Jewish adoption of philosophy, science, and medicine—philosophy serving as a handmaiden of religious truths, as it did for Islamic philosophers themselves.

▶ See Chapter IV of Part IV.

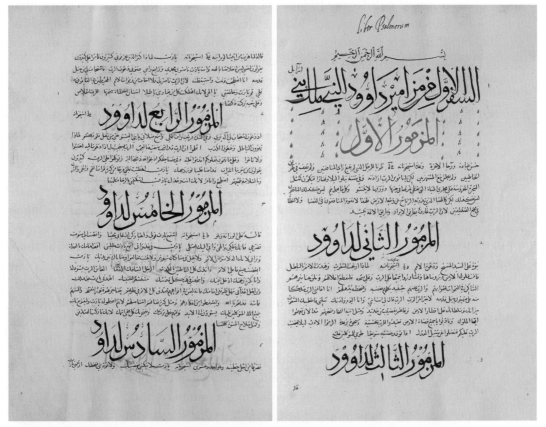

The Bible translated into Arabic by Saadia Gaon in the tenth century. Egyptian manuscript copy, first pages of the book Psalms, 1584–85. Paris, Bibliothèque Nationale de France, ms. or., Arabic 1, fol. 232 and 233 verso.

The Arabic and Islamic "renaissance" laid the groundwork for other Jewish cultural innovations. The Bible was translated into Arabic. Hebrew as a language began to be studied "scientifically," so to speak, using linguistic tools in vogue among Arab grammarians. But nearly everything Jews wrote they wrote in Arabic, and this was not limited to philosophy, for which Hebrew entirely lacked a vocabulary. Poetry, the major exception, was composed in Hebrew, but it, too, bore the stamp of Arabic culture.

Arabic poets prided themselves in writing in the language of their Holy Scripture, the Qur'an, believing Arabic to be the most beautiful of all languages. Jews followed suit by choosing biblical Hebrew for their poetry, asserting the wonderment and uniqueness of the language of their own scripture. The social setting for this new poetry also followed the Arabic model. The poems were recited and sung in gardens, like the gardens of the caliph's palace or of private homes, the physical setting for Arabic poetry. Jews continued to compose religious poetry for the synagogue, but it, too, employed biblical Hebrew and Arabic meter, and borrowed themes from Islamic pietistic thought.[17] Poetry in the Arabic mode, and the way of living that accompanied it, led many Hebrew poets, especially in their later years, to question the frivolities of their youth.[18] Judah Halevi represents the most extreme example of this rejection of the Golden Age; toward the end of his life he abandoned his native Spain and embarked on a pious pilgrimage to the Holy Land.[19]

⟩ See Nota bene, Saadia Gaon, pp. 758-761.

One of the greatest rabbis of the Middle Ages, Saadia Gaon (d. 942), rightly called the "father" of Judeo-Arabic culture, wrote poetry. He served as head of the great yeshiva located in Baghdad, one of the two most important religious centers for Jews throughout the Islamic domains. He composed the first comprehensive Jewish prayer book, writing the directions for the worshipper in Arabic (the prayers, of course, remained in their original Hebrew) and including poems of his own. Saadia also compiled monographs on Jewish law in Arabic, as did other *geonim*, or heads of the yeshiva. Even the supposedly sacrosanct realm of Jewish law was not immune to Islamic influence. In fact, in the works of some scholars, the entire structure of Jewish legal discourse was altered in accordance with Islamic categories, while some of the content of Islamic law influenced Jewish legal thought as well.[20] Saadia was also a pioneer in applying Greco-Arabic rational philosophic categories to Jewish thought in a systematic way, adopting current methods from Islamic theologians.[21] Maimonides (1138–1204), the acme of Judeo-Arabic philosophy, strove to make Judaism compatible with neo-Aristotelian philosophy.[22]

⟩ See article by Phillip Ackerman Lieberman, pp. 683-693.

Other religious developments within Judaism also drew inspiration from Islam. The Karaite movement—the first oppositional movement in Judaism since the ascendancy of the Talmudic rabbinic scholars in late antiquity over the Sadducees—arose in the eastern Islamic world at just about the same time and in the same place that Shi'ism began to flourish, in opposition to the dominant Sunni "orthodoxy."[23] Later on, Sufi pietism exerted a powerful influence on Jewish religious thought and practice as early as the eleventh century in Spain and then, beginning in the early thirteenth century, in Egypt. Abraham, the son of Maimonides (d. 1237), was a "Jewish Sufi," as were his descendants, the leaders of the Jewish community in Egypt, for several more generations.[24]

▷ See article by Elisha Russ-Fishbane, pp. 856-864.

The Arabic language gave Jews entrance to the corridors of Muslim power and made possible the remarkable careers of such luminaries as Samuel ha-Nagid ibn Naghrela in the eleventh century, head of the Jewish community, poet, Talmudist, and vizier of Granada (the father of the Jewish vizier assassinated in 1066), as well as scores of other Jewish denizens of Islamic courts, many of whom occupy pages in Islamic chronicles. Other dignitaries, as well as merchants, less well known because they did not leave books behind, but whose quotidian lives are described in minute detail in the documents of the Cairo Geniza, are no less important as Jewish exemplars of the Jewish-Muslim coexistence that reigned for several centuries during the Islamic high Middle Ages. For such illustrious figures in the Jewish elite, those centuries were indeed a Golden Age.

▷ See Nota bene, Samuel ibn Naghrela, pp. 132-133.

▷ See Nota bene, The Cairo Geniza, pp. 99-101.

---

1. Much of the first part of this essay relies on my book *Under Crescent and Cross: The Jews in the Middle Ages* (Princeton, NJ: Princeton University Press, 1984; new edition with new introduction and afterword, 2008). Much of the second part draws on my article "The 'Convivencia' of Jews and Muslims in the High Middle Ages," in *The Meeting of Civilizations: Muslim, Christian, and Jewish*, ed. Moshe Ma'oz (Brighton, UK: Sussex Academic Press, 2009), 54–65.

2. For a discussion of the debate over *convivencia* and its corollary, the tension between tolerance and intolerance in Spanish history, of which the Jewish thesis was a part, see Alex Novikoff, "Between Tolerance and Intolerance in Medieval Spain: An Historiographic Enigma," *Medieval Encounters* 11 (2005): 7–36.

3. This insight was first expressed, as far as I know, by Bernard Lewis in his essay "The Pro-Islamic Jews," *Judaism* 17 (1968): 402: "The myth was invented by Jews in 19th century Europe as a reproach to Christians—and taken up by Muslims in our time as a reproach to Jews."

4. See the representative sample of books in Arabic and other languages by Arabs and others treating the subject of the Jews of Islam, often apologetically, mentioned in the notes in chapter 1 of my *Under Crescent and Cross*.

5. The clarion call of danger from Muslim exploitation of the myth of Islamic tolerance was sounded in an essay by British historian Cecil Roth in the Zionist Organization of America's *New Palestine* (October 4, 1946), and in the British Zionist *Jewish Forum* in the same month. The essay was virtually forgotten until it was reprinted by the American Israel Public Affairs Committee (AIPAC), in the "Myths and Facts" supplement to its *Near East Report*, shortly after the Six-Day War of June 1967. Coincidentally, at exactly the same time as the Roth essay (September 1967), a more conciliatory article appeared in the magazine the *Jewish Spectator*, by Trude Weiss-Rosmarin, entitled "Toward Jewish-Muslim Dialogue."

6. See his "Ghetto and Emancipation," *Menorah Journal* 14, no. 6 (June 1928): 515–26, at the end; reprinted in the *Menorah Treasury: Harvest of Half a Century*, ed. Leo W. Swartz (Philadelphia: Jewish Publication Society of America, 1964), 59–63.

7. Mark R. Cohen, "The Neo-Lachrymose Conception of Jewish-Arab History," *Tikkun* (May/June, 1991): 55–60; also "Islam and the Jews: Myth, Counter-Myth, History," *Jerusalem Quarterly*, no. 38 (1986): 125–37; and *Under Crescent and Cross*, chapter 1.

8. Of her many books, *Le Dhimmi: Profil de l'opprimé en Orient et en Afrique de Nord depuis la conquête arabe* (Paris: Anthropos, 1980) is representative.

9. For a thoughtful discussion of Islam's pluralistic approach to religion, grounded in the Qur'an, see Abdulaziz Sachedina, *The Islamic Roots of Democratic Pluralism* (New York: Oxford University Press, 2001). See also Heribert Busse, *Islam, Judaism, and Christianity: Theological and Historical Affiliations* (Princeton, NJ: Markus Wiener, 1998), 33–35. Part 4 of my *Under Crescent and Cross* discusses sociological factors underlying this Islamic pluralism.

10. This is the view of Antoine Fattal, *Le statut légal des non-Musulmans en pays d'Islam* (Beirut: Imprimerie Catholique, 1958), 67.

11. On the Byzantine origins of stipulations in Islamic law, see A. Fattal, *Le statut légal des non-Musulmans en pays d'Islam*. On the Sasanian roots, see Milka Levy-Rubin, *Non-Muslims in the Early Islamic Empire: From Surrender to Coexistence* (Cambridge: Cambridge University Press, 2011), chapter 5.

12. See Roy P. Mottahedeh, *Loyalty and Leadership in an Early Islamic Society* (Princeton, NJ: Princeton University Press, 1980), 108–15; Cohen, *Under Crescent and Cross*, 246.

13. See Cohen, *Under Crescent and Cross*, chapter 6, and, regarding frequent non-Muslim recourse to Islamic religious courts, Uriel I. Simonsohn, *A Common Justice: The Legal Allegiance of Christians and Jews under Early Islam* (Philadelphia: University of Pennsylvania Press, 2011).

14. Among the many discussions of this episode is Moshe Perlmann, "Eleventh-Century Andalusian Authors on the Jews of Granada," *Proceedings of the American Academy of Jewish Research* 18 (1948–1949): 843–61. The poem is handily accessible in Bernard Lewis's translation in Olivia Remie Constable, ed., *Medieval Iberia: Readings from Christian, Muslim, and Jewish Sources* (Philadelphia: University of Pennsylvania Press, 1997), 96–99; excerpts from the main Arabic and Jewish sources about the event, translated by Amin T. Tibi and Gerson D. Cohen, respectively, are also found there. The Hebrew source, like the Arabic chronicle and the Arabic poem, share the view that Joseph acted high-handedly while in office.

15. For a discussion of persecutions of Jews under Islam, see *Under Crescent and Cross*, chapter 10.

16. Adam Mez, *Die Renaissance des Islams* (Heidelberg: Winter, 1922). The book has been translated into many languages.

17. This later phenomenon is discussed thoroughly by Raymond P. Scheindlin in *The Song of the Distant Dove: Judah Halevi's Pilgrimage* (Oxford: Oxford University Press, 2008). The corpus of fifty-five Geniza documents relating to Halevi was published, with a long commentary by Moshe Gil and Ezra Fleischer, *Yehudah ha-Levi u-vene ḥugo: 55 te'udot min ha-Genizah* (Jerusalem: World Union of Jewish Studies, 2001).

18. Ross Brann, *The Compunctious Poet: Cultural Ambiguity and Hebrew Poetry in Muslim Spain* (Baltimore: Johns Hopkins University Press, 1991).

19. Raymond Scheindlin, *The Song of the Distant Dove*. The more common view, that Halevi was a "proto-Zionist," is forcefully reiterated in a recent biography by Hillel Halkin, *Yehuda Halevi* (New York: Schocken, 2010).

20. The influence of formal features of Islamic law on Judaism has been the subject of much scholarship, while the most important work on the influence of the *content* of Islamic law on the Jewish legists has been dominated by the fruitful investigations of Gideon Libson, for example, "Islamic Influence on Medieval Jewish Law? Sepher ha-'Arevut (Book of Surety) of Rav Shmuel ben Hofni Gaon and Its Relationship to Islamic Law," *Studia Islamica* 73 (1990): 5–23, and his *Jewish and Islamic Law: A Comparative Study of Custom during the Gaonic Period* (Cambridge, MA: Harvard University Press, 2003).

21. A succinct introduction to Jewish philosophy in the Muslim world is found in Daniel H. Frank and Oliver Leaman, eds., *The Cambridge Companion to Medieval Jewish Philosophy* (Cambridge: Cambridge University Press, 2003).

22. Of the many works about Maimonides and his works, see, recently, Joel L. Kraemer, *Maimonides: The Life and World of One of Civilization's Greatest Minds* (New York: Doubleday, 2008).

23. An excellent overview of the "Karaite problem" in Jewish historiography is Meira Polliack, "Medieval Karaism," in Martin Goodman, ed., *The Oxford Handbook of Jewish Studies* (Oxford: Oxford University Press, 2002), chapter 12. A refined treatment of the relations between Karaites and Rabbanites, particularly as reflected in the documents of the Cairo Geniza, is contained in Marina Rustow, *Heresy and the Politics of Community: The Jews of the Fatimid Caliphate* (Ithaca, NY: Cornell University Press, 2008).

24. The foremost scholar of the Sufi phenomenon in Judaism is Paul Fenton. See his chapter, "Judaism and Sufism," in Daniel H. Frank and Oliver Leaman, eds., *The Cambridge Companion to Medieval Jewish Philosophy* (Cambridge: Cambridge University Press, 2003).

Chapter I
The Emergence of Islam

The Jews of Arabia at the Birth of Islam
Gordon D. Newby

Jews at the time of Muhammad and the rise of Islam had a long history in Arabia and were well integrated into both urban and rural environments as urban craftsmen, traders, farmers, and bedouin. Most Arab clans and tribes had Jewish members representing all facets of Arabian life.

The origins of the Arabian Jewish communities are shrouded in legend, but there were strong connections between Arabian Jewish communities and Jews in Persia and in Palestine. Arabian Jews were rabbinic in that they were organized into congregations headed by rabbis, and they were in touch, at least limitedly, with the Babylonian academies. However, it is clear that the practices and beliefs of the Arabian Jews were different from the Judaism idealized in the Babylonian Talmud, whose final redaction took place only about a century before the birth of Muhammad. During Muhammad's lifetime, Jews were integrated into the early Muslim community, established in their religious practices, but also subject to limits imposed by the ascendance of Islamic political power.

Gordon D. Newby

Gordon D. Newby is professor of Middle Eastern and South Asian studies at Emory University. His research specialties include early Islam, Muslim relations with Jews and Christians, and comparative sacred texts. His publications include *A History of the Jews of Arabia* (University of South Carolina Press, 2009).

Origins and early history: From legend to history

According to Muslim tradition, the present-day Arabs were preceded in the Hijaz by the Amalekites. When the Israelite armies, led by Moses, destroyed the Amalekites by God's command, they spared the Amalekite king's son, contrary to the divine command, and were forbidden to enter Syria (i.e., the Holy Land) and so turned to the then deserted dwellings of the Amalekites in the Hijaz. This legendary account of the origin of the Jewish settlements of Yathrib/Medina, which conflates the biblical accounts of the Amalekites, is similar to other origin legends that rely on biblical and midrashic lore for the earliest ideas about the origins of Arabian Jews. When these foundation legends are expressed in Arabic literary sources, such as the *Kitab al-Aghani*,[1] they often appear to be etiological, as in the linking of the story of Moses and the Amalekites to the two Jewish tribes of Yathrib/Medina, the Banu Qurayza and the Banu al-Nadir, who were called the Two Priestly Tribes (*al-kāhinān*)[2] "because they were descended from al-Kahin, the son of Aaron, the son of 'Amran, the brother of Moses Ibn 'Amran, may the prayers of God be upon Muhammad, his family, and the two of them. They settled in the vicinity of Yathrib after the death of Moses, upon him be peace."

Links to the temple

The second type of foundation legend links Jews in Arabia with the Diaspora after the Roman destruction of the Second Temple in Jerusalem and the Jewish wars with Rome: "Then Rome rose up over all the Children of Israel in Syria, trampled them underfoot, killed them, and married their women. Also, when Rome conquered Syria, the Banu al-Nadir, the Banu Qurayza, and the Banu Bahdal fled to the Children of Israel in the Hijaz. When they departed from their houses, the king of Rome sent after them to bring them back, but it was impossible for him because of the desert between Syria and the Hijaz."[3] This links the earlier settlement of Jews in Arabia to the later migration, bestowing a sense of both antiquity and continuity to the Hijazi Jews. While this account of Jewish origins in Arabia has historical foundation, it, too, is concerned with etiology and seems to have been used by the Jews of the Hijaz to assert their superiority over the Arabs by bestowing both nobility and antiquity on them. In one account, it was reported that "the Banu Qurayzah are a people of honor and wealth, while we are an Arab people without date palms or vineyards; we were only a people of sheep and small cattle."[4]

▶ See Counterpoint, Jewish Tribes in the *Kitab al-Aghani*, pp. 52-53.

The Jewish communities of South Arabia not only linked their origins to the Diaspora after the destruction of the Second Temple but also to the First Temple. According to Yemenite legends, the original Jewish settlers left Jerusalem forty-two years before the destruction of the Temple. When Ezra (Esdras/Uzair) called on them to return to help rebuild the Temple at the end of the Babylonian Exile, they refused to do so because they foresaw that the Second Temple would be destroyed. This provoked a curse from Ezra, condemning them to a life of poverty and intellectual privation. In return, they cursed Ezra so that he would not be interred in the Holy Land.[5] Yemenite Jews also connected their origins to the biblical legends surrounding Solomon and the Queen of Sheba that are elaborated in rabbinic midrashic literature and shared in Islamic legends as well.

Western scholars have viewed the question of Jewish origins in Arabia through a variety of lenses, including assuming some relationship between Jews/Hebrews and Arabs through a biblical perspective. For Reinhart Dozy, Jews came to Arabia during the period of the Babylonian Exile and brought with them religious practices that were established in Mecca. David Samuel Margoliouth, on the other hand, held that both Hebrews and Arabs started out in Arabia when it was the Eden-like Semitic homeland.[6] On the basis of inscriptions in Arabia and Babylon, we learn that the last king of Babylon, Nabonidus (556–539 B.C.E.), invaded the Hijaz and made his capitol at Tayma. Associated with this is an Aramaic fragment found at Qumran known as the "Prayer of Nabonidus." According to some, this was a supplication to God directed by a Jewish seer to cure a skin disorder.[7] For some, Nabonidus's sojourn in Arabia accompanied by Jews is an indication of the historical beginnings of Jews in Arabia. Even if the first Jews in Arabia did arrive with Nabonidus, we have to wait until after the destruction of the Second Temple before we have more evidence of Jewish settlements and culture in the Hijaz.

Cuneiform tablet with part of the Nabonidus Chronicle (556–530 B.C.E.), 530–400 B.C.E., probably Babylon, Iraq. London, British Museum.

Early Judeo-Arabic

Linguistic evidence for the presence of Jews in Arabia is impossible to date, but by the time of the rise of Islam, we have evidence of a specialized Judeo-Arabic and the presence of Hebrew and Jewish Aramaic terms assimilated into the Northwest Arabic of the Hijaz. Common words like *çalāt* (from the Aramaic *tzeluta*, "prayer"), *çadaqa* (from the Hebrew *tzedaqa*, "charity, almsgiving"), *zakāt* (from the Hebrew *zekhut*, "purification" or "merit"), and *nabī* (from the Hebrew *navi'*, "prophet") are all treated in the Qur'an as "clear" Arabic. Jews in Arabia spoke a variety of Judeo-

▶ See article
by Geneviève
Gobillot,
pp. 611-621.

Arabic termed *al-yahūdīyah*, "the Jewish [tongue]," and read scriptures in both Hebrew and in Arabic translations, preparing Targumim, or translations interspersed with commentaries, in the manner of other Diaspora Jews. It is the opinion of this author that most of this linguistic development took place in the centuries after the unsuccessful Bar Kokhba revolt (132–135 C.E.), which marked the end of Jewish resistance against Roman occupation, and it is in the Roman period and after that we begin to get more evidence of Jewish life in Arabia.[8]

One of the results of the Jewish conflict with Rome was the movement of Jews from the center of the Roman *oikoumene* to the periphery, Gaul, Iberia, and Arabia. We know that the Pharisaic Jew turned Christian, Paul, who had been Saul of Tarsus, spent three years in Arabia after his conversion to Christianity, presumably among possible Jewish converts,[9] and prior to the start of the Bar Kokhba revolt, the revolt's spiritual leader, Rabbi Akiba, journeyed to Arabia, as he did elsewhere, to garner Jewish support for the conflict with Rome. When the Christian missionary Theophilus traveled to Arabia two centuries later, he found a great number of Jews.[10] By the middle of the next century, the rulers of Yemen were using monotheistic formulas in inscriptions that appear to be Jewish or based on Jewish ideals.

The political role of Arabian Jews

By the beginning of the fifth century C.E., Arabia was the scene of intense missionary activity. In general, the Persian Gulf areas were under the influence of the Persians and their Nestorian clients, while the Red Sea areas were Monophysite and nominally under Byzantine control. Persia aggressively asserted itself in both the Hijaz and the Yemen, acting through local agents to collect taxes and prevent Byzantine incursions. In the Hijaz, the Jewish tribes of the Banu Qurayza and the Banu al-Nadir were set up by the Persians as "kings" of Medina to collect the *kharāj* tax. The connection was through the Lakhmid dynasty in Hira, the center of Persian clientage among the Arabs and the center of Nestorian missionary activity. According to al-Tabari, the head of the Lakhmid dynasty at al-Hira was a "governor" for the Persians in the areas of Iraq, Jazirah, and the Hijaz as early as the fourth century.[11] From the Byzantine perspective, Judaism in the Hijaz would have been identified with Persian interests and ambition in Arabia.

According to the biography of Muhammad, Judaism was introduced by missionizing rabbis connected with the Hijaz, who were invited to the Yemen by the last of the Tubba kings, Tiban As'ad Abu Karib. The son of this king was overthrown by a person with no connection to the royal family, who ruled brutally. He consolidated power by either murdering the leaders of the society or sodomizing them, rendering them unfit for rule. When he tried to sodomize Dhu Nuwas, the second son of Tiban As'ad, Dhu Nuwas killed the usurper and assumed the kingship. According to Islamic inscriptional and Christian hagiographic sources, he assumed the regnal name of Yusuf (Joseph) and reestablished Judaism as the royal religion, imposing it on the rest of his Himyarite kingdom. Yusuf appears to have had a triangular relationship involving his kingdom in the Yemen, the Jews of Yathrib in the Hijaz, and the Lakhmid dynasty in al-Hira in Iraq, just south of modern Kufa. Both Yathrib and al-Hira were under Sasanian Persian rule, and Yusuf seems to have been a significant factor in Persian/Lakhmid attempts to take the South Arabian city of Najran, which had been part of the Tubba kingdom but had fallen under the Byzantine-Ethiopian axis. His attempts to oust the pro-Byzantine Monophysite population of Najran have been memorialized in Syriac martyrologies and provoked an attack by Ethiopian forces on Arabia. He was apparently aided in this enterprise by "Jewish priests" from Tiberias, most likely part of the larger group of priests who had fled into Arabia to live in Levitical purity against the hope of a restoration of the Temple. Inscriptional evidence indicates that Yusuf was killed in battle against the Ethiopians, but literary accounts say that he rode his horse into the Red Sea and was not seen again. This literary trope is an indication that the Yusuf figure was regarded by some as the salvific Mashiach ben Yosef (Messiah descended from Joseph), the military precursor to the Mashiach ben David (Messiah descended from King David).[12] This major Jewish figure in pre-Islamic Arabia appears to have led the last attempt to establish Judaism in Arabia as part of a larger hope to ally with Sasanian forces against Byzantine control of the Palestine. The resulting Byzantine invasion, supported by the Ethiopians, was one of the factors in the rise of Islam, but Jewish communities in the Yemen persevered until modern times.

> *"This major Jewish figure in pre-Islamic Arabia appears to have led the last attempt to establish Judaism in Arabia."*

Jews in the Hijaz: Both urban and bedouin

At Muhammad's birth in 570 C.E., the Jewish communities in the Hijaz had lost their political and economic power to the rising fortunes of the Meccan Quraysh, although they were still a strong cultural presence. The *via odorifera*, which had given the Arabs their power through long-distance trade in luxury goods, was also in decline, as the constant warfare between the Byzantine and Persian Empires had exhausted their wealth. The royal titles granted to the Jews as tax collectors for the Persians had passed to the Arabs and then become empty memories for both. Muhammad was born into an age of decline and anxiety, but Judaism in Arabia was a vital Diaspora culture. Jews could be found in all areas of Arabian society. They were merchants, bedouin, farmers, poets, artisans, and warriors. They lived in castles, houses in cities, and in tents in the desert. They spoke Arabic, both formal and Judeo-Arabic, as well as Aramaic, and made use of Hebrew idioms. They were connected with the major Jewish intellectual and religious centers in Babylonia and Palestine, but they had their own Arabian practice of Judaism. Like their neighbors of the time, this age of anxiety and decline helped promote their interest in mysticism and eschatology. The early seventh century was a rich time for Arabian Jews, as well as a prelude to a fateful and sometimes fatal conflict with Islam.

For the student of the history of Jews in Arabia, it is hard to read against the grain of scholarship from the nineteenth and early twentieth centuries. The idea of Jews as warriors, farmers, and bedouin went against notions and stereotypes of the "Jewish race," which precluded such activities, even for some Jewish scholars.[13] The latter half of the twentieth century saw the notions of "Jewishness" and "Arabness" challenged in significant ways. The notion of "tribe" has been shown to be far less cohesive than earlier thought, and made up of a variety of people associated temporarily or permanently by economic interest, power politics, and geography.[14] The sources clearly show that one could be a Jew (or a Christian) while being an Arab and a bedouin. But it is through the cities that most of our information comes, so we know most about the Jews of Yathrib/Medina, a city divided in Islamic sources into a Jewish faction and an Arab faction, with three tribes, the Banu Qurayza, the Banu al-Nadir, and the Banu Qaynuqaʿ as Jewish tribes, and two tribes, the Banu Aws and the Banu Khazraj, as Arab. But another important study shows that the simplified Jew-versus-Arab construct of later historians was not based on the complexity at the time of the rise of Islam.[15] Different groups lived together based on common interest, such as occupation or social class, and occasionally pastoral nomads who wished to settle in urban areas converted to Judaism, such as the Banu Hishna ibn Ukarima ibn ʿAwf, who first settled in Tayma, a Jewish town, and then moved to Medina, remaining Jewish. Groups in northern Arabian cities, just as tribes in the desert, had Jewish and non-Jewish clans and subgroups, so the simplified and fictionalized divisions represented in the histories of the conflicts between Muhammad and the Jews are a reflection and reification of later doctrinal interpretations of the Qur'an.[16]

> "One could be a Jew while being an Arab and a bedouin."

Conversion to Judaism

Related to this question is the issue of conversion to Judaism among non-Jews in Arabia. In the Arabian milieu, as elsewhere in the premodern world, there were two types of conversion. There are examples of individual conversions, of which an example was that some of the Banu ʿAwf and the Banu Khazraj in Medina converted to Judaism or were converted by their mothers, who "used to make a vow that if their child lived they would make it a Jew, since they considered the Jews to be people of knowledge and the book (scripture)."[17] As mentioned above, there were also group conversions. Both types of conversion follow the patterns we see in Arabia of conversion to Islam during Muhammad's lifetime. Individuals convert and whole clans or tribes convert. What group conversion does underscore is that religion was part of a total life in a community, social and economic, as well as spiritual and aesthetic.

Conversion to Judaism in pre-Islamic Arabia, as well as conversion to Monophysite or Nestorian Christianity, was both a rejection of the old social order and a declaration of the individual's or group's loyalty to a particular political and social matrix connected with forces outside of Arabia. The Arabic term applied to Muhammad when he left his ancestral religion was Saba', not only implying a departure from the old but an active enmity between the old and the new: through this term, he was being accused of siding with Ethiopia, itself a satellite state of Byzantium. When Yusuf Dhu Nuwas acceded to the throne in Yemen in the early part of the sixth century C.E.,

Muhammad reveals to an assembly of Jewish converts that al-Husayn ibn Sallam has converted to Islam and taken the name 'Abd-Allah. Ottoman miniature in *Siyar-i Nabi* (Life of the Prophet). Turkey, fourteenth century, vol. 3. New York Public Library, Spencer Collection Turk. ms. 3, fol. 422.

it is said that all the Himyarites joined him in his Judaism, representing opposition to Monophysite Christianity and Ethiopian military and political control of Arabia.

Unfortunately, we do not have individual accounts similar to Saint Augustine's *Confessions* that describe the conversion process, and we will never know the psychological processes involved, but the conversion of groups to Judaism indicates that Arabian Judaism exerted a strong social force in Arabia shortly before and at the time of the rise of Islam. These Jews also had interests and concerns with other Jews outside of Arabia. From the Mishna, we know that the Arab Jews had the attention of the Palestinian rabbis since at least the second century. Issues of kosher dress and food, as well as the veiling of Jewish women, were debated by the rabbis, as was the issue of living in camel hair tents.[18]

We learn most about the beliefs of the Arabian Jews from their encounter with Muhammad as presented in the Qur'an. The terms that are used to describe those Jews contemporary with Muhammad are *rabbāniyyūn* and *ahbār*. The word *rabbāniyyūn* appears to be the term "Rabbanite," a term of self-description by the *geonim* (heads of the Talmudic academies in Babylonia) and the usual Karaite word used for the majority group of Jews who adhere to rabbinic precepts; it appears to be used in this sense in the Qur'an.[19] The *ahbār* seem to be a subclass of Rabbanite Jews, following the Talmudic use of the term *'haver* as someone who, while not being part of the rabbinical elite, is still deemed a "companion" (this is the meaning of *'haver*) of the rabbis because, among other things, he is punctilious in his tithing of agricultural products and adheres to the laws of purity.[20] The Qur'an polemicizes against statements attributed to the *rabbāniyyūn* that the hand of God is fettered and that they contend that Ezra is the son of God. Both attacks appear to be polemical readings of beliefs that, although foreign to normative rabbinical lore, were known among some Rabbanite Jews, although it appears that some of the Arabian Jews mentioned in the Qur'an were practitioners of mystical and magical practices, which are also frowned upon, if not outright forbidden, by rabbinical law.[21] Nevertheless, as mentioned above, Arabian Jews sought rabbinic advice on matters of everyday life, celebrated Passover, read the Torah in Hebrew and translated it into Arabic, and practiced the laws of *kashrut* in clothing and eating.

Arabian Jews and Islam

▶ See article by Geneviève Gobillot, pp. 611-621. Modern Western scholarship has noted that the Qur'an contains much "biblical" material and that the chief figures in Qur'anic stories are scriptural figures, such as Moses, Abraham, Joseph, David, Jonah, and Solomon from Jewish scripture and Jesus and Mary from Christian scripture. This has raised a debate about the extent and nature of influence on Muhammad by Jews and Christians. One of

The Bible

The term "Tanakh" refers to the Hebrew Bible. Tanakh is an acronym for Torah (the Pentateuch, written by Moses under divine dictation), Neviim (Prophets), and Ketuvim (Writings). The Pentateuch is what Judaism calls the written Torah. The Tanakh is also called Mikra, "reading," akin to qara, "to read," from the same root as the word Qur'an.

the earliest works to discuss this was the prize-winning work of Rabbi Abraham Geiger in 1833, the title of which translates as "What Did Muhammad Take from Judaism?"[22] During the first part of the twentieth century, European and American scholars were preoccupied with

▶ See article by Michael L. Miller, pp. 828-833.

trying to assess the degree to which either Jews or Christians were most influential on early Islam and which kinds of Jews or Christians they might have been. In trying to assess the relationship between Jews and the Qur'anic representations of biblical material, it is easy to see that some of the Qur'anic material is closer to midrashic accounts than it is to the Tanakh. But even here, it is hard to find a one-to-one correspondence between Qur'anic stories and surviving midrashim.[23] From the Muslim perspective, the "biblical" figures in the Qur'an come from a heavenly archetype (*Umm al-Kitab*, "the Mother of the Book") from which extracts were sent by God through prophets to Jews, Christians, and Muslims, the People of Scripture (*Ahl al-Kitab*).

One view of Muhammad's relations with the Jews of Northern Arabia is that he "accommodated" the Jews in hopes that he would convert them, but when they resisted, he reshaped his message to be more anti-Jewish and focused his mission on the non-Jewish Arabs. From my perspective, this universalizes some passages in the Qur'an that can just as easily be read to reflect specific historical circumstances and that address particular groups rather than all Jews in general. Muhammad appears to have operated within categories shared with the Jews of the Hijaz, even when he and his message were under attack by some of them. In his own eyes, and those of others, Muhammad was a genuine continuation of the process of divine revelation and was speaking in tones reminiscent of the biblical prophets when he spoke for widows and orphans and decried those whom he saw as hypocrites when they supported opposition groups against him. The notion of accommodation and conciliation does not reflect Muhammad's appeal and successes. Islam and Judaism in Arabia were operating in the same sphere of religious discourse: the same fundamental questions were discussed from similar perspectives; moral and ethical values were similar; both religions shared the same religious characters, stories, and anecdotes; and there is no expectation from their reception that the "biblical" material in the Qur'an was anything but familiar to the listeners of the message, be they Jews, Muslims, or Christians. And Islam and Judaism shared another fundamental worldview: both religions were from the beginning religions where practice, religious law, and ritual purity are central. When there was disagreement among Muslims and

Jews, it was over interpretation of shared topics, not over two mutually exclusive views of the world.

Jews within the Muslim community

The best-known part of the history of the Arabian Jewish community comes at the end of their influence in Arabia at the time that Muhammad moved from his birthplace of Mecca to the city of Yathrib, better known as Medina, in 622 C.E.[24] Muhammad's move, known as the Hijra, marked the beginning of Muhammad's assertion of public authority and Islam as a political entity. Much of the story of this move is shrouded in hagiographic myth, such as Muhammad's being saved from the pursuing Meccan tribesmen by a spider weaving a web over the mouth of a cave in which he was hiding (this too has a parallel in rabbinical lore, which tells the same thing about David fleeing the wrath of a mad King Saul); neverthe-

▶ See article by Mark R. Cohen, pp. 61-63.

less, early Islamic sources preserve a version of an agreement between Muhammad and the Jews of Medina that reflects the establishment of a new political order. As a result of the conflicts among the Medinan inhabitants, the two dominant Arab tribes, the Banu Aws and the Banu Khazraj, had enlisted Muhammad's help as a mediator and a figure to give them strength against other inhabitants, including some major Jewish groups. In this agreement, often referred to as the Constitution of Medina, Muhammad set himself up as *primus inter pares*: "Whenever you disagree about something," it says, "it must be referred to God and to Muhammad." In several clauses it specifies that particular Jewish groups are part of the agreement and liable for supporting the city in its conflict with the Meccans, who were bent on destroying Muhammad, his group of Muslims, and the city of Medina that had taken him in.

Most notably, the agreement says, "The Jews of the Banu Awf are one community (*umma*) with the believers. The Jews have their laws (*dīn*) and the Muslims have their laws (*dīn*)." It then goes on to list other Jewish groups, but not all the groups known to have participated in the conflicted his-

Jewish tribes in Yathrib, later Medina, sixth to seventh centuries.

tory of Medina and Arabia from 622 C.E. to Muhammad's death in 632 C.E. This has led some scholars to date the final redaction of this agreement to the period after the major Jewish elements allied with Muhammad's opposition were subdued.[25] Regardless of the historicity of all the elements of this agreement, it has been regarded by Muslims in many ages and places as the foundation for granting Jews a place in the Islamic polity with certain rights. As part of Muhammad's vision of the new community in which Jews and Christians would participate with Muslims, we see legislation in the Qur'an that tried to bind everyone together through commensality: "The food of those who have been given Scripture is lawful for you, and your food is lawful for them."[26] Dietary practices have bound Jews together and separated them from the rest of the world, and it is reasonable to expect that this legislation was intended to have the same effect in binding the new multiconfessional community.

The end and beyond

As Muhammad and the nascent Islamic community gained strength against Meccan economic and military opposition, many Arab groups joined Muhammad, submitted, and became Muslim. This included a few Jews according to Islamic sources, but three major groups, the Banu Qaynuqa', the Banu al-Nadir, and the Banu Qurayza, resisted strongly. Both the Banu Qaynuqa' and Banu al-Nadir were removed from their strongholds and disarmed, and the Banu Qaynuqa' were expelled after a number of their fighters were killed by Muhammad's forces.[27] Many modern readers, both Muslim and Jewish, reading through the lenses of later historical periods, view the actions of Muhammad as anti-Jewish, and there are certainly passages in the Qur'an and early Islamic sources to support such a view. However, many Jews remained in Medina until Muhammad's death and beyond, while in cities like Khaibar, their residency rights and religious practices were confirmed by treaty, as long as they agreed to pay an annual capitulation tax. A number of Jews migrated north to the Holy Land and were interviewed by Muhammad's biographer, Ibn Ishaq, for the first biography of the Muslim prophet. In spite of the retrospective claim that the caliph 'Umar I expelled Jews (and Christians) from the Arabian Peninsula, it appears that the process of moving Jews out of Northern Arabia was a gradual process, as Muslims acquired more and more land once held by non-Muslims. Our sources give sporadic accounts of Jewish tribes in Arabia, the last being from the middle of the twentieth century. Various travelers report the existence of tribes of Jews living as bedouin, but not pasturing their flocks on the Sabbath, a remnant of the once vibrant Arabian Jewish community.[28]

Arabian Jews left no advocates to argue for their importance in Jewish history, but Jewish presence in Arabia is felt in the development of Islam. One does not have to assume, as earlier scholars have done, that Muhammad "borrowed" from Judaism, but the development of Islam within a strongly Jewish milieu still reverberates in the early Islamic sources.

---

1. Abu al-Faraj al-Isfahani, *Kitab al-Aghani* (Cairo: Bulaq edition reprint, 1970), 19:94–98. This Islamic tradition conflates two biblical episodes: the first war against the Amalekites, when the latter attacked the Israelites just after the parting of the Red Sea (Exodus 17:8–16), and the second war against the Amalekites, commanded by God to King Saul through the prophet Samuel. Saul, contrary to the divine command, at first spared the life of the Amalekite king Agag (1 Samuel 15).

2. Ibid. In biblical sources, *kohen* is the name of the priestly function exercised by Aaron and his male descendants, the *kohanim* (priests).

3. Ibid.

4. Muhammad ibn 'Umar ibn Waqid, *Kitab al-Maghazi*, ed. Marsden Jones (London: Oxford University Press, 1966), 2:480.

5. Louis Ginzberg, *Legends of the Jews* (Philadelphia: Jewish Publication Society, 1967), 6:4311–32. This story has its roots in Midrash Tanhuma, commenting on Haggai 1:6, and is only one of the many stories showing the tension between the Diaspora and the ingathering.

6. See Reinhart Dozy, *De Israeliten te Meka* [*Die Israeliten zu Mekka von David's Zeit*] (Leipzig: W. Engelmann, 1864); D. S. Margoliouth, *Relations Between Arabs and Israelites Prior to the Rise of Islam: Schweich Lectures 1921* (London: Oxford University Press, 1924).

7. C. J. Gadd, "The Harran Inscription of Nabonidus," *Anatolian Studies* 8 (1958): 80; J. T. Milik, "Prière de Nabonide," *Revue Biblique* 63 (1956): 407ff.; David Noel Freedman, "The Prayer of Nabonidus, " *B.A.S.O.R.* 145 (1957): 31ff.

8. See Gordon D. Newby, "Observations about an Early Judaeo-Arabic," *Jewish Quarterly Review,* new series 61 (1971): 214–21; Moshe Gil, "The Origins of the Jews of Yathrib," *Jerusalem Studies in Arabic and Islam* 4 (1984): 206.

9. Galatians 1:17.

10. Philostorgius, *Ecclesiasticae Historiae* (Geneva: Chouët, 1642), 3:5.

11. Al-Tabari, *Ta'rikh*, ed. M. J. de Goeje (Leiden: Brill, 1879), 1:823.

12. See Gordon D. Newby, *A History of the Jews of Arabia* (Columbia: University of South Carolina Press, 2009), 39–48, for a discussion of the sources.

13. See, for example, the differences between Israel Friedlander, *Jewish Quarterly Review* 1 (1910): 251, 451, and Hartwig Hirschfeld, *Jewish Quarterly Review* 1 (1910): 447–48.

14. See the important study by Ella Landau-Tasseron, "Asad from Jahiliyya to Islam," *Jerusalem Studies in Arabic and Islam* 6 (1985): 1–28.

15. Michael Lecker, "Muhammad at Medina: A Geographical Approach," *Jerusalem Studies in Arabic and Islam* 6 (1985): 29–62.

16. This complexity has implications for the current debate about the origins of Islam and the dating of the Qur'an. For a good explanation of these issues, see Fred Donner, *Muhammad and the Believers: At the Origins of Islam* (Cambridge, MA: Belknap Press, 2010).

17. Gil, "The Origins of the Jews of Yathrib," 210.

18. See, for example, Shabbat 6:6 and Ohalot 18:10.

19. See Qur'an 3:79, 5:44, and 5:63.

20. Baba Batra 48b, 75a, and Kiddushin 33b.

21. For a fuller discussion of this with source references, see Newby, *A History of the Jews of Arabia*, 58–74.

22. Abraham Geiger, *Was hat Mohammed aus dem Judenthume Aufgenommen?* (Bonn, 1833; 2nd rev. ed., Leipzig: Kaufmann, 1902).

23. Some scholars have looked at Islamic materials as a source for "lost" midrashim. For examples of this and a discussion of the relationship between the Qur'anic figures and Jewish sources, see Gordon D. Newby, *The Making of the Last Prophet* (Columbia: University of South Carolina Press, 1989).

24. The oldest name of the city is Yathrib or Yathrippus in the Greco-Roman chronicles. The name Medina, which means "city or town" in Arabic, is also the name for city or town in Aramaic and Hebrew, and was likely adopted as a proper name from the common use of "city" because it was a major commercial center in the Hijaz, rivaling the cultic center of Mecca.

25. See Moshe Gil, "The Constitution of Medina: A Reconsideration," *Israel Oriental Studies* 4 (1974): 44–65, for a discussion of this and a list of the major primary and secondary sources.

26. See Qur'an 5:5.

27. The accounts of the destruction of the Banu Qaynuqa' seem to have been tendentiously reshaped in the Islamic sources during the late Umayyad and early Abbasid periods, when there were armed Jewish uprisings against Islamic rule in the areas of Iran and Syria. For a summary of arguments about this reshaping of the sources, see Barakat Ahmed, *Muhammad and the Jews: A Reexamination* (New Delhi: Vikas, 1979).

28. See Newby, *A History of the Jews of Arabia*, 97–108, for a discussion of the reports and their sources.

The Origin of the Jewish Tribes of Arabia in the *Kitab al-Aghani*

According to the Arab tradition, the predecessors of present-day Arabs in Arabia were originally known as "Amalekites." They were tyrannical, and nearly all were exterminated by Jews sent by Moses. These victorious Jews then settled in the northwestern part of Arabia (al-Hijaz). In the *Kitab al-Aghani*, written by 'Ali ben al-Husayn Abu al-Faraj al-Isfahani (897–967 C.E.), we discover the origins of the Jewish tribes established in Medina, the Banu Qurayza and the Banu Nadir. They considered themselves the two "priestly" (*al-kāhinān*) tribes, descendants of the Temple priests who had fled Jerusalem after the Romans' destruction of the Temple in 70 C.E. That story is a reworking of the biblical accounts of the Amalekites found in the book of Numbers (Bamidbar) 24:20 and in Samuel (Shmuel) 1:15, and reformulated in the rabbinical Haggadic literature. These founding legends were probably spread by the Jewish tribes of Medina to show their superiority over their neighbors and to reassert their ancient rights in Arabia.

Gordon D. Newby

The History of Aws and the Genealogy of the Jews Living in Medina, as well as Their Chronicles

Aws, son of Dana the Jew, was a member of the Banu Qurayza. It is said that the Banu Qurayza and the Banu Nadir were the two "priestly" (*al-kāhinān*) tribes, because they were descended from al-Kahin, son of Harun [Aaron], son of 'Amran, brother of Musa [Moses] ibn 'Amran—may the prayers of God be upon Muhammad, upon his family, and upon Harun and Musa. They settled near Yathrib after the death of Moses—may peace be upon him—and before the migration of the Azd, following the breach of the Ma'rib dam and the establishment of the Aws and Khazraj in Yathrib.

This account was transmitted to me by 'Ali, son of Sulayman al-Akhfash, who learned of it from Ja'far, son of Muhammad al-'Asi, who had it from Abi al-Minhal 'Uyayna, son of al-Minhal al-Muhallabi, who for his part had it from Abu Sulayman Ja'far, son of Sa'd, who received it from the mouth of al-'Ammari.

He reports: "The inhabitants of Medina in the early days, before the sons of Israel, were a people from the vanished communities called the Amalekites. They were dispersed throughout the region and were a people of great power and great iniquity. Included among these Amalekites, residents of Medina, were the Banu Haff, the Banu Sa'd, the Banu al-Azraq, and the Banu Matruq. The king of Hejaz, who was of their lineage and was named Arqam, wandered as a nomad somewhere between Tayma and Fadak.[1] These Amalekites settled in Medina in great number: there they had quantities of date palms and farms. Musa ibn 'Imran

[Moses] – may Peace be upon him – dispatched his troops against the tyrants of Ahl al-Qura, in order to launch hostilities. Musa – may Peace be upon him – thus raised an army composed of the sons of Israel to go against the Amalekites, and ordered them, should they be victorious, to exterminate them all and to leave none alive. The army of the sons of Israel penetrated into Hejaz, and God, powerful and great, gave them the advantage over the Amalekites. They exterminated all of them, except one of the sons of King Arqam: he was harmless and a beautiful boy, and so they were loath to kill him. They declared: 'Let us take him with us to Musa, who will give us his opinion on that question.' So they returned to the land of Sham, where they found Musa—may Peace be upon him – dead. The sons of Israel [living in the land of Sham] said to them: 'What have you done?' They replied: 'God, powerful and great, has granted us victory: we have exterminated them, and none of their people is still alive, save a young and beautiful boy, whom we were reluctant to have perish. We therefore decided to bring him to Musa—may Peace be upon him – so that he might give his opinion on the question.' The sons of Israel replied: 'That is an act of disobedience: you received the order to spare no one. By God, never again will you enter our country of Sham!' When they had been driven off, the war troops of the sons of Israel declared: 'How could we do better than to occupy the dwellings of those we killed in Hejaz? Let us return and establish ourselves there.' So they rejoined their rear guard and arrived in Medina, where they settled. That army constituted the first settlement of Jews of Medina. The community grew up all around Medina, even to the province of 'Aliya. They built forts, accumulated wealth, cultivated the land. They continued to live thus in Medina for a long time, until Rome rose up against all the sons of Israel in the land of Sham, trampled them underfoot, killed them, and raped their women. And so, when Rome had defeated them in the land of Sham, the Banu al-Nadir, the Banu Qurayza, and the Banu Bahdal fled to Hejaz, where they rejoined the sons of Israel [who had been living there since the war against the Amalekites]. When they left the land of Sham with their families, the king of Rome ordered that they be pursued and brought back, but the fugitives arrived at their goal. Now there is between the land of Sham and Hejaz a waterless desert. And so, when the Romans pursuing the sons of Israel reached Tamr, they perished, tormented by thirst. That is why that place was named Tamr al-Rum,[2] and that name has remained to the present."

Abu al-Faraj al-Isfahani, *Kitab al-Aghani* (Cairo, 1390/1970), 19:94ff.

---

1. Tayma is an oasis located northwest of Arabia, four hundred kilometers north of Medina; Fadak is a village near Haybar in Hejaz.

2. Tamr al-Rum: the "Tamr" of the Romans.

The Prophet and the Jewish Tribes of Arabia according to *Al-Sira*

Because the Prophet (A.D. 570–632) lived in an oral tradition society, what we know of his activities, and especially of the battles he waged, was first reported by word of mouth. Some of the accounts were set down in writing by those few of his companions who knew how to write, and they became the object of partial compilations. None of these accounts, oral or written, on the life of the Prophet gave rise to any efforts at collection, collation, or verification until the late eighth century, that is, more than a century and a half after the Prophet's death on June 8, 632. The first work with comprehensive ambitions, *Al-sira al-nabatawiyya*, was compiled by Muhammad ibn Is'haq (d. ca. 767). That title also came to be applied to later works, which complemented the first, taking up some of its themes and adding others. These are primarily the work of four major chroniclers living during the Abbasid dynasty: al-Waqidi (747–823), author of the *Kitab al-Maghazi* (*Book of Conquests*), 3 vols.; Muhammad Ibn Sa'd (784–845), author of the *Kitab al-Tabaqat al-Kabir* (*Book of the Circles of Companions*), 11 vols.; al-Tabari (839–923), author of the *Kitab al-Rusul wal-Muluk* (*Book of the Prophets and Kings*), 10 vols.; and al-Baladhuri (d. 892), author of the *Kitab Ansab al-Ashraf* (*Book of Noble Lineages*), 4 vols.

For historians, these chronicles are at once irreplaceable when taken as a whole and potentially misleading in their details. Indeed, the accuracy of the notations was necessarily compromised by the length of time that had elapsed, the technical conditions of their transmission, and the partisan preferences of the successive transmitters. For that reason, it is important to be able to compare, associate, and collate the works of the five major chroniclers, each of whom pursued his research independently of the others. The sum total of this research gives the historian valuable frames of reference by which to overcome the weaknesses of each one individually.

If we are to believe *Al-Sira*, the story of the tumultuous relations established between the Prophet and the Jewish tribes of his time is that of a religious proximity consumed by a political rivalry. During the first third of the seventh century A.D., the Jewish tribes from central Arabia were for the most part living in two large cities, Yathrib (which would later be renamed Medina, from *Madinat al-Nabi*, "City of the Prophet") and Khaybar, and in three smaller urban areas, Fadak, Tayma', and Wadi al-Qura. There is no trace of a Jewish presence in Mecca. The Prophet nevertheless had his first contact with the Jews during the Mecca period of his preaching (610–22). This was a long-distance contact. The lords of Quraysh, the dominant tribal alliance in Mecca, decided to send two of their members to Yathrib to ask the Jewish rabbis what they ought to think of the Qur'an that Muhammad was reciting. Was it possible that his Book came down from heaven like that of the Jews?

The rabbis proposed that the Prophet be tested, questioned about the history of the "Sleepers of the Cave,"[1] about the person of "Dhul-Qarnayn,"[2] and finally, about the meaning of "the Spirit."[3] If he gave the right answers, the rabbis said, he was without a doubt a prophet and had to be followed. Otherwise, he was an imposter. The Qurayshites, upon returning from Mecca, asked the Prophet the three questions. For fifteen nights, Muhammad waited for Gabriel to come and reveal the answers to him. But these answers left the Meccan lords skeptical, and they would continue to reject Islam. The Prophet finally left his native city in 622.

He settled in Yathrib, where three large tribes – the Banu Qaynuqa', the Banu al-Nadir, and the Banu

Quraydha – had established themselves several generations earlier. Were these Arab converts? Jews who had emigrated from Palestine? We do not know. But at the time of the Prophet's arrival, these tribes possessed wealth (especially palm groves), weapons, and fortified dwellings. Their political influence was exerted especially through alliances with the two principal polytheistic tribes of the city, the Aws and the Khazraj, who seem to have originally come from Yemen. All these groups were continually at war with one another. The Aws and the Khazraj had been at each other's throats for ages, and the Jewish tribes, far from remaining united, chose to support opposing camps, with the Quraydha forming alliances with the Aws, the Qaynuqa' and the al-Nadir allying themselves with the Khazraj. It was in the hope of breaking that cycle, which was draining for all parties involved, that some members of the Aws and Khazraj, at first minorities within their own tribes,[4] undertook a joint initiative that would soon turn the order of things on its head. Having embraced Islam, they appealed to the Prophet to come with his seventy or so Meccan companions and to settle among them.[5] They were wagering that he could establish peace between their two tribes by his power of arbitration, exercised not in the name of one tribe or another but in the name of a religion, which, precisely, was called on to transcend tribalism. They won that wager, since the majority of the Aws and Khazraj clans ultimately embraced Islam. But that was not the case for the Jewish tribes.

The Prophet began by proposing to the Jews a "pact of agreement and mutual support" (sometimes improperly called the "Constitution of Medina"), which all three accepted. "The Jews will pledge their own expenditures and the Muslims their own. They will support each other to fight the enemies of that pact. They will consult with each other, exchange advice, and do good, not evil, to each other. Neither will commit a crime against its ally." But the spirit of that pact was gradually abandoned, giving way to increasingly conflictual relations.

What was the crux of the problem? The Qur'an, as the Word of God, was a continuation of the Torah. Muhammad was the last in the cycle of prophets; Abraham and Moses had preceded him. A number of rabbis said at the time that they were awaiting a new prophet. Muhammad claimed he was that one and therefore asked them to embrace Islam. But the rabbis refused. For them, the awaited prophet could belong only to one of the twelve tribes of Israel.

Initially, confrontation took the form of public disputes. The rabbis would seize different opportunities to catch the Prophet off balance, to find fault with him, even ridicule him in front of his own people, while Muhammad, supported by the angel Gabriel, eluded their traps, answered their challenges, and demonstrated that he was truly the chosen of God, whose advent the Torah had predicted.

So long as the pact remained in force, the doctrinal quarrels, more or less heated, went on. But they did not completely undermine day-to-day existence, which was composed of neighborliness, visits between Muslims and Jews, and fruitful commerce. Things began to sour after the successive military campaigns that Mecca and its polytheistic allies launched against Muhammad, since the Jewish tribes chose those moments to turn against the Prophet instead of affirming their solidarity with him. But they did so separately, one after another, without conferring with or aiding one another. In the end, that would prove fatal to all of them.

The first clash took place after the Battle of Badr (624). Things were looking bad for the Muslims, who were facing Meccan troops much superior in number. In Yathrib, polytheists and Jews were already wagering on the Prophet's defeat and were openly rejoicing. But the bravery of the Muslims, sure of divine protection, turned the anticipated defeat into a miraculous victory.

Upon the heroes' return, tensions rose sharply between certain Muslim neighborhoods and the Jews of the Banu Qaynuqa' tribe. They openly challenged the Prophet, then entrenched themselves in their forts. They were expecting their traditional allies from the Khazraj tribe – some of whom, known as the Munafiqun, or Hypocrites, remained secretly hostile to Islam – to join them and deal a fatal blow to Muhammad. But neither the Khazraj nor the other Jewish tribes came to their aid. After two weeks, the Banu Qaynuqa' surrendered and were banished from the city.

After the defeat of Uhud (625), the Prophet faced a difficult period. In particular, he was urgently in need of money. Accompanied by a small number of companions, he went to the lords of the Jewish tribe of the Banu al-Nadir to ask them to advance him a certain sum. They received him well and offered to share their meal with him.

While everyone was busy with the cooking, the lords of the Jewish tribe hastily assembled and pondered whether they ought not to take advantage of the unique opportunity offered them to assassinate Muhammad. But the Prophet, having been alerted in time, hastily left the place. He let the Banu al-Nadir know that, in attempting to commit treason against him, they had violated the pact between him and them. As a result, he ordered them to leave Yathrib within ten days. The great chiefs of the tribe, believing that this time they could count on solid support, rejected Muhammad's ultimatum and retreated to their forts.

The support did not come. In particular, the Jewish tribe of the Banu Quraydha refused to aid its coreligionists, telling them that would be a flagrant violation of the pact that bound it to Muhammad. The Banu al-Nadir had to surrender in turn. They were condemned to leave the city with only what their camels could carry, excluding any war weapons.

Two years later, in 627, the so-called Battle of the Trench took place. Mecca formed a vast tribal coalition with the aim of attacking Yathrib simultaneously from all sides. The Prophet called on the whole city, including the Jewish tribe of the Banu Quraydha, to dig a trench within a few days' time around Yathrib, one deep and wide enough that neither camels nor horses could cross it. Protected by that trench, the Muslims repelled the multiple assaults of the coalition forces, even discouraging several of the enemy tribes and finally forcing Mecca to lift the siege.

The battle lasted fifteen days. In the meantime, the lords of the Banu Quraydha had committed an irreparable act. At a critical moment in the siege, secretly contacted by coreligionists in alliance with the Meccans, they suddenly changed allegiance and took the side of the Prophet's enemies. A rumor spread that they were preparing to attack certain city neighborhoods, where the warriors' families were confined. That raised a dilemma for the Prophet: either thin the ranks at the front or leave those neighborhoods unprotected.

When the Muslim victory was won, the retribution was terrible. Surrounded in their forts, the Banu Quraydha ultimately surrendered. The Prophet entrusted their fate to a member of the Aws tribe, which had previously been their ally. He ordered "all the men old enough to shave put to death, the women and children reduced to slavery, and their possessions divided up among the Muslims."

The last confrontation between Muslims and Jews took place in Khaybar. The Prophet considered that city, which had consistently supported Mecca against him, an enemy bastion. But he waited to attack it until he had concluded a truce with his native city, the famous truce of al-Hudaybiyya.

The lords of Khaybar did not learn the lesson of the defeats suffered by the Jewish tribes of Yathrib: they opted for the same defensive strategy. They retreated to their forts, which, defended separately, fell one after another. The conflicts were nevertheless extremely violent. At a crucial turning point in the war, the Prophet, to fire up his people, uttered these words, which sum up the meaning of his battle: "Satan came to whisper to the Jews that Muhammad was attacking them to seize their possessions. Disabuse them. Tell them: 'Pronounce these words: "There is no God but God." By these words alone, you will safeguard your possessions, your lives, and your credit with God."' The Jewish lords refused to embrace Islam. Their defeat culminated in their being reduced to vassals. The Prophet extended his protection to their lives and their lands, but they were required to hand over half their crops.

At the end of the Medina decade of his preaching (622–32), the Prophet thus put an end to a Jewish power that had at first been far superior to the Muslims' economically and militarily. Among the reasons for that reversal, *Al-Sira* suggests at least two factors. On one hand, in Yathrib as in Khaybar, rivalries between Jewish tribes prevailed over religious solidarity, whereas the unifying force of Islam won out over the multiple tribal allegiances of the new Muslim community. On the other, when conflicts erupted, the Jews systematically made the defensive choice to retreat to their forts, whereas the Muslim troops, charged up by the charismatic presence of the Prophet, were spurred on to attack. ●

Mahmoud Hussein is the joint pen name for Bahgat Elnadi and Adel Rifaat, who are political scientists, Islamologists, and writers. They have published, notably, Al-Sîra, *2 vols. (Grasset, 2005, 2007) and* Penser le Coran *(Grasset, 2009; Folio Gallimard, 2011).*

---

1. The Sleepers of the Cave: seven young believers from the Roman period who took refuge in a cave. God made them sleep for three centuries, so that they could witness the Resurrection and the Last Judgment (Qur'an 18:13–15).
2. Dhul-Qarnayn: a figure to whom Islam grants the qualities of a prophet and who possesses the mythified traits of Alexander the Great (Qur'an 18:83–97).
3. The Spirit: presented as a divine creation (Qur'an 18:85).
4. The residents of Yathrib who converted to Islam were called Ansars, or Partisans.
5. The Meccans who converted to Islam were called Muhajirun, or Emigrants.

Islamic Policy toward Jews from the Prophet Muhammad to the Pact of 'Umar[1]

Mark R. Cohen

The first encounter between Jews and Muslims dates back to the very beginnings of Islam. This essay discusses the foundations of the Muslim-Jewish relationship. The ambivalent attitude toward the Jews of Medina in the Qur'an, and the Prophet Muhammad's aggressive assault on some of the Jewish tribes, reflect the gulf between his expectations for their acceptance of his message and their rejection. At the same time, Muhammad guaranteed nonviolence toward the "People of the Book" (Jews and Christians) in return for payment of tribute and humbleness. Muhammad's so-called Constitution of Medina incorporated Jews either as part of the Islamic *umma* (faith community) or in a non-belligerency arrangement, but in either case granted them freedom to practice Judaism. Originally established under treaties with conquered peoples, it culminated in the pragmatic policy of *dhimma*, a word that means "protection." In its classic form, this status was enshrined in the so-called Pact of 'Umar, which guaranteed Christians, and by association Jews, security and freedom to practice religion discreetly, in return for acceptance of restrictions commensurate with the inferior status of the non-Muslim communities.

Mark R. Cohen

Professor of Near Eastern Studies at Princeton University, he holds the Khedouri A. Zilka Professorship of Jewish Civilization in the Near East. His publications include *Under Crescent and Cross: The Jews in the Middle Ages* (Princeton University Press, 1994; revised edition 2008).

The Prophet Muhammad and the Jews

The question of where Muhammad learned about Judaism can be answered through a combination of conjecture and evidence. According to the Islamic tradition, Arabia at that time was pagan, though seeds of monotheistic belief seem to have been planted there even before Muhammad entered the scene. Mecca, where Muhammad was born, was home of a great pagan shrine, the Ka'ba, later to become the focal point of the Islamic pilgrimage. Those isolated Jews residing in Mecca during his youth—Jewish wives of members of his tribe, the Quraysh, and their offspring—would not have served as a significant source of knowledge about Judaism.[2] Muhammad was more likely to have come in contact with

Jewish merchants trading in the town or during his own commercial travels to the north. From these people he would have been exposed to some Jewish beliefs and practices. He doubtless met Christians, too, whether merchants trading in Mecca, hermits living in the desert, or Christian members of other Arabian tribes. From them he would have absorbed ideas of Christianity, as well as of Judaism, filtered through Christian eyes.

▷ About Jews in Arabia, see article by Gordon D. Newby, pp. 39-51.

In Medina, by contrast, he encountered no Christians, only a large settlement of Jewish tribes, most of them affiliated with local Arabs, including three large, wealthy, and powerful Jewish tribes with typical Arab tribal names: the Banu Nadir, the Banu Qaynuqa', and the Banu Qurayza. From them he would have learned much more about Judaism, though it is uncertain how much their Judaism was informed by rabbinic law, since the Babylonian Talmud was still in the process of reaching its final form, which was not concluded until after his death. While attitudes toward the Jews expressed in the Qur'an were doubtless formed already in Muhammad's Meccan period, his Jewish *policies* were a product of his experience in Medina.

Different messages about Jews in the Qur'an

The Qur'an contains a mixed message about the Jews (as well as about the Christians). This mirrors the ambivalent feelings of the Prophet, reflecting the gulf between his high expectations and the Jews' disappointing response.

At the outset, most scholars agree, Muhammad assumed the Jews would flock to his preaching and recognize him as their own prophet—indeed, the final, or "seal" of the prophets. Fred M. Donner argues, in fact, that originally the new religion—the "community of believers," he calls them—was meant as an ecumenical community open to Jews and Christians.[3] And so the Prophet's attitude was at first largely conciliatory. In stark contrast to the Fathers of the Christian Church, who often made polemical use of the Old Testament, reinterpreting it allegorically in order to sway Jews to Christ and buttress their own new teachings, Muhammad incorporated biblical stories in the Qur'an, often with postbiblical midrashic embellishments presumably gathered from local Jewish oral traditions, to add to the store of Jewish reference points he hoped would attract the Jews.[4] He also adopted or adapted several Jewish practices in hopes of drawing Jews near. For instance, he established daily prayers as in Judaism—though five times a day rather than three. He designated Jerusalem as the direction to be faced during prayer, later switching to Mecca when the Jews failed to flock to his preaching en masse. Muhammad followed the Jewish example regarding dietary laws (the prohibition of pork, for example) and ritual slaughter of animals, and permitted Muslims to eat food prepared by the Jews or Christians (with the exception of pork). All these efforts were aimed at winning Jewish acknowledgment of his prophetic mission. Apart from religious motives, there was a more mundane reason for reaching out to the Jews. He needed the militarily powerful and wealthy Jewish tribes of Medina as allies against his enemies in

▷ About *isrā'īliyyāt*, see pp. 625-627.

Mecca. Most of the Jews rejected his preaching. His disappointment and frustration are reflected in many unfriendly verses in the Qur'an.

His policy, however, was in many ways tolerant. One of the most important Qur'anic policies regarding the Jews—indeed, all People of the Book—is summed up in the famous verse "There is no compulsion in religion" (*lā ikrāha fī dīni*) (Sura 2:256).[5] It gives voice to a realistic pluralism in early Islam. In context, as one scholar has persuasively argued, the verse seems to have been meant descriptively, not prescriptively, that is, as a statement of resignation, acknowledging that people are not likely to give up the faith into which they were born.[6] Nonetheless, over time, the verse came to be understood as a prescription forbidding Muslims to compel others to accept Islam against their will.

The "no compulsion in religion" verse should be seen in conjunction with other statements in the Qur'an that illustrate the pluralistic attitude of the nascent Islamic *umma* toward other monotheists. This pluralism is enshrined, for instance, in the ninth sura, in a verse that establishes the basis for Islamic policy toward the Jews and other People of the Book. The sura begins with a set of revelations preached to the *mushrikūn* (idolaters, polytheists). Their fate, if they fail to believe in Muhammad and the message of Islam, is to be fought to the death or until they accept Islam. This is the source of the proverbial image of "Islam or the sword." Verse 29 declares a different policy for the People of the Book. It grants the Jews, Christians, and other scriptuaries a third choice: freedom to remain in their religion as long as they pay tribute and assume a humble position vis-à-vis the majority religion. "Fight against such of those who have been given the Scripture who believe not in Allah nor the Last Day, and forbid not that which Allah hath forbidden by His messenger, and follow not the Religion of Truth, until they pay the tribute readily, being brought low."

> **" The famous verse 'There is no compulsion in religion' gives voice to a realistic pluralism in early Islam. "**

"Tribute" here translates the Arabic word *jizya*, which in time, in imitation of Byzantine and Sasanian taxation systems, evolved into a discriminatory poll tax incumbent upon every non-Muslim scriptuary once a year.[7] "Being brought low," Arabic *ṣāghirūn*, later constituted the prooftext for the regimen of humiliating restrictions (*saghār*) imposed on non-Muslims by Islamic law as it evolved in succeeding centuries. The enigmatic phrase rendered "readily," *'an yadin* in Arabic, could also be translated as "out of hand," or "with the hand," or "from what is at hand." The words gave rise to many different interpretations in medieval Qur'an commentaries, some of them prescribing harshness, others leniency, in collecting the tax. It seems that no one knew precisely what the phrase originally meant.[8]

As Muhammad's mission in Medina progressed and he steadily succeeded in spreading Islam among the pagan Arabs, Jewish rejection grated on him all the more. Lack of cooperation on the part of the Jews in the battle against Mecca further angered him. Consequently, he expelled two of the three main Jewish tribes. According to credible Islamic sources, including a possibly vague allusion to the event in the Qur'an

ممسين لم محتلطوا ابدا واصلا لسائر القبائل الا الان ابا لهب كان هاشميا فاتصل بقريش وفارق الهاشميين فاضطر منوهاشم وبنوالمطلب

The Quraysh in consultation as to the proscription of their kinsmen. Miniature from the *Jami' al-Tawarikh* of Rashid al-Din, 14th century, Edinburgh University Library, Scotland. Ms Or 20 f.54r

(33:27–28), the third tribe, the Banu Qurayza, was violently attacked because of their alliance with the polytheist Meccans.[9] Nearly all the males were killed and the women and children were enslaved.[10] What seems like a change in "policy" from the original, benign religious tolerance to violent opposition did not, however, become a precedent.

The pragmatic Constitution of Medina

Apart from the Qur'an, the most important source regarding Muhammad's attitude and policy toward the Jews is the so-called Constitution of Medina.[11] The text of this important document is preserved in two full versions, the better known of the two being the biography of the Prophet by Ibn Ishaq/Ibn Hisham.[12] It is referred to as a *kitāb*, "document," or "compact" (the translation "constitution" is a modernism with an obvious programmatic purpose).[13] The document creates a unified *umma* (Donner refers to it as the "*umma* document"[14])—"one people (*umma wāhida*) to the exclusion of others" in the introduction—based on faith rather than on separate tribal loyalties. It spells out the obligations of the various tribes toward one another and toward the general war effort against pagan enemies in the Arabian Peninsula. Since one of Muhammad's functions was to mediate tribal feuds that in ancient Arabian law were settled by vengeance and bloodshed, he appears in the document in his role as arbitrator. Jewish tribes are mentioned as well, though, problematically, the three large tribes, Banu Nadhir, Banu Qaynuqa', and Banu Qurayza, are not singled out by name.

Lecker understands the constitution as a single document containing two separate agreements, introduced by the title: "Compact of the apostle, may God pray for him and give him peace, which he wrote between the emigrants (from Mecca) and the helpers (the tribes of Medina), *and* a *muwāda'a* with the Jews." *Muwāda'a*, Lecker explains, means a non-belligerency treaty, a guarantee of security (*amān*) in return for cessation of hostilities and cooperation against the enemy.[15]

Ibn Ishaq's introduction adds the important detail that the *muwāda'a* (and compact, *'ahd*) with the Jews "allowed them to keep their religion and property (*aqarrahum 'alā dīnihim wa- amwālihim*)." The constitution itself begins with a cover statement, introducing the first part of the document, which does not concern the Jews: "This is a compact from Muhammad the Prophet between the *mu'minūn* and the *muslimūn* of Quraysh and Yathrib and those who join them as clients, attach themselves to them and fight the holy war with them." Lecker identifies the *mu'minūn* with the Prophet's own tribe, the Quraysh, along with Arabs of Yathrib-Medina, and the *muslimūn* (Muslims) with other tribes living in the oasis.[16]

Apart from one reference to the Jews in the first twenty-six clauses, where they appear as clients of particular Arab tribes, in the second part they are the main counterparties. Two important clauses at the very beginning, whose meaning is disputed, form the crux. The first is usually rendered as follows (following Ibn Ishaq's recension): "The Jews share expenditure with the believers as long as they are at war. The Jews of Banu 'Awf are *umma ma'a al-mu'minīn*," "an *umma* (community) with the believers." Almost every scholar takes this to mean that the Jews were initially part of the Muslim community.[17] The second phrase is translated, "the Jews have their religion (*dīn*) and the Muslims have theirs." This correlates with the statement in Ibn Ishaq's introduction, *aqarrahum 'alā dīnihim wa-amwālihim*, and should not be understood otherwise.[18] It gives expression to the religious pluralism in Islam mentioned before.

With some textual support from outside the constitution, Lecker emends *umma* to *amana* and translates: "the Jews of Banu 'Awf are secure (*amana*) from (*min*) the *mu'minūn*" (he leaves the last word untranslated). This emendation is orthographically plausible. Combined with a careful logical argument, Lecker's revisionist interpretation constitutes a bold suggestion. The constitution, he argues, is consistent with separate non-belligerency compacts concluded with the three large Jewish tribes shortly after the *hijra* (thus incidentally explaining their omission from the document), part of a pragmatic policy to assure Jewish loyalty and support in return for their own security and religious freedom.[19]

While Donner's theory would strengthen the case that the Prophet meant to be inclusive, incorporating the Jews into the *umma* of monotheistic believers, in Lecker's interpretation, it is not necessary to conclude that the Jews were part of the community of Islam. Hence, determining the date of the treaty or whether or not the Prophet had at first a "pro-Jewish" policy is asking the wrong question.[20] If Lecker's view is upheld, we would be entitled to conclude that Muhammad's policy in Medina—as distinct from his attitude—did not change from tolerant (in the Constitution of Medina) to intolerant, culminating in the oft-mentioned "break with the Jews." His policy, as represented already in the Constitution, was consistent, stemming from a pragmatic decision to achieve mutual non-belligerency with the Jews and to attain their cooperation in the struggle against Mecca. As part of this policy he granted the Jews security (*amān*) and religious freedom, which then became standard in subsequent conquest treaties made with native populations.[21] As we shall see, this set the stage for the full-blown *dhimma* system governing Muslim and non-Muslim relations throughout the

❯ See article by Henry Laurens, pp. 269-279.

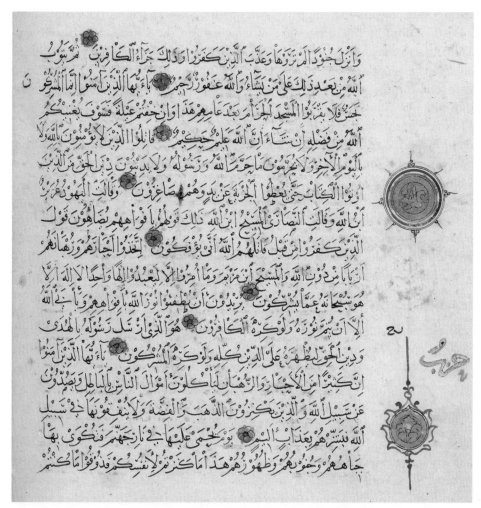

Page of the Qur'an showing the *jizya* verse, 9:29, between the third and fourth rosettes. Iraq?, thirteenth century. Paris, Bibliothèque Nationale de France, Arabic ms. 6716, fol. 67 verso.

Middle Ages (indeed, until it was abolished in the nineteenth century in the Ottoman Empire and the early twentieth century in Morocco; in Yemen it ended only with the mass exodus of Yemeni Jews to Israel in 1950).[22]

> **Taxes**
>
> Muslims fulfilled *zakat* ("purification," one of the Five Pillars of Islam), while non-Muslims (*dhimmis*) paid the *jizya* (meaning "tribute" or "compensation"), individually or collectively. Moreover, *dhimmis*, under threat of expropriation, paid a land tax called *kharaj*, calculated according to the size of the cultivated area, while Muslim landowners were subject to the *ushr*, a smaller amount.

The *dhimma* policy

The foundations laid in Medina and elaborated elsewhere in the Arabian Peninsula during Muhammad's lifetime paved the way for a policy toward the peoples subjugated during the first great wave of conquests in the Christian Byzantine and Zoroastrian Sasanian Empires after the Prophet's death in 632. This policy was based on *dhimma*, or "protection," a word appearing a handful of times in the Qur'an and later found in the phrase "the *dhimma* of God," designating a covenant relationship with man, in which sense it occurs, among other places, in the Constitution of Medina.[23] The policy grew out of the indulgent side of the Prophet's attitude toward non-Muslim People of the Book in the Qur'an and also conformed with his pragmatic policy of security (*amān*) and free exercise of religion in return for loyalty—established with respect to the Jews and then extended to other scriptuaries. Pragmatism, rather than protracted warfare, dictated policy toward the vast population of Zoroastrians as well. Mentioned only once (Arabic *mājūs*; Sura 22:17) in the Qur'an, the Zoroastrians possessed a book, the Avesta, and this admitted them to the category of protected People of the Book, despite their seemingly idolatrous worship of fire.[24]

The evolving policy is clearly evident in the conquest treaties, where the word *dhimma* sometimes occurs in the context of the security and freedom of religion offered by the Muslims to the conquered peoples in return for their non-belligerency and the payment of tribute.[25] The conquered non-Muslims eventually were called *ahl al-dhimma*, "protected people," *dhimmī*s for short. The payment of a lump sum tribute upon surrender of a town was later converted into a permanent, annual poll tax levied on each non-Muslim individual. This was construed as a fulfillment of the command of Sura 9:29. The *jizya* was considered a kind of protection money, and *dhimmī*s remitted it on the assumption that it would guarantee their security.[26] Pragmatism had its advantages for both sides. The Arabian Muslims were desert fighters, sweeping from town to town, conquering one after the other, with no time, inclination, or skills to govern them. Here and there they established separate garrison settlements in which tribes managed their own lives according to the new rule of Islam. It proved convenient and politic to leave the indigenous populations

> ❝*It proved convenient and politic to allow the religious communities to govern themselves.*❞

▸ About the modern use of the word *dhimmitude*, see article by Mark R. Cohen, p. 30.

alone and to allow the religious communities to govern themselves. Thus, the older warrant for religious freedom and *amān* came to embrace a large measure of communal autonomy, one of the hallmarks of policy toward the Jews for centuries under successive Persian, Greco-Roman, and Christian regimes.[27] The impact this had on Jewish community life in the Islamic world will be described in subsequent chapters of this volume.

The conquering Arabs were ill-equipped to administer their own new state apparatus as well, and so non-Muslim self-government on the local level was matched by the service of non-Muslims in Islamic bureaucracy. *Dhimmī* employment in Muslim administration during the first ruling dynasty, the Umayyads of Syria (661–750), had the odd result that Greek continued to be used as the language of administration for a considerable amount of time in Byzantine territories after their conquest. Even when Muslims began to assume bureaucratic control of the empire, *dhimmī*s continued to serve in positions of authority, some of them rising very high at court and in administration, even, in rare cases, to the office of vizier. This put them in situations where they exercised power over Muslims, much to the consternation of Muslim clerics and other pious figures, who chastised Muslim rulers for sanctioning this wanton violation of the right order of society.[28]

A pragmatic policy of live and let live thus governed relations between the conquered and the conquerors, a prudent alternative to stretching their relatively small forces thin in fights to the bitter end. This pragmatism was later applied to people who were not monotheists or People of the Book, such as Hindus, in some parts of India. The grant of considerable autonomy to the non-Muslim communities, alongside religious freedom, allowed them to maintain their separate identity.

Though not themselves partners to the conquest treaties—nowhere were Jews in charge of the towns they inhabited—they were nonetheless subject to the same terms as the majority conquered population. They paid the same poll tax, received the same protection in return for loyalty and proper subordination, and benefited from the same freedom of religion and community autonomy. Unlike the days of Medina, where Jews were the only representatives of the non-Muslim People of the Book and occupied center stage in evolving Islamic policy, now Jews were but one *dhimmī* group among others, at least two in the former Byzantine Empire, and sometimes, as in Iran, three. Islamic policy toward the Jews was, therefore, diffused over the entire protected non-Muslim class.

> " *In Islamic law, Jews were considered part of the* **dhimmī** *class as a whole.* "

In the Islamic world, nothing along the lines of the specific "Jewry law" of Christendom developed, the latter focusing attention upon the Jews as the single nonconforming population of the population (apart from Christian heretics) and eroding the protected status of *religio licita* they had enjoyed under pagan Roman law. In Islamic law, Jews were considered part of the *dhimmī* class as a whole. When violations of what we may call "*dhimmī* law" occurred, it was the *dhimmī*s who were prosecuted, usually Christians and Jews together, and, where they were present, Zoroastrians as well. Policy focused on the Jews qua Jews did not exist, and this had considerable importance for the relationship between majority Muslims and minority Jews.

Islamic policy toward non-Muslims in the conquered territories was not, however, dictated simply by pragmatic considerations. What we might call "sociological factors" also played a role. The heterogeneous mixture in the Islamic Empire of non-Muslim peoples professing a variety of religions—a veritable pluralism of infidels—was complemented by a mixture of ethnic Muslim or Islamized groups. There were the Arabs, of course, but also Muslim Iranians. Islamized Berbers populated North Africa. In Spain they lived alongside Islamized Slavs, Christian converts, as well as Hispano-Romans and descendants of the Germanic Goths. Turkic peoples began to arrive in Iraq as military slaves as early as the ninth century. These and others created a richly hued mosaic of peoples and religions, in which the Jews constituted just one group out of many. In this society, different religions and ethnic groups lived side by side, aware of their differences but coexisting in a more or less live-and-let-live atmosphere, each recognizing its place in the hierarchy.

Transcending the hierarchy, Jews and other *dhimmī*s could be found in nearly all categories of Islamic society, working alongside Muslims who outranked them by virtue of religion. They functioned as local and international traders, artisans, government clerks, and in a number of other professions common to Muslims. Informally, the educated elite shared intellectual pursuits such as philosophy with Muslim counterparts, and studied and practiced medicine in an interdenominational setting. In these endeavors, Jews and Muslims manifested "loyalties of category," to use terminology coined by historian Roy Mottahedeh, that straddled the Muslim and non-Muslim divide, encouraged a certain tolerance, and mitigated the discrimination inherent to the ever-present religious hierarchy.[29]

For all the reasons discussed above, it is not surprising that only rarely did the Jews suffer qua Jews in the Islamic world. The well-known persecutions of the Middle Ages, such as the destructive assault on *dhimmī*s and their houses of worship by the so-called mad Fatimid caliph al-Hakim (ruled 996–1021), were aimed at non-Muslims as a group and not at Christians or Jews per se. The same is true of the devastating conquest of North Africa and Muslim Spain in the 1140s by the puritanical Almohads, in which thousands of Jews and Christians were killed and thousands of others converted to Islam under duress, or fled. The Almohads targeted lax Muslims as well.

▶ See article by Mercedes García-Arenal, pp. 111-129. An exception that proves the rule is the notorious "pogrom" against the Jewish community of Granada, Spain, in 1066, in which the males of the community were killed and the women and children enslaved, as punishment for the haughty behavior of the Jewish vizier Joseph ibn Naghrela. The tragic episode, exceptional as it was in targeting the Jews per se, in reality represents an extreme instance where Muslims retaliated against *dhimmī*s for exceeding the accepted norms of the hierocratic Muslim-*dhimmī* relationship.[30]

The Pact of 'Umar[31]

The Granada episode brings us to the Pact of 'Umar, the most important statement of Islamic policy toward the *dhimmī*s. Notably, the pact guarantees the non-Muslims the very same *amān* that underlies the non-belligerency treaty in the Constitution of Medina, and is in direct continuity with the early policy pioneered by the Prophet and developed further in the conquest treaties.

There are many questions concerning the text of the document. Who wrote it? Was it really 'Umar ibn al-Khaṭṭāb (r. 634–644), the second caliph and companion of the Prophet, or perhaps Caliph 'Umar ibn 'Abd al-'Azīz, who reigned from 717–720 and was known for his piety and rigorous enforcement of Islamic law? What is the provenance and purpose of the stipulations? Why does the document have the strange form of a letter written by the conquered non-Muslim people themselves and listing in such detail the harsh conditions of their subordination, rather than the form of an agreement composed by the conquering caliph or general, in the normal manner of conquest treaties? Why are there different versions of the text, in some cases representing an appeal to the conquering general rather than to the caliph?

Most scholars have been skeptical about the pact's authenticity. Perhaps best known among the doubters is Arthur Stanley Tritton. In his book, *The Caliphs and Their Non-Muslim Subjects: A Critical Study of the Pact of 'Umar*, published in 1930,[32] he compared the text of the pact and its restrictive stipulations with historical evidence of treatment of non-Muslims in the early conquest period and afterward. He showed that these sources show no awareness of the document prior to the beginning of the ninth century. The fact that the pact presents the non-Muslims (Christians, in fact) dictating their own harsh terms of surrender to the caliph 'Umar, rather than the reverse, seemed an additional reason for doubting its genuineness.

The first text Tritton could find containing the elements of the pact was a formulary for a conquest treaty in the law book *Kitab al-umm*, of the jurist al-Shafi'i (767–820), who compiled that collection apparently between ca. 814 and his death. Tritton concluded that the versions of the Pact of 'Umar represented pattern treaties drawn up as an exercise by students in Islamic schools. It was attributed pseudepigraphically to Caliph 'Umar, a companion of the Prophet and one of the "founding fathers" of the Islamic state, and caliph during the earliest phase of the Islamic conquests. Tritton was followed in his skepticism by Antoine Fattal, whose book in French, *Le statut legal des non-Musulmans en pays d'Islam*, is still a standard work on the Pact of 'Umar and on the legal status of non-Muslims in general.[33]

Because of its central importance in Islamic *dhimmī* policy in the Middle Ages, we give the text here in its entirety. It is important to note that, like the conquest treaties and for the same reasons, the many versions of the Pact of 'Umar do not feature the Jews as the petitioners (it is usually Christians). But the Jews were nonetheless subject to the same rules. The division into sections is that of the present writer. Their significance will be discussed below.[34]

See Counterpoint, The Pact of 'Umar, for the text of this document, pp. 72-73.

In an important article, Albrecht Noth persuasively argued that many of the clauses in the pact reflect the early conquest period and that, in its original context, it was not devised to humiliate, let alone persecute, non-Muslims. It was meant to erect boundaries differentiating between the tiny Muslim minority and the vast majority of conquered non-Muslim peoples. In order to strengthen their own identity, the Muslims needed to distinguish themselves from the local populations, to put the non-Muslims in their place, to keep them in a humble position and ensure they remained in the low rank to which they had been assigned by the hierarchical religion.[35]

This makes sense. I have argued, further, in answer to the skeptics who dismiss the document as a forgery, that the pact as we know it, though placed in the mouth of the conquered people, actually imitates the form of a petition requesting a decree, a normal procedure in Islamic society, with the non-Muslims suing for peace and stipulating their own restrictions—in return for various guarantees of security. The caliph ʿUmar confirms their request (in the "confirmation clause"), turning the petition into a decree granting the non-Muslims' request for "security for ourselves, our offspring, our property, and the people of our religious community."[36] In her book *Non-Muslims in the Early Islamic Empire*, Milka Levy-Rubin argues that many of the regulations imposed upon the non-Muslims in the pact, in particular those regarding special clothing, honorific names, outward display of religion, showing deference to Muslims, bearing arms, and so on, are based not on Byzantine laws regarding the Jews (others, she concedes, are) but on Sasanian models. Among Zoroastrian Iranians, such rules supported a rigid, discriminatory social hierarchy separating the privileged classes from the lowly farmers, artisans, and tradesmen.

Levy-Rubin claims—not conclusively in my opinion—that the regulations in the Pact of ʿUmar, adopted from Sasanian practice, are similarly discriminatory and humiliating rather than, as Noth claims, simply a means of differentiating between Muslims and non-Muslims.[37] Levy-Rubin brings new evidence, as well, of Muslim rulers attempting to enforce the regulations of the pact.[38] The evidence, however, does not show the extent to which the enforcement was successful, that is, to what extent *dhimmīs* and others actually complied. Instances of violence against non-Muslims for violating the laws are evidence not of compliance but precisely the opposite. They indicate consistent evasion. My contention, along with other scholars with whom Levy-Rubin disagrees, is that the many attempts to enforce the rules show how often and to what extent they were observed in the breach. This must mean that local and even central authorities, as well as local Muslim populations, exercised a rather laissez-faire attitude regarding the official policy dictated by Islamic law. With general acquiescence on both sides, and absent the acute religious tension that accompanied the theologically tinged hierarchy of Christianity and Judaism, a certain permeability of the boundaries separating Muslims from their non-Muslim neighbors was possible. The Islamic model of hierarchy was also flexible, and this flexibility muted to a certain extent the stipulations of the pact, which, as time passed, became humiliating.[39]

Returning to the Pact of 'Umar itself, the earliest datable version of the standard version as we know it, with the letterform and the characteristic components, comes from the middle of the ninth century.[40] In a new hypothesis regarding its origins, Levy-Rubin contends that the standard version was but one of several alternative documents regulating the conduct of the non-Muslim subjects, some of which became absorbed into the pact proper.[41] Whatever the case, it is clear that once the pact achieved canonical status, it became part of the holy law of Islam, the shari'a, and as such, apart from minor changes or elaborations from time to time, it remained a fixed and stable guide to policy, not subject to arbitrary manipulation by rulers.[42]

Along with the annual poll tax, which, burdensome as it was for the Jewish poor (though lightened by charitable subsidies from the community)[43] functioned as a kind of guarantee of security, the *dhimma* system worked tolerably well most of the time, imparting a sense of security for non-Muslims and integration into society. When from time to time the system broke down and Jews (usually along with Christians) suffered from extreme discrimination, even physical violence and forced conversion, they understood this as a temporary lapse (on rare occasions lasting many years) of the *dhimma* system and counted on an eventual return to normalcy. This general feeling of security most of the time is what made possible the remarkable immersion of Jews in the culture of Arab-Islamic society during the high Islamic Middle Ages, which will be described in subsequent chapters of this volume.

▷ On the "lachrymose conception of Jewish history," see the prologue, pp. 29-30.

1. A longer version of this essay, entitled "Islamic Attitudes and Policies," appears in *The Cambridge History of Judaism*, vol. 5, *Jews in the Medieval Islamic World*, edited by Robert Chazan and Marina Rustow, reproduced here with permission.

2. On the Jewish wives of Qurashi pagans, see Michael Lecker, "A Note on Early Marriage Links between Qurashis and Jewish Women," *Jerusalem Studies in Arabic and Islam* 10 (1987): 17–39.

3. Fred M. Donner, *Muhammad and the Believers: At the Origins of Islam* (Cambridge, MA: Belknap Press of Harvard University Press, 2010), 68–74, based on his article "From Believers to Muslims: Confessional Self-identity in the Early Islamic Community," *Al-Ahbath* 50–51 (2002–3): 9–53.

4. In *Journeys in Holy Lands: The Evolution of the Abraham-Ishmael Legends in Islamic Exegesis* (Albany: State University of New York Press, 1990), Reuven Firestone describes what he calls a culture of biblical storytelling in pre-Islamic Arabia. Muslims were permitted, even encouraged, to relate stories handed down by the Banu Isra'il, but later this license was revoked. M. Kister, "Ḥaddithu 'an Bani Isra'il wa-la kharaja," *Israel Oriental Society* 2 (1972): 215–39.

5. See discussion in Yohanan Friedmann, *Tolerance and Coercion in Islam: Interfaith Relations in the Muslim Tradition* (Cambridge: Cambridge University Press, 2003), 87–120.

6. Rudi Paret, "Sura 2:256: Lā ikrāha fi d-dini; Toleranz oder Resignation?" *Der Islam* 45 (1969): 299–300.

7. On the Byzantine and Sasanian taxation systems, see Antoine Fattal, *Le statut légal des non-Musulmans en pays d'Islam* (Beirut: Imprimerie Catholique, 1958), 317–23.

8. M. J. Kister, "An Yadin' (Qur'an, 9:29)," *Arabica* 11 (1964): 272–78; Mark R. Cohen, *Under Crescent and Cross: The Jews in the Middle Ages* (Princeton, NJ: Princeton University Press, 2008); Uri Rubin, "Quran and Tafsir: The Case of 'an yadin,'" *Der Islam* 7 (1993): 133–43. For varying interpretations of 'an yadin by Islamic jurists and accounts in historical sources of how the *jizya* was collected at different times and different places, see Fattal, *Le statut légal des non-Musulmans en pays d'Islam*, 286–91.

9. The Qur'anic allusion is in 33:27–28. See M. J. Kister, "The Massacre of the Banu Qurayza: A Re-examination of the Evidence," *Jerusalem Studies in Arabic and Islam* 8 (1986): 61–96.

10. This event is the subject of heated polemical debate, some citing it as evidence of Muhammad's "anti-Semitic" cruelty, others denying the veracity of the story. A sampling of the literature is cited and discussed in Cohen, *Under Crescent and Cross*, 47n18.

11. See, among other studies, Michael Lecker, *The "Constitution of Medina": Muḥammad's First Legal Document* (Princeton, NJ: Darwin Press, 2004). Its authenticity seems unassailable today. Even such a normally skeptical scholar as Patricia Crone upholds the authenticity of the constitution in *Slaves on Horses: The Evolution of the Islamic Polity* (Cambridge: Cambridge University Press), 7. See also Donner, *Muhammad and the Believers*, 72.

12. The two versions, the other one being Abu 'Ubayd's *Kitab al-Amwal,* are conveniently printed together in Lecker's book.

13. See Muhammad Hamidullah, trans. and ed., *The First Written Constitution in the World: An Important Document of the Time of the Holy Prophet*, 3rd ed. (Lahore, Pakistan: Sh. Muhammad Ashraf, 1981).

14. Donner, *Muhammad and the Believers*, 72–74.

15. Lecker, *"Constitution of Medina,"* 143.

16. For Donner, in keeping with his main thesis, *mu'minūn* refers to all believers, including Jews and Christians, while *muslimūn* refers to the new converts from paganism. Later on the term *muslimūn* took on the more restrictive meaning of a new faith distinctive from Judaism and Christianity. Donner, *Muhammad and the Believers*, 57–58, 71–72.

17. Abu 'Ubayd's recension, in *Kitab al-amwal*, ed. Muhammad Khalil Harras (Cairo: Maktabat al-Kulliyat al Azhariya Dar al-Fikr, 1975), 260–64, has *min* in place of *ma'a*. Uri Rubin prefers that version and interprets it to mean *"umma* of [i.e., "consisting of"] believers," in keeping with Qur'anic usage of this preposition. "The 'Constitution of Medina': Some Notes," *Studia Islamica* 62 (1985): 14. The result, however, is the same: the Jews are part of the *umma*.

18. As does Moshe Gil in "The Constitution of Medina: A Reconsideration," *Israel Oriental Studies* 4 (1974): 44–66. The article is reprinted with some important changes, responding to his critics, in *Jews in Islamic Countries in the Middle Ages*, trans. David Strassler (Leiden: Brill, 2004), 21–45.

19. Michael Lecker, "Did Muhammad Conclude Treaties with the Jewish Tribes Nadir, Qurayza, and Qaynuqa'?" *Israel Oriental Studies* 17 (1997): 29–36. For another explanation for their exclusion, see Rubin, "The 'Constitution of Medina': Some Notes," 9–10, which argues that the *umma* constituted a unity of Arabs, including Jewish allies of Arab tribes, based on *locality*, and that the three major tribes were excluded from the document since they lived outside the central area of Medina, among their date palm groves and near their fortresses.

20. Moshe Gil buttresses his theory that Muhammad had an "anti-Jewish" policy from the very outset in Medina by dating the constitution before the battle of Badr, which took place eighteen months after the Prophet's arrival in the oasis.

21. In *Non-Muslims in the Early Islamic Empire* (Cambridge: Cambridge University Press, 2011), chapter 1, Milka Levy-Rubin claims that the term *amān,* which does not occur in the Qur'an, imitates and in effect translates the Greek *pistis* (equivalent to Latin *fides*), meaning "protection and assurance of safety," presumably the term used by conquered people in Byzantine territory in suing the Muslims for peace. I am grateful to Dr. Levy-Rubin for allowing me to read the manuscript of her book. Said Amir Arjomand adopts the view of R. Serjeant, who took the word *mu'minūn* in the constitution to be a derivative of the word *amān* and understood *mu'minūn* not as "believers," as it meant later on, but as members of a security pact, to be contrasted with "Muslims." Attempting to preserve the connotation "believers," he translates the word "faithful covenanters [under God's security]," among whom the Jews are to be numbered. Like Lecker, Gil, in *Jews in Islamic Countries* (27; in a paragraph not included in the original article, "The Constitution of Medina," 50), states that *mu'minūn* derives from the word *amān* and means "those who provide security," though he does not take the step of emending *umma* to *amana*. He believes that *umma* simply means "a group or a community" (ibid.). Nor does he claim, as does Lecker, that the second part of the document is a non-belligerency pact.

22. For a recent discussion of the Constitution of Medina, see Said Amir Arjomand, "The Constitution of Medina: A Sociolegal Interpretation of Muhammad's Acts of Foundation of the *Umma*," *International Journal of Middle East Studies* 41 (2009): 555–75. Arjomand accepts Lecker's subdivision of the documents, however, though he tentatively suggests subdividing Lecker's second part into two and considers the third section to be a supplement, a separate agreement, or "defense pact," with the client Jewish tribe of Banu Qurayza, called "the Jews of Aws" in the text; Arjomand, "The Constitution of Medina," 560. If the third section constitutes a separate agreement, in Arjomand's opinion (which differs from Lecker's), at least one of the main Jewish tribes was originally included in the *umma*. He asserts, though, that "[t]he critical division is between the first two deeds," that is, in agreement with Lecker's subdivision. Ibid., 561.

23. See the important article by Mahmoud Ayoub, "Dhimmah in Qur'an and Hadith," *Arab Studies Quarterly* 5 (Spring 1993): 172–82. Lecker (*"Constitution of Medina,"* 146) notes that the variant *dhimma* occurs in two late (fourteenth-century) recensions of that document, which could mean that later authorities recognized that there was a connection between the granting of security in the constitution and the *dhimma* policy, based on security, that became standard following Muhammad's death.

24. Jamsheed Choksy, *Conflict and Cooperation: Zoroastrian Subalterns and Muslim Elites in Medieval Iranian Society* (New York: Columbia University Press, 1997).

25. The authenticity of the conquest treaties, like the biographies of the Prophet and kindred literature, has evoked skepticism, but the very variety of details bespeaks a large measure of credibility. See Albrecht Noth, "Die literarische überlieferten Verträge der Eroberungzeit als historische Quellen für die Behandlung der unterworfenen Nicht-Muslims durch ihre neuen muslimischen Oberherren," in *Studien zum Minderheitenproblem im Islam* I, ed. T. Nagel et al. (Bonn: Selbstverlag des Orientalischen Seminars der Universität, 1973), 282–304. To my mind the case has been settled by Milka Levy-Rubin in her 2011 book, *Non-Muslims in the Early Islamic Empire*, chapter 1. Taking the longue durée approach, she shows that the treaties substantially resemble compacts with conquered peoples in Greco-Roman and Iranian antiquity – and even have distant echoes in the ancient Near Eastern past.

26. See Cohen, *Under Crescent and Cross*, 169–74, where the expression *yaḥqin dimā'hu*, "spares his life" (172n123), echoes phraseology in Islamic peace treaties. See Levy-Rubin, *Non-Muslims in the Early Islamic Empire*, chapter 1 (*ʿalā ḥaqn dimā'ihim*).

27. On *dhimmī* judicial autonomy and its limits, see Fattal, *Le statut légal des non-Musulmans en pays d'Islam*, chapter 8, and Néophyte Edelby, "L'autonomie législative des chrétiens en terre d'Islam," *Archives d'histoire du droit oriental* 5 (Brussels, 1950–51): 307–51.

28. On non-Muslims serving in Muslim government offices, comparing the normative prohibition with the abundant evidence from historical sources of rampant overstepping of the prohibition, see Fattal, *Le statut légal des non-Musulmans en pays d'Islam*, 236–263. For a recent discussion of the issue see Munʿim Sirry, "The Public Role of Dhimmīs during ʿAbbāsid Times," *Bulletin of the School of Oriental and African Studies* 74 (2011), 187–204.

29. See Roy P. Mottahedeh, *Loyalty and Leadership in an Early Islamic Society* (Princeton, NJ: Princeton University Press, 1980), 108–15; Cohen, *Under Crescent and Cross*, 246.

30. Among the many discussions of this episode is Moshe Perlmann, "Eleventh-Century Andalusian Authors on the Jews of Granada," *Proceedings of the American Academy of Jewish Research* 18 (1948–1949): 843–61.

31. See Mark R. Cohen, "What Was the Pact of ʿUmar: A Literary-Historical Study," *Jerusalem Studies in Arabic and Islam* 23 (1999): 100–57, and other literature cited there. To this should be added Milka Levy-Rubin's *Non-Muslims in the Early Islamic Empire* (see note 21 above).

32. A. S. Tritton, *The Caliphs and Their Non-Muslim Subjects: A Critical Study of the Pact of ʿUmar* (London: H. Milford and Oxford University Press, 1930; repr., London: F. Cass, 1970).

33. Fattal, *Le statut légal des non-Musulmans en pays d'Islam*.

34. Translation taken from Fattal, *Le statut légal des non-Musulmans en pays d'Islam*, 61–63.

35. Albrecht Noth, "Abgrenzungsprobleme zwischen Muslimen und Nicht-Muslimen: Die 'Bedingungen ʿUmars (aš-šurūt al-ʿumariyya)' unter einem anderen Aspekt gelesen," *Jerusalem Studies in Arabic and Islam* 9 (1987): 290–315; English translation in Robert Hoyland, ed., *Muslims and Others in Early Islamic Society* (Aldershot, Hants: Burlington, VT: Ashgate, 2004).

36. Marina Rustow discusses the decree given in response to a petition (*al-tawqīʿ ʿalā al-qiṣāṣ*) on the basis of documents from the Cairo Geniza, in "A Petition to a Woman at the Fatimid Court (413–414 A.H./1022–23 C.E.)," *Bulletin of the School of Oriental and African Studies* 73 (2010): 1–27.

37. Levy-Rubin, *Non-Muslims in the Early Islamic Empire*, chapter 3.

38. Ibid., chapter 5.

39. See the discussion in Cohen, *Under Crescent and Cross*, part 4, drawing inspiration from the book *Homo Hierarchicus* by the French social anthropologist Louis Dumont and from other social anthropologists and sociologists.

40. See Cohen, "What Was the Pact of ʿUmar," 110–16, 119–20.

41. Milka Levy-Rubin, "*Shurut ʿumar* and Its Alternatives: The Legal Debate on the Status of the *Dhimmīs*," *Jerusalem Studies in Arabic and Islam* 30 (2005): 170–206, incorporated into chapter 2 in *Non-Muslims in the Early Islamic Empire*. A similar approach is taken independently by Daniel Miller in his dissertation, "From Catalogue to Canon: The Rise of the Petition to ʿUmar among Legal Traditions Governing Non-Muslims in Medieval Islamicate Societies" (PhD dissertation, University of Missouri – Kansas City, 2000).

42. For an episode illustrating the just manner in which the Pact of ʿUmar was applied in a Jewish case from the late Middle Ages, see Mark R. Cohen, "Jews in the Mamluk Environment: The Crisis of 1442 (A Geniza Study)," *Bulletin of the School of Oriental and African Studies* 47 (1984): 425–48.

43. Mark R. Cohen, *Poverty and Charity in the Jewish Community of Medieval Egypt* (Princeton, NJ: Princeton University Press, 2005), 235.

The Pact of 'Umar:
A Controversial Document

The Pact of 'Umar ('ahd 'umar; also *al-shurut al-'umariyya*, "Stipulations of 'Umar") is the basic document outlining the obligations of the non-Muslims living in *Dar al-Islam* (territory ruled by Islam) and defining the relationship of the *ahl al-dhimma*, or *dhimmīs*, "protected people," with Muslims and with the Islamic state.

Mark R. Cohen

'Abd al-Rahman b. Ghanm related: When 'Umar b. al-Khattab, may God be pleased with him, made peace with the Christian inhabitants of Syria, we wrote to him as follows:

[Cover letter]
In the name of God, the Merciful and Compassionate.
This is a letter to the servant of God, 'Umar, the Commander of the Faithful, from the Christians of such-and-such city.

[The Letter]
When you came against us, we asked you for a guarantee of security (*amān*) for ourselves, our offspring, our property, and the people of our religious community (*milla*), and we undertook the following obligations toward you, namely:
– We shall not build in our cities or in their vicinity new monasteries, churches, hermitages, or monks' cells, nor shall we repair, by night or day, any of them that have fallen into ruin or which are located in the quarters of the Muslims.
– We shall keep our gates wide open for passersby and travelers.
– We shall provide three days' food and lodging to any Muslims who pass our way.
– We shall not give shelter in our churches or in our homes to any spy, nor hide him from the Muslims.
– We shall not teach our children the Qur'an.
– We shall not hold public religious ceremonies.
– We shall not seek to proselytize anyone.
– We shall not prevent any of our kin from embracing Islam if they so desire.
– We shall show deference to the Muslims and shall rise from our seats when they wish it.
– We shall not attempt to resemble the Muslims in any way with regard to their dress, as, for example, with the qalansuwa [a conical cap], the turban, footwear, or parting of the hair.
– We shall not speak as they do, nor shall we adopt their kunyas [honorific bynames].
– We shall not ride on saddles.

– We shall not wear swords or bear weapons of any kind, or even carry them on our persons.

– We shall not engrave Arabic inscriptions on our seals.

– We shall not sell alcoholic beverages.

– We shall dress in our traditional fashion wherever we may be, and we shall bind the zunnār [distinctive belt] around our waists.

– We shall not display our crosses or our books anywhere in the roads or markets of the Muslims.

– We shall only beat the clappers in our churches very quietly.

– We shall not raise our voices in our church services, nor in the presence of Muslims.

– We shall not go outside on Palm Sunday or Easter, nor shall we raise our voices in our funeral processions.

– We shall not display lights in any of the roads of the Muslims or in the marketplaces.

– We shall not come near them with our funeral processions [or: we shall not bury our dead near the Muslims].

– We shall not take slaves who have been allotted to the Muslims.

– We shall not build our homes higher than theirs.

[Amendment Clause]
When I brought the letter to 'Umar, may God be pleased with him, he added: "We shall not strike any Muslim."

[Forfeiture Clause]
We accept these conditions for ourselves and for the members of our religious community, and in return we are to be given protection (*amān*). If we in any way violate these conditions which we have accepted and for which we stand surety, we forfeit our covenant of protection (*dhimma*) and shall become liable to the penalties for rebelliousness and sedition.

[Confirmation Clause]
Then 'Umar, may God be pleased with him, wrote to him (to 'Abd al-Rahman b. Ghanm): "Confirm what they asked, but add two clauses, which I make conditional upon them in addition to those which they have made conditional upon themselves. They are: 'They shall not buy anyone made prisoner by the Muslims,' and 'Whoever strikes a Muslim with deliberate intent shall forfeit the protection of this pact.'"

Chapter II
In Islamic Lands

Jews and Muslims in the Eastern Islamic World
Marina Rustow

The Islamic world housed the majority of the world's Jews for most of the medieval period, and the Jewish communities of the Islamic world were responsible for many of the institutions, texts, and practices that would define Judaism well into the modern era. Islamic rule remade the very conditions—intellectual, demographic, economic—in which Jewish communities lived, and created a civilization that enabled them to thrive. But just as much of medieval Jewish history is about Jews under Islamic rule, so, too, is much of the history of the early Islamic world about non-Muslims.

In 632 C.E., when armies under the banner of Islam began conquering territories outside the Arabian Peninsula, the first caliphs found themselves ruling over a population the overwhelming majority of which were Jews, Christians, Zoroastrians, and Buddhists. Although it is common to refer to these groups as non-Muslim "minorities," in fact, Muslims were a numerical minority in their own empire for the early centuries of their rule. They would become an absolute majority only in the ninth or tenth century, depending on the region.[1] The early stages of the Islamic conquests brought the Jewish populations of the Near East under a single empire that maintained its political unity for three centuries – and its cultural unity for much longer.

Marina Rustow

Marina Rustow holds the Charlotte Bloomberg Professorship in the Humanities at Johns Hopkins University at Baltimore, where she is an associate professor in the Department of History. She is the author of *Heresy and the Politics of Community: The Jews of the Fatimid Caliphate* (Cornell University Press, 2008) and coeditor, with Robert Chazan, of *The Cambridge History of Judaism*, volumes 5 and 6 (Cambridge University Press, forthcoming).

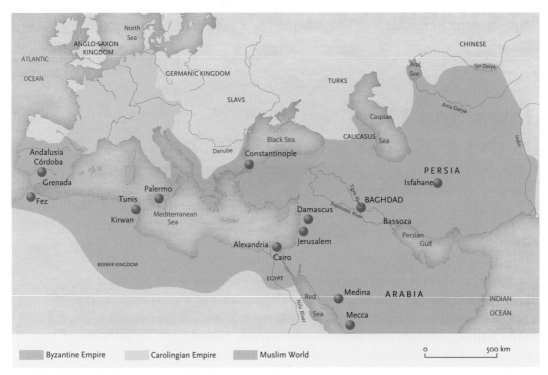

The expansion of Islam in the ninth century.

Jews and Muslims in the early Islamic Empire

The age of the unified caliphate saw the rule of three dynasties: the Rashidun, or "rightly guided," caliphs of Medina (632–661), so called because they had known Muhammad personally, belonged to the tribe of Quraysh, and were his relatives by blood or marriage; the Umayyads (661–750), who built their capital at Damascus, an ancient city with a solidly Roman core; and the Abbasids (750–1258), who founded the new capital of Baghdad on the Tigris River in 762, north of the ruined Sasanian capital of Ctesiphon. It was during this period of unity that the Islamic Empire reached its greatest territorial extent.

Under the Rashidun caliphs, Muslim armies conquered the Levant, Egypt, and coastal North Africa into Libya, dealing a severe blow to the Byzantine Empire and putting an end to the Sasanian shahs of Iraq and Iran. In the east, they pressed as far as Khorasan (modern Afghanistan and Turkmenistan), taking Balkh, an ancient center of Buddhism and Zoroastrianism, and Merv, a great emporium on the trade route to China. The Umayyads pushed the boundaries of their empire as far as the Indus River in the east and the Atlantic coasts of Africa and Europe in the west. The Abbasids extended their borders into Sicily, Crete, the Horn of Africa, and deeper into Central Asia. Each successive stage of the conquests brought the conquerors into contact with new subject peoples, and each move of the central government brought the caliphal bureaucracy into contact with the administrative and legal traditions of the previous rulers, especially those of the Byzantine and Sasanian Empires.

Conversion to the new religion was a slow, gradual, and initially restricted process. At first, the conquering Muslim armies lived in relative isolation from most of the conquered population, in garrison cities (sing. *miṣr*, pl. *amṣār*) such as Kufa, Basra, and Mosul in Iraq, Fustat in Egypt, and Qayrawan in Ifriqiya (central North Africa; today's Tunisia).[2] But there were also non-Muslims in the *amṣar*; conversion therefore began as it had several centuries earlier when inhabitants of the Roman Empire abandoned pagan worship for Christianity: in dense population centers. But as in any preindustrial society, the vast majority of people were peasants and nomads spread out across the countryside, or else nomadic pastoralists.

The Islamic conquests did not, then, have the character of an explosive or sudden transformation. There were palpable continuities between the former Byzantine and Sasanian Empires and the new Islamic one. In Egypt, the region for which the most evidence has survived, the Muslim rulers retained Christian experts to administer their bureaucracies; many early Islamic administrative documents from Egypt are written in both Greek and Arabic.[3] The vast majority of the populace—peasants who struggled to pay the tax collector—would have felt little change as they rendered old but renamed taxes to new masters.

❯ See article by Mark R. Cohen, p. 68.

For some groups, to be sure, there were radical, even traumatic changes. Zoroastrians no longer benefited from the state sponsorship their religion had enjoyed under the Sasanian shahs. Chalcedonian Christians (those in communion with the Byzantine Church) who had lived under Byzantine rule now found themselves stranded in alien territory. But for other Christian groups—the Miaphysites of Egypt (Copts) and Western Asia (Jacobites and Armenians)—and for Jews, after the initial cataclysm of conquest, Islamic rule presented a relief from theologically based oppression.[4] The conquests may have been even less traumatic for Jews than for others. Jews had lived as a tolerated minority under Christian rule since the fourth century; they continued to live as a tolerated minority under Islam. Under the Byzantines, Jewish religious practice had been legal but restricted; similar restrictions continued under Islamic law, while others were lifted. And though Sasanian Jews had found a fairly stable modus vivendi under the shahs, under the Abbasids they took an active part in the creation of a great imperial culture.

> ❝*Islamic rule not only transformed Judaism but enabled its consolidation and diffusion.*❞

For these reasons and others, Islamic rule brought a new latitude to Jewish communal life. Eventually, it would also bring about a complete revolution in Jewish culture—both the high culture of the educated elite and the everyday life of the

77

average Jewish inhabitants of cities, towns, and the countryside. By the tenth century, the rabbinic forms of Judaism that had begun to develop in Mesopotamia and Palestine in late antiquity had spread far beyond those regions and taken root in a huge swath of land, from Iberia to Khorasan. In that sense, Islamic rule not only transformed Judaism but enabled its consolidation and diffusion. The main transformations can be divided into five rubrics: politics, demography, economics, language, and technology.

Politics in a united empire

The three major Jewish communities of antiquity (in Mesopotamia, Palestine, and Egypt) had been divided between Sasanian and Byzantine rule. Now, the effects of living in a politically unified realm—one that also happened to represent, increasingly, the pinnacle of world civilization—granted them new possibilities and opportunities.

Political unity entailed, first and foremost, freedom of movement. There were fewer boundaries to cross and fewer contested zones to hinder migration and trade. During the early Islamic centuries, many Jews moved from the three historical centers to towns across the Islamic world. Because non-Muslims' legal status was now consistent across the empire, having paid one's taxes in one area entitled one to travel to another.[5] The consolidation of large areas under Islamic rule also created new means of geographic mobility. Fresh trade routes opened; the Umayyad and Abbasid caliphs built roads and other transport infrastructure in the interests of taxation, information gathering, and communication with provincial officials.[6] Private postal carriers came to use that infrastructure as well, facilitating communication in writing and travel across distances previously unimaginable.

Islamic rule thus created both the occasion and the means for Jews to found new communities, strengthen old ones, and develop new networks of exchange and mobility. The net effect on Judaism as a system of beliefs and practices was its relative standardization across a vaster territory than ever before. To be sure, in any preindustrial society, cultural integration tends to be limited, and, in any case, greater among the urban, literate elites than the rural masses. But Jews under Islamic rule became a disproportionately urban population. Despite the vast distances that divided them from one another, they developed a coherent cultural koine and a pattern of geographic mobility that is truly remarkable when compared with other premodern societies.

One measure of that cultural integration was the rise of the *geonim* of Iraq as the spiritual leaders of the Jewish world. The *geonim* (sing., *gaon*) were the heads of the two rabbinic academies (yeshivot) in the Mesopotamian towns of Sura (on a main subsidiary of the Euphrates called the Nahr Sura) and Pumbedita (far-

> ### *Responsa*
>
> The dispersion of the Jews throughout the world brought decision-makers (specialists in the law) to provide written answers to legal questions before them. These written analyses, equivalent to Islamic fatwas, were called *teshuvot* (*responsa* or "answers") or *She'elot u-teshuvot* ("questions and answers"), abbreviated *Shut*. The Latin term *responsa* is often used in the literature of European languages. Teshuvot are valuable for the researcher, since they reflect the socio-historical details of Jewish life in history.

ther north on the Euphrates, about five kilometers upstream from al-Falluja near the Nahr 'Isa). Although by the time the yeshivot begin to be mentioned in gaonic literature they are already assumed to be ancient, they owed their institutional development to the kinds of changes wrought by Islamic rule. The yeshivot came to serve as high courts, centers of learning, and bodies of governance over the Jewish communities of Iraq, Iran, and beyond; in turn, they depended on those communities to supply them with disciples and monetary contributions. Only with Islamic rule were the *geonim* able to develop significant networks of followers, and they could not survive without donations and students from abroad. Thousands of surviving letters, legal responsa, and copies of sections of the Babylonian Talmud sent throughout the Mediterranean basin attest to the influence the yeshivot developed outside their immediate geographic orbit.[7]

But that influence also had limits. The yeshivot had little say over the quotidian affairs of far-off Jewish communities: local rabbinic leaders decided pressing legal and ritual cases without waiting weeks or months for ships or caravans to bring them directives from Iraq. Nonetheless, those leaders—and many of their followers—offered the Iraqi yeshivot obeisance and fealty by sending them formal queries (often about the meaning of passages in the Talmud) together with donations. In exchange, the yeshivot composed responsa (answers to queries) and granted local scholars official titles and the authority to lead their communities independently. Responsa came to constitute the primary literary output of the yeshivot and their most important means of contact with their followers. The circulation of responsa reflects the organization of Jews into networks of towns and cities more closely linked with each other than with the surrounding countryside.

Demographic changes: Urbanization

One of the most important long-term effects of the Islamic conquests was migration to cities. The cities of the Islamic Empire became centers of territorial bureaucracies, and interurban links themselves tended to encourage geographic mobility and the tighter integration of the elites. Urbanization was a change palpable on every level of society, affecting those in the countryside as well. If the Jews of the Middle

Ages were a disproportionately urban population, the roots of that urbanization are to be sought during this period. Not all Jews moved to the major cities following the Islamic conquests, but most lived in dense settlements of some sort, be they cities or towns. Muslims, too, were disproportionately urban at the beginning of the conquest period, though soon new landholders who were connected with the ruling regime began to proliferate throughout the countryside.

In the early Abbasid period, the Jews of Iraq had tended to work in commerce, crafts, and other town-based occupations. The Iraqi belletrist al-Jahiz (d. 869) described Jews as "dyers, tanners, barbers, butchers, and tinkers," and while the generalization was typical of his literary style and cannot be taken as a literal description of all Jews, it is significant that he emphasized that Jews practiced town-based professions rather than agriculture. Al-Jahiz's point was a different one: that Jews worked in despised professions, while Christians boasted among their ranks courtiers, state officers, physicians, and money changers. But by the tenth century, the Jews also had their share of courtiers and bureaucrats in Baghdad and elsewhere. Before the end of the ninth century, there are also traces of Iraqi Jews in long-distance commerce.[8]

> "But by the tenth century, the Jews also had their share of courtiers and bureaucrats in Baghdad and elsewhere."

As to why Jews, Christians, and Zorastrians alike came to abandon the land, one spur may have been the Muslims' imposition of the *kharāj* (land tax) on non-Muslim villages. The *kharāj* was a collective tax, and that meant that when individuals fled to cities, they increased the tax burden on those who remained behind. Urbanization itself thus made life for peasants more difficult, and ultimately, the burden of subsistence farming and the increasing viability of earning a livelihood through crafts and trade encouraged many to move to towns and cities. Progressive urbanization is reflected in an important legislative change that the rabbinic authorities of Iraq promulgated a generation after Baghdad was founded. According to the Babylonian Talmud, debts on the estates of deceased persons could be collected only from real property (land). Between 786 and 787, two of the three central Jewish legal authorities, the *gaon* of Sura and the *exilarch* (who ran an academy in the shadow of Sura and was responsible for representing the Jews at the caliph's court), decreed that debts on estates of the deceased could now be collected on movable property.[9] The new law came about because so many Jews had abandoned the land for towns and cities as to make the old ruling impracticable. And even those who remained in the countryside were now well connected with urban centers: Arab geographers report, for instance, a regular mail route between Pumbedita and Baghdad, a distance of about 62 kilometers (39 miles).

▶ See Nota bene, Bagdad, pp. 102-105. The rise of Baghdad as the most important city of the Islamic world bore profound implications for Jewish culture. By the late ninth or early tenth century, the two Iraqi yeshivot left their seats in Pumbedita and Sura and moved to the capital.[10] At Baghdad, both institutions came to be headed—for the first time—by cosmopolitan and outward-looking *geonim* educated beyond their own confines. Thinkers such as Saadia, Shemu'el ben Hofni (ca. 998–1013), and Hayya bar Sherira transformed the role of the *gaon* by composing works that went far beyond the boundaries of the traditional formats of the responsum and the legal compendium. They also added new fields of inquiry to the intellectual range of Jewish religious leaders, including philosophical theology (Arabic, *kalām*), hitherto a preserve of Muslim and Jewish Karaite thinkers.

The work of the tenth-century *geonim* and other cosmopolitan Jewish intellectuals reflects a culture of exchange that took place in public and semiprivate literary salons, known in Arabic as *majālis* (sing., *majlis*). These gatherings served as forums for the patronage of poets and other writers, and for philosophical and theological debates on every conceivable question. They reflect a relative lack of boundaries between thinkers and writers of different religions, a phenomenon without parallel in the medieval Christian world in this period.[11]

Provincial Jewish life in Palestine

Palestine followed a different trajectory from Iraq. It had been more densely urbanized under Roman and Byzantine rule, and its cities were relatively well developed, even if most (except Caesarea) were relatively small; but the north, where much of the Jewish population was concentrated, had been dominated by large villages, and the Palestinian Talmud reflects this mixed urban and rural setting.[12] The Jews of Roman Palestine were in many ways provincials, embracing Roman culture in certain ways but resisting it in others.[13] Under Islamic rule, Palestine retained its provincial character. It formed a part of the much larger administrative unit of Syria (*bilād al-Shām* in Arabic, comprising modern Syria, Lebanon, Jordan, Israel, and the Palestinian territories); unlike the Jews of Iraq, those of Palestine did not have an imperial capital at their doorstep.

That said, the fairly well-developed port system on the Syrian littoral meant that Palestine housed networks of trade and commerce, both local and long-distance. The Umayyads refortified the seaports of Tyre and Acre. Although Caesarea contracted and declined under the Muslims, the notion that the early Arab rulers kept their distance from the sea in favor of inland cities is not entirely true. While the political centers tended to be concentrated inland—Ramla was founded as the district (*jund*) capital of Palestine, and Tiberias, the main center of Palestinian Jewish life after the failure of the Jewish revolt of 132–35 C.E., became the capital of the *jund* of al-Urdunn—inhabitants of the Sham had access to the sea, to shipping, and to the system of port cities in the Mediterranean basin.

Tiberias was both a center of Abbasid government administration and the most important center of Jewish culture in Palestine through the middle of the tenth century. The two facts were related. A teacher of Saadia Gaon, Abu Kathir Yahya ibn Zakariyya (d. ca. 932–33), was an Abbasid official (*kātib*) in Tiberias, and he typified the tendency of the learned elite to serve in government bureaus. He also reflects an important phenomenon among Jews under Islamic rule: religious specialists and communal leaders frequently served as government administrators and courtiers, many using their political prestige on behalf of their communities and mediating for them at the royal courts.

Tiberias was also home to the Palestinian yeshiva well into the tenth century and the city where Jewish biblical scholars undertook the most extensive and, ulti-

▶ See Nota bene, Saadia Gaon, pp. 758–761.

mately, authoritative project to stabilize the text of the Hebrew Bible and provide it with vowels and cantillation signs: the *masora*. Qur'anic scholars in the eighth century had developed some similar techniques of stabilizing their sacred text, and it is possible that the Masoretic scholars were indebted to them. But in the study of scripture and language, the influence flowed in all directions. Arabic-speaking Jews, Christians, and Muslims collaborated in gaining access to the contents of the Hebrew Bible/Old Testament; the entire project of translating the biblical text to Arabic was one shared among scholars of the three religions.

Tiberias's religious prestige ultimately ceded to that of Jerusalem. Islamic rule had allowed the Jews to settle permanently in Jerusalem for the first time since the failed revolt of 132–35 C.E., when the Roman emperor Hadrian had exiled them. While in 638, the Arab conqueror of the city, 'Umar ibn al-Khattab, had excluded the Jews from the city, drawing up a treaty that preserved the status quo ante in the interests of the Christian majority; eventually, after further negotiation, Jews resettled there.[14] Initially, they came to Jerusalem from elsewhere in Palestine, especially Tiberias; later, Jews from all over the Islamic and even the Christian world migrated there. They came in especially great numbers from the Islamic

> *Islamic rule had allowed the Jews to settle permanently in Jerusalem for the first time since the failed revolt of 132–35 C.E., when the Roman emperor Hadrian had exiled them.*

East: in the eleventh century and perhaps earlier, Jerusalem housed an entire Persian-speaking neighborhood. Around the middle of the tenth century, the yeshiva left Tiberias for Jerusalem, in circumstances poorly understood, and enjoyed a period of particular strength and stability just when the Iraqi yeshivot were being forced into temporary closure ca. 1040.

Jerusalem remained a major center for Jews and Christians, but it was also the theater of Islamic triumphalist monument-building. The Umayyad caliph 'Abd al-Malik (685–705) began building the Dome of the Rock (Qubbat al-Sakhra) on the site of the Temple Mount, and its location and physical form constituted direct challenges to Judaism, the site of whose former sanctuary it now filled, and to Christianity, whose Church of the Holy Sepulchre was now no longer the highest point in the city. The structure was a grand announcement that Islam had superseded both previous religions.

▶ See Nota bene, Jerusalem, pp. 108-110.

But the special status of Jerusalem also translated into certain advantages, first for Christians, and then for Jews, on whom the Muslim rulers imposed a taxation structure that allowed them to pay the *jizya*, the tax on condition of which they were allowed to remain non-Muslim and granted the patronage of the state, not as individuals but in one lump sum. This meant that the rich could pay for the poor. Eleventh- and twelfth-century records from Egypt attest that in practice this happened even when the tax was levied individually, but the allowance in Jerusalem was significant, since it probably attracted poor Jews to the city. It probably also facilitated the flow of Jewish pilgrims, who could avoid paying the tax levied on non-Muslim visitors. All this had a salutary effect on Jerusalem's economy, as trade records suggest for the eleventh century—a period during which Jerusalem was otherwise considered, as one merchant put it, "a weak city" for trade, except during pilgrimage seasons.[15]

Palestine eventually followed the wider Islamic-period pattern of producing an interregional network of well-connected urban population centers. Jerusalem maintained close and frequent links with the Fatimid capital of Fustat (Cairo), with the centers of provincial government in Damascus and Ramla, with the seaport of Tyre, and with Aleppo and Baghdad. Those links are attested in letters that survive from the eleventh and twelfth centuries. They are likely to have dated to the Abbasid and even the Umayyad periods.

Economics

In preindustrial societies, the broad prevalence of subsistence farming meant there was little need for precious metal coins. Peasants traded in kind or in copper; even the early Abbasids recognized that peasants were more likely to pay their taxes if they could offer produce rather than money. Together with urbanization and geographic mobility in the early Islamic heartlands came the spread of gold and silver coins and their exchange—particularly for items that brought a high profit margin, such as slaves, furs, spices, and other luxury goods.

This situation is reflected in Arabic and gaonic literature alike. A brief passage in a geographic work called *Kitab al-Masalik wa-l-Mamalik* by the Abbasid postmaster and spymaster Ibn Khurradadhbih, composed between 846 and 885, tells of a group of Iraqi Jewish merchants called *rādhāniyya*, or Radhanites, who covered staggering distances over half the vast expanse of the globe.[16] The Radhanites spoke an impressive number of languages (Arabic, Persian, Greek, French, other Romance dialects, and Slavonic—Ibn Khurradadhbih's omission of Aramaic from the list may indicate that it was assumed of Jewish traders) and traveled by land

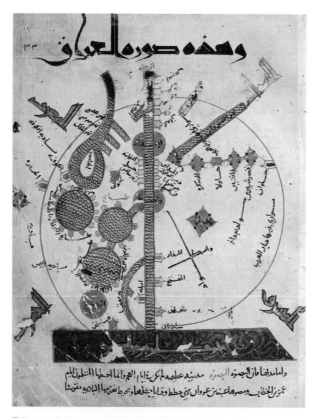

This map, by the geographer Al-Istakhri, is taken from *Livre des routes et des royaumes* (Book of Roads and Kingdoms) and shows the mouth of the Tigris River, the city of Baghdad, Kufa, and the Persian Gulf. Iraq, tenth century. Cairo, National Library.

and sea from Western Europe to India and China, including, in between, the Mediterranean Sea, the Red Sea, Constantinople, the land of the Slavs, and the Caspian Sea. Their cargoes included slaves (both female and male, including eunuchs), furs, textiles, weapons, and spices. Long-distance traders had to deal in expensive items to make the costs and risks of travel pay off. Although a dearth of corroborating accounts independent of Ibn Khurradadhbih's has made it difficult for scholars to say much more about the Radhanites, gaonic responsa offer parallel information on the traffic in slaves, textiles, and spices. In addition, the trade routes of the Radhanites were standard ones in their time—with the notable exception of the overland route to China via the Khazar kingdom; and Ibn Khurradadhbih's role in the Abbasid postal and information system would have made him privy to reliable information.[17]

▌ See Nota bene, The Cairo Geniza, pp. 99-101.

The Radhanites attest to Jewish activity in long-distance trade as much as one century before the documents of the Cairo Geniza document it in more detail and farther west.

They also demonstrate Iraq's importance as an entrepôt and staging point for great mercantile networks during the Abbasid heyday. The Abbasid court at Baghdad would have been the best conceivable market for luxury goods, since only the rulers and their immediate retainers possessed enough liquid funds to purchase such expensive items. The presence of the court was, indeed, essential in the unprecedented economic growth of early Islamic Iraq.[18] Only when the Fatimids conquered Egypt did the luxury market shift westward.

The breakup of the caliphate

The epoch of Islamic political unity did not last: a mere three centuries after the founding of the caliphate, it had split into three. The province of al-Andalus was the first to break away: when the Abbasid dynasty came to power in 750, Islamic Iberia remained under the control of the Umayyad dynasty of governors, and it remained under Umayyad control until the early eleventh century. But the biggest series of challenges to Abbasid hegemony arrived in the tenth century, along with a concatenation of military and fiscal crises at home and abroad. No sooner had the population and wealth of Baghdad grown exponentially in the late ninth century than political chaos and economic decline stunted its ascendancy.

The first crisis arrived in 909, in the form of the Fatimid dynasty, which conquered Ifriqiya and Sicily and then set its sights on the East. The Fatimids adhered to the Isma'ili branch of Shi'ism, a different legal and theological school from that of the Sunni Abbasids. The first Fatimid ruler, who took the messianic regnal name al-Mahdi, also had the temerity to proclaim himself caliph—a title reserved for the succession of rulers after Muhammad. The theology of the caliphate held that there could be only one political and religious leader (*imām*) of the Muslims at a time. Yet now there were two. The Fatimids constituted a direct affront to Baghdad both religiously and politically; and in 969, they set out eastward from Ifriqiya to conquer Egypt. They quickly subdued it, founding their palatine city of Cairo (al-Qahira, "the [city] victorious") just north of Fustat. Eventually they also conquered al-Sham. Then they set their sights on Iraq. Though they never conquered Baghdad, they retained control of Egypt for two hundred years, and of Syria until the Crusader conquests, shifting the center of the Islamic world westward.

In the late tenth and eleventh centuries, the Fatimids were the most powerful state in the Mediterranean. Rulers—Christian and Muslim alike—imitated the Fatimid style of royal propaganda, decorative arts, and administrative procedure. One imitator was the Umayyad governor of Cordoba, 'Abd al-Rahman III, who in 929 proclaimed himself caliph and commenced the building of an enormous palatine complex at Madinat al-Zahra' outside Cordoba, modeled after the Fatimid capitals of Ifriqiya.

❯ See article by Mercedes García-Arenal, p. 111.

The number of caliphs in the Islamic realm was now three.

That same year, Baghdad was the scene of a dramatic power struggle between the army and the court of the profligate caliph al-Muqtadir (908–932), who was deposed and killed. In 945, a shaken Abbasid court called upon mercenaries from Daylam, south of the Caspian Sea, to rule what remained of their realm; as the Buwayhid dynasty, they governed the Abbasid territories until 1055. The Buwayhids were Shi'a like the Fatimids, but unlike the Fatimids, they ruled in the name of the Abbasid caliphs. Nonetheless, the vast territory formerly ruled by the Abbasids would never be truly reunited: while most subsequent Islamic dynasties, up to and including the Ottomans, called their sovereigns sultans rather than caliphs and claimed to rule in the name of the Abbasid house, the caliphate would never enjoy the same authority as in its early years.

Yet the political fragmentation to which the Abbasid realm was subjected did not reverse the cultural unification of previous centuries. Paradoxically, it furthered it, for one main reason: the crisis in the Iraqi heartland sent waves of migrants westward, and those migrants brought Iraqi customs and culture with them. For the Jews, this fact was transformative. Just as the Islamic conquests of the eighth century had sent migrants westward to the Mediterranean basin and beyond, so did the collapse of the Iraqi economy in the late ninth and early tenth centuries. The presence of so many easterners in the west furthered the sense of a cultural koine. It created an intellectual ferment in the Eastern Mediterranean, and helped integrate the customs and traditions of Palestine, Egypt, and elsewhere with those of the East. This was especially true among Rabbanite and Karaite Jews. And so the center of the civilized world shifted from Baghdad to the hubs of the Indian Ocean and Mediterranean trades, Fustat and its royal city, Cairo.

Hundreds of business letters written during the Fatimid period by Jewish long-distance traders and merchants survived in the Cairo Geniza. They demonstrate an intensity of shipping centered on two main networks: in the eleventh century, a triangular trade among Egypt, Ifriqiya, and Sicily; and, in the twelfth, as Italian merchants began to dominate the Mediterranean trade, the maritime route to India via Upper Egypt, the Red Sea, and Yemen. The centrality of Egypt to both those networks offered the Fatimids a seemingly endless source of revenue, from customs and other taxes. It also made it a desirable destination for anyone in search of good markets, cultural riches, and positions in the state bureaucracy. By the eleventh century, Egypt would grow from a province to a metropole.

It also grew from a minor place of Jewish settlement to the very center of the eastern Jewish world, on a par with the Iberian Peninsula in the west. That it should do so was not obvious. Of all the places so far discussed, early Islamic Egypt had been the least important Jewish settlement when the Muslims conquered it. It had never been a center of rabbinic activity, like Mesopotamia and Palestine, but by 1127, the gaon of Palestine himself would move to Fustat, and a generation later, ca. 1165, so would the great Andalusian philosopher and jurist Moses Maimonides (1138–1204) of Cordoba.

Egypt is also justly a major player in any study of the medieval maritime world, particularly maritime commerce. Like al-Sham, Egypt had outlets onto both the Mediterranean and the Red Seas; like al-Sham, it had a network of inland waterways to move goods up and down the interior of the country, a less expensive means of shipping than over land (animals had to be fed and watered, while boats did not). But al-Sham never became as wealthy as Egypt. The explanation for this must be sought in the presence of the Fatimid court: like the Abbasids before them, the Fatimids managed and exploited the region's natural resources, especially the Nile floods, keeping it prosperous, extracting wealth from the population, and concentrating it in and around the capital. True, Syria boasted its share of wealthy centers: the port of Tyre housed a coterie of successful long-distance traders in close communication with Fustat and Alexandria; but the truly great traders were based in Fustat and Cairo.

Language

The logistical challenges involved in trade operations were not limited to transportation. Goods had to be procured at a reasonable price and their quality assured, most often by proxy. If one wished to trade over long distances—and to earn the large margins of profit long-distance trade permitted— then one needed a network of

A village bazaar, with a mosque in the background, in *Maqamat* (*The Assemblies*) of Al-Hariri. Illuminated manuscript of Al-Wasiti. Iraq, thirteenth century. Paris, Bibliothèque Nationale de France, ms. or. Arabic 5847, fol. 138.

allies and business associates with local connections abroad. Sometimes traders relied on their cousins or sons and other relatives; or they apprenticed the sons of trading partners; or they trained free servants or slaves in reading, arithmetic, and business. In all cases, one needed to issue commands and reports in writing. What was needed for this was not only a means of conveying documents but a common language.

Under Islamic rule, spoken and much of written communication took place in a language entirely new to the populations outside the Arabian Peninsula and the semiarid lands of the southern Sham: Arabic. Arabic ultimately replaced the other languages that had been spoken and written for centuries throughout the newly conquered Islamic territories, including Greek, Aramaic (though pockets of it survived and still survive today), and Persian (which experienced a renaissance in the ninth century). For the Jews, Arabic took the form of Judeo-Arabic, a range of Arabic registers and dialects written in Hebrew characters that served as a koine, enabling Jews across vast distances to communicate with each other.[19] Arabic would remain the language spoken by the vast majority of the world's Jews until the later medieval and early modern periods, when the Romance languages (including Ladino) and, finally, Yiddish eclipsed it; and it is the language in which many of the most important Jewish works of the Middle Ages were composed.

> *Arabic would remain the language spoken by the vast majority of the world's Jews until the later medieval and early modern periods.*

For Jews, Arabic also—perhaps paradoxically—proved to be an important language for the renewal of written Hebrew. Like other classicizing languages based on scriptural texts considered immutable, classical written Arabic carries a set of ideologies attached to its use. First and foremost is the belief in the perfection of the language as spoken by God directly to Muhammad (*i'jāz al-Qur'ān*). Arabic speakers attempted to adhere to the classical purity of the Arabic of the Qur'an, and developed the sciences of grammar, morphology, syntax, and lexicography in order to understand it better. Jews adapted all those sciences to the study of Hebrew and of biblical texts, in the tenth and eleventh centuries, literally inventing the field of Hebrew linguistics—a field in which Karaite Jews in particular were pioneers.

▶ See Chapter II of Part IV, pp. 653-681.

Technology: Paper manufacture and written communication

One of the most important changes in this period was a vast proliferation of written culture, especially in the ninth and tenth centuries. Written transmission as a mode of passing on knowledge constituted a veritable revolution for Jews, since the previous millennium had given rise to taboos around making official written copies of rabbinic texts. (Copies for personal use were permitted.) By the tenth century, the oral monopoly on textual transmission applied only to one Jewish text, the Babylonian Talmud, and only the Iraqi *geonim* continued to insist that it be learned orally.

The diffusion of three technological innovations made the production and circulation of written texts possible: paper, an empire-wide postal system, and the codex (the bound book as we know it today). All three helped people to exchange ideas, information, and goods over long distances, especially among the urban and literate elite; ultimately, they were Islamic-era developments that entirely transformed Jewish culture. The latter two had Roman precedents, but spread under Islam to an unprecedented extent.

Paper totally transformed written culture all over the Islamic world. Papermaking techniques had been developed in China by the first millennium C.E.; by the early eighth century at the latest, writing paper was being produced in Central Asia.[20] But the Abbasids manufactured paper on a scale hitherto without precedent because they needed large quantities of writing material to run their bureaucracy; in the second half of the eighth century, they founded the first Arab paper mills at Baghdad.

Prior to the eighth century, books in the Near East had been written on papyrus and parchment, and documents on both those materials and on clay shards (ostraca), wood, cloth, and tanned leather. Paper held distinct advantages over these media: it was lightweight, durable, and relatively simple to manufacture; it was less expensive than parchment; and, unlike papyrus, on which Egypt held a virtual monopoly, it could be made anywhere, since its main ingredients were cotton and linen rags.[21] The Abbasid administration in Baghdad understood that a local source of writing material was a good investment, and the bureaucrats appreciated one important quality of the new medium: while parchment and papyrus can be washed or scraped (palimpsested) and thus erased without significant damage to the writing surface, paper documents cannot be altered without leaving evident traces of tampering. Paper is thus an effective weapon against forgery.

From Baghdad, paper spread westward. By the mid-tenth century it had become the preferred medium for both everyday and scholarly writing in the Islamic world. Even in the latter country, which had manufactured papyrus for millennia, papyrus was reduced to wrapping paper and then, by the thirteenth century, stopped being made altogether.

▶ See Nota bene, The Cairo Geniza, pp. 99-101.

The tenth century is the period not only of the first documents on paper that survive from the Islamic world but of the first Jewish documents preserved in numbers great enough to enable us to reconstruct an entire society on their basis. Roughly 330,000 folio pages survived in the Cairo Geniza, especially during the period from ca. 950 until 1250. A sizable minority of these—more than 15,000—are letters, contracts, depositions, official lists, accounts, receipts, and other documentary sources. Most of the documents are on paper; some, such as Jewish marriage, betrothal, and divorce documents, and Islamic legal contracts, are on parchment. The Geniza texts demonstrate the role writing played in everyday life, not only

> *Written transmission as a mode of passing on knowledge constituted a veritable revolution for Jews.*

for transmitting and teaching literary works, but also for transacting business. One subset of documents—letters—demonstrates the uses of the well-organized and empire-wide postal infrastructure. Jews had certainly communicated via letter under Roman rule, as had pagans and Christians (as the Epistles of the New Testament attest). But the postal system established by the Umayyads, and developed to an unprecedented extent by the Abbasids, created a network of roads, staging points, caravanserais, and ports that made it possible to convey people, objects, and written communiqués from one place to another with relative efficiency. While the Umayyads had created the system for government purposes and restricted its use to military intelligence and administration, in the late ninth century the Abbasids centralized the system and founded a government bureau to administer it, and private postal carriers multiplied. Mailing letters seems to have been inexpensive, and it is striking how many letters were sent not only for business purposes but simply to update relatives and friends living far away.[22] Letters, too, must have contributed to the sense that the vast expanse of space ruled by Islam was relatively unified.

Paper also contributed to the spread of the codex: papyrus is not an ideal material for binding, since the fibers tend to fray at the edges, and a single parchment codex could require the hides of as many as three hundred sheep. Although the Roman republic saw the first codices of papyrus used for classical literature, eventually the medium became inextricably associated with Christian books. Jews, therefore, resisted it and, until the advent of Islam, they transmitted their religious and literary works either orally or on papyrus and parchment rolls. But Muslims' adoption of the codex from the earliest period, for the Qur'an and other texts, broke the medium's exclusive association with Christian books, and so by the ninth century Jews had begun using it too.

All the transformations set in motion by the Islamic conquests—the migration of populations, their concentration in cities, their greater mobility and communication across long distances—meant that medieval Jews lived differently from their predecessors who had produced the classical texts on which many of their religious practices depended. The literate elites who produced and consumed the new Jewish culture were also responsible for interpreting and promulgating the old texts within Jewish communities. It is to those communities and their organization that this chapter now turns.

Jewish communal life and religious leadership

The caliphs and sultans governed somewhat loosely, due not to benevolence but to a shortcoming shared with all premodern empires: lack of manpower. That left people at liberty to organize themselves into solidarity groups based on ideology or kinship, or into other reciprocity-based networks that helped them with everything from meeting basic material needs to marrying off daughters, finding apprenticeships for sons, or forging contacts in new places. As with other solidarity-based self-help groups under Islamic rule, the Jews organized themselves along religious lines. It is in that sense that the medieval sources speak of a "Jewish community." Jews also maintained networks based on professional bonds or obligations of patronage and clientele, and those often crossed religious borders, but the default sense of belonging was to the Jewish community, even if its members did not all share exactly the same religious beliefs, practices, or loyalties.

The Jewish communities distributed charity, ransomed captives, collected taxes and fees, adjudicated disputes through a system of courts and legal specialists, and elected and appointed leaders. They also held property in trust and collected contributions from their members for expenditures, such as stipends for scholars. In towns and small cities, they appointed leaders who, by the late eleventh century, had come to bear the Arabic title *muqaddam*, although the office existed before the title used in this sense; the central Jewish authorities, the *geonim* of Palestine and Iraq, often chose communal leaders from outside the place they served, presumably to keep them independent of local factions.[23] This was one way of ensuring justice and a sense of solidarity, and of offsetting the potential for private patronage outside the communal system.

There were three types of Jewish congregations: the Babylonian Rabbanites, who followed rabbinic law and tradition as promulgated by the *geonim* of Iraq; the Shami or Palestinian Rabbanites, who followed the *geonim* of Palestine; and the Karaites, who developed a school of law based on their own interpretations of biblical and postbiblical law. Throughout Egypt and al-Sham, cities of significant size, such as Fustat, housed all three types of congregation, as the Geniza documents attest; in Iraq, the same was probably true as well, at least to judge by literary sources that refer to Karaites and Palestinian-rite Jews in Iraq.[24]

The three Jewish congregations functioned as schools of thought, each with its own legal tradition—much like the *madhāhib* in Islamic law. Among Muslim scholars in this period, the label *madhhab* applied not only to the four Sunni schools but also to the Shiʿa, regardless of instances of mutual recrimination in polemics. The label *madhhab* made sense to medieval Jews as well: in documents and literary sources in Judeo-Arabic, writers from all three groups refer to themselves and other groups as *madhāhib*, with the implication that each was equally legitimate. True, Rabbanite and Karaite polemicists—and Iraqi- and Palestinian-rite polemicists, for that matter—accused each other of straying from correct belief and practice, but those kinds of disagreements were usually restricted to a handful of zealots. Most of the community, the leaders included, cooperated.[25]

▶ See The article by Phillip Ackerman-Lieberman, pp. 683-693.

Although the three Jewish *madhāhib* were each headed by a separate leader, they formed one larger community for administrative purposes. Jews everywhere had—and exercised—the option of joining any of the three groups, since membership was a matter of personal loyalty rather than territorial jurisdiction; a person from Baghdad could follow the Palestinian rite. (Indeed, the gaon of Palestine in the 1050s was a Baghdadi.) Loyalty to one group or another often hinged, in practice, on political and social alliances rather than ideological considerations. The head of the Shāmī-rite congregation in Fustat ca. 1030 received a warning from a colleague in Palestine about growing opposition to his leadership: "Haven't we here in Palestine received numerous letters, the longest of which contains [the signatures of] thirty-odd witnesses, complaining that you are alienating the congregation with your haughtiness and domineering manner? Because of you and your son-in-law, many people have switched over to the other [Iraqi-rite] synagogue and to the Qaraite congregations."[26] The three groups also competed over wealthy members, particularly the long-distance merchants engaged in the Mediterranean and Indian Ocean trades.

Wealthy members of the communal elite—long-distance traders, bankers, or physicians—often served as intermediaries between the Jewish community and the courts of the caliphs and sultans. In Iraq, this role was usually played by the *exilarch*, who occupied his position by virtue of his claims to Davidic ancestry, or by Jewish courtiers such as the Banu Natira, a dynasty of Abbasid bankers in the tenth century. In Fatimid Egypt and Syria before the Crusader conquests, numerous courtiers played the role, Karaites and Rabbanites alike. In the last decades of the eleventh century, the position was formalized and its incumbent titled *ra'īs al-yahūd*, "head of the Jews."[27]

Having an intermediary at the ruler's court was an absolutely essential asset to any community, in part because of a special feature of Islamic statecraft: the petition-and-response procedure. In principle, any subject could petition the sovereign and other members of the caliph's or sultan's court with requests in matters personal or collective. The Geniza has preserved hundreds of such petitions to caliphs, sultans, viziers, and other high-ranking courtiers and bureaucrats in Egypt and Syria. They were composed by Jews, Christians, and Muslims; the fact that non-Jewish petitions survived in a Jewish Geniza attests to cooperation among members of the three religions in lodging petitions, writing them, and handling them.[28]

The petitions fall into four general types: complaints against officials who had committed injustices (*maz.ālim*), requests for investiture by communal leaders, bids for governmental arbitration in communal disputes, and individual requests for material and other types of help. They demonstrate that the central government relied on its subjects to bring to its attention problems in governance, particularly when midlevel officials abused their power. They also demonstrate that ordinary subjects enjoyed the latitude to protest and make demands. In practice, however, the government chanceries were not consistent in answering petitions. That is where the courtly intermediaries proved useful: having a petition answered could depend on the intercession of leaders with contacts in the palaces. Those leaders themselves—some *muqaddamun*, the *ra'īs al-yahūd*, the *geonim* of Jerusalem, Muslim qadis, and Christian patriarchs and bishops—also petitioned the rulers to request investiture in their positions. Sometimes they were forced to lean on intercessors (in the eleventh century, Rabbanite leaders cultivated the patronage of Karaite courtiers). The regime, in turn, benefited from these requests because they functioned as royal propaganda, helping the ruler to secure an image as just and as the personal patron of his subjects, Muslim and *dhimmī*s alike.

Political styles and communal administration

The administrative procedures of the Jewish community were partly modeled on those of the Islamic state. Members of both religions engaged in similar styles of politics and of forging individual alliances through patronage and reciprocity. Letters exchanged among Jews use idioms of loyalty and friendship that are strikingly similar to those used among Muslim functionaries of the Fatimid and

Abbasid courts and bureaucracies. A Jew in late eleventh- or early twelfth-century Alexandria who addresses a petition for charity to a Jewish benefactor follows the standard form of petitions to Fatimid caliphs and viziers, and even the physical format of the document is similar to that of Fatimid petitions, with the name of the writer (*tarjama*) appearing at the top left of the page.[29] The same Arabic terms that express the social concepts of patronage, clientele, and loyalty in Islamic sources also pervade Jewish ones in Judeo-Arabic.[30]

None of this is surprising: the system of Islamic politics was a relatively open one, admitting participation by non-Muslims, initially as specialized bureaucrats and later as literate elites from a wide range of professions. The fact that Jews engaged in the styles of patronage and reciprocity attested among Muslim elites had repercussions for the way they administered and organized their communities. First, the fluidity of membership in the Jewish *madhāhib* led to intense competition among leaders over their followers. Despite the vigorous battles the yeshivot conducted over hegemony and followers, there is little evidence that the Diaspora communities felt obliged to commit their loyalties to one *madhhab* exclusively, like Muslims who submitted legal queries to different *madhāhib* simultaneously. In Qayrawan, Fustat, and Palermo, some rabbinic leaders, wealthy traders, and other community members who solicited responsa from Baghdad and sent donations in return also gave funds to the Jerusalem yeshiva and sought official titles from both centers. Karaites felt free to have their legal documents drawn up in rabbinical legal courts, and some rabbinic scribes obliged them by writing documents according to Karaite specifications. Karaites also donated money to the Palestinian yeshiva and assisted both Sura and Pumbedita with raising funds and having them transferred to Iraq. Such multiple allegiances are nearly impossible to explain using monolithic models of the Rabbanites as the orthodox group and the Karaites as a heretical sect (as was habitual in older scholarship on Karaism), or with a centralistic model postulating the hegemony of one *madhhab* over the others. The reality was more complex.

> ❝ *The fact that Jews engaged in the styles of patronage and reciprocity attested among Muslim elites had repercussions for the way they organized their communities.* ❞

But the progressive centering of the Jewish world on Egypt also altered this model of multiple allegiances. In both Egypt and the Sham, the three *madhāhib* came to form a single Jewish community over the course of the eleventh century. Nearly year by year, the gaonic office in Jerusalem amassed prerogatives and developed a more consistent relationship to the Fatimid court and bureaucracy in Cairo. The Jewish intercessors at court began to take on increasingly formalized roles, and this finally culminated in the creation of a new office of leadership over Jewish communities under Fatimid rule centered on Egypt: the *ra'īs al-yahūd* (head of the Jews). The position was the project of a coterie of Egyptian notables of the 1060s and

1070s, including Rabbanite physicians at the Fatimid court; ultimately, it brought the entire tripartite Jewish community (Palestinian Rabbanites, Iraqi Rabbanites, and Karaites) under the aegis of a single office that would persist until the Ottomans abolished it in the sixteenth century. For the first time since antiquity, the Jewish world was no longer linked to the central leadership in Iraq and Palestine. This turn away from the centers toward what used to be the peripheries echoed the breakup of the Abbasid realm more than a century earlier.

The strength of this centralized Egyptian Jewish community was particularly evident in its institutions of communal governance, such as care for the indigent. Although Fustat and Cairo are overrepresented in Geniza material, the community does seem to have loomed large among Mediterranean Jews seeking relief from poverty: poor people migrated to Fustat to benefit from a well-organized set of communal services. Charity lists also include numerous converts to Judaism, some of whom may have converted to benefit from the extensive Jewish system of relief for the poor, including peasants hoping to better their lot in the city.

Funds from private donors were joined with community funds—fines, taxes, foundations, bequests, and other exceptional collections. These resources were used for distributing food and clothing, scholarships, and extraordinary expenses, such as paying the ransom of captives; after the First Crusade, ransom was paid not only for persons but also for sacred books.[31] The old ecumenical method of governance centered on the yeshivot in Iraq and Palestine now gave way to a local administration centered on Egypt and transcending the interests of each congregation. The Fatimid conquests had made this possible; the rise of Egypt as an economic and political center had made it desirable; and the Crusades had made it necessary, by forcing many of the Jewish communities of al-Sham into exile, including the Palestinian yeshiva itself.

State intervention in the later Middle Ages

The Ayyubid sultans (1171–1250) recaptured large parts of al-Sham from Crusader rule, including Jerusalem in 1187. But even after the Islamic conquest of Syria and its reattachment to the Ayyubid administration in Cairo, Syria continued to exercise some measure of political independence. If from the beginnings of the Fatimid period in Egypt Jews had found it imperative to hone their expertise in negotiating with the state for privileges and offices, by the Ayyubid period, doing so had become nearly routine. Though it is common to say that the Jews formed an independent community that functioned free from the interference of the state, in fact, their leaders sought state interference and support when it served them. But it was also rare that the Islamic state intervened in Jewish matters without an invitation. Under the Mamluk sultans (1250–1517), it became less rare. But even here, despite the image depicted in both Jewish and Muslim sources of a rapacious Mamluk state determined

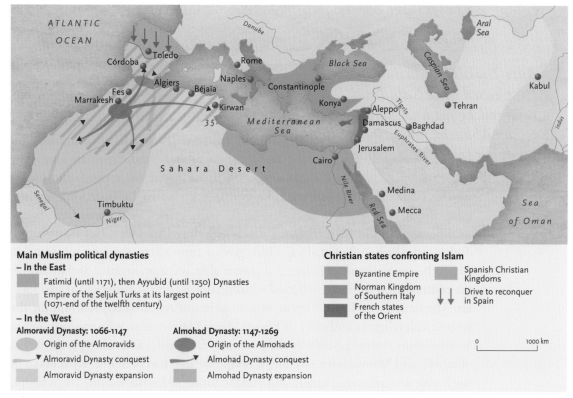

Main Muslim political dynasties
– In the East

Fatimid (until 1171), then Ayyubid (until 1250) Dynasties

Empire of the Seljuk Turks at its largest point
(1071-end of the twelfth century)

– In the West

Almoravid Dynasty: 1066-1147

Origin of the Almoravids

▼ Almoravid Dynasty conquest

Almoravid Dynasty expansion

Almohad Dynasty: 1147-1269

Origin of the Almohads

▼ Almohad Dynasty conquest

Almohad Dynasty expansion

Christian states confronting Islam

Byzantine Empire

Norman Kingdom
of Southern Italy

French states
of the Orient

Spanish Christian
Kingdoms

↓↓ Drive to reconquer
in Spain

0   1000 km

The Muslim world in the twelfth century.

to usurp Jews' and Christians' privileges and property, it was Jews themselves who had established the precedent of turning to the state with requests for interference and mediation between Jewish factions. Official Mamluk chroniclers represent the state as intervening in internal *dhimmī* communal conflicts so as to paint the regime as administratively effective and religiously zealous, but where documentary sources can offer a bit more background and detail, it is clear that *dhimmī*s took the initiative.[32]

In Iraq, it may be that such interventionist policies had begun slightly earlier, but we lack the copious documentation of Egypt to understand whether there, too, Jews had initiated it. Under the Abbasid caliph al-Muqtadi (1055–94), the Saljuq Turks wrested Baghdad and the Abbasid state from the Buwayhids; during this period there was an increase in state incursions into the Jewish community's affairs, probably a side effect of rivalry between the *atābeg* (commander in chief) Nizam al-Mulk and the assistant vizier, Abu Shuja' al-Isfahani. It may be that Jews followed the rivalry closely and used it to their advantage, as they did in Egypt on more than one occasion, but there is little firsthand evidence apart from the single eyewitness account of Johannes of Oppido, a Norman priest who converted to Judaism in the waning years of the eleventh century and took the Hebrew name 'Ovadya. This

'Ovadya visited Baghdad ca. 1105 and reported that Abu Shuja' had attempted to force Jews to wear distinguishing signs on their clothing. The decrees were alternately repealed and renewed well into the 1140s.

"Anti-Jewish legislation in Iraq eased once Saladin, restored Egypt and Syria to the Abbasid realm by pledging fealty to Baghdad."

Tensions and anti-Jewish legislation in Iraq eased once Saladin (1171–92), the first Ayyubid sultan, restored Egypt and Syria to the Abbasid realm by pledging fealty to Baghdad. But the reunification of Iraq and Egypt did not lead to a corresponding reunification of Iraqi and Egyptian Jews. The gaonate of Baghdad had been revived: the Jewish traveler Petahiah of Regensburg, who visited Baghdad in 1176, reports that the gaon Shemu'el b. 'Ali ibn al-Dastur (1164 – ca. 1194–97) possessed the power to appoint judges in Iraq, Iran, and Syria, including Damascus. But Benjamin of Tudela, who visited Baghdad ca. 1168, gives a contradictory report according to which the appointment of judges and *geonim* alike was a prerogative of the *exilarch*; the contradiction may have reflected a jurisdictional conflict between the two leaders. The same gaon, Ibn al-Dastur, was an object of repeated opprobrium for the great Jewish religious authority of Egypt, Moses Maimonides, who mocked him as an ignoramus motivated only by the pursuit of fancy titles and other perquisites of office. To read Maimonides, one might think that Iraq had been entirely eclipsed in the Jewish scholarly imagination, and that the future of Jewish learning lay in Egypt, Provence, and perhaps Yemen. The reality was probably more complex. The Iraqi *geonim* were still communicating with the West, and they received the attention and backing of the Abbasid state during the long reign of the Abbasid caliph al-Nasir (1180–1223). But the independence of the Mediterranean communities from Iraq for so many centuries could not simply be erased.

Beyond polemics

The patterns Jews followed in their trade networks, congregational organization, literary production, and personal loyalties owed much to the Islamic world. Whether Jews as a group bore a similarly palpable effect on Islamic collective life is unlikely. Jews constituted a tiny minority in a vast civilization, perhaps no more than 10 percent of the population of major cities such as Baghdad and Fustat (perhaps more in Jerusalem). But there is one sense in which Jews in medieval eastern Islamic lands are far more important than their sheer numbers suggest: the vast quantity of their written materials that have survived. These allow historians to reconstruct the texture of daily life in Islamic lands and make it clear that power relationships were often more fluid and open to negotiation than one might imagine. True, Muslim rulers and jurists in theory defined non-Muslims as subalterns and set the terms of the relationship. But a closer look at the communities through their documentary sources suggests that attempts at religious self-definition, including some of the statements one finds in polemics and other learned works, do not tell the entire story.

---

1.   Richard W. Bulliet, *Conversion to Islam in the Medieval Period: An Essay in Quantitative History* (Cambridge, MA: Harvard University Press, 1979).

2.   Chase F. Robinson, *Empire and Elites after the Muslim Conquest: The Transformation of Northern Mesopotamia* (Cambridge: Cambridge University Press, 2000).

3.   See Arietta Papaconstantinou, ed., *The Multilingual Experience in Egypt from the Ptolemies to the Abbasids* (Farnham, Surrey: Ashgate, 2010); Petra M. Sijpesteijn, *Shaping a Muslim State: The World of a Mid-Eighth-Century Egyptian Official* (Oxford: Oxford University Press, 2012).

4.   Michael G. Morony, *Iraq after the Muslim Conquest* (Princeton, NJ: Princeton University Press, 1984); Mark R. Cohen, *Under Crescent and Cross: The Jews in the Middle Ages* (Princeton, NJ: Princeton University Press, 1994); Robert G. Hoyland, *Seeing Islam as Others Saw It: A Survey and Evaluation of Christian, Jewish, and Zoroastrian Writings on Early Islam* (Princeton, NJ: Darwin Press, 1997); Milka Levy-Rubin, *Non-Muslims in the Early Islamic Empire: From Surrender to Coexistence* (Cambridge: Cambridge University Press, 2011).

5.   S. D. Goitein, *A Mediterranean Society: The Jewish Communities of the Arab World as Portrayed in the Documents of the Cairo Geniza*, 6 vols. (Berkeley: University of California Press, 1967), esp. 1:62.

6.   Adam Silverstein, *Postal Systems in the Pre-Modern Islamic World* (Cambridge: Cambridge University Press, 2007); Goitein, *Mediterranean Society, op. cit.*, vol. 1, p. 281-295.

7.   Robert Brody, *The Geonim of Babylonia and the Shaping of Medieval Jewish Culture* (New Haven, CT: Yale University Press, 1998); David Goodblatt, "The History of the Babylonian Academies," in Steven T. Katz, ed., *The Cambridge History of Judaism*, vol. 4, *The Late Roman-Rabbinic Period* (Cambridge: Cambridge University Press, 2006), 821–39, esp. 837; Sacha Stern, "Rabbinic Academies in Late Antiquity: State of Current Research," in Henri Hugonnard-Roche, ed., *L'Enseignement supérieur dans les mondes antiques et médiévaux: Aspects institutionnels, juridiques et pédagogiques,* Colloque international de l'Institut des traditions textuelles (Fédération de recherche 33 du C.N.R.S.) (Paris: J. Vrin, 2008), 221–38.

8.   Al-Jahiz, *Kitab al-radd ʿala l-Nasara*, translated in Charles Pellat, *The Life and Works of Jahiz* (Berkeley: University of California Press, 1969), 87–88; Morony, *Iraq after the Muslim Conquest*, 312.

9.   Brody, *Geonim of Babylonia*, 63.

10.   Ibid., 36–37.

11.   Hava Lazarus-Yafeh et al., eds., *The Majlis: Interreligious Encounters in Medieval Islam* (Wiesbaden: Harrassowitz, 1999).

12.   Hayim Lapin, *Economy, Geography, and Provincial History in Later Roman Palestine* (Tübingen: Mohr Siebeck, 2001).

13.   Hayim Lapin, *Rabbis as Romans: The Rabbinic Movement in Palestine, 100–400 C.E.* (Oxford: Oxford University Press, 2012); Seth Schwartz, *Were the Jews a Mediterranean Society? Reciprocity and Solidarity in Ancient Judaism* (Princeton, NJ: Princeton University Press, 2009); and Martin Goodman, *Rome and Jerusalem: The Clash of Ancient Civilisations* (London: Allen Lane, 2007).

14.   Levy-Rubin, *Non-Muslims in the Early Islamic Empire*, 53.

15.   Letter of Yisra'el b. Natan to Nahray b. Nissim, ca. 1060 (Jewish Theological Seminary of America, ENA NS 48.15, line 4), published in Moshe Gil, *Palestine during the First Muslim Period (634–1099)* (in Hebrew), 3 vols. (Tel Aviv: Tel Aviv University Press, 1983), vol. 3, doc. 477 (cited there as JTS Geniza Misc. 15), line 4; Jessica Goldberg, *Trade and Institutions in the Medieval Mediterranean: Geniza Merchants and Their Business World* (Cambridge: Cambridge University Press, 2012), 223.

16.   The name of the group indicates that they originated in Radhan, the province around Baghdad that housed the Sasanian-era city of Mahoze and other Jewish population centers. Barbier de Meynard put forward this hypothesis about the name of the Radhanites as early as 1865, and Gil has more recently argued in favor of it; Moshe Gil, *In the Kingdom of Ishmael* (Hebrew), 4 vols. (Tel Aviv: Tel Aviv University, 1997), sec. 344.

17.   Gil, *In the Kingdom of Ishmael*, secs. 344–46; Peregrine Horden and Nicholas Purcell, *The Corrupting Sea: A Study of Mediterranean History* (Oxford: Blackwell, 2000), 162–63; Adam Silverstein, "From Markets to Marvels: Jews on the Maritime Route to China ca. 850 – ca. 950 C.E.," *Journal of Jewish Studies* 58 (2007): 91–104.

18.   Hugh Kennedy, "Feeding the Five Hundred Thousand: Cities and Agriculture in Early Islamic Mesopotamia," *Iraq* 73 (2011): 177–99.

19. David J. Wasserstein, "Why Did Arabic Succeed Where Greek Failed? Language Change in the Near East after Muhammad," *Scripta Classica Israelica* 22 (2003): 257–72.

20. Medieval Arabic chronicles claim that the Abbasids discovered paper when they defeated Tang armies at the battle of Talas in Transoxiana in 751 and captured a Chinese prisoner of war who kindly taught his captors paper-making techniques, but this is probably a later legend that circulated to explain the excellence of the paper made in Samarqand. Actual samples of Central Asian paper have survived from the early eighth century, so the Abbasids would not have needed a Chinese teacher. Jonathan Bloom, *Paper before Print: The History and Impact of Paper in the Islamic World* (New Haven, CT: Yale University Press, 2001), 42–43.

21. Adam Bülow-Jacobson, "Writing Materials in the Ancient World," in Roger S. Bagnall, ed., *The Oxford Handbook of Papyrology* (Oxford: Oxford University Press, 2009), 4–5. Though Pliny mentions the existence of the papyrus plant in Syria and Mesopotamia, it requires stagnant pools of water to grow, and special manufacturing techniques perfected in Egypt. In the Middle Ages, it also grew in Sicily, but was not used for papermaking (ibid., 25n8).

22. Silverstein, *Postal Systems*; Goitein, *Mediterranean Society*, 1:281–95.

23. Goitein, *Mediterranean Society*, 2:69–70.

24. For Karaites in Iraq, see al-Qirqisani, for example, who mentions them at Baghdad, Basra, and Tustar (*Kitab al-anwar wa-l-maraqib*, ed. L. Nemoy [New York: Publications of the Alexander Kohut Memorial Foundation, 1939]), chap. 19. For Palestinian Rabbanites in Iraq, see, for example, Levi b. Yefet, *Sefer ha-misvot* (Leiden, MS Or. 4760, MS Warner 22, 19r–19v; cf. St. Petersburg, Russian National Library, MS Yevr.-Arab. I 3920).

25. Marina Rustow, *Heresy and the Politics of Community: The Jews of the Fatimid Caliphate* (Ithaca, NY: Cornell University Press, 2008).

26. Letter of Shelomo b. Semah to Efrayim b. Shemarya, Cambridge University Library, T-S 10 J 29.13.

27. Mark R. Cohen, *Jewish Self-Government in Medieval Egypt: The Origins of the Office of Head of the Jews, ca. 1065–1126* (Princeton, NJ: Princeton University Press, 1980); see further Rustow, *Heresy and the Politics of Community*, 328–40, and for the historiography, 100–107.

28. Marina Rustow, "A Petition to a Woman at the Fatimid Court (413–414 A.H./1022–23 C.E.)," *Bulletin of the School of Oriental and African Studies* 73 (2010): 1–27.

29. Cambridge University Library, T-S 13 J 18.14; see Cohen, *Poverty and Charity*, 177–85, and *Voice of the Poor*, doc. 1; cf. Khan, "The Historical Development of the Structure of Medieval Arabic Petitions," *Bulletin of the School of Oriental and African Studies* 53 (1990): 8–30.

30. Marina Rustow, "Formal and Informal Patronage in the Islamic East: Geniza Evidence," *al-Qantara: Revista de Estudios Árabes* 29 (2008): 341–82.

31. Cohen, *Poverty and Charity*, Cambridge University Library, T-S 10 J 5.6 + T-S 20.113; Rustow, *Heresy and the Politics of Community,* 341n43 and 340–44.

32. Marina Rustow, "At the Limits of Communal Autonomy: Jewish Bids for Government Interference," *Mamluk Studies Review* 13 (2009): 133–59.

The Cairo Geniza

What is now known as the Cairo Geniza came to the attention of scholars between the 1860s and 1890s. A hoard of about 330,000 separate pages of books and documents had accumulated in a storage room of a medieval synagogue in Fustat and began to find their way to dealers, private collectors, and libraries.[1]

The last decades of the nineteenth century were the great era of Egyptology and of discoveries in Pharaonic tombs. Amid Europe's fascination with the ancient world, a few intrepid scholars went to Egypt in search of post-Pharaonic material. In 1896–97, two Oxford scholars, Bernard Grenfell and Arthur Hunt, excavated a rubbish heap outside the Hellenistic city of Oxyrhynchus in the Fayyum (modern al-Bahnasa) and found it contained a half-million Greek papyri – including three pages from a lost Christian Gospel.[2] That year and in the same spirit, Solomon Schechter, reader in rabbinics at Cambridge University, tracked down the source of the Geniza documents and brought the remaining manuscripts back to Cambridge.[3]

A *beit geniza* is a storage chamber where texts in Hebrew script are deposited when they are too worn out to remain in circulation, or, in the case of documents, when the business they have transacted has been concluded. Most of what the Geniza contained were fragments of literary texts: the Hebrew Bible, biblical commentaries and translations, rabbinic literature (including some of the earliest known fragments of the two Talmuds), philosophy, science, poetry, and belles lettres. Some of these works had been transmitted well into the modern age, and the copies now found contained interesting textual variants. Other works had been entirely unknown before the Geniza's discovery, or known only from quotations in other medieval works.

One of these was a legal code by 'Anan ben David, an eighth-century Iraqi Jew who devised his own school of Jewish law, one different from the rabbinic tradition that had preceded him. The Geniza also yielded more than eight hundred works by the shadowy Palestinian liturgical poet Yannai, who probably lived in the seventh century, all of whose works had been lost except one.[4] Many of the poems of Yannai that survived in the Geniza had been copied on top of erased (palimpsested) Greek texts that themselves held clues to Egypt's pre-Islamic, Hellenistic past and that of its Jewish communities.

The Geniza also totally transformed parts of Jewish history thought to be known and understood. Moses Maimonides, who lived in Egypt from the 1160s until his death in 1204, was a member of the synagogue where the Geniza was housed. Among the finds are draft pages of some of his works in his own hand, including the philosophical masterpiece *The Guide for the Perplexed*. (One page from the *Guide* was pieced together from three fragments in two separate libraries as recently as 2004.) There are also letters from Maimonides's brother, David, an India trader whose business ventures supported the great sage's scholarship until he died in a shipwreck, forcing Maimonides to seek work at the Ayyubid court as a physician.

A sizable and significant minority of the Geniza's pages – probably more than fifteen thousand – are documents (letters, contracts, lists, accounts, children's exercise books) written by known and unknown figures. These have cast light onto entirely new realms of the Jewish and Islamic pasts, such as trade, agriculture, the roles of women, education, the history of childhood, sex, food, and the function, symbolism, and prices of textiles and clothing.[5]

Because there are no medieval testimonies on the practice of *geniza*, we will never be sure what motivated the Shami congregation of Fustat to store its papers. Based on modern practices of *geniza*, however, scholars have made some educated guesses. One reconstruction speculates that medieval Jews believed that just as the body is a container for the soul and deserves a proper burial, so too should manuscripts be buried after they've become too worn to transmit knowledge.

Indeed, some modern Jewish communities store texts in a *geniza* until they can be buried. In Ottoman Jerusalem in the nineteenth century, Jews emptied their *beit geniza* and brought it to the cemetery once every seven years in a festive ceremony, or else during droughts in an effort to bring rainfall. For unknown reasons, the members of the Shami congregation in Fustat did not bury their papers systematically, and in the eleventh century, when they rebuilt their synagogue, they provisioned it with a *beit geniza* so large that they could fill it up indefinitely.[6]

The community deposited its papers in their *geniza* chamber continuously for nearly nine centuries, but the best-documented period is 1000–1250. This is fortunate for two reasons. First, until the Geniza's discovery, this had been one of the least-known periods in Jewish history, populated only by the religious, philosophical, and literary works that happened to have been continuously transmitted rather than lost, destroyed, or confiscated and censored by the church in medieval Europe. Second, during this period Egypt happened to be the center of the Islamic world and the hub of the Mediterranean and Indian Ocean trades. Geniza documents were therefore able to illuminate not only medieval Jewish communities but the entire burgeoning society of which they were a part.

There have been other sensational finds since the Cairo Geniza. In 1945, a number of ancient Christian books came to light at Nag' Hammadi in Upper Egypt. One of them was the apocryphal Gospel of Thomas, almost in its entirety, in Coptic translation; it turned out to be the same Christian text in the

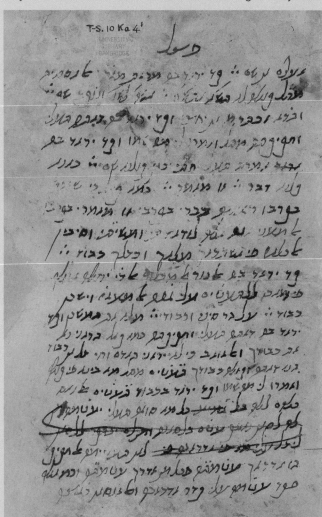

A draft of Maimonides's *Guide for the Perplexed*. Egypt, late twelfth century, Judeo-Arabic fragment discovered in the Cairo Geniza. Cambridge University Library, coll. Taylor-Schechter. By kind premission of the Syndics of Cambridge University Library.

original Greek that Grenfell and Hunt had excavated at Oxyrhynchus half a century earlier. In 1947, a Palestinian shepherd at Khirbet Qumran near the Dead Sea discovered a clay jar containing ancient Hebrew books. Excavations of the site over the next decade revealed an ancient Jewish library—now known as the Dead Sea Scrolls—containing the earliest copies of biblical and apocryphal Hebrew texts ever found. Both these finds were small compared to the riches of Oxyrhynchus and the Geniza. But while Oxyrhynchus yielded mainly documentary texts related to a provincial town, the Geniza has offered generations of scholars the opportunity to reevaluate medieval Jewish culture in the context of the cosmopolitan, urban culture that produced and consumed it. ●

Marina Rustow is the Charlotte Bloomberg Associate Professor in the Humanities at Johns Hopkins University. She is the author of Heresy and the Politics of Community: The Jews of the Fatimid Caliphate (Cornell University Press, 2008) *and coeditor with Robert Chazan of the fifth and sixth volumes of* The Cambridge History of Judaism *(Cambridge University Press, forthcoming).*

---

1. The Geniza's contents are now housed in fifty libraries and several private collections. Most are being made available online as digital images through the Friedberg Genizah Project (www.genizah.org).
2. On the excavation of Oxyrhynchus and its contents, see Peter Parsons, *City of the Sharp-Nosed Fish: Greek Lives in Roman Egypt* (London: Weidenfeld and Nicolson, 2007).
3. For a wonderful, readable account of the scholarly discovery of the Geniza, see Adina Hoffman and Peter Cole, *Sacred Trash: The Lost and Found World of the Cairo Geniza* (New York: Schocken, 2011).
4. Hoffman and Cole, *Sacred Trash*, 103, 119.
5. The classic work is S. D. Goitein, *A Mediterranean Society: The Jewish Communities of the Arab World as Portrayed in the Documents of the Cairo Geniza*, 6 vols. (Berkeley: University of California Press, 1967–88). There are now also scores of newer works by Goitein's students and their students.
6. Goitein, *Mediterranean Society*, 1:17.

Baghdad

The city of Baghdad was built in the middle of the eighth century as the capital of a new dynasty, that of the Abbasid caliphs, who took power in 750. Within a few decades, Baghdad had become the economic and cultural center of the Middle East, attracting scholars and merchants from all over the empire. Jews, Muslims, Christians, and Zoroastrians, people from Bukhara and Khorasan, from Yemen, Syria, and Egypt, flocked to the City of Peace (Madinat al-Salam, as its founders called it), contributing to one of the most diverse and dynamic cultural contexts the world has known.

The sources documenting Baghdad in the Abbasid era are ample. They attest to many of the great men of the age (though to fewer women), particularly their political activities, courtly intrigues, and cultural output. The Jewish sources take a special position among these, since they offer glimpses of life beyond political circles and the literary elite.

Baghdad housed as many as 500,000 inhabitants at its height in the late ninth and early tenth centuries.[1] What did it take for a city to sustain a population of this magnitude? Most important, a steady food and water supply. Baghdad was well situated at the northern side of the vast alluvial plain between the Tigris and the Euphrates—an area of such rich, fertile silt that the Arabs named it al-Sawad, "the black land." The Abbasids took advantage of this setting by expanding the pre-Islamic system of irrigation canals. They also ensured the food supply to Baghdad by taxing peasants in the hinterland in kind rather than coin; the peasants thus avoided borrowing tax money at ruinous rates of interest. When the Abbasids moved the capital from Damascus to Baghdad, they enabled themselves to collect more taxes and thus to harness the riches of Iraq: the Sawad yielded more than five times as much in taxation as the provinces of Syria and Palestine.[2]

The geographer al-Maqdisi (d. ca. 990) reports that in his day, Jews were the third largest population group in Iraq and Iran, after Muslims and Zoroastrians; he included rural areas in which Jews were clearly a majority, such as the Jibal in Iran and the area around Sura, which still housed mainly Jews well into the tenth century, if not later. But estimating the Jewish population of Iraq and Baghdad presents difficulties because of a severe paucity of information. The only figure that has been transmitted to us comes from the Iberian Jewish traveler Benjamin of Tudela, who visited Baghdad in 1170 and estimated 40,000 Jewish inhabitants, 28 synagogues, and 10 institutions of higher learning. These figures are plausible. At Baghdad's height in the tenth century, between 50,000 and 75,000 Jews would not be an unreasonable guess, between 10 and 15 percent of the total population.

As the Iraqi population urbanized and the Abbasids came to rule one of the largest empires in world history, Baghdad grew into the most important city in the Near East.

The burden of subsistence farming and the economic attractions of the city spurred ever greater numbers of peasants to abandon agriculture. With urban growth came vastly expanded geographic mobility and commerce; long-distance traders brought goods, information, and people (including slaves) from as far away as al-Andalus, India, Constantinople, and the land of the Slavs, and the Abbasid court served as a prime market for them. Selling luxury goods to rulers could mean gaining a permanent place at the Abbasid court or else accumulating so much capital in trade as to make a move into banking possible.

Indeed, the Abbasid court served as an economic magnet, bringing commerce to the city and the possibility of work in the bureaucracy and the army. Over the course of the ninth century the court grew into an extensive machinery, staffing thousands of employees. The caliphs retreated behind the walls of their palaces and became less accessible to the outside world. They were protected by endless numbers of guards and attendants, among whom the vizier (*wazīr*) and the main chamberlain (*ḥājib*) were the most powerful.

The bureaucracy in Baghdad was an immense apparatus with tens of specialized departments dealing, for example, with land taxes, state landholdings, military affairs, official correspondence, and the minting of coins. These bureaus were staffed by salaried professionals. Most of the high-ranking scribes – we lack information on the anonymous subordinate scribes – came from families of large landowners and merchants in the Sawad. Scribes with non-Muslim and non-Arab backgrounds were well represented in the bureaucracy. Many Christians reached high-ranking positions, becoming directors or subdirectors of administrative departments. The same was true for the Shiite minorities; one of the most famous viziers of the early tenth century, Ibn al-Furat, was of Shi'ite origin. Jews are rarely mentioned in the administrative departments, except for the position of court banker and *jahbadh*, who supplied funds for the often deficient state treasury and measured the weights and values of gold (*dīnār*) and silver (*dirham*) coins in the Abbasid Empire's bimetallic economy.

One of the most noticeable features of the Abbasid administration was its extensive use of written documents – especially when compared to the administrations of early medieval Europe. The number and types of specialized letters, surveys, registers, reports, financial accounts, and internal

A tenth-century specimen of Baghdad paper: a letter from Nehemiah, *gaon* of the Pumbedita academy in Baghdad (960–68), to an Iraqi leader in Fustat (Old Cairo) complaining that the Egyptians have ignored his appeals for donations. Cambridge University Library, T-S 12.851. By kind permission of the Syndics of Cambridge University Library.

memoranda are overwhelming. So are the references to archives. The introduction of paper manufacture from Central Asia also played a major role in the dissemination of written documents within the Abbasid administration. Unfortunately, the original documents from Iraq have been lost, though a few have been copied into narrative sources, and Abbasid documents on papyrus and leather have survived from the provincial administrations of Egypt and Khorasan.

The Abbasid bureaucracy must have required vast quantities of paper. Soon after the first paper mills in the Islamic world were founded in Iraq, Baghdad became so closely associated with the manufacture of excellent paper that Byzantine writings referred to it as *bagdatikhon*.

The availability of paper also affected the book trade. By the early ninth century, there were no fewer than one hundred bookshops in Baghdad's paper-sellers' market (*sūq al-warrāqīn*) vending and copying books. If they served a population on the order of half a million people, this is a remarkably high ratio of booksellers to inhabitants even by modern standards. The demands of literary consumers

A suftaja written by a merchants' representative (*wakīl tujjār*) in Fustat, Abu Zikri Yehudah ben Yosef ha-Kohen (fl. 1131–ca. 1149). More than eighty of his *safātij* have been preserved. Like modern checks, this *suftaja* specifies the amount to be paid to the recipient written in numerals and words. Cambridge University Library, T-S Ar. 30.184d. By kind permission of the Syndics of Cambridge University Library.

should not, however, be overstated: literacy rates in premodern societies were low.

Baghdad soon became the home of the most important scholars of the era. Literary salons multiplied, and a wave of translations from Greek, Persian, and Syriac to Arabic introduced ancient scientific and philosophical works to a new public. Cultural life was far from exclusively Islamic. Although Baghdad attracted the most important Islamic jurists and theologians from the empire, Christians played a vital role in the translation of the classical Greek heritage, and Jews are attested among the earliest exponents of *kalām*, or speculative reasoning, in the ninth century. In the ninth and tenth centuries, scholars of all three faiths evidence new interest in Arabic translations of the Jewish and Christian scriptures. Until then, Muslims had cited biblical stories only in their Islamized form, as *qisas al-anbiyā'* or *isrā'īliyyāt* (legends about pre-Islamic prophets and biblical Israelites). But in late ninth-century Iraq, they began to gain access to Arabic translations of the biblical text itself. The Iraqi polymaths Ibn Qutayba (828–89) and al-Jahiz (781–869), and the great Abbasid historian and Qur'an commentator al-Tabari (839–923), all quoted the Bible on the basis of Christian Arabic translations made from the Syriac translation of the Septuagint. That translation would also shape the Judeo-Arabic Bible translations of Sa'adya ben Yosef al-Fayyumi, *gaon* of Sura in Baghdad (928–42), who set a new standard for translation of the Hebrew Bible into Arabic; his translation would, in turn, influence Christian Arabic translations for centuries. None of this is obvious, since the Hebrew Bible and the Greek Septuagint from which the Christian Syriac translations were made are not identical; it attests to the mobility across religious boundaries of the biblical text – and of the Baghdadi scholars who studied it.[3]

Abbasid Baghdad witnessed the spread of a culture that valued literacy highly. Scribes in the bureaucracy expressed their corporate identity through their expertise in writing, producing specialized treatises; legal specialists edited and standardized model documents to make them more effective and watertight; and religious experts discussed the advantages and disadvantages of writing down traditions, prophetic traditions in the case of Muslims and rabbinic ones in the case of Jews. One of the most striking outcomes of the dissemination of literacy was the growing trust in writing and written documents.

Such a development is clearly visible in written documents supporting financial transactions, especially the *suftaja* (pl., *safātij*), a written bill of credit used in both the tax administration of the remote provinces and long-distance trade. The *suftaja* spread all over the empire. The tenth-century historian al-Miskawayh attests to the provincial administration's reliance on it during the reign of al-Muqtadir (908–32), when the vizier 'Ali ibn 'Isa and his successor Abu 'Ali ibn Muqla were sent the contents of the treasury of Ahwaz in *safātij* of 300,000 and 600,000 dirhams, respectively.[4] Trade, too, benefited from the use of the *suftaja*. The Babylonian *geonim* endorsed its use by Jewish merchants, despite a Talmudic prohibition against employing a similar antique device called a *diyoqni*.[5]

The early tenth century saw the political breakdown of the Abbasid caliphate. The state was afflicted by major financial deficits caused by wars, mismanagement, and devastation of the fragile agricultural land of Iraq. The need for immediate cash forced viziers and caliphs to introduce fiscal privileges for large landowners and to enter into unfavorable contracts with tax farmers; the caliphs borrowed money from wealthy merchants and bankers at high rates of interest. Meanwhile, faraway provinces of the empire, including Ifriqiya (central North Africa), rebelled, requiring military expeditions and thus higher expenses. The army claimed an ever-increasing role in the political arena, and the caliph came to depend on its goodwill. In 936, the military governor of Wasit, Ibn Ra'iq, came to Baghdad to take over the administration, effectively marking the end of the political and military power of the Abbasid caliphs. ●

Marina Rustow is the Charlotte Bloomberg Associate Professor in the Humanities at Johns Hopkins University. She is the author of Heresy and the Politics of Community: The Jews of the Fatimid Caliphate *(Cornell University Press, 2008) and coeditor with Robert Chazan of the fifth and sixth volumes of* The Cambridge History of Judaism *(Cambridge University Press, forthcoming).*

Maaike van Berkel is associate professor of medieval history at the University of Amsterdam. She works on the social and cultural history of medieval Islam, particularly the bureaucracies of the Abbasids and Mamluks, and the political culture of the Abbasid court.

1. Premodern population estimates are necessarily speculative. There were no census registers, the sources offer varying (usually very high) estimates, and numbers can be miscopied in manuscripts. Hilal al-Sabi' (969–1056) offered what he called a conservative estimate of 96 million (!) based on the number of public baths (see his *Rusum dar al-khilafa*, ed. M. 'Awwad [Baghdad: Matba'zt al-'ani, 1964, 18–19]). Al-Sabi' also criticizes his predecessors who have "greatly exaggerated their descriptions of Baghdad without giving us proof and without increasing our knowledge" or offering "reasonable or dependable arguments." Still others provided estimates based on the quantity of soap used in bathhouses or the number of male and female singers.

2. On the regional economic system that sustained Baghdad and benefited from its riches, see Hugh Kennedy, "Feeding the Five Hundred Thousand: Cities and Agriculture in Early Islamic Mesopotamia," *Iraq* 73 (2011): 177–99.

3. Ronny Vollandt, "Christian-Arabic Translations of the Pentateuch from the 9th to the 13th Centuries: A Comparative Study of Manuscripts and Translation Techniques" (PhD dissertation, Cambridge University, 2011), 22, 63–75, 182–204 passim.

4. Ahmad b. Muhammad al-Miskawayh, *Tajarib al-umam* (The Experiences of Nations), ed. Amedroz and Margoliouth (London: Blackwell, 1920–21), 1:187.

5. The most recent discussion of the ruling and of the Greek etymology of the word *diyoq-ni* appears in Mark R. Cohen's book manuscript in progress, tentatively titled *Law and Society in Maimonides' "Mishneh Torah": Codification on the Post-Talmudic Islamic Economy*, introduction. Thanks to Professor Cohen for making parts of this work available to us.

Persecutions under the Reign of al-Hakim

In the last quarter of the ninth century, the Islamic world was the birthplace of the Ismaili movement, a Shi'ite current whose objective was to establish an alternative to Sunni Muslim society. Propagandists spread the Ismaili doctrine, and underground groups organized throughout the Islamic world. A specific Ismaili current came into being in North Africa in 893; its followers took the name "Fatimids" (a reference to their direct ancestor Fatima, daughter of the Prophet, and to her husband, 'Ali, Muhammad's cousin). They managed to assemble an army from the local Berber tribes and formed a Fatimid kingdom in the Maghreb, centered around Kairouan and Mahdia, the port they built nearby. But the aim of the Fatimids was to conquer Baghdad, capital of the Abbasids; they wanted to impose their doctrine on the entire Islamic world. In 969 the Fatimid caliph al-Mu'izz succeeded in conquering Egypt, after an operation meticulously planned by Ya'aqub ibn Killis, a Jewish vizier who had converted to Islam. Within a year, the Fatimids added most of Palestine as well as southern Syria to their conquests and founded a new capital in Egypt: Cairo, near the former capital of Fustat. Al-'Aziz, al-Mu'izz's son, pursued the task of establishing the new kingdom. He turned away from the Maghreb to concentrate on Egypt, Palestine, and Syria. He devoted himself particularly to the kingdom's commercial development. Upon his death in 996, his eleventh son, al-Hakim Bi-Amr Allah, ascended to the throne. He had been born to a Christian mother, and his court included a large number of Christians.[1]

Traditionally, the Jews supported the power in place, which usually ensured them protection and security. In the early years of his reign, al-Hakim seems to have followed that practice. This is indicated by a Jewish text discovered in the Geniza, commonly called the "Egyptian Scroll." It mentions an event dating to the beginning of the year 1012. During formal Jewish funeral ceremonies, the populace had attacked the Jews in the cortege. The police arrested and incarcerated twenty-three Jews. Having learned of these events, al-Hakim took the trouble to make inquiries, and, after his investigations, concluded that the Jews were innocent and sent them home. The Egyptian Scroll celebrates him for that action in the following terms: "The king, may he live eternally, king of justice, who hates the wicked and whose throne offers the hope of clemency."[2]

The Islamic sources, most of them written by Sunnis, were quite naturally hostile to the Ismaili Fatimids in general, and to al-Hakim in particular. This is why the information they provide focuses especially on the repression by al-Hakim and on the decrees he promulgated during that period. The primary targets of these decrees were the Christians, beginning in about 1007, then the Jews, apparently from 1012 on; but the Sunni Muslim population was also targeted. That repression reached its peak in 1009, when al-Hakim gave the order to destroy the Church of the Holy Sepulchre and to confiscate all its property. He also ordered the destruction of all the churches and synagogues in his kingdom. He compelled the Jews and Christians to wear humiliating signs intended to set them apart from the Muslims. According to certain sources, he even made the Jews and Christians choose between converting to Islam or being expelled, an attitude in total contradiction with Muslim belief ever since its origins in the Qur'an, which proscribes constraint in religion (Qur'an 2:256). Only one allusive reference to these events appears in the documents of the Geniza, in a letter whose ending is missing, written in about 1013 by Elhanan ben Shemaria, son of Shemaria ben Elhanan, leader of the community of Fustat. It is addressed to the Jewish community of Jerusalem. Here is the end of the text as it has come down to us: "The evil things grew and the good went away. . . . Synagogues were destroyed, omens came: the scrolls of the Torah were torn up and their shreds cast to the four winds, the holy books were scattered in the streets . . . the churches were destroyed and turned into rubbish heaps, we dressed in black and our faces are dark, our houses are filled with moaning, wood is hung around our necks, we are grief-stricken and have no peace. . . . Many have abandoned their faith and turned away from religion." That is a somber evocation of the repressive measures: synagogues destroyed and profaned, Torah scrolls burned, the humiliation of wearing distinctive signs (for example, a piece of wood around the neck), forced conversion to Islam.[3]

The sources provide no clear explanation of al-Hakim's motives. A few contemporary researchers refer to mental imbalance, while others attempt to interpret his acts in the light of his fanatical desire to be the incarnation of the Mahdi (Messiah), who occupies a fundamental place in Fatimid thought. The coming of a descendant of 'Ali is expected, one who will guide the world on the right path. Regarded objectively, al-Hakim's acts can be seen as a way of imposing the Pact of 'Umar in particularly extreme ways. But in the last years of his life, al-Hakim allowed the exiles to return, and the places of worship that had been destroyed were gradually rebuilt throughout his kingdom. He even allowed the Jews and Christians who had been forcibly converted to Islam to return to their original religion (despite the fact that apostasy was punishable by death, according to most Muslim jurisconsults). The life of the Jewish community more or less resumed its normal course in 1016, some five years before al-Hakim was assassinated.

The relations between al-Hakim and the Jews and Christians were an anomaly in the Fatimid kingdom and, more generally, in the view of the world elaborated by Islam, and gave rise to strong opposition among the Sunni Muslims. Yet we have found no evidence other than the letter of Elhanan ben Shemaria, and it is impossible to know for certain what sort of relations the Jews maintained with al-Hakim. We must, however, take into account the Jews' traditional allegiance to the power in place and the praise they bestowed on the

caliph before the repressive decrees. It is true that al-Hakim's reign developed under unstable conditions. There were local revolts in Egypt and an uprising by the bedouin in Palestine. The inadequate flooding of the Nile for several years in a row plunged Egypt into famine and destitution, stirring up discontent. It is plausible that the Jews, like the rest of the population, suffered from his manner of exercising power and even more from his enforcement of the Pact of 'Umar, but we have found no written statements expressing hatred toward him. Conversely, several positive elements of al-Hakim's reign are identifiable: the construction of lavish mosques in Cairo; the founding of al-Azhar, a richly endowed study institute intended to spread the Ismaili doctrine; the establishment of political contacts and the conclusion of several treaties with Byzantium; and the maintenance of an acceptable level of order in the kingdom, despite the many revolts. Al-Hakim was nonetheless assassinated in 1021. Because his body was never found, mystic groups such as the Druze concluded that he truly was the Mahdi and that he would reappear when the time came. His son, az-Zahir, succeeded him on the throne.[4] ●

Elinoar Bareket is a lecturer at the Achva Academic College, under the aegis of the Ben Gurion University of the Negev, and at the Sapir Academic College. Her works include Fustat on the Nile: The Jewish Elite in Medieval Egypt *(Brill, 1999);* The Leaders of the Jewish Community of Fustat in the First Half of the Eleventh Century *(Research Institute on the Diaspora, University of Tel Aviv, 1995, in Hebrew); and* The Jews of Egypt, 1007–1055, Based on Documents from the Archive of Efraim ben Shemarya *(Ben Zvi Institute, 1995, in Hebrew).*

1. S. Lane-Poole, *A History of Egypt in the Middle Ages* (London: Nabu Press, 1968), 92–136.
2. Quoted in Jacob Mann, *The Jews in Egypt and in Palestine under the Fatimid Caliphs* (New York: Cornell University Library, 1970).
3. M. Gil, *Eretz Israel ba-tekufa ha-muslemit ha-rishona* [*Palestine during the Early Islamic Period, 634–1099*], part 2: *Documents of the Cairo Geniza* (Tel Aviv, Tel Aviv University, 1983), B, 43.
4. Yacov Lev, *State and Society in Fatimid Egypt* (Leiden: Brill, 1991), 25–37.

Jerusalem

The entrance of the first Muslim armies into Jerusalem is shrouded in mystery, yet we can nevertheless distinguish two stages: the first siege was carried out in the winter of 634 and the second occurred after the disastrous defeat of the Byzantines in the Battle of Yarmuk in the summer of 636. Following negotiations between the Muslims (Saracens) and the patriarch Sophronius (d. 638), who served as the head of the church of Jerusalem, the city capitulated. The account of the negotiations between the caliph 'Umar and the patriarch is merely a historical legend, while the stories on the participation of the Jews in the first phase of Islamic rule reflect an apocalyptical interpretation of the events. It seems that immediately after the withdrawal of the Byzantine army from inland Syria, the old proscription that

Fighting at the gates of Jerusalem, Ottoman painting, 1583. Istanbul, Museum of Turkish and Islamic Arts.

banned the Jews from inhabiting Jerusalem, which was confirmed in the abovementioned treaty, was lifted by the new regime.

Muslim sources tell about the participation of Jews in the excavation of the Temple Mount and the (building of the) foundation of a new sacred space (harām), that is, the al-Aqsa Mosque and the Dome of the Rock, which late Jewish sources confirm. Mention of the al-Aqsa Mosque recalls the sacred place of Jerusalem in Muslim belief. There, according to the exegeses of the Qur'an (Sura 17:1) and the hadith, one night the angel Gabriel miraculously transported the Prophet Muhammed, via a mythical steed, to "the Farthest Mosque" (al-Masjid al-Aqsa) in Jerusalem. On his arrival the Prophet met and prayed with some of the prophets, including Moses and Jesus, and also ascended to heaven and spoke with God.

Muslims and Jews shared the vision of Jerusalem as a sacred city, the place where King David and King Solomon (prophets in Islamic tradition) ruled and erected the Temple (masjid, or mosque, in Islamic tradition). Yet while the Jews envisioned the holy city as the navel (umbilicus) of the universe, the Muslims considered Jerusalem as a secondary sacred location, next to Mecca. In their prayers they turn to this sacred city, where the Caaba, the shrine of Abraham, is situated. Nevertheless, through the period covered in this article, a rich literary output of tractates that praised the merits of Jerusalem (al-Quds: "the Holy" in Arabic) was recorded.

A Jewish population flourished in Jerusalem under the aegis of the caliphs. The specific location of their neighborhood in the city is disputed. The yeshiva of Jerusalem gained wide fame and recognition. Some of the families immigrated from northern Palestine;

others migrated from all over the Islamic world. With the renewal of maritime communication between Southern Europe and the Eastern Mediterranean (in the tenth century) connections between the Jews of Europe and the Jews of Palestine were reestablished. In addition to Rabbanites, the city also housed a vibrant Karaite community.

The significance of the city in Jewish religious life under the caliphs can be deduced from the ceremony of the declaration of the new moon (month) on the Mount of Olives. On the day of Hoshana Rabbah (the seventh day of Sukkoth/Tabernacles), the chiefs of the yeshiva of Jerusalem would ascend to the Mount of Olives and make the proclamation of the calendar, that is, they gave the dates of the upcoming Jewish festivals and indicated whether the year would be a leap year. Jewish pilgrims from the East as well as the West came to Jerusalem. A ritual of circumambulating the Haram al-Sharif's walls and praying at its gates took place yearly on Hoshana Rabbah, just as in Temple times. From the southern wall, the so-called Gate of the Priest, the procession would climb to the "chair" (a long sacred stone). In addition to the proclamation of the calendar, the heads of the yeshiva would announce the nominations of new scholars and leaders. This was followed by the collection of donations from the audience and a festive meal. At that time, the early custom of contributing money to light candles at the Dome of the Rock vanished, and was seemingly replaced with the Jews contributing to communal charity institutions in the city and to the Jerusalem yeshiva.

The rich documentation found in the Cairo Geniza sheds light on Jewish life in Jerusalem during those centuries, and on communication between the local communities and other Jewish congregations and with the Diaspora. From these documents we learn that during the Fatimid period, the head of the Jerusalem yeshiva (*gaon*) served as the head (*ra'īs al-yahūd*) of the Jews of the Fatimid state.

Toward the closing decades of the eleventh century, the number of Jews in Jerusalem shrank and their economic condition went from bad to worse. The yeshiva, the heart of the intellectual and judicial community, emigrated from Jerusalem to Tyre. The Franks renewed the old Byzantine rule that banned Jews from dwelling in Jerusalem, but the Muslim sultan Saladin abolished this decree in October 1187. Following his victory in Hattin in northern Palestine, Saladin led his armies to attack the fortified cities and towns of the Latin Kingdom of Jerusalem. The sultan synchronized the recapture of Jerusalem with the Islamic calendar, and his army entered the city "in striking coincidence" with the anniversary of the Prophet Muhammad's ascension to heaven (*al-'Isrā' wal-Mi'rāj*), which is traditionally celebrated on the night of Rajab 27. During the negotiations that led to the surrendering of the city, the Franks of Jerusalem secured a treaty with Saladin. The parties agreed that the Latins would ransom themselves and go free. Following his entry, the sultan ordered the purification of Jerusalem. The Dome of the Rock and the al-Aqsa Mosque were re-Islamized. Some assume that at that event the famed volume containing all the books of the Hebrew Bible, which was revised by Rabbi Aaron Ben Asher and was considered as the most authoritative, was removed to Egypt, where Maimonides (A.D. 1138–1204) saw it. The claim that Saladin issued a call to the Jews to come settle in Jerusalem as a new Cyrus (see Ezra 1:1–3) is probably a myth.

Yet, this was a very short period of relief. The armies of the Third Crusade threatened to capture Jerusalem. Considering the advance of Richard the First (the Lionheart) as a grave menace to the city, Saladin ordered that Jerusalem should be refortified and repopulated with loyal inhabitants, among whom were probably Jews. A popular historical legend narrates that during his advance toward Jerusalem, King Richard fell ill and Maimonides turned down an invitation to travel to Palestine to treat the sick king. Yet, as Bernard Lewis has already demonstrated, this is a nice anecdote but absolutely without historical foundation.

In the wake of the truce with King Richard, Saladin returned to Damascus, where he passed away, leaving the sultanate to his Ayyubid heirs. They governed the Holy City for several decades. During these years they contributed modestly to attiring Jerusalem with an Islamic robe. Some Jews reinhabited the city.

The Hebrew poet Judah Alharizi, in his *maqāma* (Tahkemoni 16:39), mentions that he saw three Jewish communities in Jerusalem (A.D. 1216): al-Ifranj (literally "Franks," from Latin Europe), Maghribians (from North Africa/Spain), and al-Shamiyun (from Syria-Palestine). It might be that this last congregation settled in the city during the years between the victory at Hattin and the advance of King Richard. The realm of the Ayyubids stretched from southern Turkey (Ashur/Assyria) to Yemen, and presumably Jews from these lands moved to Jerusalem, too. Several letters from the Geniza tell stories of these worshippers.

The economic destitution, the arrangements concluded between the Ayyubids and the Franks, and the advance of the Mongols reduced the size of the Jewish population of Jerusalem in the last decades of the Ayyubids almost to nothing. ●

Professor at Haifa University, Yehoshua Frenkel teaches social and political history of the Arab world during the Middle Ages. His recent publications include "The Turks of the Eurasian Steppes in Arabic Geographical Literature," in Mongols, Turks and Others: Eurasian Nomads and the Sedentary World, *edited by Reuven Amitai and Michal Biran (Brill, 2005).*

The Jews of al-Andalus
Mercedes García-Arenal

The Jewish communities of al-Andalus—the part of the Iberian Peninsula under Muslim rule—were particularly illustrious between the reign of the Umayyad caliph of Cordova 'Abd al-Rahman III (912–961) and the Almohad takeover after 1140. No other medieval Jewish community had so many high-ranking personalities in the political and economic spheres; no other produced a literary culture of such breadth, revealing an intellectual life shared with the Muslims. That blossoming was all the more unexpected in that the Jews of Hispania had lived in great social and legal insecurity during the time of the Visigoths, when they were persecuted and compelled by decree to convert. Part of the Jewish population of al-Andalus, no doubt stemming from the migratory waves of the Islamic conquests, embraced the invaders' culture and language from the start.[1] The unification of the territories and the adoption of the Arabic language constituted a fundamental change,[2] since, among other things, these measures facilitated the establishment of fluid relations among the various Jewish communities. In that Arabization, what was specific to the Jews' literary culture was the extraordinary cultural vitality of the elites, combined with their material prosperity, their participation in public affairs and in the administration of the courts of al-Andalus, their responsibilities within their communities, and their importance in Jewish history. That importance is, in fact, paradoxical, given the small number of their representatives.[3]

Mercedes García-Arenal

A university lecturer and researcher at the Consejo Superior de Investigaciones Científicas (CSIC) in Madrid, the author studies Islamic minorities and Jews in the Islamic world, as well as the conversion process and messianism. She is the editor of *Conversions islamiques: Identités religieuses en Islam méditerranéen* (Maisonneuve et Larose, 2001).

An Andalusian golden age? A historiographical view

Al-Andalus does not constitute a unique example of cultural interaction between Jews and Muslims. Far from it. Various aspects of that phenomenon can also be found in other Islamic regions. Individual Jews, especially in Egypt and Iraq, had enjoyed power and wealth before the tenth century, and entire dynasties had transmitted the viziership from father to son in medieval Morocco and later, well after the eclipse of al-Andalus. In Iraq and Morocco as well, the particular character-

⟩ See the
article by
Marina
Rustow,
pp. 87–88.
istics of their literature would be affected by the use of Arabic and by an immersion in Arab-Muslim culture. This was also the case for the Jewish community of
Cairo during the early Middle Ages, which reached its peak in the twelfth century.
But nowhere else was the concentration of eminent Jewish personalities in the cultural, scientific, professional, and political realms as high as it was in al-Andalus
between the tenth and twelfth centuries, so much so that, in Jewish history, the
period came to be known as the "golden age." Naturally, the literary culture of the
Andalusian Jews, more than any other, managed to acquire an iconic value in the
later Jewish imagination.

⟩ See
the prologue
by Mark R.
Cohen,
pp. 28–38.
In the nineteenth century, that golden age was the object of marked interest from
the German intellectuals who personified the *Wissenschaft des Judentums* (science of
Judaism). The corresponding countermyth made its appearance in the mid-twentieth
century, and not only with respect to the Jews of al-Andalus. This myth, more contemporary historiographically and still robust today through various modes of diffusion,
insists on the victimization and deterioration of Judaism and the Jews under Islam.[4]

As for Spanish historiography in the nineteenth and twentieth centuries, it placed studies of that Jewish community within the context of what it considered an acute and
persistent problem: the integration of al-Andalus into the history of Spain. That episode
represented an obstruction to building Spanish nationalism, inasmuch as it brought to
the fore a foreign plurality when compared to the principles of coherence and unity
through which the other European nations were making sense of their past. In their
efforts to legitimate the study of Islamic and Jewish history, and to consolidate their
own academic discipline, the Spanish Orientalists, in both Hebrew studies and Arabic
studies, devoted themselves almost exclusively to research in cultural history, integrating the art and literature produced by the Arab Muslims and the Jews of the peninsula
into the Hispanic cultural heritage.[5] Finally, and more recently, the embrace in Spain
of a plural and "tolerant" past as a model for the present has taken the form of another
fertile myth: that of the "three cultures."[6] This means that studies of the period have
almost always been used to define and legitimate a present-day identity on the basis
of an "invented tradition." Although these myths constitute proof of the interest and
fascination exerted by the situation of the Jews in al-Andalus, they also illustrate the difficulty of addressing their status without adopting an ideological stance.

It may be for that reason that there are no recent monographs on the Jews of al-
Andalus: there do not seem to have been any social histories of that community
since the 1970s. The standard reference, Eliyahu Ashtor's *The Jews of Moslem Spain*,
published in English in 1973,[7] ends with the taking of Toledo in 1085. Only specialized studies dating back more than twenty years have complemented the pan-
oramic view of the *taifa* kingdoms or of the Nasrid kingdom of Granada.[8] That
absence of recent monographs is no doubt also attributable to the creation of a
national culture in Israel that relies on its own historiography, for which the study of
al-Andalus has remained little more than an afterthought.

In addition to these difficulties, the Jewish communities were long studied exclusively in terms of religious affiliation. They were thereby reduced to minority status and perceived only in terms of their marginality, even though the porosity among the various communities was extremely important in that context. That is why the new modes of research coming in the wake of postcolonial studies, which have taken an interest in hybridization or symbiosis, have been particularly fruitful. These studies avoid speaking of "borrowings" or "influence," terms that imply the domination or preeminence of one culture over another, and emphasize that the contact between cultures rarely occurs in a single direction, and that the dominant culture from the social and political standpoint cannot be protected from the effect of such contact. Ideas arising within one cultural context can even acquire an altogether new meaning when they are received or applied in a different context.

Eminent specialists such as Ross Brann have focused more on the process than on the result; that is, more on the evolution of a culture than on its creations, pointing to ambiguities and ambivalence.[9] Furthermore, voices warning against the threat of losing one's identity – one's "purity" and "authenticity" – through contact with other cultures often reverberate the loudest in these moments of ambiguity and ambivalence. Under Islamic rule, for example, that threat led to the recommendation that one "differentiate oneself from the Jews and the Christians" (*mukhafalat ahl al-kitāb*), which, within the intracultural dimension of the process, is an invitation to eliminate what certain groups perceive as discordances engendered by alien elements, and to define and reinforce the lines of demarcation between them.[10] These efforts arose within both the Muslim majority and the Jewish and Christian minorities.[11] All these phenomena, which occurred in al-Andalus and later in the Christian kingdoms of the north, allow us to see how misleading the polemical versions are, since one side emphasizes only victimization, violence, or subjection, and the other only harmony and tolerance. It goes without saying that violence was inherent in all medieval societies. David Nirenberg's now inescapable thesis is that in Christian medieval Aragon, harmonious coexistence and violence were part of the same system; in other words, a certain degree of violence was the guarantor of a certain degree of peace and cohabitation. Violence there was almost ritualized, manifesting itself regularly in a measured way, and reinforcing the segregation on which the coexistence between diverse religious communities was based. That system was in the interest of all parties concerned. It is to be noted that such systematic violence did not occur in al-Andalus but only elsewhere, in Aragon, for example. Isolated episodes of violence against the Jews were the means by which the boundaries between the minority group and the majority could be abolished and redefined; and, when crises occurred, they were also the vehicle for attacks against the royal power and the tax system.[12] As a result, I shall not defend the vision of al-Andalus as an *Arcadia felix* or, on the contrary, as a place where the *dhimmī*s were the target of violence and humiliation. More interesting are the perspectives introduced by such authors as Ross Brann, Esperanza Alfonso, David Wasserstein, Raymond Scheindlin, and Sarah Stroumsa, who focus on the Arabization of Andalusian Jews and the impact of that process on literary history and cultural identity. In particular, these authors demonstrate that the Hebrew language could not isolate itself from the cultural world in which it was located or from a multiethnic and religiously plural society such as al-Andalus.[13]

Recent research on al-Andalus has dealt less with the questions of cultural identity than with the social history of Muslim Spain,[14] expanding and introducing innovation into the discipline in a way extremely pertinent for understanding the life of its Jewish communities.[15] The area of extension of "al-Andalus," the name the Arab-Muslim sources gave to the Iberian Peninsula, and by which we designate the territory under Muslim rule, gradually diminished over the course of the Middle Ages. In the Arabic sources, al-Andalus is systematically characterized as an "island," a land surrounded on one side by the sea and on the other by the Christians. In reality, al-Andalus was a border territory, the western border of Islam. Straddling two civilizations, both the world inherited from the Hispano-Romans and the Arab-Muslim world originating in the East, the society of al-Andalus developed characteristics peculiar to itself. Over their eight centuries of presence on Iberian soil, the Muslims maintained close relations with the East and the Islamic community, to which they felt they belonged, through their religious obligation to go on pilgrimage and through journeys made by the educated elite to receive training in the Orient from renowned masters.

> *I shall not defend the vision of al-Andalus as an Arcadia felix or, on the contrary, as a place where the dhimmīs were the target of violence and humiliation.*

The Muslim conquest

The Muslim armies crossed the Strait of Gibraltar for the first time in 711. Within a few years, the Visigothic monarchy had fallen apart, weakened by internecine struggles. These Muslim troops were sent by the governors of North Africa, who in turn reported to the Umayyad caliphate, which ruled the Islamic Empire from Damascus. The armies were composed of Arabs and, in much larger numbers, of Berbers. The Arabs enjoyed a privileged position as such, because they had been the first to receive the message of the Prophet Muhammad. The Arab component of al-Andalus grew in number following a major Berber uprising in the Maghreb in 739. At that time, the Umayyad caliph of Damascus sent in Arab troops of Syrian origin who, after they were defeated, took refuge in al-Andalus and settled there. The contribution of the Berber populations, however, was constant throughout the Middle Ages. Divisions appeared between the Arabs belonging to the first wave of conquests and the Syrian troops who followed. A good portion of the Berber tribes

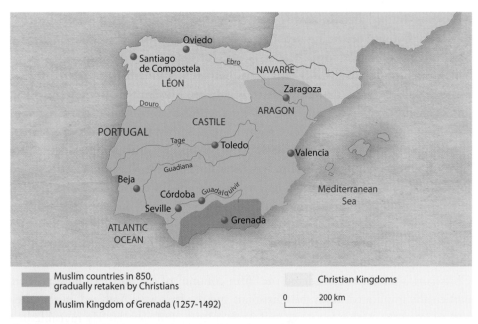

Muslim countries in 850,
gradually retaken by Christians

Christian Kingdoms

Muslim Kingdom of Grenada (1257-1492)

0   200 km

Christian and Muslim kingdoms in Spain, ninth to fifteenth centuries.

who converted to Islam during the first century of the conquest became part of the Arab clans' clientele. All these groups would insist on the place they held within a lineage in order to benefit from social consideration.[16] To these heterogeneous elements, it is necessary to add the autochthonous Hispano-Roman or Gothic populations, who were Christianized, but probably superficially, or at least not uniformly. The pace of their conversion to Islam is still poorly understood, but it seems that the authorities did not seek to accelerate it, preferring to continue collecting the taxes the *dhimmī*s were obliged to pay. Conversions increased as the central power gained in social and cultural prestige. By about the eleventh century, the majority of the residents of al-Andalus were Muslims, and only small minorities of Christians and Jews remained.[17]

Political domination and cultural influence

Despite that retreat of Christianity in the face of Islam, there was a deep fracture between the Arabs and the Berbers, who for their part felt like "second-class Muslims." Like the Hispano-Romans converted to Islam, these "new Muslims" were sometimes subjected to social, political, and economic discrimination, which led to revolts. Hence the episodes known as *fitna*, "uprisings," in the second half of the ninth century, and later the *fitna barbariyya*, or "Berber *fitna*," which in the early eleventh century put an end to the caliphate and marked the beginning of the *taifa* kingdoms. Immediately following these two *fitna*, but also over the next few centuries, the Berbers, according to the Arabic sources, were the object of denigration more often than the *dhimmīs*.[18]

The society of al-Andalus was thus very complex. On one hand, a series of what could be called vertical divisions existed within the Muslim majority; on the other, horizontal divisions into "castes" were at work within both communities of *dhimmīs*, the Christians (from among whom many administrators, functionaries, and ambassadors were recruited until the mid-fourteenth century) and the Jews. The social status of these two minority groups was determined by the Muslim majority's need for their cooperation in certain functions, and also by the convenience of appealing to courtiers who, during internal struggles for power, could not hope to engage in intrigues because of the terms of the *dhimma* pact. It was therefore imperative to involve these minorities in the conflicts proper to the Muslim majority and in the various stages of battle or negotiation with the states of the northern peninsula. The Christians, sometimes considered the "fifth column" of the northern powers, were particularly implicated. Both the Christians and the Jews were Arabized, in that they had adopted the Arabic language and Arab culture, and were largely invisible in a diverse and plural society.[19] Finally, there was a vast population of slaves of various backgrounds, both from the northern peninsula and from Eastern Europe.

At the political level, al-Andalus was initially under the power of the governors named by Damascus, then later achieved virtual independence when the Umayyads were supplanted by the Abbasids of Baghdad (750). A member of the overthrown family, 'Abd al-Rahman, took refuge in al-Andalus, where in 755 he founded an emirate. Al-Andalus truly began to thrive under the domination of his descendant 'Abd al-Rahman III, who took the title of caliph, proclaimed his right to govern as Commander of Believers on Earth (*amīr al-mu'minīn*), minted a gold coin, and had a palatine city – called Madinat al-Zahra—built near the capital of Cordova. Like the Umayyad caliphs who succeeded him, he played a role in creating an identity proper to al-Andalus, based on the Islamic religion and Arab culture. At the same time, he strove to relegate Arab ethnicity to a secondary position, so that the vertical fractures within Andalusian society would be attenuated. That effort was partly historiographical: a series of court chroniclers and compilers of biographies and bibliographies of al-Andalus scholars enjoyed the protection of the caliphs themselves. But it also entailed integrating converts and *dhimmīs* into the world of science and scholarship. The caliph's entourage included illustrious Jewish personalities. The Muslims of al-Andalus felt vastly superior to the Christians

> **Taifas**
>
> In the eleventh century, after the fall of the Caliphate of Cordoba, small kingdoms arose locally in al-Andalus. *Taifa* (from the Arabic *tâ ifah*, plural *taw âif*, "party") kingdoms were not strictly monarchical but in fact were based on a regional oligarchy. The fragmentation of these kingdoms, which never achieved political unity, contributed to the Christian reconquest.

of the north at the cultural and scientific levels, in their refinement and way of life, but inferior to their Eastern coreligionists. The Jews of al-Andalus, for their part, judged themselves markedly superior to the Eastern Jews and, of course, to those of the northern peninsula.

Classical Arabic Islamic literature was introduced into the court of Cordova, as were the manners and modes of life of the court of Baghdad, which the Umayyads of al-Andalus sought to imitate. Al-Andalus underwent remarkable literary development over the following centuries, in the areas of poetry, logic, philosophy, grammar, the sumptuary arts, and architecture.[20] The Jews participated in the cultural experience common to all Andalusians, and their names can be found in all the activities of court life. For example, Abu-al-Nasr al-Mansur was a musician working in the Umayyad court of al-Hakam I (d. 822).

'Abd al-Rahman was not the first Muslim ruler to shatter the unity of the caliphate. The Fatimids, a Shi'ite dynasty founded in Tunis whose empire extended to Egypt, proclaimed themselves caliphs in the early tenth century. 'Abd al-Rahman's decision to take the title of *amīr al-mu'minīn* may not have been unrelated to the rivalry between his family and the Fatimids for control of North Africa. That rivalry led to the establishment of ties between Cordova and Constantinople, ties that had enormous cultural and symbolic repercussions and intensified Mediterranean trade, in which the Jews of al-Andalus played a prominent role. They were the chief representatives of the elites of the Jewish communities and were very interested in cultural life; as such, they exerted a decisive influence on the political economy and were an important factor in the Jews' integration into Muslim society.[21]

Political crisis, new alliances, and the place of the Jews

The Muslim authorities on the Iberian Peninsula maintained their hegemony until the early thirteenth century. But military pressure from the Christians of the north had been felt there for nearly a century. In 1085 Toledo was conquered by Alfonso VI, king of León and Castile. The caliphate founded by 'Abd al-Rahman had collapsed, and the territory of al-Andalus had been dismembered into several *taifa* kingdoms (*mulūk al-tawā'if*), where minor local sovereigns without great legitimacy created their own courts and sought to imitate caliphal Cordova.

The divisions among these kingdoms gave the Christians an opportunity to meddle in the internal politics of the Islamic world and to levy taxes on some of these petty kings, who established relations of vassaldom with them so as to be protected from their Muslim neighbors and enemies. In other words, on that border territory of al-Andalus, it appeared legitimate to resort to alliances with non-Muslims in order to defend oneself from rivals of the same religion.

This was a politically tumultuous and culturally productive period. It was precisely during the time of the *taifa* kingdoms that the Jews experienced the greatest material prosperity and acquired the most visibility and influence in al-Andalus society. They played a preeminent role, especially in Seville, Saragossa, and Almería, where a few Jewish families had members who were viziers. The most famous case was that of the Ibn Naghrelas of Granada: according to his enemies, Joseph ha-Nagid was a vizier more powerful than the sultan, and, whatever the extent of his power, it was the reason for a popular uprising in 1066 that culminated in his execution and that of a large number of Granadan Jews, as well as the looting of their houses. This was the most serious act of anti-Jewish violence we know of in the history of al-Andalus. There was another episode of lesser scope in Cordova in 1135.[22]

In these times of political and religious crisis, a portion of the Muslim elites, especially religious elites, felt that the existence of al-Andalus was seriously threatened. Because of the circumstances, the Muslims' hostility toward the Jews increased, particularly toward those who, by virtue of their scientific knowledge, wealth, or erudition, had attained high positions. A whole tradition of negative feelings dating back to the time of the Prophet Muhammad's preaching resurfaced. The preeminence of Jewish dignitaries in some *taifa* kingdoms, such as Saragossa and Granada, was underscored at the time in the Arabic sources, which often associated it with Christian pressure. Such was the case, for example, for the chronicler Ibn al-Kardabus. Without establishing any causal relationship, he diagnosed that preeminence as the source of all the evils that placed the Muslims of his time in danger: "The affairs of the Muslims were entrusted to the Jews, who caused in their ranks the ravages of lions, now converted into chamberlains, viziers, and secretaries. During that time, the Christians went about al-Andalus every year, capturing, sacking, destroying, and taking prisoners."[23] The crises of Islam within Muslim Spain can be read through the "textualization" of the ambivalent relations between the Muslims and the Jewish elites.[24] But when an act of violence was committed against a group or against a highly placed Jewish individual, the instigators felt obliged to justify it from the standpoint of the law. They habitually argued that the Jews or Christians had violated the *dhimma* pact, contravening the clauses of their contract with Islam, so that the government and the faithful were no longer obliged to respect their pledges. That concern appears even in the literature most aggressive toward the *dhimmī*s: for example, in the poem by Abu Ishaq, a jurist from Elvira, composed on the occasion of the anti-Jewish movement in Granada in 1066.

The end of Muslim domination

The taking of Toledo by the Christians sounded the alarm, impelling the kings of *taifa*s to appeal to North Africa, where a Berber dynasty was in power: the Almoravids, originally a militant and rigorous reformist religious movement. From their territories in southern Morocco, they founded a powerful empire, of which al-Andalus became a province. So it was that in the late eleventh century, Muslim

Spain lost its political independence. That loss of autonomy would be perpetuated when another Berber dynasty, the Almohads, originally from Morocco, took power. But the Almohads would prove no more capable of checking the advance of the Christians: Cordova fell in 1236, Murcia in 1243, Seville in 1248, and after that city, the entire Guadalquivir Valley. The Islamic domination was reduced to the kingdom of Granada, which included the present-day provinces of Granada, Málaga, and Almería. It would disappear in 1492, when the Catholic monarchs Isabella and Ferdinand took the city and decreed that all Jews had to convert to Catholicism or face expulsion from the territories, a measure that would be applied to all Muslims a few years later, in 1502. There was a large Jewish population in Granada at the time of the Christian conquest. This is worth noting, since some have assumed that Judaism in al-Andalus had disappeared with the Almohad conquest. But major studies have demonstrated that such was not the case. In reality, the Jewish community had swelled in the two centuries of the Nasrids' rule, with the immigration of Jews from the Christian territories of the north, whose situation at the social and legal levels had worsened as of the mid-thirteenth century.

Audience of the Sultan of Fes comes to support the Muslims of Grenada against the Almohads. Miniature in the *Cantigas de Santa Maria*, thirteenth century. Madrid, Escurial Library, poem 181, fol. 240 recto.

There is a tendency to believe that the key date for the Jews of al-Andalus is some-where around 1146, the year the Almohad caliph 'Abd al-Mu'min decreed conversion to Islam obligatory for all *dhimmī*s living in his territory. More than a reform movement, Almohadism was a complete revolution, both in its objectives and in its achievements. Its founder, Ibn Tumart, inspired hope for a new future that would involve a total break with the ideas and practices of the past, and that would estab-lish the rule of justice on earth before the end of the world, when all humanity would embrace the same religion. Everyone, both Muslims and non-Muslims, had to convert to its doctrine, considered to be the universal religion that had existed even before the Revelation.[25] Ibn Tumart's preaching and the actions of 'Abd al-Mu'min and his descendants ushered in considerable changes not only in the areas of doctrine and jurisprudence but also in social organization: the minting of a new square coin, the reform of the writing system, the reorientation of the *qibla* in the mosques, a new formula for the call to prayer, and the abolition of the *dhimma* pact. Hence the Jews and the Christians found themselves obliged to convert to Islam, and the Muslims who were not followers of the Almohad doctrine were officially declared infidels (*kuffar*).[26] During the conquest of Seville in 1147, the Jews and the Christians, along with a large portion of the Muslim population, were the victims of massacres.[27] In al-Andalus, the Jewish population converted to Islam, and some Arabic sources record that these converts roused so many suspicions that they were obliged to wear distinctive clothing.[28]

Little is actually known about these episodes. The Arabic sources hardly mention what would have been an unprecedented event, the abolition of the *dhimma*, and provide few details about its consequences or duration. It is taken for granted that, once the first surge of Almohad power was over, things resumed their usual course, and converts were allowed to return to Judaism. We know almost nothing else, and it is strange that the Jews could have abandoned Islam without being charged with the crime of apostasy. As for the rare Hebrew sources, they are either far removed geographically or they postdate the event. What remains, therefore, is the undis-puted fact that a large number of Jews emigrated to the Christian territories in the north and to other Islamic territories, including Morocco and Tunisia, even though these areas too were under Almohad domination. The example of the philosopher Maimonides, a native of Cordova, provides a good illustration of that phenomenon.

The Jewish population

The sources available to us on the Jews of al-Andalus shed the most light on the elites. Only a few documents of the Cairo Geniza make it possible to reconstruct, directly or through generalization, certain characteristics of the economic and social life of the communities of Muslim Spain. We must therefore rely on Arabic sources. These sources indicate in particular that the Jews of al-Andalus had an important economic role. A merchant elite brought all its influence to bear on the activities linked to customs, the treasury, and taxation. But most of the communities devoted themselves to retail trade and urban artisanal crafts, especially the production of sumptuous fabrics, brocaded silks, and other brocade and trim. The Jews were also money changers and pawnbrokers, cultured milk vendors, and shopkeepers.[29]

Similarly, we have very few data on the demographic evolution and geographical distribution of that population. Both the Arabic and the Christian sources on the reconquered cities indicate that each of these cities had a Jewish quarter. Not all the Jews lived in that district, and it was not usually closed or marked off from the rest of the urban space. But the baths and the synagogue were located there.[30]

Al-Razi, the chronicler of the conquest, called Granada the "city of the Jews." 'Abdallah, the Zirid king of the *taifa* of Granada who was deposed by the Almoravids, reports in his memoirs that, under the reign of his grandfather Badis, most of the residents of Granada were Jewish; and the Arab chronicles that relate the pogrom of 1066 speak of raids and looting in "the Jewish quarters." The German traveler Jerome Münzer, who visited Granada in 1494 – which is to say, shortly after the city was taken by the Catholic monarchs – tells us that the Jewish quarter, located in the city center, had twenty thousand residents. King Ferdinand would order its demolition. Nevertheless, the city's "capitulations," signed in 1491, mention that Jews also lived in Albaicín and other outlying districts of Granada.

Lucena, one of the most active centers of trade in al-Andalus, was populated almost exclusively by Jews before the arrival of the Almohads; that city was protected by a wall and a moat. According to the anonymous chronicle *Al-Hulal al-Mawisyya*, the Almoravid caliph Yusuf ibn Tashfin went there to impose a heavy tribute on its residents. The Jews of Lucena had in fact declared that they would convert to Islam if the Messiah, expected to arrive in the year 500/1107, did not appear. When the Messiah did not come, the emir changed the conversion to financial compensation.[31]

Worship in a synagogue. Barcelona Haggadah, fourteenth century. London, British Museum.

Ibn Hayyan, a Muslim chronicler from the time of the caliphate, relates that in Toledo, the Jews resided in a "city of Jews" (*madīnat al-Yahūd*) surrounded by a wall erected in 820 by one of the men who had opposed Umayyad authority. James I, king of Aragon, also discovered an extensive and densely populated Jewish quarter in Majorca when he seized the city in about 1230. Such was also the case in Valencia. But we have no demographic data, and the archaeological research that has recently told us so much about the composition of the cities of al-Andalus and of their populations has shed little light on the size of the Jewish quarters or on the number of their residents.

The Jews: Courtiers and rabbis

As a result, any study of the Jews of al-Andalus runs the risk of becoming a catalog or list of scientists, poets, and grammarians. The information available to us about isolated individuals has a clear illustrative value, but it also has serious limitations, not to mention the risk that such information will be turned into exemplary stories in the service of the political needs of the moment.

Abu Yusuf Hasdai ben Ishaq ibn Shaprut was without a doubt the most distinguished Jew of al-Andalus: a famous physician in the Umayyad court of Cordova, he was in the service of Caliph 'Abd al-Rahman III (r. 912–961), then of his son al-Hakam II (r. 961–76)[32]

See also the Nota bene devoted to him, pp. 134-135.

He was reputed both for his traditional Jewish education (the Bible and the Talmud) and for his thorough knowledge of belles lettres (*adab*) and the "science of the ancients" (*falsafa*). Such erudition was also a distinctive trait of al-Andalus, since the conservative sectors of rabbinical Judaism shared with orthodox Islam a profound distrust of Greek knowledge.[33] In addition to practicing medicine, Hasdai held important administrative, fiscal, and diplomatic positions, as attested by Muslim and Jewish sources. According to the Arab historian Ibn Hayyan, he surpassed all the royal servants in his manners, intellectual discipline, subtlety, patience, and intelligence. Ibn Juljul's history of the physicians of al-Andalus, continued and expanded by Ibn Abi Usaybi'a,[34] also mentions him as a physician, though such works generally confined themselves to transmitting and cataloging Muslim scholars. Hasdai's role as a physician was far from unique or unusual. The number and impact of physicians on science in general can be assessed by reading the *Categories of Nations* (*Kitab tabaqat al-Umam*) by Ibn Sa'id al-Andalusi, a judge, philologist, and historian who lived in al-Andalus in the eleventh century. Among these "categories of nations" distinguished for their contributions were the Banu Isra'il. Included on that list were a large number of physicians of al-Andalus, who shone for their knowledge of logic, philosophy, Arabic, and Hebrew.

Hasdai too gave his support to Jewish belles lettres. Above all, both Ibn Sa'id and Ibn Abi Usabi'a declare that he took advantage of the respect Caliph al-Hakam had for him to import from the East all the Jewish books he needed: "Thus the Jews of al-Andalus could learn what they did not know and had less difficulty devoting themselves to study."[35]

Hasdai was entrusted with important diplomatic missions. Through members of the Byzantine embassy, he learned of the existence of the kingdom of the Khazars, a people in the southern steppes of Russia whose rulers were Jews. He corresponded with them in his own name and in that of his community, for whom the possible existence of a Jewish kingdom assumed great importance as the source of messianic hopes.[36]

The lineage of the Naghrelas, both by the extent of their power and the duration of their ministry, represented the apogee of the Jewish aristocracy in al-Andalus; the assassination of vizier Joseph ibn Naghrela marked the beginning of the Granada massacre of 1066. For nearly three decades they had been at the height of power and in the intimate circle of the Granada ruler Badis ibn Habbus. Nevertheless, that was not an isolated event or one specific to al-Andalus: recall the case of the Banu Ruqasa, who gave

> **"The lineage of the Naghrelas, both by the extent of their power and the duration of their ministry, represented the apogee of the Jewish aristocracy in al-Andalus."**

the Marinid dynasty of Fes several generations of viziers and high officials between the second half of the twelfth century and the first half of the thirteenth.

Isma'il ibn Naghrela (d. 1056), known in Hebrew by the name Samuel ha-Nagid, was a dignitary in the court of Habbus. He aided that king of the Zirid dynasty of Granada by ensuring the succession of the king's son Badis. As a result, he occupied a key position in the government. The great historian Ibn Khatib depicts him as "someone who wrote in both languages, Arabic and Hebrew. He knew the literatures of both peoples. He had penetrated deeply into the principles of the Arabic language and had familiarized himself with the works of the most subtle grammarians."[37] In fact, Samuel was one of the greatest Jewish poets of al-Andalus. His collected works fill three volumes and include his reflections on the principal military and political feats of his career, as well as some profane love poems. They were recopied by his children from their early childhood, since Samuel considered that task an integral part of their education and an introduction to the good manners of Jewish nobles. His son Joseph reports that, in his childhood, he received from his father a small collection of Arabic poems that he had to learn by heart. Such a practice, which was common in the education of young Muslims, constituted a real innovation in Jewish circles.

❯ See Nota bene, Samuel ibn Naghrela, pp. 132-133.

When Joseph was still very young, his father died, and the Zirid sovereign elevated Joseph to a position even more influential than his father's had been. He inherited an enormous fortune, coming in part from the possession of lands, and was entrusted with the country's tax system. Badis, now elderly, retired from the affairs of the court after the assassination of his son Buluggin. As a result, Joseph would become the true leader of the kingdom. Zuhayr, the vizier of Almería, which the king wanted to seize from Granada, undertook a campaign against the now-Jewish power of that neighboring *taifa*. The campaign fed Granada residents' resentment of Joseph, and he was assassinated, which triggered the uprising of the plebians and prompted the departure of many Jews from the city. Muslim viziers and courtiers had known the same fate under the reign of Badis,[38] since living on close terms with the sovereign during a struggle for power was risky, but it is undeniable that a person's Jewishness was arbitrarily pointed out whenever someone wanted to destroy a highly placed individual, or rather, a sovereign surrounded by Jewish courtiers.

> *Living on close terms with the sovereign during a struggle for power was risky.*

We know of many other Jewish courtiers and rabbis, such as Ishaq ibn Hasday and Abu Fadl ibn Hasday in the court of the Banu Hud of Saragossa, and Abraham ibn Muhajir in the court of Seville. At least six Jews served as viziers in the *taifa* kingdoms. The Muslim sovereigns often assigned their Jewish dignitaries very unpopular tasks, such as tax collection. Other high-ranking figures, such as Moshe ibn Ezra, had the title *sāhib al-shurta*, or "chief of police," conferred on them. It is worth pointing out that these Jewish dignitaries of the Muslim courts and government, following the example of Ibn Shaprut and Ibn Naghrela, assumed a preeminent role within their own communities, protecting science and belles lettres, and also among the Muslims in the scientific world. In addition, they participated in the religious and theological debates of their time.

Mention must also be made of the Muslim polymath of al-Andalus, Ibn Hazm, who was especially famous for his treatise on love, *Tawq al-Hamama* (*The Dove's Necklace*), and for his book on heretical Islamic doctrines, *Kitab al-Fisal*. Ibn Hazm also composed an important work refuting Judaism, in response to an adversary who had written a treatise on the errors of Islam. That book is known under the title *Radd ala ibn al-Nagrila*, or *Refutation of Ibn Naghrela the Jew*, in other words, a refutation of a work supposedly written by Samuel ibn Naghrela, whom Ibn Hazm claimed to have met in his youth. It is a polemical piece of writing that virulently seeks to discredit an entire religious group, and which, as a result, is laden with social content and political propaganda.[39] His condemnatory and aggressive tone, however, is not very different from that adopted in his other polemical writings on the versions of Islam he judges to be heretical. Conversely, that work is representative of the atmosphere reigning in al-Andalus, where a Jew could express his views on the errors that, in his eyes, the Qur'an contained; where Muslim and Jewish scholars knew one another, informed themselves about one another's works, and took up their pens to refute them; and where, as in the case of Ibn Hazm, Muslims could question Jewish

❯ See the Nota bene, pp. 696–700.

scholars on the details of their religion. Researchers such as Camilla Adang have suggested that Ibn Hazm must have been in contact with the Karaites, who supplied him with arguments against rabbinical Judaism on which he relied in his *Refutation*.

Both the Arabic and Hebrew sources, therefore, provide us with accounts of the close relation between physicians, scientists, and philosophers, for whom the field of knowledge was religiously pluralistic. These elites shared the same teachers, just as they had mysticism and speculative thought in common. Maimonides indicates he had "read texts . . . under the tutelage" of a disciple of the Muslim philosopher Ibn Bajja (d. 1138), known in the West as Avempace. According to Ibn Bassam, a Jew named Yusuf ibn Ishaq al-Isra'ili belonged to the literary circle of the famous poet Ibn Shuhayd. The poet appreciated the talent and intelligence of his student, who had surpassed a Muslim schoolmate in verbal sparring. Ibn Shuhayd was a close friend of Ibn Hazm, who in *The Dove's Necklace* mentions the friendly visits he made to a Jewish physician and herbalist from Almería.

Moshe ibn Ezra's references to the Qur'an in his *Kitab al-muhadara wa-l-mudhakara* indicate that the Jews had access to the Muslims' holy book. Sometimes they even made use of that knowledge in astonishingly free discussions with Muslims, as demonstrated by the famous and implicitly polemical debate between Ibn Ezra and a Muslim scholar on the problem raised by the translation of the commandments into another language.[40] Another significant example of the close ties between Jewish and Muslim intellectuals was an incident involving the Jewish physician Ibn Qamni'el. When another physician proposed an esoteric view of the Song of Songs to the Almoravid emir Yusuf ibn Tashfin, Ibn Qamni'el stepped in to deny it and to convince the emir of the appropriate spiritual reading to be made of the sacred text.

See Counterpoint for the text, pp. 636–637.

Obviously, these courtiers, viziers, secretaries, and tax agents could not have held such high positions had they not shared cultural traits with the Muslims and a common education in various disciplines: belles lettres, etiquette, rhetoric, science, and aesthetics.

Poets, grammarians, philologists

Poetry acquired as much importance for the Jewish aristocracy of al-Andalus as for the Muslim aristocracy. The principal Jewish poets composed *qasidas* and *muwashshahat* in Hebrew, reveled in poetry contests, and hired poets of their own to compose panegyrics to them and official correspondence in rhymed prose. There was in fact a small professional class of secretaries and poets; but the leaders of the community were also poets. A new profane poetry was created in Hebrew, corresponding to a process that was not only cultural but also social:

> *The Jewish elites had a tendency to adopt the manners, interests, and models of the Arab elites.*

the Jewish elites had a tendency to adopt the manners, interests, and models of the Arab elites. A remarkable aspect of that phenomenon was the deliberate adoption of Arabo-Islamic paradigms to express Jewish culture. For example, the Andalusian Jewish poets used the meters, prosody (*'arud*), and genres of classical Arabic poetry. They also erected biblical Hebrew into the equivalent of classical Arabic, granting the Hebrew language a new cultural cachet that surpassed its traditional status as a "holy language" (*Leshon haqodesh*). The pride and consideration that the Jews of al-Andalus felt for their literary successes were expressed in an edifying manner in the book Moshe ibn Ezra devoted to poetry, *Kitab al-muhadara wa-l-mudhakara*, and in the *maqāmāt* (prose narratives) of Yehuda al-Harizi. It is no coincidence that the four best-known Jewish poets of al-Andalus—Samuel ha-Nagid, Shlomo ibn Gabirol, Yehuda Halevi, and Moshe ibn Ezra—despite their differences in style and temperament, were all fine connoisseurs of Arabic and of the diverse branches of knowledge to which that language opened doors. Nor is it a matter of chance that they all included Arabic motifs in their Hebrew poetry.[41]

Similarly, grammatical and philological studies have prompted some to consider the literary heritage of the Jews of al-Andalus the most important manifestation of Jewish culture in the Islamic world. The grammatical and lexicographical studies that Arab scholars did on their own language served as a model for Jewish researchers in their study of Hebrew and the Bible. Thanks to the discovery of structural resemblances between Arabic and Hebrew and the identification of related words, the Jewish grammarians and lexicographers of al-Andalus played a prominent role in the formal legitimation of the fusion between the Hebrew language and Arabic knowledge, assimilating structures of thought, values, terms, and methodology. In other words, they demonstrated that Arabic could be an essential vehicle for transmitting Jewish culture. The linguist Yehuda Hayyuj's observation that the Arabic system of trilateral roots was also applicable to Hebrew was a methodological advance of key importance. Moshe ibn Chiquitilla (eleventh century) explained that the grammarians had to use Arabic to understand the details of Hebrew. Although a large number of Arabic and Hebrew texts have been lost, the fragments from the Geniza have made it possible to establish that the circles of philologists, grammarians, and exegetes wrote extraordinary philological studies of Hebrew in the Arabic language, not to mention commentaries on books of the Hebrew Bible and pious philosophical reflections.

From the linguistic standpoint, the legacy of Arabic translations and the adoption of clear syntactical and lexical Arabisms left a strong imprint on the character of medieval Hebrew in Spain. In addition, the religious texts of some Jews of al-Andalus, also written in Arabic, ordinarily call God "Allah," use the terms *imam* and *minbar* to designate, respectively, the officiating priest and the pulpit, and employ the word "Qur'an" for the Torah, even though the form "Tawrat" existed in classical Arabic.[42] Some Jewish texts, including pious books, though loath to conform to one of the models of the dominant Arab Muslim culture, were nevertheless written in

Arabic. They were therefore the reflection of the Jews' immersion in that culture, and especially of the inroads Arabic had made in their own existence, in their own conscience. Such is the sense of the Sufi terms and ideas strewn throughout the work of Ibn Paquda (*The Duties of the Heart*) and of the Judaization of terminology and conceptual elements from the Shi'ite tradition in Yehuda Halevi's *Kuzari*.[43] Poetry, grammar, lexicology, mysticism, and ethics, not to omit logic and rational thought, were thus the fields in which the contributions of the Jews of al-Andalus proved to be most important. For example, Shlomo ibn Gabirol, an eminent poet, presents himself as the author of speculative or ethical Arabic works in his famous *Source of Life* (*Fons vitae* in the Latin version) and, less markedly, in his *Islah al-'akhlaq, Improvement of the Moral Qualities.* According to discoveries made in the Geniza, Ibn Gabirol was also the author of an anthology of Arabic aphorisms, translated into Hebrew under the title *Mivhar ha-Peninim,* or *Selection of Pearls.* The essay on philosophical terminology, *Maqala fi sina' at al mantiq* (*Treatise on the Art of Logic*), written by Moshe ibn Maymum (Maimonides) in his youth, seems to have been dedicated to a Muslim dignitary, a specialist in religious law.[44]

Maimonides is a good example with which to conclude. He was one of the most perfect representatives of medieval Judaism and of the Almohad civilization that shaped it. Although the Almohad invasion limited the literary production of the Jews in the territory of al-Andalus, it continued in other regions for nearly a century, as indicated by the case of Maimonides, which is, moreover, not unique. The Jews who emigrated to Castile kept their ties to Arabic, continuing to write poetry in that language and to translate works from Arabic to Hebrew. In Toledo, with the support of Alfonso X the Wise, the translation activities of Jews took a different turn.

▶ See the Counterpoint devoted to that book, pp. 130-131.

1. Raymond P. Scheindlin, "The Jews in Muslim Spain," in *The Legacy of Muslim Spain,* ed. Salma Khadra Jayyusi (Leiden: Brill Academic, 1992), 188–200; and especially, by the same author, "Merchants and Intellectuals, Rabbis and Poets: Judeo-Arabic Culture in the Golden Age of Islam," in *Cultures of the Jews: A New History,* ed. David Biale (New York: Schocken, 2002), 313–88. See also David J. Wasserstein, "The Muslims and the Golden Age of the Jews in al-Andalus," in *Dhimmis and Others: Jews and Christians and the World of Classical Islam,* ed. Uri Rubin and David J. Wasserstein (Winona Lake, IN: Eisenbrauns, 1997), 179–96.

2. David J. Wasserstein, "Islamisation and the Conversion of the Jews," in *Conversions islamiques: Identités religieuses en Islam méditerranéen,* ed. Mercedes García-Arenal (Paris: Maisonneuve et Larose, 2001), 54.

3. David J. Wasserstein, "Jewish Elites in al-Andalus," in *The Jews of Medieval Islam: Community, Society and Identity,* ed. Daniel Frank (Leiden: E. J. Brill, 1995), 103.

4. See, among many other writings, Mark R. Cohen, "Islam and the Jews: Myth, Counter-Myth, History," *Jerusalem Quarterly* 38 (1986): 125–37; and Esperanza Alfonso, *Islamic Culture through Jewish Eyes: Al-Andalus from the Tenth to the Twelfth Century* (London: Routledge, 2008), 3 and references.

5. Eduardo Manzano Moreno, "La construcción histórica del pasado nacional," in *La gestión de la memoria: La historia de España al servicio del poder,* ed. Juan Sisinio Pérez Garzón (Barcelona: Crítica, 2000), 33–62.

6. Mercedes García-Arenal, "Al-Andalus et l'Espagne: La trajectoire d'un débat," in *Construire un monde? Mondialisation, pluralisme et universalisme,* ed. Pierre Robert Baduel (Paris and Tunis: Maisonneuve et Larose, 2007), 32–53.

7. Originally published in 3 volumes (Philadelphia: Jewish Publication Society, 1973).

8. See David J. Wasserstein, *The Rise and Fall of the Party-Kings: Politics and Society in Islamic Spain, 1002–1068* (Princeton, NJ: Princeton University Press, 1985); and Rachel Arié, *L'Espagne musulmane aux temps des Nasrides*

(1232–1492) (Paris: De Boccard, 1973; new ed., 1990). For a review of scholarship, see Angel Sâenz-Badillos, "Les recherches sur les juifs d'al-Andalus dans les vingt-cinq dernières années," *Revue du monde musulman et de la Méditerranée* 63, nos. 63–64 (1992): 63–79.

9. Ross Brann, *The Compunctious Poet: Cultural Ambiguity and Hebrew Poetry in Muslim Spain* (Baltimore: Johns Hopkins University Press, 1991); and especially, by the same author, *Power in the Portrayal: Representations of Jews and Muslims in Eleventh- and Twelfth-Century Islamic Spain* (Princeton, NJ: Princeton University Press, 2002).

10. Meir J. Kister, "Do Not Assimilate Yourselves . . . ," *Jerusalem Studies in Arabic and Islam* 12 (1989): 321–71.

11. Maribel Fierro, ed., *Judíos y musulmanes en al-Andalus y el Magreb: Contactos intelectuales* (Madrid: Casa de Velázquez, 2002), introduction, 10.

12. David Nirenberg, *Communities of Violence: Persecution of Minorities in the Middle Ages* (Princeton, NJ: Princeton University Press, 1996).

13. Ross Brann, "The Arabized Jews," in *The Cambridge History of Arabic Literature: The Literature of al-Andalus*, ed. María Rosa Menocal, Raymond P. Scheindlin, and Michael A. Sells (Cambridge: Cambridge University Press, 2000), 435–54; Alfonso, *Islamic Culture through Jewish Eyes*; Wasserstein, *The Rise and Fall of the Party-Kings*.

14. There are of course exceptions. See, by way of example, Manuela Marín, *Al-Andalus y los andalusies* (Barcelona: Icaria, 2000); and "Historical Images of al-Andalus and the Andalusis," in *Myths, Historical Archetypes and Symbolic Figures in Arabic Literature*, ed. Angelika Neuwirth et al. (Beirut: In Kommission bei Franz Steiner Verlag Stuttgart, 1999), 409–21.

15. See the most recent overviews for the period of interest here: Manuela Marín, *Individuo y sociedad en al-Andalus* (Madrid: Editorial MAPFRE,1992); Eduardo Manzano Moreno, *Conquistadores emires y califas: Los Omeyas y la formación de al-Andalus* (Barcelona: Crítica, 2006); or, by the same author, *Épocas medievales,* vol. 2 of *Historia de España*, ed. Josep Fontana and Ramón Villares (Barcelona and Madrid: Crítica, 2012); Maribel Fierro, *'Abd al-Rahmān III: The First Cordoban Caliph* (Oxford: One World, 2005). There is also a significantly augmented Spanish edition: Maribel Fierro, *Abderramán III y el califato omeya de Córdoba* (Donastia-San Sebastían: Editorial Nerea, 2011).

16. The bibliography on this question is vast. See, for example, Maya Shatzmiller, "Le mythe d'origine berbère, aspects historiographiques et sociaux," *Revue de l'Occident Musulman et de la Méditerranée* 38 (1983): 145–56; Elías Terés, "Linajes árabes en al-Andalus según la 'Yamhara' d'Ibn Hazm," *Al-Andalus* 22, no. 2 (1957): 55–111 and 337–376; and especially, Helena de Felipe, *Identidad y onomástica de los beréberes de al-Andalus* (Madrid: Consejo Superior de Investigaciones Científicas, 1997).

17. Mercedes García-Arenal, "Rapport entre les groupes dans la péninsule ibérique: La conversion des juifs à l'islam (XIIᵉ – XIIIᵉ siècles)," *Revue du monde musulman et de la Méditerranée* 63, nos. 63–64 (1992): 91–102.

18. See, for example, Emilio García Gómez, *Andalucía contre Berbería: Reedición de traducciones de Bey Hayyan, Saqundi y Ben al-Jatib* (Barcelona: Oriente y Mediterráneo, 1976).

19. Manuela Marín, "Signos visuales de la identidad andalusí," in *Tejer y vestir: De la Antigüedad al Islam* (Madrid: Consejo Superior de Investigaciones Científicas, 2001), 137–80.

20. Within a large bibliography, see a recent contribution: Mariam Rosser-Owen, *Islamic Arts from Spain* (London: V & A Publishing, 2010).

21. As Shlomo Dov Goitein amply demonstrates in *A Mediterranean Society: The Jewish Communities of the Arab World as Portrayed in the Documents of the Cairo Genizah* (Berkeley: University of California Press, 1967–93). See also, more recently, Olivia R. Constable, *Trade and Traders in Muslim Spain: The Commercial Realignment of the Iberian Peninsula (900–1500)* (Cambridge: Cambridge University Press, 1994), 54–62 and 85–96.

22. Ambrosio Huici Miranda, "Un fragmento inédito de Ibn Idari sobre los Almorávides," *Hespéris-Tamuda* 1, no. 1 (1961).

23. In García Sanjuan, "Violencia contra los judíos: El progromo de Granada del año 459H/1066," Maribel Fierro (dir.), *De muerte violenta: Política y religión en al-Andalus* (Madrid: CSIC, 2004), 167–206.

24. See Wasserstein, *The Rise and Fall of the Party-Kings*, 210–11; Brann, *Power in the Portrayal*, 21.

25. Maribel Fierro, "Conversion, Ancestry, and Universal Religion: The Case of the Almohads in the Islamic West (Sixth/Twelfth – Seventh/Thirteenth Centuries)," *Journal of Medieval Iberian Studies* 2, no. 2 (2010): 155–73.

26. The most recent statement of various aspects of Almohadism can be found in Patrice Cressier, Maribel Fierro, and Luis Molina, eds., *Los Almohades: Problemas y perspectivas*, 2 vols. (Madrid: Casa de Velazqu, 2005).

27. Jean-Pierre Molénat, "Sur le rôle des Almohades dans la fin du christianisme local au Maghreb et en al-Andalus," *Al-Qantara* 18, no. 2 (1997): 389–413.

28. Mercedes García-Arenal, "Jewish Converts to Islam in the Muslim West," in Rubin and Wasserstein, eds., *Dhimmīs and Others*, 227–50, esp. 238.

29. Maya Shatzmiller, "Professions and Ethnic Origin of Urban Labourers in Muslim Spain: Evidence from a Moroccan Source," *Awraq* 5 (1982): 149–60.

30. For an overall view of that question, see Leopoldo Torres Balbás, "Mozarabías y juderías de las ciudades hispano-musulmanes," *Al-Andalus* 19 (1954): 172–97; Maribal Fierro, "A Muslim Land without Jews or Christians: Almohad Policies Regarding the 'Protected People,'" in *Christlicher Norden, Muslimischer Süden: Ansprüche und Wirklichkeiten von Christen, Juden und Muslimen auf der Iberischen Halbinsel im Hoch- und Spätmittelalter*, ed. Matthias Tischler and Alexander Fidora (Münster: Aschendorff Verlag, 2011), 231–47.

31. Mercedes García-Arenal, "Messianisme juif aux temps des mahdis," in Fierro, ed., *Judíos y musulmanes en al-Andalus y el Magreb*, 217–18.

32. Philoxène Luzzatto, *Notice sur Abou-Iousouf Hasdaï Ibn-Schaprout, médecin juif du dixième siècle, ministre des khalifes omeyyades d'Espagne 'Abd al-Rahmân III et al-Hakem II, et promoteur de la littérature juive en Europe* (Paris: Impr. de mme. ve Dondey-Dupre, 1852). This little book remains of great interest.

33. See Julio Samsó, *Las ciencias de los Antiguos en al-Andalus* (Madrid: Editorial MAPFRE, 1992).

34. Sulayman ibn Hassan ibn Juljul, *Tabaqat al-'Attiba'wa-l-Hukama': Les générations des médecins et des sages* (Cairo: al-Ma'had al-'Ilmi al-Faransi li-l-Athar al-Sharqiyya, 1955); Ibn Abi Usaybi'a, *Uyun al-Anba fi Tabaqat al-Attiba'* (*Sources of the Classes of Physicians*), 2 vols. (Cairo, 1882), 2:39. A more recent edition was published in Beirut (1401/1981). See also Fuat Sezgin et al., eds., *Studies on Ibn Abi Usaibi'a (d. 1270) and His Uyun al-anba' fi tabaqat al-Attiba'* (Frankfurt-am-Main: Institut für Geschichte der arabisch-islamischen Wissenschaften, 1995).

35. Ibn Abi Usabi'a, *Uyun al-Anba fi Tabaqat al-Attiba'*, 2:48; Ibn Sa'id al-Andalusi, *Science in the Medieval World: "Book of the Categories of Nations,"* ed. and trans. Sema'an I. Salem and Alok Kumar (Austin: University of Texas Press, 1991), 80–82.

36. Eliayu Ashtor, *The Jews of Moslem Spain*, 3 vols. (Philadelphia: Jewish Publication Society, 1973–1984), 3:201. See also Douglas M. Dunlop, *The History of the Jewish Khazars* (Princeton, NJ: Princeton University Press, 1954).

37. Ibn al-Khatib, *Ihata fi tarikh Gharnata*, ed. Muhammad Inan (Cairo: Maktabat al-Khanji, 1973), 1:538.

38. See, for example, María Luisa Ávila, "Al-Yuryani e Ibn 'Abbas, víctimas de Badis," in *De muerte violenta: Política, religión y violencia en al-Andalus* (Madrid: Consejo Superior de Investigaciones Científicas, 2004), 137–66.

39. Camilla Adang, *Islam frente a Judaísmo: La polémica de Ibn Hazm de Córdoba* (Madrid: Aben Ezra Ediciones, 1994); and, by the same author, *Muslim Writers on Judaism and the Hebrew Bible: From Ibn Rabban to Ibn Hazm* (Leiden: E. J. Brill, 1996). For the large bibliography on the subject, see Brann, *Power in the Portrayal*, 76ff.

40. Brann, "Reflexiones sobre el árabe y la identidad literaria de los judíos de al-Andalus," in Fierro, ed., *Judíos y musulmanes en al-Andalus y el Magreb*, 23.

41. Arie Schippers, *Arabic Tradition and Hebrew Innovation: Arabic Themes in Hebrew Andalusian Poetry* (Amsterdam: Institute for Modern Near Eastern Studies, 1988).

42. See, for example, Scheindlin, "Merchants and Intellectuals, Rabbis and Poets," 313–88, especially 327 and references.

43. Shlomo Pines, "Shi'ite Terms and Conceptions in Judah Halevi's Kuzari," *Jerusalem Studies in Arabic and Islam* 2 (1980): 165–251.

44. Joel L. Kraemer, "Maimonides on the Philosophic Sciences in His Treatise on the Art of Logic," in *Perspectives on Maimonides: Philosophical and Historical Studies,* ed. J. L. Kraemer (Oxford: Littman Library of Jewish Civilization, 1991), 77–78.

The *Kuzari*:
Defense of the Despised Religion

Yehuda Halevi, one of the greatest poets of the Andalusian "golden age," is also the author of a treatise whose original title is *Kitab al-hujja wa-l-dalil fi nusr al-din al-dhalil* (Book on the Refutation of the Proof Concerning the Despised Religion), or *Kitab al-Khazari* (Book of al-Khazar), rendered as *Sefer ha-Kuzari* in Hebrew. The book presents itself as a dialogue between a rabbi and the pagan king of the Khazars, a Turkish people who at the time ruled a region between the Caspian and Black Seas that served as a buffer between the Byzantine Empire and the Islamic world. Historically speaking, the Khazar nobility converted to Judaism in the eighth century, as attested by the correspondence of the Andalusian Hasdai ibn Shaprut. The fictive dialogue composed by Halevi tells how the king of the Khazars, intellectually and spiritually unsatisfied with paganism, questioned a philosopher, a Christian, and a Muslim before refuting each of their claims to possess the truth and finally turning to the "despised religion" of Judaism, whose fundamental concepts the rabbi teaches him. Through the voice of the Jewish sage, it is Yehuda Halevi's own philosophy of Judaism that the author expresses. He therefore rejects the rationalist and universalist conception of religion developed by Islamic Aristotelians, which in his time was finding many followers among the Jews, who preferred it to a vision of Judaism founded on the miraculous character of the Creation and of the Revelation, on the centrality of obedience to the divine commandments recorded in the Torah, and on the uniqueness of the Jewish people in God's eyes.

"*Al-Khazari*: Believers in other faiths declare that man, by the pronunciation of one word alone, may inherit paradise, even if, during the whole of his life, he knew no other word than this, and of this did not even understand their significance. How extraordinary is that one word, which raised him from the ranks of a brute to that of an angel. He who did not utter this word would remain an animal, though he might be a learned and pious philosopher, who yearned for God all his life.

The Rabbi: We do not deny that the good actions of any man, to whichever people he may belong, will be rewarded by God as an individual for his good works. But the priority belongs to people who are near God during their life, and we estimate the rank they occupy near God after death accordingly.
Al-Khazari: Apply this also in the other direction, and judge their degree in the next world according to their station in this world.

The Rabbi: I see thee reproaching us with our degradation and poverty, but the best of Christianity and Islam boast of both. Do they not glorify Him who said: 'He who smites thee on the right cheek, turn to him the left also; and he who takes away thy coat, let him have thy shirt also'? After having endured misunderstandings, beatings, and death for centuries, Jesus, his apostles, and his followers attained their well-known fame because they glorified in their sufferings. This is also the history of the founder of Islam and his friends, who eventually prevailed, and became powerful. The nations boast of these, but not of these kings whose power and might are great, whose walls are strong, and whose chariots are terrible. Yet our relation to God is a closer one than if we had reached greatness already on earth.

Al-Khazari: This might be so, if your humility were voluntary; but it is involuntary, and if you had power you would slay.

The Rabbi: Thou hast touched our weak spot, O King of the Khazars. If the majority of us, as thou sayest, would learn humility toward God and His law from our low station, Providence would not have forced us to bear it for such a long period. Only the smallest portion thinks thus. Yet the majority may expect a reward, because they bear their degradation partly from necessity, partly of their own free will. For whoever wishes to do so can become the friend and equal of his oppressor by uttering one word, and without any difficulty. Such conduct does not escape the just Judge. . . . Besides this, God has a secret and wise design concerning us, which should be compared to the wisdom hidden in the seed that falls into the ground, where it undergoes an external transformation into earth, water, and manure, without leaving a trace for him who looks down upon it. It is, however, the seed itself that transforms earth and water into its own substance, carries it from one stage to another, until it refines the elements and transfers them into something like itself, casting off husks, leaves, and so on, and allowing the pure core to appear, capable of bearing the Divine Influence. The original seed produced the tree—bearing fruit resembling that from which it had been produced. In the same manner the law of Moses transforms each one who honestly follows it, though it may externally repel him. The nations merely serve to introduce and pave the way for the expected Messiah, who is the fruition, and they will all become His fruit. Then, if they acknowledge Him, they will become one tree. Then they will revere the origin which they formerly despised."

Judah Halevi [Yehuda Halevi], *Kitab al-Khazari (Kuzari)*, trans. Hartwig Hirschfeld (New York: Forgotten Books, 1964), part 1, § 110–15, part 4, § 23; *Le Kuzari: Apologie de la religion méprisée*, translated from the original Arabic text collated with the Hebrew version, introduced and annotated by Charles Touati (Louvain, 1994), 37–38 and 173.

Samuel ibn Naghrela

Samuel ibn Naghrela (993–1056) was born in Córdoba, where he received a thorough education in traditional Jewish learning and in Arabic letters. In his youth, he was acquainted and intellectually engaged with 'Ali ibn Hazm, a Muslim contemporary who would become an important man of letters, famous today for his legal work and for treatises on comparative religion and on love. Ibn Naghrela was a youth at the time of the Berber invasion (1013), when he fled to Malaga. After serving its governor, Ibn al-Arif, Ibn Naghrela entered the administrative service of the court of Habbus, the Berber ruler of the kingdom. According to an oft-repeated story, Ibn Naghrela first came to the attention of the court through the skill he displayed in composing a formal letter for a servant of Ibn al-Arif; but a similar story is told of al-Mansur ibn abi 'Amr, so this may be merely a topos adopted by a medieval Jewish chronicler.

On Habbus's death (1037–38), Ibn Naghrela supported the claims of Badis against Badis's brother. On Badis's accession, Ibn Naghrela enjoyed his confidence and became a trusted adviser, eventually rising to the position of vizier. As part of his duties, Ibn Naghrela accompanied the troops of Granada on their annual expeditions against neighboring *tawā'if* taifas, especially Seville and Almería. (Although it is often said that he was a general, his extensive Hebrew poems on the battles he witnessed in some official capacity only once suggest that he was in command; there is no evidence to this effect in Arabic sources.) As the most powerful Jew in the *tā'ifa* kingdom, he was accorded the title *nagid* by the Jewish community and functioned as head of Granada's Jewish community, but his activities on behalf of the Jewish community and his Jewish scholarship gained him renown throughout the Jewish communities of al-Andalus in

his own time and long after his death. Ibn Naghrela had three sons and at least one daughter, who may have composed poetry in Arabic. He was succeeded in his position at court by his eldest son, Joseph, whom he had groomed to be his successor at court. For a man so deeply engaged in public affairs, both of the court and of the Jewish community, Ibn Naghrela had a remarkably fruitful literary career, mostly writing in Hebrew or Judeo-Arabic (he may also have composed poems and a polemical treatise against the Qur'an in classical Arabic). He displayed his rabbinic learning in a treatise on the Talmud titled *Hilkhata gavrata* and his knowledge of Hebrew grammar in a work titled *Kitab al-Istighna'*. When the latter was severely criticized by Abu Marwan Ibn Janah, his contemporary and one of the greatest scholars of the Hebrew language of the age, Ibn Naghrela responded sharply with a polemical work written in Judeo-Arabic. Ibn Naghrela amassed a large library of Jewish books, including a manuscript of the Bible that he copied himself and his own abridgment of the chronicle Yossipon. The core of Ibn Naghrela's literary achievement is the large body of poetry he composed and whose collection and editing in several volumes he oversaw. These works are among the great literary achievements of the Hebrew Golden Age and justify ranking Ibn Naghrela among the most impressive Jewish literary figures of the Middle Ages. There is some doubt as to just how many volumes he compiled. Three are known by their titles, corresponding to three books of the Hebrew Bible: *Ben Tehillim* (Son of Psalms), *Ben Mishlei* (Son of Proverbs), and *Ben Qohelet* (Son of Ecclesiastes). *Ben Mishlei* and *Ben Qohelet* are extant. *Ben Mishlei* is a collection of short gnomic poems and epigrams in the spirit of ancient wisdom literature. It deals with human relations, love, and courtly life, often in a cynical vein.

Ben Qohelet is likewise a collection of short poems and epigrams in the spirit of Arabic ascetic poetry. It deals with the brevity of life, the certainty of death, and the need to lead an upright life in anticipation of judgment after death.

The status of *Ben Tehillim* is problematic, as the work published in the twentieth century under that title does not resemble its description in a biographical notice of Ibn Naghrela written in the twelfth century, nor is it similar in structure and uniformity of contents to *Ben Mishlei* and *Ben Qohelet*, as would naturally be expected, given the similarity of the three titles. Possibly, the original *Ben Tehillim* is lost, and the work known today by that title is the purported fourth work (though some poems in this work may also have been included in *Ben Tehillim*). But it is also possible that the work now known as *Ben Tehillim* is actually *Ben Tehillim* with some modification.

The work now known as *Ben Tehillim* is far more varied and more personal than either of the other works. Much of it is devoted to events of Ibn Naghrela's life, especially the approximately forty poems describing the battles of the troops of Granada in which he participated or that he observed. It also contains laments for the dead, including a poignant series of poems on the death of his brother, poems addressed to his son Joseph, and poems reflecting on his status as a Jewish courtier. Other unusual items are poetic prayers, a poem describing an ocean voyage during which the ship encountered a sea monster, a poem describing an eclipse, and a poem containing a lurid meditation on death. The volume also contains panegyrics, epigrams, riddles, wine poems, and erotic poems, such as were commonplace among Arabic and Hebrew poets.

All the poems in the three collections known to us use prosodic patterns adopted from Arabic; these are among the earliest examples of the form in the work of a Hebrew poet. ●

Professor of medieval Hebrew literature at the Jewish Theological Seminary, Raymond Scheindlin studies the encounter of Jewish and Arab cultures in Spain through poetry. His publications include The Song of the Distant Dove: Judah Halevi's Pilgrimage *(Oxford University Press, 2007).*

Hasdai ibn Shaprut

Hasdai ibn Shaprut (ca. 915–ca. 970) was the preeminent Jewish dignitary of tenth-century al-Andalus and the patron of Jewish letters who set in motion the Hebrew Golden Age, a two-century period of extraordinary literary achievement in Hebrew and Judeo-Arabic.

Hasdai descended from a family in Jaén, but his father came to Córdoba, where he became a wealthy and prominent figure in the Jewish community. Trained as a physician, Hasdai is said to have successfully compounded theriaca, a drug of wide-ranging powers reportedly devised in antiquity, whose formula had

The pharmacological reference book *De materia medica* by Dioscorides (40–90 CE) was translated into Arabic in the Middle Ages by Ibn Shaprut. Miniature taken from a copy of the manuscript from Iraq, 1229. Istanbul, Topkapı Palace Museum Library, fol. 2 verso.

been lost but that had long been sought by medical men. Hasdai entered the service of 'Abd al-Rahman III (r. 912–61) as a physician and eventually was given other responsibilities, both administrative (as head of the customs department) and diplomatic. In 953, Hasdai conducted negotiations in Córdoba with John of Gorze, the representative of the Holy Roman emperor Otto I; John later spoke with admiration of Hasdai's shrewdness. In 956, Hasdai was sent, together with a Muslim diplomat, to the king of León to negotiate a peace treaty.

In 958, Hasdai was sent on a mission to Navarre that involved both his medical and diplomatic skills. His task was to cure Sancho—the deposed king of León who had taken refuge in Pamplona, then ruled by his grandmother Toda—of his obesity, and bring him and Toda to Córdoba to negotiate Cordoban support for a Navarrese invasion of León and Sancho's restoration. In these negotiations, Hasdai gained important concessions from Toda and Sancho. It seems likely that Hasdai's suitability for such missions resided not only in his diplomatic skills but also in his knowledge of languages, particularly Latin – not a common accomplishment among Andalusian Muslims.

Another episode that involved Hasdai's knowledge of medicine, as well as Latin, was his participation in the translation by a team of scholars of the pharmacological work *Peri hyles hiatrikes* (generally known as *De materia medica*), by Dioscorides, when a manuscript was brought as a gift from the Byzantine emperor Constantine VII to Abd al-Rahman III in 948–49. After the death of the latter, Hasdai seems to have continued to serve in the court of his successor, al-Hakam II.

Like other Jewish courtiers in Muslim states, Hasdai used his position in support of the interests of the Jewish community and was recognized as head of the community, with the title *nasi*. Beyond managing the affairs of the Jewish community of al-Andalus, he corresponded with prominent figures of other Jewish communities such as Dosa, son of Saadia Gaon in Iraq, and with leaders of Byzantine southern Italy. Hasdai wrote in his own name to Constantine VII, interceding on behalf of the Byzantine Italian Jews.

Most famously, Hasdai attempted to establish contact with Joseph, king of the Khazars, a Turkic people inhabiting the region from the Caspian Sea west to the Dnieper River, whose royal house had adopted Judaism in the eighth century. His letter to Joseph is extant; there is also a response, of dubious authenticity, that includes many details about the Khazars and their kingdom. The letter to the Khazar king was composed by Menahem ben Saruq, a member of Hasdai's staff who also composed a Hebrew dictionary. Preceded by a panegyric poem, the epistle is a milestone in the development of Hebrew literature because it represents a clean break with rabbinic Hebrew style and adumbrates the new, simple, elegant, and biblicizing style that would characterize the writing of the Hebrew Golden Age. The poem, though it does not employ Arabic prosodic conventions that would soon be adopted wholesale by Hebrew writers, displays other features that are characteristic of Arabic courtly poetry.

When Hasdai, for unknown reasons, turned against Menahem, the latter sent a panegyric poem and a formal epistle to Hasdai, even more elegant than those addressed to the Khazar king, reproaching Hasdai for ingratitude and demanding justice for the physical violence that Hasdai had instigated against him. As the work's style reflects the new poetics of the Hebrew Golden Age, its content reflects a new social reality in which a Jewish grandee employs professional writers and supports literary scholars who engage in intellectual activities other than traditional rabbinic scholarship.

Hasdai also supported Jewish literary scholarship by acquiring Hebrew manuscripts from abroad. As the most powerful member of the Jewish community, he controlled the Talmudic academy in Córdoba. •

Professor of medieval Hebrew literature at the Jewish Theological Seminary, Raymond Scheindlin studies the encounter of Jewish and Arab cultures in Spain through poetry. His publications include The Song of the Distant Dove: Judah Halevi's Pilgrimage *(Oxford University Press, 2007).*

The Conversion of Jews to Islam
Mohammed Hatimi

The Islamic scholarly literature granted little place to the conversion of the Jews to Islam. Although Christians did so more often for many reasons, many Jews did convert and contributed toward shaping Muslim civilization. The absence of Jewish converts in the collective memory is linked in many cases to Islamic resentment at not having been successful in gathering the Jews, despite the fact that, early on, Muhammad had hoped to find in them an ally on which to build the new religion he was professing. It is therefore the refusal to convert that became a major theme in the Arabic sources.

Mohammed Hatimi

A professor in the Department of History in the Faculty of Arts and Humanities at the Sidi Mohamed Ben Abdellah University in Fes, the author studies primarily minorities and the Jewish presence in Morocco and in Islamic countries.

Conversions to Islam during the Muslim conquest were usually a pragmatic choice on the part of Jews, the alternative being to remain within the purview of the *dhimma*, under whose provisions they were still allowed to practice their religion. During occasional historical episodes, however, the Jews were compelled to embrace Islam.

The beginnings of Islam

The conversion of the Jews in Islamic countries was not the result of the same processes that occurred in Christian territories, even during the rare episodes of forced conversion. Until recently, proselytism as it took place in Christendom, in the form of organized brotherhoods, had no equivalent in Islamic countries. The Islamization of the largest number of the faithful was the declared objective of the founding of holy texts, and it was also the principal objective the Muslims set for themselves throughout Islamic history. At the start of the conquest, that obligation was identified with the duty of jihad, a notion with a rigid sense: war against the infidels in view of converting them, by force if necessary. During the first two centuries of Islamic expansion, therefore, political submission to the Islamic state meant joining its "community," or *umma*, and embracing the faith. The Muslims were most successful with nonmonotheistic groups. Later, the notion of jihad lost its rigor, becoming merely a defensive action that took the form of the *da'wa*, the "call" or "invitation" to join Islam.

It was primarily toward the People of the Book, Christians and Jews (whether Arabs or not), who were recognized as possessing a share of the Truth, that the Muslims expended a sustained effort at persuasion through good conduct. Over the long term, the process bore fruit with the Christians, and that became a source of community pride. By contrast, the conversion of the Jews appears to have been less successful, and even less sought after. In addition, Muslim historiography sometimes explained certain fractures of the *umma* into rival currents as resulting from the subversive action of Jewish converts. For example, although these different factions, such as Shi'ism, Mu'tazilism, and others, actually arose from internal struggles, a few historiographers went so far as to impute their advent to the maleficent actions of Jewish converts. In contemporary Islamist literature, subversion by Jewish converts is still an obsession.

Suspicions concerning the conversion of the Jews took root with the advent of Islam and can be explained by the Prophet's failure, reported in *al-Sira*, to win over the Jewish tribes in Medina. These texts serve as a major point of reference for Muslims on how to proceed and conduct themselves toward the Other. Several suras in the Qur'an warmly invite the Banu Isra'il, the "sons of Israel," to convert as a sign of acknowledgment and renewal of their covenant with Allah (Qur'an 2:40–103). The Prophet enthusiastically undertook a rapprochement with the Jews of the region. His chief asset was religious polemic. To show proof of good faith, he adopted the habit of fasting on the same days as the Jews and prayed in the direction of Jerusalem. He went to the Jewish places of prayer and study, tried to explain to his interlocutors the legitimacy of his mission, and, immediately thereafter, the aberrations to which their beliefs led. A few rabbis and clan chiefs were won over by his words, others by his conduct, and they converted to Islam. Although they were few in number, the Qur'an alludes to their unquestioned sincerity: "Some there are among the People of the Book who truly believe in God, and in what has been revealed to you and what has been revealed to them. They humble themselves before God and do not sell God's revelations for a trifling price. These shall be rewarded by their Lord. Swift is God's reckoning" (Qur'an 3:199).[1] Of all these converts, Ka'b al-Ahbar was the most venerated. In a polemical treatise that became a Muslim reference work in comparative religion, Ibn Qayyim al-Jawziyya (thirteenth century) calls him "the most learned of rabbis" and praises him as the one who best understood the Jewish writings, a gift from which the author also deduces Ka'b's aptitude for believing in Muhammad's prophecy.

The problem raised by Jewish converts was very specific in nature. They had adopted new rites, but at the spiritual level, Islam basically only reinforced what they already believed. Conversion was synonymous not with rupture but rather with continuity. That made them suspect in the eyes of their previously pagan coreligionists, who had totally broken away from their prior beliefs. An "incident" mentioned by the historiographer Tabari (838–923) attests to that problem. He reports the discussion between Ka'b al-Ahbar and the second caliph, 'Umar, when the keys to Jerusalem were handed over:

When 'Umar came . . . to Aelia [the Roman name for Jerusalem] . . . he said, "Bring me Ka'b."

Ka'b was brought to him, and 'Umar asked him, "Where do you think we should put the place of prayer?"

"By the Rock [the location of the Holy of Holies]," answered Ka'b.

"By God, Ka'b," said 'Umar, "you are following after Judaism. I saw you take off your sandals."

"I wanted to feel the touch of it with my bare feet," said Ka'b.

"I saw you," said 'Umar. "But no . . . we were not commanded concerning the Rock, but we were commanded concerning the Ka'ba [in Mecca]."[2]

▶ See also Phillip Ackerman-Lieberman's article, pp. 683–693.

That explains the decision to no longer adopt the Rock, and thus Jerusalem, as the *qibla*, but instead to pray toward the Ka'ba. The change marked the rupture with Jewish rituals.

Initially, the coexistence of the different communities was guaranteed, as indicated by one of the first documents that the Prophet approved, *Sahifa*, which attests to the Jews' observance of and respect for religious practices. A few lines of demarcation nevertheless existed: nowhere is there any mention of marriages between Jews and Muslims during that first period of the hijra. Later, the Jews' insubordination prompted the Prophet of Islam to change his policy, which put an end to dialogue. He declared them outright enemies of religion. The tone of the suras against the Jews became more violent. Beginning with the Battle of Badr (624), the issue at hand was no longer to convert the Jews but to neutralize them, then to expel them from Medina and the entire Arabian Peninsula. The use of weapons took root, and, siege after siege, the Prophet and his companions became increasingly intransigent. One of the Prophet's initiatives eased the bitter feelings. He married Safiyya Bint Huyayy, a woman from a good Jewish family. She was poorly received by the Prophet's entourage because of her origins and had trouble getting along with the Prophet's other wives. Several incidents that occurred after his death attest to the doubts surrounding her faith and also to her desire to avenge her family members killed during the Battle of Khaybar (June 628). Nevertheless, tradition considers her a "Mother of Believers," a status that confers respect and veneration. Other companions of the Prophet may have taken Jewish captives as concubines. It is easy to understand the reasons for the silence of sources on that subject, especially since it is not known whether the conversion of these captives was attested.

Conversion during the Muslim conquest

The Muslim conquest marked the shift from a purely Arab Islam to another, more diversified form, which posed the challenge of how to deal positively with populations that had little inclination to embrace the religion of the conquerors under the threat of the saber. The Islamic sources, most of them Arabic, relate the conversion of the pagan peoples in a triumphalist tone. They are more subdued when they mention the conversion of the Christians and even more so regarding that of the Jews. The Jews' conversion is not described at length: if there were truly Jewish communities in the various conquered territories, the chroniclers do not mention them by name. They confine themselves to noting the contributions of certain Jews who, on their own initiative, had facilitated the advance of the Muslim armies.

With respect to the phases of the Muslim conquest and the modalities for converting entire groups, the sources insist on the appeal of Islam, which they consider a determining factor in the voluntary and almost spontaneous choice of the new believers, but which cannot in itself account for the massive and pragmatic embrace of the new religion. Material incentives may also have been decisive. Almost everywhere, in Iraq, Syria, and Egypt, the conversion of several clan chiefs and members of the old Byzantine and Persian oligarchy allowed them to be exempt from tax obligations and from the arbitrariness of the new masters; in addition, they enjoyed advantages granted by their participation in the administrative and military management of the state. Often, the leader's conversion led to that of the community as a whole. It is likely that small, isolated Jewish communities chose to convert to ensure themselves social position and integration, since advantages falling to the leader extended to the governed.

Not all conversions can be explained by the material benefits. Faith in the coming of the Messiah persuaded a few. In fact, the victorious advance of the Arab warriors, who in record time succeeded in defeating strong and organized armies and in integrating civilized peoples, was able to spark the curiosity and admiration of a few Jewish communities, particularly those of the small towns of Palestine. The learned saw these successes as proof of the imminence of the fulfillment of biblical prophecies and the advent of the messianic era. They converted in the hope of taking part in that event.

In the large urban centers, Islamization followed a different logic. The conquest of the Bilad al-Sham had come about immediately, rapidly, and without devastation. The Arab armies were disciplined, and most of the warriors hoped to settle permanently in the conquered regions. The new arrivals, being city dwellers themselves, were inclined to preserve what Ibn Khaldun called the *umrān*, the "manifestations of civilization," and also the services of artisans, shopkeepers, and local elites. The conquerors therefore made few efforts to compel or even encourage the People of the Book to convert. Segregation and corvées, standard practice in the countryside, rarely occurred in the cities. Although it would be an overstatement to say that the state and individuals were not preoccupied with converting non-Muslims, after the first century, the conversion of large communities was conceived as a slow missionary process. Calls to convert were commonplace, but the methods employed were persuasion and incentives.

It was primarily among the Jewish elites that incentives had the most positive results. A few of these Jewish officials, surely under pressure from rivals linked to some of the ulema, ultimately converted to the state religion to protect their privileges and positions. The most famous of the vizier converts, in the East and in the Muslim West, was undoubtedly Ya'qub ibn Killis (930–91). Born in Baghdad, where he grew up and studied mathematics, he eventually left Iraq, arriving in Egypt after a short stay in Syria. Introduced into the court, he quickly won the trust of Vizier Kafur Ikhshid, who assigned him several missions, which Ya'qub successfully performed. He immediately attracted the rage of detractors, who pointed out that it was illegal to make use of the Jews' services. Ya'qub then officially converted to Islam, learned the Qur'an, and became a student of Islamic law. But that conversion did not spare him from being imprisoned after his master's death. He purchased his freedom and went to Ifriqiya (Tunisia), where he entered the Fatimids' service. He distinguished himself once more, through his skill at managing tax resources. He had the merit of allotting a portion of his wealth to the transcription of the sacred texts and founded a school where students devoted themselves primarily to Qur'anic studies. Muslim historiography draws a nuanced portrait of him, mentioning his skills but at the same time stressing the large gifts he used to corrupt both his allies and his detractors.

In addition to the sociological motives, choosing to convert was sometimes a necessity. A case in point is that of Abu al-Barakat al-Baghdadi (d. about 1150). He converted near the end of his life in the aim of avoiding the reprisals threatening him. Among other things, his detractors suspected him of providing poor medical care in his capacity as a physician. He wrote a philosophical treatise, "The Intellect and Its Quiddity," which attests to a profound knowledge of Muslim religious literature. But, because he was originally Jewish, the Muslim philosophers showed little interest in him.

> *Conversions occurred out of conviction or opportunism, under the influence of constraint —or out of love.*

Conversions occurred out of conviction or opportunism, under the influence of constraint—or out of love. At all times, conversion through marriage was a path to Islamization. It occurred in only one direction, from Judaism to Islam, and exclusively on the part of Jewish women who married Muslim men. The prophetic precedent served as a frame of reference in that matter. The number of Jewish converts was higher in the Muslim West. The historian Ibn Khaldun declared that several Berber tribes, from Libya to the Atlantic coasts and southern Spain, professed Judaism. During the early period of the conquest of Ifriqiya, Arab war leaders were preoccupied with the "pacification" of the Berbers (Amazighs), and it was imperative that these tribes convert as a means to legitimate the armies' advance. If the conquest of Spain was to continue, the adherence of the Berbers, who were considered idol worshippers, was indispensable to the *pax islamica*. But the Arabic sources mention the Arab conquerors' difficulties in converting the Berber tribes. Although the resistance in that case was political in nature, Arab historiography attributed it to the influence of the local Jewish forces, who waged battle for fear of losing face. It is within that context that we need to read the half-legendary episode of the Kahina, the "Berber queen" who led the resistance against the advance of the Arab armies and who is often presented as a Jewish figure. Subsequently, the fear of being subjected to the ravages of tribal and urban uprisings often lay behind mass conversions. During the unrest that struck several cities, the aggressors had the habit of attacking the Jewish neighborhoods, which were less protected and supposedly contained "treasures." As a result, self-protection against political vagaries became a motive for converting. In Morocco, for example, the first half of the fifteenth century was an unstable and tumultuous period, and a good number of Jewish families converted, usually for their safety. Examples can be found in Fes, Rabat, Salé, and in cities on the coast and in the interior, where a few families still have Jewish names (Cohen and Skali, for example).

The Jewish converts to Islam sometimes displayed a marked hostility toward their former faith. Two cases are worth citing here. The first is that of Ibn Yahya al-Maghribi (d. 1175),

A Jew in Medina, newly converted to Islam, urges his fellow Jews to convert as well. Ottoman painting, sixteenth century, in *Siyar i-Nabî*, volume III, folio 363 (verso). New York, New York Public Library, Spencer Collection.

better known as Samu'al al-Maghribi. Born in Fes to a pious Jewish family (his father was a rabbi), he emigrated to Iraq, where he made a name for himself with his works in mathematics and astronomy. His conversion in 1163 came about after a dream in which a voice commanded him to embrace Islam. Shortly thereafter, he wrote a few treatises critical of Judaism and Christianity. The most famous was titled *Ifham al-Yahud*, or *Confutation of the Jews*. The second case is that of Abd al-Haqq al-Islami, who was born in Ceuta during the time of the Merinids (1214–1465). His

"Sharp Retort to the Jews" became a major point of reference in confrontations with Judaism. It is to be noted, regarding these polemical treatises, that the Jews could not "retort," since religious confrontation was strictly forbidden them.

There were often suspicions that Jewish conversions to Islam were not sincere. Although, in theory, the convert could claim the same rights as his coreligionists, in practice he found various restrictions imposed on him, and his sincerity was challenged on many occasions. The misadventures of the Bildiyyin provide a good example. This group of Jewish families who converted belatedly to Islam settled in several Moroccan cities. Members of these families were also known by the name *muhājirūn*, that is, those who, like the companions of the Prophet, had made the hijira and had benefited from a spiritual journey from a "dark" age to another, better time. It was customary for their name to include a noun, *islami*, whose connotations were sometimes positive, sometimes degrading. In any case, it attested to their origins, and especially to their recent Islamization. In Fes especially, they had to fight to get a foothold as full members of the *umma* and to thwart the various attempts to exclude them from the city's major commerce and artisanal trades. They often won their case, despite harassment from rival groups who pointed with pride to their own origins or social position.

Forced conversion

Conversion of Jews by force was very rare. A few princes imposed it during reigns that the historiographers characterize as neither glorious nor praiseworthy. Of all the episodes of forced conversion, that of the Almohads in the Muslim West (North Africa and Andalusia) was the most painful. It did not target the *dhimmī*s exclusively: the wrath of the Almohads also fell on Muslim tribes who did not share their conception of Islam. Behind the "crusade" against those they considered *al mojassidoun* (anthropomorphists) and *al-mushrikūn* (polytheists) stood one man: Ibn Tumart. After a short stay in the East, where he became imbued with the ideas of orthodox scholastics and was introduced to the system of *ta'wil* (figural interpretation), Ibn Tumart returned to North Africa. What for his masters was only theology became for him a political program. As soon as he set foot in the Almoravids' territory, he began a long trek from city to city, winning *al-Muwahhidūn* (Unitarian) disciples, who considered their master "the flawless imam." His contradictory speeches dealt with all subjects of public life, and his diatribes did not overlook the place of the Jews within the Muslim city. Ibn Tumart's eschatological vision of the world ruled out any possibility of compromise: only the believer whose orthodoxy was attested without reservation had the right to live. As a result, under the influence of Almohad propaganda, the last Almoravid prince, 'Ali Ben Yusuf (r. 1106–43), took measures to move the Jewish quarter outside the city of Marrakesh. The offensive against the Jews took on tragic dimensions from the first days of the Almohad reign

('Abd al-Mu'min, r. 1130–63). The disciples of the Mahdi were obsessed with the idea of completing in the Muslim West the missions the Prophet had begun in the East: the purification of the territory and of its inhabitants entailed the conversion of the non-Muslims. These disciples quite simply abolished the *dhimma* pact, on the pretext that the community no longer needed the dividends of the *jizya* (the tax collected from the *dhimmīs*). Converts were few among the Christians, who preferred exile, since the vast majority were in any case recent immigrants (Spanish refugees, mercenaries, or merchants). Conversely, a large number of Jews did convert. For their part, they had already been integrated into the society, sometimes well before the Muslim conquest. In addition, the version of Islam proposed by the Almohads was based on the absolute oneness of God, a key concept in Judaism. Even the idea of the Mahdi was not totally alien to that religion. There is evidence that the new masters held seminars to persuade the Jews of the legitimacy of conversion.

But the Almohads still had to be assured of the sincerity of the new converts. The historiographer al-Marrakushi reports these words of Sultan Abu Yusuf Ya'qub al-Mansur: "If I were convinced of their Islamic faith, I would allow them to mix with the Muslims in marriages and in other circumstances; and if I were certain of their infidelity, I would kill their men, reduce the children to slavery, and give away their possessions as booty to the Muslims. But I have doubts about them."[3] The Jews were thus subjected to close scrutiny. Then the idea took hold of obliging these "new believers" to submit to several everyday obligations, the most conspicuous being distinctive clothing. These constraints, rigorously applied, led a learned convert (Ibn Aknin, author of the *Tibb al-Nufus*, or *Medicine of the Souls*) to say that living conditions had never been so harsh. Maimonides also describes the discomfort of the Jews under Almohad rule. Having arrived in Fes in about 1160, he probably had to convert, but did so only in appearance. In light of his later writings, it is easy to imagine that he found that decision dreadful, and he sought in Judaism itself the justification for choosing safety. In response to the question of whether one ought to "convert outwardly or face martyrdom," he wrote the "Epistle on Forced Conversion" (or "Epistle to Yemen"): "To someone who comes to ask us whether he ought to get himself killed or rather acknowledge [the prophetic mission of Muhammad], we reply: may he acknowledge and not be killed. Such a wondrous persecution has never been seen, one in which words alone are imposed on you. The advice I give myself, and the council I wish to give to myself, my friends, and those who ask for advice, is that we must leave these places and go wherever we will be able to practice our religion and the Torah, without constraint or fear." Maimonides carried out his program, while others rejected it.

After the Merinids broke away from Almohad religious strictures, most Jewish converts opted to return to their original faith, and they were not harassed. Maimonides himself benefited from that dispensation. Even in Cairo, where he was recognized by an Andalusian who denounced him for the crime of apostasy, he was defended on the premise that forced conversion cannot be considered legally valid.

143

Another instance of forced conversion occurred during the reign of the sixth Fatimid sultan, al-Hakim Bi-Amr-Allah (996–1021). Although of lesser scope, it too arose from the aberrations of an emir who pursued coercion to impose his own truth, despite religious and social resistance. The historiographical sources draw an unflattering portrait of the sultan and agree that he tended to rule by the saber. His desire to compel the Jews to convert must be cited alongside his other decisions: forcing them to work at night, prohibiting them from consuming some fruits and vegetables, and so on. Al-Maqrizi, the historiographer of the Fatimids, indicates that the wrong committed against the Jews and Christians caused a collective malaise, and that the sultan, faced with protests from all sides, reversed course.

---

1. [Verses from the Qur'an are taken from *The Koran*, trans. N. J. Dawood (New York: Penguin, 1995) – JMT.]

2. Quoted in Bernard Lewis, *The Jews of Islam* (Princeton, NJ: Princeton University Press, 1984), 71.

3. Al-Marrakushi, *The History of the Almohades* [*Kitab al-Mu'yik fi talkhis akhbar al-Maghreb*], ed. Reinhart Dozy (Leiden: E. J. Brill, 1881), 223.

Chapter III

In Christendom

The Legal Status of the Jews and Muslims in the Christian States
John Tolan

In the Muslim societies of the Middle Ages, Jews and Christians had the status of *dhimmīs*, protected but at the same time inferior. In the Christian kingdoms of the Middle Ages, Jews and sometimes Muslims lived under similar conditions with respect to the Christians. But their status became increasingly precarious in many European countries. Minorities were subjected to violence and expulsions. For example, the Jews were expelled from France in 1182, again in 1306, and once more in 1394; from England in 1290; from Spain in 1492; and from Portugal in 1497. The Muslims were expelled from Sicily in the thirteenth century, then gradually from all the Christian nations on the Iberian Peninsula.

John Tolan

A professor of medieval history at the Université de Nantes, the author works primarily on the history of the legal status of religious minorities. Among his publications: *Saracens: Islam in the Medieval European Imagination* (Columbia University Press, 2002); and *Saint Francis and the Sultan: The Curious History of a Christian-Muslim Encounter* (Oxford University Press, 2009).

The Roman foundations of the Jews' status in Christendom

The legal foundations for this minority status can be found in Roman legislation of the fourth and fifth centuries. The Theodosian Code, promulgated in 438, is a collection of laws decreed by emperors from Constantine I to Theodosius II. Book 16 of the code deals with questions of religion.[1] It marks the establishment of Christianity as an actual state religion, with, for example, privileges and exemptions for some members of the clergy. Different laws of the code deal with Judaism, often called a "superstition" or a "sect." The Jews were prohibited from proselytizing, marrying Christians, holding certain public posts, mocking the rites and certain beliefs of the Christians, having Christian slaves, circumcising their slaves, and so on. At the same time, however, other laws protected the Jewish communities: they were guaranteed the right to practice their faith and to have synagogues. The Jewish patriarch and chief rabbis were granted exemptions and privileges similar to those of the Christian clergy. The historian Amnon Linder even speaks of the establishment of a true "Jewish church."[2] Some of these laws designate Judaism not as a "superstition" but as a "religion," just like Christianity. Under the Christian Roman Empire, Judaism (unlike, for example, paganism, which was banned) became a legitimate religion, though clearly inferior to Christianity.

Roman law, of course, had a profound influence on the Christian states of the Middle Ages, especially on the Eastern Roman Empire (improperly called "Byzantine"). The reforms of Justinian (527) included a revision of legislation concerning the Jews that confirmed their minority status (protected and inferior). The Justinian Code became the foundation for Byzantine law and an important source of Latin European jurisprudence, both in canon law and civil law. Theology also contributed toward justifying and defining the inferior status of the Jew. Augustine, for example, explained that the Jews must be allowed to live in peace within the Christian community because they preserved the sacred Hebrew texts in their original language and because they were the living witnesses of the punishment God imposed on them for having refused to acknowledge Jesus as their messiah. This is the reason they were banished, exiled to the four corners of the world to live in poverty. Paradoxically, this view justified both tolerance of the Jews and oppression: they must be allowed to live in Christian lands, Augustine said, but they must also submit to the yoke of the dominant society.

In addition, they must all convert to Christianity at the end of time. This dual legacy, legal and theological, clarifies both why the Jews could live within Christian societies and the precariousness of their existence.

The Muslims in medieval Christian Europe

Beginning in the eleventh century, during the Christian conquests of Muslim territories (in Sicily, the Holy Land, and on the Iberian Peninsula), many Muslims found themselves under the yoke of Christian princes and were often granted a status analogous to that of the *dhimmī*s in the Islamic world. Various juridical texts define the legal status of the Muslim under Christian domination: capitulation treaties, municipal and royal charters, and acts of ecclesiastical councils.[3] These documents show that Muslims in the Christian kingdoms could be slaves, free peasants, artisans, or mercenaries in the royal armies. The Muslims' right to practice their faith was generally assured. Their conversion could only be voluntary and, of course, only to Christianity. The laws tried to maintain a certain level of segregation. In theory, the Muslim was to be socially inferior to the Christian, just as the *dhimmī* in Islamic countries was inferior to the Muslim – or as the Jew was in Christian kingdoms. The legislation concerning Muslim minorities was derived from the traditional laws limiting the place of the Jews in Christian society: according to canon law, the Jews were not to have the slightest power over Christians. In particular, they could not have Christian slaves or hold public positions. Later legislation extended these principles to the Muslims. The Third Lateran Council (1179) prohibited Jews and Muslims from possessing Christian slaves—a prohibition often repeated in royal legislation (for example, in the *Siete Partidas* of Alfonso X of Castile). Various *fueros* (charters granted to cities in Spain) prohibited the Jews and the Muslims from being judges in cases involving Christians.[4]

The Muslims, like the Jews, were granted the right to practice their religion and to have places of wor-

A man raising his club against a group of Jews. Margin illustration in the chronicle of Matthew Paris, *Flores Historiarum*, Westminster, fourteenth century. London, British Library, Cotton Ms. Nero D. II, fol. 183 verso.

ship. Alfonso X, king of Castile and León (r. 1252–84), affirmed, for example, that the "Moors" could live "observing their law without insulting our own." Their mosques were royal property. The sovereign could therefore do with them as he pleased. Implicitly, that provision included the possibility of turning them into churches or of setting some aside to continue to serve as mosques.[5] Such tolerance, however, tended to erode over time. A good example is the right of *adhan*, the call to prayer by the muezzin, which was often among the concessions granted. In 1311 the Council of Vienne prohibited the *adhan* in Christian territory. But that prohibition would not always be respected: in Valencia, various kings and lords in the fourteenth and fifteenth centuries refused to apply it or granted dispensations, sometimes incurring the wrath of the ecclesiastics.[6]

Limiting social promiscuity

Many laws were aimed at banning any sexual relationships between Christians and non-Christians. Marriage was prohibited, of course, except in cases where a Muslim or Jew who was already married converted to Christianity. According to Gratian's Decree (twelfth century), that person had the right to remain married to a non-Christian spouse, a right that Pope Gregory IX confirmed in 1234.[7] In Christian Spain generally, the Christian woman and Muslim or Jewish man who had sexual relations faced great risks. But that was not the case for a Muslim or Jewish woman and her Christian lover. The *fuero de Sepúlveda* stipulated that a Muslim man who slept with a Christian woman would be thrown off a cliff, and his lover would be burned at the stake; in the *fuero de Béjar*, both were to be burned. The *Siete Partidas* of Alfonso X were somewhat more merciful toward the Christian woman: the Muslim or Jewish lover was to be stoned, while his accomplice would lose half her property. If she was married, she risked the death penalty; if she was a prostitute, the two lovers would be whipped together throughout the city. In all cases, the penalties were harsher for repeat offenders.[8] Contact with a religious adversary was often seen as an element of corruption or pollution that was to be avoided. Certain *fueros* did not allow non-Christians to go to the public baths on the same days as Christians.[9] Christian wet nurses were not allowed to breastfeed Jewish or Muslim children, nor could Christians employ Muslim or Jewish wet nurses.[10] Better enforcement of sexual prohibitions was also the reason for imposing (or attempting to impose) clothing restrictions. This was particularly true in the case of the Fourth Lateran Council in 1215, which ordered "Saracens" and Jews to wear distinctive clothing in order to prevent sexual relations, or rather, to prevent Christians from using the pretext of ignorance to justify their affairs with non-Christians. These measures, which were supposed to apply to all Christendom, were very unevenly enforced. Sumptuary laws that imposed distinctive signs on the Muslims or that prohibited them from wearing "Christian" clothing were reiterated many times: at the Cortes of Seville in 1252, at that of Valladolid in 1258, and again at that of Seville in 1261, proof that the measure decreed by the council of 1215 was not respected to any great extent.[11]

> *Muslims and Jews were lumped together because of their supposed hostility toward the Christians. Both were 'blasphemers' according to the council.*

It was not only sexual corruption but also spiritual corruption that was feared. Innocent III and the Fourth Lateran Council endeavored to spare the Christians from the mockery and blasphemy of the "infidels." To protect the Holy Week rituals from such contamination, the council did not hesitate to ban Muslims and Jews from public places during that period, as Spanish legislation would also do.[12] Muslims and Jews were lumped together because of their supposed hostility toward the Christians. Both were "blasphemers" according to the council, which claimed that members of these two groups would parade during Holy Week in gaudy clothing, making fun of the Christians who were ritually expressing their sorrow in commemoration of the Passion of Christ. That hostility was specifically invoked to justify the ban on holding public positions: a "blasphemer" could not be given the slightest power over a Christian. A polemical view of Islam and Judaism fed these decisions of the Fourth Lateran Council: without enumerating or distinguishing the different "blasphemies" of the Muslims or Jews, the council affirmed that these were sufficient to justify the exclusion of the minorities from every post of authority.

The fear of apostasy

The problem of conversion recurs often in these documents. Alfonso X the Wise made it the principal subject of *título* 7.25 of the *Siete Partidas*, "On the Moors":

seven of its twenty laws are devoted to it. Five concern the punishments to be imposed on Christians who convert to Islam. Apostates would lose all their possessions, which then became the property of heirs who had remained Christian; converts could be accused of that crime for up to five years after their death. Even if they returned to Christianity, they would lose the right to hold office, to bear witness, and to enter into purchasing or sales contracts. In the political and military context of thirteenth-century Castile, the fear of conversion to Islam corresponded to a very real danger: conversions often occurred during captivity in Islamic territories or accompanied an act of political treason.[13]

By contrast, the conversion of a Jew or Muslim to Christianity was desirable, according to the *Siete Partidas*, but it had to be voluntary: Christians must try to convince by reason and example, not by violence or constraint. No one had the right to prevent a Muslim or Jew from converting to Christianity, or to call the convert *tornadizo* (renegade or traitor), or to insult him or her. It was the fear of being the object of such insults, along with force of habit, that according to Alfonso would prevent Jews and Muslims from converting. The kings of Aragon promulgated similar laws to protect converts from insults and the loss of their inheritance.

All that legislation tended at once to protect the minorities and to circumscribe their rights. The various interest groups could converge or diverge. For example, the religious authorities of the minorities (imams and rabbis) and of the majority (the Christian clergy) all sought to avoid sexual promiscuity among people of different faiths. Many a Christian king or prince granted privileges to individuals or groups (Jewish physicians or courtiers, the Muslim militia) to undermine the power of other groups (vassals with large holdings, burghers). This created tensions and jealousies that were often more than strictly religious disputes. The legal status of religious minorities in Christian countries was ultimately much more fragile than that of the *dhimmī*, which was well rooted in the founding texts of Islam. Muslims and Jews lived in the Christian kingdoms at the king's or queen's pleasure, and nothing kept sovereigns from expelling them, which they did increasingly as the Middle Ages came to an end.

---

1. *Les Lois religieuses des empereurs romains de Constantin à Théodose II, 312–438*, vol. 1, *Code théodosien*, book 16, repr., Theodor Mommsen's text with a French translation by Jean Rougé and notes by Roland Delmaire (Paris: Cerf, 2005). [English edition: *The Theodosian Code and Novels, and the Sirmondian Constitutions*, trans. Clyde Pharr (Princeton, NJ: Princeton University Press, 1952) – JMT.]

2. Amnon Linder, "The Legal Status of the Jews in the Roman Empire," in *The Cambridge History of Judaism*, vol. 4, *The Late Roman-Rabbinic Period*, ed. Steven T. Katz (Cambridge: Cambridge University Press, 2008), 128–73. See also Amnon Linder, *The Jews in Imperial Roman Legislation* (Detroit: Wayne State University Press, 1997); Daniel Boyarin, "The Christian Invention of Judaism: The Theodosian Empire and the Rabbinic Refusal of Religion," *Representations* 85 (2004): 21–57.

3. See John Tolan, "The Social Inferiority of Religious Minorities: *Dhimmī*s and Mudejars," chap. 3 of Henry Laurens, John Tolan, and Gilles Veinstein, *Europe and the Islamic World: A History*, trans. Jane Marie Todd (Princeton,

NJ: Princeton University Press, 2012), 49–69; Andrea Mariana Navarro, "Imágines y representaciones de moros y judíos en los fueros de la corona de Castilla (siglos XI – XIII)," *Temas medievales* 11 (2002–3): 113–50.

4. Navarro, "Imágines y representaciones."

5. Alfonso el Sabio (Alfonso the Wise), *Las siete partidas* (Madrid: Atlas, 1807; 1972), § 7.25.1. See John Tolan, *Saracens: Islam in the Medieval European Imagination* (New York: Columbia University Press, 2002), 174–75, 186–93; Robert Burns, "Jews and Moors in the *Siete Partidas* of Alfonso X the Learned: A Background Perspective," in *Medieval Spain: Culture, Conflict, and Coexistence*, ed. Roger Collins and Anthony Goodman (Basingstoke: Palgrave Macmillan, 2002), 46–62.

6. Maria Teresa Ferrer i Mallol, *Els sarraïns de la corono catalano-aragonesa en el segle XIV: Segregació i discriminació* (Barcelona: Consell Superior d'Investigacions Cientifiques, 1987), 88–94.

7. Gratian, *Decretum*, causa 28. For Gregory IX's confirmation of the decree in 1234, see *Responsiones ad dubitabilia cerca communicationem christanorum cum sarracenis*, in Raymond de Peñafort, *Summae*, 3 vols., in *Universa Bibliothcea Iuris*, ed. Xavier Ochoa and Aloysius Diez (Rome, 1976–1978), 3:1024–36, chap. 11; John Tolan, *Les relations entre les pays d'islam et le monde latin du milieu du Xe siècle au milieu du XIIIe siècle* (Paris: Bréal, 2000), 164–69.

8. Navarro, "Imágenes y representaciones," 144; Alfonso el Sabio, *Las siete partidas*, § 7.25.10, § 7.24.9.

9. James F. Powers, "Frontier Municipal Baths and Social Interaction in Thirteenth-Century Spain," *American Historical Review* 84 (1979): 649–67.

10. Joseph O'Callaghan, "The Mudejars of Castile and Portugal in the Twelfth and Thirteenth Centuries," in *Muslims under Latin Rule, 1100–1300*, ed. James Powell (Princeton, NJ: Princeton University Press, 1990), 11–56, esp. 31.

11. Lateran 4, canon 68, in *Les conciles oecuméniques: Les décrets*, vol. 2, part 1 (Paris, 1994), 567; O'Callaghan, "The Mudejars of Castile and Portugal," 30–31.

12. Lateran 4, canon 68. On the Crown of Aragon, see Elena Lourie, "Anatomy of Ambivalence: Muslims under the Crown of Aragon in the Late Thirteenth Century," in Elena Lourie, *Crusade and Colonisation* (Aldershot: Variorum, 1990), 52; David Nirenberg, *Communities of Violence: Persecution of Minorities in the Middle Ages* (Princeton, NJ: Princeton University Press, 1996). On Castile, see O'Callaghan, "The Mudejars of Castile and Portugal," 44.

13. See Robert I. Burns, "Renegades, Adventurers, and Sharp Businessmen: The Thirteenth-Century Spaniard in the Case of Islam," *Catholic Historical Review* 58 (1972): 341–66; Nirenberg, *Communities of Violence*, 128n4; Mikel de Epalza, *Fray Anselm Turmeda (Abdallah al-Taryuman) y su polémica islamo-cristiana* (Madrid: Hiperion, 1994); Dwayne Carpenter, "Minorities in Medieval Spain: The Legal Status of Jews and Muslims in the *Siete Partidas*," *Romance Quarterly* 33 (1986): 275–87; and, by the same author, "Alfonso the Learned and the Problem of Conversion to Islam," in *Estudios en homenaje a Enrique Ruiz-Fornells*, ed. Juan Fernández-Jiménez, José Labrador-Herraiz, and Teresa Valdivieso (Erie, PA: ALDEEU, 1990), 61–68.

Jews and Muslims in Sicily

The Muslim occupation of Sicily from 827 to 1071 led to the Arabization of the Jews on the island and their submission to the *dhimma* system. The reconquest by the Normans resulted in the establishment of a kingdom founded on an implicit but lasting pact of coexistence between communities: the Normans extended the *dhimma* to the Muslims, a minority at that time, and consolidated the foundations of jurisdictional autonomy and personal law for both the Jews and the Muslims. These minorities were considered "serfs of the Royal Chamber," that is, immediately dependent on the king; they were both subject to the *jizya* and citizens of the cities. The ecumenical kingdom of the Normans lasted more than a century, but it was swept aside by crises of succession within the Hauteville dynasty. The central power, weakened by the regencies, could not protect the Muslims, who took up arms. Their unwitting revolt ultimately led to their being forcibly displaced to Lucera, Apulia, under Frederick the Great. The emperor made some of the émigrés his Saracen guards and reconstituted an autonomous community for them. Until the end of the Middle Ages, even after the failure of the plan for coexistence, autonomy remained the rule for the Jewish community of Sicily, which displayed constant loyalty to the royal power. The state also recognized the validity of the Muslims' institutions – notarial practices and contract marriage – and the Muslims, few in number, were sometimes citizens of the cities.[1]

The conquest and famines that devastated North Africa in the ninth to twelfth centuries, as well as the ravages of the Hilalians, contributed toward a mass migration to Sicily, which continued under the Norman regime: Arabs and Berbers from Cyrenaica, Tripolitania, the Zab region, Ifriqiya, and the central Maghreb; Christians from Carthage, Mahdia, and El Gharbia; and Jews from throughout the Maghreb and even from the Draa region and Tafilalet. A final wave of Jews, fleeing the late-arriving persecution of the Almohad al-Mansur in Marrakesh in 1231, were welcomed to Sicily in 1239. Emperor Frederick II settled them in Palermo.[2]

The family names of the Jews of Sicily, fixed in the fourteenth century, allude to the origins of their ancestors and make it possible to draw an imperfect map of these migrations: Sijilmasa, the Draa, Tahert, M'sila, Tébessa, Mahdia, Sfax, Gafsa, Tripoli, Sirte, and Barqa, a string of strong communities connected to Sicily by commerce from the eleventh century on. These migrations did not end in the thirteenth century. Maghrebi Jews continued to settle in Sicily, where they retained the status of privileged immigrants.[3] The Jewish community of Trapani earned the privilege of welcoming migrants in 1474, and in 1491 Ferdinand, the Catholic king of Aragon and Sicily, granted safe-conduct to seventy Maghrebi Jews who came to settle there.

Familiarity with the language linked the Jews of Sicily to the Maghreb and thus allowed them to act as go-betweens, a role they shared with the Maltese and the Christians of Pantelleria, who were also Arabophones. They served as translators for notaries or in legal courts, or as brokers in commerce between Sicily and Tunisia. They possessed Arabic books in medicine and astronomy. In the late thirteenth century, King Charles of Anjou called upon Ferragut of Agrigento to translate al-Razi's medical manual, *Al-Hawi*, from Arabic into Latin. In 1403 Martin the Younger, king of Sicily, even chose Samuel Sala, a merchant active in Trapani, as an ambassador to conduct delicate negotiations with the Hafsid sovereign on the question of redeeming each other's captives, which involved a few bribes. The Sicilian Jews' linguistic abilities, the support provided by the network of Jewish communities, and perhaps their kinship ties also explain their important place in commerce with Tunisia. The Jews of Trapani and of Pantelleria, like the Muslims of that island, continuously enjoyed the freedom to go to Tunis, Kelibia, Sousse, Sfax, Djerba, and Tripoli. They did not have large amounts of capital at their disposal, but they associated themselves with the Christians, who financed them. These Jews participated in resupplying the archipelago with wheat and barley from the coastal cities of Ifriqiya during lean years, and brought oil, camel and ox hides, and dates back from Djerba. They also played a role in redeeming Sicilian captives after long and costly negotiations with the corsairs: this was both a good deed and good business.

Although major trade in textiles passed through the Tunisian *funduqs* of the Genoans and Catalans, the activities of the Jews remained modest. They participated as brokers, negotiators, and in networking. Some, on the fringes of that honest commerce, also trafficked in contraband: wood, iron, and weapons were the most profitable, and the most in demand by the Hafsid power. Finally, the Maghreb represented a refuge for Jewish criminals – thieves and counterfeiters – who could wait there for the outcome of a negotiation or for the conclusion of a deal with the justice system.

In Sicily, the use of a common language, Arabic, established connections between the Jews and the Muslims – usually slaves being redeemed – and with the new converts to Christianity. In the early decades of the fourteenth century, Jewish and Muslim converts, returning from Lucera after their colony had been destroyed, vouched for one another before notaries. In fact, they shared trades and techniques inherited from the world as it is known to us through the documents of the Cairo Geniza, such as how to work cotton fiber. In the following century, many Sicilian Jews worked as brokers on the slave market. At the time, slavery was a universal form of domestic labor, and the law prohibited the Jewish community from possessing Christian slaves.[4] The purchase of Maghrebi and African captives provided a solution. Since the

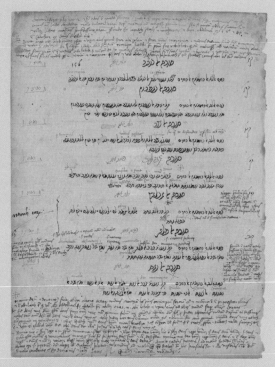

The "Mithridate Qur'an," created in Hebrew characters by a group of Jewish scholars. Sicily, early fifteenth century. Rome, Vatican Library, ms. ebr. 357 fol. 156 recto.

Jewish house was not to be desecrated by idolatry, the seven laws of the sons of Noah were applied to the Muslim slave, a "foreign guest" who was thereby integrated into the Jewish family in a subordinate position. The sons born to captives who were their masters' concubines were circumcised, and, upon their emancipation, these men joined the ranks of the community. In addition, a small but notable proportion of the wills of Jewish Sicilians stipulated that their slaves be emancipated. The former slaves then became part of the shifting population of free Muslims. The Jewish community was moved by the same humane feelings as the church (with respect to Christian slaves) and favored emancipation. In 1459, several Jews from Trapani helped Saracen slaves flee to Tunis and were imprisoned for their deed.[5] Many masters concluded *taille* (land tax) contracts with Muslim captives, who were allowed to work on their own behalf while living away from their masters, earn their freedom, and pay for their return to the Maghreb. The Sicilian documentation indicates that there was always a certain porosity – illegal and therefore rarely attested – between the different religious groups. The Cairo Geniza gives us a glimpse of conversions by Jews to Islam in the eleventh century, that of the cantor of Palermo, for example. Christians who converted to Judaism under the Norman regime had to leave secretly for Egypt. There were also conversions from Islam to Judaism in fifteenth-century Sicily, for example, that of a freedman, an isolated Muslim who married a Jewish woman.

Sicilians in the twelfth to fifteenth centuries had an unusual curiosity about nearby religions and engaged in philosophical exegeses of their content. These included "sessions" in which Frederick II and his entourage of Jewish and Christian scholars worked on an allegorical interpretation of Genesis, and the "seminar" in which the kabbalist Abraham Abulafia gathered the elite of Sicilian Jews in the late thirteenth century, leading them to the gates of Christianity.

Then there was the case of the so-called Mithridates Qur'an, which traveled from the library of Pico della Mirandola to the Vatican (Vat. Heb. 357). Indeed, the interest of Jewish scholars in Islam and the Qur'an has been the object of a recent major discovery. In the early fifteenth century, a team of scholars transliterated a noncanonical, archaic version of the Qur'an into Hebrew characters – probably in Palermo, if the watermark is any indication. The transcription demonstrated a good knowledge of Arabic, though not without some confusion between similar-looking consonants. The work required a great deal of effort and patience, and suggests an unusual intellectual curiosity. It was obviously not done as part of a controversy, since at the time there were only a handful of Muslims in Sicily, and none were scholars.[6] Pico della Mirandola probably received it from a remarkable individual who took the name "Flavius Mithridates," the son of Rabbi Nissim Abu'l-Faraj of Caltabellotta,

himself a learned astronomer. Mithridates received a meticulous education (Hebrew, Aramaic, Arabic) and training in the Talmud. He broke away from Judaism and was baptized under the name Guglielmo Raimondo Moncada in 1467. His conversion led to a brief and brilliant career – though not without obscure episodes – that took him to Rome, Germany, and Florence before his death in 1489. A translator and teacher of the Oriental languages, he translated part of the Qur'an and was one of several who participated in compiling a glossary in both Latin and Hebrew.

King Ferdinand's expulsion decree of 1492–93 – imposed on the recalcitrant Sicilians when Ferdinand became king of all Spain by marrying Isabella of Castile—put an end to that short-lived, common history. The Jewish community went into exile: Sicilian Jews took to the road in organized communities, going first to Naples, then to Ottoman Constantinople. Only a few resettled in the Maghreb, where they continued to have commercial relations with Trapani and Palermo. ●

A professor specializing in medieval Sicily at the Université de Paris X-Nanterre, Henri Bresc is the director of the Centre d'Histoire Sociale et Culturelle de l'Occident (CHSCO; Center for the Social and Cultural History of the West). His publications include Arabes de langue, juifs de religion: L'évolution du judaïsme sicilien dans l'environnement latin (XIIᵉ – XVᵉ siècles) *(Bouchène, 2001).*

1. Henri Bresc, *Arabes de langue, juifs de religion: L'évolution du judaïsme sicilien dans l'environnement latin, XIIᵉ – XVᵉ siècles* (Paris: Bouchene, 2001).
2. Giuseppe Mandalà, "La migrazione degli Ebrei del *Garbum* in Sicilia (1239)," *Materia giudaica* 11, nos. 1–2 (2006): 179–99.
3. Henri Bresc, "La Sicile médiévale, terre de refuge pour les juifs: Migration et exil," *Al-Masaq* 17, no. 1 (March 2005): 31–46.
4. Henri Bresc, "La schiavitù in casa degli ebrei siciliani del Tre e Quattrocento," *Quaderni storici* 42, no. 3 (2007): 679–98.
5. Shlomo Simonsohn, *The Jews in Sicily*, vol. 14, *Notaries of Palermo and Trapani* (Leiden: E. J. Brill, 2008), 9368.
6. Benoît Grévin, "Le Coran de Mithridate," unpublished paper for the École Française de Rome, 2005–6.

Ramón Llull and the Interfaith Utopia

Throughout the Middle Ages, the three monotheisms coexisted around the periphery of the Mediterranean, resulting in the production of a corpus of religious apologetics or polemics. These works often took the form of "dialogues" between the faithful of two or three rival religions, based on debates (sometimes fictive, sometimes real) that usually ended in the victory of one of the protagonists (the one who represented the author's religion, of course), and the rivals' conversion to the "true" faith. Among numerous examples, we could cite the debate between the Nestorian Catholicos Timothy and Caliph al-Mahdi in Baghdad in 781, Yehuda Halevi's *Kuzari* in the twelfth century (see the Counterpoint on the *Kuzari,* p. 130), and Cardinal Nicholas of Cusa's *De pace fidei* in the fifteenth. The tone of these texts varied between animosity and respect, but in general the aim was, if not to convert the rivals, then at least to reassure the faithful of the "true" religion. The *Book of the Gentile and the Three Wise Men,* written in Catalan by the Majorcan Ramón Llull in about 1274–1276, is no exception to that rule. Nevertheless, it is extraordinary for the tone of respect and balance reigning among the participants. The Gentile, a pagan in the grip of despair, begs the three Wise Men to explain the principles of their religions, which they do one by one, applying the rhetorical rules of Llull's *Ars,* a methodology he wanted to erect into a universal logic. Apart from the fact that the author, a Christian closely associated with the Franciscans, proves to be knowledgeable and well informed about the other two traditions (for example, he quotes the Talmud and the Hadith), he comes up with a particularly astonishing finale, in which the Jew, the Christian, and the Muslim decline to know which of the three "Laws" the Gentile chose, so that they might continue together to seek the path of truth.

John Tolan

Ramón Llull and the Interfaith Utopia

When the Gentile had heard all the arguments of the three wise men, he began to recount everything the Jew had said, and then everything the Christian had said, and similarly with what the Saracen had said. As a result, the three wise men were very pleased, for the Gentile had understood and retained their words; and together they said to the Gentile that it was clear they had not spoken to a man without heart or ears. After recounting the above matter, the Gentile stood up and his understanding was illuminated by the path of salvation, and his heart began to love and to bring tears to his eyes, and he worshipped God… When the Gentile had finished his prayer, he went to the lovely spring and washed his hands and face, because of the tears he had shed, and dried himself with a white cloth he carried, the one he had formerly used to wipe away his continual tears of sorrow. He then sat down next to the three wise men and said: "Through God's grace and blessing, I happened to meet you gentlemen here where God saw fit to remember me and take me as His servant. Blessed be the Lord, therefore, and blessed be this place, and may God bless you, and blessed be God for making you want to come here! And in this place, where I have received such good fortune, in the presence of you gentlemen, I want to select and choose that religion which, by the grace of God and by your words, seems to me to be true. And in that religion I want to be, and I want to work for the rest of my life to honor and proclaim it." . . .

The three wise men then stood up and most agreeably and devoutly took leave of the Gentile. Many were the blessings the three wise men wished on the Gentile, and the Gentile on the three wise men; and their leave-taking and the end of their conversation was full of embraces, kisses, tears, and sighs. But before the three wise men left, the Gentile asked them in astonishment why they did not wait to hear which religion he would choose in preference to the others. The three wise men answered, saying that, in order for each to be free to choose his own religion, they preferred not knowing which religion he would choose. "And all the more so since this is a question we could discuss among ourselves to see, by force of reason and by means of our intellects, which religion it must be that you will choose. And if, in front of us, you state which religion it is that you prefer, then we would not have such a good subject of discussion nor such satisfaction in discovering the truth." . . .

They took leave of one another most amiably and politely, and each asked forgiveness of the other for any disrespectful word he might have spoken against his religion. Each forgave the other, and when they were about to part, one wise man said: "Do you think we have nothing to gain from what happened to us in the forest? Would you like to meet once a day, and, by the five trees and the ten conditions signified by their flowers, discuss according to the manner the Lady of Intelligence showed us, and have our discussions last until all three of us have only one faith, one religion, and until we can find some way to honor and serve one another, so that we can be in agreement? For war, turmoil, ill will, injury, and shame prevent men from agreeing on one belief."

Each of the three wise men approved of what the wise man had said, and they decided on a time and place for their discussions, as well as how they should honor and serve one another, and how they should dispute; and that when they had agreed on and chosen one faith, they would go forth into the world giving glory and praise to the name of our Lord God. Each of the three wise men went home and remained faithful to his promise.

Here ends the *Book of the Gentile and the Three Wise Men* . . . which book constitutes a doctrine and method for enlightening clouded minds and awakening the great who sleep, and for entering into union with and getting to know strangers and friends, by asking what religion they think the Gentile chose in order to find favor with God.

Ramón Llull, "The Book of the Gentile and the Three Wise Men," in *Selected Works of Ramón Llull*, trans. Anthony Bonner, 2 vols. (Princeton, NJ: Princeton University Press, 1985), 1:294, 300–301, 303–4.

Jews and Muslims in the Latin Kingdom of Jerusalem
Yehoshua Frenkel

The Middle East at the closing quarter of the eleventh century was a rich multiethnic and multireligious mosaic. The Jewish population of the Eastern Mediterranean constituted one of the ancient components of this variegated society. The conquest by the Franks, that is, the Crusaders, did not change this reality; in the first decade of the Latins' rule, the Jews suffered heavily from the violence of the newcomers. This was also the fate of the Muslim communities in cities along the seacoast and in Jerusalem.

Yet, with the passing of time, the Franks adopted a sociopolitical policy that did not differ profoundly from the Islamic caliphate treatment of non-Muslims. This article aims to describe the history of the Jewish population in the Latin Kingdom of Jerusalem. Among other things, it argues that the fate of the Jews did not differ considerably from that of the Muslim population of the Crusaders' kingdom.

Yehoshua Frenkel

Yehoshua Frenkel is a professor at Haifa University. He teaches political and social history of the Arab world during the Middle Ages. His recent publications include "The Turks of the Eurasian Steppes in Arabic Geographical Literature," in *Mongols, Turks and Others: Eurasian Nomads and the Sedentary World*, edited by Reuven Amitai and Michal Biran (Brill, 2005).

The Middle East in the eleventh century

On the eve of the Frank conquest, the Jewish population of Syria and Palestine constituted one of the ancient components of this variegated society. Their legal status was that of "the protected people," namely, communities that paid poll tax and in return enjoyed restricted religious and communal freedom. Their history in those years, starting from the days of al-Hakim until the arrival of the Seljuks, is a story of decline, at least in the case of the Jews of Palestine. The Geniza documents make it clear that at the time of arrival of the First Crusade to Syria, the center of the Jewish community was in Tyre, and not in Jerusalem.

The first encounters between the Franks and the Jews

The advance of the Crusaders' armies incited panic and flight among the Fatimid garrisons who were stationed in the Syrian coastal towns and among the civil population. Their Jewish inhabitants had presumably already learned at this early date about the dreadful fate of the Jews along the routes of the advancing Crusades.

The first direct encounter in Palestine of a Jewish community with the Franks took place in Jerusalem (June–July 1099). The Jews of Jerusalem participated, along with the Muslim Fatimid garrison and the local population, in the defense efforts. The defenders knew about their prospects in case of conquest. The historian of the First Crusade Albert of Aachen (fl. ca. 1100) recounts that during the siege, Baldwin of Bourcq ordered that a Muslim prisoner who refused to convert to Christianity should be brought before the Tower of David and decapitated.

The Greek princess Anna Comnena (1083–1153), in the biography of her father, the Byzantine emperor Alexiade, says, "They [the Latins] encircled Jerusalem's walls and made frequent attacks on them and besieged the town, and within one lunar month they took it and killed many of the Saracenic and Jewish inhabitants. When they had brought all into subjection and no one resisted them, they invested Godfrey with supreme authority by unanimous consent, and called him 'king.'"

The success of the Franks in seizing cities populated by Jews, and the fate of the Jews, is reflected in contemporary documents. These sources tell of Jewish participation in the fighting and shed light on Jewish solidarity by providing shelter to refugees and by collecting money to ransom prisoners. (In accordance with Islamic legal tradition the standard sums were three captive males for one hundred golden dinars). Since the armies of the Crusaders came

> **"Sources tell of Jewish participation in the fighting and shed light on Jewish solidarity."**

from different parts of Europe, their behavior differed. It is well attested that during the first decade of the Frankish penetration into Syria, the local population suffered heavily from the brutality of the assaulters. A great number of Muslims were killed. Refugees fled for their lives. In some locations Jews were murdered and women were raped; in other cases Jews were imprisoned and enslaved. The account of the siege of Haifa by Tancred and Daimbert reveals an identical story: the Jews and the Saracens valiantly defended the city until the fall of the citadel, after which the Crusaders flocked into the city and killed whoever crossed their path.

The onslaught of the Franks and the heavy price paid by Jewish communities in Europe and the East, as well as their success at eliminating the Muslim presence in Jerusalem, provoked three reactions among the contemporary Jews: outbreaks of Messianic expectations, apocalyptical writings, and conversions.

In a long poem Baruch ben Isaac of Aleppo mourned the fate of the land and the Jews: "Bare of buttocks are they, enchained in iron; the boy is given away for a modest fee, while the girl is traded for the best price … the pain of your anxiety overwhelms your bed, the pupil of your eye pours endless tears, for there is no end to your trembling, your virgin daughters have been thrown upon the rocks like sheep for slaughter. How those who dwell at the center of the universe [Jerusalem] have become defiled and melted in the crucible of wrath, delivered into the hands of a foreign nation and made to hear an unknown language, their houses given over to those who plundered them."

Maimonides's epistle to Yemen (written ca. 1172) attested that during the eleventh century there were several outbreaks of messianic expectations. Maimonides views the Jewish suffering of his time as a prelude to the messianic age. Benjamin of Tudela reports about the messianic propaganda conducted by Menahem ben Salomon in eastern Turkey.

The scroll of Ovadyah (Obadiah) the Norman proselyte is a well-known conversion story (written in ca. 1102). Originally from southern Italy, Obadiah wandered in Syria, Palestine, Egypt, and Mesopotamia. During these years he wrote fourteen tractates to prove the truth of the Jewish religion.

Muslims in the Latin Kingdom of Jerusalem

The Latin chronicles hardly ever mention the Muslim inhabitants of the kingdom. The Latins considered both indigenous Christian communities and Muslims as heretics.[1]

Muslims, who formed a considerable part of the population in some urban centers, were nonetheless second-class citizens who apparently played no political or legal role and were not allowed to participate in the public life of the city.[2] Most of the time, they were prevented from organizing their traditional social and religious associations. The *Assises des Bourgeois* recorded severe penalties for Muslim violence against the Latins. Muslims had virtually no rights in the countryside, where they were essentially the chattel slaves of the Frankish landlords. This class of nobility did not communicate directly with the Muslim villagers. The head (*ra'is*) of community who served as the liaison between the absentee landholder and the subjected villagers served as a kind of vassal to whatever noble owned his land. Revolts of Muslim villagers were few and far between.

Jews and Muslims: A shared legal status

The Franks reinstated the old Byzantine law that prohibited the Jews from living in Jerusalem. This ban was enforced until Saladin's victorious entry into Jerusalem and the failure of the Third Crusade, as described by Judah ben Solomon al-Harizi, one of the Andalusian Jewish poets. Jews, Muslims, and Orthodox Christians were forbidden to hold or acquire manorial rights in a village.

Similarly, in order to limit contact between Christians and non-Christians, the Frankish law prohibited sexual relations between Latins and the indigenous population, hoping to prevent the type of social intermingling of which Fulcher of Chartres describes: "Some [who were Occidentals and have now become Orientals] have taken wives not only of their own people but Syrians or Armenians, or even Saracens who have obtained the grace of baptism. One has his father-in-law as well as his daughter-in-law living with him, or his own child if not his stepson or step-father. Out here there are grandchildren and great-grandchildren. ... People use the eloquence and idioms of diverse languages in conversing back and forth. Words of different languages have become common property known to each nationality, and mutual faith unites those who are ignorant of their descent. Indeed it is written (Isaiah 65:25): 'The lion and the ox shall eat straw together.'"

All other indigenous regulations were actually the continuation of the Islamic rules of the "protected people," yet with a major difference. Within the borders of the Latin Kingdom, the Muslims, the past governors, were downgraded to the status of second-class subjects. They paid a *capitatio*, a poll tax similar to the *jizyah*. A version of the *Assises de Jerusalem*, probably passed in 1192, and the *Assises des Bourgeois* (*Livre de la Cour des Bourgeois* [*1229–44*]) stipulated that all non-Franks, whether Muslim, Christian, or indeed Jewish, were lumped together as an indistinguishable second tier.

> **"All non-Franks, whether Muslim, Christian, or indeed Jewish, were lumped together as an indistinguishable second tier."**

They were subject to different penalties from Franks for the same offenses. Particular neighborhoods and marketplaces were fixed by law for the non-Frankish population. In thirteenth-century Acre, Jews possessed slaves and slave-girls.

The Jews held their own autonomous courts, which decided religious matters and other community institutions, and were allowed to have their own synagogues. The whole realm of matrimony, divorce, and inheritance remained under the jurisdiction of rabbinical courts. Yet the regulations of the Latin Court of the Market show that Jews could appeal to this court, particularly in mixed cases involving Latins and non-Latins.

From Jerusalem to Acre: The Second Kingdom

A change in the Latins' attitude toward the local population, including the Jews, can be observed in the accounts of the Frankish conquest after the year 1110. This is true in the case of villages and cities such as Ashkelon and Tyre. A Geniza document mentions negotiations in Nablus between a Jew and a Frankish knight to ensure the freedom of the former's sister. The history of the Samaritans supports the assumption that contrary to the coastal plains, the population in the mountainous regions was not affected by the Latin conquest.

In Galilee, Jewish (Hebrew) sources name about a dozen communities. An important Jewish center developed in Tiberias. The history of the Jews of Safed during the early decades of the Latin Kingdom is unclear, yet in the thirteenth century it is certain that a community inhabited the town. Acre emerged as a significant Jewish center after the Battle of Hattin (1187), with the transition of the Latin king to his new capital.

At the same time that the Franks controlled Palestine and the Syrian coast, Jews lived in the neighboring provinces of Egypt and inland Syria. These were old communities deeply rooted in the Islamic surroundings. Following the Battle of Hattin, the Ayyubid conquered a considerable portion of the Latin Kingdom. This victory certainly affected the Jewish congregations of the territories that the Franks lost.

Jerusalem was one of the regions and towns that the Ayyubids succeeded in controlling after the limited achievements of the Third Crusade and the truce of Ramla (1193). A small Jewish congregation is mentioned in Nablus. This and other communities were under the jurisdiction of the *nagid* (the head of the Jews living under the Ayyubid regime). These new geopolitical conditions offered an opportunity for Jews from around the world to visit the Holy Land. Hence, Jewish communities appear in writings from the second half of the Latin rule in Palestine, and some among them even settled in Jerusalem. The heterogeneity of scriptural traditions and approaches induced tensions and disagreements between the Jews of the Holy Land, which sometimes caused confrontation with the inhabitants of Jerusalem.

The salient feature of Jewish life in the Second Latin Kingdom is the shifting of the communal and economical centers from the interior regions of Palestine to the coastal plains, which were ruled by the Franks. The mountainous regions, now (i.e., after 1187) under the domination of the Ayyubid dynasty, witnessed a steep decline in economic life.

The community most affected by this development was that of Acre, which came to play the role of the political capital and the commercial hub of the Second Kingdom. Social and political upheavals hampered the chances of Jerusalem from serving as a home for Jewish learning and jurisdiction. In a letter to his son in Spain, Nahmanides laments the condition of Palestine in 1268: "Jerusalem is more ruined than anything else, and the land of Judaea more than Galilee ... and there are no Children of Israel in Jerusalem, because since the coming of the Tatars [Mongols in 1244] they ran away and some were killed by the sword, except two brothers, dyers."

Emigration and immigration: The land of Israel and the Diaspora

Since the arrival of the first Frankish waves to the port cities of the Eastern Mediterranean, their naval capabilities indicate a new phase in maritime transportation and navigation. This can also be seen in the growing number of Jewish travelers and pilgrims that disembarked in the ports of the Latin Kingdom and Egypt. Some among them gained fame as foremost scholars, spiritual leaders, and writers. About ten Hebrew itineraries from those years have survived.

Maimonides provides a condensed account of his sea trip from Northern Africa to Acre (in April–May 1165). From there, he and his companions made their way to Jerusalem: "I entered the Great and Holy House and I prayed in it ... and on Sunday I left Jerusalem to kiss the Tomb of the Patriarchs [in Hebron]."

Judah Halevi (1075–1141) composed the popular verses: "My heart is in the East, and I in the uttermost West ... Zion lieth beneath the fetter of Edom [Christians; i.e., Franks], and I in Arab chains." He describes pilgrimage as a spiritual journey: "the sacred place serves to remind men and to stimulate them to love God."

During the twelfth century and particularly after Saladin's success, several waves of Jewish immigrants (*olim*) settled in Palestine. This movement grew in the thirteenth century. A salient figure in this wave was Nahmanides, who departed Spain (Aragon) for the Holy Land. In his commentary he writes about the high merits of the Land of Israel.

Intellectual history

Although the Land of Israel did not become a center of study and transmission of religious knowledge, nevertheless it attracted the attention of poets and travelers who wrote their verses and itineraries in Hebrew. This last genre emerged, presumably, under the influence of the European Christian *itineraria*. This may explain the salient place given by their authors to the descriptions of mausoleums and shrines. These travelogues also contribute to our reconstruction of the map of Jewish communities in the Latin Kingdom and the Ayyubid sultanate (1171–1250).

The *Travels* of Benjamin of Tudela, in particular, describe his journey along the Lebanese coast to Acre before traveling to other locations within the Kingdom of Jerusalem. In each place he provides the number of Jews, often naming the leading personalities, which is critical information in our efforts to reconstruct the social networks and lines of communication.

---

1. See Jonathan Riley-Smith, *The New Cambridge Medieval History*, vol. 4, *ca. 1024–ca. 1198* (Cambridge: Cambridge University Press, 2008), 544.

2. Christopher Tyerman, *God's War: A New History of the Crusades* (London: Allen Lane, 2006).

Part II

The Modern World

Jews and Muslims in Ottoman Territory before the Expulsion from Spain

Gilles Veinstein

Ottoman Jewry, in the centuries preceding the large emigration of Sephardic Jews to Turkey that transformed it, already existed in communities (Romaniote, Ashkenazi, Italiote, Karaite, etc.) composed of the populations of conquered territories or of exiled European Jews. By 1453, most of these Ottoman Jews, either on their own initiative or by force, had moved to the new capital conquered by Mehmed II. The sultan recognized the usefulness of Jewish contributions to his fledgling state, and was particularly appreciative, for his personal use, of the able physicians, whom he on occasion made his advisers. A supreme representative was needed to represent each group within the empire. The sultan recognized a grand rabbi, Moses Capsali, as the representative for the Jewish community, and later made Elijah Mizrahi his interlocutor.

Gilles Veinstein (1945-2013)

Gilles Veinstein, professor at the Collège de France, held the chair of Turkish and Ottoman History and was the director of studies at the École des hautes études en sciences socials (EHESS) in Paris. His works include *Le Sérail ébranlé: Essai sur les morts, dépositions et avènements des sultans ottomans, xive-xixe siècles* (Fayard, 2003).

The multiplication of the communities

Not only had a Sephardic emigration into the Ottoman Empire begun long before the expulsion—beginning at least as far back as 1391, following the Almohad persecutions—but that empire was established through its successive conquests of lands that had previously been Roman, then Byzantine, in Asia Minor and the Balkans. These lands already had long-standing Jewish colonies of a different origin: Greek-speaking (more precisely, Judeo-Greek-speaking) Jews called Romaniotes. Thus, in Anatolia the Ottomans encountered a community in Bursa, alluded to in the account by Schiltberger (1396–1427).[1] Other communities of modest size probably existed as well. The communities encountered in the Ottomans' European conquests, at Gallipoli (Gelibolu), Adrianopolis (Edirne), and

> *Not only had a Sephardic emigration into the Ottoman Empire begun long before the expulsion—beginning at least as far back as 1391, following the Almohad persecutions.*

Sephardic

Now broadly and erroneously employed to mean all Jews originating from Islamic countries, the name "Sephardic Jews" properly means those Jews that lived in Spain (called *Sefarad* in Hebrew, from Obadya 1, 20). After resettling in North Africa and the Ottoman Empire following the 1492 expulsion, these *Megorashim* ("Expelled") often kept a separate identity from the autochtonous Jewish populations or *Toshavim*. The name *Ma'araviim*, meanwhile, was first used to designate Jews from the Syro-Palestinian region in contrast to the Babylonian Jews, but was afterward applied to Spanish and Maghribi Jews, while the Middle-Eastern communities took upon themselves, up to the present day, the name of *'edot ha-mizrach*, "communities of the Orient."

in several Bulgarian cities, were relatively larger. The conquerors, as they progressed, brought new communities under their domination in the islands of the Aegean Sea, Amarinthos, and Constantinople, conquered in 1453. When Salonika became definitively Ottoman in 1430, after an interim of Venetian domination, the city probably still had Romaniote Jews, even though they were notably absent from the population of the city in 1478.

From Byzantium, the Ottomans also inherited a few small groups of Karaites, supporters of a movement dating from the first half of the ninth century that recognized the Bible as the sole law and therefore rejected the Talmud and rabbinic authority. They were present in Adrianopolis in Thrace, Provadija in Bulgaria, Kastamonu in Anatolia, and Caffa (Feodosiya) in Southern Crimea. They underwent something of a renaissance during the fifteenth and sixteenth centuries.[2]

In Byzantium, which had once been Christianized Rome, a tradition of legal restriction against Jews—accusations and persecutions, and sometimes even forced conversions, for religious and political reasons—was well established.[3] It would continue during the Middle Ages in the Bulgarian and Serbian Empires. Under these circumstances, the transition to Muslim domination was perceived as a positive development to the communities discriminated against and always in jeopardy, and the idea—destined for great success in Christian lands—that the Jews were the natural accomplices of the Ottoman conquerors took on a certain credibility. Similarly, the Ottoman state in the process of formation soon became one place of refuge for the Jews of Western and Central Europe, who were victims of persecutions, forced conversions, and various degrees of banishment during the fourteenth and fifteenth centuries. In these conditions Ashkenazi and Italiote groups joined the existing Romaniote population. In connection

> **"The Ottoman state in the process of formation soon became one place of refuge for the Jews of Western and Central Europe, who were victims of persecutions."**

with these migratory strains, let us recall the famous letter (of which there are several versions) written sometime between 1430 and 1440 to the communities of Swabia, the Rhineland, Styria, Moravia, and Hungary in the name of the Ashkenazi rabbi Isaac Zarfati, who was educated in Germany and later settled in the Ottoman Empire, where he is said to have become the grand rabbi of Edirne.

One version of the letter reads, "Here, in the country of the Turks, we have no reason to complain. We possess great fortunes. Gold and silver in great quantities are in our hands. We are not oppressed by heavy taxes and our commerce is free and unobstructed. Rich are the fruits of the earth. Everything is cheap and each of us lives in peace and freedom."[4]

It is certain that in his desire to be convincing, the rabbi, or whoever was writing for him, is indulging in idealizing the Turkish refuge. Furthermore, it is possible that the text was put together in collaboration with, if not at the instigation of, Ottoman authorities of the time, thus making it a type of propaganda. Whatever the case, it is clear that a Jewish presence not only posed no legal problem for the Ottoman sovereigns, who conferred on such subjects the status of *dhimmī*s, but in fact provided a beneficial or even necessary contribution to society. The Ottomans needed the Jews, or at least some Jews—their capital, their knowledge of and competence in a variety of skills, their experience with an outside world that remained foreign to the Turks in large part—as an indispensable aid to the development and prosperity of their young state. Recourse to the Jews, moreover, had nothing exclusive about it; capable Christians were just as welcome. But the Jews, in addition to the fact that the fate awaiting them in their countries of origin made them available, were particularly well placed in these economic, financial, and scientific activities, which made it possible for the Ottomans to compensate for their own deficiencies.

Mehmed II and the Jewish population of Istanbul

This pragmatic policy toward the Jews is illustrated by the policy of Sultan Mehmed II to repopulate Constantinople (Istanbul) after his conquest of the city in 1453. The city had long been but a shadow of its former self, and the threat of Turkish conquest had weighed on it for decades. The sultan, as soon as he took the city, pursued the objective of repopulating it and creating all the conditions for an unequaled urban development, in order to make his new capital the city that it had once been. As part of an appeal for the return of those who had fled, the sultan launched a policy of deportations (*sürgün*) to Istanbul of populations from various parts of the empire and of all faiths.[5] Nearly all the Jewish communities existing at that time within the empire substantially swelled the two initial autochthonous communities already present in Constantinople. Thus, we find in Istanbul, in documents from the first half of the sixteenth century, Jewish congregations whose names appear to reflect the localities in Rumelia and Anatolia from which their members (at least the initial ones) had been deported.[6] Thirty Balkan towns are cited in this way, which must have represented the totality of the communities of that

> *Nearly all the Jewish communities existing at that time within the empire substantially swelled the two initial autochthonous communities already present in Constantinople.*

area. Eight Anatolian towns are also cited; only the communities of Ankara and Bursa seem to have remained in place. For example, the existence in Istanbul of a congregation referred to as "from Salonika" attests to a deportation, and explains why Jews were entirely absent from that Macedonian city in 1478. The Karaites of Edirne, Provadija, and Kastamonu were also deported to Istanbul.[7]

The gruesome connotations associated with the word "deportation" in our own time call for a clarification. Besides the fact that the Ottoman *sürgün* were not restricted to Jews or any particular population, these operations could have political motives (to purge a given region of individuals or groups considered to be dangerous by uprooting them from their original milieus to get them as far away as possible), but the intention was most often of an economic nature: to provide a

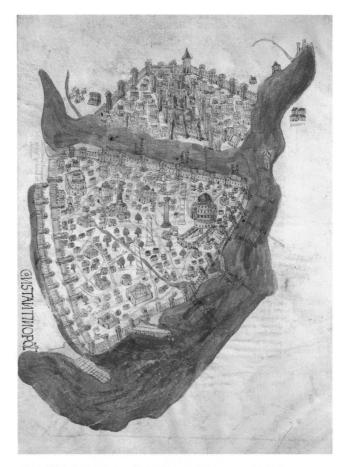

Map of Constantinople in 1420 in the Liber *insularum archipelagi of Buondelmonte*. The Jewish quarter during this period is situated in the south, at the far right of the map, according to *Encyclopedia Judaica*, p. 917. Paris, Bibliothèque Nationale Française, cod. lat. 4825, fol. 37.

given locality (a new conquest, for example) the vital forces it lacked. Moreover, while the status of *sürgün* carried an obligation to change residence, it could also include fiscal and other forms of aid intended to favor the good installation of newcomers. This clarification does not pretend to mitigate the dramatic effects of the displacements entirely, but to indicate that, at least in the best cases, they could lead the displaced to a new prosperity. Nevertheless, the Israeli historian Joseph Hacker has demonstrated that the Hebrew manuscripts of Byzantine Jews between approximately 1453 and 1470 sometimes managed to express strong though guarded anti-Ottoman feelings linked to the resentment over the deportations of Mehmed II.[8] In the decades following the conquest, the Jews of Istanbul, in addition to other factors of differentiation within this heterogeneous group, were divided between the *sürgün* and those who, attracted by the possibilities offered by the development of the capital, came to settle there of their own volition (*kendi gelen*, in Turkish).[9] Furthermore, not all the *sürgün* remained in Istanbul. As years passed, some obtained authorization to return to their original localities.[10]

The first "Great Jews" and the sultan

Beginning in this period, medical knowledge, in particular, was among the superior qualities that the Ottomans sought among the Jews. The most famous of the Jewish physicians who immigrated during this period was Jacopo de Gaete, also known as Yakub Pasha or Hekim Yakub. Having come from Gaete, a southern port in Italy, to Edirne during the reign of Murad II, he first served under that sultan before passing into the service of Murad II's son Mehmed II, who admitted him into his entourage, naming him receiver of finances (*defterdār*) and later vizier.[11] A contemporary Greek historian presented him as "a wise man . . . having attained the heights of his art, as much in theory as in practice, and who, furthermore, exerted a great influence on him [the sultan]."[12] Another Jewish physician who did not convert, and preceded by only a short time the great Sephardic court physicians in the entourage of the sultans of the sixteenth century, Rabbi Efraim ben Nissim ibn Sanchi is said to have been the physician of King Alfonso V of Portugal. Forced into exile, he returned to the court of Istanbul by 1481 at the latest. His son Abraham, in turn, became the palace physician.[13]

The desire has been attributed to Mehmed II, in his ambition to be the head of a universal and centralized empire, to bring together in his capital the supreme heads of all the great religions (who he had supposedly appointed) and gather them beneath his scepter. This allegation is partly anachronistic, since that situation was not to be realized until after his rule. But he did reestablish the patriarchate of the Greek Orthodox Church for the benefit of the monk Georges Scholarios, called Gennadios.

> " *It has even been claimed that the grand rabbi participated in the divan sessions, that is, the sultan's supreme council, which is obviously false.* "

At an unknown date, but thought to be shortly after the conquest, he also named a grand rabbi for the Jews (*haham başı*), Moses Capsali, born in Crete. We know almost nothing about the conditions of that nomination, and the account closest to the events available is suspect because it was written by one of his young relatives anxious to establish his place in history, the rabbi chronicler Eli Capsali. On the relations between the sultan and his grand rabbi, their intimacy, and the unparalleled honors the sultan is said to have granted the rabbi, a whole legend would subsequently be embroidered that does not stand up to historical criticism. In this vein, it has even been claimed that the grand rabbi participated in the divan sessions, that is, the sultan's supreme council, which is obviously false. It is likely that for Mehmed II, Moses Capsali was neither more nor less than a kind of patriarch of the Jews—that is, of all the Jews—although in the absence of any official order (*berāt*) of nomination, we have

▶ See Nota bene devoted to Eli Capsali, pp. 200–202.

no way of knowing the truth in this respect.[14] It is certain, in any case, that whatever the sultan's intentions may have been, from the Jewish perspective, the "Jewish" institution put in place by the Ottoman state was far from self-evident, quite unlike the Greek patriarchate on which it may have been modeled.

A second *haham başı* succeeded Capsali, Eli Mizrahi, who carried out his functions until his death in 1526. In the meantime, or perhaps already before Mizrahi's nomination, the function of chief rabbi had been relieved of its fiscal function (the collection of the rabbinate tax or *rav akçesi*) of the greatest interest to the Ottoman administration, henceforth entrusted to an intendant (*kahya*). The first holder of the office, Sha'altiel (Salto), incurred the wrath of the congregations for his excessively complacent relations with the Ottoman administration, to the point of being banished (both he and his descendants) by the community and forbidden from exercising any function that would put him in contact with the Ottoman authorities. But it became necessary to reverse this deci-

Haham başı or leader of the Jews, whose traditional costume remained more or less unchanged until the present day, based on drawings and watercolors from the eighteenth century, *Dessins originaux de costumes turcs*. Paris, Bibliothèque Nationale Française, Prints Department.

sion, as Sha'altiel became indispensable.[15] Mizrahi and all the heads of the congregations had to agree to release him from the oath he had taken to no longer accept the *kahyālık* of the community.[16]

After the death of Eli Mizrahi in 1526, other grand rabbis of the Romaniotes of Istanbul were named, but there was no longer a *haham başı*. The position remained vacant until 1835, when it was filled in an entirely different context, that of the reforms of the Ottoman Empire. What were the causes of the repeated failure of the position of the *haham başı*? In addition to the initial misalignment between that institution and the realities of Judaism, a new factor was the increasing heterogeneity and division among Ottoman Jewry that came with the great Sephardic immigration, beginning at the end of the fifteenth century.

---

1. Johannes Schiltberger, *The Bondage and Travels of Johann Schiltberger: A Native of Bavaria, in Europe, Asia, and Africa, 1396–1427*, trans. Philip Brunn (Cambridge: Cambridge University Press, 2010), 40.

2. Salo Wittmayer Baron, *A Social and Religious History of the Jews, vol. 18, Late Middle Ages and Era of European Expansion (1200–1650)*, 2nd ed. (New York: Columbia University Press, 1983), 163.

3. See Josua Starr, *The Jews in the Byzantine Empire, 641–1204* (Athens: Verlag der Byzantinisch-Neugriechischen Jahrbücher, 1939); Andrew Sharf, *Jews and Other Minorities in Byzantium* (Ramat-Gan: Bar-Ilan University Press, 1995).

4. See a shortened version of the letter in English, *A Treasury of Jewish Letters: Letters from the Famous and the Humble*, ed. Franz Kobler (Philadelphia: Jewish Publication Society of America, 1953), 283–85.

5. Halil Inalcik, "Istanbul," in *Encyclopaedia of Islam*, 2nd ed., vol. 4 (Leiden: Brill, 1978), 224–48.

6. Mark Alan Epstein, *The Ottoman Jewish Communities and Their Role in the Fifteenth and Sixteenth Centuries* (Freiburg: Klaus Schwarz Verlag, 1980), 178–80.

7. Ibid., 187.

8. Joseph Hacker, "Ottoman Policy towards the Jews and Jewish Attitudes towards the Ottomans during the Fifteenth Century," in *Christians and Jews in the Ottoman Empire*, ed. Benjamin Braude and Bernard Lewis, vol. 1, *The Central Lands* (New York: Holmes and Meier, 1982), 117–25.

9. Minna Rozen, *A History of the Jewish Community in Istanbul: The Formative Years, 1453–1566* (Leiden: Brill, 2002), 12.

10. Ibid., 46–47.

11. The issue has not been decided as to whether he did in fact participate in a Venetian conspiracy to assassinate Mehmed II, which would be difficult to reconcile with the fact that his descendants continued to be exempt from taxes from generation to generation. See Franz Babinger, "Ja'qub Pascha, ein Leibarzt Mehmeds II," *Rivista degli Studi Orientali* 26 (1951): 87–113; B. Lewis, "The Privilege Granted by Mehmed II to His Physician," *Bulletin of the School of Oriental and African Studies* 14, no. 3 (1952): 550–63.

12. Kritovoulos, *History of Mehmed the Conqueror*, trans. Charles T. Riggs (Princeton, NJ: Princeton University Press, 1954).

13. Rozen, *A History of the Jewish Community in Istanbul*, 203n18.

14. In an Ottoman accounting records document from the archives of the Topkapi Palace, Kamil Kepeci (KK) 2411, p. 20, Capsali is referred to as the "rabbi and metropolitan of the Jews of Istanbul." Quoted by Epstein in *The Ottoman Jewish Communities*, 58.

15. Rozen, *A History of the Jewish Community in Istanbul*, 74.

16. Ibid., 318.

Chapter I

In Ottoman Territory, Fifteenth to Nineteenth Centuries

Jews and Muslims in the Ottoman Empire

Gilles Veinstein

The great movement of the expulsion of the Jews from Spain and Portugal, taken up by several Italian states at the end of the fifteenth and the beginning of the sixteenth centuries, had important consequences for Ottoman Jewry, which would be the major recipient of these exiles. The Sephardic component, which was layered onto older, preexisting strata of Jewish populations, and would in turn be superseded by other arrivals, was henceforth dominant in population and cultural influence, in keeping with a brilliant, carefully preserved heritage. The favorable reception of Jews by Sultan Bayezid II is not a myth, even if it shows more enlightened pragmatism than a hypothetical Judeophilia. In several domains—the cloth trade, major commerce, finance, and tax farming—Jews, and specifically the Sephardi, played a dynamic though never exclusive role. Some, such as palace physi-

Gilles Veinstein

Gilles Veinstein, professor at the Collège de France, held the chair of Turkish and Ottoman History and was the director of studies at the École des hautes études en sciences socials (EHESS) in Paris. His works include *Le Sérail ébranlé: Essai sur les morts, dépositions et avènements des sultans ottomans, XIVe-XIXe siècles* (Fayard, 2003).

cians and big businessmen, even exerted a certain political influence, though one that remained semiofficial, since it was never institutionalized. All this was made possible by the attachment of the Muslim sultans to the status of *dhimmī*, with its discrimination but also its tolerance (in principle), its guarantees, and a measure of autonomy that did not, on the other hand, stand in the way of integration into the Ottoman ranks. But the question remains whether Jews with *dhimmī* status were on an equal footing with Christians or whether they were treated worse, and if so, why. After the relative "golden age" of the sixteenth century, the Ottoman Jews saw their condition worsen due to both internal and external factors. They retained remnants of their former positions, but the abolition of the Janissaries at the beginning of the nineteenth century would mean additional hardships for them.

Exile of the Spanish Jews

The expulsion of the Jews from Castile and Aragon, according to the terms of the edicts of March 31, 1492 (one for Castile and one for Aragon), and similar measures in the other Iberian kingdoms and several Italian states as a result of successive waves of immigration at the end of the fifteenth and throughout the sixteenth centuries, led to distinct changes in Ottoman Jewry. This emigration was initially made by so-called proper Jews but later included conversos, or, to use a decidedly insulting designation, *marranos* (pigs), that is, Jewish converts to Christianity. Conversion had been the condition of their remaining in their country of origin, but it also made them suspect of Judaizing—of being Crypto-Jews, those who had not sincerely forsaken their original religion. For them, emigration to Ottoman territory was a fully affirmed return to the faith of their fathers.

Before examining the details of this new avatar of Ottoman Jewry, we must bear in mind that it was by no means the last, and that during the sixteenth and seventeenth centuries this community continued to be enriched with new immigrants of various origins.

The Ottoman Army marching on Tunis in 1569. Page from the *Sehname-i Selim*, by the Ottoman chronicler Lokman (Istanbul, 1581). Toronto, Aga Khan Museum.

New Jewish arrivals

In the first half of the sixteenth century, the conquests of Selim I and Suleiman the Magnificent transformed the Arab Near East into the Ottoman Near East. These conquests offered not only new destinations to those who had chosen to seek refuge in the Ottoman Empire but also endowed Ottoman Jewry as a whole with a new component. In Baghdad, Damascus, Aleppo, Jerusalem, Alexandria, Cairo, and Basra, the Ottomans integrated new Jewish subjects who distinguished themselves from the preceding ones in language and culture, since the natives had been Arabized (*musta'ribah*) and spoke one of the variants of Judeo-Arabic. Proud of the brilliant history that they shared at the time of the great Arab empires, and not without disdain for the Romaniotes or European Jews, these Arabized Jews were themselves divided between the "Orientals" (Mizrahiyyim) from Iraq and the "Occidentals" (Ma'raviyyim) from Aleppo, Damascus, and Cairo. To these groups would be added the Jews of the Maghreb, when that zone entered the orbit of Istanbul in the sixteenth century.

In this process of the continuous creation of Ottoman Jewry by successive increments, the arrival of Ashkenazim from Poland and Ukraine in the second half of the seventeenth century must also be mentioned. But the major factor at the end of the fifteenth and beginning of the sixteenth centuries remains the arrival of the Iberian Jews.

Expulsion of the Iberian Jews

After centuries of relatively harmonious coexistence, the tensions between Jews and Christians became chronic in Spain beginning at the end of the thirteenth century, which led to regular episodes of overt persecution against the Jews. Concurrently, the conversos (also called "new Christians" or, pejoratively, Marranos), were denounced as a threat to the integrity of the Christian faith.

In 1478, the sovereigns Isabella of Castile and Ferdinand of Aragon obtained a bull from Pope Sixtus IV instituting an inquisition to that effect. Tribunals were established in the main cities of Castile and Aragon. In these circumstances of mounting persecution, the extreme measures of the expulsion of 1492 appear, in a retrospective and comprehensive perspective, as an end result, as much as an

> *"The great movement of the expulsion of the Jews from Spain and Portugal taken up by several Italian states at the end of the fifteenth and the beginning of the sixteenth centuries, had important consequences for Ottoman Jewry."*

innovation.[1] At the same time, this measure, more general in its scope than the earlier anti-Jewish provisions, was part of the general policy of institutional reform and centralization of power of the Catholic monarchs, Isabella and Ferdinand, after the fall of Grenada, Islam's last bastion on the peninsula.

The provisions of 1492 threw the Jews of the two kingdoms into shocked alarm. At least their representatives were able to obtain a stay of four months, the effect of which was to make the departure coincide with the anniversary of another catastrophe: the destruction of the Temple, on the ninth of the month of Av. Also, at first the authorities allowed the banished to sell their furniture and real estate and leave with their fortunes. But at the last moment a royal opinion voided this provision and forbade the exiles from taking any precious items, such as gold, silver, pearls, and silks, out of the kingdom. The trauma was total and brutal.

But not all Jews left. Some of the Jews of Spain preferred, at least at the first stage, to convert, and they joined the category of Marranos, the discredit and vulnerability of which has already been mentioned. Among those who chose exile, all did not initially choose faraway destinations. On the contrary, some first sought refuge in the Iberian Peninsula itself in the neighboring kingdoms that had not yet taken measures against the Jews. They probably thought that that proximity would facilitate a return in the near future, which they continued to hope for. Was it not said that they took the keys to their houses with them?

Moreover, in 1493 the monarchs, probably having considered the negative consequences of their decision, offered the banished a chance: they could return and, in theory at least, recover their goods at the price they had sold them for, provided they accepted conversion. It is estimated that a portion of those who had gone into exile in the closest places (perhaps one-third), dejected by their first tribulations, seized the chance to return.

Understandably, under these circumstances, it is difficult to definitively know how many left Spain following the edicts of 1492. None of the figures given by various historians, considering the necessarily hypothetical constructions on which they are based, has resulted in unanimity among the specialists. Reacting against the exaggerations suggesting the movement of considerable masses, others have gone too far in the opposite direction by reducing the number of émigrés to a few tens of thousands. Miguel Ángel Ladero Quesada, relying on the numbers given by Andrés Bernáldez, estimated the number of departures to have been in the neighborhood of 107,000 Jews.[2]

> *The emigration of the Marranos was a long-term phenomenon that, in the case of the Ottoman Empire, continued at least until the 1580s.*

Moreover, the question of the destinations of the exiles is complicated by the fact that these choices did not remain unchanged, as the Iberian states and several Italian states in turn took measures of expulsion in the decades following 1492. Furthermore, the chronology of those measures must be interpreted with the understanding that some were applied and others were not, or not entirely. In Navarre, under pressure from the Catholic monarchs, the expulsion was decreed in 1498. In Portugal, King Manuel I, the "Fortunate," issued a decree on December 5, 1496, banishing Jews who would not be converted. The delay of execution ended in October 1497. Furthermore, the situation of the Portuguese Marranos did not become critical until 1547, when the Inquisition was instituted in that kingdom. That jurisdiction would obtain, in 1579, the power of confiscation. The other fugitives of 1492 set out on their journey, and those who had taken to the sea risked being shipwrecked or robbed and reduced to slavery by pirates. The goal was to reach Italian cities not under Spanish jurisdiction that still seemed safe: Venice—from which the Marranos would be expelled for the first time in 1497—but also Ferraro, Rome, Ancona, and Mantua. In the kingdom of Naples, though a dependent of the Crown of Aragon, the Alhambra edict was not applied. A first measure of expulsion was taken in 1510, but the definitive expulsion did not occur until 1541. Other fugitives went directly, without intermediate steps, to the Maghreb (especially Morocco and Oran), Palestine (under Mameluke domination until 1517), and the European and Asiatic parts of the Ottoman Empire.

Installation of the Sephardi

The first mentions of the arrival of the refugees in Salonika are from 1492–93: Majorcans by 1492 and Castilians in 1493. Rules (*haskamot*) on the usufruct of land (*hazaka*), intended to avoid a "housing crisis" of refugees, were issued from Salonika by 1494. At the same time the first communal organization was put in place, headed by a triumvirate of rabbis.[3] Orders for clothing woven by the Jews of Salonika for the Janissary soldiers also quickly appeared, as they began in 1509 at the latest (therefore, sixteen years after the expulsion).[4]

But the complexity of the process of immigration in the Ottoman Empire is not only attributable to the fact that some came directly and others after intermediary stops in other countries, but the emigration of the Marranos was a long-term phenomenon that, in the case of the Ottoman Empire, continued at least until the 1580s. Those who at first preferred not to leave and were therefore resigned to conversion sometimes changed their minds over time. This could happen during their lives or skip several generations. The persecutions of the Inquisition, the discriminations of the decrees of "purity of blood" (*limpieza de sangre*) intended to bar them from a series of

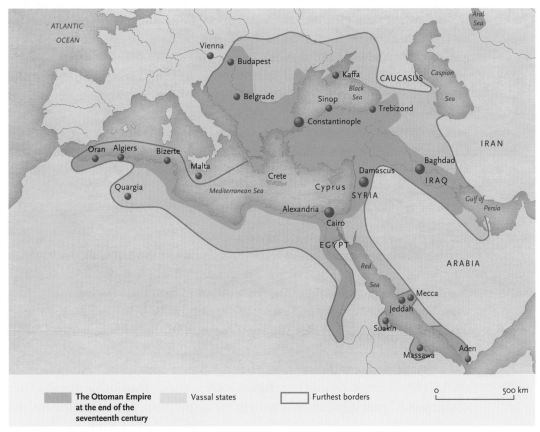

The Ottoman Empire in the seventeenth century.

functions, and still other motivations (in some cases more personal and clandestine) might lead an individual or family, at a given moment, to take the leap and leave in order to declare their Jewishness elsewhere, in the rare places in which it was still permissible to do so, particularly in the Ottoman Empire.[5] In these circumstances, if the exile of the Iberian Jews was a phenomenon circumscribed in time (enlarged only by the time lapses between the successive edicts in the different kingdoms), that of the conversos was chronologically much more spread out and remains impossible to quantify.

Regardless of the manner or the moment, once the émigrés arrived in Ottoman territory, they moved about and changed domiciles. Certain cities served as reception centers: this was the case for Istanbul, the capital, and Edirne (Adrianople), the sultan's second residence, but it was also the case for points that were, on the surface, less obvious, the success of which requires more specific geographical and economic explanation—Salonika, of course, but also Safed (Zfat in Galilee) or Avlona (Valona, presently Vlorë) in Albania.[6] For a few decades at the beginning of the sixteenth century, this last city hosted the third-largest Jewish community of Ottoman Europe, with Jews making up one-third of its population. Dissemination then took place from these two poles: the Jews left Salonika, for example—mainly for fiscal reasons—and gathered in a string of satellite towns in Greece, Macedonia, and Bulgaria. Later, in the seventeenth century, for economic reasons, the émigrés from Salonika headed in the direction of Manisa and Smyrna (Izmir), where they formed the nucleus of Jewish communities destined to become important.[7]

The Iberian emigration also spread in Anatolia, notably in Bursa and Tokat, just as it had in the Near East, which had, as pointed out earlier, become Ottoman by the first half of the sixteenth century; and in Palestine, of course, but also in Alexandria, Cairo, Damascus, and so on.

The Sultan's welcome

A myth sprang up concerning Bayezid II's reception of the Sephardic Jews, which was and always will be a part of the "golden legend" of Turkish-Jewish relations. According to it, not only did the sultan let them in but out of tolerance and charity he invited them to come and personally kept watch over their security and good treatment by his agents. Bayezid's alleged Judeophilia should be approached with circumspection, since he was known not only as a particularly pious Muslim (he was nicknamed *veli*, or "close to God") but also for the unfavorable measures toward the Jews that he took on other occasions, such as the destruction of illegally built synagogues.[8] Thus, if it is indeed a myth, its origin is the *Seder Elyahu Zuta*, the chronicle written in Hebrew some thirty years after the fact by Rabbi Eli (Eliyahu) Capsali.

▶ See Nota bene Eliyahu Capsali pp. 200–202.

Capsali writes: "Sultan Bayezid, the king of Turkey, having learned all the evil the king of Spain brought down on the Jews who were seeking a place of refuge, had pity on them and ordered his country to welcome them."[9]

In the same spirit, a historian of the Ottoman Jews at the end of the nineteenth century did not hesitate to allege the existence of a "circular order"—this is his term—from Bayezid II to all his provincial governors "not only not to drive away the Spanish Israelites, but to welcome them with affability. He even threatened with the death penalty all those who mistreated the immigrants or caused them the slightest harm."[10]

So much idealism aroused the skepticism of later historians, who pointed out that no document was ever produced to back up that irenic version of the facts.[11] But a relatively recent discovery has raised doubts—at least to some extent—on this disabused skepticism. It is true that an order corresponding to Franco's paraphrase has never been found in the archives. Still, some orders from Bayezid II dating from 1501, though limited to individual cases and clearly concerning particularly affluent individuals, do tend to support the preceding general assertions.[12] In an order of mid-June 1501, addressed to the qadis of the province of Rumelia (Eastern Europe)—consequently, an order that was indeed "circular"—the sultan expresses himself as follows: "Given that . . . the Jew named Gabriel Perviriz [?] has requested authorization to lead into my well-guarded lands his household, namely, his wife, his young children and his goods that are presently in Apulia, I have ordained that, in whatever port wherein he may disembark . . . you will make no obstacle, and that he may come and go, without your permitting the least hindrance on the highways or byways, either to himself or his children, his goods or his animals. You will chastise those who oppose this order, and inform us in writing of the names of any such as disobey."[13]

A few days later the case of a certain Baruch, son of Moses, who was in Corfu and had requested authorization to settle in the empire with his whole household, was decided: "Consequently," answered the sultan, "I have ordained that the Jew in question shall debark at the port of his choosing and settle in my well-guarded lands, without any person hindering or causing damage to himself, his sons, his daughters, his money, his animals, his goods, and his retinue."[14] Another time, the sultan intervenes in favor of the Jew, Joseph son of Abraham, pursuant to a request presented to the palace by his brother Isaac. Upon his arrival from the "land of the Franks" (Frangistan), Joseph had had to leave his two daughters in safety "somewhere in Kastoria." Now that he asks for them, they are refused him. The sultan orders the qadi of Kastoria to make an inquiry into that rather obscure affair and to order the restitution of the daughters to their father, unless they have become Muslim in the meantime.[15] One hypothesis is that he may have placed his daughters under the protection of an Orthodox monastery where they were converted or about to be converted, which would explain the refusal to return them to their father.

These various orders, accompanied by the sultan's monogram (*tuğra*), which authenticated them, were delivered to their beneficiaries so that they might in turn present them, if necessary, to the authorities for whom they were intended. The first two documents quoted are more precisely safe-conducts (*yol hükmi*) that place their bearers beneath the protection—or more precisely, the "grace" (*amān*)—of the sultan. One neither entered nor circulated in Ottoman territory without such a document, which represented a safeguard. It was indispensable, especially if one was considered an infidel and carrying money. The shari'a authorized every Muslim to seize any foreign infidel (held to be *harbi*, that is, an enemy, as opposed to the *dhimmī*) who had penetrated Muslim territory and to execute him or reduce him to slavery if he did not have a safe-conduct in valid and due form.[16] This goes against the position of those who, in their desire to be done with the myth, have pushed the paradox to the point of claiming that the Sephardic immigration took place independently of the will of the Ottoman authorities.

What lesson may we draw from the archival discoveries, if not a confirmation of the hypothesis that the sultan was probably guided not by an inveterate Judeophilia but simply by an enlightened pragmatism? He was interested in these Jews not because they were Jews and because they were persecuted or at risk of persecution, but for what they could contribute to his states, especially if they immi-

> *Ferdinand is said to be a well-advised prince, but he impoverishes his kingdom and enriches mine.*

grated with their goods and capital, as some did, especially among the Portuguese.[17] Ottoman sovereigns already knew from experience that some Jews could be useful to them. They did not need to wait for the Sephardic emigration to have among them Jewish doctors or important businessmen, Italiotes or Romaniotes, who, by the way, would never be entirely eclipsed by the success of the Sephardim. Another saying commonly attributed to Bayezid II clearly suggests this: "Ferdinand is said to be a well-advised prince, but he impoverishes his kingdom and enriches mine." In sum, Bayezid continued the straight line of pragmatism manifested by his father, Mehmed II, but whereas Mehmed II had brought that pragmatism to bear mainly for the benefit of Istanbul, his renascent capital, its effects would be more broadly disseminated under his successor. In the absence of precise documentation, however, these phenomena remain sufficiently obscure to forbid our distinguishing, in this scattering of émigrés and the proliferation of the communities that resulted, how much is attributable to a deliberate government policy and how much to an adaptation of the Jewish émigrés themselves to the conditions they encountered. Whatever processes were at work over time, the Ottoman censuses of the sixteenth century showed new Jewish immigrants in a variety of cities and regions, not only in Istanbul, Salonika, and Safed in Galilee, but in the Balkans: Artas, Patras, Euboea, Thebes, Trikala, Nikopol, Sofia,

Manastir (Bitola), Skoplje, Sérrai, Kavalla, Demotika, Xanthi, Kastoria, Volos, and Larissa. Other outcasts settled in Asia Minor, in Bursa, Tokat, Izmir, and Manisa; finally, others pressed on as far as Palestine and the rest of the Middle East. In certain cases, the census taker echoed the initial geographical origin of the membership of the different Jewish congregations in place, designating the congregation by the name of their region of origin. We find denominations such as Aragon, Calabria, Castile, Catalonia, Spain, Maghreb, Portugal, Apulia, Sicilia, or, yet again, Córdoba, Lisbon, Messina, Otranto, Sevilla, and Toledo. There is also a congregation named "of the Franks" (*Ifraniye*) in Safed and congregations called "of the Italians" (*Talyan*) in Salonika and Safed.[18]

The pragmatism of the sultans and their awareness of the needs of their states was at work in the pursuit—with varying degrees of success and to the benefit of certain provinces—of "utilitarian deportations" of Jews inaugurated by Mehmed II and Bayezid II.[19] In 1523, for example, following the conquest of Rhodes by Suleiman the Magnificent, Jewish families were transferred from Salonika to that Aegean island. Shortly afterward, the Jews of Buda, conquered by the same sultan, were transferred to the Macedonian port of Kavalla.[20] Some subsequently left Kavalla to return to their places of origin, over which the Turkish occupation had meanwhile been confirmed, the Ottoman governor having approved their return. Then, after the conquest of Cyprus under Selim II, the governor of the island planned, in 1576–77, to colonize the island with the help of rich Jewish families from Safed. But the interested parties were able to avoid the threat thanks to their support in the capital. Nevertheless, in 1579, the same governor, true to his original idea, was authorized to establish on his island a group of Jews whom he had intercepted en route from Salonika to Safed.

The place of the Jews

Before expressing general considerations on the place of Jews in the empire of the sixteenth century in general, along with an assessment of the degree to which the apprehensions of the authorities were well founded, and thoughts on the ability of the émigrés to avail themselves of the possibilities offered them, I will cite a particular case, eminently revelatory of the pragmatic relationships on both sides, of the give-and-take that came with the installation of the Sephardi in the Ottoman Empire. This example involves a phenomenon often referred to, though not necessarily from this point of view: the monopoly held by the Jews of Salonika on the production of the cloth used for making winter uniforms for the Janissaries.[21] We know that this practice was established shortly after the arrival of the Sephardi in Salonika, since, as previously stated, it was in full operation in 1509.[22] On the other hand, we have no direct tangible trace of the conditions in which that sort of an arrangement between the émigrés and the state was concluded, or in what form. But

كيم ماموسى پت اپى دوريۈغا ن

بوزنى أشوقوبى نى كيرك دوتوغا ن

Scene from the bazaar in Kufa, taken from the *Makhzen el-esrar*, Baghdad, ca. 1550. Paris, Bibliothèque Nationale Française, sup. turc. 978, fol. 41.

it is fairly easy to imagine the reasons for that situation. Textile manufacturing of cotton and silk was already active in the Ottoman Empire in the fifteenth century, but the production of wool was much less developed. Spain, on the other hand, had become famous for its wool production, a result of such technical innovations as the fulling mill. We lack specific information on the place of Jews in this industry, but it is clear that not all Spanish Jews practiced trades related to cloth, and that many who did work in that sector served in the role of *señor del paño*, that is, as financiers and merchants rather than artisans. Direct involvement in making fabric therefore required émigrés from Salonika to adapt to their new living conditions. Indeed, in their Macedonian exile, both in Salonika and in the towns and villages where cloth-making flourished, not only were the majority of Jews involved in that industry but they took up the entirety of the operations. With respect to the furnishers of cloth for the Janissary uniforms, the only parts of the process they did not manage were the raising of sheep (which remained in the hands of the Muslims) and the actual making of the uniforms, which was turned over to Muslim tailors. Hence, it would be too simplistic to assert that the Jews from Salonika—the Spanish and a fortiori those of other origins—were content to continue with their prior activity during exile.

Though we do not know how the immigrants initially became involved in this market, one particular circumstance gives us some idea. We know through the sources used by the historians Isaac Samuel Emmanuel and Joseph Nehama that the modus vivendi, to borrow an expression from the latter, between the Porte and the Salonikan community in the second half of the following century was given official recognition by the Porte's dispatching to Salonika (between 1566 and 1568) a rabbi who has remained famous for his consultations and historical works, Moses Almosnino. On that occasion, the sultan issued what Nehama, insufficiently familiar with the Ottoman institutions, dubbed a "certificate of exemption"—an inappropriate formulation that led him to hazard erroneous interpretations of the supposed independence of the Salonikan community.[23] The correct name of the act in question is *mu'afnāme-i hümāyūn*, that is, imperial exemption (the term *müsellem*, a synonym of *mu'af*, refers to the notion of exemption) in reference to fiscal exemptions in a broad sense, which were granted to the Salonikans. Unfortunately, the written act itself, given to Almosnino, has not been recovered. On the other hand, a different

> **" In their Macedonian exile…
> not only were the majority of
> Jews involved in that industry
> but they took up the entirety
> of the operations. "**

document, which dates from 1572, refers to another imperial decree of exemption granted to the Jews of Salonika—probably the one obtained by Almosnino—which interestingly reiterates the essence of the content.

On the day after the Battle of Lepanto (October 7, 1571), the Sublime Porte decided, among other measures taken after his defeat, to fend off an eventual attack by having the ramparts of Salonika repaired. To that end, "to buy lime and other necessary materials," the job required a large sum of money from the Jews and Christians "making a living within the shelter of said ramparts." At the same time, certain categories of *re'āyā* (non-Muslim subjects) were requisitioned to serve as manpower for the work. The Jews were incomparably more highly taxed than the Christians, because they were much more numerous in the city and had more rich people in their ranks: twenty to thirty thousand florins (*filori*) were required of the Jews and two thousand of the Christians. The sum appeared exorbitant to the Jews, who immediately went before the judge and local administrator, the qadi, and even deemed it necessary to have a memorandum (*rıqā'*) taken to the sultan himself.

If we follow the affair through several orders contained in volume 19 of the great series of archives of Istanbul, the *Mühimme defteri* (registers of important affairs), we find first a vehement reaction from the Porte, suggesting that the sum be obtained from the sale of the cultural objects and liturgical ornaments that the Jews kept in their synagogues. But that extreme and unusual decision was not acted upon. I will not go further into the details of that affair, in which the Porte modified the required amount and also proposed other solutions to the Jews to discharge their debt. More pertinent to my intention here are the reasons given by the Jews for refusing to pay: the heavy burden of the required contribution, and especially the fact that in its very principle, that contribution violated the exemptions accorded them by their sultan. To reinforce this claim, the community, in the memorandum it addressed to the Porte, cited the detail of the "imperial edict of exemption" that it had been granted, the description of which, in my opinion, was the charter granted a few years earlier to Rabbi Almosnino. The sultan, in turn, following the normal structure of mandates, took up this passage of the memorandum in his response, an order to the qadi of Salonika on July 9, 1572.[24] From the edict mentioned, it appears that originally the furnishing of this cloth had not constituted a constraint exerted by the sultan on that community but a market obtained by the community by its own demand, alongside a series of other exemptions, in compensation for what represented the true obligation imposed upon the community: the charge of money changers (*sarraf*) of the silver mines near Siderocapsa (Siderokastro) in Chalcidice, by investing the annual sum of 50,000 *akçes* in them. In a mining context, the money changer's function was to buy the refined silver from the foundry, transport it to the mint workshop connected with the mine, and resell it to those in charge of the minting workshop, the *sāhib-i'ayār*.[25] Due to fixed prices, there was no enrichment expected from this operation. This was part of the usual practice of requisition by the sultan of private capital—notably but not exclusively Jewish—forced to be invested in nonremunerative enterprises corresponding to public services. The appeal for Jewish capital in this context is presented as the original basis for the agreement between the sultan and the community of Salonika. But we cannot exclude the possibility that this is an a posteriori reconstruction, and that this obligation of *sarraflık* (moneylenders) in fact appeared on a later occasion, in the context of measures taken by Suleiman to relaunch the mine around the mid-1530s.[26] In any case, even if we conclude that the manufacturing of cloth for the military was not, in the beginning, an obligation but a privilege solicited by the Jewish immigrants themselves—a compensation for what was in fact the true constraint (a privilege, moreover, accompanied by a valuable right of preemption on the wools from Macedonia that went together with orders coming from the state)[27]— the fact remains that the windfall soon turned into a formidable chore (*hizmet*), as the quantities required by the state increased from 1,200 pieces annually at the start to 4,000 around 1620. A draconian production pace had to be maintained, and lapses in quality were mercilessly punished, to the point of condemnation and hanging of a representative of the Salonikan community, Rabbi Juda Covo, in 1637. "It is an iron rod that strikes Israel in the nape of the neck," another rabbi wrote around the same period.

Beyond this particular case, the totality of occupations practiced by Jews in the Ottoman context were not limited to a few specialties, as was often the case in Christendom, but were on the contrary numerous and varied, whether in commerce in all its forms, handicrafts, or even agriculture in some situations inherited from the past. Similarly, these activities were situated at very diverse economic levels, from the highest to the most modest. Moreover, none of these activities represented a Jewish monopoly either de jure or de facto, as was sometimes the case in Christendom. On the contrary, the Jews worked side by side with Christian subjects, and also, more than has been thought to be the case, with Muslims of the "Great Lord." But this did not keep them from being particularly present in certain sectors: not only in the preparation of wool, but also silverware, jewelry, tanning, and international commerce and finance. Not only was Jewish commerce welcome in the eyes of the authorities, but, although not providing it with more positive support, the regime at least cleared the way for its possibility by guaranteeing freedom of circulation and a degree of police protection for Jewish merchants of all kinds. Under these circumstances, it is rather in the renewal and revitalization of certain branches of the Ottoman economy that the Jewish contribution, particularly Sephardic, appears decisive in the sixteenth century. In international business, Jews brought capital, networks of relationships throughout Europe and the Mediterranean, and new commercial techniques: letters of exchange and credit, insurance contracts, and the anticipation of funds to producers. If they did not have exclusivity

> ❝ *Sephardic emigration included many physicians who had graduated from Iberian faculties and who were able to interrelate the ancient fields of knowledge with more recent experiments better than their Muslim contemporaries.* ❞

in financial matters, an elite group of them was very much in evidence, generally putting together financial operations and commercial enterprises. They lent at interest, after the example of Muslim religious and charitable foundations—required, as were these foundations, not to exceed under any circumstances annual charges of 10 to 15 percent.[28] They were money changers who used the diversity of currencies present in Europe. They were also involved in leasing contracts of the state, which had a bearing on tax revenue, property tax, minting workshops, mines, and so on. In these large-scale enterprises in which the backer risked his fortune and perhaps his life if he failed to meet his obligations to the treasury, they likely had Christians and Muslims as associates. Western sources have placed much emphasis on the Jewish contribution to the Ottoman artillery. This factor is difficult to measure with any degree of precision, but in any case, it was neither as exclusive nor as decisive as has been claimed, partly for ideological reasons.[29]

The role the Sephardic émigrés were prepared to occupy, and the unforeseen need that they met for the sultans of the period in the government of the empire, was that of "court Jews" or "grand Jews" (without the title). Directly inherited from the Spanish tradition, this role had had precedents among the sultans before the Sephardi. It was, in fact, at the intersection of several activities combining, to varying degrees, medicine, big business, and diplomacy.

Sephardic emigration included many physicians who had graduated from Iberian faculties and who were able to interrelate the ancient fields of knowledge with more recent experiments better than their Muslim contemporaries. Some acceded to the entourage of the sovereigns, winning their confidence and even forming veritable dynasties. This was the case with the Hamon family, originally from Grenada, representatives of which succeeded one another by the side of the sultans, from Bayezid II to Selim II.[30] But during the same period, and thereafter, not all the palace physicians were Jews: a list from about 1535, for example, mentions ten Muslim physicians to six Jewish ones. Other "grand Jews," also physicians or businessmen, played a role in Ottoman politics during the sixteenth century, giving the sovereigns the benefit of their international experience and their networks. The most famous of

⊮ See Nota bene devoted to Joseph Nasi, pp. 220–221.

them was probably Don Joseph Nasi (João Migues, ca.1514–79), whose aunt and mother-in-law, Gracia Mendes, the widow of a great Marrano businessman, had preceded him to Istanbul.[31] The favor and influence of Nasi culminated under Selim II, who made him the duke of Naxos in 1567 and the farmer of fiscal revenue of that island, as well as of other Cyclades.[32]

Other great figures of the second half of the sixteenth century included Salomon Ashkenazi (ca. 1520–1602),[33] a negotiator of the Porte with the Republic of Venice; David Passi, a mediator between Murad III and the king of Poland Sigismund III;[34] and Alvaro Mendes (1520–1603), another Marrano businessman who moved from Portugal to Turkey with an immense fortune, to return to Judaism and be circumcised at the age of sixty-five. Like Nasi, he was a fierce adversary of Spain,

"Female Jewish agent carrying merchandise to young Turkish women who are not allowed out." Print from *Recuil de cent estampes représentant différentes Nations du Levant*, by Jean-Baptiste Vanmour, engraved by Philippe Simonneau for the king's ambassador M. de Ferriol, 1714. Paris, Bibliothèque des Arts Décoratifs.

working for a rapprochement between the Ottomans and France, England, and even, in the years 1594–97, Portugal. He became the farmer of fiscal revenue for the island of Mytilene, and in turn held the title of duke.

Another way Jews were able to enter the upper levels of power, among female Jews (but not specifically Sephardic ones), was in the service of Muslim princesses—under the generic Greek name of *kira*. Some of them, women freer in their movements than their patrons, who were cut off from the world by the prescriptions of Islam, turned that circumstance to their advantage, acquiring great credit by furnishing them with the articles they avidly desired, as well as news from the outer world. The most famous of them, Esther Kira, the wife of a physician from an important rabbinical family in Istanbul, reached the height of her influence, thanks to the Sultana Safiye, the wife of Murad III. But having been accused by the Janissaries of monetary depreciations that weakened their pay, she was put to death during a rebellion in 1600. The treasury had recourse to the immense fortune she left to mollify the mutineers.[35]

If some Jews played a notable role in Ottoman diplomatic life during the sixteenth century due to their knowledge of languages, their international experience, and their network of correspondents, it must be noted, on the other hand, that this role was never made official and that they never enjoyed the equivalent of what would be, at the end of the seventeenth and beginning of the eighteenth centuries, the grand dragomanate (office of translator/interpreter) attributed to the Greeks of the Phanar. Moreover, even if the Jews were frequently polyglots and functioned as interpreters in the embassies and consulates, as well as in the seats of commerce, the imperial divan of this period did not recruit Jewish translators. It reserved that function for Muslims—in reality, for Christian "renegades."[36]

The Jews: *Dhimmī* like the others?

If the sultans were able to benefit from a Jewish population whose usefulness, or even necessity, they acknowledged without running into the judicial and religious obstacles that encumbered their presence in Christendom, and if the Muslim and particularly the Ottoman lands thus constituted a refuge for the Jews, it was thanks to the status of *dhimmī*. While historically this status was rejected by certain radical regimes, in the Ottoman Empire it was always the norm. It went together with Hanifism, a moderate judicial school adhered to by the

> *If the Muslim and particularly the Ottoman lands thus constituted a refuge for the Jews, it was thanks to the status of* dhimmī.

Turks, and appears to be a natural consequence of the great religious diversity existing in the empire, which was such that Muslims were a minority in several parts of it (particularly in Eastern Europe). But *dhimmī*s were more or less well treated in the entirety of the Ottoman territory, depending on the historical period and context. There is no doubt that the Ottomans applied this status to their Jewish subjects, as they did to Christians. I even believe that we must interpret the concern to establish a posteriori, on a legal basis, during the reign of Suleiman the Magnificent, that the Jews of Constantinople did not aid and assist the *basileus* during the conquest of that city by Mehmed II (a fact confirmed by a whole series of decrees of successive sultans) as a means to justify the attribution of *dhimmī* status to the Jews. (Similar legal fictions would, moreover, be established for the same purpose, but, more paradoxically, on behalf of the Greeks, even though they had in fact backed the Byzantine enemy.) The *dhimma* could indeed only apply to unbelievers who had not resisted the conquest and who had voluntarily recognized the domination of Islam. Only the absence of resistance allowed the conservation of their preexisting synagogues, the reading of the Torah, and "the practice of their religion according to their usages."[37] Furthermore, the specific per capita tax of the *dhimmī*, the *djizye* (from the Arabic *jizya*), was indeed required of Jews.

But Ottoman documentation shows, for inexplicable reasons, that the classification of *dhimmī* was reserved for Christians, while the Jews were designated only as *yehudi* (Jews). Beyond this terminological nuance, there are quite a few differences in their respective statuses. Jews, for example, were exempt from some of the obligations of Christians, and certain communities did not have to pay the *ispendje*—another Ottoman fee to be paid by non-Muslims.[38] Additionally, no Jew was touched by the formidable *devshirme*, the gathering up of young non-Muslim boys to serve the sultan after forced Islamization. How can we explain these differences that seem to give favorable treatment to the Jews? They may be due to the Jews' position as city dwellers more than to their Jewishness, though it appears that the *ispendje* and *devshirme* were not entirely restricted to rural populations. Or could it be that the Ottomans felt closer to their Jewish *dhimmī* than to their Christian *dhimmī* for reasons of greater theological affinities?[39] It is true that in the documentation the pejorative term *kāfir* (infidel) is used exclusively to designate Christians. Nevertheless, evidence to the contrary abounds, where Jews are even more despised than Christians and represent, in the common Muslim opinion, the most despicable and ill-treated portion of humanity.

How are we to explain this point of view on the part of Muslims who do not share the Christians' theological prejudices? Some possible answers are provided by the traveler Evliya Celebi, who represents, in the second half of the seventeenth century, what Robert Dankoff has called "an Ottoman mentality."[40] Evliya reproaches the Jews for being narrow-minded and fanatical—an opinion based mainly, as the rest of the comment explains, on "their dietary restrictions, which are stricter than with any other group." They did not eat meat slaughtered by Muslims; they would rather die than eat clarified butter (as opposed to fresh butter and sesame oil). In general, they accepted neither food nor drink from other people; in fact, they did not mingle with others, and the companionship they might have with non-Jews would only be artificial. All their acts, according to Evliya, who repeats a topos from earlier Ottoman literature, were calculated for the purpose of treachery and the killing of Muslims.[41] Evliya also mentions that some young Jewish boys played the role of prostitutes, particularly appreciated by the Janissaries.

In this situation, connected perhaps with the penury of certain Jewish families, it is the virility of the Jews that appears to be put in question, as it was de facto by their exclusion from the *devshirme*. If, surely, being Jewish and being rich could be associated in certain contexts, as during attacks of the insurgent Janissaries on Jewish residences in Istanbul or Cairo,[42] in other contexts, to be Jewish was synonymous with wretchedness and sordid poverty—and this latter equation could only be reinforced by the degradation of the material situation of the Ottoman Jews after the sixteenth century. That destitution went in tandem with a reputation for filth, impurity (Nehama described the streets of Salonika as "twisted bowels, rotten with humidity, dark and fetid"[43]), but it also had another possible origin: the Jews' involvement, since the Middle Ages, in the ill-famed production of leather. Consequently, the most repulsive tasks were assigned to them, such as burning the corpses of the tortured, for example.[44]

Finally, another factor must be taken into consideration to explain the harsher treatment of Jews as opposed to Christians: they were not protected by the "capitulations" granted foreign Christian states, whose representatives among the Ottoman authorities ensured respect.

Autonomy and integration

The Jews—more exposed than the Christians to the scorn and ill treatment by Muslims in general, who see that they are kept in their subordinate position, as well as to the abuses of the agents of the state, liable also to persecution by the Christians of the empire, the inheritors of Byzantine anti-Semitism—had no other recourse than the sultan himself, who recognized the Jews' right of petition and made it a point of honor to look upon them as his *dhimmī* and therefore as his "protégés" in the full sense of the term. Many imperial orders attest to this, even if we may assume that at least some were not obtained by the interested parties without greasing some palms in the process. The role of the sultan as protector of the Jews and benefactor of Israel is shown in a particularly significant way in his attitude toward accusations of ritual murder, made against Jews, in which the blood of the victim was supposedly used to make ritual bread during Passover. Mehmed II had already shown the way at the end of the fifteenth century by issuing an edict to the effect that similar accusations should not be heard locally by Muslim tribunals but transferred to his own council, the imperial divan, sitting next to him, just as in cases involving foreign diplomats, for example. In the known cases during the sixteenth century, the accusation comes from Muslims, but clearly reflects locally entrenched anti-Semitic traditions. This principle was regularly confirmed by the successive sultans of the sixteenth century: Suleiman the Magnificent, Selim II, and Murad III. As a basis for his involvement, the sultan ritually repeated that his Jewish tributaries were his tributaries, just like his other tributaries.[45]

> " *The role of the sultan as protector of the Jews and benefactor of Israel is shown in a particularly significant way in his attitude toward accusations of ritual murder, made against Jews, in which the blood of the victim was supposedly used to make ritual bread during Passover.* "

A first consequence of the *dhimma* was to make the Jews free to assert themselves as Jews and therefore to allow Marrano émigrés to return to the religion of their ancestors—a return that was marked, as the sources point out in some cases, by a late circumcision. If difficulties were raised to this return, they came from radical rabbis (Marranos might have non-Jewish maternal ancestors) and in no case from Muslims. Moreover, in certain cities (Salonika, Arta, Avlona, Izmir), the Marranos constituted distinct congregations. In a general sense, all the controversies of a religious, judicial, ritual, or liturgical nature that divided congregations of different origins, particularly the Sephardi from other communities, or even arising within a selfsame congregation—essentially, everything that constituted the intellectual and spiritual life of Ottoman Judaism, and that generally receives the most attention from historians of Ottoman Judaism—took place unbeknownst to or with the indifference of the Turkish masters. The Turks intervened only in cases of disturbance to the public order, as was the case, it seems, of the predication of Sabbatai Zevi, the "false Messiah" who divided the Jewish communities.

> *A first consequence of the* **dhimma** *was to make the Jews free to assert themselves as Jews and therefore to allow Marrano émigrés to return to the religion of their ancestors.*

Another consequence of the *dhimma* concerns the respect, in principle, Ottoman authorities showed to Jewish places of worship by allowing their repair or reconstruction. The theoretical interdiction against new construction after the conquest obviously was circumvented (as it was, moreover, for the Christians, as attested by the creation of churches and monasteries during the Ottoman period) since, with the arrival of newcomers and the formation of new congregations, the old synagogues no longer sufficed and new ones had to be built, even very modest ones, and even, in some cases, inside private homes. In Salonika, for example, during the eight years following 1492, seven new synagogues were added to the three original synagogues (the Romaniote, the Italiote, and the Ashkenazi). Still others would be created during the following century. On the other hand, some dispositions of the shari'a, external to the clauses of the *dhimma* proper, contributed to the Islamization of urban space, to the detriment of Christian or Jewish establishments.[46] To the question of whether, given the case of some houses that had been constructed for Jews at a distance of less than 15 *zirā'* (about eleven yards) from a mosque—the effect of which was to reduce the space allotted to the Muslim community and to inconvenience it as a result of the throwing of rocks by these Jews—the Muslims were legally authorized to expel that group of Jews, the famous mufti Ebussuud Efendi asserted that indeed they were. However, the sultan could show his concern by establishing a compromise between that imperative of the shari'a and the hereditary rights of transmission of the Jews (their right to property, essentially), which he did in fact recognize.[47]

Moreover, it was thanks to the relative autonomy granted the communities by the *dhimma* that the Ottoman Jews could locally establish their own forms of organization and government. The basic unit was the *qahal*, or congregation. In the constitution of these *qehalim*, the Sephardic émigrés merely reproduced the model of their former Castilian *aljamas* as they had last been defined by the statute of Valladolid in 1432 at the recommendation of King Juan II's treasurer Don Abraham Benveniste, several of whose descendants emigrated to Ottoman territory. This mode of organization would gradually be adopted by communities of other origins. Each *qahal* was equipped with a general assembly of taxpayers who delegated their authority to a communal "committee" of notables (*hombres buenos*) elected or co-opted among the elite of wealth and knowledge. It was meticulously regulated in all the details of public and private life by ordinances (*takkanot*) and conventions (*haskamot*) that it elaborated for its use. The *qahal* maintained a number of civil servants, beginning with the rabbi, the official leader of the community, whose powers were religious, educational, and judicial. At court, the *beit din*, he was assisted by two deputy judges. In the event of serious misconduct, he pronounced excommunications—temporary or permanent. The rabbis also furnished judicial consultations or *responsa* (*she'elot u-tshuvot*, literally "questions and answers") that, when they came from renowned doctors, could become authoritative well beyond the city of their author. In large agglomerations, such as Salonika, it became necessary to set up a federal authoritative structure above the individual *qehalim*.

▶ See article by Marina Rustouw p. 79.

This institutional edifice, which made it possible in 1560 for Rabbi Almosnino to speak of a *republica*, was built and functioned independently. The Ottoman authorities knew only the representatives of the congregations, laymen whom they designated, according to the context, as *kethüdā* (intendants), *nā'ib* (substitutes), or even, in a more military register, *yayabaşı* (head of infantrymen), *yüzbaşı* (centurion), or simply *ser* (chief). These individuals, interlocutors of the Ottomans, especially in matters of taxation, participated in two spheres—an ambiguity lending itself to abuse and exposing them to the hostility of their coreligionists—as exemplified by She'altiel (Salto) in Istanbul, or Baruch, in the years 1539–45. Originally from

Portrait of Ottoman Sultan Mehmet II the Conqueror, by Costanzo da Ferrara (ca. 1450–1524). Detail. Istanbul, Topkapı Palace Museum Library.

Portugal, this *kethüda* of the Jews of Salonika took advantage of his favor with the Turks to fiscally fleece his coreligionists on an annual basis. In these circumstances, if there was a link between Jewish populations and the Ottoman administration, it was first of a fiscal nature, since, as his first mission, the *kethüda* assessed and collected taxes for the treasury.

In fact, the Jewish taxpayers (as well as the Christian ones) were under a double tax system: that of the state and of their community. To the state, the Jews paid not only the *jizye*, the fee of building duties (*'avāriz*) and other commercial taxes—often corresponding to local customs[48]—but a specific flat fee, the *rav akçesi* (or *jizye-i rav*, which could be translated as "rabbinical license"), which is supposed to have been modeled on the flat fee paid by the Orthodox patriarch at the time of his nomination, and bearing the name *kharā*.[49] To these fundamental contributions were added, under various pretexts, a host of fees and unpaid chores imposed by the local authorities on all who were not able to

> *Acts written by qadis… reveal the frequency with which Jews appeared before the Muslim tribunals, including in cases in which the law did not oblige them to appeal to these tribunals.*

prove that they had received explicit, official dispensation. Many Jewish communities did in fact possess edicts of exemption. But the creative imagination of the tax collectors for profits was limitless, and the *dhimmī*, given their subordinate position, were particularly vulnerable to abuses.

In any case, this taxation, which tended to become heavier and proliferate, was not the only cord attaching the congregations to the apparatus of the Ottoman state. Beyond their internal rules in matters of personal or family and business law, and the imposing legal corpus elaborated by their doctors, the Jewish subjects of the sultan remained under the law of the state, as applied particularly through the clauses of the *dhimma*. Let us cite, by way of illustration, a consultation of the rabbi of Salonika, Shemuel ben Hayyon (d. 1608). He notes that the sultan forbade non-Muslims from owning slaves in principle, although he allowed it in fact, on payment of a capitation tax (*kharāj*) for every male or female slave possessed. Nevertheless, he was no less cognizant of the point of view held by one of his illustrious predecessors, Rabbi Joseph ben Lev (1502–88), according to whom the law of the state was the only valid one (in keeping with the Talmudic principle *dina de-malkhuta dina*, "the law of the land is law"), that non-Muslims did not have the right to acquire slaves.[50] Moreover, the law of the state applied in crimes involving bloodshed, commercial transactions, and also in litigation between Jews and members of other communities—Muslim or Christian. Acts written by qadis, preserved in the archives of many places in the empire, reveal the frequency with which Jews appeared before the Muslim tribunals of their districts, including in cases in which the law did not oblige them to appeal to these tribunals—for example, in litigation between Jews— even in affairs of personal rights. Hence, we may surmise that they were motivated

Jezzar Pasha, governor of Acre, was condemned as a criminal; to his right, a Jewish judge reads the sentence. Print, nineteenth century, by Edward Orme. Paris, Bibliothèque Nationale Française.

by a judicial strategy that played on the differences between Jewish and Muslim law, from which one or both of the parties thought they could draw an advantage—or that they intended in this way to obtain a judicial decision of superior weight, with which no one, official or private, could take issue.

In the courtroom protocols established by the qadis, Jews did not appear exclusively as litigants. We see them in the role of witnesses (including for Christians), and as representatives (*vekil*) of Jews or Christians. Even more surprising, in view of the normal rules of Islamic procedure, in certain contexts, we see them referred to by the qadi as among the attesting witnesses of his hearings. This recourse to Islamic courts, when it was optional, was often condemned by the rabbis (in Salonika, for example),

> **" The Ottoman Jews did not, then, live in a closed circuit but were connected by many ties to the Ottoman phenomenon in its entirety. "**

who looked upon it as treason and threatened the violators with excommunication. But that attitude does not appear to have been the general one; the documentation also reveals, for example, cases of collaboration between Jewish and Muslim judges in Jerusalem.[51] Moreover, while some of the economic activity of the Jews had religious precepts as a basis (the preparation of meat, wine, and dairy products, and the textile industry itself), in no domain was their clientele limited to their coreligionists, but it extended to nearly the whole of Ottoman society. The Muslims, for example, did not disdain purchasing the meat of animals ritually slaughtered from a Jewish butcher but revealed on examination not to meet the strict requirements of *kashrut.* In large-scale commerce or tax farming, Jews could associate with non-Jewish services, just as professional guilds could gather members of different religions.

However specific their religious and cultural domains were, and however vigorous the community institutions were that surrounded them, the Ottoman Jews did not, then, live in a closed circuit but were connected by many ties to the Ottoman phenomenon in its entirety.

Centuries of decline

If the sixteenth century represented a kind of golden age of Ottoman Jews, an apogee of their economic and financial position, and even, to a certain extent,

of their political influence, the following centuries were undeniably less favorable for the Jews, as well as for the empire altogether. From being a driving force, that component of the multireligious Ottoman society became one of its poorest, most backward, and despised parts. To explain this decline, alongside the general causes affecting the empire, more specific causes have been invoked, particularly the increasing competition in commercial and financial matters from other non-Muslim communities, namely, the Greeks and Armenians, who were more favored by international circumstances and more dynamic. In places of commerce, such as Salonika and Smyrna, the Jews tended to be reduced to the role of brokers, intermediaries between local production and business and foreign merchants. This role—a necessary one— could give certain Jews the status of protégés of the Western consuls, which permitted them to escape the Ottoman institutions and their agents. Western imported goods also constituted serious competition for Jewish production, mainly in the cloth trade. The preference henceforth given by Marrano émi-

A Jew in Constantinople. Gouache and cut paper in the Ottoman style, taken from *A Briefe Relation of the Turckes, Their Kings, Emperors, or Grandsigneurs, Their Conquests, Religion, Customes, Habbits at Constantinople, etc.,* by the British traveler Peter Mundy, 1618. London, British Museum, Add. 23880 Or. 54, fol. 58 verso.

grés to other destinations (London, Amsterdam, Hamburg, and South America) more promising than the Ottoman Empire in crisis deprived Ottoman Jewry of the new blood and international connections that had been its strong point in preceding centuries. Only the contribution of newcomers from Livorno regenerated the aging Salonikan community from the end of the seventeenth century on. Thereafter, it was no longer from the Jews that the Ottomans expected an opening onto the West. Furthermore, the Ottoman governors, under the influence of those extremists to which the name *kādızādeli* was given in the second

> **" *It was in this degraded context that the crisis of Ottoman Judaism broke out as a result of the preaching of Sabbatai Zevi, the 'false Messiah.'* "**

half of the seventeenth century, ignited, during this same time, the most rigorous and rigid forms of Islam, which only emphasized the most negative aspects of the condition of *dhimmī*. It was in this degraded context that the crisis of Ottoman Judaism broke out as a result of the preaching of Sabbatai Zevi (1626–76), the "false Messiah," a paroxysm of messianic and Kabbalistic inspiration marking Jewish thought during the last centuries. Sabbatai finally accepted, in 1666, the injunction of Sultan Mehmed IV to convert to Islam.[52]

▶ See Nota bene, Sabbatai Zevi, pp. 197–199.

But let us not paint too dark a picture. Jews were still present in the seventeenth and eighteenth centuries in large-scale commerce and the contracting out of customs fees and other revenue of the treasury. A few Jewish families, such as the Carmonas, still occupied eminent positions close to the sultans and the Janissaries (the Adjiman). The Jewish "merchant in chief" (*bāzırgān başı*), that is, the great purveyor for the Janissaries, remained rich and powerful. But the abolition of the Janissaries in 1826 would remove one of the remaining pillars of fortune for the Jews. The Jewish physicians subsisted after the sixteenth century, including within the palace. They became proportionately less numerous, but some continued to be granted the privileges that set them apart from the ordinary *dhimmī*.[53] At the height of the influence of the *kādızādeli*, in 1663 and 1671, only the Jewish physicians who converted to Islam were retained in their functions in the palace, and even they were sometimes viewed with suspicion. Such was the case of the chief physician Hayatizade Mustafa Efendi, who was dismissed upon the arrival of Ahmed II, under the pretext that he was a convert and not an *alim*, and "that he maintained good relations with the Jews and evinced treason." In short, "it was inappropriate that his impure hand should take the sacred pulse of the sultan."[54]

---

1. See Béatrice Leroy, *L'Expulsion des juifs d'Espagne* (Paris: Berg International, 1990); Cecil Roth, *A History of the Marranos* (Skokie, IL: Varda Books, 2001); Maurice Kriegel, "La prise d'une décision: L'expulsion des juifs d'Espagne en 1492," *Revue Historique* 260 (1978): 49–90.

2. M. Á. Ladero Quesada, *España en 1492* (Madrid: Hernando, 1978).

3. See Joseph Nehama, *Histoire des Israélites de Salonique*, vol. 2 (Salonika: Molho, 1935).

4. Halil Sahillioglu, "Yeniceri cuhasi ve II. Bayezid'in son yillarinda yeniceri cuha muhasebesi," *Guney-Dogu Avrupa Arastirmalari Dergisi*, nos. 2–3, Istanbul (1974): 415–67.

5. See Yosef Hayim Yerushalmi, *From Spanish Court to Italian Ghetto: Isaac Cardoso; A Study in Seventeenth-Century Marranism and Jewish Apologetics* (New York: Columbia University Press, 1971).

6. See Gilles Veinstein, "Une communauté ottomane: Les juifs d'Avlonya (Valona) dans la deuxième moitié du XVIe siècle," in *Gli Ebrei e Venezia, secoli XIV–XVIII*, ed. G. Cozzi (Milan, 1987), 781–828.

7. See Feridun M. Emecen, *Unutulmus bir cemaat: Manisa yahudileri* (Istanbul: Eren, 1997), 35–37.

8. A. Shmuelevitz, *The Jews of the Ottoman Empire in the Late Fifteenth and the Sixteenth Centuries: Administrative, Economic, Legal and Social Relations as Reflected in the Responsa* (Leiden: Brill, 1984), 31.

9. Eliyahu Capsali, *Seder Elihahu Zuta*, ed. M. Benayahu, A. Schmuelevitz and S. Simonsohn (in Hebrew) (Jerusalem: Tel-Aviv University and Ben Zvi Institute, 1976), 1:213, 239.

10. Moïse Franco, *Essai sur l'histoire des Israélites de l'Empire ottoman depuis les origines jusqu'à nos jours* (Paris: A. Durlacher, 1897), 37–38.

11. See Minna Rozen, *A History of the Jewish Community in Istanbul: The Formative Years, 1453–1566* (Leiden: Brill, 2002), 38: See also Benjamin Lellouch, "Les juifs dans le monde musulman du XVe au milieu du XIXe siècle," in *Les Juifs dans l'histoire*, ed. Antoine Germa, Benjamin Lellouch, and Évelyne Patlagean (Seyssel: Champ Vallon, 2011), 289.

12. Feridun Emecen and Ilhan Sahin, *Ahkam Defteri 2: Bayezid dönemine ait 906/1501 Tarihli* (Istanbul: Turk Dunyasi Arastirmalari Vakfi, 1994).

13. Ibid., 15, doc. no. 50.

14. Ibid.

15. Ibid., 62, doc. no. 219, and 101, doc. no. 362.

16. On the idea of *amān* in Muslim law, see art. "Amān" in *The Encyclopaedia of Islam*, vol. 1 (Leiden: Brill).

17. Rozen, *History of the Jewish Community in Istanbul*, 200.

18. See Omer Lutfi Barkan, "Essai sur les données statistiques des registres de recensement dans l'Empire ottoman aux XVe et XVIe siècles," *Journal of Economic and Social History of the Orient* 1 (1957): 9–36; Amnon Cohen and Bernard Lewis, *Population and Revenue in the Towns of Palestine in the Sixteenth Century* (Princeton, NJ: Princeton University Press, 1978).

19. See Omer Lutfi Barkan, "Les déportations comme méthode de peuplement et de colonisation dans l'Empire ottoman," *Istanbul Universitesi Iktisat Fakultesi Mecmuasi*, 11:524–69; 13:56–79; 15:209–329.

20. Istanbul, Bibliothèque du musée du palais de Topkapi, E. 12321, no. 166.

21. Nehama, *Histoire des Israélites de Salonique*, vol. 2; I. Emmanuel, *Histoire des Israélites de Salonique*, vol. 1, (40av.J.C. à 1640) contenant un supplément sur l'histoire de l'industrie des tissus des Israélites de Salonique, Thonon, 1935–1936; S. Avitsur, "History of the Woolen Industry of Salonica" (in Hebrew), *Sefunot* 12 (1971–78): 147–68; Sahillioglu, "Yeniceri cuhasi"; Bejamin Braude, "International Competition and Domestic Cloth in the Ottoman Empire, 1500–1650: A Study in Undevelopment," *Review* 2, no. 3 (1979): 437–51 and "The Rise and Fall of Salonica Woolens, 1500–1650: Technology Transfer and Western Competition," *Mediterranean Historical Review* 6, no. 2 (1991): 216–36; Suraiya Faroqhi, "Textile Production in Rumeli and the Arab Provinces: Geographical Distribution and International Trade (1560–1650)," *Osmanli Arastirmalari: The Journal of Ottoman Studies* 1 (1980): 66–71.

22. Sahillioglu, "Yeniceri cuhasi."

23. Gilles Veinstein, "La draperie juive de Salonique: Une relecture critique de Joseph Nehama," in *The Jewish Communities of Southeastern Europe from the Fifteenth Century to the End of World War II*, ed. I. K. Hassiotis (Thessalonika: Institute for Balkan Studies, 1997), 579–89.

24. *Muhimme defteri* (quoted henceforth as *MD*) 19, Basbakanlik Arsivi, Istanbul, doc. no. 418.

25. R. Anhegger, *Beiträge zur Geschichte des Bergbaus im osmanischen Reich* (Istanbul, 1943), 1:79–80; Nicoara Beldiceanu, *Les actes des premiers sultans conservés dans les manuscrits turcs de la Bibliothèque Nationale à Paris*, vol. 1, *Actes de Mehmed II et de Bayezid II du ms. Fonds turc anc.* 39 (Paris–The Hague: Mouton, 1960), 169.

26. Pierre Belon, *Voyage au Levant (1553). Les observations de Pierre Belon du Mans, op. cit.*, p. 156.

27. See, for example, *MD*, "registers of important affairs," vol. 3, f. 35.

28. A. Hananel and E. Eskenazi, *Evreiski Izvori: Fontes hebraici ad res oeconomicas socialesque terrarum balcanicarum saeculo XVI pertinentes* (Sofia, 1958), doc. 155, 369–70; Maurice Goodblatt *Jewish Life in Turkey in the Sixteenth Century as Reflected in the Legal Writings of Samuel de Medina* (New York: Jewish Theological Seminary of America, 1952, 54) cites rates of from 6 to 13 percent.

29. Gilles Veinstein, "The Ottoman Jews: Between Distorted Realities and Legal Fictions," *Mediterranean Historical Review* 25, no. 1 (June 2010): 53–65.

30. Uriel Heyd, "Moses Hamon, Chief Jewish Physician to Süleyman the Magnificent," *Oriens* 16 (1963): 152–70.

31. See Cecil Roth, *Don̄a Gracia of the House of Nasi* (Philadelphia: Jewish Publication Society of America, 1992).

32. J. Reznik, *Le duc de Naxos: Contribution à l'histoire juive du XVIe siècle* (Paris: Librairie Lipschutz, 1936); P. Grunebaum-Ballin, *Joseph Naci duc de Naxos* (Paris–The Hague: Mouton, 1968).

33. See Benjamin Arbel, "Venezia, gli Ebrei e l'attività di Solomone Ashenasi nella guerra di Cipro," in Gaetano Cozzi, *Gli Ebrei e Venezia: Secoli XIV–XVIII; atti del Convegno internazionale organizzato dall'Istituto di storia della società e dello stato veneziano della Fondazione Giorgio Cini, Venezia, Isola di San Giorgio Maggiore, 5–10 giugno 1983* (Milano: Edizioni di Comunità, 1987), 163–90.

34. See Suraiya Faroqhi, "Ein Günstling des osmanischen sultans Murad III: David Passi," *Der Islam* 47 (1971): 290–97.

35. See J.-H. Mordtmann, "Die jüdischen Kira im Serai der Sultane," *Mitteilungen des Seminars für orientalische Sprachen, Westasiatische Studien* 32 (1929): 1–38.

36. Gilles Veinstein, "L'administration ottomane et le problème des interprètes," in *Études sur les villes du Proche-Orient, XVIe–XIXe siècles: Hommage à André Raymond*, ed. B. Marino (Damascus: Institut français d'études arabes de Damas, 2001), 65–79.

37. Gilles Veinstein, "La prise de Constantinople et le destin des *zimmī* ottomans," *Archivum Ottomanicum* 23 (2005–2006): 343–46.

38. Beldiceanu, *Les actes des premiers sultans.*

39. See the reflections of Bernard Lewis in "The Pro-Islamic Jews," in *Islam in History: Ideas, Men and Events in the Middle East* (London: Alcove Press, 1973), 137.

40. Robert Dankoff, *An Ottoman Mentality: The World of Evliya Celebi* (Leiden-Boston: Brill, 2004).

41. Ibid., 68.

42. Nicolas Vatin and Gilles Veinstein, *Le Sérail ébranlé: Essai sur les morts, dépositions et avènements des sultans ottomans, XIVe–XIXe siècle* (Paris: Fayard, 2003), 103.

43. Nehama, Histoire des Israélites de Salonique, 6:192.

44. See Istanbul, library of the museum of the Palace of Topkapi, *Kamil Kepeci* 888, doc. nos. 936 and 1267.

45. See Amnon Cohen, "Ritual Murder Accusations against the Jews during the Days of Suleiman the Magnificent," *Journal of Turkish Studies* 10 (*Raiyyet Rusumu: Essays Presented to Halil Inalcik*) (1986): 73–78; repr., in Amnon Cohen, *Studies on Ottoman Palestine* (Ashgate: Variorum, 2011).

46. See the analyses on this subject by Karl Binswanger, *Untersuchungen zum Status der Nichtmuslime im Osmanischen Reich des 16. Jahrhunderts mit einer Neudefinition des Begriffes "Dhimma"* (Munich: Trofenik, 1977).

47. M. Ertugrul Duzdag, *Seyhulislam Ebussuud Efendi Fetvalari isiginda 16 Asır Turk Hayati* (Istanbul: Enderun Kitabevi, 1983), nos. 403 and 404, 94.

48. For example, there is mention in 1590 in Ankara of a tax on Jews, referred to as *ādet-i dād-ı yehūdiyān* (customary tax on Jewish commerce), of 2,100 aspers per annum. See Halit Ongan, *Ankara'nın iki numarali Ser'iye Sicili* (Ankara, 1974), doc. no.1331, 101.

49. Rozen, *A History of the Jewish Community in Istanbul*, 27–33.

50. Hananel and Eskenazi, *Evreiski Izvori*, 2, doc. no. 60, 154–56; Goodblatt, *Jewish Life in Turkey*, 125.

51. Amnon Cohen, *Jewish Life under Islam: Jerusalem in the Sixteenth Century* (Cambridge, MA: Harvard University Press, 1984), 115–17.

52. Gershom Scholem, *Sabbatai Sevi: The Mystical Messiah, 1626–1676* (Princeton, NJ: Princeton University Press, 1973).

53. *MD* 104, no. 529 and *MD* 106, no. 164: Exemption privileges for a palace physician, the Jew Levi in 1693 and 1695; 95; *MD* 106, no. 950: renewal of a *berāt* by Ahmed II authorizing the Jewish physician Musa son of Nesim to wear ermine *kalpak* and ride a horse. On the developments of the eighteenth century, see Marc David Baer, "17 Yuzyilda Yahudilerin Osmanli Imparatorlugundaki Nufuz ve Mevlilerini Yitirmeleri," *Toplum ve Bilim* 83 (1999–2000): 202–22.

54. Silahdar Findikli Mehmed Aga, *Ta'rih* (Istanbul: Devlet Matbaasi, 1928), 578.

Salonika, "the Sefarad of the Balkans"

Modern Salonika (Thessaloniki), the present capital of northern Greece and the second largest city in the country, hardly reflects (apart from a few suggestive vestiges) the past of a multi-millennial city, especially its glorious moments at the end of the Roman period and under Byzantium. A Jewish colony had existed earlier, dating back to antiquity, but as in all the other Mediterranean centers, it represented only a small minority of the population. The Ottoman period (1430–1912) would bequeath the city a singular destiny, making it the sole metropolis of the ancient world to have a mainly Jewish population, in which Saturday was the day of closure for the port and the shops, and in which the Jewish feast days were shared by the entire city. What would have been unthinkable in Christendom would continue to remain possible in the land of Islam.

Mehmed II, having conquered Istanbul in 1453, deported the Jews of Salonika to his new capital in keeping with his goal of repopulating and reinvigorating the city. In the ensuing centuries, these Jews made up a distinct, separate congregation. So thorough was this relocation that in 1478 a census of the city of Salonika no longer mentioned any Jewish residents. The expulsion of the Jews from Spain and Portugal subsequently changed the situation entirely: Salonika, following several other Ottoman cities (Istanbul, Edirne, Safed), became one of the main refuges of the exiles. Henceforth there would be talk of "the Sefarad of the Balkans," "the Jerusalem of the Balkans," or of "the Mother in Israel." By 1510, out of a total of 4,073 households in the city, 56 percent were Jewish, divided into twenty congregations. In 1530, in a total of 5,132 households, Jewish households constituted 52 percent. In 1613, the count was 7,557 households, 68 percent being Jews. With time, the ethnic composition of the population became more diversified. Nineteenth-century Salonika, besides its Muslims, who lived in the heights of the hilly city, was comprised of Greeks, Slavs (Bulgarians and Serbs), Gypsies, and Armenians, as well as a colony of Westerners, but that did not prevent the Jews from keeping their predominance, with rates of 50 to 55 percent of the population.

If that large Jewish population pursued a diverse range of trades and was situated at all levels of the social ladder, three factors accounted for the attraction that the city held for the immigrants: its geographical position, at the crossroads of major commercial routes; the raising of sheep from Macedonia, which sustained a woolen cloth industry that made the Jews from Salonika the suppliers of the Janissaries' woolen uniforms; and the gold and lead mines of Chalcidice, where Judeo-Spanish became the idiom. Thanks to the relative tolerance and partial administrative and judicial autonomy ensured to them by the status of *dhimmī*, the Jews established their own system of self-government. Their basic units were the congregations conceived on the model of the Spanish *aljamas*, which were headed by federal institutions such as the triumvirate of the "officers of the holy mission for the collective account" and the "common mission of Talmud Torah," founded in 1520. This framework was, in the sixteenth century at least, that of a remarkable cultural development in which the influence of the Sefarad dominated, and in which names like Amato Lusitano, Samuel of Medina, and Moshe Almosnino were foremost. As Samuel Usque writes, "From this famous city the law for all Israel emanates." •

Gilles Veinstein

Sabbatai Zevi, the "False Messiah," and Islam

Portrait of Sabbatai Zevi. Engraving, late seventeenth century. Paris, Musée d'Art et d'Histoire du Judaïsme.

Among the Ottoman Jews, the hardships of exile intensified the study of Kabbalah—an esoteric and mystical teaching formed in thirteenth-century Spain. During the sixteenth century the doctrine took on a messianic orientation, reflecting the tribulations of the expelled Jews and the approach of 1648, thought to be that of the Final Deliverance. Safed (Tsfat) in Ottoman Galilee—one of the rallying points of the exiles—became in the sixteenth century the center of the "new Kabbalah" with thinkers such as Moses Cordovero and Isaac Luria Ashkenazi (1534–72), whose disciples included Hayyim Vital and Israel Sarug. "Lurianism" or "Lurianic Kabbalah" was spread widely in the seventeenth century by popular preachers and (especially in Europe) by Hebrew printers. This was one key to the success of the messianism professed by Sabbatai Zevi (1626–76) in the second half of the seventeenth century. Other factors included the pogroms perpetrated in 1648 by Bohdan Khmelnytsky and his Ukrainian Cossacks, and the economic crisis that affected Polish and Ottoman Jewry at that time.

Sabbatai Zevi was born in 1626 in Izmir, a port that was beginning to develop thanks to émigrés from places of less favorable circumstances, such as Salonika. His family, possibly of Ashkenazi origin and devoted to commerce, were from the Peloponnese. Ordained a rabbi during his adolescence, he went on to dedicate himself to the study of Kabbalah, though taking a greater interest in the *Zohar*, the classic on medieval esotericism, than in the new Lurianic Kabbalah. Starting in the fateful year 1648, this man, whose mental equilibrium has raised questions among historians (Gershom Scholem diagnosed him as manic-depressive, with alternating phases of transgressive exaltation and melancholic ascesis), began to present himself as the savior of Israel and, despite the interdiction, to pronounce the ineffable name of God in public. After he and his companions were expelled from the community of Izmir, he went to Salonika, where he adopted the same behavior, which resulted in another expulsion from the council of rabbis. He then wandered about in several Greek towns, arriving in Istanbul in 1658. He stayed there for a few months, and, as elsewhere, caused a scandal through his antinomic provocations: he ate forbidden foods, transformed the days of fasting and mourning into feast days, and married a former prostitute in a mystic nuptial ceremony. These actions aroused the

197

indignation of the Jewish authorities and ended in his excommunication. He returned to his native town of Izmir, where he remained from 1659 to 1662. He then traveled to the Middle East, via Rhodes and Egypt, and spent several years in Jerusalem (which had become the center of Kabbalah in the seventeenth century after the decline of Safed), in Egypt, and in Palestine. In 1665 he met a brilliant intellectual and great connoisseur of Lurianic Kabbalah, Nathan of Gaza. Nathan recognized Sabbatai as the Jewish Messiah and became, through his works, the theorist of the movement (Sabbatai himself composed no work, with the possible exception of the *Raza de-Mehemnuta* [The Secret of the Faith]). The two men, based in Jerusalem, sent letters throughout the Diaspora in an effort to obtain support from the communities. One of Nathan's letters even predicted that the Messiah would make the Ottoman sultan his servant. On the whole, these statements were categorically rejected by the rabbis, but there were exceptions. In any case, they met with popular support, the scope of which is not agreed upon by historians, but it was enough to get the attention of the Ottoman authorities.

When Sabbatai returned to Istanbul in January 1666, preceded by all the rumors to which his messianism had given rise, he was arrested and led before the imperial divan, presided over by the grand vizier Koprulu Fazıl Ahmed Pasha, who imprisoned him. This did not put an end to the crisis, however, since from the prison of Gelibolu (Gallipoli), to which he was finally transferred, the alleged Messiah drew numerous visitors, while his secretary Samuel Primo continued to fan the fervor of the faithful with his letters. Sultan Mehmed IV then adopted a different approach: he had him appear before him in Edirne on September 15, 1666. He was summoned to prove his supernatural powers by surviving the arrows with which they threatened him. He escaped the ordeal by converting to Islam. Not only did he receive the monetary bonus normally reserved for new converts (the *kisve behāsı*, intended, as a rule, for the acquisition of new attire), but he was also given the honorific title of *kapıcı başı* (head chamberlain). The theatrics of this conversion have not lost all their mystery. Transitioning to Islam was a way for an infidel to escape judicial penalties, so this objective alone could motivate conversion. But in this particular case, something else might have been at work: the intention of the Ottoman governments, then under the influence of a radical strain of Islam (referred to as *kādızādeli*), to manipulate an emblematic convert, which would explain the honors showered upon him. If such a plan actually existed, it underestimated the psychological instability of this individual, which precluded relying on him. He was ultimately relegated to Dulcigno, in Albania, where he died in 1676.

But his adventure had consequences. Some of his disciples, an estimated two hundred families—under the influence of Nathan of Gaza, who had "theorized" the conversion of his prophet by presenting it as a messianic action of transcending the law and subverting Islam from within—converted to Islam, thus becoming the originators of what the Turks would pejoratively refer to as *dönme* ("converts," or more precisely, "turncoats"). Thus was born a group of crypto-Jewish Muslims (some of whom refused to believe in the death of their Messiah and continued to await his return), presenting a particular variant of Marranism. They were turned away by both the Muslims (in Yemen, in 1679, Sabbatai's disciples were even punished) and the Jews. In Salonika, their main center before their departure for Istanbul in 1912, they formed a kind of intermediary community, whose quarters, on a hillside, were located between the Muslim and Jewish quarters. They were divided into three groups: Izmirlis, Kunisios, and Jakubis. Externally, nothing set them apart from the Muslims. They respected all the obligations of Islam, had Muslim names, and spoke Turkish. But they had their own mosques, and they continued to secretly observe the rites of Judaism, as well as those unique to their own movement. Rejected by the other communities, they practiced strict endogamy. One of their commandments prescribed: "Practice the customs of the Turks to all appearances, but abstain from uniting with them in bonds of matrimony." They worked in small businesses and the craft industry, and as civil servants in the municipality, among other occupations. Some gained access to liberal professions. In contemporary Istanbul, they are a discreet sect, present in business as well as in intellectual and artistic life. ●

Gilles Veinstein

Eliyahu Capsali, Jewish Cantor of the Ottomans

"Behold how the Eternal has made this Turkish nation great and magnificent"

In 5283 by the Jewish calendar, or 1523 of the Common Era, Eliyahu Capsali was born of an old, rich, and learned Jewish lineage from Candia, in the Venetian land of Crete. Moshe, his great uncle, previously settled in Constantinople before becoming, after 1453, the first authority of Ottoman Jewry; but the family was tied above all to Italy and its rabbinical schools, especially that of Padua. Like several Capsali before him, Eliyahu was both a temporal leader (*condestabulo*) and spiritual leader. The rabbi would, moreover, become famous for his treatises on the Law (*halakhah*), his responses to judicial consultations (*teshuvot*), and his ordinances (*takkanot*) regulating the life of the Jews of Candia. But the long chronicle he recorded on paper that year has been transmitted by only four manuscripts, and was not published until the 1970s. Its title, *The Order of Eliyahu the Little* (*Seder Eliyahu Zuta*), sounds indeed like an *apologia auctoris*. It deals essentially with history other than Jewish history, which is quite exceptional in Hebrew letters prior to the nineteenth century. It is devoted to the House of Ottoman and its conquests from the beginning to the taking of Rhodes (1522). In the prologue, Capsali explains why he has taken on this task: "The first reason is in order that man may acquire knowledge and intelligence by hearing the stories of the kings of the Christians and Turks, and in particular that he may know the wisdom of the great king, Sultan Selim, who was unmatched among the kings of the Christians." He goes on to add: "The second is *that all the peoples of the earth may know* (Josh. 4:24) that God is the Eternal and that

there is a God who judges on earth (Ps. 58:12). For when the reader sees my stories . . . he will accept the yoke of the kingdom of heaven, and this whole people [the Jews] will understand that *the eyes of the Eternal inspect all the earth* (Zech. 4:10), *observing the evil and the good* (Prov. 15:3) *to give everyone according to his conduct, and according to the fruit of his doings* (Jer. 32:19) . . . See how the Eternal, in His wisdom and His intelligence, has made that Turkish nation great and magnificent, *has blessed its undertakings—and its possessions are increased in the land* (Job 1:10). He has sent it from a distant country and blessed it. The Turk is *the rod of His anger, in whose hand as a staff is His indignation* (Isa. 10:5), in order that with it He may mete out to the nations and the peoples, to the provinces given to debauchery, the full measure of their chastisement! *The Eternal is a God of knowledge, and by Him actions are weighed* (1 Sam. 2:3)."[1] Like Isaiah's Assyrians, the Turks were sent by Providence to punish sinners. Their elevation, particularly under Selim I (1512–20), furnishes substance for a lesson.

After the prologue, the chronicler describes the creation of the world and the beginnings of mankind, of Adam in the aftermath of the flood. Enumerating Noah's posterity, he pauses on Togarmah, the grandson of Japheth by Gomer, whose descendants the Bible does not specify. So he turns to a universal history, though centered on the period of the Second Temple, the *Sefer Yosippon* (which may be dated 953), and repeats word for word the passage on the ten clans issued from Togarmah, among which the Turks are found. These last, he concludes, "entered the same religion as the Ishmaelites, and are therefore also connected with the name of Ishmael." It is at this point that the fascinating passage on the origin of Islam begins. Here is its argument: Muhammad, a cardinal of the Church of Rome, takes power in the East by force of arms, even giving the assurance that God has sent him to found a new religion. Being illiterate, he asks Ali, a baptized Jewish Christian, to put his laws into writing, which are nothing but a translation of the biblical verses on the oneness of God. Abu Bakr, a Jewish prince who has been won over, and who is jealous of the influence exerted on the impostor by the Christian Hayya, assassinates the latter during a drinking session. Muhammad, when he sobers up, thinks he himself is the one who is guilty of murder and decides to forbid consumption of wine. Here Capsali takes up the motifs present in the epistle of Ya'aqov ben Eliyahu (thirteenth century), but that letter draws on traditions formed among the Christians of the Latin East and West who seek the origin of Islam in the Christian direction; the Hayya of Ya'aqov ben Eliyahu and of Capsali must be identified with the monk Bahira, a character from the Christian polemic against Islam.

The reader thus knows the origin of the Turks and of the "house of Ishmael" into which they entered. The history of the "kingdom of Togarmah, which rose up from the dust to the heavens and the stars" can now begin. Capsali says he has relied on the testimony of "old and learned Turks," his father, who has sojourned in Istanbul, and an Egyptian rabbi. It is equally possible that Italian, Greek, or Jewish merchants, or representatives of the Venetian power, served him as informers. Obviously, he is adapting no written source. His knowledge of Ottoman history is therefore very uneven. For the first sovereigns, the story is short and the chronology confused; from Mehmed II (1451–81) the events are dated and the narrative is clearly fuller, but the history of the ten years that preceded the writing of the chronicle is told with a very great wealth of detail.

Before the celestial court convened for the New Year, God promised Osman "a kingdom hard as iron," as the fourth kingdom of the vision of Daniel, the last before the redemption. His sons were called upon to subjugate four kings: "the king of Greece," with the taking of Constantinople in 1453; "the Sofi," in other words Ishma'el, the Safavid shah of Iran, defeated in 1514; 'Ala al-Dawla, the emir of the Dhul-Qadr principality, between Central Anatolia and Upper Mesopotamia, who was killed during the expedition of 1515; and "the Sudan," the head of the Mameluke Empire, who was conquered in 1516–17. The essential role thus fell on Selim. In the litany of his victories, the one over 'Ala al-Dawla opened the route for him to Cairo, and especially made him the depository of the Assyrian heritage, therefore the scourge of God. But his conquests were not over after the victory over the fourth king: Selim died prematurely, before having "been able to reign on the universe like Cyrus, Darius and Alexander the Macedonian." In 1522, the tenth king of Togarmah, Suleiman, took over Rhodes. Capsali assures us that he destroyed the idols that the Christians adored in the churches, then prostrated himself before the God of Heaven. Plainly, the coming of the Messiah was nigh; besides, Isaac Abravanel had calculated it in the *Migdal Yeshu'ot* (1497–98) as being 1531.

In Capsali's view, in 1453 God wanted Mehmed II to settle old scores and chastise the Greeks for the wrongs they did "since they have been a nation"; that is, since the domination of the Seleucids to Israel. According to him, the conqueror of Constantinople was a Judaizer who participated in the celebration of Pesach at the table of Moshe Capsali. The rabbi of Candia knew that he had settled Balkan Jews in Istanbul. But it was especially Bayezid II (1481–1512) who worked to bring about the "ingathering of the exiles" of Israel, the first event of the messianic times, by welcoming the Jews after the expulsion from Spain (1492): "Sultan Bayezid, the king of Togarmah, learned of all the hardships the king of Spain had caused the Jews to suffer; he knew that they sought *a place to rest the soles of their feet* (Deut. 28:65), and his eye had pity on them. He sent messengers and *made a proclamation throughout all his kingdom,*

201

and put it also in writing (Ezra 1:1) that none of the governors of the city would be authorized to repel the Jews or drive them away, but that they should all be welcomed with goodwill; whoever disobeys will be liable to the death penalty . . . The exiled Jews came to Togarmah by the thousands and by myriads and the country was filled with them . . . *Thus, the sons returned to their own border* (Jer. 31:17)."[2]

In the persecutions that Sephardic refugees related to him, Capsali probably saw, as did Isaac Abravanel before him, "the birth pangs of the Messiah." Today we know that the majority of the Spanish Jews set out for other Christian countries, and that Bayezid II's proclamation is not very credible. But for the rabbi of Candia, it was essential that the Togarmah kings should play a major role in the "ingathering of the exiles" in order that their victories might carry the messianic hope. Their religion was false, even if they were not idol worshippers. And yet the hand of God was everywhere at work in their actions, speeding the redemption of Israel, and of all mankind. ●

Benjamin Lellouch, lecturer in modern history at the University of Paris 8, is a specialist on the Ottoman Empire and author of Ottomans en Égypte: Historiens et conquérants au XVIᵉ siècle *(Peeters, 2006) and of* Juifs dans l'histoire: De la naissance du judaïsme au monde contemporain, *in collaboration with Antoine Germa and Évelyne Patlagean (Champ-Vallon, 2011).*

---

1. Eliyahu Capsali, *Seder Eliyahu Zuta*, vol. 1, ed. Aryeh Shmuelevitz, Shlomo Simonsohn, and Meir Benayahu (Jerusalem: Mekhon Ben-Tsvi, 1975), 9–10; emphasis in original.

2. *Ibid.*, 218–19; emphasis in original.

The Jews of Palestine
Yaron Ben Naeh

After the defeat of the Mamluks at Marj Dabiq in August 1516, the Ottomans occupied a Palestine that was subdivided into districts (*sandjaks*), which were part of the Bilad al-Sham (historical Syria). This was essentially an agricultural region, with a small number of urban centers. This territory, once a passage between Egypt and Syria, became a remote and impoverished province; its only interest to the central power consisted in its relative religious importance, given the presence of sacred places—Jerusalem in particular—as well as the proximity of the route to the Hajj, the pilgrimage to Mecca, via Transjordan.

Yaron Ben Naeh

Yaron Ben Naeh, professor of Jewish studies at the Hebrew University of Jerusalem, is also director of the "Misgav Yerushalayim," Center for Research and Study of Sephardi and Oriental Jewish Heritage. His publications include *Jews in the Realm of the Sultans: Ottoman Jewish Society in the Seventeenth Century* (Mohr Siebeck, 2006).

Demographic evolution

Until the nineteenth century, the population did not exceed 250,000, with very few non-Muslims, who were concentrated mainly in the cities. The Christians were grouped in Jerusalem, Bethlehem and its periphery, and in certain parts of Galilee, particularly Nazareth. Toward the end of the Mamluk period, a few hundred Jewish families resided mainly in the cities—Jerusalem, Safed, Gaza, Nablus, Hebron, and certain villages of Galilee. This community had members of various origins—Arabic-speaking natives (*musta'ribīn*); Jews from the Maghreb, who spoke an Arabic dialect; others native to the Iberian Peninsula since the end of the fourteenth century, who spoke Judeo-Spanish; and a handful of Yiddish-speaking Ashkenazi. In time, Judeo-Spanish became the vernacular. The expulsion of the Jews from Spain and Portugal increased the number of immigrants to the region, but the significant change came after the Ottoman conquest of Palestine in 1516.

Between 1520 and 1530, Safed became the center of Jewish life in Palestine. Contrary to Jerusalem, where they were a minority, the Jews in Safed represented close to half the population. Aside from a few villages, two other communities of small size but considerable importance should be mentioned: Hebron, a satellite of the community of Jerusalem, and to a lesser degree Tiberias, where the Nasi family encouraged Jews to settle.

▶ See Nota
bene devoted
to Joseph
Nasi,
pp. 220–221.

The relative but rapid growth of Jewish settlers in Palestine was accompanied by a great diversity of its ethnic components. In Safed, communities were organized in keeping with the residents' countries, regions, or towns of origin. From the end of the sixteenth century on, Palestine began to attract persons of a certain age, such as widows who wished to devote their last years to prayer and charity, and scholars who, convinced of the virtues of study and prayer in the Holy Land, aspired to die and be buried there. Others—especially natives of Syria, Palestine, and Egypt—were content to make a pilgrimage (*ziyarah*) or to have their remains brought to the Mount of Olives in Jerusalem, or to Safed.

The decline of Safed, which began around 1590, coincided with the prosperity of Jerusalem, which sheltered the largest Jewish community in the region. Jerusalem retained this status until the end of the Ottoman period, except for a brief period at the end of the eighteenth century, when Akko (Acre), the capital of the Pasha Ahmed al-Jazzar, became the country's most important and populous city.

Map of Jerusalem taken from the *Theatrum Orbis Terrarum*, Cologne, 1599. Print by Franz Hogenberg. Paris, Bibliothèque Nationale Française.

The legal and social status

Within the framework of the *dhimma*, the Ottoman state recognized the existence of urban Jewish communities in Jerusalem, Safed, Damascus, and elsewhere. Even if the Jews preferred the proximity of their coreligionists, there was no ghettoization or areas specifically set apart for Jews or for Christians. The areas of Jewish residences, which sprang up spontaneously, did not have hermetic borders. Neighborhood difficulties or conflicts generally broke out because faithful Muslims complained about the proximity of the Jewish quarter during prayers at the mosque.

At the end of the Mamluk era and a century later, from 1586 to 1588, the Jews of Jerusalem fought for legal recognition of their synagogue. They had to fight hard, often in vain, to be granted the legitimacy of their secular property rights to the building. In the second half of the sixteenth century, construction of a private synagogue began at the initiative of a rich Jew from Istanbul, David Elnekave. In Safed, at least twenty hidden places of worship sprang up during the seventeenth century, despite the ban on building new synagogues. It was not until 1584—as the result of a denunciation or an attempted extortion—that the

> **Even if the Jews preferred the proximity of their coreligionists, there was no ghettoization or areas specifically set apart for Jews or for Christians.**

sultan ordered the governor of Damascus to investigate the construction of these oratories forbidden by the shari'a. The outcome of that episode is unclear. In any case, we have no testimony of grievances about, or of the destruction of, any places of worship. Indeed, there was often a considerable gap between the official policy, the edicts of the sultan, and their application, especially in remote provinces like Palestine.

The difficulty in applying the decisions of the central power was sometimes detrimental to the interests of the population as a whole, beyond the Jewish community alone. During this period, official complaints were made denouncing the machinations of the regional directors. The sultan invariably ordered an investigation in order to prevent abuse, but the local authorities persevered in their malfeasance (which did not necessarily target Jews), knowing that they would slip through the net. With respect to the treatment of the Jews, distinctions should be made between different population groups: the governor and his entourage, coming from the center of the empire and generally motivated by the lure of gain, often behaved like arbitrary despots, while the qadi, embodying the law and justice, did what they could to temper abuse. Jews and Christians, because of their precarious status, were the targets of choice, but neither did Muslims escape the cupidity of these dignitaries. The fact that Palestine was an outlying and marginal province made its citizens easier to exploit. By the time the orders from the imperial capital arrived, the local government officials had achieved their goal and lined their pockets. If the Jews were ostensibly resigned to this state of affairs, in reality they worked to obtain edicts favorable to their own interests through corruption and pressure on the local authorities, and by the intermediary of influential Jews at the imperial court. The sultans did indeed promulgate decrees that regulated the rights of Jews and protected them from harassment or bullying. The local Muslim notables, the sheiks and the merchants, were as a rule moderating elements, although not necessarily out of conscience or religious conviction. Documents of the eighteenth and subsequent centuries attest that the distribution of gifts to key figures was a common custom intended to protect the Hierosolymitan community. But it was not a rare occurrence for the Jewish population, children in particular, to be victims of aggression—the throwing of stones or insults. Further, some devout religious Muslims would denounce the "depraved" ways of the *dhimmī*: showy dress, scorn for Muslims, disturbance of the conduct of prayers at the mosque, even forbidden construction of synagogues.

Letters of doubtful sincerity dating from the beginning of the seventeenth century relate the respect that Muslims held for their neighbors, as well as their zeal in maintaining the Jewish holy places in Galilee. On the other hand, calls for help sent by couriers express some degree of concern about the possible destruction of synagogues, the desecration of cemeteries, and the imprisonment or murder of members of the community. It is impossible to tell how much of the rhetoric is based on fact. European travelers, especially from the seventeenth century onward, stressed—not without cynicism—that the Jews of Palestine, their ancestral land, were more subject to hatred and humiliation from the Turks than were the other subjects of the empire, but that they also were regarded as a powerful community, capable of harming Christians and their holy sites.

It is important to note that all residents of the land of Islam had a basic sense of security, and the certainty of their permanence, without any threat of expulsion, forced conversion, or physical violence. They also had the assurance that the authorities—the qadi at the level of the municipal administration and the sultan as a higher authority—would support their safety and their right to justice.

One of the most significant elements of the great reforms (Tanzimat) was the granting of the same civil rights to Muslims and non-Muslims and the annulment of the per capita tax. Jews and Christians became equal before the Ottoman law, and the state recognized their status of *millet* (community of the empire). At the same time, many Ashkenazi Jews benefiting from the protection of their countries of origin chose to settle in Palestine, joining the Ottoman citizens, some of whom acquired the status of protégés of certain European powers: Great Britain, Holland, Austria, Russia, and so on. In Syria and Palestine, these transfers provoked the anger and humiliation of the Muslim population, which, feeling wronged, manifested its resentment by acts of violence toward Christians. Certain elements of the Jewish community, particularly the Francos (Sephardim settled in the Middle East, intermediaries between the Europeans and the natives) and in a broader sense those who seemed close to the Europeans, were also the object of hatred among their Muslim neighbors. An illustration of this is the affair of Damascus (1840), which began with the suspicious death of a Catholic monk and degenerated into a violent attack on the leaders and members of the Jewish community.

Economic activities

One of the characteristics specific to Jews on Islamic soil, and in the Ottoman Empire in particular, was the great diversity of their economic activities. The governments did not discriminate against minorities, with the exception of military service and administrative functions within the army, domains to which the equality of civil rights later gave them access. The activities of the Jews were determined according to their abilities, traditional trades, and the jobs scorned by Muslims, as well as the possibilities offered by local market conditions. When the Jewish population displayed a normal age distribution this simultaneously meant a solid economy in which there were more assets both in the domestic and the outside world. Not everyone competed in Palestine's job market. Widows, scholars of a certain age, and others lived on allocations and other subsidies. The fundamental employment problem in Palestine concerned the quality of immigration: the elderly, who had little disposal income, and the Ashkenazim, who were unfamiliar with the language of the country, let alone the characteristics of the local job market, and were thus incapable of taking part in it. They found work solely within their community of origin, most of them subsisting with the financial help of the Diaspora.

On these questions our knowledge of Palestine is fragmentary. The sources present the following overall picture. Some towns in Galilee housed a dozen or so Jewish families who were working the land. Others had established commercial connections between the country and the city—they bought the peasants' harvests, raw materials, and cloth, and resold them as retail goods or manufactured or imported products. The cities were populated by merchants, craftsmen, community professionals (teachers, ritual slaughterers, scribes, etc.), domestic workers, and day laborers. The workforce consisted essentially of men, but also of women employed as household help, embroiderers, spinners, and street vendors. The Jews, members of craftsmen and merchant guilds of the city, had shops next door to those of non-Jews in the marketplaces. In sixteenth-century Safed, the textile industry represented the main source of income for the Jewish community in all the stages of the processing of wool: dyeing, spinning, weaving, and printing. The decline of this sector, in competition with cheap-labor countries, brought about the collapse of the community. Jerusalem, on the other hand, offered the greatest professional diversity. The roll of the Jerusalemite Jewish taxpayers in the years 1690-91, published by Uriel Heyd, bears witness to the distribution of trades in the community (a total of 182 Jews paid their per capita tax). They worked in the textile industry (silk in particular), as goldsmiths and tanners, and they were brokers or providers of services (doctors, domestics, etc.). This list reveals the overriding importance of the dozens of students at religious schools and of administrators of the congregation. This community, like the others, included a few affluent individuals who were careful not to show off their wealth. The limited range of economic activities of the Yishuv raises the question of financial support from outside the community. The concept of Palestine as the Holy Land evolved during the Ottoman period—four Holy Cities, in which the population held fast to the country through thick and thin, despite hard times and suffering, studied and prayed for their brothers in the Diaspora, obligating the latter to bring them material help. This support, initially thought of as a philanthropic act, was transformed in the sixteenth century—and even more so during the seventeenth—into a duty of the Diaspora Jews toward the Yishuv. That evolution, of an ideological nature, persevered during the nineteenth century, until the beginning of the twentieth.

The place of Palestine (*Eretz Yisrael*) in Jewish consciousness

▶ See Nota bene, Jerusalem, pp. 218–219.

The question of financial aid to the Jews of Palestine raises a final point: the real place of the Land of Israel in Jewish life from the end of the Middle Ages to the beginning of the modern era.

What place did the Jewish Yishuv of Palestine occupy in the daily life of the Jews in the Diaspora—center or periphery? It would seem that, with the exception of a relatively brief period of the sixteenth century with the apogee of Safed, of its Kabbalistic center and its prolific masters, Palestine was a remote and wretched province of the empire. The Land of Israel, as well as Jerusalem, incarnated a far-away ideal rather than a tangible reality. At no time (including the messianic period of Sabbatai Zevi) was there any question of immigrating to Palestine to populate the land and do a mitzvah (religious precept). More than an inhabitable space, it was rather the land of holy places in which elderly believers came to live out their last days. Its geography and topography were represented as a schematic configuration of sacred sites. The pilgrimages (*ziyarah*) or burials in Palestine, which were mainly the expression of religiousness or popular faith, fulfilled an economic function. The terms Jerusalem and Zion were traditionally evoked in prayers, and on an individual basis or collectively one responded to solicitations for gifts according to one's ability, nothing more.

The Land of Israel, sacred or not, did not represent a significant factor in the rabbinical universe. In the course of the centuries, the sages of Palestine found themselves at the bottom of the ladder in relation to their eminent colleagues in Istanbul, Salonika, and later Izmir. The rabbinical schools (yeshivot) of Palestine constituted an intermediary step, a provisional stop of a few years before the students went on to occupy advantageous positions in larger cities. The community leaders succeeded, however, in forging the ideal image of a holy city and congregation, first in Safed and later in Jerusalem. The *takkanot* (ordinances) relative to religious morality, the orthodoxy, austerity, and,

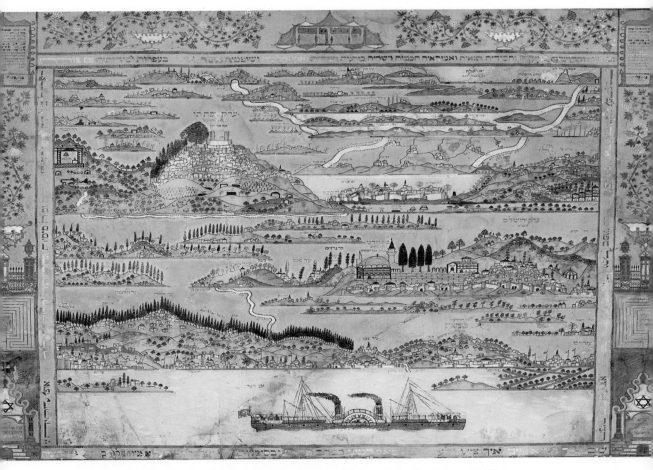

Jewish representation of the geography of Israel and Jerusalem. *Shiviti*, by Moses Ganbash—*a shiviti* being a decorative plaque serving to commemorate the omnipresence of God, according to the verse "I have set the Lord always before me" (Psalm 16:8), but also to indicate the direction of prayer, toward Jerusalem. Constantinople, 1853. New York, Metropolitan Museum of Art.

finally, condemnation of luxury delivered a message of destitution to the Muslims, justifying especially the particular status of these congregations of penniless students who dedicated their lives to an in-depth investigation of sacred texts.

Although in theory Islamic law established boundaries between Muslims and *dhimmī*s, daily life in the city eluded the most rigid dispositions of the shariʿa, and the two communities coexisted harmoniously. The Jews and their Muslim neighbors lived in close proximity, and no particular ostracism was observed. They rubbed shoulders in the urban centers where they worked side by side—as craftsmen or merchants in the marketplaces, for example. Men frequented the same cafés and hammams. There was no obstacle to women meeting in the public baths as well, but as they led a more or less reclusive life, the circle of their associations was essentially limited to their homes and inner courtyards.

From the four corners of the Ottoman Empire, testimonies evince the participation of non-Jews in Jewish holidays and vice versa. Thus, Jews were hired for their services: they had a reputation as quasi-professional mourners, and like the Christians and Gypsies, they were sought after as musicians, dancers, or jugglers to enliven the events organized by Muslim notables. The autobiographies and chronicles of the times attest to the Jews' integration into their environment. The way of life

> *Although in theory Islamic law established boundaries between Muslims and dhimmīs, daily life in the city eluded the most rigid dispositions of the shari'a.*

for needy Jews was apparently closer to that of their Muslim or Christian neighbors than to that of their more fortunate coreligionists. Perhaps the Jews recognized in themselves a Judeo-Arab (or even Ottoman, in the enlightened milieus) identity, in opposition to the new identity that colonialism and forced modernization wished to thrust upon them, as indicated by numerous texts from the beginning of the twentieth century.

The Jews in Jerusalem and Hebron during the Ottoman Era
Nazmi Al-Jubeh

We must await the period of the Mamluks—at the beginning of the fourteenth century—to see the Jews resettle in large numbers in Jerusalem and Hebron. The demography remained stable during the lengthy period from 1250 to 1516, at the end of which Jerusalem fell into the hands of the Ottomans. It is in the vast empire they formed in the sixteenth century that we find the largest Jewish communities of the era. The Ottoman Porte did not resist Jewish immigration to Jerusalem and Hebron from France, Spain, Portugal, Hungary, Germany, and Italy, as well as immigrants from Ottoman territories.

Nazmi Al-Jubeh

Nazmi Al-Jubeh is the chairperson of the Department of History and Archaeology at Birzeit University (Palestine). A graduate of Tubingen University (Germany) and an expert on cultural heritage, he has published several books and a great number of articles on history of Jerusalem, Hebron, cultural heritage, and politics.

A collective existence in the shadow of pluralism

The Jews, who were part of the tolerated minorities, were regarded as a single community, at least according to the study of Islamic court records,[1] despite divisions within the community. Naturally, one cannot give a single, fixed image of that community that would be valid for the whole Ottoman period. The real situation among the Jewish population varies with the times, from citizenship, to near-total equality, to proven persecution on occasion. But the same observation can be made with respect to Muslims and Christians. During the difficult periods—those, for example, during which a corrupt governor was installed in Jerusalem—all the residents of the city suffered the same degree of arbitrariness and persecution. These same archives of the Islamic tribunal of Jerusalem show that the Jews of the Holy City—and those of Hebron—were, at the beginning of the Ottoman period, plunged into penury. This is proven by the *jizya* tax they were required to pay: it was a very low rate—and many of them were exempt from any payment, being dependent on community aid for their subsistence.

The Ottoman regime left the Jews who lived in the two cities a remarkable degree of freedom in the management of their affairs, recognizing their hierarchy and taking care not to interfere in the government of the person they called the "sheik of the Jews," who represented his community to the Ottoman power—that is, the *cadi* or governor, with whom he was in more or less daily contact, playing the role of privileged intermediary between the central power and the community. Alongside the "sheik of the Jews," who was considered the official spokesman of the community, there was a religious representative, the *dayan*, or judge. The "sheik" was generally from the ranks of the Sephardim.

At the end of the sixteenth century, the destitution of Jerusalem's Jews increased, and the demands for help from the Jewish communities of the Diaspora grew proportionately, as did requests for a lowering of the *jizya* and other taxes. The consequence of this was a greater indebtedness of Jews to Muslims. The archives contain dozens of records on this subject, bearing witness to the difficulty the Jews had in paying their debts. The problem persisted throughout the two subsequent centuries. Internally, a sharp conflict emerged between "Eastern" Jews (*must'arabim*, those coming from the Near East, speakers of Arabic) and "Western" Jews (originating in Spain or the Maghreb), and both of these groups together against the Karaites. These divisions went so deep that these different groups refused to live in the same places, some even preferring the proximity of Muslims to that of their coreligionists of a different group. The Ashkenazim were relative newcomers to Palestine, and in particular to Jerusalem and Hebron, since they did not arrive until the end of the eighteenth century. Their arrival created problems for the Ottoman state, because they wanted to place themselves under the protection of the Western powers. That desire suited the interests of those countries, particularly Russia, which sought to insinuate itself into the domestic affairs of the Ottoman Empire in the name of the protection of minorities. In fact, the majority of Ashkenazim (60 percent) placed themselves under the protection of Austria, 20 percent under that of England, and the rest were split among America, Russia, and Holland.[2] Hence, the Ashkenazim did not go very far toward integrating themselves into the local culture. This was problematic not only for the Ottoman government but also for the Eastern Jews, who, for their part, considered themselves to be Ottoman subjects. The seeking of foreign protection seems to have weakened the control that the Sephardim exerted on the affairs of the community in the seniority of their ties with the local population and their excellent relationship with the Ottoman government. For many reasons, particularly historical and cultural ones, the Ottoman governor of Jerusalem dealt with the representative of the Sephardic Jews as if he represented all the Jews, despite the protests of the Ashkenazim.

> " *The Ottoman regime left the Jews who lived in the two cities a remarkable degree of freedom in the management of their affairs, recognizing their hierarchy and taking care not to interfere in the government.* "

Insertion into Ottoman life

The Jews during this period enjoyed great religious freedom, manifested particularly by the fact that they owned synagogues and, departing from a strict interpretation of the *shari'a*, could even build new ones as long as they obtained the necessary authorizations. They also had a great many religious schools (yeshivas). They were buried in their own cemeteries. The pilgrimage of the Jews to Jerusalem and Hebron was authorized and even encouraged by the local authorities, who provided normal conditions of security. Access to holy places varied with the sites and the times. Thus, while Jews were not allowed access to the plaza of the mosques, it was under the Ottomans, beginning with Suleiman the Magnificent, that the space in front of the Western Wall began to be developed and gradually become a major site of devotion. Jews could also go to, but usually not enter, the Cave of the Patriarchs in Hebron. The status of Rachel's tomb, on the road to Bethlehem, varied with the times.

These archives of the Islamic tribunal also show that the Jews were present at many trials, in which they brought complaints against Muslims or against coreligionists. The testimony of a Jew was received against another Jew, or against a Christian, sometimes even a Muslim; in the last case, sometimes the testimony was used, sometimes not. A Jew could take an oath before the Islamic tribunal, although certain men of religion might forbid their coreligionists from doing so. As for the Jewish woman, the same laws were applied to her as to Muslim women. Jews held many administrative positions in Ottoman Jerusalem, especially during the periods in which their community was flourishing—less when their number

Islamic representation of the city of Jerusalem, with the Dome of the Rock at the center, seventeenth century. Istanbul, Topaki Palace Museum Library.

decreased. In Hebron, Jews had always been few. The strictly economic contribution of Jews was not very large, since most of the men in the community dedicated themselves to religious practices and prayer, and were supported by social aid (*halukkah*). But there were a few butchers, shoemakers, tanners, money changers, sellers of spices (the managing agent of this guild was often Jewish), and wine merchants. Their importance in economic life increased with the approach of the nineteenth century. All trades were open to them without restriction. They were registered in all the guilds and were found even among their managing agents.

> "*The pilgrimage of the Jews to Jerusalem and Hebron was authorized and even encouraged by the local authorities, who provided normal conditions of security.* "

With Christians, relations were not good. The two communities preferred to remain separate; we see no Jew residing in the Christian quarters. Moreover, Jews were forbidden even to cross through these quarters, which they considered impure places. On the other hand, it is not rare to see Jews residing in the same houses with Muslims and sharing their daily life, sometimes even certain jobs. But the sale, purchase, and leasing of real estate were virtually reserved for Muslims. Jews entered restaurants run by Muslims, and did not hesitate to shop in their stores; Muslims, for their part, bought food from Jews, especially meat products.

In a detailed study of the life of Jerusalem's Jews—a study based on the comparison between Islamic and Jewish sources—Amnon Cohen concludes: "It was not a mingling of equals; everyone knew that the Jews were a 'protected people.' But beyond this basic understanding—and perhaps thanks to it in that it removed the element of competition from Jewish-Muslim relations—life was so arranged in Jerusalem that the Jews could survive, develop, and sometimes even prosper within the Muslim society and under the aegis of Muslim rule."[3]

It is significant to observe, for example, that many memoranda and petitions addressed to the Porte by inhabitants of Jerusalem are signed by Jews, who were not a large group in proportion to the population of the Holy City. There are even examples of correspondence with Istanbul, in which Jews complain of abuses on the part of the governor. This shows that the right of remonstrance and protest was safeguarded, and the oppression never went to the point of keeping Jews from exercising this right, and from expressing their opinions. The judicial system in Jerusalem was independent of local power, and the *cadi*, named directly by Istanbul, tried to ensure respect for the rights of inhabitants, without distinction of religion—those rights guaranteed by Islamic law, and particularly those of the weakest and most vulnerable subjects. It appears that among the Jews of Jerusalem, the *cadi* enjoyed great confidence; it is not rare to see Jews standing in justice before him, even when the opposing party is a coreligionist. In this case, it has been said, the law authorized Jews to appear before a *dayan*. The archives present hundreds of cases of Jews having recourse to the Islamic judge, the *cadi*, whether it is a civil or criminal case.

Things reached the point where Jewish jurists tried to limit this recourse, forbidding, for example, recourse to the Islamic tribunal for inheritance matters, or from giving a sworn statement. But apparently the Jews of Jerusalem did not respect these interdictions.

The tax records give a rather precise idea of the demography of the Holy City intra muros. For the year 1563, for example, the number of inhabitants is approximately 12,700, of which 1,600 are Christians, 1,200 are Jews, and 9,900 are Muslims. Jews made up less than 10 percent of the total population. That proportion was even lower in Hebron. The number of Jews in Jerusalem dwindled during the sixteenth century. In 1572, there were only 115 heads of families left; in 1606, only 60. If we take as the basis of our calculation a factor of 5 (a hypothesis accepted by demographers), we see that the total Jewish population in Jerusalem at the beginning of the seventeenth century was not above 300. Furthermore, the study of the records of home ownership shows that, due to their poverty, the Hierosolymitan Jews preferred to rent their homes rather than buy them.

For the next two centuries, contradictory figures do not allow a clear idea of the situation. These are evaluations based on the relations of the travels of Westerners. The nineteenth century constituted a decisive turn for the Jewish presence in the Old City of Jerusalem, and especially during the period of the Egyptian domination (1831–40). This can be inferred on the basis of a conversation held at that time, in June 1839, between Ahmed Dizdar, the governor of Jerusalem, and Moses Montefiore, the British Jewish philanthropist (it is the governor who is speaking):

> **The nineteenth century constituted a decisive turn for the Jewish presence in the Old City of Jerusalem.**

"You know the age when it was said, 'This is a Christian, and that a Jew, and there is a Mussulman!' but now . . . these times are past. Never ask what he is: let him be of whatsoever religion he may, do him justice, as the Lord of the world desired of us!"[4]

Demographic growth

Arabic and Hebraic archives from that time clearly show that the Jews—often of Polish origin—bought public houses or buildings (*kolel*), not only in the Jewish quarter but also in the Muslim ones. With the return of the Ottomans, the central power pursued the reforms already in process in the rest of the empire. These reforms brought with them an increase of activity among the Jews in the Old City and its environs, especially after 1860. This activity is reflected in a sustained rate of acquisitions of land and buildings, with the support of the European consulates in Jerusalem—mainly those of Russia, Great Britain, Germany, Austria, and France. Each of the European states stood behind its Israelite protégés residing in Palestine, and contributed the services of its ambassadors to Istanbul for the purpose of establishing real estate purchase contracts. This same period of the second half of the nineteenth century witnessed a growing interest in the regions beyond the walls of the Holy City.

In 1855, Montefiore acquired a piece of land near the southwest corner of the Old City, on which he built a small colony in 1859, consisting of thirty-four residences reserved for poor Jews, and known as the Mishkenot Sha'ananim, to which was added, after Montefiore's death, the Yemin Moshe quarter, named in his honor. This was the beginning of the Jewish expansion beyond the ramparts, and this establishment would be followed by many others, forming new quarters in which only Jews would settle. These Jews were represented at various administrative levels: there had been a Jewish representative on the Council of Jerusalem since 1840, and one on the District Council of Administration as well, and also in the general assembly of the *Mutasarrif* of Jerusalem. The Municipal Council, made up of five members, had one Jew, then two, when it increased its total membership to ten in 1868. Throughout the second half of the century, the rhythm of Jewish immigration to Jerusalem and Hebron accelerated. The year 1860 may be considered the decisive one in that respect.

This demographic growth was matched by urban development, both of private homes and public establishments: synagogues, religious schools, and hotels. Old synagogues were restored; others were built, such as al-Kherba in 1864, and the synagogue Tiferet Israel in 1876. The Eastern Jews restored four old synagogues: Eliahu ha-Navi (1835), Yohanan ben Zakai (1839), Kahal Tzion, and Istanbuli (1835). Some of these synagogues were built in the Ottoman style, also known as Late Byzantine. Before this period, the Jewish places of worship in the Old City were indistinguishable, from the outside at least, from other buildings; only after entering could one appreciate the interior spaciousness.

It may be said that the Jewish presence in Jerusalem was the longest and most durable during the periods of Muslim rule. This is evident in comparison with the periods prior to Islam. If, then, we consider that the presence of a true Jewish community dates from the Mamluk period (disregarding the Fatimid

In 1857, Moses Montefiore had constructed a mill on the lands he had acquired at the outskirts of the walls of Jerusalem, southwest of the port of Jaffa; then in 1860, he constructed the *Mishkenot Sh'ananim*, or "Peaceful Habitation," a collection of sixteen apartments. Photograph by John Mendel Diness, around 1860. Jerusalem, Israel Museum.

period—before the Crusades), we observe an uninterrupted presence of seven centuries under successive Muslim powers. Nowhere else in the world—not even in pre-Islamic Palestine—has Judaism known such continuity.

---

1. These registers of the Islamic ("Sharaic") tribunal of Jerusalem reflect the daily life of the community, from the beginning to the end of the Ottoman period: personal relationships, trials, decrees by the sultan, administrative measures, inheritances, marriage and divorce contracts, various grievances, management of mortmain property, and so on. These were invaluable documents, and very useful for the study of the social, economic, political, and administrative life of Ottoman Jerusalem. They also contain information on the other religious communities in Palestine.

2. See on this subject Isaiah Friedman, "The System of Capitulations and Its Effects on Turco-Jewish Relations in Palestine, 1856–1897," in *Palestine in the Late Ottoman Period: Political, Social, and Economic Transformation*, ed. David Kushner (Jerusalem: Yad Izhak Ben-Zvi Press, 1986), 280–93.

3. Amnon Cohen, *Jewish Life under Islam: Jerusalem in the Sixteenth Century* (Cambridge, MA: Harvard University Press, 1984), 225.

4. Ruth Kark, "The Question of the Exploitation of Lands during the Second Visit of Montefiore in Palestine in 1839," *Cathedra* 33 (1986): 59 (in Hebrew). [Kark's quote from Ahmed Dizdar also appears in her "Agricultural Land in Palestine: Letters to Sir Moses Montefiore," in *Transactions: The Jewish Historical Society of England* 29 (1982–86): 208.—Tr.].

Myths and Realities of Jerusalem for the Jews

During the Ottoman period Jerusalem was, for the Jews, a place of nostalgia whose name recurred in their daily prayers. Jerusalem, or Zion, represented a symbolic extension of the site of the destroyed Temple. During the Mamluk period, the site of the Mount of Olives, which faced the Temple, was replaced as a place of pilgrimage and ceremonies by the tomb of the prophet Samuel, north of the city. Beginning in the fifteenth century, this place, equally appreciated by the Karaites and considered sacred in the Muslim tradition, would become the most important site in the region for pilgrimages and the ceremonies of *ziyārah*, a popular Muslim feast day celebrated on the twenty-eighth of the month of Iyar, the anniversary of the death of the prophet Samuel. Other sacred sites of lesser importance in the city and its environs included the tomb of Rachel, the tomb of King David (which caused intercommunal strife at the end of the Mamluk period), royal tombs, the stelae on the sides of the Mount of Olives, and a portion of the Western Wall. Various circumstances caused certain sites to become more famous and others to fall into decline, among them whether Muslims had taken control of the site, problems of accessibility, or, to some degree, the influence of Kabbalah. Kabbalah took the view that the tomb of a zaddik favored the elevation of prayer. The masters of Kabbalah, beginning with Rabbi Isaac Luria (ha-Ari, 1534–1572), created dozens of religious sites in Galilee, redrawing the map of pilgrimages and placing at its center the village of Meron, site of the sepulchre of Rabbi Shimon bar Yochai, to which tradition attributes the redaction of the *Sefer ha-Zohar*.

Beyond mentions in prayers and religious ceremonies, the Jews expressed their connection with Jerusalem in various ways: immigration, pilgrimage, transfer of bodies for burial in the Land of Israel and especially Jerusalem, financial aid, and political support. With the change of regime, Istanbul, the capital of the Ottoman Empire, naturally replaced Cairo, the capital of the Mamluk sultans. Istanbul would replace Venice as the main European port from which immigrants to Palestine embarked, and it was in Istanbul that, in 1726, an institution named the "committee of officials of Jerusalem in Constantinople" (*Va'ad Peqidei Yerushalayim be-Kushta*) was created to oversee the financial affairs of Jerusalem's Jewish community, and afterward of those of the other holy cities. In the nineteenth century, this committee was supplanted in the domain of charity and financial matters by the "committee of officers and administrators" (*Va'ad Peqidim ve-ha Amarkalim*) located in Amsterdam.

The Jewish community of Jerusalem passed from a situation in which it occasionally asked for help in exceptional circumstances to a position that required permanent and continuous financial support, advancing the argument that the Jews of the Diaspora had a duty to help their brothers living in Palestine. Charity funds were created for this purpose in the Jewish communities of the Diaspora, and emissaries were sent from Palestine every two or three years to raise and collect these funds. The Jewish communities abroad did not always respond positively to the demands for aid, and they did not invariably welcome the emissaries with honor and joy. A diary kept by one of the greatest emissaries, Rabbi Haim Yosef David Azoulay, who undertook several fund-raising voyages in the second half of the eighteenth century, gives an eloquent testimony of the coldness, and even the occasional hostility, the emissaries encountered, even when they were beyond reproach. Thus, there was a discrepancy between the place of honor the Land of Israel held in the Jewish consciousness and the disposition of individuals to willingly act in its favor.

For the Jews, particularly after the beginning of the seventeenth century, Jerusalem was an idealized place, a land devoid of everything, a gathering of sacred sites. It appeared this way on maps and in illustrations: a configuration of points, without the least relation to actual topography or landscape. It was only upon their arrival there that immigrants discovered the difficulties of life in the Land of Israel ●

Yaron Ben Naeh, professor of Jewish studies at the Hebrew University of Jerusalem, is also director of the Center for Research and Study of Sephardi and Oriental Jewish Heritage. His publications include Jews in the Realm of the Sultans: Ottoman Jewish Society in the Seventeenth Century *(Mohr Siebeck, 2006).*

In the center, the Occidental Wall topped by the Dome of the Rock and the Mosque of Al-Aqsa, designed to look like the Temple and the Temple of Solomon, respectively, by superimposing topographies both real and imaginary. Around the circle are the figures of the thirteen "shrines." The majority of these places, particularly in Galilee, have been identified by the Safed Kabbalists in the sixteenth century. Tablecloth used to cover bread on the Shabbat table, from Palestine in the nineteenth century. Jerusalem, Israel Museum.

The Nasi Family, or the Dream of Tiberias

The Nasi, a family of Portuguese conversos, made a fortune thanks to Doña Gracia Nasi and her sister, Brianda Nasi, who were both wives of the Mendes brothers, owners of the second-largest European bank before the Spanish Inquisition. Exiled in Northern Europe, Doña Gracia returned to Italy, where, denounced by her sister as a "Judaizer," she was arrested.

But it was the Ottoman sultan himself who intervened several times on her behalf to the authorities of Venice, pledging himself for her to be freed and her goods returned to her. Because "Turkish policy was tolerant, liberal, and humane to a degree in comparison with that of Christian Europe,"[1] and she was thus able to return openly to Judaism, Doña Gracia left Italy and moved to Istanbul in 1554, accompanied by an impressive following of family, friends, servants, and slaves, and at the head of an immense fortune. Her cousin João Migues joined her the same year with the members of his retinue. He also returned to Judaism and was known thereafter by the Hebrew name Don Joseph Nasi. Their return to Judaism made a great impression, provoking amazement—even anger— among certain Europeans of the city.

Joseph made close contacts with the court of Suleiman the Magnificent, who hoped to obtain copious information from him on European enemies. Joseph also became closely associated with Prince Selim, who made it possible for him, when Selim ascended to the throne, to rise further in the court hierarchy. He received various marks of official honor, among them the dukedom of Naxos. An archipelago of the Aegean Sea surrounding the island of Naxos (along with a group of other Greek islands taken from the Venetians) was allotted to him, as well as the title (not, in fact, Ottoman) of Duke of Naxos.

His fortune allowed him to obtain the right to collect several of the most lucrative taxes, notably taxes on imported wines. He also engaged in the commerce of wax and honey. His aunt, Doña Gracia, for her part, conducted a maritime business of great breadth, especially with Italy, relying on a network of agents. Joseph's influence on Sultan Selim II is internationally known. Foreigners knew how to use him to serve their purposes. It is possible that he may have conducted espionage activities for Spain, or that he was a double agent.

The Nasi palace was a center of benevolence and charity, study, and the redaction and copying of manuscripts. Gracia was behind the creation of a yeshiva in Istanbul. In Salonika, she created a new community devoted to conversos returning to Judaism. Gracia became the most famous Jewish woman of her day, usually nicknamed simply "the Lady," ha-Geveret. She played a central political role in the communities of Istanbul and Salonika, and did not shrink from using her influence and from threatening to use her strength and power against anyone who did not bow to her requirements. Thus, she passed a commercial interdict against the port of Ancona after conversos were sent to be burned at the stake in that city on the pope's orders. The interdict sparked a controversy in the community and much internal tension before finally becoming inactive.

In the view of Cecil Roth, the biographer of the Nasi family, Don Joseph was no less than one of the "fathers of Zionism," who desired to obtain an independent or semiautonomous Jewish territory in Palestine. But the author also points out a historical error: it was in fact Doña Gracia, and not her nephew, who was the motivating force in the negotiations with the sultan; she demanded the right to collect the taxes of Tiberias and its environs in exchange for an annual payment of one thousand gold pieces, the construction of a rampart, and the conveyance of drinking water. It seems that her goal was to settle former conversos, who practiced various activities, especially the production of silks, in Tiberias.

After an agreement on the formal terms (around 1563), one of Joseph's agents was sent to negotiate directly. His mission did not move things forward significantly because neither the local population nor the governor of Damascus was particularly in favor of the operation. The main buildings and the synagogue were finished in the mid-1560s. The mulberry trees were planted to feed the silkworms and merino sheep —a species known for the quality of its wool—were perhaps brought from Spain. Also, date palms and citrons were planted around the city. According to the testimony of the Portuguese traveler Pantaleon de Abiero, it was rumored in Palestine that Doña Gracia intended to move to Tiberias with a number of newcomers. This rumor was perceived as a sign of the imminent arrival of the Messiah. But the end of the story was modest: in 1569, when Doña Gracia died, the rabbis could no longer rely on her help and had to appeal to wealthy patrons. During the 1570s, the dream of Tiberias ended: no crowd of people arrived to settle there, and Joseph himself, who continued to live in Istanbul, began to lose interest. At his death, the population of Tiberias was at a standstill. In the 1590s, Don Samuel ibn Ya'ish (formerly Avaro Mendès, who had received the title of Duke of Mytilene) replaced, to

Portrait of Doña Gracia Nasi, completed by Pastorino de Pasorini, medal in bronze recast in the nineteenth century after the original of the sixteenth century. Paris, Musée National du Moyen Âge, Strauss Collection, Rothschild Depot.

a certain extent, Joseph Nasi, and his son Jacob even moved to Tiberias to study the Torah there. ●

Yaron Ben Naeh, professor of Jewish studies at the Hebrew University of Jerusalem, is also director of the Center for Research and Study of Sephardi and Oriental Jewish Heritage. His publications include Jews in the Realm of the Sultans: Ottoman Jewish Society in the Seventeenth Century *(Mohr Siebeck, 2006).*

1. Cecil Roth, *Doña Gracia of the House of Nasi* (Philadelphia: Jewish Publication Society of America, 1948), 147.

Chapter II

Northern Africa

In Emergent Morocco
Emily Benichou Gottreich

Morocco as a protonational entity came into existence in the period stretching from the late fifteenth to the early nineteenth century. During this period its borders became fixed, its cities emerged as world capitals, and its defining political ideologies and institutions, including sharifism, maraboutism, the *abīd al-būkhāri,* and the *makhzen* (to name just a few), grew firmly entrenched. Meanwhile, Moroccan Jewish identity, despite its purported timelessness, likewise cohered into its recognizable form as a result of the new geopolitical and spiritual realities. The protonational identities forged during this period would be increasingly challenged by European intervention in the coming centuries, first by the Spanish and Portuguese, then more definitively by the British and French. The consolidation of the Moroccan state on the one hand and the Moroccan Jewish community on the other were not only concurrent processes but also, in many ways, contingent. The current chapter will trace these two processes, which culminated in a distinctive Moroccan culture characterized by unprecedented levels of Muslim-Jewish coexistence and cooperation.

Emily Benichou Gottreich

Is Associate Adjunct Professor of History and Middle Eastern Studies, vice chair for the Center for Middle Eastern Studies at the University of California, Berkeley, and president of the American Institute of Maghrib Studies (AIMS). Her research interests include the history of Jews in Morocco, North Africa, and the relations between Jews and Muslims. Her publications include *The Mellah of Marrakesh: Jewish and Muslim Space in Morocco's Red City* (Indiana University Press, 2006).

The Sephardic influx

The waning days of the last Zenata Berber dynasties (Marinids r. 1244–1465, Wattasids r. 1472–1554) brought great change to Moroccan society. Hitherto, Moroccans, while certainly not homogenous in terms of class or ethnicity, were nonetheless overwhelmingly of Berber (Amazigh) and/or Arabic culture and language. The majority of the Moroccan population lived in the south and the interior of the country. (Portuguese and Spanish settlements on the Atlantic

❯ See
Nota bene,
Intermediaries
between
Christians and
Muslims in
Oran, p. 233.

and Mediterranean seaboards inhibited settlement along the coast.) While most Jews lived simply, interspersed with Muslims in rural areas and villages, a few individuals had managed to ingratiate themselves with the Marinid court in Fez and were invested with greater responsibility and status. All that changed after 1492, however, when the Spanish Crown issued its writ of expulsion, jettisoning its Jews, known broadly thereafter as Sephardim, to be followed in short order by its Muslims. Although the precise number of exiles who sought refuge in Morocco is unknown, their social impact was clearly significant, particularly in the north, where Spanish is still spoken today. The Muslim immigrants were able to integrate into Moroccan society relatively quickly. The Jewish exiles (Heb., *megorashim*) had a more difficult time of it, a fact that is often glossed over in favor of the positive impact of this "precious" immigration.[1] For Moroccan Muslims, the arrival of the Sephardim meant overcrowding, competition for jobs, and increased prices in the souk. Even in the south, where far fewer Sephardim settled, their presence was destabilizing, a fact that lies behind Mawlay 'Abd al-Ghalib's creation of a walled Jewish quarter (*mellah*) in Marrakesh, where the Jews could be better contained and monitored.[2] Things were no easier for them in the Jewish microcosm. The Sephardim were a traumatized people, yet they were also extremely proud of their heritage and customs. They were distinguished by language (*Haketiya*, or Western Ladino), rituals, dress, food, and even aristocratic affectations (consistent with the Spanish emphasis on bloodlines, many prominent Sephardim identified themselves as belonging to the house of David). They were also responsible for bringing the first Hebrew printing press to Morocco, making Fez among the earliest publication centers since the end of the fifteenth century, followed by Tunis and Oran in the eighteenth and nineteenth, respectively. Seeing themselves as the inheritors of the high culture of al-Andalus, the Sephardim resisted mixing with the *toshavim*, the autochthonous Jewish population of Morocco, whom they derided

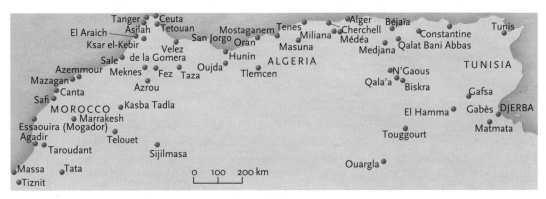

Jewish communities in North Africa in the fifteenth and sixteenth centuries.

as *foresteros*. In the capital cities, they maintained separate quarters from the indigenous Jews, and for a period did not even share the same *shkhita* (Heb., practices of ritual slaughter), making it impossible for members of the two communities to eat together, let alone intermarry. While many Sephardic practices were eventually assimilated into Moroccan Judaism, for example, the "Castilian Law" forbidding bigamy, integrating the Sephardim themselves was not easy.

Jews as intermediaries in emergent Morocco

The development of the Moroccan state during the sixteenth century provided a small cushion for these upheavals. In 1554 the Saadi dynasty came to power after a successful jihad to dislodge the Portuguese from the Atlantic coasts, something its predecessors had glaringly failed to do. This was followed in 1578 by a definitive Moroccan victory in the Battle of Ksar al-Kabir, which put an end to both the Portuguese threat from the North and Ottoman attempts at expansionism from the East. The relief felt by the Sephardic Jews of Morocco was tremendous. The threat of Christianization, which had hung over their heads for centuries, was now finally

> *" Sephardim were especially useful middlemen, thanks to their mobility, contacts, and firsthand knowledge of Europe. "*

over. Jews in the North commemorated the events with a special "Pourim de los Cristianos."[3] Most important, these victories left Morocco free to claim a more influential—and lucrative—calling as the full economic and diplomatic partner of the emerging European powers, namely, England, France, and the Netherlands. Moroccan Jews found unprecedented opportunities in the emerging new world order, which in turn brought certain of them into close contact with the Moroccan Muslim elite. The Sephardim were especially useful middlemen, thanks to their mobility, contacts, and firsthand knowledge of Europe. From their ranks came several of the outstanding diplomats of the era, including the towering figure of Samuel Pallache.[4] The Saadi state reached its apex under Sultan Ahmad al-Mansur (r. 1578–1603), who sought to link Morocco both to the Atlantic discoveries,[5] and, more successfully, to the trans-Saharan trade. Jewish and Muslim merchants alike profited from the reinvigorated economy. Though Jews tended to dominate the sugar trade and Muslims the slave trade, members of both groups collaborated in all sectors of the Moroccan economy. The most successful merchants bore the title of *tujjār al-Sulṭān* (sing., *tājir*; royal merchants), who conducted trade on behalf of the *makhzan*. The leaders of each individual Jewish community, often themselves members of the *tujjār*, were given the title *shaykh al-yahūd* (shaykh of the Jews), in which capacity they acted as intermediaries between the *makhzan* and their coreligionists on the local level. Jewish merchants were instrumental in introducing new products into Morocco at this time, including staples like tea, coffee, and tobacco. Eventually entire new cities were built to accommodate the growing mercantile economy. Mogador, later named Essaouira, once a small fishing village, was developed in the eighteenth century and quickly became a central node in Morocco's long-distance trade, much of which was conducted by Jews, who came to comprise nearly half the population.

◗ See Nota bene, Essaouira, pp. 231–232.

The emergence of the state and its power to create or consolidate Jewish communities within national boundaries was a primary influence on Muslim-Jewish relations during this period. Undergirding these developments was a movement toward, if not secularism, at least a state-centered religious identity that was less hostile to Jews than at any time previously. In the sixteenth century, Morocco began to move away from a tribal-based power system toward sharifism, which privileged those who could claim descent from Muhammad. Sharifism had functioned as a foil to authority previously, but under the Saadis it became increasingly fused with notions of authority and legitimacy. With this shift came a changed attitude toward the Jews: whereas in earlier periods sharifism had been associated with animosity toward Jews, under the Saadis, the tables had turned to the point that certain Sufi groups rebelled against the Saadis precisely because they were seen as maintaining too close relations with Jews.[6] But having conceded sharifism to the *makhzan*, they had lost an important ideological weapon in the battle.

The centralization that began under the Saadis was lended additional form and meaning by the Alawis, the succeeding sharifian dynasty (r. 1659–today), though the Alawis were able to assert their dominance over Morocco only in fits and starts. The slow collapse of Saadi rule had left Morocco deeply fragmented. While Mawlay Muhammad al-Shaykh was able to hold on to power in Marrakesh until 1655, in the North, various actors took advantage of the power vacuum to assert their independence. Salé functioned as an all but independent state populated by *moriscos*, Muslims

> *Whereas in earlier periods sharifism had been associated with animosity toward Jews, under the Saadis the tables had turned.*

from the Iberian Peninsula (and Spanish Jews), which from 1660 was ruled by the "pirate king" of the North, al-Khidr Ghaylan. Relations between the sharifs and the Sufi *tariqa*-s were particularly tempestuous, with two rival marabouts, the charismatic head of the *zawiya* of Dila and the shaykh of Massa, fighting for supremacy. The marabout of Dila conquered Fez in 1641. It fell to Mawlay Rashid to recapture it and overthrow the *zawiya*, one of his defining acts, which established his position as the true founder of the Alawi dynasty. Jews in Fez and in the area of the *zawiya* were caught in the crossfire. According to the main Jewish source of the period, the mid-seventeenth century was known as the *arba'in san'a diyal fitna*, "the forty years of chaos." It reports that in the year 546 (1645), "all the synagogues were closed and sealed by order of the sodomite of the *zawiya*," and subsequently

Synagogue in Fes. Charles Landelle, oil on canvas,
1866. Paris, private collection.

destroyed.[7] Compounding the physical destruction, Jews were also subject to excessive taxation. However, it should be kept in mind that all Moroccans, not just Jews, were victims of taxation. Along similar lines, both Jews and Muslims suffered terribly during Morocco's terrible draughts, particularly those of 1603–6 and 1662–69, which resulted in widespread hunger and famine.

Sufi groups and Sabbateans

The Sufi challenge had an interesting parallel in Moroccan Jewish society in the form of Sabbateanism, the mystical movement established in the Ottoman Empire by Shabbatai Tsvi, the so-called false messiah, who converted to Islam in 1666 and whose antinomian theology wreaked havoc throughout the Jewish world. Although Shabbatai himself never traveled as far west as Morocco, the introduction of many of the writings associated with the movement and the arrival of some of its main figures allowed Sabbateanism to establish a firm foothold. As in the Ottoman Empire, Sabbateanism found its greatest supporters among the Sephardim, especially the neo-Christians, or *conversos*. Special centers for reconversion had been established

⟩ See Nota bene, Sabbatai Zevi, pp. 197–199.

in Morocco in the sixteenth century to help *conversos* return to Judaism, but they nonetheless remained vulnerable. Decades of living outwardly as Christians had left them with a tenuous grasp on Jewish law and ritual, which they knew in an amalgamated form if at all. Thus Salé, a city dominated by Iberian exiles, both Muslim and Jewish, became the most important center for Moroccan Sabbateanism—Elisha Ashkenazi, the father of Nathan of Gaza, settled in Salé, and one of the movement's most zealous leaders, Ya'akov b. Sa'adun, lived there as well[8]—followed by Meknes, also a Sephardic stronghold, where a Sabbatean prophet by the name of Joseph ben Sur emerged in the late seventeenth century.

It is likely that links existed between Sufi groups and Sabbateans in Morocco, as they clearly did in the Ottoman Empire.[9] At the very least, we know that the previously mentioned Jewish community living in the area of the Dila *zawiya* included Sabbateans, suggesting some degree of frequentation.[10] Yet it is also true that conversion was a less prominent feature of Sabbateanism in Morocco than elsewhere, either in the form of Sabbateans converting to Islam after 1666 (i.e., following Shabbatai's example) or of Muslims joining the movement. Most important, in Morocco, the traditional Jewish authorities succeeded in controlling and ultimately assimilating the movement into normative Moroccan Judaism. Certain prayers and supplications from Sabbatean works were allowed to enter into the liturgy and prayer books, where they remain today.[11] The strong messianic yearning in Sabbateanism was consciously separated from the rest of the theology of the "cult": it was recognized as an acceptable tenet of Judaism and was allowed to persist. Thus vestiges of Sabbateanism were visible in Morocco as late as 1826: a letter from a British traveler describes an annual event whereby the Jews would select a virgin from their community and enclose her in a crate. They would then watch and wait for her to become pregnant by the Holy Ghost, which meant she would give birth to the messiah. But these behaviors were more indicative of a religious rift.[12] Even today, when the rationalist Maimonides is accepted as the ultimate legal source by Moroccan Jews, strong mystical tendencies are still apparent in many aspects of Moroccan Judaism, such as saint veneration or the offering of toys or money to children on Tisha B'Av.[13] These concessions are partly responsible for "saving" Moroccan Judaism from the fate of European Judaism, which became split between Haskalah and Hasidism in the post-Sabbatean era, while also rendering it uniquely resilient to European colonial intervention in the religious sphere.

A new order

With the ascension of Sultan Mawlay Ismail in 1672, certain practices that strongly reinforced the vertical relationship between the *makhzan* and the Jews, as well as changes that brought Muslims and Jews closer together, were instituted. For example, many ruined synagogues were rebuilt under Mawlay Ismail, bringing new spiritual (and economic) energy to the various communities. The new capital built in Meknes attracted migrants from throughout Morocco, including enough Jews for him to order the building of a *mellah* there in 1679, the third such entity in Morocco after those of Fez and Marrakesh. Muslim and Jewish craftsmen and artisans were employed for all these projects. At the same time, however, other external forces were working to pull apart Muslim-Jewish ties. Knowing that their appeal to Moroccan Muslims was limited, European powers were quick to identify the potential instrumentality of Moroccan Jews for gaining a political and economic foothold in the country. Jews were used as intermediaries in the ransoming of European captives, treaty negotiations, and the import/export trade.

As a result of increased European intervention, Morocco's port cities began to develop dramatically in the eighteenth century, a process that eventually led to their eclipsing of the traditional inland economic centers. This process was played out on the microcosmic level among the *tujjār al-Sul ān*, both Jews and Muslims, who emigrated from the inland centers to the coasts to take advantage of the new opportunities. Among the Jews, these included certain members of the Corcos family of Marrakesh, a branch of which grew to great prominence in Essaouira. On the national level, ▶ See Nota bene, Essaouira, pp. 231–232. Jewish-Muslim relations continued to ebb and flow, with a particular low point coming in 1790–92, during Mawlay Yazid's "reign of terror" as the country fell into a vicious civil war abetted by the Spanish. The atrocities committed against the Jews during this period were among the last to escape the direct intercession of outside forces, however. As the nineteenth century dawned, European organizations, including the Board of Deputies of British Jews, the Alliance Israélite Universelle, and the Anglo-Jewish Association, driven by multifaceted motives, began to take careful notice of the situation of the Jews, and Jewish-Muslim relations, in Morocco, and to take action.

---

1. The expression comes from Fernand Braudel, "Espangnols et mauresques," *Annales E.S.C.* (1947): 4:403.

2. Emily Gottreich, *The Mellah of Marrakesh: Jewish and Muslim Space in Morocco's Red City* (Bloomington: Indiana University Press, 2007), 21–25.

3. Purim was originally a biblical celebration commemorating the miraculous rescue of the Jews of Persia, as the Book of Esther recounts. Subsequently, other local Purims were born to commemorate the rescue of a particular community.

4. For a full-length study on Samuel Pallache, see Mercedes Garcia Arenal and Gerard Wiegers, *A Man of Three Worlds: Samuel Pallache; A Moroccan Jew in Catholic and Protestant Europe* (Baltimore: Johns Hopkins University Press, 2003).

5. Mercedes Garcia Arenal, *Ahmad al-Mansur: The Beginning of Modern Morocco* (Oxford: One World, 2009).

6. In 1614, the Sufi shaykh Yahya bin 'Abdallah rebelled against Mawlay Zaydan in Marrakesh to protest the presence in the court of Jews like Abraham Wa'ish, who was in charge of the treasury, and Samuel Pallache. See Henri de Castries and Pierre de Cenival, *Les sources inédites de l'histoire du Maroc*, Archives et Bibliothèques des Pays-Bas (Paris: Leroux, 1907), 2:399.

7.   *Divre ha-yamim shel Fez*, fol. 20a, as cited by H. Z. Hirschberg, *A History of the Jews in North Africa* (Leiden: Brill, 1981), 2:237–38. It should be noted that the Jews of the *zawiya* were resettled in Fez, possibly due to their relative prosperity and political neutrality. Adherents of the marabout were all killed.

8.   See the descriptions of Germain Mouette, a Frenchman captured by pirates who was held in Salé from 1670–81, in *Relations de captivité dans les royaumes de Fez et de Maroc* (Paris: Mercure de France, 2002), 47–49.

9.   See Marc Baer, *Honored by the Glory of Islam* (Oxford: Oxford University Press, 2007), 123–24, 129; and Matt Goldish, *The Sabbatean Prophets* (Cambridge, MA: Harvard University Press, 2004), 39–40. Both authors also discuss the influence of Christian millenarian movements on the development of Sabbateanism in the Ottoman Empire. This does not appear to have been a contributing factor in Morocco, where indigenous Christian communities ceased to exist after the Almohad period.

10.   See Hirschberg, *A History of the Jews in North Africa*, 2:248.

11.   Specifically those from the controversial text *Hemdat Yamim*, which, by the eighteenth century, had become a mainstay of Moroccan Jewish religious tradition.

12.   G. R. Beauclerk, *A Journey to Morocco in 1826* (London, 1828).

13.   Tisha B'Av, the ninth day of Av, normally is a day of intense mourning: it commemorates the destruction of the First and Second Temples of Jerusalem, and, more generally, the sufferings of exile. Sabbateanism, based on a midrashic story that the Messiah was born on this day, transforms the day of mourning and fasting into a celebration of the coming of the Messiah.

Essaouira

The town of Essaouira (known as Mogador to Europeans) was Morocco's principal seaport for foreign trade from the latter half of the eighteenth until the late nineteenth century. The Jews of Essaouira (Mogador) were proportionally one of the largest Jewish communities of any city of the Muslim world, about 30 to 50 percent of the population for much of the town's existence. Founded in 1764 by the sultan Sidi Muhammad ibn 'Abdallah, to serve as the port of Morocco's southern capital, Marrakesh, the town was settled by many inhabitants from the southern Atlantic port of Agadir, which was shut to commerce. Jews were among the Agadiris who settled in the new port, and they were joined by other Jews from the major Jewish communities of Morocco.

In the first decade of the town's existence, representatives from some of the major merchant families of Morocco settled there, including Macnin, Sebag, and Pinto of Marrakesh; Hadida and Israel of Tetouan; Merran of Safi; and Guedalla of Agadir. In the late eighteenth and first decades of the nineteenth century, they were joined by other Moroccan families who figured among the town's important merchants: for example, Corcos, Afriat, Ohayon, and Elmaleh. Representatives of prominent Algerian merchant families, such as Cohen-Solal and Boujnah, also settled in the new town. These Jewish merchants were key intermediaries between Morocco and Europe, connected to Jewish and Muslim traders in the interior of Morocco, especially in the Southwest (for example, Oued Noun, Iligh, and Ifrane of the Anti-Atlas), along the trans-Saharan trade routes, and to their agents in European commercial centers such as Livorno, Marseilles, Amsterdam, and London. The most important merchants in Essaouira, the *tujjār*

of the sultans, were extended credit to trade and inhabited *makhzan*-owned houses in the elite casbah quarter of the town. The majority of the twenty to thirty royal merchants, listed in the *makhzan* registers as recipients of *makhzan* credit, were Jews. The elite Jewish families maintained close connections to the sultans, who in turn protected their commercial interests as well as their property rights. This relationship was maintained through the exchange of gifts, and mutual interests in maintaining the preeminent position of Essaouira as Morocco's principal port of trade.

The affluent Jews were dependent on the mass of poorer Jews, peddlers who plied their wares in the markets, workers who prepared goods for export, such as goatskins and ostrich feathers, and

Jewish musicians in Mogador. Eugène Delacroix, 1847. Paris, Louvre Museum.

231

simple artisans. Thousands of Jews, primarily from the Sous region of Morocco, came to settle in the town and inhabited the *mellah*. Initially the Jewish community did not live in a separate quarter, but in 1807 the sultan, Mawlay Sulayman, decreed that Jews in Essaouira, and in a number of other cities that did not have *mellahs*—Rabat, Salé, and Tetouan—should be compelled to live in a separate Jewish quarter. A few Jews from among the elite Jewish merchants were able to escape the injunction, and continued to inhabit the casbah, later joined by other Jewish merchants. From the time of its foundation, the Jewish merchants bought land and property in the *mellah*, including commercial premises and synagogues, a form of investment from profits accruing from trade. The population of Essaouira doubled from the late eighteenth to the late nineteenth centuries, from about 8–10,000 to about 17–20,000; the Jewish population may have reached 10,000. The growth of the number of inhabitants put pressure on the existing neighborhoods, and in the 1860s a new casbah quarter was built for the merchants; efforts were made, however, to expand the area of the *mellah*, increasingly overcrowded by poor migrants from the Sous (the area of the *mellah* formed one-eighth or one-ninth of the town, but housed about 40 percent of the total population). Though some new shops were built by the *makhzan* in the 1860s,

the expansion of the *mellah* dwellings was vertical, with additional floors spiraling upward; only in the late nineteenth century was an adjacent area added to the *mellah*.

While Jews lived somewhat separate lives, the *mellah* was hardly a place of confinement, and Muslims and Jews interacted in the marketplace, port, and regional weekly markets. Numerous shops in the bazaar (*sūq*) were rented by Jews, many of which belonged to the *hubus* (*habous*), Muslim pious endowments, and Jewish merchants owned or rented shops and warehouses in the medina. Jews and Muslims frequently entered into business partnerships, and Jews frequently loaned money to Muslims with whom they had commercial dealings. So numerous were the Jews of the town that the rhythms of daily life were very much ordered by the Jewish weekly and annual cycle (the market closed on Shabbat and Jewish holidays). The interdependency between Muslims and Jews helped maintain a system of relative trustworthiness: Muslims depended on Jewish brokers to market their merchandise, while Jews depended on Muslim transporters to convey their goods over long distances. ●

Daniel J. Schroeter is professor of history at the University of Minnesota, Minneapolis, where he holds the Amos S. Deinard Chair in Jewish History. His publications include The Sultan's Jew: Morocco and the Sephardi World *(Stanford University Press, 2002).*

Intermediaries between Christians and Muslims in Oran

The relations between Jews and Muslims in the Maghreb during the modern period were strongly marked by the military, diplomatic, and commercial presence of the Spanish and Portuguese monarchies in the region. The Sephardim, who were able to speak Spanish as well as Arabic or Berber, acted as intermediaries between Christian and Muslim powers. The expulsion of the Jews from Spain in 1492 prompted hundreds of families to settle in the Maghreb, where many Jewish communities were established. The arrival of Spanish- and Portuguese-speaking Jews in the region came about at a time when a network of small forts and larger fortifications called Christian presidios was being consolidated. Historians disagree on the number of Jews expelled from Spain in 1492, and it is even more difficult to assess how many of those chose to settle in the Maghreb—though many sources attest to their substantial numbers. Families from Sepharad joined communities already present in Moroccan lands, particularly Fez and Salé. The Straits of Gibraltar in the last centuries of the Middle Ages no longer constituted an insurmountable barrier. The implantation of the Portuguese in Ceuta in 1415 inaugurated an era during which Portuguese, Castilians, and Genoese of Christian faith, on one side, and Muslims from Grenada and Jews, on the other, could pass from one continent to the other, depending on their objectives. For periods of varying lengths from the fifteenth to the seventeenth centuries, the Portuguese and the Spanish established a string of military presidios in Mogador, Mazagan, Larache, La Mamora, Tangiers, Ceuta, Alhucemas, Melilla, Oran-Mers el-Kébir, and as far as La Goulette.

The best-known case documented by available archives remains that of the city of Oran, where the three religions coexisted from 1507 to 1669. When the Spanish troops seized the city of Oran and the port of Mers el-Kébir from the Zayanid kingdom of Tlemcen (1507–9), many Jewish families were living there. Some of them were from Spain, which they had fled upon the expulsion of 1492, some even earlier. These people spoke both Castilian and the languages of North Africa, and so were given authorization from the Catholic kings, then from Charles V, to remain there officially. Since the city was under the dual jurisdiction of Castile and the archbishopric of Toledo, the 1492 decree of the expulsion of the Jews should have applied to it as in any other place in Spanish territory. This authorization was, at the beginning, limited to two or three individuals, along with their families: the Satorras, the Cansinos, and the Zamirous. But the reason for the exceptional case of Oran resides less in the presence of influential Jews than in the fact that the authorities of the Castilian Crown recognized this "anomaly" as a "necessary evil."

The new Spanish municipal and military institutions of Oran and Mers el-Kébir would not have been able to interact with their regional environment without interpreters. Thus, it was in their capacity as translators (*lenguas*) that influential Jews were allowed to remain within the city walls; later, some were probably able to translate not only Arab and Berber, but also Osmanlı Turkish into Spanish. The king of Tlemcen, from the beginning of the Hispanic presence in his territory, established diplomatic relations with his Spanish rivals and negotiated economic and fiscal arrangements in order to assess their respective shares of the regional agricultural production. The other Jewish families acted as Tlemcen's agents toward the Christian authorities of Oran. In order to carry out their missions, they had occasion to reside alternately in either city. Thus, at the beginning of the sixteenth century, only three families had been allowed within the presidio. But from 1527–30 on, the emperor Charles V was obliged to accept the residence of twenty-eight Jewish families in his city of Oran. Their role in diplomatic and commercial relations within the surrounding region proved indispensable. On that basis, the little community, in the course of the seventeenth century, grew to the respectable size of about five hundred people, and had a synagogue in which a rabbi, often of the Cansino family, officiated. But the real importance of the community was even greater if one takes into account the substantial population of dependents and slaves who worked in its service; in that Christian jurisdictional and religious context, the dependents of Jews could only be Jews or Muslims.

Oran was not the only place where the function of agent and interpreter for the local Christian powers in their relations with the regional populations and authorities was entrusted to prominent Jews. David el-Hatat was the interpreter of the Portuguese captain general of Ceuta; Juda Pariente and Brahim Malagui performed the same function in Melilla. But the particular strength of the Jews of Oran came from the fact that they had stable family networks in Tlemcen and Mostaganem, but also extending as far as Salé. The actual tolerance toward these Jewish families, within the legal framework of the Crown of Castile, stretched beyond the perimeter of the presidios in the Maghreb. Indeed, in certain cases, merchants belonging to these families contracted directly with Christian merchants of the ports of Malaga or Cartagena, without going through the intermediary of Christians from North Africa. The Spanish archives, especially those of the Inquisition, make mention of the presence of prominent Jews at the marketplaces of Castile in the sixteenth and seventeenth centuries. These were probably a small number of individuals who were, in addition, closely watched from the moment of their debarkation. Still, the particular

conditions of political and economic life in North Africa led the kings of Spain to accept this bending of the principle of territorial prohibition to any individual of Jewish or Muslim religion. Maghreb Muslims, too (but later), benefited from exceptions to the rule. This was the case with the arrival of hundreds of Muslim auxiliaries to the Spanish army who settled in Andalusia between 1708 and 1732, when the city of Oran fell into the hands of the Turks and the inhabitants of Algiers.

A very revealing anecdote concerning these exchanges was related by a member of the great Cansino family. Jacob Cansino was not only an interpreter and negotiator but also a collector of taxes owed by neighboring tribes to the Christian authorities of Oran. So he was constantly in contact with the Muslim pastors and farmers from the hinterlands of Algiers. He issued documents to them showing their regular payments made to the municipality. One day in October 1659, as he was camping in a tent in the farming area, he was visited by an elderly peasant: "A poor Moor from the Arab village of el-Bazasz and his wife, dressed in a *teliz*, because she did not have the wherewithal to obtain an *Al-quicel*, were in tears because the cow they owned had been stolen and because people from Uled Balegh had beaten them and tied the little shepherd of their flock to a tree; they were still looking for their sheep. To console them, I had them stay with me and had dinner given to them, continuing to speak of the incident and of others concerning complaints by people from Jaffa. Then I requested that two tales by ben Garein be read to them, as in the tragedies of Don Quixote."[1] This episode is very striking in that it shows the degree of intimacy between a Jewish agent of the Christian power and the Muslim inhabitants of the region in a generalized system of mutual negotiation and exchanges.

Among the Jews of Oran, the Cansino family was probably the best known in seventeenth-century Castile. Their greatest notoriety, in the court of Madrid at least, was attained when Isaac Cansino had an important work printed under his name in 1638: the *Book of the Splendors of the City of Constantinople*, presented as the translation of a work by Rabbi Almosnino of Salonika. The fact that it was published in Madrid is remarkable in every way. Cansino, its translator and publisher, accompanied the work with a presentation of his family, the most emblematic of the community of Oran. Through this portrait, he revealed to a public readership, which would not be well informed on the matter, the existence of a Judaism of Oran—that is, a Spanish Judaism—still quite alive. He dedicated his publication to the Count-Duke of Olivares, thus acting as any other author of the Spanish system of letters and of bookselling of his time. Finally, through Moses Almosnino, the author he translates here, he disseminates praises for the Ottoman sultan, who is capable of religious tolerance with respect to the non-Muslims of his empire. Thus the Spanish readers find, in their own language, the demonstration that the sultan, whom they considered the most despotic of sovereigns, was capable of greater goodwill than the kings of Spain were toward his infidel subjects. The message could not be clearer, but it is not certain that it was very helpful to Philip IV's favorite at the very moment when he was being attacked by his opponents, who presented him as the friend of Portuguese bankers of Jewish origin.

But we must not limit ourselves to these manifestations of openness and intimacy taken out of the larger picture of an era in which mutual contempt often overrode respect. In connection with the relations between Jews and Muslims as they may be seen in the context of the Christian presidios of North Africa, we cannot pass over in silence the intense participation of the great Jewish families in the Muslim slave trade. The two main clans of the Oran community were the two largest slave owners and traders. Of course, that activity was in no way particular to Jews: it was common to all contemporaries as well. The history

of the intertwined captivities of Jews, Christians, and Muslims in the Mediterranean in the modern era shows this quite clearly.

The history of the main Jewish community of the Hispanic Maghreb is interrupted in 1669 with the total expulsion of the Jews from Oran. They had to liquidate their goods in a few weeks and embark en masse in ships that transported them to Livorno and Nice. The expulsion was decided on in the feverish context of the crisis brought about by the mystic episode of Sabbatai Zevi and the terror inspired by the Ottoman conquest of the island of Crete in 1667. As always, this sort of event is presented from the Spanish perspective as a glorious exploit of Catholic orthodoxy, and as a tragedy by the victims. After the expulsion, we may reasonably assume that the

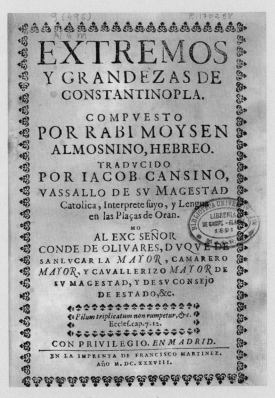

Cover of the book *Extremos y grandezas de Constantinople*, by Rabbi Almosnino of Salonika, translated by Jacob Cansino. Madrid, 1638. Madrid, Complutense University.

Spanish of Oran continued to deal with the Jews of the Maghreb. The later documentation, especially in the eighteenth century, indicates, between the lines, that prominent Jews continued to gravitate to the Christian presidios of North Africa, while at the same time retaining their bases on Islamic soil.

On one point, at least, Christians and Muslims were in agreement: the Jews were useful in facilitating their endless negotiations in a situation marked by chronic instability. But is this enough to make the case for a continuum between the experience of the Hispanic Oran of the modern period and the situation of intercommunity relations in Oran during the French Empire? That step is too hazardous to be taken without solid proof. It is preferable, pending the discovery of new documents, to assume that these two histories are in fact separate. The question of the relations between Jews and Muslims in French colonial Algeria, in both Oran and the rest of the country, is probably a totally different matter. ●

Jean-Frédéric Schaub is director of studies at the École des Hautes Études en Sciences Sociales (EHESS) in Paris. His publications include Les Juifs du roi d'Espagne: Oran 1507–1669 *(Hachette Littératures, 1999);* La France espagnole: Les racines hispaniques de l'absolutisme français *(Seuil, 2003);* Lois, justice, coutume *(EHESS, 2005);* Oroonoko: Prince et esclave *(Seuil, 2008); and* L'Europe a-t-elle une histoire? *(Albin Michel, 2008).*

---

1. Quoted and translated in Jean-Frédéric Schaub, *Les Juifs du roi d'Espagne* [The Jews of the King of Spain] (Paris: Hachette Littératures, 1999), 114.

Jews in Libya

Jews lived in Libya before the Muslim conquests of North Africa. According to the Arab historian Ibn Khaldun, tribal groups in a mountainous region of Tripolitania, Jebel Nefusa, accepted the Jewish religion before Islam arrived. There are debates about the certainty of this information, while it is likely that Jews migrated into Libya soon after Muslim presence was established there.

Historical documentation of life in Libya is thin. Gravestones in the Jebel Nefusa from the twelfth to the thirteenth centuries indicate the presence of Jewish life, and there is also evidence that Jews in the whole region suffered under the harsh rule of the Almohads at that time. Three hundred years later, when Tripoli was conquered by Spain during the first half of the sixteenth century, and the Spanish Inquisition was in force in the city, the interior mountain communities served as a refuge for the Jews, and Jewish life was able to quietly continue there.

A more continuous view of Jewish life begins toward the end of the eighteenth century. One prominent Jew, Abraham Khalfon (1741–1819), served as a head of the community, representing it to the ruler of Tripoli, and was also a scholar. He composed a history in Hebrew utilizing records in government archives and documents in the rabbinic court. In his own days, a tyrannical ruler from abroad controlled the city between 1793 and 1795, oppressing both Muslims and Jews. Members of both communities rejoiced when the invader was overthrown, and the Jews instituted a local Purim holiday to commemorate the date of his fall.[1]

Much of Khalfon's history was later lost, but part was copied into the Hebrew manuscript of Mordecai Ha-Cohen (1856–1929), a native of Tripoli.[2] Ha-Cohen described both Muslim and Jewish life in the city during the period of the nineteenth-century Ottoman reforms. In this new situation, Rabbi Yaaqov Maimon was able to participate as a judge in the reorganized court, along with Muslim judges. Ha-Cohen's portrayal of this development assumes that there was overlap in the legal understandings of Jews and Muslims regarding a range of issues that might come before the court.

Later in the nineteenth century, another rabbi, from abroad, criticized Jews in Tripoli for visiting Muslim

A Libyan rabbi. Italian postcard, 1912.
Paris, private collection.

coffeehouses upon finishing Sabbath morning prayer. This had long been the local custom, and Jews returned to the shops after the Sabbath ended to pay for what they had ordered. On the other hand, there still were occasions, like the *mawlid* (birthday celebration) of Muhammad, during which Jews and Christians in Tripoli cautiously kept off the streets lest outbursts of religious ecstasy be directed against them. By the end of the century, growing influence from Italy brought new factors into the fabric of daily life that fundamentally affected relationships between Muslims and Jews. ●

Harvey E. Goldberg is professor emeritus and the Sarah Allen Shaine Chair in Sociology and Anthropology at the Hebrew University of Jerusalem. His work has sought to combine anthropology and Jewish studies, including a translation from Hebrew of an indigenous account of the Jews of Libya: The Book of Mordechai by Mordecai Hacohen *(Philadelphia, Institute for the Study of Human Issues, 1980, 1993). He is the author of* Cave Dwellers and Citrus Growers *(New York, Cambridge University Press, 1972) and* Jewish Life in Muslim Libya *(University of Chicago Press, 1990), and editor of* Sephardi and Middle Eastern Jewries *(Indiana University Press, 1996).*

---

1. Harvey E. Goldberg, "Les jeux de Pourim et leurs déclinaisons à Tripoli: Perspective comparative sur l'usage social des histoires bibliques," *Annales: Histoire, Sciences Sociales* 49 (1994): 1183–95.
2. Mordecaï Ha-Cohen, *Higgid Mordecaï: Histoire de la Libye et de ses Juifs, lieux d'habitation et coutumes* [in Hebrew]. Edited and annotated by Harvey Goldberg (Jerusalem: Ben-Zvi Institute, 1978).

Chapter III
Asia and the Middle East

The Jews in Iran
Vera Basch Moreen

The long and complex history of the Jews in Iran dates as far back as 586 B.C.E., when Nebuchadnezzar exiled thousands of Jews from Judea to Babylonia. The late medieval and premodern period of this sojourn, dating approximately between the fifteenth and nineteenth centuries, occurred during formative centuries in Iranian history, characterized primarily by the struggle to define and consolidate the borders and character of the future state of Iran. Part of the Abbasid caliphate until the rise of the Buyid dynasty (945–1055 C.E.), vand a substantial kingdom in the realm of the Mongols and their descendants (1258–1388), Iran's distinctive identity came to prevail against the physical and intellectual conquest of both Arabs and Mongols. Thus the fate of various non-Muslim minorities,

Vera Basch Moreen

Works at the Center for Advanced Judaic Studies of Jewish Studies at the University of Pennsylvania. A specialist in Judeo-Persian studies, she is coeditor of the *Encyclopedia of Jews in the Islamic World* (Brill, 2011). Her publications include *In Queen Esther's Garden: An Anthology of Judeo-Persian Literature* (Yale University Press, 2000).

including the Jews, unfolded against a stage in perpetual political and religious turmoil. We lack information about Iranian Jews during the Timurid (1405–1506) and the Aq Qoyunlu (also called the White Sheep Turkmen, 1370–1502) periods. However, the absence of sources relative to the history of Iranian Jewry is remedied, more or less, after the advent of the Safavid dynasty (1501–1736).

The Safavid era

The Safavid dynasty's founder, Shah Isma'il I (r. 1501–24), who compelled the hitherto largely Sunni realm of Iran to become Shi'i, focused primarily on defeating the Aq Qoyunlu, the Uzbeks, and the Ottomans, his Sunni foes, rather than on non-Muslim minorities, such as the Jews. However, two European travelers attest that he certainly disliked them. Tomé Pires, the Portuguese ambassador to

China, who visited Iran in 1511–12, wrote, "He [Shah Isma'il] reforms our churches, destroys the houses of all Moors [Sunnis?], and never spares the life of any Jew."[1] And Raphael du Mans, a later traveler, wrote in the 1660s, "So deep is his [Shah Isma'il's] hate that whenever he sees a Jew he orders to put out his eyes."[2]

During the reign of Shah 'Abbas I (1581–1629), at the apex of Safavid rule, Iranian Jewish historiography got its start with Babai ibn Lutf's *Kitab-i anusi* (*KA*; The Book of a Forced Convert).[3] His chronicle relates the periodic persecution of Iranian Jews between 1617 and 1662 and describes selective events, mainly as they pertain to Jews, from the reigns of shahs 'Abbas I, Safi I (1629–42), and 'Abbas II (1642–66). Some of the external events that *KA* refers to that are not related to the Jews are actually corroborated by an Iranian chronicle, *'Abbasnama*, by Muhammad Tahir Wahid Qazvini,[4] the principal source for the reign of 'Abbas II, which is why Ibn Lutf, a native of Kashan, can be considered a reliable chronicler of events affecting the Jews. He appears to have witnessed some of the persecutions, primarily the forced conversions that occurred during the reign of 'Abbas II. But the Jews were not the only group that suffered during 'Abbas I's attempts to centralize his kingdom and grasp all

> "*Between 1656 and 1662, Muhammad Beg made an all-out effort to convert all the Jews to Shi'i Islam.*"

power in his hands. There is no information regarding the number of Iranian Jews who converted to Islam during his reign, and Ibn Lutf relates that Iranian Jews regained full religious freedom during the reign of his successor, Safi I. However, these occasional persecutions increased in number and intensity during the reign of 'Abbas II. Between 1656 and 1662, Muhammad Beg, the shah's grand vizier, made an all-out effort to convert all the Jews to Shi'i Islam. Motivated perhaps slightly more by religious zeal than by greed, at first Muhammad Beg rewarded the new converts, only to demand not only the return of the reward money but the payment of the *jizya* in full—even retroactively—by all the Jews wanting to return to Judaism. Muhammad Beg's rapacious policy, apparently not fully endorsed by the shah, did not go unopposed. The towns of Farahabad, Gulpaygan, Khurramabad, Khunsar, and Yazd, as well as some Muslim officials and divines (notably Mullah Muhsin Fayd-i Kashani [d. 1680]) refused to force the Jews to convert, thus significantly defying the central authority of Isfahan. But the larger Jewish communities of Isfahan and Kashan appear to have converted by force, and the Jews became *anusim* (Heb., forced converts) for about seven years. They complied outwardly with the tenets of Shi'ism but continued to practice Judaism in secret, a situation similar to the state of *taqiyya* (dissimulation) practiced by Shi'i minorities in many Sunni societies. Both Armenians and Zoroastrians were similarly pressured at the time, as Muhammad Beg coveted the wealth of the first and was highly intolerant of the second group. The Armenian historian Arakel of Tabriz,[5] Qazvini, and the missionary account *A Chronicle of the Carmelites in Persia*[6] confirm these events. 'Abbas II eventually reversed some of Muhammad Beg's policies, including the forced conversions, but the prolonged and widespread nature of the conversions was a dangerous harbinger that left a negative mark on Iranian Jewish communities both spiritually and materially.

Throughout the seventeenth and eighteenth centuries, the influence of the Shi'i hierocracy continued to increase, as did their intolerance toward Sufis and religious minorities, including Jews, Christian Armenians, and Zoroastrians. The concept of *najasat* (Ar./Pers., ritually impure), deeming all non-Shi'ia impure, was fully endorsed by Shi'i theologians and increasingly embraced by the populace, thus placing further social and economic obstacles in the way of these minorities. Jewish communal difficulties increased during the reign of Sultan Sulayman (1666–94) when the false Jewish messianic movement of Sabbatai Zevi (d. ca. 1676) extended to some parts of Iran so that, according to the French traveler J. Chardin, the Jews of Hyrcania (Gurgan) expected his imminent appearance and refused to pay the *jizya*.[7] ▶ See article by M. Ali Amir-Moezzi, pp. 816–823.

Economically, Iranian Jews occupied the lower strata of society involved in occupations such as weaving, farming, dyeing, minstrelsy, butchery, and so on. Their economic prowess had clearly declined from earlier medieval times from the commercial to the working class. The famous traveler J. Chardin describes them as, "ils sont pauvres et misérables partout,"[8] artisans, small-scale "usurers," purveyors of medical and magical services, with Jewish women having access to the palaces of rulers. Iranian Jews in late medieval Iran were not great financiers, and by the seventeenth century they were entirely overtaken by Hindu *banyans* (traders). Nor were they large-scale merchants, an activity in which the Armenians surpassed them. Their impoverishment is revealed by two Judeo-Persian chronicles (for the second, see below) that mention the enormous difficulties caused by the demands of the *jizya*, adding to the impression that the economic status of Jews declined continuously in premodern Iran and reached its nadir in the nineteenth century.

The years between 1662 and 1722, the period marking the end of *KA* and the beginning of the second Judeo-Persian chronicle, remain mostly obscure as far as Iranian Jewry is concerned, although at least one episode of persecution is recorded by *The Chronicle of the Carmelites*.[9] The last two decades of the Safavid dynasty were overshadowed by both foreign and internal pressures that greatly weakened the kingdom. Clearly, no social or religious group, including the Jews, could have remained unscathed in such difficult times. Another Judeo-Persian chronicle, the *Kitab-i Sar Guzasht-i Kashan dar bab-i 'Ibri va Goyimi-yi Sani* (*KS*; The Book of Events in Kashan Concerning the Jews; Their Second Conversion), written by Babai ibn Farhad, the grandson of Babai ibn Lutf, relates some of the hardships they endured at the beginning of the eighteenth century. Ibn Farhad lived through the downfall of the Safavid dynasty, as well as the invasions of the Afghans, Ottomans, and Russians. He refers to these events only briefly, primarily from the perspective of the Jewish communities and individuals that were affected directly. Most of *KS* describes selected episodes connected with the rise to power of Tahmasp Quli Khan, the future Nadir Shah (1736–47), as these came to affect the Jewish community of Kashan, the chronicler's native town, for a period of seven months in 1729–30, especially the events that led to the short-lived apostasy of its Jewish community. As mentioned above, the precedent for purchasing freedom of worship having been set in the seventeenth century, the Jews of Iran began to live under the threat of the annulment of their religious freedom. It is not surprising, therefore, to find some Jews sympathizing with the Sunni Afghan invaders in hopes that their rule would be less harsh toward the Jews.[10]

Intolerance and modernization

The Afshar (1736–95) and Zand (1750–96) dynasties provide no direct historical information about Iranian Jews, but quite a few Judeo-Persian literary texts can be traced to this period, testifying to the Jews' continued survival and even relative prosperity despite increasingly turbulent political and social conditions. The historical trail can be picked up again during the rule of the Qajar dynasty (1779–1924), in a period in which an abundance and variety of sources describe Iranian Jewry's reaching the absolute nadir, even as the dawning of the modern era initiated their gradual emancipation. During this period the internal and external problems of Iran multiplied. Famines, general physical insecurity, budgetary constraints, the loss of territories to Russia (between 1820 and 1860), and diplomatic failures against the British in Afghanistan were only some of the events that contributed to widespread popular dissatisfaction.[11]

The Qajars, of Turkoman origin, were no innovators and adhered to the governing system of the Safavids. During the first half of their rule, into the 1860s, the status of the Jews continued to decline precipitously as they became ever more socially and economically marginalized and oppressed. They were repeatedly the targets of fanatical mobs incited by intolerant mullahs. Thus the Jewish community of Tabriz was destroyed in 1791 as a result of a blood libel accusation. Most notably, the Jews of Mashhad were attacked in 1839. Those who did not flee were forced to convert and became *anusim*. Attacks on the Jews of Shiraz (1820s) and Barfurush (1866) were among the most serious bouts of persecution that led to the decline or complete annihilation of numerous Iranian Jewish communities, among them those of Ardabil, Qum, Qazvin, Rasht, and Sabzavar. The

A Jewish marriage contract (*ketubah*) that shows typical Iranian motifs such as a lion surmounted by a solar star, a Persian symbol of sovereignty and power. Ispahan, 1860, watercolor. Jerusalem, Israel Museum.

concept of *najasat*, in addition to the already demeaning requirements of *dhimmī* status, the payment of *jizya*, and restrictions dictated by the Shiʻi religious calendar, even if not uniformly enforced, created unbearable situations in many communities.

Several laws, unique to Shiʻi Iran, became ever more strictly enforced and wreaked havoc with communal life. The most onerous of these, first promulgated under ʻAbbas I, was a major change in the law of inheritance that enabled

> **It was especially during the long reign of Nasir al-Din Shah... that earnest efforts to modernize Iran led to some improvements for the Jews as well.**

converts to Shiʻism to become sole heirs of their families. Although abolished in 1880, this law continued to linger in some communities well beyond this date. Similarly demeaning was the law that prevented Jews from being witnesses in a Muslim court as late as the 1910s. And equally discriminating was the

fact that the blood money a Muslim had to pay for the killing of a Jew was less than 10 percent of what was required for killing a Muslim. Economic hardships were further compounded by periodic famines, especially the Great Famine of 1871–72 in which 20 to 40 percent of the Jews living in the south and center of Iran perished. Periodic nomadic raids, Christian conversionary efforts, and the attraction to the new faith of Bahaism, all contributed to the serious communal stresses endured by Iranian Jews in the second half of the nineteenth century.

Nevertheless, these were the decades, until 1921, that witnessed attempts at reforms within Iran, greater contact between Iran's Jews and Ottoman and West European Jewry, and the increasing positive involvement of Jewish philanthropists from France, England, and Baghdad. They all contributed to the gradual albeit uneven process of ameliorating the status of Iranian Jews. It was especially during the long reign of Nasir al-Din Shah (r. 1848–96), who visited Europe several times, that earnest efforts to modernize Iran led to some improvements for the Jews as well, notably the establishment of Western-style schools under the auspices of the Alliance Israélite Universelle of France.[12]

---

1. Tomé Pires, *The Suma oriental of Tomé Pires: An Account of the East, from the Red Sea to Japan, Written in Malacca and India, 1512–1515*, trans. Armado Cortes (London: Hakluyt Society, 1944), 1:27.

2. Raphael du Mans, *Estat de la Perse en 1660*, ed. Ch. Schefer (Paris: E. Leroux, 1890).

3. Vera Basch Moreen, *Iranian Jewry's Hour of Peril and Heroism: A Study of Babai ibn Lutf's Chronicle* (New York: American Academy for Jewish Research, 1987).

4. Muhammad Tahir Wahid Qazvini, *ʻAbbasnama*, ed. I. Dehgan (Arak: Chapkhana-yi Farvardi, 1951).

5. Arakel of Tabriz, *Livre d'Histoires: Collection d'Historiens Arméniens*, trans. and ed. M. I. Brosset (St. Petersburg: Impr. De l'Académie Impériale des Sciences, 1874–76), 1:364.

6. *A Chronicle of the Carmelites in Persia* (London: Eyre & Spottiswoode, 1939), 1:364.

7. J. J. Chardin, *Voyages* (Paris: L. Langlès, 1811), 6:135.

8. Ibid., 6:133–34.

9. *Chronicle*, 1:408.

10. Vera Basch Moreen, *Iranian Jewry during the Afghan Invasion: The Kitab-i Sar Guzasht-i Kashan of Babai b. Farhad* (Stuttgart: Franz Steiner Verlag, 1990).

11. David Yeroushalmi, *The Jews of Iran in the Nineteenth Century* (Leiden: Brill, 2009), introduction and background.

12. Ibid. See also David Yeroushalmi's article, "1787–1925 (Qajar Dynasty)," in *Encyclopedia of Jews in the Islamic World* (Leiden: Brill, 2010), 2:586–94.

A Judeo-Persian Chronicle of Forced Conversions

Babai ibn Lutf wrote *Kitab-i anusi* (The Book of a Forced Convert), the first Judeo-Persian chronicle known thus far, sometime after 1662. It describes the periodic persecution of Iranian Jews during the reign of Shah 'Abbas I (1581–1629) and especially during the reign of Shah 'Abbas II (1642–66). In the latter reign, the Jews of many major Iranian communities (such as Isfahan and Kashan) were forced to convert to Shi'i Islam in 1656 at the instigation of the grand vizier, Muhammad Beg. They adhered to Judaism in secret until 1662, when they regained freedom of worship.

Vera Basch Moreen

Come, listen and see what these afflicted [Jews] experienced and how they became Muslims ... They were brought to the palace in the presence of Asaf [Muhammad Beg, the grand vizier] and the Shah of Shahs. When they saw that entire council (you would say the Day of Resurrection arrived), they began trembling like willows. Tears stained their cheeks and fear reigned in their hearts. Suddenly, Asaf called out to Sason: "I offer you an easy solution. Take all your women by the hand and leave the realm. Leave your wealth, property, and houses behind; go thirsty until you reach a shore with water. Or else become Muslims at once, sincerely; cease being hypocrites!" Sason answered: "Asaf, my Refuge, know that I am powerless to decide in this matter. Sa'id is a *mullah* [here, a learned Jew] and learned, the teacher of our children. If he will convert now, I too will embrace the new faith." Then Sa'id was brought forth and Asaf said: "O Jew, become a Muslim that you may find honor and hasted on the road to Paradise along with friends. Become God's slave and our brother; you would be the best of Muslims!" Sa'id said to him: "O light of my eyes, I cannot deny my religion. We are already Muslims [that is, submitters to God] in the Jewish manner: we too know only one God!" When Asaf heard this speech he became angry and said to his servants at once: "Take this Jew and tie his feet firmly to a camel. Then tear up his belly; say nothing about this to anyone." The servants took the old man and tied him to a camel but God Himself became his shield. God inspired him to say then: "Grant a respite till tomorrow!" When the grandees heard this, they willingly granted his wish. The poor man thought in distress: "Perhaps tonight God, the Living Founder of the World, will grant deliverance from the hands of the council!"

O Babai, be humble before God. Who else can grant you access to the Fountain of Intercession?

From Babai ibn Lutf's *Kitab-i Anusi* (*The Book of a Forced Convert*); reproduced from Vera Basch Moreen, *Iranian Jewry's Hour of Peril and Heroism: A Study of Babai ibn Lutf's Chronicle (1617–1662)* (New York: American Academy for Jewish Research, 1987), 182, 188.

Jews of Yemen
Yosef Tobi

According to their own tradition and according to new archaeological findings, Jews lived in the country later known as Yemen at least since the seventh century B.C.E. It seems that trade was the main incentive of Israelites to immigrate to that country. Their position was so strong that around 370 C.E., the major political power in Yemen, the Kingdom of Himyar, adopted Judaism, until the Ethiopian Christians took control of the country and destroyed the Jewish state. Since 629 the country was governed by Islam and the Jews became subject to Muslim discriminatory rules of *dhimmī* and were forced to pay the protection tax (*jizya*). However, they could observe their religion and make a living. During their long stay in that country, the Jews of Yemen kept their ties with other Jewish spiritual centers, including that of the Land of Israel. Since the early 1880s they started to immigrate to their old homeland, until immediately after the establishment of the state of Israel in 1948, when most of them came to Israel.

Yosef Tobi

Yosef Tobi teaches in the department of Hebrew literature and comparative literature at Haifa University in Israel. He has written extensively on medieval Hebrew poetry and medieval Judeo-Arabic literature and is a specialist in the history of Yemenite Jews. He is the author of *The Jews of Yemen: Studies in Their History and Culture* (Brill, 1999) and a contributor to *The Cultures of the Jews: A New History*, edited by David Biale (Schocken, 2002).

Jews of Yemen under the Tahiri Dynasty (1454–1517)

The rule of the Shafi'i Rasulids in Yemen for quite a long period (1229–1454) brought political stability. During that period the Jews also enjoyed social and economic prosperity. This changed with the rise of the Tahiri dynasty, whose rule lasted until the Turkish occupation in 1517. From a note written in a Jewish manuscript of Yemen, we learn that the old synagogue of Sanaa was destroyed in 1457 under the rule of Ahmad 'Amir, the founder of the Tahiri dynasty. At the end of the fifteenth century, Yemen entered into a state of political instability, mainly due to the military activity of the Portuguese navy on the south coast of the Arabian Peninsula, bordering Hadramawt, and that of the Ottoman fleet in the area of Aden. From medieval sources it seems that there were Jewish settlements in this area, although we do not have details about their size.

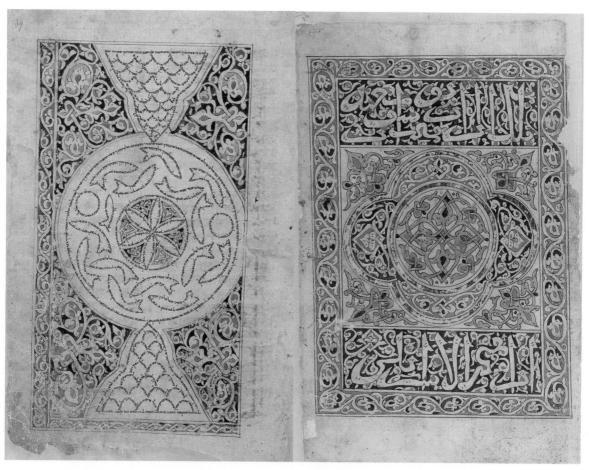

First and last folios of a Yemeni Pentateuch: on the left, verses from the Psalms are lettered according to floral motifs common in Islamic manuscripts; on the right, the colophon carries the name of the copyist and the date in Arabic. Sana'a, 1649. British Library, London, ms. or. 2348, fol. 39 and 155.

A European source indicates that Jews helped the Portuguese army to orient along the coast.[1] The Jews expected the foreign occupation and certainly hoped to change the hard conditions of life under the Tahiri dynasty.[2] These expectations had a messianic character. According to the Hadrami historian Ba Faqih al-Shihri, the Jewish Messiah was active in 1499/1500, during the rule of Amir ibn 'Abd al-Wahhab, the last king of the Tahirids.[3] The king's response was a collective punishment—the liquidation of the Jewish settlement in Hadramawt, as a response to the alleged violation of the protection agreement, a fact that canceled their right to exist anymore in this country.[4] Presumably some of them were slaughtered,[5] many converted to Islam, and others migrated to places such as Aden and Yemen or the adjacent mainland.[6] Indeed, since the end of the fifteenth century, there were no Jewish communities in Hadramawt, save along the western periphery, especially in Habban and Bayhân.[7] However, Muslim silversmiths who testified that they were descendants of Jews were certainly not descendants of the ancient Jews of Hadramawt but of Jewish jewelers who arrived there for their work two to three generations before.[8]

It seems that the liquidation of the Jewish community in Hadramawt was not immediate, since it was reported that in November 1527 a Jew of the sultanate of Fartaque was paid by the Portuguese for assistance and providing food and lodging when they were lost while looking for the way to Hurmuz.[9] However, Zakharia al-Zahiri, traveling in Hadramawt in the 1660s, did not find Jewish communities there.[10] It seems that the solution to the mysterious disappearance of the Jews of Hadramawt during the sixteenth century may come from the fatwas of the contemporary Muslim scholars in this country and Yemen, who frequently referred to the Jews.[11]

An important note about the treatment of Jews by the Tahirids is found in the colophon of a Jewish manuscript from Yemen in 1505, the year in which Amir ibn 'Abd al-Wahhab, the last sovereign of the Tahirids, took control of Sanaa from its two Zaidi governors, Imam al-Washli and Muhammad ibn al-Husayn: *dawla zālima wa-dawla zābita wa-amān fi dawlatih* (one kingdom is exploitive and another is repressive, but security exists in the Kingdom of God only).[12] Indeed, the legal status of Jews in Yemen began to deteriorate at that time, mainly because of new discriminatory regulations established by the Muslim reign. Such laws against the *dhimmī*s (the protected Jewish or Christian citizens) were not included in the Zaidi legal writings till comparatively late, as *Kitab al-Azhar* of Imam al-Murtada, of the first half of the fifteenth century. These changes also led to deterioration of the economic and social situation of the Jews.[13]

The period of the Turkish occupation (1546–1635)

The Zaidi imams, who for several centuries were completely pushed to their strongholds in the north, gained power during this time and took control of larger territories in the central plateau where big Jewish communities lived. In principle, they started to implement the new discriminatory regulations against the Jews. However, the Jews of the central plateau in Yemen probably did not share the fate of the Jews of Hadramawt because the Tahiri rule there was not strong enough. Moreover, already in the early sixteenth century, the Ottoman forces began to operate off the coast of Yemen until they completely took over the central plateau in the 1540s, which improved the legal status of the Jews. This change was part of the general policy toward the minorities in the Ottoman Empire. The change was not reflected in dismissing discriminatory laws, as they were applied throughout the empire, but the Ottoman government and courts in Yemen had implemented the principles of the Hanafi legal school, the common one in the empire, which was much more convenient to non-Muslims. But this was in contradiction to the Zaidi law, which during those days had already gone through the metamorphosis from the early phase to the late phase, and was impacted by the extremist Hanbali school of Ibn Taymiyya and Ibn Qayyim al-Jawziya. The result was more severe regulations toward non-Muslims. In any case, the aforementioned change did not lead to improved interrelations between Jews and the Muslim majority in Yemen, which disapproved of the policy of the foreign rule toward the Jews. Moreover, Muslims accused Jews of siding with Turkish rule and acting against the interests of the local population. Due to these accusations, the Zaidis treated the Jews more severely, not only in comparison to the Turks but also in comparison with the ancient Zaidi policy. The hostile attitude of the Zaidi population toward the Jews also affected the Turkish rulers in Yemen, who, under the pressure of local Muslims—especially when the Yemeni revolted against Ottoman rule—quickly repudiated the current sympathetic policy at the empire's capital toward the religious minorities. What is more, when the rebellious Zaidi imam al-Mutahhar could eliminate the Turkish army in areas adjacent to Sanaa in 1567, he renewed the tough policy toward the Jews. Deterioration in the attitude of the Turkish governors toward the Jews was repeated close to the end of their rule in Yemen during the Yemeni revolt initiated by Imam al-Qasim in 1590. The poet Shalom Shabazi (1619–ca. 1680) wrote about the cruel harassments of the leaders of the Jews, including his father, Yosef Avigad, by Fazli Pasha, the Turkish governor in southern Yemen in the 1620s. He even tried to convert them to Islam by force.[14] However, despite the hostile attitude of Turkish governors toward the Jews, there is no doubt that in principle and practically, the conditions under which the Jews lived during the Turkish rule were by and large more comfortable than during the following Imami period, when systematic policy was directed against the Jews in order to end their existence in Yemen, as we shall see.

The period of the Imami Qasimi dynasty (1635–1800)

With the expulsion of the Turks from Yemen in 1635, after having retreated from Sanaa in 1629, almost all of Yemen, including most of its Jewish settlements, came under a stable Zaidi regime for the first time. This regime was the most hostile to the Jews of Yemen as local Muslims took revenge for the relatively comfortable attitude of the Turks to the Jews and because of the aforementioned alleged argument that the Jews sided with the Turks. Imam Isma'il al-Mutawakkil (1644–76), a devout Muslim who vastly expanded the boundaries of the kingdom,

> *This regime was the most hostile to the Jews of Yemen as local Muslims took revenge for the relatively comfortable attitude of the Turks to the Jews.*

was especially hostile. It seems that only in this time period could the Zaidis fully apply the discriminatory laws against Jews, after having received a mandatory religious sanction in the writings of Imam al-Murtada of the fifteenth century, and after their rule in the sixteenth century application was rather loose. The application of discriminatory laws, such as the ban to ride a donkey, to walk to the left of a Muslim, to respect him, to be punished by flogging if these laws were violated, and the rejection of evidence of a Jew against a Muslim, should be attributed to the move from Turkish rule to Qasimi rule.[15]

The messianic activity in 1666–1667 and its consequences: The decree against headgear and the Expulsion of Mawza'

Consequent upon the Messianic outburst in Yemen in the seventeenth century, with the advent of Sabbatai Zevi in the Jewish world, unprecedented trouble descended on the Jews the like of which they had not known before. In 1665 rumors through letters and messengers began to arrive in Yemen about Sabbatai Zevi. The situation of the Jews at that time was very poor. Imam Isma'il, who was a fervent fanatic of Islam, began to persecute the Jews because of their apparent solidarity with the Turks, the foreign occupiers who were so hated by the local Muslims. No wonder, then, that the rumors about Sabbatai Zevi fell on attentive ears in Yemen, including Shalom Shabazi, although the Jewish court in Sanaa rejected all these rumors. Many Jews of Yemen began to adopt customs of repentance, used by the followers of Sabbatai Zevi in other countries, and prepared for the expected redemption. Some of them even began to sell their real and movable estates. According to Muslim sources, the Jews even behaved brazenly against Muslims. However, already at this stage Isma'il responded very sharply. He summoned the Jewish leadership and would have made the decision to destroy all Jews, were it not for the advice of one of his close associates, Qadi Shams al-Din Ahmad al-Maswari. But he dismissed the Jews' status as *dhimmīs*, the external symbol of which was removing their headgear (*'amā'im*), a respected status symbol. They were forced to walk bareheaded, the most despicable thing in Yemeni society in those days. Isma'il also put Shlomo Naqqash, the Jewish president, in prison on the desolate island of Kamaran in the Red Sea.

But the imam's response did not eliminate the messianic faith, nor did Sabbatai Zevi's conversion to Islam in September 1666. The central figure of the messianic activity at this stage was Sulaiman al-Jamal, a respected scholar in the San'ani Jewish community who delved especially into the wisdom of Kabbalah, but who did not hold any position in the official leadership. In the intermediate days of Passover in 1667, he believed he had a divine revelation, though others believed he was seized by the spirit of madness, and felt that he was doomed to detach the Muslim ruler from the throne and put himself on it on behalf of the Jewish people. This divine revelation was probably the result of a prolonged and intense contemplation in the messianic conviction. On that day he came out of the Jewish neighborhood, located within the wall of the Sanaa, dressed in finery and surrounded by enthusiastic supporters, and proceeded to the fortress that controls the city from the west (al-Qasr). His supporters dropped away one by one, and he came alone to the governor, who was in charge of the city in the absence of Imam Isma'il (who was in Suda), and asked him to come down from the throne. This stupid act astonished the governor and his entourage. They knocked him down, hit him with their shoes, and led him to jail.

When the story was brought to Imam Isma'il's attention, he turned to the clerics, and they unanimously ruled that al-Jamal's action and the messianic belief of the Jews were a violation of the protection agreement, to the effect that it was not valid anymore. The government's commitment to protect the Jews, their property, and their right to live according to their religion became completely void. Various options were supposedly possible for the imam concerning how to abolish the Jewish entity in Yemen: physical destruction, imposing Islam, and deportation. The first two options were rejected; the first presumably on simple humanitarian grounds and the second due to the clear instruction given to Muhammad not to impose Islam. The third option of deportation, therefore, remained. But even in this matter a dispute arose between the scholars of Islam in Yemen. Isma'il deliberated and did not reach a resolution but used a harsh hand with the Jews by executing al-Jamal and by collective punishments, such as the imprisonment of the leaders of the Jewish community in the Kamaran, fines, denial of rights, confiscation of property, imposition of new humiliating laws, and closure of the synagogues. However, he did not allow Muslims to attack Jews directly. On his deathbed he ordered his nephew, Ahmad al-Mahdi, who ascended him as imam in 1676, to expel the Jews from Yemen. But even the new imam did not hasten to fulfill his uncle's directive. There were several suggestions as to where the Jews of Yemen should be deported: the coastal African area on the western side of the Red Sea or the subcontinent of India ruled by Muslim Mogul. Eventually, the deportation was not carried out beyond the borders of Yemen, but to a remote place in Western Yemen, the village of Mawza', not far from the port town of Mocha. It seems that this place was chosen because there were already Christians living there, representatives of European economic companies operating in Yemen on the trade route to India. The hope was that the intolerable conditions of life in Mawza' would drive the Jews to convert to Islam or that they would even destroy them. It is possible as well that they were already on their way to Mocha, Yemen's main port in those days, to drive them out of the country, but before that took place, they were held back in Mawza' and remained there.

The decree of expulsion of the Jews in 1679 encompassed all of them who lived within the control of the central government in Sanaa. It seems that Jews living under tribal protection peripheries were not exiled. This event, known as the Expulsion of Mawza', was thus a record of consecutive events that started with the Sabbatean movement in Yemen in 1665. It is the most deep-rooted in the communal historical memory of Yemenite Jewry. But ultimately, economic considerations prevailed on religious and political decisions, and after about a year and a half, the exiles began to return slowly to the interior of Yemen, most of them not to their previous settlements, and certainly not to the neighbor-

> **" This event, known as the Expulsion of Mawza'… is the most deep-rooted in the communal historical memory of Yemenite Jewry. "**

hoods within the walls of cities such as Sanaa, Rada', and Dhamar, but outside them. There, new Jewish quarters gradually evolved, but they were subject to a course of attacks by robbers and the onslaught of tribes for many years.

The clerics claim to expel the Jews in 1725

The issue of the Jewish existence in Yemen remained in dispute among the scholars of Islam there, such as in the writings of the jurisprudent Muhammad al-Shawkani (1759–1834). Like some Zaidi scholars, who affirmed the expulsion of the Jews when asked by Imam al-Mahdi, Shawkani rejected the opinion of Imam al-Murtada in *Kitab al-Azhar*, and in his commentary *al-Sail al-Jarrar* on this work, he ruled that indeed the traditions brought by the name of the Prophet Muhammad on the expulsion of the Jews were referring to the entire Arabian Peninsula. However, there was no reason not to allow them to live in their towns, provided they paid the *jizya*.[16] Shawkani's ruling appears to be purely academic, but it turns out that during the eighteenth century, Yemenite Jews were in danger of deportation twice: in 1725 and in 1762.[17]

The Jewish community had begun to recover, partly thanks to Imam Muhammad al-Mahdi (1687–1716), known as Sahib al-Mawahib: he took care of the Jews, protected them, and allowed them to return to their previous status.[18] The rulers of Yemen in the eighteenth century, first al-Mahdi and then al-Mutawakkil, rejected the insistent pleading of the clerics (such as Muhammad ibn Isma'il al-Amir, known as al-Badr [1688–1768]) to enforce the deportation of the Jews because of their strengthening ties with the Jews, especially with the 'Iraqi family, which was in charge of the mint house.[19] As is known, at least since the end of the seventeenth century, the Jews ran the imami mint house (where coins were made). It was not only due to their expertise as professional silversmiths but also because they were much more trustworthy than the Muslims in the eyes of the imams regarding the highly important legal tender in Yemen, which symbolized the authority of the government. A minor change in al-Mutawakkil's stand took place following a severe, scathing violation of the protection agreement by the Jews—selling wine to Muslims. In 1725 a drunk Muslim sexually assaulted a boy at a restroom in a mosque in Sanaa.[20] Although the boy was not abused, the rumors about the affair reached al-Mutawakkil, who was then obliged to defend Islam from the Jews, who had sold wine to Muslims and who had furthermore, it transpired, been building new synagogues in violation of the discrimination laws. The imam at first had no choice but to follow al-Badr's advice to imprison the 'Iraqi and to command the closure of the synagogues, until the scholar's son Yusuf came in during the prayers in the mosque with a religious legal ruling that rejected the closure of synagogues on the grounds that they were built by permission of the preceding imams.[21]

The Jewish community, headed by Shalom 'Iraqi, recovered from this affair. 'Iraqi's status strengthened during the reign of Imam al-Mansur, al-Mutawakkil's son, who was his age and was assisted by him to gain the imamate.[22] This was the period when Yemenite Jewry flourished, economically as well as otherwise, in part because of the role it played in the international trade to India when passing through the most important Yemeni port in those days: Mocha. This town had an important Jewish community, which deteriorated as a consequence of the Egyptian invasion to the west of Yemen in the 1810s and the British occupation of Aden in 1839.[23]

The plan of Imam al-Mahdi to expel the Jews and the closure of the synagogues in 1762

In 1763 the German researcher Carsten Niebuhr, heading a scientific delegation sent by the Kingdom of Denmark, visited Yemen. He left his impressions in a detailed and important travelogue.[24] He reports that two years before his visit, Shalom 'Iraqi was put in jail with a high penalty imposed upon him, and twelve out of the fourteen synagogues of the Jews in their village near the city of Sanaa were shut down, and the Jews were required to lower the height of their homes,

Jewish marriage contract (*ketubah*), Sana'a (Yemen), eighteenth century. Jerusalem, Israel Museum.

which were more beautiful and taller than those of the Muslims. Just two weeks before Niebuhr arrived at Sanaa, 'Iraqi was released.[25] Jewish sources relate the change in al-Mahdi 'Abbas's attitude to 'Iraqi with the change of regime, but this is not compatible with reality;[26] the matter should be attributed to the ceaseless pressure of the clerics on the imams over the years. Unlike his father al-Mansur Husain and his grandfather al-Mutawakkil Qasim, 'Abbas al-Mahdi was an eminent scholar of Islam and Arabic literature, religiously devout, and an associate of clerics, in particular those whose relationships with his father and grandfather were not of high quality.[27] His mentor was the *sayyid* 'Abd Allah Lutf al-Bari al-Kibsi (1700–1701 to 1759–60), and one of the scholars who supported him for the imamate after the death of his father was the experienced al-Badr.[28]

This ideological affinity between the ruler and the clerics created an atmosphere of extreme religious fanaticism in the country that was not in favor of religious minorities. Apart from the Jews there were the Indian merchants (*banāyina*), settled in port towns in the southwest and west of Arabia, who were tremendously hated by the Muslim scholars because their religion included symbols of idolatry. Inspired by the clerics, 'Abbas al-Mahdi worked to remove their houses of worship in Mocha.[29] But the clerics were not satisfied with that and wished to fulfill the old dream of eliminating the existence of two religions in Yemen. The result was that al-Mahdi "banned some of their [the Jews] leaders and intended to fulfill the messenger of God's will ... but it did not work out."[30]

Despite the pressure of the clerics to expel the Jewish religion, and the imams' intentions to comply with their demands, he eventually decided to avoid this situation, possibly due to practical economic considerations. However, he accepted al-Badr's opinion concerning the closure of the synagogues. They remained in this situation for thirty years, until Imam 'Ali al-Mansur (1775–1809), al-Mahdi's son, permitted them to be reopened—for a huge fee.[31] But still, the idea of the expulsion of the Jews was not removed from the minds of the rulers of Yemen and its Muslim clerics. The eighteenth century ended with Napoleon's invasion of Eastern countries, an action that drew intense renewed activity of foreign powers in Southern Arabia, first Britain and then the Ottoman Empire. Yemen found itself in a harsh governmental and economic instability, which had direct results on the Jewish communities. But this is beyond the confines of this study.

---

1. Francisco Alvares, *The Prester John of the Indies*, vol. 2 (Cambridge: Hakluyt Society, 1961), 482–83; R. B. Serjeant, *The Portuguese off the South Arabian Coast* (Oxford: Clarendon Press, 1963), 32.

2. Information on Jewish life in Yemen during the Tahirids is very scarce. See Yosef Tobi, "Arabic Writings of Yemen," *Reports on the Jews of Yemen*, in *Pe'amim* 2 (1995): 28–31; see also Yosef Tobi, *Studies in Megillat Teman* (Heb.) (Jerusalem, 1986), 71.

3. R. B. Serjeant, *Materials for South Arabian History*, BSOAS 13 (1950): 581–601.

4. Hayyim Habshush, *The History of Israel in Yemen*, ed. Yosef Qafih, in Yosef Qafih, *Collected Papers*, ed. Yosef Tobi (Jerusalem, 1989), 2:700.

5. The Hadrami chronicler al-Shihri reports that supporters of the Jewish Messiah were destroyed by the army of the Muslim ruler after they were slyly surrounded while parked safely in their place. See Yosef Tobi, in "Arabic Writings of Yemen, " *Reports on the Jews of Yemen*, *Pe'amim* 1, 64 (1995): 68–102, 30–31.

6. A fatwa from 1517 of the faqih Ba Makhrama, dealing with payment of *jizya* by the Jews, teaches that the Jewish community in Aden counted thousands of people, a huge inexplicable number, only if there was a quick migration from just before this year. See R. B. Serjeant, *The Portuguese off the South Arabian Coast* (Oxford: Clarendon Press, 1963), 138–40; Yosef Tobi, *Reports on the Jews of Yemen*, *Pe'amim* 2, 65 (1995): 18–56, 29–31.

7. On the Jewish settlements in Habban, see Laurence D. Loeb, *Jewish-Muslim Socio-Political Relations in Twentieth Century South Yemen*, in *Judeo-Yemenite Studies: Proceedings of the Second International Congress*, ed. Ephraim Isaac and Yosef Tobi (Haifa: Princeton University Press, 1999), 71–99; Renate Meissner, *Die südjeme-*

nitischen Juden: Versuch einer Rekonstruktion ihrer traditio-nellen Kultur vor dem Exodus (Frankfurt am Main: Peter Lang, 1999).

8. R. B. Serjeant, "A Judeo-Arab House Deed from Habban (with notes on the former Jewish communities of the Wahidi Sultanate)," *Journal of the Royal Asiatic Society* 85, new series (1953): 117–31; Mikhail Rodionov, "Silversmiths in Modern Hadramawt," *Erythraeum* 1 (1997): 124.

9. Alvares, *The Prester John of the Indies*, 482–83.

10. Zakharia al-Zahiri, *Sefer Ha-Musar*, ed. Yehuda Ratzaby (Jerusalem, 1966), 220.

11. Two compilations of the Hadrami Ba Makhrama's fatawa in manuscripts are kept in the School of Oriental and African Studies, London, and one of Ibn Ju'man, who was the mufti of Zabid, was in possession of Serjeant. See *The Portuguese off the South Arabian Coast*, 28n3, 168, 219.

12. Yehuda Ratzaby, "Documents about the History of the Jews of Yemen," *Sefunot* 2 (1958): 289–90; Tobi, *Studies in Megillat Teman*, 43–44.

13. Murtada 1972, p. 322.

14. Shalom Shabazi, *Hemdat Yamim (a commentary of the Pentateuch)* (Jerusalem, 1955), 447.

15. Habshush, *The History of Israel in Yemen*, 706–8.

16. See Shawkani 1985, op. cit., IV, 570; cf. Husayn 'Abdullah al-'Amri, *The Yemen in the 18th & 19th Centuries: A Political Intellectual History* (Ithaca, NY: Cornell University Press, 1985), 163; Husayn 'Abdullah al-'Amri, *Al-Imam al-shawkani Ra'id 'asrihi: Dirasa fi fiqhihi wa-fikrihi* (Beirut, 1990), 315–18. On Shawkani, see al-'Amri, *Al-Imam al-shawkani Ra'id 'asrihi*; Bernard A. Haykel, *Revival and Reform: The Legacy of Muhammad al-Shawkani* (Cambridge: Cambridge University Press, 2003).

17. Muhammad ibn Muhammad Zabara al-San'ani, *Nubala' al-yaman bi-al-qurn al-thani 'ashar li-al-hijra: Nashr al-'urf li-nubala' al-yaman ba'd al-alf.* (Sanaa, 1985) (d. 1960). The book is a compilation of Yemeni personalities in the Hijri twelfth century (1689–1785).

18. Tobi, *Studies in Megillat Teman*, 152; 'Amram Qorah, *The Tempest of Yemen*, ed. Shim'on Greidi (Heb.; Jerusalem, 1954), 13.

19. On the rise of the family of 'Iraqi, the service of Aharon and his son Shalom in the courts of the imams, and their involvement in the political intrigues, see Tobi, *Studies in Megillat Teman*, 151ff.

20. All related here is based on the biography of al-Badr; see Zabara, *Nubala' al-yaman bi-al-qurn al-thani 'ashar li-al-hijra*, 36–37.

21. Ibid., 328.

22. Tobi, *Studies in Megillat Teman*,166–67.

23. On the wealth and economic welfare of the Jews in those years, see Shalom Qorah, *Wrath of Time*, ed. Yosef Qorah, in *The History of the Jews of Yemen from Their Writings*, ed. Yosef Tobi, 126–44 (Heb., Jerusalem, 1980),140.

24. On the mission and the details regarding the Jews in that book, see Aviva Klein-Franke, "The First Scholarly Missionary to South-Arabia as a Source for the History of the Jews of Yemen" (Heb.), *Pe'amim* 18 (1984): 80–101.

25. For details of these events in the Jewish sources, see Yosef Tobi, "The Appeal of the Officers of Constantinople to R. Shalom 'Iraqi, the President of the Jews of Yemen in 1742," *Shalem* 1 (1974): 257–69; Klein-Franke, *The First Scholarly Missionary to South-Arabia*, 88–94.

26. Habshush, *The History of Israel in Yemen*, 26; Qorah, *Wrath of Time*, 140.

27. On al-Mahdi 'Abbas, see Zabara, *Nubala' al-yaman bi-al-qurn al-thani 'ashar li-al-hijra*, 19–28.

28. Ibid., 19–20. Al-Kibsi was a renowned Zaidi family (ibid., 135–38).

29. Ibid., 41.

30. Ibid., 136.

31. Qorah, *The Tempest of Yemen*, 22.

Jews and Muslims in Central Asia
Catherine Poujol

The history of the Jews in Central Asia (in Bukhara in particular) and their relation to the Muslim majority in the oases of Turkistan from the second half of the nineteenth century until 1917 is an often neglected field of research.[1] Yet it is one of the fundamental keys to an understanding of the breaks and continuities that mark that region of the world, visited by the colonial and then the Soviet tempests, in which the local Jews were both witnesses and protagonists. The Jews of Bukhara present the peculiarity of having crossed the centuries in a generally peaceful cohabitation with the Sunni Muslims of the Hanafite persuasion—with the exception of a few episodes of forced conversion, especially in the eighteenth and nineteenth centuries.[2] Exploited by the czarist power in its strategy of fostering settlements in the area, they constituted for several decades one of the poles, essential yet unrecognized, of a triangular relation with the Russian and Uzbek powers in which their economic and cultural importance amply made up for their small numbers—about ten thousand in 1873 out of a total population of about three million.[3]

Catherine Poujol

Catherine Poujol is a professor of the history and civilization of Central Asia at the Institut National des Langues et Civilisations Orientales (Inalco). Her publications include *Le Kazakhstan* (Paris, 2000) and *Dictionnaire de l'Asie centrale* (Paris, 2001).

The specificity of a minority community

Judaism is the only religious current that preceded the Islamization of Central Asia in the eighth century and continued until the fall of the Soviet Union. The Bukharan Jews—mentioned by Benjamin of Tudela, who puts the number of Jews in Samarkand in the year 1167 at fifty thousand—spoke Judeo-Tajik, a local variant of Judeo-Persian. They were a branch of Persian Jewry that had pursued a process of historical demarcation from their coreligionists of Iran from the beginning of the sixteenth century, after the advent of the Safavid dynasty in Persia and the adoption of Shi'ism as the state religion in 1501. The resulting political, economic, and cultural break isolated the Jews of Transoxiana (Turkistan), settled in the large oasis cities along the Silk Road (Bukhara, Khiva, Balkh, Merv), from their original homeland of Meched, Isfahan, Tabriz, and Herat, while at the same time producing a steady stream of emigration. Indeed, the Persian Jews, subject to recurrent persecutions, often took refuge beyond the Amu River, where the Sunni Uzbek khans of Bukhara and Khiva proved more tolerant.[4] Hence, they came to reinforce a community of a few thousand people on the road to "dejudaization," swept up by an infatuation with Sufi spirituality, the rare intellectual elites being more attracted to the works of Hafez or Omar Khayyám (transliterated in Hebrew letters) than to the study of the Torah. The historical split was further amplified when they became the object of a religious reactivation at the end of the eighteenth century, at the instigation of the Jews of Ottoman Palestine who were seeking the "ten lost tribes of Israel," or at least decentered or lost communities.[5] When Rabbi Yusuf Mamon Mogribi, born in Tétouan in 1773 and settled in Safed in Palestine, was charged with the mission to spiritually revive Central Asian communities in 1793, he probably did not know that he would spend sixty years there, initiate the custom of pilgrimages to the Holy Land, and awaken a form of Zionism before its time. Arriving in Bukhara in 1793,[6] he founded religious schools (*ḥadarim*) and went so far as to modify the ritual (*minhag*) of the Bukharans: he praised the Sephardic ritual instead of the Persian one, asserting that the Bukharans descended from the Jews of Spain. Here is what the European traveler Meyendorff says about him: "The rabbi of Bukhara . . . told me that when he arrived in Bukhara, he had found his coreligionists plunged in the deepest ignorance; only a very small number knew how to read; they had only two copies of the Holy Writ, and their manuscript only contained the first three books of the Pentateuch. The rabbi assured me that it was not more than a hundred years old, and that it did not differ at all from the printed ones. This Algerian Jew, an old man full of wit, who nearly wept with joy at seeing Europeans again, overlooked no opportunity to spread the instruction of his religion among men; he founded a school, and had books sent from Russia, Baghdad, and Constantinople. Presently all the Jews of Bukhara can read and write; they study the Talmud." He left Bukhara to "die in Jerusalem," leaving a religious community that was reconstructed, ready to welcome the modernity brought in by Russian colonization.

The situation of the Bukharan Jews at the time of the czarist colonization

In the middle of the nineteenth century, the Jews of Bukhara lived in compact groups in the large oasis cities of old Transoxiana—Bukhara, Samarkand, Merv, Shakhrisyabz, Panjakent—and were beginning to settle in the dynamic valley of Fergana: Kokand, Andijan, and Margilan.[7] The ethnologist-jurist Zalman Lvovitch Amitin-Shapiro even believes that the "ghettos" of the cities of Central Asia were organized at their request for security purposes.[8]

In Bukhara, they were grouped into three adjacent quarters near bazaars: the *Mahalla i-kohne* (or "old mahalla"), the oldest and largest, and the most homogeneous until 1991; the *mahalla i-now* (or "new mahalla"), built in the first half of the nineteenth century; and the extension of the Amirabad quarter.[9] Essentially shopkeeper-craftsmen (tailors, hatters, dyers of silk and cotton,[10] carders, barbers, cobblers), some entered socially important professions as physicians, dentists, makers of talismans and potions,[11] and musicians.

Until the emirate was made into a protectorate by Russia in 1873, the Bukharan Jews constituted the sole religious minority of consequence to be in close contact with the Muslim majority. The handful of civilian and military Orthodox Russians, installed in the colonial city of Kagan, fifteen kilometers (about nine miles) from Bukhara under the authority of the resident-general, were not subject to the power of the emir. The emir continued to apply shari'a law until the takeover of Bukhara by the Red Army in September 1920. It was not until 1928 that shari'a was replaced by Soviet law.

> *The Bukharan Jews constituted the sole religious minority of consequence to be in close contact with the Muslim majority.*

As elsewhere in Muslim lands, the Bukharan Jews were regulated by their status as *dhimmī* and enjoyed a distinct community organization placed under the direction of a *kalontar* (in Tajik) or *nasi* (in Hebrew), the equivalent of the Tajik or Uzbek *aksakul*, elected by the community (in reality by its richest members—the leader himself being the most wealthy), and whose function was confirmed in writing by the emir in the form of a document called an *elik*. The *nasi* also functioned as community judge of family and religious questions, or conflicts within the community.[12] This relative juridical autonomy presupposed that shari'a law would apply to acts that were more important (concerning real estate and commercial or private leases), or insufficiently recognized by the community jurisdiction, particularly in cases of conflicts and dispositions involving inheritance.

It is especially in the fiscal domain that the status of the Jews most closely resembled that of their coreligionists in Islamic territory. The paying of the *jizya* (canonic tax allowing them to practice their religion) was regulated by twelve "inspectors," the *kalontar-jizya*; prior to 1917, all Jews over twelve years of age had to pay it once per trimester in the synagogue, in the presence of the representative of the *kush-begi* (a sort of prime minister) and of the *kalontar*. Amitin-Shapiro, having conducted his own investigation in the 1920s, established that there were three tariffs: twelve *tenga* per annum for the neediest, twenty-four for the middle class, and forty-eight for the most well-to-do.[13] Each one of them received two slaps in the face after paying, a gesture symbolically performed on the neck of the wealthiest, and less symbolically for the others.[14]

It is in their relations with the surrounding majority that the Jews of Bukhara have had a particularly bitter experience compared to the Jewish minorities of the rest of the world, especially since the beginning of the nineteenth century, in the form of the so-called twenty-one obligations.[15] The Bukharan Jews had to be identifiable by their attire. Their houses were marked by a rag, so that Muslims would not come to beg. They did not have the right to wear a turban or lavish coats outside—such as the *chapan* with brocades—which well-to-do families did, nevertheless, wear at home. They were recognizable by their astrakhan caps, lined with a wide band of black fur. Their belts had to be a cord and not a strip of silk, their mount an ass, not a horse. They had to walk through the city on foot, and before sunset, unless they could ride behind a Muslim. Their quarters were closed off by a wire stretched between two stakes (*eruv*) by nightfall. Their women had to wear a veil if they went out on the street.

Apart from these various forms of discrimination, they were generally only occasionally bothered by their Muslim neighbors, Hanafi Sunnis,[16] who considered the Bukharan Jews to be very conservative and feared them because of their "ability to cast evil spells," while at the same time respecting them for their musical talents, recruited for celebrations of all kinds. They did not practice usury, which was in the hands of Hindu or Afghan money changers, who were plentiful in the bazaars of Turkistan; the hostility toward them, traditional in other places in the Diaspora, was considerably lessened as a result.[17] Still, depending on the goodwill of the successive emirs and the ascendency of whatever particular Muslim dignitary was in power, campaigns of forced conversions to Islam took place beginning in the second half of the eighteenth century, both in groups and individually.[18] These forced conversions are the origin of the small community of Chala Jews whose housing is still recognizable today at the end of dead-end streets in the far end of the old Jewish quarters of Bukhara.[19] There were six or seven Chala quarters in Bukhara (*mahalla-i callaho*) for a total number of 2,500 people in the region in 1865. Today a few families still remain who declare themselves officially as Muslim, but who have preserved the memory of Judaism, as reflected by the fact of their being rejected by the neighborhood with respect to intermarriage.[20]

On the status of preferential subjects by Russian powers

Long before the actual conquest of the states of Turkistan (Bukhara, Khiva, and Kokand), the czarist colonial powers had devised a strategy to penetrate the zone by favoring, in the form of a preferential legal status—in an ostentatious and paradoxical fashion, considering their "interior Jewish policy"[21]—a community whose particularly trying legal and societal situation under Muslim power was known to them. Once the British intentions with respect to the oases of Central Asia, unequivocal since 1840, had heightened the awareness of a Russian general staff that was previously little inclined to actually intervene in the Central Asian theater of Anglo-Russian rivalry,[22] the idea of colonizing Central Asia and of advancing the Russian strategic lines in the direction of India became self-evident. But it was based on experience accumulated by centuries of difficult diplomatic contacts with the Uzbek states—hence the idea of using a target population that would serve as an intermediary and facilitate a less frontal clash.

Accordingly, the Russian legislators, despite their ingenuity in restricting the rights of Jews within the empire, agreed as early as 1842 on special measures favoring Bukharan Jews who wanted to do business with Russia and who had formerly been obliged to go through a Muslim intermediary. Thus, the decree of July 4, 1833, forbidding Asiatic Jews from belonging to the commercial guilds of the districts, was lifted. In 1835, they were allowed to go to the Nijnyj-Novgorod fair; in 1842 they were permitted to transport their merchandise to the Russian cities of the Orenburg line; then, in 1844, to all the cities of Siberia. Perhaps they were aware of the pro-British position of the local Jews of both Iran and Turkistan, with respect to the question of the Holy Land and the anticipated help from Britain to get it back.[23] These legislative dispositions, which were in fact taken on behalf of the Jews of Bukhara, led them to consider the arrival of the Russians in the region as their salvation.

> " *The czarist colonial powers had devised a strategy to penetrate the zone by favoring a community whose particularly trying legal and societal situation under Muslim power was known to them.* "

Such a favorable status thus corresponded to the demand of the colonial military administration to win allies in a region thought to be difficult. Moreover, the Russian industrial elite wanted to turn a profit from an area rich in raw materials indispensable to Russia's economic development (cotton, silk, coal, copper, and petroleum). But everyone agreed that the protectorate of Bukhara constituted a potential seat of resistance, similar to the khanate of Kokand in the valley of Fergana, which would be annexed to the general government of Turkistan in 1876, due to endemic revolts. Therefore, it was necessary to get the upper hand by creating a migratory flow that would drain Bukhara of its most active human resources.[24] This relatively liberal policy focused in its first phase on (1) making available the status of Russian subjects,[25] *poddanstvo* (decree of April 29, 1866), the obtainment of which was facilitated by joining a Russian merchant guild, and (2) the opening up to local Jews of rights to residency and access to real estate outside Bukhara. Thus, less than a century after the religious resurgence of the Bukharan Jewish community, the economic circuits of Turkistan were reactivated. A new layer of well-to-do entrepreneurs appeared, profoundly modifying the sociological stratification of the community. The Vodiaev family (father and sons), who called themselves "the Rothschilds of Turkistan," were members of the first guild of Moscow and possessed silk mills, cotton carding enterprises, the facilities for production of karakul skins, railway cars, and important interests in the exportation of cotton to Russia and England. The Vodiaev family lived in Kokand, like the Simkhaev and Potilahov families, by contrast with the Davydovs (Davidoffs), members of the second guild of Tashkent, where they were based:[26] in June 1865, at the time of the takeover of Tashkent by Russia, the records show twenty-seven Jewish families, that is, 150 people; in 1901 there were 534 in the old city and 921 in the new, out of a total population of 163,342 inhabitants. All attempted to practice a strong endogamy in order not to split up their capital.[27]

Thus, one of the goals of Jewish emigration from Bukhara to Russian Turkistan was the possibility for the most affluent to acquire real estate and develop large commercial family firms. In present-day Kokand, the town hall and post office buildings that once housed the commercial enterprises of these great families, who concentrated in their hands a considerable portion of the exports and commercial exchanges with Russia and various European countries, can still be seen.[28] Thus, Tsion Vodiaev sold his cotton directly in Liverpool, using his own railway cars.[29] It is not surprising that the Russian administration had to reverse its policy in Turkistan completely by attempting to retract formerly granted advantages, or at least stopping the outstanding success of some of them.[30] Thus, a certain Nathan Davidoff, having acquired coal mines in the region of Andijan (not without difficulty before 1917), found himself at odds with the

Wealthy Jewish merchants of Tashkent, Uzbekistan. Nineteenth-century engraving, drawing by E. Ronjat. Paris, Bibliothèque Nationale Française.

czarist administration, which refused him the concession of a railroad track to connect his mine to the closest station.

Birth of a "Jewish question" in Turkistan

The Russian regime, after having sought to win over an enterprising religious minority (the only one available) well disposed toward it, got caught up in the "Jewish question": it had to protect the interests of the Russian traders and entrepreneurs while at the same time avoiding the displeasure of the urban Muslim elites and the rural poor, who had been impoverished by nascent capitalism and the lack of arable land. It is within this context that the prohibition against Jews settling in the rural areas must be placed—a ban that was rarely circumvented, except in the case of factories or businesses built by local Jews along the train lines.

Thus, beginning at the end of the 1890s, Russian policy began to harden toward them. This is due especially to the climate of insurrection maintained by certain local Muslims whose undeclared longing for a holy war against the Russian power had manifested itself on several occasions in the Fergana valley, which prompted that power to spread the notion that the Jews "were oppressing the Muslims" in order to deflect animosity from itself.[31] Another cause concerned the waning influence of the local Jews in Turkistan. A disagreement developed within the seat of Russian power, in which the War and Justice

Ministries opposed those of Commerce and Industry concerning the decisions to be taken with regard to the minority whose economic importance was on the rise. That opposition had "vertical" repercussions in the relationships between the cabinet and the Governor-Generalship of Turkistan, founded in 1867 and directed at the time by General von Kaufman, the *yarim padshah* of Turkistan (half Padishah). Their rights of residency were therefore revised in keeping with the Regulations on the Management of Turkistan, enacted in 1887 by the colonial administration of Turkistan and supplemented by a provision of the senate of 1889. Threatened from this point on by expulsion, Jewish residents had to prove by the testimony of two witnesses that they had settled in the territory of Russian Turkistan (or of their ancestors) before the czarist conquest.

Furthermore, the Jews "of neighboring countries," namely, Bukhara (in which there remained no more than 2,800 Jews in 1914[32]) and Afghanistan, were henceforth divided into two categories. The first was made up of those who had not become Russian subjects (i.e., who had not obtained *poddanstvo*), called "foreign Jews," and had not had access to real estate. They had five years, starting from 1901, to settle in Och, Katta-Kurgan, or Petro-Aleksandrovsk, a deadline extended to 1909, then 1910, with the later addition of three other cities: Samarkand, Margilan, and Kokand.[33] The second group (less numerous) comprised those who had obtained the Russian

Jewish children with their instructor in Samarkand. One of the first color photographs from the explorer Sergei Prokudin-Gorskii, from his documentary on the Russian Empire in the years 1909–15. Sergei Mikhailovich Prokudin-Gorskii Collection, Library of Congress, New York.

poddanstvo, which included an authorization of residency in one of the cities open to Jewish settlement and an enrollment (difficult to obtain) in the trade guild of that same city, which allowed them to buy real estate. But it was absolutely forbidden for them to take part in the commerce of alcohol and wine production (as they traditionally had in the emirate of Bukhara).[34]

Beyond these legal restrictions, the quasi-monopolies on commerce held by a Jewish oligarchy, even on a reduced scale, could not fail to displease the Muslim majority—as was well understood by the colonial power. Anti-Semitic campaigns were launched, relayed by the local Muslim press, which railed against the Jews and the Armenians. The military authorities raised a state of alarm, and especially after 1910–11, the czarist government mobilized to pit the Turkistani peasants, ruined by years of consecutive drought, against the large Jewish concerns, like that of Nathan Davidoff,[35] who was accused of charging excessive loan rates or loans impossible to repay other than by the sale of land.

The archives of the chancelleries of Samarkand, Jizzakh, and Kokand are rich in documents, reports, secret circulars, and attestations dating back to the beginning of the twentieth century in which Jewish families from Turkistan attempted to prove that they had lived there for a long time and requested residence permits for Jews from the protectorate of Bukhara and foreign Jews who had been arrested without papers upon the expulsion of the Jews from Persia, Afghanistan, or Bukhara.[36] This issue of obtaining residency authorization was important enough that it was often treated in secret files and became an inducement for pogroms as a solution to the difficulties of the Russian powers in Turkistan.[37] It is true that the Jews of Central Asia spread Russian influence in the region (Russian merchandise, the Russian language) and that their offspring attended Russo-indigenous business schools,[38] dressed like Russians, and bought their real estate from Russians—in excessive numbers, apparently.

Moreover, the disputes between Jews and Muslims were settled by what the colonial administration called courts of the people (*narodnyj sud*), whose judges were chosen from among "politically appropriate men": that is, Muslims well disposed toward Russia.[39] On the other hand, as soon as a conflict arose in which the opponent was a Russian subject, an "international tribunal" (an expression foreshadowing a Sovietism waiting in the wings of history) was assembled.

Future ruptures

The Revolution of 1917 required the Jews of the Russian Empire to choose between Zionism and communism. Many Bukharan Jews chose the "ascent" to Palestine (aliyah) to realize the Zionist dream (founding the *rehovot* quarter outside the precinct of Jerusalem), while oth-

> **"The Revolution of 1917 required the Jews of the Russian Empire to choose between Zionism and communism. Many Bukharan Jews chose the 'ascent' to Palestine."**

265

ers joined the communist structures of *Yevsektsia* (Jewish section of the Communist Party of the Soviet Union). Many Bukharan Jewish families who remained in Turkistan were ruined by the civil war and collectivization. Some managed to immigrate to Europe or the United States via the Caucasus and Turkey (as did the Vodiaev, Simkhaev, and Potilakhov families), while others remained, which brought about an economic restructuring.

The Soviet regime undertook the secularization of Bukharan Judaism by dismantling the educational system, constructing a proletarian Jewish culture (later destroyed by Stalin), and establishing Jewish kolkhozes in Uzbekistan. During the Soviet period, the situation of the Jews became as complex from the point of view of religious practice as that of the Muslim majority. The official atheist ideology necessitated adaptations for both religious communities—a new social contract and secret practices. Its application varied according to the directors in place in the Kremlin. Beyond the fluctuations in the dialogue between the state and religions in the USSR, the independence of 1991 was not reassuring for the Bukharan Jews, who feared they might become scapegoats in the economic crisis brought on by the dislocation of the socialist system. But the diplomatic and economic relations between independent Uzbekistan and Israel were excellent, which was displeasing to neighboring Iran. Of the 36,568 Bukharans tallied in 1989, most have left Central Asia.In Bukhara today there remain only a few families. The Jewish community of Bukhara has disappeared from its original land and brought about a veritable renaissance, as a diaspora of the Diaspora, in Israel and especially in the United States—specifically in New York, where the borough of Queens alone has 40,000 Bukharian Jews.

1. See the studies by Albert Kaganovitch, including his doctoral thesis on the relations between the Russian administration and the Jews of Bukhara, their legal status from 1868 to 1917 (in Russian; Jerusalem, 2003) and *Bukharan Jews in the 20th Century: History, Experience and Narration*, ed. I. Baldauf, M. Gammer, and T. Loy (Wiesbaden: Reichert-Verlag, 2008).

2. Ibid., 307, on the 800 to 1,000 Jewish families living in Bukhara at the beginning of the nineteenth century, 300 of which, according to the English missionary J. Wolff, were forced to convert to Islam, and went under the name of Chala (or Anusim, "the forced," in Hebrew), in *Researches and Missionary Labours among the Jews, Mohammedans and Other Sects, by the Rev. J. Wolff during His Travels between the Years 1831 and 1834* (London: J. Nisbet & Co., 1835; repr., Philadelphia: O. Rogers, 1837).

3. They would number 22,000 in 1914, of which 2,800 were in Bukhara, after decades of economic development, but only 24,500 in 1926, because of the civil war. See A. Kaganovitch, "Bukhara," in *Encyclopaedia of Jews in the Islamic World*, ed. Norman A. Stillman (Leiden: Brill, 2010), 510.

4. W. Fischel, "The Jews in Medieval Iran from the Sixteenth to the Eighteenth Century: Political, Economic and Communal Aspects," in *Irano-Judaica* (Jerusalem: Ben-Zvi Institute, 1982), 265–91.

5. See C. Poujol, "Les relations entre l'Asie centrale et la Palestine ou les voies d'un sionisme affectif, 1793–1917," *Cahiers du Monde russe et soviétique* 32, no. 1 (Jan.–Mar. 1991): 33–42.

6. When he arrived there, the Jews were eating the meat of the Muslims, no longer observed Shabbat, and possessed only the first three books of the Bible. See G. de Meyendorff, *Voyage d'Orenbourg à Boukhara fait en 1820* (Paris: Librairie Dondey-Dupré, 1826), 175.

7. On their settlement in the Fergana valley, see C. Poujol, "Approaches to the History of Bukharan Jews' Settlement in the Fergana Valley, 1867–1917," *Central Asian Survey* 12, no. 4 (1993): 549–56.

8. Zalman Lvovitch Amitin-Shapiro (1893–1970?), an Ashkenazi Jew, born in Bielorussia, was the first professor at the Soviet school created for the Jewish children of Bukhara in 1918, where the national language was Hebrew from 1922 to 1923. Arrested in 1938, he moved to Bishkek after five years of detention, and spent the remainder of his life as a historiographer there. His most complete work is "Essay on the Jurisdiction of the Jews of Central Asia" (Tashkent, 1931) (in Russian).

9. O. D. Soukhareva, "The Quarter Community in the Post-Feudal City of Bukhara" (in Russian) (Moscow: Nauka, 1976).

10. They had a monopoly, until 1865, on the blue dyeing of silk and cotton thread for the cloth known as *kalgay*, used to produce women's undergarments; M. Zand, "Bukharan Jewry," *Pe'amim* 35 (Jerusalem, 1988), 74–75.

11. Z. L. Amitin-Shapiro, "On the Folk Medicine of the Bukharan Jews" (in Russian), *Bjulleten' SAGU*, no. 13, *Tashkent* (1926): 13–14.

12. The following pages draw some of their inspiration from my article published in *La revue du Monde Musulman et de la Méditerranée*, 107–10, "Les juifs de Boukhara ou la fin d'un double enclavement minoritaire, 1897–1918," in *Identités confessionnelles et espaces urbains en terres d'Islam* (Aix en Provence: Edisud, 2005).

13. Which, in his terms, corresponds to the canonic tax set by Abu-Hanifa, given the correspondence between the *tenga* (2.975g) and the silver dirhem; see Fischel, "The Jews in Medieval Iran from the Sixteenth to the Eighteenth Century."

14. Baruch Moshavi, *Customs and Folklore of Nineteenth-Century Bukharan Jews in Central Asia* (microfilm in Hebrew, doctoral thesis) (New York: Yeshiva University Press, 1974).

15. See Amitin-Shapiro, "Essay on the Jurisdiction of the Jews of Central Asia."

16. This is not the view of the research scholar Albert Kaganovitch, who insists mainly on the antagonism between the two communities, specifically in his academic work titled "The Relations between the Jews of Bukhara and the Muslims of Central Asia from the Beginning of Islamization to Our Times," at the Vidal Sassoon International Center for the Study of Antisemitism in Jerusalem. The historian David Ochildiev introduces a case-by-case approach: depending on the emir in power, and depending on the importance of the individual to be converted. Thus, the court physician or the singer would be a Muslim, as verified by the investigations of the author between 1985 and 2007.

17. They would not be able to be exploited by the Russian general staff to deflect Muslim anti-Russian sentiment when the state of emergency was decreed in Turkistan; see below.

18. *La vie de Yakuv Samandar ou les revers du destin*, a historical novella by Mordekhai Batchaev, translated from Tajik and introduced by Catherine Poujol, preface by Michael Zand, Papers in Inner Asia 19, Indiana University, Research Institute for Inner Asian Studies (1992).

19. *Encyclopaedia Iranica*, vol. 4, col. 535; S. Vajsenberg, *Evrej v Turkestane* [The Jews in Turkestan] (in Russian), *Evrejskaja starina*, no. 3 (St. Petersburg, 1912), 394.

20. Successive surveys by C. Poujol in Bukhara between 1979 and 2007. M. Zand, "Conversion of Jews to Islam in Central Asia in 18–19 Centuries and the Formation of the Chala (Central Asian Crypto Jews Group)," Fourteenth International Congress of the International Association for the History of Religions, Abstract, Winnipeg, Canada, 1980, 94.

21. The bibliography on this subject is considerable. See the *Systematic Index of Studies on the Jews in the Russian Language from 1708 to December 1889* (in Russian) (St. Petersburg, 1892).

22. On the Anglo-Russian rivalry, see G. N. Curzon, *Russia in Central Asia* (London, 1889), and V. I. Lebedev, *Russes et Anglais en Asie centrale, vers l'Inde* (Paris: Nabu Press, 1900).

23. Nahum Sokolow, *History of Zionism* (London: Longmans, Green, 1919), 1:101–32.

24. See C. Poujol, "Approaches to the History of Bukharan Jews' Settlement in the Fergana Valley, 1867–1917."

25. M. I. Mys, *Manuel sur les lois russes sur les juifs*, 4th ed. (in Russian) (St. Petersburg, 1914); *Journal de Nathan Davidoff, Le Juif qui voulait sauver le Tsar*, translated from Russian and Hebrew by Benjamin Ben David and Yankel Mandel (Paris: Gingko éditeur, 2002), 185–214.

26. Dmitriev-Mamonov, *Putevoditel' po Turkestanu i Sredneaziatskoj zeleznoj dorogi* (Collection on Turkestan and the Great Siberian Railway (in Russian) (St. Petersburg, 1903), 379–89.

27. The practice of consanguine marriages to preserve the family patrimony was current among Muslims as well as among the Jews of Central Asia. This tendency holds true in the case of the Davidoff family, which had two hundred members at the beginning of the twentieth century (*Journal de Nathan Davidoff, Le Juif qui voulait sauver le Tsar*, 194).

28. C. Poujol, "Les relations entre l'Asie centrale et la Palestine ou les voies d'un sionisme affectif 1793–1917," 33–42. In the *Catalogue des archives centrales de l'Ouzbékistan* (in Russian) (Tashkent, 1948), we find that out of seven large companies that existed in Turkistan at the end of the nineteenth century, three belonged to the great Jewish Bukharan families (124–28). Similarly, out of 67 commercial companies, "27 belonged to Jews divided into 20 families" (Dmitriev-Mamonov, *Putevoditel' po Turkestanu*, 379–89).

29. Information given by one of his children who lived in Istanbul, met by the author during the year 1986–87.

30. Binyamin Ben David, "Nathan Davidoff, Industrialist of Russian Turkestan," *Les cahiers d'Asie centrale*, no. 8 (Aix en Provence: Tashkent): 171–86, and *Journal de Nathan Davidoff*, 43–48.

31. According to the terms used by the czarist bureaucrats, especially under the influence of the governor-general of Turkistan A. I. Samsonov (1909–14) and of the regional administration of Fergana, very sensitive to the rise of Zionism among the Jews of Bukhara (Amitin-Shapiro, "Essay on the Jurisdiction," 23).

32. A. Kaganovitch, doctoral thesis on "The Relations between the Russian Administration and the Jews of Bukhara, Their Legal Status from 1868 to 1917" (in Russian) (Jerusalem, 2003), 38–39.

33. S. Vajsenberg points out the illogical nature of the Russian jurisdiction that considers the Jews originating in the protectorate of Bukhara as foreign, while at the same time forbidding Russian Jews to move there under the pretext that it was a portion of the empire outside of their authorized "zone of residency" (Amitin-Shapiro, "Essay on the Jurisdiction of the Jews of Central Asia"), 20–21.

34. Mys, *Manuel sur les lois russes sur les juifs*, 304–7.

35. For more information on the Nathan Davidoff trial and the exploitation of anti-Semitism in Turkistan, see "Journal of Nathan Davidoff," 208–11, in documents from the Davidoff Collection of the Central Archives of Uzbekistan.

36. State Archives of Uzbekistan, consulted by the author between 1999 and 2001.

37. "Secret Circular of 12/4/1910 to the military governors of the regions of Syr-Daria, Samarkand and Fergana on the differences of approach of the Tsarist administration concerning the classification of Jews according to their place of settlement and real estate" (State Archives of Uzbekistan, old collection, collection 21, register 67/1903, collection 300, register 1). It is during the following period that this sort of problem takes on importance in Turkistan. See A. Kaganovitch, "The Jews of Bukhara facing Soviet Realities, 1920–1930," to appear in Russian in *Ab imperio*.

38. See A. Kaganovitch, "The Education of Bukharan Jews in Turkestan Province, 1865–1917," *Irano-Judaica* 5 (Jerusalem, 2003): 212–13.

39. In the archives of the Jizzakh police, files mention that it is forbidden to choose as a judge of the people a "Sufi propagandist" who had participated in the uprisings of Andijan in 1895.

Chapter IV

Relations with the European World

Judaism and the Religious Denominational Community in the Near East
Henry Laurens

Jews enjoyed a protected status in the Ottoman Empire. In the capital as in the provinces, extending from Algeria to the Caucasus at the Danube, they played an important role in finance. But the rise of Christians in the East, beginning in the eighteenth century, proved detrimental to the Ottoman Jews. The modernization of society in the nineteenth century overtook the established institutionalized religious communities (*millet* in Turkish). This system, which set rules for the emancipation of non-Muslims in the Empire, was born simultaneously from the internal evolution of Ottoman society and European intervention. The Ottoman Jews, although they benefited from a type of "Golden Age" from the Levantine era until the end of the nineteenth century, found themselves further marginalized by the emergence of nationalism.

Henry Laurens

Henry Laurens is a professor at the National Institute of Oriental Languages and Civilizations (INALCO) and the Collège de France, where he holds the chair of History of the Arab World. His publications include a history of Palestine in three volumes—*La question de Palestine* (Fayard, 1999, 2002, 2007)—and *Orientales* (CNRS Éditions).

A hierarchized society

The period of the Ottoman Empire traditionally called classical (sixteenth and seventeenth centuries) is now considered a prolongation, or even a consummation, of medieval Islamic society, while the nineteenth century, under the impact of European imperialism, constitutes the genesis of a new world. Therefore, the period prior to 1800 may be considered that of an ancien régime analogous to that of Europe—a regime in which the primary distinction was not between "orders" but between the governors and the governed. The governors had the theoretical status of "slaves of the Sultan" (*kul*), which gave the master of the empire control over their life and death, as well as the eventual disposition of their property, while the life and property of the governed were considered

The city of Damascus was one of the major centers of the Ottoman Empire. View of the city from the Great Mosque, seventeenth century. Damascus, National Museum of the Arts and Popular Traditions.

to have the protection provided by Islamic law. The society of the governed was organized into a hierarchy of bodies or groups (*taifa*) according to a principle of distinction in terms of honor and dishonor, or of purity and impurity. Thus, although non-Muslims were at the bottom of the social hierarchy as being protected, disarmed, and subject to a special taxation, they had their place in the social order nonetheless. Non-Muslims, then, constituted specific *taifa* by reason of their particular tax status, their specific organization into instituted religious groups, and the distinctions and protections allotted to them. These groups existed in fact, and in social practice, without being recognized as exclusive by the state. Religious courts existed for matters of personal status (marriage, inheritance), but nothing stood in the way of a non-Muslim appearing before a Muslim court if he believed it to be in his best interests, and historical archives suggest that practice was fairly common.

Centralization seems to have worked to the advantage of the religious authorities of the Greek Orthodox and Armenian Churches. The former benefited from a "Byzantinizing" of the Ottoman Empire. The conquest of the Arab Near East at the beginning of the sixteenth century reestablished contact between the patriarchate of Constantinople and those of Antioch and Jerusalem that had been interrupted by the Arab conquests of the seventh century. Similarly, the Holy See had undertaken a vast missionary effort directed at the Eastern churches. The battle between Rome and Constantinople ended in a schism at the beginning of the eighteenth century and the establishment of a Greco-Catholic Church. Orthodox Arabs were dominated by the ethnic Greeks, while the Maronites recognized the authority of Rome. The non-Chalcedonian churches had undergone the same evolution with the creation of Uniate churches (united with Rome). These Catholic churches were the beneficiaries of a de facto protection from France, by virtue of a broad interpretation of the capitulation treaties. The Armenians, thanks to their increasing role in the finances of the Ottoman Empire, had attained a certain degree of power. Because of this, in the seventeenth and eighteenth centuries, a triangular conflict existed among Greek Orthodox, Armenians, and Catholics over the control of Christian holy places in the Holy Land.

Contrary to these three large groups, it seems that there was no centralized and influential Jewish community within the empire. It is true that in the sixteenth century a massive number of Jewish immigrants arrived from Spain, expelled by the Catholic monarchs, and certain important Jewish figures had various forms of political influence, but that golden age did not last long. In the Near East, the Jews had economic specialties, in particular, custom duties

> **" The first difference between the Jews and the Christians is that the Christian populations were generally rural. "**

and the finance of local potentates, but they were always in a triadic relation with the Muslims and the Christians—quite the opposite of their status in the Maghreb, where they constituted the only indigenous non-Muslim group.

The Ottoman conquest seems to have made possible a demographic reawakening of non-Muslims after their numerical decline during the preceding centuries. The only reliable data we have are for the sixteenth and nineteenth centuries. In the Fertile Crescent around 1580, Christians represented approximately 7.3 percent of the total population and Jews 0.9 percent. In 1880, Christians and Jews represented 18.1 percent and 2.4 percent of the population, respectively, and two-thirds of the Jewish population was concentrated in the territories that make up present-day Iraq. (The specific situation of Yemen is not taken into account here.) The growth of the Iraqi Jewish population seems to be connected with waves of immigration from Iran, where conditions for the Jews had deteriorated considerably. Thus, the natural growth of the Jewish population was weaker than that of the Christian.

The first difference between the Jews and the Christians is that the Christian populations were generally rural, often mountain-based, while the Jewish population was essentially urban. In ancient societies, urban populations most often diminished over time, largely due to recurrent epidemics. The second difference is that the Catholics had growing support from Christian Europe, thanks to the work of missionaries and the action of Catholic states. The tenor of life among the Eastern Christians, Catholics primarily, developed in increasing harmony with European society; Eastern Jews did not dispose of any such advantage. The increasing dynamism of the Catholic Greeks worked to the detriment of the Mediterranean Jewish communities, who, from the middle of the eighteenth century, lost their positions in finance and custom duties. In Constantinople we find similar developments, this time to the advantage of Gregorian Catholic Armenians. The Jews fell victim to their traditional association with the Janissaries, who, until their brutal suppression in 1826, were considered adversaries of the first Ottoman reforms.

As a result, the Jews of the Near East were in full social and economic decline at the beginning of the nineteenth century, at a time when the direct influence of Europe was becoming stronger. Nevertheless, certain Jewish notables had European consular protection. The Iraqi Jews seem to have been untouched by this trend, but their region was considered "backward" by the Ottoman reformers. On the other hand, the economic relations of that region with India, which was in the process of being taken over by the British, became more intense. In the nineteenth century, Great Britain favored this trade between Iraq and India and the settlement of "Baghdadi" Jews in its possessions on the Indian Ocean, even as far as Singapore and Hong Kong.

The Ottoman reforms

From the second half of the eighteenth century, the ruling Ottoman circles became aware of the increasing imbalance of power between them and a Christian Europe, in which a carving up of the Ottoman Empire is mentioned publicly. This was the beginning of what would later be called the "Eastern question." Napoleon Bonaparte's Egyptian expedition of 1798–1801 marked the beginning of European power confrontations surrounding the route to India. Contrary to popular belief, Bonaparte never considered establishing a Jewish state in Palestine, even if certain others did so for him in Protestant England and among Frankist messianic circles in Central Europe. Despite his declarations of friendship toward Islam, Bonaparte appeared to count on the support of the local Christians, Copts, and Greek Catholics (the Maronites maintaining a wait-and-see position). He did not try to make Eastern Jews political players, probably because they did not seem to him to represent a force of consequence. For this reason they escaped the reprisals and exile that followed the French expedition to Egypt.

Contrary to popular belief, Bonaparte never considered establishing a Jewish state in Palestine.

The first Ottoman reforms tended to favor a return to the old institutions of the empire, then toward the adoption of the forms of the modern European state, characterized by a rationalized administration and fiscal system, as well as by the adoption of a military draft. The Greek revolt of 1821 challenged the relations of subordination between Christians and Muslims. In the Near East, the period referred to as the "Syrian wars" (1833–41) between the Egypt of Mehmed Ali and the Ottoman

Empire witnessed a de facto emancipation of non-Muslims. The 1839 edict known as "of Gülhane" abolished the distinction between "governors" and "governed" according to the principles of European economic liberalism: "If there is an absence of security for property, everyone remains indifferent to his state and his community; no one interests himself in the prosperity of the country, absorbed as he is in his own troubles and worries. If, on the contrary, the individual feels complete security about his possessions then he will become preoccupied with his own affairs, which he will seek to expand, and his devotion and love for his state and his community will steadily grow and will undoubtedly spur him into becoming a useful member of society."[1]

Fiscal reform was announced as follows: "It is therefore necessary that henceforth each member of Ottoman society be taxed at a determined rate, according to his fortune and his faculties, and that nothing beyond that can be required of him."

The same equality was announced with respect to military recruitment. While the aim of the edict was for the governors to free themselves of domination by the sultan, by extension or by intellectual necessity the reforms extended to non-Muslims: "These imperial concessions extend to include all of our subjects; of whatever religion or sect they may be, they will enjoy them without exception. A perfect security is therefore granted by us to the inhabitants of the Empire, in their life, their honor and their fortune, as is required by the sacred text of our law."

This edict, in terms of the expression of principles, was the Eastern equivalent of the Night of the Fourth of August.[2] It put an end to a traditional social order, which, though shaken, had existed for more than a thousand years. In the view of the authorities,

Jewish woman. Miniature taken from the *Zanannameh* (Book of Women) by Fazil Enderuni, showing a woman dressed in the French fasion. Istanbul, eighteenth century. London, British Museum.

the requirement of statutory equality of all replaced the old system of protection while appealing in theory to the same religious rules that had given the old order legitimacy.

This secondary aspect of the edict of Gülhane took on prime importance due to the growing interventions of the Europeans in favor of non-Muslims. The Damascus affair of 1840 is emblematic in this respect.

While clearly the accusation of ritual crime belongs to the last stage of the elimination of the Near Eastern Jews from their positions in the Ottoman system, to the benefit of the Greek Catholics, it is also clear that the mobilization of the Jews of Western Europe under the leadership of Crémieux and Montefiore introduced the fate of non-Muslim Ottomans into international politics. Every intervention in favor of non-Muslims was responded to by reference to the edict of Gülhane.

Nonetheless, the essential question remained that of the Ottoman Christians, who were in full economic, social, and cultural development. Catholics enjoyed support from France; the Orthodox had protection from Russia. While Great Britain outlined a similar strategy toward the Jews, the desire of the Protestant missions to convert them raised implacable suspicion. As a result, while Jews received increasing consular protections, the will among European countries to establish a religious protectorate for the Jews of the empire as a whole was absent or considered impracticable.

Consequently, Jews were kept at a distance from the mid-nineteenth-century religious denominational tensions in the Syrian provinces. Muslims viewed the Christians, in addition to their violating the traditional order that relegated them to a secondary position, as agents of the European powers. Thus, the Jews escaped the Aleppo riots of 1850 and the massacres of Mount Lebanon and Damascus in 1860. They were not considered violators of the traditional order or a threat to the upholding of Islam.

The Crimean War (1854–56) challenged the survival of the Ottoman Empire and the status of non-Muslims. France and Great Britain, allied with the Ottomans, imposed an edict of emancipation. But they chose emancipation at the level of the community, not the individual, in contrast to the emancipation of non-Christians in Europe. The Hatti Humayoun of February 18, 1856, was presented by the Porte as consistent with the Ottoman administrative tradition; it founded the system of the *millet*, or nation (taken in the sense of community): "Every Christian or other non-Muslim community shall be bound, within a fixed period, and with the concurrence of a commission composed ad hoc of members of its own body, to proceed, with my high approbation and under the inspection of my Sublime Porte, to examine its actual immunities and privileges, and to discuss and submit to my Sublime Porte the reforms required by the progress of civilization and of the age. The powers conceded to the Christian patriarchs and bishops by the Sultan Mehmed II and his successors shall be made to harmonize with the new position which my generous and beneficent intentions ensure to these communities. The principle of nominating the patriarchs for life, after the revision of the rules of election now in force, shall be exactly carried out, conformable to the tenor of their firmans of investiture. The patriarchs, metropolitans, archbishops, bishops, and rabbis shall take an oath on their entrance into office according to a form agreed upon in common by my Sublime Porte and the spiritual heads of the different religious communities. The ecclesiastical dues, of whatever sort or nature they be, shall be abolished and replaced by fixed revenues of the patriarchs and heads of communities, and by the allocation of allowances and salaries equitably proportioned to the importance, rank, and dignity of the different members of the clergy."[3]

The entire system of protection, without ever being explicitly named, was abolished, and full freedom granted to the exercise of worship: "Each sect, in localities where there are no other religious denominations, shall be free from every species of restraint as regards the public exercise of its religion. In the towns, small boroughs, and villages where different sects are mingled together, each community, inhabiting a distinct quarter, shall, by conforming to the above-mentioned ordinances, have equal power to repair and improve its churches, hospitals, schools, and cemeteries. When there is a question of the erection of new buildings, the necessary authority

> **" The edict of emancipation concerned first and foremost Christians, and it was for the purpose of consistency that it was broadened to include Ottoman Jews. "**

must be asked for through the Sublime Porte, which will pronounce a sovereign decision according to that authority, except in the case of administrative obstacles. The intervention of the administrative authority in all measures of this nature will be entirely gratuitous. My Sublime Porte will take energetic measures to ensure to each sect, whatever be the number of its adherents, entire freedom in the exercise of its religion."

As a result, public posts were open to non-Muslims: "The nomination and choice of all public servants and other employees of my Empire being entirely dependent upon my will, all the subjects of my Empire, without distinction of nationality, are admissible to public positions and qualified to hold them, according to their abilities and merits, and in conformity with regulations of general application."

With respect to military recruitment, the principle of a replacement tax for conscription was allowed; this was more a privilege than discrimination, given the human cost of the wars of the Ottoman Empire at the approach of its demise.

The edict of emancipation concerned first and foremost Christians, and it was for the purpose of consistency that it was broadened to include Ottoman Jews, who did not count as political entities in their own right. It is significant that the Treaty of Paris of 1856, in article 9, says nothing about Ottoman Jews: "His Imperial Majesty the Sultan, in his constant care for the well-being of his subjects, having granted a firman that, in improving their lot without distinction of religion or race, devotes his generous intentions to the Christian populations of his Empire, wishing to give a new testimony of his feelings in this respect, had resolved to communicate to the concerned parties of said firman, spontaneously issued from his sovereign will. The concerned parties see the high value of this communication. It is understood that it cannot, under any circumstances, give the right to the said powers to involve themselves, either collectively or separately, in the relations of His Royal Majesty the Sultan with his subjects, nor in the interior administration of his Empire."

▶ See article by Catherine Poujol, pp. 258–268. It was difficult for Russia to recognize the emancipation of the Ottoman Jews while its domestic politics remained discriminatory. Moreover, in Great Britain, Austria-Hungary, and the German states, the emancipation of the Jews had not yet been accomplished.

"Jerusalem, Wailing Wall," indicates the inscription at the base of this photograph, taken around 1870, by Félix Bonfils of France. Paris, Musée d'Art et d'Histoire du Judaïsme.

Levantine society

The consequence of the Hatti Humayoun was to structure the Jewish *millet* on the model of the Christian denominational community. The regulation was adopted in 1856. The grand rabbi of Constantinople was granted the status equivalent to that of a Christian patriarch. It was a relatively artificial construction, and the Jewish community never attained the degree of coherence and centralization of Christian communities. The *millet* concerned above all the Jewish population of the capital, but the grand rabbi was considered the spokesman of the entirety of the rabbis of the empire, and as such became the interlocutor of the authorities. Despite the assurances of the Treaty of Paris, the system of consular protection, with its fiscal and juridical principles, continued to spread in the Jewish population.

The next step was the constitution of the Alliance Israélite Universelle in 1860. Despite its plan of concentrating all its vital forces on Judaism, the new institution was a sure indicator of French influence. It was, in fact, the Israelite counterpart to the French Catholic missions. Its working language was French and its scholarly work considerable. As in the case of Catholic missions, a specific pedagogy was conceived for use with Eastern populations. At the end of the nineteenth century, Muslim students were admitted into the schools of the Alliance, esteemed for the high quality of their instruction. Conversely, some Israelites frequented Catholic schools, which were considered to be at a higher level, particularly Jesuit colleges. Periodically, issues of conversion provoked strong tension.

> *"At the end of the nineteenth century, Muslim students were admitted into the schools of the Alliance, esteemed for the high quality of their instruction."*

Thus, there was no contradiction between a project that wished to be assimilationist in the Ottoman sphere and the growing Gallicization of the new Jewish elites of the empire. This was because French was the language of modernity in the Ottoman Empire, and the administrative second language. It was the main language of communication and sociability of the Levantine society of the Eastern Mediterranean, the high point of which was between 1860 and 1914. One could express oneself in French and proclaim oneself to be an "Ottomanist," that is, a citizen of the Ottoman Empire. But the Levantine Jew, like the Levantine Christian, also tried to acquire one or several consular protections, a step leading to the adoption of a European nationality.

However, contrary to the Christian Arabs, the Jews, barring a few brilliant exceptions (such as James Sanua [Yaqub Sanu] in Egypt), steered clear of the Arab cultural renaissance of the second half of the nineteenth century, the Nahda. Their modernization essentially took place in French. In Iraq, Arabization was relatively stronger, and English, the language of business, was in vigorous rivalry with French, but that country only played a secondary role in the Nahda. Without any territorial base, the Ottoman Jews seemed destined to escape the trap of nationalism. They were both faithful to the empire and desirous of acquiring foreign protection.

The appearance of Zionism upset this precariously balanced system. Obviously, the emergence of a Jewish nationalism was associated with the multiple national affirmations that began to fragment the delicate Levantine society at the beginning of the twentieth century. In the Balkans, the Orthodox *millet* was divided into nations with territorial orientations (ethnic Greeks, Serbs, Bulgarians, and Romanians). In this Balkan context, Zionism was in competition with the assimilative project of the Alliance. In Anatolia, the opening of the "Armenian question" in the 1890s, and the Greek project of reconquest, announced an extension of Balkanization. Violence of various kinds, massacres, and terrorism foreshadowed a relatively somber future. In the Arab East, the Israelites stayed away from the Arab autonomist movement, made up of Muslims and Christians who rose up in the wake of the Young Turk Revolution of 1908.

In Palestine, the confrontation between the old Eastern Jewish communities and the newly arrived Zionists was direct. The Arab population and the Ottoman authorities learned by reading the European press about the territorial ambitions of Zionism, though these were downplayed by its local representatives in Palestine. Ottomanism remained the official discourse, just as the attachment to Levantine indecision allowed the relatively peaceful coexistence of communities, but the Ottoman Jews were on their way to becoming political players.

The importance of the third party

In the Near East and the Ottoman Empire, the evolution of the Jewish communities is to be understood in a triadic relation with the Christians and the Muslims. In the new society that was emerging in the process of reform and modernization, the Jews were led to mold themselves within the system of *millets*, which were defined according to Christian communities. Also, the Levantine moment, with its indeterminations and foreign protections, was of great help to the Jewish communities in the process of economic and cultural renascence after the decline of the preceding period. The "apoliticism" of the Ottoman Jews, in contrast with the clamorously demanding Christians, had the appearance of a pledge of faithfulness toward the Ottoman authorities.

> *"In the Near East and the Ottoman Empire, the evolution of the Jewish communities is to be understood in a triadic relation with the Christians and the Muslims."*

Nevertheless, the new culture disseminated in particular schools of the Alliance, if it was adapted to the then triumphant Levantine model, was combined with the legacy of the preceding period, which set the Jewish communities apart from the Arab cultural renaissance of the second half of the nineteenth century. Modern Arab culture, which prefigured nationalism, was a common creation of Christians and Muslims, without any marked Jewish participation. The same is true of the Arab movement of independence after the Young Turk Revolution. Only Zionism, as much among its partisans as its adversaries, politicized the Jewish communities, who were caught up in the discourse of Ottomanism and the practice of foreign protections.

The fall of the Ottoman Empire put an end to the Sunni caliphate authority and the centralized religious administration accompanying it. It allowed for the emancipation of the non-Sunni Muslims, making the Sunnis one community among others. The model of the religious denominational community was generalized to include all Muslims in the aftermath of the First World War, at a time when Muslim demographic growth was becoming

School for Boys, Baghdad, 1898. Archives of the Alliance Israélite Universelle.

stronger than that of non-Muslims. The formation of the local modern state clashed with that reality—the generalization of the religious community that acquired a political representation de facto or de jure (seats reserved for a community).v

Based on the reality of their own society, the Arabs of the Near East interpreted Zionism as the will of a religious community to become territorialized, which could only lead to an ethnic homogenization and prompt similar callings on the part of other communities, as attested by the theme of the "national Christian homeland" in the Lebanon of the 1930s. Thus, we enter the infernal process of the suspicion of disloyalty directed against the Jews of the Near East, who were suspected of being hidden partisans of Zionism. This mechanism was one of the emerging factors of anti-Semitism in the Muslim population of the 1930s, particularly in the Sunni religious movement, which is found in the Muslim Brotherhood. The so-called Wailing Wall riots of 1929 were a pivotal moment, because they heralded the clash between the Jewish and Muslim worlds in the worst of historical contexts, that of the accession of Nazism to power. The dynamics that were in the process of being put into place would lead inexorably to the disappearance of the Jews from the lands of Islam. ❱ See article by Mark R. Cohen, pp. 546–553.

1. [This quotation, with slight modifications, and the two following from the Gülhane Decree are available at the site http://sitemaker.umich.edu/emes/sourcebook/da.data/97045/FileSource/1839_gulhane.pdf—Trans.]

2. [This is an allusion to the unanimous abolition of feudal rights and privileges by the National Constitutional Assembly during the French Revolution of 1789.—Trans.]

3. [This quotation, with slight modifications, and the two following from the Hatti Humayoun are available at the site http://www.anayasa.gen.tr/reform.htm.—Trans.]

In Alexandria, the New Cosmopolitan Reality

At the beginning of the nineteenth century the Jewish population of Alexandria, a community with roots going back thousands of years, was just beginning to emerge from a long decline. It appears to have consisted of no more than a few dozen families in 1820, and in 1830 it still had fewer than four thousand members, a situation reminiscent of the one in 1481, when, a few years before the arrival of a new Jewish population fleeing persecution on the Iberian Peninsula, between sixty and seventy Jewish families were settled there, according to the Tuscan traveler Meshullam da Volterra. A considerable surge had ensued, further reinforced during the Ottoman period by the arrival of Jews from the Maghreb. But at the turn of the nineteenth century, signs of vitality were still infrequent despite strong Jewish involvement in local business, as well as in the Ottoman administration—in customs, for example. The situation of the Jewish community was still, at the beginning of the nineteenth century, governed by the principles of the Old Regime: an imperial Ottoman interpretation of Egypt's medieval Islamic precepts and practices.

Coexistence rested on the recognition of a certain number of prerogatives of local communities, among them the Jewish one, which was dominated by the Karaites. This community, endowed with its own institutions of representation and distribution of the tax burden, was directed by the council of notables, in which the principal families were represented. Directed by the "head of the Jews" (ra'īs al-yahūd), it represented one of the voices within the urban civic organization of the Ottoman Old Regime, which meant participation in the council of notables of the city, the right to address the sultan, and the right to petition. Thus, coexistence was organized at the intersection of the local and imperial spheres. The Jews of Alexandria spoke mainly Arabic, Hebrew being the ritual language and Osmanli the language of the administration. At a moment of confluence traversed by a period of French occupation, the Ottoman restoration, followed by the reign of Mehemet Ali, and finally by British colonization, we should not read Old Regime coexistence solely from the angle of the protection granted to dhimmīs, but also see it as a system of governance of diversity. Places of residence reflected, at least in part, the community's lines of division. Alexandria had a Jewish quarter, hārat al-yahūd, but not all Alexandrian Jews lived there. At the turn of the nineteenth century, some Muslims and Christians also lived in that quarter, which was not closed. Wealthy Jewish merchants and businessmen generally lived in the business district of the souks, and the poor sometimes lived just outside the city in precarious habitations. Daily life reflected a coexistence in which religious lines of division were bridged by other forms of sociality: neighborhoods, trades, or affinities also regulated relations. There were mixed corporations in which Jewish, Muslim, and Christian artisans rubbed shoulders. Of course, we should not have an unduly irenic view of that coexistence, since urban life in Alexandria was marked by many incidents, revolts, and injustices, but rather integrate that interpretation with a global reading of Ottoman Islamic societies. The Old Regime managed a governance of diversity based on essentially nonegalitarian principles, which recognized the plurality of communities, trades, and social statuses and organized a hierarchy of them, but that at the same time guaranteed a certain form of self-government and representation.

Beginning in the mid-nineteenth century, many elements of this secular reality were confronted with the sudden appearance of new elements. First, there was the arrival of a massive number—given the size of the local community—of Jews in the city, most from other provinces of the Ottoman Empire. The number of Jews in Alexandria multiplied tenfold in a few decades, reaching about forty thousand. Among them, the Greek Jews from Istanbul and the Ionian Islands were the most prevalent, but Levantine Jews from Anatolia and from the Arabian Peninsula were also attracted by Egypt's new prosperity. Many Ottoman Jews also fled the Maghreb, which was in the process of being colonized, and settled in Alexandria, thus retracing the traditional routes of migration. At the same time, the city, clearly growing from the 1840s, received a large European immigration comprised of many Jews from Romania and the margins of the Russian and Austro-Hungarian Empires, but also from Alsace and, later, Germany. This change accentuated the diversity of a community that was by no means homogeneous to begin with. The caesura was clear, both (sociologically) between the poor common people or artisans of the traditional community and merchants or contractors from other cities of the Ottoman Empire or Europe, and between Arabic speakers or Ottomans and European migrants. The sociability and traits of daily life among these new populations differed from those of the Ottoman legacy of the Old Regime: the Jews of Alexandria who belonged to these new classes devoted themselves to international business and to transforming the city into a bourgeois space in which housing was reconfigured by a whole generation of architects. They participated in a new form of cultural sociability, with its theaters, coffeehouses, and magazines. Coexistence was organized according to new codes: those of the bourgeois urban life in the nineteenth century—a model that gradually disseminated within the community, including the wealthiest Arabic-speaking Jews.

From the time of the French expedition (1798), which devoted no specific attention to Jewish political representation, Alexandria became the stake of geopolitical rivalries, mainly between France and Great Britain. Indeed, the consuls used their protected status to reinforce their influence among the various factions of the city and the new institutions of city

12376. Zaoud-el-Mara, Jewish Quarters, Alexandria, Egypt.

Copyright 1898, by B. W. Kilburn.

The Jewish quarter of Zaoud-el-Mara, in Alexandrie, photographed by the American B. W. Kilburn. Washington, D.C., Library of Congress.

management. In this context, in which municipal power was concentrated in the hands of merchants and proprietors, the influence of a number of prominent Jewish families grew considerably, alongside that of the great European and Muslim merchants. It would be appropriate to speak of an ephemeral cosmopolitanism, not only cultural and entailing mixed-dwelling neighborhoods in the city but also in respect to governance and urban modernization. The discriminating element was not religion but money, in the framework of a system that entrusted the management of the city to a group of merchant proprietors, within which the Jews showed a large measure of convergence with the views of their Muslim and Christian counterparts. Together, they worked to transform Alexandria into a model municipality. This was, then, the time of a society, if not authentically cosmopolitan—since the poll tax system excluded the majority, including the majority of Jews—then at least of diverse middle classes, with an intense cultural, communal, and commercial life. Under Ismail Pasha (r. 1863–79), a sovereign who fostered the development of the Jewish community, financing was put in place for the reconstruction, in neo-Gothic style, of the Eliyahu Hanavi Synagogue, which had been destroyed by a French bombardment in 1798. This synagogue was rebuilt under the Muhammad Ali Dynasty (Ismail Pasha's grandfather's reign). The Jews of Alexandria occupied an important place in the management of the city and participated in its exceptional expansion. Great families, such as the Aghions and the Menasces, financed schools and community initiatives. The Jewish works of charity, such as those of the Eliyahu Hanavi lodge (1892) or Ezrat Achim (1885), marked the social landscape of the city and reinforced the internal cohesion of the community. These Jewish initiatives lasted throughout the Khedival period and British colonization until formal independence in 1921. During

Eliyahu Hanavi synagogue in Alexandria. Postcard published on the occasion of Rosh Hashanah, early twentieth century.

the same time period, however, there was a noticeable fascination with the European way of life, despite the involvement of many Alexandrian Jews in the birth of the Egyptian nationalist movement.

At the moment of independence, the status of Jews diverged between former Ottoman subjects becoming Egyptian and European Jews either remaining stateless or reverting to the citizenship of their country of origin. To this must be added the legacy system, which gave the protection of European citizenship to many Alexandrian Jews. In the twentieth century, in which identities paradoxically polarized around strong ideologies in 1948—and even more so in 1967—the fragile compromise that resulted from the cosmopolitanism of the nineteenth century entered a time of crisis. In an international geopolitical situation and an Egyptian political one that placed the Alexandrian Jews—not previously active in the Zionist movement—in an untenable situation, this was in many ways the end of coexistence. ●

A historian at the Zentrum Moderner Orient in Berlin, Nora Lafi is a specialist on the Ottoman Empire and urbanism in the Arab world during the Ottoman period. She is the editor of Municipalités méditerranéennes: Les réformes urbaines ottomanes au miroir d'une histoire comparée (Moyen-Orient, Maghreb, Europe méridionale) *(Klaus Schwarz Verlag, 2005), and* The City in the Ottoman Empire*, with U. Freitag, M. Fuhrmann, and F. Riedler (Routledge, 2011).*

Part III

The Present

The Crémieux Decree
Benjamin Stora

In the late nineteenth century, the fate of the Jews of Algeria, inscribed within the vast history of Mediterranean Judaism, hinged on the relations between Jews and Muslims during the colonial period of the Maghreb, a situation that had consequences in the following century. When the first French soldiers landed in the bay of Sidi Ferruch, the Jews of Algeria constituted an organized "nation," or *millet*, of the Ottoman administration. In 1830 the Jewish community of Algeria was 25,000 strong, and most of its members were poor. The reactions of the Jews to colonial development varied a great deal by region. Those living near Algiers, and later, Oran, unlike their nomadic and rural coreligionists from the Constantine region, were well positioned

▶ See article by Henry Laurens, pp. 269–279.

Benjamin Stora

A specialist in the history of the Maghreb, Benjamin Stora is a professor at the Université Paris-8 and at the Institut National des Langues et Civilisations Orientales (INALCO). He is the author, notably, of *La gangrène de l'oubli: Mémoire de la guerre d'Algérie* (La Découverte, 1991); *Imaginaires de guerre: Algérie-Vietnam* (La Découverte, 1998); *Algérie-Maroc: Histoires parallèles* (Maisonneuve et Larose, 2003); and *Les trois exils des juifs d'Algérie* (Stock, 2006). He is coeditor of the present book.

to accept the French presence. While those the French called Muslim "natives" (*indigènes*) withdrew to the interior of the country so as not to have contact with the occupying forces, the Jews of Algiers quickly made an effort to mingle with the French soldiers in order to trade with them.

King Louis-Philippe's government had kept in its memory the example of the European Jews' assimilation during the French Revolution, and the attitude of neutrality the Jews adopted during the conquest of Algeria prompted the French authorities to pay a great deal of attention to that minority, from whom they hoped to garner support. On November 9, 1845, the royal order of Saint-Cloud made Algerian Judaism fit the French mold. It created a central consistory in Algiers, just as Napoleon had done in France in the early nineteenth century. This order also established a provincial consistory in Oran and another in Constantine.

France truly set out on the path to assimilate the Jews of Algeria with the Crémieux decree, which would cause a tremendous stir. This decree of October 24, 1870, bore the signatures of Gambetta, Glais-Bizoin, Crémieux, and Fourichon. It came at the end of a long fight.

Synagogue in Algers displaying Islamic architectural motifs, lithograph, nineteenth century. New York, Granger Collection.

Battles for a decree

In 1847 Louis de Baudicourt wrote, in *La colonisation de l'Algérie* (*The Colonization of Algeria*), that the "French government had a major interest in attaching the Algerian Jews to itself." In 1859 the man responsible for reporting on that question to the General Council of Algiers noted: "It is obvious that a declaration making the Israelites French en masse would remove all difficulties and would be welcomed by them as a blessing." In May 1860, when Jewish notables from Algiers presented the mayor of that city with a petition in favor of collective nationalization, he promised to support it before the government. And in Oran, during Napoleon III's second trip to Algeria in 1865, the emperor gave this response to a speech by Grand Rabbi Mahir Charleville: "Soon, I hope, the Algerian Israelites will be French citizens."

Then, on July 14, 1856, Napoleon III issued a senatus consultum that opened the possibility of naturalization to the "natives" of Algeria: members of the Muslim and Jewish communities could become French, provided they *made a request.* That senatus consultum offered several prerogatives to the Jews and Muslims: they could now obtain French citizenship on an individual basis, could freely enter some public service jobs, and could serve in the army. But interminable administrative procedures stood in the way of attaining French citizenship. In addition, in order to become naturalized, Jews were required to entirely renounce their native culture. Up until that time, the reforms undertaken by the French administration had targeted only religious institutions (secularization) and, as a result, the religiously observant. The notion of emancipation based on an act of will failed to be convincing.

In the Jewish community, citizenship remained the privilege of the wealthy elites. But large numbers of Algerian Jews, to prove their allegiance to the nation and their desire for integration, and to escape adverse living conditions, joined the public sector and the military, the only state institutions available to them. Even when assigned to subordinate positions in the machinery of the administration, the Jews thus took their place within colonial society, with which they gradually grew familiar.

Reformist circles considered the senatus consultum of 1865 an insufficient measure and pleaded relentlessly for the collective naturalization of the Algerian Jews. Every year between 1856 and 1869, the General Councils of Algeria's three administrative departments expressed their wish for the mass naturalization of indigenous Israelites.

The year of the decree

In March 1870, Comte Léopold Le Hon, a member of the legislature, after an agricultural survey of Algeria, adopted the view of certain Algerian colonists and became a proponent of mass naturalization.[1] Sarlande, the mayor of Algiers, believing that "to keep the Israelites away from public affairs was a mistake and a pity," also called for naturalization as a necessary measure.[2] General Wimpffen asked that "they be given by decree the same rights as their coreligionists in France."[3]

On the eve of the War of 1870, at the insistence of the representatives of the French population of Algeria (including some colonists) and with the support of civil and military high officials (including the prefect of Algiers and the generals of Algiers and Constantine), the imperial government was about to yield on the question of naturalization. On March 8, 1870, Minister of Justice Émile Ollivier transmitted the following text to the Council of State:

Art. 1—In application of the senatus consultum of July 14, 1865, the Israelites native to Algerian territory are hereby authorized to enjoy the rights of French citizens.
Art. 2—Any native Israelite, within a year of the promulgation of the present decree, may declare to the appropriate authorities that he does not accept the benefits of naturalization.

On July 19, 1870, Ollivier declared before the legislature that he "wished to naturalize the Israelites." He wondered "whether naturalization can be achieved by decree or whether it requires a law," and affirmed that there was only a "question of form" to be settled. Then the Franco-Prussian War broke out. Three months later, the government of National Defense, sitting in Tours after the disaster at Sedan and the threats to Paris, decided to reorganize the regime and administration of Algeria.

The personality of Adolphe Crémieux

Adolphe Crémieux, the spokesman for the movement in support of the Jews of Algeria, was in the forefront of that battle for emancipation. Born Isaac-Jacob Crémieux on April 30, 1796, in Nîmes, in the department of Gard, he died in Paris on April 30, 1880. A lawyer in Nîmes and later in the capital, he was also a politician and the longtime president of the Central Consistory and of the Alliance Israélite Universelle. And he was a Freemason: initiated in 1818, he left the Grand Orient of France in 1860 to preside over the Supreme Masonic Council of France. A deeply rationalistic Jew, Adolphe Crémieux aspired to be a universalist and rejected political communitarianism. Passionately in love with the Republic and with citizen emancipation, he was profoundly attached to the principles advocating the liberation of society, without guillotines and without mass graves. He glorified his homeland of France in all his acts and writings. When the Republican Revolution won its victory in Paris on February 24, 1848, Crémieux joined the provisional government, which had proclaimed the Second Republic, as minister of justice (he held that post until June 7, 1848). On March 3, he secured from the Cour de Cassation (final court of appeals) the abolition of the last legal forms of discrimination against the Jews of France. A few days later, Crémieux received "a delegation of blacks and mulattoes from the French colonies" and told them: "The new Republic will

The Zaouis, a Jewish family in Algeria, in 1914.
Private collection of Benjamin Stora.

accomplish what the Republic of '92 proclaimed: You will be free once more."

At the instigation of Crémieux—though he did not officially appear among its founders—the Alliance Israélite Universelle was created in 1860. Crémieux became its president in 1864. Elected a member of Drôme to the legislature he served from 1869 to 1870. He again became minister of justice after the fall of the Second Empire, under the government of National Defense, serving from September 4, 1870, to February 17, 1871. He promulgated six decrees regulating life in Algeria, including putting an end to the military administration of Algeria, and, especially, automatically granting French citizenship to the 35,000 Jews of Algeria. This last decree would be known to posterity as the "Crémieux decree," and it was the crowning achievement of his life. Enacted on October 24, 1870, it stipulated that "the Israelites native to the departments of Algeria are declared French citizens; as a result, their real status and their personal status are, from the promulgation of the present decree, regulated by French law, with all rights acquired to this day remaining inviolable. Every contrary legislative provision, senatus consultum, decree, regulation, or ordinance is hereby abolished." The application decrees were issued on October 7, 1871. Adolphe Crémieux served as a member of the department of Algiers from 1872 to 1875.

The consequences of the decree

In 1871, native Algerian Jews therefore became French persons of Jewish descent. This collective naturalization separated them from the other indigenous people, the Muslims, who saw this demarcation as the beginning of disunity. It established the first preconditions for confrontations between the two communities. The end of *dhimmī* status shattered the traditional legal framework within which the two communities had moved. The Jewish community of Algeria, joined by that of Tunisia, and later by that of Morocco, built its unity around a secularized version of traditional religion, a strong sense of itself as a minority, and a profound attachment to the liberal image of France. The Muslims of the Maghreb and the Mashriq, who were not invited to join the colonizers' societies, remained attached to their religious customs and criticized the Jews for abandoning their long history in Islamic territory. This naturalization was also harshly criticized by a few army leaders and by a portion of the European population. The Jews' entry into French society allowed them to make a tremendous social leap forward, but things did not always go smoothly. Twenty years after the promulgation of the Crémieux decree, Algeria experienced an extremely violent wave of anti-Semitism. The "anti-Jewish crisis" began in Oran, culminating in riots there in May 1897, and was accompanied by persecution of various kinds, in both everyday life and officially. In Algiers, the agitators demanded the abrogation of the Crémieux decree "in the name of the enraged people." The Jews were accused of being "capitalists" who oppressed the common people, even though the overwhelming majority lived in a state of enormous insecurity: of the 53,000 Jews residing in Algeria at that time, 44,000 lived in poverty, their needs met by some 10,000 proletarians. In reality, these anti-Jewish campaigns masked a denunciation of the "native" who had been elevated to French nationality. Behind the declared anti-Semitism of the Europeans in Algeria, the fear of the "Arab peril" was lurking.

> **In 1871, native Algerian Jews therefore became French persons of Jewish descent. … The Muslims … saw this demarcation as the beginning of disunity.**

---

1. Speech of March 7, 1870, in Claude Martin, *Les Israélites Algériens de 1830 à 1902*, doctoral thesis (Paris: Heracles, 1936), 129.
2. Ibid., 130.
3. Ibid., 131.

The Invention of the Holy Land
Elias Sanbar

It was certainly not in the nineteenth century that Palestine added to its name the epithet "the Holy Land." This title of nobility—burdensome and costly for the people of an area henceforth permanently targeted for conquests—had already been applied to it for centuries. It designates the crucible of the two monotheisms, Judaism and Christianity. Later, Islam, for which Palestine was to become the Muslim Holy Land, was added to the two others—three sanctities existing in the same place.

Elias Sanbar

Elias Sanbar, a historian and writer, has taught at the University of Paris 7 (Jussieu) and at Princeton University. He was the editor in chief of the *Revue d'études palestiniennes*, which he founded at Éditions de Minuit press, and is also the translator of the poetry of Mahmoud Darwish. His many works include *Le Bien des Absents* (Actes Sud, 2001); *Figures du Palestinien: Identité des origines, identité de devenir* (Gallimard, 2004); and *Dictionnaire amoureux de la Palestine* (Plon, 2010).

For Palestine, this did not mean a new status but a radical transformation of the very concept that we are witnessing today: modern explorations were paradoxically legitimized by archaic notions that would prepare the way for the tragedy that is currently playing itself out in the Middle East. The process consisted first in fusing myth and history, rendering them virtually interchangeable. Its starting point was the controversy between the partisans of the theory of Darwinian evolution and the Anglican Church, whose dogma maintained that the Bible was not only a source of faith but also a historical narrative, with the Genesis story as its founding episode. This confrontation between Science and Faith shifted naturally to the physical locations in which the Church, through archaeological excavations and observation of the ways and customs of the Palestinian population, could prove that Darwin had erred. This precipitated a rush to Palestine in the form of countless expeditions, assembling a potpourri of pastors, preachers, archaeologists, evangelical missions, and aspiring photographers who sought to provide proof of Darwin's error thanks to the realism of photography—and it also brought consuls and emissaries from various Western and Eastern powers. This rush to Palestine, referred to as a "Peaceful Crusade," brought about a tipping point: to historical science it opposed "genealogical proof." Theoretical debates between theologians and modern men of science, far from taking place behind closed doors, galvanized a real country.

Czarist Russia's approach to the future dismemberment of the Ottoman Empire was not complicated—far from it—by any conflicting interests and ambitions. The Ottoman Empire itself, resisting its programmed disappearance and amalgamating the upholders of modernity and the objective allies of the "infidels," would exemplify the claim that Palestine was the battlefield between Christianity and Islam.

"Lydde, 'Lot' of the Old Testament," says the caption on this stereoscopic image; Tiberias, Jewish fishing village. Photographs published by Underwood and Underwood, 1900.

Going beyond the simple conflict between two interpretations of evolution, a political premise emerged from these multifaceted confrontations: *anteriority* in a place establishes future legitimacy based on these premises. Thus, whoever was there before others would have rights to an eternal and exclusive presence. Before the birth of Theodor Herzl's Zionist project, Palestine had been prepared to receive a historic-religious ideology according to which it belonged to a people chosen thousands of years earlier who were bearers of an exclusive right of property from a divine source.

This matter-of-fact statement must never be perceived as the result of a plot, a Machiavellian plan cooked up by "foreigners" practicing a kind of prelude to Zionism. What is being described here is in reality the consequence of the conjunction of a desire for imperial conquest and a discourse strongly anchored in Anglican Protestantism, which asserted its faith as the fulfillment—a kind of "superior form"—of Judaism for "the greater glory," not of God but of Victorian England. Since England had proclaimed itself to be the protector of the Jewish communities in the empire, some practices, taken very seriously at that time, came to light. For example, the founding of a society for the conversion of Jews to the Anglican religion would prompt one of its prominent members, James Finn, the English consul to Jerusalem, to develop a theory according to which it would suffice to celebrate the Anglican services in Hebrew to get the Jews of Palestine to convert to the Anglican faith. The temple in which this "experiment" was carried out stood within the walls of Jerusalem, near the Jaffa Gate. The building today, near the Swedish Cultural Center, is the seat of a Christian fundamentalist millenarian organization.

Anteriority, as a source of exclusive legitimacy, began shifting, imperceptibly at first, then radically: from being a *Holy* Land promised to a chosen people, Palestine itself would become a *Chosen* Land. Hence, it was not at all surprising that the watchword *redemption of the land*, a novelty that would automatically transform the inhabitants into sources of contamination, should appear. We read, for example, in the work of Claude Reignier Conder, one of the protagonists in the British Palestine Exploration Fund, of this dream of a land that could "be once more a land rivaling in fertility and opulence its ancient condition, as it appears through the attentive study of the passages that have been left us by the Bible or later Jewish writings.... It is man, and not Nature, who has ruined the good land."[1] Here we have the prelude to the idea of the future displacement of the Arabs, so that the earth—the places, not the human beings—may recover its original purity. Palestine, now chosen, is required to measure up to its supposedly thousand-year-old image. The "Peaceful Crusades" get to work making the real country correspond to the earlier decor—humans, flora and fauna, and landscapes. Now, Palestine is a simple, humble land, unwilling to seem physically worthy to serve as a setting for the Divine Message. The scene needs to be reinvented. A new one will be fashioned, creating from the ground up a country that does not exist in reality.

All this is discernible (with a few exceptions) in the immense body of texts left by the scientists, travelers, and archaeologists of that time. It is particularly noticeable in the images produced by photography, a new medium, boasted of as being perfectly realistic, as opposed to painting, which, so it was said at the time, was deformed by the subjectivity of the painters who projected their emotions on their canvases.[2] Boasting of the qualities of the new invention, confident that at last they had the means to provide irrefutable proof that the positions held by the Anglican Church were well founded, some would go as far as to declare that it was now possible to see with their own eyes what the prophets saw. The Scottish reverend Alexander Keith, who traveled to Palestine with his doctor/photographer son, expressed perfectly this relation to the photographic image, which he used to illustrate the thirty-sixth edition of his book— clearly committed to the crusade against Darwin—entitled *Evidence of the Truth of the Christian Religion derived from the Literal Fulfilment of Prophecy Particularly as Illustrated by the History of the Jews and by the Discoveries of Recent Travellers.*[3] The photography, he wrote in his introduction to the work, henceforth enriched with a score of engravings reproduced in daguerreotype, is "a mode of demonstration that could neither be questioned nor surpassed; as, without the need of any testimony, or the aid of either pen or pencil, the rays of the sun would thus depict what the prophets saw." But the *view* of Palestine would prove to be terribly disappointing for the proponents of this theory of a land that was, in a sense, naturally extraordinary. According to these ideologues, this land, tarnished by the presence of Islam, was waiting to be restored to its origins, an absolute requirement for its redemption. Palestine was approached as a space committed to emptiness, awaiting the departure of its secular inhabitants. The anteriority/exclusivity formula was applied to all the

Palestinian communities, including Eastern Christian Palestinians, who, "contaminated" and fallen, were not seen as different from the Muslims of their country. ❯ See article by Nadine Picaudou, pp. 329–339. Thus, shift by shift, the nineteenth century would be that of the entrance of Palestine into a particular colonial history, because, as opposed to other colonizing conquests, this one was not about the conquest and subjugation of an autochthonous population but the effort to gradually displace a people from its national territory and to replace it with communities that did not "come" but "returned" to Palestine. This politics of expulsion in gestation would be accompanied by a redefinition of "the Arab," who was no longer referred to as a "Palestinian." So what is a "real" Arab? The answer, intended to disqualify the real Palestinians, is the fascinating and unreal figure of the *Bedouin*. The noble nomad of the desert, the only Arab worthy of the name—does

> **The Palestinians would soon be "studied" in the same way as were archaeological ruins—living relics of a glorious biblical heritage.**

he not have the precious advantage of being nomadic? Is it not enough for him to cross through the landscape, to come in through the courtyard and leave through the garden? Paradigm of transience, nobly mounted on his charger, always on the

The Jordan, photographed by Bonfils; color added through a very elaborate process. Published by the firm Photoglob Zurich and signed "PZ," around 1888. This technical feat introduced a profound change in perspective. Paris, private collection of Elias Sanbar.

Holy Thursday foot-washing ceremony in Jerusalem. Maison Bonfils, around 1880.

move atop his thoroughbred steed, this desert wanderer possesses the great virtue to his admirers (quite ignorant of the real Bedouins' lives) of not claiming any territory. Consequently, the sedentary ones, whether town or country dwellers, who make up the majority of Palestinian society, would be the negative version of the object of pseudoscientific or ethnological works that abound in racist remarks. We read, for example, the following words of the famous American writer Mark Twain, widely disseminated at the time: "They reminded me much of Indians, did these people.... They sat in silence, and with tireless patience watched our every motion with that vile, uncomplaining impoliteness which is so truly Indian, and which makes a white man so nervous and uncomfortable and savage that he wants to exterminate the whole tribe.... Oriental scenes look best in steel engravings."[4]

Approached as living vestiges of a past all the more grandiose for being part of the past, the Palestinians would soon be "studied" in the same way as were archaeological ruins—living relics of a glorious biblical heritage they had unconsciously carried forward in the form of body language, imitated fragments, bits of language—in short, shards of a bygone world, a paradoxical approach showing that the Palestinians were, despite their defects, indeed the inhabitants of that land whose traces are in their genes, according to their detractors.

These three elements—anteriority, redemption of the land, illegitimate presence of Palestinians in Palestine—are the fundamental components of the pre-Zionist period. Later becoming arguments often used by the protagonists of the Zionist project, they were forged, essentially, in the Christian world.

1. Claude Reignier Condor, *Tent Work in Palestine* (London: Bentley, 1879).
2. Elias Sanbar, *Les Palestiniens: La photographie d'une terre et de son peuple de 1839 à nos jours* [The Palestinians: The Photographing of a Land and Its People from 1839 to Our Time] (Paris: Éditions Hazan, 2004).
3. Published in Edinburgh by William Whyte, 1848.
4. Mark Twain, *The Innocents Abroad* (Hartford, CT: American, 1869), 472–73, 544.

Chapter I

The Beginnings of the Separation

From Coexistence to the Rise of Antagonisms

Michel Abitbol

Long before the French occupation of Algeria in 1830, the eruption of Europe into the Levant and the Maghreb alienated the Jews from their Muslim neighbors. It thoroughly transformed their relationship, which, essentially religious in nature, became one of political and social antagonism. This trend increased with the extension of European colonization, the rise of nationalism, and the expansion of Zionism in Palestine. The Jews were not well viewed by a population violently shaken in its convictions by foreign occupation and modernization, and the years 1870–1948 were hardly propitious—except in Iraq—for their integration. As a general rule, they did not share their neighbors' fears with respect to the West, or their dread of European imperialism. The Mediterranean Jews, already suspect in the eyes of the Muslims because of their generally positive attitude toward Europe, were rendered even more so given the sponsorship they received from European Jewish institutions such as the Universal Israelite Alliance, which intervened in their favor at the least incident. As Arab countries were struggling toward independence, Muslim opinion tended to consider them ungrateful collaborators of the colonialist powers and agents of the world Zionist organization aspiring to drive the Arabs out of Palestine.

Michel Abitbol

Michel Abitbol, an Africanist and Orientalist, is a professor emeritus at the Hebrew University and former director of the Ben-Zvi Institute in Jerusalem. He has taught in Paris at the École des Hautes Études en Sciences Sociales (EHESS), at Paris 8, the Institut d'Études Politiques, and at Yale University. He has contributed to *Histoire Universelle des Juifs* (Hachette, 2002) and *Encyclopedia Judaica* (Coronet Books, 1972–1991). His publications include *Le Passé d'une discorde: Juifs et Arabes depuis le viie siècle* (Perrin, 1999; Perrin Tempus, 2003); *Les Amnésiques: Juifs et Arabes depuis 1967* (Perrin, 2005); *Les Juifs d'Afrique du Nord sous Vichy* (Riveneuve, 2008; Éditions du CNRS, 2012); *Histoire du Maroc* (Perrin, 2009); and *Histoire des Juifs* (Perrin, 2012).

The beginning of European influence

It is well known that the European colonization of the Muslim-Arab world began with the French conquest of Algeria in 1830, followed more than half a century later by that of Tunisia in 1881, the Italian entry into Libya in 1911, the conquest of Morocco by France and Spain in 1912, and the placing of all the Levantine countries at the end of the First World War under British and French mandate. It is less well known that it was

> **It was essentially under the pretext of defending Jewish and Christian minorities in Muslim countries that Europe ... began ... to impose its will.**

essentially under the pretext of defending Jewish and Christian minorities in Muslim countries that Europe, confident of its overwhelming military and economic superiority, began, in the middle of the nineteenth century, to impose its will in North African and Near Eastern countries. It was in reaction to European pressure that in February 1856 the Sublime Porte published an imperial edict (Hatt-i Humayun) announcing the abolition of the *jizya* and establishing the equality of all the subjects of the Ottoman Empire, Muslims and non-Muslims. This text allowed Christian and Jewish *dhimmī* to serve in the army and construct new religious buildings—which con-

▶ See article by Mark R. Cohen, pp. 67–69.

stituted, at least in theory, a flagrant attack on the ʿUmar Pact, concurrently in vigor. Tunisia, following the Ottoman example, engaged in a similar reform movement, and on September 9, 1857, Mohammed Bey, taking the Hatt-i Humayun as his model, promulgated the ʿAhd al-Aman, or "Fundamental Pact," guaranteeing equal rights for all Tunisian subjects, without religious distinctions, and eliminating the requirement for Jews to wear distinguishing marks on their clothing and to pay the *jizya*.

The publication of the ʿAhd al-Aman was precipitated by a relatively minor incident that degenerated into a brief diplomatic confrontation between the Regency and the European powers. This is known as the Batto Sfez affair, after the name of a Jewish wagoner who was sentenced to death in 1857 and executed for having cursed the name of the Prophet—which gave rise to a very acute upsurge of violence against the Tunisian Jews, who barricaded themselves in their neighborhood while their leaders roused the European consuls installed in the Regency. Using these events as a pretext, the English and French governments required Bey to apply the same texts concerning the non-Muslims as those adopted in Istanbul, and at the same time Napoleon III commanded the French Mediterranean squadron to cruise the waters in front of Tunis. This deadlock is explained by the Tunisian chronicler Ibn Abi Dyaf in the following terms: "It is reported that when the Jews of Paris who enjoyed freedom and embalmed themselves in its perfume learned what had happened to their coreligionists, they addressed one of their notables who was in power, telling him: 'Our Tunisian brothers suffer from insecurity because of their religion.' That is when the French fleet landed at the beginning of Muharram 1274 [1857 C.E.]. It consisted of seven ships, with about nine hundred cannons, and was commanded by one of the most prominent officers, named Tréhouart."[1]

As during the Damascus affair in 1840, marked by the intervention of the Jews of France and England in favor of the Syrian Jews,[2] the incidents of Tunis confirmed to the Tunisians the new image they began having of "their" Jews: that of a minority belonging to a powerful and turbulent group, world Judaism, with great centers in Europe, capable of using its immense influence on the European governments to intervene at the slightest complaint of the Jews in Muslim countries. Another fact corroborated that nascent popular opinion: the visit to Marrakesh in 1864 of the philanthropist Moses Montefiore, who hurried aboard the British frigate *La Magicienne* to help the Jews of Morocco and to demand that the sultan modify their legal status in compliance with the egalitarian clauses of the Ottoman Tanzimat.[3] The result was slight—being reduced to the proclamation of a *dahir* as a reminder of the rights recognized for Jews in Islamic lands, and the request that the agents of the Makhzen treat them appropriately, "as stipulated by God, by applying to them, in the administration, the balance of justice and equality between them and those who are not Jewish, so that none of them should be the victim of the slightest injustice." This directive (rather innocuous, after all) aroused the anger of the local chronicler Al-Nasiri al-Slawi, who, after having reviled the Jews of Mogador for having manifested their joy at seeing the Judeo-British emissary, could not find words harsh enough to criticize the Western notion of freedom from which the new rights applying to Jews derived: "This freedom established by the Europeans in these last years is the absolute work of irreligion, for it carries with it the complete destruction of the rights of God, the rights of parents and the rights of humanity."[4]

▶ See article by Henry Laurens, pp. 269–279.

Little by little, beginning in the middle of the nineteenth century, a deep change in the image of the Jew began to take shape in the Arab-Muslim world: beyond traditional religious contention, the Jew was henceforth considered a political adversary who traded the "dhimma" of Islam for that of Christianity, to borrow the words of a contemporary Moroccan historian, ʿAbd al-Wahab al-Mansour. It was indeed the case that the Eastern Jews, who, since 1860, had been taken under the wing of powerful European Jewish organizations like the Universal Israelite Alliance and the Anglo-Jewish Association (ready to intervene on their behalf with the powers in case of incidents involving their Muslim neighbors), availed themselves of these circumstances

> **"Beyond traditional religious contention, the Jew was henceforth considered a political adversary."**

to escape, as far as possible, from their condition as *dhimmī*. Thus, long before European colonization itself, the legal and political status of Jews indeed evolved in many Muslim countries to the point of becoming incomparably better than that of their coreligionists in Poland, Ukraine, and Russia, then prey to the worst pogroms in their history.

Equality without integration

Once "emancipated," the Jews of the Muslim countries, contrary to those in Christian countries, did not generally show a strong desire for cultural and social integration.

Teachers and rabbis of the Alliance Israélite Universelle in Tunisia.
Archives of the Alliance Israélite Universelle.

The Ottoman Jews continued as a group to use Judeo-Spanish as a vernacular language (or more precisely Judezmo) after the Tanzimat, while the Westernized Jews of the Maghreb simply dropped Arabic for French with an eagerness that made them suspect in the eyes of Muslim intellectuals. Though in most countries Westernization reduced the legal barriers separating Muslims from their fellow Christian and Jewish countrymen, it did generate new types of interethnic tensions everywhere. Segregated living quarters continued to be the rule, and it was unusual for the children of one group to attend the schools of the other, or take part in their leisure activities.

By 1830, Algerian Judaism was thus squarely in the hands of the Jews of France, who, by their own initiative, would lead it along the path of emancipation and assimilation that they themselves had traveled beginning in 1791. Rapidly "consistorialized" (1845), then naturalized French (1870) and stripped of all their traditional community structures, the Algerian Jews ended up becoming "expatriated" inside the very country in which they had lived for centuries. Their accession to French nationality was a new "exodus from Egypt," as Adolphe Crémieux, the main force behind that naturalization, would say of them, without having the least suspicion that not all Algerian Jews agreed with him. The Algerian example has no parallel elsewhere from the point of view of its scope, but from Morocco to Syria the energetic outreach of Europe did indeed cut the Jews off from their Muslim neighbors, along the lines of a mechanism meticulously exposed by Albert Memmi in his famous sociological novel, *The Pillar of Salt.*

Thus the Jew became an adversary, not only more "visible" but also more turbulent than usual, due to his concentration, since the beginning of European expansionism, in a restricted number of urban areas. In Morocco, where Jews represented no more than 3 percent of the overall population, they constituted, by the end of the nineteenth century, 20 percent of the inhabitants of the port cities—in which the main economic exchanges with Europe took place—and 25 to 40 percent of the population of cities such as Tangiers, Mogador, Tetouan, and Casablanca. In Tunisia during these same years, half of the 30,000 Jews of the country lived in the capital, Tunis. Similarly, 40 percent of the 16,000 Jews of Libya resided in Tripoli; 80 percent of the 10,000 Jews of Egypt, just before the British occupation in 1882, lived in the two towns of Cairo and Alexandria; almost all of the 15,000 to 20,000 Jews of Syria-Lebanon lived in Damascus, Aleppo, and Beirut; and most of the Jews of Iraq lived in Baghdad, where they made up, in the middle of the nineteenth century, about one-third of the city's population.

▷ See Nota bene on Albert Memmi, pp. 589–591.

Demographic Evolution of the Jews of North Africa in the 19th–20th Centuries

	Morocco	Algeria	Tunisia	Libya
1830		17,000		
1871		34,600		
1881			35,000	
1891		47,500		
1901		57,100		
1911	110,000 *(1912)*	70,300	50,500	14,200
1921		74,000	54,000	
1926	125,000		60,000	
1931	143,000	114,000	70,000	24,100
1936	186,000		80,000	27,600
1941		123,000	89,700	30,400 *(1939)*
1946	230,000 *(1947)*	130,000	100,000	31,800 *(1945)*
1951	199,200			

This disproportion, in addition to influencing the perception that Jews began to have of themselves and their importance in the economic life of the country, contributed above all in distinguishing them demographically and sociologically from their neighbors. At the end of the nineteenth century, more than 80 percent of the population of the Maghreb and the Mashriq was rural, while the Jewish population was 75 percent urban. More and more Jews left their traditional neighborhoods—*haras* and *mellahs*— and distanced themselves from the Muslim populace to live in new neighborhoods populated by Europeans. In Libya, by 1917, 40 percent of the Jews of Tripoli lived outside the traditional quarters of Hara al-Kabira and Hara al-Saghira; in Morocco, almost half of the Jews living in large cities abandoned the *mellah*, with its decrepit houses and narrow streets, for the "new city"

> **At the end of the nineteenth century, more than 80 percent of the population of the Maghreb and the Mashriq was rural, while the Jewish population was 75 percent urban.**

before the Second World War. The same situation was prevalent everywhere: the Harat al-Yahud of Old Cairo had been abandoned since the end of the nineteenth century by the affluent, Westernized sectors of the community—who had decided to settle in the new residential neighborhoods of Ismailiya, Tawfiqiya, Abbasiya, and Heliopolis, where many Copts and Europeans of the same social circumstances resided.

On the social level, the emergence of a Jewish middle class of civil servants, technicians, and liberal professions, as well as the spread of European education, are among the major changes in the colonial era that progressively widened the gap between Jews and Muslims. In Morocco and Tunisia, the level of school enrollment of school-age children was about 13 percent for Muslims at the end of the colonial era, while for Jews it was 60 percent and 90 percent, respectively, during the same years. In Algeria, it was virtually 100 percent among Jews of French nationality, while it barely reached 8 percent among Muslims in 1944. The same gap existed in Libya: barely 5 percent of Muslims spoke and wrote Italian in 1931, as opposed to 44 percent of Jews in Tripoli and 67 percent in Benghazi. Other statistics are no less revealing: in 1914 in Tunis, ninety students received bachelor's degrees. Among these there were twenty-seven Jews—twelve of whom would go on to become doctors, and nine lawyers. In comparison, only five Muslims earned a degree.[5]

In Egypt, where about 75 percent of Jewish children were enrolled in schools around 1937, Arabic was not the language of culture for the vast majority of the Jews of the country, who spoke mainly French. It was only beginning with the Second World War that Arabic—totally absent from the curricula of the Universal Israelite Alliance in the Maghreb—became one of the three official languages of the community in Cairo, the two others being French and English. Aside from the exceptional case of the Iraqi Jews, to be discussed later, the situation was about the same elsewhere—as in Syria and Lebanon, for example, where French was still the main language of communication for the Jews of both countries.[6]

The Jews of the Near East from 1917 to 1947

	1917	1947
Iraq	85,000	125,000
Egypt	60,000	66,000
Syria-Lebanon	35,000	35,000
Yemen	45,000	54,000
Iran	75,000	90,000
Turkey	100,000	80,000

Whether we consider Sadia Lévy, Raymond Bénichou, and Elissa Rhaïs in Algeria; Blanche Bendahan and Carlos de Nesry in Morocco; Albert Hadas, Carlo Suarès, and Elian Finbert in Egypt; or Vitalis Danon, Raphaël Lévy (Ryvel), and especially Albert Memmi in Tunisia, it was mainly in French that the first Jewish writers of these countries published their works.[7] French was also the language chosen by the

The rabbis of Fes (Morocco), during an award ceremony in 1931.
Archives of the Alliance Israélite Universelle.

main emerging print media, such as *La Justice* and *L'Égalité* in Tunisia; *Le Réveil juif*, the *Gazette d'Israël*, *l'Union marocaine*, and *L'Avenir illustré* in Morocco; and *Israël* and *La Revue sioniste* in Egypt. The journal *Al Shams*, published in the 1930s and 1940s in Cairo, was virtually the only important work published in literary Arabic by Jews on Islamic soil. It is as if during the colonial period, with the exception of Iraq, Jews and Muslims made up two separate worlds, each living at its own political and social pace, and little informed on the debates of conscience and trends of thought of one another.

> " *It is as if during the colonial period, with the exception of Iraq, Jews and Muslims made up two separate worlds, each living at its own political and social pace.* "

Nationality and nationalism

The eyes of the Jews were turned toward Europe, and obtaining a foreign passport continued to galvanize their minds. The Egyptian community, less rooted in its country than all the other North African communities, continued to be mainly made up of those coming from foreign countries who shared neither the language nor the conditions of life of the surrounding society. Quai d'Orsay [the seat of the French administration] showed great generosity toward the Egyptian Jews, who, opting for French nationality, contributed to the reinforcement of the French presence in the Nile Valley, opposing Great Britain. In 1917, only 22 percent of the Jews of the country were of Egyptian nationality; that figure would rise to 22 percent ten years later, and it was only with the annulment, in 1937, of the capitulation and the elaboration of new definitions of Egyptian citizenship that the number of naturalized citizens and of stateless persons would diminish substantially.[8]

Movement of the Jewish Population in Egypt between 1800 and 1947[9]

Year	Jewish Population	Growth	Total Population
1850	7,000		5,500,000
1882	10,000	43%	7,600,000
1897	25,200	152%	9,734,000
1907	38,635	53%	11,190,000
1917	59,581	54%	12,709,000
1927	63,550	7%	14,218,000
1937	62,953	– 1%	15,921,000
1947	65,639	4%	18,967,000

In Tunisia, about seven thousand Jews obtained French nationality from 1911 until the outbreak of the Second World War, and until the end of the protectorate, about a quarter of the Jews of the country went from the status of "indigenous" to that of French citizen, thus breaking all political attachment to the overall Muslim society, though they were not sure of being "welcomed" into European colonial society. Here, again, what is at stake for France is to counter foreign influences—Italian in this instance. Fearing no danger of this kind in the Cherifien Kingdom, the French obstinately refused to grant their nationality to the Jews of Morocco. Moreover, as astonishing as it may seem, they even tried to slow the expansion of French education among the Jews of that country. Too rapid a Europeanization of the Jews—or so it was said in the entourage of Marshall Lyautey, the resident general of the French protectorate in Morocco—besides risking being ill-viewed by the Muslims, could also be prejudicial to the future of the protectorate. The Moroccan Jew—as George Hardy, charged with public education, explains in strong imagery—is a butterfly that has barely emerged from its black chrysalis, but "a butterfly tipsy from the sudden light, and that, ill prepared for its happiness, would soon become a nouveau riche and young Israelite butterfly, in sum a very nasty and very bothersome insect."[10] This ill will toward them by the French colonial authorities hardly discouraged the new generations of Jews in their enthusiasm for France and its culture. Even the Moroccan Zionists who, in theory at least, should have practiced a different form of worship, shared that unshakable faith in France, as we may read in 1926 in *L'Avenir illustré*, the newspaper of the Moroccan Zionists: "It is in Morocco, on this ground freed from so much oppression by the generosity of France, that Moroccan Jews must accomplish their own modernization. The Zionist ideal that we have not ceased bringing to life in their eyes agrees perfectly with the inspiration that they draw from the French traditions implanted in Morocco, and to speak to them of their other spiritual fatherland, blessed Jerusalem, is still another way of making them love France." The readers of *L'Avenir illustré* and those of *L'Union marocaine*, the second most important Jewish newspaper (openly "assimilationist"), probably represented a very small part of the whole of Moroccan Judaism: large sectors of the Jewish population were hardly touched by French influence in the period between the two world wars. But for them as well, the colonial period was no less a period of "de-Moroccanization," to use a term of the Tangiers essayist Carlos de Nesry, a period of breaking away from the overall society. Ethnically compartmentalized, the exchanges between the Jewish and Muslim colonized groups were reduced to those deriving from the necessities and contingencies of daily life. Now living far from the medinas and having largely abandoned the use of Arabic, the Jews for the most part lost the opportunity to follow the intense intellectual activity as it was developing in reformist Muslim circles—activity giving rise, at the beginning of the 1930s, to the Moroccan national movement, following closely upon the promulgation of the Berber *dahir*, which allowed the Berbers of the country to return to anti-Islamic practices. Moroccan nationalism, which presented itself more like a movement defending Moroccan Islam than like a political emancipation movement, could not attract militants of Jewish faith into its ranks; no more, for that matter, than could the Tunisian Destour, which was also solidly rooted in the Islamic tradition.

In a more general sense, Muslim intellectuals excluded the Jews from the ideas of *watan* (fatherland) and *umma* (nation) that began to take shape in the nineteenth century. But thanks to the expansion of general education and the formation of the first modern Jewish and Muslim elites, the mutual interest in each other's civilizations became more widespread than ever: the foundation of the Jewish religion and the origins of the Hebrew language intrigued the collaborators of the reformist Egyptian journal *Al-Manar*, created in 1898 by Rashid Rida.

There were other exceptions to that general separation of the elites. For example, when, at the end of the 1870s, Egypt fell into the grip of its European creditors, it was a Jewish journalist, James Sanua or Jacob Sanua, alias Abu Naddara, who proclaimed the slogan loud and clear to the world: "Egypt for the Egyptians." Born in Cairo in 1839 and a very close friend of Jamal al-Din al-Afghani and Muhammad ʿAbduh, he would be, until his death in exile in Paris in 1912, the indefatigable opponent of the British conquest of the Nile Valley. As has already been remarked by his biographers, there is nothing in the writings, friendships, or private life of Sanua that betrays his Jewish origin. It is true that in this he is not very different from the majority of the contemporary Christian Arab nationalists, incomparably more numerous than their Jewish counterparts.

▶ See article on James Sanua, pp. 934–939.

At left , John Bull, representing Great Britain, says to a resistant fellah (peasant), representing Egypt, "I am here; I will stay here." The latter replies, "You will not stay here." Cover of *Le Journal d'Abou Naddara*, 1886.

The tradition begun by Jacob Sanua was resumed in the period between the two world wars by a certain number of Jewish figures leading a "Pharaonic" and not Islamic strain of the national Egyptian movement, open to Egyptians of all origins and faiths. Thus it was, for example, that Leon Castro, Félix Benzakein, Vita Sonino, and David Hazan were active members of the nationalist Wafd Party, created in the aftermath of the First World War by Saad Zaghlul, and that Joseph Cattaoui went from the Wafd to the Liberal Party in 1922, and from the latter to the Ittihad Party in 1925.[11] But when, around the mid-1930s, these lay and liberal groups gave way to more radical organizations, such as the student association Misr al-Fatat (Young Egypt), created by Ahmad Hussein in 1933, or to other movements more oriented toward Islam, such as that of the Muslim Brotherhood, founded in 1928 by Hasan al-Banna, the Egyptian Jews followed the path taken by all the other North African Jews and dropped out of all active participation in the political life of their country.

But even before that, the majority of Egyptian Jews, handicapped by their status of state-less persons or foreigners, felt little attraction to the political life of the country. This was also true for the Jews of the other Arabic countries, who, as a rule, turned away from nationalist ideologies. It is true that on the eve of the colonial era, all is not yet definitively played out, and the new identities are still very blurred. Proof of this is that in the aftermath of the first Arab Congress of Paris in 1906, *Al-Hayat*, the nationalist journal of Damascus, chose quite naturally a chief editor of the Jewish faith, Elias (or Eliyahu) Sasson, who would fulfill that function until 1923—before settling in Palestine in 1927 and ending up as Israel's minister of police in 1967. When Sasson left *Al-Hayat*, the Balfour Declaration was six years old, and Jews and Muslims had long since entered the colonial era. These two factors, colonialism and Zionism, added to the sudden rise of Arab nationalism and would inexorably distance the Jews from the Arabs during the period between the two world wars.

Pan-Arabism, Zionism, and anti-Semitism

This mutual political alienation was probably accentuated as the Westernized elites of both populations put their faith in Pan-Arabism and Zionism—two nationalist ideologies, fundamentally hostile to each other, claiming their rights to the same soil: Palestine. Whether in Syria, Iraq, or Egypt, or yet again Morocco, Tunisia, and even Algeria, the Palestinian question would poison the relations between Jews and Arabs to the point of becoming, by the 1930s, the main nexus of intercommunity tensions in these countries. The Pan-Islamic Congress of Jerusalem held in 1931 marks a true turning point in the relations between Jews and Muslims, both in the Levant and in the Maghreb. It was followed just about everywhere by violent anti-Jewish demonstrations, the most serious of which—those of Constantine in August 1934—killed or wounded dozens on both sides.[12] Considered as zealous helpers of European colonialism, the Jews were also accused of not having lifted a finger to assist the Muslims, who were struggling beneath the yoke of European domination: "You are sensitive to all the sufferings of humanity—except ours," says the very moderate Ferhat Abbas in 1935, addressing the Jews of Algeria.[13] In measured terms, he put his finger on the main element in the drama already playing itself out between Jews and Arabs: the insensitivity of one group toward the other. The future president of the provisional government of the Republic of Algeria openly pointed out the existence of Jewish-Muslim conflict that, generated in part by the imbalances resulting from the colonial situation, was not (far from it) simply an emanation of the anti-Jewish fermentation prevalent in the world of the *pieds-noirs* [French colonists living in Algeria before independence], and even less a repetition of the old, traditional ostracism based on religion.

Still other elements must be taken into account in this development. Besides the anti-Zionist slogans that had become common in the Arab demonstrations of the

1930s, the appearance of new themes, such as "Jewish usurer" or "arrogant Jew," coming straight from the arsenals of European anti-Semitism, were beginning to appear. This peregrination of the anti-Semitic phraseology from the Christian cultural domain to that of the Muslims was especially conspicuous in the Middle East, where the *Protocols of the Elders of Zion* were broadly disseminated beginning in the 1920s, followed a few years later by the translation into Arabic of Hitler's *Mein Kampf*, available in Baghdad bookstores by the mid-1930s.

The Jews, while voluntarily excluding themselves from Muslim society overall, were not welcomed by the European colonialist community, as demonstrated by the violent wave of anti-Semitism that followed the general naturalization of Algeria's Jews in 1870. Born of the encounter between a certain logic of republican exclusion and the colonial situation based on a rigid ethnoreligious hierarchy between colonialists and colonized, Algerian anti-Semitism was destined to become a true mass ideology, mobilizing all segments of the *pied-noir* population and established on the absolute and permanent negation of the Frenchness of Algerian Jews. "Trying to make a Frenchman out of a Jew is like trying to change a sack of coal into flour," read one anti-Semitic pamphlet from 1883 entitled *The Indigenous Algerian Kosher Voters*.

> **The Jews, while voluntarily excluding themselves from Muslim society overall, were not welcomed by the European colonialist community.**

Thus, while clearly respecting Arabs and Kabyls—see the lovely pages written on the native-born Muslims of Algeria by the anti-Semitic author of *La France juive*, Édouard Drumont, and his Algerian rival Georges Meynié, the author of the insipid *Algérie juive*—what the anti-Semitic Algerians hated most about the Jews was, paradoxically, their manners, accent, and dress as "Arabs of [the] Mosaic faith." "Israelite Algerians are not Frenchmen," one of their first detractors, the prefect Charles du Bouzet, had written in a petition against the Crémieux Decree, addressed to the National Assembly in 1871. "Their mother tongue is Arabic, which they speak poorly and write in Hebrew letters…. Their ways are Eastern and almost all of them dress like Easterners. No intellectual culture, one sole profession, business, one sole passion, that of amassing money by piling up little profits and living in a sordid manner. Foreign to the traditions of the French nation, remaining outside European civilization, these Easterners have no fatherland."[14]

This point of view was embraced in 1895 by the socialist Jean Jaurès: "The Jews of Algeria, who have been naturalized en masse twenty-five years ago by the Crémieux Decree, are, in short, foreign to the traditions, ideas, and battles of France," he wrote in *La Dépêche de Toulouse*. "They vote as Jews en bloc for the opportunist candidates because opportunism developed the power of finance, and it is thus, so to speak, the political form of the Jewish mind."[15]

Organized through numerous radical, socialist, and anti-Jewish leagues, communicated in dozens of newspapers—a hundred or so being openly anti-Jewish dailies published during the 1880s and 1890s, inviting their readers to smoke "anti-Jewish" cigarettes, drink absinthe and "anti-Jewish" anisette, wear "anti-Jewish" head coverings, and boycott Jewish businesses and Judaizing employees—the anti-Semitism of Algeria's Europeans was a heavy, concrete, daily phenomenon, irremediably affecting the material and moral situation of the fifty thousand Jews of the colony at the end of the nineteenth century. A natural child of the colonial situation, the anti-Semitism of the Europeans of Algeria persisted as long as the French presence in that part of the Maghreb. True, there were some eclipses—as in 1900, when the Waldeck-Rousseau government took energetic measures against the anti-Jewish leagues, or yet again during the First World War, during which the sacred entente (*entente sacrée*, the peaceful coexistence between all components of French society during the war) was initiated in the interethnic relations in Algeria. But, all things considered, the *pied-noir* anti-Jewish ostracism did not disappear entirely from Algerian politics until the onset of the Second World War, when a new threat, far more dangerous than the "Jewish peril," loomed on the horizon of French Algeria: the Algerian national awakening, destined to call into question the very presence of France on Maghreb soil.

The Iraqi exception

Colonialism was unfavorable to cultural exchanges between Jews and Muslims, other than those inherent to the necessities of life. But there was one notable exception: the case of the Iraqi Jews, who demonstrated a true desire for symbiosis with the surrounding Arab society. On the one hand, the relative freedom from restrictions under the British colonial regime, which ended in 1922, and on the other, the adoption, by the responsible parties in the Jewish community, of Arabic as the main language of culture (whereas everywhere else in the East, Jews had preferred the colonialist languages), probably determined the specificity of the historical path taken by Iraqi Judaism. There was a reason why its writers and leaders stressed, along with their adherence to Arabism, the ancient origins of the Jews in that country, which date back to the destruction of the First Temple, that is, before the sixth century C.E. Consequently, as they emphasize, Iraq is the fatherland of the Jews as well as of the Arabs. "My Iraqi identity comes from my ancestors," states the Baghdadi Shalom Darwish, who left Iraq against his will in 1950. "It grew, matured and was nourished, like me, from the waters of the Tigris…. That identity is not clothing that can be removed like a snakeskin. It was born 2,500 years ago, before the coming of the ancestors of those who call themselves Iraqi today." The poet Anwar Shaoul goes further in quest of his identity:

> From Moses I received my faith
> But I live beneath the aegis of that of Mohammed
> Generous, Islam has granted me its hospitality
> And it is from the rhetoric of the Koran that I draw my knowledge
> I adore the Creator as an adept of the religion of Moses
> But that does not affect my love for the people of Ahmad

▶ See Nota
bene on
Samaw'al,
pp. 940–942.

Like Samawwal I will always keep faith with them
Whether I am in Baghdad or elsewhere.[16]

The ideology of the "Arabism" or of the "Iraqism" of the Jews continued to have emulators within the Jewish elite of the country until the mid-1930s, when the increased Jewish-Muslim tension in Palestine sounded the death knell of the myth cleverly maintained by King Faisal (who himself died in 1933) of an interfaith Iraq. This dream, seriously called into question by the massacre of the Assyrians in 1933, was definitively interred after the massacre of the Jews of Baghdad, that is, the Farhud, which was perpetrated in June 1941 by the Iraqi army, routed before the British troops of General Wavell.

▶ See article
by Michel
Abitbol,
pp. 356–357.

Triumphal arch erected by the Jewish community of the city in honor of King Faisal I in 1928, Baghdad, Iraq.

This dramatic event occurs in the last chapter of the history of the Jews in the Islamic lands: the one concerning their uprooting and departure from those countries. The "dejudification" of the countries of the Levant and the Maghreb took effect at the same time that a new map of the Near East was being sketched out after the birth of the State of Israel in 1948 and the triggering of the process of decolonization.

‣ See article by Michael M. Laskier, pp. 415–433.

The end of the history of the Jews in the Islamic lands, neither the consequence of diabolic machinations nor a simple emigration in search of better living conditions, is part of the vast movement of populations that, for more than a century, has moved in one and the same direction: that of the ethnic, cultural, and religious homogenization of the Arab-Muslim world. Under the pressure of standardizing the nation-state and nationalism, that hitherto pluralistic space has been emptying itself for decades of its Armenian, Greek, Assyrian, Copt, Maronite, Jewish, or Kurdish minorities, to which the *pied-noirs* of Algeria must be added—and also, paradoxically, the Palestinian refugees of 1948. Thus, the Maghreb and the Mashriq have long ceased being that richly variegated, ethnically diverse Tower of Babel that enchanted ethnologists in the early 1960s.

---

1. Ibn Abi Dyaf, *Athaf Ahl al-Zaman bi-Akhbar Muluk Tuns wa 'Ahd al-Aman* (1962), 235.

2. On the affair of accusation of ritual murder against the Jews of Damascus, the best study to date is Jonathan Frankel's *The Damascus Affair: Ritual Murder, Politics and the Jews in 1840* (Cambridge: Cambridge University Press, 1997).

3. On Moses Montefiore and his trip to Morocco, see Michel Abitbol, *Le Passé d'une discord* (Paris: Perrin Tempus, 2003), 166–73.

4. Al-Nasiri al-Slawi, *Kitab al-Istiqsa*, French translation, *Archives marocaines* 9 (1906): 258.

5. See Elie Cohen-Hadria, "Les juifs francophones dans la vie intellectuelle et politique de Tunisie entre les deux guerres," in Michel Abitbol, *Judaïsme d'Afrique du Nord aux XIXᵉ–XXᵉ siècles* (Jerusalem: Ben-Zvi Institute, 1980), 52.

6. See, for more details, *Le Passé d'une discorde*, 269–87.

7. On this literature, see especially Guy Dugas, *La littérature judéo-maghrébine d'expression française—entre Djéha et Cagayous* (Paris: L'Harmattan, 1990).

8. Sergio Della-Pergola, "Jewish Population in the 19th and 20th centuries," (Hebrew) in *The Jews in Ottoman Egypt (1517–1914)*, ed. J. M. Landau (Jerusalem: Misgav Yerushalaim, 1988), 52.

9. According to the data published by Sergio Della-Pergola, "Jewish Population in the 19th and 20th Centuries," 29.

10. Quoted by Mohammed Kenbib, *Juifs et musulmans au Maroc* (Rabat, Morocco: University Mohammed-V of Rabat, 1994), 426.

11. Gudrun Kramer, *The Jews of Modern Egypt, 1914–1952* (London: I. B. Tauris, 1989), 124–28.

12. Charles-Robert Ageron, "Une émeute antijuive à Constantine, août 1934," *Revue de l'Occident musulman et de la Méditerranée* (1973): 23–40.

13. *La Dépêche Algérienne*, November 13, 1935.

14. Charles du Bouzet, *Les Israélites indigènes de l'Algérie* (Paris: Impr. de Schiller, 1871), 4.

15. Jean Jaurès, "La question juive en Algérie," *La Dépêche de Toulouse*, May 1, 1895.

16. Quoted by Nissim Kazzaz, *Les Juifs d'Irak au XXᵉ siècle* (in Hebrew) (Tel Aviv: Ben-Zvi Institute, 1989), 62.

Constantine: A Judeo-Muslim City

In his wonderful "Petit guide pour des villes sans passé" (A Short Guide to Cities without a Past, 1947),[1] Albert Camus, with passion and melancholy, evokes Algiers, Oran, and Constantine. For each of the three principal cities of Algeria, just a few years before the start of the War of Independence, he relates his memories and sensations: "The mildness of Algiers is somewhat Italian. The cruel brightness of Oran has something Spanish about it. Perched on a rock above the gorges of the River Rummel, Constantine is reminiscent of Toledo." A few lines later, he describes each city's singularity by neighborhood: "For local color, Algiers offers an Arab city, Oran a Negro village and a Spanish neighborhood, Constantine a Jewish quarter." Albert Camus was right: Constantine is a city distinguished for the size of its Jewish population, clustered in the Charrah neighborhood and mixed in with the Muslim population. In 1941, the city counted 30,640 Muslims, compared to 50,232 Europeans; but under the rubric "Europeans," the figure of 14,000 Jews is mentioned. The very official *Encyclopédie coloniale* notes: "Constantine is the Algerian city in which the Jews have attained the highest proportion: 13 percent, based on the total population of the commune; at least 18 percent, if one does not take into account the so-called scattered population but only what is concentrated in the city. It is certainly indebted to them for a large part of its commercial activity."[2]

Constantine, presented as a robust, rebellious, and mystical city, is an old citadel perched on an enormous rock, surrounded by ravines. With its bridges and walkways suspended in midair, the city has the extraordinary appearance of a "peninsula." Alexandre Dumas compared it to "a fantastic city, something like Gulliver's floating island." The entire city is packed onto the summit of a stone block and surrounded by the gorges of the river Rummel, which are about two kilometers long and a hundred meters deep. At its highest point, "the Rock" reaches an altitude of 644 meters, and it is there that the first refuge, the Casbah, stands. About sixty kilometers as the crow flies separate it from the sea. The suspension bridge, built by the French, is the city's most popular emblem. That unique, strange, and impressive location is rich with history.

A religious city, long the intellectual center and flourishing marketplace for the entire eastern part of Algeria, Constantine was the capital of Numidia under King Masinissa and under King Jugurtha, who long held out against the Romans before yielding. The city took the name "Cirta," a Roman designation from the Punic "Kirtha," which means "city" in the language of the Carthaginians. It is evident that Berber Jews from Palestine were living there three centuries earlier. In fact, the old Berber stock constitutes the city's original demographic bedrock, since Constantine is not far from the region of the Chaouis in the Aurès, where legend places the battles of al-Kahinat, queen of a Berber tribe that faced Arab horsemen in the seventh century.

In 311 C.E., the city revolted against Rome. The price it paid was to be destroyed by Emperor Maxentius. Emperor Constantine rebuilt it in 313, bestowing his own name on it. After the Arab conquest and the establishment of Islam as the dominant religion, Constantine was first a dependency of Petite Kabylie, then placed itself within the sphere of influence of Tunis under the Hafsid Dynasty. When the Ottomans arrived in the sixteenth century, it came under the trusteeship of Algiers. At the time, Constantine had about forty thousand residents, including a large

Sanya (?), *Vue de l'intérieur de la synagogue de Constantine*, 1841. Oil on canvas. Paris, Musée d'Art et d'Histoire du Judaïsme, gift of Georges Aboucaya, in memory of Colette Aboucaya-Spira.

Jewish community. Under the Hafsids, the Jews seem to have lived in groups scattered among the Muslims. There was in Constantine an old Muslim middle class made up of notable families, each of them jealous of its centuries-old prestige. In the sixteenth century, Constantine was chosen as the capital of the Beylik of the East. During the Turkish occupation, Salah Bey (r. 1771–92) put his own stamp on the city as a capital and provided it with such structures as the Sidi El-Kettani mosque and madrasa (school), formerly on Place Négrier. Better known as Jamaa El Kettani or El Kettania, it still exists and has never closed its doors. Salah Bey confined the Jews to the Charrah neighborhood (with Grand Street at its heart).

When the French undertook the conquest of Algeria, Constantine was the last large city to resist them. It fell on October 12, 1837. Jewish families took part in the battles alongside the Turkish troops led by Salah Bey. He was very popular among the Jewish community, since he was recognized as being more liberal than his predecessors. At that time, the indigenous population of Constantine differed in composition from that of the other cities of the country. It had only a small number of Turks and Kouloughlis (the descendants of mixed marriages between Turks and Arabo-Berbers) and few Moors. It was composed almost exclusively of Arab or Berber families, coming from nearly all the tribes in the province, and of Jews.

After the raids on Jewish shops in Istanbul on August 5, 1934. Private collection of Benjamin Stora.

An order of June 9, 1844, divided the city into two parts, one European and the other Muslim. In the European zone, located in the west, rectilinear streets running north to south were constructed, whereas the Judeo-Muslim zone retained its prior appearance. In the indigenous neighborhoods, the Muslims were located in the south and east, the Jews in the northeast. The army took over the Casbah, where barracks and a hospital were erected. Private construction and a few public buildings huddled between narrow streets, where it was difficult for traffic to circulate. The squares were minuscule. Muslims and Jews lived together in that atmosphere, moving to the beat of the same music in the city where malouf, or Arabo-Andalusian music, developed. They adopted the same culinary practices and the same respect for religious traditions. In the early twentieth century, Constantine had about a hundred Jewish places of worship and more than twice that many mosques.

The Crémieux Decree, which naturalized the Jews in 1870, making them French citizens, would gradually separate the two communities throughout Algeria. The decree would be the focus of an extremely virulent anti-Semitism, especially in European milieus and at the time of the Dreyfus affair. Unlike other cities such as Oran, Constantine did not have that experience, however, despite the fact that its mayor, Émile Morinaud, was known for his anti-Semitism. It is true that, among the large cities of Algeria, it was in Constantine that the Muslim Algerians had the greatest influence. In 1876 there were 34,700 Muslims to 17,000 Europeans; in 1936, 56,000 Muslims and 50,000 Europeans, including 14,000 Jews of French nationality. In 1941 Algiers counted 25,474 Jews, Constantine 12,961, and Oran 25,753. Orléansville, Bougie, Bône, Mascara, and Sétif also experienced growth in their Jewish populations, sometimes in proportions higher than those of the three major cities.[3]

The separation between the Jews and Muslims of Constantine came about violently. It took place on August 5, 1934. That day, a pogrom broke out in the city and its surrounding area, and neither the police nor the army intervened to stop it. Twenty-seven died, twenty-five of them Jews (five children, six women, and fourteen men). It began with a dispute between an intoxicated Jewish soldier, accused of having urinated on the wall of a mosque, and a group of Muslims. The violence of the unrest indicates how fragile the harmony between the communities had been. Prominent Jewish and Muslim personalities hastened to preach moderation to their coreligionists. On one side was M. Lellouche, president of the consistory and regional councillor, and Chief Rabbi Halimi. On the other was the grand mufti of Constantine, Sheikh Ben Badis, a major religious reformer and founder of the Association of Ulema; and Dr. Bendjelloul, regional councillor and one of the leaders of the national movement of the Constantine region. But the harm had been done. The city, a capital of culture that had produced major writers, such as Kateb Yacine and Malek Haddad, and the painter Jean-Michel Atlan, would become even more divided during the Algerian War. The assassination on June 21, 1961, of Cheikh Raymond, a great Jewish singer of malouf music, would precipitate the departure of the entire Jewish community. In 1962–63, all traces of a community that had called its city the "Little Jerusalem of the Maghreb" would be erased. ●

A specialist in the history of the Maghreb, Benjamin Stora is a professor at the Université Paris 8 and at the Institut National des Langues et Civilisations Orientales (INALCO). He is the author, notably, of La gangrène de l'oubli: Mémoire de la guerre d'Algérie *(La Découverte, 1991);* Imaginaires de guerre: Algérie-Vietnam *(La Découverte, 1998);* Algérie-Maroc: Histoires parallèles *(Maisonneuve et Larose, 2003); and* Les trois exils des juifs d'Algérie *(Stock, 2006). He is coeditor of the present book.*

1. Published in Albert Camus, *Noces, suivi de l'Été* (Paris: Les Éditions Gallimard, 1959; reissued 2010), 124.

2. *L'Encyclopédie coloniale et maritime*, ed. Eugène Guernier (Paris: Institut de l'Encyclopédie Coloniale et Maritime, 1948), 137.

3. For the demographic figures, I have relied on the impressive work of Maurice Eisenbeth, chief rabbi of Algiers, especially his long article "Les Juifs, esquisse historique depuis les origines jusqu'à nos jours," published in *L'Encyclopédie coloniale et maritime*, 143–58; on the social data, see Jacques Taieb and Claude Tapia's "Portrait d'une communauté," in *Les nouveaux cahiers*, 29 (1972): 49–61; and, on the statistical data and analysis, see Doris Bensimon, "Mutations sociodémographiques au xixᵉ et xxᵉ siècle," *Histoire* 3 (November 1979): 200–210 (issue devoted to the Jews in France).

The Case of Tunisia

On the eve of the establishment of the French protectorate over the kingdom of Tunis, several laws had introduced a degree of equality, at least at the level of the texts of the law, with respect to the status of the Jews. Several factors had contributed to these positive changes, especially outside pressure from the European states with which the Regency maintained commercial exchanges at the time. This period had been marked by the economic ascendency of a local Jewish elite that had become very active in commerce with Europe, thus offering it the opportunity for privileged relations with the beys and allowing it to improve the status of its coreligionists. These changes were also the result of the desire for reform among the political elites of the country and among certain reigning beys. Ahmed Bey (1837–55), whose reign was marked by several modernist and reformist measures (the creation of the École polytechnique of Le Bardo, the abolition of black slavery, a visit to France), took several measures dictated by the *maslaha* (interests of the state), according to the chronicler Ben Diaf, in favor of Christians and Jews. Beginning at this time, travelers and chroniclers agree that the fate of the Jews began to improve.[1]

During the reign of his successor, Muhammad Bey (1855–59), the Fundamental Pact was enacted on September 10, 1857, which abolished the status of *dhimmī*: the bey promised that "All our subjects, Muslim or other, will submit equally to the regulations and usages in vigor in the country. None, in this respect, will enjoy any privilege over another." The Fundamental Pact provided that "when the criminal court has to decide on the sentencing of an Israelite subject, it will include Israelite assessors."[2] The following year, on September, 14, 1858, Muhammad Bey allowed Jews to wear the red fez.

Although the constitutional reforms of 1861 did not grant specific representation for Jews on the new Great Counsel, that question had occasioned much debate among the members of the Muslim elite, which were split between partisans and opponents to the integration of the Jews in the new representative body.

The period of the French protectorate in Tunisia (1881–1956) was a distinct moment in the history of the relations between the Jews and the Muslims of that country. During that time, the two communities lived peacefully together under the supervision of the French colonial authorities, henceforth present in the country by virtue of the Treaty of Bardo (May 12, 1881), which placed the Regency under French protection. The Jews, by and large, gave a favorable reception to the French troops arriving in Tunis in 1881 in the hope that it would contribute to their legal status, after the example of their coreligionists in France. The regime of the protectorate definitely offered new work opportunities for the Jewish elite in the economic, administrative, and political domains. But colonization did not affect all communities and all classes in the same way.[3] If most Jews continued to live in the same conditions as the Muslim population, the Jewish elite identified more closely with the French elites settled in Tunisia, requesting French nationality, in keeping with the Algerian Jews after the Crémieux Decree. A portion of this elite, being Francophile, wished to see the arrival of France as "the incarnation of an event founding law and justice."[4] Order and security having been ensured by the new colonial regime, hundreds of Jews from Tunis and other centers in which they had long been established settled in the interior of the country, in cities in which there had been few Jews (Gabès, Gafsa, le Kef, Bizerte, Tala, Mactar, Tataouine, Gardane, etc.) or in new centers created by colonization (Ferryville, the towns in the mining basin of Gafsa, etc.). This settling on the entirety of the territory was thus the opportunity for more and more contact with the Muslim population. From the north to the south of the country, most of the urban centers had their little Jewish community with its rabbis, rites and traditions, synagogues, cemetery, and school, and Jews in the city practiced a certain number of specific activities, involving commerce, jewelry, moneylending, handicrafts, and so on.

The introduction of these modifications did not change the daily life of the Jews, which was rooted, as was the case with Muslims as well, in its traditions and identity markers. Within a two-year period, Muslims and Jews, in April 1885 and March 1887, respectively, reacted violently to the new regulations on burials that the municipality of Tunis wished to establish. Both groups refused to submit to the measures, which tended to municipalize funeral services. The violent protests of the Muslim and Jewish populations forced the authorities to abolish most of the decisions made, and the burial of the dead remained essentially a private affair within the province of the family or the community.

The show of conservatism did not always resist modernist temptations that crossed Muslim and Jewish elites, even though they were expressed differently. Thus, at the beginning of the twentieth century, a part of the Jewish elite, considering Tunisian justice archaic and decayed, conducted a campaign to extend French jurisdiction to the Tunisian Jews. Their Muslim counterparts confirmed the backward character of Tunisian justice, but urged their Jewish countrymen to join them in the struggle necessary to develop and modernize it.[5] Some Jews decided the defects of the judiciary system were beyond reform and needed to disappear. Others,

like Nessim Samama in his intervention in 1908 at the North African Conference, refused to consider its suspension and demanded only its reform.[6]

The First World War brought loss of lives among the Muslims as well as the Jews in Tunisia—in unequal numbers, it is true, but both communities were indeed stricken by that tragedy. Despite the development of legal rights for Jews, making obsolete the clauses of inferiority imposed on them by their *dhimma* status, the Fundamental Pact had maintained the beys' tradition of excluding Jews from the army; this continued under the French protectorate regime. According to the letter of the law, only young Muslims were forced into military service in the army. But several hundred young Israelites from Tunisia volunteered.[7] The first to leave were those in the Jewish community of Livorno, who joined the Italian army, and others, subjects of the bey who were won over to the French cause, joined the French army. A total of 500 Jews served, enlisted under the flag, out of a population of 40,000.[8] Some, like Sergeant Bismuth, distinguished themselves in 1916 in the Battle of Verdun.

But the wave of anti-Semitism that spread during the war in France and Algeria did not spare Tunisia. In those difficult times, both in France and in the colonies, the Jews were suspected of having little involvement in the great patriotic battle of France. During the summer of 1917, the return of soldiers on leave in Tunisia was accompanied by several incidents and attacks against the Jews in La Goulette, Tunis, Bizerte, and Sousse. The French authorities gave free rein to these acts of violence and even seem to have favored these outbursts against the Jews in hopes of appeasing the Muslim populations, who were severely affected by shortages and rising food prices. Most often, the French police did not intervene until long after the civil attackers, directed by soldiers on leave, had completed their extortions and ransacked Jewish-owned stores. The same harassment against Jews took place the following year, in November 1918, during the celebration of the armistice, giving rise to physical attacks by Frenchmen, with young Muslims from Tunisia mixed in, on Jewish populations in Tunis and several other cities. According to the testimony of Elie Cohen-Hadria, nothing happened without the complicity of the colonial authorities: "Since the French occupation," he writes, "very limited pogroms have been carried out in North Africa, and Muslims have begun massacring Jews. But on each occasion, without exception, it has been possible to demonstrate that the massacre was only possible thanks to the tolerance, if not satisfaction and suggestions, of the French authorities."[9]

Just after the First World War, intellectuals from both communities tried to move toward a meeting of the minds and perform reconciliatory acts. Tunisian Jews, though not very numerous, took part in the preparatory meetings that would lead to the creation of the Destour Party in June 1920. To compensate for the failure of their first mission to Paris, leaders of the young nationalist party attached Elie Zerah, a Jewish lawyer, to their second delegation sent to Paris in 1920. Toward the end of 1920, the Judeo-Muslim Union was constituted in Tunis. The attempted reconciliation was the result of meetings held at the office of the Alumni Association at Sadiki College. Expressing a desire for unity, a short-lived committee of mixed composition was formed, made up, among others, on the Muslim side, of Tahar Ben Ammar, Hassen Guellaty, Noomane, and Ayachi, and on the Jewish side, Albert Bessis, Mardoché Smaja, and Drs. Hayet and Bulakia. The stated purpose of the committee was "to expose the aspirations of the Jews and the Muslims and to seek solutions acceptable to both, in order to work together toward the building of a new, fraternal Tunisia within the framework of the Protectorate." The weekly *La Tunisie nouvelle* took on the task of defending these values and principles in thirteen issues published between October 1920 and March 1921. In this same context of reconciliation, in January 1921, Elie Uzan joined the delegation that met with the new resident general,

Lucien Saint, to present the Tunisian demands to him. The executive commission of the Destour Party, from its third congress held in Tunis on May 29, 1921, elected Albert Bessis to the post of treasurer and Elie Zerah and counselor Uzan as members of that commission. Even though the existence of such unified structures, bringing together elites from both communities, was only temporary, their appearance at the propitious moment during periods marked by tensions constituted an expression of the desire for appeasement and united Muslims and Jews in their actions surrounding common demands, which helped avoid flare-ups and exploitation of these divisions by the colonial authorities.

But beyond these attempts to overcome tensions, the daily life of the towns and villages was experienced as a sharing, in exchanges and the adoration of Jewish singers who sang in dialectical Arab, drawing crowds of Jewish and Muslim fans. The 1920s saw the sudden rise to fame of Leila Sfez, and, above all, of the diva Habiba Msika, who drew crowds during her musical and theatrical performances, and plunged Tunisia into mourning when she suddenly disappeared, the victim of a crime of passion.

During the 1930s, in a context marked by the consequences of the great economic crisis, violent acts and attacks were perpetrated during the months of July and August 1932 against the Jewish neighborhoods of several cities: Ariana, Moknine, and Sfax. The memory of these events, and the fear of seeing the violence of 1934 in Constantine (Algeria) repeated in Tunisia, encouraged further attempts to reconcile Jews and Muslims. In May 1935, the eight-hundredth anniversary of the death of Maimonides provided the opportunity for a two-week period of displays, encounters, and ceremonies organized at the Alliance Israélite Universelle and the headquarters of the cultural association Khaldounia. Muslim and Jewish intellectuals seized the opportunity to recall a long history of peaceful coexistence between the two communities. In November of the same year, a collaborative ceremony was organized in memory of the victims of the First World War. The coming to power of the Popular Front government in 1936 and the freedom of political life favored the creation of a Judeo-Muslim league, presided over by Haj Abdelaziz Mehrezi. Its objective was to overcome tensions between Jews and Muslims that had developed in the course of that same year—echoing the events in Palestine.[10] ●

Habib Kazdaghli is a professor of contemporary history at the Manouba University in Tunis. He has worked for many years with a team of historians connected with the group France Méridionale et Espagne (FRAMESPA), of the University of Toulouse–Le Mirail (UTM). He is currently dean of the Faculty of Letters, Arts, and Humanities at Manouba University. His works include Le tourisme dans l'empire français: Politiques, pratiques et imaginaires (xixᵉ–xxᵉ siècles): Un outil de la domination coloniale? *with Colette Zytnicki (Publications de la Société française d'histoire d'outre-mer, 2009), and articles on Tunisia during the colonial period.*

1. Jacques Taieb, "1881, année zéro," *Archives juives*, no. 32/1 (1999): 20–31.

2. Ibid.

3. Claude Nataf, "La communauté juive de Tunisie sous le protectorat français," *Archives juives*, no. 32/1 (1999): 4–19.

4. Abdelkarim Allagui, "L'État colonial et les juifs de Tunisie de 1881 à 1914," *Archives juives*, no. 32/1 (1999): 32–39.

5. Ibid.

6. Ibid.

7. Landau E. Philippe, "Les Juifs de Tunisie et la grande guerre," *Archives juives*, no. 32/1 (1999): 40–52.

8. Ibid.

9. Elie Cohen-Hadria, ed., *Du Protectorat français à l'indépendance tunisienne, souvenirs d'un témoin socialiste* (Nice: Centre de la Méditerranée moderne et contemporaine, 1976).

10. Allagui, "L'État colonial."

The Balfour Declaration and Its Implications
Denis Charbit

Three paragraphs, twenty lines, one hundred twenty-eight words: never in the annals of European diplomacy would so short a text have such great consequences for the political future of a region of the world. Thanks to this declaration, the name Arthur James Balfour (1848–1930) has been passed down to posterity. Neither his philosophical essays, his leadership in the British conservative party, his management of the affairs of Ireland as secretary of state, nor his legislative work in the field of education as deputy of the House of Commons has left an imperishable trace. He was prime minister from January 1902 to December 1905, during which time the Entente Cordiale was concluded between France and the United Kingdom, but the action of Lord Balfour as the head of the government has been eclipsed by the declaration that bears his name, dated November 2, 1917, on the letterhead of the Foreign Office, since he served in that capacity from 1916 to 1919. This won him both gratitude—there were Balfour Streets in most of the Israeli neighborhoods—and notoriety, as the Arabs of Palestine and the Muslims regarded him as the one through whom scandal and misfortune befell them.

Denis Charbit

Denis Charbit, senior lecturer in political science at the Open University of Israel, is the author of *Sionismes: Textes fondamentaux* (Albin Michel, 1998); *Qu'est-ce que le sionisme?* (Albin Michel, 2007); and *Les intellectuels français face à Israël* (Éditions de l'Éclat, 2009).

The content of the declaration

What is the substance of this declaration? Besides the goodwill expressed in favor of "the establishment in Palestine of a national home for the Jewish people," the British government declares its readiness to endeavor "to facilitate the achievement of the object." These words were chosen with prudence. They could always be interpreted by the British authorities in a restrictive or an extensive sense; the die was cast, to the great dismay of the Arab nationalists, who considered themselves swindled, and to the great satisfaction of the Zionist leaders, who fully understood the importance of the historical step forward that had been accomplished. It is true that a "national home" is not a state, but the project was approved, and its definitive legal status could wait. For the first time, in a text with obvious political implications, the Jewish

▶ See article by Denis Charbit, p. 340.

community was defined as a people—which was not self-evident at that time, including to a number of Jews who identified with an exclusively religious definition of their particularism. While the declaration specified that this home would be established in Palestine to the exclusion of any other territory, it did not necessarily mean all of Palestine, whose borders had yet to be determined. The two brief and formal concessions—stipulating that "nothing shall be done which may prejudice the civil and religious rights of [autochthonous] non-Jewish communities in Palestine," or the political rights and legal status enjoyed by Jews in any other country in which they were established—did not alter in the slightest the essential diplomatic confirmation granted to Zionism.

Nearly one hundred years

Foreign Office,
November 2nd, 1917.

Dear Lord Rothschild,

I have much pleasure in conveying to you, on behalf of His Majesty's Government, the following declaration of sympathy with Jewish Zionist aspirations which has been submitted to, and approved by, the Cabinet.

"His Majesty's Government view with favour the establishment in Palestine of a national home for the Jewish people, and will use their best endeavours to facilitate the achievement of this object, it being clearly understood that nothing shall be done which may prejudice the civil and religious rights of existing non-Jewish communities in Palestine, or the rights and political status enjoyed by Jews in any other country".

I should be grateful if you would bring this declaration to the knowledge of the Zionist Federation.

Letter from Arthur James Balfour, of the British Foreign Office, to Lionel de Rothschild, head of the representative body of the Jewish community in Great Britain, dated November 2, 1917, called the "Balfour Declaration."

after its promulgation, the controversy still has not cooled off. In a parallel history of the conflict written by a group of teachers, which presents side-by-side narratives from the perspectives of Israelis and Palestinians, the gap remains considerable.[1]

Zionist versus Arab reactions

From the Zionist perspective, the letter addressed to Lord Lionel Rothschild, the leader of the organization representing the Jewish community of Great Britain, attests to the sympathy that its author, Arthur James Balfour, felt for a generous cause compatible with British interests and correcting a historical injustice. Heir to the Roman Empire, which had subjected the Jewish kingdom to its authority, destroyed the Second Temple, and changed the name of Judea to Palestine, Great Britain made honorable amends, eighteen and a half centuries later. The lay Zionists looked upon the letter as a Magna Carta of their cause,[2] while the religious Zionists, sensitive to the repetition of history when the initial model was of biblical origin, saw in the Balfour Declaration a new edition of the decree of the Persian emperor Cyrus in 538 B.C., which authorized the Jews who had been exiled to the shores of the waters of Babylon after the destruction of the First Temple to return to Judea to reestablish their former independence.

For the Arabs, preeminently the Palestinians, the Balfour Declaration remains the most unreasonable expression of Western imperialism, the most manifest negation of their existence, since it is their very identity and their political rights that are being assassinated: they are designated only as non-Jewish populations, unable to claim anything beyond civil and religious rights. The Balfour Declaration was neither the first nor the last intervention of Great Britain in the region, but by contrast with the fate of so many other British decisions that the Arabs either came to terms with or managed to circumvent, all the efforts to suppress the Balfour Declaration, to change its direction or diminish its importance, never succeeded in reversing the momentum it had unleashed. The decree had promoted and privileged a new political actor—the Zionists—bearers of claims competing with their own.

For the Zionist movement, the Balfour Declaration undoubtedly inaugurated a new era, that of "the state on the march," but it also corresponded to the ultimate outcome of a diplomatic strategy that Theodor Herzl, the father of Jewish nationalism, had elaborated during his ten years of Zionist activities. After having vainly implored Jewish philanthropists to forgive the debts of the Ottoman Empire in exchange for a territorial concession in Palestine, which the sultan would have granted them, Herzl concluded that the only way to concretize the "modern solution" of a state for the Jews was to obtain the help of a great power. Such a power would proclaim a charter favoring a Zionist movement—that is, it would bring to the international scene its moral, political, and financial support for the reconstruction of a Jewish national home in

> *For the Zionist movement, the Balfour Declaration undoubtedly inaugurated a new era, that of 'the state on the march.'*

Palestine. The measures taken by Herzl in this direction during his lifetime had proven ineffectual: neither the German emperor William II, with whom he obtained a brief interview during the magnate's official visit to Palestine, nor the minister of the Interior Plehve under Czar Nicholas II took his proposition seriously. Only the minister of the British colonies, desirous to avoid a new flood of Jewish immigrants following the Kishinev pogrom, conceived the project, in 1904, of redirecting that flow toward Uganda and of creating, to that end, a Jewish republic under Herzl's supervision. The offer went no further, but it pushed the Zionist movement to the brink of a schism. To turn one's eyes away from Zion was a reprehensible infidelity, if not treason. Herzl, exhausted, died a few months later.

But the controversy clarified once and for all a debate internal to the Zionist movement, at the conclusion of which it was decreed that henceforth there would be "no Zionism without Zion": only a territory located in the region corresponding more or less to ancient Palestine should be considered for the ingathering of the Jews. The diplomatic strategy having failed, the partisans of practical Zionism recommended the acquisition of lands and their development, lot by lot, rather than putting their hopes in improbable outside support, which did not materialize. Chaim Weizmann, leaving aside the vain quarrels between Zionists who were all motivated by the same ultimate objective, argued for a "synthetic Zionism": the key to success for the Zionist undertaking rested upon combined efforts, both in situ and in the international arena.

The solemn declaration not only constituted recognition in principle but it stood within a context that gave it an operational political meaning and an imminent performative value. Since the Ottoman Empire had sided with Germany as early as 1914, the British decided to open an eastern front, convinced that that zone was a weak link in the German defense. To break the deadlock of military forces in Europe, now bogged down in trench warfare, the United States had to be convinced to throw its weight into the balance, and while waiting for them to come on board, another front had to be opened against Germany and the Austro-Hungarian Empire, pushing up from the Middle East to the Balkans. These military calculations, aimed at hastening the victory, included long-term strategic considerations: to secure the British positions throughout the East—in Egypt and India—and to consolidate their empire in the region, it was quite useful to take over the Middle East. For the Zionist movement, the First World War reestablished the priority of diplomatic action and the need for making choices. The first choice was to break with the neutrality that had been proclaimed at the onset of hostilities. Weizmann bet on the victory of

> *The accommodation of the British appetite for power, French claims, Jewish national aspirations, and indigenous Arab demands—such were the stakes in that essential decade for the Middle East.*

Great Britain, and since that country defined the goal of the war as the dismantling of the Ottoman Empire, it was important to put oneself beneath England's protective wing in order to be invited to the table of the victors. Weizmann, associated with the drafting of the Declaration, could avail himself of a result that accomplished the strategy recommended by Herzl. In declaring war on the Ottoman Empire, the British offered the nationalist Arabs, as well, grounds for hope: the Revolution of the Young Turks in 1908 having aroused vain hopes for autonomy, they could henceforth catch a glimpse of the realization of their national aspirations with the suppression of the Ottoman obstacle that was their first adversary.

In exchange for participation, even if only symbolic, in the large-scale military maneuvers in preparation, Jews and Arabs bought their right to enter the dance of grand diplomatic maneuvers. The scenario was clear: the military coup de grâce would bring about the agony, final this time, of the "sick man of Europe," the Ottoman Empire, out of which would be born, besides the independent Turkish Republic—reduced to its territorial sanctuary by the Treaty of Sèvres of August 10, 1920, revised in 1923—a new political creation destined to fix the fate of the Arab provinces of the moribund ex–Ottoman Empire. What form would it take? One state or many? A federation or protectorates? The answer was decisive for the Arabs but secondary for the Zionists, who desired above all to be associated with the destinies of a territory in Palestine. The accommodation of the British appetite for power, French claims, Jewish national aspirations, and indigenous Arab demands—such were the stakes in that essential decade for the Middle East. Between 1914 and 1923, the Arab provinces would go through their most formidable political mutation since the advent, in 1453, of the Ottoman Empire, under whose authority they had hitherto remained.

Great Britain's intentions

It was on the eve of that great territorial redistribution that British power published the Balfour Declaration, offering the Jewish community of Palestine and the leadership of the Zionist movement favorable treatment that was far from being realized. From the British point of view, the Balfour Declaration corresponded to several interests. Raised in 1915, the proposition appeared in many reports and memoranda submitted to the government, and represented a conjunction of favorable opinions stemming from religious motivations. Preoccupied with convincing the United States to enter the war on the side of the Allies, the British had to overcome an isolationist tendency quite widespread among Americans, including its Jews. These Jews, mainly of Russian provenance, could not accept that their new country should become an ally of the czar, whom they detested because of his anti-Semitic policy, which had pushed them into exile and continued to plunge their brothers, who had stayed behind, into misery. As it was out of the question to intervene in the domestic affairs of the czar, it was by backing the Zionist cause that Great Britain could count on a change of attitude on the part of the American Jews, whose influence it overestimated. The Russian Revolution of February 1917 in no way diminished the relevance of an opportune declaration—quite to the contrary: the British feared the Russian temptation of a separate peace with Germany. A clear backing of Zionism might incite the Jews of Russia to encourage the provisional revolutionary government to continue the war.

Competing demands

Besides encouraging America's entry into the war and keeping Russia in the Allied camp, the British intent in backing the development of a Jewish national home in

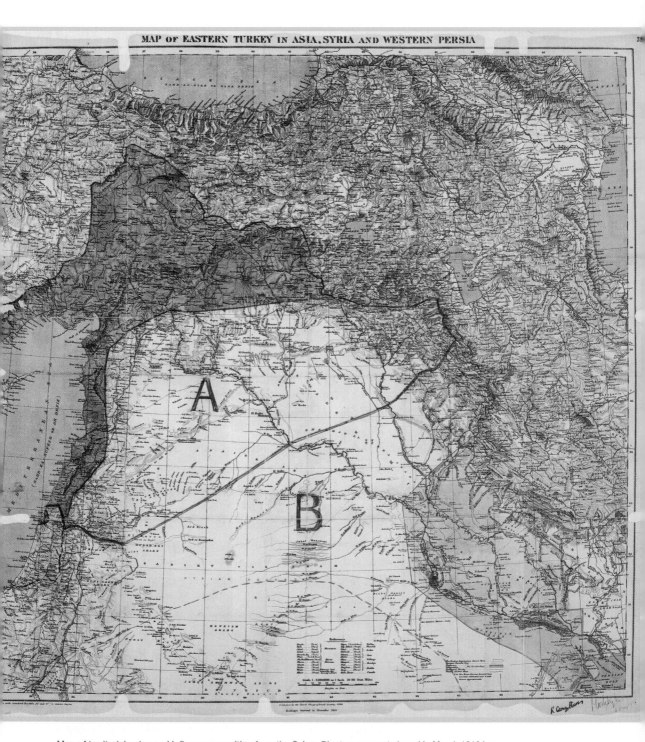

MAP OF EASTERN TURKEY IN ASIA, SYRIA AND WESTERN PERSIA

Map of territorial gains and influences resulting from the Sykes-Picot agreement signed in March 1916 by France and Great Britain: two zones of control (or protectorate, blue for the French zone and pink for the British zone), two zones of influence (A for France, B for Great Britain), and one yellow zone under international administration. Paris, Archives of the Ministry of Foreign Affairs.

Palestine was above all to have an edge over the French. Had not these last been the first to express their desire to "assist the renaissance… of the Jewish nationality, on that land from which the people of Israel have been driven so many centuries ago?" This diplomatic message, addressed to Nahum Sokolov on June 4, 1917, by Jules Cambon, the secretary of Foreign Affairs, which ended with a solemn engagement ("The French government… can feel only sympathy for your cause, the triumph of which is bound to that of the Allies. I am happy to assure you of this here"),[3] was interpreted as a warning: four months later, the British government published the Balfour Declaration, similarly inspired for the purpose of blocking France's designs on Palestine. Last, it was important to be in tune with the evolution on the ground by giving moral legitimacy to the imminent military occupation of Palestine. The conquest would be based not on force but on rights; not on an imperial whim but on a project of eminently respectable self-determination, conforming to the international norms defined by President Wilson for the postwar period. A month and one week after the Balfour Declaration, on December 11, the commander of the armed forces of His Majesty, General Allenby, entered Jerusalem. A year later, on December 7, 1918, the cease-fire was signed.

The Balfour Declaration was not the only project involving the future of Palestine. It was, in fact, only the most recent of the promises made by the British during the war. Two others had preceded it: the first had been made by the British governor of Egypt, Henry McMahon, to Sharif Hussein, offspring of the prestigious Hashemite dynasty dating back to Muhammad. A Muslim became the ally of a Christian to struggle against the Muslim power constituted by the Ottoman Empire: this was made even more spectacular by the fact that the Muslim in question was the protector of Mecca and Medina. In return for a victorious general insurrection against the Ottoman Empire, he would get a kingdom.[4] In the first letter, McMahon was evasive on the question of borders of the said kingdom granted Hussein. McMahon eventually gave way to Hussein's insistence, but rather than sending a specific map, or even designating in writing the regions that would be included, he listed the territories that would be excluded: in the East, Mesopotamia (corresponding to present-day Iraq); in the Northwest, the region of Mersin and Alexandretta; the Syrian and Libyan coast from Latakia to Beirut; and "the Syrian zone to the west of the districts of Damascus, Homs, Hama, and Aleppo." Palestine was not mentioned as such, thus opening a Pandora's box: being in Southwestern Syria, was it outside of the kingdom or a part of it?

The second promise was not an offer made to a third party but secret agreements duly signed in March 1916, with supporting maps, this time by Great Britain and France, to divvy up the spoils of war. The negotiators, Mark Sykes and Georges Picot (from the British Foreign Office and the French Office of Foreign Affairs, respectively) had established on a Levantine map an initial distinction between zones of control and zones of influence, depending on the kind of domination, rigid or more lax, that the two powers intended to hold. They had also agreed on the setting up of an international condominium, mainly Franco-British, over Palestine, Jerusalem, and the Holy Places.

The Hussein-McMahon correspondence, the Sykes-Picot agreements, and the Balfour Declaration had occurred in wartime, to respond to the political pressures and interests of the times. Once the hostilities were over, the Allies, having won the war, could now take action, availing themselves of their victory. But the context was somewhat different than they had anticipated: the French had not participated in the battles, which diminished their claims; the Bolsheviks—plunged in civil war with the White Russians and at war with the international coalition that had assembled against them, preoccupied with holding on to their power—were out of the running; the Americans had once more retreated into their isolationism; Great Britain was the only real power on the ground. But it fell to this last to manage and harmonize, as much as possible, the vying claims of the Zionists, the Arabs, and the French.

Weizmann protested against the Sykes-Picot agreements that divided the territory of Palestine into four zones, intended, respectively, for France, Great Britain, the Arab kingdom, and joint international authority. Hussein railed against the Balfour Declaration, which in his view amputated the future Arab kingdom from Palestine and Jerusalem, the third most holy city of Islam.

Abdullah ibn Hussein, Emir of Transjordan (1921–46), and Emir Shakir, during the visit of Sir Herbert Samuel, the British high commissioner of Palestine, in Transjordan. Photographed on April 19, 1921.

Nevertheless, if the Hashemite dynasty was hardly indifferent to the fate of Palestine for reasons much more religious than political, the essential objective of Emir Hussein and his sons, as leaders of Arab nationalism, was the advent of the great kingdom promised by McMahon. In an initial phase, the British seemed to be determined to go through with it: Emir Faisal, having their consent, went to Damascus in June 1918 to establish his authority in situ. For the Arabs of Palestine, between the Balfour Declaration and an Arab kingdom in gestation, the choice was made: on November 2, 1918, they marked the first anniversary of the British Declaration with a mass demonstration followed by a petition to the government of His Majesty signed by the city fathers and notables to demand the integration of Palestine into the body of Syria, since it constituted its southern flank, as they loved to repeat. In that respect, the seeds of conflict were sown. On January 3, 1919, in an event often forgotten, Emir Faisal, careful to take the Zionist aspirations into account, signed, under the auspices of Colonel Lawrence, an agreement of mutual cooperation with Weizmann, including a demarcation of borders between the Arab kingdom and the Jewish national homeland. But Great Britain and France, reversing the decision to support Faisal's reign in Syria in the month of September 1919, and attributing "mandates" to themselves over the provinces of the ex–Ottoman Empire, decided to rewrite a new page of history, from which that promised Arab kingdom was definitively erased.

---

1. See *Side by Side: Parallel Histories of Israel-Palestine* (Beit Jallah: PRIME [Peace Research Institute in the Middle East], 2003), 6–10.

2. Simha Flapan, *The Birth of Israel: Myths and Realities* (New York: Pantheon Books, 1987), 16.

3. See Renée Neher-Bernheim, *La Déclaration Balfour* (Paris: Julliard, coll. "Archives," 1969), 254–55.

4. It consisted in the exchange of ten letters by the two men between July 1915 and March 1916, known as the Hussein-McMahon correspondence.

"The Arabs" as a Category of British Discourse in Palestine

Nadine Picaudou

During the Mandate period, in an attempt to reconcile various interests, the British political discourse commonly had recourse to the category "Arabs" to designate Muslim or Christian Palestinians. Various pseudoethnic or pseudopsychological distinctions, such as the figure of the fellah or the Bedouin, were also pressed into service. These designations, both bearers of colonial categories and heirs to the nomenclature of national minorities of the Ottoman reforms, influenced the fate of relations between Jews and Muslims in the ensuing years. They also furnished ideological material from which the Zionist discourse would make decisive borrowings. In a context no longer consonant with the usual categories of colonization, Great Britain experienced (particularly during episodes of revolt in Palestine) the contradictions inherent in its project for this territory by intending to earmark a Jewish national home while at the same time guaranteeing justice for the indigenous populations.

Nadine Picaudou

Nadine Picaudou, a historian specializing in the Middle East and professor emeritus of the University of Paris 1 (Panthéon-Sorbonne), is the author of *La Déchirure libanaise* (1989); *La Décennie qui ébranla le Moyen-Orient (1914–1923)* (1992); and *Les Palestiniens, un siècle d'histoire* (1997, 2003), all published by Éditions Complexe, and *L'Islam entre religion et idéologie: Essai sur la modernité musulmane* (Gallimard, 2010).

Two irreconcilable obligations

The first years of British presence in Palestine just after the First World War took on two successive roles: that of a provisional military occupation, between 1917 and June 1920, followed by that of the civil High Commission, before the League of Nations Mandate took effect in 1923. The first British high commissioner, Sir Herbert Samuel, remained in his position until July 1925, and it was in the course of those founding years that a central concept imposed itself into British discourse, which probably owes a good deal to his vision and personal ethics: the *dual obligation* to which a Mandate power would be subject. It would have to support and promote the building of a Jewish national home in Palestine, in accordance with the commitments made in the

Balfour Declaration, and at the same time progressively endow the country "with free institutions of government" within the framework of a political unity of Palestine, and in compliance with the requirements of justice toward all populations.

In 1937, the British report by the Royal Commission of Inquiry, presided over by Lord Peel, into the "troubles" in Palestine in 1936 explicitly destroyed the dual obligation concept and emphasized the structurally irreconcilable nature of the two requirements. On the one hand, the very nature of British domination would make any true allegiance of the population to the state impossible, and on the other, community antagonisms would not have allowed the creation of a "representative" government.[1] Furthermore, this irreconcilable nature of the two obligations has been frequently stressed in the historical account of Mandate Palestine, whether it was a version favorable to the Zionist theories, denouncing the politics of appeasement toward the Arabs and decrying the betrayal of the promises made to the Jews, or, on the contrary, a version favorable to the positions of the Palestinian Arabs, who were anxious to show the structural collusion between British and Zionist interests. The account most concerned with offering an equitable version of what was at stake recognized the constant difficulty the British had in prioritizing the two obligations.[2]

In reality, the ambition of providing the country free governmental institutions within a united framework while respecting the requirements of justice toward all populations harbored deep ambiguities, as attested to by the divergences internal to the British political class. Two main points engender controversy. The first concerns the status granted to the Jewish segment of the population of Palestine. Should it be considered a component of the Palestinian community of citizens or a separate *national* entity? The second involves the implications of the principle of representation, given the demographic structure of the country: applied in a unitary framework, such a principle would necessarily lead to imposing the dominance of an Arab majority on a Jewish minority. Sir Herbert Samuel summarized the dilemma clearly just after the 1921 Jaffa riots. Suggesting enlarging the participation at the consultative council created in October 1920, and electing local members who had hitherto been named by the high commissioner, he underscored on that occasion the "serious objections" raised by the "division of the electorate into separate religious communities," but also the no less serious objections to adopting "the 'ordinary geographical basis… for that would result in the minorities being swamped.'"[3] In other words, the problem was the following: how to reconcile a logic of political representation of these groups in a Judeo-Arab national unitary framework, which would inevitably lead to the assertion of an Arab majority, and a community logic of functional partition in which the British authority would arbitrate between Jews and Arabs while at the same time seeking to satisfy each of the

> " *A logic of political representation of these groups in a Judeo-Arab national unitary framework … would inevitably lead to the assertion of an Arab majority.* "

two camps independent of each other. Formulated in this way, the dilemma was not only insoluble but it led to masking the discrepancies that existed in the very nature of the policies followed with respect to the two communities, and even more so in the way of understanding the "requirements of justice" concerning them apart from each other.

Figures of the native

It is within this general framework that the following reflections are situated. Their object is a pure fact of discourse, the notion of "Arabs" as a category of British political discourse, the postulates on which it is based, and the stock of representations in which the British action is rooted with respect to the Palestinian Arabs in the course of the first years of the Mandate period. An inquiry into the meaning and uses of that category leads first to the observation that the Arabs constitute the "indigenous" or native figure par excellence, and belong, as such, to a classic colonial ethos. But this also leads to the observation that the Arabs are not always assimilated to simple natives, pure passive objects of colonialist intervention, because the qualification of "Arab" acquires, in a time of crisis, another meaning and is laden with another weight, designating a political community capable of becoming an obstacle to British policy in Palestine.

The indigenous figure can be understood in various ways. Most frequently, the *natives* are assimilated to a heterogeneous assemblage of faith groups juxtaposed as attested by the nomenclature of British censuses that, after the example of Ottoman classifications, categorize populations according to their religious identity, distinguishing between Muslims, Christians, Druzes, Jews, and "others." Moreover, the indigenous Palestinians are not generally considered as being "true" Arabs, but as mixed or "Arabized" populations, and it would be easy to assemble an anthology of commonplaces that adorn British discourse in this respect. John Shuckburgh, an authority in the Middle East Department at the Colonial Office, writes as follows in December 1922, in the margin of a memorandum drafted by Sir Herbert Samuel: "The majority of them, at any rate in the large towns and on the Mediterranean coast, are not Arabs at all."[4] Gilbert Clayton, formerly the head of Military Intelligence in Cairo, later secretary general of the mandate, well disposed to Arabs in general, wrote to his friend Gertrude Bell in June 1918: "The so-called Arabs of Palestine have nothing in common with the true desert Arabs, or even with those of the other civilized regions of Syria and Mesopotamia."[5]

The British view, in reality, assigns to the populations of the two banks of the Jordan differentiating identities, which Sir Ronald Storrs, the first military governor of Jerusalem, would later summarize as follows: "While the Arabs East of the Jordan were a splendid people and the real thing, those West of the Jordan were not Arabs at all but merely Arabic-speaking Levantines," a thesis he himself considers to be "ethnologically correct, but nationally misleading."[6] Elie Kedourie

Bedouin, photograph from the American Colony, around 1880. Private collection.

has long since shown the doctrinal importance of the Levantine in the modern British way of envisioning the Middle East. It is known that this term first designated a European resident of the Levant, then, specifically, an individual indigenous to the south of Europe, most often Greek or Italian, before finally being extended to include non-Muslims of the East acting as intermediaries between Europe and the Middle East, and, as such, conveyors of the deleterious effects of a materialist and vulgar Western modernity come to contaminate the purity of the East. The term "Levantine," which initially designated a functional group of intermediaries within Ottoman society, finally came to define a human type, contrasting with the Arab of pure race as the hybrid stands in contrast with the authentic. The British way of seeing things, however, not only includes the indigenous Arab of Palestine in the stereotype of the degenerate Levantine but also the archetypal peasant opposed to the free Bedouin of Transjordan—a "gentleman by birth,"[7] if we are to believe Sir Alec Kirkbride—as if the difference in the way of life went hand in hand with the racial criterion, or was synonymous with it.

But the figure of the Arab peasant of Palestine cannot be reduced to the opposite of that of the Bedouin, transfigured by romanticism, because the ethnicizing vision soon gives way, in British discourse in Palestine, to a more sociological perspective that organizes Palestinian society in terms of a different dichotomy, opposing peasantry to rural aristocracy (feudal gentry), a recurrent theme in Zionist literature as well. Sir Ronald Storrs consummately summarizes the argument, here again to distance himself from it: "The Fellah, the peasant, was a fine fellah, a stout fellah, with all the bluff and blunt virtues conventionally ascribed to peasantry by those who know it least. He was also unorganized and inarticulate. The Effendi on the other hand was a decadent 'capitalist' parasite, a selfish obstructive agitator of an Arab majority not ill disposed if only 'left to themselves.'"[8]

Natural rights in question

Such a conventional view of society, contrasting the positive figure of the peasant with the negative image of a small clique of effendis, is clearly not without political implications. How could the virtuous and nonpoliticized peasant follow the exploitative owner whom he hates? All of these categories, whether pseudoethnic or pseudosociological, that tend to depersonalize the Arabs of Palestine contribute to confining them to indigenous status. We must determine the ways in which this status is subject to being used in the specific case of Palestine. To confine the Arabs within the framework of the "indigenous" is to say that their sole legitimacy is based on their being there—on a simple reality that implies no "natural" right to the homeland, particularly since they are deemed to have neglected to develop it, a recurring argument in all colonial discourse, the political implications of which are obvious. For legitimacy of being there is implicitly contrasted with a superior form of legitimacy, which comes from a principle and not just from a simple reality—a principle that is none other than the British commitment to favor the establishment of a Jewish national home in Palestine. Storrs's words are, once again, very enlightening on this point, even though he does not explicitly hierarchize the respective degree of legitimacy of Arabs versus Jews: "While the rights of the Arabs are based on their residence in the country, the rights of the Jews are independent of this qualification, for the trust being held by Great Britain for the Jewish National Home to be established in Palestine for the benefit of the Jewish people... does not depend on the numerical strength of the present Jewish population of Palestine."[9]

> **To confine the Arabs within the framework of the 'indigenous' is to say that their sole legitimacy is based on ... a simple reality that implies no 'natural' right to the homeland.**

The fact is, the British White Paper of 1922 would use a formula incessantly repeated thereafter: "the Jewish people... is in Palestine as of right and not on the sufferance." Therefore it is Britain's promise that grounds the legitimacy of the Jewish presence, and it is the honor of the country and its credibility, a major asset of its imperial policy, that is committed in respect to that promise. To an Arab delegation that reminded Churchill, in August 1921, of the British commitment to protect the rights of the "non-Jewish communities of Palestine" according to the terms of the Balfour Declaration, Churchill replied that the British had never promised the Arabs "self-government," to which he added: "We promised that you should not be turned off your land,"[10] as if native presence on the land only inferred the maintenance of the status quo, while the commitment made to the Jews implied recognition of their national rights. The British promise, moreover, concerned potentially all Jews, whatever their place of residence might be, so when the British administration referred to Palestine "as a whole," it intended, in the words of John Shuckburgh in a memorandum of November 7, 1921, "not only the existing population of Palestine, but also those future citizens of the country to whom the Balfour Declaration had promised a National Home."[11]

There is, then, a structural divergence in the basis recognized by the British Mandate for the respective rights of Jews and Arabs in Palestine; that is, the nature of the requirements of justice with respect to the two groups is defined differently. In the case of the indigenous Arabs, these requirements are derived from a classical colonial ethics that could be summarized in three axioms: to put into place an efficient and honest administration, defined negatively by the rejection of the convenient bad example constituted by the Ottoman administration; to maintain the social and religious status quo; and to ensure the well-being of the various populations. It is, in sum, in order to ensure the maintenance of the established social order that the British will make the urban notables their legitimate interlocutors and natural intermediaries with the population. In reality, it was less a question of associating the Arab elites with power than with pursuing a policy of patronage intended to keep in contact with Arab society in the absence of truly representative institutions. Such is the spirit that presided particularly over the establishment in 1922 of the Supreme Muslim Council, an organization that gave Muslim notables an alternative to an overt political cooperation with the British, which their rejection of the Balfour Declaration made impossible. Thus, the religious field replaced the political one, which contributed to a form of communitarianism unique to Muslims.[12] As for the promotion of the well-being of the populations, that was the responsibility of colonial ethics, and Sir Herbert Samuel, in his interim report on the first year of civil administration in Palestine, very explicitly connected that obligation with the indigenous Arabs: "It is the clear duty of the Mandatory Power to promote the well-being of the Arab population, in the same way as a British administration would regard it as its duty to promote the welfare of the local population in any part of our Empire. The measures to foster the well-being of the Arabs should be precisely those which we should adopt in Palestine as if there were no Zionist question and if there had been no Balfour Declaration."[13]

> ❝ *In British discourse, the backwardness of the indigenous population was always assessed by comparison with the images of modernity and progress associated with the new Jewish pioneers.* ❞

Thus, the colonial imperative of development was applicable in Palestine as it was everywhere in the empire, and the natural target for it was the indigenous population—in this case the Arabs. Still, there did not seem to be, within the political action of the Mandate, an absolute separation between what related to a classic colonial enterprise and what was in support of the national Zionist project. For there was a common conviction, originating in the Zionist argument, that won overriding consensus in the British political class beyond differences of sensibility: the Zionist program would contribute to the development of Palestine for the greater good of all its inhabitants, Jews and Arabs. In British discourse, the backwardness of the indigenous population was always assessed by comparison with the images of modernity and progress associated with the new Jewish pioneers, and the argument in favor of development, the ultimate moral justification for domination, made the Zionist enterprise coincide with the British one, as if the "sacred mission of civilization" were in this case taken charge of by both the British and the Zionists. Sir Herbert Samuel, in his famous speech of June 3, 1921, in the aftermath of the Jaffa riots, which was a rude awakening from his dream of harmonious community coexistence, actually took up once more the Zionist argument that would become a commonplace of British political discourse when he asserted: "Certain [Jews] should come to Palestine in order to help by their resources and efforts to develop the country, to the advantage of all its inhabitants."[14] Let us note that this repeated way of claiming to give an economic response to a political problem, a very long-term promise, provoked the sarcasm of the newspaper *Filastin*, which published an Arabic translation of the speech and emphasized that a population in need of reassurance about the Zionist ambitions had just heard a talk devoted to improving the roads, the telephone, the telegraph, and even the food for asses.[15]

Visit of Lord Balfour, British minister of Foreign Affairs, to a kibbutz in Palestine, then in the British Mandate. Photograph taken around 1925.

"The Arab scarecrow"

The Palestinian Arabs are not, however, purely indigenous, or even passive objects of colonial action, since we observe that the explicit characterization, "Arab," becomes generalized, and particularly prominent in times of crisis. Then the Arabs are defined as a community having the ability to block British policy, and the fear of Arab violence appears as one of the major forces hampering it throughout this period. The fear of community confrontations is old, and it is in the constant risk of Jewish-Arab violence that the very justification of British domination resides. It is by pleading the exceptionality of Palestine and invoking the power of the "racial and religious passions"[16] that are unleashed there that the British retain that direct hold on Palestine, unparalleled in the rest of the empire. But the representations of Arab violence in the British political class waver between two registers: now pure irrationality (the image of a retarded, childish race, combined with the indigenous dimension), now the manifestation of a latent political hostility. In the first case, Arab violence is considered to be both inevitable and incapable of questioning the British policy. In the second, it constitutes, conversely, a symptom of the political failure of the Mandate holder (Great Britain). The crisis of May 1923 is an example of the second position: the community confrontations of Jaffa dictate to Sir Herbert Samuel a policy of appeasement, or at least of a discourse of appeasement intended to regain the confidence of the Arabs. The high commissioner, in his address of June 3, proposed a reinterpretation of the Balfour

> *The Arabs hold, in the eyes of the British, a decisive political arm—that of consent—which is both the weapon of the weak and a determining factor in the success of the Mandate policy.*

Declaration: "[T]he terms of the Declaration referred to do not contemplate that Palestine as a whole should be converted into a Jewish National Home, but that such a Home should be founded in Palestine.... Nevertheless, it is the intention of His Majesty's government to foster the establishment of a full measure of self-government in Palestine."[17] That is to say, the Arabs hold, in the eyes of the British, a decisive political arm-- that of consent--which is both the weapon of the weak and a determining factor in the success of the Mandate policy.

In the course of that initial phase of the presence in Palestine, which preceded the enforcement of the Mandate, the British hesitated on how to secure the consent of the Arabs—first, because the category "Arabs of Palestine" was not clearly defined for them from the beginning. During the beginning of the 1920s, the tie between Palestine and its regional environment remained ambiguous. Great Britain was tempted, at first, to pressure its allies in the national Arab movement to give up Palestine officially. It was this sort of strategy that led to the secret agreement signed under the patronage of the British between Emir Faisal and the representative of the Zionist Federation of Great Britain, Chaim Weizmann, in January 1919, an agreement that the emir would accept the Balfour Declaration and the activation of the Zionist program in Palestine in exchange for economic aid to "the Arab State" to come into being and subject to the recognition of an Arab independence. The text designated the *ashraf* as the only legitimate Arab political agents, and made the mistake of believing that an agreement negotiated with the national Arab movement in Damascus would suffice to defuse the local rejection of Zionism. What is more, it incurred the risk of radicalization, since the best arm of Palestinian anti-Zionism was the dream of uniting with Syria, which would not leave the Arabs of Palestine standing alone before the Zionist threat.[18] Sir Herbert Samuel was entirely aware of this risk. In a report sent to the Foreign Office on April 2, 1920, on the basis of an initial visit to Palestine, even before his nomination to the post of high commissioner, he wrote: "The movement in Palestine for its union with Syria springs from several sources. There is a natural patriotic sentiment among the small class of politically conscious Arabs in favour of an independent Arabia which should be extensive and as important as possible.... A united and independent Syria is regarded as being the only means of combating Zionism."[19]

Indeed, the British promptly undertook to isolate the so-called minority of ideologues in Palestine in order to rely rather on the notables who, for their part, were trying to negotiate the positions of power in the new post-Ottoman, postwar context. Later, during negotiations on the Mandate, which were long delayed by the objections of France and the Vatican, one of the major stakes for the British was to legitimize the separate future of Palestine and to justify its dissociation from the Arab environment. They did so on the basis of a deliberately biased rereading of the Hussein-McMahon correspondence, intended to show that Palestine had been excluded from the British promises made to the Arabs in 1915. That rereading was driven by internal British controversy, especially during the rejection of the Palestinian Mandate by the House of Lords, on June 21, 1922, a rejection explicitly motivated by the commitments made toward the Arabs in 1915 and 1918. But the House of Commons approved the Mandate, and the White Paper of 1922 finally gave the official version of the promises made to the Arabs and the territorial reservations contained therein. "This reserve (territorial) has always been considered as covering the vilayet of Beirut and the independent Sanjak of Jerusalem. The whole of Palestine west of the Jordan was thus excluded from the commitment of His Majesty."[20]

In 1923, Lord Devonshire, secretary of the Colonial Office, summarized the situation in these terms: "The Arabs as a whole have acquired a freedom undreamed of before the war. Considering what they owe us, they may let us do have our way in one small area, which we do not admit to be covered by our pledges and which, in any case, for historical and other reasons stands on wholly different footing from the rest of the Arab countries."[21]

> **During negotiations on the Mandate ... one of the major stakes for the British was to legitimize the separate future of Palestine and to justify its dissociation from the Arab environment.**

The exceptional nature of Palestine, and its exclusion from the promises made to the Arabs, joined forces to legitimize the British position. From then on, the Arabs of Palestine were clearly distinguished from the other Arabs, which came down to two things: they could not base their political claims on some British promise; and, consequently, there was no symmetry between Jews and Arabs. Simply residents on Palestinian soil, and unable to assert British promises on which to base their political rights, the Arabs lacked a solid foundation for their national claims and could not hope to enjoy the benefit of authentic political representation. They were nonetheless recognized as ipso facto political entities, as they held the arm of consent and the power to obstruct British policy. Arab violence thus saw that it had political significance. By revolting, the Palestinian Arabs ceased being pure natives and rose to the level of political actors aware of their interests, which had to be taken into account. Sir Herbert Samuel expressed this very clearly in a dispatch sent to Winston Churchill at the Colonial Office in June 1921: "I must regard, however, that a new factor has entered into the political situation of this country, and that is the interest for public affairs in the minds of the population in general, that has been disclosed by the events in Jaffa and in the neighborhood. They are now seen to be race-conscious in a more definitive manner than they were before, and, for the time being at least, they are impressed by the power which they find that they possess to resist and obstruct the government."[22]

But in this respect a distinction must be made between the British analysis on the ground and that of the national leaders in London, less sensitive to what certain Zionists called "the Arab scarecrow," which they did not perceive as a major political danger, because they cordoned off Arab violence in Palestine as being at the level of purely local reactions of natives, and incapable of affecting Anglo-Arab relations at the regional level. In the summary of British policy already quoted, the new secretary of the Colonial Office, Lord Devonshire, wrote in 1923, "So long as the general body of Arab opinion is not against us, the dangers resulting from local dissatisfaction ought not to be serious."[23]

As early as 1922–23, however, the Palestinian political leaders, and particularly the Supreme Muslim Council, tried to appeal to Arab and Muslim solidarity, availing themselves of the pilgrimage and sending delegations to neighboring countries. The British civil servants of the India Office expressed repeated concerns in this regard, while the High Commission in Palestine followed very closely the discussions within Palestinian circles concerning the opportunity to solicit Islamic military aid both from Kemalist Turks and Saudi Ikhwani(s). But these attempts to mobilize Arab and Islamic opinions on the subject of defending Islam's holy places—threatened by Zionism—do not constitute, in the course of the period we are considering, a major issue that would weigh heavily on British policy.[24] The pressure exerted is not at all comparable to the ability the Zionist movement has to give an international dimension to the Jewish question. It was not until the second half of the 1930s—by the combined effects of the Great Revolt of the years 1936–39 in Palestine, the war in Ethiopia, and the heightened threats in Europe—that Great Britain was forced to consolidate its Arab alliances in the Middle East. From then on, imperial interests took definitive precedence over internal Palestinian ones. In 1937, the Middle East department of the Foreign Office, henceforth charged with the region as a whole, asserted that "to look at the Palestine problem in the light of our alleged commitments to the Central European Jews, while refusing to look at it in the light of the situation, and of our vital imperial interests, in the neighbouring Arab countries and the Middle East as a whole, can only lead to a catastrophe."[25]*

*The present article by Nadine Picaudou, included here with the permission of the IFPO Press, was originally published as "'Les Arabes' comme catégorie du discours mandataire britannique en Palestine," in *Temps et espaces en Palestine,* ed. Roger Heacock (Beirut, Lebanon: Institut français du Proche-Orient ["Contemporain publications," no. 25], 2008), 235–45.

---

1. On the British Mandate in Palestine, see, especially, Henry Laurens, *La Question de Palestine,* vol. 2: *Une Mission sacrée de civilisation, 1922–1947 (*Paris: Fayard, 2002).

2. On this point, see especially Gabriel Sheffer, "Principles of Pragmatism: A Reevaluation of British Policies toward Palestine in the 1930s," in *The Great Powers in the Middle East 1919–1939,* ed. U. Dann (New York/London: Holmes and Meier, 1988).

3. Quoted by Sahar Huneidi, *A Broken Trust: Herbert Samuel, Zionism and the Palestinians, 1920–1925* (London/New York: I. B. Tauris, 2001), 145.

4. Ibid., 61.

5. Quoted by Bernard Wasserstein, *The British in Palestine: The Mandatory Government and the Arab-Jewish Conflict, 1917–1929,* 2nd ed. (London: Basil Blackwell, 1991), 13.

6. Ronald Storrs, *Memoirs of Sir Robert Storrs* (New York: G. P. Putnam's Sons, 1937), 378. This thesis is also present in *The Handbook for Syria and Palestine* (London: Foreign Office, 1920), 56–57.

7. The National Government of Moab (Jordan, 1920–21), Sir Alec Seath Kirkbride, *A Crackle of Thorns: Experiences in the Middle East* (London: John Murray, 1956), 69.

8. Storrs, *Memoirs,* 377.

9. Ibid., 379.

10. Quoted by Huneidi, *A Broken Trust,* 151.

11. Ibid., 55.

12. On the SMC, see Bernard Wasserstein, *British in Palestine*; Y. Porath, *The Emergence of the Palestinian Arab National Movement, 1918–1929* (London: Franck Cass, 1977).

13. Quoted by Huneidi, *A Broken Trust,* 102.

14. Ibid., 131. On the same theme, see also the report from R. Meinertzhagen to Lord Curson, March 31, 1920, quoted by Doreen Ingrams, *Palestine Papers, 1917–1922: Seeds of Conflict* (London: John Murray, 1972), 83.

15. Quoted by Huneidi, *A Broken Trust,* 132.

16. The expression is from William Deedes in a letter of June 2, 1922, quoted by Bernard Wasserstein, *British in Palestine,* 168.

17. Excerpt from British White Paper of 1922. See above, note 15.

18. On a global treatment of this period, see, especially, Nadine Picaudou, *La décennie qui ébranla le Moyen-Orient, 1914–1923* (Brussels: Complexe, 1992).

19. Quoted by Ingrams, *Palestine Papers,* 82.

20. On the 1922 White Paper, see, especially, Henry Laurens, *La Question de Palestine,* vol. 1: *L'Invention de la Terre sainte, 1799–1922* (Paris: Fayard, 1999), 610–13.

21. Quoted by Ingrams, *Palestine Papers,* 174.

22. Ingrams, *Palestine Papers,* 129–30.

23. Ibid, 174.

24. On the attempts at pan-Islamic mobilization, see Basheer M. Nafi, *Arabism, Islamism and the Palestine Question, 1908–1941: A Political History* (London: Ithaca Press, 1998).

25. Quoted by Aaron S. Klieman, "Bureaucratic Politics at Whitehall in the Partitioning of Palestine 1937," in *The Great Powers in the Middle East,* 133.

Zionism and the Arab Question
Denis Charbit

In 1920, the British government obtained authorization from the League of Nations to administer a mandate over Palestine in order to foster the development of a Jewish national home by virtue of the Balfour Declaration, which it had promulgated three years earlier. The convergence between its strategic interests and the furtherance of historical justice for the Jewish people of the Bible, scattered and persecuted through the centuries, would be disrupted by an element that, excluded from the arrangement, would stridently voice its opposition: the Arab population of Palestine. Jewish and Muslim communities thus became actors not just in the religious domain but also in the form of national collectivities.

Denis Charbit

Senior lecturer in political science at the Open University of Israel, Denis Charbit is the author of *Sionismes: Textes fondamentaux* (Albin Michel, 1998); *Qu'est-ce que le sionisme?* (Albin Michel, 2007); and *Les intellectuels français face à Israël* (Éditions de l'Éclat, 2009).

The end of the British promise of an Arab kingdom

On April 24, 1920, during the peace conference that met in San Remo to determine the fate of the provinces of the former Ottoman Empire, which the Versailles Conference had been unable to accomplish, Great Britain, with the complicity of France, recommended the carving up of the former Ottoman possessions into four distinct entities: Lebanon, Syria, Palestine, and Mesopotamia (present-day Iraq). As it was unthinkable to annex them, which would contradict the self-determination principle that was supposed to govern postwar international diplomacy, France and Great Britain committed to administering nothing more than a provisional mandate, with the official objective of preparing the local elites to take charge of their respective territories. The two powers seem to have dropped the distinction between zones of influence and zones of control, as provided for in the Sykes-Picot Agreement, but globally they awarded themselves mandates over the territories they coveted (Lebanon and Syria for France, Mesopotamia and Palestine on both banks of the Jordan for Great Britain).

▶ See articles by Elias Sanbar, pp. 292–296, and Denis Charbit, pp. 320–328.

With the recommendation for the breakup of the Arab provinces, the original promise to create a great Arab kingdom was officially buried. After having initially supported the installation of Emir Faisal, who had been the political and military head of the Arab revolt in Syria, the British had withdrawn their troops in September 1919 to the benefit of the French, then disavowed (in March 1920) the proclamation made by the

Syrian Congress on the independence of an Arab kingdom on a territory comprising Lebanon, Syria, and Palestine. Giving up the plan of awarding Emir Faisal a large state that would place the Arabs under the authority of a unified sovereign political structure alongside a Jewish national home in Palestine, the British and French preferred to divide and rule. This unified Arab nationalism, sacrificed in the name of Western interests, would become a great political myth of contemporary Arab history, invested with all the hopes of grandeur and renascence. At the same time, on the ground, that unrealized dream would be replaced by Lebanese, Syrian, Iraqi, and Palestinian nationalisms, corresponding to the respective mandate territories—tainted, despite their political importance, by that ambiguous origin, since they owed their actual formation to this mandate-determined carving up imposed by the West. The disappointment was a cruel one: the Arabs learned, at their expense, what retractions and treason the Great Powers were capable of.[1] While the explicit mission of the European powers was to facilitate the process toward independence—they were required to give an accounting of its progress at regular intervals in reports filed with the League of Nations—they took care

not to set an end date for their departure. The "provisional" was made to last. The frustration of the Hashemite family was considerable, but the British did not fail to show their gratitude: Faisal, driven out by the French, fallen out of favor in Syria, was immediately crowned, by way of recompense, king of Iraq, where he reigned until his death in 1933. Abdullah, his brother, was named emir of Transjordan, while Sharif Hussein presided over the fortunes of the Hijaz (the Arabian Peninsula) before being overthrown by Ibn Saud.

The Palestine question

What of Palestine? While the Sykes-Picot Agreement had provided for an Anglo-French condominium to be established in the Holy Land, the conjunction of the Balfour Declaration and military presence on the ground put the British in a position of strength to obtain an exclusive mandate over Palestine. In that connection, the Zionist interests converged with those of the British, which were bent on dislodging all French authority in Palestine, despite the traditional

Proclamation of the British Mandate of Palestine in 1922 by Sir Herbert Samuel, Lord Allenby, and Emir Abdullah. Mary Evans Picture Library.

role of France in the protection of the Christian holy places. Better yet, the Balfour Declaration was incorporated in the legal document, making the British Mandate over Palestine official. As the Zionist thinker Ahad Ha'am wrote, "it went from the stage of governmental *promise* to the status of international *commitment*," ratified by the League of Nations.[2] Thus, the Palestine Mandate was different from other mandates: bound to the Balfour Declaration, the British could not open up a perspective of independence for the Arabs of Palestine (even a distant one) that would be identical to the one that had been planned for the indigenous Arab populations of neighboring entities. Palestine did not participate in the same process, because, politically speaking, the place was already taken by the Jewish national home. The Arabs of Palestine violently rejected what was, to them, a confiscation and a dispossession; the Jews persisted in making good use of what the Declaration guaranteed them—especially since, to replace the military authority, the civil government was placed under the authority of the high commissioner, Sir Herbert Samuel, the first within the British political class to have supported the Zionist project with ardor. The Syrian kingdom having turned into a failure, the Arabs of Palestine formulated their political revindication by demanding the abolishment of the Balfour Declaration, the end of the British Mandate, and Palestinian Arab independence for all of Palestine. To dissipate the ambiguity and circumscribe a potential conflict, Great Britain decided in 1922 to distinguish between Palestine to the west and Palestine to the east

> *For the Arabs of Western Palestine ... their land had been allotted by a foreign imperial power to a colonial force they considered just as foreign.*

of the Jordan, and to give Emir Abdullah the east side, or Transjordan, which was thereby excluded from Zionist colonization. The tension, even reduced to restricted territorial dimensions, remained as acute as ever. For the Arabs of Western Palestine, the evil remained undiminished: their land had been allotted by a foreign imperial power to a colonial force they considered just as foreign, without their ever having been consulted. Because they were unable to make their voices heard, the immediate objective was to put a stop to all Jewish immigration to Palestine and all land transactions by means of which the Jews might succeed progressively and pacifically in transforming the nature of the country in such a way as to make it into a Jewish national home, and ultimately a Jewish state—as soon as a Jewish majority was reached.

From religious to national communities

Beginning in 1920, the relations between the Jewish and the Muslim communities underwent a double transformation: on the one hand, because of the primacy of the political stakes, they were no longer established between religious communities in the strict sense but between national ones. The transformation was not clear-cut, because in both camps national and religious identities overlapped—without merging. At the heart of the Jewish community, the old anti-Zionist ultraorthodox Yishuv resisted this progressive hegemony of the national project. On the other hand, the birth of a national Arab community entailed the suspension of the religious separation between Arab-speaking Christians and Muslims. The accession of Haj Amin al-Husseini to the head of the national Palestinian movement was indicative of the inability to undo the intermingling of national and religious causes: the political representative of the Palestinian Arab nation, the mufti of Jerusalem, was also the supreme Muslim religious authority. Moreover, there was no longer an Ottoman Empire but a British authority to head both communities. The Ottoman Empire had protected the Muslims of Palestine by virtue of their shared religious affiliation; now the British, while disposing of an authority that put them in fact above all communities, including the Yishuv, were trying to fulfill the promises of the Balfour Declaration to the benefit of the Yishuv. The triangular relation was far from being symmetrical: in the eyes of the Jewish authorities in Palestine, the British combined power and sympathy for the Zionist cause, while the Arabs, openly hostile to their [Jewish] political aspirations, constituted, in relation to British authority, their direct political competitor, whose rivalry was on the increase. In this context, the main concern of the Yishuv was to preserve the climate of entente necessary for Great Britain to remain true to its commitments and resist the pressure of the Arab party. Ben-Gurion, at the head of the Jewish Agency for Palestine, played the card of submission and cooperation. Very rare were the voices warning of the long-term consequences of an alliance with the British Empire—voices like that of Gershom Scholem,

▶ See Nota bene on the Mufti of Jerusalem, pp. 360–361.

a historian of Kabbalah and an exacting Zionist, who worried that the Zionist movement, by hitching its star to the colonial empire, had "eaten of the forbidden fruit of Versailles" and taken its side: "Zionism has forgotten the powers of tomorrow—powers that are hidden, repressed, but capable of emerging tomorrow."[3]

Yishuv

A Hebrew term for "housing settlement," which designates the Jewish community established in Palestine before the creation of the State of Israel. The *yishuv* distinguishes itself by its social composition, its recent formation, and the nationalist and political ambitions that recall the *yishuv hayashan*, or "old community," established in Palestine centuries ago.

Antagonisms

Proclaiming their anteriority and their modernity, their goodwill and their firmness, the Jews asserted that they had a right *to* Palestine and conceded rights to the Arabs *in* Palestine. They also adduced the fact that the 25,000 square kilometers (about 9,600 square miles) granted to the Jewish people after the departure of the Ottomans—in order that it, too, might enjoy political sovereignty over the land of Eretz Israel, which was its original birthplace—reduced the territory at the disposal of the Arab nation for its future political independence by only 3 percent, whether that nation were to take the form of one sole state or of several states. To the Arabs of Palestine, the land was one and indivisible.

In 1920 and 1921, it was still in connection with the holy places that tensions mounted: the demonstration of young Jews at the West Wall (the remains of the Second Temple) was perceived by the Muslims as a call to take over the esplanade where it was built and on which the Dome of the Rock and the Al-Aqsa Mosque had stood since the seventh century. In 1929, a new cycle of violence broke out in Hebron and Jerusalem, and then again in 1936, no longer from any religious motivation but at the conclusion of a general strike by the Arab party.[4] These repeated tensions more or less forced the Yishuv to pronounce itself on what has been termed in Zionist discourse "the Arab question." Without reviewing the positions of the various political factions represented by the institutions with which the Jewish community was endowed, we can discern the dominant views of the question. Let us first note, as a dominant trait, the denial of conflict: in order not to drive the Yishuv to despair, some persuaded themselves that the conflict was minor, that it was a diversionary tactic to attenuate the class war within Palestinian Arab society, and that the economic growth stemming from the dynamism of the Yishuv would have beneficial fallout for everyone. Others capitalized on the violence perpetrated against private individuals in order to deny its actual political significance and consider only the cultural dimension, either to stress the savagery and barbarity of an entire community or to interpret it as the work of Jew-haters. Did they truly not understand the political nature of Arab hostility, or were they pretending not to see it? Is this attributable to the spatial separation of the two groups? The absence of a common language, perhaps, curtailing communication and mutual understanding? Or was there, despite real but sporadic tensions, the maintenance of a real coexistence among elites, but also among businessmen, and even workers, who, on several occasions, showed active and real class solidarity in the face of the British master?[5]

▶ On Brit Shalom, see article by Denis Charbit, p. 471.

More lucid perceptions were also formulated and discussed. Recognizing an authentic attachment of the Arabs to their native soil, some urgently demanded a solution that took into account their fears and their demands, such as the binational state recommended by Brit Shalom (the Alliance for Peace); others, like Jabotinsky, on the basis of the same premise of a visceral Arab attachment to their native soil, excluded the possibility of a compromise without armed combat. On the Palestinian side, there was also a pragmatic-minded group attempting to side with the British; but that group was a minority when compared with

Waqf

An Arabic term designating, within the scope of the Muslim legal system, the inalienable endowment of land and property for religious or charitable purposes. Such endowments confer a certain power, particularly in a religious sense, to the families that hold them, such as the Hussein dynasty in Palestine for the *waqf* of the tomb of Moses, or the Khalid or Dajani families, for example.

those opposing all concessions—toward the Jews as well as the British, as long as the latter did not definitively break with the Balfour Declaration. The 1936 revolt, which was both a protest against the immigration of Jews fleeing Nazi Germany (whose arrival en masse destroyed the demographic equilibrium) and a rebellion against British authority at an opportune moment for the revision of the mandates, was also the occasion of a settling of scores between the two camps associated with great family lines, the Husseini and the Nashashibi, holders of a certain number of *waqf,* or religious properties held in mortmain (without power of resale).

The British, wanting to preserve the stability of an area at the brink of the Second World War, published a White Book in May 1939, announcing their decision to reduce their commitment toward the Jewish community of Palestine in order to take into account Arab claims concerning immigration and land transactions. Avoiding both refusal and unlimited authorization, a quota of 75,000 Jews for the next five years was adopted. For the mufti who had been expelled from Palestine, it was too little too late.[6] Meanwhile, the Jewish population had climbed from 70,000 to almost 600,000. (On the other hand, land acquisition was ridiculously small, despite the aura surrounding the pioneers: 1,000 square kilometers [about 386 square miles], amounting to scarcely 6 percent of Mandatory Palestine.)

The power relations that had allowed the British to impose their diktat after the First World War were swept away soon after the end of the Second World War, making the mandate system obsolete. If the system of mandates definitively compromised the creation of a unified Arab state, in the long view it only slowed down their access to independence. In 1943, after a quarter-century's delay, the Arabs of Lebanon proclaimed their sovereignty; then it would be the turn of the Arabs of Syria, and finally those of Transjordan—the Iraqi Arabs having already been authorized to do so in 1930.

1. Zeine N. Zeine, *The Struggle for Arab Independence: Western Diplomacy and the Rise and Fall of Faisal's Kingdom in Syria* (Beirut: Khayat's, 1960).

2. Ahad Ha'am, "La véritable signification de la Déclaration Balfour" (1920), in *Sionismes: Textes fondamentaux,* ed. Denis Charbit (Paris: Albin Michel, 1998), 611.

3. Gershom Scholem, "Changing One's Orientations" (1931), in *Sionismes: Textes fondamentaux,* ed. Charbit, 631.

4. On the National Palestinian Movement, see the pioneer work by Ann Mosely Lesch, *Arab Politics in Palestine, 1917–1939: The Frustration of a Nationalist Movement* (Ithaca, NY: Cornell University Press, 1979).

5. See Zachary Lockman, *Comrades and Enemies: Arab and Jewish Workers in Palestine, 1906–1948* (Berkeley: University of California Press, 1996).

6. See Neil Caplan, *Futile Diplomacy,* vol. 2: *Arab-Zionist Negotiations and the End of the Mandate* (London: Frank Cass, 1986).

Martin Buber: A Spiritual Zionism

A philosopher of German language and a promoter of the dialogical approach, with the goal of fostering an authentic relationship and mutual recognition between individuals (*I and Thou*, 1922), Martin Buber (1878–1965) is considered the leading figure of Jewish personalism. Close to Jewish socialism and the anarchism of Gustav Landauer, Buber was far from making the creation of a sovereign state the ultimate goal of Zionism, to which he adhered very early. Facing the growing reality of hostilities between Jews and Arabs in Palestine, he established as a political principle that their national causes were both legitimate. The inspirational force of Brit Shalom (Covenant for Peace), founded in 1925, and then of Ihud (Unity) in 1942, he recommended the establishment of a binational state. In the following text of 1929, bearing the mark of renewed Jewish-Arab confrontations in Hebron and Jerusalem, Buber issues a warning against the tendency toward ethnocentrism, which consists in attributing to one's own nation all the virtues and in transforming the defects found in the opposing nation into a negative and definitive essence. In this he sees the process of dehumanization that fuels all conflict and precipitates the opposing parties into a spiral of violence. By contrast, Buber advocates an ethical approach that tends to conceive of the other in the same way we would like him or her to judge us.

Denis Charbit

We have the right to live out our existence as a people. We even have the obligation to do so, because the goal of that existence is our eternal mission. It is the very essence of that existence, ever inscribed within us.

Those who rely solely on force will counter with the objection that the requirement formulated by the sense of responsibility toward our national existence is "only a moral one." In fact, it is a political requirement, in the broadest extent of this term.

When, after the war, we resumed our work of reestablishment in Palestine, in new forms and dimensions, "under the aegis of the British Empire," few among us (precisely those same few who, today, our patriots accuse of betraying our national interests) had foreseen that this "aegis" would entail concrete obligations, with all their consequences, for us alone. It was inevitable that we would be accused of sowing the seeds of imperialism and that the hatred of imperialism would be redirected toward us.

A few years ago, I had a conversation on the Arab question with the director of a great cultural institution of the Yishuv. What he told me was more or less the following: "You know me, and you know that I am no chauvinist: but they are an inferior race." We ourselves are spoken of in similar terms in certain parts of Europe. So who is right? As long as we have not imagined to ourselves the inner reality of a nation whose life is motivated by other factors and whose principles are different in nature from our own, as long as we do not come to know and understand what goes on in that nation's heart of hearts and what is expressed by those factors and principles, we shall always consider what is different as inferior. The inner reality of every nation has its own value, and any external criterion by which you come to judge it can only be erroneous.

… The close-minded attitudes inform the dominant type of nationalism, which has gained so many adherents among us—the most worthless assimilation—which teaches that everyone must consider his or her own nation as an absolute and all other nations as something relative; that one must evaluate one's own nation on the basis of its greatest era, and all other nations on the basis of their lowest points. If this idea continues to gain acceptance it will lead to a worldwide disaster.

The open-minded attitude of humanitarian nationalism, which claims supporters from our midst who have been "fighting for the Arabs," as long as Zionism has been a political doctrine, demands of us that we judge other nations as we would wish to be judged ourselves, not by our own baser needs, nor by our greatest acts, but by those that are characteristic of us, which reflect our character. Only a system of this nature can educate mankind, guaranteeing its stand in face of the dangers that are likely to assail it in the generation to come and that no words can express.

I doubt that there is any more harmful thing, for any public action, than this attitude toward an ally or an adversary consisting in considering him as marked with a particular, immutable character. Once we adopt the idea that he is "this or that," we fall into the trap of an irrational view of his nature. It is only when we have realized this that we will be able to claim to work in harmony with reality.

We are not settled in Palestine with the Arabs but rather alongside them. Settlement "alongside" [*neben*], when two nations inhabit the same country—which fails to become settlement "together with" [*mit*], must necessarily become a state of "against." This is bound to happen here, and there will be no return to a mere "alongside." But despite all the obstacles in our path, the way is still open for reaching a settlement "together with." And I do not know how much time is left to us. What I do know is that if we do not attain [such a relationship with the Arabs of Palestine], we will never realize the aims of Zionism.[1]

---

1. [This translation combines elements from the translations of Denis Charbit ("Le Foyer national et la politique nationale en Palestine," speech, Berlin, October 1929, in *Martin Buber, Mission et vocation*, vol. 2: *Peuple et monde: Essais sur les problèmes de l'heure*, chap. 8, "Jerusalem," ed. La Bibliothèque sioniste, Organisation sioniste mondiale [1984], 308–16); and Gabrielle H. Schalt, in *The Martin Buber Reader: Essential Writings* (New York: Palgrave Macmillan, 2002), 285–86.—Trans.]

Chapter II
Confronting Nazism

The Diverse Reactions to Nazism by Leaders in the Muslim Countries
Michel Abitbol

Nazi anti-Semitism is alien to Muslim cultures. That said, it would be an offense to history to overlook the fact that during World War II a number of authorities in Islamic territories hoped for the victory of the Axis powers. Apart from a few isolated cases we will discuss, these positions were not reached out of ideological sympathy with Nazism, the substance of which was generally unknown to the population.

Rather, these authorities hoped that the defeat of France and England at the hands of Nazi Germany and Fascist Italy would precipitate the end of Western colonialism, which the two major European democracies embodied. Nevertheless, during the first two years of the Second World War, when the Jews of North Africa were victims of Vichy's anti-Semitic legislation, the Muslim population on the whole, with rare exceptions, refrained from any attacks on them. The same was true during the occupation of Libya between 1941 and 1942, when General Rommel's German troops passed through. This was also the case in Tunisia during the six months of German occupation following the Anglo-American landing on the coasts

Michel Abitbol

An Africanist and Orientalist, professor emeritus of Hebrew University of Jerusalem, and the former director of the Ben-Zvi Institute in Jerusalem, Michel Abitbol has taught in Paris at the École des Hautes Études en Sciences Sociales (EHESS), the Université Paris 8, the Institut d'Études Politiques, and Yale University. He collaborated on *Histoire universelle des juifs* (Hachette, 2002) and on the *Encyclopedia Judaica* (Coronet Books, 1972–1991). His publications include *Le passé d'une discorde: Juifs et Arabes depuis le viie siècle* (Perrin, 1999; reissued by Tempus, 2003); *Les amnésiques: Juifs et Arabes depuis 1967* (Perrin, 2005); *Les Juifs d'Afrique du Nord sous Vichy* (Riveneuve, 2000; reissued by Éditions du CNRS, 2012); *Histoire du Maroc* (Perrin, 2009); and *Histoire des Juifs* (Perrin, 2012).

of Algeria and Morocco, known as Operation Torch, in November 1942. The notorious exception was the Baghdadi Farhud of June 1941. At that time, dozens of Jews were massacred by rogue units of the Iraqi army, following its rout at the hands of the British expeditionary force that had landed in Basra and Baghdad to drive Rashid 'Ali al-Gaylani's pro-Nazi regime from power.

French Algeria under Vichy

The Statut des Juifs (Statute on Jews) of October 1940, amended in June 1941, was the touchstone of Vichy's anti-Jewish legislation. It defined a Jew as "any person of the Jewish religion," as well as "any person descending from three Jewish grand-parents." It was applied in full in Algeria but only partially in Tunisia and Morocco, where the French authorities displayed a great deal of caution, especially regarding the religious implications of the new anti-Jewish policy. For example, in order not to offend the king of Morocco and the bey of Tunisia, the "racial factor" was not taken into account for Moroccan and Tunisian Jews who had converted to Islam. In Algeria and France, by contrast, Jews who had converted to Islam or Christianity continued to be considered Jewish.

No German pressure compelled Marshal Philippe Pétain to promulgate the racial laws of autumn 1940 or to extend them to North Africa, much less to abrogate the Crémieux decree. The abolition of French citizenship for the Jews of Algeria, a measure hailed by Charles Maurras as "the end of a seventy-year scandal," had the aim, according to comments by the Vichy leaders themselves, of "indirectly easing Muslim demands," it being understood that the decree had clearly favored the Jews over the Muslims. The officials at Native Affairs in Algeria therefore received the directive to examine the repercussions within the Muslim population of abrogating the Crémieux decree. The results of these surveys were mixed, to say the least: in the rural areas, the reactions seem to have been very favorable, but it was an entirely different matter in the urban zones. The anti-Jewish measures brought no joy to Muslim city dwellers. This was later confirmed in a letter sent on November 29, 1942, by Dr. Boumendjel, one of the principal leaders of the Algerian national movement, to the leaders of Algerian Jewry:

I can assure you that, in general, the Muslims have understood that it would be inappropriate for them to rejoice in the special measures of which the Jews of Algeria are the victims. They cannot reasonably get behind those who are attempt-ing to practice a racial policy when they themselves are struck down on a daily basis in the name of racism. Our adversaries did not suspect that in making the Jews inferior, they could only bring them closer to the Muslims. Most of them believed that the Muslims would be delighted with the abrogation of the Crémieux decree, whereas they may simply have realized that a citizenship that can be withdrawn after seventy years of being exercised was questionable, through the fault of the very ones who had granted it.... They refuse to be "overgrown children," dupes, or bargaining chips.[1]

The Muslims' disaffection with the anti-Jewish measures was deeply lamented by the French authorities, who had a tendency to see it as the result of Jewish propaganda. According to some police reports, the Jews had tried to persuade the Muslims that the abolition of the Crémieux decree had been decided by Pétain "to avoid giving rights to them, the Muslims." "On good authority," it was believed that, "in their resentment," the Jewish leaders would go so far as to "provide funds" to the Algerian nationalists. Among the indications of "connivance" that were considered particu-larly convincing: in Sidi Bel Abbès, the traders in Muslim fabrics no longer had to wait too long to receive the merchandise ordered from wholesalers in Oran; and, in Algiers, the Jews had supposedly recommended that their Muslim domestics cut back on expenses, "because life is going to become increasingly difficult, and French rule in this country will not last much longer."[2]

> **" The Muslims' disaffection with the anti-Jewish measures was deeply lamented by the French authorities, who had a tendency to see it as the result of Jewish propaganda. "**

In reality, though it is undeniable that under the new circumstances efforts at Judeo-Muslim rapprochement certainly took place, these rarely went beyond the very platonic stage of "monotheistic brotherhood." One widely known exception: the underground Communist cells in which Christian, Jewish, and Muslim militants dreamed together of a radiant future for Algeria. Furthermore, having long since acquired its own acclaim, Algerian nationalism hardly needed any assistance—very shaky, moreover—from the Algerian Jews. Even stripped of their French nationality, the Jews continued to consider themselves French patriots through and through. It was only after 1943 that a few Jews would join the ranks of the Algerian nationalist movement.

❭ See Nota bene on Messali Hadj, pp. 365–366.

The Maghreb caught between resistance and collaboration

In the two protectorates of Morocco and Tunisia, the Muslim leaders' benevolent attitude toward the Jews of their countries is a well-attested historical fact. When, as in Tunisia, the goodwill of a profoundly religious resident general, Admiral Esteva, was factored in, the anti-Jewish measures ultimately lost most of their bite. Everyone was well aware that the status of protectorate would leave little freedom of action to Moncef Bey and Mohammed V, who were, in fact, only the executors of the orders of the residencies. When Moncef Bey took power on June 19, 1942, he was anxious to assure "the Jewish population as a whole" of his solicitude; and, at a time when a general debasement of the Jews was the rule, he judged it opportune to award some twenty Jewish personalities with the highest Tunisian decoration, the Nishan Iftikhar. He would pay a high price for that discreet disavowal of French policy: after the Liberation, General Juin had him deposed and exiled to France, reproaching him in particular for having awarded the same decoration to about fifty SS leaders during the German occupation of the country.[3]

In Morocco, the sultan as well found himself politically obligated to place his signature on different decrees presented to him by the residency, in application of the Vichy legislation. At the same time, he was intent on expressing, at a more personal level, his sympathies toward distinguished Jews, who came to visit him several times in 1941 and 1942. He told them that he considered them full-fledged subjects of the kingdom, and that neither their property nor their persons would be attacked.

▶ See Nota bene on Mohammed V, pp. 362–364.

That attitude, which enormously irritated the French authorities, was all the more remarkable in that the sovereign was surrounded by advisers whose feelings toward the Jews were not always friendly. In 1941 one of them, Grand Vizier Al-Muqri, explained to Paul Baudouin, Pétain's minister of foreign affairs, how the Jewish problem had always been "treated" in Morocco: "Before the Protectorate, the Jews took about twenty years to make a huge fortune. They enjoyed it for ten years, and, at that moment, a small revolution occurred and wiped out their fortunes. The Jews started up again, and again they enriched themselves for thirty years, ultimately having their excess property confiscated. Now that the Protectorate exists, we fear that that thirty-year pattern will be broken. The Protectorate has lasted for twenty-eight years. We therefore have two years to confiscate the fortunes of the Israelites following the age-old rule, which seems very wise to me."[4]

That said, unlike these messages, it does not seem that the anti-Jewish themes conveyed by German propaganda in Morocco, and in the rest of the Arab countries, had an immediate effect on relations between Jews and Muslims. Nonetheless, the German broadcasts directed at the Maghreb, relayed by *Paris-Mondial*, intensified a few weeks after the 1940 armistice. Striving especially to lend credence to the idea of an imminent victory by the Third Reich, they made the English and the Jews their daily targets, presenting them as the common enemies of the Arab-Muslim world and of Germany. In fact, many popular songs in honor of "*Hajj* Hitler" or "*M'allem* Hitler" were composed in the North African countryside and in the shantytowns of the big cities during those years.[5] But in daily life, the population did not modify their practice of coexisting with their Jewish neighbors. In addition, the Germans, respectful of the armistice accords that had allowed France to keep its entire empire, refrained from inciting the North African population to revolt. Similarly, they curbed the appetites of Franco and Mussolini, who wanted to seize French Morocco and Tunisia in the wake of the debacle.

> " It does not seem that the anti-Jewish themes conveyed by German propaganda in Morocco, and in the rest of the Arab countries, had an immediate effect on relations between Jews and Muslims. "

That did not prevent a few Maghrebi nationalist militants—they belonged to the Algerian PPA, to the two Tunisian Destour parties, or to the Moroccan reformist nationalist current—from working openly for the Axis powers. A very well-documented example is that of the Moroccan 'Abd al-Khaliq Torres, who went to Berlin in January 1941 to meet with Marshal Hermann Göring, Hitler's designated heir, and with Heinrich Himmler, head of the Gestapo. The Germans promised arms, munitions, and financial assistance in view of preparing, at the appropriate time, the German invasion of French Morocco through Spain and Gibraltar.[6] In that aim, Torres formed an underground organization to liberate Morocco. Its principal members were Ibrahim Wazzani, Makki al-Nasiri, and Ahmed Balafrej, who himself had made frequent trips to Berlin since the Nazis' accession to power. In accordance with the plan of action that Admiral Wilhelm Canaris, commander of the Abwehr, personally communicated to Torres a few days later in Madrid, a German submarine laden with weapons and munitions was supposed to drop off its cargo in a well-sheltered inlet not far from Ceuta. At the same time, a large sum of money would be made available to Torres at a bank in Tangiers, to be used to instruct guerrilla fighters recruited from among the tribes of Northern Morocco. At the agreed-upon date, neither German money nor armaments arrived. There is every reason to believe that the plot was uncovered after a joint action by the espionage services of Franco and the French Second Bureau, neither of which really wanted to see the Führer get his hands on Morocco.

In fact, after the defeat at the Battle of Britain, the Germans themselves abandoned their plan to intervene in Morocco, a plan Hitler had never considered seriously. More wrapped up than ever in his expansionist aims to the East, he really became interested in the south bank of the Mediterranean only after the difficulties faced by his Italian ally, Mussolini. And it was to save him from a sure rout at the hands of the English general Wavell's troops that, in spring 1941, he sent Field Marshal Erwin Rommel's Afrika Korps to the Libyan desert.

In the East, pro-German leaders

Did the pro-German maneuvers in the immediate entourage of King Farouk of Egypt give sufficiently precise indications about the state of mind of the Egyptian public vis-à-vis Germany? Such, in any case, was the view professed by Farouk. His chief of staff, General 'Aziz 'Ali al-Misri, tried to enter into direct contact with German agents in Baghdad, using, notably, the services of Anwar El Sadat, the future Egyptian head of state. As Farouk wrote in a secret message to Hitler during the Afrika Korps's speedy advance toward the Egyptian border, "90 percent of the Egyptian people" wanted the German victory. They were waiting for the German army to enter Egypt and liberate them from what they considered the brutal yoke of the English.[7] Begun on April 3, 1941, the reconquest of Cyrenaica by German tanks was achieved in less than a week. But despite that remarkable success, the Desert Fox could not retake Tobruk, the last obstacle before the Egyptian border, until January 1942. Expecting the Germans' imminent entry into the Nile Valley, demonstrators paraded in the streets of Cairo to shouts of *Ila al-Aman Ya Rumil* (Onward, Rommel), while the Jews of Alexandria, terrified, began to flee the city en masse. The English, however, quickly retaking control of the situation, forced King Farouk to moderate his pro-German zeal and to install, on February 4, 1942, a new Wafdist cabinet. Headed by Mustafa Nahhas, it was in full agreement with the Allied camp. The Germans found a prestigious ally in the person of the mufti of Jerusalem, Hajj Amin al-Husayni. Very early on, he offered his services to the Axis powers to establish a center for propaganda and sabotage operations in North Africa, "behind enemy lines."[8] In addition, his many visits to Berlin and Rome, and his declarations about the "Judeo-Bolshevik" and "Judeo-British" conspiracy, were skillfully exploited by German propaganda. On his own initiative, he also set up a regiment of Muslim volunteers to fight alongside the Wehrmacht in Serbia and Croatia. These actions would once and for all ingrain the image of the Nazi collaborator that Jewish public opinion has retained of him—and of several other Arab leaders considered national heroes by their people. In July 1940, the mufti wrote in one of his first messages to the Führer: "Palestine, which over the last four years has fought against democracies

▶ See Nota bene on the Mufti of Jerusalem, pp. 360–361.

> **The Germans found a prestigious ally in the person of the mufti of Jerusalem, Hajj Amin al-Husayni ... who offered his services to the Axis powers.**

and world Judaism, is ready to play an active role [alongside the Axis powers] at any moment and to redouble its efforts both within its borders and with the other Arab countries. The Arab peoples, exploited, mistreated, and disappointed by our common enemy, confidently hope that your final victory will promote their independence and complete liberation, as well as their unity."[9] This message further casts into relief the "connivance" between Hitler's Germany and the Palestinian leader. All the same, it is important to point out that the mufti was not authorized by anyone to speak in the name of the Arab people.

In Iraq during that time, Prime Minister Rashid Ali al-Gaylani, in power since September 1939, had never concealed his sympathies for the Axis countries. Their victory appeared to him as desirable as it was ineluctable, especially after the French débâcle of June 1940. Close to the mufti of Jerusalem, he was very active within the Pan-Arab Committee created by the Palestinian leader upon his arrival in Baghdad. One of its principal objectives was precisely to promote the rapprochement of the Arabs with the Axis powers in exchange for a Germano-Italian proclamation in favor of the independence of the countries of the Maghreb and the Mashriq. The emissaries of Rashid Ali—in the first place, his minister of justice and chief collaborator, Naji Shawkat—thus shuttled between Baghdad, Rome, Berlin, and secondarily, Ankara, flanked by the mufti's private secretary, 'Uthman Kamal Haddad, or preceded by him. There they had many meetings with Franz von Papen, German ambassador to Turkey, who played a prominent role in the Germano-Arab negotiations in the early 1940s.

The Germans were handicapped by their alliance with the Italians, to whom they had left preeminence in the Mediterranean. The Italians' colonial aims became even clearer after the collapse of France and the English setbacks within Egyptian borders during the summer of 1940. Under the circumstances, the Germans could not make

Rashid Ali al-Gaylani (speaking), former prime minister of Iraq, in Berlin, May 2, 1943. Ali al-Gaylani, who organized a failed rebellion against the British, is accompanied here by the Grand Mufti of Jerusalem, Haj Amin al-Husseini, and the Iraqi general Ibrahim Pasha al-Rawi. Archives of Süddeutsche Zeitung.

up their minds to satisfy the demands of the mufti and of Rashid Ali, or even to send him the weapons he was requesting to hold off the English. After many secret meetings, they finally agreed to publish, on October 18, 1940, a declaration of friendship addressed to the Arab countries. But they carefully avoided any reference to Arab independence, so as not to elicit the wrath of their Italian ally.

In late November 1940, the English, having gotten wind of the details of these negotiations, demanded that Rashid Ali be deposed.[10] After a little temporizing, he was obliged to give up power on January 31, 1941. Surrounded by his pan-Arab friends and anti-Western officers of the Golden Square, Rashid Ali did not declare defeat, however, and began to conspire openly against the new pro-Allied government of Taha al-Hashimi and Nuri al-Said. At the same time, the mufti appealed to Hitler, telling him that the Arab countries were ready to align themselves "enthusiastically" with the Axis powers and to do their part in "the well-deserved defeat of the Anglo-Jewish coalition,"[11] provided that Germany and Italy would take their political and military needs into consideration.

The Farhud of Baghdad

Disappointed by the unpromising situation of their Italian allies, to whom the English had just dealt bitter defeats in Egypt and Libya, the Germans decided to take the initiative in Iraq. On April 1, 1941, Rashid Ali once more seized power. Wishing to vanquish once and for all the new "illegal" Iraqi government, Winston Churchill then resolved to apply the clauses of the Anglo-Iraqi accord of 1930, which allowed British troops to pass through Iraq and to be stationed there. The first units of the British expeditionary corps landed in Basra on April 17. Rashid Ali, though he had not opposed their arrival, refused to allow new units through before the first contingent had departed. On April 28, the English disregarded that refusal and sent new units to the Habaniya air base east of Baghdad. Unwilling to lose face, Rashid Ali then turned to the Germans, hoping that this time they would not back down and would provide him with the necessary aid to counter the English. Joachim von Ribbentrop, German minister of foreign affairs, who had had supreme control of Iraqi affairs since the beginning of the year, intended to do just that. He initiated negotiations with France on May 5 to deliver German military materiel to Iraq via Syria.

It was not until May 15, after the taking of Basra by the English, that German planes dropped their first bombs over Habaniya. In the absence of adequate coordination with the Iraqi general staff, however, their contribution to the military deployment set in place by Rashid Ali was almost nil. Several German aircraft were destroyed on the ground in the Aleppo airdrome in Syria. In addition, the English no longer had to worry about the Luftwaffe or the Italian air force. The Italians, latecomers on the scene, hardly had time to carry out even the most insignificant air raid against the British, who completed the conquest of the entire country on May 30. Rashid Ali and the mufti of Jerusalem, compelled to take flight for Iran, found themselves back in Italy a few weeks later, then in Germany. The Palestinian leader was received at length by Hitler on November 28, 1941. Rashid Ali reiterated his request to Hitler concerning Germany's recognition of Arab unity and the constitution of a single Arab state encompassing Iraq, Syria, Lebanon, Palestine, and Transjordan.[12]

The Iraqi capital, left practically on its own, was the theater of very serious unrest against the Jews on June 1 and 2, 1941. These riots, which occurred during the Jewish holiday of Shavuot, called Farhud in Iraq, do not seem to have been premeditated by Rashid Ali's government before it fell apart, nor do they seem to have been organized by his followers after he fled. Although making no mystery of their pro-German and anti-Jewish feelings, his supporters had generally refrained from attacking the Jews. According to most testimony collected after the fact, the first assaults were provoked by rogue soldiers, who, at the sight of Jewish civilians dressed up for the holiday, believed they were dealing with a demonstration of support for the English.[13] Calling on the assistance of the Kata'ib al-Shabab (Youth Brigade) militiamen from Futuwwa (the Iraqi equivalent of Hitler Youth), the rioters, armed with revolvers, knives, and clubs, surged into the old Jewish quarter and onto neighboring streets. Without being hindered in the slightest by the police, they sacked synagogues, houses, and Jewish shops and massacred their inhabitants. Least affected by the unrest were the residents of mixed residential neighborhoods. Unlike their coreligionists in working-class areas, they could count on the protection of their Muslim neighbors or, at the very least, could effectively surround themselves by guards, paying

> **" The riots came as a rude shock to the community as a whole and its assimilated elites in particular, who had believed in the full integration of Jews into Iraqi society. "**

whatever was required. In any event, never since the Middle Ages had the Jews of Iraq been subjected to a pogrom of such gravity: 150 to 180 dead, several hundred wounded, and a very large number of residences and businesses destroyed. Nearly 15 percent of the Jewish population of the capital was affected by these riots. Similar but less serious events took place in other cities of the country, especially Basra.

The riots came as a rude shock to the community as a whole and its assimilated elites in particular. Having believed in the full integration of Jews into Iraqi society, they were stunned to observe how quickly public opinion had labeled them collectively as "traitors" and "English imperialists." The Jews were forced to seek their salvation in the support of the regime in place, which the English had put back in charge. They would find themselves cut off from a wider and wider swath of public opinion, which, extremely shocked by the defeat of their country by the British, became more radicalized than ever. The Iraqi Jews, seeing their dream of being "Iraqi citizens of the Jewish religion" evaporate, would take refuge in the Zionist ideal or in Communism.

The failure of Germany's Arab policy

At the political level, the situation of the Axis powers in Tunisia was no less complicated following Operation Torch in late 1942. As in the former free zone of metropolitan France—now occupied—the Germans continued to recognize French sovereignty in the former regency and allowed the residency general to survive, just as they tolerated the continuation of the Laval-Pétain government.

Within the Tunisian population, the Muslim majority was undoubtedly the first object of German and Italian solicitude. Under the friendly gaze of the Axis powers, Moncef Bey took advantage of the new set of circumstances to put a nationalist stamp on his public declarations. At the same time, Habib Bourguiba and the leaders of his Neo-Destour Party were released from their Marseilles prison and taken to Rome before being repatriated to Tunis. The Germans even allowed the publication of a new Arab nationalist newspaper, *Ifriqiya al-Fatat*. They authorized a Destourian youth congress and the creation of the Tunisian Red Crescent, which was rapidly infiltrated by the nationalists. So, too, was the leadership of Radio-Patrie, which began its broadcasts in January 1943.[14]

In the aftermath of Operation Torch in November 1942, Jewish men of Tunisia are conscripted for forced labor by Germans occupying the country. Photo by Lüken, December 1942, French Army Communications Audiovisual office (ECPAD).

The mufti of Jerusalem was one of the few to grasp that the U.S. armada, spotted in the vicinity of Gibraltar, was preparing to land on the coasts of the Maghreb and not in Dakar, Corsica, or Sardinia, as Berlin and Paris believed. On September 27, he expressed his worries to his Italian hosts in Rome regarding the imminence of an Allied landing in North Africa "and its potential repercussions for the Jewish problem." To ward off such a danger, he declared himself ready to organize, in liaison with the Neo-Destour Party, resistance to the Allies and also to constitute what was called an Arab legion "of unified liberation."[15]

Following the arrival of the Axis forces in Tunis, the mufti had his brother deliver a long letter to Moncef Bey, in which he vouched for the pro-Arab and pro-Tunisian sentiments of the Germans and Italians. The war against the Jews—and no longer only against the Zionists—is one of the most recurrent motifs of that missive, whose content was approved by Berlin and Rome before it was sent on November 22. "I am sure the Tunisians will be unable to draw any benefit from the Allies. On the contrary, the Jews' influence over them will grow and [will] intensify the calamity they face. The Tunisians, now taking the side of the Axis army in the struggle against common enemies, contribute toward repelling their domination, the Communist peril, and the Hebrew influence. We all know how much the Americans and the English use the Jews and help them realize their ambitions and aspirations in the Maghreb and the entire Arab East. The participation of Tunisia in that struggle will constitute a serious factor in laying the first solid foundations and in obtaining a much better future within the new order to come."[16]

Wasted effort: neither the repeated interventions of the mufti nor the pressures of the German generals could overcome Moncef Bey's reservations, even though his eldest son, Ra'uf, was infamous for his pro-German ideas. Nor could they win over most of the other principal Muslim leaders of the regency or Habib Bourguiba, who refused a rapprochement with the Axis powers. In fact, the Arab policy of Germany, which renounced any initiative of that type and was visibly concerned not to irritate the French of Vichy or the Italians, was paralyzed by its own contradictions. As a result, it was unable to attract the massive and active support of the Muslim population. Only a few dozen Tunisians enlisted in the Wehrmacht's Arab legion, formed in Germany (the Deutsch-Arabische Lehrabteilung, or DAL), or in the detachments of the African Phalange, which was constituted in Tunisia itself by French officers under the aegis of the Germans. Few—in fact, very few—people read the Paris newspaper *El-Rachid*, created in January 1943 by the Algerian Mohammed El-Maadi on behalf of the German-leaning Comité Musulman de l'Afrique du Nord (Muslim Committee of North Africa).

In Palestine, finally, the Jews generally considered themselves the natural allies of Germany's enemies from the start. By contrast, their Arab neighbors adopted a wait-and-see attitude during the first years of the war and generally showed a great deal of reluctance to cooperate with the British. There were a few exceptions among the Jews: in particular, the small far right Fascist group Brit Habiryonim (literally, "covenant of the hooligans") and the handful of militants of Lehi, headed by Abraham Stern and Yitzhak Shamir (future prime minister of Israel in the 1980s), which considered entering into contact with Fascist Italy and even Nazi Germany. On the whole, however, the Jews swallowed their anger and sided with the English "occupier," taking an active part in the British war effort. The most eminent leader of the Palestinian national movement, the mufti of Jerusalem, while absent from his country, had thrown in his fate with that of the Axis powers. By contrast, the Zionist leadership, at the instigation of David Ben-Gurion, had the good luck of making a "winning" choice by associating itself with the Allies and, especially, remaining in place to adapt the needs of the future Jewish state and its political and ideological orientations to the imperatives of the moment.

---

1. Michel Ansky, *Les Juifs d'Algérie du Décret Crémieux à la Libération* (Paris: Éditions Du Centre, 1950), 296–97.
2. Michel Abitbol, *Les Juifs d'Afrique du Nord sous Vichy* (Paris: Maisonneuve et Larose, 1981), 64–66.
3. Juliette Bessis, *La Méditerranée fasciste: L'Italie mussolinienne et la Tunisie* (Paris: Éditions Karthala, 1981), 340–41.
4. Quoted in Robert Assaraf, *Mohammed V et les juifs du Maroc à l'époque de Vichy* (Paris: Plon, 1997), 140.
5. Charles-Robert Ageron, "Les populations du Maghreb face à la propagande allemande," *Revue d'Histoire de la Deuxième Guerre mondiale* 29, no. 114 (April 1979): 1–39.
6. Jean Wolf, *L'épopée d'Abd El Kooleq Torres* (Paris: Eddif-Balland 1994), 217–31.
7. Gudrun Kramer, *The Jews of Modern Egypt, 1914–1952* (London: I. B. Tauris, 1989), 157.
8. See Italian diplomatic sources cited in Daniel Carpi, "The Mufti of Jerusalem, Amin el-Husseini and His Diplomatic Activity during World War II (October 1941–July 1943)," *Studies on Zionism* 7 (Spring 1983): 118.
9. Quoted in R. L. Melka, "The Axis and the Arab Middle East, 1930–1945," PhD dissertation, University of Minnesota, 1966, 117.
10. On these events, see Majid Khadduri, *Independent Iraq: 1932–1958* (London: Oxford University Press, 1960), 193–98.
11. Ibid., 378–80, esp. 380.
12. On this subject, see Carpi's "The Mufti of Jerusalem," 101–31. This article is based on Italian sources.
13. On these events, see Esther Meïr, "The Baghdad Pogrom, June 1–2, 1941" (in Hebrew), *Pe'amin* 8 (1981): 21–37; Yehuda Taggar, "The Farhud in Arabic Texts by Iraqi Statesmen and Authors" (in Hebrew), *Pe'amim* 8 (1981): 38–45; Nissim Kazzaz, *The Jews in Iraq* (in Hebrew) (Jerusalem: Ben-Zvi Institute, 1991), 238–44.
14. Rahn report, in L. Hirszowicz, *The Third World and the Arab East* (Toronto: University of Toronto Press, 1966), 268–89; M. Kraiem, "CGT et syndicalisme après la prise de Tunis par les Alliés, 1943–1944," *Revue Tunisienne de Sciences Sociales* (April 1975): 273–308.
15. Quoted in Bessis, *La Méditerranée fasciste*, 334.
16. Ibid., 335.

The Mufti of Jerusalem, Opportunism and Anti-Semitism

Hajj Amin al-Husayni, born in 1895, was the son of one of the distinguished Muslim families of Jerusalem. He received his early education in Jerusalem, where he attended the schools of the Alliance Israélite Universelle—a common choice in the world of notable Muslim families—then in Cairo and Istanbul. He made his pilgrimage to Mecca in 1913, thereby acquiring the title "Hajj." He was an Arab nationalist who served as an officer in the Ottoman army during World War I before moving on to the Arab Revolt. He participated in the venture of the Arab kingdom of Damascus. The British accused him of inciting the Nabi Musa riots of 1920. He was convicted, then pardoned.

In 1921 the British named him grand mufti of Jerusalem, the highest position in the Islamic religious hierarchy of Palestine. He collaborated with the Mandatory power, while at the same time taking a resolutely anti-Zionist line. He played the religious card, claiming that he was defending the Muslim holy sites against the Zionist threat, which led to the unrest of August 1929, known as the "Wailing

Haj Amin al-Husseini, Grand Mufti of Jerusalem, reviewing Bosnian volunteers for the Waffen-SS at an army training camp, 1944. SV-Bilderdienst.

Wall Riots." He then became the chief figure in the Palestinian national movement. The mass arrival of Jewish immigrants beginning in 1933 made any compromise impossible. He supported the general strike of summer 1936, which accounts for his break with the British. He planned a general uprising, but the Mandatory power caught up with him and attempted to arrest him in September 1937.

He then took refuge in Lebanon, which was under the French Mandate. From there he organized the Palestinian Revolt, while at the same time offering his services to France. Placed under house arrest, he escaped in October 1939 and returned to Iraq. There he participated with the Arab nationalists in the spring 1941 uprising against British rule. After its failure, he took refuge in Iran, which was soon invaded by the Soviets and the British. He fled first to Turkey, then to Nazi Germany. At the time, he styled himself the leader of "Free Arabs" against French and British colonialism. He met with Hitler and attempted to negotiate a recognition of the independence of the Arab countries on the part of the Axis powers. His chief act of collaboration was his participation in the propaganda broadcasts to the Arab world. At the time, he adopted a radical anti-Semitic discourse. By his own admission, he learned of the Shoah in summer 1943.

In 1945 he was arrested by the French and placed under house arrest in the Paris region. He again escaped in May 1945 and settled in Egypt, where he reassumed leadership of the Palestinian national movement. He defended the plan for a unified Palestine in which the Jews would constitute a minority. During the 1948 war, he attempted to establish a government over all of Palestine. Afterward, first in Cairo and then in Beirut, he headed an Arab High Committee seeking to represent the Palestinians. He participated in the Bandung Conference of April 1955. In the early 1960s, he opposed Nasser, which led him to a rapprochement with Iraq, then to the creation of the Palestine Liberation Organization (PLO). He died in Beirut in 1974.

A religious and political leader, he was close to the Muslim Brotherhood movement. Having been born into a family of notables, he became radicalized in order to assume leadership of a popular movement. His behavior in international and inter-Arab relations was perfectly opportunistic. He was a nationalist and an Islamist above all. Anti-Semitism came later, as a consequence of his battle against Zionism.

Propaganda, first Zionist and then Israeli, has sought to make him out to be one of the principal accomplices of the Shoah, which considerably exaggerates his importance. This view has recently been adopted by those who argue for the existence of an "Islamofascism." ●

Henry Laurens is professor at the Institut National des Langues et Civilisations Orientales (INALCO) and at the Collège de France, where he occupies the chair of history of the Arab world, Henry Laurens is a specialist in the Middle East and the author, notably, of a three-volume history of Palestine: La question de Palestine *(Fayard, 1999, 2002, 2007), and of* Les Orientales *(CNRS Éditions, 2004).*

Mohammed V,
Protector of Moroccan Jews

Sultan Sidi Mohammed ben Youssef, who became King Mohammed V in 1957, has symbolized, particularly after the speech he gave in Tangiers in April 1947, the Moroccan aspirations for independence. His dethronement and exile to Madagascar in August 1953, due to his refusal to make what the French insisted were "reforms" but that he viewed as a move toward an anachronistic regime of "co-sovereignty," had created a climate of millenarian tension to such a degree that some of his subjects, from one end of the country to the other, claimed to have seen him "riding a white horse on the moon." Considered by his people as the liberator of Morocco and the architect of the recovery of national sovereignty, he has remained in the collective memory of Moroccan Jews—or Jews of Moroccan origin—the ruler who bravely opposed the application of measures inspired by the racial laws of Vichy between 1940 and 1942. And he did so despite being shackled by the protectorate regime. Indeed, the protectorate treaty, signed on March 30, 1912, conferred the prerogative of laws and their promulgation to the high commissioner of France, and not to the sultan.

Thus, it was General Charles Noguès, the resident-general appointed to Rabat by Léon Blum, who, at the instigation of the Vichy government and under pressure from its many partisans among the colonialists and other elements of the European colony who had also caught the Pétainist fever, submitted texts of *dahirs* (decrees) inspired by racial laws enacted by Metropolitan France to the sultan. These royal decrees, providing specifically for a *numerus clausus* and the Aryanization of Jewish goods in the French zone of the protectorate, were promulgated on October 30, 1940, and August 22, 1941.

Faced with the enactment of discrimination and the threats to their property, the prominent Jews of various communities sought whatever means of shelter they could. First they tried to plead their cause with the resident-general, reminding him of the services rendered by Moroccan Jews to the French cause before 1912, and reaffirming their "faith in the French conscience [which] has always been the guide of humanity." Their petitions emphasized their condition as Moroccan subjects, under the exclusive jurisdiction of their country. One of them, dated June 23, 1941, specified that "the Muslim tradition [had] always made it a point of honor to protect the Jews, and the Moroccan sovereigns [had] never failed to do so. It is in the shadow of their palace that the mellahs were built. Since the protectorate, and while at the same time becoming...a frequently distinguished element of French influence, the Moroccan Jews have not ceased being good and loyal subjects of the Sharifian Empire." The notables did in fact evoke "the marks of attachment [of the Moroccan Jews] to France, ever great in times of misfortune." They expressed their "despair before a horizon so charged with threats, in which idleness and suffering, with their inevitable aftermath of progressive degradation, dominate," and beseeched the resident-general "to ward off the irremediable catastrophe looming before us."

The hope of the Jewish notables to see their grievances prevail was all the keener because General Noguès, the holder of real power in the protectorate, had tolerated, before September 1939, the presence on Moroccan territory of many German, Austrian, and other Israelite refugees who had fled the Nazi terror. Furthermore, he had permitted their fellow Moroccan Jews to come to their aid. But though careful to avoid zeal in carrying out the instructions from Vichy, and not wanting to push the Jewish elite over to the Gaullist and English camps, which could have stirred the Muslims to rise up against the French authority, it was difficult for the resident-general to suspend the measures enacted on instructions from Vichy. In June 1940, he had, moreover, opted for Pétain instead of de Gaulle, who had proposed that he take over the direction of the Resistance in his capacity as head of the theater of operations in North Africa. It was precisely to shelter the Moroccan protectorate from a German invasion that the resident-general had yielded to the conditions of the armistice, while at the same time not ruling out the possible future eventuality of a return to combat in the not-too-remote future.

After the failure of their demands addressed to the resident-general, the notables resolved to appeal even more forcefully to the sultan, reminding him of their status as Moroccan subjects and their canonical condition as *dhimmī*s with the right to the sovereign's protection in his capacity as spiritual head of the country. A report from the French military intelligence service dated July 11, 1941, indicates that these notables explained, "His Sharifian Majesty would be infringing on Qur'anic law if he approved by *dahir* measures contrary to the spirit and the letter of the Qur'an. Christians and Jews can live in Muslim territory and freely pursue all the noncanonic professions on condition that they pay the tax and respect the Muslim religion." Recourse to the ritual traditionally accompanying requests for "protection" (*zouag*, *'ar*), and the announcement of the requisite sacrifice of bulls in such circumstances, bestowed an even greater symbolic meaning to this reminder of the sultan's canonical obligations in his capacity as imam. The supplications passed upward to the sultan, and the entreaties made to him in the palace itself by Muslim notables and persons of high standing in the Makhzen on behalf of their Jewish friends could do no more than prompt Sidi Mohammed to make "gestures" along the lines of the expectations of both parties. In the context of the upheavals that shook the world stage since the Munich crisis (1938) and its potential effects on the development of the

General Charles de Gaulle shakes the hand of Mohammed ben Youssef (future King Mohammed V of Morocco) at Rabat, Morocco, August 1943.

colonies, these "gestures" on the part of the sultan could only reinforce his status as the ruler of a state that had retained, despite the protectorate, its legal and political personality. Thus, in the eyes of his subjects and of French and world authorities, Sidi Mohammed was within the long-standing tradition of the protection of *dhimmī*s that distinguished his predecessors.

Furthermore, having been informed of the comings and goings of American agents in the country, ostensibly charged with carrying out the Murphy-Weygand Agreement on supplying products of prime necessity to North Africa but in reality preparing an eventual debarkation of the Allies on Moroccan coasts, it was difficult for the sultan not to consider the reactions of the United States to everything concerning the Jews. Indeed Robert Murphy, President Roosevelt's special envoy, visited synagogues in Casablanca and elsewhere "to express American government sympathy for the Jews."

Thus, Sidi Mohammed made many gestures of concern with respect to his Jewish subjects. In May, June, and August 1942, in the palaces of Rabat and Fez, he received delegations that had come to communicate grievances of various communities to him. He reaffirmed the right of these subjects to the protection of their sovereign and insisted that they receive equal treatment with their Muslim compatriots. He also invited Jewish notables to the official ceremonies for the presentation of good wishes on the occasion of Muslim religious holidays or the Feast of the Throne.

The anti-Jewish measures were very unpopular among the Muslim populations, as witnessed by Xavier Vallet, the Vichy government's commissioner-general for Jewish affairs. The resident-general, who knew better than anyone that an understanding with the sultan represented the keystone of the protectoral edifice and one of the most efficient ways to block the machinations of the Axis powers, consequently avoided pressuring Sidi Mohammed directly. He had to slow down the application of the measures inspired by the laws of Vichy and introduce all kinds of derogations and exceptions. The schools of the Alliance Israélite Universelle continued to function normally, and were sometimes able to recruit teachers of Jewish descent who had been dismissed from French secondary schools. As for the expulsion of the Jews from European neighborhoods, it was limited to families having acquired houses in those areas after September 1, 1939. The obligation of the declaration of goods applied only to "inheritance with a value above 5,000 francs": furniture, personal belongings, and personal jewelry were exempt.

It is in these circumstances that the Jews of Morocco escape the tragic fate of their coreligionists in Europe. The fact that, compared with their fellow Jews in Algeria and Tunisia, they underwent neither the trauma felt by the former as a result of the abrogation of the Crémieux Decree nor the sufferings inflicted on the latter by the forces of German occupation explains the deep veneration in which they hold Sidi Mohammed ben Youssef. ●

Mohammed Kenbib, a historian and a professor at the Mohammed-5 University of Rabat, is the author of numerous books and articles, including Juifs et Musulmans au Maroc, 1859–1948 *(1994),* Les Protégés *(1996), and* Temps présent et fonctions de l'historien *(2009), all published by the Mohammed-5 University of Rabat. He has contributed to the* Encyclopedia of Jews in the Islamic World *(Brill, 2010).*

Messali Hadj, the Refusal to Collaborate

When World War II broke out in 1939, Messali Hadj, forty-one years old at the time, was already a well-known political figure in both Algeria and France. Born in the city of Tlemcen in 1898, he emigrated to France after World War I. Messali participated in the creation of Étoile Nord Africaine (ENA; North African Star) in 1926, the first organization to demand independence for Algeria. When the French government dissolved ENA in 1929, Messali fell out with the Communists, who had supported him until that time. He launched a new Étoile Nord Africaine in 1933. Its newspaper was called *El Ouma* (The Community of Believers), and it pronounced itself in favor of a government formed through the election of a constituent assembly. Messali became the leader of a nationalist movement with a working-class base, supported by an Arabo-Muslim ideology. After the Popular Front's electoral victory in 1936, he held on to the objective of independence and announced his opposition to the Blum-Viollette plan, which advocated giving twenty thousand Muslim Algerians access to French citizenship.

Although Messali Hadj separated from the Communists, who had been behind the creation of ENA, he continued to lean to the left throughout the interwar period. He established close contacts with leftist militants in the Socialist Party, such as Marceau Pivert; with the Trotskyists; and with anarcho-syndicalists such as Robert Louzon, director of the review *La révolution prolétarienne*. These choices clearly indicate Messali Hadj's political position: he refused to support the French parties located on the far right. He was clearly anti-Fascist, despite the dissolution of his organization by the Popular Front government in January 1937.

In March 1937, Messali Hadj launched the Parti du Peuple Algérien (PPA; Algerian People's Party). It claimed to adhere to the democratic left and persistently refuted all attacks that sought to conflate it with Jacques Doriot's Parti Populaire Français (PPF; French People's Party). The organization headed by Messali Hadj found widespread support among the youth of Algeria and made staggering progress in that country.

Militants in France wrote articles favorable to Germany. This Germanophilia worried Messali Hadj, who decided to create a bimonthly, *Le Parlement algérien* (The Algerian Parliament), which did not close the door to "overt collaboration with the French people, at a time when so many threats are taking shape in North Africa." But the pro-German group was not to be discouraged. In spring 1939, Yacine Abderrahmane, Ouamara Rachid, and Mohamed Taleb went to Germany to request financial and military aid. Messali, upon learning of their mission, immediately disavowed the militants, who had been active in the PPA's Fédération de France. He then named a new French leadership. On July 26, 1939, the PPA was banned. Messali Hadj was arrested on October 4, 1939. In late 1939, those ousted from the PPA formed the Comité d'Action Révolutionnaire Nord Africain (CARNA; North African Revolutionary Action Committee). They believed that the incipient war was not their fight, and that it was necessary to work with the adversaries of colonial France, which was considered the principal enemy. When the Germans entered Paris, they therefore opted for overt collaboration.

During that time, Messali rejected the Vichy regime's proposals for collaboration. With close ties to personalities such as Bernard Lecache, founder of the Ligue Internationale contre le Racisme et l'Antisémitisme (LICA; International League against

Racism and Anti-Semitism), Messali always firmly condemned the regime's discourses. During his prison term, he received Colonel Schoen, a specialist in North African issues at the Ministry of the Interior, who promised to have him released in exchange for a declaration in support of Marshal Pétain; Messali categorically refused. In March 1941, he was therefore sentenced to sixteen years at hard labor and twenty years of banishment. He was interned in various camps in Southern Algeria, the Lambèze penal colony in particular. With his head and eyebrows shaved, a ball and chain on his feet, he was put in solitary confinement, "exposed" in a cage placed in the prison yard. He would later be deported to French Equatorial Africa. During that time, the leaders of the underground PPA were divided on the measures to be taken: some would support the policy of the Axis powers; others, increasingly numerous, ascribed to Messali's position, advocating independence while remaining in the camp of the Allies and Free France. After the Anglo-American landing of November 1942, Messali Hadj's political perspicacity and loyalty to democratic principles made him very popular in Algeria. He was again imprisoned, however, at the end of World War II; and the demonstrators in Sétif on May 8, 1945, who demanded his release, were harshly repressed. ●

A specialist in the history of the Maghreb, Benjamin Stora is a professor at the Université Paris 8 and at the Institut National des Langues et Civilisations Orientales (INALCO). He is the author, notably, of La gangrène de l'oubli: Mémoire de la guerre d'Algérie *(La Découverte, 1991);* Imaginaires de guerre: Algérie-Vietnam *(La Découverte, 1998);* Algérie-Maroc: Histoires parallèles *(Maisonneuve et Larose, 2003); and* Les trois exils des juifs d'Algérie *(Stock, 2006). He is coeditor of the present book.*

The Tunisian Jews in the German Occupation

The defeat of France in 1940 and the establishing of the Vichy regime further complicated the relations between Jews and Muslims. Several grave incidents were reported, specifically during the summer of 1940, when the town of Kef was the scene of tensions between Muslims and Jews for almost a week (from August 3 to 8, 1940). Often rumors, purposely spread, began the disturbances, such as one involving a "rape committed by a Jew" or simply a "relationship between a young Jewish man and a young Muslim woman." The very idea was enough to increase tensions and trigger attacks against Jews. Thus, the rumors in Kef spread to Oued Meliz, Souk El Arbaa, Tala, and Silian. There were attacks on Jewish neighborhoods, and Jewish stores were ransacked. Sometimes lives were lost, as in Gabès on May 18, 1941. This breakdown in relations between the two communities can be explained largely by the context of war and the unleashing of Nazi ideology.

The Jews of Tunisia, from October 1940 to the liberation of Tunis in May 1943, were subjected

Jews of North Africa were subjected to forced labor by the Germans occupying Tunisia, December 1942. Archives of Süddeutsche Zeitung.

to the racial laws of the Vichy government. Their population, livelihoods, possessions, and political affiliations were assessed by census. They had been barred from practicing several professions, particularly the liberal ones, on which a *numerus clausus* had been imposed, to reduce their numbers as much as possible. Similarly, the number of Jewish children allowed in public schools was limited. It was hoped that such vindictive measures taken in an international context marked by strong anti-Jewish propaganda led by the French government and its press, and by German and Italian radio, would foster an outbreak of hatred on the part of the Muslim population against the Jews. While it is true that acts of vandalism of Jewish stores were reported, it must be noted that during the period of the German occupation of Tunisia, which lasted from November 1942 to May 1943, there was no reported anti-Jewish action led by Muslims.

Quite the contrary. The bey, Moncef, who acceded to the throne in June 1942, a few months before the arrival of the German troops, repeatedly made assurances that His High Solicitude was directed to all elements of the population. In the course of a meeting with a delegation of dignitaries who had come to visit him at the end of June 1942, he assured them that they were his subjects, on a par with the Muslims.[1] Moreover, the historian Michel Abitbol notes: "Faithful to the Bey tradition, the new sovereign keeps up very constant relationships with several notable Jews and, at a time when the degradation of Jews was the general rule, he deemed it the right moment to decorate some twenty Jewish figures with the highest Tunisian distinction, the Nishan Iftikhar."[2]

The Germans, immediately upon their arrival in Tunis, had imposed forced labor on the Jews, and several camps were set up in various regions of the country, containing a total of three thousand requisitioned workers. Attempts were made by certain Muslim elements and particularly by the French Right of the French Popular Party to take advantage of German hatred for Jews, but according to the historian Paul Sebag, "manifestations of hostility were, in sum, rather rare. The vast majority of the Muslim population displayed the greatest restraint."[3] There were even several cases in which Muslims showed active support for groups of Jewish workers, saving them from forced labor or protecting families from the exactions of the German forces. Such was the case of Khaled Abdelwahab, who later was nominated for the title "Righteous Among the Nations" for having sheltered Jews during the German occupation.[4]

Even if there is no comparison between what happened in Tunisia and the fate of millions of Jews and other minorities in Europe, it must be remembered that seventeen Jewish deportees from Tunisia never returned to their homes, and that the Jewish communities of Tunis, Djerba, Sfax, and Gabès were forced, under the threat of collective liquidation, to pay high fines in cash and gold to the German troops.

But we must also mention the failure of attempts by the Nazis to drive the Muslim population to organize pogroms against their Jewish fellow citizens. These failures were made possible thanks to the firm position of Moncef Bey and the actions of clear-sighted men such as the prime minister, Mohamed Chenik, and the ministers Mahmoud El Materi and Aziz Jallouli. Tunisian political leaders such as Habib Bourguiba called out, from the depths of their cells, to their fellow countrymen to get in contact with the representatives of the Allies in Tunisia and to abstain from all collaboration with the Germans. Networks of resistance fighters, inspired by communists, socialists, and Gaullists, were formed in Tunisia to sabotage the Germans and pave the way for the victory of the Allies, who were advancing from Algeria. The Communist Party of Tunisia was a mixed-faith and multinational party, comprising Muslims, Christians, and Jews who had contributed together, and in a perfect brotherhood, to the struggle against the racial laws decreed by the Vichy government and the edicts of the German occupier, until the liberation of Tunis by the Allied forces in May 1943. ●

Habib Kazdaghli is professor of contemporary history at the Manouba University in Tunis. He has worked for many years with a team of historians connected with the group France Méridionale et Espagne (FRAMESPA), of the University of Toulouse–Le Mirail (UTM). He is currently dean of the Faculty of Letters, Arts, and Humanities at Manouba University. His works include Le tourisme dans l'empire français: Politiques, pratiques et imaginaires (xixᵉ–xxᵉ siècles): Un outil de la domination coloniale? *with Colette Zytnicki (Publications de la Société française d'histoire d'outre-mer, 2009), and articles on Tunisia during the colonial period.*

1. The June 2, 1942, edition of the newspaper of the Jewish community, *Le Petit Matin*, gives large coverage to this statement and its commentary. See Michel Abitbol, *Les Juifs d'Afrique du Nord sous Vichy* (Paris: Riveneuve Editions, 2008), 110.

2. Ibid.

3. Paul Sebag, *Histoire de juifs de Tunisie des origines à nos jours* (Paris: L'Harmattan, 1991).

4. See the testimony of small children collected by Robert Sattloff, *Among the Righteous: Lost Stories from the Holocaust's Long Reach into Arab Lands* (New York: Public Affairs, 2007).

Taha Hussein: An Arab Writer Denounces Nazi Barbarism

In 1940, the great Egyptian intellectual Taha Hussein reviewed Hermann Rauschning's *Hitler Told Me*, published in 1939. The author of the book was at first a member of the Nazi Party, before opposing it from 1935 on. On that occasion, Hussein publicly protested against the face Nazi barbarism was assuming.

Abdelwahab Meddeb

If you took it upon yourself to lift the lid concealing the conscience of that man, you would see that it is scarlet in color, dripping with blood, even though he does not acknowledge the existence of an agency called the conscience. He maintains that to believe in it is mere illusion, to obey its injunctions mere weakness, and any compassion felt at the sight of blood mere folly. And if you opened his heart, you would see only a hard, impenetrable, unfeeling, inert rock, a sterile, crude block, cruel with a gratuitous cruelty. He considers the heart, like the conscience, an object unworthy of interest, and the emotions the fruit of a degenerate nature, like the vagaries of this decadent civilization destined to disappear, whose disappearance he himself desires and which he will do his best to make disappear. If you open up his brain, you will see a diminished organ, weakened, flickering uncertainly, incapable of fixing its attention, of reflecting on a difficult problem. But there again, he does not believe in the mind, he sees it as mere foolishness, frenzied discourse, a poisoned gift that the Greeks and Romans made to us before vanishing. Their culture was destined to collapse, to be replaced by a new civilization that will have emancipated itself from morality, philosophy, and revealed religions — a civilization that will know nothing of the mind and of conscience, that will know only instincts, and that, pushed forward by a blind and stupid force, will go wherever its wild fantasies lead it.

That is the idea I formed of the man, after reading the book whose title appears at the top of this little discussion. The author of the book is a German, a friend of Hitler's, one in his close circle. He met him at the time of the struggle he was waging to seize power, he delighted in his victory, worked to harvest the fruits of that victory and to exploit all its potentialities. Mr. Rauschning was among those sincere, patriotic Germans who were profoundly saddened by the defeat of their country during the last war, and even more than the defeat itself, by the disastrous consequences it had for the country. […] Hitler is an intellectually limited man who does not like to delve deeply into problems or to reflect in any depth. He hates books and culture, he is superbly ignorant about what science and experience could offer him, and he resorts only to wild fantasies that have no precise aim. He has only contempt for philosophers, politicians, and thinkers. He thinks he has come into existence to lead Germany, and with it the world, toward a new phase of their destiny. Every means can be used to that end, whatever the difficulties and obstacles. Everything that will allow the achievement of that goal is permitted and licit, even if it goes against morality and conscience. Furthermore, he

wants to liberate men from the dual burden of morality and conscience, which only hampers their will and makes them hesitant, unfit for action. And he wants to act, to forge ahead relentlessly. He also wants to liberate them from revealed religion, which for him has the flaw of having founded existence on the principles of justice, duty, the good. In reality, in matters of right and justice, he knows only the right of Germany, and in the matter of the good, he sees only what Germany can obtain through the exertion of its power. He acknowledges no legal system except the one his country will impose on the world by force. It is for that reason that he wants to give it the means to crush all resistance, wherever it may come from. The individual exists only insofar as he places himself in the service of the German people. What does it matter if he suffers from hunger, thirst, woes of every kind? What does it matter if he is sacrificed, if he dies or is subjected to a thousand atrocities, provided the Hitlerian regime takes root in Germany? What does it matter if millions of others are also sacrificed so that German domination of the world can be established?
In fact, he does not hesitate to confront even men of religion, whom he brutalizes until they submit and believe in him, making religion an instrument of his power. Nor does he have any scruples about shutting down the universities, persecuting scholars, in order to place scholarship and instruction in his exclusive service. [...]
The man of good faith, having arrived at this point in my report, stops reading, wondering whether this is not a delirium brought on by fever. And yet these are Hitler's own words, faithfully recorded by his friend Rauschning.
The summary I have given in my turn attenuates a great deal the violence of the remarks, since I fear being poorly regarded by reasonable people. And yet everyone is well aware that the person who quotes an atheistic remark is not an atheist himself, and the person who evokes madness is not himself mad. [...]
All in all, the image one takes away from reading this book is foul and repulsive, and if the book proves anything, it is that lack of instruction and a neglected education produce despicable results in some individuals, who take advantage of a crisis situation to seize power and to exercise it in a despotic manner. Another lesson to be drawn is that true civilization does not lie in the material progress of industry, commerce, agronomy, and scientific research, but above all in a morality diffusing itself to souls, hearts, and intelligences, one that prepares them to resist evil and to shun it. [...]
I give thanks to God that I did not wait until the declaration of war to hate Hitler and his regime. In fact, I have hated them both since they made their appearance; I have resisted them with all my strength. I have always envisioned Hitler as a man whose conscience drips with blood, who considers nothing respectable or sacred, an enemy of the spirit, of humanity, of all the ideals of civilization. And now his acts and words confirm in everyone's eyes what I had understood from the beginning of his fateful rise. It is therefore a duty more than a right for anyone who believes in spiritual, moral, and religious values, and in liberty, to stand up as the adversary of that man and that regime, and to mobilize every resource against both so that humanity may one day recover its civilization intact and its conscience in integrity.

Hitler Told Me, review of Rauschning's book by Taha Hussein, March 18, 1940.

Muslim Righteous Among the Nations

The murder of the Jews during the Holocaust was perpetrated in Europe—a continent with a predominantly Christian population. Although Nazi ideology was a new form of anti-Semitism, it used elements of traditional Christian anti-Judaism and heavily built on deeply rooted anti-Semitic sentiments in the attempt to destroy the Jews. Thus, the majority of Europe's population was indifferent to the fate of the Jews, acquiesced, or even collaborated with the regime that sought to destroy every Jew, only because he was born Jewish. Only a small minority resisted and stood at the side of the persecuted Jews. Some of these courageous men and women were even willing to take great risks to save their Jewish neighbors. Since 1962 Yad Vashem, the Holocaust Memorial Center in Jerusalem, on behalf of the Jewish people and the State of Israel, bestows the title of Righteous Among the Nations on these rescuers.

It is only natural that the very large majority of more than twenty-four thousand men and women recognized as Righteous to date are Christians of the different denominations, and that only a small number of recognized rescuers are Muslims. Among these Muslim Righteous we find, among others, a Turkish diplomat who saved Jews on the island of Rhodes, Tatars from the former Soviet Union, who themselves belonged to a minority in their countries of residence, as well as Muslims from areas with a large Muslim presence, mainly Bosnia and Albania. In view of the role Christian anti-Semitism played in the attitude toward Jews during the Holocaust, and its contribution to the fact that large portions of Europe's populations were hostile or indifferent to the persecution of the Jews, the examination of these Muslim rescuers is of special interest and may shed light on this highly debated question.

In 1934, Herman Bernstein, the U.S. ambassador to Albania, wrote, "There is no trace of any discrimination against Jews in Albania, because Albania happens to be one of the rare lands in Europe today where religious prejudice and hate do not exist, even though Albanians themselves are divided into three faiths." This is probably the reason that Albania became a safe haven for more than a thousand Jews, and that, contrary to the situation in other countries, many of the Jews who were saved in Albania were not local Jews but refugees who had arrived from Yugoslavia, Greece, and other countries in the 1930s and early 1940s. In their testimonies, the rescued describe their lives in Albania until September 1943, when the Germans occupied the country, as being relatively safe; some of them were even able to operate small businesses, and their children integrated and learned the local language. Many factors obviously impacted the attitude toward Jews; one of them certainly was the small size of the Albanian Jewish community—only some forty families.

In September 1943 Albania came under German control, and at the beginning of 1944, Jews were ordered to register. This order was not implemented by the Albanians, and many Jews fled from Tirana, finding refuge with Albanian families or joining the partisans. Only two Jewish families were captured and deported. Even though in Albania, too, there were collaborators, and survivors' testimonies mention fear and the occasional use of derogatory terms for Jews, the accounts generally praise Albanians' attitude toward Jews.

According to accounts of both Jews and their Albanian protectors, the assistance afforded to the Jews was grounded in an Albanian code of honor—"Besa"—literally meaning "to keep the promise."

According to this code, which sprouted from the Muslim faith as interpreted by Albanians, one who acts according to Besa is someone who keeps his word, to whom one can entrust one's life and the lives of one's family. "Our parents were devout Muslims and believed, as we do, that every knock on the door is a blessing from God. We never took any money from our Jewish guests. All persons are from God. Besa exists in every Albanian soul," explained the brothers Hamid and Xhemal Veseli, who were recognized as Righteous Among the Nations by Yad Vashem.[1] "Besa was the key which saved the Jews," explained Marco Menachem, who was saved by Righteous Among the Nations Vasil and Kelkira Nosi.[2]

In 1987, Gavra Mandil, a well-known Israeli photographer, turned to Yad Vashem with a request to recognize his Albanian rescuers. "Albanians are simple people, but very kindhearted, warm, and humane. They may not have been educated on the heritage of Goethe and Schiller, but they attach the greatest importance to human life in a most natural and unquestioning way. In those dark days when Jewish life in Europe didn't count [for] much, Albanians protected the Jews with love, dedication, and sacrifice," Gavra Mandil wrote to Yad Vashem.[3] The Mandil family had fled from Yugoslavia to Kosovo, from which they had been brought to Albania in the summer of 1942. The family father found work in a photo shop in Tirana, where he met Refik Veseli, an apprentice. When the Germans occupied Albania, Refik took the Mandil family to his native village of Kruja, where they were hidden with another Jewish family by his parents and siblings. After liberation the Mandil family returned to Yugoslavia and invited Refik Veseli to complete his apprenticeship. In 1987 the Veseli family became the first Albanians to be recognized as Righteous Among the Nations by Yad Vashem. Gavra Mandil appealed to Albania's president, and despite the harsh restrictions on travel, permission was given

During the Nazi occupation of Albania, the Mandils sought refuge in.the village of Kruja with the Veseli family. In 1987, the Veselis received the title of Righteous among the Nations from Yad Vashem. Jerusalem. Collection of the Yad Vashem. Museum.

to Refik Veseli to travel to Jerusalem, where he planted a tree in the Avenue of the Righteous at Yad Vashem.

Since then approximately seventy Albanians have been recognized as Righteous Among the Nations. Due to decades of an extreme communist regime, and the high occurrence of mixed marriages, the rescuers' religion is not always noted in the files, but more than half of these Albanians are probably Muslims. Together with the Bosnian Muslims and those of other countries, the number of Muslim rescuers recognized by Yad Vashem is somewhere around seventy. They come from all walks of life, but their stories are inspiring and teach us that the ability to overcome prejudice is within the grasp of every individual, notwithstanding their religion or nationality. Such is the story of Righteous Among the Nations Dervis Korkut, the curator of the municipal museum in Sarajevo, who not only saved a young Jewish woman but also hid the famous fourteenth century Sarajevo Haggadah, a beautifully illustrated manuscript, and thus saved a unique treasure of Jewish culture from falling into the hands of the Germans.[4] At a time when anti-Semitism prevailed, Korkut, Veseli, and

373

Refik Veseli with the Mandil son, Grava, who became
a famous Israeli photographer and advocated for his saviors
to be recognized by Yad Vashem. Jerusalem. Collection of
the Yad Vashem Museum.

the other Righteous extended a helping hand to the persecuted Jews.[5]

Director of the Righteous Among the Nations Department at Yad Vashem, Irena Steinfeldt published How Was It Humanly Possible: A Study of Perpetrators and Bystanders during the Holocaust *(Yad Vashem, 2002), and was coeditor of* The Holocaust and the Christian World *(Kuperard 2000, Continuum 2002).*

1. Yad Vashem M.31/3768.
2. Yad Vashem M.31/5368.
3. Yad Vashem M.31/3768.
4. Yad Vashem M.31/6323.
5. For further reading, see *The Encyclopedia of the Righteous Among the Nations, Europe Part II*, ed. Israel Gutman (Jerusalem: Yad Vashem Publications, 2011); Norman H. Gershman, *Besa: Muslims Who Saved Jews in World War II* (Syracuse, NY: Syracuse University Press, 2008).

Chapter III

The Great Rupture in the Middle East

Al-Nakba: A Few Keys to Reading a Catastrophe

Elias Sanbar

Al-Nakba, or "the Catastrophe," is what the Palestinians call the expulsion from their ancestral land in 1948, which created the problem of refugees and its corollary issue, al-'Awda, the "battle for the return to Palestine." As the moment of origin of the conflict, al-Nakba remains the most complex and the most emotionally charged of all the issues now being addressed by the Israeli-Palestinian peace process.

The right of return is demanded as a fundamental right of displaced persons, but the Israelis see it as a negation of their future legitimacy and existence. That right is most

Elias Sanbar

A historian and writer, Elias Sanbar has taught at the Université Paris 7 Jussieu and at Princeton University. He was editor in chief of *La revue d'études palestiniennes*, which he founded at Éditions de Minuit, and also the translator of the poetry of Mahmoud Darwish. His many works include *Le bien des absents* (Actes Sud, 2001); *Figures du Palestinien: Identité des origines, identités de devenir* (Gallimard, 2004); and *Dictionnaire amoureux de la Palestine* (Plon, 2010).

often demanded, and also most often denied, by the other side. It is therefore fitting to propose a few keys to reading that episode of 1948, which saw the disappearance of the Palestinians from Palestine, the prelude to exile.

The year 1948, the two wars

The soldiers in the regular Arab units of Lebanon, Syria, Iraq, Transjordan, and Egypt, who crossed the borders of Mandatory Palestine on May 15, 1948, did not realize that the first act of the Palestinian tragedy was already over, and that the overwhelming majority of those they came to assist were already "refugees" massed on the borders of their country. Apart from a few episodes, the expulsion had already been carried out when David Ben-Gurion proclaimed the State of Israel on that date. It therefore cannot be said—contrary to the official Israeli account—that when the Arab countries went to war following the proclamation, they were simply sending in reinforcements to assist other armies, this time Palestinian, engaged in a battle to destroy the newly born Jewish state. In presenting the facts this way, Israel designated itself as a state under assault, forced to defend itself against adversaries much greater in number and with far more weapons and equipment. Not only does the statistical data on the Arab forces engaged in this war contradict this assertion, so too does the lack of resolve on the part of some Arab kings and heads of state. It is not sufficient to argue, however—as is often done—that "the Palestinians lost their homeland because corrupt Arab regimes had not really wanted to save it." In reality, the united Arab armies were defeated by the formidable war machine of the Haganah, in what must be considered the war of the *reconquest* of Palestine, not that of its *preservation.* Two wars took place in 1948. The first ended on May 15 with the expulsion of the Palestinians and the installation of Israel in their place, while a second pitted Israel against the armies of the neighboring Arab countries. The Israeli account, to which the entire world subscribed at the time, amalgamated these two wars into a single one—the second, to be precise. What was the political interest in making such an amalgam? In systematically conflating the first war of Palestine with the second, in reducing it to merely an episode of this second war, Israel could make people believe that no expulsion had taken place and that the Palestinians had "left" of their own free will, at the appeal of Arab heads of state. The other advantage of

> " *Two wars took place in 1948. The first ended on May 15 with the expulsion of the Palestinians and the installation of Israel in their place, while a second pitted Israel against the armies of the neighboring Arab countries.* "

that "confusion" was that it established the belief that the State of Israel had merely waged a legitimate war of defense for its survival. To minimize the existence of hundreds of thousands of refugees massed on the borders, to conceal the destruction of the cities and of hundreds of villages—more than four hundred localities razed—the discourse of basic self-defense played fast and loose with the dates of operations conducted by the Jewish units before May 15, 1948. It also presented the refugee question as a consequence of the assault conducted by the Arabs, who were made to bear full responsibility for the disaster.

And yet the first war, considered in terms of its real chronology, was the arena for a completely different history. When they set out to conquer the Mandatory territory of Palestine in late March 1948, the units of the Haganah, the Palmach, and other Jewish combatant groups all proceeded from a presupposition, that of a threatened space. From the start, then, the offensive presented itself as a strictly defensive action, even though that country/national territory did not yet exist: it was a dream country, not a real one. Of course, the Jewish settlements had been targets of the Palestinians throughout the British Mandate, just as the Palestinian localities had regularly been subjected to attacks from the Zionist movement. But the important thing is that Zionist colonization did not yet possess a physical, defined territory to be defended.

> ### Haganah
>
> The Haganah refers to a clandestine Zionist paramilitary organization created in 1920; it was the most active and best trained organization during the British Mandate of Palestine. During the Second World War, Haganah units served in the ranks of the British army, which supported the creation of an elite unit, the Palmach. The Haganah, which dissolved in 1948, was the predecessor of the Israeli Defense Forces. The creation of the Israeli army put an end to the rivalries between the Haganah and other paramilitary organizations (the Irgun, formed in 1931 from a schism with the Haganah, and the Stern, or Lehi, group that formed in 1940 and declared itself a "terrorist" organization).

The military leaders of the Haganah who launched Plan Dalet—as Ben-Gurion's staff named the general military operation, which was developed well before the events—fought for an *open plan*, territory that was ill-defined, especially since it had no preestablished or declared limits. To be sure, the war began on the basis of the "geography" set out in the UN Partition recommendation of November 29, 1947, but neither the Zionists nor the Palestinians waged it in terms of that configuration. On the contrary, with the Zionists hiding behind the claim of self-defense and the Palestinians committed to safeguarding a land they considered national and indivisible, they waged total war on each other.

Thus, of the thirteen operations defined by Plan Dalet, eight occurred within the territory allocated, in principle, to the Palestinian state. Some of the code names of these major operations speak volumes, expressing the desired aim. "Operation Yevusi" had clear historical connotations—it referred to David's battle to take Jerusalem away from the Jebusites—but other operations bore more explicit names: "Misparayim," or "scissors" (objective: the capture of Haifa and the expulsion of its population); "Yiftah," "to open" (objective: the "cleansing" of Eastern Galilee); "Hametz," or "leavening," an allusion to the obligatory Passover ritual of *cleaning* one's house of the slightest impurity (objective: the conquest of Jaffa and surrounding villages); "Matateh," "broom" (objective: empty all the Arab villages between Tiberias and Eastern Galilee); and so on. All these code names or watchwords proclaimed what was truly at stake in this supposed defensive war: de-Arabization.

This war, which left no room for the sharing of space, could have only one of two outcomes: either the Palestinians would succeed in preserving their presence in their homeland, or the Zionists would manage to deprive them of it. This is the "geography" of the disappearance that arose de facto from the boundaries of the territories. In 1947–48, many military observers who followed the development of the conflicts based on the territorial logic of the UN Partition recommendation were intrigued by the fact that Ben-Gurion's staff had not ordered the evacuation of the settlers in the high-density Arab zones. Were they not threatened? Only in 1958 would Yigal Allon, head of the Palmach in 1948, respond: "The strategic considerations which had underlain the plan of Zionist settlement decided in large measure the fate of many regions of the country, including areas largely or entirely settled by

Arabs, such as Tiberias, Tsemah, Beit She'an, Acre, Haifa, and Jaffa.... Those areas of Jewish settlement further inland, in the heart of Arab-controlled territory, constituted forward bases, whose function was to hold out at all costs until the advance of the main body of troops."[1]

But there were no "inland" Jewish areas in Palestine before May 15, 1948. On the contrary, the country in its totality constituted the Palestinian interior, itself populated in some places by outsider Jews who kept to themselves. The conquest of the country would therefore come about by joining together these settlements, rear or forward. The empty space of Palestine emerged as a result of these links, which, each time they were established, allowed armed units to carry out the expulsion of the surrounded populations. And it was on the basis of this multitude of zones, emptied of their inhabitants, that the physical and material demarcation of the Jewish state began to take concrete form. From one advance to the next, a line came into being—that of the "borders" of the State of Israel in 1948. That state was *proclaimed* on the morning of May 15, 1948, but it was *founded* before that date. Nearly everything was already played out with the first Israeli-Palestinian war, *before* the second war of Palestine, which was the first Israeli-Arab war.

> " *Nearly everything was already played out with the first Israeli-Palestinian war, before the second war of Palestine, which was the first Israeli-Arab war.* "

Why did the Palestinians leave?

The official Israeli account has long claimed that the Palestinians obeyed the orders of their leaders and the appeals broadcast by the Arab radio stations, despite the fact that some Jewish leaders called upon them to remain. This allegation, which was taken at face value, has been invalidated by Erskine B. Childers, a UN official at the time, who, one by one, verified and contradicted each of the cases where the Jewish armies claimed they did not seek to make the Palestinians leave. In particular, he listened to all the Arab radio broadcasts between November 29, 1947, and May 15, 1948, which were recorded in full by BBC Monitoring. He did not find a single Arab or Palestinian call for people to leave.[2] The question remains, however, why the Palestinians left, why they bowed to the will of their adversaries and not to that of their own leaders. The question, approached in this way, becomes that of the success of the expulsion.

Before seeking a response, we need to set aside the case of the Palestinians from the Gaza Strip and Cisjordan. Their territories, as a result of the armistice accords concluded in 1948–49, were *detached* from Palestine. In some sense, then, these Palestinians found themselves outside Palestine "without budging from it."

The question of the imbalance of forces between the two camps must also be given its due. It is evident that the supply corps, the stock of weapons, and the standing of the units gave a clear advantage to the Haganah. But we may also wonder whether, in 1936–39, the forces of the Palestinian rebels possessed the slightest material advantage over the formidable colonial troops of the empire. These three years, known as the "Great Revolution of '36," culminated in nearly 80 percent of the territory escaping the grasp of the British colonial power, until the Palestinians were finally defeated. That defeat came at the end of a true war of reconquest waged by the empire's armies under the command of Rommel's future conqueror, General Montgomery. Did not the Palestinians, despite the imbalance of forces, stand up to the most powerful of colonial armies, forcing the British to dispatch to Palestine what was at the time the largest expeditionary corps in the world? The question, "Why did the Palestinians leave?" then becomes "Why did the Palestinians lose 'their' war, the first therefore, the one that unfolded between the UN Partition recommendation on November 29, 1947, and the proclamation of the Jewish state on May 15, 1948?"

At this point, we must go back a few years to reflect upon the consequences of the collapse of the 1936–39 revolution. One of the first consequences of the defeat of the Palestinian national movement at that time was that the Palestinians again found themselves prisoners to their internal divisions, which in fact coincided with a territorial regionalism. Opposition to both the colonial power and to the expulsions would

The "arrivals" in neighboring Arab countries, here in Zarqa, Transjordan, 1948 (UN). UNRWA Archives.

henceforth be notable for its fractured quality, its divisions. In 1936–39, the movement that constituted the Palestinian national corps had developed, thanks to a dual "circulation," both in social relations and in physical places. That circulation brought together two dynamics, one internal to the social forces of each region, the other operating at the level of Palestine as a whole. The defeat in 1939 marked the end of the second dynamic, widespread until that time. That left the resistance on the ground localized and isolated. The national leadership of the mufti of Jerusalem bore a heavy responsibility for that historical setback. The dual-circulation mechanism, so effective against the Mandate, was no longer in place, and society confined itself to a static, strictly defensive resistance. It was as a result of that new reality, that "geography of isolation," and by virtue of it, that the expulsion strategy worked. It was therefore not the offensive of Plan Dalet that placed the Palestinians on the defensive; on the contrary, it was the existence of that defensive approach that allowed the plan to find fertile ground for its actions. This tactic, repeated by the Zionists throughout the first war of 1948, serves as a good illustration. It consisted of always encircling isolated Palestinian positions, then giving the besieged the choice between departure and massacre, such as the one that took place in Deir Yassin on the night of April 8, 1948. The work of encirclement by the units of the Haganah took advantage of the extreme fragmentation of the Palestinian points of resistance: the Palestinian forces of Tiberias were fighting in Tiberias, those of Safed in Safed, those of Haifa in Haifa, and so on. The Jewish units succeeded in assembling the maximum number of forces for each operation, against an isolated and, as it were, amputated adversary, one cut off from its rear bases. It was therefore not a small number of Jewish forces who crushed an enormous Arab majority but rather the reverse, each time in a restricted operation: about a hundred rifles in Tiberias against Allon's brigades; a few hundred men in Haifa facing several thousand, dispatched to the field on the eve of the battle to take the city; and so on. To make a population of more than 1.4 million spill out onto the roads in panic, it would never have sufficed to launch all at once the threat of a fate identical to that of the residents of Deir Yassin. But, by repeating the threat every time that one village, one neighborhood, or one town was defeated, the Israeli forces, much greater in number than the Arab residents, were able to empty the village, the town, and the city from one neighborhood to the next. That is how the expulsion came about; that is how the defeat and the departures that accompanied it can be explained.

> *It was therefore not a small number of Jewish forces who crushed an enormous Arab majority but rather the reverse, each time in a restricted operation.*

How did that departure come about?

What happened between the moment a village emptied out and the moment its residents crossed the border? The received idea is that the Palestinians left their villages and cities and walked in unison to the frontier. The thousands of statements and accounts of those who left, and the family histories of thousands of people, tell a completely different story. With the exception of rare cases where villages were completely evacuated by the residents at the mere approach of danger, almost all the Arab cities and villages fell and emptied out after battles. Of the few localities that avoided expulsion, some owed that escape only to their isolation, their situation far from the major operations. In other cases, the Jewish units quite simply did not have time to empty them before May 15. Some sites were also "spared" because of their special status: Nazareth, for example, a holy site under French protection.

As the war spread, all the Palestinian localities became convinced that each in turn would have to confront the opposition forces. As a result, every time a place was attacked, its closest neighbors, those who knew "their turn" was imminent, moved their women and children to a safe place in a neighboring village or neighborhood, one that, though close to the front, had the advantage of not being on the front lines. These endless trips to the back lines, not outward from Palestine, invariably stemmed from the network of alliances or solid kinship ties between the communities concerned. One village or another placed its women and children under protection in another village, at a distance from the immediate combat sector, but the men remained in place to defend their village.

The same thing would occur in cities, where the noncombatant population moved from one neighborhood to another, more protected one—or, quite simply, to a "more Arab," less mixed neighborhood. As for the men who remained in place, they waged battle, then retreated, if beaten, to the refuge village or neighborhood. Then that refuge, because of the fall of the front line positions, became the front line in turn. Nevertheless, the two united villages did not constitute a larger group of men—with, as a result, a greater capacity to defend themselves—since a new departure was under way. With the successive setbacks and the discouragement of the freshly arrived combatants, a certain panic began to overtake the population and swelled as the torrent of arrivals grew. These factors, combined with the ineluctable consequences of the defensive operation and of the fragmentation of the Palestinian camp, led the entire first village—that is, the women, children, *and* the defeated defenders this time—to accompany the women and children of the second village to a third one. Only the men from the second village remained in place.

This new development, apparent in several regions simultaneously, culminated in an exodus of greater scope, still within Palestine, which converged on the cities of each region. Departure after departure, the future refugees crammed together. The displaced persons thus began by being refugees *in Palestine* before moving on to the neighboring Arab countries. The various offensives waged within the framework of Plan Dalet culminated not in an expulsion from their homeland but in a regrouping in the coastal cities, from which the great exodus would for the most part occur. It is precisely because it occurred in two stages that the final departure was able to come

The fall of Jaffa, April 1948. UNRWA Archives.

about so quickly. If expulsions across the border had occurred in great numbers, they would have taken months to complete and would doubtless have been accompanied by international complications for the Ben-Gurion movement.

It also happened that some major regions of the country, because of the way the battles of the second war of 1948 unfolded, and, subsequently, because of the armistice accords concluded between Israel and the United States, again "found themselves" detached, as such, from Palestine. Such was the case for Cisjordan and the Gaza Strip. Having welcomed numerous refugees from the other regions, they nonetheless remained Palestinian, even though Cisjordan was under Jordanian power and the Gaza Strip under Egyptian. Two types of exiles therefore coexisted in such regions: that of the inhabitants, who discovered from one day to the next that they were "Jordanians" or "Egyptians"; and that of persons displaced from the sectors that, in the meantime, had become Israeli territory. Although expelled, they remained in a part of what had been Palestine.

Palestinian exile was peculiar in nature. The Palestinians were certainly forced to leave because they were beaten, but they were also convinced that their fate would be temporary. This conviction made it easier to leave, because departure was perceived as provisional, especially since the host territories were other Arab territories; that is, lands considered by the Palestinians to be an extension of their "home." What was the source of the conviction that the Zionist victory would be short-lived? Did the Palestinians not realize the scope of the national catastrophe they had just been through? They certainly did not. They remained sure, in spite of everything, that they were not alone and abandoned to the adversary. When the departure occurred, the Palestinians were convinced that the Zionist project would be swept aside by the Arab armies. This false hope made the idea of a temporary absence from their native country bearable. Above all, it at first instilled in them the sense that they were displaced persons, not exiles. How could it be otherwise? Despite their enormous sorrow, they could not experience their arrival in neighboring "fraternal countries" as an exile in the full sense of the term. And, finding themselves once more in an Arab country, they did not—not yet—register the loss of the homeland but simply remained patient and took cover on a new rear line.

Hence, these thousands of people, after crossing over, did not head toward the interior of the host countries. Before going into the camps, tens of thousands of Palestinians remained for several months on the border of their homeland, waiting. But the Arab armies were in turn defeated, and the sense of provisional absence gave way to that of a terrible misfortune, al-Nakba, the Catastrophe of 1948. At that time, a new national ideology came into being, taking root in those who would later engage in what would become the Palestinian national movement in exile, dedicated to al-'Awda, the battle for the return to Palestine.

---

1. Yigal Allon, in *Siege in the Hills of Hebron: The Battle of the Etzion Bloc*, ed. Dov Knohl (New York: T. Yoseloff, 1958), 376. The first war of 1948 is almost summed up in these words of Allon.

2. Erskine Childers, "The Wordless Wish: From Citizens to Refugees," in *The Transformation of Palestine*, ed. Ibrahim Abu-Lughod (Evanston, IL: Northwestern University Press, 1972), 165–202.

From the Judeo-Palestinian Conflict to the Arab-Israeli Wars
Denis Charbit

The Arab-Israeli conflict has lasted a long time: nearly seventy years, if one considers its beginning the outbreak of the war of independence in 1947, which the Palestinians call al-Nakba. And if one situates its origin just after World War I, when the political interests of the two communities found themselves facing off in a mimetic rivalry, whose object of dispute was the same land, it is, so to speak, a hundred-year war. Israeli collective psychology forged a representation of the enemy that was consistent with the collective mobilization of society the state required. Over the course of the conflict, that hegemonic representation was called into question: the more the figure of the Arab adversary faded out and that of the Palestinian came into focus in his place, the more the initial monolithism fissured—though it never crumbled altogether—making it possible for concurrent, intermediate, minority-view, or dissident representations to force their way through. The representation of the enemy also has a history.

Denis Charbit

Senior lecturer in political science at the Open University of Israel, Denis Charbit is the author of *Sionismes: Textes fondamentaux* (Albin Michel, 1998); *Qu'est-ce que le sionisme?* (Albin Michel, 2007); and *Les intellectuels français face à Israël* (Éditions de l'Éclat, 2009).

The year 1947: The shock therapy of the partition plan

After World War II, British support for the national Jewish homeland was not a matter of course. That is attested to by Britain's refusal to authorize the landing in Palestine of survivors of the concentration camps who had embarked on the ship *Exodus* in July 1947. A special United Nations commission, charged with calming tensions between Jews and Arabs after the departure of the British, recommended the creation of two sovereign states in Palestine, with economic union added on and a *corpus separatum* for Jerusalem. It stipulated the formation, if need be, of a binational state in which each of the two communities would possess specific prerogatives concerning the management of its own interests.

The partition plan for Palestine, proposed by the commission and submitted to a vote of the UN General Assembly, had the effect of electroshock therapy on the *yishuv* (the Hebrew term for the Jewish community established in Palestine before

November 29, 1947: A Jewish crowd cheers after the vote in favor of the plan to partition Palestine, providing for the creation of a Jewish state. Photograph by Pynn.

the creation of the State of Israel). None of the political groups of the Jewish community of Palestine had advocated a solution of that kind; and yet, as it turned out, the majority of them aligned themselves behind that recommendation. The coalition of the leftist parties (Mapai, Ahdut HaAvoda) and of the centrists (General Zionists), which had called for a Jewish state in all of Mandatory Palestine, now agreed to a state extending over only 55 percent of the territory. Was this a definitive revision or a provisional accommodation? A strategic decision or a tactical measure? For David Ben-Gurion, head of the provisional government, the recognition of a sovereign entity, even on a limited territory, was better than a binational solution that would limit the Jewish community's freedom of action. Furthermore, since he sensed that the Arabs would oppose it by force, he could hope, in the case of victory, to expand the territory that had been allocated by the UN. This was also the moment of truth for the Hashomer Hatzair, a party of Zionist and Marxist inspiration, and for the two branches, Jewish and Arab, of the former PKP, the Communist Party of Palestine. Although they had consistently supported a binational solution in the name of worker solidarity, they consented to the partition of the two states, which was also approved by Moscow.

For diametrically opposed reasons, two parties persisted in their refusal. The Ihud, which had taken over from the Brit Shalom movement, still considered the partition a "moral defeat," proof of the political immaturity of two national movements incapable of suppressing their appetite for exclusive power to participate in good faith in constructing a binational state. The Revisionist Party, founded by Vladimir Jabotinsky in the early 1920s to contest the British decision (which the Zionist movement accepted) to remove Transjordan from the national Jewish homeland, saw the nearly unanimous adherence to the partition of 1947 as a further betrayal. It was even more unacceptable since, this time, the plan supported the exclusion of Jerusalem from the future Jewish state.

The partition plan was approved by the General Assembly on November 29, 1947, with thirty-three votes in favor, thirteen against, and ten abstentions. The idea of sharing the land or of sharing power had been conceived to guarantee that war would not take place. But a vote would not be enough to prevent it.

The years 1948–1949: Al-Nakba and Tkuma, the trauma of war

Al-Nakba and Tkuma, "the Catastrophe" and "Independence," or dispersal and liberation: it is impossible to imagine two more antinomic terms. In the wake of the hostilities, which were declared in two stages, the State of Israel succeeded in holding on to and even extending its territory beyond the limits assigned by the UN (from 55 to 78 percent). The war unleashed by the armies of five Arab countries in May 1948 was an extension of the war that the Palestinian militias had already been waging since November 1947, despite the differences in means, operations, and actors involved in the conflict: the objective was the same, and the Arab countries took up the slack in the hope of succeeding where the Palestinians had failed.

Although the Israelis were the victors in the test of strength, the price they paid in blood was no less heavy: their losses reached six thousand men (1 percent of the Jewish population). An Israeli ethos came into being: the Jewish state, which had been recognized in principle by the international community, could emerge only with the aid of its soldiers' determination, in unison with the civilian population. The lesson drawn from the 1948 conflict has fueled the collective Israeli consciousness to this day. Although the Jews may well be threatened, as they were in other times and places, a qualitative difference confers on the State of Israel its intrinsic value and raison d'être: they now have the means to defend themselves and to retaliate.

By its force of conviction and persuasion, however, that undeniable truth —experienced as such by the Jews of Israel—conceals the situation on the other side. The defeat inflicted by the Tzahal (an acronym for the Hebrew Tzva Hagana L'Israel, "Israeli defense army") on the Palestinians was not a military defeat like any other, as it was for the Arab states involved in the conflict. For when the war was over, no independent Palestine, as stipulated by the partition plan, had come into being. Egypt and Transjordan had seized half the territory, Israel the rest. And in addition to the military defeat and the deferral of the advent of the Palestinian state, more than half the Arabs of Palestine (700,000 out of 1.2 million) had lost their homes and personal property. Having sought refuge, primarily in Cisjordan and Gaza but also in Lebanon and Syria, they could not establish a substitute homeland in the territory of Palestine that had been granted them. They could not make it a sanctuary that would have compensated for the loss of the native land through the construction of a national homeland.

What was al-Nakba? The proclamation of the Jewish state, as the date of its commemoration (May 14) seems to indicate? The suspension of political independence? The exile of half the Palestinian people, the source of the present-day Palestinian diaspora? Or all three at once?

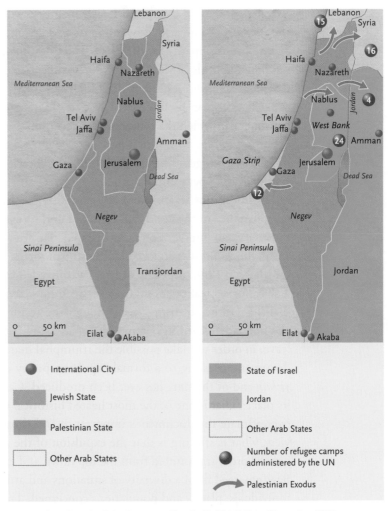

Left: Partition Plan for Palestine passed by the United Nations (November 1947).
Right: Situation resulting from the 1948 Arab-Israeli War (1948–49).

The Israelis, to escape morally unscathed, elaborated the following argument: the Zionist movement's consent to the partition plan of Palestine passed by the UN cleared the State of Israel a posteriori of all responsibility. Conversely, the Palestinians wanted the war, and the Palestinians lost the war: they had to accept the consequences. Any military confrontation necessarily produces a winner and a loser at the end of the battles. And in the case of 1948, the winner was not the aggressor but the object of aggression. Just

> **"Conversely, the Palestinians wanted the war, and the Palestinians lost the war: they had to accept the consequences."**

because the aggressor lost does not make him a victim and cannot erase his responsibility qua aggressor. Added onto that ironclad conviction was the Manichaean narrative conveyed by official Israeli memory, which consists, if not of "blaming the victims," to borrow Edward Said's expression, then at least of preventing any expression of empathy for their fate. The Palestinian refugees voluntarily obeyed the reiterated appeals of their leaders to evacuate, so as to facilitate the reconquest. In that case, Israel argues, the fault of the Palestinians is twofold: their leaders rejected the partition plan by force (which is true), and their departure corresponded to a conspiracy in which the refugees were accomplices (which is false). So much for the expulsion *manu militari* of a portion of them; so much for the constant efforts to prevent the refugees from returning home. The Palestinian narrative focuses on the results of the operations conducted by Israel and obscures the Palestinian leaders' responsibility for its outbreak. By contrast, the Israeli narrative obscures its own responsibility in the conduct of the war and its consequences, focusing instead on the dual Arab intervention at its origin: a day after the UN vote, on November 30, 1947, the *yishuv* was attacked by Palestinian forces; and a day after its proclamation, on May 15, 1948, the State of Israel was invaded by five Arab states.

The historical reality lies midway between these two narratives. There was no Israeli plan for ethnic cleansing, even though the result came close to it. Just as we do not have any recordings of appeals broadcast over the radio exhorting the Arabs to leave, in order to make possible the triumphal march of the Arab armies, so too, no document attesting to a formal expulsion policy decreed by the leadership of the *yishuv* and of the state has ever been produced. Can the Haganah's Plan Dalet take its place? That is one of the most heated historical controversies between those who overestimate the document's importance and those who underestimate it.[1] In my view, what is striking is that the expulsion of the Arabs, far from resulting from a general order transmitted from the top down and executed to the letter and without flaw, emerged from a diversity of situations and attitudes. These were specific to the individuals, places, and populations concerned. The military leaders on the ground played the decisive role: some zealously executed the orders; others took no account of them. For fear of diplomatic reprisals from the Catholic countries of Europe and the Vatican, the Christian Arabs, in Nazareth especially, were not harassed. Conversely, most of the villages overlooking the main roads were emptied of their inhabitants in anticipation of battles with the Arab armies. The Arabs' ability to distance themselves momentarily from the theater of battle, the fear of massacres, the ambient panic, and the contagion effect that generally turned the exodus of a few thousand into a mass movement, but also no doubt (in Haifa, for example) the incapacity of the Muslims to conceive of their existence as a religious minority under Jewish domination, led a number to leave without an expulsion in the strict sense.[2]

Whatever the circumstances and causes of the Palestinian exodus, it is indisputable that every measure was taken by the Israeli army to keep the refugees out. This was true until the end of hostilities and after the cease-fire. Despite their hopes, the refugees were unable to take advantage of the truce that the UN imposed on the belligerent

⟩ See the position of Elias Sanbar on this point, pp. 292–296.

parties in June 1948 and to return home. The Israelis' objective was as political as it was military: having already adopted a postwar perspective, the state was counting on as small a non-Jewish population as possible—about 160,000 in 1949. The matter at hand was to reduce the potential demographic pressure and the security risks stemming from a fundamentally refractory minority. The silence about Palestinian refugees was scarcely broken. The philosopher Martin Buber, addressing Prime Minister Ben-Gurion directly in March 1949, warned him of the moral dimension of the problem: "The possibility existed for the government, and perhaps it still does now, of doing a great moral act, which could bring about the moral awakening of the public, and its influence on the world would certainly not be bad…. The main point is that something be done on our own initiative. Were we not refugees in the diaspora? … And if 'raison d'état' argues against such an initiative, then it suffers

▶ See Counterpoint on Martin Buber, pp. 346–347.

from myopia."[3] In the boon of the voluntary and involuntary departure of the Palestinians, Buber identified a conflict between morality and reason of state, already fearing that the Jewish state's behavior, despite Jewish history, was that of a "state like any other." A year later, S. Yizhar, one of the most important prose writers of Hebrew literature, published a novella, *Hirbet Hizah*, whose title is taken from the name of a fictive Arab village. Long taught in school, the book relates the moral dilemmas of a young officer who is hesitant to execute the evacuation order given to Palestinian villagers—men, women, and children.[4] He finally resigns himself to doing so under pressure from his comrades, who reassure him that the houses evacuated by their residents will soon be reoccupied by other equally destitute refugees, flooding in at that very moment from Europe, Asia, and Africa.

The new Jewish arrivals, in fact, numbered close to a hundred thousand for the single year 1948, and nearly a million between 1948 and

Jewish refugees arriving in Haifa in 1949. Archives of Süddeutsche Zeitung.

1951. Half of them, most from Germany and Poland, had survived the Shoah and wanted to rejoin their loved ones, when they still had any, who had settled in Palestine before World War II. The other half came from the Arab countries, especially Iraq, Yemen, and Morocco.

See article by Michael M. Laskier, pp. 415–433.

The ethnic cleansing—since the term has been introduced into the historiographical debate—was reciprocal. Without consulting each other, the two sides tacitly proceeded to an exchange of populations. For Israel, that was only right and proper: the Jewish refugees became part of the Jewish state; the Arab refugees were in either Cisjordan or the Gaza Strip (hence in Palestine) or they were established along the border, in neighboring states whose language, religion, and culture they shared. They were exiles, no doubt, but not foreigners, less foreign in many respects than those who, having remained in their native land, would become a part of a Jewish state, whose culture, language, and faith were not their own.

From the Judeo-Palestinian conflict to the Arab-Israeli wars

After the cease-fire was signed between the belligerent parties (the Rhodes Armistice Agreement), a peace conference was held in Lausanne between April and September 1949, with the aim of moving from an armistice to a peace treaty. It was unsuccessful. The failure of negotiations meant that the Arabs would give priority to revenge; as for the Israelis, they granted preference to the status quo. A peace treaty would have obliged the Arab camp to formalize political and diplomatic recognition, of which it was literally incapable, just as it would have forced Israel to give up the territories acquired during the war and to reintegrate the refugees into their homeland, which the Israelis hardly wanted.

For Israel after the war, the Arab enemy, Muslim for the most part, had three faces. Within its borders, there were those who had remained. On the other side of the border, there were the refugees, some of whom were trying to infiltrate the country. And always, on all sides, nearly surrounding Israel, were the Arab countries, which conferred on Israeli society its siege mentality. In terms of its area and population, the Jewish majority that had gathered in Israel turned out to be very relative. The official designation for the Arabs within national borders was "the Arabs of Israel" (Arviyei Israël), which for a long time the people in question adopted. A different terminology accentuated their inferior numbers: "the minorities" (Beney Mioutim). It was not until the late 1980s that these Arabs began to publicly use a self-designation that reestablished an openly assumed national affirmation: "The Palestinian citizens of Israel."

See articles by Eliezer Ben-Rafael, pp. 445–451, and Laurence Louër, pp. 452–457.

The attitude of the Israeli authorities was ambivalent. On one hand, citizenship was granted to all Arabs present, by virtue of their residence in the territory, and has since been transmitted to their direct descendants. The Arabs in Israel are equal before the law: they formally enjoy all social, civil, and political rights; they have parliamentary

The New Historians

This title refers to a group of Israeli researchers whose work in the Israeli and British archives, opened to the public in 1978, led them to reinterpret the events of 1948 and to question the founding myths of the State of Israel. Among this group were Avi Schlaïm, Ilan Pappé, Benny Morris (before his reversal in 2004), and Tom Segev.

representation fulfilling a tribunal function; and their distinctive linguistic, cultural, and religious personality is recognized. Their fate is of national interest both in terms of public policy and for democratic legitimacy of Israel in the eyes of the Western world. Nevertheless, the persistence of the conflict on the borders of Israel has led the Arabs of Israel to be assimilated to a potential "fifth column" of Pan-Arabism or irredentism. The establishment of a military administration in 1949 to control their fundamental freedoms—of movement, expression, and association—was confirmation of that. One of Ben-Gurion's advisers for Arab affairs provided its raison d'être: "Ben-Gurion always reminded us that our policy cannot be defined in terms of the Arab minority's de facto inability to destroy the country but must rather take into account what they could do if they had the opportunity."[5] Even the abolition of the military administration, approved by the Knesset in 1966, did not eliminate suspicions about the Arabs' loyalty. Few of them have taken action, but their solidarity in principle with the Arab cause troubles the Israeli public.

Were the refugees ignored? For the "New Historians" and for Palestinian historians, it is important to relate in detail and on a case-by-case basis the circumstances, motivations, and methods that set the Palestinians on the path of exile. Fundamentally, however, a refugee is someone who, once a cease-fire is in place, cannot return home. And the proximity of the refugee camps to the State of Israel made the prospect of return all the more tangible. The homeland was within reach; one had only to cross the border. For Israel, both those who sought to strike the enemy and those who wanted to try their luck at returning home were infiltrators.[6] The famous funeral oration delivered in 1956 by Moshe Dayan, chief of staff at the time, attests to a sincere understanding of the motivations of the Fedayeen, who had killed the young Roi Rothberg: "Let us not blame the assassins. Why should we be angry with them for the entrenched hatred they feel for us? They have been living in refugee camps around Gaza for eight years already and have seen with their own eyes how we have taken possession of the land and the villages where they and their ancestors used to live." That apparent understanding actually served to reinforce the military ethos and to consolidate the state of mind of an entire generation: "The responsibility for Roi's spilt blood does not rest with the Arabs but with us. Are we blind to the sense of our destiny? Do we not see in its full cruelty the mission our generation bears? Have we forgotten that that group of young people living in Nahal Oz carries on its shoulders the weight of the gates to the city of Gaza, behind which hundreds of thousands of eyes and hands pray that our weakness may come and that they may finally be able to tear us to bits? The quest for peace deafened Roi's ears, he did not hear the voice of the coming massacre."[7]

Confrontations with Palestinian commandos were not rare, but that was hardly the main front. Since May 1948, the previously interethnic civil war has been transformed into a conventional war between two states, fought by regular armies. Within that perspective, Israel truly appeared to be a state defending its private preserve against the repeated attacks of its adversaries, determined to do battle. Meanwhile, the Palestinian problem was becoming marginal, if not completely overshadowed. Allied with France and Great Britain to wage the Sinai campaign in 1956, Israel no doubt demonstrated brilliant offensive capacities, but its "collusion" with waning colonial powers led to mediocre diplomatic results. On the orders of the United States, Israel quickly had to withdraw to the international border. Israeli socialism and Arab socialism, far from reaching a convergence of some kind, faced off in the Third World: Nasser took charge of the nonaligned countries, while Ben-Gurion made the most of Israeli expertise in agricultural development to establish fruitful relations with the young nations of sub-Saharan Africa and Asia.

---

1. For example, the historian Benny Morris considers it a military plan of action that was to be carried out before the invasion of the Arab countries, not a political program. See Benny Morris, *The Birth of the Palestinian Refugee Problem, 1947–1949* (Cambridge: Cambridge University Press, 1991), 92–108.

2. Tamir Goren, "Why Did the Arab Residents Leave Haifa? Return to a Controversy" (in Hebrew), *Cathedra* 80 (1996): 175–208.

3. Paul R. Mendes-Flohr, ed., *A Land of Two Peoples: Martin Buber on Jews and Arabs* (New York: Oxford University Press, 1983), 244.

4. S. Yizhar, *Convoi de minuit*, trans. from the Hebrew by Laurent Schuman (Paris: Actes Sud, 2000).

5. Shmuel Dibon, quoted in Yair Bauml, *A Blue and White Shadow: The Israeli Establishment's Policy and Actions among Its Arab Citizens: The Formative Years 1958–1968* (in Hebrew) (Haifa: Pardes, 2007).

6. Those who managed to escape the vigilance of the border guards were allowed to stay in Israel. They did not obtain Israeli nationality, only the status of "absent-present" residents.

7. Moshe Dayan, *Avnei Derech* (in Hebrew) (Jerusalem: Edanim / Tel Aviv: Dvir, 1976).

Israel in the Face of Its Victories
Denis Charbit

The Six-Day War of 1967 ought to have been the crowning achievement of the pan-Arab strategy of reconquest: despite their differences of regime, leadership, and diplomatic orientation, and the rivalries between one state and another, a coalition linking Egypt, Syria, and Jordan galvanized the crowds. The response of Israeli public opinion tended toward panic in the face of that increasing tension, that unprecedented anti-Zionist and anti-Semitic provocation, after ele-

Denis Charbit

Senior lecturer in political science at the Open University of Israel, Denis Charbit is the author of *Sionismes: Textes fondamentaux* (Albin Michel, 1998); *Qu'est-ce que le sionisme?* (Albin Michel, 2007); and *Les intellectuels français face à Israël* (Éditions de l'Éclat, 2009).

ven years of implicit peaceful coexistence. But the top advisers favored a preemptive war (which consisted, in this case, in anticipating the enemy attack by a few weeks, or even a few days), for which the Americans gave the green light.

Far from realizing its initial ambitions, the pan-Arab cause ended in a defeat even more bitter than that of 1948. Beaten after only six days of battle, the states involved in the conflict had parts of their territories amputated: the Sinai (including the Gaza Strip); Cisjordan, with East Jerusalem at its heart; and the Golan Heights. The year 1967 marked a major turning point in the history of the conflict.

The rise of the Palestinian national movement

Israel and the Israelis, victors in quick succession on every front, gave in to euphoria after the Six-Day War: Jerusalem was "reunified," Hebron and Jericho recovered, the Sinai reconquered. Such a spectacular reversal of the situation defied reason and made the messianic chord vibrate anew. Israeli discourse invoked the intervention of divine Providence and hailed the alliance with the United States. Two thousand years of Jewish history, summoned forth by the greatest writers in the country in the *Manifesto for Greater Israel*, called on the government not to give an inch. In succinct terms, the Arabs were wrong because they had lost. The three "nos" of the Arab League meeting in Khartoum—no negotiation, no peace, no recognition of Israel—eliminated any dilemma for Israel and justified its firmness. The victory had erased all cleavages and all dissension: a "sacred union" was achieved.

Only a few resisted the ambient triumphalism. There was, to be sure, the far left group Matzpen, which denounced the occupation, but its general challenge to Zionism, and its objective of a democratic and secular Palestine, deprived it of any significant impact, except among the student sector. Yeshayahu Leibowitz, the famous Hebrew University professor who combined academic knowledge and religious tradition, warned his fellow citizens against turning Israel into a police state entirely absorbed in its repressive task against the Arabs. Sooner or later, he said, the Arabs would not fail to rise up in rebellion.[1] The younger generation of writers, including Amos Oz and Abraham B. Yehoshua, was also quick to assume its responsibilities. As the novelist Yitzhak Orpaz forthrightly declared: "I know of no role nobler for an intellectual than that of addressing the man in the street and the writer from the Movement for Greater Israel, to tell them: 'You are drunk!'"[2] Young demobilized soldiers who had grown up in the kibbutz expressed their uneasiness and discomfort, though without the firm tone and lucidity that marked Leibowitz's provocative prophecy. The remarks and statements collected in *Siach Lokhamin* (Warriors' Words) shook more than one reader attuned to that internal balancing act between patriotic duty and conscience.[3] Was that rift, summed up by the expression "We shoot and we weep" (*Yorim ve-Bokhim*), deeper than that of the hero of S. Yizhar's novella *Hirbet Hizah*?

❯ See article by Denis Charbit, pp. 384–392.

The 1967 victory had delivered Israel from the feared destruction, but it placed under its control a civilian population that already looked on the occupier with hatred and fear. How would the monolithic narrative that had represented the Arab exclusively as a sworn enemy designate these new subjects, both similar to and different from the Arab population of Israel? Although they possessed passports from the Hashemite state, it would have been anachronistic to call them Jordanians. Palestinians? That was a new word, and even today there are two ways of transcribing it in Hebrew, one referring to Mandatory Palestine, Palestinim, the other to the Philistines of the biblical era, Pelishtim. "Until the Six-Day War, my generation did not know there was something called Palestinians," attests, for example, Orly Yadin, daughter of the chief of staff [of the Israel Defense Forces] and archaeologist Yigael Yadin. "We had grown up in a state in which there were Arabs."[4]

> *For a long time, Israeli consensus could be summed up in this quip from Golda Meir, who declared in Russian 'There is no such thing as a Palestinian people.'*

It is undeniable that the defeat of Pan-Arabism in 1967 allowed Palestinian nationalism to flourish. After the war, the Palestine Liberation Organization (PLO), founded in 1964 and instrumentalized by the Arab states, was able to recover its decision-making autonomy from the "fraternal countries" that had exploited its dependence for their own interests. Retaking control of the Palestinian cause was undoubtedly the most arduous fight the PLO waged. But the major accomplishment achieved by its historic leader, Yasir Arafat, was to reformulate in national and political terms a problem that international consensus had been content to hold in check —without solving it, moreover—within a humanitarian context. In their own eyes, the Palestinian refugees were becoming, or becoming again, a nation in quest of a homeland and a state. In the place of Israel or alongside it? Such was the alternative for the Palestinians. The first option was faithful to the original aim of the Palestinian national movement, but it was conceivable only if the Palestinians managed to conquer Israel—which was unrealistic if the balance of power was any indication. The second, which entailed a historic compromise on the dimensions of the territory, had the major virtue of providing a homeland and a state in Palestine for the Palestinians.

For the Israelis, the dawning awareness of the existence of a Palestinian people came about slowly and with difficulty—one step forward, one step back—with nadirs of aversion and zeniths of acknowledgment. For a long time, Israeli consensus could be summed up in this quip from Golda Meir, who declared in Russian: *Palestinaïm yok* ("There is no such thing as a Palestinian people"). Political leaders (such as the militant pacifist on the radical left Uri Avnery or the leftist Lova Eliav) took up the challenge, calling the Palestinians by their name and distinguishing them as a people in their own right within the Arab nation. The first step toward that recognition consisted of admitting that the violence of the armed struggle against Israel could not erase the reality of the Palestinians' tragic fate. As the columnist Boas Evron wrote in 1968: "That people were defeated. They were the victims of the Egyptians and the Hashemites, the Iraqis and the Syrians, and of us, the Israelis, of course. It is the Arab people alone who are unable to raise an army worthy of the name against us, and

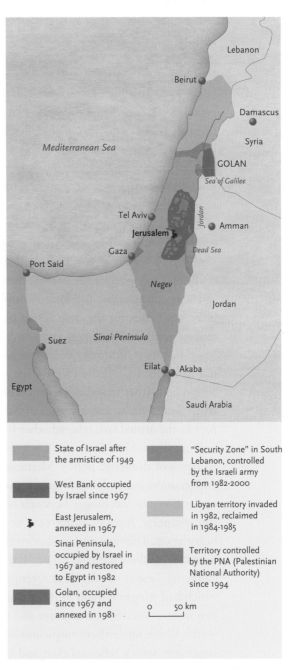

From the "Greater Israel" (1967) to the recognition of Palestinian authority (1995).

State of Israel after the armistice of 1949

West Bank occupied by Israel since 1967

East Jerusalem, annexed in 1967

Sinai Peninsula, occupied by Israel in 1967 and restored to Egypt in 1982

Golan, occupied since 1967 and annexed in 1981

"Security Zone" in South Lebanon, controlled by the Israeli army from 1982-2000

Libyan territory invaded in 1982, reclaimed in 1984-1985

Territory controlled by the PNA (Palestinian National Authority) since 1994

0   50 km

it is the Arab people alone whom we are not able to beat. We have occupied the Palestinians, we have uprooted them; they do not have tanks, cannons, or airplanes. And yet they persist in making life difficult for us…. The problem is political, and it cannot be solved except by a political solution."[5]

The other turning point

In 1973 the Yom Kippur War undermined the myth of an invincible army and swept aside Israeli smugness. Israel became aware of its fragility. In signing the first peace treaty with Israel four years later, President Anwar El Sadat removed Egypt from the field of battle. Would the unanimous admiration for the *rais*'s courage lead to a different perception of the Arab world? No, he was singled out as an extraordinary individual, not as the leader of a nation aligned behind him. The classic model of Israeli-Arab confrontation was now past however. The Arab states, either because they did not want it (Jordan, for example) or because they were incapable of it (Syria), never again waged battle against Israel (an exception in many respects was the bombing of Israel by Iraqi scud missiles during the First Gulf War in 1991). And yet, although Egypt, but also Jordan and Morocco, no longer fell within the traditional category of the enemy, the place of the barbarous and bloodthirsty Arab did not stand vacant for long. Coupled with the PLO Charter, which called in black-and-white for the destruction of the State of Israel, the long series of hostage-takings, airplane hijackings, and bomb attacks, which mowed down civilians in Lod, Ma'alot, Kiryat Shmona, Jerusalem, and Tel Aviv, had only one meaning for a large number of Israelis. If the Palestinians achieved their ends, their actions and ideology would be neither national liberation nor a Third-Worldist revolution but rather the repetition of the worst: a replica of Nazism. By extension, any Palestinian who took part in the armed struggle, whether he targeted military personnel or civilians, was without distinction a terrorist (*mehabel*).

▶ See Nota bene on Sadat and Begin, pp. 401–402.

In terms of domestic policy, Menachem Begin's accession to power in 1977, after twenty-nine years of Labor government, restructured the left/right cleavage. The opposition was no longer between labor and capital, collective property and private property, but lay along two revived axes: secular/religious and annexation/negotiation. The new coalition offered a voice to a social group—the "Eastern communities" (Edot Hamizrach), or "Easterners" (Mizrachim), from the Muslim Arab countries—eager to take their revenge on the Ashkenazi and secular establishment, which had relegated them to the social margins. Their nationalist vote was driven by two motivations: first, a negative and painful knowledge and experience of the Arab world, which made them suspicious of it; and second, a tenacious resentment of the Israeli left, which reflected class and ethnic tensions. In a survey done by Amos Oz in the summer of 1982, one of these Eastern Jews made the connection between ethnic stratification and social status: the use of a cheap Palestinian labor force from the occupied territories provided the Easterners with the opportunity to rise in the ethnic and social hierarchy. "I'm a supervisor. And he's a contractor, self-employed. And that guy there has a transport business. Also self-employed.... If they give back the territories, the Arabs will stop coming to work, and then and there you'll put us back into the dead-end jobs, like before. If for no other reason, we won't let you give back those territories. Not to mention the rights we have from the Bible, or security. Look at my daughter: she works in a bank now, and every evening an Arab comes to clean the building. All you want is to dump her from the bank into some textile factory or have her wash the floors instead of the Arab. The way my mother used to clean for you. That's why we hate you here. As long as Begin's in power, my daughter's secure at the bank. If you guys come back, you'll pull her down first thing."[6]

The end of consensus

If the Yom Kippur War of 1973 had sowed doubt about the Israeli authorities, the Lebanon War of 1982 for the first time shattered the national consensus regarding a military operation. Not only was the political leadership accused of malfeasance but the legitimacy of war was also called into question. The perception of the conflict began to erode: Israel was no longer the weak and frail state of earlier times, besieged on all sides, simultaneously confronting several countries on several different fronts. Rather, it was a regional power supported by the United States, and one, moreover, that possessed nuclear weapons. At stake was no longer Israel's existence but rather the Palestinian problem. That was now the heart of the conflict. The asymmetry between David and Goliath had been reversed: the Jews had their state; the Palestinians scarcely had any. The controversy was without nuance and unyielding: Begin had called the Palestinian fighters "two-legged beasts"; Yeshayahu Leibowitz baptized the Israeli soldiers in Lebanon "Judeo-Nazis." Ariel Sharon had sought to eliminate Arafat in his bunker; Uri Avnery decided to go there to meet with him publicly.[7]

Within a decade—between the massacre of Israeli athletes at the Munich Olympic Games in 1972 and the massacres of Palestinian civilians in the Sabra and Shatila camps, perpetrated in 1982 by Lebanese Phalangists under the protection of the Israeli army—a large part of the international community had made an about-face and now supported the Palestinian cause. In Tel Aviv, four hundred thousand people, that is, 8 percent of the total population of the country, came together at the appeal of the Shalom Akhshav (Peace Now) movement in the largest demonstration in the history of Israel, demanding an independent judicial commission to investigate Israel's responsibility. In the end, Menachem Begin gave in to pressure, though not without claiming that, in Sabra and Shatila, "goys massacred goys, and they accuse the Jews."

The intifada that exploded in 1987 led to another critical look at Israeli occupation. Having been managed "liberally" for about fifteen years (the "open bridges" policy, the free and democratic municipal elections held in 1976), the occupation could no longer keep its hands clean and now required the massive use of repressive measures. It denied two million people the enjoyment of their fundamental rights. Eventually, the Israeli democracy itself was threatened. Controversy raged in Israel on the significance of the intifada: Was it the insurrection of a people whose rights had too long been denied, or a new phase in a permanent conflict? Did the "settlements" (as they were called on the right; the left used the term "colonization"), created little by little in the first decade (1967–77), then multiplying in the second (1977–87) —and which would continue to develop—truly correspond to the security needs of the army? Were they still a potential bargaining chip in political negotiations that would open one day or another? Or was their aim to make any territorial restitution impossible, improbable, or superfluous, by virtue of their dissemination and rapidly expanding demographic importance? In short, was Israel still waging a battle to protect its existence and guarantee its defense, or was it conducting a different strategy to keep Cisjordan, called "Judea-Samaria" within that context, inside Israel? The uncertainties also had to do with the adversary's intentions: Would the Palestinians be satisfied with a state next to Israel, or were they still true to their historic mission of liberating all of Palestine in stages, beginning with the weak link of the territories? Through these diametrically opposed fears, these perceptions of self and other, an entire relationship to the Shoah was surfacing: the fear of becoming, the refusal to become, the executioner ("Never again"); or the fear of being, the refusal to be, the victim a second time ("Never again to us").

During the Algiers conference in autumn 1988, the PLO, exclusive representative of the Palestinian people, approved UN Resolution 181 forty years after the fact, acknowledging the legitimate coexistence of a Jewish state and an Arab state in Palestine. The United States immediately established relations with the PLO.

> *The time had come to work toward making Palestinian and Israeli aspirations compatible, instead of holding fast to their intrinsic and definitive contradiction.*

Mutual recognition between the Israelis and the Palestinians was now only a question of time. After secret negotiations conducted in Oslo between the two parties, that recognition was made public and celebrated at a White House ceremony on September 13, 1993. The handshake between Yitzhak Rabin and Yasir Arafat—between, that is, the former general of the Tzahal, who had ordered the expulsion of the residents of Lod in 1948, and the head of the PLO, who had sponsored so many attacks—was not a matter of course. It symbolized the long path traveled from violence to recognition, and the no less long path that remained to be traveled from recognition to reconciliation, from mutual suspicion to mutual trust. The fall of the Berlin Wall and the Gulf War had no doubt created a suitable international climate. The moral cost of Israel's repression of the intifada had led a number of Israelis, beginning with Rabin, to judge that the security of Israel no longer entailed the army's continued presence in the territories. The time had come to work toward making Palestinian and Israeli aspirations compatible, instead of holding fast to their intrinsic and definitive contradiction. Israeli historians, looking again at the entire history of the conflict from its origins, revised the official views of the refugees, thus inaugurating the "New History" of Israel.[8] Has not the spread of that new approach contributed toward the view that, since the Jews are not as good and pure as they thought, and since the Palestinians are not as evil and wicked as believed, the two peoples ought to find an honorable compromise? To this day, the Oslo Accords of 1993 have been the only attempt at negotiation between the two parties in conflict. They culminated in the creation of a Palestinian Authority, established temporarily, in anticipation of a definitive peace treaty that would stipulate the formation of a Palestinian state alongside Israel and the definition of its economic, diplomatic, and security modalities.

Peace short-circuited by religion

A young Israeli in tears on Rabin Square, where Yitzhak Rabin was killed. Photo by Abbas, Tel Aviv, 1995.

That transitional phase, intended to test the capacity of both parties to get along, was exploited by those political powers within each population that opposed an end to the conflict as a threat to their objectives. The abandonment, by both the Israeli government and the PLO, of the maximalist territorial objectives that the two national movements had set for themselves—a Jewish state on Eretz Israel, an Arab state on all of Palestine—was, for Jewish ultra-nationalism and radical Islamism, more than a betrayal of national aspirations. It was in their view an intolerable and illegitimate violation of a sacred commandment, the plenitude of Eretz Israel or the integrity of Dar al-Islam, as taught by the Torah or the Qur'an. The margin for maneuvering for those on both sides who supported political compromise shrank even further, since neither succeeded in providing what they had pledged to obtain through negotiation: for the Israelis, the end of terrorism; for the Palestinians, the end of the occupation and the creation of a sovereign state. The assassination of Yitzhak Rabin on November 4, 1995, was the tragic symbol of that rejection of peace by the advocates of violence.

The negotiation at the Camp David Summit in 2000, which might have brought results, in fact failed. After that, the Second Intifada plunged both sides, regardless of their leanings, into a new cycle of deadly violence. Between 2000 and 2005, it resulted in more than 6,600 dead—5,500 Palestinians and 1,100 Israelis. Since then, negotiations have resumed, but the mutual distrust has never really been overcome. Israel persists in pursuing the colonization of the very territory on which a Palestinian state could still be created, which leaves doubts about its intentions for peace. The Fatah, for its part, whether from lack of clarity or lack of political capacity, remains resistant to any treaty that would not include the recognition of the Palestinian refugees' right of return to the State of Israel.

Is it the trauma of the Shoah and of al-Nakba that haunts the leaders and the two peoples and that prevents them from escaping the vicious cycle of their history, a repetition of which seems still possible to them? Such are the major problematics, rooted in precise historiographies, that the historian must bring to light. His aim is to read, in the enormous variety of discourses produced in Israel in our time, either the marks left behind or their dissolution, from the most virulent and alarmed reactions to the efforts driven by the most conciliatory wishes.

---

1. Yeshayahu Leibowitz, *Judaïsme, peuple juif et État d'Israël* (Paris: J. C. Lattès, 1985).

2. Yitzhak Orpaz, "La rue a rugi," *Haaretz*, September 8, 1967, in Yona Hadari, *Messiah Rides a Tank: Public Thought between the Sinai Campaign and the Yom Kippur War, 1955–1975* (in Hebrew) (Tel Aviv: Ha Kibbutz ha-Meuchad, 2002).

3. A French translation was published under the title *Le septième jour: Dialogues de combattants de la guerre des Six-jours* (Paris: Plon, 1972).

4. Orly Yadin, quoted in Yehouda Shenhav, *The Time of the Green Line: A Jewish Political Essay* (in Hebrew) (Tel Aviv: Am Oved, 2010), 44.

5. Boas Evron, in *Yediot Aharonot*, September 12, 1968, cited in Hadari, *Messiah Rides a Tank*.

6. Amos Oz, *In the Land of Israel*, trans. Maurie Goldberg-Bartura (San Diego, CA: Harcourt, 1993), 36.

7. Uri Avnery, *Mon frère, mon ennemi* (Paris: Liana Levi, 1986).

8. See the excellent overview by Ilan Greilsammer, *La nouvelle Histoire d'Israël* (Paris: Gallimard, 1998).

Sadat and Begin:
The Men behind a Historic Peace Treaty

When Anwar El Sadat and Menachem Begin came to power – Sadat succeeded Nasser (d. 1970) in Egypt, and Begin won the Israeli parliamentary elections in 1977 after twenty-five years as head of the opposition – it was inconceivable that these two men would be the signatories of a historic peace treaty. Sadat was still crowned in the glory of the surprise attack he had inflicted on Golda Meir during the Yom Kippur War; Begin, for his part, laid claim to a "Greater Israel" and postulated that the Arabs aspired to only one thing: the destruction of the Jewish state by any means.

Some explain this historic event in terms of the impact of détente within the international system. Others argue that Sadat's strategic choice to ally himself with the United States and to break ties with the USSR ultimately implied the end of hostilities. The national interests of Israel were obvious: in signing a separate peace with Egypt, it would change the nature of the Israeli-Arab conflict. And, in fact, to this day there has been no further military confrontation between the states in the region. A psychological hypothesis provides one last explanation: the two men's audacity may be explained by their personal motivation to belie the negative image of "eternal seconds in command," which pursued them both. Sadat may have avenged the Arab humiliation suffered in 1967, but in the eyes of his people, he remained a pale shadow of Nasser. Begin, meanwhile, suffered from the suspicion that he was an extremist hawk, compared to his former rival, the charismatic David Ben-Gurion, who had proclaimed the creation of the State of Israel.

Although their respective faiths were not the principal driving force of their action, it is undeniable that Sadat and Begin shared the certainty that they had a mission to fulfill: change the course of history for their people and for their country. Sadat was a faithful Muslim, and Begin demonstrated a sincere respect for the Jewish tradition. No doubt as well, President Jimmy Carter harnessed his deep Christian convictions to incite the leaders to respond to the redemptive challenge that history placed before them at the Camp David Summit in September 1978. And whatever their personal ideals, it is undeniable that at the different stops of Sadat's visit to Jerusalem, there was something on the order, if not of the prophetic, then at least of political lyricism: the landing of the plane at Lod airport on the evening of November 19; prayers among the faithful at al-Aqsa Mosque, Sadat's hands open, eyes looking toward the ceiling and beyond; the speech in Arabic delivered at the Knesset before

Collaboration between two leaders, Anwar Sadat and Menachem Begin, November 1977. Photograph by Alon Reininger.

the 120 dumbfounded legislators; the huge crowd of jubilant Israelis pressing around him, sensing that history was breaking free from its ordinary violence. That evening, the whole world held its breath: even the most rational minds vibrated with emotion.

Politics very quickly reasserted its rights, leading to a more arduous, down-to-earth negotiation. The Israeli side had wrongly believed that because of his isolation in the Arab world, Sadat would give in on his territorial demands, provided an accord was signed. Begin had initially wanted to share the Sinai, primarily to hold on to the Israeli settlements created there as of 1967. But precisely because the Sinai was a desert, an agreement was possible: in accepting the principle of demilitarization in return for complete Israeli withdrawal, Sadat turned the Sinai desert into a buffer zone, thus offering Israel the best guarantee possible to satisfy its demands for security.

Egypt was immediately ousted from the Arab League and lost its role as dominant leader in the region. In privileging a "Pharaonic" orientation in the service of the Egyptian nation's interests, Sadat had sacrificed the Palestinian cause, the unity of the Arab nation, and Islam. He paid with his life for his political courage: he was assassinated in 1981 by a member of the Egyptian Islamic, which considered reconciliation with Israel high treason. Peace was stronger than the throes resulting from his death, however. Hosni Mubarak, who became president of Egypt, put the peace accords into practice, though he confined himself to minimal normalization with Israel.

Sadat's initiative, followed by Begin's reaction, underscores the relativity and versatility of the representations current in public opinion. Even though, in the eyes of the Israelis, Egypt was the enemy par excellence, much more so than Yasir Arafat's Fatah or Hafez al-Assad's Syria, Sadat became, through the magic of his words – "No more war, no more bloodshed" – the most admired Arab leader in Israel. •

Senior lecturer in political science at the Open University of Israel, Denis Charbit is the author of Sionismes: Textes fondamentaux *(Albin Michel, 1998);* Qu'est-ce que le sionisme? *(Albin Michel, 2007); and* Les intellectuels français face à Israël *(Éditions de l'Éclat, 2009).*

The Mobilization of Religion in the Israeli-Arab Conflict

Alain Dieckhoff

The conflict in the Middle East that, with varying intensity, has torn the region apart for a hundred years is not fundamentally religious but rather political. The Jews oppose not the Muslims but the Arabs (a minority of whom are Christian), and the two sides fight over a land on which they both aspire to realize their national projects. Nevertheless, religion plays a role in that struggle, shifting with the times but undeniable. How could it be otherwise? The dispute concerns the Holy Land, a place to which all three monotheisms are attached. The Jews are combating Muslims, and a large number on both sides embrace their respective religion, as both practice and belief. That religious identification is neutral in itself: it produces effects only in certain historical contexts, when it is mobilized for political purposes by those involved.

Alain Dieckhoff

Director of research at the Centre d'Études et de Recherches Internationales, Sciences Po (CNRS), Alain Dieckhoff teaches at the École Doctorale of Sciences Po. He edited the book *L'État d'Israël* (Fayard, 2008), and is the author, notably, of *Israéliens et Palestiniens: L'épreuve de la paix* (Aubier, 1996); *L'invention d'une nation: Israël et la modernité politique* (Gallimard, 1993); and *La nation dans tous ses États: Les identités nationales en mouvement* (Flammarion, 2000).

During the Mandatory period, the Islamization of the Palestinian struggle occurred under the aegis of the mufti of Jerusalem. On the Jewish side, it was primarily the nationalist right that played the religion card. In the 1950s and 1960s, the dominant rhetoric was that of secular nationalism; but, beginning in the 1970s, the politicization of religion increased continually, both on the Jewish side (the development of an active messianism to legitimate the colonization of Cisjordan and Gaza) and on the Muslim side (calls for jihad to defend the Islamic identity of Palestine).

The Mandatory period

It was indisputably the Zionist project of reconstructing a Jewish nation as a political state that profoundly transformed relations between Arabs and Jews in Palestine. The Arabs had hoped to achieve their national independence on the rubble of the Ottoman Empire within the framework of an Arab kingdom. They saw their dream of unity obliterated by the Franco-English colonial division of the region.

In addition, they found themselves in competition with Jews of a new kind, very different from the small community of pious Jews with whom they had coexisted until then. These new Jews, most of them from Eastern Europe, were secular and driven by national ambitions. The dispute with them was political, not religious. The two major points of friction during the time of the British Mandate (1920–48) had to do with immigration and the purchase of land. Even in those founding years, however, a politicization of the religious developed, a process pursued by very different kinds of actors.

On the Palestinian side, the dominant figure during the interwar period was Hajj Amin al-Husayni, grand mufti of Jerusalem from 1921 to 1948. Despite his title, Amin al-Husayni, who came from a prestigious family of notables, was much more than an ordinary religious dignitary. He was above all an Arab nationalist—he had founded a nationalist club in 1918 at the age of twenty-three—who quickly understood the considerable potential for the political mobilization of the religious. In April 1920, the first major riot against the Jews in Jerusalem erupted at his instigation, during the Muslim celebration of Nabi Musa (the pilgrimage to the tomb of Moses, near Jericho). This was the thunderous beginning of Amin al-Husayni's long career as a political agitator. With the support of the British, who encouraged the institutionalization of Palestinian Islam, he quickly constituted a base of power, getting himself named mufti of Jerusalem in May 1921—even though he was far from having all the required religious qualifications—and then chair of the Supreme Muslim Council, a new institution that oversaw all religious positions and managed

▶ See Nota bene on the Mufti of Jerusalem, pp. 360–361.

mortmain properties (*waqf*). To the great displeasure of the Nashashibis, his everlasting rivals, Amin al-Husayni, henceforth the official representative of the Muslim community, methodically set out to use Islam as a political resource. In September 1928, a minor incident—the installation of a partition to separate men and women at the Western Wall (known as the Wailing Wall)—offered him an opportunity to style himself the supercilious guardian of the Islamic identity of Al-Quds, the Arabic name for Jerusalem. Hajj Amin saw the measure as a violation of the status quo and an attempt to encroach on Muslim property, which was in fact the case for the space opposite the wall. That trivial incident, judiciously exploited, instilled in a number of Muslims a fear that persists even today: that of a gradual takeover by the Jews of the Esplanade of the Mosques, in the aim of building the Third Temple there.

The dispute around the wall inevitably gave rise to a countermobilization in the Jewish sector. It emanated not from religious circles but from the "secular" Zionist

▶ See Nota bene on Jerusalem, pp. 410–414.

groups that made defense of the wall a national duty. This situation, surprising at first glance, can be explained by the fact that most pious Jews had gathered under the banner of ultra-Orthodoxy. They championed a rigorous practice of Judaism, but, at the same time, they were completely opposed to Zionism, which they considered a rebellion against God's plan. The wall, a holy site, ought not to be transformed into a national attribute: such was their credo. Yet that is precisely what the Jewish nationalists were bound and determined to do, particularly those on the right, who had rallied behind Ze'ev Jabotinsky. In mid-August 1929, during the Jewish holiday commemorating the destruction of the Temple of Jerusalem, these militants on the Zionist right paraded to the wall, singing patriotic hymns and carrying a large deployment of flags printed with the Star of David. Immediately, the craziest rumors, relayed by the passionate sermons of Muslim clerics, circulated in Jerusalem and throughout the country. The resulting unrest lasted for a week. In a tragic irony of fate, most of the 133 Jews killed by Muslim rioters belonged to the ultra-Orthodox, non-Zionist communities of Hebron and Safed. The events of 1929 contributed toward the increasingly religious turn of the conflict in Palestine. A striking demonstration of that shift was the convocation, in December 1931, of a World Islamic Congress under the auspices of the grand mufti, which brought together 130 delegates from some twenty countries. Palestine became not only an Arab cause but an Islamic one.

> **Religion is a tool used by certain actors to make policy in specific circumstances. At other times, it plays only a secondary or even altogether marginal role.**

This significant development in no way implies that the Judeo-Arab conflict must be seen solely through a religious prism. Religion is a tool used by certain actors to make policy in specific circumstances. At other times, it plays only a secondary or even altogether marginal role.

From secular nationalism to religious nationalism

On the Arab side, the dominant rhetoric in the 1950s and 1960s was "anti-imperialist." The State of Israel was denounced in the PLO Charter of 1968 for its organic connections to global imperialism. Zionism was vilified as a colonialist force, and the armed struggle presented as the sole path to the liberation of Palestine. The language was politically extremist, but it belonged to the register of national liberation movements. On the Israeli side, in a country governed by the Zionist left since the creation of Israel in 1948, the absolute priority was to consolidate a modern state and to ensure its continued existence in the region. That assertive nationalism also entailed the denunciation of "progressive" Arab regimes (especially Nasser's Egypt) and of the Palestinians, who were characterized as "terrorists." It is striking to observe the near absence, on both sides, of any discourse appealing to religion in the strategies of self-legitimation and of delegitimation of the other. That would gradually change in the 1970s, on both the Israeli and the Arab sides. From the early twentieth century, within the Zionist organization, there was a small current of Orthodox Jews and their rabbis, who, having broken away from the majority of the "men in black," attributed a religious meaning to Zionism. Encouraged by the first chief rabbi of Palestine, Avraham Yitzchak Hacohen Kook

(1865–1935), these religious Zionists saw a true messianic dynamic at work in the rebuilding of a Jewish nation. Since, in their eyes, the creation of the State of Israel marked "the dawn of redemption," they considered it perfectly legitimate to participate in the operations of that state by holding ministerial posts or doing military service, for example. For the first two decades, they privileged a strategy of accommodation with the state, even though, at the time, that state was closely associated with a Zionist left with little inclination for religious effusiveness. All that changed after the Six-Day War. The younger generation of religious Zionists perceived the Israeli victory of June 1967 as a miraculous event through which the divine presence had stunningly manifested itself.[1] How else to interpret a military victory that had allowed Israel to reestablish its foothold in such centers of Jewish memory as the Old City of Jerusalem and Hebron? In the eyes of these religious Zionists, taking possession of the land of Israel as a whole (from the Mediterranean to the Jordan) marked qualitative progress on the path of messianism. Henceforth, the Jewish people were supposed to be in the midst of the redemptive process.

Beginning in the mid-1970s, that ideo-theological perception, popularized by Rav Kook's son Zvi Yehuda Kook (1891–1982), was advanced by the Gush Emunim, or

In Jerusalem, during the celebration of Yom Yerushalayim ("Jerusalem Day"), which commemorates the victory of the Israeli forces during the Six-Day War in 1967, Israeli nationalists dance in front of the Damascus Gate. Photograph by David Silverman, May 21, 2009.

"Bloc of the Faithful," the activist wing of religious Zionism. The movement had become famous because of the boost it gave to the colonization of Cisjordan and Gaza. The advance of the Jewish presence was seen as a true religious imperative with the capacity to hasten the end of time.[2] That conviction led the majority of religious Zionists to shift toward a messianic fundamentalism fraught with danger. If the possession of Eretz Israel as a whole marked an advance in the messianic process, then any retrocession of territory (within the framework of accords with the Palestinians) could only constitute an intolerable regression. Such an eventuality had to be denounced, even combated by force. It was precisely in the name of that messianic absolute that Baruch Goldstein massacred twenty-nine Muslims at prayer in Hebron in February 1994 and that Yigal Amir assassinated Prime Minister Yitzhak Rabin in November 1995. Both actions were an attempt, by violent means, to put an end to a peace process discredited from the start because it compromised messianism in a lasting way. Subsequently, the religious Zionist camp confined itself to protesting peacefully against the unilateral withdrawal from Gaza (summer 2005). But this evacuation was experienced as a trauma. According to some settlers (particularly the youngest of them), it also initiated the process of the state's delegitimation. Indisputably, the existence of a religious norm held to be superior (in this case, the "sanctity of the land") justifies challenging the political order, which raises the issue of the democratic principle and whether it is to be fully recognized.

At the same time, certain fringe elements of ultra-Orthodoxy underwent an evolution, which led them to a rapprochement with religious Zionism on the territorial question. Clearly, the ultra-Orthodox Jews (*haredim*) all share the conviction that the land of Canaan was given by God to the Jewish people as a perpetual and irrevocable possession. This certainty is combined, however, with a pronounced providentialism: only divine intervention will allow the Jewish people to recover the Land of Israel as a whole. Although, for pragmatic reasons, ultra-Orthodoxy renounced its militant anti-Zionism after the creation of the State of Israel, it continued to grant no religious meaning to the historical events and to champion the virtues of political passivity. Two Hasidic faiths deviated from that rule, however: the Lubavitchers and the Breslovs. Messianism is particularly strong in these groups, and their members considered it a religious obligation to increase the Jewish presence in "Judea-Samaria" (which, more prosaically, also allowed their large families to find affordable housing). This explains the appearance in Cisjordan over the last fifteen years of a large ultra-Orthodox population (ninety thousand settlers; that is, a third of all those outside East Jerusalem), who share, at least in part, the inflexible nationalism of the followers of religious Zionism.

> **The politicization of religion we see in Israel has had its counterpart on the Palestinian side.**

The politicization of religion we see in Israel has had its counterpart on the Palestinian side. In the late 1970s, the Muslim dimension of Palestinian identity, largely ignored by the PLO's "liberation nationalism," resurfaced. As elsewhere in the Arab East, this revival was expressed as an intensification of religious practices but also as a gradual political mobilization of Islam. In Palestine during the 1980s, this occurred within the Muslim Brotherhood movement. Before that time, the Muslim Brothers had advocated the Islamization of society only through patient labor in the field; henceforth, they accompanied that work with a political Islamization of the Palestinian cause. The change resulted both from developments specific to the Palestinians (disillusionment with the PLO's strategic deadlocks) and from regional events (the Islamic Revolution in Iran, Hezbollah's rise to power). Islamism thrived in Israel proper, around Sheikh Darwish, but especially in the territories occupied in 1967, around Sheikh Ahmed Yassin of Gaza. He brought about a decisive shift in the political involvement of the Muslim Brotherhood: in December 1987, Hamas (the Islamic Resistance Movement) was created within the context of an uprising (intifada) against the Israeli occupation. Hamas spelled

Sheikh Ahmed Yassin, a founder of Hamas, presides over a gathering of Hamas in Gaza on August 1, 1998, before a poster of Yasir Arafat, his political adversary and then-president of the Palestinian Authority. Photograph by Antoine Gyori.

out its ideological orientations in a founding text, its charter of August 1988. This long document, composed of thirty-six articles, is filled with religious references but also with anti-Semitic rhetoric (the theme of a Jewish conspiracy). It defends an extremist vision of Palestine, which is defined as an Islamic mortmain property for all eternity that cannot be divided. As a result, the State of Israel, a joint creation of the "forces of infidelity" (the capitalist West and the communist East) has no legitimacy: only armed jihad will put a definitive end to the "Zionist invasion." Unquestionably, the Hamas charter is radical both in its objectives (to recover all of Palestine) and in its means (recourse to armed struggle, in practice primarily suicide attacks). Such fundamental intransigence does not prevent a certain pragmatic evolution (purely tactical, perhaps) of many Hamas leaders, who have brought up the idea of concluding a lasting truce with the Jewish state in exchange for its withdrawal from all the territories occupied in 1967.[3]

"A land of two peoples": that is how the Austrian-born Israeli philosopher Martin Buber aptly summed up the essence of the

Israeli-Arab conflict. It is already very difficult in itself to reach a lasting peace settlement founded on constructive compromise, because certain central questions (the status of Jerusalem, the future of the Palestinian refugees) are unusually complex. The introduction of religion into that equation and its excessive politicization only complicate matters indefinitely, since the combination of religious fundamentalism and nationalism inevitably supports the logic of war.

▶ See Counterpoint on Martin Buber, pp. 346–347.

---

1. Alain Dieckhoff, "Les visages du fondamentalisme juif en Israël," *Cahier d'études de la Méditerranée orientale et le monde turco-iranien (CEMOTI)* 28 (1999): 85–94.

2. David Newman, "From Hitnachalut to Hitnatkut: The Impact of Gush Emunim and the Settlement Movement on Israeli Politics and Society," *Israel Studies* 10, no. 3 (Fall 2005): 192–224. See also Ehud Sprinzak, *The Ascendance of Israel's Radical Right* (New York: Oxford University Press, 1991).

3. On the history of Hamas, see Khaled Hroub, *Le Hamas* (Paris: Demopolis, 2008); and Aude Signoles, *Le Hamas au pouvoir: Et après?* (Toulouse: Editions Milan, 2006).

Jerusalem, a Political and Religious Issue

In establishing its mandate over Palestine (1920–22), Great Britain made every effort to institute a new golden age of harmony between its Jewish, Christian, and Muslim "citizens," both "real" and "spiritual," one founded on respect for the rights and traditions of all. Within the framework of the status quo, it endeavored to oversee impartially the Christian holy sites and the sacred sites of the other religions (giving Muslims exclusive rights to the Haram esh-Sharif, granting Jews limited right of use of the Western Wall, and so on). It reaffirmed the validity of the Ottoman community organization, the traditional prerogatives of the religious leaders, and the authority of their tribunals in matters of personal law, this time including the Muslims. It was within this context that Hajj Amin al-Husayni, son of one of the notable Muslim families of the city, was promoted to grand mufti in 1921. He headed the Supreme Muslim Council, which administers the rich *waqf* of the Haram esh-Sharif (that is, the mortmain property of that Islamic holy site, which his family holds, along with the responsibility for administering it).

At the same time, the British established Jerusalem as the capital of the Mandatory power. As a result, Al-Quds, the "Holy City" for Muslim and Christian Arabs, became the nerve center of a diverse Arab Palestinian nationalism founded in large part on Islam, a reality that was embodied in the grand mufti's accession to leadership of the city in the 1930s. At the same time, the Jewish Agency, an organization representing Zionist interests, installed itself in "Yerushalayim," the city's Hebrew name, which can be literally translated as "City of Peace." Of course, unlike the *haredim* (God-fearing) Jews and the Zionists of other allegiances, the leadership for the Jews of Palestine—that is, the Labor Zionists—clearly preferred Tel Aviv, the city

of Jewish modernity, to Jerusalem. But the more bitter the Judeo-Arab conflict of legitimacy became, the more value the Holy City, the irreplaceable link between national ideology and Jewish tradition, assumed in their eyes.

This new context made the city the focal point of a national-religious antagonism between its Jewish residents, who were in the majority by far (34,000 in 1922 and 80,000 in 1948, including a strong and very divided *haredim* minority), and its Christian and Muslim residents. Among the 28,000 Arabs living in the city in 1922, the Muslims were at first in the minority, but by 1948, they constituted the majority of the 39,000 Arabs of Jerusalem. The city's residential organization was gradually altered by the antagonism. Every flare-up of intercommunity violence—in 1920, 1929, 1933, and 1936–39—translated into a reduction of social interrelations and a more rigid "mosaic" of Jewish and Arab "neighborhoods." Finally, during the Battle for Jerusalem (1948–49), the violence resulted in the nearly absolute division of the populations into two separate urban spaces.

From 1949 to June 1967, Jordanian East Jerusalem, which included the Old City, was separated from Israeli West Jerusalem by the "Green Line." That cease-fire line marked the failure of the 1947 UN plan for a *corpus separatum* and for an internationalization of Jerusalem. East Jerusalem (47,000 Arab residents in 1948, 66,000 in 1967), merely an administrative center for Cisjordan, suffered as a result of the growing importance of Amman as the capital of the Hashemite Kingdom, even while remaining a symbol dear to a resurgent Palestinian nationalism. Despite the distrust of the Jordanian authorities, this is where the constitutive congress of the Palestine Liberation Organization (PLO) was held in 1964. Furthermore, the

Hashemite sovereigns, descendants of the Prophet and solicitous of international opinion, aspired in their turn to be the guarantors, albeit selectively, of the religious status quo: the Christian and Muslim holy sites were entrusted to the care of a state minister; pilgrimages were welcomed there, as was Pope Paul VI in 1964; but the Jewish holy sites, abandoned to looting and dereliction, were de facto barred to the faithful.

From 1949 to 1953, by contrast, the successive Israeli Labor governments, flying in the face of international decisions, transferred all state institutions with the exception of the Ministry of Defense to West Jerusalem, which was proclaimed the capital of a new Jewish state. There it built commemorative sites celebrating the Zionist epic, the heroes who had died for the nation, and the victims of the Shoah. Conversely, though the city (196,000 residents in 1967, most of them Jewish) retained its religious centrality for Israeli Jews, its spiritual aura suffered in Israel and in the Diaspora from the amputation of the Western Wall. In addition, the question of observance of the Shabbat gave rise to frequent tensions between its ultra-Orthodox residents, a handful of whom were resolutely opposed to the Jewish state, and their "secular" fellow citizens, who were considerably more numerous and supported a secular conception of the state and of society.

On June 8, 1967, East Jerusalem had scarcely been conquered when the Israeli victors of the Six-Day War rushed to declare the city "reunified" and entirely subject to the law of Israel. They assigned it a municipal boundary that extended considerably east of the old Green Line and entrusted its management to the former Labor Party mayor of West Jerusalem (beginning in 1965), Teddy Kollek. He served until 1993. The Arab residents of the former Jordanian sector were granted the status of "permanent residents" and allowed to participate in the municipal elections, which, however, they almost unanimously boycotted. They also enjoyed freedom of movement and retained their Jordanian passports and their religious and legal autonomy at the personal level. As religious Jews returned to pray at the Western Wall and Israelis again frequented the Old City, a number of East Jerusalem Palestinians took jobs in the western sector. But these contacts, largely one-sided or unequal, were also short-lived.

The objective of all the Israeli governments, on both the left and the right (as of 1977), was to make Israel's control of the city irreversible in the face of Palestinian protests and international pressures, especially from the United States. This objective was supported almost unanimously within the country. The separation of the question of political sovereignty from that of religious sovereignty—it alone was deemed negotiable—was one of the means implemented to achieve that goal. The Israeli government refrained from evoking the status quo of the holy sites, since the wall was immediately declared property of the Jewish state and under its management. But it left the administration of the holy sites of the other religions to their traditional leaders. It simply reserved for itself the right to monitor security of the sanctuaries and freedom of worship. There were no major problems for the Christian holy sites, despite the fact that the Vatican did not recognize the State of Israel until 1993. But things proved much trickier in practice for the Muslim holy sites, especially the Haram esh-Sharif. It was a site of prayer but also of demonstrations by Palestinian nationalists, and the target of "Third Temple" Jewish zealots. Serious unrest occurred on several occasions, including the gun battle of 1990 and the al-Aqsa Intifada of 2000. The Israeli authorities, to maintain or reestablish order, were thus led to closely regulate visits to the site and to call in the army. Although the Israelis had not recognized the Higher Islamic Council, created by the Muslims of Jerusalem and of Cisjordan in 1967 to oversee their religious interests, they did collaborate with it. Above all, they preserved the right of the secular powers of

Jordan to designate the grand mufti and to oversee management of the *waqf.*

Apart from its functional import, that decision had the advantage of maintaining the animosity between the Hashemite dynasty and the Palestinians. Indeed, the Jordanian influence, thus preserved, was an argument in favor of Amman's claims to recover East Jerusalem and Cisjordan. Yet, until 1988, the PLO and its leader, Yasir Arafat, laid claim to the city as a whole as the future capital of a State of Palestine that would encompass all of the former Mandatory Palestine. At that date, realism led the Palestinian leader to confine his aspirations to the old eastern part of the city, future capital of a state to be founded on "every free part of the territory of Palestine." King Hussein of Jordan, in fact, had just renounced his political claims on Jerusalem and Cisjordan, but not his religious prerogatives. That reservation would fuel a muffled but persistent disagreement during the Israeli-Palestinian peace process, known as the Oslo talks (1993–2001), since the Palestinian Authority of Gaza wanted to claim those prerogatives in the name of the Palestinian people.

Since the First Intifada (1987–93), moreover, the PLO had been competing with an Islamist Palestinian movement composed of the Islamic Jihad and especially of Hamas, which would not compromise on Al-Quds. They considered it the holy city that Providence had promised in its totality to a Muslim power. Between 1990 and 2000, the Palestinian CEC (Central Elections Commission), rapidly discredited in Palestinian public opinion for its management and for the failure of the peace process, was for that reason prohibited from any further retreat on the Jerusalem issue, which had become one of the bones of contention between the two enemy Palestinian factions. The question of sovereignty over the Holy City, increasingly more complex, thus contributed notably toward blocking all efforts to settle the Israeli-Palestinian conflict (the Oslo process, the road map for the Annapolis conference in late 2007, and so on).

The de facto situation created on the ground by the Israeli authorities further contributed to that deadlock. Their aspirations had been given a firm push in the 1980s and 1990s by the rise of a national-religious Jewish sphere of influence with a determining political weight at both the national and local levels. Since 1967, the Jewish state had tirelessly developed, in the city reunified by law, a methodical urbanization and Judaization process in the west as well as the east. In the eastern zone, a new fundamental law of 1980 proclaimed Jerusalem the "capital of Israel," "full and reunified," which further encouraged Jewish ascendancy. The Old City was the arena for highly symbolic operations, such as stewardship over the esplanade in front of the Western Wall and the restoration of the Jewish quarter. At the same time, on the northern, eastern, and southern fringes of the new municipal boundaries, fortress-like Jewish neighborhoods (Neve Yaakov, Ramot, Ramat Eshkol, French Hill, East Talpiot, Gilo) multiplied atop the hills of Judea, on lands that were usually confiscated in the name of the "public interest." Such neighborhoods were also wedged between Arab neighborhoods and villages, so as to create a "territorial continuity" between the Jewish neighborhoods, impede development of Arab neighborhoods, and cut them off from the Cisjordanian hinterland.

In the early 1990s, the population of Jerusalem surpassed 500,000, of which 360,000 were Jews. Jews therefore outnumbered Arabs, even in the eastern sector (175,000 to 170,000), where they were attracted by financial incentives. The programs for creating or extending Jewish settlements there now belonged to the context of a "metropolitan Jerusalem" that extended well into Cisjordan. In the settlements (Ma'ale Adumin Bloc, Ariel, Gush Etzion), there were generally three Jews for every Arab. In addition, the Israelis' hold on the land was furthered by the construction of special service road networks. Finally, in the 1990s–2000s, a growing number of nationalist and religious-nationalist Israelis moved

In the foreground, the Western Wall, and in the background, the Dome of the Rock, on Haram al-Sharif. Photo by P. Deliss, September 2007.

into houses in the heart of the Arab sectors (Sheikh Jarrah, Silwan), acquired under the table by private associations or requisitioned. Jerusalem, having become the most populous and spread-out city in Israel, now counts 800,000 residents, 530,000 of them Jews, including 190,000 ultra-Orthodox. The ultra-Orthodox Jews are particularly prolific and poor. When they are united, they have the ability to win the mayor's office, which they held from 2003 to 2008. In any event, their vote carries a great deal of weight in the municipal elections.

In this maelstrom, the PLO could not maintain—at least, not after the 1990s—the few governmental or paragovernmental institutions opened in East Jerusalem to aid in the peace negotiations, such as the famous Orient House, its unofficial headquarters. As for the Arabs of Jerusalem (numbering 270,000 at present), they have been reduced to poverty and cloistered in neighborhoods neglected by the city. Most hang on to their overcrowded housing, however, despite the increasingly nitpicking regulations and the incessant harassment by omnipresent Israeli police and military forces to limit their movements. This is because Palestinian unrest and terrorism, which resurfaced in Jerusalem in 1968, reached a first peak at the turn of the 1990s during the First Intifada (shopkeeper strikes, stone throwing, knife attacks, torching of vehicles, demonstrations). It peaked a second time in the 1990s, with a series of terrible suicide attacks, which Hamas set off by remote control to sabotage the peace process. Still others followed in the early 2000s during the al-Aqsa Intifada. In the eyes of many Israelis, and also of Ariel Sharon's government, this last wave of violence justified the construction in 2003 of a "security barrier." It marked the triumph of the policy of separating the Jewish and Arab populations, a policy that had been prevalent at least since the end of the Oslo process. In Jerusalem, the security barrier includes Ariel, Ma'ale Adumin, and Gush Etzion, and, with them, the Arab neighborhoods of East Jerusalem, which explains the suicide attacks of 2008, perpetrated by Arab residents, whose connections to the Islamist parties are not clear. As for the "war of the cradle," there are now some doubts that despite what was previously believed, it is turning to the advantage of the Muslim Arabs of Jerusalem (the number of Christians having fallen there). Their fertility rate has, in fact, been slowing since 2000, compared to that of the *haredim*.

Have the Israelis achieved a fait accompli? With a few rare exceptions, they are counting on it, though many "secular" Jews (who are in the majority), on the right and especially on the left, find the "haredization" of the city oppressive, which has translated into a negative rate of Jewish migration to Jerusalem. The Palestinians increasingly fear it, for though the principle is broadly accepted on both sides, the resolution of the Israeli-Palestinian conflict through the creation of two states, each with Jerusalem as its capital (by virtue of modalities yet to be invented), now seems extremely remote, if not hypothetical. ●

Catherine Nicault is professor of contemporary history at the University of Reims. Her publications include Une histoire de Jérusalem, 1850–1967 *(CNRS Éditions, 2008); and "1850–1967: Genèse d'un divorce,"* Qantara 73 (Fall 2009), *issue on "Jérusalem, la ferveur de la guerre."*

The Emigration of the Jews from the Arab World

Michael M. Laskier

While Jewish communities had lived for centuries within various Muslim societies, for the majority of them the second half of the twentieth century was the theater, sometimes brutal, of their departure. Of the 750,000 Jews in Muslim countries, 550,000 were Maghrebi. In these countries, the Jews did not always participate in the same way in the various strains of Zionism, nor did they adopt the same positions on the aliyah, immigration to Israel. Similarly, the locations of the Jews shifted in accordance with the reconfiguration of maps within the framework of Arab nationalisms—even if, at first, the Jews identified with them, as in Iraq.

The reasons for their departure were multiple—economic or political—as were the contexts in which they took place. The destinations of the departing Jews were also multiple, and for some of them it was Israel, either directly or via Europe. The Jewish Agency, which had the mission, among others, of organizing the emigration of Jews of all ages (of the young, in particular), was especially active, whether secretly, as in Morocco, Egypt, Iraq, and Syria, or tolerated and legal, as in Lebanon, Yemen, Algeria, and Tunisia, from 1949 to 1962. But always the question of Jewish emigration was twofold for the Arab governments—inextricably linked to increasing tensions brought about by the conflicts in the Middle East between Arabs and Israelis, and also by the desire of the Arab League to keep the Jews from leaving Arab countries in order not to strengthen the nascent State of Israel.

Michael M. Laskier

Michael M. Laskier is professor of history at the Bar-Ilan University (Israel) and director of the Menachem Begin Institute for the Study of Resistance Movements. His research focuses on contemporary Israel and the Arab world and the history of the Jews of the Mediterranean region, as well as in France. His works include *Israel and the Maghreb: From Statehood to Oslo* (University Press of Florida, 2004) and *North African Jewry in the Twentieth Century: The Jews of Morocco, Tunisia, and Algeria* (New York University Press, 1997).

From secrecy to laissez-faire in Egypt

On May 15, 1948, Egypt, along with four other Arab countries, went to war against the new neighboring State of Israel. The authorities imposed a series of restrictions on the entire population, including the censoring of mail and the control of telephone communications. Then a wave of arrests among the Jews began

415

> ### Jewish Agency
>
> A nongovernmental organization, created in 1929 and based in London and Jerusalem, that worked for the development and colonization of Palestine. During the 1930s, the government of Jerusalem, headed by David Ben-Gurion, played a decisive role in relations with the Diaspora and Mandate power. In May 1948, the Jewish Agency transferred its powers to the newly created provisional government of the State of Israel, and served as the official link between the government and the Jews of the Diaspora.

without advance warning—with accusations of Zionist and communist machinations. The offices of the Jewish Agency and of the Jewish federations in Cairo and Alexandria were closed, and the Zionist youth movements went underground. Also, most Jewish-owned goods were temporarily requisitioned. In June, July, and August, violent riots broke out against the Jews at the instigation of extremist groups. Attacks in Jewish and Karaite neighborhoods in Cairo left dozens dead or wounded. At first, the regime prevented emigration in general, and the aliyah to Israel in particular, because of the war in the Middle East and for fear of reprisals by the recently formed political opposition of the Muslim Brotherhood. At this point, the Egyptian royal house attempted to stifle this movement: its founder, Hassan al-Banna, and several others of its members were arrested—and held in the same prisons, by the way, as the arrested Jews.

With time, the authorities ended up closing their eyes, on condition that the Zionist activities fostering Jewish emigration took place discreetly. And shortly after the accession to power of the Wafd Party in January 1950, the Jews obtained the restitution of the goods that had been confiscated from them, the prisoners were freed from the camps in which they were being held, and the anti-Zionist attacks on them became infrequent. In 1952, Gamal Abdel Nasser overthrew King Faruk I and the previous regime by a military coup. Beginning in 1955, the situation of the Jews of Egypt deteriorated significantly for two essential reasons. The first concerned the policy of the new Egyptian leader, which took a direction favorable to national pan-Arab homogeneity, marginalizing the non-Muslim minorities, who were suspected of perpetuating European colonialism. The second reason was the Suez War of the autumn of 1956, when France, Great Britain, and Israel united to launch a vast military offensive against the Egyptian leader, with the goal of weakening his actions and influence in the Middle East and the Maghreb, and regaining control of the Suez Canal after its nationalization in July of that same year. Immediately following the beginning of hostilities, the Egyptian government published decrees announcing a state of emergency, imposing censure, and putting in place a legal basis for massive detentions, the dismissal of public and private mail services, and the forfeiture of nationality of large groups of the population. Many Jews were even thrown out of the country. With the help of the French consul of Port Said, they embarked for Toulon, then Marseilles, and finally, for some, Haifa, between November 1956 and May 1957: in all, 14,000 of the 23,000 Jewish refugees reached Israel, while the others were dispersed in various countries (France, but also Brazil and the United States).

In Egypt, the situation of the Jews worsened after the alliance concluded with Syria in February 1958 and became the United Arab Republic (UAR). After the Egyptian defeat during the Six-Day War, the authorities took steps that made the lives of some 2,500 Jews remaining in Cairo and Alexandria more precarious. Two or three days after the beginning of the struggles that broke out at the beginning of June 1967, the police arrested several of them, among them the rabbi of Alexandria and the president of the community of Cairo. In all, 425 men were jailed in the Abou Zaabal prison near Cairo. Shortly afterward, they were expelled from the country with their families. The detainees and their families left for various destinations in Europe and elsewhere, including Israel. In September 1970, there were only 250 Jews left in Egypt.

⟩ See Counterpoint on the departure of Jews from Egypt, pp. 434–435.

The different phases of the departures from Libya

Once Libya was freed from the grip of the Axis countries, Germany and Italy, the arrival of the British military administration scarcely improved the situation of the thirty thousand Jews living there. On November 4, 1945, an anti-Jewish riot broke out in Tripoli after rumors concerning confrontations between Arabs and Jews in Palestine, and of false accusations about the profaning of Muslim holy places and the Mosque of Omar. These rumors proliferated in the nearby villages and Tripolitania, and the British government did not intervene to quell them. The consequences were disastrous: 132 deaths, most of them old men, women, and children; hundreds of wounded; widespread material damage; pillaging; and theft. Several members of the community, having lost their houses and means of subsistence, were forced to seek assistance from the committee of the Tripoli community. At the end of the 1940s, the growth of migratory streams from Libya toward Israel and Italy resulted from the riots, the creation of the State of Israel, its victory in the 1948 war, and the radicalization of nationalism within Libyan political circles (for example, in Egypt and various other points of the globe), but also from the Libyan Jews' mistrust of the British, who, according to them, had made no attempt to protect them.

Great Britain concluded an agreement with Israel stipulating that it would coordinate the departure of Jews based on quotas set by the Jewish Agency, in order to allow for the reception and integration of the immigrants into Israeli society in an orderly and nontraumatic fashion. In 1949, the Immigration Department of the Jewish Agency in Libya, which exercised the function of a consular office, conducted its work openly and legally.

At the end of December 1952, the Bureau of Emigration and the Israeli consulate of Tripoli closed their doors, while the Israelis were leaving the country. After having rejoined the Arab League in March 1953, the government of independent Libya, under the authority of King Idris al-Sanusi and of the Istiqlal Party, took a series of measures against the Jewish community. On December 31, 1952, the committees of the communities were dissolved and replaced by Muslim representatives;

the Alliance Israélite Universelle was closed in Tripoli in 1960, and on March 21, 1961, a special law was adopted according to which "all goods and property located in Libya belonging to institutions or persons residing in Israel or maintaining ties to such country or business will be placed under government stewardship." The Jews left the country with Italian visas; once they arrived in Italy, the Jewish Agency transferred them to Israel. Between 1948 and 1967, a considerable number of Jews decided to remain in Italy.

The Six-Day War induced the Libyan government to declare that it associated itself "with the Arab war of defense" and made its resources available for the struggle to liberate Palestine. The nationalist press published articles tainted with anti-Semitism, quoting entire paragraphs from Hitler's *Mein Kampf.* The Jews desperately tried to head off the danger by sending telegrams to the king, expressing their neutrality and their loyalty to the royal house.

But the hostilities, which began with the Israeli attack, reinforced the demonstrations, riots, and violence against the Tripolitan Jews, and entailed the destruction of businesses and private homes. The great synagogue of Tripoli, Beit El, was burned, with hundreds of sacred books, including ancient volumes, reduced to ashes. Finally, the authorities declared a state of emergency and a curfew to avoid chaos. The appeal sent by Lilo Arbib, one of the leaders of the Jewish community, to the mufti of Tripoli, requesting that he obtain from the Muslims an immediate stop to all violence, remained a dead letter. The inhabitants of the Jewish quarter then turned to the commissariats, then to Camp Gurgi on the outskirts of the city.

> " *The Moroccan sultan had rallied the entire population to Judeo-Muslim solidarity, despite the war between Israel and the Middle Eastern Arab countries.* "

After the riots, the Libyan government tried to gild its seriously tarnished image by alleging that only four people had been killed during the disturbances. At Arbib's request, the Libyan authorities agreed to let the Jews leave for Italy until the return to calm. Beginning on June 12, 1967, and continuing for several weeks, the majority of the Jews were thus able to leave the country. They were authorized to take no more than twenty pounds sterling and twenty kilograms of personal items. Several hundred Jews decided to remain in Tripoli, and two hundred in Benghazi. In September 1969, following the rise to power of the military junta and the fall of the monarchy, the Jews lost all hope of retrieving their possessions. In the 1970s, only a few dozen Jews remained in Libya. Today there are none.

The different stages of the departure of the Moroccan Jews

In June 1948, during the most intense time of the war in the Middle East, riots against the Jews broke out in Oujda and in the neighboring town of Djerada, well known for its coal mines. The toll was at least forty-two dead and twenty wounded,

Jews and Muslims combined, in a span of thirty-six hours, as well as the attendant material damage. This region, along the border with French Algeria, was at that time the point of passage for the clandestine emigration of Moroccan Jews. It was also an area marked by the activities of Moroccan nationalists who, present in the miners' unions, had organized several strikes that the French residential authorities had tried to foil. These nationalists maintained, for political purposes, a detrimental atmosphere by means of anti-Zionist propaganda, even though, a month before the violent outbursts, the Moroccan sultan had rallied the entire population to Judeo-Muslim solidarity, despite the war between Israel and the Middle Eastern Arab countries. These riots of 1948 marked the deterioration of relations between Muslims and Jews, and swelled the wave of immigration of the lower classes and the Jewish petite bourgeoisie, who, concerned for their social status, saw in the birth of the State of Israel a way out of their precarious situation.

After the de facto recognition of the State of Israel by France (January 24, 1949), which continued to maintain its protectorate of Morocco, an agreement was reached to set up a channel for organizing the aliyah under the cover of a publishing house called Kadima. The office was in Casablanca, with affiliates in Marrakesh, Fez, Meknès, and Tangiers. Israeli emissaries directed the operations in collaboration with local Zionist activists under the sponsorship of the Mossad le Aliyah Bet

(the organization charged with the secret immigration of Jewish refugees to Palestine beginning in 1938) and the Aliyah Department of the Jewish Agency. In coordination with this, a transit camp was established in El Jadida, near Casablanca. After a temporary stay in this camp, the immigrants boarded French boats headed for transit camps in Marseilles before continuing toward Israel. At the beginning, the number of immigrants was limited to six hundred people per month (set in relation to the natural growth of the Moroccan

Arrival of immigrants in Haifa, 1962. Photo by Keren Hayessod, Brussels, Center for Judeo-Moroccan Culture.

Jewish population), but with time the quota was increased. In 1955, under pressure from the Jewish Agency, from 2,500 to 3,500 people left the country each month—depending on Israel's capacity to receive the immigrants and the flexibility of French policy. In autumn 1956, approximately 90,000 people had already emigrated, most of them to Israel. Independent Morocco forbade the Jewish Agency to pursue its activities. Besides Israel, Jews emigrated by the thousands to France, Belgium, and Spain, as well as North America (particularly Canada) and South America.

The situation between the representatives of the different Moroccan and French parties and movements calmed down after the conference at Aix-les-Bains in August 1955, opening the way to Moroccan independence, which was declared in 1956. Jewish leaders and intellectuals established ties with their Muslim counterparts, members of the Istiqlal Party, and other forums in order to reflect on the construction of a new, progressive Morocco. Some Jews remained skeptical, expressing reservations about the declaration by the sultan Mohammed Ben Youssef (the future Mohammed V) after his return from exile to Madagascar, on the subject of the guarantee of the rights and duties of Jews. Others, on the contrary, chose to join ▶ See Nota bene on Mohammed V, pp. 362–364. the nationalists. The state of Morocco, moreover, showed a series of positive signs, including the nomination of a Jewish minister of government, Dr. Léon Benzaquen, charged with mail and telegraph communications.

The *makhzen* (royal power), fully informed of the actions of the Jewish Agency, preferred to ignore the departure of the Jews under his jurisdiction, as long as it took place discreetly. But between May and December 1956, the Moroccan government took steps to slow down that emigration, which had taken on ample proportions: 36,301 persons had succeeded in leaving for Israel that year.

Given the impossibility of arranging for the departure of Jews legally, a vast secret network was put in place at the end of 1956 and charged with Jewish interests at all levels. The Misgueret (Framework) had been created under the control of an Israeli intelligence agency, the Mossad le-tafkidim meyuhadim (Special Operations Organization); one of its main tasks was to instruct young Jews in self-defense, including the use of weapons. When a third of the schools of the Alliance Israélite Universelle were nationalized, this network also contributed to making the other establishments function under its aegis and strict control of the authorities.

In January 1961, two noteworthy events evinced the increased tensions: the persecutions of Jews during the visit of the Egyptian president Gamal Abdel Nasser to Casablanca, and the sinking of a ship of clandestine passengers chartered by the Misgueret in the region of Al Hoceima, bound for Gibraltar, which caused the deaths of forty-two migrants. The Misgueret used this to encourage Jews to go to Israel. The interior minister of Morocco, facing the protests of the leaders of the Moroccan community and international pressure, declared on February 24, 1961, that the Jews were "free to settle anywhere, with the exception of Israel." Since Morocco did not recognize the State of Israel, it was obviously impossible to get a passport for that country. The Moroccans who helped Israel "would lose their nationality." That declaration, after all, represented a significant turn in the Jews' favor: officially, they were forbidden to go to Israel, but the government did not intervene in their comings and goings after their arrival in Europe or America.

Hassan II, on his advent to the throne in March 1961, after the death of Mohammed V, granted amnesty to all the prisoners of the opposition. This measure included the local activists of the Misgueret who had been arrested in the past. At the same time, the representative of the Mossad responsible for the Misgueret in Morocco developed connections with the royal power between May and October 1961. Secret encounters took place in Europe to find agreement between the two parties to resume legal or semilegal immigration. Since Israel had promised the throne a financial "compensation," it was agreed that the formulation "immigration to any country with the exception of Israel" would be maintained. But it was clear that Israel was the real destination of the majority of immigrants, for whom the Old Continent was no more than a temporary step. This great wave of immigration that took place with the greatest of discretion and the complicity of the Moroccan authorities was called Operation Yakhin, from the name of one of the two columns of the Temple of Jerusalem. On December 16, 1961, the leftist opposition newspaper *Al-Tahrir* did not abstain from criticizing the government, which it reproached for having turned their backs on the Palestinian refugees.

> ❝ *This great wave of immigration that took place with the greatest of discretion and the complicity of the Moroccan authorities was called Operation Yakhin.* ❞

With the exception of a few interruptions in Operation Yakhin, based on political considerations, the departure of the Jews continued to proceed with regularity. The selection of the immigrants of Operation Yakhin was made according to strict criteria, with the goal of eliminating small communities, in order to reduce the "Jewish map" of Morocco, while at the same time maintaining the security of the Jews. Hence, priority was given to communities of fewer than three hundred families.

From November 1961 to December 1964, more than 92,000 Moroccan Jews immigrated to Israel. Most left Morocco with their families. Single immigrants were a minority, made up of those going to join their parents already settled in Israel, students, or young people from the *aliyat hanoar* (an organization charged with the immigration and integration of the young). The Six-Day War did not cause a panic, as the Jews were given immunity, thanks to the efforts of the government and the palace. (The economic embargo on Jewish-owned businesses was temporary.) It is clear that the secret connections developed between the Israeli Mossad and Morocco for security, at the beginning of the 1960s, played a significant role in this. Still, the war increased Jewish desire to leave the country. Their uneasiness increased in proportion to the aggressive behavior of nationalist elements who took advantage of Gamal Abdel Nasser's rout and Israel's territorial expansion to increase anti-Jewish activity. From 1967 to 1979, the yearly average of Jewish immigrants was 47,000. In 1971, there were only 42,000 left, as a result of departures for Israel and other countries. In 1975, there were only 22,000 left. Today there are scarcely 3,000; they enjoy royal protection, which ensures them freedom of worship and education.

Despite tolerance: The case of Tunisia

On the eve of the birth of the State of Israel, a Jewish community, 110,000 strong, was living in Tunisia, where they represented nearly 3 percent of the population. The city of Tunis had 65,000 Jews, Sfax 4,500, and Sousse 4,000; the rest were in Djerba, Nabeul, and the northern towns. Historically, relations there were, on the whole, more harmonious than in other regions, the nationalist groups having been more open than elsewhere to the Jews; the Neo-Destour Party, founded by Habib Bourguiba and Salah Ben Youssef in 1934, even encouraged them to join.

▶ See Nota bene on Tunisia under the Protectorate, pp. 316–319.

The desire to immigrate to Israel manifested itself between 1945 and 1948, and the departures to France accelerated at the beginning of the 1950s with the intensification of the struggle for independence, though Jewish involvement in these events was rare. Between 1948 and 1950, Israel organized the departure of Tunisian Jews through the Mossad le Aliyah Bet. Beginning in 1950, the Aliyah Department of the Jewish Agency took over. The Israeli emissaries and their local adjuncts worked in collaboration with the American Joint (American Jewish Joint Distribution Committee), the dispensers of the Œuvre de Secours aux Enfants (OSE), the Department of Education and the *aliyat hanoar*, under the auspices of the Jewish Agency, and the professional schools of the ORT network. The French authorized the activities connected with the Zionist movement, and the departures via Algeria (until 1950–51) and via France and Italy, on the condition that the greatest discretion be exercised. In summer 1955, the movement of emigration of Jews to Israel and other destinations increased, with the formation of an autonomous administration. After

> *The Jews felt more and more marginalized in the public and economic domain, although, officially, there had been no notable changes in the position of the authorities respecting them.*

the birth of an independent government around Bourguiba and the Neo-Destour Party, the Jewish Agency continued to organize immigration without restriction or exception. In 1958, in the wake of the admission of Tunisia and Morocco to the Arab League, Israel and Tunisia reached an agreement to modify the name of the Aliyah Department of the Jewish Agency, known henceforth as the Swiss Jewish Association, in order to avoid embarrassing incidents and pressures coming from the opposition to the regime. Until autumn 1956, Tunisia allowed Jews to emigrate with a Tunisian passport mentioning their destination—Israel. After the Suez War and under pressure from the Egyptian government, France or Italy replaced Israel under the heading "destination," even though the Tunisians knew that the Jews then left Europe to settle in Israel.

The undeniable tolerance practiced by Tunisia was insufficient, however, to alleviate the concerns of the Jews, uneasy about their future if, for one reason or another, Bourguiba were to disappear from the political scene. They felt more and more marginalized in the public and economic domain, although, officially, there had been no notable changes in the position of the authorities respecting them. On the contrary, the officials lost no occasion to emphasize the complete equality of the Jews with the Muslims. In reality, however, Jews were progressively ousted from key positions, and the only ones that retained their posts were those who could not be replaced. Jewish merchants had the greatest difficulty in obtaining authorizations for import-export businesses, and there were scarcely any Jews in the important administrative posts, with the exception of the minister of economy. In 1960, the municipal council of Tunis had only two Jewish members out of a total of sixty, even though Jews represented 14 percent of the city's population. Few Jews were affiliated with the Neo-Destour, either because the party was no longer particularly disposed to welcome them or because the Jews themselves expressed serious reservations about local politics.

The increasing difficulties that the Jews, even of the middle or upper classes, encountered at the social level stepped up emigration. France became, little by little, the main destination of the emigrants who left by their own means or with the help of the Hebrew Immigration Aid Society (HIAS), active in Tunisia as of 1956. Due to serious incidents arising during the summer of 1961 between France and Tunisia involving the naval base in the port of Bizerte in the northern part of the country, the 1,200 Jewish inhabitants found themselves in a particularly dangerous situation. Their Muslim neighbors accused them of collabora-

Israeli stamp that commemorates the twentieth anniversary of the Youth Aliyah, a Jewish organization founded in 1933 that saved Jewish children from Nazi Germany by sending them to Palestine. The organization continued its activities after 1945 by serving to integrate young Jews coming from North Africa and Asia. May 10, 1955.

ting with the French, which was in fact the case with certain Jews, particularly the employees of the shipyards of the French navy. A large number of Tunisian Jews emigrated for fear of riots. In September 1961, there were 250 Jews living in Tunis; these Tunisian citizens, who were originally from Bizerte, were evacuated during a joint rescue operation carried out by agents of the Misgueret (which also operated in Tunisia), the French government, envoys from the Jewish Agency, and the Israeli military attaché in Paris. The refugees embarked on French barges leaving for Annaba, in Algeria; from there they were flown to Marseilles, and then to Israel. Bourguiba's efforts in 1965 to lead Israel and its neighbors to the negotiation table to find a solution to the Israeli-Arab conflict and the Palestinian refugee problem reinforced Jewish confidence in the Tunisian president, despite his policy of economic austerity. The Six-Day War, however, tested Bourguiba's goodwill toward the Jews severely. Riots broke out in Tunis on June 5, accompanied by slogans such as "Long live Nasser," "Long live the Arab people," and "Down with Israel and Imperialism." The rioters marched on the American Information Center and the British Embassy, ransacking their offices. Then they attacked Jewish shops and the Grand Synagogue on Avenue de la Liberté.

Bourguiba was not notified of the events until that evening. According to a member in his close circle, certain ministers were aware of the situation, but no one took the initiative of stopping the riots. At eight, Bourguiba spoke on television and the radio. In his speech, he strongly condemned the violence against Americans, British, and Jews, and declared that he would take draconian measures to prevent further outbreaks of violence. A few days later, the minister of the interior and the local police chief were relieved of their duties, and forty-five participants in the riots were arrested and brought to trial. The damaged buildings were promptly repaired.

Things returned to normal in August 1967. Jewish businesses reopened their doors. Despite the efforts by the authorities to restore calm, however, the Jews remained alarmed. They had discovered that the rioters, among whom were Algerians and Egyptians, had followed the specific orders of a blacklist establishing a distinction between Jews and other citizens. The Jews left the country en masse. At the end of the 1960s, half of the Tunisian Jews had immigrated to Israel, while the other half chose to settle in France. Today, several thousand Jews still live in Tunisia. Their fate will be one of the tests of the new Tunisian democracy, and of the government directed by the Islamist party Ennahda.

Algeria torn apart

The leaders of Algerian Judaism maintained that only prudent neutrality and a discreet loyalty to France would make it possible for the Jews to avoid being swept into the bloody maelstrom that was about to engulf the French colonial power and those under its administration, the Muslims. When, in November 1954, the armed struggle conducted by the National Liberation Front (FLN) began, that ambiguous neutrality ended in failure. The Jews became a vulnerable population. Before the insurrection, the city of Medea, in the department of Algiers, was home to an active and flourishing community of about a thousand Jews. In 1957, there were only seven families left. That community was the target of several organized attacks in which some of its members were killed, including Rabbi Yaakov Choukroun, assassinated on the steps of the synagogue. This was also the case in larger communities in the departments of Oran and Algiers. Beginning in 1956, certain Jewish merchants and community leaders received threatening letters from the FLN telling them to finance the revolutionaries, and specifying that they would pay with their lives and those of their families if they refused.

The party line of the FLN, as shown by appeals addressed to the grand rabbi of Algeria in August and November 1956, solemnly requesting the Jewish community to show its allegiance to the Algerian nation, did not necessarily exclude the Jews from the national Algerian scene. But added to the intercommunity tensions was the Israeli-Palestinian conflict: in April 1958, the Jewish community of Algiers took the initiative of celebrating the tenth anniversary of the State of Israel; its president received a threatening letter from the nationalists, accusing him of not being able to choose which side he was on.

The precarious living conditions of the Algerian Jews prompted the Mossad to increase the activities of the Misgueret in Algeria in 1956. In the storm of the civil war, Jewish cells, trained by the Mossad, took up "self-defense" actions, attacking cafés or businesses held by Muslims, such as in Constantine, on May 12, 1956.[1] The conflict was equally violent with the activists for French Algeria, who also represented a threat to the Jewish communities. The situation deteriorated around 1961, when a group of Fascist-leaning Europeans, hostile to any Franco-Algerian agreement, and to de Gaulle, founded the Organisation de l'armée secrète (OAS). From the

> *The party line of the FLN, as shown by appeals addressed to the grand rabbi of Algeria in 1956, did not necessarily exclude the Jews from the national Algerian scene. But added to the intercommunity tensions was the Israeli-Palestinian conflict.*

beginning of 1961 until March 18, 1962, the date of the signing of the Évian agreements between France and the FLN that paved the way to Algerian independence, violence spread throughout the country. Jewish victims were numerous. Oddly, Jews approached the extremists (just as some of their coreligionists, a few years earlier, joined the FLN) and joined the ranks of the OAS, despite the anti-Semitism displayed by several members of the organization.

Given the increase in violence, the community leaders opened up discussions with the French government. In December 1961, Jacques Lazarus, a former member of the Resistance and director of the World Jewish Congress for North Africa, called upon the appropriate French government officials to take drastic measures to end Muslim and European abuses against Jews; if not, he threatened, the Jewish organizations of Algeria would urge their coreligionists to leave the country and invade mainland France by the tens of thousands. Immigration to Israel was scarcely considered. Besides, there was no massive immigration of Algerian Jews to Israel, with the exception of the Jews from Oran, of Moroccan origin, not possessing French nationality, and Jews of Constantine (about 5,000). In all, 130,000 people emigrated. Most disembarked on the other side of the Mediterranean, in France, where they arrived, in total disarray, at the end of the summer of 1962.

Arrival of Jews and Pieds-Noirs in the camp of Grand Arénas, Marseille, 1962. Photograph by Daniel Franck.

Secret action in Syria

In 1947, the Jewish community of Syria numbered between thirteen and fifteen thousand. After independence, the authorities watched the movement of the members of the Jewish community with particular attentiveness. The delivery of passports or exit visas from the territory was delayed for administrative reasons, or even refused. Those who tried to cross the border with Lebanon secretly were arrested under the accusation of trying to get to Palestine. We now know that the secret networks were connected with emissaries of Zionist institutions active in Syria and Lebanon, as well as in North Africa and Iraq. Between 1943 and 1948, the Mossad le Aliyah Bet arranged, with the help of indigenous youths, to get more than five thousand Jews to Palestine.

Beginning in 1948, the network intensified its activities to accelerate immigration. These actions took place in an increasingly tense context, marked by brutal upheavals in the region and by anti-Jewish riots (in Aleppo in December 1947, in 1948 when a bomb exploded in the Alliance Israélite Universelle of Damascus, and then in July and August, when bombs killed dozens of Jews in that same neighborhood).[2] The Mossad le Aliyah Bet enrolled Shula Cohen, who was living in Beirut, as a liaison agent in Syria and Lebanon, where she was charged with contacting Lebanese and Syrian smugglers. With time, she became an essential link in the clandestine immigration of Syrian Jews to Palestine via Lebanon. The network was discovered in 1961 and its members arrested. Until its dismantling in 1952, the Mossad le Aliyah Bet, and the Aliyah Department of the Jewish Agency, which then took over that function, kept up good relations with Lufthansa Airlines, which took charge of the departure of a portion of the Beirut Jews. Its employees also transmitted mail and other documents to the agents of the Aliyah Department in Beirut, as well as information concerning Syrian Jews. The immigrants disembarked in Turkey and continued their trip to Israel from there. A total of 5,630 Jews immigrated to Israel between 1948 and 1950. The clandestine immigration also took place via the Mediterranean. Other Lebanese Jews left for the United States and Latin America, especially Argentina and Colombia.

The situation of the Jews worsened at the end of the United Arab Republic (UAR) of Egypt and Syria in September 1961, and particularly in 1963, with the accession to power of the Ba'th Party, supported by the army. The policy of emigration became more restrictive then, and freedom of movement inside the country was limited. Hostility toward the Jews increased after the discovery and execution of an Israeli spy, Eli Cohen, in 1965, and after the military putsch of 1966, which allowed the accession to power of the radical left wing of the Ba'th Party led by the Alaouite minority. The Six-Day War, in 1967, placed the Jews before the same dilemma as in 1948: how to come to terms with a weakened power and the weakened population in the midst of which they lived. In mid-July, the Jewish faculty of the community schools were dismissed and replaced—temporarily at least—by Muslim professors. Members of the military and their families were forbidden to socialize with Jews, who could not renew their driver's licenses once expired, for example. The Palestinian refugees in Syria encouraged the local population to attack the Jews. But the Sunni Syrian Muslims and the minorities showed a surprising tolerance. At the end of the Six-Day War, 4,300 Jews were still living in Syria: 2,500 in Damascus, 1,500 in Aleppo, and 300 in the northeast of the country. After the 1970 putsch, the Alaouites held on to power, headed by the al-Assad family. The situation of the Jews improved with the arrival of Hafez al-Assad, even though freedom of movement and the right to emigrate, to whatever destination, including Israel, was still limited. Jewish defectors were killed by smugglers, and others were turned in to the authorities. Some were tortured or subjected to interrogation.

> **The situation of the Jews [in Syria] improved with the arrival of Hafez al-Assad, even though freedom of movement and the right to emigrate ... was still limited.**

After the fall of the Soviet Union in 1991 and the attempts by Hafez al-Assad to build closer relations with the West, Syria authorized the Jews who were still living there to leave the country. Between April and October 1992, approximately 2,600 Jews left Syria. Some went to the United States and Latin America, others to Israel.

A later exile than elsewhere for the Lebanese Jews

In Lebanon, contrary to what occurred in Egypt, Syria, and Iraq, the Palestinian Arab question and the exacerbation of Arab nationalism did not have, at first, the same disastrous consequences for the situation of the Lebanese Jews. It was the Lebanese civil war of 1958 that brought on an initial wave of emigration among Jews, even though they were absolutely none the worse for it, for Christian

Lebanese, and even Muslims, put up a human protective wall to protect the Jewish neighborhoods in Beirut. The Jews, who were free to leave Lebanon, chose Europe or the American continent, even though the Lebanese authorities did not forbid departure for Israel. The 1948 and 1956 Middle East wars did not affect the Jews, who constituted a decisive element in the Lebanese economy. After the Six-Day War, the establishment of the Palestine Liberation Organization (PLO) in Lebanon, and its infiltration into the military and political establishments, in which it became a dominating factor, the situation of the Jews began to deteriorate. The Muslims began to suspect the Jews, though demographically marginal, of being "agents of the Israeli-Christian-Maronite axis," as a result of PLO propaganda.

The perennial nature of the prosperous little Jewish community was threatened. In 1970, there remained only approximately one thousand Jews in Lebanon after a vast emigration toward the West. Subsequently, the relations between Jews and Muslims worsened during a long civil war from 1975 to 1990, in which the Palestinian factions played a preponderant role with respect to its outbreak and length. Acts of sabotage and attacks on schools, religious institutions, and Jewish properties accelerated their departure. Today, only a few dozen or so remain in the Country of the Cedar.

❿ See article by Kirsten E. Schulze, pp. 436–443.

In Iraq: The shock of departure

While the Jewish community of Iraq, 130,000 strong and relatively well integrated into public administration, finance, and trade, was still just recovering from the trauma of the Farhud—a massacre of great violence and without precedent, in which it is estimated that as many as 180 Jews perished, and perpetrated by the Iraqi nationalists in 1941—it had to face, after a short period of relative calm, the brutality of decisions that hastened its departure.

In September 1948, Shafiq Ades, a rich businessman accused of Zionist activism and arms trafficking with Israel, was executed. Other arrests followed, orchestrated by the minister of defense immediately after the 1948 war, targeting Jews and communists. In 1949, insecurity intensified and the community grew apprehensive when the eventuality arose of an exchange, either voluntary or forced, of one hundred thousand Iraqi Jews for the same number of Palestinian refugees. When Iraq—the only state having taken part in the war to have adopted that position—refused to sign the Rhodes armistace agreement, the Jews understood that the future of their community was in serious jeopardy. On March 9, 1950, the Iraqi parliament adopted the "law of denaturalization," authorizing Jews to leave the country definitively on the condition that they give up their citizenship. The law did not mention a destination, but it was clear that the majority of the Jews would immigrate to Israel, the only country whose doors were open to them.[3] But neither the Iraqi authorities nor the Israelis ever imagined that so many Jews would, in fact, leave for Israel.

At the beginning of May 1950, after a secret agreement between Israel and Iraq on the evacuation of Jews, the local responsible body—the movement for Zionist pioneer youth, which had 2,000, members, and the Mossad le Aliyah Bet—announced the figure of 47,000 potential candidates for emigration in the country as a whole. In September 1950, there were 70,000, and 104,000 by the end of 1951, to which there must be added those who left the country through Iran, as in the past. Their departure was made possible thanks to discreet negotiations between the Israeli representatives and Prime Minister Tawfiq al-Suwaidi. The transportation of the émigrés who participated in that secret (or rather semisecret) operation, called Operation Ezra and Nehemiah, was expedited by the Near East Air Transport, in collaboration with El Al [Airlines].[4] The attacks on Jews, their generalized dismissal from employment, the nationalist propaganda of the members of the Iraqi Istiqlal (Independence) Party that dominated the political scene at that time, and the attacks on Jewish economic interests—the freezing or confiscating of their real estate and other property—accelerated their departure.

At the end of 1951 or the beginning of 1952, about ten thousand Jews were still in Iraq, in Baghdad for the most part. The process of emigration, whether legal or clandestine, continued uninterrupted during the 1950s. It should be pointed out that some succeeded in crossing the Iraq-Iran border with the complicity of the shah of Iran and the help of Kurdish smugglers, who benefited from the support of Israel in their fight against the military regime of Baghdad. At the end of the 1960s, three thousand Jews were still living in Iraq. Today, only a few hundred remain.

From Yemen, a messianic (and economic) departure

A unique phenomenon: the Jewish community left Yemen for reasons that were equally religious, spiritual, and messianic. According to Dov Levitan, a specialist on the Jewish Yemenite community, on September 19, 1949, Israel authorized the publication of information about emigration organized by Yemenite Jews under the authority of the Jewish Agency.[5] During 1949 and 1950, the transportation of more than 45,000 Yemenite Jews to Israel took place. The repatriation of refugees by air was baptized Flying Carpet in reference to the biblical verse "I bore you on eagles' wings and brought you to Me" (Exodus 19:4), after the example of the Iraqi Operation Ezra and Nehemiah.

> **" A unique phenomenon: the Jewish community left Yemen for reasons that were equally religious, spiritual, and messianic. "**

Earlier in the modern era, the first waves of Yemenite Jewish immigration to Palestine coincided with the arrival of European Jews there at the beginning of the 1880s. Toward the end of the 1930s, the census showed approximately 30,000 Yemenite Jews in Palestine. Despite restrictions imposed beginning in May 1939 by the English, who set up immigration quotas in Palestine (75,000 refugees for a five-year

▶ Voir See article by Yosef Tobi, pp. 248–257.

Yemeni Jews studying a map of Israel, Lod (Israel), around 1948. Hulton-Deutsch Collection.

period), after pressure brought to bear by the Palestinian Arab leadership, which they based on the British White Book, more than 4,000 Yemenite Jews disembarked in Palestine during the Second World War. The Jewish Agency succeeded in obtaining entry certificates to Palestine within the framework of the White Book—the authorities gave them preferred status because of their precarious economic situation. But, in 1945, the Yemenite imam closed the doors to the country—a measure that effectively prevented the departure of Jews.

After the birth of the State of Israel, negotiations were set in motion for the purpose of evacuating Yemenite Jews and their compatriots who had been blocked in Aden since 1945. But, as Levitan explains, the negotiations failed for two essential reasons: the British, who controlled Aden and the local port, were categorically opposed to the departure of young men of military age, and they also cited the failing health of certain potential candidates for emigration.[6] The arrival en masse in Camp Hashed in 1948–49 of Jews wishing to return to Zion, and their deplorable socioeconomic condition, forced the Israeli government and the Jewish Agency, confronted with this situation of deep distress and great overcrowding, to work toward a speedy evacuation. After lengthy negotiations, the British wound up agreeing to collaborate by authorizing Israel to move on to the operational phase—negotiating with Imam Yahya and his government to reach an agreement for the transfer of Jews. Contrary to the case of Iraq, in which the Israeli emissary negotiated directly, though privately, with the prime minister on Operation Ezra and Nehemiah, it was impossible to establish direct links with the imam of Sanaa. For this reason, Israel charged the World Jewish Congress to begin negotiations on the spot. The imam and his representatives made their position more flexible especially after the armistice agreement signed in Rhodes between Israel and the Arab countries. Around April 1949, the Yemenite regime finally authorized the Jews to leave the country freely, passing through Aden. Their destination, without it being made specific, would be Israel. The departure of the Jews had its advantages from the point of view of the government, which took control over their goods and, being emigrants, the *jizya* (a poll tax that non-Muslims still paid in Yemen) and fees for the right to leave the country. Levitan identifies three steps in the Yemenite Jewish emigration: the first, from December 1948 to March 1949, consisted of 5,550 refugees who went to Israel by way of Aden; the second, from June to September 1949, in which 41,092 Jews left from Yemen, and 1,770 from the little community of Aden; and the third, from October 1950 to April 1956, during which 1,344 Jews left from Yemen and 449 from Aden. The British closed the transit camp of Hashed at the end of Operation Flying Carpet, and before the imam authorized the departure of Jews without restrictions, 4,000 of them entered Israel secretly until the end of February 1949. Unlike Operation Ezra and Nehemiah, it was a nonstop trip. From the end of 1950 until 1956, when the operation was practically over, a number of Jews continued to leave Yemen by various means. In 1954, three emissaries from the Aliyah Department of the Jewish Agency were still in Aden. And, in the 1990s, the Israeli government, in collaboration with Western Jews, arranged for most of the Jews who remained in Yemen to go to Israel; others settled in the United States with the help of American Jews.

The reasons for leaving

More than the worsening of the Palestinian question and hostility toward Zionism, what opened the path for Jewish emigration beginning in the 1940s was the ascendency of Arab nationalism. This phenomenon, more widespread in Egypt, Libya, and Iraq than in the French Maghreb, was less prevalent in Tunisia. By the end of the 1940s, the Israeli-Arab conflict precipitated the disintegration of the Jewish communities of the Middle East and Egypt—even those in the Maghreb and Yemen, despite their being far from the theater of confrontations—because that conflict served to cement pan-Arabic solidarity.

The arrival in Israel of the Jews referred to as Sephardim was not without its problems. One cannot suppress the fact that certain key figures in the Jewish Agency, the Knesset, the government, or in the Israeli media belittled the Jews of the Arab countries, forming negative judgments about them even before their arrival, and giving preference to the Jews coming from the United States or Eastern Europe. Nevertheless, aliyah should be understood globally, through a thorough analysis of the decisions reached during meetings of the directors of the Jewish Agency—and one should not make an assumption based on small phrases with racist undertones that were obviously not the general policy.

But these criteria—which sometimes induced Israel to slow down the immigration of Jews coming from Arab countries—should also be offset by economic considerations, which were largely decisive for people desirous of coming to Israel. In a period of economic recession, such as the era of the *tsena* (dearth) at the beginning

The American photographer Robert Capa follows the arrival of thousands of Jewish immigrants in the port of Haifa, May–June 1949.

of the 1950s, during the grave crisis that struck in the mid-1960s, or after an improvement in the economic, political, and security situation in their respective countries, it was not rare for those eligible to emigrate to defer their departure, or even cancel it definitively. The generally accepted idea that the Jews of the big cities of North Africa or of the Middle East—with the exception of Egypt, Iraq, and Lebanon, where most Jews were city-dwellers—emigrated less to Israel than did the villagers or inhabitants of little provincial towns is untrue. The data we possess reveal that most of the emigrants lived in large cities. While the Jews from Atlas or the southern valleys of Morocco, from villages in Tripolitania, from Cyrenaica in Libya, from the south of Tunisia, or from Iraqi Kurdistan may have been full of enthusiasm at the idea of the aliyah, they represented less than a third of the emigrants.

1. See Benjamin Stora, *Les Trois Exils: Juifs d'Algérie* (Paris: Stock, 2006), 152–55.
2. Michael M. Laskier, *À l'ombre du conflit arabo-israélien et le nationalisme arabe: Les relations entre musulmans et Juifs de Syrie entre, 1948–1970, Peamim* 66 (1996).

3. Esther Méïr, "L'Opération Ezra et Néhémie: L'émigration des Juifs d'Irak," in *Ouvertement et en secret: Les grandes vagues d'immigration des Juifs issus des pays musulmans, 1948–1967*, ed. Haïm Saadoun (Jerusalem: Institut Ben-Zvi, 1999), 61–78.

4. Ibid.

5. Dov Levitan, "Sur les ailes des aigles: L'alya en provenance du Yémen et d'Aden," in *Ouvertement*, ed. Saadoun.

6. Ibid.

"They Called Us Blue Muslims"

In *Une enfance juive en Méditerranée musulmane* (A Jewish Childhood in the Muslim Mediterranean), the French writer Leïla Sebbar, born in Algeria, collected the statements of more than thirty Jewish authors, who recount their childhood in Islamic countries, then their departure from Morocco, Algeria, Turkey, or Egypt. One such author is Mireille Cohen-Massouda, who was born into a Karaite Jewish family in Cairo in 1940. In 1956 her family was exiled to France. This collection is, in the words of its orchestrator, the exploration "of a Southern Mediterranean that was cosmopolitan, a Jewish and Muslim Mediterranean, now orphaned by the Jews who inhabited it alongside Islam. A perfectly joyful, sometimes cruel history recounts it. Individual stories remember another time."

I was born in Cairo, Egypt, into the oldest and largest community of Arab Jews, called the Blue Muslims. "Muslims," because they remove their shoes and prostrate themselves during their prayers, and "Blue" because of the blue threads woven into the fringe of their prayer shawls, or tallith. It is within that community that I grew up. Arabic was the language spoken by my grandparents. A language I experienced as forbidden....
My father, from a Karaite family of eight children, was transformed by fate and by his mother's love into a gentleman, a *khawaga*, a *doktor*. He spent nearly twenty years in Paris, where he had gone to study dentistry. In late 1938, on the advice of a Russian Karaite dentist well informed about the Nazi threat, he left France and returned to Egypt. He did so as well "to marry the woman intended for him." Although he fulfilled his mother's wishes in marrying a Karaite woman, he rejected the confinement of the community and moved to the heart of the city, to the Groppi Building (named after the most exclusive tearoom in the capital, founded by the Swiss, which was sacked and burned on January 26, 1952, along with many other middle-class residences and businesses in Cairo),[1] on Soliman Pasha Square. He selected places frequented by the upper middle class, whether Christian, Jewish, Copt, or Muslim, whose preferred language was French. Arabic, the language of his ancestors, the language of his brothers, those who had worked to pay for his education, became the language of the street, the language of the servants. He made it a point of honor, however, to get his brothers out of the Hara [the Jewish quarter]. The youngest, Habib, converted to Islam for love and kept the name Cohen....
In 1948, upon the creation of the State of Israel, my father was ordered to leave Egypt within forty-eight hours. He had to appeal to the king, at whose table he sat every evening in his gambling club, to have it declared void.
In 1949 he decided to take us, my brother Elie and me, on vacation to Europe. It was our first trip away from our homeland. I was nine years old, my brother four. A certain Maurice Cohen,

my father's namesake, suspected of being a Zionist spy, was blacklisted. At customs, we were all body-searched....

It was only as an adult that I understood why, during my childhood, I often saw my lawyer grandfather, *Maître* Khadr Massouda, engrossed in the Qur'an. In the *mehkemehs*, the tribunals, he, a Jew, was arguing in Arabic in accordance with Qur'anic law to defend Muslim subjects. A man of law, my grandfather was also a man of peace. I do not know how to sort out what I experienced from what I heard. But echoing inside me are warnings that sent everyone from all sides to the cellars, safe from the bombings. I still feel the warmth of the blanket and the arms surrounding my child body. I see silhouettes of my grandparents, ears glued to the radio set, listening to Radio London.

Despite all the internal quarrels concerning the alliances, or rather, the misalliances between Karaites and Rabbanites, the war brought my grandfather closer to Chief Rabbi Nahum. In Egypt, the only differentiation among Jews was between Karaites and Rabbanites. It was only in Europe that I discovered the distinction between Ashkenazi and Sephardim. In Israel, the Karaites are not considered Jews. As Josy Eisenberg put it so aptly in one of the four broadcasts devoted to them in 1988, they are "the Jews of the Jews."

Offering assistance to the Jews of Europe was their foremost objective: the Nazis, in fact, did not identify the Karaites as Jews until 1944, which allowed a certain number of them to escape extermination. From his position as president, *Maître* Khadr Massouda made certificates of membership in the Karaite community for Rabbanites, false certificates for real lives. It was to him, president of the Karaite Community of Cairo, that members of the community turned in 1948, when the State of Israel was created, and in 1952, when Cairo burned and Colonel Naguib came to tell the Karaites that Egypt was their home and they had nothing to fear—the rumor circulated that Nasser had had a Karaite nurse. I have a precise memory of that January 26, 1952. We had been prevented, my brother Elie and I, from going to school. Over the course of the day, the streets turned black with people, the commotion of the street turned into shouts, screams. Hateful slogans rose up to us. Cairo was burning.

Mireille Cohen-Massouda, "Les musulmans bleus," in *Une enfance juive en Méditerranée musulmane*, ed. Leïla Sebbar (Saint-Pourçain-sur-Sioule: Bleu Autour, 2012).

---

1. *Editor's Note*: On that day, popular riots targeted the buildings in the modern neighborhoods of Cairo, easily identifiable as possessions of the British and their supposed Jewish supporters.

The Case of Lebanon: Contemporary Issues of Adversity

Kirsten E. Schulze

Jewish-Muslim relations in Lebanon before the twentieth century on the whole were characterized by amicability. Jews lived among Sunnis, Shi'a, and Druze, and had well-functioning trade and communal relations with all of them. The nature of Jewish-Muslim relations, however, changed with the emergence of the Palestine conflict. The first strains in Sunni-Jewish relations appeared with the 1936–39 Arab Revolt. This set the pattern for sporadic violence against Lebanon's Jews, which was motivated by solidarity with the Palestinians from the 1930s onward. The rise of pan-Arabism further underlined these sentiments, particularly among Sunni politicians. Shi'a-Jewish relations did not become strained until much later. This was partly due to the fact that Jews at the end

Kirsten E. Schulze

Kirsten E. Schulze is senior lecturer in international history at the London School of Economics. She is the author of *The Jews of Lebanon: Between Coexistence and Conflict* (Sussex Academic Press, 2001, 2009) and "Point of Departure: The 1967 War and the Jews of Lebanon" (*Israel Affairs* 14, 2009). She has written extensively on the Arab-Israeli conflict, including *The Arab-Israeli Conflict* (Longman, 1998, 2008) and *Israel's Covert Diplomacy in Lebanon* (Palgrave Macmillan, 1998).

of the nineteenth century had started to migrate from the rural areas to the Sunni and Christian urban centers of Saida, Tripoli, and Beirut. Thus, Shi'a-Jewish intercommunal contact was limited. Shi'a political marginalization until the 1970s also played a role. Indeed, it was only with the outbreak of the 1975 Lebanese Civil War, the Palestinian guerrilla presence in Southern Lebanon, and the 1982 Israeli invasion that Shi'a became openly hostile toward Lebanese Jews, whom they associated with Israeli aggression.

The Jews of Lebanon in the early twentieth century

In the first half of the twentieth century, Lebanon saw some dramatic changes: the First World War, the collapse of the Ottoman Empire, the French Mandate, and Lebanese independence. Lebanon was modernized, centralized, and democratized. Beirut transformed itself from a sleepy port town into one of the most culturally, intellectually, and economically vibrant cities in the Middle East. These developments were echoed among Lebanon's Jews. The Jewish communities on the periphery in Hasbaya and Tripoli were the first to decline. In 1913 all but three of the Jewish families living in Hasbaya moved to the Galilee and settled in Rosh Pina on the initiative of Baron Rothschild.[1] Tripoli's community started to shrink after the First World War as the younger generation migrated to Beirut, drawn by the excitement of cosmopolitan life.

The Beirut community had grown steadily in size from the mid-nineteenth century onward, absorbing the Jews who had fled the Druze-Maronite war in the Chouf in 1860, where they used to live during the modern period, under Druze protection, as farmers. This explains why this place has been called *al-arz al yahud*, "the cedars of the Jews," up till now. Those who had fled Damascus in the context of blood libel accusations went to Beirut, as did those who left Tripoli in search of greater opportunity. As the community expanded, they also moved out of their traditional neighborhood around Souk Sursock and Dalalin into Wadi Abu Jamil, which became known as the Jewish quarter. Community life was vibrant, religiously traditional, and revolved around trade and finance. Notable for this period were the *maisons commerciales* of Joseph David Farhi and Co. Ltd., Joseph Dichy Bey, and Anzarut and Sons, and the two Lebanese Jewish banking houses of Safra and Zilkha. The community also boasted a small number of writers and poets, such as Esther Azhari Moyal,[2] as well as a number of Jewish newspapers and magazines such as *Al-Alam al-Israili*, *Le Commerce du Levant*, and the *Jewish Voice*.

After the First World War, the Beirut community also assumed political prominence. This was the result of the organizational reforms introduced by the community pre-

Lebanese Jews in their apartment. Photograph by Micha Bar Am, 1982.

437

sident, Joseph Farhi, which included establishing an elected community council that became the central body in Lebanon.[3] Thus, the Beirut community became synonymous with the Lebanese Jewish community and became the interface for the

> *Lebanon's Jews were fully integrated into a state that defined itself as multicultural, multireligious, tolerant, and pluralistic.*

newly established Lebanese government and other ethnic and religious communities in Lebanon.[4] Relations with the government were amicable. High officials, such as the Maronite Christian president, the Sunni Muslim prime minister, the Shi'a Muslim speaker of parliament, and the Druze minister of defense, were regularly invited and indeed attended Jewish holiday receptions such as the annual Passover reception at the Magen Avraham synagogue. Relations with Lebanon's other religious and ethnic communities were equally good, both on a business and a social level. Lebanon's Jews were fully integrated into a state that defined itself as multicultural, multireligious, tolerant, and pluralistic.[5]

The Arab-Israeli conflict and its impact

Jewish-Muslim relations throughout Lebanese history had been mostly amicable. Even Zionist-Arab tensions in neighboring Palestine were initially seen as an essentially local problem and did not have an impact on Jewish-Muslim relations in Lebanon. This changed with the 1936–39 Arab Revolt. When its leader, Haj Amin al-Husayni, fled from the British authorities to Lebanon in 1938, he started to agitate among the Sunni Muslims against the Zionists and Jews more generally. Muslim demonstrators took to the streets of Beirut, and on July 14 and 26, 1938, bombs were thrown into Wadi Abu Jamil, but no one was hurt.[6] In November 1945, Jews in Tripoli became the targets of anti-Jewish riots in which some fourteen Jews were killed.[7] These riots prompted the Tripoli Jewish community to publicly disassociate itself from Zionism. Tensions again arose in 1947 following the UN resolution to partition Palestine. On December 4, 5, and 6, bombs exploded on the outskirts of Wadi Abu Jamil in Beirut, causing some property damage.[8] On the night of January 7, 1948, an arms cache was discovered in the Jewish quarter, and rumors circulated that it belonged to Zionist agents. This resulted in the stabbing of a Jewish merchant and explosions on successive nights in Wadi Abu Jamil.[9] On April 16, a strike was called in Beirut and in Tripoli to protest the Deir Yassin massacre. This resulted in some damage to Jewish property in both cities.[10] Anti-Jewish demonstrations were held on May 15 after the declaration of the State of Israel. While these incidents were indicative of Sunni Muslim sympathy with the Palestinians, and a tendency by some to take out their frustration on the local Jewish population, it was also very clear that the Lebanese government did not approve of such actions. Indeed, during all these disturbances the Lebanese government was quick to send in the police or army to protect Lebanon's Jews from what it saw as un-Lebanese behavior.

After the 1948 Arab-Israeli War, Jewish-Muslim relations returned to their friendly character. Indeed, Lebanon became the destination of many Syrian and Iraqi Jews fleeing the less tolerable environment of their home countries. Thus, Lebanon became the only Arab state in which the number of Jews grew after 1948 from 5,200 Jews to 9,000 in 1950, and by 1958, it had reached 14,000. During this period, life was easy and exciting. The established Lebanese Jewish bourgeoisie moved out of Wadi Abu Jamil into more fashionable areas of Beirut. Summers were spent in the mountains, where two beautiful synagogues had been built, one in Aley and the other in Bhamdoun.

When the first Lebanese civil war erupted in 1958, pitting Muslims against Christians and shaking the foundations of the Lebanese state, some Jewish families decided to leave Beirut and move to Kisrawan, but most stayed. They did not, however, leave Lebanon, unlike the Syrian and Iraqi Jewish refugees. With the departure of the latter, the Jewish community shrank from 14,000 to 6,000 in a steady trickle over the next decade. This period was also marked by an increased migration of Jews from Sidon to Beirut. Between 1959 and 1968, the Sidon community shrank from 1,000 to 150 Jews. Similar to the migration of the Tripoli community in the 1940s, Sidon's younger generation was attracted by the greater opportunities in Beirut.

Point of departure

The 1967 war was a turning point for Lebanese Jewry, as well as for Jewish-Muslim and, indeed, Christian-Muslim relations. The war itself was almost a nonevent. While Lebanon expressed formal solidarity with the Arab side, it stayed out of the fighting. Lebanon's president, Charles Helou, took great care not to entangle the Lebanese army in the conflict, not to allow the other Arab armies to utilize Lebanese territory in their war efforts, and not to allow the war to threaten Lebanon's Jews. However, Lebanon was not spared the impact of the war. Indeed, the war ensured that Lebanon's

> **" The 1967 war was a turning point for Lebanese Jewry, as well as for Jewish-Muslim and, indeed, Christian-Muslim relations. "**

fate and the fate of its Jews became inextricably linked with the Palestinian refugees and guerrillas. Some 200,000 to 350,000 Palestinians were displaced, and many of these eventually ended up in Lebanon either directly or by way of Jordan, from which they were expelled after Black September (1970). The 1967 war, more than anything, politicized Muslims in Lebanon, Lebanese and Palestinian alike.[11]

Palestinian commando operations, which had been sporadically launched from Lebanon and Jordan into Israel since 1965, became a regular feature after the war. They resulted in an Israeli reprisal policy aimed at "convincing" Lebanese authorities that they should prevent the commandos from operating out of their territory. The increased Palestinian presence, their newfound Palestinian confidence, their military operations, and Israeli reprisals set the ball rolling for the disintegration of Lebanon. It radicalized Lebanese Muslim opinion and reopened the sectarian wounds from the 1958 civil war. Shi'a, Sunni, and Druze, who felt that the Maronite Christians had an unjustly large share of the economic and political pie, lined up behind the Palestinians. Lebanon became awash with Muslim grievances and Christian fears. Lebanon's Jews were severely shaken by the rapid political changes, so much so that for the first time in Lebanese history, they started to consider emigration. After the war, the community, which hitherto had had a fairly high profile, virtually disappeared from public life. The Lebanese government felt forced to make adjustments, advising the very small number of Jews working in the municipality or as contractors to ministries to resign, as "it could not deal with mounting Arab and Palestinian pressure."[12] In 1969 the Lebanese government, at the behest of the Arab League, concluded an agreement with the Palestine Liberation Organization (PLO). Palestinian refugee camps were transformed into guerrilla training camps while Muslim prime minister Karami argued that Palestinian commando activity on Lebanese territory was compatible with the sovereignty and security of the country. Anti-Jewish incidents increased during this period. Some Muslims called for the boycott of Jewish shops. Palestinian guerrillas targeted the community for extortion. On January 19, 1970, a dynamite explosion took place in the Khaddouri Louis Zilkha Charity Foundation School at the edge of the Jewish quarter. While Lebanese interior minister Kamal Jumblatt condemned the attack and quickly assured the Jewish community of government protection, the explosion left the community shaken. Five weeks later, on February 28, the assassination of Eduard Sasson sent more shock waves through the Jewish community. Sasson had been a prominent member of the community who managed a theater in Beirut. According to Jewish community president Joseph Attie, Sasson was asked to rent a theater to the *fedayeen* group and checked with his superiors, who reacted negatively; when he told this to the interested people, they said "this will cost you heavily."[13] Sasson was not the only Lebanese Jew to be on the receiving end of *fedayeen* extortion attempts or threats. In April 1970, Attie was advised by both the French and Spanish embassies that he had been marked for assassination by radical Palestinian elements and that he would be well advised to leave the country. Attie stayed, but many others did not. Between August 1967 and 1970, almost half of the community, some 3,000, decided to emigrate "because of fear for the future and/or for the negative effects of bringing up children in such an uncertain atmosphere,"[14] and fear that they may be killed.

In 1970 the vast majority of synagogues in Beirut closed. Only Magen Avraham remained open. The year 1970 also signaled the end to the yearly pilgrimages to Saida to the tomb of Ben Abisamak and the mausoleum of Zebulon. Jewish emigration continued, motivated not only by the push factor of the changing political landscape in Lebanon and the economic decline but also by the pull factors of the attractions of life in Europe and the Americas, and the already existing Lebanese Jewish émigré communities. In 1972, the community declined to less than 2,000.[15] The Alliance schools were still running, with an estimated 350 pupils, while another twenty attended other schools, but the atmosphere was very much one of what Attie called "a community in liquidation."[16]

In October 1973 another war between Israel and its Arab neighbors broke out. In 1974 hardly a week passed without some villages in South Lebanon being hit by Israeli raids. Between June 1968 and June 1974, the Lebanese army counted more than 30,000 Israeli violations of their national territory. Clashes between Palestinians and Lebanese Christians were also increasing, while the political situation was deteriorating rapidly. This ultimately led to the second civil war in 1975. The Beirut Jewish community was caught in the crossfire by virtue of the geographic location of Wadi Abu Jamil, which was right on the green line dividing Muslim West and Christian East Beirut. In a round of extremely bitter fighting in autumn 1975, large parts of Wadi Abu Jamil were destroyed, an estimated 200 Jews were killed, and community life came to a complete standstill. By the end of 1976, another 2,000 Jews had left the country. Only 60 remained in Beirut and another 500 in the mountains. In 1978 chief rabbi Chaoud Chreim emigrated to São Paulo, leaving the dwindling community without a rabbi.[17]

Israel's 1982 invasion of Lebanon marked a new phase in the Lebanese Civil War and came as a mixed blessing to Lebanon's Jews. In their siege of Beirut, Israeli planes destroyed the roof of Magen Avraham. At the same time the Israeli presence restored a semblance of security to the community and opened access across the border. Many Jews went to visit relatives. Others left Lebanon to Israel or via Israel to the United States, South America, or Europe. However, as Israel became embroiled in Lebanon's sectarian conflict, the hitherto neutral Jews became associated with Israel and started to be targeted by the newly

Cover of the book *Wadi Abou Jamil: Stories of the Jews of Beirut*, by Lebanese journalist Nada Abdelsamad (Beirut: Dar al-Nahar, 2009). Muslim neighbors and friends reflect on Jewish residents and history in this section of the Lebanese capital and the secrecy that surrounded the departure of the Jews in the 1970s.

formed Shi'a resistance movement Hezbollah. Until this point Jewish-Muslim tensions had come from Lebanese and Palestinian Sunni Muslims. Now the Shi'a, who had become politicized in the 1970s, became the primary source of anti-Jewish hostility.

Between 1984 and 1987, eleven leading members of the community were kidnapped in an attempt to compel Israel to withdraw from Lebanon. Following the kidnappings, the remaining Beirut Jews were evacuated to the Christian enclave.

In 1989 the civil war came to an end. However, the presence in Lebanon of some 22,000 Syrian troops for more than another decade deterred both Christian and Jewish Lebanese émigrés from returning. There were still a few Jews in areas such as East Beirut, Broumana, Bikfaya, and Jounieh, but they were dispersed and had ceased to function as a community. Lebanon was no longer the center of Lebanese Jewry. However, Lebanese Jewish life continued in the Lebanese diaspora. Indeed, the vast majority of Lebanese Jews decided to settle among other Lebanese émigrés in Paris, Montreal, São Paulo, and New York rather than immigrating to Israel.

The Jews of Lebanon today

In the summer of 2009, Lebanon's Jews were propelled into public view with the beginning of the reconstruction of the Magen Avraham synagogue. Until that point they had maintained an extremely low profile. The reconstruction of the synagogue sparked interest in Lebanese Muslims in the history of the Jews of Lebanon and prompted both Sunni Lebanese prime minister Fuad Siniora and Shi'a Hezbollah spokesman Hussein Rahhal to welcome its reconstruction and highlight amicable relations of the past. A return to the amicable past of Jewish-Muslim relations, however, remained circumscribed by the realities of the Arab-Israeli conflict and Israeli policy toward Lebanon. It would require the return of a significant number of Jewish émigrés, as hoped for by the community itself, in order to assume real meaning.

---

1. *Encyclopedia Judaica*, 1543. See also Heskel Haddad, *Jews of Arab and Islamic Countries: History, Problems, Solutions* (New York: Shengold, 1984), 59.
2. Hayyim J. Cohen, *The Jews of the Middle East, 1860–1972* (Jerusalem: Israel University Press, 1973), 141.
3. Tofic Attiie, "Joseph David Farhi," in *In Memoriam: Hommage á Joseph David Farhi*, ed. Abraham Elmaleh (Jerusalem: La Famille Farhi, 1948), 27.
4. Joseph Schechtman, *On Wings of Eagles: The Plight, Exodus, and Homecoming of Oriental Jewry* (New York: Thomas Joseloff, 1961), 167.
5. Kirsten Schulze, *The Jews of Lebanon: Between Coexistence and Conflict*, 2nd ed. (Eastbourne, UK: Sussex Academic Press, 2009), 37–40.
6. A. Rahmany, Director of the Alliance, Liban I.C.4, AIU Archives. See also E. Penso, Director of the Alliance Israélite Universelle (Beirut) to His Excellency Monsieur Puaux, High Commissioner of Lebanon and Syria, July 27, 1939, Liban I.C.1, AIU Archives.
7. Hayyim J. Cohen, *The Jews of the Middle East*, 44.

8. Houston-Boswell to Foreign Office, December 9, 1947, FO 371/61743, Public Record Office.

9. Joseph Schechtman, *On Wings of Eagles*, 176.

10. Summary for April 1948, May 28, 1948, FO 371/68489, Public Record Office.

11. Kirsten E. Schulze, "Point of Departure: The 1967 War and the Jews of Lebanon," *Israel Affairs* 15, no. 4 (2009).

12. *The Jerusalem Report*, October 24, 1991.

13. Summary of Remarks by Dr. Attiyeh, September 2, 1970, Box 80, HIAS Archives.

14. Ibid.

15. Kirsten Schulze, "Point of Departure," 350.

16. Lottie Levinson (HIAS Geneva) to Gaynor Jacobson (HIAS NY), October 13, 1970, Met with Dr. Attie, Box 80, HIAS Archives.

17. Kirsten Schulze, *The Jews of Lebanon*, 153–56.

Chapter IV

Spaces of Cohabitation

Muslim-Jewish Relations in Israel

Eliezer Ben-Rafael

The Israeli Declaration of Independence promised that the State of Israel ensures complete social and political equality for its citizens, irrespective of religion, race, or sex, and guarantees freedom of religion. There is no declared official religion, and each religious community has jurisdiction over its internal affairs and matters of personal status.[1] All religious courts are recognized, autonomous, and supported by government budgets; accordingly, Israel funds more than one hundred mosques and their imams. The government also finances numerous extracurricular Islamic studies. Nevertheless, Israel's definition as a Jewish state implies a privileged link to the faith attached to Jewishness, and manifests this in the choice of flag, emblem, and anthem. Moreover, the Law of Return grants Jews throughout the world the special right to settle in the country.[2] All these are received with mixed feelings by Arabs, Muslims, and Christians, who commemorate the Jews' Independence Day as their Nakba Day.

Eliezer Ben-Rafael

Eliezer Ben-Rafael is professor emeritus of sociology at Tel Aviv University and is a past president of the International Institute of Sociology. He received the Landau Prize for Life Achievements in Sociology. His works include *Jewish Identities* (2001), *Is Israel One?* (2005), and *Jews and Jewish Education in Germany Today* (2011), all published by Brill, and *The Kibbutz on Ways Apart* (Mossad Bialik and Yad Tabenkin, 2009, in Hebrew), and *Ethnicity, Religion and Class in Israel* (Cambridge University Press, 2007). His edited works include *Transnationalism: The Advent of a New (Dis)order* (2009) and *Comparing Modernities* (2005), both published by Brill.

Demography

Those who remained in the country in 1948 were about 150,000 out of an original population of 900,000—mostly villagers, besides the residents of Nazareth and a few neighborhoods in predominantly Jewish cities. Until 1966, Arabs (or Palestinians) in Israel were subject to military rule, which restricted their freedom of movement around the country.

This population has long had an unusually high rate of natural increase: 43.4 per thousand, at its peak in 1966.[3] In 2009, out of an Israeli population estimated at 7,552,000 people, of whom 5,703,700 were Jewish, 17 percent were Sunni Muslims, 2 percent were Christians, 1.65 percent Druze, and others 3.85 percent. These figures included the Arab population of East Jerusalem (about 250,000) and the Druze (30,000) residing in the Golan Heights—a region annexed to Israel after the 1967 Six-Day War, the inhabitants of which mostly refused the offer of Israeli citizenship. Except for these groups, Arabs in Israel speak Palestinian Arabic and Hebrew. They live throughout the country but form a slight majority in the Galilee (the Northern District).

▶ See article by Laurence Louër, pp. 452–457.

Nazareth is the largest Arab city, with a population of 65,000, while most of the 170,000 Bedouin and Sunni live in the Southern Negev.[4]

In the north of Israel, near the town of Baaneh (foreground), where Arabs live, and the city of Karmiel (background), which has a Jewish majority. Photograph by Lefteris Pitarakis, August 27, 2002.

Jewish multiculturalism

Israel is defined as a Jewish state. Since many Israeli Jews are not observant, defining Jewishness is a cause of division revolving around the question of the public status of religion. A status quo regarding religion's public role was decided on in 1947 and remains in place. Its main provisions are that the chief rabbinate has authority over matters of personal status, and that public transportation will not run on the Sabbath.[5] Notwithstanding this agreement, a whole series of disputes unfold on practical grounds, though in Israel religiosity is by no means a dichotomy (12 percent of

Israeli Jews define themselves as ultra-Orthodox, 12 percent as religious, 13 percent as traditional-religious, 25 percent as traditional, and 42 percent as secular).[6] The veteran contenders against the Zionist establishment are the ultra-Orthodox Jews, a small but very active public whose party fights both for specific demands and for strengthening religious law in the constitutional order. For this party, Israel qualifies as a Jewish state only according to its response to those exigencies. The Orthodox—principally the "National Religious"—primarily aspire, grounded on their reading of the Bible, to the annexation of the West Bank, conquered in 1967, and the increase of Jewish colonies there. One more cleavage, also marked by religious references, involves the Mizrahi communities (Mizrahim [sing., Mizrahi], Jews of Middle Eastern and North African origins). While the vast majority of the Mizrahim have integrated into the middle class and secularized, many others belong to underprivileged strata and cling to some of their traditions. In many cases, they find it difficult to abandon, in the Land of the Jews, the practices they upheld in "foreign" lands as symbolizing their Jewishness. It is in this spirit that the Shas Party, headed by rabbis, enlists many traditional-minded Mizrahi Israelis, and aspires to imprint the Mizrahi heritage on mainstream culture. These tensions stem from the fact that Zionism draws its themes from Jews' heritages and cannot completely separate religion from the national identity; as a result, the role of religion in the social order sparks incessant debates.

Another Jewish component of Israeli society is the Russian-speaking immigrants who arrived en masse in the 1990s with strong human capital. They draw their cultural perspectives mainly from the Russian language and culture, and remain at a distance from Jewish religion or tradition. They aspire to become Israelis but without renouncing their Russian identity. But more than a few are politically close to the National Religious via their ultranationalist approach to issues of national security.[7]

A national minority

Under Israeli law, Arabs are a national minority. Arab institutions are autonomous in various domains. Arab colleges train teachers for Arab state schools (although Hebrew is the rule in the universities) where Arabic is the teaching language. Hebrew is taught in these schools as early as third grade, while in Hebrew schools, Arabic is mandatory in junior high classes. The quality of education is unequal compared with Jewish frameworks, and the dropout rate for Arab secondary pupils is twice as high as among their Jewish counterparts.

Arabic is the second official language of the country; it appears on road signs and in governmental publications. There are radio and TV broadcasts in Arabic, and several Arabic dailies, weeklies, and other magazines are published regularly. The increasing majority speak both Arabic and Hebrew. The primary language of Arabs in Israel is Arabic, but with Jews, they use Hebrew. Hebrew words have entered their Arabic language, and people often describe it as "Israeli Arabic" or "Arabrabya."[8]

Hybridization is also visible in other domains of culture. While Israel's Arab citizens are influenced by the Jewish mainstream, especially in housing, the number of children, women's status, and educational careers, they tend to retain characteristic models in given activities. The *hamula*, the patriarchal extended family, is still a principle of social organization,[9] even though most people now work individually outside the community, and nuclear families have their own homes. Yet, although most Arabs in Israel earn their living in the all-Israeli economy—industry, education, or social services—the living standards of Arabs are quite far from those of Jews. About 6 percent of civil servants are Arabs, though they constitute 20 percent of the general population. Arab towns form the majority of those with the highest unemployment rates. And, on average, Arab workers earn about 70 percent of Jews' earnings. This is connected to lower educational achievements, insufficient opportunities in the vicinity of their places of residence, and unofficial discrimination by Jewish employers.

Non-Druze Arab citizens do not serve in the military. Seeing the symbolic role of the military in a society at war, Arabs are perceived as second-class citizens. As a state commission confirmed, "The Arab citizens of Israel live in a reality in which they experience discrimination as Arabs."[10] These difficulties find direct expression in the area of politics.

Transnational and religious dimensions

As elicited in a wide-ranging survey,[11] when asked about their major collective identity, nearly half the Jewish respondents (46 percent) answer "Israeli" and more than a third (36 percent) "Jewish"; less than one-fifth (17 percent) opt for other allegiances. In contrast, the answer given by almost half (45 percent) of Arab respondents is "Arab," and, by slightly more than a quarter, "Israeli citizen" (28 percent) or "Palestinian" (27 percent). The contrast between Jews and Arabs is surprisingly moderate in view of the saliency of the "Palestinian" token in Arab leaders' public discourse.[12] Nevertheless, "Arab" ranks first among Arabs while "Israeli" is first among Jews; the Palestinian token also appears more widespread among Muslims (29 percent) than among Christians (15 percent). Christians tend more than Muslims to see themselves as "Israeli citizens" (40 percent vs. 26 percent). Less surprising, the Palestinian token is more frequent among the younger than the older. Thus, when summing up the Arab respondents' first two choices, the Israeli component is present in 68 percent of responses, either as the first choice (41 percent) or as the second (26 percent). The Arab component figures in 72 percent of responses (30 and 42 percent, respectively). The Palestinian component is present in 44 percent of responses (21 and 23 percent, respectively). Thus, "Israeliness" is, after all, important in the identities of Arabs in Israel, though "Arab" prevails and "Palestinian" is not negligible. On the other hand, about three-quarters report wide social distance from Jews, despite the fact that many do socialize with individual Jews as friends or colleagues. Far fewer Jews report similar relations with Arabs, which, among other reasons, is due to the fact that Jews are four times more numerous than Arabs.

At the same time, Arabs and Jews also seem ready to learn from the other about their respective life experiences, though Jews show less openness than Arabs in this respect. These tendencies, however moderate, fluctuate with political events, and each new wave of hostility on the Israel-Palestine scene has an impact on the reciprocal feelings of Israelis. This again confirms that Jewish-Muslim relations in Israel strongly depend on developments in the external conflict, which does not contradict that the commitment of Arabs in Israel to the Palestinian cause does not exclude familiarity with, and attraction to, Israel. They feel like Arabs and not Jews; many see themselves as Palestinians and not just Arabs; and a great number are Israelis and not just "Middle Easterners."

> *Jewish-Muslim relations in Israel strongly depend on developments in the external conflict.*

Perspectives

Multiculturalism is a characteristic of contemporary Israel, and Arabs constitute a highly salient facet of it. As non-Jews, Arabs are peripheral in this setting, but the rules of this cleavage lead to the polity, where the minority is unavoidably influenced by the majority but still has its own impact. The importance of this factor is directly anchored in the protracted conflict with the Arab world in general, and with the Palestinians in particular.

Actually, the very existence of Arabs in Israel as a national minority was the direct outcome of the earliest stage of this conflict. As the conflict continued, it had many more consequences; one of the most important of them is Israelis' permanent concern with security issues. In comparison, all other facets of Israel's multiculturalism are confined to a secondary significance. It is against this backdrop that one measures the predicament of Arabs in Israel. Their collective identity is divided between their "Palestinian" collective identity and Israeli citizenship, but their ultimate inclination is to be a part of the country, even if and when Palestinians establish their own state and Israel retains a Jewish majority. It appears that they basically support the claims of Palestinians elsewhere, and they themselves are divided into different orientations.

That such developments potentially exist is shown by many frameworks created by Jews and Arabs in recent decades to forward understanding and cooperation. One

Hebrew and Arabic words on the blackboard of a bilingual school, where Jewish and Muslim children study together. Jerusalem, November 4, 2002. Photograph by David Silverman.

illustration is the program known as Kedem (the Hebrew acronym for Kol Dati Mefayeis [Voices of Religious Reconciliation]), which attempts to penetrate different Jewish and Arab communities and emphasize the imperative of coexistence, which, as research confirms, may be grounded in the common values they share.[13] This has led some to suggest that the clergy might outdo politicians at peacemaking.[14]

In the final analysis, all surveys show that both Arabs and Jews are committed to coexistence and democracy.[15] Israel could accommodate the Arab minority without losing its character as a Jewish and democratic state. The Arabs could fulfill most of their demands without transforming Israel into a full binational state. At the time of writing this chapter, it seems, however, that much depends on the dynamic of the Israel-Palestine relationship. Once this issue is settled, Jews and Arabs in Israel may find a way to a satisfying coexistence. Though once the external conflict is no longer an impediment for a fair settling of minority-majority relations, the Jewish state should confront its ultimate trial: being at the same time a Jewish state and a democracy.

---

1. Alisa Rubin Peled, *Debating Islam in the Jewish State: The Development of Policy toward Islamic Institutions in Israel* (Albany: State University of New York Press, 2001).

2. The Law of Return does not strictly follow traditional Jewish religious law (*halacha*) in relation to the definition of who is a Jew. Individuals who would be considered Jewish under *halacha* are excluded from the rights under the Law of Return if they converted to another religion; others, not defined as Jews, are entitled to immigration if they are related by marriage to a Jew or have a grandparent who was a Jew. Steven V. Mazie, *Israel's Higher Law: Religion and Liberal Democracy in the Jewish State* (Lanham, MD: Lexington Books, 2006).

3. Julian J. Landau, Raphael Israeli, Daniel Rubinstein, Arik Rudnitzky, Mahmoud Abass, and Shmuel Moreh, "Land of Israel: Arab Population," in *Encyclopaedia Judaica*, 2nd ed., ed. Michael Berenbaum and Fred Skolnik (Detroit: Macmillan, 2007), 10:710–40.

4. Israel Central Bureau of Statistics (ICBS), *Israel Annual Statistical Report*, Jerusalem, 2010. Israeli Raphael, *The Islamic Movement in Israel* (Jerusalem: Jerusalem Center for Public Affairs, 1999), available at http://www.jcpa.org/jl/jl416.htm.

5. Except for Haifa, where a large Arab population lived at the time of the agreement (1947). Charles S. Leibman, *Religious and Secular: Conflict and Accommodation between Jews in Israel* (New York: AVI CHAI, 1990).

6. According to the ICBS (2010).

7. Eliezer Ben-Rafael and Yochanan Peres, *Is Israel One? Religion, Nationalism and Multiculturalism Confounded* (Leiden: Brill, 2005).

8. Ilan Pappe, *The Forgotten Palestinians: A History of the Palestinians in Israel* (New Haven, CT: Yale University Press, 2011).

9. Maha T. El-Taji, *Arab Local Authorities in Israel: Hamulas, Nationalism and Dilemmas of Social Change*, PhD dissertation, University of Washington, 2008.

10. This refers to the Orr Commission appointed by the government after the 2000 riots; its report was publicized in the media.

11. Ben-Rafael and Peres, *Is Israel One?*

12. It may be suggested that Arab leaders in Israel and members of Knesset (MKs) tend to include their counterparts outside Israel in the audience they refer to in their public intervention as participants in the Palestinian transnational elite.

13. Ron Kronish, *The Holy Land for Jews, Christians and Muslims*, www.mfa.gov.il/NR/rdonlyres/E0399E1C-CF36-4806.../ch6.pdf; and IBOPE Zogby International, *Jews and Muslims in Israel Share Values*, April 2006, http://www.ibope.com.br.

14. Robert Eisen, "Muslims and Jews: Common Ground," *Washington Post*, May 9, 2006.

15. Sammy Smooha, "Arab-Jewish Relations in Israel: Alienation and Rapprochement," *Peaceworks*, no. 67, United States Institute of Peace, 2010.

The Arabs in Israel

Laurence Louër

The State of Israel has an Arab minority that represents 20 percent of its total population, which is to say, 1,500,000 people. It is composed of the Palestinians who did not leave the territory of what became Israel in 1948, and of their descendants. The vast majority are Sunni Muslim: 84 percent, versus 8 percent Christian of various denominations and 8 percent Druze. At the institutional and legal levels, Arab citizens of Israel have never enjoyed recognition as a collective entity. To discourage any form of political action on the basis of a national Arab and Palestinian identity, the state has preferred to consider them a collection of religious minorities, each possessing a particular institutional status.

"Israeli Arab" is the translation of the official designation (Ha'Aravim Ha'Israelim in Hebrew) for the Arab minority living in Israel. But the vast majority more readily define themselves as "Palestinians" or "Arabs in Israel." They thus reject the term "Israeli." Their Israeli citizenship, then, is purely formal in their eyes: it amounts to nothing but a legal status and entails no sense of belonging to a state, which is the state of the Jews.

Laurence Louër

A researcher at the Centre d'Études et de Recherches Internationales (CERI) at the Institut d'Études Politiques de Paris (Sciences Po) and the Centre National de la Recherche Scientifique (CNRS), Laurence Louër is also editor in chief of the review *Critique Internationale* She teaches at Sciences Po and served as a permanent consultant to the Direction de la Prospective (prospective office) at the Ministry of Foreign Affairs in France between 2004 and 2009. Her publications include *Les citoyens arabes d'Israël* (Balland, 2003), translated into English as *To Be an Arab in Israel* (Columbia University Press, 2007); and *Chiisme et politique au Moyen-Orient: Iran, Irak, Liban, monarchies du Golfe* (Autrement, 2008), translated into English as *Shiism and Politics in the Middle East* (Columbia University, 2012).

The different "nationalities" of the Arabs in Israel

The Druze, who profess a heterodox doctrine derived from Shiʻite Islam and have a presence in Syria and Lebanon as well, were offered recognition in Israel as a community in their own right. Among other things, they were granted an assembly that represents their interests vis-à-vis the state, a religious tribunal responsible for some family matters, and their own educational system. Within the framework of the unusual nationality system in Israel, which distinguishes between citizenship —Israeli for all—and different nationalities (*leʻom*), the Druze are recognized as a nationality distinct from the Jews and the Arabs. This recognition came on the heels of a pledge by their notables to support a policy of extraordinary loyalty to the state. In particular, they agreed to obligatory military conscription for all men, to which Muslim and Christian Arabs are not subject.

The various Christian denominations also have their own institutions, including religious tribunals and community agencies that enjoy wide-ranging autonomy in the management of religious affairs. They have also been able to conserve ownership of a large number of lands, as well as a large network of private schools, most of them founded before the creation of Israel.

Although the Muslims have not benefited from collective forms of recognition as advanced as those of the Druze and Christians, they too possess religious tribunals. Unlike the other two groups, who were able to keep their religious hierarchies almost intact after the creation of Israel, the Muslims suffered from the exodus of almost the entire religious elite. Only one religious judge (qadi) remained, in the city of Tiberias. That very specific situation contributed toward the initial poor institutionalization of Muslims as a collective entity and the subsumption of their religious affairs by the state. It is the government that names religious judges, through an interministerial committee. The state has also confiscated most of the mortmain properties; that is, the religious foundations that represented the principal means of subsistence for Muslim religious.

The Arabs in Israel thus live on the periphery of Israeli society at every level. Economically, they are among the poorest sectors. Half may live under the poverty line. They have a very high unemployment rate and a low educational level.

Young Arabs in Israel pass by electoral posters in the predominantly Arab city of Umm al-Fahm, February 2, 2009. Photograph by Tara Todras-Whitehill.

Political representation of the Arabs in Israel

Until the mid-1980s, the overwhelming majority of Arabs voted for the Labor Party, the victor in all Israeli elections until 1977. Subsequently, Labor, despite alternating with the Likud as the party in power, continued to receive the majority of the Arab vote. The other influential parties among the Arab population were the Mapam (the Unified Workers Party, ancestor of the Meretz, a party to the left of the Labor Party) and the National Religious Party. The Mapam mobilized Arabs around an egalitarian discourse of class, inviting them to ignore their ethnic identities and to concentrate on socioeconomic status.

The Arab vote for the National Religious Party may come as more of a surprise, since this party spearheaded the colonization of the occupied territories beginning in 1967. As it happens, this vote followed a clientelist logic. The National Religious Party, a pillar in the government coalition, held ministerial portfolios beneficial to the interests of the Arabs: Interior, Education, and Religious Affairs. The Ministry of the Interior decided, almost at its discretion, budget allocations to the municipalities, and it was therefore important for the Arab municipalities to have good relations with it. In the same way, it was of interest to the Arabs to have contacts within the Ministry of Education, since the majority of Arab graduates were recruited from the Arabic-language educational sector. The same clientelist logic applied to the Ministry of Religious Affairs, which financed the construction of mosques in Israel and paid the salaries of some imams.

Things changed radically in the mid-1980s. The Arabs began to vote for Palestinian nationalist parties, that is, parties that rejected the identity of "Israeli Arab." They claimed membership in the Palestinian nation and the status of a Palestinian minority in Israel. Before this time, there was only one protest party for the Arab population: the Israeli Communist Party. It was not formally Arab, its leadership being Jewish, but the militant base and the overwhelming majority of electors were Arab. Then, new parties emerged that placed a strong emphasis on Palestinian identity by reappropriating the nationalist discourse of the PLO. However, they emphasized that they did not want the destruction of Israel but rather total equality between Jews and Arabs, and the establishment of a Palestinian state within the 1967 borders.

> " *In the mid-1980s ... the Arabs began to vote for Palestinian nationalist parties ... that rejected the identity of 'Israeli Arab.'* "

At present, three major slates attract most of their votes: the United Arab List for Renewal (Raam-Taal in Hebrew), a coalition of socially conservative movements; the Arab Movement for Change, headed by Ahmed Tibi, a former adviser to Yasir Arafat; and the Islamic Movement, which first appeared in the 1980s. The Islamic Movement, a political party that embraces the ideology of the Muslim Brotherhood, initially focused on the Islamization of Arab society by creating pietist associations, collecting funds to construct mosques, and encouraging several dozen young people to go off and train in the Islamic sciences in the Islamic legal institutes of Cisjordan. Upon returning to Israel, most of these young people found positions as imams in the recently built mosques. At first paid by the community of the faithful, many later acquired the status of public employees, either at the Ministry of Religion or at the Ministry of Education. They served as teachers of Islamic religion in the Arabic-language public education sector, which provides schooling to Muslim and Christian Arabs.

It was only later that the Islamic Movement became interested in the national political arena, choosing in 1996 to participate in the legislative elections for the first time. That choice was the source of a schism within the movement: one faction rejected integration into the Knesset on the grounds that Israeli "pseudo-democracy" would never really make room for its Arab citizens. That radical faction, led by Raed Salah, preferred to concentrate on local politics. It won several municipalities but had a brush with the Israeli justice system, which suspected it of financing Hamas under the cover of charity assistance. As a result, Raed Salah was himself imprisoned for two years, between 2003 and 2005.

The Arab minister Raleb Majadele (on the left), the first Muslim to become minister in an Israeli government, takes the oath in the Knesset, Israel's parliament, with Secretary General Arie Hahn (right), January 29, 2007. Photograph by Sebastian Scheiner.

Muslims at the Knesset

At the Knesset, the moderate faction rapidly established itself as a key player in the political life of the Arabs in Israel. Its great pragmatism has no doubt been a contributing factor. The party has not hesitated to participate in the parliamentary elections as part of a coalition of small Arab parties aggregated around clientele of local notables. The United Arab List, frequently reorganized but with a stable core, has regularly topped the three competing Arab slates since the second half of the 1990s (the other two slates are the Democratic Front for Equality and Peace, one of the avatars of the Israeli Communist Party; and the Democratic Patriotic Assembly, long headed by Azmi Bishara, who has been in exile in Qatar since 2007). The

Islamic Movement has proved very flexible in its relations with the Jewish political parties. Its leaders display a certain fascination with the ultra-Orthodox Sephardim Jewish party Shas, which in their eyes embodies an effective model of adaptation to the Israeli political system. Paradoxically, the Shas was able to become part of the system based on what was at first an anti-Zionist ideology. The legislators from the United Arab List even made headlines in the late 1990s by joining forces with ultra-Orthodox Jewish legislators to fight a bill that stipulated the extension of military conscription to all Israeli citizens, including students at Jewish religious schools and Christian and Muslim Arabs.

Ties with the Palestinians of Cisjordan and Gaza

The Palestinians of Israel maintain family ties primarily with those of Cisjordan and Gaza. In 1948, whole families were separated, villages cut in two by the armistice line, especially in the zone of Israel called the "Little Triangle," populated by an Arab majority. After 1967, the Green Line was reopened, a move that promoted contact between families. These contacts have been maintained over the years, including with family members living in refugee camps in Syria, Lebanon, and especially Jordan. Since the Oslo Accords, it has become easier to travel in these countries.

There are also intensive economic relations, though the outbreak of the Second Intifada in 2000 changed the rules of the game and made the border less permeable. Israelis now prefer to turn to Asian workers rather than a Palestinian labor force. For a very long time, however, Palestinian laborers from the occupied territories came to seek work in Israel, even in the Arab zones. The Palestinians of Israel, for their part, do their shopping in the markets of Cisjordan, and shopkeepers stock up on manufactured products and fresh produce in the Palestinian territories because of their lower cost.

Links to Palestinian political organizations exist and are no secret. The legitimacy of Arab leaders in Israel, in fact, depends on demonstrations of friendly ties with those they call their "brothers" on the other side of the Green Line. But beyond such posturing, there are no organizational connections between the Arab political groups in Israel and those in the Palestinian territories. This is even true for Hamas and the Islamic Movement.

As a result, the situation is rather complex. Beyond the declarations of solidarity, suspicions remain on both sides of the Green Line. Some young people who went to train in the religious studies in the territories were left with a rather mixed view of their stay, especially after the outbreak of the First Intifada in 1987, since they were systematically suspected of being Israeli spies. In fact, the Israelis have often used the Arab population of Israel, especially the Druze, to infiltrate the Palestinian resistance movements in the territories. Arabs of Israel are therefore often suspected in the territories of being enemy agents. Supposedly, they have become "Judaized," that is, acculturated in contact with Israeli society, and have forgotten their roots. Conversely, in the 1990s the Palestinian Authority (Sulta Falestinya) was often called the "Salata Falestinya" (Palestinian Salad) by the Arabs of Israel to emphasize how corrupt and ineffective it was, and how different they, the Palestinians of Israel, were from it. After all, they possessed their own political organizations and projects. Their desire to maintain political autonomy and their own identity has translated into a political objective, which is neither to annihilate Israel nor to become Palestinian citizens when a state is created, but to remain Israeli citizens, with the same rights as the Jews. That project is now the object of a consensus among the Arabs of Israel, who wish to be recognized as an autochthonous national Palestinian minority. The strategy, in operation since the 1990s, rests on an identification with the new concept of "indigenous people" that emerged in international agencies and that has come to legitimate their demand for recognition of collective rights. Although the situation of the Arabs of Israel corresponds a priori to that of a national indigenous minority, Israel, as well as the United Nations, has denied them that recognition. Political organizations, as well as many associations of Arab civil society in Israel, also demand the de-Judaization of the state, on the grounds that the discrimination from which they suffer is a direct result of the Jewish character of the State of Israel. That demand is encapsulated in the slogan invented by Azmi Bishara in the 1990s: "The state of all its citizens." In reality, that demand for de-Judaization contradicts the demand for a recognition of the status of an indigenous national minority. Only if the state is Jewish is it possible to recognize a special collective status for non-Jews. By contrast, the demand for de-Judaization refers to a universal citizenship blind to national and religious affiliations and based on the individual.

Ultimately, the question of the status of the Arabs in Israel will no doubt emerge as a major problem, even if an Israeli-Palestinian accord ultimately leads to the creation of a Palestinian state, homogeneous at the ethnonational level, which, by its very existence, will make the Arab minority of Israel look like an incongruity.[1]

---

1. This article is a considerably augmented version of "Les Arabes Israéliens: Un enjeu pour Israël et le futur État palestinien," which appeared in *Moyen Orient* 5 (April–May 2010). See also my *Citoyens arabes d'Israël* (Paris: Balland, 2003).

Shari'a Jurisdiction in Israel

Michael Karayanni

Shari'a courts are an integral part of the Israeli judiciary.[1] Indeed, Islamic law as applied by the shari'a courts—and that can be applied at times even by the regular civil courts—is taken to be within the judicial notice of each and every Israeli judge. The jurisdiction accorded to shari'a courts and issues governed by Islamic law are mainly within the domain of family law pertaining to local Muslim subjects.[2] Israel's Jewish state officially recognizes these Muslim institutions. The judicial jurisdiction of shari'a courts has been brought under statutory regulation in some areas, but in others, Israeli law limits the application of certain Islamic norms.

Michael Karayanni

Michael Karayanni holds the Edward S. Silver Chair in Civil Procedure and is director of the Harry and Michael Sacher Institute for Legislative Research and Comparative Law at the Hebrew University in Jerusalem. His publications include *Conflicts in a Conflict* (Oxford University Press, 2012) and *"The Palestinian Minority in Israel,"* in *Family Law and Gender in the Modern Middle East,* ed. Hisham Kassim and Adrien Wing (Cambridge University Press, 2013).

To be Muslim in Israel

The Muslim community in Israel represents 1.2 million inhabitants. Most of them are Sunni, and the school of Islamic jurisprudence that dominates the shari'a, as applied by the shari'a courts, is that of the Hanafi school.

One's religious affiliation in Israel can have major ramifications on one's legal status. For example, while a Jew has an almost absolute right to immigrate to Israel and acquire Israeli citizenship upon arrival, no such right exists for members of other religious groups.[3] Another important ramification of religious affiliation that is more relevant for our present discussion is in the sphere of family law.[4] Until the present day, the law governing marriage and divorce of local Israeli citizens is the law of the relevant religious community,[5] and the courts of such communities have the exclusive jurisdictional competence to handle such matters.[6] Local citizens who belong to one of the recognized religious communities cannot opt for a civil marriage or divorce but need to resort to the local religious institution.[7] In an effort to avoid the jurisdiction of religious institutions in matters of marriage, some Israelis seek to solemnize their marriage abroad.

In other family law matters, such as inheritance, alimony, and guardianship of children, the religious courts can have jurisdiction to adjudicate such matters if all of the concerned parties provide their consent.[8] Such jurisdictional capacity is referred to as "concurrent jurisdiction." If such consent is absent, the ordinary civil court (today the Court for Family Affairs) will have the jurisdictional capacity to adjudicate the matter.

Whether the religious court is operating within its exclusive jurisdictional authority or within its concurrent jurisdictional authority, the assumption is that it can apply its own religious norms, which in the case of shari'a courts is the shari'a itself.[9] In certain matters, however, especially those within the concurrent jurisdiction of religious courts, the Knesset (the Israeli legislature) has limited the application of certain religious norms by mandating the application of secular territorial norms instead, even by the religious courts themselves. As we shall see later on, this was done in an effort to safeguard the interests of women and children in matters coming before the religious courts.[10]

This state of affairs, under which religious courts are accorded jurisdiction to deal with family law matters of local subjects, is a legacy of the Ottoman *millet* system. Israel, like the British Mandate over Palestine (1922–48) before it, maintained the basic features of the Ottoman design of relegating local subjects to their respective religious institutions for determining their personal status and any other derived entitlement. The Ottomans, who had taken Islam to be the official religion of their empire, accorded non-Muslim subjects of a monotheistic religion, namely, Jews and Christians, special concessions. Among these was the capacity to handle and adjudicate their adherents' personal status matters. At the time, the shari'a courts assumed the role of official state courts, and thus had the residual judicial capacity in all other matters not under the jurisdiction of any of the recognized *millets*. The Ottoman *millet* design underwent major reforms, especially in the nineteenth century. The end result of these reforms (also known as the Tanzimat) was limiting the jurisdiction of shari'a courts and the creation of other state courts instead (Nizamia courts).[11] However, given the original preferred status of the shari'a courts, they have managed to maintain a wider jurisdictional capacity in personal status issues than other religious courts, even after the establishment of the State of Israel.[12]

> *"This state of affairs, under which religious courts are accorded jurisdiction to deal with family law matters of local subjects, is a legacy of the Ottoman millet system."*

▶ See article by Henry Laurens, pp. 269–279.

Muslim institutions in Israel

In light of the fact that Israel as a nation-state and as the state of the Jewish people was not interested in assimilating its non-Jewish population or working toward constructing an all-inclusive civic identity, but was officially committed to Zionist political ideology, it was accepted that certain communal recognition needed to be accorded to the non-Jewish population of the country.

Given the perceived security threat of the Muslim minority just alluded to, this recognition was of a controlled nature: to give a measure of recognition and autonomy to the Muslim minority only to the extent that such recognition did not hinder national state interests.

One of the first manifestations of this policy of controlled recognition was in respect to the Supreme Muslim Council. This body, instituted by the British in 1921, had wide-ranging administrative authority, primarily in handling Muslim religious endowments—*awqaf* (sing., *waqf*) and the administration of the shari'a courts, including the appointments of qadis (judges of shari'a courts).[13] In 1948, the council was dissolved and most of its members left the country. Israel was determined not to reestablish this body, fearing that it would become a springboard for nationalistic activities.[14]

Another important manifestation of this policy of controlled recognition was precisely the fate of the *waqf* property. Through carefully designed legal instruments, the bulk of this property, including the enormous revenues that it generated, was taken over by an Israeli government organ, the Custodian for Absentee Property.[15] With control over the affairs of the Muslim community now within state hands, the government, through the Ministry of Minority Affairs and then through the Ministry of Religious Affairs, reestablished the operation of shari'a courts and appointed qadis to adjudicate matters of personal status previously entrusted to the jurisdiction of such courts.[16] Interestingly, such appointments were made at the time without any specific authorization, for the Supreme Muslim Council no longer existed. In order to fill this legal vacuum, the Knesset enacted the Shari'a Courts (Validation of Appointments) Law in 1953,[17] under which formal recognition was accorded to them. Other Muslim

Jews and Muslims pass one another in the streets of Jerusalem. Photograph by JR.

religious officials like imams and *khatibs* came under the supervision of the Ministry of Religious Affairs. The budget for the operation of the shari'a courts, as well as the salaries paid to these officials, also came from this ministry's budget. Another step of recognition was to permanently regulate the appointment of qadis. For this purpose the Knesset enacted the Qadis Law in 1961.[18] Under this law, those with the following qualifications are eligible to be appointed as a qadi: (a) is a Muslim citizen of Israel who is more than thirty years old; (b) has proper shari'a or Islamic studies higher education or who is a licensed Israeli lawyer with at least five years of practice; (c) leads a way of life and has a character that suits the status of a qadi in Israel; and (d) has successfully passed a written exam administered by a special examination committee. The official appointment of the qadi is by the president of the State of Israel, after being nominated for the post by a nine-member committee headed by the Israeli minister of justice and representatives from the government, Shari'a Court of Appeals, Knesset, and the Israeli bar. In the swearing-in ceremony, the qadi needs to take an oath, under which he promises to be loyal to the state and to dispense justice among the people in a neutral manner.

The amount of recognition and funding of Muslim religious institutions has been the source of much dissatisfaction. For example, though a statute, the Protection of Holy Sites Law of 1967,[19] protects all religious sites in Israel without distinction, regulations issued by the Ministry of Religious Affairs in accordance with the law name only certain Jewish religious sites as protected.[20] In a series of petitions filed in the High Court of Justice during the second half of the 1990s, it was revealed that at the time the share of all the non-Jewish religious communities in the budget of the Ministry of Religious Affairs was barely 2 percent, while these communities account for about 20 percent of the population.[21] The great disparity in government recognition and funding of non-Jewish religious institutions has been admitted in an official government report.[22]

> **" *Petitions ... revealed that the share of all the non-Jewish religious communities in the budget of the Ministry of Religious Affairs was barely 2 percent, while these communities account for about 20 percent of the population.* "**

The judicial jurisdiction accorded to shari'a courts

The jurisdictional framework for shari'a courts in Israel is still found in a British Mandate enactment entitled the Palestine Order in Council, 1922–1947. Among the preserved sections of this semiconstitutional document is section 52, which grants Muslim religious courts exclusive jurisdiction in all matters of personal status of local Muslim citizens and even foreigners "who under the law of their nationality are subject in such matters to the jurisdiction of Muslim religious courts." The list of personal status matters that came under the exclusive jurisdiction of the shari'a courts was the one found in an Ottoman enactment that listed a broad spectrum of issues like marriage, divorce, alimony, maintenance, guardianship, inheritance, and more.[23] As a result, the shari'a courts enjoyed the broadest jurisdictional capacity in matters of personal status, even when compared to rabbinical courts.[24] However, as time went by, this jurisdictional capacity was limited, due in large part to new Israeli legislation that was meant to apply on a territorial rather than personal-religious basis.[25] This territorial quest mandated that the primary jurisdictional authority be granted to civil courts who would apply civil secular norms to all Israelis in a uniform fashion. So as things stand today, shari'a courts have exclusive jurisdiction only in matters of marriage and divorce.[26] On the contrary, in certain matters, such as inheritance, alimony, custody, and maintenance of children, shari'a courts can have the jurisdictional capacity to adjudicate such matters if the concerned parties agree.[27] In some issues the Israeli civil courts are instructed to apply the shari'a. This is certainly the case if an issue of marriage or divorce needs to be resolved in an incidental manner in proceedings duly brought before a civil court.[28] For example, if the wife sues to receive her share as an heir in the husband's estate in the civil courts, but the other heirs object, arguing that she was never married to the deceased or has long been divorced by him, then the civil court would have to resort to shari'a in order to resolve the issue of marriage or divorce. Another section in the above-mentioned Palestine Order in Council that was also preserved (section 47) designates a local citizen's religious law as the governing law in matters such as marriage and divorce,[29]

Muslim court in Tayibe, Israel.

which in the case of Muslim citizens is shari'a. The application of shari'a by civil courts occurs also in cases of alimony and maintenance among local Muslim family members, for once again the law designates local citizens' personal-religious law as the governing law in such matters.[30]

Shari'a Courts of First Instance exist in Jerusalem, Acre, Nazareth, Jaffa, Tayyibah, Baqa Al-Gharbiyya, and Beer Al-Sabea. Above these courts sits the Shari'a Court of Appeals in Jerusalem. Religious courts generally, including shari'a courts, have been accorded the power of ordinary civil courts to summon parties and witnesses to appear before them.[31] In certain proceedings shari'a courts are also empowered to issue an arrest warrant if a party or a witness does not appear before the court, and under certain conditions even attach a party's assets as a means of securing appearance and compliance with the court's orders. Additional powers are given to the shari'a court for the purpose of keeping order in the courtroom.[32] Judgments of the shari'a courts are executed like any other judgment by a civil court. The Israeli Supreme Court, sitting in its capacity as the High Court of Justice, can apply a certain measure of judicial review over the judgments of the shari'a court.[33] As state institutions shari'a courts need to abide by certain rules, especially of administrative law. Therefore, the High Court of Justice can invalidate a judgment rendered by the shari'a court if it comes to the conclusion that the court lacked proper jurisdiction or conducted the proceedings before it, contrary to the rules of natural justice.

> *In some issues the Israeli civil courts are instructed to apply the shari'a, [particularly] if an issue of marriage or divorce needs to be resolved in proceedings duly brought before a civil court.*

Setting limits for shari'a norms

After the establishment of the State of Israel, there was a movement to reform some aspects of the law governing personal status directly, rather than just restricting the jurisdictional competence of the religious courts. The desire to totally modernize the law in this area was countered by different political considerations, one of which was not to offend Jewish religious parties that were part of the government coalition.[34] Thus, certain pressing issues were singled out and legislation was passed restricting the application of certain religious norms, even when the matter was under the exclusive jurisdiction of religious courts. Such a movement, as far as the Muslim community was concerned, was also backed by the fact that at the time other countries in the Middle East also pushed for certain modernization in the law of personal status.[35]

The first enactment in this respect was the Age of Marriage Law in 1950.[36] This law set the minimum of marriage at seventeen in an effort to prevent the practice of child marriage. The law does not, however, invalidate the marriage itself if it is otherwise valid under the relevant religious law of the parties. Yet, in the case of a marriage of a minor, the law does give standing to a welfare official with a special appointment to petition the relevant religious court to dissolve the marriage because it is forbidden under the law. The parties themselves, as well as their guardians, have also been given the status to petition for the dissolution of such a marriage—a circumstance that can mitigate their criminal liability. As a result of pressure exerted by shari'a court officials, exceptions to the law were recognized in due course.

> *A unilateral divorce, like a polygamous marriage, is still binding as far as Israeli law is concerned, notwithstanding its criminal nature.*

For example, the civil court—nowadays the Court for Family Affairs—can grant permission for the marriage of a minor if she has been found to be pregnant or given birth to a child conceived by her marriage partner, or if the minor is sixteen years old and under the circumstances there is a just cause to permit such a marriage to take place.[37]

In the same perspective, the Women's Equal Rights Law in 1951 ceremonially proclaimed that a man and a woman are entitled to equal treatment,[38] and that any provision that discriminates against a woman just because of her gender is not to be followed.[39] The law did not go as far as restricting the application of discriminatory religious law, at least not in matters that were under the exclusive jurisdiction of religious courts. As it explicitly stated, it does not purport to change the law governing marriage and divorce. Nonetheless, the law did include two major provisions that criminalize a polygamous marriage and the unilateral repudiation of marriage (*talaq*) against the will of the wife.[40] Another modification brought about by the law was in respect to a woman's capacity to be the guardian of her children.

Concerning polygamous marriage, the Women's Equal Rights Law makes offenders liable for up to five years in prison if they contract such a marriage and up to six months if they participate in its solemnization. There was opposition to such an enactment by certain quarters within the Muslim community in Israel. In fact, a few years after the law was enacted, a Muslim citizen who asked the shari'a court in Acre to grant him a special permission to marry a second wife but was denied petitioned the Israeli High Court of Justice, claiming that the criminalization of polygamy constitutes an improper infringement upon his freedom of religion.[41] The court denied the petition, explaining that Islamic norms do oblige a man to take more than one wife but only permit it under certain conditions. The discomfort with the crime of bigamy now applied to Muslims was softened in 1959 by permitting a polygamous marriage in the case when the spouse had been absent for seven years without a word or had suffered from mental illness.[42] Whether this legislation had any effect on polygamy among the Muslim community is another matter. About the same time, polygamy was decreasing for social, economic, and cultural reasons anyway.[43]

As to unilateral divorce, the Women's Equal Rights Law required the husband to first seek the permission of the shariʻa court in order to absolve himself from criminal liability. The other constitutive element of the crime that needs to be established is that the divorce took place against the will of the wife. It is interesting to note that this latter condition has its origin in the Jewish divorce (*get*), which must be accepted by the wife for it to dissolve the marriage.[44] But given the fact that the Women's Equal Rights Law did not seek to alter the substantive law of marriage and divorce, such a unilateral divorce, like a polygamous marriage, is still binding as far as Israeli law is concerned, notwithstanding its criminal nature.[45] It is important to add, though, that a crime now defined by the Women's Equal Rights Law can give rise to a civil action for compensation against the husband.[46]

Different scholars have doubted whether the Age of Marriage Law and Women's Equal Rights Law had any real impact.[47] In terms of age of marriage, authorities, including the qadis, did little in enforcing the norms.[48] A more direct intervention in the religious norms, including the shariʻa, is to be found in fields such as the inheritance rights of minor females, maintenance for children, and custody of children. The Succession Law of 1965 allows the religious courts to divide the estate among minors and incompetent persons according to the religious norm, only as much as the norm in respect to this group of heirs does not grant them less than what they are entitled to under the Succession Law itself.[49]

> " *If under the shariʻa the female heir is entitled to half the share of a male heir, the shariʻa court will nonetheless need to grant a minor female heir a share equal to that of the male heir, for such is the norm under the Succession Law.* "

Thus, if under the shariʻa the female heir is entitled to half the share of a male heir,[50] the shariʻa court will nonetheless need to grant a minor female heir a share equal to that of the male heir, for such is the norm under the Succession Law. The Family Law Amendment (Maintenance) Law of 1959 stipulates that if a minor is not entitled to maintenance according to his or her personal law, which in the case of local citizens is their religious law, then maintenance should be provided in accordance with the secular provisions of the law itself. The Capacity and Guardianship Law of 1962 instructs religious courts to take into consideration the best interests of the child as a guiding principle.[51]

---

1. Aharon Layish, "Qadis and Shariʻa in Israel," *Asian and African Studies* 7 (1971): 237, 238.

2. Yitzhak Reiter, *Islamic Institutions in Jerusalem: Palestinian Muslim Organization under Jordanian and Israeli Rule*, Arab and Islamic Laws series 15 (The Hague: Kluwer Law International, 1997).

3. Laurence Louër, *To Be an Arab in Israel* (New York: Columbia University Press, 2003), 11; David Kretzmer, *The Legal Status of the Arabs in Israel* (Boulder, CO: Westview Press, 1990), 36.

4. See Pinhas Shifman, "Religious Affiliation in Israeli Interreligious Law," *Israel Law Review* 15, no. 1 (1980): 1.

5. See Ruth Halperin-Kaddari, "Women, Religion and Multiculturalism in Israel," *UCLA Journal of International Law and Foreign Affairs* 5 (2000): 339, 343.

6. Asher Maoz, "Religious Human Rights in the State of Israel," in *Religious Human Rights in Global Perspective: Legal Perspectives*, ed. Johan D. van der Vyver and John Witte Jr. (The Hague: Martinus Nijhoff, 1996), 349, 355; Henry E. Baker, *The Legal System of Israel* (Jerusalem: Israel Universities Press, 1968), 159–60; Amnon Rubinstein, "Law and Religion in Israel," *Israel Law Review* 2 (1967): 380, 384–88.

7. See Marc Galanter and Jayanth Krishnan, "Personal Law and Human Rights in India and Israel," *Israel Law Review* 34 (2000): 101, 122–23. See also Menashe Shava, "Civil Marriages Celebrated Abroad: Validity in Israel," *Tel Aviv University Studies in Law* 9 (1989): 311–46.

8. The shari'a court's jurisdictional capacity to issue adoption orders is theoretical, for shari'a does not recognize adoption to begin with. See Ella Landau-Tasseron, "Adoption, Acknowledgement of Paternity and False Genealogical Claims in Arabian and Islamic Societies," *Bulletin of the School of Oriental and African Studies* 66 (2003): 169–72.

9. Aharon Layish, "Muslim Religious Jurisdiction in Israel," *Asian and African Studies* 1 (1965): 49, 57–58.

10. Ibid., 60.

11. Alisa Rubin Peled, *Debating Islam in the Jewish State: The Development of Policy Toward Islamic Institutions in Israel* (Albany: State University of New York Press, 2001), 6.

12. Layish, "Muslim Religious Jurisdiction in Israel," 50–51, 58.

13. See Uri Kupferschmidt, *The Supreme Muslim Council: Islam under the British Mandate for Palestine* (Leiden: E. J. Brill, 1987); Edoardo Vitta, *The Conflict of Laws in Matters of Personal Status in Palestine* (Tel Aviv: S. Bursi, 1947), 102–3.

14. Peled, *Debating Islam in the Jewish State*, 7.

15. Rubinstein, "Law and Religion in Israel," 389; Maoz, "Religious Human Rights in the State of Israel," 356; Peled, *Debating Islam in the Jewish State*, 50–51.

16. Robert H. Eisenman, *Islamic Law in Palestine and Israel: A History of the Survival of Tanzimat and Shari'as in the British Mandate and the Jewish State* (Leiden: E. J. Brill, 1978), 169.

17. 8 Laws of the State of Israel (hereafter LSI) 42 (1953–54).

18. 15 LSI 123 (1960–61).

19. 21 LSI 76 (1966–67).

20. Gad Barzilai, *Communities and Law: Politics and Cultures of Legal Identities* (Ann Arbor: University of Michigan Press, 2003), 109.

21. Michael Karayanni, "Living in a Group of One's Own: Normative Implications Related to the Private Nature of the Religious Accommodations for the Palestinian-Arab Minority in Israel," *UCLA Journal of Islamic and Near Eastern Law* 6, no. 1 (2007): 12. See also Ilan Saban, "Minority Rights in Deeply Divided Societies: A Framework for Analysis and the Case of the Arab-Palestinian Minority in Israel," *NYU Journal of International Law and Politics* 36 (2004): 885, 943.

22. State of Israel, *Implementation of the International Covenant on Civil and Political Rights (ICCPR): Combined Initial and First Periodic Report of the State of Israel* (Jerusalem, 1998), 228.

23. Moussa Abou Ramadan, "Judicial Activism of the Shari'a Appeals Court in Israel (1994–2001): Rise and Crises," *Fordham International Law Journal* 27 (2003): 254, 264n50.

24. Ido Shahar, "Legal Reform, Interpretive Communities and the Quest for Legitimacy. A Contextual Analysis of a Legal Circular," in Ron Shaham (ed.), *Law, Custom and Statute in the Muslim World. Studies in Honor of Aharon Layish*, Studies in Islamic Law and Society vol. 28 (Leiden: Brill, 2007), 205.

25. Menashe Shava, "Connecting Factors in Matters of Personal Status in Israel," *Tel Aviv University Studies in Law* 5 (1982): 103, 105–6.

26. Mousa Abou Ramadan, "Divorce Reform in the Shari'a Court of Appeals in Israel (1992–2003)," *Islamic Law and Society* 13 (2006): 242, 246.

27. Succession Law, 5725-1965, section 155(a), 19 LSI 58 (1964–65).

28. Layish, "Qadis and Shari'a in Israel," 267.

29. Menashe Shava, "Matters of Personal Status of Stateless Persons in Israel," *Israel Yearbook on Human Rights* 9 (1978): 149, 155.

30. Family Law Amendment (Maintenance) Law, 5719-1959, 13 LSI 73, sections 2 and 3 (1958–59). An exception exists in the case of children (see below).

31. Religious Courts (Summons) Law 5716-1956, 10 LSI 34 (1956).

32. Religious Courts (Prevention of Disturbance) Law, 5725-1965, 19 LSI 114 (1964–65).

33. Daniel Friedmann, "Independent Development of Israeli Law," *Israel Law Review* 10 (1975): 515, 559–60.

34. Eisenman, *Islamic Law in Palestine and Israel*, 156.

35. Ibid., 157–58, 169, 171n6.

36. 4 LSI 158 (1949–50).

37. Marriage Age (Amendment) Law, 5720-1960, 14 LSI 52 (1960).

38. 5 LSI 171 (1950–51).

39. See Layish, "Muslim Religious Jurisdiction in Israel," 60–61.

40. Until the enactment of the Women's Equal Rights Law, women suffered from an inferior status in this respect, but with its enactment they were guaranteed equal status. See Layish, "Muslim Religious Jurisdiction in Israel," 72.

41. HCJ 49/54 *Melhem v. Shari'a Judge in Acre* (1954) IsrSC 8 910.

42. Penal Law Amendment (Bigamy) Law, 5719-1959, 13 LSI 152 (1958–59).

43. Layish, "Muslim Religious Jurisdiction in Israel," 66–67.

44. Eisenman, *Islamic Law in Palestine and Israel*, 187.

45. See Layish, "Muslim Religious Jurisdiction in Israel," 64, 68, 76. However, some doubts were recently cast on whether a unilateral divorce by a Druze husband can be validated in a civil proceeding given its criminal nature. See HCJ 2829/03 *Plonit [Jane Doe] v. Druze Appellate Court in Acre* (2006) IsrSC 60 (4) 159 (per Justice Salim Jubran).

46. CA 245/81 *Sultan v. Sultan* (1984) IsrSC 38(3) 169.

47. See Zeina Ghandour, "Religious Law in a Secular State: The Jurisdiction of the Shari'a Courts of Palestine and Israel," *Arab Law Quarterly* (1990): 25, 30–31.

48. Martin Edelman, *Courts, Politics, and Culture in Israel* (Charlottesville: University of Virginia Press, 1994), 83; Eisenman, *Islamic Law in Palestine and Israel*, 172; Layish, "Qadis and Shari'a in Israel," 260.

49. Succession Law, section 155(d).

50. Layish, "Muslim Religious Jurisdiction in Israel," 279; Andrew Treitel, "Conflicting Traditions: Muslim Shari'a Courts and Marriage Age Regulation in Israel," *Columbia Human Rights Law Review* 26 (1995): 403, 424.

51. See 16 LSI 52 (1961–62). For the reaction of shari'a courts on this issue, see Moussa Abou Ramadan, "The Transition from Tradition to Reform: The Shari'a Appeals Court Ruling on Child Custody (1922–2001)," *Fordham International Law Journal* 26 (2003): 595, 614–15.

Mixed (Interreligious) Marriages in Israel

In present-day Israel, the law of marriage is under the exclusive jurisdiction of local citizens' respective religious law and religious institutions; so, at least, is the case for those Israelis that belong to one of Israel's fourteen recognized religious communities (the Jewish, the Muslim, the ten official Christian communities, the Druze, and the Baha'i). Israel has no civil institution of marriage that these citizens can choose if they so desire. It is also important to note that under the existing jurisdictional design, none of these recognized religious communities have the legal power to solemnize a marriage unless both parties belong to that specific religious community. Therefore, a mixed marriage between a Muslim and a Jew, or even among Christians that belong to denominations that are not officially recognized (say, a Greek Orthodox and a Melkite Catholic) cannot take place in Israel, as no single religious community has the jurisdiction to formalize such a marriage. It is irrelevant in this respect whether either of the parties regards itself as a religiously observant individual. In principle, religious identity is imputed to local Israeli citizens according to the internal rules of the recognized religious communities, irrespective of their degree of religiosity. Under these conditions, for the mixed marriage to take place in Israel, one of the parties needs to convert and become a member of his or her spouse's religious community. They then can conclude the marriage under the law and jurisdiction of the chosen religious community. Interestingly, the rules that govern this process of religious conversion exist in a civil, territorially applicable enactment adopted during the British Mandate over Palestine, large portions of which are still in effect.[1] According to this legislation, the conversion must be registered in a public record, which can be done only after an appropriate certificate from the head of the religious community to which the local citizen has converted is provided to the registrar.

Another option for a mixed Israeli couple is to travel outside of Israel and marry in a country that recognizes civil marriage. Under two Israeli Supreme Court judgments handed down in 2006, there is good reason to believe that the formal validity of such a marriage would be recognized in Israel if it is valid under the laws of the country in which it was celebrated.[2] In fact, this rule has long applied in Israel if the mixed couple married in another country while they were citizens of that country. If this couple then immigrated to Israel and acquired the status of Israeli citizens, their foreign marriage would be regarded as valid under Israeli private international law.[3] Another long-held precedent of the Israeli Supreme Court is that the Ministry of Interior official in charge of the population registrar is under obligation to register a foreign marriage if presented with a foreign public certificate that is prima facie authentic. Such registration is not considered proper evidence in a court proceeding for the validity of such marriage but is regarded as providing notice for statistical purposes.[4] However, a number of institutions in Israel might regard this registration as sufficient evidence for their own purposes.

The Israel Bureau of Statistics, the central government agency in charge of collecting and publishing different statistical information about Israel, does not have specific numbers on mixed interreligious marriages. The data it collects on marriages contain only the numbers reported by the local religious communities, and, as explained earlier, these communities lack the jurisdiction to conduct mixed marriages.[5] Available data in unofficial reports indicate that mixed marriages

2008: Tomas was born

I AM ADRIANA,
DID ALYAH
10 YEARS AGO
FROM ARGENTINA.
HERE I MET MOJI,
ARAB FROM
EAST JERUSALEM
GROWN UP IN SPAIN.

2004: WE MET, FALL IN LOVE AND MOVE IN TOGETHER

2012: Juan was born

2006: got married in Argentina

2013: continue enjoying our family and being happy :) ♥ ISRAEL PEACE IRAN FACTORY ♥

At the launch of the movement "Israel Loves Iran," started in March 2012, numerous Internet users subscribed to the intercultural message of peace and shared their photos on social networks. Here Adriana, an Israeli Jew, and Moji, an Arab from East Jerusalem, demonstrate their union, formalized in Argentina in 2006. Israel Peace Iran Factory, 2012.

in Israel in which one spouse is Jewish are about 5 percent of all marriages.[6] Even then, most of these marriages occur when both spouses are immigrants from the former Soviet Union.[7] This, in turn, leaves the percentage of marriages among Israelis who are not affiliated in one way or another with the former Soviet Union a very rare event. As I have explained elsewhere with respect to mixed interreligious adoptions in Israel, which are also restricted, the governing norms are grand social structures informed by a code of separation between the different religious communities integral to the local society for centuries and reinforced by the existing conflict.[8]

There is yet another route that deals with mixed relationships in Israel, even if the marriage relationship is not considered valid under the existing rules. A large number of laws in Israel recognize spousal partnerships that have some of the same rights and obligations as legal marriages. This de facto marriage requires a number of conditions that can vary from one law to another, mainly a continuing joint cohabitation. If such a condition is present and seems to be permanent, then the couple acquires rights and obligations in relation to each other as if they were legally married. For example, they can inherit from each other as if they were married and can owe alimony if they separate. The recognition in this de facto marriage is independent of the religious affiliation of the parties and can certainly be applied to a religiously mixed couple. ●

Michael Karayanni holds the Edward S. Silver Chair in Civil Procedure and is director of the Harry and Michael Sacher Institute for Legislative Research and Comparative Law at the Hebrew University in Jerusalem. His publications include Conflicts in a Conflict *(Oxford University Press, 2012) and* "The Palestinian Minority in Israel," in Family Law and Gender in the Modern Middle East, ed. *Hisham Kassim and Adrien Wing (Cambridge University Press, 2013).*

1. Religious Community (Change) Ordinance, 2 Laws of Palestine 1294 (1934).

2. See, for example, LFA 9607/03 *Ploni* (*John Doe*) *v. Plonit* (*Jane Doe*) (Nov. 29, 2006), Nevo Legal Database (by subscription); HCJ 2232/03 *Plonit* (*Jane Doe*) *v. Regional Rabbinical Court*, Tel Aviv–Jaffa (Nov. 21, 2006), Nevo Legal Database (by subscription).

3. CA 191/51 *Skornik v. Skornik*, 8 PD 141 (1954).

4. HCJ 143/62 *Funk-Schlesinger v. Minister of Interior*, 17 PD 225 (1963).

5. Zvi Triger, "Love and Prejudice: Interfaith Marriage in Israel" (in Hebrew), in *Law and Gender*, ed. Daphne Barak-Erez et al., College of Management Academic Studies (July 10, 2007): 733, 753.

6. Ibid.

7. See Daphna Hacker, "Inter-Religious Marriage in Israel: Gendered Implications for Conversion, Children and Citizenship," *Israel Studies* 14, no. 2 (2009): 178, 179.

8. See Michael M. Karayanni, "In the Best Interests of the Group: The Religious Matching Requirement under Israeli Adoption Law," *Berkeley Journal of Middle Eastern & Islamic Law* 3, no. 1 (2010). It should be noted that these grand social norms do not encompass the various Palestinian-Arab Christian communities with respect to marriages among their members; these indeed occur in relatively substantial numbers. However, the existing social barriers do include mixed marriages among Palestinian-Arab Christians and Muslims in spite of the common national identity.

Judeo-Arab Associations in Israel

Denis Charbit

Within the context of a long-lasting Israeli-Arab conflict, and given the country's identity as a "Jewish and democratic state," Judeo-Arab associations play a crucial role in the struggle against inequality and prejudice. Since 1967, some have been involved in the defense of the Palestinians' rights in the occupied territories. Perceived as an indispensable tool of democratic society, they are also the target of nationalist groups. Community networks are very dense in Israel. Inspired by practices of sociability tested in the Diaspora, and with the recent development of civil society and of the "third sector" to complement the political and economic spheres, they now tend to supplant membership in the traditional political parties when it comes to militant engagement.

Denis Charbit

Senior lecturer in political science at the Open University of Israel, Denis Charbit is the author of *Sionismes: Textes fondamentaux* (Albin Michel, 1998); *Qu'est-ce que le sionisme?* (Albin Michel, 2007); and *Les intellectuels français face à Israël* (Éditions de l'Éclat, 2009).

Brit Shalom, the Peace Alliance

Even before the creation of the state, the *yishuv*'s cultural, social, and political development rested on the wide-ranging activities of organizations founded on volunteer service. Of these, let us note the creation in 1926 of Brit Shalom (the Peace Alliance) by the sociologist Arthur Ruppin and the philosopher Martin Buber. This was the first association within the Zionist movement to postulate that Palestine belonged to both peoples, unambiguously and without any hierarchization. It belonged to the Jews, by virtue of their spiritual and memorial fidelity to the Land of Israel, promoted and maintained by Judaism both during the exile and during times when they were established there, and it belonged to the Palestinians, by virtue of their ancient and long-lasting presence and their attachment to the land, also founded on Christian or Muslim religious fidelity. All the same, Brit Shalom was not a Judeo-Arab association in the strict sense. Its members were Jews, which did not detract from their solid commitment to a peaceful solution that respected Palestinian national authenticity. Brit Shalom recruited its members from among jurists, high officials, and academics. Several scholars specializing in Islam, who could hardly be suspected of "Orientalism" in the sense denounced by Edward Said, gave their intellectual support to the political objectives of the movement. Nevertheless, the many attempts to establish a credible and sustained dialogue with the Arab leaders of Palestine, both Muslim and Christian, in order to propose an alternative to the conflict for both peoples, and to replace competition with cooperation, were rarely crowned with success. This relative failure inevitably limited Brit Shalom's ability to convince the Jewish community in Palestine of the pertinence of a binational political solution, especially since the organization was inclined to restrict the freedom of Jewish immigration to Palestine and declared itself indifferent to the objective of a Jewish majority.

The weight of the independent actors

With the establishment of the State of Israel, and until 1967, the Judeo-Arab associations that took over from Brit Shalom shifted their field of action. It was no longer the resolution of the conflict as such that motivated them (though they were in favor of it) but rather a concern to promote the rights of the Arab minority that had remained in Israel after 1948, and a determination to fight the discrimination from which that minority suffered. They took part in struggles to abolish the military administration, which exercised its prerogatives over the Arab population of Israel until 1966, and in the demonstrations against the expropriation of lands belonging to Arabs, which was ordered by the public authorities to create new Jewish localities in Galilee.

Before considering the activities and achievements of the existing associations, we need to grasp in the first place the determining role of the Six-Day War in 1967, and then the long-term impact of the war of October 1973 in the rapid expansion of civil society in general and of the Judeo-Arab associations in particular.

Israeli domination, exerted in 1967 over a million and a half Palestinians in the Gaza Strip and Cisjordan, opened a new field of action whose importance would grow continually: the struggle against the occupation and the defense of the fundamental rights of the Palestinians. The October War played a key role inasmuch as it undermined the omnipotence of the government and called into question the centralization of power, which, in the name of nation-building, had dominated the early decades. Actors independent from the government demanded their autonomy at that time: the general public, the press, the justice system. In 1974, for the first time in the political history of Israel, demonstrations—organized by demobilized reservists—succeeded in forcing Golda Meir to resign as prime minister. As for the press, which until that time had been docile and "responsible," it came to believe that it had fallen short of its mission, because it had not uncovered the malfeasance cruelly revealed by the war. It began to take its investigative work seriously and opened its columns to voices other than those of the government and the parliamentary opposition. In 1978, in an unprecedented decree, the High Court of Justice ordered the minister of defense to evacuate a Jewish settlement on land that belonged to a Palestinian private individual. A few years later, it extended to associations the right to file petitions against the government, which had previously been restricted to individuals directly affected by a decision of the public authorities.

On the basis of that threefold shift, social and political change was taken in hand by extraparliamentary organizations that capitalized on the challenge to governmental authority and the decline of the traditional political parties by putting forth their own demands. If one adds the crisis of the revolutionary paradigm in the Western world to the benefit of the humanitarian paradigm and the cause of human rights, it becomes easier to understand, within Israel's inescapable ideological context, the rise of civil society and the intervention of NGOs in the public sphere, including associations devoted to Judeo-Arab rapprochement.

A typology, a typography

Since it would be tedious to identify and enumerate all the organizations involved in this dialogue, I shall first establish a typology of these associations based on definite criteria before highlighting their strengths and weaknesses, and evaluating their impact within Israeli society and vis-à-vis the public authorities.

First, let us distinguish between Judeo-Arab and Israeli-Palestinian organizations. Judeo-Arab associations bring together Jews and Palestinians of Israel who live inside the Green Line (the cease-fire line established in 1949), whereas Israeli-Palestinian groups have the aim of establishing a dialogue with Palestinians in the occupied territories, and therefore attract people living on both sides of the Green Line. This spatial cleavage is essential. The first group of organizations, placing the emphasis on the ethnocultural dimension, seeks to strengthen ties between Israeli citizens with little knowledge or understanding of one another. Such associations also seek to improve conditions of coexistence and to comprehend and defend the demands of

Rabbi Menachem Froman of Tekoa, holding his tallit, works for peace and favors dialogue between Israeli Jews and Palestinians. Photograph by Rina Castelnuovo, *New York Times*, December 5, 2008.

the Arab minority in Israel. The second type of organization, giving precedence to the political dimension through a joint fight against Israeli military occupation—its oppression and repression—aims to reestablish a political separation that the Six-Day War had obliterated, in the form of two sovereign states living side by side in peace.

In the interest of strengthening the social bond and joint citizenship, the Judeo-Arab associations, as indicated by their generic name, do not seek to call into question the primacy of fundamental solidarities, that of the Jewish people and that of the Arab nation. Differences in identity at the linguistic, religious, ethnocultural, and historical levels constitute an initial given that the associations accept, especially since, in Israel, living space is communal and homogeneous. This provides each community, especially the Arab minority, with autonomy in the management of its local public space. In Israel there are Arab cities and towns, and Jewish cities and towns. Even in so-called mixed urban areas, such as Haifa, Jaffa, and Saint-Jean d'Acre, each community congregates in its own neighborhoods. Nevertheless, the Judeo-Arab associations are fully aware that this community structure generates inequalities and prejudices. These two evils are at the heart of their activities. Sometimes they work in both areas at once, when their complementarity is evident. Usually, however, they privilege one set of issues, since each implies a specific mode of action. If concerned with inequalities, they wage *struggles for redistribution*; if concerned with prejudices, they wage *struggles for recognition*. In the first case, they privilege the vertical dimension, since they point an accusing finger at the successive governments and uncover their discriminatory practices. With the aid of regularly published statistical surveys and qualitative reports,

> *The Judeo-Arab associations are fully aware that this community structure in Israeli society generates inequalities and prejudices. These two evils are at the heart of their activities.*

Jewish and Arab sociologists, economists, and jurists provide a systematic and exhaustive assessment of social inequalities. They do so by measuring the gap between the Jewish population and the Arab population in every domain—from the number of high school graduates to life expectancy, from the overrepresentation of Arabs in penal institutions to their underrepresentation among the economic and academic elite. They all emphasize the need to improve the integration of Arabs in Israel into the business, high-tech, and public sectors. They recommend affirmative action measures borrowed from the American model. And they also call for radical resolve on the part of the government in favor of the Arab minority, through the financing of local collectivities, national education, professional training, and central planning. Sometimes they target specific groups: the Bedouins and their fundamental opposition to the state's plans to relocate them to the cities; the villages—still unrecognized by the state—where refugees who succeeded in returning to Israel in the early 1950s, unbeknownst to the authorities, have congregated. Struggling to find interlocutors within the administration's political class, they broadcast their activities to the general public, and these activities are then relayed by the press. When inequality is not merely statistical in nature but actually constitutes a violation of the law, they often appeal to the justice system. Operating as think tanks and advocating a reformist approach, these organizations are persuaded that the realm of social justice within which they situate themselves is more favorable to change than are struggles for recognition, where issues of identity are liable to raise roadblocks. Most of the Judeo-Arab associations, however, privilege the horizontal dimension. Challenges to the government, though not absent, are optional and depend on the pedagogical or explicitly political nature of the association. Since the principal objective is to fight prejudice—in other words, to battle racism—the principal activities center on intercommunity gatherings intended to replace mutual ignorance with knowledge of the other on a human scale. The aim is twofold: first, to discover and reinforce similarities between people who have an occupation or a pastime in common, or who belong to the same age cohort; and second, to normalize differences instead of apprehending only their threatening aspects. In short, they seek to transform coexistence from a simple contiguity in space to the sharing of values and practices on an equal footing. A large proportion of these associations work in the field of education (the Givat Haviva Institute, the Adam Institute) and offer seminars that bring together Jewish and Arab school directors and instructors. The aim is to establish personal and professional friendships that will lead to cooperation between scholarly institutions located in border areas. In the interest of going

Daniel Barenboim directs the West-Eastern Divan Orchestra in the Waldbühne in Berlin on August 23, 2008. This symphony orchestra, which Barenboim founded with Edward Said in 1999, brings together young musicians from Israel, Palestine, and surrounding Arab states. Photograph by Miguel Villagran.

further than that type of rapprochement, initiatives have recently been set in place to create bilingual schools (three so far, in Jerusalem, Kfar Qara, and Séguev) where Arabs and Jews can study together. Classes are to be given simultaneously in Hebrew and Arabic. Since the early 1970s, the village of Neve Shalom/Wahat al-Salam has brought together some fifty Arab and Jewish families. A School for Peace welcomes students from both communities for joint workshops, where they learn to handle the identity-based conflicts that do not fail to arise. Let us also recall the audacious project headed by Jewish and Arab instructors: together they wrote the history of the Israeli-Palestinian conflict (*Side by Side: Parallel Histories of Israel-Palestine*)[1] in order to compare the two accounts and the two historical memories. Finally, let us note a few sporadic or long-term Judeo-Arab artistic experiments in the fields of art, music, and theater. For example, the symphony orchestra known as the West-Eastern Divan Orchestra, formed at the initiative of the conductor Daniel Barenboim and of Edward Said, continues to bring together musicians from Israel and from Muslim countries.

Such encounters, once they have reached a certain stage, allow people to compare painful family memories of the Shoah and of al-Nakba, or, in the more recent past, to mourn the loss of soldiers who died at the front, civilians who were victims of attacks, and Israeli Arabs killed by security forces in 1956, 1976, and 2000. The reactions, variable and unpredictable, may range from empathy to identification, or they may be unyielding. The Zochrot association, for example, collects testimony from Palestinians about al-Nakba of 1948 and seeks to raise the awareness of the Jews about the denial of that span of history. It is not unusual in such cases for the Jewish side to take its distance from Zionism. Some associations, in fact, refrain from venturing into these high-risk zones and confine themselves, for example, to promoting the teaching of Arabic in Jewish schools and to encouraging school directors to hire Arab instructors, so that young students may rid themselves of their prejudices through contact with adults on the other side.

Assessment and prospects

Any assessment of the activities of these associations is a Sisyphean labor. Although the gains are far from negligible, they still appear insufficient. They are a drop in the ocean compared to the challenges that need to be met, especially among the young. The participants' goodwill and good faith cannot dissimulate the structural problems these associations face. Most are not subsidized by the government or by public funds but are dependent on donations from Jewish philanthropic organizations in Israel or the Diaspora, and on projects approved and financed by the United States (USAID) and the European Union. Furthermore, these associations struggle to keep up their numbers and to diversify the sociological profile of their members. Finally, the Jews occupy a preponderant share of the leadership positions, even though the number of Arab participants is often higher than that of Jewish members. This attests to a need for cooperation and asymmetrical exchange. It is true that a number of Jews responsive to the cause prefer to get involved in Israeli-Palestinian dialogue because of the urgent situation in Cisjordan or Gaza. Since the First Intifada, a few dozen NGOs originating in Israeli civil society, more audacious than the timorous opposition parties, were created to uncover and denounce the structural vices and practices of the occupation. The association B'Tselem publishes legal and statistical documentation and reports on the state of human rights in the territories. Physicians for Human Rights regularly sends doctors and nurses to provide care to the Palestinians and to thereby show a different face of Israel. Sometimes symbolic actions have appeared more subversive. The group Women in Black, for example, gathers at intersections of large cities to commemorate in silence the Jewish and Arab victims of the occupation, thus transgressing Jewish women's traditional role, which is to wear mourning clothes only for Israeli soldiers. Neither funders of the revolt nor accomplices of the occupation, these militants have shifted the traditional lines of the Israeli political field. Winning the battle of ideas, however, is insufficient for the political objectives pursued: the end of Israeli occupation and the creation of a Palestinian state alongside Israel. The members of these associations, though stirred by the same battle, are not of a single mind. The reformists want to restore the pre-1967 "paradise lost," Israel before the occupation, and return to a humanistic and secular Zionism. For the radicals, the worm is in the fruit: from the military administration imposed on the "Arabs of '48" to the military administration imposed on the "Arabs of '67," Israeli domination has been the rule, not the exception. For them, the obstacle is Zionism.

The religious question

Let me also mention the interfaith dialogue between Jewish and Muslim religious leaders. This dialogue is of particular merit in that, for the last few years, religion has been considered a factor that has intensified discord and fanaticism more than it has promoted concord and moderation. Interfaith dialogue is limited to official meetings between clerics of the two monotheistic faiths, such as the one in Alexandria in 2001, at which Eliyahu Bakshi-Doron, the Sephardim chief rabbi, and Sheikh Tantawi of Al-Azhar University in Cairo took part. Although the long-term results are hardly conclusive at this time, the potential impact of such dialogue should not be underestimated, given the authority spiritual leaders possess. Just as a fatwa or a *psaq halakha* is likely to galvanize passions, declarations made by venerated authorities could be decisive at the right moment.

▶ See article by Alain Dieckhoff, pp. 403–409.

This public and conspicuous dimension of interfaith dialogue at the highest levels hardly exhausts the other aspects of this type of dialogue, which are characterized by the establishment of study circles and regular support groups. There is no syncretism or ecumenicalism at the heart of this approach. It simply highlights the complementarity of spiritual quests, rather than emphasizing their rivalry. The association Rabbis for Human Rights, which seeks to make heard a voice of Judaism that differs from the proclamations of religious nationalism, organizes one-day workshops that bring together religious leaders from the two faiths. Those who participate refrain from publicizing the meetings to avoid being co-opted by the media and to remain discreet, so that the authenticity of the measures pursued can be assured.

That these associations work in a different arena than the one the media present daily to viewers worldwide is certainly an occasion for hope. These movements that cross Israeli and Palestinian societies do the field work necessary to overcome obstacles that impede the resolution of conflicts.

---

1. *Side by Side: Parallel Histories of Israel-Palestine* (New York: New Press, 2012).

In the Territories

Aude Signoles

The Israeli occupation of the West Bank and the Gaza Strip in 1967 led to day-to-day links between the dominating and the dominated societies at all levels, whether administrative, economic, or cultural. Conversely, and paradoxically, the period of the Israeli-Palestinian peace process that began with the signing of the Oslo Accords of September 13, 1993, was accompanied by a policy of separate living spaces for Israelis and Palestinians, initiated by Israel. This policy took several forms: the withdrawal of the Israeli army from certain areas of the occupied territories; the transfer of management of the occupied populations to a Palestinian authority vested with civilian power; the nearly airtight sealing off of the Gaza Strip; on the West Bank, the construction of permanent "walls" and border-crossing points, intended to filter and regulate movements of populations toward annexed East Jerusalem and the Israeli settlements; and also the barring of Palestinian workers from commuting daily to Israel. In the long run, the combined effect of these steps, all of which were intended to produce an effective physical barrier between the two populations, tended to transform the state of Israeli-Palestinian relations at the political-administrative level, as well as the territorial, economic, and cultural levels. It also led to the development of antagonistic views of the Israeli and Palestinian "worlds" at the very moment when the imbrication of population zones and the existence of common economic and security interests had never been stronger, and zones and agents of mediation existed.

Aude Signoles

Aude Signoles, associate professor at the Institute of Political Science (Sciences Po) in Aix-en-Provence, teaches Middle Eastern international relations and political sociology. She is the author of *Le Hamas au pouvoir: Et après?* (Éditions Milan, 2006); *Le Système de gouvernement local en Palestine* (Agence française de Développement, 2010); *Les Palestiniens entre État et diaspora: Le temps des incertitudes* (with J. al-Husseini; Karthala/IISMM, 2012); and *Vivre sous occupation, quotidiens palestiniens* (with V. Bontemps; Ginkgo, 2012).

The administration as a space of encounters:
Relations of dominance and mediation

The signing of the Oslo Accords consecrated the emergence of the Palestinian Authority, a new institution in the Palestinian territories whose mission was to manage the civil affairs of the populations of the West Bank and the Gaza Strip (2.6 and 1.6 million inhabitants,[1] respectively, the majority being Sunni Muslims). This creation constituted a turning point, since these populations would be, for the first time in their national history, governed by an authority of properly Palestinian central power. Until then, and since 1967, the inhabitants of the Palestinian territories were primarily administered by the Israeli occupation authorities. This meant, concretely, that their daily lives were governed by the promulgation of military orders—orders that led to the establishment of power relations of the dominant/ dominated sort, to the advantage of the Israelis, since all the individual or collective Palestinian initiatives were contingent on prior Israeli authorization in order to be carried out.

In 1982, an Israeli civil administration replaced the army in processing applications for authorization from Palestinians in the occupied territories for foreign emigration (for whatever reasons—family, medical, professional, etc.), the construction of private or public buildings, the implementation of projects of public infrastructures (such as water or electricity supplies, but also roads, slaughterhouses, cemeteries, primary schools, etc.), or the opening of professional offices for nonprofit associations. From the Israeli point of view, the creation of the Israeli civil administration, with its central offices located in Beit El, a settlement near the city of Ramallah, corresponded to the desire to make domination less visible by diminishing the incidences of direct, face-to-face contact between the population and the soldiers. Beyond that point, the administrative procedures that the populations in the Palestinian territories had to follow were generally handled through local political Palestinian officials (mayors or town representatives) who interceded with the Israeli civil administration. These contacts between Israelis and Palestinians were accepted by the population of the occupied territories, because they served the interests of the local collectivity as a whole. But everyone knew that these Palestinians, placed in a situation of intercession or of forced demand, sometimes also functioned as informers for the occupier.

The First Intifada, in 1987, changed everything. This popular Palestinian uprising, originating in the Gaza Strip and initially carried out by the youths of the refugee camps, advocated a "break" with the occupation and called for acts of civil disobedience. These acts included setting up Palestinian institutions that would be alternatives to those of the occupier, the rejection of co-opted municipal teams, and the refusal to pay Israeli taxes. Under these circumstances, anyone suspected of maintaining ties with the civil administration of the occupier was threatened (verbally or physically) in the name of the struggle for the recognition of the national rights of Palestinians.

The institution of the Palestinian Authority in 1993–94, on the other hand, led to the official formalization of the administrative ties between Israelis and Palestinians. The Palestinian Authority thereafter fulfilled the function of managing the civil

affairs of the populations of the Gaza Strip and
the West Bank, in place of the Israeli civil administration. The transfer of power brought about by
the Oslo Accords was partial, however, in that it
included neither the Israeli settlers residing in the
Palestinian territories nor the Israeli inhabitants of
East Jerusalem—nor even the Palestinians of the
Holy City, who were subject to national Israeli law
since the annexation of its eastern part in 1967.
Furthermore, the effectiveness of the functional
sovereignty of the Palestinian Authority was
hindered by the very small, vague, and discontinuous nature of its territorial basis. The zones of
Palestinian autonomy on which the Authority
could exert its full jurisdiction were not extensive,
and already densely populated. Most of the land
available for future infrastructure projects lay in
the vicinity of Palestinian towns and villages, in
rural or pre-urban zones in which all local public
intervention (road construction, schools, municipal sewage disposal, electric power grids, etc.) was
subject to an Israeli procedure of prior approval.
Thus, the period of the Oslo Accords contributed
to making the Palestinian Authority and its agents
intercessors between the demands made locally by
the different administrative and political authorities
responsible for the conception and implementation
of the public Palestinian policies and the Israeli civil
administration, which remained. The joint Israeli-
Palestinian liaison committee for the management
of civil matters (or CAC) was the specific forum

Israel and the Palestinian territories.

for discussion intended by the promoters of the agreements to receive these kinds
of demands, and to resolve the eventual disagreements they might engender. It was
symptomatic of the inequality of the existing power relations between the two parties, since practically all the demands came from the Palestinians, and because the
Israelis had the ultimate decision-making power.

Parallel to this, the transfer of civil powers to the Palestinian Authority also implied
the deployment of large Palestinian police forces, in place of Israeli soldiers. In 1998,
their number was estimated between thirty-five and forty thousand. At first, these
Palestinian police forces were seen as guarantors of political stabilization by the State
of Israel and the American sponsor of the peace process, who wanted them to devote

481

a major part of their activity to the surveillance of Palestinian political opponents (Islamists, especially) and, if necessary, their arrest. This conception of the role of the Palestinian police incurred the displeasure of the president of the Palestinian Authority at the time, Yasir Arafat, as well as of the main leaders of his movement, Fatah.

But the existence of security interests shared by Israelis and Palestinians declined in the wake of the Second Intifada, as Yasir Arafat was accused by the State of Israel of pushing his militants and the police forces of the Palestinian Authority along the path of political violence. Then a conjunction of events and circumstances brought about a resurgence of the desire for Israeli-Palestinian cooperation on the issue of security. In January 2005, there was the accession to the head of the Palestinian Authority of Mahmoud Abbas, a leader hostile to the pursuit of armed violence against Israel; then, even more importantly, there was the nomination of an emergency government in 2007 with Salam Fayyad as prime minister (a politician who cultivated his label as an independent and was particularly well viewed by the Americans for his professional past at the IMF and the World Bank) in the context of a political and territorial split between Hamas (which controlled the Gaza Strip) and Fatah (which held the West Bank). And the fact is that since then the Palestinian police have worked regularly with Israeli military intelligence to find the networks and individuals tied to Islamist movements on the West Bank.

The management of the Palestinian territories:
Closing off of Palestinian living spaces and colonization by Israeli settlers

In 1967, a Palestinian from Ramallah, Gaza, Hebron, or Nablus could go to the beach in Tel Aviv or visit friends in Jerusalem. In 1993 this was no longer possible. The "peace process" increasingly meant a diminishment of living space and increased isolation for most Palestinians.

Various texts delineate the concrete picture of Palestinian autonomy on the ground, beginning with the signing of the Oslo Accords. The Cairo agreement of May 1994 set out the precise conditions of withdrawal of the Israeli army from the Gaza Strip and the Jericho enclave. The Taba agreement of September 28, 1995, organized the redeployment of the Israeli army out of six urban population centers in the West Bank (Tulkarem, Kalkilya, Jenin, Nablus, Ramallah, and Bethlehem). The cities from which the Israelis withdrew, referred to as Area A of Palestinian autonomy, were transferred to the control of the Palestinian police, while the rural districts (Area B) were placed under mixed Israeli-Palestinian supervision. Area C, made up of Israeli military bases, Jewish settlements, and so-called bypass roads (which connected the settlements to the main Israeli population cen-

> *In 1967, a Palestinian ... could visit friends in Jerusalem. In 1993 this was no longer possible.*

ters, Jerusalem and Tel Aviv, avoiding Palestinian localities) continued to be subject to the authorities of the Israeli occupation. In 1997, the city of Hebron, with a population of 130,000, in which 450 settlers lived in the shadow of the Caves of the Patriarchs, was cut in two, in accordance with the terms of an agreement negotiated separately: the peripheral neighborhoods were transferred to Palestinian autonomy (Area A), while the historical heart of the old city remained under the control of the Israeli army.

Altogether, these Israeli withdrawals from the occupied territories were far from answering the expectations of the Palestinian population and direction. Being partial, they led to Israeli control of 60 percent of the West Bank and the Gaza Strip, as well as all the outside borders (land, shoreline, and naval), and a good part of the Palestinian water resources, by the end of the interim period of the 1999 peace agreements. Since then, the situation on the ground has not changed very much—with respect to the West Bank at least.

In the Gaza Strip, Ariel Sharon's government opted for a unilateral strategy of territorial withdrawal in August 2005. This involved the five to eight million settlers established on this small piece of Palestinian territory. This act of withdrawal, unanimously hailed by the international community as a gesture of "goodwill," was far from leading to the total "liberation" of the Gaza Strip, since the Israelis remained masters of the control of the sea, land, and airspace borders, as well as of the flow of goods and services in and out of Gaza. Their domination was felt even more strongly after the electoral victory of Hamas in January 2006. Since then, the population of Gaza has been subjected to a political boycott by Israel, but also by the United States and the European Union, accompanied by the nearly total shutdown of the borders of that area.

In the West Bank, the application of the Oslo Accords has led to a situation of extreme discontinuity for the Palestinians. Area A of Palestinian autonomy, far from being contiguous, is made up of very small, disconnected pieces. This process of cutting up the living space of Palestinian life, which concerns mainly the West Bank, is largely the result of an Israeli policy of fostering the settlement of the occupied territories—particularly intensive during the last twenty years. Thus, while in 1992 the number of settlers on the West Bank was estimated to be 112,000 (as opposed to 1,500 in 1972, and 23,000 in 1983), it reached 180,000 in 1999, and exceeded 300,000 in 2012—to which must be added 250,000 Israelis residing in annexed East Jerusalem. Today, West Bank settlers, divided across more than 120 official sites (without counting the illegal settlements; that is, not authorized by the successive Israeli governments), make up 4.1 percent of the Israeli population,[2] but—and this is especially important—more than 16 percent of the total population of the West Bank, and take up more than 42 percent of its space. The living space of the Palestinians on the West Bank was thus fragmented during the 1990s into 180 enclaves, while the space totally under Israeli control—mainly located in the Jordan Valley, in and around East Jerusalem, as well as along the Green Line (the 1949 line of military demarcation that functions as the national border)—is quite continuous. At the same time, the miles of bypass roads built by the Israeli authorities on the West Bank, mainly for the benefit of the settlers, have contributed considerably to excluding Palestinian cities and towns from the Israelis' field of vision and to including, within the space-time of the settlers, the centers of Israeli life in the State of Israel itself.

Along these same lines, the construction of "apartheid walls" (to use the Palestinian expression) or of "security barriers" (to use the Israeli expression) by Ariel Sharon's Israeli government beginning in 2002 contributed to the idea of a hermetically sealed border, from the point of view of the Israeli side. The ostensible concern, from the start of the project, was mainly one of security: to put up an impermeable barrier along the border to avoid the perpetuation of Palestinian suicide attacks in Israel. But these walls, which in 2008 ran about 250 miles long and in some areas rose to a height of more than twenty-six feet, were particularly useful in making it possible to contain more settlers and blocks of settlements within the borders of Israel. Thus, in 2007, more than 65,000 settlers distributed over seventy-two settlements were able to live east of the wall of demarcation, while 35,000 Palestinians found themselves hemmed in on the Israeli side of the wall.[3]

The West Bank walls, declared illegal by the International Court of Justice on July 9, 2004, surrounded several large Palestinian agglomerations (Bethlehem and Qalqilya), separated certain market towns from their rural hinterland, and isolated others or

Aerial view of the West Bank where a wall built by Israel separates a Palestinian village (left) and an Israeli colony (right). Photograph by Lefteris Pitarakis, July 29, 2003.

split them in two. In East Jerusalem, these walls cut off several peripheral neighborhoods from their nerve centers (universities, hospitals, commercial zones, etc.), ipso facto preventing the city from playing its role as a political, economic, social, religious, and cultural crossroads for the Palestinians.

Last, the process of territorial disintegration and of exclusion/inclusion of Israeli and Palestinian populations was represented by Israeli military checkpoints set up at the entry and exit gates of Palestinian cities and towns. These checkpoints, part of the daily life of these populations, were the occasion for arbitrary, sometimes long, often humiliating checks, emblematic of the asymmetric power relations and the perpetuation of Israeli domination. The first were installed during the First Intifada (1987–93) with a view to security, but also to represent a border between the (Palestinian) West Bank and the municipal territory of greater Jerusalem (annexed by Israel); thus, they gave rights to the use of space and rights of circulation between these distinct spaces, depending on whether one was a Palestinian from Jerusalem, a Palestinian residing in a different city of the West Bank, or an Israeli. The number of military checkpoints has not ceased growing since then. It reached historic highs beginning with the Second Intifada (in 2000), as attested by the official statistics of the OCHA (a United Nations organization), which counted nearly seven hundred (seventy-six being permanent) in the West Bank in June 2009.

The combination of these devices of control of the flow of populations has produced relations to time and space on the West Bank that differ sharply for Israelis (for whom circulation is fluid) and the Palestinians of the territories (for whom the uncertainty of passage is the rule). They do not, however, create an absolute line of separation, since many "between-the-two" groups exist (such as the Palestinians of East Jerusalem and the Israeli Palestinians, who can circulate freely within the West Bank and Israel), and because the inhabitants of the West Bank and the Gaza Strip since then have acquired the habit of getting around these checkpoints that violate their freedom of circulation. But the period of the Second Intifada stiffened Israeli security practices and led to the existence of "no-rights" zones targeting the two main population groups and leading to a use of highway networks that borders on segregation. Indeed, since 2000, Israeli citizens (Jews) are forbidden to enter the autonomous Palestinian cities (classified as Area A), while access to numerous portions of bypass roads or areas classified as C areas is restricted for Palestinians: this is notably the

> *The Israeli figures in everyday Palestinian life consist of no more than the soldier and the settler.*

case with the Jordan Valley, and, in the western part of the territory, Palestinian spaces that have been hemmed in between the Green Line and the Israeli wall.

The increasingly close spatial imbrication of the areas of Israeli and Palestinian populations on the West Bank is therefore accompanied by a process of confinement and separation of the spaces of Palestinian and Israeli life—which has become increasingly acute since the early 2000s.

An economy under dependency

The economy has led to extensive and frequent exchanges since 1967 between Israelis and Palestinians—but of unequal nature. Palestinian society serves mainly as a reservoir of manual labor and easy markets for the Israeli economy. There were 100,000 Palestinians working in construction and public works, manufacturing, housework, and agriculture at the beginning of the 1990s. During the entire period of occupation, working in Israel was considered an act of treason, though it was acknowledged that the financial gain it made possible was important for maintaining the family economy. This widespread opinion became less absolute with the opening of peace negotiations. Beginning in 1994, the economic activity of the Palestinian territories was framed by the Paris Protocol. This text perpetuated the unequal system of exchanges that existed during the occupation years, to the detriment of the Palestinian economy. In the commercial domain, it imposed a quota system on the Palestinians for both exported and imported products. It also required that Palestinians respect restrictions on the volume of goods exchanged. The administrative procedures this involved were often long and costly, and with no guarantee of results. They induced most Palestinian entrepreneurs to work through the intermediary of Israeli import-export subcontractors to facilitate the process.

Parallel to this, the Palestinians' freedom of circulation was also restricted by the institutionalization of a system of work permits. This system was introduced beginning with the First Intifada for "security" reasons. It allowed Israeli management to profile individuals allowed to enter Israeli territory to work. The criteria for giving work permits evolved according to the changing political situation, but the overall tendency was always to keep politically militant Palestinians (current or past) out of the Israeli labor market. This is probably why the inhabitants of Gaza were kept much more "under surveillance" by means of this control device than those of the West Bank—the State of Israel having always considered the Gaza Strip as harboring more "undesirables" than the West Bank. Moreover, this system of work permits has also been used by the Israeli army as a means of collective punishment regarding the populations of the Palestinian territories. Indeed, whenever an attack was perpetrated on Israeli territory, the flow of workers was considerably slowed down. Similarly, since the takeover of control of Gaza by the Islamists in June 2007, no inhabitant of that territory has been allowed by Israeli security services to cross the border.

Thus, in the long run, this system of work permits—the acquisition of which was made obligatory during the Oslo period—has brought about a recurrent fluctuation of work mobility from Palestine toward Israel and has considerably reduced the number of Palestinian workers used in Israel. In 1996, this number was 25,000, due to the closing off of the Palestinian territories; in 1999, in an "enabling" political context, it reached about 140,000, plus 60,000–90,000 clandestine workers and some 10,000 skilled workers in the settlements. In 2002, after two years of Intifada, it fell to 16,000, and, in 2007, oscillated between 63,000 and 67,000 (only the inhabitants of the West Bank being relevant since that year).

Beyond the negative impact that these restrictions of circulation had on the economic development of the Palestinian territories (which had a decrease of GNP of 30 percent between 1993 and 2000), the marginalizing of the Palestinians from the Israeli workforce increased mutual ignorance—especially among the younger generations. Thus, while during the preceding generation the parents rubbed shoulders in the factories and Israeli kibbutzim, and could share both moments of conviviality and struggles stemming from their common membership in the same workaday world, their children's generation was stricken with massive unemployment (even for the most educated) and the absence of economic perspectives. Above all, that younger generation no longer shared spaces of daily socializing with the Other—in which the values of solidarity or mutual assistance could be put into practice. Hebrew, a language assimilated in the workplace, in daily exchanges with the Israeli civil administration, or through the Israeli media or a (long) stay in prison, was less and less known by young Palestinians who henceforth had "native-born" intermediaries charged with translating (in all senses of the word) their demands to the Israelis, satellite television in Arabic, and spaces for socialization and transmission of their identity, more and more "virtual" and full of imagery.

Palestinians wait for permission to cross the wall separating the city of Bethlehem, in the West Bank and Jerusalem, in order to attend Friday prayer at Al-Aqsa Mosque. Photograph by Oded Balilty, October 6, 2006.

As for the Israelis, they would sometimes shop in the more or less informal markets of the Palestinian cities along the border during the first years of Oslo. They used to buy all kinds of things (fruits and vegetables, sundries, portable phones, etc.), attracted by the low prices. Some Israelis would go for treatment on the West Bank because of the low cost of medical care from the Palestinians, relative to Israel. Others, less numerous, went to spend their evenings in Ramallah in the "with-it" bars of the city. But the Second Intifada put a sudden end to the visits of those Israeli citizens to the interior of the Palestinian territories.

Militant sociability and spaces of cultural encounter

Assistance to Palestinian political prisoners and the denunciation of civil rights violations perpetrated in the occupied territories have, since 1967, been the result of joint Israeli-Palestinian actions taken by associations or collectivities of lawyers. B'Tselem, Hamoked, and the Alternative Information Center are the main NGOs opposing targeted assassinations, arbitrary arrests, forced deportations, house arrests, and collective punishments of populations. They often acted in concert with their Palestinian counterparts, al-Haq in Ramallah, "Law" in Jerusalem (now closed), and the Palestinian Center for Human Rights in Gaza. These NGOs are supported by Israeli pacifist associations, such as Women in Black, which demand the respect of humanitarian rights and international law; from 1970 to 1980, they represented a very small minority of the Israeli population, their actions largely viewed as illegitimate. After the Oslo Accords, the base of these NGOs broadened somewhat. Since 2002, some Israeli-Palestinian actions against the construction of the Wall have helped raise international awareness of the cause, but remain very marginal.

As for the culture, it unites a small fraction of Israeli and Palestinian intellectuals. During the period of the occupation, writers, journalists, and academics from both sides have exchanged views on the future of the territories by the intermediary of the press or in private meetings. Several local individual initiatives have also promoted mutual exchanges and understanding. The Israeli film *Arna's Children* (2004) bears testimony to this. It tells the story of a Jewish woman who arrives in Israel in the 1950s and devotes herself to the children of the refugee camp of Jenin (West Bank), imbuing them with her passion for the theater.

> *After the signing of the Oslo Accords, cultural exchanges have become more frequent and official.*

See article on Judeo-Arab associations, pp. 471–478.

After the signing of the Oslo Accords, cultural exchanges have become more frequent and official. For example, there are many research seminars organized around the themes of peace, refugees, and also of Jerusalem. These meetings follow closely in tandem with the agenda of diplomatic negotiations. Some artistic initiatives have left a deep impression on many, such as the jazz evenings of the Flamingo Club in Ramallah, which attract Jewish and Palestinian musicians around the Israeli-American saxophonist Arnie Lawrence and his group Blues for Peace. These initiatives have, in their time, made less of a stir than the media-intense concert given in Ramallah on August 21, 2005, by the West-Eastern Divan Orchestra, the Israeli-Arab musical ensemble of Daniel Barenboim, conductor of the world-famous Argentine Jewish orchestra. But they have touched a more popular audience.

---

1. According to the Palestinian Central Bureau of Statistics (PCBS) of 2012.

2. According to the figures of the Israeli Ministry of the Interior, more than 300,000 Israelis were living on the West Bank in 2009; that is, 4.1 percent of the total population of the State of Israel.

3. Source: Office for the Coordination of Humanitarian Affairs (OCHA), 2007.

Survival of the Jewish Community in Turkey

Nora Seni

In 1923, the year Mustafa Kemal Atatürk's Republic of Turkey was created, there were 78,000 members of the Jewish community in Turkey. By the 2000s, the figure had fallen to 17,000. That demographic decline, which even now continues at a slower pace, stands in contrast to the rather prosperous situation of the Jewish population, whose institutions have experienced a clear revival since the late 1990s. That paradox is an expression of the complex relations between the Turkish nation and its Jewish community, and it demonstrates equally complex connections between history and memory. Despite the drop in its population, the Jewish community of Turkey remains the largest in the Balkans region, the Middle East, and the Caucasus.

Nora Seni

A professor at the Université Paris 8, director of the "Mediterranean and Cities" program, Nora Seni was director of the Institut Français d'Études Anatoliennes in Istanbul from 2008 to 2012. Her works include *Les inventeurs de la philanthropie juive* (La Martinière, 2005).

The preoccupation with demographics: Minorities in Turkey

Immediately following the creation of the secular Republic of Turkey by Mustafa Kemal, the Jewish community represented nearly 90,000 of the 14 million inhabitants; by 1955, it represented only 46,000 of Turkey's 24 million residents. The largest emigration occurred with the creation of the State of Israel, and that trend, whose driving force was primarily economic, continued into the 1960s. At present, departures for Israel and other countries are estimated at about a hundred a year.[1] It is customary to distinguish the economic motives for exile from the motives of persecution and segregation. This distinction overlooks the fact that an economic situation that impels someone to leave is at times the result of segregation, so-called national preferences. Such was the case, especially in the public sector, upon the creation of the Republic of Turkey, even though the republic was established on secular foundations that theoretically endowed everyone with citizenship and equal rights. Hence, in a book published in 2011, Vitali Hakko, a Jewish retailer and industrialist, founder in the 1960s of one of the first department stores in Istanbul and of the Vakko clothing line, tells the story of the abrupt dismissal of his father in 1925, following the nationalization of the Compagnie Française des Chemins de Fer (French Railway Company).[2]

In fact, at the end of World War I, the multiethnic, multinational Ottoman Empire disappeared, in favor of a Muslim Turkish national state that established itself on the entire territory of the Anatolian peninsula and on a part of Thrace, where the Muslim element, including Kurds, was in the majority. Muslims became an even larger majority as a result of the massacres and forced exodus of the Armenians in 1915. Gaining strength after the founding of the republic through population exchanges with Greece, the demographic "preoccupation" in the last decades of the Ottoman Empire would lie behind the Kemalist policy of homogenization, or "Turkification."[3] Sometimes endeavoring to appropriate, with greater or lesser brutality, the patrimony held by the non-Muslim minorities and to encourage them to leave, sometimes using linguistic constraints (campaigns to ban in public spaces the use of Greek, Armenian, and Judeo-Spanish, the language used by the Jews in Turkey), this policy of homogenizing the population would be modulated as a function of the political context (World War II, the application for admittance to the European Union, the new regional policy that took shape in Turkey in the 2010s, relations with Israel).

The end of historiographical amnesia

Since the 1990s, there has been a clear reorientation in the historiography of the Jews of Turkey. Scholarly concerns about historical truth have supported the recent rise in research and the increase in publications by Turkish Muslim academics on one hand and, on the other, by the businessman turned essayist, historian, and editor Rifat Bali. These works are dissipating the amnesia of the official history of contemporary Turkey, as it is transmitted in textbooks and in the interdicts of nationalism. They report both on the "events of Thrace,"[4] that is, the pogroms of 1934 that led Jewish families of Edirne, Tekirdag, and Kirklareli to flee Istanbul, and on the wealth tax (1942),[5] which particularly affected the Jews and bankrupted many of them.

> **Scholarly concerns about historical truth have supported the recent rise in research and the increase in publications by Turkish Muslim academics.**

They provide information on the violence of September 1955,[6] which targeted the shops and offices of the Greeks, Jews, and Armenians. The truth about Nazi sympathies during World War II among the magnates of the Social Democratic press—the Nadi family, owners and columnists of the daily *Cumhuriyet*, who were close to the Kemalist government—was no doubt more difficult to establish.[7] It was equally difficult to determine the proportion of reality contained in the image of "Turkey as the savior of European Judaism" during World War II. The German historian Corry Guttstadt's *Turkey, the Jews, and the Holocaust*, translated into Turkish and published in 2012, arrived at an opportune moment and shed light on Turkey's role vis-à-vis the Jews during that war.[8] These aspects of scholarly literature, which have raised overall awareness, continue to be ignored by official history and are not always taken into account in the educational materials of the national education system.

Turkish "tolerance"

Parallel to that rapid expansion in scholarship, an official rhetoric is being elaborated, primarily targeting international opinion. Turkey, claiming to be heir to the Ottoman Empire in terms of its multinational composition, emphasizes the tradition of "tolerance" in that country, its "mosaic" of religions, its "multicultural rainbow" society. The AKP (Adalet ve Kalkinma Partisi [Justice and Development Party]), in power since 2002, which defines itself as "conservative Muslim," is exploiting that claim, both to support its application for membership in the European Union and to make the best of the virulent anti-Israeli declarations of Prime Minister Tayyip Erdogan. The image of the mosaic of cultures also functioned as a major talking point of the Istanbul 2010 European Capital of Culture Agency. For the first time in the Turkish public space, in the media and on billboards, you could hear and see Greek-, Armenian-, and Jewish-sounding names of people being thanked for their presence on Turkish soil.

These new dynamics are converging with a sincere nostalgia on the part of Turkish intellectuals for the lost cosmopolitanism of cities such as Istanbul, Izmir, Antioch, and Edirne. Such longing pervades the novels and novellas of Turkish writers.

In addition to this set of factors, the published memoirs of Jewish businessmen are joining the passel of success stories by Turkish industrialists that highlight their philanthropy.[9] Although hagiographic, these works teem with details of interest to historians.

Convergences, alliances

Apart from the historiographical boom, other developments make it possible to fend off the catastrophic view that the end of Judaism in Turkey is inexorably approaching. Jewish community institutions are becoming more diverse and are opening up to Turkish society as a whole, presaging better integration into European and international Judaism. Lines of convergence with the official policies of Turkey are appearing. The relations between contemporary Jews and Turks are not heir to a legacy of armed conflict or massacres, as is the case for Greek-Turkish and Armenian-Turkish relations. As a result, the survival of the Jewish community has widely been put forward to bear witness to the tradition of "Turkish tolerance." The Quincentennial Foundation (marking the arrival of the Iberian Jews in the Ottoman Empire) was created in 1992, specifically to allow the Jewish elites of Turkey associated with the business world to raise inter-

> *The relations between contemporary Jews and Turks are not heir to a legacy of armed conflict or massacres, as is the case for Greek-Turkish and Armenian-Turkish relations.*

national awareness about the hospitality of the Turks. The Jewish community is therefore expected to lobby, especially in the United States, to deny the status of genocide to the massacres of the Armenians of Anatolia in 1915.

The Turkish-Israeli rapprochement also dates to the 1990s and included military cooperation. It was brutally suspended in the wake of the Gaza War in December 2008. Since then, Prime Minister Tayyip Erdogan's anti-Israeli harangues have become constants of the new regional Turkish policy and have won over "the Arab streets." Immediately following that war, the prime minister made a declaration that chilled members of the Jewish community: he conflated Jews and Israelis, regretting that "the Jews of Spain were welcomed into the Ottoman Empire five hundred years ago." Since then, however, he has continually specified that his invectives are not about "Jewish citizens of Turkey." But the affair of the Turkish ship *Mavi Marmara*, en route to Gaza and violently taken over by the Israeli army on May 31, 2010, resulting in nine dead, deepened the fracture.

Culture

Parallel to the new openness of the Jewish community in the 1990s, a movement has been attempting to revive Judeo-Spanish. A French–Judeo-Spanish dictionary was published,[10] the Jewish community weekly *Salom* added a supplement in Judeo-Spanish called *El Amaneser*, and the Sephardim Cultural and Research Center of Istanbul was created.

Furthermore, the Jewish primary school and high school buildings in Ulus (a residential neighborhood in Istanbul) were renovated in 1994. Six hundred and twenty students were enrolled there in 2012. The Quincentennial Foundation also created the Museum of Turkish Jews.

Although these institutions rely solely on the devotion of a few, it is possible to believe that the linguistic and educational aspect of the "Turkification" policy has run its course, and that the Jewish community is mobilizing to save parts of its cultural heritage from oblivion.

Since 2005 the Jewish community of Istanbul, like the Jews of England who came up with the idea, have held Limmud Days, a demonstration aimed, among other things, at "learning and teaching" and at "broadening the horizons of Judaism." On these occasions, meetings take place with invited Turkish Muslim

Salom, the weekly paper of the Jewish community in Turkey (since 1947), in Turkish, and the monthly *El Amaneser* in Judeo-Spanish.

academics, journalists, and artists. All these participants assure communication between worlds that have until now been somewhat isolated from each other.

Convergences, alliances (continued)

Turkey was spared by World War II, which stopped at its borders. Its intellectuals did not participate in the horror, doubts, and questions resulting from the discovery of the death camps in Europe. The Turkish intellectual world has remained rather remote from the work of conscience that followed, and from its effects on contemporary thought. The Jews of Turkey were no exception, even though they mourned their cousins and families by marriage, deported from Salonika in 1944, primarily to Treblinka and Auschwitz-Birkenau. They are now gradually associating themselves with European Jewish memory and are adopting the memorial rituals. The Jewish community has religiously commemorated Shoah Day since 1980. And, since 2011, in memory of the liberation of the Auschwitz camp, it has held a public ceremony, covered by the media, at which representatives of the Turkish Ministry of Foreign Affairs, the governor of Istanbul, academics, and intellectuals participate. This event arose from the desire of the Turkish government to join the Task Force for International Cooperation on Holocaust Education, Remembrance, and Research (ITF). Thirty European countries, the United States, Canada, Israel, and Argentina are members of this group. The Stockholm Declaration (2000) was its founding act, and it made the signatory countries pledge to encourage research on the Shoah and to teach it. It also stipulates that all archives in the signatory nations having to do with World War II be opened. At the same time, since 2010, Turkey has welcomed the events of the Aladdin Project, an international organization based in Paris whose purpose is to provide, in the different languages in use in Muslim countries, a corpus of eyewitness statements and historical documents on the Shoah. In addition, state television purchased, translated (with the aid of that same organization), and, in spring 2012, broadcast in its entirety Claude Lanzmann's film *Shoah*.

---

1. Interview on July 28, 2012, with Sami Herman, president of the Jewish community of Turkey.
2. Vitali Hakko, *My Life: Vakko* (Istanbul: Libra, 2011), 23.
3. Rifat Bali, *Model Citizens of the State: The Jews of Turkey during the Multi-Party Raid* (Lanham, MD: Rowman & Littlefield, 2012).
4. Rifat Bali, *Trakya olaylari* (Istanbul: Libra Kitap, 2012).
5. Ayhan Aktar, *Varlik vergisi ve "Turklestirme" Politikalari* [The Wealth Tax and "Turkification" Policies] (Istanbul: Iletisim Yayinlari, 2008); Rifat Bali, ed., *The "Varlik Virgisi" Affair: A Study on Its Legacy—Selected Documents* (Istanbul: Isis Press, 2005).
6. Dilek Guven, *6–7 Eylül olaylari* [The Events of September 6–7, 1955] (Istanbul: Iletisim, 2005); Rifat Bali, ed., *6–7 Eylül olaylari 1955 Olaylari: Taniklar-Hatiralar* (Istanbul: Libra, 2010).
7. Cemil Kocak, *Turkiye'de Milli Sef donemi (1938–45)* (Istanbul: Iletisim, 1996).
8. Corry Guttstadt, *Die Türkei, die Juden und der Holocaust* (Berlin: Assoziation A, 2008).
9. Mehmet Gundem, *Luzumlu adam Ishak Alaton* (Istanbul, 2012); Hakko, *My Life: Vakko*; Bernar Nahum, *Koc'ta 44 yilin* (Istanbul: Milliyet Yayinlari, 1988).
10. Klara Perahya and Eli Perahya, eds., *Dictionnaire français–judéo-espagnol* (Paris: Langues et Monde, 1998).

Iranian Paradoxes
Katajun Amirpur

Iran is a country that eludes any simple explanatory model. This is equally true for the relations that the state and the society maintain with the Jewish minority. Although the positions that President Mahmoud Ahmadinejad has taken are violently anti-Zionist and openly negationist, Iran remains one of the only countries in the Muslim world to be inhabited by a substantial Jewish community, estimated at about 25,000. That remnant is most certainly linked to the antiquity of the Jewish settlement in Persia, which dates to the sixth century B.C.E., and to the Jews' active social and cultural involvement and participation. As a religious minority, the Jews

Katajun Amirpur

Professor at the University of Hamburg in Germany, Katajun Amirpur is a specialist in Islam and in Muslim societies, particularly Iran. Her publications include *Die Entpolitisierung des Islam: Abdolkarim Soruss Denken und Wirkung in der Islamischen Republik Iran* (Ergon-Verlag, 2003); and *Schauplatz Iran* (Herder, 2004).

are subjected to the discriminatory rules formulated by the Islamic Republic of Iran. So too are other religious minorities, in some cases even more rigorously. In a country officially hostile to the State of Israel, a distinction is repeatedly made, not only at the political level but also within civil society, between "its" Jews, therefore Iranians, and the Zionists.

The political roots of anti-Zionism

The prehistory of the current state of anti-Zionism goes back to the 1960s. On July 24 of that year, Shah Mohammad Reza Pahlavi recognized the State of Israel, if not de jure then at least de facto. That recognition was condemned by the Arab League and led to a diplomatic break with Egypt. Subsequently, Iran sought to cooperate with the Jewish state, purchasing Israeli arms and seeking out a large number of Israeli experts, who also provided expertise and were involved as military advisers and instructors for SAVAK, the shah's ill-famed secret service. In a different arena, Iran had welcomed the Jewish nationals of Iraq who were fleeing persecution and dictatorship.

⟩ See article by Michael M. Laskier, pp. 415–433.

Ruhollah Khomeini, the future guide of the Islamic revolution, harshly criticized that close cooperation with Israel and attacked the shah, calling him a "crypto-Jew" and Israel's lackey. Khomeini held the West, the Jews, and their henchman Mohammad Reza Pahlavi responsible for the problems of Iran.[1] This polemic resonated deeply with the detractors of the regime, for whom the shah was the real adversary. According to them, the fight against the shah entailed a critique of Israel and the United States. This was the beginning of the resentment against America and the State of Israel, still so strong today. The harshness of this polemic is also reflected in the literature written about those years. It shows that the population did not often make the distinction between the Jews of Iran and the Israelis, supporters of the shah. The Iranian novelist Gina Nahai, living in the United States, has offered an example in *Caspian Rain*,[2] which depicts the frictions within late-1970s Iranian society as they related to the Jews. After the 1978 (or 1979) revolution, the condemnation of the Iranian Jews encompassed without distinction the collaboration between the shah's regime and Israel and the lucrative business affairs of some Jews under his reign. The reproaches were similar: spying for Israel, sympathy for Zionism, corruption, and treason.[3] Tens of thousands of Iranians of the Jewish faith left the country at the time, in fear of an uncertain future. Ruya Hakkakiyan, the author of *Journey from the Land of No*, the story of a young girl in Khomeini's Iran, provides a concrete illustration. When the family discovers anti-Semitic inscriptions painted on the wall of their house ("a plus sign gone awry, a dark reptile with four hungry claws," and, beneath it, the warning "Johouds Get Lost"), they decide to leave the country.[4] Most Iranian Jews went to the United States. Their number, previously 60,000 (other estimates range from 80,000 to 100,000), dropped to 25,000 or 30,000.

A relatively large proportion remained in Iran, however, which can be explained primarily by their deep attachment to the country, an attachment built up and reinforced over the course of history. In various interviews, many people hammer home again and again that there is no comparison between what the Jews endured in Iran and the persecutions in Europe. And they evoke the enormous nostalgia for Iran that gnaws at their relatives who have immigrated to Israel. This is shown by the results of a survey taken among the members of the Iranian community established there, whose data, when it became known, caused great astonishment in the Israeli press.[5]

> ‘We consider our Jews different from those Zionists.’ These were Khomeini's decisive words, which Iranian Jews repeat even today.

The appearance of the distinction between Zionist and Jew

Shortly after the Iranian Revolution, the new official government established a distinction between anti-Zionism, immanent to its state ideology, and the Jews living in Iran.[6] As explained by David Menashri, professor of Iranian studies at the Dayan Center at Tel Aviv University and president of the Central Organization of Iranian Immigrants in Israel, Khomeini thereby renounced his anti-Semitic remarks for more balanced and more tolerant positions.[7] The leaders of the Jewish community pledged their loyalty to Khomeini, emphasizing that Jewishness and Zionism were two completely different things. This is why, even in our own time, the Jewish community

Prayer in a mosque in Tehran with anti-Zionist posters in the background. Photograph by Paolo Pellegrin, October 2006.

sends messages of solidarity to the Palestinians, and the welcome page of the Tehran Jewish Committee website continually publishes directives in which it takes its distance from Zionism.[8] The Iranian state, when articulating its fundamental attitude toward the Jews, generally makes the distinction between Jewishness and Zionism.

"We consider our Jews different from those Zionists." These were Khomeini's decisive words, which Iranian Jews repeat even today, on the many occasions when they are dealing with the authorities of the Iranian state. The words appeared so important for the security of the Jews of Iran that, the same day they were uttered, they were inscribed on the facade of every Iranian synagogue. Although they did not prevent the Jews from being downgraded to second-class citizens, they did recognize the legitimacy of the Jews' existence in Iran and authorized the community to maintain its traditions. The Jews face the same discrimination as the other officially recognized religious minorities in Iran: they are free to exercise their religion but cannot participate in political events with the same rights, and they are also at a disadvantage from a legal standpoint. In concrete terms, this means that the Islamic Republic guarantees them a limited autonomy. They have their own places of worship, and there are Jewish schools and hospitals; the state pays a considerable share of the costs necessary for the operation of Jewish retirement homes; and the Jews have a representative in the parliament who defends their interests. A few years ago, Maurice Motamed, their legislator at the time, managed to get the "blood price" for Jews—that is, the expiatory financial compensation that the justice system allots to a crime victim's family—raised to the same level as what the Muslims receive. It had previously been half as much.

If we consider the years since the Islamic Revolution as a whole, it was during the presidency of Mohammad Khatami (1997–2005) that the Jewish community of Iran fared the best, even though his opponents within the country imprisoned many Jews in 1999 to sabotage his openness policy. Khatami intervened in favor of the Jews kept in detention in Shiraz and obtained their release. In 2004 he was the first president since the revolution to visit a synagogue, a gesture that the Jewish community interpreted as a mark of respect.

The complexity of "state" anti-Semitism

After certain circles, to which Ahmadinejad also belongs, became more invested in a policy to scuttle the broad social openness that Khatami had initiated, the situation of the Jews worsened appreciably. One example is the incarceration of the Jews of Shiraz already mentioned. At that time, the number of anti-Semitic declarations in the media also increased. Among many others, an article published on May 4, 2002, in the newspaper *Jomhuri-ye eslami* repeated the anti-Semitic cliché of ritual murder: a physician living in England spoke of an old Jewish custom, according to which the Jews supposedly used human blood to prepare their feast meal at Pesach (Passover).[9] The review *Ofoq-e bina*, edited by the cultural committee of the Jewish society of Tehran—a reliable barometer, since it frequently publishes different reactions to the anti-Semitic declarations—reported for its part a growing number of anti-Semitic attacks.

Indeed, Ahmadinejad is not the one who invented this particular form of hostility to Israel, combined with anti-Semitism. He is not the one responsible for the habit in Iran of disputing Israel's right to exist. And he is also not the one behind "Jerusalem Day," celebrated once a year, during which anti-Semitic insults have been uttered for decades. What is new about Ahmadinejad is that he is fanning the flames and seems obliged to fan them more and more, in response to the Western world's reactions to his outbursts.

I cannot fail to mention at this point the declaration that Israel had to be "wiped off the map," in the English-language quotation so often cited in the West, ever since a *New York Times* article published the translation of Ahmadinejad's remarks in its pages in October 2005. The translation is wrong, but it is interesting to analyze the reasons why the Iranian president let it circulate for so long. No doubt the main reason was his ambition to occupy the leading position of opinion among the Arab masses. He wants—as a Persian, by the way—to play a leading role in the Arab world, and the only way he can succeed is through the sole connection between him and them: rejection of the State of Israel.

The escalation of his discourse, bordering on revisionism in recent years, can also be explained in terms of domestic politics. The president of the Islamic Republic needs television images, such as those of autumn 2010, which showed him being jubilantly welcomed in Lebanon. In May 2005, scarcely a few months after his election, Ahmadinejad's domestic policy already faced enormous obstacles. It already appeared that his promises could not be kept. This accounts for his concern to shine in the foreign policy arena. Like Khomeini, he uses the theme of Israel to achieve that end. There is no doubt that in doing so his invectives have gone too far and have lapsed into anti-Semitism. Nevertheless, it is a fairly certain hypothesis that he is not guided by ideological or religious hatred of the Jews, which would lead to a desire to annihilate the Jewish people. In reality, his religious hatred is directed against a different minority, the Baha'i. Ahmadinejad's attitude toward the Jews of Iran speaks for itself: however brutal his policy against any initiative or person contradicting his revolutionary doctrine—cultural centers, women's rights militants, young people, students, Sufis, and so on—he leaves the Iranian Jews in peace. The fact no less remains—and this is an alarming reality—that through him and those close to him, anti-Semitic discourse is gaining in "respectability," though the opposition that is forming at the same time, and that criticizes anti-Semitism, may take the upper hand.

In 2006 Ahmadinejad called the Shoah into doubt for the first time, before proceeding to deny it altogether. It was at this moment, when he publicly disputed the reality of the Shoah, that the conflict erupted between him and the Iranian Jews. For by his words Ahmadinejad had entered a "no-go area" (restricted zone) in their eyes. Maurice Motamed, the Jewish representative in parliament, vehemently protested, as did Harun Yashayayi, leader of the Jewish community at the time. Yashayayi called on Ahmadinejad to take back his words, formulating his criticism in terms that could not be clearer: "Dear Dr. Ahmadinejad, the Holocaust is no more a legend than the Halabja poison gas attack by Saddam Hussein."[10]

> *[It was only when Ahmadinejad publicly disputed the reality of the Shoah in 2006] that the conflict erupted between him and the Iranian Jews.*

The circle surrounding Ahmadinejad includes people who are well informed on the substance of anti-Semitic ideas. It is probable that Ahmadinejad's remarks about the Germans are to be imputed to Mohammad Ali Ramin, an academic trained in Germany, who presents himself as the president's adviser on German affairs. The president claimed that it would be wrong to try to persuade the Germans, even sixty years after the end of the war, that their fathers were criminals. Written communications, behind which Ramin's hand is recognizable, betray an intimate knowledge of European negationist discourse, a knowledge, by the way, that is hardly widespread in Iran. They concern, for example, the Institute for Historical Review, founded in the United States in 1978, and its standard reference work, *Dissecting the Holocaust*. Note that it was also Ramin who organized the Tehran conference on the Shoah in 2006. This part of Ahmadinejad's attacks, inspired by the ideas of the negationist European right, is new. The rest is old wine in new bottles. Nevertheless, the reality of Iranian society cannot be conflated with the positions of its president alone. Although the Iranian president, Mahmoud Ahmadinejad, dis-

Madare sefr daraje (*Zero Degree Turn*), an Iranian television series on the Holocaust, aired in 2007.

putes the reality of the Shoah, it is also true that Iranian public television broadcast a series on the Shoah during his term. That fictional series, comprising more than forty episodes, retraced the story of Abdol Hossein Sardari, the "Iranian Schindler," who, in his capacity as a diplomat posted in Paris during the 1940s, saved the lives of hundreds of French Jews by providing them with Iranian passports. *Zero Degree Turn* (Madare sefr darajeh) captivated millions of television viewers in 2007, with an episode every week for months. No doubt the program did not omit the regime's anti-Israeli propaganda: in particular, it exploited the well-known anti-Semitic cliché that Jewish Zionists collaborated with the Nazis. But, for the first time, the history of the extermination of the European Jews was evoked in Iran's public space, and it reached a broad audience. Before that time, the Shoah had rarely been at issue in the media, and school textbooks gave practically no information on the subject. It is a fact: the film stirred compassion for the fate of the Jews during World War II. It resonates more with the population, it seems, than do the tirades of Ahmadinejad, who, while claiming to confine himself to anti-Zionism, often slips into anti-Semitism.

Abdol Hossein Sardari, the main character of this series, and Ahmadinejad are the two facets of Iran, which has always been and which remains, in a paradoxical and contradictory fashion, the homeland and the place of refuge for tens of thousands of Jews. To an equal degree, it is also a country where discrimination against the Jews, for the most diverse reasons—religious, political, and racial—is not uncommon.

---

1. Ruhollah Khomeini, *Hokumat-e islami* [The Islamic State] (o.O. 1971), 175.

2. Gina Nahai, *Caspian Rain* (San Francisco: MacAdam/Cage, 2007), 137.

3. David Menashri, *Iran: A Decade of War and Revolution* (New York: Holmes and Meier, 1990), 238.

4. Roya Hakakian, *Journey from the Land of No: A Girlhood Caught in Revolutionary Iran* (New York: Three Rivers Press, 2004), 134–35.

5. David Oren, "Longing for a Lost Country," *Ha'aretz*, April 9, 1982; Orly Halper, "Immigrant Moves Back 'Home' to Tehran," *Jerusalem Post*, November 4, 2005, http://www.jpost.com/servlet/Satellite?cid=1131043721479 &pagename=JPOst/JPArticle/SHowFull.

6. David Menashri, "The Jews of Iran: Between the Shah and Khomeini," in *Anti-Semitism in Times of Crisis*, ed. Sander Gilman and Steven Katz (New York: New York University Press, 1991), 353–71.

7. Interview with David Menashri on hagalil.com, http://www.nahost-politik.de/iran/juden.htm.

8. See http://www.iranjewish.com/News_F/news_40_ghodsi.htm.

9. On this subject, see Walter Posch, "Juden im Iran: Anmerkungen zu einem antizionistischen Brief an Mahmoud Ahmadinejad," in *David—Jüdische Kulturzeitschrift* 84 (2010); and http://www.davidkultur.at/ausgabe. php?ausg=84&artikel=107#top. In 2005, when a televised series repeated and dramatized that same cliché, the Jewish legislator Maurice Motamed protested before the Iranian parliament. See http://www.iranjewish.com/News_F/news_25_2.htm.

10. See http://www.iranjewish.com/News_F/news_29_03-holocaust/.htm.

In the Shadow of the Republic: A Century of Coexistence and Conflict

Ethan B. Katz

From their very inception, Jewish-Muslim relations in France were a triangular affair. That is, the French state and questions of national belonging within the republic were always at the heart of these relations. Three components of identity and status defined Jews' and Muslims' relations with one another and the French Republic: the place of each group in France's colonial empire, Jews' and Muslims' positions as religious minorities in an officially secular France, and the complex attachments of members of both groups to transnational entities. Jews and Muslims consider one another from various angles: as, for instance, citizens and subjects, fellow Mediterraneans, political opponents and allies, shopkeepers and patrons, neighbors, and even friends and lovers. Their interactions occurred in two spheres: politics and sociocultural settings. Until 1962, political relations revolved largely around the question of colonial Algeria. Particularly in the years following the 1967 Six-Day War, however, the issue of the Arab-Israeli conflict took on increasing importance. Sociocultural relations, often separated from politics in earlier decades, also became more politicized. Increasingly, Jews and Muslims sought to navigate public ethnoreligious identities that seemed at odds with the notion of republican *laïcité*. In this context, Jews and Muslims came to see one another in narrower, more ethnic, and often more conflictual terms.[1]

Ethan B. Katz

Ethan B. Katz is assistant professor of history at the University of Cincinnati. He specializes in Europe and the history of modern Judaism, and is the author of a doctoral thesis entitled "Jews and Muslims in the Shadow of Marianne: Conflicting Identities and Republican Culture in France, 1914-1975."

In early twentieth-century France

In early twentieth-century France, Jewish-Muslim interaction was largely nonexistent. On the eve of World War I, France's 110,000 Jews were mainly either from families who had lived in France for centuries or recent immigrants from Eastern Europe. The Jewish community was highly established and structured, and many Jews were well integrated into France's economy, society, and politics.

Muslims had just begun to settle in metropolitan France. Primarily Algerians from the northern mountainous region of Kabylia, they worked as rotational manual laborers or itinerant merchants, making meager wages and living in isolation. Muslims in France numbered between 4,000 and 5,000 in 1912 and 15,000 by 1914.[2] The First World War changed that dramatically. From 1914 to 1918, nearly 400,000 North African Muslims came to France as soldiers or laborers.[3] Meanwhile, about 38,000 Jews from France and North Africa served in the armed forces, and 85,000 Jewish civilians resided in the metropolis.[4] As Jews and Muslims began to interact in significant numbers, the war's particular circumstances would set the terms of their relations for decades to come.

Two key components of status and identity already shaped Jews' and Muslims' wartime interactions: first, the position of the two groups as religious minorities in a historically Catholic and legally secular country; second, many Muslims' and Jews' position and roots in French colonial North Africa, particularly Algeria. The majority of Jews and Muslims who fought together in World War I were Algerian natives.[5] Jews and Muslims in the same regiment had to encourage, protect, or assist one another in the heat of battle. Many Jewish medics in largely Muslim regiments, for instance, received citations for rallying or protecting their comrades under enemy fire.[6] As victims of discrimination but believers in the promise of republican universalism, both Muslims and Jews repeatedly underscored their service to bolster their credibility as French patriots. In a crucial distinction, however, Jews in Algeria, "emancipated" en masse in 1870

> *Jews and Muslims in the same regiment had to encourage, protect, or assist one another in the heat of battle.*

with the Crémieux Decree, did so as French *citizens* affirming their belonging. Muslims in Algeria, by contrast, still governed by the Senatus-Consulte of 1865, could apply for French citizenship only if they agreed to surrender their *statut personnel* as Muslims; most viewed such a step as a religious betrayal and therefore still lacked French citizenship.[7] Thus, in highlighting their wartime devotion to France, they made a plea for equal rights.

Indeed, World War I established that interactions between Jews and Muslims in France were not a binary but a triangular affair. That is, the French state played a pivotal role in defining the early terms of Jewish-Muslim relations. Likewise, Jews and Muslims perceived and articulated their initial relations principally through the lens of each group's relationship to the French nation. The role of many Jews in Algeria as military interpreters highlights this triangular relationship. Interpreters acted as critical intermediaries between French personnel and Muslim soldiers.[8] The position meant intimate contact with numerous Algerian Muslim soldiers. These Jewish interpreters became Muslims' confidants and caretakers but also monitored their conduct, morale, and private lives as state-employed surveillance agents.[9]

While it is difficult to determine the exact number of Jews and Muslims who fought side by side, an incomplete memory book from the Jewish community in Algeria suggests that more than 1,500, or roughly 12 percent of Jewish soldiers in Algeria, served in the same regiments as Muslims.[10] With Jews in nearly all heavily North African Muslim units, a far higher proportion of Muslims served in a regiment that included Jews.[11]

Opportunity and crisis between the wars

Following World War I, most Muslims were "repatriated" to North Africa. Within a short time, however, many returned to France as workers. Their number continued to grow, and by the late 1930s, about 140,000 resided in France.[12] Most were laborers who sent much of their salary back to their family in North Africa and returned home periodically. Meanwhile, large numbers of Jewish immigrants swelled France's Jewish population to more than 300,000 by 1939. While most of the newcomers were from Eastern Europe, growing numbers arrived from North Africa and the Levant, bringing the population of Mediterranean Jews to roughly 35,000 by 1939.[13] Paris and its environs housed the largest population of both Jews (150,000–200,000 by 1939) and Muslims (60,000 as of the early 1930s),[14] but the two groups settled throughout France. Marseilles, a magnet for immigrants, became an important site of Jewish and Muslim communal life and interaction; by the late 1930s, the city was home to 12,000–15,000 Jews, about half from the Mediterranean, and about 17,000 mostly Algerian Muslims.[15]

> *Paris and its environs housed the largest population of both Jews and Muslims, but the two groups settled throughout France [particularly in Marseilles].*

Such a widespread and varied presence led to interactions in two principal spheres: national politics and shared sociocultural spaces. In the first instance, Jews and Muslims found themselves implicated in the larger political battles of the 1930s; these centered on the boundaries of belonging within the French nation and empire. The Jewish-Muslim riots in Constantine, Algeria, on August 3–6, which left twenty-five Jews and three Muslims dead and dozens more injured, marked a crucial awakening that produced lasting reverberations in the metropolis.[16] Thereafter, the question of Algeria's future became even more central to Jewish-Muslim relations in France. Muslim and Jewish groups in France expended enormous energy through speeches, the press, and public reports that presented radically opposed versions of the violence in Algeria. On a larger scale, the events in Constantine combined with the growing threat of fascism (revealed by the antiparliamentary riots of February 6 of the same year) to create a sense of crisis regarding the place of Algeria, its Muslim inhabitants, and immigrants in the French Republic.

In this context, from 1934 to 1936, a countermobilization led to the formation and triumph of the Front Populaire, wherein many politically engaged Jews and

Muslims on the left found themselves allied. The Popular Front's leader, Léon Blum, was a visible French Jew; with the coalition's election in 1936, he became prime minister and lent his name to the Blum-Viollette project, a reform bill to give full French citizenship to more than 20,000 Algerian Muslims (which was finally unsuccessful).[17] Still, the modesty of the Blum-Viollette project reflected an imbalance of influence between Jews and Muslims, and even many Jewish reformers saw Muslims as marginal to French nationhood.

> " *The modesty of the Blum-Viollette project reflected an imbalance of influence between Jews and Muslims.* "

With the growing disappointments and divisions of the Popular Front (PF), the nascent Algerian nationalist party, the Étoile Nord-Africaine (ENA)—a onetime member of the PF, then dissolved by it—became radicalized and increasingly popular.[18]

Even in these initial decades, developments such as the Arab-Jewish riots of 1929 and the Arab Revolt of 1936–39 showed how the question of Palestine could complicate the terms of Jewish-Muslim relations in France. Around both of these events, small numbers of Jews and Muslims spoke or wrote about the possibility of spillover, some seeking to inflame conflict and others to extinguish it. In this way, in addition to the aforementioned religious and colonial elements of status and identity, a third transnational element began to define Jews' and Muslims' relationships to France and to each other.[19]

Meanwhile, during the interwar period, small numbers of North African Jewish and Muslim immigrants to France began to establish shared sociocultural settings. The largely Jewish Saint-Gervais quarter in the lower Marais in Paris, and the distinctly Muslim Rue des Chapeliers in the Belsunce in Marseille, became sites of Jewish-Muslim interaction. Muslims and Jews ate, drank, and played cards together in North African cafés, shopped in the same Maghrebi food and clothing stores, and sang and danced together at Judeo-Arabic musical gatherings.[20] By the mid-to-late 1930s,

Caricature of a "demonic" politician from the extreme right addressing Jews and Muslims. *Le Droit de Vivre*, April 4, 1936.

however, the rise of the anti-Semitic extreme right (whose cynical politics are portrayed in the accompanying cartoon), which undertook heavy propaganda among Muslims, challenged the basis for this environment. Occasionally, acts of violence by members of right-wing leagues even produced altercations between participating Muslims and Jewish defense groups.[21]

Jews and Muslims under the Occupation (1940–1944)

Between 1940 and 1944, occupation, the Shoah, and France's internal struggles upended many of the preceding dynamics in Jewish-Muslim relations. Under Vichy and Nazi racial laws, Jews in France became "non-Aryans" and struggled for their very survival. Muslims, while still mostly noncitizens, were considered in Nazi and Vichy racial law as akin to "Aryans."[22]

▶ See article by Michel Abitbol, pp. 297–311.

As Jews sought to evade persecution, many of those from the Maghreb or Levant presented themselves as Muslims, using Muslim cultural places in an effort at disguise. Muslim authorities, such as Si Kaddour Benghabrit, head of the Grand Mosque of Paris, had the opportunity to assist or thwart such efforts. Benghabrit did help a certain number of Jews. Yet, on several occasions, he assisted Vichy's Commissariat Générale aux Questions Juives by identifying Jews claiming to be Muslim as in fact Jewish.[23]

▶ See Nota bene, pp. 516–519.

Significant evidence reveals wider Muslim support for Vichy and/or Germany, particularly during the first two years of the Occupation. In many cases, anti-Semitic attitudes were not necessarily the primary motivation. Optimistic that the advent of Vichy might improve their status, and eager to show their devotion to France, many Muslims chose to join ultranationalist, procollaboration, anti-Semitic groups like the Parti Populaire Français.

Others were drawn to Germany by its propaganda and promises. Yet my research also demonstrates how, particularly in certain quarters of Paris and Marseille, shared sociocultural spaces remained places of daily interactions. Small numbers of Muslims joined the Resistance, occasionally helping to save Jews. Many more Muslims fought as soldiers in the liberation of France in 1944–45, sometimes alongside Jewish soldiers or *résistants*.[24]

Muslim leaders of the French Popular Party (PPF) speak during a large party gathering for North Africans in Paris, March 29, 1942. Centre de Documentation Juive Contemporaine.

Decolonization as rupture and cultural catalyst (1945–1962)

The events of World War II helped to generate greater enthusiasm for Zionism among French Jews, and for anticolonial nationalisms among France's Muslims. Yet the First Arab-Israeli War in 1947–48 did relatively little to affect the two groups' relations. The Jewish community emphasized material and political support for the new Jewish state; Muslim activists articulated their solidarity with the Arab side as part of broader pro-Arab and anti-Western positions. With rare exceptions, neither community's engagement during the 1947–48 war touched substantially on the question of Jews and Muslims in France or its colonies.[25]

Yet decolonization in North Africa, especially the Franco-Algerian War, soon marked a key turning point for Jewish-Muslim relations. The defining question of the day remained one's relationship to the French Republic and Empire, with a choice between separation and some form of ongoing affiliation. In the course of the war, increasingly large numbers of Muslims lent support to the independence movement of the Front de Libération Nationale (FLN). Meanwhile,

> *The Algerian Jewish community responded to the Call of Soummam with a statement of strict neutrality that upheld Jews' attachments to Algerian soil, their Muslim neighbors, and France.*

beginning with the "Call of Soummam" in August 1956, the FLN appealed to Jews in Algeria as spiritual and ethnic brethren.[26] The Algerian Jewish community responded with a statement of strict neutrality that upheld Jews' attachments to Algerian soil, their Muslim neighbors, and France. In the course of the war, the FLN expressed increasing impatience with the lack of clear Jewish communal support for its cause, and FLN attacks provoked increasing numbers of Jewish victims. Jewish leaders in Algeria reiterated their community's neutrality while emphasizing Jews' attachment to France.

Jewish individuals and smaller groups in Algeria and France made a range of choices about which side to support. Tiny numbers of Jews in Algeria joined the FLN.[27] In France, left-wing Jewish organizations like the Union des Juifs pour la Résistance et l'Entraide and the Union des Étudiants Juifs de France mobilized support for Algerian autonomy and a just end to the conflict.[28] Beginning in 1960, as it became clear that the French would leave Algeria, a significant number of Jews in Algeria supported the violent paramilitary Organisation de l'Armée Secrète (OAS), which sought to keep Algeria French at all costs.[29] At the same moment, as the violence of the OAS intensified and spread to France itself, many Jews in the metropolis condemned the group bitterly, comparing its tactics and ideology to those of the Nazis.[30] For the leaders of the French Jewish community, the war posed a tremendous challenge. In my own research, I have found that in vigorous internal debates, the Conseil Représentatif des Israélites de France (CRIF) struggled to balance French patriotism, growing fears for the security of Algeria's Jews, and sympathy for the cause, if not the methods, of the Algerian revolutionaries.

❯ See Nota bene by Benjamin Stora, p. 365–366.

Meanwhile, in 1958 the French state capped a series of reform efforts by granting all Algerian Muslims full French citizenship *without* requiring a change to their *statut personnel* as Muslims. Yet, as Todd Shepard has persuasively argued, in the war's closing months and immediate aftermath, the state sought to redraw the contours of French nationhood in a way that would allow for the forgetting of the history of French Algeria. At the same moment when de Gaulle's government assured that Jews in Algeria would retain full rights as French citizens, it effectively stripped Algerian Muslims of their recently acquired citizenship.[31]

Meanwhile, since the 1950s, the massive immigration of Jews and Muslims from Algeria and newly independent Morocco and Tunisia had also created new sites of sociocultural interaction. In neighborhoods like the Saint-Gervais and the Belsunce, but also Belleville in Paris and Cronenbourg in Strasbourg, new North African cafés, markets, neighborhoods, and sports leagues became meeting points for sizable numbers of Jews and Muslims. The Algerian War—through ideological choices imposed on everyone, brutal violence from both sides, changes of legal status, and massive Jewish and Muslim migration—became

> ❝ *The question of Algeria would no longer dominate Jewish-Muslim political interaction as it had for thirty years. Yet the war's memory and impact would endure.* ❞

a decisive turning point in Jewish-Muslim relations in France. The question of Algeria would no longer dominate Jewish-Muslim political interaction as it had for thirty years. Yet the war's memory and impact would endure.

The year 1967 and after: Israel, Palestine, and narrowing terms of interaction

The June 1967 Arab-Israeli War marked another important moment of destabilization for Jewish-Muslim relations in France. The war, and Israel's stunning victory, prompted an unprecedented outpouring of visible pro-Israel sentiment from French Jewry in the form of communal declarations, rallies, fund drives, and visits to the Jewish state.[32] Meanwhile, the Algerian government and the associated Amicale des Algériens en Europe called Algerians everywhere to take up arms, donate blood, and organize on behalf of their Palestinian coreligionists.[33] Soon after the war, French president de Gaulle's November 1967 press conference, in which he started a shift in French foreign policy away from support for Israel and toward closer ties with the Arab world, provoked strong reactions in both communities. De Gaulle's new policy, but more so his description of Jews as "an elite people, sure of itself and domineering," left many Jews feeling shocked and betrayed. The Algerian government tried to seize the moment as an opportunity for Franco-Arab reconciliation.[34] During the 1970s, Jews and Muslims increasingly publicly expressed attachments to their ethnoreligious identities, according to the evolution of the Middle East conflict. Such displays challenged the long-standing ethos of French republican *laïcité* in new ways; they also placed many of France's Jews and Muslims in a face-to-face situation, defined by international and interethnic tension. As Joan Wolf has shown, Jews developed greater consciousness, which frequently linked Holocaust memory to support for Israel.[35] Some Jewish groups drew this connection to critique the increasingly pro-Arab posture of French foreign policy.

During the same period, important changes occurred in France's Muslim demography and politics. By 1974, a series of measures from the Algerian and French governments instituted bans on Algerian migration to France. In 1975–76, however, the French government introduced family reunification laws, enabling North African workers to bring their wives and children to mainland France in large numbers for the first time. Meanwhile, the 1967 war and the uprising of May 1968 had brought new attention to the Palestinian cause among Muslims in France. By late 1968, the Palestinian organization El Fatah sought to make inroads among Muslims in France; Trotskyites, Maoists, and other "leftists" also took up the Palestinian cause. In time, a homegrown pro-Palestinian movement began to emerge. Following the massacre of Black September in 1970, several groups calling themselves "Committees for the Support of the Palestinian Revolution" emerged across France. By October, they were publishing their own newsletter, *Fedai: Journal for the Support of the Palestinian Revolution*. These movements called for immigrant working-class mobilization both on behalf of the Palestinian cause and to fight discrimination against North African laborers in France. These committees (which by 1972 gave

The Rabbi Emmanuel Chouchena, of Algerian birth, and the Tunisian Ambassador Mohammed Masmoudi meet in Belleville to help reestablish calm after the riots of June 1968. *L'Arche*, June 1968.

way to the Mouvement des Travailleurs Arabes, or MTA) demonized Zionism as synonymous with imperialism and the oppression of North African workers. They valorized the Palestinian resister, or *fedai* in Arabic, as a model linked to the struggle of these workers for better living and working conditions in France.[36]

More than any previous event, the 1967 war seemed to threaten Jewish-Muslim sociocultural interactions. In June 1968, riots between Jewish and Muslim residents of Belleville erupted in the days before the anniversary of Israel's victory. Jewish-Muslim interactions were overrun not only by politics but soon by transnational allegiances connected to the Palestinian-Israeli conflict. Regardless of the actual origins of the riots, the nearly immediate *perception* of their connection to the Middle East conflict, one that quickly colored the events themselves, suggested the beginning of a transformation of the terms of Jewish-Muslim interaction even in the sociocultural sphere.[37] Yet Jewish and Muslim leaders quickly restored order.

In the period that followed, continuing relative harmony in interethnic neighborhoods from Paris to the provinces signaled that these riots marked more of a parenthesis than a turning point. Notably, however, many such neighborhoods did take on a more territorialized character, with Jews, Muslims, and other immigrant groups using visible community institutions, shop windows, and ethnic attire to claim distinct spaces for themselves and their community.[38]

Cooperation and conflict in multicultural France (1981–2000)

The 1981 election of President François Mitterrand of the Socialist Party ushered in an era of republican pluralism, wherein public manifestations of transnational, (post)colonial, and religious differences seemed to become more widespread. The new government quickly recognized second-generation North African immigrants as full French citizens, revitalized the Parisian *banlieues*, and permitted the establishment of foreign associations on French soil. Equally important, the Socialist Party supported the rise of the "Beurs." This movement marked a generational rupture whereby many young people from North Africa (the "second generation" born in France) sought to articulate a set of hybrid identities that embraced Frenchness while maintaining strong cultural connections to the Maghreb.[39] The movement also sought to improve the quality of life and opportunity for those residing in the *banlieues*, the often poor, violent, and run-down neighborhoods where many Muslims lived on the outskirts of Paris and other French cities.

In time, however, a growing backlash emerged on the right, particularly from Jean-Marie Le Pen's new Front National Party. In response, many Beurs and other young Muslims teamed with the Union des Étudiants Juifs de France and a number of left-wing Jewish intellectuals in 1985 to found the group SOS-Racisme, a grassroots antiracism organization. The group explicitly defended a "right to difference," underscoring the multicultural character of shifting contemporary ideas about republican inclusion. At the same time, from the start, within SOS-Racisme, tensions existed between the effort to unite around a "pluriculturalist" conception of France and the particularist identity politics of various factions within the group, including certain Beurs and young Zionists.[40]

In time, though, a number of Muslims came to feel that the Beur movement and SOS-Racisme represented paternalistic attempts by the Socialist Party or other elites to control them. Moreover, throughout the 1980s, when Jews and Muslims teamed on the left to defend French universalism, the shadow of the Middle East conflict often hung over the actions. During the 1982 Lebanon War, for example, violent altercations in the streets occurred between Jewish and Muslim activists. Anti-Israel protests during the same war invoked comparisons between Zionism and Nazism. This latter development showed the Holocaust to be an increasingly asserted and contested object of memory often linked to debates about Israel-Palestine.[41]

▶ See article by Esther Webman, pp. 533–542.

Still, the 1990s appeared to bring increasing intercommunal cooperation. The (post) colonial and transnational dimensions of relations appeared to move toward resolution, while the religious took on a more ecumenical character. During the 1991 Gulf War, as Maud Mandel has demonstrated, significant Jewish-Muslim tensions surfaced, and many feared violence, but ultimately calm prevailed.[42] The 1990s produced significant watersheds of recognition for France's Jews and Muslims around the public memory of the Holocaust and the Algerian War. The period saw a number of local dialogue initiatives among Jewish, Muslim, Christian, and other ethnic and religious leaders. The seemingly imminent prospect of Middle East peace also augured well for the future of interethnic relations in France.

Crisis in the twenty-first century

Yet the first decade of the twenty-first century witnessed new transnational and religious tensions, which fueled outbreaks of both anti-Semitism and Islamophobia. A series of challenges emerged concerning the relationship of Jews and Muslims with the French nation-state, and with one another. The first and most obvious was the outbreak of the Second Intifada in Israel-Palestine in autumn 2000. In the weeks and months that followed, more than 700 recorded anti-Semitic incidents occurred in France.[43] During the first decade of the twenty-first century, France witnessed an average of more than 600 recorded anti-Semitic incidents each year. These can be divided roughly into 75 percent "threats" and 25 percent "violent actions."[44] Escalating conflict in the Middle East has often—but by no means always—produced the most intensified periods of anti-Semitism in France. A clear linkage occurred at several moments during the Second Intifada, at the start of the American War in Iraq, and in response to both the Israeli War in Gaza of December 2008 to January 2009 and the so-called Flotilla Incident of May 2010. Yet other periods show the correlation is only partial. Since late 2003, there have only intermittently been clear links between events in the Middle East and anti-Semitism in France.[45]

Other important, more local (and perhaps more underlying) factors have also driven recent Jewish-Muslim conflict. The first is the continuing high levels of poverty, discrimination, crime, and unemployment experienced by many Muslims in France, particularly by those living in the *banlieues*.[46] Second, France has witnessed a newly militant French secularism, highlighted by the controversial so-called headscarf law of 2004 that banned "conspicuous religious symbols" from French public schools.[47] Such an atmosphere has often stigmatized Islam and Muslims in a manner that has encouraged more radical, often anti-Western and anti-Semitic, movements.

Yet another key factor has been the changing dynamics of education for Jewish and Muslim children more broadly in France. Since 2000, the French public school in a number of neighborhoods has become a site where Jews feel vulnerable due to anti-Semitic attacks that range from graffiti to bullying. Again, the *banlieues*, where many North African Jews and Muslims continue to live in close quarters, have been the most frequent sites of trouble. Under such circumstances, by 2002, the number of Jews in private Jewish schools had almost doubled (to 28,000) from the figure of the 1980s (16,000).[48] One researcher found that this has in turn led to a defensive atmosphere in many Jewish schools that promotes a highly ethnic Jewish identity that sees itself as less integrated in France and innately hostile toward Muslims and

In 2006, the Judeo-Muslim Friendship Association of France began its annual "Tour de France" bus tour to promote dialogue among Jewish and Muslim communities. Photograph by Pierre Andrieu.

Arabs.[49] At the same time, new initiatives of institutional Jewish-Muslim dialogue have emerged. The most notable and sustained example has been that of Rabbi Michel Serfaty and other Jewish and Muslim leaders in France. In 2004, Serfaty and about thirty other Jewish and Muslim communal figures created the Amitié Judéo-Musulmane de France (Muslim-Jewish Friendship of France) (A.J.-M.F.). The group aimed to effect greater understanding, knowledge, and respect between France's Jews and Muslims, and to undertake cultural, sporting, and travel events as a means of improving relations. Beginning in 2006, each year the A.J.-M.F. has organized a Jewish-Muslim "Friendship Tour" by which a bus visits Jewish and Muslim sites and speaks and listens to community members all across France.[50]

At other levels, more positive contacts and images have also emerged. These have ranged from Jewish-Muslim mixed marriages, which remain infrequent but not unheard of, to a spate of successful Francophone films showing Jews and Muslims interacting on more complex, richer terms than those of ceaseless conflict.[51] Furthermore, credible surveys of Muslim public opinion repeatedly show a mixed picture, with many positive signs in terms of Muslim integration in France, and indicate that even at the moments of the greatest rate of anti-Semitic incidents, hostility to Jews is only harbored by a distinct minority of the French Muslim population.[52]

During the twentieth century, Jews and Muslims in France had "learned," according to the historian Maud Mandel—through frequent contrasts in legal and socioeconomic status in France, the international context of the Arab-Israeli conflict, and the discourses of communal, associational, and political leaders—to think of one another only in conflictual terms.[53] As we have seen, now they express their mutual hostility more widely and commonly. But institutional dialogue efforts, popular culture images of more hopeful relations, and mixed neighborhoods remain part of a complex picture. To what degree this crisis of relations marks another turning point for Jews and Muslims is a question that only future historians will be able to assess.

---

1. Until quite recently, very little scholarship had existed on the history of Jewish-Muslim relations in France. Two recent books offer the first major accounts of the subject, and treat most of the topics discussed here in much greater depth. Maud S. Mandel, *Muslims and Jews in France: The Genealogy of a Conflict* (Princeton, NJ: Princeton University Press, forthcoming); Ethan Katz, *Burdens of Brotherhood: Jews and Muslims, from North Africa to France* (unpublished manuscript under revision). I have relied heavily upon both of these works, particularly the latter, in much of what follows.

2. For figures of Jews, Philippe E. Landau, *Les Juifs de France et la Grande Guerre: Un patriotisme républicain, 1914–1941* (Paris: Editions CNRS, 2000), 13–14, 33. For Muslims, see Benjamin Stora, *Ils venaient d'Algérie: L'immigration algérienne en France (1912–1992)* (Paris: Fayard, 1992); Pascal le Pautremat, *La politique musulmane de la France au XXᵉ siècle: De l'Hexagone aux terres d'Islam; Espoirs, réussites, échecs* (Paris: Maisonneuve et Larose, 2003), 279.

3. For overall figures of colonial workers and soldiers during the war, see Tyler Stovall, "The Color Line behind the Lines: Racial Violence in France during the Great War," *American Historical Review* 103 (1998): 741–42, 766. Among soldiers, 173,000 were Algerian, 50,000 Tunisian, and 37,000 Moroccan. Le Pautremat, *La politique musulmane de la France au XXᵉ siècle*, 146 and 173. The 132,321 laborers comprised 78,056 Algerians, 35,506 Moroccans, and 18,249

Tunisians. Stora, *Ils venaient*, 14. Some 200,000 West Africans also fought in the war, but it is unclear how many were Muslim. Unless otherwise indicated, when I refer to Muslims, I mean those from the Maghreb and their descendants.

4.   Jewish soldiers comprise 16,000 native-born French Jews, 8,500 Jewish immigrants, more than 13,000 Algerian Jews, and several hundred Tunisian and Moroccan Jews, mostly in the Foreign Legion. For the numbers of native-born and Algerian Jews, see Landau, *Les Juifs de France et la Grande Guerre*, 26 and 33; for the number of Jewish immigrants, see Esther Benbassa, *The Jews of France: A History from Antiquity to the Present*, trans. M. B. DeBevoise (Princeton, NJ: Princeton University Press, 1999), 137. In order to determine the number living in the metropolis, I have subtracted those native and immigrant Jews in the French armies from the commonly given population estimate of 110,000 for the eve of the war.

5.   On "mixed" regiments, in which Jews and Muslims often fought together, see Richard S. Fogarty, *Race and War in France: Colonial Subjects in the French Army, 1914–1918* (Baltimore, MD: Johns Hopkins University Press, 2008), 68–71.

6.   Several examples can be found in *Livre d'Or du Jüdaisme Algérien* (Algiers: Comité Algérien d'Etudes Sociales, 1919).

7.   On the complexity of legal status in nineteenth-century Algeria, see Laure Blévis, "Les avatars de la citoyenneté en Algérie coloniale ou les paradoxes d'une catégorisation," *Droit et Société*, no. 48 (2001): 557–80.

8.   H. Prague, "Revue de l'Année Israélite," *Annuaire des Archives Israélite*, 1929–30; Gilbert Meynier, *L'Algérie révélée, la guerre de 1914–1918 et le premier quart du siècle* (Geneva: Librairie Droz, 1981), 85.

9.   See Meynier, *L'Algérie révélée*, 416, 438–39, 455; Fogarty, *Race and War*, 141–49.

10.   The exact breakdown would be 6.2 percent, or 806, in the first category, and 5.9 percent, or 767, in the second. Compiled from *Livre d'Or*.

11.   See ibid.; Anthony Clayton, *France, Soldiers and Africa* (London: Brassey's Defence, 1988), 248.

12.   Neil MacMaster, *Colonial Migrants and Racism: Algerians in France, 1900–62* (New York: St. Martin's Press, 1997), 223.

13.   Benbassa, *The Jews of France*, 148–49.

14.   For Jews, see Paula Hyman, *From Dreyfus to Vichy: The Remaking of French Jewry, 1906–1939* (New York: Columbia University Press, 1979), 30, and David H. Weinberg, *A Community on Trial: The Jews of Paris in the 1930s* (Chicago: University of Chicago Press, 1977), 4. For Muslims, see *Archives de la Préfecture de Police* (APP) (Paris), DA 768, Official Municipal Bulletin of December 14, 1932.

15.   For numbers of Jews, see Florence Berceot, "Renouvellement socio-démographique des Juifs de Marseille, 1901–1937," *Provence historique* 175 (1994): 39–40, 44. For Muslims, see Michel Renard, "Aperçu sur l'histoire de l'islam à Marseille, 1813–1962: Pratiques religieuses et encadrements des Nord-Africains," *Revue française d'Histoire d'Outre-mer* 90, nos. 340–41 (2003): 279–80.

16.   On the riots and their significance in Algeria, see Joshua Cole, "Antisémitisme et situation coloniale pendant l'entre-deux guerres en Algérie," *Vingtième siècle*, no. 108 (October–December, 2010): 3–23; and Charles-Robert Ageron, "Une émeute anti-juive à Constantine (August 1934)," *Revue de l'Occident Musulman et de la Méditerranée*, nos. 13–14 (1973): 23–40.

17.   For manifestations of this sentiment, see Mahieddine Bachetarzi, *Mémoires, 1919–1939* (Algiers: Editions Nationales Algériennes, 1968), 277–78.

18.   In January 1937, the Popular Front dissolved the ENA.

19.   See Ethan Katz, "Tracing the Shadow of Palestine: The Zionist-Arab Conflict and Jewish-Muslim Relations in France, 1914–1945," in *The Israeli-Palestinian Conflict in the Francophone World*, ed. Nathalie Debrauwere-Miller (New York: Routledge), 18–30.

20.   Beyond my own research, I have drawn on Jean Laloum, "Des Juifs d'Afrique du Nord au Pletzl? Une présence méconnue et des épreuves oubliées (1920–1945)," *Archives Juives* 38, no. 2 (2005): 47–83 for the Marais; and Émile Temime, *Marseille transit: Les passagers de Belsunce* (Paris: Éditions Autrement, 1995) for the Rue des Chapeliers.

21.   Robert Soucy, *French Fascism: The Second Wave, 1933–1939* (New Haven, CT: Yale University Press, 1995), 66, 80, 329–30.

22.   For the status of Muslims in Nazi racial law, see Jeffrey Herf, *Nazi Propaganda for the Arab World* (New Haven, CT: Yale University Press, 2009), 17–24. Muslims occupied a more ambiguous place in Vichy's racial conceptions, but still one superior to Jews. See Pascal Blanchard and Gilles Boëtsch, "La France de Pétain et l'Afrique: Images et propagandes coloniales," *Canadian Journal of African Studies* [*Revue Canadienne des Etudes Africaines*] 28, no. 1 (1994): 1–31.

23.   For the most thorough discussion on this issue, see Ethan Katz, "Did the Paris Mosque Save Jews? A Mystery and Its Memory," *Jewish Quarterly Review* 102, no. 2 (Spring 2012): 256–87.

24.   For a good discussion of Muslim collaboration and motivations, see Charles-Robert Ageron, "Les populations du Maghreb face à la propagande allemande," *Revue d'Histoire de la Deuxieme Guerre mondiale*, no. 114 (April 1979):

1–39. On Muslim soldiers in the Liberation armies, see Belkacem Recham, *Les musulmans algériens dans l'armée française, 1919–1945*, Histoire et perspectives méditerranéennes (Paris: Harmattan, 1996).

25. On the impact of the 1947–48 war in France and the Francophone world, see Mandel, *Muslims and Jews in France*, chapter 1.

26. For useful discussions of Jewish challenges and choices during the Algerian War in previous scholarship, see, in particular, Sarah Sussman, "Changing Lands, Changing Identities: The Migration of Algerian Jewry to France, 1954–1967," PhD dissertation, Stanford University, 2003; Richard Ayoun, "Les Juifs d'Algérie pendant la guerre d'indépendance (1954–1962)," in *Archives Juives*, special issue: *Les Juifs et la Guerre d'Algérie* 29, no. 1 (1996): 15–29; and Benjamin Stora, *Les trois exils: Juifs d'Algérie* (Paris: Stock, 2006), part 3.

27. For an example, see Jean Laloum, "Portrait d'un Juif du FLN," *Archives Juives* 29, no. 1 (1996): 65–71.

28. See Philippe Boukara, "La gauche juive en France et la guerre d'Algérie," *Archives Juives* 29, no. 1 (1996): 72–81.

29. This argument has been made most strongly in Todd Shepard, *The Invention of Decolonization: The Algerian War and the Remaking of France* (Ithaca, NY: Cornell University Press, 2006), chapter 6.

30. On this point, see Boukara, "La gauche juive en France et la guerre d'Algérie," and Stora, *Les trois exils*.

31. Shepard, *The Invention*, especially chapter 9.

32. For numerous examples, see the issues of the *Journal de la Communauté* from June through December 1967. Here I have also drawn from Mandel, *Muslims and Jews in France*, chapter 4.

33. See, for instance, "Le FLN au peuple algérien: La cause palestinienne est la tienne," *El Moudjahid*, June 3, 1967. On this issue, see also Mandel, *Muslims and Jews in France*.

34. See, in particular, "La France contre le fait accompli au moyen-orient," and "Accord algéro-français sur le gaz," *El Moudjahid*, June 16, 1967.

35. Joan B. Wolf, *Harnessing the Holocaust: The Politics of Memory in France* (Stanford, CA: Stanford University Press, 2004).

36. On the development of the Palestinian movement in France during these years, see Abdellali Hajjat, "Aux origines du soutien a la cause palestinienne en France," *Europe Solidaire Sans Frontieres*, February 1, 2006, http://www.europe-solidaire.org/spip.php?article3675. On the Palestine committees and the MTA, see Rabah Aissaoui, *Immigration and National Identity: North African Political Movements in Colonial and Postcolonial France* (London: Tauris Academic Studies, 2009), chapters 8 and 9.

37. Daniel Gordon, "Juifs et musulmans à Belleville (Paris 20e) entre tolérance et conflit," *Cahiers de la Méditerranée* 67 (December 2003), http://cdlm.revues.org/document.html?id=135.

38. For an excellent analysis of this phenomenon in the Belleville case, see Patrick Simon and Claude Tapia, *Le Belleville des Juifs tunisiens* (Paris: Éditions Autrement, 1998).

39. On the Beurs, see Paul Silverstein, *Algeria in France: Transpolitics, Race, and Nation* (Bloomington: Indiana University Press, 2004), chapters 5–6.

40. For the relations of Jews and Muslims within SOS-Racisme, see Mandel, *Muslims and Jews in France*, chapter 6.

41. On this point, see Wolf, *Harnessing the Holocaust*.

42. Maud S. Mandel, "The War Comes Home: Muslim-Jewish Relations in Marseille during the 1991 Gulf War," in *Israeli-Palestinian Conflict in the Francophone World*, ed. Nathalie Debrauwere-Miller (New York: Routledge, 2010), 163.

43. For statistics here and below, I have drawn upon annual reports of the Commission Nationale Consultative des Droits de l'Homme [National Consultative Commission on Human Rights (hereafter CNCDH)] on Racism, Anti-Semitism, and Xenophobia in France, 2000–2010 (http://lesrapports.ladocumentationfrancaise.fr/), and the reports of the Service de Protection de la Communauté Juive [Service for the Protection of the Jewish Community (hereafter SPCJ)] on Anti-Semitism in France, especially for 2010 (www.spcj.org).

44. The first category has included anti-Jewish graffiti; verbal threats against Jews, chants like "Death to the Jews" at political rallies; leaflets denying the Holocaust or making outlandish claims about Jewish power; and menacing mailings targeting Jewish individuals or institutions. Anti-Semitic violent actions in France have included desecrations of Jewish cemeteries, firebombs of synagogues, attacks on the homes of individual Jews, pushing Jews in the street and the schoolyard, violent assaults on Jews, and occasionally homicides against Jews.

45. See Jonathan Laurence and Justin Vaisse, *Integrating Islam: Political and Religious Challenges in Contemporary France* (Washington, DC: Brookings Institution Press, 2006), 226–28.

46. With regard to anti-Jewish violence, the tragic embodiment of this factor was the late January 2006 episode in which Ilan Halimi, a twenty-three-year-old French son of Moroccan Jewish immigrants, was abducted, brutally tortured, and eventually killed over twenty-four days. The perpetrators were a group calling itself the "Gang of Barbarians" (consisting largely of young men from Muslim Arab or black African descent) in the Parisian *banlieue* of Bagneux.

47. See, especially, Joan Scott, *The Politics of the Veil* (Princeton, NJ: Princeton University Press, 2007).

48. Laurence and Vaisse, *Integrating Islam*, 228, 230–31, 238–39.

49. Kimberly Arkin, Rhinestones, Religions and the Republic. Fashioning Jewishness in France, Stanford, Stanford University Press, forthcoming.

50. Interview with Michel Serfaty, April 12, 2007; Michel Serfaty, "Juifs et musulmans de France: Une relation à construire," unpublished paper.

51. In the first instance, see the findings of Isabelle Levy, *Vivre en Couple Mixte* (Paris: L'Harmattan, 2011); on the second point, for many interesting examples, see Dinah Assouline Stillman, "Muslims as Jews, Jews as Muslims, and Both as the Other in Recent French Cinema," *AJS Perspectives* (Spring 2012): 32–37.

52. On the Union des Étudiants Juifs de France and SOS-Racisme, see, for instance, *Les Antifeujs: Le Livre blanc des violences antisémites en France depuis septembre 2000* (Paris: Calmann-Lévy, 2002), appendixes; *Muslims More Moderate: The Great Divide; How Westerners and Muslims View Each Other*, Pew Global Attitudes Project (Washington, DC: Pew Research Center, 2006), 46, 49–50; and the *Gallup Coexist Index 2009: A Global Survey of Interfaith Relations* (Gallup and the Coexist Foundation, 2009).

53. This argument and formulation are among the most important ideas laid out in Mandel's book *Muslims and Jews in France.*

The Mosque of Paris and the Saving of the Jews: An Unresolved Question

Did the Jews of Île-de-France find asylum, aid, and assistance within the walls of the Muslim Institute of the Mosque of Paris occupied by the Germans? In other words, what was the official position of the Muslim community in the capital at that time, represented for the most part by Si Kaddour Benghabrit, the rector of the Muslim Institute of the Mosque of Paris? These questions, and the answers that have been given to them, go back to the time in question. Two opposing claims have surfaced. The debate continues.

The first answer is that the majority of Muslims present in the French capital during the occupation collaborated with the Germans, going so far as to denounce Jews. The second asserts that the Muslim community, by the intermediary of its representative, Si Kaddour Benghabrit, saved hundreds of Jews from death in the camps. Both of these claims are unfounded, since they draw their arguments from German propaganda (mainly in the press and other media archives) and the extravagant rumors originating during that period, thus producing a distorted, or at best anachronistic, reading of the historical facts.

The Muslim community in the French capital just before the outbreak of the Second World War was mostly Algerian, male, working-class, and well integrated with the French working class, whose ideas and political comportment adopted, and only occasionally frequented, the Mosque of Paris: for important Muslim holidays such as the Aid el Kebir or during ritual funeral services.

On the other hand, the Muslim Institute of the Mosque of Paris, particularly its annexes—the restaurant, the Hammam (communal bathhouses), and the shops— was one of the most cosmopolitan and exclusive places in the capital, where worldly Parisian and foreign figures, such as politicians, intellectuals, artists, and students from North Africa, the Middle East, and Europe, individuals of all faiths, mingled freely. Si Kaddour Benghabrit devoted himself to giving a twofold image of this place: that of the lost Andalusia and that of the court of the Moroccan sultan. In less than ten years, he succeeded in making the Muslim Institute of the Mosque of Paris (inaugurated in 1926 by the Republic as a tribute to Muslim soldiers of the First World War) the center for dialogue and understanding between the three religions of the book, particularly between Judaism and Islam, due to the presence of many North African Jews who frequented this location. He quickly became a recognized and indispensable figure in this Judeo-Arab dialogue in the city. In 1935, Senator Justin Godart invited him to the celebration of the eighth centenary of Maimonides, and asked him to give a short speech, invoking, with his "habitual authority, the golden age of Arab-Israelite spiritual collaboration, the benefits it brought to Western civilization, and the perspective of seeing it reborn."[1]

At the moment of the occupation of the capital by the German army, Benghabrit, along with the entire staff of the Muslim Institute of the Mosque, like many Parisians, took the path of exile and settled in Dax. But in June 1940 he wanted to return to Paris with the staff who had withdrawn with him, to restore services at the Mosque and its annexes, and he submitted a request to this effect to the Ministry of Foreign Affairs at Vichy.[2] On the way back, he was arrested with his son, three employees, two imams, and the Mosque guide and his family, all North Africans, on the basis of a German directive forbidding people of color to enter the occupied zone,[3] which had been abusively extended to include North Africans.

By January 31, 1941, a telegram from Algiers arrived from General Weygand: "I learn via private sources [of the] arrest of Si Kaddour Benghabrit in Paris. Re serious repercussions [of] that news on all North African Muslims, [I] will keep secret as long as possible. [I] wish to know ASAP whether General Nogues [has been] informed, and Si Kaddour Benghabrit's relatives." The same day, another telegram from Rabat, from General Nogues, said: "A lawyer named Krachling…has remarked that Si Kaddour Benghabrit was jailed at Cherche-Midi and turned over to the German military. Before answering General Weygand, who gave me this information, I would like to know whether the facts [are] accurate." On April 1, 1941, a telegram from Vichy informed General Weygand that Fernand de Brinon, the delegate general of the government in Paris, being interrogated by the department, formally denied the arrest of Benghabrit. The incident was closed. But it was the origin of the rumor according to which Benghabrit was arrested by the German authorities on suspicion of having come to the aid of Jews. A second rumor, originating during the same period, purported that Benghabrit was a collaborator with the Germans and an anti-Semite.

Back in Paris, Benghabrit resumed his main function as adviser to the government on Muslim policy. Being a high-level civil servant experienced in the service to the French state, he recognized Vichy as a legitimate government of France and expressed his loyalty to Marshal Pétain.[4] Three difficulties concerning the Muslim community exclusively prompted him to make direct contact with the German authorities of the occupation. First of all, there was the issue of the wounded Muslims in the capital and environs,

Ceremony at a mosque in Paris with the rector Si Kaddour Ben Ghabrit (center, in white with a gray mantle) to celebrate Eid al-Kabir, December 1942.

numbering between 1,300 and 1,400 in 1941; second, there was the question of the Muslim prisoners in the German camps in Metropolitan France, numbering 80,000 at the beginning of the war; third, the issue of ritual slaughter, completely secondary for the Germans, and a point on which they were willing to yield without much difficulty.

Islam and the Muslims of North Africa and the Middle East were a major factor in the war for the Germans, who saw the benefit they could eventually derive from the situation of the Muslims present in France. For one thing, they represented a way to establish direct contact with the sultan of Morocco in order to win him over to the cause of the Reich—Benghabrit also being the sultan's chief of protocol; for another, they offered a way of making Benghabrit play a role analogous to that of Haj Amin al-Husseini in the Middle East. Thus, the German authorities used propaganda to the fullest to push through their solutions to problems concerning mainland French Muslims. Every visit and interview in the Muslim Institute of the Mosque was filmed or broadcast and made the object of much publicity in the Paris press.

The Franco-Muslim hospital, requisitioned by the German military staff on their arrival in the region of Paris (on the assumption it was to be given back) and intended to serve as an annex to Saint-Lazare as a place to provide medical care for Paris prostitutes under the aegis of the police headquarters of the Department of the Seine,[5] was returned to the authority of Benghabrit on March 5 during a very solemn ceremony with intense media coverage, and was attended by Prince Ratibor, chief commander of the troops in Paris, and several high-ranking German officers. The next day Commander Ratibor made a surprise visit to the Mosque and expressed his personal desire for a Moroccan decoration, the Order of Ouissam Alaouite, while at the same time promising to consider the requests made by the Muslim Institute of the Mosque of Paris—ritual slaughter, forbidden by the Germans— and to address the issue of the admission of imams

into the German camps to help the Muslim prisoners, who were the only ones not to receive spiritual support, unlike prisoners of other faiths.

Benghabrit obtained the Vichy government's agreement to recruit four imams in North Africa (two Algerians, one Tunisian, and one Moroccan), and the agreement of the Germans for their eventual access to the Muslim prisoners in the camps. Three imams were recruited and arrived in Paris on May 24, 1941. This was the occasion chosen by the Germans to begin an odious blackmail against Benghabrit. The first step was to ask him to write a letter of thanks to the Führer in the name of the Mosque. Benghabrit informed the Vichy authorities—according to a report of June 12, 1941—of the pressure exerted upon him by Prince Ratibor and the representative of the German Embassy charged with Muslim affairs, Adolf Mar. This demand was finally abandoned, but he was required to take part in a ceremony improvised and filmed in the Mosque, during which he had to present the designated imams—an occasion for the German authorities to reaffirm the supposed allegiance of the Muslim community of France to the Reich. Benghabrit was at the time suspected by the Vichy authorities of collaboration with the German authorities, and was made the object of a meticulous investigation that established his innocence: "Captain HUAUX, attaché of the Résidence General in Rabat, returned to Paris where he saw Monsieur Rageot. The latter told him that the Germans were becoming increasingly interested in the Mosque, which they wanted to make into a propaganda center. Si Kaddour Benghabrit resisted that tendency as much as he could, and his attitude is beyond suspicion. But the Germans, after having made advances to him, now seem to have decided to treat him coolly. It is rumored that Haj Amin al-Husseini is being considered to come to the Mosque."[6]

The service of the imams desired by Benghabrit was reduced to the visiting of the prisoners in the hospitals, because the German authorities were afraid to let the imams have direct contact with the Jewish prisoners from North Africa. That prudence on the part of the Nazi authorities proved to be without effect. The Muslim and Jewish prisoners, enduring the same horrors in the German camps, helped one another survive together.

As for the rescue of the Jews, I myself, in 1944, collected testimony from a French Jew, Albert Assouline, who for many years has strenuously advocated for the recognition of the rescue of the Jews by the Mosque of Paris. The story of his escape from Drancy and his going to the Mosque of Paris to hide—thanks to an Algerian, Mohammed Ben Zouaou—until he joined the Foreign Legion and sailed to Tunisia, was as precise in its details as painful and moving because of the thankfulness he showed toward that Muslim who had saved him by carrying him on his shoulders. According to him, several North African Jews had taken refuge within the walls of the Mosque and been helped by Muslims of Algerian origin, in particular. The case of the Jewish Algerian singer Simon Halali, known as Salim Halali (1920–2005), is also well known: he testified that he was saved by the personal intervention of Si Kaddour Benghabrit, who is said to have even had a tombstone engraved with his [Halali's] father's name on it in the Muslim cemetery of Bobigny. But inevitably, such testimonies, by their very nature as personal testimonies, are difficult to corroborate by written sources, let alone official ones, especially since still today the Mosque of Paris has not yet opened its archives for consultation. Without further documentation and testimonials, we can hypothesize that the enclosure of the Mosque functioned during those dark days as did all the religious sanctuaries in the Muslim world: anyone who took refuge in a sanctuary, whatever his or her origin or religion, and with no questions of any sort being asked, received what the Muslims call *amān*, or "security." ●

Associate chair of Contemporary History of the Arab World at the Collège de France, Jalila Sbai is the author of the articles "La République et la Mosquée: Genèse et institutions(s) de l'islam en France," in Pierre-Jean Luizard, Le Choc colonial de l'islam *(La Découverte, 2006), and "Organismes et institutions de la politique musulmane,"* Maghreb-Machrek *[Paris], no. 152 (April–June 1996).*

---

1. Justin Godart, Senator, Former Minister to Si Kaddour Ben Ghabrit, Head of Protocol of His Majesty, Paris, May 6, 1935, M.A.E. [Ministry of Foreign Affairs, Diplomatic Archives, Centre de La Courneuve Colmar, France—Trans.].
2. The Secretary General, "Note d'audience," Vichy, June 26, 1940, M.A.E.
3. The Adjunct Political Director, Note for the Minister, Vichy, September 23, 1940, M.A.E.
4. "The Marshal [Pétain] thanks the President and members of the Society of Habous of the Holy Places of Islam—Algerians, Moroccans, and Tunisians—for the sentiments of faithfulness and confidence that they have expressed with respect to him; he was particularly moved by them." Dispatch from the Director of the Civil Cabinet of Marshall Pétain to General Weygand, Vichy, December 13, 1940, M.A.E.
5. Note from Ch. Saint to Colonel Otzen, January 22, 1941, Vichy, M.A.E. See also note of February 22.
6. Note for the Political Director, December 16, 1941, Vichy, M.A.E.

Chapter V

Tense Conversations

Muslim Arab Attitudes toward Israel and the Israeli-Palestinian Conflict: Variable and Contingent

Mark Tessler, Alex Levy

Many people in Western countries, or at least in the United States, believe that the attitudes of Muslim Arab publics toward Israel and the Israeli-Palestinian conflict are one-dimensional and unchanging, and, more specifically, that they are unreservedly and consistently hostile.

Frequently associated with this belief is a judgment that antagonism toward Israel is rooted in Arab culture and, even more, in the doctrine and historical experience of Islam. Expressions of this view may readily be found in the writings and statements of many conservative and Christian fundamentalist personalities.[1]

While there is considerable antipathy toward Israel in the Arab world, with statements occasionally blurring the distinction between Zionism and Judaism and some-

Mark Tessler and Alex Levy

Mark Tessler is professor of political science at the University of Michigan. He specializes in comparative politics and the Middle East. His publications include *A History of the Israeli-Palestinian Conflict* (Indiana University Press, 1994). Alex Levy holds a degree in political science and Middle Eastern studies from the University of Michigan, where she worked with Mark Tessler on several research projects. She is pursuing a career in these fields of study.

times expressed in ways that suggest an association with Islam, this is at best only one part of the story. Far from being uniform and unrelentingly hostile, and also the product of a religious or cultural determinism, Muslim Arab attitudes toward Israel and the Israeli-Palestinian conflict are diverse and change in response to circumstances and events. They are best described as variable and contingent.

The popular discourse

Assertions about an Islam fundamentally hostile to Israel have also been put forward by prominent intellectuals, most notably in the "Clash of Civilizations" thesis first advanced by Bernard Lewis and later amplified and popularized by Samuel Huntington. Lewis, who has taken strong pro-Israel positions in recent years, wrote as early as 1990 that Muslim rage against the West, including Israel, reflects a "perhaps irrational but surely historic reaction of an ancient rival against our Judeo-Christian heritage."[2] Huntington's influential 1996 book discussed "Islam's bloody borders," and stated specifically that Muslim aggressiveness toward the West is rooted in the very nature of Islam and should not be understood as a product of Islamic fundamentalism or the militancy of a few Muslim extremists.[3]

Such sentiments have become even more widespread in the wake of the attacks of September 11, 2001. It is against this background that U.S. President Barack Obama acknowledged in his June 2009 speech in Cairo, addressed to the Muslim world, that violence against civilians carried out by extremists claiming inspiration from Islam "has led some in my country to view Islam as inevitably hostile not only to America and Western countries, but also to human rights. This has bred more fear and more mistrust."

Statements alleging anti-Western sentiment among Arabs and Muslims, including those that attribute this hostility to Islam, do not necessarily focus on Israel and the Arab-Israeli conflict. Many do, however, and these receive particular emphasis in the assessments advanced by those with strong pro-Israel attachments. A recent article posted by the *Jewish Virtual Library*, for example, asserts that "public comments [about Israel and Jews] by Arab officials and media publications" are "often incendiary and sometimes outright anti-Semitic," and adds that "more moderate tones are adopted when speaking to Western audiences, but more accurate and heartfelt views are expressed in Arabic to the speaker's constituents."[4]

All of this makes it important to ask about the degree to which these various analysis and assessments offer an accurate picture of the nature and determinants of the views held by Muslim Arabs.

Evidence from public opinion research

Public opinion surveys carried out in several Arab countries in the late 1980s and during the 1990s, long before the present-day anger fostered by the Al-Aqsa Intifada and Israel's wars in Lebanon in 2006 and Gaza in 2008, offer clear evidence of the diversity of Arab views. Further, several studies that investigate the determinants of the attitudes reported by these surveys show, more often than not, that considerations pertaining to Islam do not play an important role in shaping the views about Israel held by Muslim Arabs.

Public opinion surveys conducted in Egypt and Kuwait in 1988, based on representative quota samples, reported that only 14 percent of the Egyptian respondents opposed peace with Israel, whereas 70 percent believed peace to be possible and favored diplomatic overtures to Israel.

An Egyptian puts the finishing touches on a decoration symbolizing peace on the gate of the Suez Canal Authority building in Ismailia (Egypt) in 1977, on the eve of a meeting between the Egyptian president Anwar Sadat and the prime minister of Israel Menachem Begin. Photograph by Peter Hillebrecht.

The remainder, 16 percent, took an intermediate position and were neither consistently in favor nor consistently opposed to peace. Opposition to peace with Israel was more common in Kuwait. Surveys conducted in Lebanon and Jordan in 1994, based on random samples in major cities, reported a similar diversity of views. A survey in Palestine conducted in 1995 during the early and hopeful years of the Oslo peace process, and based on multistage area probability

> **" *Taken together, the surveys show that there is no single or consistent 'Arab attitude' toward Israel. "***

samples in both the West Bank and Gaza, found 33 percent in favor of peace with Israel, 48 percent somewhat in favor, and 19 percent opposed.[5] Taken together, the surveys show that there is no single or consistent "Arab attitude" toward Israel, but rather that there is significant variation both within countries and across countries.

Data from these early surveys were used not only to show the nature and distribution of attitudes toward Israel but also to investigate the factors that incline men and women toward one view or another. Three of the surveys—those in Egypt, Kuwait, and Palestine—included questions about religiosity and personal religious attachments, and a careful multivariate statistical analysis showed that in none of the three countries did the views of more religious individuals differ from those of other individuals to a statistically significant degree. Thus, as noted in the study in which these findings were published, "attachment to Islam, defined in terms of piety, observance,

Attitudes toward Peace with Israel*

	Favors Peace	Intermediate	Opposes Peace
Egypt 1988	70%	16%	14%
Kuwait 1988	25%	16%	45%
Jordan 1994	35%	21%	44%
Lebanon 1994	46%	16%	39%
Palestine 1995	33%	48%	19%

* Ratings are based on two items asking about the possibility and desirability of peace with Israel. "Favors Peace" indicates a positive response on both items; "Opposes Peace" indicates a negative response on both items; "Intermediate" indicates a positive response on one item and a negative response on one item.

and an inclination to seek guidance from religious sources, bears no relationship to attitudes about the most important inter-state conflict in the Middle East." The study also notes that its findings "derive additional significance from the national and temporal differences encompassed by the data," and specifically that "confidence in both the accuracy and generalizability of the relationships reported is enhanced by the fact they were observed in three very different political and social settings and both before and after watershed events in recent Middle Eastern history," including the 1990–91 war in the Gulf and the 1993 Oslo Accords.

An additional finding from this research is also of interest. In three of the surveys —those in Egypt, Jordan, and Palestine—economic and political orientations have a significant measure of explanatory power. Specifically, again based on multivariate analyses in which each relationship is assessed with others held constant, individuals are more likely to oppose peace with Israel to the extent they are discontent with their own and their country's economic situation, and also to the extent they believe that Islam should play an important role in political affairs. While the latter finding might suggest an Islamic influence on attitudes about Israel, this is best understood, together with the findings about personal religiosity and perceived economic security, not as opposition to peace fostered by religion but as dissatisfaction with the status quo and the desire for economic and political change.

A subsequent study based on two additional Palestinian surveys—one in 1999 and another in 2001—provides yet additional evidence for the preceding conclusions. Both surveys are based on large and representative national samples. In one instance, the survey of 1999, personal religiosity was found to have some, albeit very limited, explanatory power. Specifically, men and women who are more pious and have stronger attachments to religion were somewhat more likely than others to oppose peace with Israel. Much more important, however, was the robust and consistent finding that economic and political judgments played a critical role in shaping attitudes. Respondents who are more dissatisfied with national or personal economic circumstances were much less likely than others to support peace negotiations and Arab-Israeli reconciliation.

Of perhaps even greater relevance, those who believe that a peace settlement will worsen the condition of the national economy or their personal economic status were disproportionately opposed to peace negotiations and compromise. This suggests that during the Oslo peace process, and even in 2001, after the Al-Aqsa Intifada had begun, Palestinian views were shaped at best only secondarily by considerations of religion and culture. Rather, large numbers of Palestinians were apparently making cost-benefit economic calculations when formulating political opinions. Assessments of the Palestinian Authority (PA) were also part of the equation, with favorable assessments of the PA —both independently and when reinforced by positive economic judgments—leading to support for the peace process and peaceful coexistence with Israel. As with the study described previously, it is significant that the same pattern was observed under different circumstances, both before and after the outbreak of the Al-Aqsa Intifada.[6]

More recent surveys carried out by Zogby International in Egypt, Jordan, the United Arab Emirates (UAE), and Lebanon between 2002 and 2008 provide additional information about Arab attitudes toward Israel and the Israeli-Palestinian conflict. The surveys asked respondents the following question: "How important is the issue of Palestine in your priorities?" The following table presents responses to this question, with percentages showing whether either "The Top Priority" or "One of the Top Three Priorities" was the chosen response. As explained by Shibley Telhami, the author of a Brookings Institution study in which findings from the Zogby surveys were presented, "How people rank an issue in their priorities is central to knowing whether or not their opinion matters much in politics."[7]

Proportion Responding that Issue of Palestine is an Important Priority

	Egypt	Jordan	Lebanon	UAE
2003	66%	85%	85%	67%
2004	86%	92%	94%	80%
2005	49%	85%	57%	42%
2006	75%	94%	75%	59%
2008	88%	100%	99%	83%

The Zogby surveys do not specifically ask respondents how they feel about peace with Israel. Nevertheless, events during this period, including the ongoing Al-Aqsa Intifada and Israel's military campaigns in Lebanon in 2006 and in Gaza in 2008, all of which received intense media coverage throughout the Arab world, make it likely that attaching "priority" to the issue of Palestine implies an unfavorable attitude toward Israel.

Again, however, there is more to the story. Data from another Zogby survey, carried out in late 2006, and with interviews conducted in Morocco and Saudi Arabia, as well as the four countries listed in the table above, suggest that findings should be interpreted with caution. A question that asked respondents to rank the issues that are "of greatest concern to you" found little significance attached to "regionally and internationally induced political instability." The five issues that respondents were asked to rank were financial well-being, social values, employment, national instability, and regionally and internationally induced political instability. The last, which almost certainly led respondents to think of the Israeli-Palestinian conflict, as well as the war in Iraq and other regional problems, was ranked last in Egypt, Jordan, Lebanon, and Morocco, and next to last in Saudi Arabia and the UAE.[8]

These findings from the Zogby surveys are not entirely consistent, possibly because of some imprecision in sampling or other methodological aspects of the research. Even allowing for some inconsistency, however, these surveys leave little doubt that Arab attitudes toward Israel vary both over time and across countries. Moreover, the surveys offer clues about some of the relevant contingencies. As shown in table 2, the importance attached to the Israeli-Palestinian conflict declined in all four countries between 2004 and 2005, and then increased in all four between 2005 and 2006. Although a detailed assessment of the reasons for these changes is beyond the present report, it seems highly likely that the decrease from 2004 to 2005 was at least in part a response to the Israeli withdrawal from Gaza, and that the increase from 2005 to 2006 was at least in part a response to the Israeli war against Hezbollah in Lebanon.

> **Arab attitudes toward Israel vary both over time and across countries.**

There have been numerous high-quality surveys among Palestinians in the West Bank and Gaza during the last decade, and these surveys provide additional evidence for the assessments advanced above. First, there is broad and generally consistent support for a two-state solution to the conflict with Israel, with surveys usually reporting that about two-thirds of those interviewed support negotiations with Israel and reconciliation in the context of a two-state solution. The proportion who believe Israel is not serious about compromise and peace is also high, and some surveys show substantial support for armed attacks against Israelis, especially if taken at a time when there have been Israeli attacks against Palestinians. Nevertheless, there is clear evidence that a significant majority of West Bank and Gaza Palestinians are not rejectionists but rather support peace with Israel. The following findings from a poll taken in May 2009 illustrate a number of these tendencies.[9]

– Sixty-one percent support the two-state solution, 23 percent support the one-state solution, and 9 percent support other solutions.

– Seventy-eight percent prefer a comprehensive peace settlement rather than an interim one, and 18 percent prefer an interim settlement.

– Fifty percent accept a mutual recognition of Israel as the state for the Jewish people and Palestine as the state for Palestinian people after all issues of the conflict have been resolved.

– Sixty-nine percent believe that the chances for establishing an independent Palestinian state next to the State of Israel in the next five years are slim to nonexistent and 28 percent believe they are medium or high.

– Fifty-one percent support and 46 percent oppose launching rockets from the Gaza Strip against Israeli communities across the border inside Israel.

Second, there is little evidence that Islam plays a critical role in shaping attitudes or accounting for the views of those who reject peace with Israel. The table below presents findings carried out by the author using data from a survey conducted by the Palestinian Center for Policy and Survey Research (PCPSR) in September 2007. In response to a question about negotiations leading to a two-state solution, 62 percent expressed support for such talks and 38 percent expressed opposition—and only one-quarter of the latter, or 10 percent of all respondents, expressed strong opposition. The table shows that personal religiosity does not have a significant impact on attitudes toward negotiations leading to a two-

" Only education bears a statistically significant relationship, with support disproportionately likely among individuals who are better educated. "

state solution. Only education bears a statistically significant relationship, with support disproportionately likely among individuals who are better educated.

Factors Related to Attitudes toward Peace Talks and a Two-State Solution

Model	Unstandardized Coefficients		Standardized Coefficients		
	B	Std. Error	Beta	T	Sig.
1 (Constant)	2.343	.127		18.388	.000
More religious	– .043	.038	– .035	– 1.135	.257
Higher education	.066	.031	.067	2.123	.034
Older	– .021	.030	– .021	– .682	.496
Higher income	– .010	.012	– .026	– .834	.404
Not refugee status	.040	.045	.026	.877	.380

Dependent variable: "There is currently talk about conducting Palestinian-Israeli negotiations with the aim of establishing a Palestinian state in the Gaza Strip and about 80% to 90% of the West Bank. Do you support such negotiations?"

A final point worth noting is that support for Hamas does not necessarily reflect opposition to peace with Israel. The victory of Hamas in the Palestinian elections of January 2006 was a response to many factors, including anger at the authoritarianism and corruption of the Palestinian Authority, the nature of the electoral system, and the more effective campaign run by Hamas.[10] Thus, the report of a poll taken by PCPSR two weeks after the election concluded that the victory of Hamas "should not be interpreted as a vote against the peace process." According to the report, "about 60 percent of all voters identified themselves as supporters of the peace process, while only 17 percent saw themselves as opposed to it and 23 percent saw themselves somewhere in the middle." Moreover, the report added, "the vote does not mean that all those who voted for Hamas are opposed to the peace process. To the contrary, findings show that 40 percent of Hamas voters support the peace process and only 30 percent oppose it." In addition, a PCPSR poll taken a month later reported that 75 percent of the Palestinian public wanted Hamas to conduct peace negotiations with Israel, while only 22 percent were opposed to such negotiations, and that 64 percent expressed support for the peace process and only 14 percent opposed it.[11]

The views of leaders and elites

The attitudes toward Israel of Arab elites, like those of Arab publics, are both diverse and influenced by events. As noted earlier, supporters of Israel have collected many statements by Arab officials and media outlets that are negative and sometimes inflammatory.[12] Thus, for example, a 2006 article in the *Middle East Review of International Affairs*, published in Israel, reported that Arab reaction to a 1993 proposal for a Middle East economic initiative put forward by Shimon Peres,[13] who at the time was Israeli foreign minister, was not only unfavorable but also deeply suspicious, with the proposal "viewed in most sectors of the Arab world as a plot to shift Israel's military domination of the region toward economic hegemony."[14] Yet, once again, this is not the whole story, and in recent years has not even been the most important part of the story.

The 1993 Oslo Accords dramatically reinforced a more conciliatory attitude toward Israel that was already taking shape in many Arab countries. Although hostility toward Israel persisted in some countries, expressions of a desire for peace were widespread and significant, coming not only from officials and policymakers but also from prominent scholars and artists. Among the latter were Najib Mahfouz and Tawfiq al-Hakim of Egypt, Zelika Abu Risha of Jordan, and Adonis of Syria, all of whom publicly expressed support for the Oslo Accords and Arab-Israeli peace.[15] Moreover, these expressions were reflected in actions as well as words. Jordan signed a peace treaty with Israel; Israelis established new cooperative relationships with a number of Arab countries in the Maghreb and the Gulf; and Israeli representatives regularly interacted with officials from still other Arab countries in Washington, DC, at the United Nations, and elsewhere in meetings addressed to regional development and security.[16] In still other developments, Saudi Arabia and other Gulf Cooperation Council countries ended their secondary and tertiary boycotts of Israel, and Arab states ceased their practice of challenging Israeli credentials at the United Nations.

There were also pronouncements of support for peace from Muslim clerics during this period, the most important being a December 1994 declaration by Sheikh Abd al-Aziz ibn Baaz, Saudi Arabia's highest theological authority. Citing a verse from the Qur'an, the fatwa affirmed the right of Saudi rulers to pursue normal relations (*tatbi'* in Arabic) with Israel. Indeed, Sheikh al-Baaz added that it would be against the religion to oppose Saudi Arabia's steps toward normalizing relations with Israel.[17] Finally, new and unprecedented business relationships developed during this period. As summarized in a 1994 article in the *International Herald Tribune*, "Millionaire businessmen from Saudi Arabia, Kuwait, Qatar and Bahrain [are] jetting off to London, Paris, and Cairo to meet Israelis, while Jordanians, Egyptians, and Lebanese are rushing to Jerusalem for similar contacts."[18]

Many in the Arab world have become disillusioned with the peace process, given the continued expansion of Israeli settlements in the West Bank and recent Israeli military actions in Lebanon and Gaza, which they consider disproportionate if not completely unjustified. But this does not mean that Arab leaders reject Israel's right to exist or that they no longer support peace based on a two-state solution. In 2002, an Arab League summit endorsed a peace proposal introduced by Crown Prince Abdullah of Saudi Arabia. The proposal, which called for a two-state solution and offered Israel not only peace with the Arabs but also normal relations, was approved unanimously by all twenty-two of the Arab states at the summit.[19] Further, the Saudi plan was formally reintroduced and approved at a summit meeting in March 2007, with Arab nations stating that the plan offered Israel "the option of peace and co-existence."

All of this suggests that the attitudes toward Israel and the Israeli-Palestinian conflict held by Arab leaders and other Arab elites are both diverse and responsive to regional developments. Arab attitudes also reflect the influence of important events in the international and regional environment. The Oslo peace process and the opportunity it introduced were important in shaping Arab attitudes. Also important, and perhaps even more important in some Arab circles, have been concerns about the growing regional power of Iran. Indeed, a recent survey of one thousand people in eighteen Arab countries, commissioned by Qatar's Doha Debates and published in December 2009, found that most see Iran as a bigger threat to security than Israel, and this has most likely contributed, at least in part, to

> **"Arab attitudes reflect cost-benefit calculations rather than primordial sentiments rooted in religion and culture."**

an increase in Arab interest in resolving the conflict with Israel and, in the process, shoring up support from the United States and other Western nations.[20] To the extent this is the case, supporters of Israel may argue that Arab leaders have not had "a change of heart" and do not *truly* accept Israel's right to exist, but that would seem to miss the point. Arab attitudes are not immutable but conditioned by events, and reflect cost-benefit calculations rather than primordial sentiments rooted in religion and culture.

The attitude of the press in the Arab-Muslim world

The attitudes toward Israel held by Arab journalists are similarly variable. Although Arab media continue to be highly critical of Israeli policies and actions, devoting substantial attention to Israel's settlement activity and military campaigns, pre-occupation with Israel has diminished in recent years, and the harshest criticism is frequently directed at other targets. Thus, a 2007 survey of 601 Arab journalists in fourteen Arab countries, the United States, and Europe found a pre-occupation among those interviewed with political and economic change. Most of these journalists covered news in the Arab world, and 75 percent of them ranked "encouraging political reform" as their "most significant" role; of the twelve issues respondents were asked to rank, the Palestinian problem ranked only fifth.[21]

In another survey, conducted in 2005 and 2006, a preoccupation with the Palestinian problem ranked even lower: "supporting the Palestinian cause" was ranked eighth on a list of contributions that journalists should aspire to make. Significantly, the survey was taken during a period marked by fighting between Israel and the Palestinians, the Israel-Lebanon War, and an international boycott led by the United States against the Hamas government. Even in this context, however, a majority of the journalists stated that their most important task was to contribute to political and social reform in the Arab world.[22]

This trend is reflected in the changing media environment in the Arab world, as well as in the evolving preoccupations and priorities of individual Arab journalists. On the one hand, the proliferation of satellite television—it is estimated that more than two hundred Arab satellite televisions operate at present—provide Arab publics with a diverse array of voices and perspectives. These media sources not only report the news, they also broadcast documentaries, investigative reports, movies, and soap operas. And among the subjects to which these programs increasingly give attention are politics, religion, and sex, the so-called triangle of taboos.

On the other hand, reinforcing this trend, many stations operate outside the scope of Arab government control or in countries where there has been a decline in government censorship. Arab media have increasingly had the political space, as well as the motivation, to do more than criticize Israel and the United States, and to focus their attention on controversial topics much closer to home, including government corruption, human rights violations, and political extremism. This applies to print as well as broadcast media and, even more important, to Internet-based social media, which permit ordinary citizens to establish networks for sharing information and complaints about domestic political and economic conditions, and other factors that impact them on a daily basis.

> *Arab media have increasingly had the political space, as well as the motivation, to do more than criticize Israel and the United States, and to focus their attention on other controversial topics.*

Even if they acknowledge the changing character and priorities of Arab journalism in general, supporters of Israel frequently contend that Arab media remain biased when it comes to Israel. Criticism has been directed at the Qatari channel Al Jazeera in particular, especially because of its wide audience across the Arab world. It is true that this channel does often shine a spotlight on Israeli actions that the Arab world, and others, find troubling. But this does not mean that its harsh treatment is limited to Israel. On the contrary, Al

Gigantic Palestinian flag transported by the crowd outside a demonstration in support of the Palestinian Territories. Sharjah, United Arab Emirates, January 9, 2009. Photograph by Kamran Jebreili.

Jazeera regularly directs the same kind of harsh criticism toward Arab politics and society that it directs at Israeli policies and actions. Further, with respect to accuracy and impact, an indication that Al Jazeera does not promote a distorted view of Israel comes from a study that compared persons who watched Al Jazeera to persons who watched CNN and found no statistically significant difference in the knowledge gained from watching the two networks.[23]

In the end, although there is certainly room for additional data and analysis, all of this challenges the simplistic, one-dimensional, and frequently stereotypical judgments about Muslim Arab attitudes that one frequently encounters in Western countries. There is no shortage of Arab statements expressing hostility to Israel, of course. But neither is there any shortage of statements expressing support for peace and reconciliation. Equally important, available evidence makes it clear that religion and culture play at best a secondary role in shaping views about Israel. Attitudes respond to events, to perceptions of circumstances, and to the way people understand the reasons for these events and circumstances. Political, economic, and strategic calculations play a leading role in shaping views and accounting for variance, and thus, like attitudes everywhere, Arab attitudes are contingent as well as variable. Attributions of a preordained or unthinking determinism are just as erroneous as one-dimensional characterizations of the attitudes themselves.

---

1. For a sample of such statements, see Mark Tessler, "Arab and Muslim Political Attitudes: Stereotypes and Evidence from Survey Research," *International Studies Perspectives* 4 (May 2003): 175–80. Although this article does not focus on attitudes toward Israel and the Israeli-Palestinian conflict, it does present evidence to show that many Western stereotypes about the nature and determinants of other Arab and Muslim attitudes are incorrect.

2. Bernard Lewis, "The Roots of Muslim Rage: Why So Many Muslims Deeply Resent the West and Why Their Bitterness Will Not Be Easily Mollified," *Atlantic Monthly* 266 (September 1990): 60. A more recent and fuller account by Lewis is provided in *What Went Wrong: Western Impact and Middle Eastern Response* (New York: Oxford University Press, 2002), especially the concluding chapter.

3. Samuel Huntington, *The Clash of Civilizations and the Remaking of World Order* (New York: Simon and Schuster, 1996), 210 and 217.

4. Mitchell Barb, "Arab/Muslim Attitudes toward Israel," *Jewish Virtual Library*, available at http://www.jewish virtuallibrary.org/jsource/myths/mf25.html.

5. Mark Tessler and Jodi Nachtwey, "Islam and Attitudes toward International Conflict: Evidence from Survey Research in the Arab World," *Journal of Conflict Resolution* 42 (October 1998): 619–36. For findings from additional surveys in Palestine, see Mark Tessler and Jodi Nachtwey, "Palestinian Political Attitudes: An Analysis of Survey Data from the West Bank and Gaza," *Israel Studies* 4 (Spring 1999): 22–43. This article reports that in March 1998, 67 percent of the Palestinians in the West Bank and Gaza supported the peace process and 29 percent opposed it, and that in November 1998, 75 percent were in favor and 21 percent were opposed.

6. Jodi Nachtwey and Mark Tessler, "The Political Economy of Attitudes toward Peace among Palestinians and Israelis," *Journal of Conflict Resolution* (March 2002): 260–85.

7. Shibley Telhami, "Does the Palestinian-Israeli Conflict Still Matter? Analyzing Arab Public Perceptions," Saban Center for Middle East Policy, Analysis Paper (Number 17, June 2008); available at http://www.sadat.umd.edu/pub/Does%20the%20Palestinian-Israeli%20Conflict%20Still%20Matter.pdf. A 1999 survey of Syrians, Lebanese, Jordanians, and Palestinians also asked respondents about the importance of the Israeli-Palestinian conflict, with 45 percent indicating that the Palestine question was of concern to the entire Arab world. See Hilal Khashan, "Arab Attitudes toward Israel and Peace," Washington Institute for Near East Policy, Policy Focus #40 (2000).

8. Findings from the 2006 Zogby survey are based on an analysis of the data by the author.

9. Findings from this and many other Palestinian surveys can be found on the website of the Palestinian Center for Policy and Survey Research, http://www.pcpsr.org.

10. For additional discussion, see Mark Tessler, *A History of the Israeli-Palestinian Conflict* (Bloomington: Indiana University Press, 2009), 841–42.

11. The surveys were taken on February 15, 2006, and March 16–18, 2006. Details are available on the Palestinian Center for Policy and Survey Research website, http://www.pcpsr.org.

12. See note 6.

13. Shimon Peres, *The New Middle East* (New York: Henry Holt, 1993).

14. Ohad Leslau, "The New Middle East: From the Perspective of the Old Middle East," *Middle East Review of International Affairs* 10 (September 2006). Leslau reports that only a minority of Arab academics took an official, public position in favor of the Peres plan and explicitly rejected the claim that Israel constitutes an economic or cultural threat to the Arab world.

15. Ibid.

16. For details, see Tessler, *History of the Israeli-Palestinian Conflict*, 767–70.

17. Arabic- and English-language media accounts of the fatwa are given in the *Journal of Palestine Studies* 95 (Spring 1995): 169.

18. Caryle Murphy and Nora Boustany, "When Former Enemies Turn Business Partners," *International Herald Tribune*, May 24, 1994. See also Peter Waldman, "Guns and Butter: Khashoggi is Back, Angling for a Profit from Middle East Peace," *Wall Street Journal*, February 4, 1994.

19. The proposal called upon Israel to return to its pre-1967 borders; to agree to the establishment of a Palestinian state in the West Bank and Gaza, with East Jerusalem as its capital; and for a just solution to the Palestinian refugee problem to be agreed upon in accordance with United Nations General Assembly Resolution 194.

20. "Iran Woos Arab States as Sanctions Loom," *Financial Times*, December 14, 2009. For a fuller discussion, see Marc Lynch, *Voices of the New Arab Public: Iraq, Al-Jazeera, and Middle East Politics Today* (New York: Columbia University Press, 2005). Lynch noted as early as 2005 that many Arab countries fear Iran's Islamic regime and see peace with Israel as more urgent.

21. Lawrence Pintak and Jeremy Ginges, "The Mission of Arab Journalism: Creating Change in a Time of Turmoil," *International Journal of Press/Politics* 13, no. 3 (2008).

22. Ibid.

23. Lynch, *Voices of the New Arab Public*.

Perceptions of the Holocaust in the Arab World: From Denial to Acknowledgment?
Esther Webman

The collapse of the Soviet Bloc in the early 1990s and its impact on world affairs, including the Middle East; the emergence of the notion of a new world order; the signing of the Israeli-Palestinian Accords; and the 1994 Israeli-Jordanian peace agreement served as pretext for a revision of the traditional Arab approach toward the Jewish Holocaust among liberal Arab intellectuals. Criticizing the prevalent Arab perceptions of the Holocaust, they called for the unequivocal recognition of the suffering of the Jewish people, which eventually led to the recognition of the Palestinian tragedy by the Israelis and facilitated reconciliation and coexistence between the two peoples. Despite its relatively limited number of propagators, this approach diversified the mainstream discourse while increasingly confining denial to Islamists. The vantage point of the discourse returned to, as in the early period prior to the establishment of Israel, the acknowledgment of the Holocaust as a horrible historical fact, albeit without relinquishing other persistent themes, such as relativization of the Holocaust or equating Zionism with Nazism. Hence, in the first decade of the twenty-first century, the mainstream Arab discourse accepts the occurrence of the Holocaust but strives to challenge its uniqueness and scope while delegitimizing Israel and Zionism.

Esther Webman

Head of the Zeev Vered Desk for Tolerance and Intolerance in the Middle East, Esther Webman is a senior research fellow at the Dayan Center and the Stephen Roth Institute in Tel Aviv University. She is the head of the Zeev Vered Desk for the Study of Tolerance and Intolerance. Coauthor of *From Empathy to Denial: Arab Responses to the Holocaust* (Columbia University Press, 2009), she also edited *The Global Impact of a Myth: The Protocols of the Elders of Zion* (Routledge, 2011).

Contesting the traditional Arab approach toward the Holocaust

The traditional Arab approach toward the Holocaust stemmed from the viewpoint that it did not concern the Arabs. The scene of the disaster was Europe, and the perpetrators of the extermination acts were European, but "the Jewish problem" and its solution were exported to the Middle East. Europe relieved its feelings of guilt through the establishment of the State of Israel, and the Palestinians paid the price, becoming refugees in their own land. The initial responses to the Holocaust in the years immediately after World War II were not monolithic, but they underwent a swift change in the course of three years, up to the establishment of the State of Israel in 1948, moving from an empathic and humanitarian approach toward the suffering of the Jews and the Holocaust victims to their representation

> "*The Holocaust ... was perceived as the major factor in the Zionist success in luring the international community into accepting the establishment of the Jewish state.*"

as the major cause for the injustice that befell the Arabs. This shift was the result of the growing political controversy over the fate of Palestine, which was linked with the problem of the Jewish displaced persons. The linkage between the solutions of the two problems led to the need to obfuscate, deny, or ignore the Holocaust, since it was perceived as the major factor in the Zionist success in luring the international community into accepting the establishment of the Jewish state.

Since then, up until the mid-1990s, the Holocaust was rarely raised as an independent subject in Arab public discourse, yet it was frequently invoked, explicitly or implicitly, in the writings on and discussions of historical and political issues, such as Jewish history and the Jewish problem, the Palestine problem, and the Zionist enterprise. The context affected the nature of the reference to the Holocaust. For example, in the discussion of the Palestine problem, the comparisons between the Nakba or the Palestinian "catastrophe" and the Holocaust, and between the attitude of the Jews toward the Arabs and Nazi behavior toward the Jews, were eminent.

The traditional Arab arguments in the debate about Jewish history and Nazi atrocities ranged from justification to denial: the Jews deserved it; it is regrettable that "the job" was not completed; the Palestinian people paid its price and became the victims of the victims; Zionism effectively exploited the Holocaust to realize its goals; Zionism collaborated with Nazism in the extermination; racism is the basic tenet of both Zionism and Nazism; the numbers of the exterminated Jews were inflated and many more non-Jews were killed during the war; there were no gas chambers; starvation, conditions of war, and diseases were the causes of death; the Holocaust was a Zionist hoax.[1]

In the Arab context, the discussion of the Holocaust always revolved around its political implications and thus evaded the event itself. The flow of information about the Holocaust was deliberately limited after the establishment of the State of Israel, and hence there existed a great deal of ignorance. Moreover, few original Arab studies were done on the Holocaust. The most notorious one was the doctoral dissertation of Mahmud 'Abbas (Abu Mazin), long before his accession to the presidency of the Palestinian National Authority, on "the secret relations between Nazism and Zionism."[2] The Arabs were on the borrowing side, selecting motifs in the European literature on the Holocaust that could easily be incorporated into the anti-Jewish, anti-Zionist, and anti-Semitic discourse in order to delegitimize the State of Israel and Zionism. The basic Arab anti-Zionist stance determined the attitude toward the Holocaust, as toward anti-Semitism in general,[3] and created a unanimous discourse.

The issue of mutual recognition

Although there were just a few Arab intellectuals and activists, such as the Israeli Arab author and communist activist Emile Habibi and the Palestinian Christian theologian Naim Stifan Ateek, who spoke of the Jewish tragedy before the 1990s,[4] acknowledging its occurrence and importance to the Jews, it was not until 1997 that a debate triggered by Arab intellectuals living in the West and closely familiar with Western culture created a wide range of reactions.

Most prominent among these thinkers were the late Palestinian professor of comparative literature at Columbia University, Edward Said, and the liberal Lebanese writer and editor of *al-Hayat* daily, Hazim Saghiya. Both of them challenged the notion that "the Holocaust does not concern the Arabs." Saghiya contended, in his book *Defending Peace*, that this notion resulted from a limited understanding of European history and modernity, and from laziness, lack of curiosity, and a certain degree of opportunism. He accused the Palestinians of concentrating on the adverse political consequences of the Jewish tragedy and failing to show any empathy for the Jewish community.[5] Saghiya also claimed that, as members of the international community, the Arabs could not exclude themselves from responsibility for the calamity. In order to understand Western and world sympathy toward Israel, he insisted, the Arabs should try to understand the Holocaust, and should show more sensitivity toward and understanding of this tragedy in order to gain worldwide respect and sympathy for the Palestinian tragedy. Mutual empathy would help overcome the barriers on the road to peace.[6]

> **It was not until 1997 that a debate triggered by Arab intellectuals living in the West and closely familiar with Western culture created a wide range of reactions.**

Similarly, Edward Said linked the attitude toward the Holocaust to the general Arab political and social situation. In 1998, he wrote, "The history of the modern Arab world—with all its political failures, its human rights abuses, its stunning military incompetence, its decreasing production, the fact that, alone of all modern peoples, we have receded in democratic and technological and scientific development—is disfigured by a whole series of outmoded and discredited ideas, of which the notion that the Jews never suffered and that the Holocaust is an obfuscatory confection created by the elders of Zion is one that is acquiring too much, far too much, currency."[7] Said called for an act of comprehension that "guarantees one's humanity and resolve that

❯ See Nota bene on Edward Said and Avraham Burg, pp. 543–545.

such a catastrophe should never be forgotten and never again recur." Seeking bases for coexistence, he claims that a link exists between what happened to the Jews in World War II and the catastrophe of the Palestinian people, and unless this connection is recognized, there would be no foundation for coexistence. He does not attach conditions to the comprehension of and compassion for the Jewish tragedy; however, he believes that "such an advance in consciousness by Arabs ought to be met by an equal willingness for compassion and comprehension on the part of the Israelis and Israel's supporters."[8] However, the recognition of the realities of the Holocaust, he added, does not constitute "a blank check for Israelis to abuse us, but as a sign of our humanity, our ability to understand history, our requirement that our suffering be mutually acknowledged."[9]

The motif of mutual recognition of the Jewish and the Palestinian tragedies as a paramount element in any reconciliation between the two peoples is central to this approach. It was even formally expressed in the official Palestinian People's Appeal on the fiftieth anniversary of the Nakba published in May 1998, which stated that "while we extend a compassionable recognition of the unspeakable Jewish suffering during the horror of the holocaust [*sic*], we find it unconscionable that the suffering of our people be denied or even rationalized."[10] A historical reconciliation does not only mean recognition of past suffering and its importance to the collective memory of each people but requires the creation of a new narrative that takes into account the histories of both peoples, and necessitates the assimilation of the history of each other and of their respective tragedies.[11]

Another dominant theme in this approach is the universalization of the Holocaust. The lessons from the Holocaust, it had been argued, became universal moral values that serve as a bulwark for democracies against the threats of fundamentalism, extremism, and racism, which target Jews and Muslims alike. The increasing recognition of the Holocaust's significance, the expansion of the sphere of memory, and the participation of other peoples in it all point to the expropriation of the Holocaust from the limited Jewish possession and its assuming a meaning and a message for all humanity. Only this broader perception of the Holocaust by the Jews, accompanied by a similar recognition by the Arabs, can lead to a real reconciliation in the Middle East. In pursuing this theme, as well, it had been emphasized that the acknowledgment of the Holocaust "does not free the Jewish state or the Jews of accountability" for the Palestinian tragedy. Any denial of the Palestinian rights "will be tantamount to an infringement of the sanctity of the Holocaust, which has become a yardstick for universalistic values."[12]

Revival of debates

In 1999, young Palestinians admitted in an interview to an Israeli paper that only after the beginning of the peace process did they begin to realize and understand the human tragedy experienced by the Jewish people.[13] Concurrently, in Egypt, Amin al-Mahdi, a writer and one of the founders of the small peace movement, proposes, in his book *The Democracy Crisis and Peace*, the formation of a parliament for peace that will adopt in its founding proclamation an unequivocal denunciation of the "Holocaust and the suffering inflicted on the Jews."[14]

The new Arab approach gradually gained the support of additional Arab intellectuals and writers and evoked intensive debates on the Holocaust in the Arab press, which proved that the readiness to accept the occurrence of the Holocaust was gradually infiltrating into the mainstream Arab discourse, although not necessarily acknowledging its dimensions, uniqueness, and meaning. These debates were triggered by certain events since the first half of 1998, such as the controversy over the proposed visit of President Yasir Arafat to the Holocaust Memorial Museum in Washington in January 1998; Roger Garaudy's trial in France in February that year, and his subsequent tour to the Middle East; the pope's document "We Remember: Reflections on the Shoah" of March 16;[15] the restitution of Jewish property; and the international initiatives to commemorate the Holocaust in 2005.[16]

> **The readiness to accept the occurrence of the Holocaust was gradually infiltrating into the mainstream Arab discourse, although not necessarily acknowledging its dimensions, uniqueness, and meaning.**

In the discussions around those events and a few others,[17] the traditional themes of the representation of the Holocaust continued to dominate the discourse. However, they also consistently contained dissenting voices challenging the traditional Arab approach and suggesting an alternative reading of the Holocaust, mainly out of a belief that denial of the Holocaust is detrimental to the Arabs and weakens their cause.

The debate over Roger Garaudy and his book *The Founding Myths of Israeli Politics*, for example, and the manifestations of solidarity with him, did not stem solely from a deep belief in his views denying the Holocaust. His attack on Zionism attracted much more attention and was readily incorporated in the hostile discourse against Israel. The stalemate in the peace process polarized the dichotomy between "us" (the Arabs and Muslims on the defensive) and the "others" (Israel, Zionism, and the West), which encouraged identification with Garaudy's cause. The debate went beyond a mere discussion of the trial. It dealt with the theoretical aspects related to the trial—freedom of expression, freedom of research, the legitimacy of historical revision, and the role of intellectuals in public life—but even these discussions were not free from political implications. The trial was perceived as part of a larger political struggle between Israel and Zionism, on the one hand, and the Arabs and Muslims, on the other hand. "His views are an inspiration for the Arab struggle against religious extremism and the Zionist occupation," concluded Egyptian intellectual Salah 'Izz.[18] The positions expressed reflected also on the moral values of the writers. "We are with Zola in his defense of Dreyfus as we are with Garaudy for his right to expose the myths and deceptions on which Israel bases its policy, regardless of who is the persecuted, the Jews in the case of Dreyfus or the Palestinians in the case of Garaudy," argued Egyptian leftist Sid Ahmad.[19] "As Arabs and Muslims," explained 'Izz, "our approach to the Holocaust derives from the Islamic tenet that whether one million were killed or 6 millions or more, the crime against humanity is the same."[20] Iranian president Mahmoud Ahmadinejad's approach to the conflict and to the Holocaust, expressed in his statements and interviews following his election in June 2005, had been rejected by several Arab writers, who in some cases intertwined their denunciation with criticism of Arab society, regimes, and culture, and particularly Islamist movements. Thus, the Lebanese Hazim Saghiya deplored the fact that Ahmadinejad's words had been received enthusiastically by many Arab writers and expressed his disappointment that Holocaust denial had become "a disease" that infected the Middle East rulers, whereas in the past it had been confined to the fanatic margins of society.[21] Holocaust denial, warned another writer, exonerated Adolf Hitler and was antithetical to Islamic values. "We should differentiate between the innocent Jews who were exposed to death and the exploitation of the Holocaust by the Zionist movement… The Islamic political contentions about the Holocaust aim at patting the people's sentiments, while damaging our reputation and moral standing," he stated.[22] A similar view was voiced by others, such as Palestinian intellectual George Catan, Lebanese writer Nissim Dhahir, and Egyptians Murad Wahba and 'Amr Hamzawi, who acknowledged the significance of the Holocaust as a moral lesson for all humanity in dealing with contemporary human tragedies.[23]

> " *The stalled peace negotiations and the growing antagonism between Israelis and Palestinians curtailed the continued development of the new Arab approach to the Holocaust.* "

The outbreak of the Al-Aqsa Intifada at the end of September 2000, the stalled peace negotiations, and the growing antagonism between Israelis and Palestinians curtailed the continued development of the new Arab approach to the Holocaust. The voices propagating it were on the defensive but did not disappear. Their impact has been reflected in statements by Arabs visiting Auschwitz and Holocaust museums and participating in conferences dealing with the Holocaust.

Upon becoming the PA's prime minister in 2003, Mahmud 'Abbas (Abu Mazin), whose PhD dissertation accused Zionism of collaborating with Nazism and contested the number of Jewish victims, backed off from his thesis's assumptions in an interview with Israeli daily *Ha'aretz*. "The Holocaust was a terrible, unforgivable crime against the Jewish nation," he said, and added that it "was a terrible thing that nobody can claim I denied it." Abu Mazin reiterated this view in his concluding statement on June 4, 2003, at the end of the Aqaba summit between him and Israeli prime minister Sharon.[24]

The event that symbolizes more than any other the acceptance of the Holocaust for what it is was the trip to Auschwitz on May 26–30, 2003, by a group of Arabs and

Jews from Israel and France who defied significant criticism, particularly by Israeli Arabs.[25]

In December 2002, Christian Arab educator Fr. Emile Shoufani, a Greco-Catholic priest and an Arab school director, declared in Paris his initiative to launch a campaign "memory for peace" to learn "the Jewish pain" and "the origins of anxiety" that determined the Israelis' attitude toward the "other," to share the pain and eventually pave the way for better understanding and coexistence. Realizing the significance of the Holocaust in the Israeli psyche, Shoufani believes that "the memory of the Holocaust is the key for reopening the dialogue" between the Palestinians and the Israelis, which had been severed due to the intifada. He embarked on a venture that brought together 250 Arab and Jewish Israelis and a group of Muslims, Christians, and Jews from France to the concentration camps of Auschwitz-Birkenau. The trip took place after a period of joint learning about the Holocaust and exposure to the personal experiences of Jewish survivors. This event received the blessing of Egyptian as well Palestinian officials, including Yasir Arafat.[26]

Emile Shoufani, a priest in Nazareth, during a trip he initiated to Auschwitz-Birkenau that drew more than four hundred Jews and Arabs from Israel and France, May 2003. Photograph by Philippe Lissac.

Shoufani's views were not only a natural outcome of the new Arab approach to the Holocaust but a further extension of its limits. Inspired by the philosophical writings of Emmanuel Levinas, particularly his conception of one's ethical obligation to the Other, the Arab educator rejected any link between his will to share the Jewish pain and the acknowledgment of Palestinian suffering. He insisted that the act of compassion should be unilateral in order to "break the cycle of give and take that proved to be a vicious circle."[27] Similarly, Palestinian activist Ata Qaymari suggested that the Palestinians learn not to mix up their anger against occupation with a human reaction to the suffering of the Other. "Such an attitude will help Jews not only overcome their trauma, but also to identify with the three forms of the Palestinian agony, namely, racial discrimination, occupation and exile."[28] Another step toward acknowledgment was Israeli Arab lawyer Khaled Kassab Mahamid's initiative to erect the first and only Arab Holocaust museum in April 2005 in Nazareth. Unlike Shoufani, however, Mahamid links the acknowledgment of the Holocaust with the recognition of the Palestinian tragedy. In the one-room museum in his law offices hang posters from Yad Vashem exhibiting the horrors of the Holocaust, as well as posters displaying the flight of Palestinian refugees during the 1948 war and symbols of the Nakba, such as the key. He urges Palestinians, as well as all Arabs, to learn about the Holocaust in order to understand the Israeli deep concern with security, assuming that such an understanding will enable them to counter Israeli arguments and thus help the Palestinians achieve their political objectives.[29] Mahamid's instrumentalization of the acknowledgment of the Holocaust accurately reflects the new Arab approach.

End of unanimous Holocaust denial

The discussion among intellectuals has evolved into an unprecedented examination of the Arab attitude toward the Holocaust, and especially its denial, in an attempt to explain its origins and motives. From the particularity "of being totally innocent of any responsibility for the Holocaust, that terrible catastrophe of the Jewish people, which ended with a metaphorically identical Catastrophe of their own," expounded Ata Qaymari, "stems the whole reaction, response and stand of the Palestinian people."[30] Leipzig-based Egyptian scholar 'Umar Kamil explained that the Arab intellectual refused to acknowledge the Holocaust out of the erroneous perception that acknowledging the suffering of the Other diminishes the meaning of the Palestinian suffering,[31] whereas others, such as Ray Hanania and Joseph Massad, Palestinians living in the United States, contended that the Arab attitude toward the Holocaust, and particularly denial, was a counterreaction to the use of the Holocaust in justifying Israel's existence and political stand vis-à-vis the Palestinians.[32]

Moreover, analyzing the Arab approach toward the Holocaust reflected on the image of Arab societies and occasionally incorporated harsh criticism of their social, political, and moral situation. The debates revealed that the unanimity of the traditional Arab discourse on the Holocaust has been broken, and that a growing number of writers dare to defend its universal meaning and to call for its recognition as a traumatic Jewish experience that shapes the Jewish people's psyche. This group of writers has been consistent in defending Arafat's decision to accept the invitation to the Holocaust Museum; in condemning the Arab embrace of Garaudy, Irving, and Ahmadinejad; in welcoming the pope's document about adopting "constructive moral and political guidelines" as a standard of behavior and universal morality for all human beings;[33] and in recognizing the International Holocaust Remembrance Day. They have also rejected Holocaust denial and criticized the indiscriminate translation of Western deniers' publications into Arabic.

Retrospectively, the new approach seems to be a return to the early diversified discourse of the 1940s, when the Arabs desperately attempted to separate the Palestine problem from the issue of the displaced European Jews after the war. Realizing the potential gains that Zionists could derive from the Jewish tragedy, they also tried to disconnect the causal link between the establishment of the State of Israel and the Holocaust.

Khalid Kassab Muhammad (left), an Arab lawyer in Israel, founded in 2005 the first and only museum dedicated to the Holocaust in the Arab world, in Nazareth. Photograph by Eitan Hess-Ashkenazi, May 24, 2005.

1. On the representation of the Holocaust in the Arab world, see Meir Litvak and Esther Webman, *From Empathy to Denial: Arab Responses to the Holocaust* (London: Hurst; New York: Columbia University Press, 2009); Gilbert Achcar, *The Arabs and the Holocaust: The Arab-Israeli War of Narratives* (New York: Metropolitan Books, 2010); Azmi Bishara, "The Arabs and the Holocaust: An Analysis of the Problematics of a Conjunction" (in Hebrew), *Zmanim*, no. 53 (Summer 1995): 54–71. See also Yehoshafat Harkabi, *The Arabs' Position in Their Conflict with Israel* (New York: Hart, 1972), 254–58; Bernard Lewis, *Semites and Anti-Semites* (London: Phoenix, 1997), 203–18.

2. Mahmud 'Abbas Abu Mazin, *The Other Side: The Secret Relations between Nazism and Zionism* [*al-wajh al-aakhar: Al-'alaqat al-sirriya bayna al-naziya wal-sahyuniya*] (Amman: Dar Ibn Rushd lil-Nashr wal-Tawzi', 1984). See also Yahya Faris, *Zionist Relations with Nazi Germany* (Beirut: Palestinian Research Center, 1978); Mu'in Ahmad Mahmud, *Zionism and Nazism* [*al-sahyuniyya wal-naziyya*] (Beirut: Al-Maktab al-Tijari lil-Taba'a wal-Nashr wal-Tawzi', 1971); 'Abd al-Wahhab al-Masiri, *Zionism and Nazism and the End of History* [*al-sahyuniyya wal-naziyya wa-nihayat al-tarikh*] (Cairo: Dar al-Shuruq, 1997).

3. Bishara, "The Arabs and the Holocaust," 54.

4. Emile Habibi, "Your Holocaust Our Catastrophe" (in Hebrew), *Politica*, no. 8 (June–July 1986): 26–27; Naim Stifan Ateek, *Justice and Only Justice: A Palestinian Theology of Liberation* (New York: Orbis Books, 1990), 168–70. See also Stephen Wicken, "Views of the Holocaust in Arab Media and Public Discourse," *Yale Journal of International Affairs* 1, no. 2 (Winter/Spring 2006): 108–14.

5. Hazim Saghiya, *Defending Peace* [*Difa'an an al-Salam*] (Beirut: Dar al-Nahar, 1997), 63–69. Faysal Jalul, a Lebanese journalist living in Paris, agreed with this criticism in his review of Saghiya's book, *Al-Nahar*, December 29, 1997. See also Samir Kassir, "La Nakba recommence?" *Revue d'Études Palestiniennes* 17, no. 69 (Autumn 1998): 61–63.

6. Saghiya, *Defending Peace*, 63–94; *Ha'aretz*, March 21, 1997; *al-Hayat*, November 10, 14–15, 18, and 28, 1997; December 18, 1997.

7. *Al-Ahram Weekly*, June 25, 1998; *al-Hayat*, June 30, 1998.

8. *Al-Hayat*, November 5, 1997; *al-Ahram Weekly*, November 6, 1997; *Ha'aretz*, February 20, 1998; *Le Monde Diplomatique*, August–September 1998.

9. *Al-Ahram Weekly*, June 25, 1998; *al-Hayat*, June 30, 1998.

10. PNA, Ministry of Information, the Palestinian People's Appeal on the 50th Anniversary of the Catastrophe "Al-Nakba," www.pna.org/mininfo/nakba.

11. Rashid Khalidi, "Fifty Years after 1948: A Universal Jubilee?," *Tikkun* 13, no. 2 (March/April 1998): 55; *al-Hayat*, December 18, 1997; May 15, 1998; *al-Ahram Weekly*, January 14, 1999.

12. *Al-Hayat*, December 18, 1997; *Ha'aretz*, February 21, 2000. See also Azmi Bishara, "Response," *Zmanim* 54 (Spring 1996): 104; Salma Khadra Jayyusi, "The End of Innocence," in McGowan and Ellis, *Remembering*, 33; Matthijs Kronemeijer, *An Arab Voice of Compromise: Hazem Saghieh's "In Defence of Peace" (1997)*, student thesis, Ultrech University, 2006, 46–50, igitur-archive.library.uu.nl/student-theses/2006-0324-082630/UUindex.html.

13. *Ha'aretz*, May 28, 1999.

14. Amin al-Mahdi, *Azmat al-dimuqratiyya wal-salam* (Cairo: Dar al-Maarif, 1999), 258; *Ha'aretz*, May 28, 1999.

15. For a discussion of the Arab response to these issues, see Esther Webman, "Rethinking the Holocaust: An Open Debate in the Arab World, 1998," in *Anti-Semitism Worldwide 1998/9*, ed. Dina Porat and Roni Stauber (Lincoln: University of Nebraska Press, 2000), 16–30.

16. For information on property restitution and commemorating the Holocaust, see Litvak and Webman, *From Empathy to Denial*, 326–66.

17. See chapters on Arab countries at the Stephen Roth Institute's site, http://www.tau.ac.il/Anti-Semitism.

18. *Al-Nahar*, January 10, 1998.

19. *Al-Ahram*, January 22, 1998.

20. *Al-Hayat*, February 12, 1998. See also memorandum of the Palestinian writers, *al-Risala*, January 22, 1998.

21. *Al-Hayat*, December 24, 2005.

22. *Al-Sharq al-Awsat*, December 24, 2005.

23. George Catan, "The Jewish Holocaust: Reality or Myth," http://www.metransparent.com, May 25, 2005; *al-Hayat*, February 8, 2005; *al-Musawwar*, March 25, 2005; *al-Sharq al-Awsat*, January 1, 2006.

24. *Ha'aretz*, May 28, 2003; *The Guardian*, May 29, 2003; "PM Abbas and Israeli PM Ariel Sharon Statements following the Aqaba Summit," Aqaba, Jordan, June 4, 2003, *Journal of Palestine Studies* 33, no. 1 (Fall 2003): 150.

25. *Fasl al-Maqal*, February 21 and 28, 2003, and March 7, 2003.

26. *Ha'aretz*, February 3, 5, and 7, 2003, and May 27, 2003; *al-Sinara*, February 7, 2003, and March 14, 2003; *Kul al-'Arab*, February 7, 2003, and June 5, 2003; *Panorama*, February 7, 2003, May 30, 2003, and June 11, 2003; *al-Mashhad al-Isra'ili*, May 2, 2003; *al-Sharq al-Awsat*, May 25, 2003; *Ma'ariv*, May 28, 2003; and *Yedi'ot Aharonot*, May 30, 2003. For a comprehensive account of Shoufani's worldview and initiative, see Jean Mouttapa, *Un Arabe Face à Auschwitz: La mémoire partagée* (Paris: Albin Michel, 2004).

27. Mouttapa, *Un Arabe Face à Auschwitz*, 271.

28. Ata Qaymari, "The Holocaust in the Palestinian Perspective," in *Shared Histories: A Palestinian-Israeli Dialogue*, ed. Paul Scham, Walid Salem, and Benjamin Pogrund (Jerusalem: Left Coast Press, 2005), 152–53.

29. Khaled Kassab Mahamid, *The Palestinians and the Holocaust State* [*Al-Filastiniyyun wa-dawlat al-muhraqa*] (Umm al-Fahm, self-published, 2006); *Jerusalem Post*, March, 18, 2005; *Boston Globe*, May 6, 2005; *Independent*, May 17, 2005; *Ha'aretz*, February 24, 2006. Robert Satloff, *Among the Righteous: Lost Stories from the Holocaust's Long Reach into Arab Lands* (New York: Public Affairs, 2006), 184–85. Satloff's book deals with another, and relatively unknown, aspect of the subject: Arab sympathy with Jewish suffering in the slave-labor internment camps in North Africa during the Second World War and efforts by Arabs to hide and rescue Jews from Nazi, Vichy, and Italo-fascist persecution.

30. Qaymari, "The Holocaust," 148.

31. *Al-Sharq al-Awsat*, January 30, 2004; Joseph Massad, "Palestinian and Jewish History: Recognition or Submission?," *Journal of Palestine Studies* 30, no. 1 (Autumn 2000): 53. For similar opinions, see Muhammad Haddad, *al-Hayat*, February 8, 2004; Nail Balawi, *al-Quds al-'Arabi*, May 4, 2006.

32. Ray Hanania, "Morality and Principles in the Palestinian Struggle for Nationhood," August 5, 1998, http://www.hanania.com; Massad, "Palestinian and Jewish History."

33. *Jordan Times*, April 21, 1998; *Ha'aretz*, April 23, 1998.

Edward Said and Avraham Burg:
Two Free Voices

There can be no true dialogue without a mutual understanding that allows everyone to properly capture the point of view of the other. This is why the minimum requirement for a true dialogue between Palestinians and Israelis is a recognition by each party of the trauma that lies at the heart of the psyche of each of the two peoples: the Shoah, the genocide of the Jews by the Nazis in 1941–45 for the Israelis; and the Nakba, the taking of their territory and their uprooting in 1948 for the Palestinians.

On the Palestinian side, that recognition is less of a problem than it is on the Israeli side, for the obvious reason that the Palestinians feel no responsibility for the Shoah, while the recognition of the Nakba by the Israelis amounts to the admission of the historical responsibility of the Zionist movement in the uprooting of the Palestinians, and strengthens the claims by the latter of historical and current rights.

The widespread refusal among the Palestinians to recognize the magnitude of the terrible tragedy of the Shoah, as well as the increasing Shoah denials seen among them in recent years, constitute most often a purely reactive attitude, a senseless response to the Israeli refusal to recognize the Nakba and an expression of exasperation at the deteriorating condition of the Palestinians living under Israeli rule as citizens of the State of Israel or that of the Palestinians living in the territories that Israel occupied in 1967.[1]

But the Palestinians have officially recognized the importance of the Shoah. They did so in 1998, on the occasion of the fiftieth anniversary of the Nakba, in the solemn and official address delivered by Mahmoud Darwish on May 15, 1998. That "Appeal of the Palestinian People" was drafted by a committee of fifty members representing the entirety of the Palestinian political forces and factions, with the

Edward Said. Photograph by Ulf Andersen, Paris, November 25, 1996.

Avraham Burg. Photograph by Philippe Matsas, Paris, March 2008.

exception of Hamas and Islamic Jihad, which were less powerful than they would be during the following decade. It assigned to the Palestinians a duty of recognition of the "Jewish narrative" of the Shoah, while at the same time claiming their freedom to require of the Israelis that they recognize Palestinian rights: "If it is our moral duty to accept the Jewish story of the Holocaust as is, without intervening in the discussion on the statistical aspect of the crime, and to increase the degree of expression of our compassion for the victims, it is also our right to demand on the part of the children of the victims a recognition of the condition of the Palestinian victims and their right to life, deliverance, and independence."[2]

The 1998 appeal, in presenting the recognition of the Shoah as a "moral duty," did not qualify that duty with any condition, while at the same time inviting the Israelis to make a reciprocal gesture. In this, it conformed to the example given the preceding year by the most famous of Palestinian intellectuals, Edward Said, in an article that aroused great interest, in which he asserted: "[T]here is no reason at all, in my opinion, not to bow respectfully before the horror and particular tragedy that has haunted the Jewish people. As an Arab, in particular, I think it's important to understand this collective experience in as much of its terrible concrete detail as one is capable: this act of comprehension guarantees our humanity and our determination that such a catastrophe is never forgotten and never repeated."[3] He goes on to say, "I attach no conditions to such understanding and compassion: one feels them for their own sake, not for political advantage. Yet such an advance in consciousness by Arabs ought to be met by an equal willingness for compassion and comprehension on the part of Israelis and Israel's supporters, who have engaged in all sorts of denial and expressions of defensive non-responsibility when it comes to Israel's central role in our historical dispossession as a people.... We must think our histories together, however difficult that may be, in order for there to be a common future. And that future must include Arabs and Jews together, free of any exclusionary, denial-based schemes for shutting out one side by the other, either theoretically or politically. This is the real challenge. The rest is much easier."[4]

On the Israeli side, the most striking recognition of the historical responsibility of the Zionist movement in the Nakba has come from the relatively marginal group of "new historians," who, at the end of the 1980s, made a decisive contribution to the confirmation of the Palestinian narrative.[5] But there has never been an official Israeli acknowledgment of that responsibility, or even a repudiation of the official discourse, which, since the foundation of the State of Israel, has denied it categorically and attributed the 1948 Palestinian exodus to a voluntary departure in response to a so-called appeal by Arab leaders. Now, that allegation, even if it were true, would not change the fact that the Palestinians were denied the right of return to their lands after the end of the hostilities. The Israeli denial, far from diminishing over the years, has hardened to the degree that Israeli authorities currently forbid Palestinians to even use the term Nakba in their textbooks, and have criminalized the commemoration of the event.[6]

Avraham Burg, in his book *The Holocaust is Over; We Must Rise from Its Ashes*, which appeared in Hebrew in 2007 and in English the following year, sounded the alarm at the shift of Israeli society toward the extreme right—a shift beginning with the electoral victory of the Likud in 1977 and ending, in the Eighteenth Knesset elected in February 2000, with the Zionist Labor Party, founders of the State of Israel, in fourth position, behind two parties representing the heritage of the Zionist tradition called "revisionist" ("revising" the original Zionism and radicalizing it in an ultranationalist direction). This shift toward the extreme right found its counterpart in the progression of the influence of the Palestinian Hamas and the electoral victory of the Islamic Movement in 2006.

It is this context of the hardening of positions that makes the examination of conscience recently carried out by Burg quite remarkable—all the more so in view of his having been an eminent member of the Israeli and Zionist establishment, where he served as president of the Jewish Agency and the World Zionist Movement, vice president of the Jewish World Congress, and member of the Knesset.

Burg saw the danger that this fatal spiral represented. He understood that the key to it was the Israeli attitude toward the Palestinians. This ex-member of the Knesset (between 1999 and 2003) spoke about them in the following terms, permeated by very strong emotion: "Therefore we must stand on the tallest mountain and declare clearly and loudly we know that solving the Shoah refugee problem directly and indirectly caused the Palestinian refugee problem. Only by acknowledging our responsibility first will we be given the opportunity to explain and justify ourselves then can we give our excuses and explanations…. We have to admit that, post-Shoah, we valued our lives because we wanted to live after so much death. We were not sufficiently sensitive to the lives of others and to the price that they paid for our salvation. Please forgive us, and together we will put an end to the evil that torments us all."[7]

The day negotiations between Israelis and Palestinians are discussed by emulators of Avraham Burg and Edward Said, a just and durable peace in the Middle East will truly be at hand. ●

Professor of international relations at the School of Oriental and African Studies (SOAS), University of London, Gilbert Achcar is the author of The Clash of Barbarisms: The Making of the New World Disorder *(Paradigm, 2006);* The Arabs and the Holocaust: The Arab-Israeli War of Narratives *(Metropolitan Books, 2010); and "Eichmann in Cairo: The Eichmann Affair in Nasser's Egypt,"* Arab Studies Journal 20, no. 1 (Spring 2012).

---

1. See, on this subject, Gilbert Achcar, *The Arabs and the Holocaust: The Arab-Israeli War of Narratives* (New York: Metropolitan Books, 2010) and *Eichmann au Caire* (Paris: Sinbad-Actes Sud, 2012).

2. "Nida' al-Sha'b al-Filastini fi al-Dhikra al-Khamsin lil-Nakba" (excerpts), *Majallat al-Dirasat al-Filastiniyya* 9, no. 35 (Summer 1998): 219–21, available online at http://www.palestine-studies.org/files/pdf/mdf/8232.pdf.

3. Edward Said, "Bases for Coexistence" (1997), in *The End of the Peace Process: Oslo and After* (New York: Vintage, 2001), 205–9.

4. Ibid., 209.

5. A presentation and discussion in French of the works of the Israeli "nouveaux historiens" appears in the works of Dominique Vidal with Sébastien Boussois, *Comment Israël expulsa les Palestiniens: Les nouveaux acquis de l'Histoire (1945–1949)* (Ivry-sur-Seine: Atelier, 2007) and *Israël confronté à son passé: Essai sur l'influence de la "nouvelle histoire"* (Paris: L'Harmattan, 2007).

6. See "Israel Bans 'Catastrophe' Term from Arab Schools," *Reuters,* July 22, 2009, and Rebecca Stoil, "'Nakba Bill' Passes Knesset in Third Reading," *Jerusalem Post,* March 23, 2011.

7. Avraham Burg, *The Holocaust Is Over; We Must Rise from Its Ashes* (New York: Palgrave Macmillan, 2008), 83–84.

Muslim Anti-Semitism: Old or New?
Mark R. Cohen

The anti-Semitism that is so widespread in the Muslim world today first came to the attention of Israelis and the Diaspora thanks to Yehoshafat Harkabi's pathbreaking 1968 book, *Arab Attitudes to Israel*, published in both English and Hebrew.[1] He called it *Arab* anti-Semitism, but today in the wake of Islamist anti-Semitism, and in light of its presence in Iran and other non-Arab Islamic countries, had he been revising his book, it is likely that Harkabi would have named it *Muslim Attitudes toward Israel*.

Muslim anti-Semitism in Europe is of more recent vintage. The survey by the European Union Monitoring Centre on Racism and Xenophobia of the rise in anti-Semitism in Europe following September 11, 2001, revealed that Muslims were more prominent than any other single group in propagating this hatred, which contradicted the expected findings that it was fringe fanatics like skinheads who were the main culprits.[2] A study by the German Ministry of the Interior published in 2007 came to a similar conclusion about Muslim anti-Semitism in Germany. The data about Muslim anti-Semitism in Europe, like the better known anti-Semitism in the contemporary Islamic world, are shocking in themselves, but they raise the question, whence this Jew-hatred? Where does it come from?

Mark R. Cohen

Professor of Near Eastern Studies at Princeton University, Mark R. Cohen holds the Khedouri A. Zilkha Professorship of Jewish Civilization in the Near East. His publications include *Under Crescent and Cross: The Jews in the Middle Ages* (Princeton University Press, 1994; rev. ed. 2008).

Myths and countermyth

Many modern myths swirl around this volatile issue. Is this anti-Semitism something new, incited initially by Zionism and more recently by the policies and actions of Israel in the Middle East, particularly as applied to the Palestinians? Many Europeans believe this to be the case, recognizing a similar motivation underlying the "new anti-Semitism" of the European Left, which is in part a protest against the State of Israel and its policies since the occupation of the West Bank and Gaza in 1967. Others, European and American Jews and Israelis, for whom the findings of the EU commission were less surprising, believe that the new Muslim anti-Semitism is nothing new at all. In their view it is part of an age-old Jew-hatred ingrained in the religion of Islam and traceable to the Qur'an itself. Muslims, for their part, have always denied that anti-Semitism is a Muslim phenomenon. In a well-known refrain, they claim that Muslims oppose Zionism and the State of Israel, *not Jews*, with whom they have always lived in harmony. In this they have found support in the old Jewish myth about an "interfaith utopia" in medieval Islam. The response of the Jewish side is an equally exaggerated "countermyth" of age-old Islamic Jew-hatred and persecution.[3]

It is, of course, dangerous to indulge in sweeping judgments about the sources of Muslim attitudes toward Jews and Israel today. The picture is far too complex and the circumstances in which manifestations of hatred rear their head in the Muslim world far too encumbered by political issues and international affairs to lead to facile conclusions about the past. The efforts of certain Islamophobic writers to prove from history that Muslim jihadists are about to take over the world—an ironic inversion of the classic anti-Semitic calumny about the Jews—are, to my mind, a distortion of the past and incendiary.[4] The most extravagant recent book on this subject is *Eurabia*, by the prolific countermyth writer Bat Ye'or, a book based on years of publishing about Islamic persecution of non-Muslims in past times.[5] She endeavors to "expose" what she thinks is an invidious European plot to conspire with Arab countries in an anti-American, anti-Israel, and anti-Semitic campaign, which will, in the end, backfire by reducing Europe to what she calls by the misleading term "dhimmitude." This servile state of sufferance and suffering under Islamic dominion will reproduce, on an international plane, the subservient condition of persecuted Jews and Christians in the medieval Islamic world. The Islamophobic obsession is spread widely today in Europe, Israel, and, most recently, the United States, as a reaction to the tragic events of 9/11. It even insinuated itself into the U.S. presidential election in 2008, when

⟩ See article by Mark. R. Cohen, pp. 28–38.

> ❝ *Like Islamophobia, the question of Muslim anti-Semitism needs to be addressed dispassionately, because, together, they have become a force behind thinking about policy issues in the Israeli-Palestinian arena.* ❞

rumors flew of Barack Obama being a secret Muslim and a terrorist sympathizer. Like Islamophobia, the question of Muslim anti-Semitism needs to be addressed dispassionately, because, together, they have become a force behind thinking about policy issues in the Israeli-Palestinian arena.

A Muslim "anti-Semitism"?

In presenting my own views, I should first define what I mean by anti-Semitism because of the fuzziness that prevails in contemporary discussions of anti-Semitism in Islam. This fuzziness emanates especially from representatives of the countermyth school, for whom every nasty expression about Jews in the Qur'an, the *ḥadīth*, and other Arabic literature, and every instance of harsh treatment or violence experienced by Jews in the past, is deemed anti-Semitic. But this is decidedly not anti-Semitism. It is, rather, the typical, though nonetheless unsavory, loathing for the "other" found in most societies even today, a disdain that, in the Middle Ages, was shared by all three Western monotheistic religions in relation to pagans and rival monotheist claimants to divine exclusivity and the right to dominate society.[6]

The proper definition of anti-Semitism, which is shared by most students of the subject, is a religiously based complex of irrational, mythical, and stereotypical beliefs about the diabolical, malevolent, and all-powerful Jew, infused, in its modern, secular form, with racism and the belief that there is a Jewish conspiracy against mankind. Defined this way, I can say with a great deal of confidence, in agreement with other seasoned scholars, that such anti-Semitism did not exist "under the crescent" in the medieval Muslim world.

If, as I and many other seasoned scholars contend, modern views of a primeval, anti-Semitic Islam are a myth, why is anti-Semitism so widespread in the Islamic world today? There are, of course, many complex and interrelated reasons, beginning with the hardening of Muslim attitudes toward Jews against the background of political developments in the last two centuries. The first is colonialism, which disrupted traditional Muslim society and engendered resentment against those Jews who identified with the European colonizers and the "civilizing mission" that seemed to be the path to modernization and an improved way of life. This drove a wedge between Arab Jews and Arab Muslims, who resisted colonialism. Another is nationalism, influenced by European secular nationalism and imported into the Middle East in the nineteenth century, where it undermined some of the pluralism and relative tolerance that marked Muslim society in earlier centuries and pitted Arab against Jew as rival claimants to the same land. Yet another cause is the emergence of Islamist movements, responding to the birth pangs of modernization imposed by European foreigners. We need to remember, however, that the early Islamist movements were inner-directed, striving to reform latitudinarian and secularizing trends of Westernizing and modernizing Arab regimes.

> *The Islamic world never experienced an Enlightenment ... opening the door to critical, transformational change, ... and to acceptance of Jews as fully tolerated citizens of a secular society.*

Jewish-Muslim relations deteriorated at an accelerated pace in the first part of the twentieth century with the Arab belief that the new political Zionism was simply another form of European colonialism robbing them of their right to self-determination in a modern state. After the Second World War, relations were eroded by Jewish fear that Arab and Muslim hostility, and, more recently, suicide terrorism against civilians, could lead to something akin to another Holocaust. All of these factors have dramatically degraded Muslim-Jewish relations.

On a larger canvas, we should recognize in the background of Arab resistance to Western modernization and to Western Jewish "incursion" in Arab lands the fact, often mentioned, that the Islamic world never experienced an Enlightenment or a modern scientific revolution challenging the old ways and opening the door to critical, transformational change, to liberal republican forms of governance, and to acceptance of Jews as fully tolerated citizens of a secular society.

All this erupted in a frenzied and irrational *new* Muslim anti-Semitism, which is not, however, indigenous to Islam; nor is it rooted in theology, as has historically been the case in the Christian world, though it is as frightening to Jews as if it were.

Christian world's influence

Muslims first came into contact with European-style anti-Semitism in the Ottoman period, when the Islamic world absorbed new Christian populations.[7]

It took off later, in the nineteenth century, during the colonial period, when European missionaries, doubtless out of zeal to promote Christianity at the expense of any other option, fostered Western-style anti-Semitic Jew-hatred in the Middle East. This propaganda supported Arab Christian aspirations for a nondenominational, pan-Arab nationalism, a secular Arab world in which Christians would enjoy full equality with ▶ See article by Henry Laurens, pp. 269–279. Muslims. Many must have felt that anti-Semitism, deflecting Muslim enmity away from themselves and onto a—to them—familiar enemy, would advance the nationalist cause in which they played such a prominent role. The outbreak of blood libels in the Ottoman Empire in the nineteenth century is suggestive in this regard.

Anti-Semitism in the Arab Middle East grew in intensity after the rise of political Zionism at the end of that century, when Jewish nationalism began to clash with nascent nationalism in the Arab world, and when Jewish immigration to Palestine, growing in numbers in the first decades of the twentieth century, came to be viewed by the Arabs as a neocolonial encroachment on Muslim soil. The flames of the new Arab/Muslim anti-Semitism were fanned in the 1940s by Nazi propagandists currying favor with Arab leaders to gain support against the Allied powers. It found expression in anti-Semitic propaganda dissemi-

An Arab cartoon applies the medieval Christian anti-Semitic cliché of the Jew as Christ-killer to the Arab-Israeli conflicts. Boukhari, from the website Arabia.com, April 7, 2002.

nated in Arabic and Persian radio broadcasts and linked to anti-Jewish themes in the Qur'an.[8]

Nazi anti-Semitic propaganda about an impending Jewish takeover of the world resonated with the infamous early twentieth-century European anti-Semitic tract in Russian, the "Protocols of the Elders of Zion," which had been translated into Arabic in the 1920s by an Arab Christian translating it from the French. The Protocols depict Jews in consort with others plotting to undermine society and conquer the world for themselves. Today, the Arabic Protocols are the most popular anti-Semitic text in the Muslim world, and they are widely believed to be true. They seem almost Islamic in origin because they resonate with old themes in the Qur'an and other early Islamic literature about Jewish treachery toward the Prophet and about Jewish assistance to Muhammad's pagan Arab enemies. Other anti-Semitic themes dredged up from classical Arabic texts have come to the fore in a process of "Islamization" of Christian European Jew-hatred.[9] This effort has not been easy, since there is relatively little hard-core anti-Semitic material in classical Islamic literature, including the Qur'an.

Some of the themes taken from original Islamic sources are interpreted more severely than they are meant in their original context. There is, for instance, the dehumanizing calumny in the Qur'an, calling the Jews "apes and pigs," a folkloristic motif present in, and apparently borrowed from, other non-Islamic cultures, and coming very close to the irrational beliefs of Christian anti-Semitism.[10] In Qur'an commentary the apes and pigs theme is applied to Christians as well, which reduces it from a specifically anti-Jewish libel to one aimed at non-Muslims in general.

> *Some of the [anti-Semitic] themes taken from original Islamic sources are interpreted more severely than they are meant in their original context.*

The indictment is based on three verses in the Qur'an proclaiming that the Jews, or in one case the People of the Book as a whole, were turned by God into apes and pigs as punishment for their sins:

And ye know of those of you who broke the Sabbath, how We said unto them: *Be ye apes, despised and hated!* (Sura 2:65 [author's emphasis])

Shall I tell thee of a worse [case] than theirs for retribution with Allah? [Worse is the case of him] whom Allah hath cursed, him on whom His wrath hath fallen and of whose sort *Allah hath turned some to apes and swine*, and who serveth idols. Such are in worse plight and further astray from the plain road. (Sura 5:60, referring to the People of the Book [author's emphasis])

So when they took pride in that which they had been forbidden, We said unto them: *Be ye apes despised and loathed!* (Sura 7:166, referring to the Sabbath breakers [author's emphasis])

The language of the verses does not actually imply that the Jews are innately inhuman, only that they were transformed into animals for their misdeeds. In an eschatological context in post-Qur'anic sources, it is Muslim sinners and heretics, adversely infected by imitation of Jewish and Christian ways, who will be turned by God into apes and pigs, a warning and a threat aimed at shoring up Islamic identity.[11] This recalls the famous homilies of the early Christian preacher St. John Chrysostom of Antioch in the fourth century against Christian "Judaizers" who imitated Jewish practices, a tactic aimed at strengthening an independent Christian identity.[12]

On rare occasions in the Middle Ages, the apes/pigs theme in the Qur'an reared its head, urging repression, even violence, against the Jews, notoriously by the Spanish Arabic poet Ibn Hazm, who used this motif in a poem inciting a "pogrom" against the Jews of Granada, Spain, in 1066.[13] But it never enjoyed the centrality as an anti-Jewish polemic that it has been given today. Taken out of its original context in the Qur'an and recast in an irrational, racial mold, it is regularly preached today from mosque pulpits, in Hamas publications, and on the Internet, and has entered popular Muslim consciousness in the form of an irrational belief that contemporary Jews are the descendants, or brothers, of apes and pigs.

▶ See article by Mercedes García-Arenal, pp. 111–129.

The components of Muslim anti-Semitism today

In the absence of a storehouse of anti-Semitic texts in classical Islam, anti-Semitism is frequently expressed in cartoons depicting Judaism, often identified by symbols of the State of Israel and infused with images recalling Nazi anti-Semitic iconography. In its most recent phase, following the establishment of the State of Israel, the military defeats in wars with Israel, and Israeli occupation of lands claimed by the Palestinian people as their own, Arab/Muslim anti-Semitism has reached a fever pitch, accompanied by terrorism aimed mainly at Israelis but also at Jews throughout the world. As for the Islamist movements, they themselves did not turn outward toward Zionism and Israel until relatively late, in the 1970s, following the debacle of the Six-Day War, the Egyptian peace treaty with Israel, and the Khomeini revolution in Iran. Only then did they begin to place Zionism and Israel firmly at the forefront of their radical mission, accentuating anti-Semitic propaganda that was only latent or secondary in importance in the earlier phase of their reformism.[14] The most recent and current flare-up of Muslim anti-Semitism, enmeshed with anti-Zionism, followed the eruption of the Second Intifada (the Al-Aqsa Intifada) in late 2000 and the events of September 11, 2001.[15]

Of late this has brought to the fore a wave of Israeli and Diaspora-Jewish fear, accompanied by prejudice that looks down upon Arabs and Muslims in invidious, stereotypical, even irrational ways. This is accompanied by amnesia on the part of many Jews from Arab lands, who no longer remember the friendly, if ambivalent, relations with Muslims that Arab Jews knew in the "old country." They have forgotten that until the twentieth century, in some cases right up until the 1940s, many in the Arabic-speaking Jewish middle class were deeply embedded in Arab society and culture, much like their ancestors in the medieval world, who wholeheartedly embraced Arabic and the Islamic culture of philosophy, science, and medicine in what was, if not an interfaith utopia, then an era of wide-ranging coexistence.

One positive sign in all this is the growing literature of nostalgia by Jews from Arab lands living in Israel and elsewhere. The description of the relative comfort and good relations with Muslim neighbors and friends in the lands of emigration, right down into the middle decades of the twentieth century, belies the narrative of Islamic persecution and expulsion promoted by so many Jews from Islamic lands. It is fitting to close with some hope. I quote from the pen of Naguib Mahfouz, the Egyptian writer and winner of the Nobel Prize for Literature. In a letter to his friend Professor Sasson Somekh, the noted Israeli scholar of modern Arabic literature and himself a native-born Iraqi Jew, Mahfouz wrote: "Our two peoples knew extraordinary partnership for many years—in ancient days, in the Middle Ages, and in the modern era, with times of quarrels and disputes few and far between. Unfortunately, we have documented the disputes one hundred times more than the periods of friendship and cooperation. I dream of the day when, thanks to the cooperation between us, this region will become a home overflowing with the light of science, blessed by the highest principles of heaven."[16,17]

❱ See article by Abdelkarim Allagui, pp. 985–989.

---

1. The Hebrew title of the book, less evocative, was ʿEmda ha-ʿarvit ba-qonflikt ha-ʿarvi-yisraeli [The Arab Stance in the Arab-Israeli Conflict].

2. The report was suppressed until interested parties got hold of it and made it public. It was widely suspected that the EU had been reluctant to publish the results for fear of antagonizing the growing Muslim population in European countries.

3. See my essay "The 'Golden Age' of Jewish-Muslim Relations" at the beginning of this book, and *Under Crescent and Cross: The Jews in the Middle Ages*, new edition with new introduction and afterword (Princeton, NJ: Princeton University Press, 2008).

4. Holocaust denial figures prominently in contemporary anti-Jewish and anti-Israel sentiment in the Muslim world. For a nuanced, contextualized history of this phenomenon, see Meir Litvak and Esther Webman, *From Empathy to Denial: Arab Responses to the Holocaust* (New York: Columbia University Press, 2009).

5. *Eurabia: The Euro-Arab Axis* (Madison, NJ: Fairleigh Dickinson University Press, 2005). Most of Bat Ye'or's books have been translated into Hebrew and some into Russian, and most of them were written originally in French.

6. See, for instance, Bernard Lewis, *Semites and Anti-Semites: An Inquiry into Conflict and Prejudice*, new edition with new afterword (New York: W. W. Norton, 1999), and, more recently, "The New Anti-Semitism," *American Scholar* 75 (Winter 2006): 25–36.

7. Lewis, *Semites and Anti-Semites*, 132.

8. See Matthias Kuentzel, *Jihad and Jew-hatred: Islamism, Nazism and the Roots of 9/11*, trans. Colin Meade (New York: Telos Press, 2007). Kuentzel puts too much emphasis on the role of the Nazis in *precipitating* (he would say) modern Arab anti-Semitism without acknowledging the longue durée of the phenomenon, reaching back to the nineteenth century, with antecedents in the Ottoman period. See also Jeffrey Herf, *Nazi Propaganda for the Arab World* (New Haven, CT: Yale University Press, 2009). Herf writes only about radio transmissions in Arabic. According to

Matthias Kuentzel, "Iranian Antisemitism: Stepchild of German National Socialism," *Israel Journal of Foreign Affairs* 4, no. 1 (January 2010): 43–51, the Nazis broadcast in Persian as well.

9. Michael Kiefer, "Islamischer, Islamistischer oder Islamisierter Antisemitismus," *Die Welt des Islams* 46 (2006): 277–306; Lewis, *Semites and Anti-Semites*, 267 (in the afterword). This was already recognized by Harkabi, writing in the late 1960s; see *Arab Attitudes to Israel* (Jerusalem: Israel Universities Press, 1972).

10. Ilse Lichtenstaedter, "And Become Ye Accursed Apes," *Jerusalem Studies in Arabic and Islam* 14 (1991): 153–75.

11. Uri Rubin, "Apes, Pigs and the Islamic Identity," *Israel Oriental Studies* 17 (1997): 89–105. The apes/pigs threat is used today by Muslim preachers to discourage their congregants from transgressing, for instance, by listening to musical instruments. See http://www.islam-qa.com/en/cat/2008#2022.

12. See Cohen, *Under Crescent and Cross: The Jews in the Middle Ages*, new edition with new introduction and afterword (Princeton, NJ: Princeton University Press, 2008), 72–73.

13. Ibid., 338–40.

14. Emmanuel Sivan, "Islamic Fundamentalism, Antisemitism, and Anti-Zionism," in *Anti-Zionism and Antisemitism in the Contemporary World*, ed. Robert S. Wistrich (Houndsmill, Basingstoke: Macmillan in association with the Institute of Jewish Affairs, 1990), 74–84.

15. Esther Webman, "Anti-Zionism, Anti-Semitism, and Criticism of Israel: The Arab Perspective," *Tel Aviver Jahrbuch für Geschichte* 33 (2005): 306–29.

16. This letter is excerpted in Sasson Somekh's memoirs, *Baghdad, Yesterday: The Making of an Arab Jew* (Jerusalem: Ibis Editions, 2007), 175.

17. A longer version of this essay was published in Hebrew in the Israeli journal *Politika* 19 (Spring 2009): 121–40, and in English in *Muslim Attitudes to Jews and Israel: The Ambivalence of Rejection, Antagonism, Tolerance and Cooperation*, ed. Moshe Ma'oz (Brighton and Portland: Sussex Academic Press, 2010). A few changes, for instance, regarding bibliographical references in French, have been made.

The Anti-Semitic Obsession of al-Qa'ida

Al-Qa'ida emerged in the particular environment of the Islamist Arabs installed in Pakistan to help the anti-Soviet jihad in Afghanistan. These expatriate militants contributed little to the war of liberation of the Afghan mujahidin, which did not prevent their claiming a large role in the defeat of the Red Army. The major personality of the exiled community was a charismatic Palestinian sheik, Abdullah Azzam, who denounced the compromises of Yasir Arafat and the Palestine Liberation Organization (PLO) with the hated USSR. Azzam openly turned away from the struggle against Israel, and he justified the priority given to the Afghan jihad by reason of opportunity: the borders with Pakistan were open to foreign volunteers, while Jordan and the Golan had become impenetrable for the Palestinian commandos.

Azzam, referred to by his partisans as "the imam of jihad," established a Bureau of Services in Peshawar in 1984; to run its international network, he chose the young and rich Saudi activist Osama Bin Laden. But Bin Laden subsequently developed a close relationship with Ayman al-Zawahiri, an Egyptian jihadist, hardened by years of clandestine subversion, who advocated, far beyond the anti-Soviet struggle, the confrontation with America the "infidel" and its Arab allies. It was in the spirit of this global jihad that al-Qa'ida was secretly founded in August 1988. Azzam, kept at a distance from the new structure, died in an attack in November 1989. The range of possible sponsors of such a murder was broad, from the CIA to the KGB, not to mention Zawahiri himself, determined to remove any eventual obstacles to the global jihad. But Bin Laden repeatedly accused the Mossad of having eliminated his former mentor. Thus the founding crime of al-Qa'ida was ascribed to the Jews, by a compensatory mechanism honed to perfection at other times and in other places.

The Soviet withdrawal from Afghanistan dispersed the Arab community of Peshawar, which Bin Laden strove to mobilize on other fronts—against the Marxist regime of South Yemen, and even against the Iraqi invasion of Kuwait. These projects fell short, and the head of al-Qa'ida, strategically retreating to the Sudan, sharpened his criticism of the Saudi monarchy, which froze his assets and stripped him of his nationality. Bin Laden and Zawahiri attributed the dissolution of the USSR to its humiliation in Afghanistan, and they believed the global jihad to be capable of inflicting a comparable defeat on the United States. With this in mind, al-Qa'ida tried to infiltrate Somalia in 1993–94, to harass the Western troops there, but the adventure was inconclusive. It would take more than that to keep Bin Laden from intensifying his warlike rhetoric. Al-Qa'ida regrouped in Afghanistan in the summer of 1996, and Bin Laden, uplifted by this return to the theater of his first battles, solemnly declared war on America, whom he accused of occupying the Holy Land of Arabia.

It was "the Jewish-Crusader alliance" that the head of al-Qa'ida singled out for trial by the mob: "The Muslims have realized that they were the main target of the Jewish-Crusader coalition, and all that false propaganda about human rights has given way to blows and massacres against the Muslims in every part of the world. The latest calamity incurred by the Muslims is the occupation of the land of the two Holy Mosques, the foundation of the house of Islam, the cradle of the prophecy and source of the divine message." That is why Bin Laden, in this militant manifesto of August 23, 1996, called for the lifting of "the iniquity imposed on the Muslim nation by the Jewish-Crusader alliance."

This symbolic irruption of the Jewish figure was all the more troubling given that the global jihad had until then been mobilized against the "infidel" imperialisms or against the "apostate" Muslims. As for Bin Laden's indictment of the Saudi regime, it was based on his rejection of all Western presence in Arabia, at the very moment when Riyadh was soliciting the deployment of American forces, in August 1990, to face the Iraqi threat. The military engagement of the United States continued after the liberation of Kuwait and helped to protect the fragile Gulf regimes from being overturned from within and without. In demanding the retreat of the U.S. forces outside his native land, Bin Laden was betting on the destabilization of the Saudi regime that such a withdrawal might bring about.

But al-Qaʻida innovated by recasting its revolutionary project on a global scale: now the Muslims of the entire world would become the target of a generalized, implacable, and methodical campaign of aggression and humiliation. The Jewish-Crusader alliance, according to Bin Laden, was motivated by an implacable hostility against Islam. The groundwork for the modern "Crusades," conducted by the United States, was laid by the "Jewish" plundering of Palestine. The head of al-Qaʻida thus endorsed the anti-Zionist theme, popular in the Islamist camp, and gave it his own strategic priority, the expulsion of the American forces from Arabia, as a prelude to the eventual overthrow of the Wahabite monarchy (just as the Soviet retreat from Afghanistan had sealed the fate of the communist regime of Kabul).

This Jewish-Crusader amalgamation allowed Bin Laden to connect, in the dynamics of his global jihad, the three holy places of Islam—Mecca, Medina, and Jerusalem—the first two under "crusade" occupation, the third under "Jewish" occupation. But he also based his manifesto on the invocation of one of the last wishes attributed to the Prophet Muhammad: "Expel the Jews and the Christians from the Arabic

Peninsula." While Muhammad had granted protective pacts to the Jewish and Christian minorities of Arabia once Islam had been installed in Mecca and consolidated in Medina, this posthumous hadith justified the religious homogenization of the Arabic Peninsula by his successors. This cornerstone of the Wahabite dogma was turned against the Saudi family by Bin Laden.

During the following eight years, that is, from 1996 to 2004, the head of al-Qaʻida mentioned the Jews, or the Jewish religion, about two hundred times. But the Jews were associated in three-fourths of these citations with the "Crusaders," America, or the Christians, who were their "brothers," protégés, or even mentors. Bin Laden identified the Jews with Israel or Zionism only about forty times, and referred even less frequently to classical sources, suras or hadiths, concerning the Jews. Thus, al-Qaʻida's hostility toward the Jews had a decidedly modern tone. It emanated neither from religious Judeophobia nor from an exacerbated anti-Semitism: it followed from a frontal opposition to an America that was irreducibly opposed to Islam.

The theme of the manipulation of Washington by the Jews became increasingly frequent with Bin Laden. On March 18, 1997, he told the Pakistani press that the "present government of the United States is under the influence of the Jews" and that "dealing with the United States comes down to dealing with the Jews." On May 12, 1997, he amalgamated the two "Jewish Crusade" occupations in an interview with CNN: "The American army came to Saudi Arabia to divide the Muslims and the people, in order that there would no longer be a governing by the law of Allah there, and also to support the Israeli forces in occupied Palestine."

On February 23, 1998, Bin Laden and Zawahiri announced the foundation of the "World Islamic Front for Jihad against the Jews and Crusaders." Al-Qaʻida succeeded on this occasion in rallying to its global jihad other groups implanted in Egypt, Pakistan, and

Bangladesh, but this gathering, rather a loose one at that, was less important than the consolidation of the Jewish-Crusade theme: "If the Americans' war goals are religious and economic, they also happen to serve the little state of the Jews, its occupation of Jerusalem, and its liquidation of the Muslims. Nothing shows this more clearly than their ardent desire to destroy Iraq, the most powerful Arab state in the region, and their preoccupation with dismantling all the states in the region and transforming them into cardboard imitations, like Iraq, Saudi Arabia, Egypt, and the Sudan, which will, by their division and weakness, ensure the survival of Israel, as well as the continuation of the crusader and iniquitous occupation of the Arabic Peninsula."

Bin Laden, who had no words harsh enough to thrash "the apostate" Saddam Hussein, could not be suspected of the least complacency toward the Iraqi dictator. But the ruthless fury of Washington toward Baghdad seemed to him proof of the Jewish hold on the American decision-making process. He hammered away at this on Al Jazeera on December 20, 1998, after three days of Anglo-American bombings of Iraq: "The Jews managed to get the Christians, the Americans, and the British to take charge of attacking Iraq. The United States pretends it is in command of the operations against Iraq. But the obvious reality is that the Jews and the Israelis dominate the White House. The secretary of defense is Jewish, the secretary of state is Jewish, the responsible parties in the CIA and the National Security Council are Jewish, and other prominent responsible parties of the first order are Jewish. They have led the Christians to break the wings of the Arab world." Carried away by his enthusiasm, Bin Laden later said that President Clinton himself was Jewish. In any case, the idea of the manipulation of the Crusaders by the Jews at the expense of the Muslims became an obsession, and the head of al-Qa'ida went so far as to denounce the "Jewish Crusade."

The paradoxical flip side of such a redundant discourse was that the anti-American jihad absorbed all the other forms of jihad, and that al-Qa'ida thus avoided fighting concretely against Israel. The September 2000 outbreak of the Second Intifada, though placed beneath the symbol of Al-Aqsa, changed nothing with respect to that abstention of al-Qa'ida from the Palestinian struggle. Bin Laden often claimed his ideological affinity with Sheikh Safar al-Hawali, one of the figures in the Saudi Islamist protest movement, who at the time characterized "Christian Zionism," in vogue in the United States, as a far more dangerous enemy than Jewish Zionism, which had a more circumscribed influence. That fixation on America oriented the planning of the attacks of September 11, 2001, and the disowning of these attacks by Sheikh Hawali did not modify the strategic posture of al-Qa'ida.

The rapid collapse of the Taliban Emirate seemed to amaze Bin Laden, who was betting on the long-term resistance of his Afghan allies and on a bogging down of the American army at the gates of Kabul, or at least of Kandahar. Al-Qa'ida lost an exceptional sanctuary, and a significant number of its cadres and members were killed or imprisoned, while the jihadist elite was split apart in different countries of refuge. Bin Laden and Zawahiri, falling back into the tribal zones of the Pakistan border, were criticized for having precipitated the fall of the mulla Omar and the Taliban regime. The head of al-Qa'ida concentrated most of his resources on the preparation of a long-term terrorist campaign in Saudi Arabia, but would resume efforts against the Jewish Crusaders as soon as possible.

The chosen target was the El Ghriba synagogue, the oldest on the African continent, located on the Tunisian island of Djerba. Al-Qa'ida's intent was to strike a historical symbol of peaceful coexistence between Jews and Muslims, but also a pro-Western regime opposed to all forms of political Islam. The Tunisian suicide bomber, in cooperation with the leadership of al-Qa'ida in Pakistan, had intended to carry out the attack during the annual pilgrimage, which draws thousands of participants, but was asked to act rapidly. On April 11, 2002, al-Qaʻida sent a truck wired with a bomb to the synagogue, which crashed through a previously hollowed-out wall. Twenty people, a majority of whom were German tourists, died in the explosion. In a recording broadcast shortly afterward, Bin Laden declared that "the war has pitted us against the Jews, and any country that engages itself in the same trenches as the Jews will regret it."

Al-Qaʻida, unable to repeat the carnage of September 11 and powerless against the American steamroller in Afghanistan, intensified its search for highly visible Jewish targets in order to symbolically relaunch its worldwide jihad. The recentering was accompanied by a renewed media mobilization. On October 26, 2002, Bin Laden addressed an open letter to the "American people," in which he feigned to warn against Jewish manipulation: "The Jews began by taking control of your economy, then your media, and henceforth they control all the aspects of your life. They have subjugated you, and they reach their goals at your expense." That is why, he argued, the United States has become the seat of the "worst civilization in the history of the human race."

The "hard targets," with a military component, remained beyond the operational reach of al-Qaʻida—hence the choice by default of "soft targets" of the tourist sort. After the Djerba synagogue, the city of Mombasa, in the south of Kenya, was chosen; it was a popular destination among Israeli travelers, and small, dormant al-Qaʻida cells had been implanted in the country for many years. The operation carried out on November 28, 2002, was ambitious, with a simultaneous strike on two objectives: an Israeli charter plane (which escaped two surface-to-air missiles) and a hotel frequented by Israeli tourists. There a suicide bombing killed fifteen people, mostly members of a Kenyan troupe of folklore performers.

Al-Qaʻida demonstrated the enduring nature of its terrorist threat a year after the loss of its Afghan bases, but these attacks were insufficient for global jihad to get back on its feet in the arena of confrontation with the "infidels." On March 1, 2003, Bin Laden directed his coreligionists to "kill the Americans and Jews with bullets, knives, or stones." But two months later he launched al-Qaʻida into an exhausting conflict with Saudi security, while at the same time the American invasion of Iraq offered a Jordanian adventurer, Abu Musab al-Zarqawi, a chance to develop his own network. Al-Qaʻida and the Zarqawi group collaborated in the planning and financing of an attack on two Istanbul synagogues on November 15, 2003. The massacre was followed, five days later, by a new wave of explosions in the Turkish city, this time targeting British interests. Bin Laden thus succeeded in demonstrating that two years after 9/11, and six months after the fall of Saddam Hussein, the "global war against terror" was far from being won.

Zarqawi hoped to integrate al-Qaʻida with his followers. He wrote at length to Bin Laden and Zawahiri to that effect, and planned his anti-American jihad within the perspective of a global confrontation: "The Americans entered Iraq in order to carry out the contract of building the Great Israel from the Nile to the Euphrates, because that Zionized American government thinks that to hasten the establishing of that state will hasten the coming of the Messiah." Only the Sunni minority of Iraq was prepared to stymie this satanic plan, because the Shiʻite majority, a true "fifth column," was at the mercy of its "Jewish masters," and the Kurds had "opened their land to the Jews." Bin Laden had extended the struggle against the Jews into the jihad against America: Zarqawi transformed it into a campaign of liquidation of their Iraqi "agents," with a particular ferocity directed against the Shiʻite "heretics."

The strategic option of anti-Shiʻite terror was validated by Bin Laden in fall 2004, and Zarqawi was promoted to head of al-Qaʻida in Iraq. The escalation of horror culminated in 2006 in a real civil war, which bloodied Baghdad and the Iraqi provinces, whose populations were still mixed. Al-Qaʻida wanted to be the avant-garde of the most intolerant Sunnism, and it accused Iran and Hezbollah of playing the game of "Jewish Crusaders." (Saddam Hussein's propaganda had already qualified the Iranian military as "Zionist" during the first Gulf War in 1980–88.) This outbreak of anti-Shi'ism, however, did not succeed in protecting al-Qa'ida from the vindictive fury of the Iraqi tribes, who, frightened by that politics of making things worse in order to achieve an eventual long-term improvement, turned their arms against the partisans of Bin Laden.

From 2008 on, al-Qa'ida found itself on the defensive everywhere. Its networks, very much weakened in Iraq, were breaking down completely in Arabia and they did not succeed in extending beyond the jihadist fallback positions in Algeria. The obsessive indictment of the Jews by al-Qa'ida propaganda could not hide the reality of a blind terror whose overwhelming majority of victims were Muslims killed in Islamic lands. Even the Hamas movement was stigmatized by al-Qa'ida, which was denounced for having tacitly recognized the State of Israel (in accepting to participate in elections in the West Bank and Gaza), and accused of having compromised with the Jews. Global jihad continued on its homicidal hunt for the

Jewish scapegoat. But this Jew, with his multiform and nefarious influence, existed only in the anti-Semitic imagination. Al-Qa'ida sought to associate America with other symbolic targets, and it castigated President Barack Obama with the term "slave." According to al-Qa'ida, Bill Clinton was surrounded by too many Jews not to be one himself, and Obama was reduced to the supposed fate of his skin color. This headlong rush into racial slurs speaks volumes on the deep crisis of al-Qa'ida—disavowed and driven out by those whom it claimed to defend. The planetary struggle against the Jewish Crusaders brought with it nothing but ruin and desolation for the Muslims themselves. It is as if the real war waged by al-Qa'ida had never been against anything but Islam. ●

Jean-Pierre Filiu is associate Professor at Sciences Po, in charge with Middle East Studies and has held visiting professorships at Columbia University and Georgetown University. His publications include Apocalypse in Islam *(Fayard, 2008; University of California Press, 2011), which was awarded the Augustin-Thierry Prize of the French History Convention in Blois.* La véritable histoire d'al-Qaida *(Fayard, 2011) and* Le Nouveau Moyen-Orient *(Fayard, 2013). His books and articles have been translated into a dozen languages.*

Chapter VI
Looking at the Other

Relations between Jews and Muslims in Hebrew Literature
Françoise Saquer-Sabin

Modern Hebrew literature, which emerged in Central and Eastern Europe in the late eighteenth century, developed concomitantly with the emancipation and modernization of European Jewry. That literature took root in Palestine in the first third of the twentieth century. It both reflected and fueled the pioneer ideology that sprung up from Zionism and socialism. In other words, religion and tradition, vestiges of a rejected world, are absent from all the artistic and cultural expressions of that new identity construction. As a result, the representation of an Arab world, or of relations between Jews and Arabs in Palestine and Israel, was generally articulated at a national or even nationalist level, and in no case at a truly religious level. Nevertheless, religious affiliation is mentioned in certain works. I shall not give an exhaustive account of them here but shall rather consider a few trends in the treatment of the theme.

Françoise Saquer-Sabin

Françoise Saquer-Sabin is a professor of modern Hebrew literature at the Université Charles-de-Gaulle Lille 3. A member of the staff at the Centre d'Études en Civilisations, Langues et Littératures Étrangères (CECILLE, Center for Studies on Foreign Civilizations, Languages, and Literatures), she directs the Mediterranean Worlds research program. She is the author of *Le personnage de l'Arabe palestinien dans la littérature hébraïque du xxᵉ siècle* (CNRS Éditions, 2002), and of many articles, particularly on representations of the Israeli-Palestinian conflict and on women's literature.

Expressing the Arab world

The most significant works, inasmuch as they clearly define a religious identity or, more exactly, a socioreligious affiliation, are set in the diaspora within an Arab and/or Muslim sphere. They come from Israeli authors who themselves grew up in these environments: Sami Michaël (b. 1926 in Baghdad), with *Victoria* (1993) and *Aïda* (2008);[1] Shimon Ballas (b. 1930 in Baghdad), with *Outcast* (1991);[2] and Dorit Rabinyan (b. 1972 to an Iranian family in Israel), with *Persian Brides* (1995).[3]

Abraham B. Yehoshua (b. 1936 to a Sephardic family in Jerusalem) sets *A Journey to the End of the Millennium* in Ashkenazi Europe.[4] And Alon Hilu (b. 1972 in Israel to Syrian parents), after depicting a historical trial for ritual murder in nineteenth-century Damascus (*Death of a Monk*, 2004),[5] returns to the origins of the colonial enterprise in Ottoman Palestine in the early twentieth century (*The House of Rajani*, 2008).[6]

For Shimon Ballas, Sami Michaël, and Dorit Rabinyan, the description of a Jewish world in Baghdad (*Outcast, Victoria*) or in the suburbs of Isfahan (*Persian Brides*) attests that that world has been pervaded by the Orient, and it is difficult to determine how that influence is entangled with religious sources. In the Iran of Reza Shah, before the advent of a certain modernity on the model of Atatürk's Turkey, women's lives, though described with humor and sensuality, belong to a different era and primarily involve the marrying off of nubile girls (*Persian Brides*). In both Iraq and Iran, the Jews wear traditional clothing and women the chador. In Ballas's novel, the father smokes a narghile in the village and wears traditional clothes, but in Baghdad he wears European clothing. At home, the children must eat with forks (*Outcast*).

Mastery of Arabic is another factor that promotes cultural integration. Victoria's Arabic is said to be superior to that of the Muslims (*Victoria*); the Jews who remained in Baghdad adopted the Arab accent at the expense of Jewish Arabic (*Aïda*). As for the Maghrebi Jews, they feel more at ease in the "rich, vigorous, and expansive Ishmaelite language," as Yehoshua writes in *A Journey to the End of the Millennium*.

In the Arab Muslim environment, the neighborhoods of the city are segregated: Muslim, Christian, or Jewish. In Iran, the Jews' houses are lower than those of the Muslims (*Persian Brides*). In Iraq, some cafés are reserved for the Muslims, and the Jews and Muslims do not share food, even when they are friends (*Outcast*). Although the Jews bow to the laws of the state (*Persian Brides*), they are loath to turn to the authorities to settle their personal problems (*Victoria*).

In relations between Jewish and Muslim characters, social background is decisive. The Jewish main characters are usually well-off, and in some cases maintain more or less close connections to the representatives of power (*Victoria, Aïda, Outcast, Journey to the End of the Millennium*). A Jew may be so thoroughly embedded in society that he is taken for a Muslim (*Aïda*); an

Cover of the English translation of the novel *Outcast*, by the Iraqi-born Jewish writer Shimon Ballas, published by City Lights in 2007.

Easterner educated in America may be mistaken for a Westerner (*Outcast*). In spite of everything, however, integration is always subject to the vicissitudes of political life and the complex relationships between the different communities (*Aïda, Outcast*). Furthermore, social interactions are often vitiated by power relations and deceit, which do damage to loyal friendships (*Aïda, Outcast, A Journey to the End of the Millennium*). Religion is one of the most ambiguous factors, since, apart from *A Journey to the End of the Millennium*, relationship markers in these novels are more often established at the ethnosociopolitical level. In Yehoshua's book, however, the three religions are placed on equal footing, inasmuch as the date is given in accordance with all three calendars: the Hebrew, the Islamic, and the Gregorian. The God of the Jews and that of the Muslims are on friendly terms and complement each other, even in Abou Loufti's expression of thanks: he is grateful to "the God of the Jews, who had not prevented the great Allah from bringing his dear ones back safely, Jews and Ishmaelites alike, from the Black Forest of the Rhineland."

> **In relations between Jewish and Muslim characters, social background is decisive.**

The fate of minorities

Even conversion to Islam is portrayed not as a religious aspiration but rather as a means for establishing an identity or as a factor in integration, possibly pragmatic in nature (*Aïda*). For example, the choice of Islam is the driving force in Ballas's *Outcast*. In that novel, the protagonist's conversion to Islam appears to be a necessity linked to the choice that he, an intellectual from a good family educated in Western schools, makes about his identity. The successful integration that results does not resolve his sense of being an outcast. "No longer the outcast," he is "already inside." Rejected by his own people, he establishes his own Muslim family and strives to defend Islam against the West, calling on the Jews to abandon their particularism and to support their Muslim and Christian brothers against Zionism, a symbol of Western domination and "ethnocentric and xenophobic mentality that characterizes Judaism." His proposal to counter Khomeini's Islamism with a secular and modern manifesto founded on a national, cultural, and moral approach is, however, akin to the Zionist ideology he abhors.

Shimon Ballas has always portrayed the uncomfortable position of the "Arab-Jew" from the point of view of the Easterner confronted with the voluntarism of Zionist ideology.[7] Here, however, he reverses the identity model. The Arab-Jew becomes the Jew-Arab, who chooses to remain in the diaspora.

Sami Michaël's *Aïda* also disregards the Zionist illusion and privileges the choice of the diaspora.

Zaki did not follow his family to Israel, and he dreams of being "the last Jew [in Baghdad] in what used to be a paradise." The structure of the novel establishes a par-

Cover of the novel *Aïda*, by Sami Michael, published by Kinneret Zmora-Bitan Dvir in 2008. Cover designed by Imri Zertai. Photograph by Ziyah Gafic.

allel between his fate and that of the Shi'ite woman Samia, to whom he had been close since childhood. The Shi'ites, though in the majority, constitute a political minority persecuted by the Sunni authority. Zaki, faithful to the relationships established between the two families, saved Samia and her loved ones from destruction, thanks to his connections to powerful authorities. But as the regime becomes more rigid, a third minority arrives in their personal space, embodied by the Kurdish woman Aïda. The Jew finds himself caught between warring poles: the authorities and the rebels. The conclusion offers no hope: Zaki will not be the last Jew left in Baghdad.

The East versus the West

Yehoshua's *A Journey to the End of the Millennium* transposes the relationship between East and West to the time of the Crusades in Ashkenazi Europe. The Easterners from Tangier, both Jews and Muslims, unite against the Christian West. The Eastern environment is described positively in every particular: the "cramped and sad" cathedral of Rouen, "sad in its dark severity," is overpowered by the "spacious mosques" in North Africa and Andalus. The solidarity between Jews and Muslims, united by their daily proximity to each other, runs in both directions. They exchange their colorful clothing for more discreet attire and, in the Rouen church, all pass themselves off as Muslims. Later, in his speech in support of bigamy, the rabbi protects the "Ishmaelites" from the Ashkenazi Jews, by focusing on Ishmael, Abraham's elder son. Toward the end of the voyage, those who define themselves as "subjects of Ishmaelites living very far from here" mark their difference from their Ashkenazi brothers, and the land of Islam, compared to the land of the Crusaders, looks like a refuge: "There you shall live."

Although *A Journey to the End of the Millennium* presents a spatiotemporal context remote from the two works discussed previously, the narrative approach is similar: the novel deals with a problem in the here and now from a different perspective, on occasion by revealing its opposite. In every case, the work leads us back to contemporary history and to its author's sociopolitical choices. Ballas and Michaël, who were closely associated with the Communist Party in the 1950s—at a time when it constituted a place for Arabs and Jews to come together—both explore their common ground, though in different ways. Conversely, Yehoshua revisits the relationship between Ashkenazi and Sephardic Jews, inverting the system of qualifiers.

In Israel, from the political Other to the religious Other

The works written before 1948 did not take into account the religious dimension of the relationship between Jews and Muslims to any great extent, since at the time religious affiliation was perceived only from the angle of national identity. In these novels, a certain diversification of the Arab world (citizens of Israel, nationals from the territories of Cisjordan or Gaza, Christians, Muslims) corresponds to an attempt to move from a flat and unilateral metonymic representation to three-dimensional characters moving through a vast universe. The crossing of borders and the acknowledgment of the multiple components of Palestinian society came about belatedly, at the end of the 1970s, with Sami Michaël's *Refuge* (1977).[8] Mentions of religious affiliation have no function other than to situate the character in his environment, whereas the relationship with the Jewish character is established on ethnic and political grounds. In Yehoshua's *The Liberated Bride* (2001),[9] the Jewish Orientalist spends his day at the home of Muslims in Galilee and his night at the home of Christians in Samaria. The religious aspect is one variant in a world he aspires to blend into, so as to know it from the inside. Thus Michaël's *Refuge* and Yehoshua's *The Liberated Bride* attempt to restore the diversity of the Arab world. But only Itamar Levy (b. 1956 in Israel) places Islam at the center of a novel in the postmodernist vein, which unfolds in the midst of the Intifada: *Otiyot ha-shemesh, otiyot ha-yareah* (*Sun Letters, Moon Letters*).[10]

This book is constructed as a kind of puzzle composed of Arabic letters and Islamic legends. The narrative follows the order of the Arabic alphabet, with letters punctuating each chapter. The narrator, a faithful Muslim, tries to learn and locate them in the sacred texts. His unwavering faith in the omnipotence of scripture confers on it the virtue of providing the answer to everything and the determination for all of life's events: "If only I had a Qur'an, I would open it randomly to any page, I would blindly put my finger on one of the verses, and I would know by the first letter which of us will soon die by the soldiers' bullets." But the closer he comes to the end of his study, the more he understands that his possibilities for action are limited, and he dies before reaching the end of the alphabet. As a result, the wondrous epic of the return to Jerusalem, which the hero experienced as the ultimate escape, comes to look like a

> **"Mentions of religious affiliation have no function other than to situate the character in his environment."**

mise en abyme of his ineluctable fate: "Walking around, I realized that we were going in circles and that the Jerusalem I had dreamed of existed only in my imagination." The author delivers no political message, but he does attempt to give an identity to a different people, through a point of view in which reality and the fantastic, personal experience and the Oriental imaginary, religious visions and a restrained eroticism combine in a sort of churning and uncontrollable stream of consciousness.

In Alon Hilu's *The House of Rajani*, which retraces the establishment of the first pioneers in Jaffa in the early twentieth century, the representation of Islam is rendered through two narrative consciousnesses, that of a Jewish pioneer and that of a young Arab boy, heir to the fertile lands of the Rajani family. The Jewish point of view evokes somewhat anecdotally the religious aspect (funerary rite, mourning, the wearing of the veil). Nevertheless, the enlightened Westerner's perspective is not lacking in contempt for the superstitions surrounding the evil jinn who leave the Egyptian tenant farmers and the Muslim population as a whole paralyzed with fear.

One of the metaphorical components of the novel is the sexualization of the relation to the land. In contrast to the Hebrew narratives of the time, which placed the sickliness of the Diaspora Jew in opposition to the robust health of the Bedouin,[11] virility and beauty are here on the side of the Jew. The Arab men are weak (the son), effeminate (the father), homosexual (the two brokers), and in fact powerless to control their fate. The young Salah laments that Allah did not create him like the other boys: they know how to fight, whereas he writes poems and stories and falls into a deep sadness and nostalgia. The Arab narrative consciousness presented through that character portrays a romantic and idealized view of the Qur'anic sources and of ancestral customs. The dichotomy between the reality of the opposing armies and the boy's desire to save his people and his land by "a sharp dagger blade" while invoking Allah, as well as the references to the Muslim's traditional virility, only confirms the inevitability of defeat. The metaphorization of the conquest ends with the Muslim's inability to make use of his traditional weapons. The child becomes a preacher, but his prophetic visions of a people driven from their native land make him appear to be mad.

The author, who knows how the events will play out, presents two apparently contradictory perspectives on history, which, however, reflect the everyday experience of each of the protagonists. The posited system of relationships tends to represent metonymically the mechanism of power relations in operation since the origin of the Zionist enterprise in Palestine.

A study of these different novels thus brings to light an imbalance between the representation of Israeli reality and that of an Arab Muslim society. In no case, however, is the representation of Islam linked to a quest of a religious nature. In the "Iraqi" works, the choice of Islam as a revolutionary aspiration is placed side by side with the Communist struggle; conversely, conversion to the dominant religion is a means of preserving and strengthening national unity. In Israeli reality, the system of relationships is not fundamentally modified by the fact that the Arab is Muslim or Christian, and it seems that explorations of that other side, long schematic and two-dimensional, do not venture beyond the ethnosocial aspect. Nevertheless, these different approaches trace a path toward a broader view of the relations between Judaism and Islam in the contemporary Near East.

---

1. Sami Michaël, *Victoria*, translated into French by Sylvie Cohen (Paris: Denoël, 1996); translated into English by Dalya Dilu (London: Macmillan, 1995).

2. Shimon Ballas, *Outcast*, translated into English by Ammiel Alcalay and Oz Shelach (San Francisco: City Lights, 2007; 1st ed., 1991; original Hebrew ed., Tel Aviv: ha-Qibbutz ha-Méuhad, 2005).

3. Dorit Rabinyan, *Larmes de miel*, translated into French by Arlette Pierrot (Paris: Denoël, 2002); translated into English by Yael Lotan as *Persian Brides* (Edinburgh: Canongate, 1998).

4. Abraham B. Yehoshua, *Voyage ver l'an mil*, translated into French by Francine Lévy (Paris: Calmann-Lévy, 1998); translated into English by Nicholas de Lange as *A Journey to the End of the Millennium* (New York: Doubleday, 1999).

5. Alon Hilu, *La mort du moine*, translated into French by Emmanuel Mosès (Paris: Editions du Seuil, 2008); translated into English by Evan Fallenberg as *Death of a Monk* (London: Harvill Secker, 2006).

6. Alon Hilu, *La Maison Rajani*, translated into French by Jean-Luc Allouche (Paris: Editions du Seuil, 2010); translated into English by Evan Fallenberg as *The House of Rajani* (London: Vintage, 2010).

7. "Arab-Jew" is a designation embraced by the Eastern Jews. See also Hanan Hever's afterword to the novel (165–72): "A Jewish convert to Islam will always be suspect."

8. Sami Michaël, *Hasut* (Tel Aviv: Am Oved, 1977), translated into English by Edward Grossman as *Refuge* (Philadelphia: Jewish Publishers Society, 1988).

9. Abraham B. Yehoshua, *La mariée libérée* (2001), translated into French by Francine Lévy (Paris: Calmann-Lévy, 2003), 225; translated into English by Hillel Halkin as *The Liberated Bride* (London: Peter Halban, 2004).

10. Itamar Levy, *Lettres de soleil, lettres de lune* (1991), translated into French by Laurent Schuman (Arles: Actes Sud, 1997).

11. In Yossef Haïm Brenner (1881–1921), for example. See Françoise Saquer-Sabin, *Le personnage de l'Arabe palestinien dans la littérature hébraïque du XXᵉ siècle* (Paris: CNRS Éditions, 2002), 24, 93.

Jewish Figures in Modern Arabic Literature

Sobhi Boustani

Contemporary Arab writers consider the Arab-Israeli conflict a major subject, but the Jewish figure in modern Arabic literature seems relatively limited. It is true that only an exhaustive analysis of that literature would be able to reveal all the elements of that figure, but such an approach is far beyond the means of a lone researcher. Nevertheless, the examination of a large body of work and a number of studies on the subject allow us to observe that the evolution of the Jewish figure in modern Arabic literature is closely linked to developments in the geopolitical situation in the Near East.[1] In approaching this set of problems, we may consider various temporal and spatial boundaries: (a) literature from before and after 1948; (b) Palestinian literature of the "inside" and of the "outside"; and (c) literature of other Arab countries.

Sobhi Boustani

Professor of language and Arabic literature at the National Institute of Oriental Languages and Civilizations (INALCO), Sobhi Boustani specializes in the stylistics and poetics of modern Arabic literature. His recent publications include "Arabic Literature in Israel," in *L'Etat d'Israël*, ed. Alain Dieckhoff (Paris: Fayard, 2008), and "The Biblical Symbol in Modern Arabic Poetry," in *Tsafon, Journal of Jewish Studies North* 51 (2006).

A recurrent categorization

In the literature of the Arab Nahda (renaissance), the Jewish figure conforms perfectly to a stereotype transmitted by popular imagery through the ages. Although the story is set in the ninth century, the Jewish character in *al-Abbasa, sister of al-Rashid* (1906), by Lebanese author Jurji Zaydan (1861–1914), is a rich and greedy slave trader. Making money is his only goal, and by any means possible. The Palestinian writer Khalil Baydas (1875–1949), in his novel *al-Warith* (The Inheritor; 1920),[2] reproduces the same traditional image: the Jew who gets rich through usury and the exploitation of decent people. That image begins to change with the acceleration of Jewish immigration to Palestine between the two wars. The new social and political landscape inspired the Palestinian author Ishaq Musa al-Husayni (1904–90) in his novel *Memoirs of a Hen* (1943). As in fables, the story unfolds between two groups of hens who must live together. With fine subtlety, the text suggests the devastating and invasive force of the Zionist Jews,

Scene from the play *Return to Haifa*, adapted for the theater by Boaz Gaon from the novel by Ghassan Kanafani, directed by Sinai Peter, produced by the Cameri Theatre in Tel-Aviv, and performed at Theater J of the Jewish Community Center in Washington, D.C., during the festival "Voices from a Changing Middle East: Portraits of Home," January 2011. Photograph by Stan Barouh.

who, with no desire to share, take over the space and express their penchant to dominate.

The creation of the State of Israel in 1948 coincided with the expansion of realism as a literary current in modern Arabic literature. The Jewish figure took on new orientations. In the writings of Ghassan Kanafani (1936–72), the Jewish characters, often anonymous, are divided into two categories: the Palestinian Jews, which he calls the "old Jews," and the new Jews, who are presented not only as strangers to Palestine but as a factor of destabilization whose arrival ended the understanding that existed between the Palestinians and the "Arab Jews" due to their names and their culture.[3] In Kanafani's novel *'A'id ila Hayfa* (Return to Haifa; 1969), the character Khaldun-Dov is an example of this dichotomy. Born to an Arab family in Palestine and raised by a Jewish family, this character is the perfect illustration of an aggressive, arrogant, and hegemonic Zionist formation.

This image of the Jew, the fruit of a sectarian ideological system and highly interventionist maneuvering, is broadly distributed in Palestinian literature and Arabic literature in general. The Jewish protagonists, always secondary in the literature of Sahar Khalifa, fall into this category.[4]

The different cycles of violence in the Near East brought out the military Jewish figure, who is often the ally and inevitable instrument of Zionist ideology. That figure is marvelously described by the Palestinian Emile Habibi (1921–96) in his novel *The Secret Life of Saeed: The Pessoptimist* (1974). Saturated with Zionist ideology, this character cynically projects suspicion and violence.

In this framework, the play *al-Ightisab* (The Rape; 1990),[5] by the Syrian playwright Sadallah Wannus (1941–97), establishes a parallel between Palestinians and Israelis in Israel but also shows the gap between Israeli Zionists and humanist Jews living in the same territory. The traditional dichotomist vision—"we" Palestinian Arabs and "you" Israeli Jews—is bisected by another: "we" pacifist Jews and "you" military ones, blind instruments of the Zionist machine. Isaac, forced by his superiors to torture mercilessly, manifests psychological disturbances and sexual impotence, symptoms of regret he cannot admit. He castrates Ismail, an imprisoned Palestinian, and violently tortures Ismail's wife, Dalal, during an act of collective rape in front of her husband. Wannus associates the Jewish military-Zionist figure with an "absolute hatred" that destroys Being. Against the enormous violence of Isaac stands Dr. Abraham Menuhin, who denounces violence and resists hatred. He diagnoses, through the evils of the protagonists, the evils of society. The dramatic end of the play shows the heavy price paid by all the protagonists. Isaac, a victim of the military-Zionist alliance, is considered a traitor and is killed by his chief. Rachel, Isaac's wife, raped in turn by her husband's colleague, leaves the country.

The last scene is a dialogue between Wannus, author and protagonist, and the doctor. This dialogue, of a moralizing tone, asserts that the character of the doctor is not an isolated case. It concludes that this Israeli Jewish figure, just and peace-loving, is largely present in the society, but his voice is stifled by the power of violence.

Figures of male and female lovers

The Jewish figure as the partner in a love relationship is a common image in modern Arabic literature. In the poetry of Mahmud Darwish (1941–2008), for example, a Palestinian poet is hopelessly in love with an Israeli Jew named Rita. Rita reappears symbolically at different times in the poetic life of Darwish, tracing the evolution of a subtle, complex, and strongly desired relationship.

Modern Arabic literature often presents the amorous Jewess of an Arab as a character who departs from the traditional laws of the community. She is stigmatized by her people. In his novel *Chicago* (2007),[6] the Egyptian Alaa Al Aswany describes a love relationship between Salah, the hero, and Wendy, a Jew, when they are students in Chicago. Wendy is determined to hide their relationship for fear of retaliation from her family. Astonished at being obliged to "hide a love relationship in the United States," the hero realizes that every Jew feels concerned by the relationship. When it is divulged, the behavior of all his Jewish comrades, once cordial, becomes aggressive and virulent. Verbal and physical altercations follow.

This scenario, only briefly evoked in *Chicago*, constitutes one of the main axes of the novel *al-Sayyida min tel Aviv* (The Lady from Tel Aviv; 2009) by the Palestinian Rabai al-Madhoun.[7] Dana Ahuva, whose real name is Dana Newman, is a comedienne and rising star in the Israeli artistic milieu. She returns to Tel Aviv after a failed rendezvous in London with Nour ed-Dine, the son of an important Arab accountant. On the plane she finds herself sitting next to Walid Dahman, a Palestinian and the hero of the novel, who is returning to Gaza after a thirty-eight-year absence. The story, which unfolds in 2005, fifty-seven years after the Nakba (1948), reveals the figure of an open, captivating, and sensitive Jewish woman. She admits that it is the first time she has met a Palestinian and spoken "closely" with him, but she realizes that this encounter "reconciles her with her-

Cover of the novel *al-Yahudi al-hali* (The Handsome Jew), by Ali al-Maqri, published in 2009 by Dar al-Saqi (Beirut).

self, with her past and her present." The two protagonists return to London almost at the same time. Walid calls Ahuva and they agree to meet the following evening. The next day Ahuva is found dead in her apartment.

The author leaves the door open to all suggestions and inscribes the death of Ahuva within the framework of a military-political system that opposes openness and conciliation. All the Jewish characters, security agents Walid meets as soon as he arrives, are anonymous, identical, and presented as the product of the same school. "Samples of hatred," he says in an ironic tone, "distributed to the Palestinians by successive Israeli governments."

The story of the novel *al-Yahudi al-hali* (The Handsome Jew; 2009),[8] by the Yemenite Ali al-Maqri, unfolds far from the present-day Near East. Salim, a Jew and the hero of the novel, decides in 1644 to write his story in Yemen, specifically in Rida, a village in which the Jewish quarter is close to the Muslim quarters. An amorous and cultural relationship develops between Fatima the Muslim, the daughter of the mufti, and Salim, nicknamed "the handsome Jew." Fatima teaches him to read and write Arabic, as well as the Hebrew that he learns in his quarter. A deep love is born between them; although their meetings are rare, they sustain their love in a society that is hostile to any marriage between the two communities. Other little stories in the same vein are joined to the main story. Qasim, the son of the muezzin, and Nashwa, the daughter of Assad the Jew, commit suicide when their two respective families forbid their marriage. Saba, another daughter of Assad, flees with Ali, another son of the muezzin, an act that is perceived as avenging their brother and sister. Salim, after the death of his father and mother, leaves the village in secret with Fatima. With no specific destination in mind, they leave on a donkey and arrive in Sanaa. Fatima dies in giving birth to their first child, Sa'id.

The author exploits the history of the Yemenite Jews in order to create a novel that brings to mind the current political situation. Despite the romantic tone that runs through the novel, the author succeeds in creating, parallel to the figure of Fatima, a Jewish figure committed to openness and to his faith at the intersection of cultures. Their love is born of a mutual cultural recognition. Faithful to the memory of Fatima, their son, Sa'id, has no other allegiance than to human values, independent of religious association.

His descendants follow the same path, despite the fierce hostility of the two opposing camps.

The love relationship between Jews and Arabs is a favorite theme in modern Arabic literature, although it is regarded from a political point of view rather than a religious one. In these works, despite their determination, the lovers fail to impose their values on the whole community. On the contrary, being isolated, they often pay the price of that openness with their lives.

The Jewish figure and identity crisis

This theme is marvelously present in the novel *Haris at-tabgh* (The Tobacco Keeper; 2008) by the Iraqi Ali Badr.[9] Against the background of an intertextuality with "Tobacco Shop" by the Portuguese poet Fernando Pessoa, the author retraces the steps of Kamal Midhat, an enigmatic figure and famous eighty-year-old Iraqi musician who was kidnapped and killed in 2006. His body was found a month later on the shores of the Tigris in Baghdad. His name is one of the three masks of the Iraqi Jew Yusuf Salih, who had been forced to leave Iraq for Israel in the 1950s. Salih, unable to bear life in Israel, leaves it for Iran under a different name/mask: Hayder Silman, a Shi'ite musician. He flees Iran and returns to Iraq through Syria under a different identity: Kamal Midhat, a Sunni born in Mosul. During the 1980s he plays an important role in the cultural milieu of Baghdad. The novel ends with the return of his three children, born to different mothers, to Iraq.

The presentation of that Jewish figure is inscribed within the nostalgia of a time when Jewish minorities lived on peaceful terms with their fellow Muslim country-men. It is in this context that the Arabic novel *Shlomo al-Kurdi: Ana wa-al-zaman* (Shlomo the Kurd: Myself and Time),[10] by the Jewish Iraqi Arab-speaking writer Samir Naqqash (1938–2004), relies heavily on that nostalgic tendency. Making an allusion to the peregrinations of its author, the novel retraces the journey of a Jewish merchant, Shlomo Kattani, called al-Kurdi. Born in the Kurdish region disputed by the neighboring countries, he leaves his region for Baghdad, where he starts a used clothing business. Forced again to leave Iraq for Israel, he persists in proclaiming his Iraqi identity, and in holding on to the dream of returning to the land of his childhood.

Writing at the borders of fiction

Literature, primarily referential, portrays a Jewish figure that intersects with several aspects of the previous images. The novella *Khulwat al-Ghalban* (Poor Man's Hermitage) by the Egyptian Ibrahim Aslan relates the meeting of the narrator, during a reception given by the French Writers of Paris, with the famous Jewish psychologist of Egyptian origin, Jacques Hassoun (1936–99).[11] Hassoun, strongly asserting his Egyptian identity, expresses regret that he is unable to fulfill his father's wish: to bring a handful of soil from Egypt to spread on his tomb. He later is able to fulfill his mother's similar wish when he returns to Egypt after forty years of exile, to visit the house of his birth in the Khilwat al-ghalban quarter. It should be noted that this image of the Jew is often perceived through the prism of the Arab-Israeli conflict. The ambiguity of the borders between the Jew and the State of Israel is at the origin of a mistrust implicitly or explicitly expressed with respect to this protagonist. The narrator and his Egyptian colleagues invent numerous pretexts to decline a dinner invitation addressed to them from Hassoun.

This same mistrust is present in the novel *Warda* by Sonallah Ibrahim, in which the ambiguous behavior of Julia the Jewess leaves the narrator puzzled and mistrustful. Mistrust and deception may be read between the lines of the novella *The Stories of My Mother* by the Moroccan writer Abd al-Munim Shantuf.[12] It relates the discreet departure for Israel of the Moroccan Jewish family Hayim, tied to the narrator's family by strong bonds of friendship. The family's moving away modifies the manner in which the community regards Jews: the confidence and friendship of the past are replaced by the suspicion of the present.

Similarly, *Wadi abou Jamil, histoires des juifs de Beyrouth* by Nada Abd al-Samad,[13] which is based on "real events, thanks to the memories of the inhabitants of the Wadi Abou Jamil quarter, and narrated in a novelistic style," tells the story of several Jewish figures who left the country in large numbers, but discreetly, especially after 1967. These figures, who played a very important role in the country's economic

▶ See the article by Kirsten E. Schulze, pp. 436–443.

and social life in the middle of the last century, are often presented through the secrecy that enveloped their departure. Their portrayals vacillate between images of nostalgia and mistrust (for example, espionage for the benefit of Israel), the Jew with his rifle on the other side of the border, and the Jew who revisits his neighborhood as an "occupant."[14]

1. See, for example, ʿAdil al-Usta, *al-Yahud fi-al-riwaya al-ʿarabiyya* [The Jews in the Arabic Novel] (Ramallah: Raqmiyya, 2005).

2. Khalil Baydas, *al-Warith* [The Inheritor] (1920); new ed. (Ramallah: Raqmiyya, 2010).

3. *al-athar al-Kamila* [Complete Literary Works], 3 vols. (Beirut: Muʾassasat al-abhath al-ʿarabiyya, 3rd ed., 1987), vol. 2, *al-Qisas al-qasira* [Short Stories], 658.

4. See S. Boustani, "L'Etranger dans la littérature palestinienne," *Arabic and Middle Eastern Literature* 3, no. 2 (2000).

5. Sadallah Wannus, *al-Ightisab* [The Rape] (Beirut: Dar al-Adab, 1990). [Trans. into German by Friederike Pannewick, *Die Vergewaltigung* (Bremen: Litag-Theaterverl, 1996)—Trans.]

6. Alaa Al Aswany, *Chicago* (Cairo: Dar al-Shuruq, 2007).

7. Rabai al-Madhoun, *al-Sayyida min tel Aviv* [The Lady from Tel Aviv] (Beirut: al-Muʾassasa al-ʿarabiyya li-al-dirasat wa-al-nashr, 2009).

8. Ali al-Maqri, *al-Yahudi al-hali* [The Handsome Jew] (Beirut: Dar al-Saqi, 2009).

9. Ali Badr, *The Tobacco Keeper* (Doha: Bloomsbury Qatar Foundation, 2011).

10. Samir Naqqash, *Shlomo al-Kurdi: Ana wa-al-zaman* [Shlomo the Kurd: Myself and Time] (Cologne: Dar al-Jamal, 2003).

11. Ibrahim Aslan, *Khulwat al-Ghalban* [Poor Man's Hermitage] (Cairo: Dar al-Shuruq, 2002).

12. Abd al-Munim Shantuf, *Recueil al-Khuruj min al-sulala* (Morocco: Manshurat wizarat al-thaqafa, 2005).

13. Nada Abd al-Samad, *Wadi abou Jamil, histoires des juifs de Beyrouth* (Beirut: Dar al-nahar, 2009).

14. Allusion to the 1982 war.

Figures of the Israeli in Palestinian Literature

Kadhim Jihad Hassan

Apart from its plurality, the image of the Israeli in Palestinian literature is noteworthy for its evolution in concert with historical events. In addition, the writers—the talented ones at least—approach and describe this image without any racist or discriminatory projections. Above all, they present a nuanced image, dependent on the level and nature of the relations between the two camps: between the Palestinians and the Israeli authority, for example, or between individuals in everyday life within mixed populations and mixed organizations, such as Maki, the political party that unites Jewish and Arab Communists. Immediately after the creation of the State of Israel, in fact, that party founded social clubs and a large Arabic-language press network (Al-Ittihad, Al-Jadid, Al-Ghad). It also incited people to combat the cultural deficiencies from which the Arab population might be suffering. At the same time, it encouraged gatherings between Jews and Arabs to celebrate the anniversary of the annihilation of Nazism, for example, or May Day.[1] But as the State of Israel intensified its expansion policy at the expense of the Palestinians, relations with political institutions became increasingly tense. Palestinian poets and prose writers began to denounce the violence being done to their people.

Kadhim Jihad Hassan

A poet, essayist, and translator, Kadhim Jihad Hassan is a university professor in the Department of Arabic Studies at the Institut National des Langues et Civilisations Orientales (INALCO) in Paris. He has published several works of criticism, including *La part de l'étranger: La traduction de la poésie dans la culture arabe* (Sindbad/Actes Sud, 2007), and *Le labyrinthe et le géomètre, essais sur la littérature arabe classique et moderne, suivi de Sept figures proches* (Aden, 2008).

The stands taken by the poets

Palestinian poets—Rashid Hussein, Michel Haddad, Tawfiq Ziad, Mahmoud Darwish, and Samih al-Qasim—at the very height of their anger or indignation, chose to call the Israelis to account, reminding them of their history and demanding that they examine their consciences. Examples abound, including these lines from Samih al-Qasim (b. 1939), in which he reproduces a dialogue with an Israeli interlocutor:

– My grandparents were burned alive at Auschwitz.
– My heart shudders for them; remove the barbed wire from my skin.

— What about my long-ago wounds?
— Leave them signs of infamy on the assassins' faces over there.[2]

But it was clearly Mahmoud Darwish (1941–2008) who granted the most space in his poems to such exchanges. Combined with his unparalleled effort, beginning with his collection *Awraq al-Zaytun* (*Leaves of the Olive Tree*, 1964), to bestow on his people an entire poetic language in which they could recognize themselves and defend their identity, in his writings he courageously and lucidly introduced a dialogical dimension, without which no true poetry could likely come into being.

> **"*[Mahmoud Darwish] courageously and lucidly introduced a dialogical dimension, without which no true poetry could likely come into being.*"**

In his first collections of poems, written while he was still living in Haifa, he says that the experience of prison and house arrest, which he lived through more than once, radicalized his relationship to words and taught him to savor freedom. He deplores the mistreatment the Palestinians endure on a daily basis and criticizes the propensity among those he calls "Israeli archaeologists" for making the country's cartography coincide with biblical descriptions, which, according to him, entails modeling reality on myth. But it is also through the experience of intimate exchanges of love or friendship that he expresses the singular nature of the ordeal his people have been through. The poems devoted to Rita, an Israeli Jew, are widely known, but a different poem shows Shulamith waiting at length, and in vain, at the entrance to a bar for the return of her friend Shimon, an Israeli soldier sent to the Sinai front. She "knows now that war songs / do not express the heart's silences or loving words to those they address," and she nostalgically recalls the Palestinian friend she once knew:

▶ See article by Elias Sanbar, pp. 375–383.

▶ See Counterpoint on Mahmoud Darwish, pp. 580–581.

> She believed what Mahmoud told her, a few years ago,
> Mahmoud was a good-hearted friend,
> And he was shy. He only wanted her
> To understand that refugees
> Are a nation that suffers from cold
> And from the lack of a stolen land. [...]
> She believed what Mahmoud told her, a few years ago,
> They became lovers.
> And at their first embrace, she wept.
> From pleasure... and from her neighbors' gaze.
> All our nationalisms are not worth a banana peel,
> She said to her arm one day.
> Then came Shimon, who protected her from her old love
> And from the repudiation of her people.

Mahmoud was a prisoner at the time.[3]

In a famous poem inspired by the experience of an Israeli friend of the poet, we hear a soldier who "dreamed of white lilies / of an olive branch / of the breasts of his beloved blooming at night." He now considers leaving the country, because out there, on the front, he noted that he was "only a machine spitting red fire / and changing space into a black bird."[4]

In the following phase of his poetic itinerary, after he joined the Palestinians of the diaspora in 1971, Darwish's writing became elegiac.

His poet's voice accompanied the great losses of the Palestinians (the assassination of various leaders and the forced evacuation of Lebanon in 1982, followed by the massacres of Sabra and Shatila, for example). Nevertheless, the dialogical dimension only intensified and grew more profound. Taking as his opportunity the five-hundredth anniversary of the

Portrait of Mahmoud Darwish. Photograph by Hannah Assouline, August 1989.

conquest of America, in 1992 he devoted an entire collection of poems, *Ahada 'ashara kawkaban* (*Eleven Stars*), to a meditation on the ordeal of the American Indians and the concomitant ordeal of the Moors driven from Spain. And he traced disturbing parallels between these historical antecedents and the tragedy of the Palestinians. Having served notice to the conqueror of the relativity of his "victory," this poem attempts to make the victor understand that exile is a condition common to all men, and takes the initiative in inviting him to a dialogue, so as to transform, in René Char's expression, "old enemies into loyal adversaries": "Has not the time come to meet again, Stranger? Two strangers in a single time, in a single country, the way Strangers meet over an abyss?"[5]

The gesture of short story writers and novelists

⟩ See article
by Laurence
Louër,
pp. 452–457.

Palestinian prose has also evolved in its portrayal of Israeli figures, following the course of history and the nature of the conflict. Between 1948 and 1967, Palestinian writers of the diaspora described the misfortunes of Palestinian refugees in Arab countries and elsewhere. Conversely, those who remained within the borders of the State of Israel took on the task of describing the displacements imposed on the Palestinians and the humiliation they endured in Israeli factories, schools, and administrations. Those writers who remained in Israel call themselves "Palestinians of the interior" or "Palestinians of '48" and reject the designation "Arabs of Israel," which according to them is intended to obscure their national allegiance and to erase their identity.

As the critic Ra'ida Yasin recalls,[6] these writers treated their reality somewhat symbolically at the time, as in Tawfiq Fayyad's play *The House of Madness*. In 1967, following the Israeli annexation of Palestinian lands, which since 1948 had been under Jordanian and Egyptian authority, a new Palestinian literature was born. More critical and more artistically coherent, it approached the Israeli characters in terms of their actions, without being blind to certain human realities. This literature is represented by many voices from the interior and the diaspora, but the short stories and novels of Ghassan Kanafani and Emile Habibi achieve heights that have thus far never been equaled.

As Najima Khalil Habib points out in a work of criticism,[7] Kanafani (born in Saint Jean d'Acre in 1936 and assassinated in Beirut in 1972) distinguished in his short stories and novels between Arab Jews and Ashkenazi Jews. The former have Arab names, speak and write Arabic, and share a set of customs and a real social life with the rest of the population. The Ashkenazi character, by contrast, is one whose presence is at first imperceptible, but who in a short time becomes the head of a business or the owner of a hotel, pharmacy, or shop. Above all, it is later revealed to everyone's surprise that he has always been an activist in the Haganah or the Irgun, concealing weapons and planning operations. He is an unpredictable enemy, well protected by the organization to which he belongs, and which the British Mandatory force usually lets be. During the battles of 1948, such an activist proved to be brutal with the Palestinians, not hesitating, as in the short story *Ila an na'ud* (*Until Our Return*), to strip a woman naked and whip her. And so that she will serve as an example, he lets her die attached to a tree trunk before the eyes of her husband, who has also been abused.

Characters who are capable of positive reactions or who display humanity are nevertheless present in Kanafani's writing. The most eloquent example is Myriam in *'A'id ila Hayfa* (*Return to Haifa*).[8] In that short novel written in 1969, Sa'id and his wife, Safiyya, after the defeat of the Arabs in 1967, are allowed to visit their home in Haifa, which they were forced to evacuate in 1948. Above all, they go in the hope of finding their son, Khaldun, who was lost in the rush of the expulsion when he was only a newborn. They find their house occupied by Myriam, an Israeli woman from Poland. With her husband, Ephrat Koschen, who has since died on the Sinai front, she had adopted Sa'id and Safiyya's son. The boy, raised as an Israeli, is now named Dov and ultimately refuses to acknowledge his real parents. In retracing the story of Myriam and her husband, who came to Haifa in 1948 after losing part of their family at Auschwitz, Kanafani shows us Myriam thinking seriously about leaving Israel after she sees activists from the Haganah indiscriminately throwing Palestinian corpses into a truck. And when Ephrat gets tears in his eyes upon attending their first Shabbat in Haifa—"a real Shabbat," he tells her—she starts to cry, retorting, "It's a real Saturday, yes, but there will no longer be a true Friday or a true Sunday here!"[9]

A brilliant journalist and communist militant who became a novelist at the age of fifty, Emile Habibi (1921–96) spent the greater part of his life in Haifa. The constant need he faced (as did all the Palestinians who refused to leave) to seek some modus vivendi with the Israeli authorities inspired his first novel. It appeared in 1974 and has remained the most famous: *Al-Waqa'i' al-ghariba fi-ikhtifa' Sa'id abi l' Nahs al-Mutasha'il* (*The Secret Life of Saeed the Pessoptimist*).[10] When the State of Israel is created in 1948, Saeed the Pessoptimist is impelled to flee Palestine, but later returns secretly to live in Saint Jean d'Acre, then in Haifa. At that time, he collaborates with the nascent state and is sure he can get along using his cunning or even by betraying his loved ones (he informs the Man, who is pretending to protect him, of communist activities). Through strange, even zany situations, and through other extremely violent ones, which the protagonist is able to bear only because of his ironic stance, the whole novel demonstrates the impossibility of such a stratagem.

> "*The constant need [Emile Habibi] faced (as did all the Palestinians who refused to leave) to seek some modus vivendi with the Israeli authorities inspired his first novel, ... which appeared in 1974.*"

The new Palestinian prose

Since the First Intifada in 1987 and the second in 2000, and especially since the halting of the peace process and Israel's pursuit of its colonization policy, a new wave of Palestinian prose has arisen. Written by such authors as Ahmad Harb, Yahya Yakhlif, Hussein Barghouti, Ibrahim Nasrallah, Mourid Barghouti, Huzama Habayeb, Samiya 'Isa, Walid al-Hawdali, and Ahmad Rafiq 'Awad, these works may not always have the profundity or the aesthetic qualities of those of Kanafani and Habibi. But they generalize the critique, applying it both to Israel's security and expansionist policy and to the Palestinian administration and the society itself. Palestinian institutions are suspected of being corrupt and passive, while its society is viewed as backward and superstitious.

In the post-1948 and post-1967 literature, the dominant Israeli character in Palestinian literature is still the armed settler. He is identified by his acts (as a member of the Haganah or of the Irgun during the British Mandate, then as a soldier in the Tsahal). In particular, in this new literature, the character of the Israeli investigating officer charged with interrogating Palestinian prisoners is de rigueur. The characters range from the phlegmatic officer who acts coolly and methodically, to the one who issues threats and carries them out, to the ironic officer who is never short of jokes, to the one who knows Arabic perfectly and continually quotes the Qur'an and Arabic proverbs. Taken together, however, they constitute a well-oiled machine. These writings also introduce us to the prison doctor, whose role is confined to carrying out what is asked of him; to the Israeli soldier who imposes curfew when he feels like it and shoots real bullets at stone-throwing children; but also to the Palestinian informer or traitor and to certain Palestinian businessmen, who use the peace talks as an alibi to conclude licit and illicit deals.

> *The dominant Israeli character in Palestinian literature is still the armed settler.*

Within this world, there are still Israeli characters capable of openness and exchange. They are found especially among the workers, the intellectuals, and the women. Some workers close to the Palestinians represent the Jewish proletariat, who have known all kinds of privation since early childhood and have been thrown into a historical experience beyond their control. Among the intellectuals, some believe in the possibility of a peaceful coexistence with the Palestinians, but they are at times incapable of treating them other than with condescension. Finally, among the Israeli women, there are some who show understanding toward the Palestinian, some who can even share an intimate life with him. It may last, or it may be damaged by the tensions generated by the conflict and the extreme difficulties of daily life.

---

1. See the account of the Palestinian poet Faruq Mawasi, "Curat al-yahudi fi-l-shi'r al-'arabi fi Isra'il" [The Image of the Jew in Arabic Poetry in Israel], published online at http://www.faruqmawasi.com.
2. Samih al-Qasim, *Al-A'mal al shi'riyya al-kamila* [*Poetic Works*] (Beirut: Dar al-Awda, 2000), 1:182.
3. Mahmoud Darwish, "Kitaba 'ala daw'bunduqiyya" [Written by the Light of a Rifle] (1970), translated into French as "À la lumière d'un fusil," in *La terre nous est étroite et autres poèmes*, trans. Elias Sanbar (Paris: Gallimard, 2000), 51–52.
4. Mahmoud Darwish, "Jundi yahlum bil-Zanabiq al-Bayda'" [The Soldier Who Dreamed of White Lilies] (1967), in *La terre nous est étroite et autres poèmes*, 26 and 28.
5. Mahmoud Darwish, "Khitab al-hindi al-ahmar qabl al-akhir amam al-rajul al abyad" (The Red Man's Next-to-Last Speech to the White Man), trans. Elias Sanbar as "Le dernier discours de l'homme rouge," in *La terre nous est étroite et autres poèmes*, 287.

6. Ra'ida Yasin, "Curat al-yahudi fi-l-adab al-filastini fi-l-dakhil al-muhtall" [The Image of the Jew in the Palestinian Literature of the Occupied Territories], published online at http://www.diwanalarab.com.

7. Najma Khalil Habib, *Al-numudhaj al-insani fi adab Ghassan Kanafani* [*The Human Figure in the Literary Production of Ghassan Kanafani*] (Beirut: Bissan, 1999).

8. Ghassan Kanafani, *Retour à Haïfa et autres nouvelles*, translated into French by Jocelyne and Abdellatif Laabi (Arles: Actes Sud, 1997); translated into English as *Palestine's Children: Returning to Haifa and Other Stories* by Barbara Harlow and Karen E. Riley (Boulder, CO: Lynne Rienner, 2000).

9. Ibid., 105.

10. Emile Habibi, *Les aventures extraordinaires de Said le Peptimiste*, translated into French by Jean-Patrick Guillaume (Paris: Gallimard, 1987); translated into English as *The Secret Life of Saeed the Pessoptimist*, by Salma Khadra Jayyusi and Trevor Le Gassick (Northampton, MA: Interlink, 2001). As in the original title, the word "pessoptimist" is a contraction of "pessimist" and "optimist."

Darwish and Rita, the Jewish Lover

The first poem that the Palestinian Mahmoud Darwish devoted to Rita, the Israeli lover, is entitled "Rita and the Rifle" and dates to 1967. The divine representation of that figure intimates a separation in which the winds of destruction shatter the hymn to love. Rita is freed from her personal image, acquiring in Darwish's poetry a symbolic dimension that illustrates an entire aspect of the poet's relation to the Jewish other. All the poems that mention Rita, explicitly or implicitly, display a profound lyricism, a melancholic nostalgia in which two dimensions of that love intersect and confront each other: a human dimension ready to abolish all borders standing between the poet and the other, the beloved; and a real and disappointing dimension, where evil carefully prepares the way for the lovers' tragedy. The image of Rita returns twenty-five years later in the collection *Ahada 'ashara kawkaban* (*Eleven Stars*). In the poem entitled "Rita's Winter," the two lovers assure each other of their indissoluble bond and sing of their fusional love. Nevertheless, questions about the world surrounding them multiply, and the two dreams shatter.

Sobhi Boustani

"You who are haunted by sign and word,
 What do you say?
 Nothing, Rita. I imitate the valiant knight of song
 Who speaks of the curse of love besieged by mirrors...
 Is it about me?
And about two dreams on a pillow, which intersect or flee,
One draws a knife, and to the flute the other entrusts the commandments.
I don't understand, she says.
Nor do I, and my tongue is made of shards
Like the outburst of a woman of sense. And horses commit suicide at the far end of the track
[...]
... Rita breaks open the almonds of my days, and the fields grow wider.
For me this tiny land shrinks to a bedroom overlooking the street,
On the ground floor of a building on a mountain's flank
Open to the sea air. And I possess a wine-colored moon and a smooth stone.
I have my share of the spectacle of waves bound for the clouds, and a share
Of the Book of Genesis, of the Book of Job, and of
The Harvest Festival, and a share of what I possessed and bread from my mother
And a share of the iris of the valleys in the poems of old lovers.
I have my share of the wisdom of lovers: the dead man would be in love with the assassin's face

If only you crossed the river, Rita.
And where is it, this river? She replied…
I said: A single river, in you and in me,
And I flow in blood and I flow in memory.
The guards have left me no door to enter by.
And so I leaned against the horizon
I looked down,
Up,
All around,
And found no horizon for viewing.
In the light, I found only my gaze coming back to me.
I said: Come back to me again and perhaps I shall see
A horizon that a prophet restores
With a two-word missive: You and me,
A little joy in a narrow bed… a minimal joy.
They have not killed us, not yet, Rita. Heavy
Is this winter, Rita, and cold."

Mahmoud Darwish, *Ahada ʿashara kawkaban* [*Eleven Stars*] (Beirut, 1992), translated from the Arabic into French by Elias Sanbar in
La terre nous est étroite et autres poèmes, 1966–
1999 (Paris: Gallimard, 2000), 304–9.

Writing Difference in French-Language Maghrebi Literature

Beïda Chikhi

In French-language Maghrebi literature, the relationship between Jews and Muslims is a question of particular resonance, in that the colonial past weighs heavily on contemporary history. Both Jewish and Muslim writers have achieved fame in the field, weaving, in the same language, connections based on places that, despite antagonisms, have sometimes shaped shared spaces. Since the conflictual alterity of the 1950s, that literature has evolved toward new dialogical expressions imposed by the rise of the different fundamentalisms, by way of the trials of nationalism in the 1960s and the international issues associated with the Israeli-Palestinian conflict. These writers, whether stemming from a Jewish culture like Albert Memmi and Edmond El Maleh, or from a Muslim culture like Kateb Yacine and Abdelkebir Khatibi, have placed the memories of their peoples in dialogue. They have also elaborated on the subject of difference and its resonances, as illustrated, for example, by the reflections of Jacques Derrida.

Beïda Chikhi

Beïda Chikhi is a professor of French and Francophone literature at the Université Paris 4-Sorbonne, where she directs the Centre International d'Études Francophones (CIEF) and the "Lettres francophones" series at Presses de l'Université Paris-Sorbonne (PUPS). She has published, notably, *Maghreb en textes: Écriture, histoire, savoirs et symboliques* (L'Harmattan, 1996), and served as editor for *Destinées voyageuses: La patrie, la France, le monde* (2006) and *Figures tutélaires, textes fondateurs: Francophonie et héritage critique* (2009), both published by PUPS.

The 1950s: Political disjunction and problematic alterity

The contradictions of nineteenth-century French colonial democracy,[1] and, above all, the violent repression that took place in Algeria on May 8, 1945, gave rise to polemical expressions and at the same time led to forms of community isolationism on both sides of the colonial conflict. The early novels reacted first and foremost against the colonial ideology and the damage it had done to Maghrebi societies: Mouloud Feraoun's *The Poor Man's Son*, Mohammed Dib's *Algeria* trilogy, Albert Memmi's *The Pillar of Salt*, and finally, Driss Chraïbi's *The Simple Past*.[2] Cultural codes, instituted as marks of the characters' religious affiliation, are disseminated

▶ See article by Benjamin Stora, pp. 286–291.

throughout the narrative structure to shape a communitarian vision.[3] In Algeria, the Crémieux decree made Jewish alterity a touchy subject for Muslims, who did not enjoy the same status as Jews, and their otherness is kept at a distance by allusive terms and evasive formulations. In general, that tendency became stronger throughout the 1950s. Nevertheless, in *Nedjma*,[4] Kateb Yacine notes

> **"In Nedjma, *Kateb Yacine notes the French and Jewish aspects of Algerian identity.* "**

the French and Jewish aspects of Algerian identity. The mother of the heroine, Nedjma, is a Jewish Frenchwoman from Marseilles. Kateb Yacine exploits the genealogical tangle within the context of a history made more dynamic by the caesuras. This novel of the Algerian nation broadens the historical perspective by shifting points of reference and by weaving family connections. The figure of the Kahina, the Berber queen of the Aurès who battled the Arab conquerors in the seventh century and supposedly converted to Judaism, is evoked in the novel as a female incarnation of the resistance, within a chronology that begins with Jugurtha the pagan and ends with Abd el-Kader the Sufi Muslim.

> ▶ See Nota bene by Abdelmajid Hannoum, pp. 994–998.

The 1960s: The trials of nationalism

After Algerian independence, expressions of a communitarian identity faded to the background in favor of national concerns. Literature adapted to the new themes: social criticism, exile, sexuality, the conflict between elite culture and popular culture, the role of the sacred, and so on. The mass departure of the Jews in 1962 in no way impaired the genealogical inscription of Jewishness, which appears in Mohammed Dib's *Cours sur la rive sauvage* (*Course on the Wild Shore*),[5] a poetic narrative laden with metaphors and symbols, and a utopian projection of Algeria in which the Kabbalistic tradition, combined with Sufi mysticism, seems to be running the show.

In Tunisia, Albert Memmi, who had been living in France since 1956, pursued his exploration of identity in a series of book-length essays: *Portrait of a Jew*, *The Liberation of the Jew*, and *Dominated Man*.[6] These essays, somewhere between analysis, elucidation, and defense plea, posit a European reader as much as a Muslim one and center on the status of the Jews within nation-states. The logic they develop leads their author to defend his positions on Israel. It goes without saying that these essays are not considered "must-reads" by Maghrebis, who clearly prefer the "imaginary confession," laid out like a literary "puzzle," which can be heard in *The Scorpion*.[7]

> ▶ See Nota bene on Albert Memmi, pp. 589–591.

The 1970s–1980s and the new international issues

Memmi persevered, writing a controversial essay called *Jews and Arabs*,[8] which established an accord protocol that began with the Yom Kippur War and ended with "the open recognition of nationhood." For him, the Arabs' misfortune did not come from the existence of Israel. Edmond Amran El Maleh, a Moroccan Jewish writer who focused his work on evolving Judeo-Arab relations in the grip of political conflicts, was more warmly received by critics. In an effective poetics, *Parcours immobile* (*Motionless Journey*) and *Le retour d'Abou el Haki* (*The Return of Abu el Haki*) relate the disappearance of the Moroccan Jewish community,[9] which, however, seemed to be living in harmony with the others. *Mille ans, un jour* (*A Thousand Years, One Day*) clearly identifies the Palestinian tragedy as a source of anxiety,[10] and displays uneasiness and incomprehension regarding Jews who abandon a millennial homeland to return to Israel. The problem thus raised is accompanied by a profound meditation on the value granted hospitality in Islamic civilization.

▶ See Nota bene on Edmond El Maleh, pp. 592–593.

On that subject, Khatibi undertook an epistolary exchange with Jacques Hassoun, an Egyptian-born Jew and psychoanalyst living in Paris. In 1985 that correspondence appeared in print under the title *Le même livre* (*The Same Book*).[11] Referring to the biblical source, this book indicates that the bond that united the Jews and Muslims has deteriorated over the centuries, through the mirror effect of substitute objects of identification, including the State of Israel, which has become a substitute nation for the Arab Jews: "Something was lost between Jews and Muslims, something terribly old…and which was distorted in an extraordinary misunderstanding." Khatibi develops his thinking in *Paradoxes du sionisme* (*Paradoxes of Zionism*),[12] an essay that points out the contradictions internal to Zionism and how its discourse has drifted toward a domination of the other. More recently, the Tunis-born writer Abdelwahab Meddeb took up the question again, turning it into self-criticism: "For their part, the Muslims must find inspiration in the advances that their own tradition holds, in order to find again the conditions for moving beyond their irredentism directed at the Christians, and especially, at the Jews."[13]

Mohammed and Moses in the play *Boucherie de l'espérance ou Palestine trahie* (Slaughter of Hope or Palestine Betrayed) by Kateb Yacine, staged by the theater troupe Les Ateliers de Lyon in 2001.

In Algeria, the Palestinian question was addressed in Kateb Yacine's popular theater.[14] *Palestine trahie* (*Palestine Betrayed*; 1977) returns to the origins of the religious conflict and reconfigures values. The Jews who possess knowledge and long exemplary experience are therefore distinguished from those who have repudiated their heritage. Kateb toured with his plays throughout Algeria, and though the word "Israel" cannot be pronounced—since even to utter it would signify "recognition"—the Moses who appears onstage has enormous stature. A triangular verbal structure—Moshe/Shalom/Israel—sets up a skillful and humorous mise-en-scène of the contrasting effects of Zionism and latent Arab anti-Semitism. In the end, the spectator more clearly apprehends the conflict as political rather than ethnic or religious.

Dialogues to the letter

What Kateb inaugurated in the historical mode of interwoven family relationships will be taken up in the same terms by Nabile Farès in *L'État perdu* (*The Lost State*): "A sculpture that accompanies my lips and my mutism: in the Creole, the Berber, the Arab, the Jew, the black, the Indian, the Frenchman that 'I' am: my tongues of shadow and of life, words reddened by every form of servitude."[15] As for Dib, he has continued his meditation on exile and on writing, against a Kabbalistic backdrop. Especially in *Les terrasses d'Orsol* (*The Terraces of Orsol*), *Neiges de marbre* (*Marble Snows*), and *Le désert sans détour* (*Desert Straight Ahead*),[16] he cultivates enigma and formulates questions reminiscent of those in Edmond Jabès's *The Book of Questions*.[17] The mosaic of proper names adorning the works—Hellé, Lily, Aëlle, and Lyyl in Dib; El, Elya, Yaël, and Aely in Jabès—sheds light on a dialogical transmission that establishes a relationship with writing and, beyond it, with *El, Elohim, Elleh*, God.[18] For both authors, these names are the founders of a spoken word to be inscribed in the quest for the primary meaning signified by the root word *El*. A similar approach is elaborated in Abdelwahab Meddeb's *Phantasia* (*Fantasia*), especially his treatment of the three initial letters, the incipit, of "The Cow," the first sura in the Qur'an: *alif lām mīm*. "These three orphaned letters suggest the triliteral letter that distributes most of the root words appearing in the language. They lord it over the words; when you pronounce them, flesh trembles and thought places the first stone. In each of these letters, word becomes flesh. In them, Hebrew haunts."[19] The enigma of the letters is not separation and exile but active memory, which reinscribes history, inasmuch as it is an incitement to reread. For Meddeb, the texts intercede on behalf of a semitheoretical composition. Reference to the other is mentioned precisely in the two genealogies. The relation to Jewish alterity is truly a relation of "correspondence," as opposed to the "divergence" effect of "Catholic pomp, triumphant since Abbot Suger."[20]

As intersubjective dialogue, that approach seems to be the last resort. It also allows certain writers to move on to questions they could not raise before, or that they had

> **The mosaic of proper names adorning the works ... in Dib and ... in Jabès sheds light on a dialogical transmission that establishes a relationship with writing and, beyond it, with El, Elohim, Elleh, *God*.**

addressed in a discreet, concealed, even secret manner, in the interstices of the philosophical texts. Such was the case for Jacques Derrida, who had undertaken a reflection on his own Jewishness in *Writing and Difference.* His interpretation of the tradition intensifies the question of identity elaborated through writing, as in Jabès, who, say his commentators, discovered his Jewishness in becoming a writer. That question is also developed through what Derrida himself calls "the somnambulistic displacement of the Jabesian question/assertion."[21] Derrida also finds that displacement among Maghrebi writers, through the linguistic detour. *Monolingualism of the Other, or, The Prosthesis of Origin* undertakes a diachronic questioning based on a problematic specific to Francophone writers,[22] namely, the prosthetic figure "I have a language, but it does not belong to me,"[23] which becomes, in Derrida's text, "I have only one language, it is not mine." Derrida associates himself with the Maghrebi Francophone community at a colloquium in Louisiana. In a friendly dialogue with Khatibi, he attempts to delineate his Franco-Maghrebi identity on the basis of his own history as a French Jew from Algeria. He finds the opportunity in reading Khatibi's commentary on the chiasmus taken from Kateb Yacine's *Le polygone étoilé* (*The Star Polygon*)—"I lost my mother and her language, the only inalienable and yet alienated treasures"[24]—as demonstrated by the transcription of the proper name, "between a diglossia and a dead language."[25] Let us recall that Derrida, inspired by Lacan, had already engaged in that transcription of the proper name, transformed and inverted into anagrams. Claude Lévesque, having analyzed the specular inversion of the letters composing Derrida's two signatures in *Writing and Difference*—Reb Rida and Reb Derrissa—concludes: "One must acknowledge here the presence of the anagram: the *berbère J. Derrida*, in that dual simulacrum of a signature (where the double disseminating *s* is also found)."[26] Derrida's original Berber identity is evoked in Mohammed Dib's *L'arbre à dires* (*The Sayings Tree*), in reference to an encounter in Strasbourg:

> "*A Judeo-Franco-Maghrebi genealogy does not clarify everything, far from it. But could I explain anything without it, ever?*'
> —*Jacques Derrida.*

"I also learn that, like me, he was born in Algeria, he into a Jewish family, and that he may be descended from Berbers, perhaps even from that old and noble tribe of the Derraders."[27] Derrida would later say: "The legacy I received from Algeria is something that has inspired my philosophical work, all the work I pursued with respect to Western thought. The questions I have been led to ask, to a certain degree, with a certain exteriority, would not have been possible if, in my personal history, I had not been Algerian."[28]

The philosopher wonders: "A Judeo-Franco-Maghrebi genealogy does not clarify everything, far from it. But could I explain anything without it, ever?"[29] No, of course not, especially since it prompts him to mark his own difference as a Jew of Algeria, which "makes it possible to repoliticize what is at stake,"[30] and to reread his history within the register of colonial exclusions: identities by decree and ethnic and religious separatism. In short, everything leads us back to the social space of the Algerian novels of the 1950s: "For I lived on the edge of an Arab quarter, at one of its nighttime borders both invisible and almost impassable: there, segregation was as efficient as it was subtle."[31]

The exiles

The founding chiasmus of French-language Maghrebi literature shapes Derrida's philosophy as much as it does the imagination and thought of the Maghrebi writers, with a more or less marked oscillation between politics and symbolism. Although communitarian representations have become passé in the most recent literary works, interpersonal relationships between Jews and Muslims tend to multiply, somewhat like reunions in a shared exile. In Assia Djebar's *Les nuits de Strasbourg*

Derrida in a street of Algiers at the end of the 1940s. Jacques Derrida's personal archives.

(*Strasbourg Nights*),[32] Theldja, an Algerian art historian, and Ève, her Jewish friend from Tébessa, meet and exchange memories that will be crowned by the lexeme *Alsagérie*.[33] Strasbourg will have brought about a transcendence of the initial wound, called "Hagar" in Assia Djebar's earlier novel *Far from Medina*.[34] Hélène Cixous also reminds us of the force of political injunction that that city carries for Derrida: "In 'Le lieu dit: Strasbourg' ('Said Place: Strasbourg'), he confides that he never felt so *Algerian-exile* as in that refuge city of Strasbourg. Not a negative exile because Algerian. Said place. Exile gives."[35]

Exchanges of love and friendship, intellectual exchanges as well, bring into being a human crossroads that expands so that both sides may open themselves to existential reflection and may seize the opportunity for a new history (a chosen history this time), along the lines highlighted by Abdelwahab Meddeb in *Pari de civilisation* (*Wager of Civilization*): "An advance of civilization of any sort no longer belongs to its inventors: it must become the property of every human who proposes to acquire it."[36] That means banishing the obsessive repetition of dogma, throwing wide the doors of interpretation, and transforming all legitimacy into a "becoming."

[All quotations from the French are my translation. When a work has been translated into English, I use the English title in the body of the text but give the French-language source in the notes. If the work has not been translated, I give the French title in the text, followed by my English translation of the title.—Trans.]

1. On this subject, see "Aperçu historique et statistique de la Régence d'Alger," in Hamdan Khodja, *Le miroir* (repr., Paris: Sindbad, 1985). This book, published in Paris in October 1833, reveals the profound divisions affecting the spirit and values of the French nation when it became a colonizer. Hamdan Khodja's ideas would be adopted by the accusatory discourse of the Maghrebi writers of the colonial period.

2. Mouloud Feraoun, *Le fils du pauvre* (Le Puy: Cahiers du nouvel humanisme, 1950); Mohammed Dib, *La grande maison* (1952), *L'incendie* (1954), and *Le métier à tisser* (1957), all published by Éditions du Seuil in Paris; Albert Memmi, *La statue de sel* (Paris: Gallimard, 1953); and Driss Chraïbi, *Le passé simple* (Paris: Gallimard, 1954).

3. [Throughout this essay, the term "communitarian" should be understood to mean "characteristic of a particular (ethnoreligious) community," in this case, Muslim or Jewish.—Trans.]

4. Kateb Yacine, *Nedjma* (Paris: Éditions du Seuil, 1956).

5. Mohammed Dib, *Cours sur la rive sauvage* (Paris: Éditions du Seuil, 1964).

6. Albert Memmi, *Portrait d'un Juif* (1962), *La libération du Juif* (1966), and *L'homme dominé* (1968), all published by Gallimard in Paris.

7. Albert Memmi, *Le scorpion ou la confession imaginaire* (Paris: Gallimard, 1969).

8. Albert Memmi, *Juifs et Arabes* (Paris: Gallimard, 1974).

9. Edmond Amran El Maleh, *Parcours immobile* (Paris: Maspéro, 1980); *Le retour d'Abou el Haki* (Grenoble: La Pensée sauvage, 1991).

10. Edmond Amran El Maleh, *Mille ans, un jour* (Grenoble: La Pensée sauvage, 1986).

11. Abdelkebir Khatibi, *Le même livre*, correspondence with Jacques Hassoun (Paris: Éditions de l'Éclat, 1985).

12. Abdelkebir Khatibi, *Paradoxes du sionisme* (Rabat: Al Kalam, 1989).

13. Abdelwahab Meddeb, *Pari de civilisation* (Paris: Éditions du Seuil, 2009), 173.

14. The plays, written between 1972 and 1988, are collected in *Boucherie de l'espérance* (Paris: Éditions du Seuil, 1999).

15. Nabile Farès, *L'État perdu*, ed. Hubert Nyssen (Paris: Actes Sud, 1982), 94.

16. Mohammed Dib, *Les terrasses d'Orsol* (1985), *Neiges de marbre* (1990), and *Le désert sans detour* (1994), all published by Sindbad in Paris.

17. Edmond Jabès, *Le livre des questions*, 7 vols. (Paris: Gallimard, 1963–73).

18. See "La mosaïque des noms propres," in Beïda Chikhi, *Littérature algérienne, désir d'histoire et esthétique* (Paris: L'Harmattan, 1998), 129–32.

19. Abdelwahab Meddeb, *Phantasia* (Paris: Sindbad, 1986), 25.

20. Ibid., 127.

21. Jacques Derrida, *L'écriture et la différence* (Paris: Éditions du Seuil, 1967), 116.

22. Jacques Derrida, *Le monolinguisme de l'autre, ou, la prothèse d'origine* (Paris: Galilée, 1996).

23. See Beïda Chikhi, *Maghreb en textes: Écriture, histoire, savoirs et symboliques* (Paris: L'Harmattan, 1996), 9.

24. Kateb Yacine, *Le polygone étoilé* (Paris: Éditions du Seuil, 1966).

25. Abdelkebir Khatibi, quoted in Jacques Derrida, *Le monolinguisme de l'autre* (Paris: Galilée, 1991), 120.

26. Claude Lévesque, *L'étrangeté du texte* (Paris: Union générale d'éditions, 1978), 146–47.

27. Mohammed Dib, *L'arbre à dires* (Paris: Albin Michel, 1998), 33–34. Derrida will later say: "The heritage I received from Algeria is something that probably inspired my philosophical work." Mustapha Chérif, *Islam et Occident, conversation avec Jacques Derrida* (Paris: Odile Jacob / Algiers: Barzakh, 2006).

28. Cited by Mustapha Chérif in *Derrida à Alger, un regard sur le monde* (Paris: Actes Sud et Barzakh, 2008), 16.

29. Derrida, *Le monolinguisme de l'autre*, 133.

30. Ibid., 121.

31. Ibid., 66.

32. Assia Djebar, *Les nuits de Strasbourg* (Paris: Actes Sud, 1997).

33. [*Alsagérie*: a portmanteau word combining "Alsace" (where Strasbourg is located) and "Algérie" (Algeria).—Trans.]

34. Assia Djebar, *Loin de Médine* (Paris: Albin Michel, 1991).

35. Hélène Cixous, "Celle qui ne se ferme pas," in *Derrida à Alger*, ed. Mustapha Chérif (Arles: Actes Sud / Algiers: Barzakh, 2008), 55.

36. Abdelwahab Meddeb, *Pari de civilisation*, 119.

Albert Memmi, or the Reconciliation of Identities

Albert Memmi (b. 1920), a sociologist and novelist nurtured by the East and the West, a former resident of Tunisia who has lived in France since 1956, an anticolonialist and a Zionist, a Jew who is neither observant nor a believer, was the lucid witness to the political and cultural transformations that have caused upheaval in the Maghreb generally and in Judeo-Muslim relations in particular. His personal history, far from being a unique and singular destiny, is emblematic of his generation of Jews from the Maghreb. At the religious level, they were the last to inherit a spiritual tradition in decline and the first to mark themselves off from it. At the political level, meanwhile, they lived through the often violent jolts of decolonization and witnessed the birth of independent nation-states, in which they did not find a place.

A child of the *hara*, the impoverished Jewish quarter of Tunis that borders on the Arab quarter, Memmi grew up in the enclosed space of the ghetto and broke free by attending the schools of the Alliance Israélite Universelle. Brought up in religious traditions and superstitions before adopting the openness of a rational, critical mind, he learned the Tunisian patois, then the French of Malherbe. He could have acculturated himself completely to the West, could have blended in with the majority group, fleeing the stigma that afflicts the minority. He could have resolved not to look back, not to be turned into a "pillar of salt," the title of his first book. Despite that strong temptation, Memmi preferred to reconcile the multiple facets of his identity, to accept the pangs and rifts it produced, to cultivate the wisdom of mediation among the three groups to which he belonged: the Jews, the Arabs, and the French. His achievements as a writer and as a sociologist attest to that refusal to exclude the various strata constitutive of his personality.

In *Pillar of Salt* (1953), prefaced by Albert Camus, Memmi provided the postwar impetus to a Maghrebi literature written in French, which he contributed toward diffusing and whose specific value he grasped. Although it marks a break from exoticism, since all the authors are autochthonous, this literature is written in the language of the colonizer, which these authors have appropriated. Memmi's actions and thoughts, though they do not constitute the origin of multiculturalism, argue in favor of the intercultural. And yet, dismissing both irenicism and Manichaeanism, he fully acknowledges that exchange and enrichment can also be the source of potential conflict, and vice versa (see his novel *Strangers*, published in 1955, on the fate of an exogamous marriage).

That shifting back and forth between cultures is also found in the diversity of the written forms he has adopted. Is he not one of the rare, if not the only, sociologist to have published novels not divorced from his sociological reflections yet still autonomous? When he describes universal types—the colonized, the colonizer, the dominated, the dependent, the racist—his raw material has always been his closest, most intimate field of study, accurately translated by the term "portrait," which he has used in the title of several of his works. Although *Portrait du colonisé* (literally, *Portrait of the Colonized*, translated into English as *The Colonizer and the Colonized*; 1957) is a valid portrait of all the world's colonized, it is, in fact, especially that of the Arabs of Tunisia and Algeria, just as the colonizer he depicts is the French colonist rather than his British or Dutch counterpart.

Memmi was the first to propose the term "Arab-Jew" to define himself, even though he and his family had been uprooted from their native country, either of their own free will or by force. For Memmi, the use of the controversial term was neither a slogan nor a provocation. That compound word, for which, he acknowledges, he has not found a more adequate substitute, is indicative of his predilection for multiple identities. Memmi deliberately embraces the hyphen but cannot be counted on to mask the intrinsic ambivalence that has characterized relations between the two communities: "For us, the Arabs were at once brothers and enemies, hostile cousins. Of course, there was a commonality of customs. Like them, we ate couscous, we liked fish, we went to the beach... but each in his own place. We did not form mixed marriages, or very few....Yet we had the same sensibility, the same songs, the same singers."[1] In that respect, an "Arab-Jew" is not at all a "Jewish Arab": the first term refers to someone who participates in a civilization to which two collectivities have contributed; the second is a political affirmation that reduces Jewishness to its religious dimension. A fortiori, Memmi would never have described himself as a Muslim-Jew. Looking at his surroundings with a sociologist's eye, he readily concedes that religion is an important, sometimes paramount reference point in the conduct of the daily life of the commonwealth. Yet he remains wary of the danger religions pose when they intervene in the political arena or exert undue influence on mores. He therefore prefers, to the strictly observant Judaism of Eastern Europe, the serene and more flexible Judaism of North Africa, just as he has more sympathy for Italian Catholicism than for Spanish rigor. That reassessment of the Arab dimension in the ethos of the Jews of the Maghreb does not imply any rejection of the West as such. Precisely because it revealed its dark side with respect to colonialism, founded on the established privilege of the colonizers and on structural discrimination against the colonized, Memmi does not fail to identify, by way of compensation, the Western contribution to a life in common, especially secularism. Finally, while laying claim to a common patrimony, Memmi does not give in to the temptation to mythologize Judeo-Muslim relations: they belong to the sphere of history, with its ebbs and flows. Without ever falling into the opposite excess, which consists of claiming that the Jewish condition in Islamic countries has been nothing but continual oppression and servitude, he vigorously contests the stereotype of an "idyllic coexistence." The aim of that representation, propagated by the detractors of Israel, is to demonstrate that Zionism disrupted a preexisting harmony and therefore constitutes the sole and exclusive cause of the break between Jews and Arabs. Far from considering the ambient hostility irreversible, Memmi believes that the participation of the Jewish Diaspora and of the Arab nation is indispensable for smoothing out the

albert memmi
juifs et arabes

idées/gallimard

Cover of the novel *Juifs et Arabes* by Albert Memmi, published in 1974 by Gallimard.

tensions that accumulated in the twentieth century and which were channeled entirely toward the Israeli-Palestinian homeland. According to Memmi, that four-party dialogue—among Palestinians, Israelis, the Arab nation, and the Jewish Diaspora—will be the guarantee of a true and authentic reconciliation, more imperative than the signing of a peace treaty. ●

Senior lecturer in political science at the Open University of Israel, Denis Charbit is the author of Sionismes: Textes fondamentaux *(Albin Michel, 1998);* Qu'est-ce que le sionisme? *(Albin Michel, 2007); and* Les intellectuels français face à Israël *(Éditions de l'Éclat, 2009).*

---

1. Albert Memmi, *Le Juif et l'autre* (Paris: Éditions Christian de Bartillat, 1995), 61.

Edmond Amran El Maleh
and the Palestinian Question

Albert Memmi, born in Tunis in 1920, and Edmond Amran El Maleh, born in Safi, Morocco, in 1917, both claimed to be "Arab Jews." Anticolonialist militants from the very start, they were wholeheartedly engaged in the liberation struggles of their countries, Memmi as an intellectual, El Maleh within the Moroccan Communist Party. But it is from their memories of Maghrebi Jewry that they draw the material for their novels. Whereas Memmi's novels examine different aspects of the history of the Jews of Tunisia, El Maleh, who came to literature late in life, reanimates the Moroccan Jewish community in four novels that have appeared since 1980.

Although both these "Judeo-Maghrebi" writers look back nostalgically at a forever-vanished world,[1] they propose radically different interpretations of the events that led to the mass emigration of the Jews from the Maghreb. For Memmi, the principal cause was the status of *dhimmi* to which the Jews were relegated in Muslim countries, a manifestation in his view of a universal anti-Semitism. El Maleh, by contrast, proposes two causes remote from the Maghreb: French colonialism and the creation of the State of Israel. The particular status of the Jews of Morocco, protected by the Alawite monarchy, does not entirely explain that difference. In fact, the Jewish exodus was as pronounced in Morocco as it was in Tunisia: the more well-to-do families opted for France, the more destitute for Israel. Although El Maleh went into exile only after being harassed by Hassan II's repressive regime because of his communist past, the great majority of Moroccan Jews left the country of their own free will. It is only by analyzing the political positions El Maleh takes with respect to Israel and Palestine that we can understand how he looks on the relations between Jews and Muslims in the Maghreb.

In his novels, El Maleh depicts the tragic separation between the Jews and Muslims,[2] a tragedy that took shape during the colonial period, with "divide and conquer" policies. El Maleh thus evokes the break (*inshiqaq* in Arabic, a term that recurs often in his works) within a community that shares a common fate.[3] Without idealizing their coexistence, which he refuses to call tolerance, he portrays the intimate connections between Jewish and Muslim Moroccans, relations that gradually grew more distant during the colonial era. But El Maleh does not confine himself to that observation. The break, initiated by the colonial policy of separation, became definitive as a result of Zionist proselytism, which sought to persuade the Moroccan Jews to emigrate to the Promised Land. For El Maleh, the exodus of the Jews of Morocco was a result of that dual historical process: colonialism and Zionism. In an irony of history, it was a liberation project developed in Europe that destroyed the Jewish communities of the Maghreb, with the help of French colonial policies.

El Maleh's view is part and parcel of his original perspective on Jewishness and its relation to the nation, which he conceives as a political entity, not an ethnic or religious one. Challenging what he calls "Judeocentrism," he refuses to write the specific history of a Moroccan Jew, reconstituting instead a plural Judeo-Muslim world. It is therefore as a "Jewish Moroccan" and not as a "Moroccan Jew" that he evokes the Jewish communities of Morocco;[4] it is in this capacity as well that he denounces the Jewish state. El Maleh's political support for Palestine comes in response to that dual heritage: as a Jew, he believes he must speak out against those who claim to speak in his name; as a Moroccan, he marks his solidarity with the colonized.

In *Mille ans, un jour* (*A Thousand Years, One Day*), a novel that appeared shortly after Israel's invasion of South Lebanon, El Maleh links the tragedy of the Jews of Morocco to that of the Palestinians. Written in an oneiric style strewn with Judeo-Arabic words, the novel does not obey the logic of a historical argument. El Maleh, in any case, does not aspire to be a witness, not even in a personal capacity. Nevertheless, *Mille ans, un jour* attests to a twofold loss: that of the Jewish community of Morocco and that of the Palestinians killed in their name. That loss is mourned through the intermediary of the Kaddish, the Jewish prayer for the dead, which recurs constantly in the narrative to accompany the image of Hamad, a Palestinian child burned by Israeli bombs. Through that literary testament, El Maleh brings the Jews and Muslims together in the same text, despite the historical separation of these two communities in the Maghreb and its tragic outcome in Israel. For that Jewish Moroccan writer, Palestine may represent a way of repairing the breach between Jews and Muslims but also of restoring the Arab identity of the Jews. ●

Olivia C. Harrison received her doctorate in French and comparative literature from Columbia University. A specialist in the Maghreb, she currently teaches at the University of Southern California.

1. In the expression of Guy Dugas; see his *La littérature judéo-maghrébine d'expression française: Entre Djéha et Cagayous* (Paris: L'Harmattan, 1990).
2. See esp. Hélène Cixous, *Les rêveries de la femme sauvage: Scènes primitives* (Paris: Galilée, 2000) and *Si près* (Paris: Galilée, 2007); Jacques Derrida, *Le monolinguisme de l'autre, ou la prothèse d'origine* (Paris: Galilée, 1996); and Benjamin Stora, *Les trois exils: Juifs d'Algérie* (Paris: Stock, 2006).
3. Marie Redonnet, *Entretiens avec Edmond Amran El Maleh* (Paris: La Pensée Sauvage, 2005), 81.
4. Edmond El Maleh, "Juifs marocains et Marocains juifs," *Les Temps Modernes*, no. 375 (October 1977).

Looking at the Other: Israeli and Palestinian Cinemas
Yael Munk

As a chronological survey of some key feature films in both Israeli and Palestinian cinemas, this article discusses the influence of nationalism on the representation of Jews and Muslims in each of these, and the ways these two national cinemas have attempted to invent in order to acknowledge the religious Other, beyond that of the nationalist labeling. Doing so, they reveal an alternative, and frequently subversive, way of conceiving the Other. Analysis of filmic representation offers a very effective way by which to interpret how a nation imagines itself. While early Israeli cinema related to Israelis as Jews, often ignoring that the State of Israel is also occupied by Muslims and Christians (among others), Palestinian cinema chose to refer, with few exceptions, to Arabs as a categorical name for all those dwelling in Palestine, generally indicating Muslims. Consequently, one might assume that both Israeli and Palestinian cinemas engage with the theme of wars of religion. However, the opposite is the case: while the entire area is being torn by nationalism and religion, the two cinemas of the region seem to keep searching for ways to reach out to the religious Other.

Yael Munk

Yael Munk teaches cinema at the Open University of Israel. Among her publications are "On Ruins, Trauma and Cinema" (with Eyal Sivan), *Makhbarot Kolnoa Darom* 2 (Pardes Publishers, 2008), and "Frontières de conflit, frontières de représentation: Sur le film d'Anat Even et Ada Ushpiz 'Enchaînées,'" in *Israéliens, Palestiniens: Que peut le cinema?*, edited by Janine Euvrard (Éditions Michalon, 2005).

Pre-state Israeli cinema: The impossible dialogue

A close reading of the early films produced in Palestine prior to the establishment of the State of Israel often reveals the constant anxiety associated with a war of religion. The political standpoint of these films, however, needs to be clarified, as the first Jewish films produced in Palestine (such as *Oded the Wanderer* [Oded HaNoded], dir. and prod. Haim Halachmi, 1932; and *My Father's House* [Beit Avi], dir. Herbert Kline and Joseph Lejtes, 1947) were enabled through American Jewish funding. Their narratives represented Muslims as hostile and dangerous, whereas the Bedouin were represented according to traditional Orientalist perceptions[1]—namely, through nomadism and polygamy. As such, both these films represented the ultimate Other of the Jew who, in pre-state cinema, was associated with the Western world, thus intimating the Jew's superiority and leaving no room for dialogue.

▶ See article by Elias Sanbar, pp. 292–296.

Seven years after the establishment of the State of Israel, *Hill 24 Does Not Answer* (Giv'a 24 Eina Ona, 1955), made by British director Thorold Dickinson, offered a new cinematic angle to the Jewish-Muslim relationship. Though Israeli cinema history relates to Dickinson's film as an integral part of the national filmic production during Israel's first decade, one cannot ignore its unique foreign gaze on major national issues—the most important one being the conflict over the land. The film's episodic narrative is built around the testimonies of three men of different nationalities, all fighting for Israel's independence, who encounter each other on their way to the eponymous Hill 24. The first one is an Irish soldier who has left the British Mandate forces in order to join the Jewish underground; the second is a Jewish American tourist who has accidentally found himself in the midst of the fighting and decided to join the Jewish forces; and the third, David Amram, is a *tsabar* (Israeli-born Jew) whose parents had immigrated to Palestine from Eastern Europe. The latter's testimony remains, in my opinion, the most interesting in terms of the Jewish-Muslim conflict. His testimony is presented as a flashback, in which he tells about a military operation at the end of which he was asked to take one of the enemy soldiers prisoner. When he finally approached a wounded soldier and offered him his assistance, he discovered a swastika engraved on the latter's arm. It turns out that this was not an Egyptian soldier but, rather, a German who had joined the Egyptian army after the defeat of the Nazi forces at the end of World War II. For Amram, this appearance of the German immediately generates a vision in his mind, in which he sees himself, dressed in a heavy black coat, wearing a hat just like his ancestors in the European ghettos, standing helplessly in front of the German soldier. The wounded German recognizes his surprise, reverts to his previous identity as a persecutor of Jews, and starts cursing Amram.

This scene is paradigmatic of the early Israeli national narrative that constructed an analogy between Nazis and Arabs, between those who apparently share nothing in common but a blind hatred of all Jews. This scene, though not reflected in later Israeli films, provided a narrative basis for a religious hatred of the Jew, a hatred that crosses historical and national boundaries. According to this scene, the diasporic Jew did not disappear with the establishment of the State of Israel but merely reappeared in the guise of a national entity. In retrospect, one might say that the importance of *Hill 24 Does Not Answer* resides not only in its desire to establish the conflict between Jews and Arabs in terms of land (the Land of Israel/Palestine) but also in terms of religion: just like the Old Jew, the New Jew too remains humane in his attitude toward his opponent, even when his own life is in danger.

Israeli cinema

As noted above, *Hill 24 Does Not Answer* was not followed by any ideologically similar text in Israeli cinema, which deliberately sought to avoid the issue of religion in order to achieve the dream of normalization: to become a nation like all other nations. This approach led most early Israeli cinema to create a symbolic bridge between the glorious biblical times and the Jewish renewal in the Land of Israel,[2] with one exception—Uri Zohar's satire *A Hole in the Moon* (Hor BaLevanah, 1965). This experimental film retraces the establishment of the State of Israel as perceived through the eyes of a newcomer, Zelnick (who seems to have arrived from a Western country). The uniqueness of this character lies in his Hollywood-like behavior, which leads him to seek to make the desert bloom as if it were a huge production company.[3] One important

> *Israeli cinema [created] a symbolic bridge between the glorious biblical times and the Jewish renewal in the Land of Israel.*

scene shows Arab horsemen wearing the traditional *kefiyeh* (headdress), carrying weapons, and riding toward the film set of *A Hole in the Moon*. They address the director and implore him to be given, at least once, the role of the "good guys." This scene, which is shot entirely in negative in order to emphasize the absurd situation, reverts to "normal" when the director, surprised by their request, answers, "Are you crazy? You are Arabs!"[4] Director Zohar, known as the "enfant terrible" of Israeli cinema, succeeded here in expressing the Israeli wariness of the Arab, a wariness that at the time was expressed by the decision to cast Oriental Jews rather than Arab actors in the role of Arabs.[5]

Israeli cinema's interest in the representation of the Palestinian/Arab and the national conflict in general had gradually disappeared by the late sixties. The few films that did return to deal with the conflict in the late seventies did not approach it through the lens of religion, as is the case with Ram Loevy's *Hirbet Hizah* (1977), an adaptation of Israeli writer S. Yizhar's eponymous novel based on his memories of his part in Israel's War of Independence and published immediately after it (1949).[6] Loevy's adaptation, directed almost thirty years after the novel's publication, can be seen as influenced by the political events of the time: namely, the Six-Day War and the ensuing Israeli moral deterioration.[7] *Hirbet Hizah* narrates in first-person singular the story of what seems to be a minor event during the 1948 war: a small group of young Israeli soldiers is ordered to take the Palestinian village of Hirbet Hizah,[8] blow up its houses, and expel all the women, children, and old men remaining there. Director Loevy's film parallels the book's narrator with the voice-over of Micha, the handsome, fair-haired, and blue-eyed *tsabar* soldier. Conforming to the image of the New Jew, Micha is mostly invested in describing the beautiful landscape, seemingly ignoring, at least at the film's beginning, the moral implications of his acts. In spite of his small involvement in the mission, his moral conflict grows. The camera shows him standing aside from the invasion of the village, silently following his friends, at most trying to show some human compassion, particularly in the final sequence when he decides to bring water to the evicted Palestinians being loaded onto the truck. But even this purely humanistic act fails to attain its goal: when he runs back to the truck with the jerricans of water, he finds that it has already departed.

Recalling the biblical prophet Micah, who predicted the downfall of Jerusalem but could not prevent it, *Hirbet Hizah*'s hero should be understood through his confession, as the bystander who could not prevent the cruel acts in real time. Obedient to the national consensus, Micha understands that the destruction of the village is necessary since the land will serve for the settlement of new Jewish immigrants, those same Jews with whom the new country will be built. His stream of consciousness (in the novel and in the film) nonetheless hints at an analogy between the expelled Palestinians and the expelled Jews of Europe, as both have become refugees as a result of historical circumstances.

Hirbet Hizah's remorseful hero may be considered as one of the first Israeli cinematic protagonists to express a clear moral attitude toward the Israeli-Palestinian conflict. Loevy's film was followed by a number of Israeli feature films (referred to as "the Palestinian wave in Israeli cinema"[9]) that were critical vis-à-vis the state's ideology, and expressed this by showing the Muslim Palestinian Other's point of view regarding the occupation.

Israeli filmmaker Rafi Bukai's first feature film, *Avanti Popolo* (1986), is emblematic of this "Palestinian wave" in Israeli cinema.

Challenging the interchangeability device, based on the traditional casting of Jews as Arab characters in Israeli cinema, Bukai made a film in Arabic telling the story of two

Scene from the film *Avanti Popolo*, the first feature film of Israeli director Rafi Bukai, 1986.

Egyptian soldiers lost in the Sinai desert on the day following the end of the Six-Day War. As they desperately try to make their way home, sometimes terrified and at other times drunk (while well aware of Islam's prohibition of alcohol), they dare to approach a group of Israeli soldiers and ask for water. Facing the Israelis' hesitant response, one of them, an actor in civilian life, decides to recite the most famous lines of his last theatrical role, as Shylock in Shakespeare's *Merchant of Venice*.

> "I am a Jew! hath not a Jew hands, organs, dimensions, senses, affections, passions? Fed with the same food, hurt with the same weapons, subject to the same diseases, healed by the same means, warmed and cooled by the same Winter and Summer as a Christian is? If you prick us, do we not bleed? If you tickle us, do we not laugh? If you poison us, do we not die? And if you wrong us, shall we not revenge?"

The Israeli response is swift, and the two receive the water for which they thirst. It should be noted that in this scene Bukai went beyond the well-known Israeli device of interchangeability.[10] By creating the character of an Egyptian soldier who is an actor who has just been given the role of Shylock, the most famous Jew in Western literature, director Bukai uses the interchangeability feature in order to vividly illustrate his political viewpoint: since the Jews have been persecuted for centuries in the Diaspora, they must not now become persecutors themselves and ignore the suffering of the Other.

The "Palestinian wave" in Israeli cinema, as reflected in films such as *Hirbet Hizah* and *Avanti Popolo*, nonetheless did not attempt to decipher the Muslim or Christian identity of the Other but rather limited itself to empathy toward any person oppressed for reasons of belonging to a different religion. It was this uncommitted position, I believe, that has been responsible for the appearance of Palestinian cinema, a cinema that has introduced, for the first time, the Palestinian narrative as it coincides with the disappearance of the Palestinian representation from Israeli cinema,[11] when, for the first time, Israeli cinema turned to its long-repressed Jewish roots. Indeed, by the end of the twentieth century, Israeli cinema had produced a series of films that examined, extolled, or criticized the place of Judaism in Israeli existence, this same religion that had once been considered as irrelevant to the Jewish Zionist renewal in the Land of Israel/Palestine. Films such as David Volach's *My Father, My Lord* (Hofshat Kaits; 2007) or Joseph Cedar's *Time of Favor* (Ha-hesder; 2000), as well as his latest feature film, *Footnote* (Hearat Shulayim; 2011), all profoundly meditate on the place of (Jewish) religion in the

> **By the end of the twentieth century, Israeli cinema had produced a series of films that examined, extolled, or criticized the place of Judaism in Israeli existence.**

State of Israel, this same state that had wanted to be secular but apparently could not prevent religion from staking its claim.

Palestinian cinema

Interestingly, most Palestinian films do not represent Jews. Assuming an equivalence of meaning between Jews and Israelis, Palestinian cinema prefers to refer to the suffering of the oppressed Self, that is to say, the Palestinian. It presents this as a fact of everyday life in today's Israel/Palestine: Israeli checkpoints, soldiers, and routine controls are here to remind us of the Muslim's trauma, that same trauma that had led to their dispossession from their own land. Indeed, this

> *❝ Israeli and Palestinian cinemas are still adopting an ambivalent moden translating their hero's hesitation in front of the ultimate Other—the Jew, the Arab. ❞*

Jewish/Israeli presence that pervades Palestinian cinema can be defined as a structuring absence: Israeli Jews, though hardly represented except for a few soldiers whose faces remain blurred, are nonetheless felt everywhere, as is their possibility of controlling Palestinian lives.

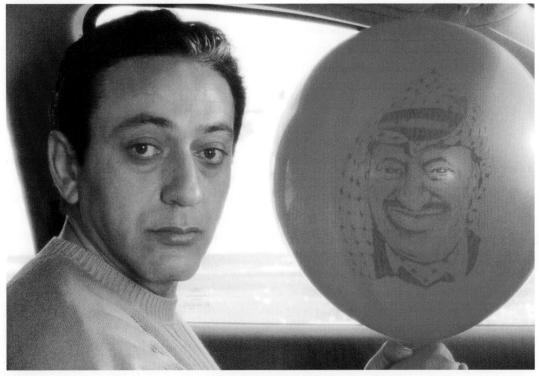

Elia Suleiman in *Intervention Divine*, a Palestinian film he directed in 2002 and in which he plays the main character.

599

In fact, Palestinian cinema seems to create no site for dialogue. The reason for this lack of communication can be found in a historical impasse in the Muslim dialogue with the Judeo-Christian discourse, as demonstrated in Jayce Salloum and Elia Suleiman's experimental film *Introduction to the End of an Argument* (1990), shot against the background of the First Intifada (1987).

In this film, Jayce Salloum, a Lebanese Canadian video artist, and Elia Suleiman, a Palestinian filmmaker, attempted to retrace the Western sources of racist approaches to Arabs. The film edited a series of dramatic scenes taken from prominent Hollywood classics such as *Exodus* (Otto Preminger, 1960) and *Lawrence of Arabia* (David Lean, 1962), and interwove them with international news coverage from the First Intifada and bold captions of the key words used in this specific discourse, which they considered to form the basis of the West's racial stereotyping of Arabs.

> *Many recent Palestinian films have chosen to focus on the difficulties inherent in adapting to the new world, difficulties that are particularly complicated for women.*

As such, this was the first film to draw attention to the racial and religious segregation between Jews/Christians and Arabs, and that returned to the ancient discourse on Judeo-Christian ethics and the subsequent negative views of Islam.

Twenty years later, Suleiman released his latest film, *The Time that Remains* (2009), a tragicomedy covering the lives of residents in Nazareth, from Israel's independence in 1948 to the present day, representing, more than any of his previous films, an attempt to come to terms with time and history. Considering that Suleiman, like most Palestinians, recognizes the Israeli-Jewish control of time, this film's title plays on its ambivalent meaning. What does "time" refer to here? The traumatic events of the Nakba (literally, "the catastrophe," that is to say, the establishment of the State of Israel in 1948) that continue to haunt Palestinian cinema in general, or the time left until the next and inevitable uprising? Certainly a highly intellectual Palestinian filmmaker, Suleiman does not hesitate to stage seemingly historical situations in order to demonstrate the hopelessness and the dead end that the Palestinian condition has reached in Israel. Are the Jews responsible for this situation? As opposed to his first film, *Introduction to the End of an Argument*, this is certainly not proven. However, throughout the narrative, Suleiman succeeds in recreating the overwhelming presence of the Israeli occupation, which is far more oppressive than any other Palestinian tradition.

Palestinian cinema has demonstrated, since as early as the beginning of the 1980s, a profound tendency toward ambivalence. Though differing from Suleiman's film, Michel Khleifi's *Fertile Memories* (1980), focusing on two Palestinian women— grandmother Romia, who remained in Palestine after the occupation, and Sahar, a single-mother novelist living in the West Bank—already introduced one of the most prominent Palestinian internal conflicts: traditional life vs. modernity. Khleifi's

Paradise Now, a Palestinian film from director Hani Abu Assad, 2003.

women depict the changing atmosphere in Palestinian society as a result of the changes that took place in Arab society following the Israeli occupation. Certainly not perceived as a blessing, the Israeli occupation nonetheless did not only oppress the Others but also revealed to them aspects of modern Western life. Many recent Palestinian films have chosen to focus on the difficulties inherent in adapting to the new world, difficulties that are particularly complicated for women. Ibtisam Mara'ana's documentaries—*Paradise Lost* (Fureidis, 2003), *Al-Jisr* (2004), *Badal* (2005), *Three Times Divorced* (2007), and *Lady Kul al-Arab* (2009)—all deal with this new situation faced by Palestinian women, a situation that keeps her torn between the traditional patriarchal society and the new world. In this new world, the place of the Jew is omnipresent though not represented, because the Israeli Jew has brought modernity to the old Muslim tradition. As a woman filmmaker working in Israel among Israeli Jews, Mara'ana's revelations of the problematics of the New Palestinian woman have become her emblem.

Other Palestinian films have engaged with the impossible condition of the occupied Palestinians. Hany Abu-Assad's *Paradise Now* (2003) presented for the first time the dilemmas of Palestinian suicide bombers, thus undermining the "semireligious" notion of the heroic death promised to those who would commit this act.

In a brilliant reflexive move, the film creates a parallel between these young men's growing hesitation and the viewer's identification with their desire to live. The film also hints that their mission as suicide bombers has in fact been imposed on them due to their straitened socioeconomic circumstances. By the end of the film, the two finally arrive in Tel Aviv with the intention of carrying out their suicide mission: they are shown wearing black suits, anxiously looking at the innocent civilians around them. Not a word is spoken. The film ends on this silent note, with the two still sitting in the taxi, before the act is committed, if it ever is.

Abu-Assad's film is crucial for the understanding of the representation of Israelis and Palestinians in today's Palestinian cinema. No Jewish character is represented on-screen (except for the taxi driver who takes the two Palestinian suicide bombers to Tel Aviv), and in fact the film seems more concerned with depicting the younger Muslim Palestinian generation's ambivalent condition. These young men, who are desperate enough to be willing to die, are finally condemned to suicide by their elders, with no possibility of objecting to this decision. In this sense, *Paradise Now* depicts the Palestinian misfortune not as a result of the Jewish Israeli occupation but rather as a misreading of the Palestinian political map that imposes tragic choices on young and innocent people.

In spite of all the good intentions, Israeli and Palestinian cinemas are still far from truly seeing the religious Other. Whether this is a result of years of nationalist discourse that have turned the Other into the enemy or the inability to dare to change an ingrained mental structure among their viewers, it seems that most Israeli and Palestinian films prefer to refer to Muslims and Jews as their traditional antagonists in a political context. Though a few films have adopted an ambivalent mode, translating their hero's hesitation in front of the ultimate Other—the Jew, the Arab—it seems that both cinemas are still hesitant about engaging with the religious issue, which is perhaps the only truth that hides behind the Israeli-Palestinian conflict.

---

1. Edward W. Said, *Orientalism* (New York: Vintage Books, 1978).

2. See Yael Zerubavel, *Recovered Roots: Collective Memory and the Making of Israeli National Tradition* (Chicago: University of Chicago Press, 1995).

3. This analogy is not completely far-fetched, as Hollywood itself was created by Jewish immigrants who wished to make the American desert bloom. See Neal Gabler, *An Empire of Their Own: How the Jews Invented Hollywood* (New York: Anchor Books, 1988).

4. See Regine-Mihal Friedman, "De l'arabe au palestinien: Le nouveau regard israelien," in *Israeliens-Palestiniens: Que Peut le Cinema?*, ed. Janine Halbreich-Euvrard (Paris: Edition Michalon, 2005), 187–95.

5. This tendency would be inverted in later Israeli films dealing with the Israeli-Palestinian conflict, when Palestinian actors would be cast in the role of Jews—as is the case in Shimon Dotan's *The Smile of the Lamb* [Hiuch HaGdi] (1986), in which Palestinian actor Makram Khoury played the role of a Jewish-Israeli IDF officer; or in Benny Toraty's *Desperado Square* [Kikar Ha-Halomot] (2001), in which Palestinian actor Muhamed Bacri played the role of the Israeli Oriental Jew who returns to his neighborhood after a long absence.

6. This same period is related to twenty-five years later in Amos Gitai's *Kedma* (2002). However, the main difference lies in the narration's point of view, as Gitai tells this historical moment from the point of view of the immigrants who had just fled Europe after World War II and been sent to the battlefield in Palestine.

7. See Tom Segev, *1967: Israel, the War, and the Year that Transformed the Middle East*, trans. Jessica Cohen (2005; New York: Metropolitan Books, 2007).

8. Anita Shapira raises the possibility that the fictional village of Hirbet Hizah may in fact be a reference to all the Arab villages that became abandoned during the Israeli War of Independence in "Hirbet Hizah: Between Remembrance and Forgetting," *Jewish Social Studies: History, Culture and Society* 7, no. 1 (2000): 9–57.

9. See Ella Shohat, *Israeli Cinema: East/West and the Politics of Representation* (Austin: University of Texas Press, 1987).

10. See note 8.

11. In this respect it is important to quote Palestinian director Nizar Hassan, born in Nazareth, who, in an interview with Israeli curator Tal Ben Zvi, effectively articulated: "Go and tell the world your story the way you want. I will not touch it—but I, and only I, will tell my story, and I will never let anyone compare it to anything. Even if humanity thinks it's a small story, for me this is the story of my people's transfer, this is the largest story, because this is my experience" (*Plastica* [Summer 1999]: 81).

Part IV

Transversalities

Prologue

Recapitulating the Positives without Giving in to Myth

Abdelwahab Meddeb
Sylvie Anne Goldberg

After more than fourteen centuries of living together, Jews and Muslims now find themselves in a historical context in which their relationship has profoundly changed. The Jewish presence in Islamic territories has been receding since the second half of the twentieth century, and the Jews are now almost completely absent. The majority (four-fifths) now live in North America or Israel. The fear, therefore, is that the imaginary Jew will replace the real Jew in Islamic representations. The effect of the separation between the two groups can be felt on the other side as well. Jewish consciousness is not free from an outlook that disfigures the Muslim.

The purpose of this section is to correct the mutual misunderstandings that currently dominate and to begin the process of remembrance

Abdelwahab Meddeb

A writer and academic, Abdelwahab Meddeb has taught comparative literature at the Université Paris-10 Nanterre and edited the review *Dédales*. He was also a visiting professor at Yale University, the University of Geneva, and the University of Berlin. He is the author of some thirty books, including *Talismano* (Christian Bourgois, 1979), *Tombeau d'Ibn Arabi* (Fata Morgana, 1987), *La maladie de l'islam* (Seuil, 2002), *L'exil occidental* (Albin Michel, 2005), *Pari de civilisation* (Seuil, 2009), and *Printemps de Tunis* (Albin Michel, 2011). He is also the producer of the broadcast "Culture d'Islam" on France Culture radio.

and anamnesis. To counter forgetfulness, we are obliged to note that, from the birth of Islam in the Hejaz, and particularly during the Medinese episode, relations between Jews and Muslims constituted the very testing ground of otherness.

From that time until the colonial period and the emergence of nation-states, these relations were characterized by a game of give-and-take. A network of mutual influences resulted in a comparative approach that took note of similarities and of differences. Historically, Judaism preceded Islam, which, to constitute an identity of its own, was prompted to mark itself off from previous systems of belief. At the same time, however, Islam laid claim to these systems and took inspiration from them, even while rectifying, redirecting, redeploying, reinterpreting, and reconsidering what it had inherited. Then, during the time of Muslim cosmopolitanism and cultural and religious creativity, Islam exerted an impact on Jewish society and culture. Influences worked in both directions and remained complex, sometimes intractable. Identifying their traces is often a matter of conjecture and is probably subject to the tropism that has oriented discourse on both sides.

But it is necessary to identify, in both the structure and content of the two religions, the points in common as well as the differences. These have to do with their formulation, operation, and casuistics, as well as their jurisprudence, which the sages constructed through a process of identification and differentiation. On matters of dogma, a Muslim could adopt in its entirety the long and rigorous demonstration of divine unity that appears in the first part of Maimonides's *Guide for the Perplexed*—all the more easily, in fact, given that the Muslim reader would have identified in that work, composed in Arabic, continuities with the Islamic philosophy of al-Farabi, from whom the Andalusian Jew Maimonides borrowed a large share of his vocabulary. Indeed, *tawhīd* (unity) lies at the foundation of both forms of monotheism. Differences

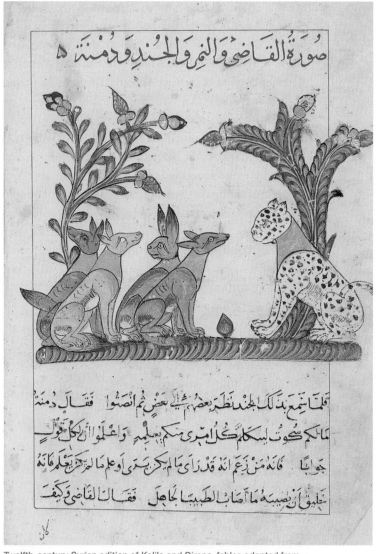

Twelfth-century Syrian edition of *Kalila and Dimna*, fables adapted from Persian into Arabic by Ibn al-Muqaffa around 750. These fables had a large influence in the Latin West through their Hebrew and Castilian translations. Here Dimna, one of the jackals, appears before the leopard judge after Dimna conspired to depose the lion from his throne. Oxford, Bodleian Libraries, ms. Pococke, 400, fol. 75 (verso).

arose as soon as the question of the true religion made its appearance. In those theocentric times, it was difficult to endorse every claim of the religion of the other.

The play of identity and difference can also be seen through a comparative linguistics focused on Arabic and Hebrew, their genesis and their diachronic development. These two languages influenced each other, as is evident in certain religious notions. But they differ in the realms of theological, philosophical, scientific, and poetic discourse.

We also sought to return to what was known as the age of *convivencia*. We have identified a number of positivities that are worth recalling today, at a time when adversity and hostility dominate. Ideologues on both sides want to obscure history and promote ignorance, so that misunderstandings will thrive in the affected communities, who will be force-fed phobias that alienate people disfigured by prejudice. That *convivencia*, whether in Baghdad, Andalusia, Cairo, or Istanbul, must be rekindled, but without being sublimated. In calling it to mind, we may effectively revive the pact of hospitality and the opulent welcome reserved for the other. Two examples illustrate that *convivencia*: first, the paean to the Arabic language by Moses ibn Ezra (eleventh century) and his celebration and grateful adoption of it; and second, the anecdote reported by Ibn ʿArabi (at the very end of the twelfth century), which depicts a Jew granting a fatwa to a Muslim.

Nevertheless, in order to avoid all irenicism and not endorse an Andalusian myth based on lies, we have found it helpful to return to the fate of the greatest Jewish success story of eleventh-century Iberia, which has been likened to a lost paradise. We consider the person of Ibn Naghrila (993–1056), prime minister, commanding general of the armies, poet, man of the sword and of the pen. He was in the service of the Berber dynasty of the Zirids, which ruled Granada during the era of the *taifa*s. Ibn Naghrila received the worst of insults in the course of his theological polemic with Ibn Hazm. In addition, his descendants were massacred. His success must have been judged illegitimate, as he was a Jew who had overstepped the bounds of the *dhimma*. Emir Abdallah (r. 1077–91), the last prince of that dynasty, even denigrated, defamed, and heaped abuse on Ibn Naghrila. In his autobiography, did not Abdallah liken him to a pig that, by means of an ill-intentioned seduction, had led his grandfather astray?

The Muslim's representation of the Jew was therefore never univocal but remained

Fifteenth-century copy of the Hebrew translation of *Kalila and Dimna* from Jacob ben Eleazar of Toledo, done in rhyming prose and completed in the thirteenth century. In the margin is the figure of one of the jackals from the fable. Oxford, Bodleian Libraries, ms. opp. add. 4°101, fol. 44 (verso).

ambivalent. This was the case in Sufi literature, in long fiction, and in short stories. Visual iconography took on a similar hue.

But what is most important is that a number of practices were shared by the Jews and the Muslims. Some remain even today. They appeal to common values in both the ethical and aesthetic senses, as attested by the architecture of synagogues in Islamic territories. Grounded in medieval archaeology, these practices are still vital, especially in music and the culinary arts. Perhaps it is in the gatherings that mold taste through food, words, or melodies that a commonality dating to ancient times is revealed, one that we recognize as a promise.

Abdelwahab Meddeb

This section follows the traces of the remarkable cultural exchanges between Jews and Muslims across time. The foundations of Jewish philosophy took shape against the backdrop of theological debates between men of letters of both religions, whether in dialogue with one another or along parallel paths. The intellectual affinities between Kalam, Sufism, and Shiʿism become clear, even as the interconnectedness of mores and of customs attests, across the centuries, to the proximity between Jews and Muslims. It is that unity, both cultural and social, that has shaped the specificity of Eastern Judaism over its long coexistence with Islam. At a time when cultural distinctions are fading away in a vast world where people

Sylvie Anne Goldberg

Director of studies at the École des Hautes Études en Sciences Sociales in Paris (at the Centre for Jewish Studies), a researcher at the Centre Marc Bloch in Berlin, and a visiting professor at the Hebrew University of Jerusalem and the University of Pennsylvania, Sylvie Anne Goldberg is the author of many works on the history of Judaism, including *La clepsydre I: Essai sur la pluralité des temps dans le judaïsme* (2000), and *La clepsydre II: Temps de Jérusalem, temps de Babylone* (2004), both published by Albin Michel. She also edited the French version of the *Dictionnaire encyclopédique du judaïsme* (Robert Laffont/Éditions du Cerf, 1996).

uprooted from their places of origin mingle together, all that remains is the transmission of particularities, buried deep in customary practices. Jews of the East, the West, and elsewhere still preserve the particular melodies of their centuries-old cantillations, their recipes for holiday meals, and certain customs associated with the rituals of the life cycle, stemming from a fount of traditions developed in common with their neighbors. Nevertheless, in contemplating the chasm that separates the Muslims and the Jews in our own time, we might almost forget that they formerly shared the same geographical and cultural space, and were woven into the same social fabric.

For centuries, Jews, Christians, and Arabs lived together, producing a specific culture and civilization. Islam drew from that culture to construct itself, starting with the religions of the Book. Although influenced by Judaism, it distinguished itself from that faith so as to better achieve its own singularity. Later, the Muslim environment had an impact on developments in the intellectual history of Judaism. The Jewish communities of longest standing were those that had settled around the Mediterranean basin, beyond the deserts of Arabia.

The Babylonia of Jewish history (which began with the First Exile in the fifth century BCE), replaced much later by Muslim Baghdad and Tehran, thus remains one of the most ancient sites. Jews lived there continuously until the twentieth century, having arrived long before the advent of Christianity and then of Islam. The influence of that major intellectual center on the entire Jewish Diaspora owes a great deal to the Muslim conquest, which, for the first time since Alexander the Great, united all the Eastern and Middle Eastern communities within a single cultural and political sphere. The status of "protected foreigner" (*dhimmī*) that was granted the Jews allowed them to preserve their religion and their institutions, even while enjoying the freedom to travel from one province to another, and, incidentally, to again journey to Jerusalem. Gradually, the Arabic language replaced vernacular Greek and Aramaic and became the language of culture, identity, and transmission. It was at that time, between the eighth and tenth centuries, that the major developments in forms of thought appeared, ultimately exhibiting what some have called a Judeo-Muslim cultural symbiosis.

Discernible in the norms of religiosity and piety, in the approach to texts, and in social structures, Jewry's contact with Islam was one of the essential vehicles for its transition from antiquity to the Middle Ages. Furthermore, the role the Jews played in transmitting Arabic sciences to the Latin countries by means of Hebrew translations, far from being negligible, made it possible to build bridges, assuring the circulation and exchange of knowledge between East and West. A second center of Judaism had developed in Christian Europe, having constituted itself by adopting other forms of thought. Eastern Jewry's differences from that community are perceptible in the realms of philosophy and science, in the relationship to study and to biblical exegesis, and in profane literature and poetry. Above all, however, it was in the practices of everyday domestic life, hidden away in the less visible, private realms overseen by women, that interactions between Jews and Muslims most clearly appeared. The place of women, the relationship to the body, culinary traditions, and the sexual division of labor between outdoor and indoor spheres are markers of these connections, which persisted until the migrations of the twentieth century.

Sylvie Anne Goldberg

Chapter I

Founding Books, Mirror Images

Qur'an and Torah: The Foundations of Intertextuality

Geneviève Gobillot

For a long time, the historical precedence of the Bible vis-à-vis the Qur'an polarized the question of their interrelationship, reducing it solely to influence and borrowing, or even, in the case of extreme polemics, to plagiarism and parody. And yet, a simple shift in perspective allows us to view the question in a completely different light. In fact, the Qur'anic text elaborates a discourse on its own status as scripture and on its relation to previous revelations. By starting with what the Qur'an says about scriptural context, we find a whole universe of thought opening up to us, one that reflects the culture surrounding the holy books and theology in the broad sense, as it is activated by reading. That cultural baggage was apparently available only to the inner circle of faithful; those who, it is said, apprehended the Qur'an as clear and luminous, the bearer of obvious meanings. It is incumbent on twenty-first-century readers to rediscover these "hermeneutic thresholds," canonical and apocryphal texts or inspired commentaries that can restore that primordial light to the message. It then appears in all its dimensions as a search for universality, ethical rigor, and respect for nuance.

Geneviève Gobillot

A professor of history of Arabo-Muslim ideas at the Université de Lyon-III, Geneviève Gobillot devotes most of her research to the principles of Qur'anic theology in the light of the "hermeneutic thresholds" constituted by the major inspired commentaries of Judaism, Christianity, and Judeo-Christianity. She recently co-authored *Islam et coran: Idées reçues sur l'histoire, les textes et les pratiques d'un milliard et demi de musulmans* (Le Cavalier Bleu, 2011).

The Qur'an as commentary on the scriptures

As I have demonstrated elsewhere,[1] the Qur'an uses three terms to characterize itself, each designating a particular mode of exegesis: *tafsīr* (commentary; Qur'an 25:33), *ta'wil* (unveiling of the original intent of the text, 3:7), and *tafsīl* (detailed explanation, 7:52). These self-definitions make it clear that what it is commenting on, unveiling, or interpreting is nothing other than the Book, the set of revealed scriptures transmitted since the beginning of the Revelation, whose perfect celestial archetype dwells with God. This archetype is the "mother of the Book," which contains the Qur'an itself (43:1–4). By referring to it, the Qur'an corrects passages from earlier scriptures that, for various reasons, have undergone modifications and alterations (*taḥrīf*) and clarifies certain of their parables (*amthāl*). Understanding the Qur'an, therefore, often consists of considering it in terms of its references to the earlier scriptures, which means that any variant it introduces in relation to the letter of the text it mentions must be read as an intentional modification, a hermeneutic process. As the Qur'an says: "This [the Qur'an] is a blessed Book which We have revealed, bringing out the truth [*muçaddiqan*] of what came before it [the scriptures]" (6:912);[2] "People of the Book! Our apostle has come to reveal to you much of what you have hidden of the Scriptures, and to forgive you much" (5:15); "To you We have revealed the Admonition (*dhikr*) [or the "reminiscence," which is to say, the Qur'an] so that you may proclaim to men what was sent down for them [the previous scriptures], and that they may give thought" (16:44).

These references fall into various categories. In the first place, there are explicit, direct quotations that refer to a precise and clearly identifiable content, accompanied by the title of the book in which it is found, for example, Qur'an 21:105: "We wrote in the Psalms after the Torah was revealed: 'The righteous among My servants shall inherit the earth.'" That is an Arabic translation in extenso of Psalm 37:29, transcribed almost

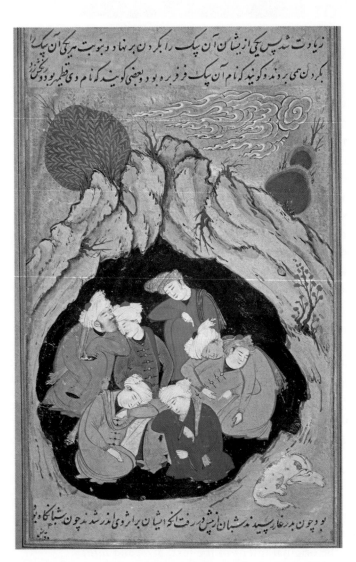

The Seven Sleepers of Ephesus, illustrated miniature in a Persian manuscript from the sixteenth century. Paris, Bibliothèque Nationale de France. Photo Josse.

word for word. This type of quotation refers to biblical passages, especially to the Torah and the Gospels. That method always serves to confirm the authenticity of the quoted passage, which is taken as a witness to prove the validity of a position that the Qur'an itself is defending. Such is the case for the verse "Bring the Torah and read it, if what you say be true" (3:93), relating to alimentary prohibitions.

Second, there are implicit quotations, evocations, or allusions to the content of a passage but without any mention of the book in which it appears, such as, "Have you heard the story of Abraham's honored guests?" (51:24), which refers to the episode of Mamre (Genesis 18:2). Finally, there are references of the kind that Michel Cuypers discovered during a rhetorical reading of the text of the sura titled "al-Ma'ida." He refers to an allusion in sura 5:28–29 to two passages from the Old Testament (Genesis 4:1–16 and Samuel 26:9–11) that links them to an excerpt from the New Testament (Matthew 23:33–36), an illusion aimed at establishing a parallel among Abel, David, Jesus, and the Qur'anic Messenger. The reference to David evokes his refusal to raise his hand to Saul, who is pursuing him (5:28). The Gospel verse, recalled in 5:29, is found in a sermon by Jesus that, according to Matthew's account, took place in the very last moments of his life, just as sura al-Ma'ida is said to have been recited shortly before the Prophet's death. Both texts, then, evoke a violently conflictual situation between certain Jews and an innocent prophet—Jesus in one case, Muhammad in the other—symbolized by Abel, who, unjustly attacked by Cain does not defend himself.[3]

Sometimes these implicit quotations or allusions, like the explicit quotations, are presented as authentic material, but often they undergo more or less extensive modifications vis-à-vis the source. It is here that the notion of a clarification provided by the Qur'an comes into play. This may be either the addition of a precise detail, the suppression of part of the text, or the establishment of new associations. One of the most remarkable modifications consists of identifying two figures as the same person—Mary, mother of Jesus, and Mary, sister of Aaron (Qur'an 19:28; 66:12; 3:35–36). This clarification has sometimes been wrongly considered an error, a misunderstanding of the Bible. In reality, the only hypothesis that would allow us to account plausibly for the matter is that, in this case, the Qur'an is using a method well known from the midrash (ancient rabbinical commentary) and the Targumim, which consists of proposing that type of an identification with a precise hermeneutical aim in view. For example, the Targum equates certain figures (Shem = Melchizedek; Laban = Balaam, Jobab = Job), when it does not simply confuse them.[4]

Midrash

From the root *d-r-sh* (*cf. madrasa*), the Midrash is the rabbinical exegesis of the Bible that occurred during antiquity and the Early Middle Ages. Its aim is not to clarify the obvious meaning of the text but to highlight the connotations, secret correspondences, unspoken aspects, and so on. It also clarifies the text with the aid of a vast oral tradition that contextualizes the biblical account.

Indeed, the Bible is not the only corpus explicitly quoted in the Qur'an and presented as the authentic words of God. The Qur'an treats a number of apocryphal texts in the same way. Not only does it quote them, but it also puts into practice methods identical to those of these other writings, methods they sometimes clearly theorized. For example, that form of intertexuality, which could be called "to the second degree," relies, like the Talmud, on examples drawn from the *Romance of Alexander* to shore up its teachings. In both texts (Qur'an 18:60–65 and Babylonian Talmud, *Tamid*, 31b–32a), the same passage from the Alexanderepic—concerning the search for the water of life eternal—serves as an edifying model to be meditated upon.

Targum

The targum (*cf. tarjama*, "translation," the origin of the English word "dragoman" and of the French *truchement* [interpreter]) is a translation of the Bible into Aramaic that incorporates a great deal of exegetical material. It originated in a synagogal practice during antiquity that sought to combine the public reading of the Torah with a verse-for-verse translation into the vernacular language. There are several targums, the best known being the Targum Onkelos and the Targum Jonathan.

The Bible and intertestamental texts in the Qur'an

The Qur'an explicitly quotes two bodies of literature that it designates by the term *suhuf*, "leaves" or "pages," generally translated into English as "scriptures": the "scriptures of Moses and Abraham" (53:32–41), the "previous scriptures" (20:133), or the "earlier scriptures" (87:16–19). As I have had occasion to point out,[5] everything seems to demonstrate that at issue in this instance are at least three apocryphal Old Testament writings: the *Testament of Abraham*; the *Testament and Death of Moses*, chapter 19 of the *Book of Biblical Antiquities*; and the *Apocalypse of Abraham*. We possess two versions of the *Testament of Abraham*. The short version dates to about CE 70 and is contemporaneous with Esdras 4 and the Apocalypse of Baruch, which belong to the fragmented Essenic movement. The long version, quoted here, goes back to the mid-second century. The *Book of Biblical Antiquities* dates to the mid-first century BC and was transmitted in a Latin version in the second to third centuries CE. The Apocalypse of Abraham, finally, dates to the first century CE.[6] The first two of these writings tell how God convinced Abraham and Moses to "go out of this futile world" by promising them "fervent joy and life without end,"[7] a promise that corresponds term for term with Qur'an 87:16–19. The *Testament of Abraham* (12:12–15) also has a description of the angels

> *The Qur'an therefore grants to these three apocryphal writings of the Old Testament the status of authentic revelation.*

placed on the right and left of every man, angels who inscribe his acts at the Last Judgment. They also appear in the Qur'an (53:32–41).

It seems that because the Torah contains no precise indications about the resurrection and the Last Judgment,[8] the Qur'an was intent on referring readers to texts on these essential subjects, placed under the aegis of Abraham and Moses. It therefore grants to these three apocryphal writings, or at least to their subject matter, the status of authentic revelation. Certain other passages from these texts were not accepted word for word, nor were other passages from the Torah. The Apocalypse of Abraham is also quoted, both explicitly (concerning a sign that confirms the veracity of the Messenger, who arose from among the Gentiles: Qur'an 20:133, Apocalypse of Abraham 29:3),[9] and implicitly, for example, regarding the famous episode in which Abraham, initially tempted to consider the stars deities, one by one denies them that honor when he observes that they do not always remain visible in the firmament (Qur'an 30:30–31, Apocalypse of Abraham 7:1–7). But one of the most significant intertextual references concerns Abraham's encounter with the angel who comes for his soul in the *Testament of Abraham.* It shows how the understanding of a single passage from the Torah could evolve over time in different contexts.

Genesis	18:2–3. And he lifted up his eyes and looked, and, lo, three men stood by him: and when he saw them, he ran to meet them from the tent door, and bowed himself toward the ground, and said, "My Lord, if now I have found favor in thy sight, pass not away, I pray thee, from thy servant." 8. And he took butter, and milk, and the calf which he had dressed, and set it before them; and he stood by them under the tree, and they did eat. 22. And the men turned their faces from thence, and went toward Sodom.
Testament of Abraham	2:2–3. When Abraham saw the Commander-in-chief Michael coming from afar, looking like a most handsome soldier, then the most holy Abraham rose and met him in accord with his custom of greeting and welcoming strangers. [The Commander-in-chief greets Abraham, who returns his greeting.]

Testament of Abraham	4:9. And the Commander-in-chief said: "Lord, all the heavenly spirits are incorporeal, and they neither eat nor drink; and he had set a table with an abundance of good things that are earthly and corruptible. And now, Lord, what shall I do?" . . . 10. The Lord said: "Go down to him, and do not worry about this; for while you are sitting with him I shall send upon you an all-devouring spirit, and it will consume from your hands and through your mouth all that is on the table." [Sarah recalls that things occurred in the same manner with the visitors of Mamre.] 6:4–5. Sarah said, "You must know, my Lord, the three heavenly men who were entertained in our tent beside the oak of Mamre, when we slaughtered the calf and readied a table for them. After the prepared meat had been eaten, the calf rose again and suckled its mother joyfully."
Qur'an	11:69. Our messengers came to Abraham with good news. They said: "Peace!" "Peace!" he answered, and hastened to bring them a roasted calf. 51:24–26. Have you heard the story of Abraham's honored guests? They went in to him and said: "Peace!" "Peace!" he answered and, seeing that they were strangers, betook himself to his family and returned with a fatted calf. 11:70. But when he saw their hands being withheld from it, he mistrusted them and was afraid of them. They said: "Have no fear. We are sent forth to the people of Lot." 51:27–28. He placed it before them, saying: "Will you not eat?" He grew afraid of them, but they said, "Have no fear," and told him he was to have a son endowed with knowledge.

Let us first note the differences in the exchange of greetings between Abraham and the angels. In the Torah, Abraham rises and advances toward the visitors, then greets them without delay. In the *Testament of Abraham*, he rises and advances, but it is the angel who greets him first. In the Qur'an, it is the angels who advance and are the first to give a greeting, thus indicating Abraham's high station. But the most interesting passage has to do with the meal. In the Torah, the three visitors, who are not explicitly identified as angels, quite simply eat the calf prepared by Abraham. In the *Testament of Abraham*, the visitor expresses the awkwardness of his position by recalling that heavenly spirits cannot touch earthly food. God then sends him the all-devouring spirit to make the food disappear. In that case, the letter of the Torah is preserved, even though the reality it refers to has changed. In some sense, then, the Qur'an draws the logical conclusion of the theorizing in the *Testament of Abraham*: heavenly beings do not eat, and therefore Abraham's visitors do not touch the food. At that moment, the Qur'an shifts from the role of commentary to that of rectification of both the Torah and the apocryphal text. It invalidates the letter of that text, even as it confirms its spirit.

The theological principle of abrogation and its repercussions

It is easy to see that the foregoing process of rectification corresponds point for point with the definition the Qur'an gives of abrogation (2:106): "If We abrogate a verse or cause it to be forgotten, We will replace it by a better one or one similar. Did you not know that God has power over all things?" My research on this question has led me to conclude that abrogation can in no case concern the Qur'an itself, despite what has long been believed.[10] The view I hold is the same one that a number of Muslim commentators adopted in the early centuries of the hijra. It is still the minority opinion, but it is gaining ground. It alone is in harmony on every point with the role of the Qur'an as interpreter of scriptures, of which I have just shown a few applications. Such a reflection is also of interest because it shakes off the prejudice that the Torah, marred with deformations (*tahrīf*) like the Gospels, is entirely replaced by the Qur'an for Muslims. Insofar as it is now possible to point out precisely the corrections of details in the scriptures—Old and New Testament—that the Qur'anic text provides, the most elementary logic allows us to deduce that a large portion of these texts is not the object of correction. Otherwise, these texts too would have to be replaced in full, verse by verse. And we know that they are not. An entire portion of the earlier scriptures, the largest portion, is thus not within the purview of Qur'anic rectification. Its status remains to be determined, of course, and this must be done in the light of historical sources on the concept of abrogation.

> **Such a reflection is also of interest because it shakes off the prejudice that the Torah, marred with deformations (tahrīf) like the Gospels, is entirely replaced by the Qur'an for Muslims.**

But before addressing that point, let me make a second observation. A perfect knowledge of the earlier texts at issue is indispensable for understanding the Qur'an's approach. Anyone who does not know that, according to the Torah, the

נחש הנחושת

In this Iranian miniature, from a Bible made by Muslim artists and given to a Jewish community, Moses refers the Hebrew people to the brazen serpent. Milan, collection of the Grand Rabbi Eliahu Khodabash Karmili, nineteenth century.

three visitors to Mamre ate and that, subsequently, they were definitively identified as being angels,[11] cannot grasp all the dimensions of the theological lesson of the Qurʾan relating to the corporeal status of celestial beings. Further evidence can be found in a verse (2:102) that the Qurʾan presents as an example of abrogation (it is introduced just before the Qurʾanic definition of that process), and which has to do with another part of the Old Testament. It concerns the assertion that Solomon was never an unbeliever, that is, that he never worshipped foreign gods: "Some of those to whom the Scriptures were given . . . accept what the devils tell of Solomon's kingdom [*mulk*]. Not that Solomon was an unbeliever: it is the devils who are unbelievers." This passage clearly stands as a correction to 1 Kings 11:4: "When Solomon was old . . . his wives turned away his heart after other gods: and his heart was not perfect with the Lord his God, as was the heart of David his father." The Qurʾan considers Solomon a prophet, thus infallible with regard to the oneness of God.

It is also not possible to truly grasp the principles governing that type of abrogation in the Qurʾan unless one addresses the history of religious ideas. A reflection on the historical context surrounding the concept of abrogation allows us to note that the Qurʾan puts into practice certain exegetical principles known at the time, especially in Gnostic, Judeo-Christian, and Manichaean circles. The oldest evidence that has come down to us can be found in the Pseudo-Clementine Homilies, an inspired Judeo-Christian text dating to the second century,[12] which claims that the Torah must be reread in the light of the teachings of Jesus, the True Prophet. The principles that are to guide that reading are given in 2 Homilies 38—"[Shortly after its revelation to Moses,] the written law had added to it certain falsehoods contrary to the law of God, who made the heaven and the earth, and all things in them; the wicked one having dared to work this for some righteous purpose"—and especially, in 3 Homilies 55:2: "And to those who suppose that God tempts, as the Scriptures say, He said, 'The tempter is the wicked one,' who also tempted Himself." ("God did tempt"; see Genesis 22:1).

It is easy to recognize the Qur'an's methods, particularly the following argument: it is not God (or a prophet) who is responsible, it is the devil who dictated these errors to those who put the Revelation in writing. In both sets of writings, what is precisely at stake is to never allow anyone to speak ill of God, or of the prophets, or even of the angels, and to never even allow hints of a flaw to remain. The Homilies (book 2, 52:1–3) theorize that position: "Assuredly, with good reason, I neither believe anything against God, nor against the just men recorded in the law [that is, the revelation made to Moses], taking

The prophet Musa (Moses), by divine order, throws his stick to the ground and it turns into a serpent. Ottoman painting, fifteenth century, Istanbul, Topkapi Palace Museum Library.

for granted that they are impious imaginations. For, as I am persuaded, neither was Adam a transgressor, who was fashioned by the hands of God; nor was Noah drunken, who was found righteous above all the world; … nor was Moses a murderer, nor did he learn to judge from an idolatrous priest—he who set forth the law of God to all the world."

Nevertheless, according to such a theological conception, which is also that of the Qur'an, the texts of the Torah and the Gospels as a whole must be respected, including the passages abrogated by the Qur'an. Even in those cases, their continued existence constitutes, for believers, an irreplaceable witness to the Qur'an's raison d'être. In addition, like the Homilies, the Qur'an explains that these interpolations must be preserved in the texts concerned, if only to make distinctions among individuals, who are all free in their choices and determinations (see 2 Homilies 38, immediately following the passage cited above): "The wicked one... dared to work this [the lying interpolations of the scribes] for some righteous purpose. And this took place in reason and judgment, that those might be convicted who should dare to listen to the things written against God, and those [might be recognized] who, through love toward Him, should not only disbelieve the things spoken against Him, but should not even endure to hear them at all."

> **According to the Qur'an, the texts of the Torah and the Gospels as a whole must be respected, including the passages abrogated by the Qur'an.**

Finally, according to the Qur'an, which goes further than the Homilies into the subtleties of that question, these passages themselves are not entirely cut off from the Truth, and their readers can eventually have access to it through a righteous interpretation: "There is no god but Him, the Mighty, the Wise One. It is He who has revealed to you the Book [Torah, Gospels, Apocrypha of the Old and New Testament, and Qur'an]. Some of its verses are precise in meaning—they are the foundations of the Book [*muhkama*, the Mother of the Book]—and others ambiguous [*mutashabbiha*, literally, able to cause confusion in the mind]. Those whose hearts are infected with disbelief follow the ambiguous part, so as to create dissension by seeking to explain it. But no one knows its meaning except God" (Qur'an 3:6–7). The Qur'an gives the example of the rabbinical commentary that accurately interpreted Solomon's attitude toward his excesses regarding possessions in the world here below: Solomon took the path of repentance after terrible ordeals (*Gittin*, Babylonian Talmud, fifth century, 68b; and the midrash *Tehillim* 78:353).[13] That interpretation implicitly evokes Qur'an 38:21–24, turning it to its own advantage. As for all the passages from scriptures that the Qur'an does not consider, we may wonder whether believers are not invited to meditate on them in the light of the principles it has given, as in 2 Homilies 51:1, where Jesus addresses his disciples, asking them to be "money changers." "If, therefore, some of the Scriptures are true and some false, with good reason said our Master, 'Be ye good money-changers,' inasmuch as in the Scriptures there are some true sayings and some spurious."

In any case, it is certain that the Qur'an requires from its readers culture and knowledge unsuspected by most commentators, which, however, will allow them to receive it as a clear text, corresponding to the definition of the *bayān*, as it recurrently characterizes itself.

I have presented only a brief glimpse of the Qur'an's approaches to the Torah. I have not come close to taking into account those of Qur'anic theology as a whole, since I would have had to add, among other things, the positions of the Qur'an toward the New Testament and toward Judeo-Christian thought, from which it also sometimes takes its distance. It is nevertheless possible to have some idea of the importance of the results accessible through an intertextual analysis within this problematic.

1. G. Gobillot, "Le Coran, commentaire des Ecritures," *Le monde de la Bible* (May 2006): 24–29; and Michel Cuypers and Geneviève Gobillot, *Le Coran* (Paris: Cavalier Bleu, 2007), 54–56.

2. [Verses from the Qur'an are taken from *The Koran,* trans. N. J. Dawood (New York: Penguin, 1995). Here the translation has been modified to conform to the French.—JMT.]

3. Michel Cuypers, *Le festin: Une lecture de la sourate al-Ma'ida* (Paris: Lethielleux, 2007), 153.

4. *Targum du Pentateuque: Traduction des deux recensions palestiniennes complètes,* with introduction, parallels, notes, and index by Roger Le Déaut, 5 vols. (Paris: Le Cerf, 1978), 1:49. See also Roger Le Déaut, "Myriam, soeur de Moïse, mère de Jésus," *Biblica* 45 (1964): 198–219; and Édouard-Marie Gallez, "Le Coran identifie-t-il Marie, mère de Jésus, à Marie, soeur d'Aaron?" in *Enquêtes sur l'islam,* ed. Anne-Marie Delcambre and Joseph Bosshard (Paris: Desclée de Brouwer, 2004), 139–51.

5. See Geneviève Gobillot, "Apocryphes de l'Ancien et du Nouveau Testament," in *Dictionnaire du Coran,* ed. Mohammad Ali Amir Moezzi (Paris: Robert Laffont, 2007), 57–63.

6. French translations of these texts appear in *La Bible, écrits intertestamentaires,* ed. André Dupont-Sommer and Marc Philonenko (Paris: Gallimard, 1987), 1282–87 (*Testament and Death of Moses*), 1655–90 (*Testament of Abraham*), 1693–1730 (*Apocalypse of Abraham*).

7. *Testament of Abraham* 1:7 and 20:12 [English translations taken from *The Testament of Abraham,* trans. Dale C. Allison (Berlin: Walter De Gruyter, 1982)—JMT]; see also *Testament and Death of Moses,* 12.

8. See, for example, Ibn Kammuna's explanations for that absence, in the Arabic text edited by Moshe Perlmann under the title *Sa'd b. Mansur Ibn Kammuna's Examination of the Inquiries into the Three Faiths: A Thirteenth-Century Essay in Comparative Religion* (Berkeley: University of California Press, 1967), 40–41.

9. See Gobillot, "Apocryphes de l'Ancien et du Nouveau Testament," 59.

10. Geneviève Gobillot, "L'abrogation (*nasihk et mansuhk*) dans le Coran à la lumière d'une lecture interculturelle et intertextuelle," special issue of *Al-Mawaqif* (2008): 6–19, Proceedings of the First International Colloquium on "The Religious Phenomenon, New Readings in the Social and Human Sciences," Mascara, April 14–16, 2000.

11. See the Targum by Pseudo-Jonathan on Genesis 18:8; Philo, *Quaestiones in Genesim,* 4:9; *De Abrahamo,* 118; Flavius Josephus, *Jewish Antiquities* 1.11.196–97; *Justin,* "Dialogue with Triphon," 57, quoted by Francis Schmidt in Dupont-Sommer and Philonenko, eds., *La Bible, écrits intertestamentaires,* 1661nn9–10.

12. *Pseudo-Clementine Literature, the Clementine Homilies,* trans. Thomas Smith, vol. 8 of *The Anti-Nicene Fathers: The Writings of the Fathers down to A.D. 325,* edited by A. Cleveland Coxe (New York: Hendrickson, 1885–96), http://en.wikisource.org/wiki/Ante-Nicene_Fathers/Volume_VIII/Pseudo-Clementine_Literature/The_Clementine_Homilies.

13. Louis Ginzberg, *Les légendes des juifs* (Paris: Cerf, 2004), 5:122–24 and 248–49n93.

The Jews in the Fifth Sura, *al-Ma'ida*

The fifth sura is of particular interest for the study of the Jews in the Qur'an because it presents itself as a conclusive text of Qur'anic revelation:[1] "This day I have perfected your religion for you and completed My favor to you. I have chosen Islam to be your faith" (5:3).[2] It is therefore possible to believe that we will find in this sura the Qur'an's last word on the question. An overly rapid reading of *al-Mai'da* might lead one to think that the Qur'an is fundamentally hostile toward the Jews. There is no dearth of invectives and condemnations against them, but these bear an obvious mark of circumstantial historical situations. The sura repeatedly notes that the condemnation applies not to all Jews but only to "some" or "many" of them. It rules out any rejection on principle of Judaism and the Jews, since it recognizes the authenticity of the Jewish covenant and the salvation granted to Jewish believers, and it authorizes conviviality between Muslims and Jews, and marriages by Muslim men to Jewish women.

The Qur'an's position toward the Jews evolved with the changing relations between the first Muslims and the Jewish population of Medina. These relations, peaceful at first, deteriorated when the Jewish tribes of Medina rejected Muhammad's authority. At that time, the Qur'an's tone became very harsh. The Jews are said to be deep-seated enemies of the Muslims: "You will find that the most implacable of men in their enmity to the faithful [the Muslims] are the Jews" (82). They mock the religion of the Muslims (57), believe in neither God nor the Prophet, nor his Revelation (81). They kindle the fire of war (64) and betray the Prophet: "You will ever find them deceitful, except for a few of them" (13). Note the exception, "except for a few," which recurs several times. Elsewhere it is said that the Jews' rebellion concerns "many among them"

(32) or "many of them" (81), which means it does not concern all of them. The Qur'an never condemns the Jews en bloc. As for the ones who betrayed him, God explicitly invites the Prophet to forgive them: "But pardon them and bear with them. God loves those who do good" (13).

Nor does the Qur'an condemn the Jewish religion as such. It fully recognizes the authenticity of the Jewish covenant ("God made a covenant with the Israelites"; 12) and the salutary validity of Judaism (and of Christianity): "Believers [Muslims], Jews, Sabaeans, and Christians—whoever believes in God and the Last Day and does what is right—shall have nothing to fear or to regret" (69).

The fundamental reproach made of the Jews, the source of all their rebellion, is that they violated their covenant, essentially by giving a distorted reading of the Torah: "Because they broke their covenant, We laid on them Our curse and hardened their hearts. They have tampered with words out of their context and forgotten much of what they were enjoined" (13). They have distorted or misinterpreted certain passages of their Book, and especially, they have neglected, "forgotten," some of its precepts, such as that of the *lex talionis*, which they refuse to apply, even though it is inscribed in the Torah. The Prophet is sent precisely to remind them of the fullness of their law and to give the proper interpretation of it (this is also true for the Christians): "People of the Book! Our apostle has come to reveal to you much of what you have hidden of the Scriptures, and to set aside much" (the texts falsified or abrogated by the new Law) (15). Among the dogmatic errors introduced by the Jews (and Christians) into their Book, the Qur'an cites their claim to be the children of God:[3] "The Jews and the Christians say: 'We are the children of God and His loved ones.' Say: 'Why then does He punish you for your sins? Surely you are mortals of His own creation'" (18). That text, paradoxically, recalls a passage from the Psalms (82:6–7), which can be read, as the King James Version would have it: "I have said, Ye are gods; and all of you are children of the most High. But ye shall die like men." Or, in an alternate reading: "I have said: Ye are gods? And all children of the Most High? And yet ye shall die like men!"

History repeats itself. Well before they rejected Muhammad's teachings, the Jews had already rejected the prophets who preceded him: "Our apostles brought them veritable proofs: yet it was not long before many among them committed prodigious evil in the land" (32). Because they "make war against God and His apostle and spread disorder in the land," they deserve the harshest punishments: execution, crucifixion, banishment (33).

Muhammad, rejected as a prophet by the Jews, is also rejected as supreme judge of the city. Rather than accept Muhammad's righteous judgment over their affairs, the Jews prefer to turn to their rabbis: they "listen to lies and listen to others who have not come to you" (41). And these rabbis interpret the Torah in their own way (41), refusing in particular to apply the *lex talionis*, even though God prescribed it in that book (45). The refusal to "judge according to God's revelations [the Torah]" is the same as unbelief and iniquity (44, 45). Does that mean that the Qur'an quite simply reintroduces an eye for an eye, the *lex talionis* in its harshest form, which the Jews had not applied for a long time—since the rabbinical tradition interpreted it as a financial compensation? Not really: although it accepts that law as a revealed legal principle (since it indisputably appears in the Torah), the Qur'an immediately accompanies it with an invitation to renounce it through ethical transcendence: "If a man charitably forbears from retaliation, his remission shall atone for him" (45).

"Take neither the Jews nor the Christians for your allies" (51): that recommendation has to do with the political realm (since forming alliances with the Jews would be the same as becoming one of them; 51) and not with personal friendship, as the Arabic term is often wrongly translated. Indeed, principles of conviviality are set out in the very first verses of the sura: the Muslims can share the Jews' (and the Christians') food without restriction, and they can invite them to their table, just as they can marry Jewish women (5).

The complexity of the sura's view obliges us to distinguish a vehement hostility toward the Jews, attributable to circumstantial historical situations, from the conciliatory attitude of the Qur'anic principles, both theological (recognition of the Jewish covenant, salvation for the Jews) and social (conviviality and

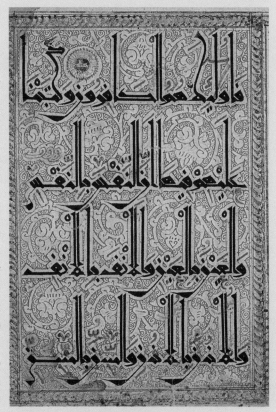

Extract from the fifth sura, al-Ma'ida, of the Qur'an in the Qarmatian calligraphic style. Iran, mid-twelfth century.

marriage with Jewish women). The harsh judgments of the hostile Jews are often tempered by restrictive terms ("some" or "many among them"). Alongside often brutal expressions, the Qurʾan is also full of nuances.

A member of the Institut Dominicain d'Études Orientales (IDEO; Dominican Institute for Oriental Studies) in Cairo, Michel Cuypers is a specialist in the literary study of the Qurʾanic text, especially from the perspective of its composition and its intertextual relations to earlier sacred literature. His publications include Le festin: Une lecture de la sourate al-Mâ'ida *(Paris: Lethielleux, 2007).* ●

---

1. See Michel Cuypers, *Le festin: Une lecture de la sourate al-Māʾida* (Paris: Lethielleux, 2007).
2. Verses from the Qurʾan are quoted from *The Koran*, trans. N. J. Dawood (New York: Penguin, 1995).
3. Cf. Deuteronomy 14:1; Psalms 73:15; Isaiah 1:2, 30:1, and 9, and 63:8 and 16; Hosea 2:1; and passim.

The *Isrāʾīliyyāt*

The *isrāʾīliyyāt* are remarks, stories, and traditions, Jewish or Christian in origin or having to do with the Children of Israel (*Banu Israʾil*), that Muslim scholars use in their writings. Ignác Goldziher, one of the pioneers in studies of the *isrāʾīliyyāt*, divided them into three categories. First, they may be remarks and narratives that complement and explain information provided in the Qurʾan on biblical themes. This type of *isrāʾīliyyāt* can be found in all genres of Muslim literature. Second, they may entail narratives in the genre known as *ʿahd banī isrāʾīl* (in the time of the Children of Israel). Despite this name, there is often no allusion to even the most minor Israelite figure. And finally, they may be folkloric and miraculous narratives that come only in part from Jewish sources.

Isrāʾīliyyāt in the first category play a particularly important role. Information on the biblical figures and themes that appear in the Qurʾan is generally elliptical and laconic, and it is no easy matter to extract details about important events in the history of the people of Israel or about central figures, such as the patriarchs, biblical prophets, or kings of Israel. Sometimes the Qurʾan does not even mention central figures, for example, the prophets Isaiah, Jeremiah, and Ezekiel, and many kings. It only briefly evokes important events (such as the exodus from Egypt, the crossing of the desert, the entry into the Holy Land, and the history of the Jewish people in their own land for more than a millennium). The same is true for the history of Christianity. Later generations were keenly aware of these silences. When we read the history books, Qurʾanic exegesis, collections of hadith, and especially works belonging to the genre of the Histories of the Prophets (*Qiçaç al-anbiyā*), we find that their Muslim authors used an abundance of materials, both Jewish (Talmudic and Midrashic) and

Christian (taken from the canonical and apocryphal Gospels). Jewish converts to Islam, as well as Muslim scholars in contact with their Jewish and Christian colleagues, were the links in the chain of transmission for these narratives.

Usually, these Muslim sources do not mention the origin of the *isrāʾīliyyāt* they report. Like biblical narratives that appear in the Qurʾan as paraphrases and not as literal translations, the *isrāʾīliyyāt* clearly resulted from an editorial labor of rewriting and adaptation, which makes it particularly difficult to trace their sources. References are sometimes vague and general, for example: "I found in the Torah," "It is written in the Torah," "It is written in the books [*maktūb fī-l-kutub*]." Such expressions do not necessarily mean that the sources are to be found in the Pentateuch or the Bible in general; they may also refer to the postbiblical literature, the Talmud and Midrash especially. A precise identification of the Jewish or Christian sources of these narratives thus requires an exhaustive knowledge of the literature.

To judge by the Muslim historical sources, these traditions had already begun to be put into writing in the late first (seventh) century. These sources attribute to Wahb ibn Munabbih (110/728), the famous Jewish convert to Islam, the *Kitab al-mubtadaʾ*, also known as the *Kitab al-israʾiliyyat*, apparently the first piece of writing in the genre. Over time, the Muslim scholars' use of extensive material drawn from the religious heritage of Judaism and Christianity gave rise to controversies and polemics. Some referred at length to the *isrāʾīliyyāt*, without seeing any problem therein. Others virulently rejected this attitude. Many sources report the story of ʿUmar ibn al-Khattab (a future caliph who would reign from year 13 to year 23 of the Hegira, that is, from 634 to 644 CE), who asked

the nations, and I am your portion among the prophets." In other words, the truth in its fullness is found in Muhammad's religion, and there is no need to turn to the sacred writings of other religions.

The refusal to rely on Jewish or Christian sources is sometimes explained by the fact that these have been falsified. According to one tradition, the Jewish convert Ka'b al-Ahbar went to visit 'Umar at home one day, a Jewish holy book in his hand, and asked for his permission to read it. 'Umar replied, "If you know this book contains elements of the Bible that God revealed to Moses on Mount Sinai, then read it day and night." This response implies that the Jews were suspected of possessing falsified writings, and one must therefore abstain from reading them.

An illustration of the controversies between the opposing camps with regard to the use of the *isrā'īliyyāt* can be found in a tradition from the time of Muhammad himself: "Transmit [teachings from] the Children of Israel and [know that] this is not reprehensible [*haddithū 'an*

Ottoman painting of Adam and Eve in paradise, in Zubdat al-Tawarikh, "The Best of Stories," 1593. Istanbul, Museum of Turkish and Islamic Arts.

a Jew of Medina to copy out certain passages from the Torah for him. When 'Umar asked Muhammad for permission to read these passages, the Prophet became angry with him. 'Umar then apologized, saying, "It is enough that Allah be my God, Islam my religion, and Muhammad my prophet." When the Prophet's wrath subsided, he said, "I swear by the One who holds my soul in his hand that, even if Moses were among you and you left me to follow him, you would be going astray. You are my portion among

banī isrā'īla wa-lā haraja]." As Meir Jacob Kister has pointed out in his study of this tradition, two opposing parties relied on it, each interpreting the tradition to justify its respective position. The defenders of the use of the *isrā'īliyyāt* translated the expression *wa-lā haraja* as indicated above. Their adversaries, however, understood it not as an affirmation but as a prohibition: "and do not commit any errors!" that is, by propagating false accounts. In general, it seems that opposition to the use of Jewish or Christian traditions was not rigid, especially in cases where their content was in harmony with Muslim notions. These traditions were obviously rejected when they contained elements likely to influence questions of Muslim faith and customs.[1] ●

Meir Bar-Asher teaches in the Department of Arabic Language and Literature at the Hebrew University of Jerusalem. He directs the Asia and Africa Institute at the same university and is a specialist in Qur'anic exegesis, especially in the field of Shi'ism.

_____

1. This article was originally published in French in M. A. Amir-Moezi, ed., *Dictionnaire du Coran* (Paris: Robert Laffont, 2007).

Arabic Translations
of the Hebrew Bible
Hanan Kamel Metwali

The Hebrew Bible has been translated many times since antiquity, by both Jews and Christians. In the third century BCE, the Torah was rendered into Greek for the Hellenophone community of Alexandria: this was the famous version known as the Septuagint. The tradition of the Targum developed concurrently in the Jewish communities of the Middle East, whose vernacular language had been Aramaic in its various dialects since the Babylonian exile in the sixth century. The biblical text was translated into Aramaic and was recited verse by verse at the synagogue, alongside the liturgical reading of the Torah. The Targums we know, and that date to late antiquity, are in some cases very close to the original text—the *Targum Onkelos*, for example. Others, such as the Targum Yerushalmi (or Pseudo-Jonathan), incorporate a great deal of Midrashic material into their paraphrases. The Christians, for their part, translated the Old Testament into Latin, Syriac (a form of written Aramaic with its own alphabet used by the communities of Syria and Iraq), and then into a multitude of languages. According to the census of the Bible House, the Old Testament has now been translated in full or in part into 1,946 languages or dialects. Most are the work of Christian organizations wishing to provide Christian communities with scriptures in the local language and also to use them as tools of evangelization.

Hanan Kamel Metwali

Hanan Kamel Metwali is a professor in the Department of Hebrew Studies at the Ain Shams University in Cairo.

The first translations

Most specialists agree that the need for an Arabic version of the biblical text was not perceived until after the death of the Prophet of Islam. From that moment on, the majority of the Jews found themselves subjects of an Islamic government. It was also at that time that the controversies between Jews and Muslims surfaced and that the debate between the two religions took root. The Bible was exposed to criticism, and Arabic translations made it possible to reply to that critical examination.

The Christians, too, seeing that the Arabic language was becoming dominant, became interested in translating the Bible into Arabic. The Melkite monks (that is, those attached to the Byzantine church) who had settled in Palestine played an important role in that translation movement, which resulted in the first Arabic version of the biblical text in about 675 (some incline toward the eighth century, however). It was translated by John, bishop of Seville, who used Jerome's Latin Vulgate as his source text. We may assume that the Jews themselves, having undertaken to translate the Hebrew Bible into Arabic, benefited from the work the Christians had done in that field. There are also indications that, in the ninth century, a Muslim by the name of Ahmad b. ʿAbdallah b. Salam set out to produce an Arabic version of the Old Testament.

The first Arabic translation done by a Jew is cited by the Karaite Yaʿqub al-Qirqisani (that is, "the Circassian") in his *Al-Anwar wa-l-maraqab* (*Lights and Guard Posts*). This is the version by Daʾud b. Marwan al-Muqammas, which dates to the ninth century. The translator had received instruction from the Christians, and it is said that his translation was influenced by them. For example, to transcribe the word "Messiah," which comes from the Hebrew *mashiah*, משיח, with a *Shin*—*masīh*, مسيح, in Arabic—

into an Arabic written in Hebrew characters, he uses the spelling מסיה (with a *Samekh*), following the Christian usage in that respect. By contrast, Saadia Gaon, a little later, would write משיח (with a *Sin*) to remain as close as possible to the original spelling, even while respecting the Arabic pronunciation. In reality, al-Muqammas's aim was to strip away any anthropomorphism from the divine figure (a method already found

> **" *Saadia Gaon was responsible for the most important Arabic translation of the Hebrew Bible before those of the modern period, and the only one that was accepted as more or less canonical by the Jews themselves.* "**

in the Targums) and to lay the theological foundations for the doctrine of Revelation, as it is formulated in the Torah.[1] There are no traces left of that translation, not even somewhat lengthy quotations from it. It was undoubtedly one of a series of Arabic versions that appeared before that of Saadia al-Fayyumi (882–942), known as Saadia Gaon. The director of one of the principal rabbinical academies in Baghdad, Saadia, a grammarian, philosopher, and commentator, was responsible for the most important Arabic translation of the Hebrew Bible before those of the modern period, and the only one that was accepted as more or less canonical by the Jews themselves. Saadia's translation is known to posterity simply as *Al-Tafsir*, "The Commentary." As the Israeli orientalist Yossef Yoel Riveline (1889–1971) wrote, "every translation is at bottom a commentary, especially if the translator is himself a commentator."[2]

Saadia Gaon's translation

The causes and circumstances surrounding the publication of Saadia's *Tafsir* can therefore be summarized as follows. In the first place, it was intended to provide the proponents of other religions with the ability to read the biblical text in Arabic, so that they could understand the truth of the Jewish religion. In addition, the texts that the Jews, especially those living in Mesopotamia and Palestine, possessed at the time were written almost exclusively in Arabic and no longer in Hebrew or Aramaic. This was the case even for those works that had to do with Jewish doctrine. Furthermore, a large number of Jews had succumbed

> **Tafsir**
>
> From the root *f-s-r*, "to comment, to make explicit," *tafsīr* means "exegesis" in Arabic, and refers especially to Qur'anic exegesis, which was contemporaneous with the Revelation itself, the Prophet having been led to clarify for his audience the meaning of the *ayāt* that were revealed to him.

to philosophical doubt, even atheism: many controversies and debates arose on the nature of divinity, giving rise to many heresies, and those who did not want to break away from Judaism expected their learned men to provide them with satisfying answers to these questions. Another motivation that encouraged Saadia to compose his *Tafsir* was the controversy with the Karaites, who wrote in Arabic. An Arabic translation would be of great help to the Rabbanites in their opposition to Karaism. Saadia therefore devoted the entire introduction to the book of Psalms to a discussion with the Karaites on the subject of prayer.[3] Saadia Gaon's disciples and readers were also very interested in Arab culture, and especially in the philosophical currents pervasive in Islamic society at the time. Jewish culture, however, was limited to the rabbinical literature and did not in itself allow for a dialogue with that philosophical culture; nor did it provide satisfying answers to their questions. Some Jews went so far as to separate themselves from their ancestral culture, which was not meeting their expectations. This is why Saadia took on these philosophical questions in the introductions he composed for each of the books of the Bible. Finally, through this Arabic version of the biblical text, he wanted decisively to

> " *Saadia Gaon's style is characterized by its elegance and literary quality. It greatly resembles that of the Christian and Muslim commentators and thinkers of the time.* "

counter the traditional attitude of his fellow directors of the yeshivas, who were interested only in legal questions and in the means for establishing their own religious authority. They adopted an attitude of distance and rejection with respect to Arab culture, which was dominant at the time, for fear of finding themselves dragged into intellectual debate and, finally, into impiety.

The language and style of the translation

Saadia's *Tafsir* was both translation and commentary: the author took a group of verses constituting a unified set, translated them, and then wrote a commentary, which was in turn discussed and explained. Although the translation of the Five Books of Moses has been preserved, especially in the tradition of the Yemeni Jews—who even today accompany the reading of the Torah at the synagogue with both the

Targum Onkelos and with Saadia's Arabic translation—the translations of the other biblical books and the commentaries pertaining to them were long lost. Fragments of them have been found among the scrolls of the Cairo Geniza. The most complete of these scrolls are those of the Torah, Psalms, Job, and Proverbs; there are also large fragments from Isaiah and Daniel. Based on their language and style, these seem to be originals. They cannot be attributed with certainty to Saadia himself, however; it may be that his disciples worked with him. Specialists have gone to great lengths to collect and organize these copies, especially Moshe Zucker, who took an interest in the book of Genesis and the Psalms. The famous twelfth-century Spanish commentator and grammarian Abraham ibn Ezra (1089–1169)

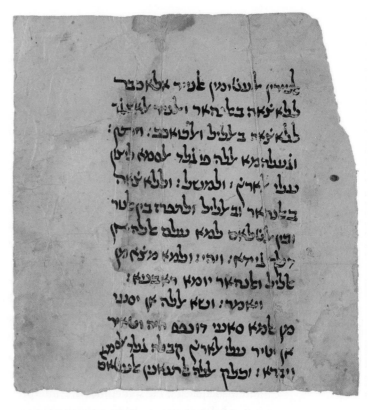

Translation of the Bible (Genesis 1:16–25) by Saadia Gaon. Fragment from the Cairo Geniza. Cambridge University Collection: Mosseri IV.81.1.

already noted that the translation was written in Arabic characters: "[Saadia] translated the Torah into the language of Ishmael, using its characters." It may have been only later that the text was transposed into Hebrew characters. Some, however, think it was written that way from the start. In any case, Saadia relied on previous versions, and especially on the Targums, particularly the *Targum Onkelos*. He also benefited from the Mishnah, the Talmud, and the Midrashim. But in his commentary, he never indicates his sources, confining himself to citing "a sage" or "Elders." On rare occasions, he compares his view to that of one of these sources.

Saadia Gaon's style is characterized by its elegance and literary quality. It greatly resembles that of the Christian and Muslim commentators and thinkers of the time. In particular, the translator is careful to render faithfully the sacred character of the Hebrew text. In addition, the Arabic used by the Jews preserved syntactical traits and vocabulary of the classical language, as Joshua Blau has pertinently noted.[4] In his concern for conciseness, Saadia strives to render every Hebrew word by a single Arabic word, and, if possible, by one with the same root. Later translators would to a great extent follow him in this. For example, Saadia uses the root *afal*, which pertains to the cosmic setting of a star, to render the Hebrew *afela*, darkness. Since this word appears in Exodus 10:22 in the expression *hoshekh-afela*, "thick darkness" (King James Version), Saadia's very use of the Arabic root has the value of commentary: we are to understand it as "crepuscular shadow." Similarly, "flesh," *bassar* in Hebrew, used to refer to the generation of the Flood—we are told that "all flesh had corrupted his way upon the earth" (Genesis 6:12)—is rendered by the Arabic *bashari*, "the human," thus making explicit the meaning of that verse. Otherwise, it would be difficult to know whether the verse is speaking solely of humanity or of all living beings. Saadia does not hesitate to make use of Arabic roots that are uncommon or even unknown in everyday language, translating the Hebrew *rogez*, "[divine] wrath," as *rigz*, "punishment" (thereby avoiding anthropomorphism), or rendering *hityahad*, "became Jewish," by the neologism *tayahad*.

> ❝ *'Priest,' or more exactly 'parish priest' in charge of worship of the divine, is translated as* imām; *while* sharīʿa *is translated* torah. ❞

Saadia also proffers subtle commentaries and interpretations of letters or polysemous words, thus displaying his great linguistic proficiency. In addition, he seeks to establish stable correspondences between the Arabic and Hebrew terms. *Kohen*, "priest," or more exactly "parish priest" in charge of worship of the divine, is translated as *imām*; the term *fiqh* is used to render "Mishnah," "Talmud," and "halakha," while *sharīʿa* is translated *torah*.

Despite all its positive qualities, Saadia's translation is marred by a number of defects and inadequacies. He sometimes overinterprets the biblical text, attributing a sense to it that belongs more to interpretation than to translation alone. For example, in Esther 8:3, he renders the Hebrew word *mahshava* (thought, intention) by the Arabic *tadbir*, which signifies something closer to "plan" or even "plot." More radically, he replaces the geographical names in the biblical text with the names those places bore at the time the translation was done. The Hebrew names "Massa" and "Sur," for instance, become "Mecca" and "Hejaz." Abraham ibn Ezra notes that Saadia Gaon attempted, for each Hebrew word, to find a corresponding Arabic term that, if possible, resembled the Hebrew in its pronunciation, even if there was no proof that the two terms were truly equivalent. This is especially true of proper names. For example, there is no conclusive evidence that the Pison (or Pishon) River in Genesis 2:11, which the Targum does not translate, corresponds to the Nile, as Saadia says. He adopts the same approach for the names of cities, animals, birds, and minerals, "to give the impression that, of all the terms that appear in the Torah, there is none that is not known and familiar." He therefore transposes the names of aromatics used in sacrifices based on the Arabic sciences of the time. When the biblical text lists the commodities, bearing obscure names, that were transported by an Egyptian caravan in the story of Joseph (Genesis 37:25), Saadia translates the terms with Arabic words for commodities whose existence is not attested in the Near East, and in Palestine in particular, until much later: *nekhot* (which *Onkelos* translates as "wax") is translated as *khurnub* ("carob," which was in fact used for therapeutic purposes in Saadia's time); *tseri* ("balm," that is, the sap of the balsam tree) is translated as *tiriāq* (from the Greek *theriakon*, a remedy made with snake and scorpion venom); and the word *lot* (lotus?) is translated as *shāh-ballūt* (chestnut), simply through the addition of a *b*, even though it is unlikely that chestnuts could be found in the cargo of a caravan going from Palestine to Egypt at that time. Another of Ibn Ezra's reproaches is that Saadia sometimes uses literary and mythological terms, such as *al-ʿanqā* ("griffin" or "phoenix") to translate *ha-ʿozniya*, one of a list of birds it is forbidden to eat (Leviticus 11:13).[5]

There is no denying the importance of that translation, however. By the richness of its vocabulary, it attests to the cultural, literary, and medical developments taking place in the Islamic countries of that time. The researcher Yehuda Ratzaby was even able to compile a *Dictionary of the Arabic Language in the "Tafsir" of Saadia Gaon*,[6] in which each word is accompanied by its contextual reference. Saadia's book was widely diffused among the Arabophone Jews, especially the Yemenites, who combined the Hebrew text, the Arabic text, and the *Targum Onkelos* into a single book called the *Taj Teimani* (*Crown of Yemen*), each verse written out in all three versions. That text was also in use among the Samaritans and the Christians. The first printed edition of the *Tafsir*, which includes only the Pentateuch and Isaiah, dates to 1983. Rabbi Yosef Kafah, a famous emissary of the Yemeni Judeo-Arabic tradition, provided a Hebrew retroversion of it.

The other Arabic translations

An Arabic translation is also attributed to Yafeth b. Ali al-Qaraʾi ("the Karaite," tenth century). Many partial translations followed, all of which have the flaw of taking as their starting point not the original Hebrew text but other Syriac, Greek, or Coptic translations. This prompted a Copt, Hibatallah b. al-ʿAssal, to propose a corrected version (in 1252 or, according to some sources, a century earlier) intended to serve as the standard text for his church. It is that version, further revised by other ecclesiastics, which, under the name Alexandrine Vulgate, remains in use in the Coptic Orthodox Church. From that time on, it was usually Christians who translated the Old Testament, either for the Eastern churches, sometimes in communion with Rome, or in an evangelical aim—the latter enterprise being for the most part pursued by Protestant organizations.

In the twelfth century, a new Arabic translation of the Old Testament appeared, done by Abi Saʿid Abi-l-Barakat. In the sixteenth century, an Arabic translation of the Psalms appeared in Genoa, Italy; during the same period, the Bible as a whole (Old and New Testaments) was published in Arabic, based

> " *From that time on, it was usually Christians who translated the Old Testament, either for the Eastern churches, sometimes in communion with Rome, or in an evangelical aim.* "

on a large number of previous versions, especially Syriac and Greek. The manuscript is now in Saint Petersburg. In 1526 an Arabic translation of the entire Old Testament

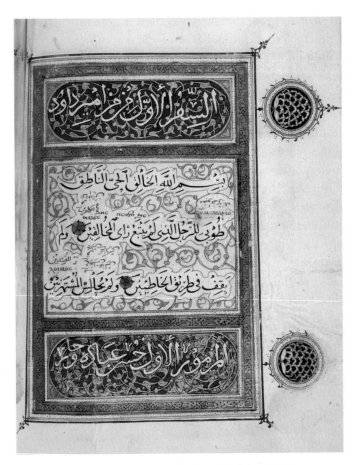

Illuminated page showing a psalm in Arabic, from a work reproducing the Psalms of David. Egypt, 1400. Collection of the British Library.

appeared. It was printed in London by William Watts in 1866, and it remains the standard version for the Eastern churches. In 1654 an Arabic edition of the Pentateuch was published in Paris in nine volumes (now held at the British Museum); it also contains versions in other languages. Another translation appeared a few years later in London, accompanied by versions in Hebrew, Samaritan (in Paleo-Hebrew characters), Syriac, Latin (the Vulgate), Greek, and, finally, by the *Targum Onkelos*. The Syriac and Greek versions were also translated into Latin. This work is also in the British Museum. Specialists tend to think that both the Paris and the London editions owe a great deal to Saadia Gaon's translation or may even be his version.

In 1620, the metropolitan of Damascus, Sarkis al-Razi, undertook a new translation of the Old Testament, welcoming the advice of a large circle of scholars, so that the result would meet expectations. The Hebrew text of reference was an exemplar provided by Pope Urban V. The translation was in fact printed in Rome in 1666, but the work was marred by a large number of errors, and many passages remained obscure or unreadable. By contrast, the Arabic version of the entire Bible that appeared in Rome a few years later (1671), accompanied by the Vulgate, is of much higher quality; it would serve as the basis for nineteenth-century Arabic versions. In 1706 an Arabic translation of the Psalms appeared in Aleppo, Syria, followed by another version of the same book, published in London in 1725 by the Society for Promoting Christian Knowledge. Ten years later, a third version of the same book appeared in Lebanon. This interest in the Psalms, more than in any other book of the Old Testament, lies in the fact that, for Christians especially, the Psalms are used as a prayer book. In 1752 an Arabic translation of the Old Testament appeared. It was prepared by Rufa'il al-Tukhi, who relied on the Coptic version, and was printed in Rome.

Contemporary Arabic versions

Currently, the most popular Arabic version, called "Smith–Van Dyck" or "Beirut," is the work of two men: Eli Smith and Cornelius Van Dyck. Smith, born in the United States in 1801, moved to Beirut in 1827 to learn Arabic. In 1837 he was entrusted by the Syria Mission and the American Bible Association with the task of publishing a Holy Book in the Arabic language. Cornelius Van Dyck, also an American (b. 1818), decided to go to Syria in 1839 after studying medicine, and from there to Beirut, where he participated in the founding of what would later be called the American University of Beirut. This institution was known at the time as the Syrian Protestant College. In 1842 Smith undertook the translation of the Old Testament, assisted in that task by Butrus al-Bustani (b. 1819), who knew several ancient languages, including Syriac and Latin. He also sought out the advice of Sheikh Nasif al-Yaziji for corrections of the language. Smith died in 1854, after completing the translation of the Pentateuch and publishing Genesis and Exodus. Van Dyck then took over, assisted by Sheikh Yusuf al-Asir, and the completed translation was published in 1865. This edition also included the New Testament, in a version Smith had left behind in manuscript form.

In 1881 members of the clergy associated with Sheikh Ibrahim al-Yaziji, the son of Smith's friend, published a new Arabic translation, which is remarkable for its elegance and literary quality, and is not at all literal. This version was commissioned by the Jesuits of Beirut as a response to Smith and Van Dyck's Protestant translation.[7] After that, other versions appeared in the twentieth century, especially that of the Union of Associations of the Holy Book in Beirut in 1978, as well as the "annotated translation" entitled *Book of Life* (*Kitab al-hayat*) in 1988. It was accompanied by a commentary intended to facilitate an understanding of the biblical text (Old and New Testaments) for a vast audience of readers.

---

1. See Ezra Zion Melamed, *Biblical Commentaries: Methods and Approaches*, 2nd ed., 2 vols. (Jerusalem: Hebrew University Magnes Press, 1978, in Hebrew).

2. Yossef Yoel Riveline, "The Biblical Exegesis of Saadia Gaon Based on His Translation," *Tarbiz* 20 (1938): 133–66 (in Hebrew).

3. Moshe Zucker, "Remarks on Saadia Gaon's Introduction to the Psalms," *Leshonenu* 33 (1969): 223–30 (in Hebrew).

4. Joshua Blau, *The Emergence and Linguistic Background of Judeo-Arabic: A Study of the Origins of Neo-Arabic and Middle-Arabic* (Oxford: Oxford University Press, 1965; repr., Jerusalem: Ben-Zvi Institute, 1981).

5. Cf. Yehuda Ratzaby, "A Study of Saadia Gaon's *Tafsir*: The Verse on Forbidden Foods," *Tarbiz* 3–4: 363–67 (in Hebrew).

6. Yehuda Ratzaby, *Dictionary of the Arabic Language in the "Tafsir" of Saadia Gaon* (Ramat Gan: Bar-Ilan University, 1985), 151–55 (in Hebrew); Yehuda Ratzaby and Michael Schwartz, "Dictionary of the Arabic Language in the *Tafsir* of Saadia Gaon," *Leshonenu* 52 (1988): 200–206 (in Hebrew).

7. *Al-Kitab al-mukaddas* (*The Holy Book*) (Beirut: Dar Al-Mashreq, 1989), introduction, 1–60.

Moshe ibn Ezra:
The Impossible Task of the Translator

Moshe ibn Ezra (1055–1135) is one of the great Jewish poets of Al-Andalus. In his *Kitab al-Muhadara wal-Mudhakara*, a work on poetry and rhetoric,[1] composed in Arabic using Arabic script (only biblical quotations are left in Hebrew letters), he cites the maxim of a poet (fol. 16): "Arabic is among the languages as spring is among the seasons."

> *He attributes that genius to the dry climate of the Hejaz, with reference to the climate theory he finds both in Galen and Hippocrates and among the Ikhwan al-Safa* (Brethren of Purity). *He writes:* "That is why these Yishma'elim [descendants of Ishmael], because they used to live on the peninsula [the Hejaz] neighboring Persia, Babylonia, and Syria, use a more agreeable language, sweeter songs, and more pleasing words than the Qahtanites [the Arabs of the South in the traditional Arab genealogy], who live in tents in the desert. These Qahtanites are the descendants of Abraham [not through Ishmael but] through his union with the concubine Ketura" (fol. 19).
>
> *He explains how the Arabic language was considerably enriched by the Islamic conquest:* "It is thanks to the excellence of their poetry and their discourse that these tribes [the Yishma'elim and the Qahtanites] came to extend their power over many languages and to subjugate many peoples, obliging them to accept their rule. They conquered the Persian Empire in Khorasan, the Roman Empire in Syria, and the Coptic kingdom in Egypt. They obliterated the borders but filled their cities and towns with wisdom and knowledge. They translated all the sciences, ancient and modern, assembled them all, and added to them their own clarifications and commentaries. Everything that had been compiled and translated in all areas of knowledge, they compiled and translated into Arabic, since God gave the Arabs the gift of a rich, poetically superior language" (fol. 21).
>
> *He also notes the linguistic proximity between Hebrew, Syriac, and Arabic, and continues:* "It is because these peoples are neighbors and have common borders. That is why, as regards most of the vocabulary, there are no differences between these languages. The difference resides solely in the greater 'aridity' or 'humidity' [of the phonetic palette], caused by climatic changes, as I have explained" (fol. 21 verso).
>
> *It is only after expounding at length on the innate poetic superiority—a true gift from God—of the Arabic language that he comes to consider the nature of ancient Hebrew poetry, the reasons for its apparent inferiority, and the task of the translator. Hence he writes, at the end of the third chapter (fol. 23 verso–24):*

"Because we have ceased using our language [Hebrew], its beauty has faded; it has been considered minor, because of the poverty of its vocabulary, or at least of what remains of it. Therefore our books have been translated into two languages, that is, Arabic and Latin, not to mention Syriac. Now, in any one given language, there are words and verbs that are missing in the other, and it is the role of the translator to borrow words in the course of his transposition, to orient them as he wishes, as well as their accents. Still, the connotations do not correspond perfectly, and this is why translation has difficulty in transposing the beauty of the source language and the images it naturally carries. As Jafiz al-Quti quite rightly says in his poetic translation of the Psalms [into Arabic]: 'In one language one finds things that have no name in another, and the things translated in this way look topsy-turvy.' He who wishes to reach the clarity of poetic intention has the obligation of not making the reading difficult by the choice of his words; he must not weigh his reader down by his writing: indeed, when we seek wisdom, the essential is to go to the heart of things. As Galen says in his book called *Of the best forms [De optima doctrina liber*?]: 'I do not suffer those who call known things by different names; let each one give a thing the name he likes: the essential is what you are talking about, not what you call it.' He returns on many occasions to this idea throughout his work, particularly in book 3 of the *Maladies and Afflictions.*

"One day, when I was young, and lived in my native land, one of the great sages among the Muslims, very knowledgeable about their laws (and who happened to be one of my Maecenas and benefactors), asked me to recite the Ten Commandments to him in Arabic. I understood that his intention in so doing was to diminish their purity, and that is why I, in turn, begged him in exchange to recite the Fatiha of the Koran to me in Latin (a language he spoke and had mastered): as he tried to translate the Fatiha, its expressivity became laughable and its beauty faded. This is when he understood my intention, and did not repeat his request."

---

1. Critical edition and translation into Spanish by Montserrat Abumalhan Mas, Consejo Superior de Investigaciones Cientificas, Instituto de Filología (Madrid, 1985). Translated into Hebrew as *Shirat Israel (Hebrew Poetry)* by Benzion Halper (Leipzig, 1924). The present translation is based on both versions. Page numbers are those of the manuscript used for the critical edition; French trans. by Julien Darmon.

Judeo-Persian Translations of the Hebrew Bible

Iranian Jews translated the Hebrew Bible into Judeo-Persian probably very early in their ancient sojourn in Iran, but written evidence of this activity, which was undoubtedly intended to educate a Jewish population whose Hebrew language was no longer strong, appears only in the fifth century. However, surviving Judeo-Persian manuscripts testify that the millennium between the ninth and nineteenth centuries kept on producing a steady stream of Judeo-Persian translations of the Hebrew Scriptures. The present state of research does not allow for determining when precisely Iranian Jews began translating the Hebrew Bible into Judeo-Persian. Since the Jewish community of Iran is perhaps the most ancient of all Jewish diasporas, dating back as far as 722 BCE, or 586 BCE, it is quite likely that knowledge of the Bible and transmission of its contents in the vernacular are quite ancient in Iran. According to evidence from the Babylonian Talmud, Iranian Jews were deeply acculturated by the Sassanian era (224 CE–636 CE) and may well have begun translating the Bible into Middle Persian (Pahlavi) for the benefit of their coreligionists and, indirectly, for their Zoroastrian and Christian neighbors as well. The fact that a few Pahlavi works, such as the ninth-century *Shkand Gumanig Wizar* (Analytical Treatise for the Dispelling of Doubts), whose contents may be earlier (Sassanian), shows an acquaintance with the Hebrew Bible and the Gospels, confirms that knowledge of the Bible among non-Jewish Iranians was available at least as early as the fifth century, and thus predates the Arab conquest of Iran (651 CE). However, written traces of this possible transmission (which may have had an important oral dimension) appear only later. In the famous Cairo Geniza, fragments have been found of some Judeo-Persian Karaite commentaries of the biblical books Ezekiel, Psalms, and Daniel dating from the ninth and tenth centuries.

The earliest known Judeo-Persian manuscript consisting of a translation and commentary of the Pentateuch is dated 1319, but at least six other fragments are fairly well known. The first printed Judeo-Persian Pentateuch was the translation of Jacob ben Tavus published in 1546 for the Constantinople Polyglot Bible. In 1657 Thomas Hyde transcribed this version and translated it into Latin for the London Polyglot (Brian Walton, ed.). Yet another famous Judeo-Persian translation of the Pentateuch, as well as the book of Psalms, was prepared by Babai ben Nuri'el, a rabbi from Isfahan, for Nadir Shah (r. 1736–46). This monarch, whose religious beliefs remain controversial, was not particularly impressed by those parts of the Bible that were made known to him. However, Ben Nuri'el's translation is decisively superior to earlier ones and is an interesting indicator of the level of Jewish knowledge among Iranian Jews in the eighteenth century.

Clearly an aid to helping Jews learn their religious tradition, the effort of translation continued into the nineteenth century. Shim'on Hakham, a Bukharan scholar residing in Jerusalem, published in 1904 a Judeo-Tajik (the Bukharan pronunciation of Persian) translation of the Pentateuch accompanied by notes derived from traditional Jewish commentaries, such as the *Targum Onkelos*, Solomon b. Isaac (Rashi; d. 1105), David Kimhi (Radak; 1235), and Abraham ibn Ezra (d. 1167). He also translated and published Judeo-Tajik translations of the books of Joshua, Judges, 1 and 2 Samuel, 1 and 2 Kings, Isaiah, and the Song of Songs. Several other Judeo-Persian translations of individual books of the Hebrew Bible, housed in public and

Queen Esther demands clemency from King Xerxes (Ahasuerus) for the Jews of Persia. From a Judeo-Persian copy of the Book of Esther, Iran, eighteenth century. New York, Library of the Jewish Theological Seminary.

private collections, have been published, including the books of Isaiah, Hosea, Jonah, Psalms, Proverbs, Job, Song of Songs, Lamentations, Ecclesiastes, and Esther.

The study of Judeo-Persian biblical translations and commentaries provides important information regarding the development of orthography, phonology, morphology, syntax, lexicon, and dialects of the Persian language by virtue of the fact that they preserve many archaic features that can be traced to Pahlavi. Perhaps these translations also acted as a bridge between Judeo-Iranian poets (such as Shahin, Imrani, Khwajah Bukhara'i, Elisha b. Samuel, and Benjamin ben Misha'el ["Amina"]), who flourished between the fourteenth and eighteenth centuries, and wrote inspired narrative verse accounts based on biblical events in conformity with the rhetorical features of Persian epic literature. ●

Vera Basch Moreen is an independent scholar and a specialist in Judeo-Persian studies, she coedited The Encyclopedia of Jews in the Islamic World *(Brill, 2011). Her publications include* In Queen Esther's Garden: An Anthology of Judeo-Persian Literature *(Yale University Press, 2000).*

Hebrew Translations and Transcriptions of the Qur'an

Aleida Paudice

The extremely broad subject of the translation of the Qur'an into Hebrew has not been studied in sufficient detail. Further study would undoubtedly shed valuable light on the relations between the Jews and Islam during the late Middle Ages and the Renaissance. Little is known of the context that produced the Hebrew translations, nor their purpose. One of the reasons is, perhaps, the often ambiguous relationship between the Jews and Islam's sacred text. This relationship speaks directly to issues of religious identity and ethnic belonging, as expressed in the theological and philosophical debate, and implies the acceptance of another conceptual and religious world that also claimed to be the true and last. A translation is never a mechanical process; the translator has choices and linguistic selections to make that often reveal something about his/her world, way of thinking, and the context in which he/she lives.

Aleida Paudice

Aleida Paudice is in the Department of Latin Language and Roman Culture at the University of Heidelberg. Her publications include *Between Several Worlds: The Life and Writings of Elia Capsali* (Peter Lang, 2010).

Since it was forbidden for non-Muslims not only to translate the Qur'an (whose translation presented the problem both of reproducing in languages different from Arabic its stylistic inimitability and of the recitation of the word of God, given in Arabic, in other languages) but also to learn and study it, it is evident that the Hebrew translations of the Qur'an can be particularly revealing about their reasons, purposes, and the context in which they originated.[1]

What, then, was the attitude of the Jews toward Islam, and what did they know of the Qur'an? During the late Middle Ages and the Renaissance, the Jews played a great role in Europe in the teaching of the Arabic language since they were often the only ones able to read it, because they had lived under Islamic rule and worked as traders and merchants in the Ottoman and Arab world.[2]

Here we do not attempt to answer the complex question of the relations between the Jews and Islam insofar as their holy texts are concerned, but we aim to supply a few areas for further investigation toward a better understanding of Jewish knowledge of the Qur'an. What did the Jews know of Islam's holy text and how did they relate to the Islamic faith?[3]

We have to look at the changes that took place in late twelfth-century Iberia and Provence, where it is possible to talk about a "Jewish intellectual revolution," which involved the translation of Arabic and Judeo-Arabic texts into Hebrew.[4] The translation of Arabic texts became more ambivalent and complex when the holy texts of Islam were translated. Jewish translators often replaced Qur'anic quotations with biblical allusions—effectively de-Islamicizing the texts—in order to acknowledge the Bible alone as the unique source of revealed truth.[5] Jewish anti-Muslim polemics, like Christian polemics, denied the status of the Qur'an as divine revelation and the prophetic role of Muhammad.[6] Although this argument is often disguised in Jewish writings, it is always implied and hinted at by different rhetorical and linguistic means, and it is reflected in the rendering of Qur'anic quotations and Qur'anic language.

As already mentioned, Jews were prohibited from learning the Qur'an, but nevertheless, Jews who lived under Islamic rule and spoke Arabic often knew the Qur'an and quoted from it in everyday life, either consciously or unconsciously, because it was a part of their culture. It is difficult to establish how the Jews studied the Qur'an and how much they knew of it, but they clearly had some knowledge of the Qur'an, as the references and quotations in Judeo-Arabic texts in particular show.[7] Most quotations of the Qur'an in Hebrew characters are, in fact, found in Judeo-Arabic works. Moses Ibn Ezra and Bahya Ibn Yossef Ibn Paquda quote Qur'anic verses maybe because of their literary and rhetorical value but also with polemical purposes.[8]

> *Jews were prohibited from learning the Qur'an, but quoted from it in everyday life, either consciously or unconsciously, because it was a part of their culture.*

Hebrew translations of the Qur'an

Hebrew translations of the Qur'an are rather late. Let us say a few words on the political and cultural setting that produced the sixteenth-century translation of the Qur'an that served as a model for the Hebrew translations.

During the fifteenth and sixteenth centuries, the expansion of Ottoman power, its threatening conquests in the Mediterranean, and its increasingly powerful commercial presence in the West were among the causes of the flourishing of Christian and Jewish historiography on the Ottomans, their traditions, and their beliefs. The first half of the sixteenth century is a key period for the creation and development of the image of the Turk in Venice. Prior to the sixteenth century, Venetian readers had to look at works written elsewhere to know about the Turks, but in the sixteenth century many famous historical works on the Ottomans were written and created an image of the Ottomans that lasted for two centuries.[9] Therefore, it is no wonder that the Italian translation of the Qur'an was printed in Venice. This translation, *L'Alcorano di Maometto*, though claiming to be a translation from the Arabic is nothing but a translation into Italian of the Latin version of the Qur'an made by Robert of Ketton in 1143 under the orders of Peter the Venerable.[10] The Italian translation, probably produced in the cultural milieu of Italian Reformers, relies on Theodor Bibliander's translation of the Qur'an of 1543.[11] Overall, Christian knowledge of Islam and its doctrine, both among the Catholics and the Protestants, was very poor, and that is why Bibliander's work represents a great novelty.[12]

Bibliander, orientalist and successor of Zwingli as professor of the Zurich Academy, also based his translation on Robert of Ketton's version, but the most interesting part of Bibliander's translation is its commentary.[13] Through Bibliander's work, the Protestant world shows a more open attitude toward Islam and attempts to understand it by means of a more scientific approach rather than by relying on medieval polemical or apologetic writings.[14]

The first translation of the Qur'an into Hebrew dates back to the sixteenth century (Heb. Ms. Brit. Mus. 111, Nr 1156/ British Library 6636), and it is a translation from the 1547 Italian edition of the Qur'an published in Venice by Andrea Arrivabene. In the seventeenth century, Jacob Levi ben Israel from Salonika (d. Zante 1636), a halakhist and rabbi famous for his responsa, wrote another translation, now in Oxford (Cat. Bodl. Hebr. Ms. No. 2207), identical to the above-mentioned sixteenth-century translation. In both manuscripts the Qur'an is divided into 124 suras instead of 114.[15] Two more manuscripts depend on these translations: one found in the Oriental Studies Center, part of the Russian Academy of Oriental Studies in Saint Petersburg (B155, 234), and the second at the Library of Congress in Washington (MS Hebr. 99).[16]

> *The Jews read the sacred texts of their neighbors, Muslims and Christians, to find confirmation of the truth of their faith.*

The translations found in the British Library (Ms. Brit. Mus. 111, Nr. 1156) and those found at the library of the Russian Academy of Oriental Studies in Saint Petersburg (B155, B234) also contain material on the life of Muhammad and the first caliphs following the Italian edition.[17]

A later manuscript translation of the Qur'an into Hebrew was written in Kochi, the southwest coast of India, in 1757, and it is now found in the Library of Congress in Washington (LC, Hebr. Ms. 99). It is a translation from the Dutch into Hebrew (previously translated from the French).[18] It is probably the translation of Jan Hendrik Glasemaker's Dutch translation of the Qur'an, which itself aimed at correcting the mistakes found in the French translation by André Du Ryer (1647).[19] This translation was probably made by an Ashkenazi Jew in Kochi, outpost of the Dutch East India Company in South Asia, around 1757, and according to Weinstein's detailed and fascinating explanation, this could be the same manuscript described by Joseph Wolff in 1831 in Meshhed in the Persian milieu of Jewish Sufis.[20] Weinstein stresses that the translation probably served polemical purposes: the Jews read the sacred texts of their neighbors, Muslims and Christians, to find confirmation of the truth of their faith.[21] The history of Hebrew translation of the Qur'an becomes clearer in the nineteenth century, when Z. H. Reckendorf published the first direct translation of the Qur'an from the Arabic into Hebrew (Leipzig, 1857), later to be followed by J. Rivlin (Tel Aviv, 1936–41) and Aharon Ben-Shemesh (Ramath Gan, 1971).[22] The most recent and scientifically accurate translation is that by Uri Rubin, who has also supplied important material and a detailed and rich commentary for the interpretation of the text.[23]

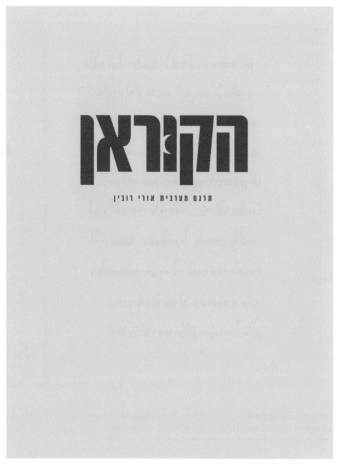

Translation of the Qur'an in Modern Hebrew by Uri Rubin. University of Tel Aviv, 2005.

Transcriptions of the Qur'an in Hebrew script

Alongside translations of the Qur'an there are also transcriptions in Hebrew script.[24] Most of the transcriptions of the Qur'an were also late, and the majority of them were written in countries under Muslim rule where Arabic was the spoken language. Bodleian Manuscript Hunt 529 is the only complete transcription of the Qur'an and the most precise and accurate from the point of view of the Hebrew and Arabic language.[25] The Bodleian manuscript was written in the fourteenth or fifteenth century, probably in the south of Iraq. It also contains a prayer in Arabic and several notes, which has led scholars to advance various hypotheses on the identity of the copyist who inserted polemical notes both against Christianity and Islam: maybe he was a Jew who converted to Islam but kept good relations with Jewish laws and customs, or a Jewish copyist who copied both the Gospels and the Qur'an and attacked

Transcription of the Qur'an in Hebrew characters. Manuscript "Arab 5," Crimea, eighth to ninth centuries. Halle, Library of the Deutsche Morgenländische Gesellschaft.

both religions. Sometimes a Jewish copyist addressed his polemical comments, like the Karaite al-Qirqisani, both against Christianity and Islam.[26]

Ms. Arab 5 from the library of the Morgenländische Gesellschaft in Halle contains another transcription, and it was described for the first time in detail by Emil Rödiger in 1860.[27] The manuscript, written on linen paper and consisting of eight folia, was found in the Crimea and donated by Pinsker in Odessa to the Morgenländische Gesellschaft in Halle in 1859.[28] It is a fragment of the Qur'an written in Oriental handwriting containing eighty-five āyat starting from sura 42:13 (14 in the Egyptian standard edition of the Qur'an) and ending at sura 43:45. The manuscript does not present notes or indications about the identity of the copyist; it is written in a rather clear hand, but it is partially damaged. The transcription was written between the late thirteenth century and the middle of the fourteenth century. The text is vocalized, although the Arabic vocalization is neither precise nor correct, and the transcription of Arabic consonants is at times inconsistent. Rödiger identifies two hands, both Jewish; the second hand wrote a comment on the margin of folio 6a. The manuscript was written for a Jewish audience and reminded them of

Fragment of the Qur'an in Judeo-Arabic from the Cairo Geniza. Cambridge University Library, Taylor-Schechter Geniza Collection, T-S Ar. 51.62.

the uniqueness of their religion as opposed to the Muslim faith.[29] Ms. Arab 5 is only one example of several Hebrew transcriptions of the Qur'an.[30]

Treasures of the Geniza

In the Cairo Geniza other transcriptions of the Qur'an in Hebrew characters are preserved, in addition to fragments of the Qu'ran in Arabic.[31] The Cairo Geniza is one of the richest and most precious sources of Arabic and Judeo-Arabic manuscripts on all kinds of subjects from theology, the Bible, and the Masora to philosophy, literature, and medicine.[32] The language of the Arabic fragments in general is a "form of Middle Arabic that deviates from Classical Arabic in that it reflects some Neo-Arabic dialectic features and pseudo-corrective elements."[33]

The Geniza manuscripts show how the Jews of Egypt (Fustat) enjoyed relative freedom compared to Jews in medieval Europe. They were not confined in a Jewish quarter and entertained lively and intense relations with the Muslims; in some cases they even turned to Muslim authorities to solve disputes and matters in which only

Jews were involved.[34] The manuscripts also reveal frequent religious contacts and influences between Muslims and Jews. For example, manuscript T-S AS 182.291 concerns the practice of genuflection and prostration introduced by the circle of Jewish pietists, whose most famous leader during the thirteenth century was the son of Moses Maimonides, Abraham Maimonides (1186–1237).[35] The pietists adopted some practices of Sufism, claiming them to also be ancient Jewish practices, but were opposed by other members of the Jewish community.[36] This document shows how Jewish mysticism was influenced by Muslim mysticism. Moreover, it also proves how the Muslim rulers were asked not only for rulings on Islamic practice but also on the rituals and liturgy of the other faiths of the *dhimmī*, like the Jews.[37]

> *" Considering the prohibition on using the Arabic script, the presence of fragments of the Qurʾan in the Geniza lets us suppose that this prohibition was not so strict. "*

From the manuscripts, it emerges that the Jews were acquainted with the Qurʾan, although it is not possible to establish to what extent and how they learned it, since the majority of the Jews "were not proficient in the reading and writing of Arabic script," as the much greater number of fragments written in Hebrew characters shows.[38] This can also be explained by the later prohibition on using the Arabic script imposed upon the *dhimmī* by their Muslim overlords.[39]

Nevertheless, in all the collections of the Taylor-Schechter Genizah Collection (Old, New, and Additional Series), a number of fragments of the Qurʾan have been preserved. The majority of them are in Arabic script, but there are also a few fragments in Judeo-Arabic. Although the presence of Arabic fragments is neither exceptional nor extraordinary, the Arabic fragments of the Qurʾan found in the Geniza raise important questions: How did they become part of the Geniza and why? Were they studied and then transcribed into Hebrew characters? Considering the prohibition on using the Arabic script, the presence of fragments of the Qurʾan in the Geniza lets us suppose that this prohibition was not so strict. Skimming through these fragments, I have noticed that many of them are written only on one side, which means that they were not reused for Hebrew writings, and some of them are written in a neat and clear handwriting, often without vocalization, but in some cases with clear vocalization, along with red dots to indicate the end of the *āya*.[40] T-S Ar. 39.460 is a fragment with writing exercises and jottings that include verses from the Qurʾan. T-S NS 305.210 and T-S NS 306.145 contain theological texts with references to Qurʾanic verses, and T-S NS 306.206 includes variants of the Qurʾan 2:19, 17–18, and 172. These are only a few examples of Arabic fragments of the Qurʾan found in the Cairo Geniza, and they are most fascinating and of great interest for scholars of various disciplines. Their characteristics are interesting because sometimes Qurʾanic verses are included in a tale (T-S Ar. 40.197), in other cases they are quoted in a theological work (T-S NS 305.210), or they are cited for the purposes of grammatical analysis (T-S NS 327.62). The best-preserved and clearest Judeo-Arabic fragment of the Qur'an is T-S Ar. 51.62, which is reproduced in the catalog Arabic and Judaeo-Arabic Manuscripts in the Cambridge Genizah Collections Arabic Old Series (T-S Ar. 1a-54), edited by Colin F. Baker and Meira Polliack (Cambridge, 2001), plate 20.

The Mithridates Qur'an

Vat. Ebr. 357 is a product of a very different environment, and it is unique in many ways. It is probably the most complex of the manuscripts examined here from the point of view of its redaction and the cultural environment that produced it. In fact, it should be examined within the context of the study of the Qur'an and of the Hebrew and Arabic languages by Italian Renaissance humanists. Vat. Ebr. 357 takes us into a very broad field of investigation of the social and cultural environment within which the knowledge of Arabic was exchanged: Who were the protagonists of this renewed interest in Arabic, and what purpose did it serve?[41] The codex consists of the Qur'an (ff. 51–156) and of two Arabic treatises on herbal remedies and medicine (ff. 1–50).[42] It is written on watermark paper of the Palermo 1409 type. We can therefore say that it was written sometime in the fifteenth century in Sicily.[43] The Arabic text is transcribed into Hebrew characters and is not vocalized. The titles of the suras were added later in red ink. The text of the Qur'an is mutilated and starts at sura 2:85, and due to the misplacing of some pages, the order of the suras is not respected (ff. 51 and 52v are between ff. 141v and 142). The most important characteristic of this manuscript is the presence of at least two hands that translate the Qur'anic text and comment on it. It is possible to detect four different hands at work and to identify two of them with that of Giovanni Pico Della Mirandola and of Flavius Mithridates (Guillelmus Raimundus Monchates).[44] The manuscript bears the signature of Flavius Mithridates; it probably belonged to Mithridates's father and was sold thereafter to Pico Della Mirandola.[45] The annotations and the commentaries, written in brown ink in distinction to the interlinear Latin translation, which is written in red ink, are of a different nature, consisting of historical, philological, exegetical, theological, and even mythological notes. They examine different aspects of the suras, make reference to Islamic tradition (hadith), and analyze in particular the most significant aspects of the Qur'an for a comparison of the Islamic faith to the Christian doctrines. It is, in fact, one of the most important commentaries of the Qur'an in Renaissance Europe. Italian humanistic culture was familiar with Islamic literature, and in particular with the Qur'an, since the role of Islam and the importance of Christianity in the Muslim faith, the prophetic role of Muhammad, and so on were at the center of theological and philosophical debates.

The transcriptions of the Qur'an examined here show how each one was produced in a different milieu and served specific purposes. While we can compare those fragments from the Cairo Geniza and the Halle manuscript that served similar polemical purposes and were written in countries under Muslim rule, where knowledge of Arabic was important for the relations with the authorities and, certainly in Egypt, was a part of everyday life, the Vatican manuscript places itself in a very different context, that of the cultural milieu of Jewish and Christian philosophers and scholars in the period of the Italian Renaissance.

---

1. On the translation of the Qur'an, see the entry by R. Paret, *Encyclopedia of Islam* (Leiden: Brill, 2003), 44–45. See also the entry by Hartmut Bobzin, "Translations of the Qur'an," in *The Encyclopaedia of the Qur'an* (Leiden: Brill, 2006), 5:340–58. On the prohibition of the study of the Qur'an, see Hava Lazarus Yafeh, *Intertwined Worlds, Medieval Islam and Bible Criticism* (Jerusalem: Mosad Byalik. 1998), 157. Jews and Christians nevertheless acquired knowledge of the Qur'an but not in public nor openly.

2. This was the case especially during the Middle Ages. See Karl H. Dannenfelt, "The Renaissance Humanists and the Knowledge of Arabic," *Studies in the Renaissance* 2 (1995): 96.

3. See Hava Lazarus Yafeh, *Intertwined Worlds*, 156–64.

4. Judeo-Arabic is an ethnolect (a linguistic entity with its own history and used by a distinct language community) that has been spoken and written in various forms by Jews throughout the Arabic-speaking world. Two main distinguishing features of Judeo-Arabic are the use of the Hebrew script and the frequent occurrence of Hebrew (and Aramaic) words and phrases. See J. Blau, *The Emergence and Linguistic Background of Judaeo-Arabic* (Jerusalem: Ben-Zvi Institute, 1985), 215. See also Jonathan P. Decter, "The Rendering of Qur'anic Quotations in Hebrew translations of Islamic texts," *Jewish Quarterly Review* 96, no. 3 (2006): 336.

5. Decter, "The Rendering of Qur'anic Quotations," 338. An example of this practice is found in a Hebrew manuscript, Ms. Dd.4.1, in the Cambridge University Library. See *Hebrew Manuscripts at Cambridge University Library: A Description and Introduction*, ed. Stefan C. Reif (Cambridge: Cambridge University Press, 1997), 397.

6. On Jewish polemics against Islam, see M. Steinschneider, *Polemische und apologetische Literatur in arabischer Sprache zwischen Muslimen, Christen und Juden* (Hildesheim: Olms, 1966 [1st ed., 1877]), 244–387.

7. See Lazarus Yafeh, *Intertwined Worlds*, 158.

8. See the article by Ryan Szpiech, "Citas árabes en caracteres hebreos en el Pugio fidei del dominico Ramón Martí: Entre la autenticidad y la autoridad," *Al-Qantara: Revista de Estudios Árabes* (Madrid: CSIC, 2011).

9. On the history of the Venetian historiography on the Ottomans, see Paolo Preto, *Venezia e i Turchi* (Florence: Sansoni, 1975), 13–22.

10. On the Italian translation, see Carlo De Frede, *La prima traduzione italiana del Corano sullo sfondo dei rapporti tra Cristianità e Islam nel Cinquecento* (Napoli: Istituto Universitario Orientale, 1967).

11. See the entry by Hartmut Bobzin, "Translations of the Qur'an," in *The Encyclopaedia of the Qur'an*, 346.

12. See Victor Segesvary, *L'Islam et la Réforme: Etudes sur L'Attitude des Reformateurs Zurichois Envers l'Islam, 1510–1550*, 13. Islam was considered a Christian heresy by the Christian world, and it was believed that people of the Arabian Peninsula were Christians before the advent of Muhammad. For a brief study on Latin translations of the Qur'an, see Ulli Roth and Reinhold Glei, "Die Spuren der lateinischen Koranübersetzung des Juan de Segovia: Alte Probleme und ein neuer Fund," *Neulateinische Jahrbuch* 11 (2009): 109–53.

13. See Victor Segesvary, *L'Islam et la Réforme*, 13.

14. Ibid., 15. See Roth and Glei's study on the earlier translation of the Qur'an by Juan de Segovia and its novelty, "Die Spuren der lateinischen Koranübersetzung," 113–20.

15. See Hava Lazarus Yafeh, "Jewish Knowledge of the Qur'an," *Sefunot* 5 (1991): 6.

16. Ibid., 42, and see *Intertwined Worlds*, 165. On Jacob ben Israel, see the entry by Joseph Hacker in *Encyclopaedia Judaica* (Jerusalem: Keter Books, 1971), vol. 11, col. 83, and also "Patterns of the Intellectual Activity of Ottoman Jewry in the 16th and 17th Centuries," *Tarbiz* 53, no. 4 (1984): 590. On this translation, see also M. Steinschneider, *Polemische und apologetische Literatur in arabischer Sprache zwischen Muslimen, Christen und Juden*, 315.

17. See Lazarus Yafeh, *Intertwined Worlds*, 165.

18. See Myron M. Weinstein, "A Hebrew Qur'an manuscript," *Studies in Bibliography and Booklore* 10 (1971): 19–52.

19. Ibid., 29.

20. See Weinstein, "A Hebrew Qur'an manuscript," 38–40. We do not know how the manuscript reached Meshhed from Kochi.

21. Ibid., 39–40.

22. See the entry by J. D. Pearson, *Encyclopedia of Islam* (Leiden: Brill, 2003), 48, and Lazarus Yafeh, *Intertwined Worlds*, 165, where she also mentions the first partial Yiddish translation of the Qur'an.

23. See Uri Rubin, *The Qurʾan: Hebrew Translation from the Arabic, Annotations, Appendices and Index* (Tel Aviv, 2005).

24. On the Qurʾan in Hebrew writing, see E. Mainz, "Koranverse in hebräischer Schrift," *Der Islam* 21 (1933): 229.

25. For a detailed description of the manuscript, see Lazarus Yafeh, *Intertwined Worlds*, 166–72; the same description is also found in "Jewish Knowledge of the Qurʾan," 43–47.

26. See Yafeh, *Intertwined Worlds*, 171–72.

27. See Emil Rödiger, "Mitteilungen zur Handschriftenkunde: Über ein Koranfragment in Hebräischer Schrift," *ZDMG* 14 (1860): 485–89 and *ZDMG* 13 (1859): 341, no. 271. See also the short description by Ernst Roth, *Verzeichnis der Orientalischen Handschriften in Deutschland* (Wiesbaden: F. Steiner, 1965), 110.

28. See also Hans Wehr, *Verzeichnis der Arabischen Handschriften in der Bibliothek der Deutschen Morgenländischen Gesellschaft* (Leipzig: Kommissionsverlag F. A. Brockhaus, 1940), 2. On the role played by Simhah Pinsker in the study of Karaism, see Haggai Ben-Shammai, "The Scholarly Study of Karaism in the Nineteenth and Twentieth Centuries," in *Karaite Judaism*, ed. Meira Polliack (Leiden: Brill, 2002), 12.

29. For a more detailed analysis, see my article "On Three Extant Sources of the Qurʾan Transcribed in Hebrew," *European Journal of Jewish Studies* 2, no. 2 (2008): 213.

30. See M. Steinschneider, Hebräische Bibliographie (Berlin: Benzian, 1860), 3:113.

31. For a list of the manuscripts of the Qurʾan in Judeo-Arabic and Arabic in the Cairo Geniza, see my article "On Three Extant Sources." I am indebted and grateful to the late Dr. Friederich Niessen from the Taylor-Schechter Genizah Research Unit for the dating of the fragments.

32. The Taylor-Schechter Genizah Collection contains about 140,000 fragments, of which a considerable proportion is in Judeo-Arabic. Most of the fragments date from the tenth to the thirteenth centuries, but there are also examples of late Judeo-Arabic from the fourteenth to the nineteenth centuries. See Colin F. Baker, "Judaeo-Arabic Material in the Cambridge Genizah Collections," *Bulletin of the School of Oriental and African Studies* 58, no. 3 (1995): 445–54.

33. See the introduction by Meira Polliack in *Arabic and Judaeo-Arabic Manuscripts in the Cambridge Genizah Collections Arabic Old Series (T-S Ar. 1a-54)*, ed. Colin F. Baker and Meira Polliack (Cambridge: Cambridge University Press, 2001), 9.

34. See Paul Fenton, "Jewish-Muslim Relations in the Medieval Mediterranean Area," in *The Cambridge Genizah Collections: Their Contents and Significance*, ed. Stefan C. Reif (Cambridge: Cambridge University Press, 2002), 152–59.

35. See Geoffrey Khan, *Arabic Legal and Administrative Documents in the Cambridge Genizah Collections* (Cambridge: Cambridge University Press, 1993), 293–94.

36. See Paul Fenton, "Jewish-Muslim Relations in the Medieval Mediterranean Area," 158.

37. On liturgical disputes, see T-S Ar. 41.105, also described by G. Khan in *Arabic Legal and Administrative Documents in the Cambridge Genizah Collections*, 293–94.

38. See Paul B. Fenton, "Judaeo-Arabic Literature," in *Religion, Learning and Science in the Abbasid Period* (Cambridge: Cambridge University Press, 1990), 464.

39. Ibid., 465. The prohibition became stricter in the sixteenth century in the Ottoman Empire. See M. A. Epstein, *The Ottoman Jewish Communities and Their Role in the Fifteenth and Sixteenth Centuries* (Freiburg im Breisgau: Klaus Schwarz, 1980), 38: "Despite the desire to expose the Jews to the correctness of Islam, late in the sixteenth century, when restrictions on protected persons were being more rigorously enforced than before, it was ordered that all copies of the Koran or Muslim religious tracts in the possession of Jews be seized."

40. For unvocalized fragments, see, for example, the well-preserved and ornamented fragment T-S Ar. 20.1 (photo published in *Arabic and Judaeo-Arabic Manuscripts in the Cambridge Genizah Collections Arabic Old Series (T-S Ar. 1a-54)*, ed. Colin F. Baker and Meira Polliack (Cambridge: Cambridge University Press, 2001), plate 11, but also T-S Ar. 38.39. For vocalized fragments, see, for example, T-S NS 183.79 and the three fragments that form part of the same manuscript T-S NS 192.11A, T-S NS 192.11B, and T-S NS 192.11C, where the red dots often indicate the end of the *āya*.

41. See A. M. Piemontese, "Le iscrizioni arabe nella Poliphili *Hypnerotomachia*," in *Islam and the Italian Renaissance*, ed. C. Burnett and A. Contadini (London: Warburg Institute, University of London, 1999), 199–217.

42. See A. M. Piemontese, "Il Corano latino di Ficino ed i Corani arabi di Pico e Monchates," *Rinascimento* 36 (1996): 227–73. Piemontese gives a detailed description of the manuscript and of its history.

43. Ibid., 64: "Testo arabo in elegante, nel carattere ebraico di tipo rabbinico a inchiostro marrone, linee 27."

44. On Flavius Mithridates, see the introduction by Haim Wirszbuski in Flavius Mithridates, *Sermo de Passione Domini*, ed. with introduction and commentary by Haim Wirszbuski (Jerusalem: Israel Academy of Sciences and Humanities, 1963), 49–50 and 93–94.

45. Benoît Grévin published, together with Giuseppe Mandalà, the first detailed critical edition and analysis of Vat. Ebr. 351. See also Benoît Grévin, "Un témoin majeur du rôle des communautés juives de Sicile dans la préservation et la diffusion en Italie d'un savoir sur l'arabe et l'Islam au xvᵉ siècle: Les notes interlinéaires et marginales du 'Coran de Mithridate' (ms. Vat. Ebr. 357)," in *Chrétiens, juifs et musulmans dans la méditerranée médiévale: Etudes en hommage à Henri Bresc*, ed. B. Grévin-Annliese Nef-Emmanuelle Tixier (Paris: De Boccard, 2008), 45–56, and "Le Coran de Mithridate (ms. Vat. Ebr. 357) à la croisée des savoirs arabes dans l'Italie du xvᵉ siècle," *Al Qantara* (forthcoming).

Jewish Views on the Birth of Islam

Jews witnessed the emergence and development of Islam and therefore had an inside view: their position was, by force of circumstance, ambivalent. Jews wrote about Islam and about the Muslim communities in which they lived, but like all minorities that suffered from limited legal and social rights, they were scant with praise and cautious in their critique. Islam emerged into history within a religious context. Jews were a part of that context and thus experienced the birth of Islam in relation to paradigms with which they were already familiar. Because the first Muslims were Arabs and the great conquest of the early period of Muslim expansion occurred under Arab military and religious leadership, Jews experienced that great success according to their traditional understanding of Arab peoples. Jews knew about Arabs from as early as the Torah, which identifies Abraham's firstborn son Ishmael as a progenitor of Arab peoples. His genealogy in Genesis chapter 25 contains Arab names such as his son Hadad, a common name to this day that means "smith" in Arabic. Other sons' names relate to geographical locations in Arabia, such as Dumah, perhaps Dumat al-Jandal, a stop on the ancient caravan route to the east of the Nabataean city of Petra in today's Jordan. Another son is named Yetur, which corresponds to an oasis in the Nejd region of Arabia. Another set of Arab names derives from Abraham's offspring through Qeturah in the same chapter, and together they reappear later in the Hebrew Bible among peoples who are identified clearly as Arabs. This is one of the reasons that the sages of the Talmud tended to identify Qeturah with Hagar, Ishmael's mother.[1]

The early Muslims were therefore identified and typed by Jews according to their experience and knowledge of Arabs in general. Some Arabs are depicted in the Bible as enemies of Israel. One group, called Hagarites after their matriarch, Hagar, are identified according to names of Ishmael's sons and lived east of the Jordan River in today's Jordan (1 Chronicles 5:10–22). Others are depicted positively in visions of redemption, such as those leading the camel caravans of Midian and flocks of Qedar, both of whom were progeny of Ishmael and Hagar/Qeturah (Genesis 25:4, 13), and who were expected to herald the glories of God according to Isaiah 60:4–7. The Talmud contains stories and references to Arabs as well, and identifies them also as Ishmaelites or Tayay'e, probably originating from the Arab Tayyi' tribe.[2] As in the Bible, some Arabs are depicted negatively as uncivilized, violent, and sexually aggressive.[3] In other references, however, Arabs are associated with messianic redemption (Jerusalem Talmud, Berakhot 2:4) and the wisdom of the desert (Baba Batra 73b). The Talmud was completed just about the time of the Muslim conquest, so it predates Islam, as does the Bible. However, some early post-Talmudic Jewish texts view the appearance of the Muslim armies in a very interesting light. Living a second-class legal status for centuries under the rule of the Christian Byzantines or Zoroastrian Persians, Jews yearned for a time of redemption. The arrival of the rapid and extremely successful military advance of a new community of monotheists from Arabia looked to some as if it were the vanguard of that redemptive process.

The setting of the following text is Roman Palestine after the destruction of the Jerusalem Temple, where the second-century Palestinian sage and mystic Rabbi Shimon bar Yochai is pleading with God to respond to his prayer for redemption. Suddenly the secrets of the end time are revealed to him, and he sees visions of the coming of the "kingdom of Ishmael," a common Jewish reference for the Muslim world:

When he saw the kingdom of Ishmael that was coming, he began to say: "Was it not enough, what the wicked kingdom of Edom[4] did to us, but we must have the kingdom of Ishmael too?" At once, Metatron,[5] the prince of the [divine] countenance, answered and said, "Do not fear, son of man, for the Holy One only brings the kingdom of Ishmael in order to save you from this wickedness. He raises up over them a Prophet according to his will and will conquer the land for them and they will come and restore it in greatness, and there will be great terror between them and the sons of Esau. . . . when he, the rider on the camel, goes forth, the kingdom will arise through the rider on an ass."[6]

Another text found in the Cairo Geniza, *Hizayon 'al hamilchamah ha'acharona* (*Vision of the War of the End Times*),[7] has also been considered by some to be a witness to the early conquests, though others consider it to refer to the Crusader wars that some Jews hoped would result in a destruction of both Christian and Muslim powers as part of the final redemption.

The case of Yemen might be particularly instructive, since a number of Jewish writings from Yemen have been preserved that articulate Jewish attitudes toward Islam. Jews had lived in Southern Arabia for many centuries prior to the rise of Islam,[8] and Jews continued to live there throughout the entire period of Muslim rule to this day. A very old tradition that is codified in a series of Jewish texts written in classical Arabic teaches that Jews in Arabia supported the Prophet Muhammad and fought on his behalf during his lifetime. The earliest version of this tradition is dated from the tenth century,[9] and it is found in at least four other versions, all of which come from Yemen.[10] The tradition asserts that Jews assisted Muhammad when he was weak and suffered attacks from Arabian polytheists. They could accept his prophetic leadership over the Arabs though not over themselves, and because both communities were monotheist in the face of the physical oppression of polytheists, they supported one another:

The Children of Israel fought on [Muhammad's] side until Friday noon, when the Prophet forbade the Children of Israel from fighting, saying to them: O Children of Israel, go and observe your Sabbath as God has commanded you through Moses the son of 'Imran, the one who conversed with God, peace be upon him. Do not be negligent of the law of Moses, peace be upon him. Then the Children of Israel accepted from him that which God commanded him to do, and they departed to keep their Sabbath. But after that, the enemies wanted to be victorious over the Prophet, him and his people, so the Children of Israel went out alone on their Sabbath day and prevailed [*jādū*] over the heathens, and killed of them seven thousand horsemen and five hundred infantrymen. Then the Prophet came to know about this and he rejoiced and laughed, and said: You strove well, O Children of Israel! By God the great, I shall reward you on this good deed, by God's will. And I shall grant [lit., "write"] you my protection, my covenant, my oath and my testimony, as long as I live and my people endure on the face of the earth.[11]

The tradition is interesting for many reasons that cannot be examined adequately due to the limitations of this general overview. Nevertheless, it is worth mentioning that it serves to overturn the limitations of second-class status imposed by Islamic law through the laws of the *dhimma*, and, in fact, the manuscript translated above is entitled, "This is the Writ of the *Dhimma*." It reverses virtually all of the social restrictions of the Islamic sumptuary laws, and one version actually lists some twenty individual privileges or protections that Muhammad decreed for the Jews in gratitude for their vital support in time of crisis. Historians and critical scholars consider the writ to have been fabricated by Jews in order to protect themselves against the legal restrictions and physical abuse that was the normal status of being a minority in the medieval world in general, and being Jewish in Yemen in particular. When trouble would arise, they could bring out the

Writ of Protection that they claimed was dictated by the Prophet to his son-in-law, ʿAli, and even signed by Muhammad himself, in order to demand protection.

The document can thus be seen as a complex statement that attests to the ambivalent situation of Jews living in the Muslim world. It can be read as evidence that Jews suffered so much they needed to concoct a potentially dangerous forgery to relieve the difficulties of their life under Islam. On the other hand, the document appears to attest to Muhammad's true monotheism and authentic prophethood in Jewish eyes. While most Jews in the medieval world would have agreed that Islam is indeed an expression of true monotheism, it was rare for Jews to consider Muhammad a true prophet. The disagreement over the prophethood of Muhammad would be the greatest theological bone of contention between Jews and Muslims throughout the centuries. Nevertheless, occasional Jewish voices are willing to ascribe a limited prophetic status to Muhammad, and one of those voices is a Yemenite scholar and community leader of the twelfth century named Nathanael Ibn al-Fayyumi. Al-Fayyumi wrote an introduction to Jewish theology in which he quotes not only the standard Jewish authorities of the Bible, Talmud, and responsa literature, but also the Qurʾan and a number of other sources that cannot be identified today.[12] In his work "The Garden of Intellects," Ibn al-Fayyumi writes:

The Creator—magnified be His praise!—knows the ruin of this world and the abode of the future world. He therefore sends prophets in every age and period that they might urge the creatures to serve Him and do the good, and that they might be a road-guide to righteousness . . . It is incumbent, then, upon every people to be led aright by what has been communicated to them through revelation and to emulate their prophets, their leaders, and their regents. . . . All call unto Him, all turn their faces unto Him, and every pious soul is translated to Him, as it is written, "And the spirit returns unto God who gave it" (Ecclesiastes 12:7).[13] ●

Reuven Firestone is professor of medieval Judaism and Islam at Hebrew Union College in Los Angeles, and a member of the Center for Religion and Civic Culture (University of Southern California). He is also the founder and codirector of the Center for Muslim-Jewish Engagement, whose mission is to promote dialogue and scientific collaboration between the two communities. His publications include An Introduction to Islam for Jews *(Jewish Publication Society, 2008).*

1. See Fred V. Winnett, "The Arabian Genealogies in the Book of Genesis," in *Translating and Understanding the Old Testament*, ed. H. T. Frank and W. L. Reed (Nashville, TN: Abingdon, 1970), 171–96; James Montgomery, *Arabia and the Bible* (Philadelphia: University of Pennsylvania Press, 1934); D. S. Margoliouth, *The Relations between Arabs and Israelites Prior to the Rise of Islam* (London: Humphrey Milford, 1924).

2. See Richard Kalmin, *Sages, Stories, Authors, and Editors in Rabbinic Babylonia* (Atlanta: Scholars Press, 1994), 263–72; Michael Sokoloff, *A Dictionary of Jewish Babylonian Aramaic* (Ramat Gan: Bar-Ilan University, 2002), 501–2.

3. Ketubot 36b, Sukkah 52b, Kiddushin 49b.

4. The kingdom of Edom is a reference in rabbinic literature to the Roman Empire, and later, the Christian Byzantine Empire. Edom is associated with Isaac's older son Esau in Genesis 36:1, and both serve as a type of code for Christians or Christian rule.

5. Metatron does not occur in the Bible, but in rabbinic literature, he is the highest of angels.

6. The text cited here is found in Adolph Jellinek, *Bet ha-Midrasch: Sammlung kleiner Midraschim und vermischter Abhandlungen aus der ältern jüdischen Literatur* (Vienna, 1853–78; repr., Jerusalem: Wahrmann, 1967), 3:78.

7. In *Ginzey Schechter*, 1:310–12; English translation is "On That Day: A Jewish Apocalyptic Poem on the Arab Conquests," trans. Bernard Lewis, in *Mélanges d'islamologie: Volume dédiés à la mémoire de Armand Abel* (Leiden: Brill, 1974), 197–200.

8. Gordon Newby, *A History of the Jews of Arabia: From Ancient Times to Their Eclipse under Islam* (Columbia: University of South Carolina Press, 1988).

9. Hartwig Hirschfeld, "The Arabic Portion of the Cairo Genizah at Cambridge," *The Jewish Quarterly Review* 15 (January 1903): 167–81.

10. Reuben Ahroni, "Some Yemenite Jewish Attitudes towards Muhammad's Prophethood," *Hebrew Union College Annual* 69 (1998): 49–99.

11. Ibid., 94, with minor adjustment for clarity.

12. Nathanael Ibn al-Fayyumi, *The Bustan Al-Ukul*, trans. David Levine (New York: AMS Press, 1966), x–xi.

13. Ibid., 108.

Chapter II
Mirrored Languages

Hebrew, Arabic: A Comparative View
Lutz Edzard

Modern linguistics groups a certain number of related languages under the name "Semitic languages." The family comprises three main branches: East Semitic, represented by Akkadian or Assyro-Babylonian; South Semitic, represented by the Ethiopian languages (Geʿez, Amharic, Tigrinya, etc.), as well as by the South Arabic languages (which are not derived from Arabic); and Central Semitic, which has two subgroups—Arabic and the Semitic languages of the northwest. It is this last subgroup that includes Aramaic, Ugaritic, and the Canaanite languages such as Hebrew, but also Phoenician and Moabite.

On the strength of this proximity, many parallels can be observed between Hebrew and Arabic, which are, moreover, the two languages of the sacred texts of Judaism and Islam.

Lutz Edzard

Lutz Edzard is a professor with the Department of Culture and Oriental Languages of the University of Oslo. He teaches comparative Semitic linguistics, Classical Arabic, the history of the Hebrew language, and Judeo-Arabic.

History of the two languages

Languages evolve through time. Historically, then, we distinguish several periods in the evolution of the Hebrew and Arabic languages. The oldest state of Hebrew is known to us through the books of the Bible; it is followed by the Hebrew known as Mishnaic, that is, the variety in which the Mishnah was composed (around 200 CE). Historians of the language have dedicated numerous works to the question of the extent to which Mishnaic Hebrew, but also biblical Hebrew, such as they are transmitted to us through the texts, reflect the language spoken on a daily basis, and to what extent they belong primarily to literary genres with their own syntax and vocabulary. In the decades following the closure of the Mishnah, or even before, Hebrew ceases entirely to be a vernacular language and is confined to the rabbinic disciplines. The two Talmuds (of Jerusalem and Babylon) are written in a learned language halfway between Hebrew and Aramaic, and the masters of the following generations communicated among themselves in Aramaic, and later in Arabic. It is largely the commentators and Talmudists of medieval Europe who, rather than writing in the local languages, take up once more the *leshon ḥakhamim* or "tongue of the Sages" of the Mishnah and the Talmud, thereby giving birth to a rabbinic Hebrew that is still practiced in our time in religious literature. This medieval Hebrew is further enriched, as we will see, by contributions from Arabic (morphology, meter) in the scientific, philosophical, and poetic domains. Beginning at the end of the eighteenth century, the Haskalah, a movement of revitalization of classical thought following the model of the Enlightenment, attempted to bring about a "return to the sources" of the biblical language in its literary compositions, while at the end of the nineteenth century Eliezer Ben-Yehuda tried, within a Zionist framework, to restore to Hebrew its status as a "living" language by enriching its vocabulary considerably, normalizing its morphology and syntax along the lines of the European languages. Although there are fine distinctions in phonology, morphology, and syntax between these periods, these differences are minimal in comparison with the development in the Romance languages, for example. If, for a modern Israeli, biblical Hebrew presents a sufficient number of archaic forms to be difficult to understand, the gap is comparable to the one separating a French reader from the language of Montaigne (and not of the language of Cicero). As for Mishnaic Hebrew, it will "sound" to his ears more or less like Quebec French to a Frenchman from France. That is why it will be possible to speak, within the limits of this article, of "Hebrew," without further specification, referring to a "classical" state of the language, except for a few Modern Hebrew words.

An adequate definition of Arabic is more complex.[1] Already in cuneiform documents we find nouns that we would classify as Arabic today; similarly, several inscriptions, for example Al-Namara, dated 328 CE, presents elements characteristic of Arabic as we know it. The expression "Classical Arabic" designates the state of the language attested in pre-Islamic poetry beginning in the sixth century, and later in the Qur'an, a linguistic canon par excellence, and subsequently in classical works. Modern Standard Arabic, used today in formal written and spoken usage, is the result of a modernization of Classical Arabic undertaken by the intellectuals of the Nahda (the Arab "Renaissance" of the nineteenth century). We thus observe, as in Hebrew, a considerable degree of stability in the higher levels of the language—perhaps even more in Arabic, since that language has not known the phenomenon of "hybridization" with Aramaic that Talmudic and post-Talmudic Hebrew experienced. On the contrary, as opposed to Hebrew, which for over a thousand-year period knew only a lettered and written usage, Arabic never ceased being spoken, and spoken in a very extensive geographical area, which ended in a situation of diglossia or rather of "polyglossia," with each region and each religious

Inscription in Arabic and Nabatean characters on the tombstone of Imru'u al-Qays, "Son of 'Amr, king of the Arabs." Al-Namara (southeast of Damascus), 328 CE. Paris, Louvre Museum, Departement of Oriental Antiquities.

community developing "its own" particular Arabic, both at the level of pronunciation and at the level of vocabulary and syntax: whence the flourishing multiplicity of so-called dialectical varieties of Arabic, often barely intelligible between one another, and coexisting with "written " Arabic (an expression that groups together Classical Arabic and Modern Standard Arabic). In the framework of this article, we will take Classical Arabic as the language of reference.

Writing and phonology

The system of consonants in the two languages is comparable, although the Arabic phonological range is a little more complex (or, according to some scholars, archaic) than that of Hebrew. If most of the phonemes of Hebrew may be found in Arabic, the establishing of an unequivocal correspondence is more complex than it might appear, for two major reasons. First, the series of Hebrew plosives (*b̲, g, d̲, k̲, p, t̲*) is phonemically and in writing identical to the series of spirants (v gh, dh, kh, f, th, which are noted as b, g, d, k, p, t): thus, a כ (*kaf*) is pronounced *k* at the beginning of a word, but *kh* in the middle or at the end of a word (רוכב *be̲kor*, "eldest son," דלמ *mele̲k*, "king"). In Arabic, on the other hand, *k* (*kaf*) and *kh* (*ḫā'*) function as two different phonemes, just as do *d* (*dāl*) and *dh* (*d̲al*), while the *v* does not exist, nor does the *p*. Second, phonetic correspondences do not always match the etymological ones: thus, the ז and the ز are both pronounced [z], but etymologically the ז sometimes, even most often corresponds to ذ (*d̲al*) [ð] ("gold" is בהז *zaha̲b* in Hebrew, ذهب *d̲aha̲b* in Arabic—comp. בהד *daha̲b* in Aramaic). The ח is pronounced classically more or less like the ح, an emphatic *h*, but etymologically it can also correspond to the خ (*ḫā'*), which is close, for the ear, to the spirantized כ (*kh*), although in terms of phonemic value the כ, spirantized or not, is equivalent to the ك. Finally, it should be noted that only the Jews of Islamic countries, the Yemenites in particular, have retained the full phonetic palette of Hebrew, whereas the European Jews, and the Israelis after them, have lost the pronunciation of the emphatic consonants. Similarly, the pronunciation of the Arabic presented here is intended to be normative, but in actual fact it has many regional variants, the ق (the *qāf*) in particular being pronounced in some places [q], in others [g], and still elsewhere [k], or even [ʔ].

Arabic, like Hebrew, is written not in an alphabet (in which consonants and vowels alternate) but in an *abjad*, that is, a system of writing that only notes the consonants and the semivowels [y] and [w]. If the *abjad* are poorly adapted to the Indo-European languages, they are perfectly well suited to the writing of the Semitic languages, in which, as we shall see, the vocalization of the words is largely dependent on their grammatical and syntactic function, which gives them a specific vocalic pattern. The order of the letters in Hebrew is the same as that of Phoenician, which, moreover, has produced the Greek and Latin alphabets. Arabic writing, derived from Nabataean writing, shares the same genealogy via Aramaic. For this reason, its letters were originally set in the same order as Hebrew, and that order continues to be maintained when numeric values are attributed to the letters, particularly in the esoteric discipline called *ʿilm al-ḥurūf*, "science of letters." The other order, more familiar since it is that of the dictionaries, takes as its basis that "Aramaic" order, but regroups the letters by their graphic proximity; indeed, in the course of the formation of Arabic writing, letters that originally were very different have ended up being written in an identical fashion, which subsequently led the scribes to add diacritical points—which did not exist, for example, at the time of the commitment to writing of the first collections of the Qurʾan.

The vocalic systems of Hebrew and Arabic are, here again, at the same time close and different. To the extent that the writing of Hebrew, like that of Arabic, does not note most of the vowels (with the exception of certain long vowels that are indispensable to the

Fragment of an ancient syllabary found in the Cairo Geniza. University of Manchester.

Hebrew		Arabic		Phonemic Value	Phonetic Value
Sign	Name	Sign	Name		
א	*ʾālep̄*	١/ﺀ	*ʾalif*	/ʾ/	[ʔ]
ב	*bēt̠*	ب	*bāʾ*	/b, ḇ/	[b, v]
ג	*gīmel*	ج	*ǧīm*	/g, ḡ; ǧ/	[g, ɣ or ʁ; dʲ]
ד	*dālet̠*	د	*dāl*	/d, ḏ/	[d, ð]
—	—	ذ	*ḏāl*	/ḏ/	[ð]
ה	*hē(ʾ)*	ه	*hāʾ*	/h/	[h]
ו	*wāw*	و	*wāw*	/w/	[w]
ז	*záyin*	ز	*zāy*	/z/	[z]
ח	*ḥēt̠*	ح	*ḥāʾ*	/ḥ/	[ħ]
—	—	خ	*ḫāʾ*	/ḫ/	[x]
ט	*ṭēt̠*	ط	*ṭāʾ*	/ṭ/	[tˤ]
—	—	ظ	*ẓāʾ*	/ẓ/	[zˤ]
י	*yōd̠*	ي	*yāʾ*	/y/	[j]
כ	*kap̄*	ك	*kāf*	/k, ḵ/	[k, x or χ]
ל	*lāmed̠*	ل	*lām*	/l/	[l]
מ	*mēm*	م	*mīm*	/m/	[m]
נ	*nūn*	ن	*nūn*	/n/	[n]
ס	*sāmek̠*	س	*sīn*	/s/	[s]
ע	*ʿáyin*	ع	*ʿayn*	/ʿ/	[ʕ]
—	—	غ	*ġayn*	/ġ/	[ɣ]
פ	*pē(h)*	ف	*fāʾ*	/p, p̄; f/	[p, f]
צ	*ṣād̠ē(h)*	ص	*ṣād*	/ṣ/	[sˤ]
—	—	ض	*ḍād*	/ḍ/	[dˤ]
ק	*qōp̄*	ق	*qāf*	/q/	[q]
ר	*rēš*	ر	*rāʾ*	/r/	[ʀ or ʁ; r]
שׁ	*šīn*	ش	*šīn*	/š/	[ʃ]
שׂ	*śīn*	—	—	/ś/	[s]
ת	*tāw*	ت	*tāʾ*	/t, t̠/	[t, θ]
—	—	ث	*t̠āʾ*	/t̠/	[θ]

understanding, for which both languages mobilize the semivowels), the classical vocalization of Hebrew as it is written and spoken at the present time is based on the work of normalization of the reading of the biblical text, with the help of vowel points added above or below letters, carried out by the Masoretes of Tiberias. The vowels of the Tiberian system include /a, ā, e, ē, i, ī, o, ō, u, ū/, as well as a reduced vowel /ə/ called *šəwā* (*shwa*, the Aramaic word for "nothing"). By contrast, the vowels of Classical Arabic only contain /a, ā, i, ī, u, ū/. The Arabophone milieu of the Jews of the Islamic world, in the same way that it was a factor for the preservation of the consonantal palette of "eastern" Hebrew, ended up with a relative impoverishment of its vocalic richness if we compare it to the Hebrew of the Ashkenazi, which, if it knew phenomena of *vowel shift*, nevertheless retained the phonetic distinction between "short" and "long" vowels. Again, only the Yemenites succeeded in keeping both the consonantal and the vocalic distinctions. Conversely, Dialectal Arabic, probably under the influence of the local languages (Amazigh, Turk, Persian, and others) has a tendency to modify, sometimes substantially, the vocalic system of Classical Arabic.

Elements of a comparative grammar of Hebrew and Arabic

If we leave conjunctions, prepositions, and particles aside, the words (nouns and verbs) in the two languages are built on a system of roots typically triconsonantal,[2] the vocalic system of which has a grammatical function (for example, transforming a verb into a substantive) and to which prefixes, suffixes, and infixes marking the gender, number, the determination, and (in Arabic only) the case of nouns, and the person, gender, number, tense, aspect, and mood of verbs. The comparison of the various words formed from the root *k-t-b*, associated with the concept "writing" and common to Hebrew and Arabic, makes clear the morphological proximity of the two languages.

Hebrew	Arabic	Gloss
kātab	*kataba*	"he wrote"
yiktōb	*yaktubu*	"he writes/will write"
kətōb	*(ʾu)ktub*	"write!"
kōtēb	*kātib*	"writer"
kətāb	*kitāb*	"book, writing"
kətubbā	—	"marriage contract"
miktāb	—	"letter"
—	*maktab*	"desk"
—	*maktaba*	"library"

The nouns and pronouns in Hebrew and Arabic have masculine and feminine gender. The feminine gender can be marked by a suffix -*a*(*t*) *or* -*t* (with allomorphs). The gender may also be lexicalized, especially in cases of natural gender, for example *'āb* "father" vs. *'ēm* "mother" in Hebrew and *'ab* "father" vs. *'umm* "mother" in Arabic.

Hebrew, like Arabic, has three numbers: singular, dual, and plural. But although any noun or verb can take the dual form, for example, the Arabic *malik* "(a) king" versus *malikāni* "two kings," that form is limited in Hebrew mainly to periods of time and parts of the body that exist in pairs, for example, *šānā*(*h*) "(one) year" versus *šənātáyim* "two years," and *yād* "(one) hand" versus *yādáyim* "two hands." The plural is marked in Hebrew by the suffix -*īm* (masculine) and the suffix -*ōt* (feminine), often with internal phonological changes, for example, *melek* "king" → *məlākīm* "kings," and *malkā*(*h*) "queen" → *məlākōt* "queens." In Arabic, the plural may be marked by the suffix -*ūn*(*a*) (masculine) and by the suffix -*āt*(*un*) (feminine), but in most cases what is used is an internal or "broken" plural, which is not always predictable, for example, *malik* "king" → *mulūk* "kings."

The nouns in Semitic languages have different "states" according to the determination: the absolute state (unmarked: *melek*, *malik* "a king"), the determined state (*ham-melek*, *al-mali* "the king"), the construct state ("king of"), and the pronominal state ("king + pronominal suffix"). As shown in the example, determination is realized by the invariable prefix *ha-* in Hebrew, followed by a gemination of the initial consonant of the word (except guttural consonants), and by the invariable prefix *al-* in Arabic, the *l* of which is assimilated to all coronal consonants (articulated against the teeth or the palate), by which the following noun begins (for example *an-nabī* "the prophet"). Finally, Hebrew, like Dialectal Arabic and Modern Arabic as it is generally spoken, has no cases, while Classical Arabic has the nominative, the genitive, and the accusative.

The verbal system is at the core of both Arabic and Hebrew grammar. It functions by the joint use of regular vocalic patterns (except in the case of phonological accommodation, as Hebrew has difficulty in accepting quiescent gutturals, particularly) and a twofold series of prefixes and suffixes. In Arabic as in Hebrew, and as opposed to Akkadian, in particular, the imperfect is marked by prefixes and the perfect by suffixes. (Contrary to Western usage, conjugation tables begin with the third person, since that form is the basic one.)

Hebrew and Arabic verb paradigms

While European languages have three "voices" (active, passive, and reflexive), the Semitic languages use "diatheses" (*binyanim*, "constructions" in Hebrew), which are also manifested by an inflection of the vocalic pattern and/or by the addition of a prefix. These *binyanim* express not only the voice, but also the intensive character of the action (*šāḇar* "he broke," *šibbēr* "he shattered into pieces"), sometimes with an important nuance (*lāmad* "he studied," *limmēd* "he taught"), or yet again the causative (*šāmaʿ* "he heard," *hišmīaʿ* "he caused to be heard").

	Perfect		Imperfect	
	Hebrew	**Arabic**	**Hebrew**	**Arabic**
3ms	*kāṯaḇ*	*kataba*	*yiḵtōḇ*	*yaktubu*
3fs	*kāṯəḇā(h)*	*katabat*	*tiḵtōḇ*	*taktubu*
2ms	*kāṯaḇtā*	*katabta*	*tiḵtōḇ*	*taktubu*
2fs	*kāṯaḇt*	*katabti*	*tiḵtəḇī*	*taktubīna*
1cs	*kāṯaḇtī*	*katabtu*	*ʾeḵtōḇ*	*ʾaktubu*
3md	–	*katabā*	–	*yaktubāni*
3fd	–	*katabatā*	–	*taktubāni*
2cd	–	*katabtumā*	–	*taktubāni*
3mp	*kāṯəḇū*	*katabū*	*yiḵtəḇū*	*yaktubūna*
3fp	*kāṯəḇū*	*katabna*	*yaktubna*	
2mp	*kəṯaḇtem*	*katabtum*	*tiḵtəḇū*	*taktubūna*
2fp	*kəṯaḇten*	*katabtunna*	*tiḵtōḇnā(h)*	*taktubna*
1cp	*kāṯaḇnū*	*katabnā*	*niḵtōḇ*	*naktubu*

A large shared lexical fund

Hebrew and Arabic share a considerable fund of common vocabulary, as in the well-known example *šālōm* – *salām* "peace." The numbers from 1 to 10 illustrate this circumstance (the following list shows the numbers in the masculine form in both languages):

#	Hebrew	Arabic
1	*ʾeḥāḏ*	*wāḥidun*
2	*šənáyim*	*iṯnāni*
3	*šālōš*	*ṯalāṯun*
4	*ʾarbaʿ*	*ʾarbaʿun*
5	*ḥāmēš*	*ḫamsun*
6	*šēš*	*sittun*
7	*šeḇaʿ*	*sabʿun*

#	Hebrew	Arabic
8	*šəmōne(h)*	*ṯamānin*
9	*tešaʿ*	*tisʿun*
10	*ʿéśer*	*ʿašrun*
100	*mēʾā*	*miʾatun*
1000	*ʾelep̄*	*ʾalfun*

Here are a few more examples of nouns taken from the lexical domain of men/ women and of relatives, animals, parts of the body, and objects of nature.[3]

Hebrew	Arabic	Gloss
šēm	*ʾism*	"name"
ʾĕnōš / nāšīm	*(ʾu)nāsun / nisāʾun*	"man, human being / women"
zāḵar	*ḏakarun*	"male"
ʾiššā	*ʾunṯatun*	"female"
ʾāḇ	*ʾabun*	"father"
ʾēm	*ʾummun*	"mother"
bēn	*ibnun*	"son"
baṯ	*bintun*	"daughter"
ʾāḥ	*ʾaḫun*	"brother"
ʾāḥōṯ	*ʾuḫtun*	"sister"
nāmēr	*namirun*	"leopard"
zəʾēḇ	*ḏiʾb*	"wolf"
kéleḇ	*kalb*	"dog"
ḥăzīr	*ḫinzīr*	"pig"
šōr	*ṯawrun*	"ox"
ḥămōr	*ḥimārun*	"ass"
ʿaqrāḇ	*ʿaqrabun*	"scorpion"
rō(ʾ)š	*raʾsun*	"head"
ʿáyin	*ʿaynun*	"eye"
ʾōzen	*ʾuḏnun*	"ear"
ʾap̄	*ʾanfun*	"nose"
lāšōn	*lisānun*	"tongue"
lēḇ	*lubbun*	"heart," "innermost"
šāmáyim	*samāʾun*	"sky"
kōḵāḇ	*kawkabun*	"star"

Hebrew	Arabic	Gloss
šémeš	*šamsun*	"sun"
ṣēl	*ẓillun*	"shadow"
yōm	*yawmun*	"day"
láylā	*laylatun*	"night"
ʾereṣ	*ʾarḍun*	"land"
máyim	*māʾun*	"water"

Two languages in contact

Given the grammatical and lexical similarity between Hebrew (as well as Aramaic) and Arabic, it is not surprising that phenomena of mutual linguistic contact and influence have existed from the earliest hours of classical Islam, especially since the Muslims of that period were in direct contact with the Jewish and Christian communities.[4] The development of the Qurʾanic language is therefore not independent of influence from these cultural and linguistic milieus. The term *tawrāh* (Torah) is obviously borrowed from the Hebrew *tōrā(h)* (literally, "religious direction"). The term *ṣalāh* (prayer) and the term *qurʾān* (Qurʾan) even owe their phonological structure to the Aramaic terms *ṣəlōṭā* and *qeryānā*. The epithet *raḥmān* (merciful) is also borrowed from the Aramaic form *raḥmānā*, attested in the Talmud.

The golden age of Judeo-Muslim coexistence before the Reconquista fostered a number of important works that focused on the linguistic context between Hebrew and Arabic. Grammarians and lexicographers like Saadia Gaon, Judah ibn Quraysh, David ben Abraham al-Fasi, Menahem ben Saruq, Dunash ben Labraṭ, Yehuda Hayyuj, Yona ibn Janah, Hai Gaon, ʾAbu l-Faraj, Samuel ha-Nagid ibn Naghrila, Abraham ha-Bavli, Moshe ibn Gikatilla, Judah ben Balʿam, and Isaac ben Barun developed intra-Semitic comparisons and thus stand among the true founders of comparative Semitic linguistics.

❱ See article by Djamel Kouloughli, pp. 664–669.

Finally, Modern Hebrew borrowed many nonexistent (or rather, nonattested) lemmas in Classical Hebrew from Arabic, on the basis of shared roots: thus *taʾrikh < taʾrīḫ* (date calendar), *adiv < ʾadīb* (polite), ou *mehager < muhāǧir* (immigrant).[5] This process continues down to our own time with many borrowings in such areas as food (for example, *ḥúmus* or *falafel*) and even salutations (*ʾahlan*, "hello"). In return, Palestinian Arabic has borrowed words from Modern Hebrew and has especially formed whole calques based on Hebrew models, as, for example, *ʿabar il-imtiḥān*, "he passed the test," a calque of *ʿavar et ha-beḥina*, instead of the equivalent in Standard Arabic *naǧaḥa fī l-imtiḥān*, "he had success in the test."[6]

1. See Jan Retsö, *The Arabs in Antiquity: Their History from the Assyrians to the Umayyads* (London/New York: Routledge, 2003).

2. We know that there is a minority of biliteral roots and that there are a few quadriliteral ones. Beginning with the medieval period, during which this triliteral conception of the roots of Hebrew and Arabic was normalized, the tendency of grammarians has often been to explain biliteral and quadriliteral roots as variants of known triliteral roots.

3. See Gotthelf Bergsträsser, *Introduction to the Semitic Languages: Text Specimens and Grammatical Sketches*, translated with notes and bibliography and an appendix on the scripts by Peter D. Daniels (Winona Lake, IN: Eisenbrauns, 1983), 210–23.

4. See, for example, Noam Stillman, "Yahūd," in *The Encyclopaedia of Islam*, new ed., vol. 11 (Leiden: Brill, 2002), 239–42.

5. See, for example, Aharon Geva-Kleinberger, "Ivrit," in *The Encyclopedia of Arabic Language and Linguistics*, ed. Kees Versteegh et al., vol. 2 (Leiden: Brill, 2007), 461–64.

6. See Muhammad Hasan Ammara, "Ivrit loanwords," in *The Encyclopedia of Arabic Language and Linguistics*, vol. 2, 465.

The Arab Inspiration of the Beginnings of Hebrew Grammar

The search for the origins of a linguistic reflection on a given language presupposes the identification of the first indications of a metalinguistic attitude toward that language. In the case of Hebrew, we must go back at least a millennium before the Christian era. It must have been around that time that the alphabetic system of writing, referred to as Phoenician, was adapted in order to fix the texts of the Jewish tradition. We are unfortunately too ill-informed on the history and the conditions of that work to be able to do more than take note of it as the first step in the linguistic reflection on Hebrew. In any case, it must be stressed how much the writing system to which this anonymous labor gave birth—a system characterized essentially by the notation of the consonantal ductus alone, that is, the stroke forming the letters of the words without any vocalic information—will weigh decisively on the entirety of subsequent linguistic research in the domain of Hebrew.

The second major step in the formation of a linguistic reflection on the Hebrew language is that which constitutes the development of the Masora,[1] that is, the set of traditions concerning the fixing of the text of the Bible and how it is to be read. The precise origin of Masoretic literature is not known. This domain of activity must have been constituted progressively as a specialization of the activity of certain scribes (*soferim*) who devoted themselves to the scrupulous reproduction of the Torah. We may assume that in the beginning the essence of their knowledge, with respect to the precise reading of the text (which consisted, as we will recall, solely in the consonantal ductus of the words), was transmitted in an exclusively oral manner. Vigilance was required not only to see to the rigorous restoration of the traditional vocalization but also to respect the rules of accentuation, pauses, and cantillation. Technically, Masoretic literature covers two large domains: (1) the graphic techniques for implementing the transformation of the original *scriptio defectiva* into *scriptio plena*, and (2) what might be called the critical apparatus, making it possible either to respect certain conventions relative to the realization of the text, or to understand the text's content on certain critical points that may influence its reading.

The first attempts at written incorporation of Masoretic knowledge were made in the margin of the sacred text, to which any direct addition was out of the question. Moreover, as far as we know, the versions of the Torah acceptable for use during liturgical service still cannot include the vowel or cantillation marks invented by the Masoretes, which are found in the study versions of scripture. Subsequently, the accretion of the commentaries handed down from one generation to the next has allowed the establishment of autonomous Masoretic works. This gradual accumulation has remained essentially anonymous. It was not until the tenth century that a name, that of Aaron Ben Asher, was associated with that immense enterprise of codification of the text of the Bible. Descended from a long line of Masoretes originally from Tiberias, and considered the last great representative of the Masoretic trend, Ben Asher left a work that is in fact a vast compilation of rules present in the marginal notes of Bibles, as well as in various independent Masoretic works.[2] This work made the codified text of the Tiberian Masora the definitive reference for all subsequent research on Biblical Hebrew. Roughly contemporary with Aaron Ben Asher, Saadia Gaon signals the birth of the third and most decisive step

Double-sided page from an alphabet book, designed to teach reading, eleventh to twelfth centuries. Cambridge University Library, Taylor-Schechter Geniza Collection, T-S K5.13.

in the constitution of a metalinguistic reflection on Hebrew. He is considered the true founder of Hebrew linguistics.[3] The appearance of Saadia Gaon on the scene, and the radical novelty of his way of speaking about the Hebrew language, can only be understood in relation to his historical and cultural context. This context is that of Jewish communities in the Arab world of the tenth century. Three important factors in the cultural lives of the Jewish Arabs of that era played an essential role in the intellectual evolution of Saadia Gaon, and consequently in the constitution of his grammatical reflection. The first two concern the overall intelligentsia of the Arab world of the period: this involves, very briefly, the systematization of the Arabic conceptions of language and grammar under the influence of Greek logic,[4] and the consequences that the theological-political debates brought

about by Mu'tazilism had on the development of linguistic reflection.[5] The third is peculiar to the Jewish community itself. It concerns the ideological-religious conflict between the Karaites and the traditionalists on the sources of religious law: for the former, the law must have as its sole source the sacred texts themselves, excluding tradition, considered by Jewish orthodoxy as essential, if only because without it many biblical passages would be obscure or even incomprehensible.

Saadia Gaon was an anti-Karaite; therefore, he argues in his *Kitab al-Sab'in lafza al-mufradah* (Book of the Seventy Hapax) that, without the help of tradition, it would be impossible to determine the true meaning of a great number of words of rare occurrence in the Bible. As an intellectual bound to his era, he was seduced by Mu'tazilite theses,

665

and introduced, in his reading of the sacred texts, the subtle distinctions established by that school between *proper* and *figurative* meaning, in order to prevent any and all anthropomorphic reading of the texts relative to the divinity in the Bible. Finally, the logico-grammatical conceptions of the times led him to formulate, with respect to the Hebrew language, rules, generalizations, and laws that markedly break with the methods and results of any prior metalinguistic reflection. With Saadia Gaon, the living connection to the narrow philological approach of the Masoretes is definitively broken, and the foundations for a genuine Hebrew linguistics are discarded. Two essential works are attributed to Saadia Gaon, both written in Arabic: the first, often designated by the Hebrew title *Agron*, is considered the first work of Hebrew lexicography; the second, generally known by its Arabic title as *Kutub al-Lughah*, is the first known grammar of Hebrew.

The *Agron*, to judge by the arrangement of its lexical units, appears to have been conceived of as a working tool intended for the poets (*paytanim*). Its first part is organized mainly, despite certain inconsistencies, by the alphabetical order of the first two initials, while the second part is based on the alphabetical order of the last part of the words. This makes the work both a dictionary of alliterations and of rhymes. Two important characteristics show that the *Agron* is, despite its shortcomings and blunders, the product of a systematic, metalinguistic reflection, and thus represents a break from the purely philological approach of the Masoretes. For one thing, there is the distinction it makes between *essential letters* (the radicals of the words) and *servile letters* (the components of patterns). Furthermore, there is the fact that in this work certain combinations of letters are explicitly characterized as nonexistent. Such considerations were unknown in the Masoretic compilations, which were closely tied to linguistic data already documented. As for the *Kutub al-Lughah*, its structure and organization reveal a conception that is already technical, but still not very systematic of the linguistic organization of the language. The study of phonetic, phonological, and morphophonological questions takes up a large part of the collection, but it is apportioned in a discontinuous manner, intimating a nonunified conception of this domain. Similarly, the treatment proposed for numerous morphological alternations is relatively superficial—naive, as it were. The syntax, which strictly speaking has no autonomy, seems essentially conceived as the study of the latitudes of inflection of the parts of speech;[6] thus, the noun and the verb accept combination with the servile (derivation) letters, and the verb, additionally, accepts combination with the indicators of "time." Nouns and particles can be combined with indicators of possession. From a strictly linguistic point of view, this work was largely surpassed in rigor, technical sophistication, and completeness in scarcely a century. But it continued to be valid from the point of view of the methodological distinctions established by Saadia, most of which were adopted by later grammarians. Among the most significant, we must mention the fundamental dichotomy between *ussūl* (underlying forms) and *furū* (derived forms)—a dichotomy whose role in morphology is essential, but which has proven to have its value in other grammatical domains as well. After Saadia Gaon, in the tenth century works of lexicography and lexicology flourished. In the second quarter of the century, the *risālah* of Judah Ibn Quray appeared, the first comparative study on the vocabulary of Hebrew (Biblical, Mishnaic, and Talmudic), Aramaic, and Arabic. At about the same time, Ibn Tamim also took an interest in the lexical relationship between Hebrew and Arabic. Around the middle of the century, David ben Abraham al-Fasi composed (in Arabic) *Jami ʿal-Alfaz*, the first great dictionary of biblical language (Hebrew and Aramaic). Finally, in the course of the third quarter of the century, Menahem Ibn Saruq produced his *Mahberet*, a work of the same sort as that of al-Fasi but, and this is the first time in the history of Hebrew linguistics, written in Hebrew. The *Mahberet* was also the first linguistics work composed in Spain, which marks a change in the center of gravity of that discipline toward the western Arab world.[7] In the last quarter of the century, Dunash ben Labrat wrote nearly two hundred objections to Menahem. Menahem's students responded, and then Dunash was in turn defended by one of his disciples. Thus, there sprang up, around the *Mahberet*, the first of the great controversies that marked the development of Hebrew linguistics, which further deepened and systematized the insights of that work.

At the end of the tenth century, the most important author in the Hebraic linguistic tradition in the domain of morphology appeared: Judah ben David Hayyuj. Originally from Fez, in Morocco, but established in Cordova by 960, he began by backing Menahem against Dunash in the *Mahberet* controversy. But his two major works are the "Treatise on Verbs with Weak Radicals" and the "Treatise on Verbs with Two Identical Radicals," in which he proposes a treatment of the "irregularities" of the morphology of Hebrew, which radically modified the conception of them held up until then. In order to do this, he advanced six methodological postulates. Every Hebrew verbal root is made up of at least three radical consonants. All the verbs of the same type have, at the level of their theoretical basic form, the same conjugation, but certain verbs may present an actual form differing from the underlying form due to the presence of "weak" consonants (*aleph*, *vav*, *yod*, and, in the final position, *he*) in their root. The differences between the underlying and the actual form can be just phonetic or both phonetic and graphic. The processes that govern these differences are essentially mutation (one consonant changing into another), elision (the dropping of a consonant), and assimilation (this last leading to the phonetic reinforcement of the adjacent consonant with the graphic introduction of a *dagesh*). These processes

are all explained by one general principle, the desire to avoid the pronunciation of weak consonants in the configurations in which they would be *quiescent*, that is, unaccompanied by vowels. Finally, discrepancies between the underlying and the actual form also occur if the second and third radicals are identical. The second treatise by Hayyuj is specifically dedicated to this class of verbs. The reader familiar with the Arabic linguistic tradition will have no difficulty recognizing in the works of Hayyuj an application of the theoretical model used successfully in Arabic to Hebrew morphology. It should be noted, however, that this *transfer of theory* was not without its problems, and required substantial adaptation, if for no other reason than because Hebrew morphology is far less conservative than that of Arabic, and therefore in the course of history underwent erosion and reconstruction, making the thesis of the "regular triconsonantic underlying structure" much more difficult to substantiate for that language than for its southern sister. It should also be stressed that this theory upset previously held ideas, including those of Saadia Gaon. Many roots traditionally considered biconsonantic or even monoconsonantic by Hayyuj's predecessors were reclassified, after his analysis, as triconsonantic with one or more weak radicals. Moreover, Hayyuj produced a lexicon of verbal roots with weak radicals, each case being accompanied by attested forms and the explanation, according to his rules, of the discrepancy between the postulated underlying form and the one actually attested.

The work of Hayyuj, though fully accepted by the scientific community of his day, gave rise, on many points of detail—and sometimes substantial issues—to the second great controversy in Hebrew linguistics. That controversy was triggered by the critical observations made by Jonah ibn Janah (in his *Kitab al-Mustalhaq*) on certain points in Hayyuj's analysis. Samuel ibn Naghrila retorts to some of these observations in his *Rasa'il al-Rifaq*. Ibn Janah responds to his objections in another work.

It is remarkable that, in all these debates, it is not the "new" methodology advocated by Hayyuj that is challenged, but the treatment of certain specific, isolated questions. These discussions often led to a deepening of the analysis and a clarification of methodological points that had become obscure.

Samuel ibn Naghrila and Ibn Janah are not known solely for their polemic talents. The former has left a dictionary that is considered one of the best for the quality of its documentation and its richness. As for the latter, in the first half of the eleventh century, he produced a work that in the domain of grammar has attained a renown comparable to that of Hayyuj in morphology. The two essential works of Ibn Hayyuj, sometimes subsumed under the title *Kitab al-Tanqih*, are a dictionary, the *Kitab al-Usul*, and what may be considered the first complete grammar of Biblical (and, secondarily, Mishnaic) Hebrew, the *Kitab al-Luma ͑*. The first covers the entirety of the domains of lexicography of Hebrew, with the exception of toponyms and anthroponyms. It contains a chapter for each letter of the Hebrew alphabet, and the words are grouped by the alphabetic order of the roots. In keeping with a widespread trend of the period, the treatment of a given lexical unit may occasion developments, sometimes quite lengthy, of an exegetic or grammatical nature. There are also many references to other works by Ibn Janah, and even of Hayyuj. The metalanguage of explanation used is Arabic. As for the *Kitab al-Luma ͑*, it contains almost fifty chapters and has a rather disconcerting structure for the modern reader. This is because Ibn Janah seems more interested in what may be called the "transversal" study of certain processes than in the (from our point of view) methodical exposition of the assemblage of facts at a given "level": phonology, morphology, syntax, and so on. Thus, in three successive chapters, he approaches the process of substitution (*badal*) first at the level of consonants, then at the level of vowels, and finally at the level of

words (which we would call "apposition"). Similarly, in two successive chapters, he approaches the contexts in which processes of elision occur, followed by the contexts in which these processes are obstructed. Elsewhere, he enumerates (again, in successive chapters) all the methods of forming questions, or yet again all the processes modifying the normal order of constituent parts (of phonemes in a word, of words in a sentence). It is interesting to note that the influence of the theoretical model of Arabic grammar, though manifest in the works of Ibn Janah, takes on a far less systematic guise than in the works of Hayyuj. Thus, we do not see, in the *Kitab al-Luma ͑*, the overall structure of the great treatises of Arabic grammar, entirely organized according to the theory of case government (*͑amal*). The reason for this situation seems to be bound up with the major typological difference separating the two sister languages: Arabic is a case-declined language, and the entire metalinguistic edifice elaborated by the Arab-speaking grammarians gravitated around that aspect of the language. Hence, a large part of that edifice had no use for a language practically devoid of case markers such as Hebrew. Therefore, it is not in the general organization of grammar that the influence of Arab linguistics on Hebrew linguistics is to be sought. Rather, it is to be sought in the domain of syntax: for example, in the analytic tools, such as the *taqdīr* (supposition), of which Ibn Janah appears to make the same use as his Arab-speaking colleagues.[8] ●

Djamel E. Kouloughli, a grammarian and linguist, is a director of research at the Centre National de Recherches Scientifiques. He is the author of Grammaire de l'arabe d'aujourd'hui *(Presses Pocket, 1994) and* L'Arabe, *in the collection* "Que sais-je?" *(Presses Universitaires de France, 2007).*

---

1. Various etymologies have been proposed for the term *Masora*: some connect it with the idea of "transmission" (of the tradition of reading), others to that of "tying" (the text by means of commentaries?), and still others to that of counting (the occurrences of letters and words).

2. The original version of his *Diqduqe ha-Teʿamim* was published by Dotan in 1967.

3. See Wilhelm Bacher, *Die Anfänge der hebräischen Grammatik* (Leipzig: Brockhaus, 1895); Salomon L. Skoss, *Saadia Gaon: The Earliest Hebrew Grammarian* (Philadelphia: Dropsie College Press, 1955).

4. See Cornelis H. M. Versteegh, "Logique et grammaire au dixième siècle," *Histoire Épistémologie Langage* 2, no. 1 (1980): 39–52.

5. See J.R.T.M. Peters, "La théologie musulmane et l'étude du langage," *Histoire Épistémologie Langage* 2, no. 1 (1980): 9–19.

6. The conception of the parts of speech borrows whole cloth the Arab tripartite division (noun, verb, and particle). In the Hebrew translations the term used to convey the Arab *harf* (particle) is *milah*, which means, in nontechnical language, "word." This constitutes an indirect argument in favor of the thesis that, in the Arabic tradition itself, *harf* must have taken on the technical meaning "particle" on the basis of the idea of "word that is neither noun nor verb."

7. Carlos del Valle Rodriguez, "Die Anfänge der hebraischen Grammatik in Spanien," in *The History of Linguistics in the Near East*, ed. Versteegh et al. (Amsterdam: J. Benjamins, 1983), 155–66.

8. This article appeared in *Histoire des idées linguistiques*, book 1, ed. Sylvain Auroux (Paris: Pierre Mardaga Editeur, 1989).

Judeo-Arabic

Judeo-Arabic, along with Hebrew, Aramaic, and Greek, should be considered one of the oldest languages used by Jewish communities, if only in their daily interaction. Indeed, this language was spoken as early as the first centuries of the Christian era in the Jewish communities spread throughout North Africa and certain countries of Southern Arabia (today's Yemen), far before the advent of Islam in the seventh century. After the extinction of the Judeo-Arabic speakers of the north, due to the wars of the Prophet and the refuge that some found in the south, Judeo-Arabic spread to the Middle East and North Africa, as well as to Andalusia, or the Muslim Spain of the Middle Ages, and to Sicily, in the wake of the Arab conquests. The old communities, as well as the new, which were formed after that conquest, adopted Arabic as the language of interaction with the new dominant power, and also, progressively, as the language of internal interaction. It is during this time that the different varieties of Judeo-Arabic we know today were formed, spoken as well as written, with varying degrees of differentiation between them. Like all Jewish languages, Judeo-Arabic was formed as a spoken language, before and after the Islamic era, through the addition and integration of a major Hebraic and Aramaic component into a matrix of basic Arabic borrowed from Arabic-speaking neighbors. This complementary component comes from the fundamental diglossia of linguistic practices of all traditional Jewish communities, which basically used the Hebrew and Aramaic of biblical and postbiblical texts in their intellectual, cultural, and liturgical activities while employing the different local dialects for everyday interaction. The integration of the Hebrew component, in addition to other phenomena of linguistic adaptation to the traditions of the community, made Judeo-Arabic, like other Jewish languages, necessarily a hybrid, differentiated language, the use of which, moreover, varied, with the rabbinic elite using it proportionately more than the majority of male and female speakers. It was also the basis of secret Jewish languages, used by men in the presence of strangers, or of their young children, when they wanted to hide the meaning of their speech. Furthermore, the language of women was different from that of men by its frequent use of fixed formulations and proverbial sayings, which made it a highly empathetic and metaphoric language.

This sociolectal diversification of Judeo-Arabic within each community was added to the great diversity of communal Judeo-Arabic dialects in the Middle East and North Africa, on the one hand reflecting the great diversity of neighboring local Arabic dialects of the various Jewish communities, and on the other translating the cultural independence of the different Jewish communities. This great dialectal diversity was also inscribed within the different geopolitical areas that made up, in a noncontinuous way since the caliphate, the different Muslim political entities in which Arabic was instituted as the main language. The dialects of a given area were differentiated, to varying degrees, at the level of vocabulary and morphophonetic realizations from those of the other areas—more specifically, the dialects of North Africa and Andalusia from those of the Middle East, primarily because of the Berber substratum with its specific vocalic and consonantal system, which served in the formation of the North African dialects and the Roman substratum of Andalusia.

To this sociolectal and dialectal diversity of spoken Judeo-Arabic, another sort of diversity should be added: that of texts and discursive genres produced or used by the Jewish communities in both the Islamic east and west. This textual and discursive diversity consists, first, in the natural discourse exchanged in daily or professional interaction by Jewish speakers, of an underlying rabbinic exegetic and homiletic discourse as well as of literal translations of biblical and postbiblical texts used both in paraliturgical practices in the synagogue or at home, and in the educational system of children that prepared them mainly for these practices. Apart from these discursive or textual activities specific to the different communities, other textual varieties were largely borrowed from Muslim

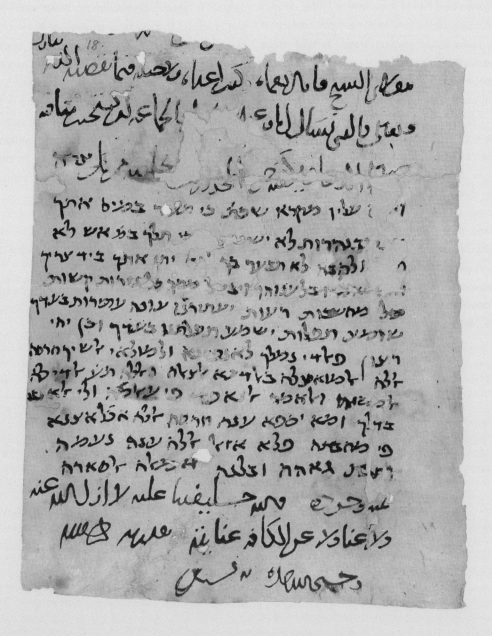

Letter with an introduction and conclusion in Arabic, quote from the book of Isaiah in Hebrew, and blessings in Judeo-Arabic. Cambridge University Library, Taylor-Schechter Geniza Collection, T-S 10J11.18.

oral traditions, and particularly from the body of songs with melodies and lyrics, and other marvelous tales, proverbs and formulaic sayings, enigmas and riddles, more or less adapted to Jewish realities.

These textual borrowings from the oral tradition were also transcribed into Hebrew letters in the different communities, particularly from the ninth century on, when Judeo-Arabic literature began to take shape, modeled initially on classical Arabic but transcribed in Hebrew letters. Contrary to common opinion, this Judeo-Arabic literature, initiated by Saadia Gaon, does not appear in the first attempts at written Judeo-Arabic, because both Sabaic inscriptions and fragments of texts discovered in the Cairo Geniza attest to phonetic writing in Hebrew letters much earlier than Judeo-Arabic, which has continued up to our own time, in a nonhomogenous manner, including poetic writing. This is what constitutes the popular, written Judeo-Arabic. As for literary or average Judeo-Arabic, during the Middle Ages it sustained a vast Jewish intellectual creation of a philosophical, linguistic, exegetic, or Halakhic nature, which developed both in Andalusia and in the great urban centers of the Middle East (such as Baghdad, Cairo, and Aleppo) and North Africa (such as Kairouan or Fez). This literary Judeo-Arabic had its moments of expansion in the tenth, eleventh, and twelfth centuries, but it persisted into the twentieth century in rabbinic circles, among those who knew and practiced this medieval creation, or in the circle of poets, and later journalists, who kept current with contemporary Muslim writing and adopted certain linguistic structures to enhance their own writing. This happened particularly at the end of the nineteenth century in Tunisia, where Jewish authors and journalists forged a new Judeo-Arabic, written in their narratives or journalistic texts, directly imitating contemporary Muslim writing and thereby arousing linguistic controversy among insiders. ●

Joseph Chetrit is professor emeritus of linguistics and sociopragmatism at the University of Haifa, where he is dean of the Faculty of Social Sciences. His publications include Diglossie, hybridation et diversité intra-linguistique. Études socio-pragmatiques sur les langues juives, le judéo-arabe et le judéo-berbère (*Peeters Leuven, 2007*).

Judeo-Persian

The ancient Jewish communities of Iran were the first in the Persianate world to write in New Persian, although they did so in the Hebrew alphabet with which they were familiar. This gave birth to "Judeo-Persian," a written language close to Classical Persian, despite significant archaisms, which has remained in use from the eighth to the twentieth centuries. The Jews of Iran spoke many Persian-Jewish dialects influenced by local Persian dialects, as well as Lotra'i (Lotorai), a hybrid dialect peculiar to them.

The antiquity of the Jewish community of Iran is best attested to by Judeo-Persian, the written language of the community. This community, the oldest-known Jewish diaspora, dates back at least as far as 586 BCE, and perhaps as far as 722 BCE. While it is not possible to document that Jews lived everywhere in the vast Persianate world (which includes Afghanistan, Kurdistan, Central Asia [Bukhara (Uzbekistan) and Tajikistan], and the Caucasus),[1] their presence in Iran and beyond is proved by tombstone inscriptions in Afghanistan dating between the eighth and thirteenth centuries,[2] two commercial documents from the eighth century,[3] and a number of early biblical commentaries.[4] Interestingly, this corpus also forms the earliest written records of New Persian, albeit in the Hebrew alphabet, before its embrace of the Arabic alphabet.

Written Judeo-Persian

A distinction needs to be made between written Judeo-Persian, which is, essentially, New Persian (Farsi) written in the Hebrew alphabet, and the numerous dialects spoken by the Jews of Iran. The retention of the Hebrew alphabet for written communication in the vernacular is familiar from

other Judaic languages, such as Judeo-Italian, Judeo-Spanish (Ladino), and so on. They were used in environments where Jews maintained a distinct religious and cultural identity in the midst of cultures less literate at the popular level and in which they endeavored to maintain their connection to the Hebrew Bible, as well as a degree of privacy from their non-Jewish neighbors. The earliest dated Judeo-Persian documents retain a number of features from Middle Persian (Pahlavi) and are therefore of great interest for the development of New Persian. They include few Hebrew words (except for the tomb inscriptions). It would appear that most of these early texts come from either

The Book of Moses, a poetic compilation of the Bible in Judeo-Persian, completed in the fourteenth century by Mawlana Shahin-i Shirazi. Jerusalem, Museum of Israel.

the regions of Fars and Khuzistan or Bukhara (resembling Judeo-Tajik).[5] After the hiatus caused by the Mongol invasion of Iran, Judeo-Persian texts reappeared in the fourteenth century with the works of Mowlana Shahin, the author of a number of Judeo-Persian epics based on biblical themes. They then continued, virtually uninterrupted, until the beginning of the twentieth century. Although these texts try to adhere to Classical Persian (*dari*), they are characterized by the absence of orthographic uniformity (they were written mostly in square, "Oriental" Hebrew and some in Rashi scripts), the fact that they contain a larger number of Hebrew, especially religious, vocabulary, and their idiosyncratic spellings, which indicate the influence of the colloquial, spoken language (such as the ending *un* for the plural *an*) rather than deep involvement with written Persian texts. In the twentieth century, Judeo-Persian was written in the Cyrillic alphabet as well as in Bukhara.

Spoken Jewish languages

The Jews of Iran, like their Muslim neighbors, spoke many Persian dialects that were mutually intelligible within the groupings outlined below but not necessarily to non-Jews. Additionally, they spoke their own Jewish version of local dialects, and these fall into two major groupings: (1) Southwestern or Persian, which stem from Old and Middle Persian and continue into present New (Modern) Persian. The dialects of the Jews of Shiraz, Afghanistan, Tajikistan, and Bukhara fall into this category, and (2) Central (or Median) dialects, which form the majority of the dialects spoken by Iranian Jews. Originating in the heart (center) of Iran, these are spoken by the major Jewish communities of Isfahan, Kashan, Hamadan, Natanz, Nahavand, and others.[6] In addition to these numerous dialects, Iranian Jews also spoke a dialect highly peculiar to themselves, which had many variations, and was known as Lotorai, Loterai, and so on, all variations of *lo-Torah*[*i*] (Heb. + Pers. suffix of abstraction), meaning "non-Torahic," and referring to its hybrid nature of combining both Semitic [Hebrew and Aramaic] and Persian elements. The purpose of this distinct dialect was to ensure private, secretive communication intelligible only to Jews.[7] Beginning in the twentieth century, Iranian Jews began to abandon their peculiar and regional dialects in favor of the Modern (Muslim) Persian spoken by the population at large.

In Kurdistan and Western Azerbaijan, many Aramaic dialects were spoken by Jews distinct from those spoken by non-Jews. ●

Vera Basch Moreen is an independent scholar and a specialist in Judeo-Persian studies, she coedited The Encyclopedia of Jews in the Islamic World *(Brill, 2011). Her publications include* In Queen Esther's Garden: An Anthology of Judeo-Persian Literature *(Yale University Press, 2000).*

1. This term is coined after the definition of "Islamicate," proposed by the historian Marshall G. S. Hodgson in his *Venture of Islam* (Chicago: University of Chicago Press, 1974), 1:56–60, to refer to geographic areas to which Persian culture and civilization spread beyond the borders of present-day Iran.

2. Benzion D. Yehoshua Raz, *From the Lost Tribes in Afghanistan to the Mashhad Jewish Converts of Iran* (in Hebrew) (Jerusalem: Bialik Institute, 1992), figs. 53–67.

3. Bo Utas, "The Jewish-Persian from Dandan-Ujlik," *Orientalia Suecana* 17 (1968): 123–36; Zhang Zhan, "Jews in Khotan in Light of the Newly Discovered Judaeo-Persian Letter," *Irano-Judaica* 7 (Jerusalem: Ben-Zvi Institute, forthcoming).

4. Thamar E. Gindin, *The Early Judaeo-Persian Tafsirs of Ezekiel: Text, Translation and Commentary*, 3 vols. (Vienna: Austrian Academy of Science, forthcoming); Shaul Shaked, "Early Judaeo-Persian Texts with Notes on a Commentary to Genesis," in *Persian Origins: Early Judaeo-Persian and the Emergence of New Persian*, ed. L. Paul (Wiesbaden: Harrassowitz Verlag, 2003), 222–50.

5. Thamar Gindin, "Judaeo-Persian Language," *EJIW*, 63.

6. Haideh Sahim, "Languages and Dialects of the Jews of Iran and Afghanistan," in *Esther's Children: A Portrait of Iranian Jewry*, ed. H. Sarshar (Beverly Hills, CA / Philadelphia: Center for Iranian Jewish Oral History / Jewish Publication Society of America, 2002), 283–93.

7. Ehsan Yarshater, "The Hybrid Language of the Jewish Communities of Persia," *Journal of the American Oriental Society* 97 (1977): 1–7.

Semitism: From a Linguistic Concept to a Racist Argument
Gabriel Bergounioux

The term "Semite" gained scientific justification in the nineteenth century, in the opposition between a different family of languages and the one that comparative grammar had brought to light and circumscribed under the name "Indo-European." This name, developed outside of the people it designated, and after it had been extended to an anthropological characterization in terms of races, was exploited in order to justify colonial domination by the European powers in the Mediterranean region. The exacerbation of nationalism and the biologization of politics led to its application against European Jewish communities at the very moment when the works of Saussure annihilated the morphosyntactic distinction postulated by Bopp between the two linguistic groups.[1]

Gabriel Bergounioux

Gabriel Bergounioux is a professor of linguistics at the Institut des Lettres of the University of Orléans. His publications include "L'orientalisme et la linguistique: Entre géographie, littérature et histoire," *Histoire Épistémologie Langage* 23, no. 2 (2001), and "'Aryen,' 'indo-européen,' 'sémite' dans l'université française," "La linguistique de l'hébreu et des langues juives" (ed. J. Baumgarten and S. Kessler-Mesguich), *Histoire Épistémologie Langage* 18, no. 1 (1996).

The definition of languages: An internal or an external process?

For a society that engages in the symbolic definition of its hierarchies, it becomes necessary, at a certain moment, to stabilize a state of language to be used for prestigious communication. That image of language, often fixed by a transcription, rejects the dialects (be they geographical or societal) in a growing number of situations. Such an image is the result of a compromise between those who assure the reproduction of cultural capital (priests, scholars, men of letters, etc.) and the civil or religious authority, desirous of extending its control by delegation to collective linguistic usage. This process may be observed in the modern age in the nations that, in order to further their consolidation, undertake the validation of a language norm that will serve to identify them. Such has been the case with the countries of Europe from the eighteenth to the twentieth century, in their claim to national unity and independence.

In a majority of cases, it has not been the internal dynamic of an emerging institutionalization in a centralized power or in the urban bourgeoisie that has triumphed in characterizing and fixing languages, specifically in questions of orthography. The decision is imposed from the outside, independently of the community of speakers, if not in opposition to it. The inequality of conditions of economic and technological development has allowed a small number of countries to exert their power over allophone populations. Even within the imperialist nations themselves, decisions concerning the treatment of language processing, especially their writing, were made by very small groups of administrators and scholars. Thus, the scriptorial notation of many languages was carried out by the spread of Islam or the agents of the colonial powers in Africa.

Whether considered on the basis of individuals or nations, the relation to other languages, that is, to the languages of others, was based above all on the perception of differences—more or less marked, more or less amplified—between what was spoken and what was meant. Generally, the assessment was disempowering.

Semitism and Orientalism

Such is the case with "Semitism," a designation from Europe with a unique history. The presence of lettered Jewish communities and the biblical reference of Christianity preserved the study of Hebrew in the West during the Middle Ages.

The Mountains of Ararat, or The Manner How the Whole Earth was Peopled by Noah and his Descendants after the Flood, engraved for the "Universal Magazine," London, 1749 (engraving), English School (18th century) / Private Collection / Ken Welsh /.

Beyond the close connections brought out by exegesis between related languages (Aramaic, Chaldean, Syriac, and others), similarities of vocabulary were found with Arabic. These rapprochements, systematized by Angelo Canini in his *Institutiones* (1554), were taken up anew in the following centuries,[2] thus contributing to the challenge to Catholic dogma, which based the sacred commentary on the Latin translation, the Vulgate.

Hebrew, thought of as the primitive language, and Aramaic being confined to theology, a different tripartite division of languages, continents, and races prevailed. After a reinterpretation of the division of the world between the descendants of Noah, the progressive elaboration of the story of the Magi (making it coincide with that imagery) confirmed the significance of a conception that brought together skin color, the shape of continents, economic activity, cultural territories, and languages.

In this model, and until the beginning of the nineteenth century, when the use of the term *Semite* in the sense that has remained attached to it became established in Europe, a geographical criterion redefined a confessional community (Islam) and a scriptorial one (Arabic script) and regrouped Turkish, Iranian (Persian), and Arabic into "Eastern languages." The perception of the Near East was transformed, as shown by the discussions of the Asiatic Society of Paris (created in 1822), which focused successively on the reading of hieroglyphics during the 1820s (Champollion), the deciphering of cuneiforms around 1850–60 (Renan contra Oppert), comparative mythology between 1860 and 1880—which introduced a confessional atmosphere into the debates—and, beginning in 1874, the classification of Sumerian, which Halévy saw as the conventional notation of a Semitic idiom, a conception rightly rejected by Oppert. The repercussions of this are that the definition of Semitism, first reconsidered on the basis of decryptions, takes a religious turn before ending up, at the end of the nineteenth century, especially after Gobineau, as a racist stigmatization based on the Aryan/Semitic opposition.

Comparative grammar and the classification of languages

The lexical similarities between Greek, Latin, and Sanskrit, pointed out by Father Coeurdoux (1767), the extension of the systemization of comparison by William Jones (1786), and the analysis in terms of the correspondence of grammatical forms by Franz Bopp (1816), made it possible to define a family of Indo-European languages on an objective basis. All external considerations of the structure of the languages were banished in favor of equivalences postulated between phonetic forms reestablished on the basis of transcriptions. A historical and phonetic model (comparative grammar) supplanted the geographical and scriptorial vision (Orientalism). The circumspection of the founder of the discipline, Franz Bopp, concerning possible inferences between a family of languages and a race, has remained constant, as has his prudence shown in the reconstruction of Proto-Indo-European

(PIE)—the putative mother-language underlying language families. But the history of comparativism is also that of its errors. A fair number of linguists, often the most prestigious, deduced, from the resemblances between languages, conclusions about the peoples speaking them: "The general trend of today's studies makes grammar history's auxiliary, from which we can deduce the most ancient, certain and precise facts about times prior to all chronicles and even all writing; facts about the origin and migrations of peoples, their intermingling and reciprocal influences."[3]

Historical grammar was subordinated to a racial anthropology based on a migratory model. The science of language lost its autonomy, and the statutes of the Linguistic Society of Paris, adopted in 1866, had as their first article: "The Linguistic Society has as its goal the study of languages, and of legends, traditions, costumes, and documents able to enlighten ethnographic science. All other object of study is strictly forbidden."

Comparative grammar began with the study of the Indo-European languages. The relationship to PIE was conceived on the model of the relationship of Latin to the Romance languages. Morphology postulates the addition of affixes to monosyllabic roots, which carry the meaning, composed of a vowel and one or several consonants that follow or precede it. This process separates the Indo-European languages, isolating them from Chinese, agglutinative languages such as Turkish, and languages that intercalate vowels between the three consonants of their lexical roots, vowels whose transformation (apophony) determines the grammatical oppositions. The Semitic languages are distinguished by this process of Indo-European languages.

From linguistic difference to racial opposition

The drifting from a linguistic conception to an ethnic one took place in three stages, beginning with Bopp's propositions. First, etymology, beginning in the 1830s, illustrated by August Friedrich Pott, established an inventory of the forms attested in the different languages of the group and prefigured the reconstruction of PIE carried out by Schleicher (1868). Then the linguistic paleontology of the 1850s, exemplified by Adolphe Pictet, deduced the conditions of life of the "primitive Aryans" from their reconstituted vocabulary. In matching up the designations for trees, animals, and topography, the original location of speakers of PIE was hypothetically determined, and from that a map of migrations was deduced. As a last step, comparative mythology, the best-known representative of which is Max Müller, broadened the terminological analysis to include social organization and mental representations, feelings, and beliefs. This approach was criticized by Antoine Meillet, and then by Émile Benveniste, in his response to Georges Dumézil.[4]

The representation of the civic order (Are the Indo-Europeans conquerors led by chiefs who subdued less warlike native inhabitants?) and the interpretation of the sacred (What do the Indian, Greek, and Germanic pantheons mean vis-à-vis biblical doctrine?) took on a particular importance at a time when the European nations dominated the world and claimed to justify slavery and colonization by a racial superiority proven since prehistoric times. How can we explain, in this context, that Christianity originated from Judaism, outside the European sphere? Or that the first announcement of the Gospel was not reserved for the nations God had chosen to distinguish in offering them the empire of the world?

With comparative grammar, the partition of the world between peoples might appear to meet scientific criteria. Phyla are established, including that of the Semitic languages, which limits the southern Indo-European family. Since these groups overlay geographical and anthropological areas, the theory of races found a supporting argument there. The reconstruction had united languages that had never been grouped together before: Sanskrit, Latin, Old Slavic, and Gothic. Conversely, no "black" population in Africa, or "yellow" in North Asia, used an Indo-European language before the arrival of the Europeans. The superimposition of languages and cultures onto territories ended up, combined with biology—either Darwinian or creationist—endorsing a racial way of thinking that served as a justification for imperialism.

Between languages and races: The nation

Still, between the "languages" (assimilated to civilizations or cultures) and the "races," the reference to the "nation," which had become the central political concept, was to reconfigure the divisions and impose itself as the essential principle of organization into states. The countries would draw their borders according to the perimeter of a language, which, as a means of communication, was being transformed into the expression of an identity. In the second half of the nineteenth century, the German and Italian units had anticipated that conception, sanctioned by the peace treaties of the end of the First World War.

The work of Renan stressed the ambivalence of a conception of nation that holds on to an ethnic element based on membership in a linguistic family.[5] His inaugural lecture at the College de France endorsed that opposition,[6] though his contractual vision of the nation qua social contract attenuated the validity of the criteria Prussia would make use of to annex Alsace-Moselle.

Bismarck's Germany, the country most involved in the research of comparative grammar, projected the superimposition of the division into languages (Indo-European against Semitic, Germanic against Latin and Slavic) onto races and nations in the project of making the three align. There, anti-Semitism took on its modern form, in continuity with the Kulturkampf, at the end of the 1870s, during which Adolf Stoecker and Wilhelm Marr, resuming Heinrich von Treitschke's *Berliner Antisemitismusstreit*, developed the arguments for a racism opposed by such scientists as Bastian and Virchow. The equivalent may be found in France, more psycho-physiological than social, in the work of Jules Soury.

The reversal of the linguistic arguments

Parallel to the anthropological critiques of the concept of race, or of some of its uses, the linguistic critique was carried out in two directions. On the one hand, external linguistics differentiated the ethnic or religious characteristics of peoples and their languages. Chajim H. Steinthal,[7] along with the ideologues of the French Third Republic, defended the idea of a shared destiny—cultural acquisition—the opposite of Maurice Barrès's transmission conditioned by "the land and the dead." The dissemination of languages does not require a massive transfer of population, and substitution can be accomplished without large-scale migration. Along these same lines, the insistence on the role of contacts between languages by Hugo Schuchardt (mixed languages, or *Sprachmischung*), Lazare Sainéan (study on Yiddish), and Nikolai Trubetzkoy (the convergence of languages, or *Sprachbund*) attenuated the conception of languages that would remain impermeable to borrowing, let alone to fusion. On the other hand, in identifying the presence of apophony in PIE (Saussure,[8] taken up by Kurylowicz) and the existence of subjacent consonantal roots (Benveniste), internal linguistics invalidated the morphological distinction traditionally made between the Indo-European languages, whose roots were considered to be of the form /C(C)V(C(C))/, with prefixes and suffixes to expand it, and the Afro-Asiatic languages, built on roots /CCC/, with vocalic insertion according to apophony. Certain linguists, such as Hermann Möller, followed by Albert Cuny and Kristian Sandfeld, proposed reuniting the two families into one; at the same time the perimeter of the Hamito-Semitic group, reformulated by Carl Brockelmann and Marcel Cohen, was reconfigured by Joseph Greenberg under the name "Afro-Asiatic."

Thus, the linguistic concept of Semitism, elaborated by linguists and exploited by racist ideologies, is today invalidated by the assurance of an independence of morphophonological principles and anthropological considerations.

1. See Ferdinand de Saussure, *Mémoire sur le système primitif des voyelles dans les langues indo-européennes* (Leipzig: B. G. Teubner, 1879), and Franz Bopp, *Über das Conjugationssystem der Sanskritsprache in Vergleichung mit jenem der griechischen, lateinischen, persischen, und germanischen Sprache* [On the system of conjugation of the Sanskrit language, compared to those of the Greek, Latin, Persian, and Germanic languages] (Frankfurt: Araeae, 1816).

2. Daniel Droixhe, *La Linguistique et l'appel de l'histoire* (Geneva-Paris: Droz, 1978), 36–42.

3. Jules Mohl, *Vingt-sept ans d'histoire des études orientales: Rapports faits à la société asiatique de Paris de 1840 à 1867* (Paris: Reinwald, 1879–1880), 452.

4. Antoine Meillet, *De indo-europaea radice *MEN, "mente agitare"* (Paris: Bouillon, 1897), and Émile Benveniste, *Le Vocabulaire des institutions indo-européennes* (Paris: Minuit, 1969).

5. Maurice Olender, *Les Langues du paradis* (Paris: Gallimard-Le Seuil, 1989), 75–126.

6. Ernest Renan, *De la part des peuples sémitiques dans l'histoire des civilisations* (Paris: Michel Lévy, 1862).

7. Heymann Steinthal, "Dialekt, Sprache, Volk, Staat, Rasse," in *Festschrift für Adolf Bastian für seinem 70 Geburstag*, ed. Thomas Achelis (Berlin: Verlag von Dietrich Reimer [Ernst Vohsen], 1896), 47–52.

8. Ferdinand de Saussure, *Mémoire sur le système primitif des voyelles dans les langues indo-européennes* (Leipzig: B. G. Teubner, 1879).

Chapter III
Two Religions of the Law

Comparison between the Halakha and Shariʿa
Phillip Ackerman-Lieberman

Despite many differences in detail, Judaism and Islam have much in common in their reliance on law as an organizing framework. Both legal systems turn to canonical textual sources (both scriptural and nonscriptural), as well as the interpretation of these texts, for the foundations of practice. Questions of legal method animated much early debate within each tradition; in Islamic law, distinctive legal schools persist to this day, which maintain such debate. Over time, narrative codes emerged in each tradition that established communal norms; these codes negotiated and at times vindicated local customary practice. As Judaism and Islam encountered modernity, both legal systems were transformed by both progressive and reactionary reform movements.

Phillip Ackerman-Lieberman

Phillip Ackerman-Lieberman is an assistant professor of Jewish studies and law and Islamic studies at Vanderbilt University. His research focuses on the social, economic, and legal history of the Jewish community of medieval Egypt based on documents of the Cairo Geniza. He was a member of the editorial board and a contributor to *The Encyclopedia of Jews in the Islamic World* (edited by Norman Stillman).

The early period: Sources and methods

Jewish and Islamic law share much in terms of structure and content, which must be ascribed at least in part to the mutual influence of each system on the other, though the direction of this influence from one system to the other has changed over the course of Islamic and Jewish history. In the early period, even before the birth of the ʿumma (the Islamic body politic), Muhammad, his companions, and followers interacted with and reacted to Jewish conceptions of law and Jewish practices prevalent in the Hijaz. Thus, for example, the *qibla* (the direction one is to face during prayer) is understood to have been established by Muhammad directly after the hijra, concurring with the Jewish practice of

> ### *Shari'a, fiqh,* Torah, *halakha*
>
> Shari'a, which signifies etymologically "path to follow" and, more precisely, "path that leads to water," designates divine law such as is expressed in the Qur'an and the Sunna. As such, it refers to a standard too general to be applicable in practice. The *fuqahâ* (sing. *Faqîh;* or jurists) are tasked with deducing practical law, called *fiqh,* from this ideal.
>
> The Torah refers to the Five Books of Moses in the strictest sense, and the combination of divine law and rabbinic commentary in a larger sense. It is, moreover, translated as *sharia* in the *tafsir* of Saadia Gaon. The Torah is expressed in particular in the Talmud, but often fails to decide on the law; it is the work of the *poskim* that interprets the Talmud to determine practical law, or *halakha,* which signifies "the way of going," and is therefore close, in this sense, to shari'a.

facing Jerusalem, though roughly a year and a half later he realigned the *qibla* to point to Mecca (cf. Qur'an 2:142–43). The Qur'an, understood to have been revealed directly to Muhammad over approximately twenty-two years (from 610 till his death in 632), alludes to the promulgation of a distinctive "law and normative way" (Qur'an 5:48, "shir'a wa minhaj") for the Muslim community. Muhammad played an active role in the development of that law, acting as *hakam* (arbitrator) to the residents of Yathrib (later renamed Medina) and establish-

ing precedents that grew in importance and standing with the rise of the *'umma.* Significantly, the role of the *hakam* in pre-Islamic Arabia was independent of any organized political leadership; as Islamic law took shape, jurisconsults would also stand independent of political elites. As the *'umma* expanded, Muhammad appointed *qādīs* (judges) as local administrators; the early caliphs also acted as *qādīs*. These *qādīs* relied on the revealed text of the Qur'an and biographical anecdotes about Muhammad and his companions for precedent, though they often maintained justice through recourse to local custom. Discretionary opinion (*ra'y*) also emerged as an independent source of law in the early period, though it would in time be rejected as a source of law by traditionalists. Jewish law understood a similar tension between precedent (textual or otherwise) and discretionary opinion from its earliest stages; rabbinic literature often vindicates a ruling both in terms of "tradition" (*shemu'a*) or "scripture" (*qerā'a*) and logical deduction (*sevara*).

According to the traditional Islamic narrative, the Qur'an was redacted shortly after Muhammad's death, giving unity and fixity to the revelation and conferring upon the early Islamic community a scripture that would carry great import as a legal source. By the end of the first Islamic century, the aforementioned biographical anecdotes had grown greatly in number and spiritual significance, being collected by caliphs and *qādīs* alike, though as the memory of Muhammad gained prominence, anecdotes about his companions eventually lost prestige relative to those about the Prophet himself. In order to assure the reliability of these anecdotes (*hadīth*; pl., *ahadith*), the names of the authorities transmitting these anecdotes were preserved; by the end of the second Islamic century, hadith collections emerged that retained both the chain of transmission (*isnād*) and the substance (*matn*) for each hadith. Likewise, the Mishnah—the first rabbinic legal code, redacted in the land of Israel in the late second century by Rabbi Judah the Patriarch)—retains substantive oral statements as well as ascriptions of those statements to rabbinic figures. The Hadith literature functions in a similar fashion, insofar as it confronts many self-contradicting *matns* and that such contradictory *matns* can also be inscribed in the same *isnad*. Over time, the validity of hadith reports would come to be judged on the basis of the chain of authorities who transmitted them, as a way of rooting out spurious traditions. As the practice of collecting hadith and the corollary science of transmission-criticism developed, a number of canonical hadith collections (generally understood to be six) emerged whose traditions were understood to be trustworthy. The Talmudic analysis of the rabbinic traditions is also often anxious to identify the go-between who transmitted

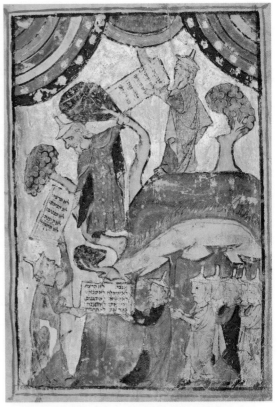

Moses receives the Ten Commandments from God and passes them to the masters, bottom right. Regensburg Pentateuch, around 1300, fol. 154 (verso). Jerusalem, Museum of Israel.

a particular tradition. The Talmud often tries to harmonize the reports based on the authority of a particular rabbinic figure, because such individuals were supposed to have occupied positions that confirmed their statements. Nevertheless, when the Talmud harmonizes antagonistic traditions, it frequently does so by looking at the content of a tradition (for example, "Here Rabbi Judah is considering a holiday; there he is considering Shabbat") rather than at the transmission of these statements—though it does not refrain completely from calling into question tannatic declarations (that is, the words of the first rabbinic sages). The Talmud's analysis of rabbinic traditions is often similarly concerned with identifying the tradent responsible for transmitting a particular tradition; and the Talmud often attempts to harmonize various reports given on the authority of a particular rabbinic figure, because such figures are presumed to have held positions that cohere across their statements. However, when the Talmud harmonizes conflicting traditions, it frequently does so by addressing the substance of a tradition (i.e., "Here, Rabbi Judah is concerned with a festival; there, he is

> ### Talmud
>
> The Talmud, from the root *l-m-d,* "to study," consists of an abundance of commentary on the first code of oral Jewish law, the Mishnah, compiled around 200 CE. It draws on the theoretical debates of the sages and their judgments, but also on a large amount of non-judicial material called *aggadot,* or "accounts." There exist, in reality, two Talmuds: the Jerusalem Talmud, finished circa 350–400 CE, which collects the debates of Palestinian academics; and the Babylonian Talmud, completed around 500 CE, which concerns itself with the debates of Mesopotamian scholars, and includes the Palestinian material. It is the second, more complete, Talmud that is considered the authority today. It is the subject of much exegetical literature that still endures and constitutes the principal text studied in the traditional religious curriculum.

concerned with the Sabbath.") rather than the transmission of those statements—though the Talmud does not entirely refrain from questioning the transmission of *tannaïtic* statements (that is, statements of the early rabbinic transmitters). The expansion of Islamic transmission-criticism fostered a detailed science of prosopography, through which medieval scholars sketched out the biographies of transmitters and, particularly, enumerated the teachers and students of these transmitters so that the plausibility of every stage in an *isnād* and the moral uprightness (and hence reliability) of its transmitters could be verified.

Early rabbinic literature maintained two distinct models of legal material: *Midrash halakha*, which turned to the Torah text for its organization and structure, and vindicated its rulings through exegesis of the Torah text; and Mishnah, which restructured Jewish law topically into six orders (each of which is divided further into tractates and chapters), which generally reproduce the opinions of rabbinic authorities apodictically (that is, without rationale) and make recourse to the Torah only infrequently. The Mishnah's lack of connection to the Torah is often addressed by the Talmud, which frequently seeks the scriptural source for *tannaïtic* rulings. Yet the authority of the Mishnah ultimately derives neither from the logic of its opinions nor from any basis in scripture that those opinions might have; in this sense, hadith literature (which derives its authority from its tradents and their *isnād*s) can be seen as akin to the statements preserved in the Mishnah. Yet the statements in the Mishnah derive their authority from the identity of the transmitters as *tannaïm* (that is, as sages of the early period, as opposed to post-Mishnaic sages or *amoraïm*); while hadith statements derive their authority from the soundness of the chain of their transmission. Thus, statements ascribed to *tannaïm* preserved outside the Mishnah (so-called *baraïtot*, many of which are quoted in the Talmud but some of which are also collected in a quasi-canonical collection called the *Tosefta*) bear equal authority with statements preserved in the Mishnah. In contrast, the emphasis on transmission history in compiling the canonical hadith collections gives the material preserved in those collections a primacy not accorded to hadith from outside the canon.

The development of schools

Some of the *tannaïm* seem to have organized themselves into disciple circles that maintained different approaches to the exegesis of scripture. Two of these circles ("schools") may be identified by their putative eponyms Rabbi Akiva and Rabbi Ishmael; the latter of these schools is understood to be more reserved in its exegesis than the former. With time, each congregation (and the same congregation could be counted several times) had to develop an allegiance toward the academies of either Palestine or Babylonia; in the eleventh century one could still observe the coexistence of such "Palestinian" or "Babylonian" congregations. Islamic law would also see distinctive methodological strains emerge over the course of the eighth century, which would coalesce in the ninth and tenth centuries into distinctive legal schools (*madhhab*). As the science of Islamic jurisprudence (*uṣūl al fiqh*) developed, these schools identified distinctive approaches to the interpretation of scripture (particularly in their use of analogy in scriptural interpretation) and the role of hadith. These schools also came to differ in their willingness to appeal to broader principles such as "justice," "equity," "the public good," or "logic," and in their reliance on custom and on communal consensus (and the definition of precisely which "community" should be relied upon when defining "communal consensus"). Four primary Sunni schools of law emerged and were sustained into the modern period. These are called the Maliki, Shafi'i, Hanafi, and Hanbali schools. As it emerged, Shi'i law came to rely on the textual sources of the Qur'an and hadith (although Shi'i scholars had their own distinctive collections of hadith), and added to these textual sources both the practice of the imams and "logical deduction."

Tannaïtic disciple circles gave way to full-fledged Talmudic academies; the lectures and discussion of *tannaïtic* and *amoraïc* material in these academies were redacted into the

A Sufi (Bayazid al-Bistami?) faces representatives from the four Islamic schools of jurisprudence (*madhhab*). From *The Lives of Saints* by Farid al-Din 'Attar, calligraphy by Said Aziz al-Din, eighteenth century. Tashkent (Uzbekistan), Institute of Oriental Studies.

Madhhab

A *madhhab* (from the verb *dh-h-b*, "to go": cf. Hebrew, *halakha*, from the verb *h-l-kh* in the same sense) refers to a legal school in Islam. Each school defines itself by the relative weight it accords to the various non-textual sources of *fiqh* and the practical differences that result. Traditionally, one counts four principal Sunni *madhahib* (Malikite, Shafi'ite, Hanbalite, and Hanafite), to which we can add two Shiite *madhhabs* (Zahiri and Ja'fari Zaidi) and Ibadi (for the Kharijites). In addition, these last three groups recognize a different body of Hadith than do the Sunni *madhhab*.

For the Jews of the Fatimid dynasty, the Islamic government recognized three *madhahib*: the Palestinian rabbinate (referring to the authority of the Talmud of Jerusalem and the Geonim of the Holy Land); the Babylonian rabbinate (referring to the authority of the Talmud of Babylon and the Geonim of Iraq); and the Karaites. Today, the Karaites have practically disappeared and all Jews recognize the Talmud of Babylon as the premier source of *halakha*. In practice, however, the divergent interpretations between medieval schools in France and Germany and from one coast of Spain to the other led to differences in practice between Ashkenazi Jews, who claim the former, and Sephardic Jews, who claim the latter. The Yemenites, isolated from the rest of the Jewish world after the Maimonidean codification, can be considered a third "Jewish *madhhab*."

Talmud. Both the Palestinian and Babylonian communities had their own Talmud. Yet the differences between the Talmuds are not primarily methodological per se, and there is also substantial overlap in material between the two Talmuds. On the other hand, the narrative works of Islamic law that emerged from the various Islamic schools of law reveal differences in substance and method alike, from the more legally conservative Hanbali school, which eschewed the use of analogy in favor of the direct exegesis of text, to the Hanafi school, which grants an expansive role to local custom, creative exegesis relying on analogy, and even legal devices that seemed to circumvent the literary sources of the law. The Hanafi school even produced compendia enumerating such

legal devices, called *hiyal*, and the success of this literature led other schools to produce similar works. Medieval Islamic jurisconsults were generally independent of political elites, although judges were appointed from the early period by local governors or caliphs. On the other hand, political power was shared in the Jewish community between jurisprudential elites, who derived their authority by virtue of their position in the Talmudic academies of Babylonia and the land of Israel, and political elites, who relied on putative Davidic descent for their authority. The heads of the Talmudic academies (*geonim*) and the official "head of the Jews" (*resh galutha* or exilarch) maintained local courts, and also held sway over distinct geographic areas of religious and political hegemony. Up until their influence waned in roughly the eleventh century, they appointed judges that served local communities throughout the Diaspora. Both Islamic and Jewish legal authorities split judicial functions in two: judges were responsible for implementing the law, while legal authorities interpreted it. Islamic jurisconsults (muftis) wrote responsa to questions of Islamic law, while *qādīs* applied those responsa. During the hey-

▶ See box on responsa or *teshuva*, p. 79.

day of the academies, the Jewish community as a whole addressed its questions to the *geonim*, who in turn publicly disseminated their responsa; those responsa were then used as briefs that were applied by local judges in actual cases. Multiple rabbinic authorities were sometimes presented with the same question; at times, a single rabbinic authority was even asked to compose a responsum by both parties to a dispute. In the early period, the authority of muftis rested solely on their reputation and not on any official position, though over time (particularly in the late medieval period) more structured roles for muftis seem to have emerged. Yet even when they lacked official position, jurisprudents gained followings and disciple circles morphed into formal madrasas (teaching institutions); even from the ninth century, collections of traditions and narrative discussion of the primary literary sources of the Qur'an and the hadith were aggregated into comprehensive legal compendia. Some of these collections reproduce questions and answers, while others present material in a statutory format. Despite the key role of fatwas in establishing precedent, neither Islamic law nor Jewish law should be seen as common law per se, since responsa are quasi-theoretical compositions or legal briefs implemented by the *qāḍī* and not by the mufti himself.

Further medieval developments

In addition to responsa, individual authorities composed self-contained monographs on specific topics, such as Abu Yusuf's eighth-century *Kitab al-Kharaj* (*Book of Land Taxation*); such monographs appear in halakhic literature as well from the time of Saadia Gaon (882–942), perhaps the most famous of which is his prayer book. These monographs point to a sea change in Jewish legal literature, as they represent restatements of the law organized topically rather than commentaries on or digests of Talmudic material. Saadia may have been influenced by a group of Jewish sectarians called Karaites who emerged around the

> **" Both Islamic and Jewish legal authorities split judicial functions in two: judges were responsible for implementing the law, while legal authorities interpreted it. "**

time of Saadia; these sectarians rejected the Talmud and rabbinic literature generally, ostensibly relying on the direct exegesis of the Bible. Karaites themselves appear to have acted as conduits of Islamic literary models into Jewish thought; the proto-Karaite 'Anan Ibn David is said to have met Abu Hanifa, eponym of the aforementioned Hanafi school, while imprisoned by the Abbasids in Baghdad at the behest of the Jewish exilarch in the late eighth century. 'Anan's *Sefer ha-mitsvot* (Book of Commandments) established a model enumerating Jewish law as a list of commandments rather than as a topically organized narrative, which was subsequently adopted by rabbinic jurists as well. Roughly a century after the rise of the Karaites, a movement similar to Karaism sprouted in Islamic law, called the Zahiri school, which rejected analogical and systematic reasoning as well as the exercise of personal opinion, turning exclusively to the reading of the Qur'an and the hadith; although this school of law would eventually fade from view, it inspired and influenced a conservative trend and was particularly influential in the thought of the fourteenth-century Hanbali scholar Ibn Taymiyya.

In addition to the study of Talmud, the writing of responsa, and the composition of halakhic monographs, the *geonim* contributed to the development of Jewish law by promulgating enactments (*taqqanot*) that responded to the economic and social transformations of an urbanizing populace during the Islamic commercial revolution of the eighth and ninth centuries. These social pressures also led to the development of widely held customs that were often subsequently vindicated through recourse to biblical proof texts. Custom was also a vehicle through which Islamic law absorbed local pre-Islamic practices in the wake of the early conquests, often also out of practical concerns. For instance, early Islamic doctrine accepted oral testimony alone and rejected the use of written documents as legal proof. However, the use of such documents not only gained prominence over time as Islamic hegemony expanded, but the eventual importance of document-writing led to the development of an entire branch of Islamic legal literature concerned with notarial practice (*'ilm al shurūt*). Formularies bridged the gap between narrative works of law and daily life in both traditions.

> *Karaites appear to have acted as conduits of Islamic literary models into Jewish thought.*

Diversity and dispersion

Concomitant with the disintegration of *geonic* authority, local centers of Jewish learning developed, and the role of local custom also expanded. From these local centers emerged some jurisprudents whose prominence gave their works a broader halakhic authority. These works include the Talmudic digest of the eleventh-century North African scholar and jurisconsult Isaac Ibn Jacob al-Fasi, and the extensive Talmudic and biblical commentaries of al-Fasi's French contemporary Solomon ben Isaac (popularly styled "Rashi"). Two competing trends responded to the rise of local custom: one, an attempt to restore the centrality of a universal, normative practice by means of a comprehensive code designed to remediate the low level of Talmudic learning in the Diaspora; and, two, an attempt to preserve local tradition through the proliferation of works that recorded that tradition. The first of these trends is exemplified by Moses Ibn Maimon (1138–1204), who composed his *Mishneh Torah* in a clear Hebrew, which reached an audience well beyond his own North African community (he had resettled in Egypt following the Almohad persecutions in Spain), and made the law accessible without the extensive study of difficult Talmudic material. The second of these trends was particularly developed among the scholars of Provence, who produced a number of compendia collecting local customs from the twelfth to the fourteenth centuries. Amid the development of local customs, two distinctive primary Jewish strains developed that fell along the geographical division of those areas under the hegemony of Western Christendom (so-called Ashkenazic Jewry) and those of Iberia and the lands of Islam. Although the Jewish communities of the Islamic Mediterranean atrophied in the thirteenth to fifteenth centuries, the renaissance of these communities with the influx of Iberian expellees at the end of the fifteenth century led to their dominance by Iberian (so-called Sephardic) traditions. The encounter of expellees from Iberia with diverse local communities in the Mediterranean Littoral led Joseph Ibn Ephraim Caro (1488–1575) to compose a code entitled *Shulhan 'Arukh*, which captured Sephardic practice; this code was subsequently integrated with a commentary by the Polish scholar Moses Isserles (1520–72), which recapitulated the corresponding Ashkenazic practice. The Shulhan 'Arukh gained widespread (but not universal) acceptance in the Jewish world as a whole and continues to animate traditional Jewish legal decision-making into modernity. Roughly half a century before the emergence of Caro's work, the Maghribi (Northwest African) Maliki jurist Ahmad Ibn Yahya al-Wansharisi strove to maintain Islamic Iberian legal and cultural heritage. Contemporaneous with the disintegration of the Nasrid kingdom

The image of the crescent as personification of shari'a. Miniature from *Kitab al-Diryaq* (Book of Theriac or Book of Antidotes), Pseudo-Galen, copy from Iraq, 1199, fol. 37. Paris, Bibliothèque Nationale de France.

of Granada, Islam's final political foothold on Iberia, al-Wansharisi collected some 6,000 fatwas from hundreds of muftis throughout North Africa and Iberia spanning the previous half millennium. Wansharisi removed many of the concrete historical details in his sources and reduced their length, a practice often noted in collections of Islamic and Jewish responsa alike.

Islamic law did not maintain geographic divisions in the same manner that such divisions are seen in the development of Jewish law.

Practices did vary by locale, but the distance between jurisconsults and officialdom often lent a competitive nature to jurisprudence, and in many cases even the courts were largely independent of rulers. In such cases, litigants had their choice of courts, which represented the various schools of Islamic law. From the early stages of Islamic law, jurisconsults collected the opinions of their colleagues from other legal schools; some of these collections were redacted into handbooks of comparative law. At times, these handbooks would serve as a systematic justification of the writer's own *madhhab*. Although legal pluralism was common, there were some geographic areas in which one *madhhab* or another held sway; and in some of these regions specific schools had the support of local rulers. Thus, al-Andalus (Islamic Iberia) bore the stamp of Maliki jurisprudence, and the Ottoman Empire had the Hanafi school as its official *madhhab*. State support of the Hanafi school became particularly important after the Ottoman conquest of the Mamluk sultanate in 1517, as Ottoman rulers attempted to limit the role of the other legal schools in local jurisprudence.

In the modern period

Both Jewish law and Islamic law have been transformed by their engagement with modernity, leading in both cases to both progressive and traditional/conservative responses. Along with the emancipation of Jews in Europe and the breakdown of the traditional self-governing *kehilla* (community) system, the nineteenth century saw the emergence of Reform Judaism in Germany. Although the initial changes implemented by reformers were largely cosmetic, to bring ritual observance in line with European Christian practice as Jews became politically and socially emancipated, Reform Judaism developed into a movement that rejected the normative force of traditional Jewish law in favor of a model that defined practices and behavior more broadly in terms of Jewish ethics. Roughly contemporaneous with the rise of Reform Judaism, Egypt saw the rise of Muhammad 'Abduh (1849–1905), whose proposals for reform included the rejection of traditional Islamic law in favor of a quasi-legal system that conjoined reason and ethics with revelation. Yet while Reform Judaism grew in Europe, and particularly flowered in North America, nineteenth-century Islamic reform was dwarfed by the rise of secular nationalism, which crystallized in the twentieth century amid the disintegration of the Ottoman Empire and the emergence of modern states in the Middle East. Although the

Ottoman Empire itself had given Hanafi law an air of officialdom, rising European influence in the nineteenth century saw significant legal reform along the lines of Western legal codes, which represented a departure from traditional Islamic law in form and substance. As part of broader legal reforms, the Ottoman Council of Ministers (deciding not to translate and adopt the French Code Napoléon) commissioned a commercial code that was based on Hanafi law but departed in several significant aspects—including its very promulgation as an official code. This work, entitled *Mejelle*, wkas implemented between 1869 and 1876, and established foundations of commercial law that persist in much of the modern Middle East.

At the same time as movements emerged that sought to incorporate Western legal, ethical, and scientific elements into Jewish and Islamic law, traditional/conservative responses to modernity inspired groups that eschewed such changes. The Austrian Hungarian Jewish legal authority Moses Schreiber (popularly known as the "Hatam Sofer," 1762–1839) spearheaded a movement that rejected the liberalizing innovations of Reform Judaism and pursued a narrow, reactionary legalism, which also drew support from conservative elements rejecting the pietistic (and at times antinomian) reforms of the rising Hasidic movement. Likewise, the Arabian Peninsula saw a conservative revivalist movement in the eighteenth century called Wahhabism, which rejected the mystical innovations of Sufism and turned to Hanbali jurisprudence seen through the lens of Ibn Taymiyya. The support of Wahhabism by Muhammad Ibn Saʿud in the eighteenth century facilitated the movement's expansion in the twentieth century as the Hanbali school became established as the official school of the kingdom of Saudi Arabia.

Ibn Khaldun: The Jews and the Political

In the Muqqadima—or Prolegomena, the introduction to his universal history, written in the fourteenth century—Ibn Khaldun analyzes, at the heart of the three monotheisms, the relation between the political and the religious. For Islam, he stresses the alliance of the two, for which the vocation is the universal propagation of religion. For Christianity, he analyzes the fundamental distinction between the figures of the pope and the emperor, which marks both the separation between the two domains and their convergence. Finally, for Judaism, he sees in the status of "kohen" the proof that the political and the religious are fundamentally separate, the former being, in this relation, neutralized.[1]

"The Israelites after Moses and Joshua had little interest in the affairs of power for about four hundred years, with their sole aim being to establish their religion. The person from among them who was in charge of their religion was called the *kohen* [priest]. He was in a way the representative (caliph) of Moses and was responsible for leading the prayers and presiding over the sacrifices of the Israelites. They made it a condition for him to be a descendant of Aaron, as it had been destined for him and his children by divine revelation. In regard to the political matters that naturally arose among human beings, the Israelites selected seventy elders who were entrusted with a general legal authority. The *kohen* had a religious rank that was superior to theirs, and more remote from the turmoil of law enforcement. This was so until the Israelites' esprit de corps was fully developed and they were rendered fit for power. The Israelites dispossessed the Canaanites of the land that God had given them as their heritage in Jerusalem and the surrounding region, as it had been explained to them through Moses. The nations of the Philistines, the Canaanites, the Armenians, the Edomites, the Ammonites, and the Moabites fought against them. During that time political leadership was entrusted to the elders among them. The Israelites remained in that condition for about four hundred years. They did not have any royal power and were harassed by attacks from foreign nations. Therefore, they asked God through Samuel, one of their prophets, that He permit them to make someone king over them. Thus, Saul became their king. Under his rule, they defeated the foreign nations and killed Goliath, the ruler of the Philistines. After Saul, David became king, and then Solomon. His kingdom flourished and extended to the borders of the Hejaz and further, to the borders of the land of the Byzantines. After Solomon, the tribes split into two dynasties. This is, as noted earlier, an inevitable consequence of esprit de corps in the context of evolving dynasties. One of the dynasties was that of the ten tribes in the region of Nablus, the capital of which is in Samaria (Sabastiyah), and the other that of the children of Judah and Benjamin in Jerusalem. Nebuchadnezzar, the king of Babylon, then deprived them of their kingdoms, addressing first the ten tribes of Samaria, and then the sons of Judah in Jerusalem, whose reign had lasted for nearly a thousand years. He then destroyed the Temple, burned their Torah, and destroyed their religion. He deported the people to Isfahan and Iraq. They were eventually brought back to Jerusalem by one of the Persian kings, Kayyanid (Achaemenid), seventy years after they had left it. They rebuilt the Temple and reestablished their religion in its original form with priestly authority; temporal power remained in the hands of the Persians. Alexander and the Greeks then defeated the Persians, and the Jews came under Greek domination. The Greek rule then weakened, and with the help of their natural esprit de corps, the Jews rose against the Greeks and put an end to their domination over them. Power was then exercised by the priests of the Hasmonean family, who fought the Greeks until the power of the latter was destroyed and they were conquered by the Romans. The Jews then came under the Roman yoke. The Romans marched on Jerusalem, the seat of the children of Herod, relatives by marriage to the Hasmoneans and the last remnant of the Hasmonean dynasty. They laid siege to them for a time, finally conquering Jerusalem by force, and spread murder, destruction, and arson. They laid Jerusalem in ruins and exiled the Jews to Rome and the regions beyond. This was the second destruction of the Temple. The Jews call it "the Great Exile." After that, they never managed to regain their power because they had lost their esprit de corps. They remained thereafter under the yoke of the Romans and their successors. Their religious affairs were taken care of by their head, called the *kohen*.[2]"

---

1. Introduction by Abdelwahab Meddeb.
2. Ibn Khaldun, *The Muqaddimah: An Introduction to History*, translated from the Arabic by Franz Rosenthal; ed. and abridged by N. J. Dawood (Princeton, NJ: Princeton University Press, 2004), 183–85.

Ibn Hazm and Maimonides and the *Fiqh*

The Muslim ʿAli ibn Hazm (b. Córdoba 994–1064) and the Jew Moses ben Maimon, known as Maimonides (b. Córdoba 1135–d. Egypt 1204), have both combined logical, theological, and juridical excellence in their works. To the daring philosophical synthesis *Moreh Nevukhīm* (*The Guide for the Perplexed*) by Maimonides corresponds the *Fical fi l-milal wal-ahwaʾ wa-l-nihal* (Critical Examination of Religions, Heresies, and Sects) by Ibn Hazm, while the great code of the Law, *Mishneh Torah* (Repetition of the Torah), is comparable to the *Kitab al-Muhalla bi-l-Athar* (Book Adorned with Traditions) both in its form and purpose. It is even probable that this last work, *Al-Muhalla*, represented, for Maimonides, a novel contribution, traces of which can be found in the *Mishneh Torah*.

The great classical treatises of *fiqh* are not simply collections of jurisprudence. On the contrary, they attribute great importance to what are called *uçūl al-fiqh*, literally, the "roots" of the *fiqh*; in other words, the methodological principles at the basis of Islamic law. This legal theory recognizes four sources of the *fiqh*: the Qurʾan, the Sunnah (recorded in hadith recognized as being authentic), the consensus (*ijmā*), and analogy (*qiyās*), as is established beginning with the first essay of *uçūl al-fiqh*, the *Risala* of Al-Shafiʿi (767–820).[1] Most of the treatises of Islamic *fiqh*, including that of Ibn Hazm, are organized by thematic books: *al-tahāra* (legal purity), *al-salat* (prayer). Each of these books contains the legal stipulations concerning the subject, whether they are positive or negative commandments. On the other hand, both the way of treating the subject and the exposition of the legal dispositions vary according to the juridical school (*madhhab*) to which the author belongs. Another difference comes from the fact that the classical treatises, such as *Al-Umm* (the Mother), by Al-Shafiʿi, begin directly with the treatment of juridical themes and rituals, while the works of Andalusian *fiqh* open with theological considerations. Indeed, these authors believe that the knowledge of the origin of divine messages, divine uniqueness, divine names, and the attributes of God must precede the evidence, which makes it possible to corroborate the laws to guarantee the veracity of the Messengers.

Al-Muhalla, a work in eleven thematic books, is one of four treatises of Ibn Hazm in which the author sets forth his conception of the *fiqh* and his juridical affiliation. It is also his last work, left unfinished at his death. His expository method is the following. He begins by defining the object of the chapter, then states his juridical opinion by prefacing it with the formula "Abu Muhammad said" or "ʿAli said," thus designating himself. He then supports that opinion with a verse from the Qurʾan or a hadith that he connects with the Prophet by a chain of guarantors. He may also make use of a consensus (or *ijmā*) on the point being treated. He also invokes the opinion of the Companions, and of those who followed them, down to the imams Abi Hanifa, Al-Malik, and Al-Shafiʿi. Only rarely does he mention the opinion of Ibn Hanbal, since he was, among Andalusians, considered only as an authority of the hadith and not as the originator of the juridical school he founded, Hanbalism. After having related all these opinions, he decides on the validity or weakness of the versions of hadith, passes judgment on the value of the transmitters, and ends by comparing his own opinion with that of his predecessors.

Still today, Maimonides's *Mishneh Torah* on the halakha constitutes a major reference. Already at the moment of its composition (in 1177), it appeared as very innovative, daring even, in form and intention. The Babylonian Talmud, which records the legal debates of the Jewish masters and analyzes their conceptual presuppositions, was closed in the sixth century and constituted the last word in legal authority—the written Torah itself being read through the prism of the Talmudic interpretation, but not constituting an immediate source of law. The codes composed since then consisted in legal abridgments of the Talmud (such as the *Sefer ha-Halakhot* by Isaac al-Fassi), monographs (*Sefer ha-Mekah ve-ha-Memkar* by Hai Gaon, on business law), or descriptive lists (*Sefer ha-Mitzvot*, by Saadia Gaon), and it was understood that jurists had to return to the Talmudic source to support their opinions, despite the growing luxury of divergent interpretations. Maimonides is the first to have proposed a systematic exposition of the Law according to logical principles. He explains in the introduction that he had a choice between two possibilities: either to follow the method and the divisions of the Mishnah (and the Talmud) or compose his book according to a different expository order and take up the subject matter of the Mishnah anew, in chapters arranged otherwise, according to a different logic—one that would be better adapted to study and more easily assimilated. Thus, each of the fourteen books is divided into chapters, each in turn containing a certain number of articles, according to an analytic approach that reflects neither the way these subjects are approached in the Talmud nor the list that it itself establishes of the 613 mitzvot, or biblical "commandments," but an a priori logical architecture: one sole mitzvah, such as that of the recitation of the Shema Yisrael, is the object of four chapters, while the twelve chapters devoted to the interdictions against idolatry cover fifty-one mitzvot.[2] Here we may well see an influence of the Islamic *fiqh.* Another clear relationship may be seen in the fact that Maimonides begins the first book of his *Mishneh Torah*, the *Sefer ha-Madda*, with a chapter on the "fundamental laws of the Torah," which he identifies as the commandments to know the existence of God, to profess his oneness, to love him, to fear him, and so on. In other words, he opens with theological and metaphysical principles that are only treated incidentally in the Talmud, but that are strongly reminiscent of Ibn Rushd [Averroes]. In choosing this order of exposition, Maimonides broadens the gap distancing himself from the Mishnah, and comes closer to the procedure followed in the treatises of the Islamic *fiqh.*

In Ibn Hazm's treatise, *Al-Muhalla*, the rules are explained immediately following the profession of monotheistic faith. In the chapter entitled "Questions on the Principles," the author states eighteen questions, through which his allegiance to the Zahiri school, which reads texts according to their immediate or obvious meaning, is manifest. Accordingly, in treating the first question, he says that the Islamic religion can only be understood on the basis of the Qurʾan, as well as on the unanimous consensus of all the religious authorities (*al-ijmāʿ*), or a large group of them (*al-kāffah*), guarantors worthy of faith (*al-thiqah*), claiming a chain of transmission reaching back to the Prophet.[3] The *ijmāʿ* transmit what all the Companions of the Prophet of God have said and known of him, without exception or divergence—which thus implies that all the believers, and not a part of them, can adhere to the content of the *ijmāʿ al-sahābah*, the unanimous consensus of the Companions.[4]

In the ninth question, on the other hand, Ibn Hazm rejects the method of analogy (*qiyās*) in these terms: "One cannot resolve a problem by analogy or by opinion; in the case of divergence of interpretation of a commandment of God, one must have recourse to his Book and his Prophet. To resort to the *qiyās*, to personal reasoning, or to an opinion is to disobey God's commandment."[5] But it is not that he advocates an irrational approach, since, in question twelve, he similarly forbids recourse to imitation (*taqlīd*), which consists in a blind respect: "It is not permitted to follow anyone, dead or alive. It is for each one to practice reflection on his own, and according to his capacities."[6] What Ibn Hazm targets in his condemnation of the *qiyās* is recourse to the analogy of principles (*al-qiyās al-uçūlī*), practiced by scholars and rationalist philosophers, on the basis of personal opinion. On the other hand, he does not reject reasoning by Aristotelian analogy, *al-qiyās al-aristī*, considering that the logic (*mantiq*) of Aristotle can be of great service in all the sciences, whether it be Qur'anic science, the science of hadith, or consultation on the questions of the licit and the illicit, the obligatory and the permitted.[7] Thus, in *Al-Fiçal*, he praises the usefulness of the Aristotelian corpus in the domain of jurisprudence, and asserts that these books are indispensable to the conscientious jurist, who will learn to construct a syllogism, distinguish the general from the particular, and put the premises and the conclusions in their proper place.[8] The reason he accepts Aristotelian logic and rejects analogy by the principles has to do with the fact that logic is quite compatible with his Zahiri approach: Ibn Hazm stays close to the text, and to its obvious meaning, forbidding anyone to interpret a verse or passage of hadith otherwise than according to its straightforward meaning, or by appealing to another valid text or to the irrefutable unanimity of the scholars.[9] In refusing the analogy principle, which would extend the judgment made in a precise context in the Qur'an and the Sunnah to a case stripped of all reference, Ibn Hazm shows that he is a good disciple of Aristotle, according to whom the conclusions must necessarily issue from the premises; he is faithful to the same method when he passes from the general to the particular, from the summary to the detail, from the genus to the species, and from the species to individuals.[10] Similarly, Ibn Hazm agrees with Aristotle on the subject of the end pursued. With the Greek philosopher the approach essentially attempts to prove a truth that is already known, and not to discover a new truth; it is a method by which one tries to convince the person whose opinion differs from ours, by explaining the premises on which our opinion is based. The Uculiyyun, on the other hand, established their method of analogy to find solutions to legal questions that were imperative in their time.[11] And it was for this reason, in order to draw from questions stripped of references a judgment that would be analogous to the one drawn from known references, that they established rules and conditions that Ibn Hazm considered too far from the obvious interpretation of the texts to be able to accept them. In Maimonides, this concern is also reflected, to distinguish clearly between what is proper to the obvious meaning of the sacred text and what to the rabbinic legislation. If he does not reject the latter out of hand, he makes a point of

Mishneh Torah by Maimonides, illuminated manuscript, around 1351, Jerusalem. Paris, Bibliothèque Nationale de France.

always specifying whether such and such a rule is a commandment of the Torah of a general or a particular nature, a commandment of the Torah that is deduced by the canonic methods of exegesis (the Thirteen Rules of Rabbi Yishmael), an obligation of rabbinic nature for which the sages of the Talmud have found an allusive support in the biblical text (*asmakhta*), or a pure novation of the rabbis, such as the reading of the Scroll of Esther during Purim. (The book of Esther is indeed part of the biblical canon, but only the Pentateuch of Moses, the Torah, is the source of Law; the celebration of Purim was instituted by the Sanhedrin, the supreme rabbinical court, during the time of the Persian domination.) All this hierarchy of norms is already present in the Talmud, but Maimonides gives it a systematic formulation, even going so far as to apply the Mishnaic expression *divrei sofrim*, "words of the scribes," to the laws of the Torah learned by exegesis, thereby suggesting that they make up an intermediary category between the biblical and the rabbinical laws. In this we may also discern a trace of the Zahiri approach, which rejects putting all the rules on the same plane by an abusive use of the analogy or *qiyās*. Similarly, in refusing to repeat verbatim the Talmudic passages, which are his source textually, and preferring to reformulate them in analytic terminology, Maimonides closes off the *taqlīd* path in favor of logic (*mantiq*).

Where Maimonides and Ibn Hazm diverge is in their approach to consensus (*ijma*) and the chain of transmission (*ʾasnad*, the certification of the chain of transmission), two major methods of establishing the *fiqh*, which is intimately linked to the science of hadith. Hence, Ibn Hazm, in the introduction to *Al-Muhalla*, writes that the goal of his work is to inventory the provisions of a juridical nature that may be found in the Qurʾan and in the established corpus of the Tradition of the Prophet, in order to distinguish them carefully from those not having an indisputable value. Maimonides is also concerned with identifying, among those who transmit the words and deeds of the Prophet, only those who may be considered worthy of confidence.[12] On the other hand, Maimonides is obviously not concerned with rejecting certain opinions expressed in the Talmud as untrustworthy, regardless of whether or not the halakha would endorse them. Indeed, a cardinal principle of the Talmudic method is to constantly confront the divergent approaches of the sages in order to bring to light the reasons for their disagreement, and, hence, the conceptual issues of each rule. But if Maimonides repeats, in the introduction to the *Mishneh Torah*, the classic *shalshelet ha-kabbalah* (chain of transmission) that extends from Sinai to the closure of the Talmud, an ancient model of which is found in the first chapter of the *Pirkei Avot* (*Sayings of the Fathers*, or *Chapters of Fundamental Principles*), in the body of his text he never mentions the names of the sages, who, in the Talmud, expressed the opinion retained by the halakha. He gives the reason in a letter: "It is in order to withdraw from the *minim* [the heretics, that is, the Karaites, who at that time played a very influential role], who reproach us for relying on individual versions, while in truth we rely on thousands, on tens of thousands of testimonies, themselves issuing from tens of thousands of other testimonies. This is why I used, in the preamble of my book [*Mishneh Torah*] the expression: 'such and such a one and his tribunal (*beit din*) received from such and such a one and his tribunal,' so that it would be very clear that we are speaking of a transmission from group to group and not from individual to individual. The Law is thus explained in itself, stripped of all personal mention. This has been done in order to have done with the *minim*, who reject the oral Torah, on grounds that it is carried by the mouth of one individual, as if that individual expressed his own opinion, and did not transmit the Torah of someone else, who himself received it from someone else."[13] ●

Layla Ibrahim Abu al-Majd is professor of Judaic and Talmudic studies at the University of Ayn al-Shams in Cairo. Among his publications (in Arabic) are Women in the Talmud *(2005) and* Women between Judaism and Islam *(2007).*

_____

1. Al-Shafi'i, *Risala*, ed. Khaled al-Saba' al-ʿIlmi and Zoheir Shafiq al-Kebbi (Beirut: Dar el-kitab al-ʿarabi), 6–7.

2. Maimonides, *Sefer ha-Mitsvot* [*Book of Commandments*] (in Hebrew), translated from Arabic with comments by Yosef Kafah (Jerusalem: Mosad ha-Rav Kuk, 1971), 2–3.

3. Ibn Hazm, *Al-Muhalla*, ed. Ahmed Mohammed Shaker (Cairo: Al-Muniriyya, 1929), 1:50.

4. Ibid., 1:54.

5. Ibid., 1:56.

6. Ibid., 1:66.

7. Ibn Hazm, *Preamble to Logic* (in Arabic), ed. Ihsan Abbas (Beirut), 9.

8. Ibn Hazm, *Traité des sectes et des communautés* [Treatise on Sects and Communities], with comments by Ahmed Shamseddin, 1st ed. (Beirut: Dar el-kutub el-ʿilmiya, 1996), 2:95.

9. Ibn Hazm, *Critique de ceux qui comprennent mal les principes du fiqh zaheri* [Critique of Those Who Do Not Understand the Principles of the Fiqh Well], ed. Mohammed Zaher el-Kawthari (Cairo: 1940), 24.

10. Daoud (Mohammed Soleyman), *La Théorie de l'analogie par les principes: Un exemple de méthode expérimentale islamique* [The Theory of Analogy by the Principles: An Example of the Islamic Experimental Method] (Alexandria: Dar el-Daʿwa, 1984), 239.

11. Ibid., 355–57.

12. Ibn Hazm (Abu Mohammed Ali bin Ahmed bin Said), *Al-Mohalla*, 1:2.

13. Maimonides, *Responsa of Rambam* (in Hebrew), quoted in the *Introduction to the Mishneh Torah* (Leipzig), 73.

Rituals: Similarities, Influences, and Processes of Differentiation
Reuven Firestone

Judaism and Islam are mutually recognized as genuine monotheisms. Despite this general recognition, Muslim and Jewish religious scholars have critiqued each others' religion over the centuries by calling into question both the authenticity of the other's scripture and the efficacy of its religious practice. This basic critique is quite similar on both sides, yet despite significant and sometimes severe disapproval, each party recognizes the essential theological and moral-ethical soundness of the other. This basic respect, though sometimes reluctant, does not apply equally to other religions, certainly not to the Oriental traditions, and for the most part, not even Christianity.[1] The most fundamental reason for the undeniable mutual recognition (and perhaps also for the need for critique) is exactly the recognizability of the other. So many aspects are familiar and decipherable, from the nature of revelation to the principles of interpretation, centrality of law, and articulation of prayer.

Reuven Firestone

Reuven Firestone is a professor of medieval Judaism and Islam at Hebrew Union College in Los Angeles, and a member of the Center for Religion and Civic Culture (University of Southern California). He is also the founder and codirector of the Center for Muslim-Jewish Engagement, the mission of which is to promote dialogue and scientific collaboration between the two communities. His publications include *An Introduction to Islam for Jews* (Jewish Publication Society, 2008).

Religious similarity has always raised the question of originality and influence, which in turn raises the question of religious legitimacy. The foundation of religious authority is its claim to reflect God's will, and the core argument between religions and between streams within religion is over which most faithfully reflects this will. When a new religion emerges into history, it inevitably criticizes the established religions, usually attacking what it defines as their hypocrisy and lack of relevance. Established religions in turn accuse new religions of banality or lack of legitimacy and of having copied or borrowed from previous religions. Mutual criticism is a common phenomenon of religious relationship, and it reflects the economics of religious competition for the souls of believers who not only seek solace and redemption within the religious framework, but also provide critical human and material resources that are necessary for the enduring success of religion.

Influence and absorption are generally mutual and analogically follow the simple Newtonian principle that action stimulates reaction. When human communities interact they influence one another through the contact of culture, language, and custom. Because religious realia are a central part of human civilization, religion is deeply involved in the process. While the directionality of impact is never one-way, one direction may be more pronounced at one time than at others, and the force of stimulus between Judaism and Islam changed over time. Religious parallels and similarities, however, do not necessarily point to borrowing and influence. Some patterns reflect common cultural contexts or simply natural human patterns of response to the transcendent or other stimuli. It is with this background that we delve into some examples of ritual in Islam and Judaism, with an eye to similarities and distinctions, possibilities of influence, and processes of differentiation. Limited space allows only a limited overview, but one that reflects the trends of relationship.

Early period parallels and similarities

Religion is impossible without some form of prayer. The earliest versions of the Qur'an refer to divine supplication, sometimes associated with offerings and sacrifice (Q. 108:2; 9:99), which was a virtually universal form of worship in the ancient world. Obligatory Islamic prayer is called *ṣalāt* (*ṣlw*), which derives from an Aramaic/Syriac term for prayer (*ṣelōṯā*) that came into Arabia before the emergence of Islam.[2] Its original meaning was to bow, and most scholars believe that it came into Arabic through Syriac Christians, though the Aramaic term continues to be used in the traditional Jewish liturgy to this day.[3] Other foreign vocabulary for religious terminology may be identified by unique word structures (morphology) that are not found in native Arabic. Some examples include terms such as *tawrāt* (Torah), *furqān* (redemption),[4] and *zakāt* (required almsgiving).[5] Islamic prayer includes bowing, kneeling, and prostration, all terms that are found in the biblical Psalms as well as extrabiblical literature, and were once a part of Jewish ritual but dropped from practice for reasons that are not clear (see below).[6]

⏵ See article by Mohamed Howary, pp. 713–719.

The liturgical core of obligatory daily prayer in Islam is the *fātiḥa* or opening of the Qur'an, represented as its first chapter. This prayer includes terms and phrases that are reminiscent of Jewish literature and prayer. The very title of *fātiḥa* echoes the Hebrew *petīḥāh*, a term used in earlier rabbinic discourse to distinguish the opening prologue of a text from the text itself. So, too, the first chapter of the Qur'an functions as a liturgical proem to the revelation that follows. It begins with praise, *al-ḥamdu lillāhi* = "praise be to God," as do many biblical Psalms and every benediction of rabbinic Judaism (*barukh attah…* = "praised are You [God]"). In the same line, God is "Lord of the universe" (*rabb al-'ālamīn*), which represents a semantic and conceptual parallel with a section of the standard Hebrew benediction "King of the universe" (*melekh ha'olam*),[7] and God is "the Merciful and the Compassionate," a phrase that finds close linguistic and semantic parallels in the Bible and in early rabbinic prayer.[8] Many more parallels may be adduced from the remainder of this required liturgical core of daily Islamic prayer.

The other ubiquitous recitation within daily Islamic prayer is "God is most great" (*Allāhu akbar*). The expectation to "magnify" God is found very early in the Qur'anic revelation, appearing already in the early sura *al-mudaththur* (74:3): "And magnify your Lord" (*warabbuka fakabbir*). It finds a direct semantic parallel with the Jewish term *gaddel* (magnify), most familiar from the series of liturgies of praise found throughout all Jewish obligatory prayers in the *Qaddish* (*yitgaddal . . . shemey rabbah*, "magnified . . . is [God's] great name").

The expectation to face "God's house" in prayer is found in both Islamic and Jewish ritual practice. In Judaism this may be traced as far back as Solomon, who is depicted repeatedly extolling the efficacy of directing prayer toward Jerusalem and its Temple (1 Kings 8:35,44, 48; 2 Chron. 6:34). While formal prayer during the period of the Temple was based on the Temple offerings, references to personal prayer occur as well, and one such case is that of the prophet Daniel, who prayed three times daily to God by facing Jerusalem from his home in Babylon.[9] The passage occurs in biblical Aramaic and is especially interesting because it uses the term *qabel*, "facing" (from the verb *qabal*, "to correspond to"), like the Arabic *qibla*, to denote directionality. The Qur'an mentions that God changed the direction of prayer (*qibla*) from an unnamed location to the Sacred Mosque, which caused some friction with the People of the Book in Medina (Q. 2:142–45). While the Qur'an does not identify the earlier direction of prayer that was replaced, Muslim commentators identify it universally as Jerusalem, toward which early Christian communities prayed as well.

A specially designated weekly prayer is another parallel between Judaism, Islam, and Christianity. As is well known, the Jewish day is Shabbat (on Saturday),[10] the Christian day is the "Lord's Day" (on Sunday),[11] and the Islamic day is "Day of Congregation" (on Friday).[12] And in traditional postbiblical Judaism and Islam, the leader of prayer may be any fit male whose piety and knowledge enables them to represent the community.

▶ See article by Mohamed Hawary, pp. 720–724.

We have observed parallels in liturgy, phraseology, body movements and their sequence, and in the representational role of the prayer leader. Even the custom of turning to the right and left and reciting "peace to you" at the end of the complete Islamic prayer cycle finds a parallel in Jewish tradition. The Talmud records a discussion among the sages in which the core section of the repeated daily service known as the *'amidah*, or "eighteen benedictions," is ended with "the giving of peace to the right and thereafter to the left" (*Yoma* 53b).

Fasting, or abstention from all food intake, is a religious requirement in both Judaism and Islam. Fasting occurs in both religions as a ritual obligation, as a form of penitence, to help raise consciousness of the plight of the unfortunate, and also as an ascetic act, and these aspects of fasting overlap in a variety of ways. The ritual obligation of fasting is established as a requirement in both scriptures (Q. 2:183–85; Lev. 16:29–31/23:27–32). The Qurʾanic reference states unambiguously that fasting is required (*kutiba ʿalaykum al-ṣiyām*), whereas in the biblical verse an idiom is used that is understood universally in Jewish tradition to require fasting, as well as abstention from sexual relations and other activities of sensual pleasure:

> *The liturgical core of obligatory daily prayer in Islam is the* fātiḥa *or opening of the Qurʾan. The very title echoes the Hebrew* petīḥāh, *a term used to distinguish the opening prologue of a text from the text itself.*

veʿinitem et nafshoteykhem—literally, "you shall afflict yourselves."[13]

Both, furthermore, establish the fast according to the calendar. The Qurʾan establishes a daylight fast during the month of Ramadan, while the Bible requires a sunset-to-sunset fast on the tenth day of the seventh month: this is the fast of Yom Kippur. It is quite clear, moreover, that the early Muslims were accustomed to fasting on the tenth day of the month of Muharram, called Ashura, which is confirmed by authoritative Islamic tradition in the hadith.[14] There can be little doubt that this custom was influenced by the Jewish practice, but it dropped from required behavior in Islam when it was replaced by the Ramadan month of daylight fasting.[15]

The people used to fast on ʿAshūrāʾ (the tenth day of the month of Muḥarram) before the fasting of Ramaḍān was made obligatory. And on that day the Kaʿba used to be covered with a cover. When Allah made the fasting of the month of Ramaḍān compulsory, Allah's Apostle said, "Whoever wishes to fast (on the day of ʿAshūrāʾ) may do so; and whoever wishes to leave it can do so."[16]

Reading from the Torah in a synagogue in Jerusalem. Photograph by P. Deliss, September 2007.

It remains a major occasion of self-affliction among the Shiʿa to this day in the *taʿziyya* ritual among the Twelver Shiʿa, because the tenth of Muharram marks the martyrdom of al-Husayn b. ʿAli.[17]

A second sunset-to-sunset fast occurs in Judaism on the ninth day of the month of *Av* (*tishaʿ beʾav*), which commemorates the destruction of the Jerusalem Temple first by the Babylonians and then the Romans. Four other public fasts in Judaism are limited to the period from sunrise to sunset as in the Ramadan fast, three commemorating a sequence of events that eventuated in the destruction of the Temple, and one commemorating the fast of Esther and the Jews of ancient Persia in solidarity and prayer to avert an attempt to destroy them.[18] Both Judaism and Islam have other nonobligatory fast days for a variety of purposes, including some in common, such as the custom of fasting on Mondays and Thursdays.

Numerous additional parallels and commonalities are found in dietary laws,[19] ritual purity,[20] ritual slaughter,[21] circumcision,[22] holy day rituals, and so forth.[23] Much could be noted about them. I limit my final comments here to one small aspect of an issue that is striking because of a curious Islamic custom treating purity. Muslims are required by religious law to ensure that they are in a state of ritual purity before engaging in prayer by engaging in some form of ritual washing (Q. 5:6). A parallel is found also in Judaism, especially after waking and beginning the morning prayers,[24] but the ritual washing in Judaism is customary rather than required. Required ritual purity presents a potential problem in the dry and arid desert environment of Arabia and much of the Middle East and North Africa, where water is scarce. The problem is resolved in Islam with the custom of *tayammum*, rubbing the hands and face with clean earth in the absence of water, and authorized by the same Qurʾanic verse requiring ritual cleansing. Discussion of *tayammum* is then expanded in the canoni-

Reading from the Qurʾan in Penang, Malaysia. Photograph by Fred de Noyelle, March 2006.

Mihrab (prayer alcove) in the Tilla Kari Mosque in Samarkand, Uzbekistan. Photograph by Gérard Degeorge.

cal hadith.[25] In a Babylonian Talmudic discussion about ritual washing, one rabbi asks another about a young student from the West whose custom was to rub his hands with earth or a pebble or sawdust in the absence of water. It is agreed that this custom is acceptable as a means of ritual washing before worship.[26]

Differences and differentiation

While many other parallels and similarities may be cited, differences are also important to note. In fact, it is just as easy to stress differences as similarities, which explains why as strong a case can be made for the distinctiveness of Judaism and Islam as for their commonalities. One could easily make the case, for example, that many more differences than similarities may be found between Jewish and Islamic prayer, from liturgy to choreography, length, number, and content. One could begin almost anywhere. Jews are expected to pray three times per day, while Muslims are expected to pray five times. Muslims bow, kneel, and prostrate themselves fully and repeatedly in every prayer service. Jews bow in the prayer service, but while the Talmud and especially the Bible contain many cases of and references to kneeling and full prostration, these fell out of practice in rabbinic Judaism. They did not fall out of practice in Karaite Judaism, however. According to the fifteenth-century Karaite scholar Elijah Bashiatsi of Adrianople (today's Edirne in western Turkey), eight body movements are indispensable forms of adoration in prayer. These include bending the head, bending the upper body until it touches the knees, kneeling, violent bowing of the head, complete prostration, raising the hands, standing, and raising the eyes to heaven.[27]

One of the most striking verbs associated with God and prayer in Judaism is *qaddesh* (sanctify). The core of the Jewish prayer service is called the *qedushah*, and

God is praised and adored through the use of this term as absolutely sacred and incomparable. The important repeated litany of praise mentioned above is called the *qaddish*, and the term is used in many forms throughout Jewish liturgies. While the same word (*qaddasa*) is common in Islam, it did not enter the prayer tradition, even though the Qur'an describes the angels as sanctifying God (*wanuqaddisu laka*) in 2:30. While this image immediately recalls Isaiah 6:1–4, which imagines the divine angels known as *serafim* crying out *qadosh, qadosh, qadosh*, "Holy, Holy, Holy is the Lord of Hosts," it is both interesting and somewhat surprising that the term is not found in Islamic liturgy.

Ark of the Torah in the Grand Choral Synagogue, Saint Petersburg, Russia. Photograph by Pascal Deloche.

Even the obvious parallels can be observed in terms of difference. For example, although Judaism and Islam each emphasize the requirement of a weekly congregational prayer of "gathering" (*kanas* in Hebrew, *jama'* in Arabic), the content of that prayer service in each religion is significantly different, as are their respective views of the special nature and significance of the day upon which the congregational prayer must be held.[28]

And despite the many similarities in fasting, nearly all of the most important calendrical fasts in Judaism are engaged for purposes of historical mourning, which is absent ▶ See article by Mohamed Howary, pp. 713–719. from Islam. And while burial rites and mourning customs find many parallels—in the immediacy of burial, strict requirements for ritual washing of the body, burial in shrouds and without embalming, the emphasis on simple coffins or no coffin at all, a mourning period during which the bereaved avoid wearing jewelry or even clean clothes—so many details vary between the two traditions that one could easily emphasize the similarities or the differences in order to stress their commonalities or their divergences. It all depends on what one wishes to highlight. Many of the similarities between Judaism and Islam can be found in Christian traditions as well.

One more example is instructive in this regard. While it is true that both Jews and Muslims pray in the direction of their most sacred site, they turn toward differ-

"Although Judaism and Islam each emphasize the requirement of a weekly congregational prayer, the content of that prayer service in each religion is significantly different."

ent locations. The importance of this distinction is articulated well in the story of the important Jewish convert to Islam Kaʻb al-Ahbar and his advice to the caliph ʻUmar. The story is found repeated in Islamic sources where the caliph, after conquering Jerusalem from the Byzantine Christians, asks Kaʻb where he should build the al-Aqsa Mosque. Kaʻb immediately suggested that it be positioned to the north of the site of the ancient Temple (and the rock upon which it rested). That way, when Muslims prayed in that mosque toward Mecca, which is situated directly southward, they would be praying toward the Jewish Temple as well. ʻUmar understood Kaʻb's intention of inserting a traditional Jewish sensibility and practice into Islam and vigorously objected to the suggestion. The al-Aqsa Mosque would be built on the southern edge of the Temple Mount (in Arabic, the Noble Sanctuary [al-ḥaram al-sharīf]), so that when facing Mecca in the proper direction of prayer, worshippers would turn their backs in the direction of the old Temple of Jerusalem.[29]

This story suggests a number of important observations about religious relationship. On the one hand, the convert naturally feels comfortable with some of the ancient traditions of his previous religion and may wish to incorporate certain of them into his new faith. On the other, the leaders of the newly emerging religion need to assert their independence from the earlier faith traditions and the institutional powers that control them. Thus, we can observe the conscious effort to distinguish between "the old" and "the new" in religion. The tension between the old and the new has always played an important part in development and change within religion and between religions.

Later parallels and similarities

With the establishment of empire and consolidation, the Muslim world reached its acme of civilization and development, and its cosmopolitan nature encouraged the many peoples and religious communities within it to compete and contribute to a common society. Muslim leaders were concerned that Islamic religious practice not be influenced by ritual or custom of the Jewish and Christian communities living among them.

The powerful Islamic influence in the disciplines of science, philosophy, grammar, and poetry, which this volume describes in great detail, had little impact on Jewish ritual, however, for two major reasons. The first is that Jewish religious ritual had become largely standardized by the triumph of rabbinic Judaism, which occurred shortly before the emergence of Islam, and the second is that a significant portion of the Jewish world lay outside the boundaries of the Muslim empires and was thus immune from the undeniable attraction of Islamic religious culture. Some movements occurred in Judaism that were deeply affected by Islamic ritual, but their impact on Judaism did not endure. One was among Karaite Jews, who, as noted above, responded favorably to some Islamic ritual styles. These include, among other things, the removal of shoes when entering the house of prayer and open space without chairs or pews to allow prostrations in prayer.[30]

Another was the pious movement that emerged in Fostat/Cairo, led or deeply influenced by Abraham Maimuni (son of Maimonides), which became influential in Egypt and some other areas of the Middle East. Abraham's father, Moses Maimonides, already required that Jews wash their face, hands, and feet before the morning prayers (*Hilkhot tefillah* 84:3), which seems to reflect an earlier custom of Jews in Baghdad under the influence of Hai Gaon.[31]

Abraham Maimuni claimed that the changes he introduced were not innovations but rather a return to authentic Jewish practice that had fallen away, but any comparison of his changes with contemporary Islamic practice would note the latter's powerful influence. What Abraham called restorations include prostrations in prayer,[32] sitting on the knees in kneeling position, facing eastward (symbolically toward Jerusalem) not only during the central prayer of the eighteen benedictions but also during other prayer times, standing closely together in rows during prayer,[33] and spreading the hands in prayer.[34] His "restorations" were, in fact, practiced by some followers, but others accused him of copying Karaites, Muslims, or both, and most of the changes were eventually rejected. Some members of his own congregation filed a complaint against him with the ruler of Egypt for forcing upon them forbidden innovations. He was eventually forced to apologize for his acts and agreed not to abuse his authority further with such demands.[35]

▶ See article by Elisha Russ-Fishbane, pp. 856–864.

Finally, the power of the Arabic language deeply affected Jewish religious terminology in a reversal of the earliest period of Islamic emergence when Jewish and Christian terms in Aramaic/Syriac entered into early Arabic religious discourse. Unlike in the Christian world, where Latin was eschewed by the Jews, Arabic was embraced by the Jews of the Arabic-speaking Muslim world, and Arabic religious terminology was commonly applied to Jewish realia even when an authentic term existed in Hebrew. The Torah could be referred to by the

> **"The Torah could be referred to by the Arabic terms al-sharīʿa (the Law), al-kitāb (the book), and even al-qurʾān (related linguistically to a Hebrew word for Bible, miqraʾ)."**

Arabic terms *al-sharīʿa* (the Law), *al-kitāb* (the book), *al-muṣḥaf* (the book of pages), *al-nuzūl* (the revelation), *umm al-kitāb* (mother of books), and even *al-qurʾān* (related linguistically to a Hebrew word for Bible, *miqraʾ*).[36] Chapters of the Torah were called by the term for chapters in the Qurʾan known as *sūra*s, the leader of prayer could be called *imam*, and "Jerusalem" was written as *dār al-salām* (the abode of peace).[37] A Jewish judge (Hebrew *dayān*) was called *qādī* or even *muftī*, a responsum (*teshuva* in Hebrew) was often called a *fatwā*, Moses was referred to as *al-rasūl* or *rasūl Allah* (messenger of God, a term used in Islam for Muhammad and other prophets), the messiah called by the Islamic term *al-qā'im al-muntaẓar* (the awaited one), and God is not infrequently referred to simply as Allah (*the* God). Sometimes the two languages were combined in phrases such as *ṣalāt al-shaḥarīt* (the morning prayer) or *laytal-al-pesaḥ*, and sometimes even the Qur'an and hadith could be cited in Jewish religious works.[38] The custom of using Arabic-Islamic terminology did not end the use of more traditional Hebrew terms, but the two often existed together. Islam-influenced terms tended to fall out of use, however, as demographic changes and migrations altered the linguistic base-languages of Jews. Today in the West, for example, local language customs have infiltrated Jewish language in a way similar to that experienced by premodern Jews in the Muslim world. In the United States such common English terms as *judge, cantor, prayer leader, Bible, Pentateuch*, and *law* may replace or exist in parallel with the traditional Hebrew terminology. A similar trend is emerging also in the American Muslim community as English words infiltrate Islamic religious language. It is fitting to conclude with the observation that in America and much of the West, the unprecedented comfort with which Jews have been accepted into the larger culture was matched most closely, though not as thoroughly, under the rule of Islam. Future historical-anthropological studies of both Jewish and Islamic contemporary ritual in the United States will likely investigate similarities, influences, and processes of differentiation in relation to Western culture and public and civil religion.

---

1. Jacques Waardenburg, ed., *Muslim Perceptions of Other Religions* (New York: Oxford University Press, 1999); Alan Brill, *Judaism and World Religions: Encountering Christianity, Islam, and Eastern Traditions* (London: Palgrave Macmillan, 2012).

2. Arthur Jeffrey, *Foreign Vocabulary of the Qur'an* (Baroda: Oriental Institute, 1938), 198–99; Arne Ambros, *A Concise Dictionary of Koranic Arabic* (Weisbaden: Reichert, 2004), 163.

3. The best-known use is in "kaddish titqabel" found near the end of the morning service: "titqabal Ṣelothon," "May their prayer be accepted," though the Aramaic root is found elsewhere in the liturgy as well.

4. The Qur'an as redemptive revelation, related to Hebrew/Aramaic *purqān, purqanā*.

5. Related to Hebrew *zekhūt*.

6. Psalm 95:6: *bo'u nishtaḥaveh venikhra'ah nivrekhah*, "come let us prostrate and bow, kneel."

7. BT *Shabbat* 137b; *Soferim* 13:6, 7, 8, and so on.

8. Ex. 34:6; Deut. 4:31; Joel 2:13; Jonah 4:2; Psalms 78:34, 86:15, 103:8, 111:4, and so on. The sages of the Talmud constructed the prayer service requiring this phrase to be part of the liturgy (Mishnah *Makkot* 3:14), and the Hebrew *haraḥamān*, which is exactly equivalent to the Arabic *al-raḥmān* of the *fātiḥa*, is found in the many later, well-known liturgical settings attached to the blessings after meals.

9. Daniel 6:11. Some do not consider Daniel a prophet because he is not described as such in the Hebrew Bible, and his book appears not in the section called "Prophets" (*nevi'im*) but in Writings (*ketuvim*).

10. Gen. 2:3; Ex.16:23–26, 20:8–11.

11. *Kyriake hemera* in Rev.1:10.

12. Qurʾan 62:9–10. For a range of views on why the Islamic day of congregational prayer is Friday, see S. D. Goitein, "The Origin and Nature of the Muslim Friday Worship," in S. D. Goitein, *Studies in Islamic History and Institutions* (Leiden: Brill, 1968), 111–25.

13. Fasting in Islam, as in Judaism, also includes abstention from sexual relations and other forms of sensual pleasure, such as smoking.

14. Bukhari, *Sahih* (Lahore: Kazi bilingual edition), Fasting, 218–25 (3:122–25).

15. The Hebrew term for the tenth of the month is *ʿasor*, and the Aramaic translations of Lev. 23:27 have *ʿasra*. In rare cases, Jewish Aramaic has the form *ʿisora* (*Ketubbot* 50a), but with the meaning of a fraction, one-tenth.

16. Bukhari, *Sahih* (Lahore: Kazi), Hajj, 662 (2:388). Other authoritative hadith mention that Muhammad personally observed the Ashura and that it may have been a custom among the Meccan tribe of Quraysh in pre-Islamic times (Kazi, Fasting, 117–18 [3:65]).

17. Moojan Momen, *Introduction to Shiʿi Islam: The History and Doctrines of Twelver Shiʿism* (Oxford: George Ronald, 1985), 240–43.

18. Esther 4:15–17, 9:31.

19. Michael Cook, "Early Islamic Dietary Law," *Jerusalem Studies in Arabic and Islam* 7 (1986): 217–77 (esp. 260–77); David Freidenreich, *Foreigners and Their Food* (Berkeley: University of California Press, 2011).

20. Marion Holmes Katz, *Body of Text: The Emergence of the Sunni Law of Ritual Purity* (Albany: State University of New York Press, 2002); Hyam Maccoby, *Ritual and Morality: The Ritual Purity System and Its Place in Judaism* (Cambridge: Cambridge University Press, 1999).

21. Freidenreich, *Foreigners and Their Food*, especially 144–96; John Cooper, *Eat and Be Satisfied: A Social History of Jewish Food* (New York: Jason Aronson, 1993), 24–28.

22. David Gollaher, *Circumcision: A History of the World's Most Controversial Surgery* (New York: Basic Books, 2000).

23. Reuven Firestone, *Children of Abraham: An Introduction to Judaism for Muslims* (Hoboken, NJ: Ktav, 2001) and *An Introduction to Islam for Jews* (Philadelphia: Jewish Publication Society, 2008).

24. Maimonides, *Hilkhot Tefilah*, 84:3.

25. Al-Bukhari, *Sahih*, Book of *Tayammum*, vol. 1, book 7 (Kazi), 1:198–210.

26. *Berakhot* 15a.

27. Elijah Bashiatsi, *Aderet Eliyahu* (Odessa: Y. Beim, 1870), 104b, as cited in Louis Ginsberg, "Adoration," in *The Jewish Encyclopedia* (New York: Funk and Wagnalls, 1925), 1:211. For illustrations of these forms, see *An Introduction to Karaite Judaism: History, Theory, Practice, and Custom*, ed. Yosef Yaron (Troy, NY: Al-Qirqisani Center for the Promotion of Karaite Studies, 2003), 130–36.

28. See Goitein, "The Origin and Nature of the Muslim Friday Worship," in Goitein, *Studies in Islamic History and Institutions*, 111–25.

29. Muhammad Ibn Jarir al-Tabari, *The History of Al-Tabari*, trans. Yohanan Friedmann (Albany: State University of New York Press, 1992), 12:194–95; S. D. Goitein, "The Sanctity of Jerusalem and Palestine in Early Islam," in Goitein, *Studies in Islamic History and Institutions*, 140n3; F. E. Peters, *Jerusalem: The Holy City in the Eyes of Chroniclers, Visitors, Pilgrims, and Prophets* (Princeton, NJ: Princeton University Press, 1985), 189.

30. Daniel Frank, "Karaite Ritual," in *Judaism in Practice*, ed. Lawrence Fine (Princeton, NJ: Princeton University Press, 2001), 248–64, and "Karaite Prayer and Liturgy," in Meira Polliack, *Karaite Judaism: An Introduction* (Leiden: Brill, 2003); and *An Introduction to Karaite Judaism*, ed. Yaron, 122–234.

31. Naphtali Wieder, *Islamic Influences on the Jewish Worship* (in Hebrew) (London: Oxford, East and West Library, 1947), 21. Wieder notes also a medieval Yemenite custom of washing the hands, face, and feet after having a bowel movement (13).

32. Ibid., 52–53.

33. Abraham notes the identical root of *sff* in the Hebrew and Arabic terms for standing closely side by side and attributes its meaning from the well-known and oft-used Arabic version (Lazarus-Yafeh, *Some Religious Aspects of Islam*, 89; see Mishnah *Avot* 5:5 and Qurʾan 37:1, 165).

34. Wieder, *Islamic Influences on the Jewish Worship*, 31.

35. Lazarus-Yafeh, *Some Religious Aspects of Islam*, 89.

36. Aside from the first, all these terms continue to be used in Islamic contexts to refer to the Qurʾan.

37. A Hebrew-Jewish folk etymology of Jerusalem has long been "city of peace" (*ʿir shalom*).

38. Joshua Blau, *The Emergence and Linguistic Background of Judaeo-Arabic* (Oxford: Oxford University Press, 1965), 159–60; Lazarus-Yafeh, *Some Religious Aspects of Islam*, 81–82.

Ibn ʿArabi and the Jew's Reply to the Muslim Pilgrim

The Andalusian mystic Ibn ʿArabi (1165–1240), nicknamed in the Islamic world Sheikh al-Akbar, "the greatest master," illustrated the obligation of otherness as practiced in a city founded on *convivencia*. In this text, a Jew, responding to a Muslim who has asked him a question, refers to Qurʾanic material. We thus learn that a Jew knows the Qurʾan by heart and can make detailed use of it. In playing the role of an imam granting a fatwa for a Muslim, he is in the same position as a rabbi formulating a *teshuvah* for a Jew. Even in complying with the Islamic frame of reference, he remains faithful to the method of his own tradition. In his Qurʾanic interpretation, adapted to the case at hand, he engages in a midrashic exercise. The method is the same, but the scriptural material has changed to conform to the horizon of belief. And it is no accident that, as confirmation of that convergence of hospitality and respect for the other, the person who reports that edifying story to Ibn ʿArabi goes by a name (Musa ibn Muhammad) that combines those of the prophets Moses and Muhammad.

Abdelwahab Meddeb

This wonderful story of a Jew was reported to me by Musa ibn Muhammad al-Qabbab the Cordoban, the muezzin at the minaret between Bab al-Hazura and Bab Ajyad, in the Holy Mosque of Mecca, may God have mercy upon it. The year was 599. He told me that a man in Kairouan had decided to complete the hajj, and, for his journey, he hesitated between land and sea. Sometimes he leaned toward land, sometimes toward sea. He therefore decided that early the next morning he would ask the first person he met and would adopt the other's preference as his own. Now the first man he encountered was a Jew. Initially, he was troubled by this. But then he took heart and said to himself: "By God, I shall be quick to question him." He said: "O Jew, I wish to consult you about the journey I am undertaking. Should I go by land or by sea?" The Jew replied: "Glory be to God! Is that the kind of question that concerns someone like you? Do you not see that God tells you in your book: 'It is He who guides them by land and sea' (Qurʾan 10:22)?[1] He put land first and sea second. God deposited a secret there, and he knows you to be worthy of it. He put it in front and the sea behind, so that the traveler would make his way on land." The man said: "I was filled with wonder at his words, I journeyed on terra firma and, by God, I have never had such a journey. God granted me a greater blessing than I had wished for."

Ibn ʿArabi, *Al-Futuhat al-Makkiyya* (*The Meccan Illuminations*), chap. 161

----

1. [Passages from the Qurʾan are taken from *The Koran*, trans. N. J. Dawood (New York: Penguin, 1993)—JMT].

Prayer in Judaism and Islam
Mohamed Hawary

Prayer holds a central place in both Judaism and Islam. It is at once an eminently spiritual and a very codified rite that places the emphasis on the proclamation of divine unity and the glorification of God. It has its source in the Holy Scriptures and represents an important point of reference for the Jewish and Muslim communities and a factor of unity for believers throughout the world. As is often the case in the two religions, the proximity between the discourses and prescriptions is striking, though major differences also exist. For example, there are parallels in the phases of prayer and the gestures that accompany it, in its public character, and in the preliminary rituals of purification it requires, as well as in the central importance of the intention of the one who prays. Understood more as a form of worship rather than as the expression of a request, prayer demonstrates a specifically monotheistic conception of religion, which entails directly addressing the divine, without intermediary or intercessor.

Mohamed Hawary

A professor of Jewish religious thought and comparative religion in the Department of Hebrew Studies at Ain Shams University in Cairo, Mohamed Hawary has published, notably, "Language and Identity: Arabic and Hebrew as a Model," presented at the International Conference on the theme of "Culture of Communication in the Era of Globalization: An Arab Vision," Faculty of Arts, Ain Shams University, April 2007 (in Arabic); and *Sabbath and Friday in Judaism and Islam, Comparative Religions* (Dar El-Hani, 1988) (in Arabic).

Jewish prayer: Biblical origins and rabbinical injunctions

No specific prayer rituals are known to have existed among the Israelites before the establishment of places specially dedicated to these rites, the Tabernacle and the Sanctuary. It is clear from Isaiah (1:15; 29:13; 58:5) that it was only in the time of the prophets that ritual prayers were set in place. We may surmise the hours for prayer from the book of Daniel (6:11). The prophet Daniel is depicted in the act of prayer, bowing at the waist and giving thanks three times a day, a number that also appears in Psalm 55:17. First Chronicles mentions a twice-daily prayer (23:30). Prayer is among the biblical obligations of Judaism, at least in principle. In Exodus 23:25 we read: "You will worship Yahweh your God" (New Jerusalem Bible). By "worship," we are to understand "prayer." In Deuteronomy we find: "[May you love] Yahweh your God and serve him with all your heart and all your soul" [6:5, 10:12, 11:13]. The Jews in exile did not neglect prayer: even in the lands of their enemies, they acted in such a way as to preserve that ritual, in fidelity to the Lord's commandments, taking care to turn their faces and hearts toward their "point of focus," located in Jerusalem. A verse from 1 Kings says: "And [they] turn back to you with all their heart and soul in the country of the enemies who have taken them captive, and pray to you, turning towards the country which you gave to their ancestors, towards the city which you have chosen and towards the Temple which I have built for your name" (8:48). This is why the rabbis have always firmly insisted on this obligation, which appears explicitly in the Holy Book.[1]

The sages of antiquity differed on the number of prayers that had to be performed each day. Some called for as many as seven, referring to Psalm 119:164: "Seven times a day I praise you for your upright judgments." Others limited the number to three—evening prayer, morning prayer, and midday prayer—in reference to Psalm 55:17: "Evening, morning, noon, I complain and I groan. He hears my cry." Some added a fourth prayer, because of Psalm 119:62: "At midnight I rise to praise you for your upright judgments." Still others, finally, reduced the number to two, on the authority of 1 Chronicles: "They have to be present every morning to give thanks and praise to Yahweh, and also in the evening" (23:30). The Talmud determined that the prayer ritual had replaced the offering of sacrifices morning and afternoon in the Temple, when the Temple still existed (Leviticus 20:26). That was the basis for setting the number of daily prayers, the prayer at nightfall having originally been supernumerary.[2] Ideally, the morning prayer is performed at sunrise or, at the latest, during the first third of the day; afternoon prayer is performed between noon and sunset, evening prayer at nightfall, and definitely before midnight. On Shabbat and on holy days, since they were the occasion for a supplementary sacrifice at the Temple, a fourth prayer, called *mussaf* (addition), was added after the morning prayer. Yom Kippur, which is devoted entirely to prayer, includes a fifth ceremony at the end, called *ne'ila*, "closing."

It was under the leadership of Esdras and the Anshei Knesset HaGedolah, "Men of the Great Assembly"—the rabbinical college of the Achaemenid period—that, according to tradition, the ritual of prayer in its current form was instituted. The heart of the liturgy was composed of prayer in the strict sense (*'amida* or *shemoneh 'esreh*, made up of eighteen paeans and requests addressed to God), preceded by the profession of faith in divine unity, the Shema Yisrael (Hear, O Israel), composed of three biblical passages (Deuteronomy 6:4–9 and 11:13–21, and Numbers 15:37–41). Between late antiquity and the early Middle Ages, various paeans, series of biblical psalms, confessions, and recitations of biblical and rabbinical texts were added to that corpus. On holy days, the ceremony was further supplemented by liturgical poems called *piyyutim*, composed by authors from medieval Andalusia, such as Solomon ibn Gabirol, Yehuda Halevi, Abraham, and Moses ben Ezra.[3]

❯ See article by Masha Itzhaki, pp. 943–951.

Prayer of *Tashlich*, in which one "casts off" one's sins at the end of Rosh Hashanah, the Jewish New Year. Photograph by P. Deliss, September 2007. Netanya, Israel.

Prayer, an essential rite of Islam

Prayer occupies a central place in Islam as well. It can even be said that this first ritual commanded by God is the pillar of the Muslim religion. We read, therefore, in the collections of hadith: "The messenger of God said: the first thing for which the servant must account on Resurrection Day is prayer. If it is valid, all the rest of his actions are also valid; if not, the rest of his actions are invalid as well."[4] And: "The messenger of God said: the first obligation given to my nation by God are the five prayers. He also said: prayer is the key to Paradise. Asked which is the best action, he replied: prayer, said at the appointed time. And also: he who deliberately neglects prayer will lose the Prophet's protection."[5] That last precision is interpreted strictly by the Hanbalite school to mean that anyone who neglects prayer is not only a sinner but loses his status as a Muslim.

The commandment of prayer is issued in the sura "Abraham": "Tell My servants, those who are true believers, to be steadfast in prayer and to give alms in private and in public, before that day arrives when all trading shall cease and friendships be no more" (14:31).[6] And in "Ta' Ha'": "I am God. There is no god but Me. Serve Me, and recite your prayers in My remembrance" (20:14). Also, in the same sura:

715

"Enjoin prayer on your people and be diligent in its observance. We demand of you no provision: We shall Ourself provide for you" (20:132). In "Pilgrimage" we read: "He will assuredly help those who, once made masters in the land, will attend to their prayers and render the alms levy, enjoin justice and forbid evil" (22:41). And finally, in "Luqman": "My son, be steadfast in prayer, enjoin justice, and forbid evil. Endure with fortitude whatever befalls you. That is a duty incumbent on all" (31:17).

Muslim prayer consists of an alternation between formulations glorifying God, especially readings from "The Exordium," or "Al-Fatihah" (the first sura in the Qur'an), at the beginning of each phase of prayer,[7] and the recitation of other suras. The choice of texts is freer than it is in Judaism. During silent prayer, the faithful recite "Al-Fatihah" behind the imam; when the prayer is said out loud, it is preferable that only the imam be audible.[8]

Before the Night Journey, Muslims prayed only twice a day, at dawn and at day's end, before sunset. This can be deduced from the sura "Qaf": "Bear then with what they say. Give glory to your Lord before sunrise and before sunset" (50:39). A famous tradition, reported under the name of Anas, recounts that, when the Prophet made the Night Journey:

I was prescribed fifty [daily] prayers. I descended until I met Moses, who asked me: "What did you do?" I said: "Fifty prayers were prescribed me." He told me: "I know the people better than you do, since I had the greatest difficulty leading the children of Israel to obedience. Your disciples cannot bear such an obligation. Therefore, return to your Lord and ask him [to reduce the number of daily prayers]." I returned and asked Allah [to reduce their number] and he reduced it to forty. I descended again and had a similar discussion [with Moses], then returned to Allah, to ask him to reduce it, and he reduced it to thirty, then twenty, then ten. I went back to Moses, who repeated his advice to me. Finally, Allah reduced the number to five daily prayers. When I again met Moses, he asked me: "What did you do?" I said: "Allah reduced the number to only five." He repeated his advice to me [to negotiate further], but I told him that I was submitting [to the definitive command of Allah].

> *Judaism and Islam accord great importance to the gestures and attitudes of prayer.*

Anas concludes his narrative by saying that "the Messenger of Allah heard Allah tell him: 'I have decreed my obligation and have relieved the burden of my servants: I will reward every good action as if it were worth ten.'"[9]

Whereas rabbinical Judaism set aside three moments of the day for prayer, Islam set aside five: dawn prayer, between the moment the eastern horizon turns bright and the moment immediately preceding the sunrise; midday prayer, between the moment the sun begins to decline and the moment when every object projects a shadow equal to itself; late afternoon prayer, between the moment when the shadows are equal and at least half an hour before sunset; dusk prayer, between the moment following sunset and the end of twilight; and night prayer, between the end of twilight and the moment preceding dawn.

Ritual aspects of prayer

Judaism and Islam accord great importance to the gestures and attitudes of prayer. The Muslim ritual places a good deal of emphasis on preliminary ritual purification. For every adult, the state of ritual purity is an essential condition for the validity of the prayer at the moment prescribed for it.[10] All ablutions are performed with water fallen from the sky or coming from a spring, with seawater, or with the water of a river or a well or a pond. Visible purity pertains to the body, to

Ritual prayer facing the direction of Mecca, in a mosque in the province of Balkh, in the north of Afghanistan. Photograph by R. and S. Michaud.

the place of prayer, and to clothing. There are two sorts of purity: that which comes from having been cleansed of bodily pollution, through the act of washing or rubbing oneself with sand, or by simple ablutions; and that which comes from having been purified of external pollution, such as menstrual blood, the blood of childbirth, urine, dog drool, pork meat, or bone, hair, or excrement from the same animal. All these can be washed away with water.

The state of ritual purity is an obligation decreed both in the Qur'an and by tradition and consensus. We read in the sura "The Table": "If you are polluted, cleanse yourselves" (5:6). The ulema used that verse as support for the view that ablutions must be performed before every prayer. But there is a difference of opinion about when that obligation was decreed. Some say it was a custom predating Islam, and that the custom became a ritual obligation. Others, the majority, maintain that it had always been an obligation.[11] The verse cited, which requires anyone who is polluted to wash, clearly indicates what sort of ablutions must be performed before prayer, and in what order: the face, both hands to the elbows, the top of the head, and both feet to the heels.

In Judaism, two orders of purification rites are to be distinguished. Ritual purity in the strict sense occupied an absolutely central place in ancient Judaism during the era of the Temple. It is the object of complex and abundant prescriptions in the Torah, regarding contact with a human or animal corpse, skin diseases such as leprosy (*tsara'at*), and genital fluids (*ziva*), menses, or seminal emissions. Purification in a *mikveh*, that is, a spring, lake, river, or basin of rainwater, is the central element of this ritual, to which others were added, such as anointing the hands, feet, and ears with oil, or even, when an impurity is contracted through contact with a human corpse, sprinkling what is called "lustral" water, that is, water into which the ashes of a perfectly red heifer have been mixed (Numbers 19). It is this prescription that gave its title to the longest sura in the Qur'an, "The Cow" (2:67–73). Since such ritual purity in the biblical sense was intimately connected to the Temple (in strict terms, it was required only before entering the Temple enclosure or performing sacrifices), it fell into disuse with the destruction of the Temple, and, especially, when the ashes of a red heifer ceased to be available, making any true purification impossible. Only two rituals endured, both involving immersion in a *mikveh*. The first concerns a woman whose menstrual period has just ended or who has just given birth: she must soak in a *mikveh* before resuming conjugal relations. This impurity, however, is confined to the sphere of the married couple and, in its current practice, does not affect the food the woman prepares, for example. Nor does it prevent her from praying. The second concerns a man who has had a seminal emission, whether intentionally or not. According to a rabbinical decree instituted by Esdras,[12] such a man has the obligation to immerse himself in a *mikveh* before studying the Torah or praying. Although the majority of those who have made rulings agree that this edict, having never been followed by the masses, is no longer obligatory,[13] this is still a commendable practice. In some communities, especially among the Hassidim, it is the custom for men to immerse themselves in a *mikveh* every morning in preparation for prayer, thereby keeping the neighbors from surmising whether they had a seminal emission during the night.

Even in the absence of observable impurity, there are purification rituals preliminary to worship and prayer,[14] which originated as part of the Temple ritual (ablutions of the hands and feet by the *kohanim*).[15] At present, they can also be found in ablutions of the hands upon rising in the morning, after the satisfaction of biological needs, before eating bread, and, in theory, before prayer, though that is seldom practiced in many communities. The Karaites wash their hands and feet in imitation of biblical ablutions but also under the influence of the Islamic environment.[16]

For prayer in the narrow sense, Jews and Muslims agree on the importance of intention: the person praying must intend to obey the commandment of prayer. He must not pray mechanically but must think about what he is saying. Judaism and Islam both prescribe standing prayer, as well as precise moments for bowing during the prayer. Although ancient Judaism had a great variety of prostrations, post-Talmudic Judaism has lost the habit of prostration with face to the ground, except in symbolic form (the face is pressed into the hollow of the arm during supplications after the main phase of prayer). By contrast, prostrations are a fundamental element of Muslim prayer. Finally, Jews and Muslims conclude the prayer by taking their leave, bowing to one side, and then the other. Jews say: "May he who makes peace on high [bowing to the left] / make peace among us [bowing to the right] and among all the children of Israel—Amen [bowing straight ahead]." Similarly, Muslims follow the example of the Prophet, based on the testimony of Waʾil ibn Hajar: "I prayed with the Messenger of God. At the end of the prayer, he said, turning to his right: peace be upon you, and the mercy of God and his blessings! He said the same thing in then turning to the left."[17]

---

1. Eliyahu Bashiasti (a standard Karaite reference), *Sefer ha-Mitsvot ha-nikraʾ Aderet Eliyau* (Odessa: Y. Beim, 1870), 57–58.

2. Aaron Ben Eliyahu (another standard Karaite reference), *Sefer Mitsvot gadol ha-nikraʾ Gan ʿEden* (Yevpatoria, Ukraine: Gozlov, 1864), 64; Maimonides, *Mishneh Torah, sefer Ahava, hilkhot Tefila,* 1.8.

3. Hasan Zaza, *Jewish Religious Thought: Emergence and Doctrines* (in Arabic) (Cairo: Library of Said Rafat, 1975), 172–73.

4. As reported by al-Tabarani in al-Saʾid Sabiq, *Fiqh al-shana* (Cairo: Darr al-Kitab al-islami / Dar al-hadith, n.d.), 1:78.

5. Al-Ghazali, *Revival of the Religious Sciences,* part 1 (Cairo: Dar al-Fikr al-ʿArabi, n.d.), 132 (in Arabic).

6. [Passages from the Qurʾan are taken from *The Koran,* trans. N. W. Dawood (New York: Penguin, 1995)—JMT].

7. Al-Nawawi, commentary on the *Sahih Muslim* (Beirut: Dar al-kutub al-ʿilmiyyah, n.d.), part 4, 100.

8. Ibid., part 1, 115.

9. *Sahih Bukhari,* 4.54.429.

10. Sabiq, *Fiqh al-shana,* 36.

11. Al-Nawawi, commentary on the *Sahih Muslim,* part 4, 100.

12. Cf. Talmud of Babylon, *Berakhot* 22a.

13. Cf. Maimonides, *Mishneh Torah, sefer Ahava, hilkhot Tefila,* 4.4; Joseph Caro, *Shulhan ʿArukh, Orah Hayyim,* 88.

14. Cf. esp. Mishnah Hagigah, 2:5–7.

15. Cf. Exodus 30:18–19.

16. Bashiasti, *Sefer ha-Mitsvot,* 58; Ben Eliyahu, *Sefer Mitsvot,* 70; and Abraham Korman, *Jewish Sects and Currents Reflected over the Centuries* (Tel Aviv: Sifriyati, 1966), 241 (in Hebrew).

17. Sabiq, *Fiqh al-shana,* part 1, 119.

Shabbat and Friday in Judaism and Islam
Mohamed Hawary

Both Islam and Judaism established a time of weekly rest for their faithful: for the Muslims, it is Friday; for the Jews, Shabbat, which also includes part of Friday, beginning after sunset and lasting until the next day when the stars come out. That proximity of the periods of rest is undoubtedly part of a more general kinship between the two religions and, to a lesser extent, between them and the other form of monotheism, Christianity, which chose Sunday as its day of rest. Beyond the similarities in their weekly calendars, however, these two religions of the Law have different emphases. For Judaism, the day of rest is a sanctified moment in remembrance of Genesis; for Islam, it is a time to gather together.

Mohamed Hawary

A professor of Jewish religious thought and comparative religion in the department of Hebrew studies at Ain Shams University in Cairo, Mohamed Hawary has published "Language and Identity: Arabic and Hebrew as a Model," in *Culture of Communication in the Era of Globalization: An Arab Vision* (Faculty of Arts, Ain Shams University, 2007); and *Sabbath and Friday in Judaism and Islam, Comparative Religions* (Cairo, 1988) (both in Arabic).

Shabbat in Judaism

Shabbat, which designates the weekly day of rest, is the principal holy day of Judaism. As expressed in the words recited to welcome and sanctify it on Friday evening, Shabbat is "in memory of creation because it is the first day of our holy assemblies, in memory of the exodus from Egypt."[1] Its origin can be found in Genesis 2:1–3: "Thus heaven and earth were completed with all their array. On the seventh day God had completed the work he had been doing. He rested on the seventh day after all the work he had been doing. God blessed the seventh day and made it holy, because on that day he rested [*Shabbat*] after all his work of creating" (New Jerusalem Bible). The unique status of Shabbat is dictated by the fourth of the Ten Commandments pronounced at the Revelation on Sinai: "Remember the Sabbath day and keep it holy. For six days you shall labor and do all your work, but the seventh day is a Sabbath for Yahweh your God. You shall do no work that day, neither you nor your son nor your daughter nor your servants, men or women, nor your animals nor the alien living with you. For in six days Yahweh made the heavens, earth and sea and all that these contain, but on the seventh day he rested; that is why Yahweh has blessed the Sabbath day and made it sacred" (Exodus 20:8–11).

The "rest" prescribed for Shabbat is defined primarily by a series of prohibitions against certain types of labor, "labor" being understood not as effort but in terms of its effect, the transformation of nature. Of these labors, one stands out: the transportation of objects in public. The various groups and sects that compose Judaism have differed on the modalities for observing Shabbat prohibitions. The strictest were the Ananites, the disciples of Anan ben David, whom the Karaites would later embrace as one of their precursors. Anan proved very rigorous in his interpretation of the divine commandment: he prohibits the taking of remedies, the performance of the rite of circumcision—which is deferred until sunset—and even the act of leaving the house in countries where the Jews live among strangers. It is also forbidden to eat hot food and to light candles, even if a non-Jew performs that task.[2] The Rabbanites, by contrast, while maintaining the gravity of the prohibitions (which, for the most part, are not spelled out in the Torah) and even adding to them rabbinical decrees to ensure that they are observed, differ in that they allow hot food

to be prepared a day early and left on the fire until the arrival of Shabbat.[3] That is the origin of the practice of eating dishes Saturday at noon that have been simmering since the previous day. The Rabbanites were joined on that point by certain Karaite or proto-Karaite authors, such as Benjamin Nahawandi, who rely on a passage from the Torah: "On the sixth day, however, when they prepare what they have brought in, this must be twice as much as they collect on ordinary days" (Exodus 16:5). That preparation is a sign of respect for and sanctification of Shabbat. Some carefully distinguish between what is permitted upon the arrival of Shabbat and what is not.[4]

The Rabbanites and the Karaites differ, however, on the atmosphere to be cultivated on Shabbat.

Among the Rabbanites, the day is not only free from worldly concerns but is also a joyful occasion, in keeping with the verse from Isaiah 58:13–14: "If you refrain from breaking the Sabbath, from concerning yourself with your own affairs on my holy day, if you call the Sabbath 'Pleasure,' and the day sacred to Yahweh 'Honorable,' if you honor

Jewish women in Jerusalem welcome Shabbat by saying a blessing over candles. Photograph by Z. Radovan, Jerusalem.

it by abstaining from travel, from pursuing your own concerns and from too much talk, then you will find true happiness in Yahweh, and I shall lead you in triumph over the heights of the land."[5] For that reason, conjugal relations on Shabbat are encouraged.[6] By contrast, the Karaites, placing the emphasis on the holiness of the day, prohibit such relations: for them, men must remain in a state of purity, in particular by abstaining from contact with women.[7]

Although group prayer requires that the men go to synagogue in the morning and in the late afternoon or evening even during the week (afternoon and evening prayers are often combined for the sake of convenience), attendance at synagogue takes on greater importance on Shabbat. The ceremony for each prayer is longer, and in both morning and afternoon there is the formal reading of a weekly pericope from the Pentateuch. Various parts of the service are also chanted; in certain communities, especially in Syria, every Shabbat during the year has its own *maqām* (melodic mode). It is also customary for the community's rabbi to deliver a sermon related to the weekly reading. Because the halakha requires that three meals be consumed on that day, the light meal after the morning service (*kiddush*) and the third meal (*se'uda shelishit*), between afternoon prayer and that marking the end of Shabbat, are grand occasions for socializing within the community. But most of Shabbat is spent within the family, around plentiful meals, with various hors d'oeuvres (*kemia*), fish, meat platters, and dessert following one after another, all accompanied by wine, as befits a holiday feast. At present, the prohibition against lighting fires, which has been extended to include the use of electrical appliances (though the Rabbanites leave on the lights on Friday), contributes toward fostering an "unplugged" atmosphere, ideally devoted to rest and to study of the Torah.

Friday in Islam

Friday, which no doubt was originally called *jum'ah* in Arabic,[8] is known in the Hejaz as *jumu'ah* (from the root *j-m-'*, "to gather"), a term emphasizing that this is the day when people congregate. Among pre-Islamic Arabs, that day was called al-'*aruba*, which has been interpreted to mean "mercy."[9] Friday took its present name, tradition tells us, because the people of Quraysh gathered at the home of Qusay on that day.[10] Some say it was the Ansari, the Prophet's first supporters in Medina, who gave it that name, because they con-

> "*[Muhammad asked] to gather together their women and their sons, as the Jews and the Zoroastrians did on Saturday, when the sun began to set on Friday.*"

gregated on Friday to pray.[11] Ibn Hazm sums up the debate as follows: it is a word of clearly Islamic origin, and it replaced '*aruba*, which was common before Islam.[12] A tradition reported under the name of Ibn Sirin[13] explains that "the people of Medina celebrated Friday before the Prophet arrived in their city, even before the 'Friday' sura came down (sura 62). It was they who had given it the name *al-jumʿa*. The Ansari said: The Jews have a special day, which returns every seven days, and at which time they congregate. The Christians have an equivalent day. Let us also consecrate one day of the week, on which we will gather and invoke the name of God. . . . Then they congregated at the home of Asad bin Zarara, who on that day prayed briefly with them—two phases

Women participate in a collective prayer to celebrate the thousandth anniversary of the arrival of Islam in the Urals and the area around the Volga, in 1989.

of prayer only—and delivered a homily. The day took the name of that gathering (*ijtamaʿu*). He sacrificed a kid, from which they ate twice, there being few of them. Then God sent down this verse: 'Believers, when you are summoned to Friday prayers hasten to the remembrance of God' (62:9)."[14]

Note that this first Friday prayer occurred in the Prophet's absence. Nevertheless, tradition judged it impossible that the Muslims who gave that day a special status could have done so without the Prophet's agreement. In fact, a hadith reported by Ibn ʿAbbas says: "The Prophet authorized the celebration of Friday before his *hijra*. He could not do so in Mecca, for reasons of discretion. He wrote a message to Musʿab ibn ʿUmair, asking him to gather together their women and their sons, as the Jews and the Zoroastrians did on Saturday, when the sun began to set on Friday. May they draw close to God through prayer."[15] The first Friday the Prophet celebrated with his companions was also his first day in Medina.

The Friday collective prayer is obligatory, according to the Qurʾan: "Believers, when you are summoned to Friday prayers hasten to the remembrance of God and cease your trading. That would be best for you, if you but knew it. Then, when the prayers are ended, disperse and go your ways in quest of God's bounty. Remember God always, so that you may prosper. Yet no sooner do they see some commerce or merriment afoot than they flock eagerly to it, leaving you standing all alone. Say: 'That which God has in store is far better than any merriment or any commerce. God is the Most Munificent Giver'" (62:9–11).

Apart from the Shafiʿi school, all the *madhhabs* believed that Friday prayer was an obligation falling not only to the community as a whole but also to each Muslim individually. The modalities of prayer in particular distinguish Friday noon prayers from those on the other days. Responsible adult Muslims living in the village or the city congregate only once a week in a precise place, in order to hear all the news related to their public lives, as well as the latest decrees and decisions concerning them, from the leader of the community (in the early days of Islam, it was the leader's representative, the caliph). During that weekly assembly, the Muslims listen to a homily intended to exhort or enjoin them, promises and warnings likely to prompt them to perform their duties with all the appropriate resolve in the following week. We may better understand the meaning of the celebration by examining the conditions for its validity: a precise place (the village), an assembly, a mosque (always the same one), a homily that expresses the ideas of the leader of the community, silence imposed while the homily is being delivered, and the fact that this homily is not of concern to servants, women, young boys, or the sick, all groups who are considered irresponsible and thus lacking the capacity to act in accordance with the speaker's directives.[16]

Two times are allotted for Friday prayer. The obligatory time is that of the call to prayer, after the imam has taken his seat at the pulpit (*minbar*). The other time is for those faithful who could not be present at the call to prayer, for all sorts of reasons:[17] rain, mud, fear, illness, or the need to stay with someone who is ill. Under these circumstances, a postponement of the moment of prayer until the end of the day on Friday may be authorized. Conversely, the presence at Friday prayer of someone who is ill, or who is a traveler, a servant, or a woman, though not obligatory, is still laudable.[18] As concerns the homily, it must come immediately before the prayer, in the early afternoon. As soon as the imam has taken his seat at the pulpit, individual prayer ends, with the exception of the first words of salutation; conversations may continue until the start of the homily. The imam begins by greeting the congregation while facing them directly, turning neither to the right nor to the left. He grasps a sword handle or the elbow rest of the pulpit. He does not wave his hands about and, to avoid doing so, may put one hand on top of the other.[19] He begins to preach by praising God and his Prophet, and continues, his voice gradually rising, by invoking the commandments and prohibitions, exhortations and warnings, promises and cautions. Then, after briefly sitting down, he rises again and resumes the sermon to its end. Then he descends from the pulpit, and the muezzin issues the call to prayer. The imam leads the abridged prayer, which has only two phases, one of the characteristics of Friday prayer.

---

1. [Translation in "Shabbat Evening Home Ritual," http://www.jewfaq.org/prayer/shabbat.htm—JMT].

2. Tsvi Graetz, *Divrei Yemei Israel*, trans. A. Kamenetzky (Warsaw, 1930), 3:207.

3. Ya'qub al-Qirqisani, *Kitab al-anwar wa-l-Maraqib* [*Book of Lights and Watchtowers*] (Karaite legal code), ed. Leon Nemoy (New York: Alexander Kuhut Memorial Foundation, 1942), 1:18. Cf. Mordekhai Yaffe, *Levush Malkhut*, part 2, *Levush ha-Hur* (Berdychev, Ukraine; reissued in Israel, 1968), 67b–68a.

4. Al-Qirqisani, *Kitab al-anwar wa-l-Maraqib*, 3:508–10; Yaffe, *Levush Malkhut*, 67a–b.

5. [Translation modified to conform to the French.—JMT].

6. Leon Nemoy, "Ibn Kammunah's Treatise on the Differences between the Rabbanites and the Karaites," *Jewish Quarterly Review* 63, no. 2 (October 1972): 129; Mohammed Bahr Abdelmajid, *Judaism* (Cairo, 1975), 149 (in Arabic).

7. Al-Qirqisani, *Kitab al-anwar wa-l-Maraqib*, 3:511–13; Mohamed Hawary, *Shabbat and Friday in Judaism and Islam* (Cairo, 1988), 91, 97–98 (in Arabic). See also Tobia Simha Levi Popovic, *Rosh Pina* [*The Cornerstone*]: *The Origin of the Karaites* (Cairo, 1947), 45–46 (in Arabic; 19–20 of the Hebrew version); Deborah HaCohen and R. Menahem HaCohen, eds., *Hagim u-mo'adim: Shabbat, rosh hodesh* [*Feasts and Celebrations, Shabbat, Neomenia*], ed. Keter Yerushalayim (Jerusalem, 1979), 16–17.

8. Al-Suhayli (Abu al-Qasim 'Abd al-Rahman b. Abd Allah b. Ahmed b. Abil-Hassan al-Khatha'mi), *Commentary on the Life of the Prophet by Ibn Hisham—presented by Taha Abderra'uf Saad* (Beirut, n.d.), part 2, 198 (in Arabic).

9. Al-Asqalani (Abul-Fadl Shihabeddin Ahmad b. 'Ali b. Mohammed b. Hajar), *Explanatory Commentary on Bukhari*, part 2, 353 (in Arabic); Al-Nawawi, *Commentary on Sahih Muslim* (Beirut: Dar al-Fikr, 1981), part 6, 3:130 (in Arabic); Al-Qastillani (Abul-Abbas Shihabeddin Ahmad b. Mohammed), *Commentary on "Sahih" by Bukhari, with Marginal Commentary on "Sahih Muslim" by Al-Nawawi* (Beirut, 1984), 2:156 (in Arabic); Al Mubarakfuri (Imam al-Hafiz Abul-'Ali Mohammed Abderrahman b. Abderrahim), *Commentary on Al-Tirmidhi*, revised by 'Abdelwahab 'Abdellatif, 3rd ed. (Beirut, 1979), part 2, 613 (in Arabic); Al-Qurtubi (Abu 'Abdullah Muhammad ibn Ahmad Ansari), *The Complete Qur'an* (Beirut, 1952), chap. 18, 97–98 (in Arabic); al-Suhayli, *Commentary on the Life of the Prophet*, 196.

10. Al-Kandahlawi (Mohammed Zakaria), *Introduction to Imam Malik,* 3rd ed. (Beirut, 1980), part 2, 200 (in Arabic).

11. Ibid., al-Qurtubi, *The Complete Qur'an*, chap. 18, 97; Al-Asqalani, *Explanatory Commentary on Bukhari*, 353.

12. Al-Asqalani, *Explanatory Commentary on Bukhari*, 353; Al-Kandahlawi, *Introduction to Imam Malik*, 200.

13. See Al-Qurtubi, *The Complete Qur'an*, chap. 18, 98; Al-Suhayli, *Commentary on the Life of the Prophet by Ibn Hisham*, 197; Al-Qastillani, *Commentary on "Sahih" by Bukhari*, 156.

14. [Passages from the Qur'an are taken from *The Koran*, trans. N. W. Dawood (New York: Penguin, 1995)—JMT].

15. Al-Suhayli, *Commentary on the Life of the Prophet by Ibn Hisham*, 197.

16. Al-Jazairi (Abu Bakr Jabir), *The Muslim's Method*, 5th ed. (Jeddah, Saudi Arabia, 1984), 324 (in Arabic).

17. Al-Baji, *Commentary on the* Mawta' *(Introduction) of Imam Malik*, 3rd ed. (Beirut, 1983), part 1, 1:194–95 (in Arabic).

18. Al-Ghazali, *The Revival of the Religious Sciences* (Beirut, 1980), 132 (in Arabic).

19. Al-Jazairi, *The Muslim's Method*, 329.

Jewish and Muslim Charity in the Middle Ages: A Comparative Approach
Yaacov Lev

Christianity, Judaism, and Islam consider the three "theological virtues" of faith, hope, and charity to be the foundational stones of their value systems. Contrary to what some may think, charity is as essential to Jewish and Islamic life as it is to the Christian worldview. Between pure generosity and social redistribution, it deeply structures traditional societies by defining the respective roles of the rich and the poor, the use of money, and the legitimacy of the institutions that have taken up the task to collect and redistribute it.

Yaacov Lev

Yaacov Lev is professor of Middle Eastern studies at the University of Bar-Ilan. He is the author of *Saladin in Egypt* (Brill, 1999), *Charity, Endowments and Charitable Institutions in Medieval Islam* (University Press of Florida, 2005), and editor of *War and Society in the Eastern Mediterranean, 7th to 15th Centuries* (Brill, 1996).

A practice rooted in scriptures

The Jewish notion of charity is rooted in biblical teachings and conveyed by a variation of word pairs, such as "justice and righteousness" and "mercy and kindness." Both concepts are perceived as virtues and equated with a meritorious way of life.[1] In practical terms, the Bible singles out the poor, widows, orphans, and the stranger as deserving beneficiaries of charity and refers to four types of agricultural charity that involve, for example, crops left at the corners of the field, grain that falls during harvesting, and a tithe for the poor paid at the end of a three-year cycle. The Bible is also solicitous of the wage earner of any kind and his right to receive payment on time. The Talmudic discourse on charity (*tzedaka*) endows charity with redemptive powers and also deals with such issues as the definition of poverty, the order of priority in which charity should be dispensed, and the amount of charity to be given. In addition, much attention is devoted to the ethical question of how to ensure the dignity of those who receive charity. The Talmud also sets forth how charity should be administered: every town should have people who are responsible for charity (*gabba'ei tzedaka*), and the dispensation of charity should be carried out through the *tamhuy*, a daily distribution of bread for the wayfarer, and the *qubba*, a weekly distribution of bread or money to the local indigents. Talmudic concepts of charity and the practical arrangements for its distribution must be understood against the shifts that affected the Jewish life in the postbiblical period. Outside the land of Israel, in the Diaspora, the biblical agricultural charity ceased to apply as the Jewish communities became predominantly urban and oriented toward craft and commerce.

The Islamic notion of charity is embodied in the Qur'anic teachings and expressed by the terms *sadaqa* and *zakat*, which have a wide range of meanings and sometimes are used interchangeably. The Qur'an urges believers to pray and to give charity, which also signifies redemption and purification. Charity should go to the needy, referred to by the terms *fuqara* and *masakin*—wayfarers, debtors, captives—and for the purpose of God (Q. 9:60). The Qur'an also singles out orphans and kinsmen as deserving of support, and exhorts its readers to provide sustenance for the needy. A clear division between voluntary charity (*sadaqa*) and obligatory alms-tax (*zakat*), with rates and methods of payment delineated in the legal writings, evolved over time and was virtually crystallized in the writings of the great sage Ghazali (d. 1111). Irrespective of this long process, on the personal level, charity signified for medieval Muslims their quest to communicate with God, to implore him for deliverance, to thank him for success, and to expiate sins. This religious meaning of charity was understood by all, and its manifestations are attested to across the whole social spectrum from the powerful and rich to the common folks. Medieval people, for example, gave charity during illness, a notion expressed by the Arabic phrase "he was cured through charity" and the Hebrew maxim "charity delivers from death." Monotheistic charity, however, not only served to communicate with God but also enhanced the position of the donor in his or her society. This applied especially to the powerful: Muslim rulers and members of the ruling class, as well as Jewish communal leaders. Although the charity of this class always had political meaning, in medieval Islam, as well as in the world of Jewish communities, politics and religion were inseparable.[2]

> **Writing about the social function of charity in the context of the Jewish communities of medieval Islam, Mark R. Cohen has stated that 'Charity acted as one of the major agglutinates of Jewish associational life.'**

Ritual, ethical, and social functions of charity

The ethical dimension of the monotheistic charity as illuminated by the practice of Jews, Christians, and Muslims shares many similarities. In Judaism and Islam, for example, secret giving is perceived as a higher moral deed, and both religions emphasize the meritorious value of charity given to neighbors and relatives, a concept embodied by such sayings as "charity begins at home" and "the poor of your city take precedent." In Islam, giving on Ramadan and in the holy cities of Mecca, Medina, and Jerusalem exceeds giving on other occasions or in other places. One can argue that Jerusalem became the focal point of monotheistic charity as Muslims,

Jews, and Christians showered extensive charity on their institutions and coreligionists in the city. These similarities are not entirely surprising. Although Islam was born in Arabia, it crystallized as a religion and civilization in the Middle East in constant interaction with Judaism and Christianity, as well as Greek and Persian lore. Writing about the social function of charity in the context of the Jewish communities of medieval Islam, Mark R. Cohen has stated that "Charity acted as one of the major agglutinates of Jewish associational life."[3] This centrality is powerfully attested to in writings of Maimonides (1138–1204), who was the first to codify the biblical and postbiblical laws on charity into a legal chapter entitled "Hilkhot Mattenot ʿAniyyim" (laws of giving to the poor) included in the *Mishneh Torah*. The relevant passage of the *Mishneh Torah*, in Joel L. Kraemer's translation, runs as follows: "The throne of Israel cannot be established, nor true faith made to stand up, except through charity, nor will Israel be redeemed, except through the practice of charity . . . He who has compassion upon others, others will have compassion upon him."[4] Maimonides's writings on charity reflect both the local practices of the

❯ See article by Marina Rustow, pp. 75–98.

Miniature of the great Iranian painter Behzad illustrating the practice of almsgiving, fifteenth century. Cairo, National Library.

Jewish community of Fustat, as borne out by the Geniza documents, and Islamic influence, especially in the discourse of poverty and the division of the poor into two categories: the conjectural poor, or shamefaced poor, and the structural poor.[5]

The documents of the Cairo Geniza studied by S. D. Goitein and Mark Cohen have thrown light on a wide range of charitable services provided by the Jewish community of Fustat (eleventh to thirteenth centuries), which included the distribution of bread, wheat, and clothing. The community also helped the needy with the poll tax (it paid the poll tax for its officials), covered the costs of education for poor and orphan boys, assisted travelers, and paid for the burial of indigents.[6] In addition, the community was actively involved with the ransom of captives captured by pirates or the Franks during the wars of the Crusades. This activity greatly strained the limited resources of the communities of Fustat and Qayrawan, which, after the ransom of the captives, bore additional expenses for providing them with the necessities of life.[7] The ransoming of captives was elevated by Maimonides to the status of the most meritorious religious duty, which even takes precedence over providing the poor with food and clothing.

There is a great similarity between the practical aspects of Jewish and Muslim charity, and in both civilizations the focus was on providing the poor with food, drinking water, and clothing.

Medieval Muslims and Jews assisted travelers and pilgrims, and in both societies many communal services were maintained through the pious endowment system (Arabic: *waqf/awqaf, hubs/ahbas*; Hebrew: *qodesh/hekdesh*). In Muslim societies the pious endowment system proliferated and became the main tool for supporting mosques, learning, mystics, urban infrastructure, and warriors of the holy war.[8]

The *waqf* institution

The Islamic pious endowment system is not rooted in the Qurʾanic teaching, and the extent to which it was a "borrowed" or an "original" institution is much debated. However, as Peter C. Hennigan has noted, institutional correlation does not necessarily imply borrowing.[9] The question of the origin of the *waqf* becomes less significant when the religious role and the social functions of this institution in medieval and premodern Islam are considered. *Waqf* is charity par excellence, and this is explicitly stated in the endowment documents, which also express the yearning of the founder for proximity to God and rewards in the afterlife. There were two types of *waqfs*: a *waqf* created for family members and a public *waqf*. Both types were perceived as acts of piety and charity, and the creation of a family *waqf* reflected the prevailing attitude that "charity begins at home."[10] Family *waqfs* were quite frequently used to circumvent the Muslim inheritance laws, and, therefore, the jurists set limits on the amount of property that was allowed to be converted into a *waqf*, and the same limitations applied to charitable legacies.

The creation of a *waqf* required ownership of urban or rural property, and the patrons of *waqf* foundations necessarily were people of considerable means. The establishment of *waqf*-supported institutions such as Qurʾanic schools for ten orphaned and poor boys, or a drinking fountain, was not prohibitively expensive and was open to patronage of the middle or upper-middle class. A Qurʾanic school (*kuttab/maktab*) reflected the religious-cultural significance of learning, a value shared by both Judaism and Islam, frequently described as text-oriented, bookish civilizations, as well as the religious injunction to take care of orphans. On the practical level, the impact of a Qurʾanic school was immense. Given the widespread poverty typical of medieval towns and the society at large, a school that offered standard education, and in many cases also a daily ration of bread and two sets of clothes per year, made a great difference to the recipients of these benefits. It was perhaps one of the cheapest *waqf*-supported charities, yet it was effective. The wish to secure an education for orphans was often combined with the will to provide drinking water for the urban population. These two charitable drives created a unique Middle Eastern institution: a drinking fountain and a Qur'anic school for orphans (*sabil kuttab/maktab*).[11]

Other *waqfs* dedicated for large mosques, law colleges, and hospitals required immense wealth, and patronage of these institutions was limited to caliphs and sultans, women of their households, and other high-ranking people of the ruling circles, such as emirs, viziers, and top administrators. Other less expensive *waqfs* were set up for a diversified range of purposes, such as distribution of food to the poor, providing for widows and female mystics, and the proper burial of indigents. Some of the female royal foundations offered housing and food to the aging eunuchs who had served those patronesses.[12]

There were also Jewish and Christian pious endowments permitted by Islamic law. Non-Muslim *waqfs* served the same range of social functions as their Muslim counterparts: Jewish pious endowments, for example, supported the local poor and the poor of Jerusalem. Other donations were made for the support of the yeshivas of Iraq and Jerusalem. The history of the Fustat Jewish community's pious endowment has been studied by S. D. Goitein and Moshe Gil, and by the 1180s this endowment included houses, shops, and commercial buildings. Few of these endowments were of the family type, whose first beneficiaries were the descendants of the founder. The typical ends served by these pious endowments included the support of communal officials, scholars, and teachers, the sick, indigent foreign Jews, and extensive distribution of bread. According to Gil's calculations, however, only 10 percent of the revenues of the Jewish pious endowment of the Fustat community benefited the poor directly. The rest went to support learning and education, in the broadest sense of these terms, and community officials.[13]

> *There were Jewish and Christian pious endowments permitted by Islamic law that served the same range of social function as their Muslim counterparts.*

Although the pious endowment of the Jewish community of Fustat is the best-known one, it was by no means unique. The pious endowments of the late medieval Karaite community of Cairo, for example, were dedicated to the poor Karaites of Fustat and Cairo, and occasionally for the Karaites and Jews in general, meaning both the Jewish Karaite and rabbinic communities. In the wider Mediterranean context, the pious endowment of the Jewish community of Qayrawan in Tunisia was used to support learning and the poor, and bequests for the *hekdesh* became popular with the Jews of thirteenth-century Christian Spain.[14]

Conclusion

The notion of salvation has a central role in monotheism, and charity was a way of achieving this goal. The quest for nearness to God and salvation symbolized the deepest meaning of medieval sacred charity. It can be said that medieval Judaism and Islam were "charitable societies," but this does not mean "welfare societies." In both civilizations the orientation of charity was focused on the scholar and the world of learning, not on the poor. Monotheistic medieval charity was an inadequate tool for dealing with welfare problems, but was better suited to providing religious services and learning.

---

1. Moshe Weinfeld, *Social Justice in Ancient Israel and in the Ancient Near East* (Jerusalem: Hebrew University Magnes Press, 1995).

2. For Jewish communal leaders and their instrumental use of charity, see Miriam Frenkel, *"The Compassionate and Benevolent": The Leading Elite in the Jewish Community of Alexandria in the Middle Ages* (in Hebrew; Jerusalem: Ben-Zvi Institute, 2006), 222–27. For the use of charity by private people—men and women—to enhance their standing within their community, see Miriam Frenkel, "Charity in Jewish Society of the Medieval Mediterranean World," in *Charity and Giving in Monotheistic Religions*, ed. Miriam Frenkel and Yaacov Lev (Berlin: Walter de Gruyter, 2009), 343–64.

3. Mark R. Cohen, *Poverty and Charity in the Jewish Community of Medieval Egypt* (Princeton, NJ: Princeton University Press, 2005), 252.

4. Joel L. Kraemer, *Maimonides: The Life and World of One of Civilization's Greatest Minds* (New York: Doubleday, 2008), 347.

5. Mark R. Cohen, "Maimonides and Charity in the Light of the Geniza Documents," *Studia Judaica* 30 (2005): 65–81; Kraemer, *Maimonides*, 269–73.

6. S. D. Goitein, *A Mediterranean Society* (Berkeley: University of California Press, 1971), 2:121–38; Mark R. Cohen, *The Voice of the Poor in the Middle Ages* (Princeton, NJ: Princeton University Press, 2005), 32–95.

7. For Qayrawan, see Menahem Ben-Sasson, *The Emergence of the Local Jewish Community in the Muslim World: Qayrawan, 800–1057* (in Hebrew; Jerusalem: Hebrew University Magnes Press, 1996), 181–83.

8. For *waqf* and its role in medieval Muslim societies, see, for example, Ana María Carballeira, "Pauvreté et fondations pieuses dans la Granade nasride: Aspects sociaux et juridiques," *Arabica* 52 (2005): 391–416; Alejandro García Sanjuán, "Les awqaf à Damas à la fin du XIIᵉ siècle à travers la relation de voyages d'Ibn Gubayr," *Bulletin d'Études Orientales* 56 (2004–5): 49–63.

9. See Peter C. Hennigan, *The Birth of a Legal Institution: The Formation of the Waqf in Third-Century A.H. Hanafi Legal Discourse* (Leiden: Brill, 2004), 50, 52, 61, 62, 67.

10. For a broader discussion, see Norman A. Stilman, "Waqf and the Ideology of Charity in Medieval Islam," in *Hunter of the East: Studies in Honor of Clifford Edmund Bosworth*, ed. Ian Richard Netton (Leiden: Brill, 2000), 357–75.

11. For this institution in Mamluk and Ottoman Cairo, see André Raymond, "Les fontaines publiques (Sabil) du Caire à l'époque Ottomane (1517–1798)," *Annales Islamologique* 15 (1979): 235–86.

12. Yaacov Lev, *Charity, Endowments, and Charitable Institutions in Medieval Islam* (Gainesville: University Press of Florida, 2005), 53–144.

13. See *Documents of the Jewish Pious Endowment from the Cairo Geniza* (Leiden: Brill, 1976), 117.

14. The Karaite pious endowment documents are from the years 1274, 1324, and 1513. See D. S. Richards, "Arabic Documents from the Karaite Community in Cairo," *Journal of the Economic and Social History of the Orient* 15 (1972): 110–11, 137, 138–39; Judah D. Galinsky, "Jewish Charitable Bequests and the Hekdesh Trust in Thirteenth-Century Spain," *Journal of Interdisciplinary History* 35 (2005): 423–40.

The Names of Jerusalem

A name expresses how an individual is situated within the chain of generations, by means of which a group defines itself. It is a vector of specification, identification, and unification, but also a marker of separation that establishes borders, limits, demarcations, and boundaries, and thus, as a result, can be the source of conflicts about legitimacy. The proper name, insofar as it is bound to a specific history, society, space, and temporality, assumes an obvious importance, especially for plural, complex, fragmented, and tattered identities like those of Jerusalem. The designation of that city varies depending on the place where one is situated, the culture from which one observes it, the religion to which one belongs, and the community from which one regards it. If, according to the adage, "the plurality of names proves the excellence of the one that bears them," then Jerusalem, given the multiplicity of its names, possesses a very particular historic weight, religious force, and symbolic charge for the peoples of the earth. Each religious tradition has provided Jerusalem with a plurality of names to make explicit its uniqueness and holiness. The great Arab historian of Jerusalem Mudjir al-Din al-ʿUlaymi (fifteenth century) recalls in his chronicle of the city the tradition of Fadaʾil, or Paeans to the Excellence of the Holy City, which bears witness to the centrality of Jerusalem. In the same way, each community—in a kind of war of names—lays claim to its own designations, which contradict, clash with, and enter into conflict with one another. Struggles between different sects, beliefs, and religious traditions have led to an escalation in the acts of naming. That act of producing one's own proper names, and as many names as possible, seems to confer might, power, and a new legitimacy with respect to the holy city.

In Hebrew, the sacred language of Judaism, the most common form is Yerushalayim or Ir ha-kodesh ("holy city" or "city of the sanctuary"). The Hebrew Bible alone contains more than 650 mentions of Jerusalem, testimony to the particular status of the city, its importance, and the vital issues associated with its history, its space, and its designation. The oldest mention of Jerusalem is found in the cuneiform tablets known as the Amarna letters (1369–1353 BCE), the diplomatic archives of correspondence between the Egyptian administration and its representatives in the land of Canaan. The name appears in Akkadian as urusalim and, in Assyrian, as ursalimmu (from ur, "city of . . ."). Note, too, the inscription from the archaeological site in the Judean Desert called Khirbet Beit Lei, or Khirbet Beit Lehi (1160 BCE): "Yhwh, God of the whole earth, the mountains of Judah belong to him, / to the God of Jerusalem."

The precise source of the name Yerushalayim is not known, but many explanations have been offered.

Some think that the name originated in the words Yeru (he founded) and Shalem, the name of the local God, the God of origins, who is said to have founded the city. In Genesis, during Abraham's time, Salem or Shalem (fullness) was the name or nickname for the city, whose ruler was then Melchizedek (literally, "righteous king," from Genesis 14:18: "Melchizedek king of Salem [Melekh shalem] brought bread and wine; he was a priest of God Most High" [New Jerusalem Bible]). The same diminutive form, Salem, appears in Psalm 76:1–2: "God is acknowledged in Judah, his name is great in Israel, his tent is pitched in Salem, his dwelling is in Zion."

Some also believed that the origin of the name was ir ha-shalom, "city of peace," which appears in Arabic as Dar al-salam (dwelling of peace). In

The western wall of the Temple and its surroundings by Samuel Schulman, 1895. Jerusalem, Museum of Israel.

documents of the Cairo Geniza, that name is evoked as *neve tsedek*, "home [or oasis] of saving justice" (from Jeremiah 31:23). Talmudic accounts say that the name was constructed from two words, *yara*, "he founded, built" and *shalem*, which produced the epithet "foundation of peace." Or that it came from *yire*, from *Adonaï-yir'eh* (Genesis 22:14): "God saw" or "God will see" (*Dominus videt* in Latin), the phrase spoken by Abraham after sacrificing a ram in place of his son Isaac, combined with the word *shalem*. Another midrashic source says that the word comes from *yerusha* (inheritance). Jerusalem is God's inheritance, *yerusha le-olam* (inheritance for eternity).

The Bible has multiple designations for the "holy city" or "city of holiness," including *Tsion* (fortress of David); *Ariel* (from Isaiah 29: "Woe, Ariel, Ariel, city where David encamped"), which may allude to *are'el* (the base of a sacrificial altar) or *ari'el* (lion of God); and *Moriah* (mountain of myrtle), the site of the sacrifice of Isaac, where the Temple would later be built, which becomes *Muriyyā or Murayyā* in Arabic. The name *Yebus*, or *Yabus* in Arabic, from the name of the Jebusite people, also appears. David conquered that Canaanite fortress, which became the capital where he would build the Temple. As a result, Jerusalem is also called *ir david* (the city of David) or *kyriat* (city of the great king), for which an equivalent in Greek exists: *polis megalo basileus* (Matthew 5:35).

From that litany of images, metaphors, and similes, let us recall, in Second Isaiah [Deutero-Isaiah] and Lamentations, the antithetical categories that attest to the ambivalence that marks Jerusalem as an intersection of stark oppositions: it is celestial and material, a city of holiness and of pollution, a city destined for unification and for fracture, a city of peace and a battlefield. Let us note, first, the series of laudatory names touting the exceptional holiness of Jerusalem, which is symbolized by gold, peace, and justice. The mystical texts insist on the femininity of Jerusalem, which is associated with the maiden, the fiancée, the beloved, and the wife: "My delight is in her," it is called in Isaiah (62:4). Based on a verse from Ezekiel (48:35), "Yahweh is there," the Talmud says *Adonaï shema*, "Her name [*shema* is feminine in Hebrew] is God."

But Jerusalem is also associated with evil, sin, and the fall. Many biblical books, haunted by the destruction of the Temple and the exile, associate the city with those who wander and go astray, with fractiousness and a penchant for evil (*Yetser hara*), conduct that unleashes divine wrath. As "the place which [Yahweh] will choose [or chose]" (*ha-makom asher yvh'ar hashem*, Deuteronomy 12:5), every transgression, every violation of the divine commandments, is perceived as a direct affront to the deity and a breach of the covenant between God and the children of Israel, the source of punishment and suffering. A good example of these antithetical lists is provided in the treatise *Avot de rabbi Nathan* (ARN, version B, chap. 39). That commentary lists "ten names of grace and ten names of disgrace": "In its praise, Jerusalem is called by ten names: town, city, faithful, wife, sought-after, my delight is in her, YHWH is there, justice, peace, and Jebus [Judges 19:10]. For its shame, Jerusalem is called by ten names: widow, prostitute, barren, recluse, exile, wanderer, abandoned, despised, afflicted, and storm-beaten." But of all these lists, no doubt the most imposing remains that of the biblical commentary *Midrash shir ha-shirim zuta*, which lists seventy names for Jerusalem, of which we note only the most remarkable: City of God (*Ir Elokim*); throne of God (*kisse Adonai*); city of holiness (*Ir ha-kodesh*);

paradise of God (*Gan eden Adonai*); garden of God (*Gan Adonai*); mountain of holiness (*Har ha-kodesh*); city of gathering (*Kiriat moëd*); city of Israel (*Ir Israël*); city of justice (*Ir ha-tsedek*); city of truth (*Ir ha-emeth*); joy of the whole earth (*Mesus kol ha-arets*); place of rest (*Menuha*); city of the tombs of the fathers (*Ir kivrot avot*); city of harmonious unity (*Ir hubra yahdav*); city of the dove (*Ir ha-yona*); city where David encamped (*Kiriat hanna David*); faithful city (*Kiria neemana*); joyful city (*kiria aliza*); beautiful landscape (*Yefé nof*); the densely populated (*Rabati am*); great among nations (*Rabati ba-goyim*); the princess of states (*sarti be-medinot*); gates of peoples (*delatot ha-amim*); peaceful residence (*Neve sha'anan*); the desired one (*Heftsiva*); the beloved (*Yedidut*); the sought-after (*derusha*); inheritance (*Yerushh, Nah'ala*); life (*Haïm*); bliss (*Gila*); eye of the world (*Eyn ha-olam*); light of the world (*Or h-aolam*); house of God (*Beth El*); city of gold (*Ir shel zahav*); paragon of beauty (*kelilat yofé*).

The names have always varied depending on the era, on who was occupying the city, and on who was in power. For example, after the destruction of the Second Temple, the Roman emperor Hadrian rebaptized Jerusalem "Aelia Capitolina," to mar its character as a holy city, and had a temple built to the glory of Jupiter. Every religious or cultural tradition bestowed a specific name on Jerusalem, derived from a common root. In biblical Greek and Latin, we find *Salem, Solyma, Hierousalēm,* and *Hierosolyma,* which means "holy city of peace"; in Syriac, *Ūrišlem*; in Armenian, *Erusalem*; in Latin, *Hierosolyma*; in Old French, *Hiérosolyme* or *Solyme*.

In Arabic, it is *al-Quds,* "the holy," or *al-Sharīf d'al-Quds,* "holy and noble place," from the Aramaic *kudsha,* as in *Karta d-kudsha* (in Hebrew, *Ir ha-kodesh,* from Isaiah 48:2), which means "holy city," "city of holiness," and also "city of the sanctuary."

There is also a poetic designation, *al-Balāt,* "the palace." Forms derived from Hebrew exist as well, such as *Ūrshalīm, Ūrshalaymi, Ūrushalīm,*

Islamic miniature representing the Dome of the Rock in Jerusalem, nineteenth century. Cairo, National Library.

or *Ūrushalaym*. In the early days of Islam, the full name of Jerusalem was *Iliya, bayt al-makdis*, "city of the temple," in reference to the Roman Aelia. It was also called, by analogy to the Qurʾanic form of the name of Elijah the Prophet (*Ilyas*), the "sanctuary of Elijah," or the "house of God," which corresponds to the Aramaic form *beth makdesha*, and also *bayt Al-Muqaddas* (Chamber of Holiness). There are a number of other epithets, all attesting to the prestige, ascendancy, and special status of Jerusalem. In the Qurʾan (10:93), it is called the "secure haven," which recalls the definition in Jeremiah 31:23, *neve tsedek har ha-kodesh* (home of saving justice [or haven, or oasis], holy mountain). In Arabic there is *salam* or *salim*, which is close to the Hebrew *shalem*, "city of the sanctuary" and "holy land," a designation shared by all three forms of monotheism.

In Islam, two aspects confer an undeniable centrality on Jerusalem: first, the mention in the Qurʾan of the Prophet Muhammad's vision or Night Journey to the "farther temple," the "heavenly Jerusalem," or the "Jerusalem on high." The first, earthly stage—the Night Journey, *al-Isra*—takes him from the sacred mosque of Mecca to the Bayt al-Maqdis (Jerusalem), where he descends from his mount to lead a prayer in the presence of all the prophets who have come to honor him (Abraham, Moses, and Jesus, among others): "Glory be to Him who made His servant go by night from the Sacred Temple to the farther Temple whose surroundings We have blessed, that We might show him some of Our signs. He alone hears all and observes all" (Qurʾan 17:1).[1] The second, heavenly stage— the Ascent, *miʿrāj*—transports him, by means of a precious and shining ladder, from Jerusalem to

735

the "carpet of intimacy." He passes through "seven heavens," then through the many successive spaces of seventy thousand veils, finally descending to the heaven of this world and returning to Mecca (Qur'an 53:1–18). Let us also mention the first *qibla* (kiblat or kiblet means "direction"), the orientation of prayer toward the East and toward Jerusalem, before prayers were directed toward the Kaaba, that is, toward the central sanctuary of Mecca. In mosques, this orientation is indicated by the *mihrab*, a niche often flanked by two columns supporting an arcature. According to the hadith that constitute the Sunnah, Muhammad, prophet of Islam, at first recommended directing prayers toward Jerusalem. That prescription was modified at the time of the hijra, when Mecca became the direction of prayer. A sura in the Qur'an confirms that obligation: "Turn your face towards the Holy Mosque; wherever you be, turn your faces towards it" (2:144). Note that the Karaite scholars (fourth to tenth centuries) adopted the Arabic appellation *Bayt ha-makdis* and named the temple enclosure *al-kuds*. ●

Director of research at the Centre National de la Recherche Scientifique (CNRS; National Centre for Scientific Research) at the École des Hautes Études en Sciences Sociales (EHESS; School for Advanced Studies in the Social Sciences) in Paris, Jean Baumgarten focuses his work on ancient Yiddish literature and the cultural history of the Ashkenazi world. He is the author of Naissance du hassidisme (2006) and of Le peuple des livres, les lectures populaires dans la société ashkénaze, XVI–XVIIIᵉ siècle (2010), both published by Albin Michel.

1. [Passages from the Qur'an are taken from *The Koran*, trans. N. W. Dawood (New York, Penguin: 1995), with modifications when necessary.—JMT]

Chapter IV

Philosophy, Science, and Intellectual Movements

Jewish and Muslim Philosophy: Similarities and Differences
Steven Harvey

Muslim and Jewish philosophers not only studied, interpreted, and commented upon the writings of Aristotle, but also played an important, indeed crucial, role in transferring his philosophy and science to the Christian West. Indeed, the emergence of Aristotle as the philosopher in thirteenth-century Scholastic philosophy is due in great measure to the Latin translations from Arabic of the writings of Avicenna, Averroes, Maimonides, and others. The Middle Ages was the golden age for both Muslim and Jewish philosophy. It was a period of significant contributions in science, as well as in the development of a rational explication of revealed religion. It was also the period in which Muslim and Jewish philosophers had the greatest impact on their own religion and on other cultures. Often these philosophers were the outstanding, best-known, and most interesting personalities of their time. They were not only philosophers and scientists but physicians, judges, poets, ministers, political advisors, and legal and religious authorities. This essay focuses on these important medieval Muslim and Jewish philosophers, their similarities, and their differences.

Steven Harvey

A professor in the Department of Philosophy at Bar-Ilan University in Israel, Steven Harvey is chair of the Jewish Philosophy Commission of the International Society for the Study of Medieval Philosophy (SIEPM). He has published *Falaquera's "Epistle of the Debate": An Introduction to Jewish Philosophy* (Harvard University Press, 1987) and edited *The Medieval Hebrew Encyclopedias of Science and Philosophy* (Kluwer Academic, 2000) and *Anthology of Writings of Avicenna* (2009, in Hebrew).

The first philosophers

The beginnings of Islamic philosophy and Jewish philosophy in the medieval world may be traced to the same century and the same country. This is no coincidence, for the literary language of the Jews of the East, just like that of their Muslim neighbors, was Arabic. Thus Muslims and Jews savored at the same time the fruits of the translation movements from the middle of the eighth to the end of the tenth centuries, centered in newly founded Baghdad, the capital of the Abbasid caliphate, where numerous Greek philosophic, scientific, and medical works were translated into Arabic. The Jew's new interest in philosophy was a direct result of these translations, along with the rise of Mu'tazilite *kalām*, the most famous early stream of Islamic theology, under the caliph al-Ma'mun in the first third of the ninth century in Baghdad, and the influence of Al-Kindi, the first Muslim philosopher, in the first half of the ninth century, also in Baghdad. Thus, among the best-known early Jewish thinkers, Dawud al-Muqammas (ninth century) was a *mutakallim* whose views were similar to those of contemporary Mu'tazilite theologians; Isaac Israeli (ca. 855–ca. 955) was a Neoplatonic philosopher, influenced directly or indirectly by Al-Kindi, among others; and Saadia Gaon (882–942) was an eclectic thinker whose major theological-philosophical work, *Kitab al-amanat wa'l-'itiqadat* (Book of Beliefs and Opinions), exhibits knowledge of a wide variety of Greek and Islamic philosophical teachings, while adopting the structure and many arguments of the Mu'tazilites. In short, Jewish philosophical and theological thought developed from the ninth to the thirteenth centuries along with and under the direct influence of contemporary Islamic philosophy and theology, but the two traditions were, as we shall see, not in perfect harmony with each other.

Muslim philosophy began in the ninth century with Al-Kindi, the "philosopher of the Arabs," a well-known and prolific author (d. ca. 870). Al-Kindi wrote nearly three hundred works on a wide variety of subjects that, as his recent biographer Peter Adamson observes, show the "astonishing range of his interests."[1] The subjects include logic, physics, psychology, metaphysics, ethics, politics, arithmetic, geometry, music, astronomy, spherics, the measurement of distances, astrology, medicine, and pharmacology, and topics such as jewels, glass, swords, perfumes, tides, and mirrors. While Al-Kindi himself often seems to be a Neoplatonist, there are clear Aristotelian influences upon his philosophy, and he himself adopted doctrines of the Mu'tazilite theologians. Adamson explained the "irenic attitude towards kalām" of his followers as "part of their general eagerness to engage in all the

Aristotle teaching physics to students. Miniature in "The Choicest Maxims and the Best Sayings," by Al-Mubashshir, copy from the thirteenth century. Istanbul, Topkapı Palace Library, ms. Ahmet 3, 3206.

intellectual activities of their culture."[2] After Al-Kindi, philosophy in Islam developed in different directions with various Islamic sects and schools turning to Plotinus's teachings as more compatible with Islam than those of Aristotle, and indeed as a guide for understanding their own theological doctrines. In particular, they were influenced by and struggled to understand the so-called *Theology of Aristotle*, which was not a work by Aristotle, but an Arabic version of the last three books of the *Enneads.* The central role of Al-Kindi in the development of Muslim philosophy, through his own writings, through the many important Greek philosophical and scientific works that were translated for him and his circle, and through his efforts to legitimize the philosophical teachings of the ancients is now well known.[3]

What is surprising is that despite his very many achievements, Al-Kindi is often overlooked in medieval Arabic listings of the leading Muslim philosophers.[4] Rather, Al-Farabi (ca. 870–950) is considered the first eminent Muslim philosopher. He is the founder of the tradition in Muslim philosophy rooted in the orderly study of Aristotelian logic, physics, and metaphysics, but influenced by Plato's *Republic* and *Laws* in the field of political philosophy. Al-Kindi may have been familiar with Aristotle's writings, but he was not an Aristotelian; and Al-Farabi may have employed Neoplatonic language and imagery, but he was not a Neoplatonist.[5] Al-Farabi was followed by Avicenna (Ibn Sina in Arabic; 980–1037) a half century later in the East, and Ibn Bajja (1085–1138), Ibn Tufayl (1110–1185), and Averroes (Ibn Rushd in Arabic; 1126–98) in the twelfth-century Spanish West. While these philosophers do not always agree and each is known for his own particular teachings, they all belong to the tradition of Muslim philosophy founded by Al-Farabi. This strand of Muslim thought, the great tradition of rigorous Muslim Aristotelian philosophy that begins with Al-Farabi, comes to an abrupt end, or at least is muted, with the death of Averroes at the end of the twelfth century.

Medieval Jewish philosophy, as we have seen, begins with thinkers such as Isaac Israeli and Saadia Gaon. While Israeli is a philosopher who rarely cites Jewish works and makes little effort to harmonize Judaism with philosophy, Saadia states explicitly that his aim is to prove rationally the theological truths of Judaism and show the weaknesses of the arguments of those who counter those truths. For Saadia, philosophy is at the service of religion, but for him logical reasoning is also a valid source of truth in its own right. Indeed, Saadia maintained the absolute power of the intellect to attain truth independent of revelation, if one is certain of one's premises and careful in one's argumentation. For him, such rational truths will accord with those of Judaism.

Philosophical truths and revealed truths

It is useful to reflect upon this distinction between the philosophical perspectives of Israeli and Saadia for understanding why Jews—and for that matter their Muslim sources—turned to philosophical inquiry. The fundamental point is: If scripture provides truth, why need the believer, be he Muslim or Jew, turn to alien wisdom? Israeli does not address this question, but his answer to the question of why man is rational suggests his own reasons for engaging in philosophical inquiry: [Man is rational so] that he may discern with his intelligence and investigate with his deliberation and cogitation, in order to understand the truths of things and do what corresponds to truth in justice and rectitude, follow the good and keep away from the evil, so that he should obtain the reward of his Creator, may He be exalted.[6]

In other words, we engage in philosophy in order to attain truth and thereby discern how to follow the path of good, know the Creator, and obtain his eternal reward. A bit later he explains that the soul and body come together "to the end that the truths of the subject of science may become clear to man ... that

> *It is useful to reflect upon this distinction between the philosophical perspectives of Israeli and Saadia for understanding why Jews—and for that matter their Muslim sources—turned to philosophical inquiry.*

he may do what corresponds to truth ... in order thereby to obtain the reward of the Creator."[7] While Israeli rarely cites Jewish sources, his *Book on Spirit and Soul* is an exception, and is replete with biblical proof texts and refers, among other things, to a "proof from the Torah for the existence of reward [in the next world]."[8] This text has been described as a "[Jewish] theological work providing biblical foundation for the Neoplatonic teaching of Israeli."[9] The Jewish aspect is the biblical support for the belief in an eternal spiritual reward of the Creator. Israeli's description, at least in the *Book of Definitions*, of this "paradise and the goodness of the reward" as the "union with the upper soul, and the illumination by the light of the intellect and by the beauty and splendor of the wisdom" is a classic Neoplatonic expression of the ascent of the soul to the Divine as found in Arabic texts available to him.[10] In his various philosophical writings, Israeli speaks of the Creator and his creation, and of religious concepts such as prophecy, but there is little to suggest a particular concern to harmonize his philosophy with Judaism. His primary goal seems to derive from the curiosity and passion of the philosopher to attain knowledge of what he is capable of knowing.

In contrast, Saadia, in his book *Beliefs and Opinions*, directly confronts why, if scripture provides truth, the Jew should turn to wisdom:

> We inquire into the matters of our religion with two objectives in mind. One of these is to have verified in fact what we have learned from the prophets of God theoretically. The second is to refute him who argues against us in regard to anything pertaining to our religion.[11]

For Saadia, God has informed us that "if we would engage in philosophical speculation and diligent research, inquiry would produce for us in each instance the complete truth, tallying with His announcements to us by the speech of His prophets."

If this is true, one could then ask why divine wisdom was transmitted via prophecy when it could be attained via rational proofs. Saadia's response is that the All-Wise knew that philosophical reasoning takes much time and many might never attain truth because of confusion or faulty reasoning or insufficient intelligence. God therefore sent his prophets so that we would not be without truth and religious guidance while we sought to establish the truth rationally.[12] Saadia's explicit goal is to remove doubts and guide the reader to truth regarding religious teachings—such as those concerning the existence of God, his unity, his knowledge, creation, prophecy, Divine Law, free will, the nature of the soul, and reward and punishment—so that "he who believes out of sheer authority [*taqlīd*] will come to believe out of philosophical inquiry and understanding."[13]

In traditional *kalamic* fashion, Saadia discusses the sources of knowledge in the introduction to his book before his philosophic-theological discussions. He expounds three sources of certain knowledge: sense perception, intuition, and logic (or, literally, the knowledge that follows necessarily), to which he adds—also following the Muslim theologians—a fourth authentic tradition (*al-khabar al-ṣādiq*). The fourth source, which includes the books of prophetic revelation, is brought in his discussions as a further support of conclusions of the first three.[14] Saadia wishes to make clear that Judaism does not go counter to reason but harmonizes perfectly with it. In contrast, Israeli, as we have seen, has little use for biblical proof texts in his philosophical writings. In this, he is like Al-Kindi, who, as the scholar Alfred Ivry has claimed, attempts in "most of his philosophical writings to prove his case without resort to extra-philosophical means."[15] Of course, the use of biblical proof texts does not in itself establish the aims or even the orthodoxy of the author. The mysterious group of Neoplatonic philosophers who compiled the book *Risalat Ikhwan al-safa'* (Epistles of the Brethren of Purity) filled it with Qur'anic citations, but these proof texts often "provided an excellent smoke-screen for doctrines which were entirely un-Quranic."[16] Notwithstanding, in the case of thinkers like Israeli and Saadia, Israeli, like Al-Kindi, seems most interested in using philosophy to discover truth, while Saadia, like the Muslim *mutakallimūn*, is intent on using reason to prove and clarify the true teachings of religion. Yet Al-Kindi, like Saadia, believed in the essential harmony of the truths of philosophy and those of religion, and held that the prophets did not "have access to any more or different knowledge from that attained in philosophy ... [but] to precisely the same truths, but instantly and without effort or study."[17]

Saadia's conviction that philosophy is a source of truth, no less so than scripture, is maintained by later Jewish thinkers even in anti-Aristotelian works such as the *Kuzari* of Judah Halevi (ca. 1074–1141), whose protagonist proclaims, "God forbid that Scripture should contradict what is manifest or demonstrated."[18] Jews turned to philosophy for different purposes, but for whatever reasons, it is striking that few Jewish philosophers or theologians from Saadia and Israeli to

Falāsifa

This technical Arabic term (literally, "the philosophers") refers to thinkers of the Islamic philosophic tradition initiated by Al-Farabi.

the second half of the twelfth century exhibit any influence or interest in Al-Farabi, Avicenna, Ibn Bajja, or any of the other Muslim philosophers in the Farabian tradition of Aristotelian philosophy. In fact, although Halevi's *Kuzari* is in part a critique of that stream of Aristotelian philosophy,[19] we do not know what occasioned it. His accounts of the teachings of the philosophers are based on those of Avicenna and Halevi's contemporary, Ibn Bajja,[20] but we cannot point to any Jewish philosophers of Halevi's day who were knowledgeable about them or any other Muslim Aristotelians. Halevi's young friend Abraham ibn Ezra (1089–1164) seems to have been influenced by some of Avicenna's writings—for example, in his treatment of God's knowledge of particulars and in the distinction between necessary and possible existence—but he is an exception and, in any case, cannot be considered an Aristotelian. In fact, virtually all the Hispano-Jewish philosophers of the eleventh and first half of the twelfth centuries, such as Solomon ibn Gabirol (d. ca. 1058) and Joseph ibn Saddiq (d. 1149), may be characterized as Neoplatonists, with little interest in the *falāsifa*.

It was not until Abraham ibn Da'ud (ca. 1110–80) completed his *Ha-Emunah ha-Ramah* (Exalted Faith), the first book of Jewish Aristotelianism, in 1161 that we encounter a Jewish philosopher with intimate knowledge of Aristotelian philosophy and science who strives to show the harmony between the principles of Judaism and what he calls "true philosophy," that is, Aristotelian philosophy and science. Ibn Da'ud's main philosophical sources were Al-Farabi and, in particular, Avicenna,[21] and he is the first Jewish philosopher to be significantly influenced by these thinkers. Ibn Da'ud's place in history as the first Jewish Aristotelian is almost immediately overshadowed by Maimonides (1138–1204), the best-known and perhaps greatest of the medieval Jewish thinkers. Maimonides makes clear that the true science is Aristotelian, and that his works are the "roots and foundations of all the works on the sciences." As we will see, he praises the Muslim *falāsifa*, but makes no explicit mention of Ibn Da'ud.

After Maimonides, Hebrew replaces Arabic in the West as the main language of Jewish philosophical discourse. The works of the Muslim *falāsifa*, most notably virtually all the commentaries of Averroes on Aristotle, are translated into Hebrew, and the Aristotelianism of Maimonides and Averroes becomes the dominant school of the leading thirteenth- and fourteenth-century Jewish philosophers. Most Jewish philosophers of this time do not strive for originality but rather to convey and explicate the true teachings of philosophy and science. One major exception is Gersonides (1288–1344) who focused in his *Milhamot ha-Shem* (Wars of the Lord) on those important problems such as the immor-

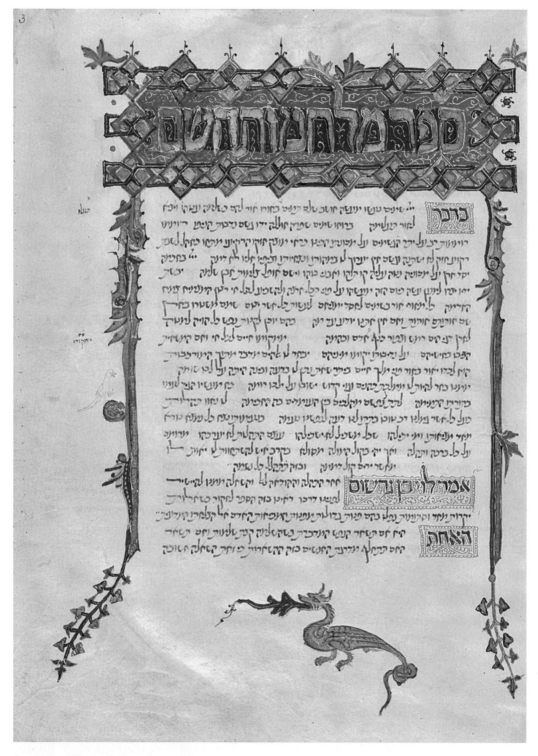

Gersonides, *Milhamot Hashem*, Spain, 1391.

tality of the soul, God's knowledge, his providence, and the creation of the world, which he believed had not been treated philosophically and correctly.[22] His target is often Maimonides, the Jewish philosopher he admired most, whose views he claims are not always based on philosophical principles, but sometimes on "theological considerations."[23] Another major exception is Hasdai Crescas (ca. 1340–1410/11), who wrote a bold critique of Aristotelian physics based on the principles of that science. Like Gersonides, he criticized Maimonides, not for being blinded by theological considerations but rather for being "seduced by the discourses of the philosophers."[24] In general, the Jewish philosophers in the centuries following Maimonides accepted Aristotle and the Muslim *falāsifa* as the leading philosophical authorities. There were Neoplatonic trends within post-Maimonidean Jewish thought, but these were peripheral and had little impact.[25]

◗ See article by Gad Freudenthal, pp. 796–815.

> " *The Jewish philosophers in the centuries following Maimonides accepted Aristotle and the Muslim* falāsifa *as the leading philosophical authorities.* "

In short, the Farabian tradition of Aristotelian philosophy, which virtually comes to an end with Averroes's death in 1198, begins at about this time in Judaism with Ibn Daʾud and Maimonides.

Medieval assessments of the Muslim and Jewish philosophers

It has been mentioned that, despite his significant place in the history of Muslim philosophy, Al-Kindi is usually ignored by the leading Muslim philosophers. In his stead, Al-Farabi is counted as the first great philosopher in Islam. The first to ignore Al-Kindi is Al-Farabi himself. In his well-known account of the transmission of Greek philosophy from Alexandria to Baghdad from the surviving fragments of his lost book, *On the Rise of Philosophy*, Al-Farabi is completely silent about Al-Kindi. True philosophy, rooted in the writings of Aristotle, comes to Baghdad via a tradition of master-student philosophical study that extends to the academy in Alexandria. Al-Farabi tells us that his master was a certain Christian, Yuhanna ibn Haylan, with whom he learned Aristotelian logic up to the end of the *Posterior Analytics*, the book that teaches how to distinguish an argument that is demonstrative and certain from one that is not.[26] Muhsin Mahdi has described Al-Farabi's tradition of philosophy: "These philosophers, commentators, and thinkers … were the ones who handed down to the Muslims the books and the tradition of reading and studying these books and interpreting them; this took the form of a clearly defined scholarly tradition."[27] The careful study and analysis of these books that characterize this tradition are evident to us from the extant long commentaries on them. Al-Kindi and the other early Muslim thinkers were not part of this tradition, but rather are connected with the Hellenistic Roman Athenian school and its Neoplatonic cosmologies.[28] It is thus not surprising that

Al-Farabi does not mention Al-Kindi or any other Muslim philosopher here, for it seems quite likely that he saw himself as the first representative of the authentic tradition of philosophical learning in Islam. In fact, Al-Farabi's only reference to Al-Kindi in his writings is in a book on music, and it is not at all favorable.[29] Similarly, Avicenna does not mention Al-Kindi's philosophy, nor does Al-Ghazali (who considered Al-Farabi and Avicenna "the most reliable transmitters and verifiers among the Islamic philosophers"[30]). In the West, Ibn Tufayl does not mention him in his brief account of philosophy in Islam in his philosophical novella *Hayy ibn Yaqzan*, but rather focuses on Al-Farabi, Avicenna, Al-Ghazali, and Ibn Bajja, while Averroes's known reference to him is a harsh critique "of the man known as Al-Kindi ... who wrote a treatise in which he sought to speak about the rules by which the nature of a compound drug may be known.

But he went astray in speaking about the art of numbers and the art of music, in the matter of someone who looks into something only incidentally. This man adduced in that book senseless and hideous things."[31] Similarly, when in the fourteenth century Ibn Khaldun lists the greatest Muslim philosophers, he mentions Al-Farabi, Avicenna, Ibn Bajja, and Averroes; that is, only philosophers from the Farabian tradition. These men, he tells us, enjoyed special fame and prestige.[32]

▶ See Nota bene on *Hayy ibn Yaqzan*, pp. 853–855.

Within Judaism Maimonides, as stated above, saw himself as part of this same tradition, and—as is clear from the opening letter and introduction to the *Guide for the Perplexed*—appreciated the importance of the master-student tradition of learning.

▶ See article by Makram Abbés, pp. 764–777.

In his famous letter to Samuel ibn Tibbon, translator of the *Guide*, in which he recommends which philosophers are worth studying, he has the highest praise for Aristotle, whose works are the "roots and foundations of all the works on the sciences." He explains that Aristotle can only be properly understood with the commentaries of Alexander of Aphrodisias, Themistius, and Averroes. The only other philosophers he praises are Al-Farabi, Ibn Bajja, and, to a lesser extent, Avicenna. Al-Kindi is not mentioned, and Isaac Israeli and the pre-Farabian Muslim philosopher Al-Razi are dismissed as "mere physicians," and their philosophical works as of no benefit. Maimonides does not recommend a single Neoplatonist, and he does not recommend a single Jewish philosopher.[33] For Maimonides, like Al-Farabi and Ibn Khaldun, the only true philosophy, the only philosophy worth doing, was the logic-based, systematic, and orderly inquiry of the Farabian tradition. Later Jewish philosophers would be even more discriminating, avoiding those philosophers of the tradition, such as Avicenna, whom they felt strayed from Aristotle's path.[34]

A different assessment of the great *falāsifa* was provided by those—exceptionally learned in this tradition of philosophy—who chose to critique it in defense of religion. The critique of Al-Ghazali (d. 1111) of the *falāsifa*, *Tahafut al-falasifa* (The Incoherence of the Philosophers), was perhaps the most influential of these critiques and the most damaging to philosophy. Al-Ghazali held that

Maimonides, *Guide for the Perplexed*, copy from a Hebrew translation of the fourteenth century. The person helping at right is probably Aristotle. Copenhagen, Royal Library, cod. Hebrew 37, fol. 114r.

one cannot properly critique something unless one understands it well and has become an expert in it. He believed that some of the teachings of the *falāsifa* were subversive, and tells us in his autobiography, *al-Munqidh min al-dalal* (Deliverance from Error) that he was surprised that none of the theologians had attempted to refute these teachings intelligently. Unlike Avicenna, who was nurtured in the sciences and philosophy from his youth, Al-Ghazali claimed he knew virtually nothing about these disciplines when he began to study them in his thirties. He tells us he read and studied the books of the philosophers in the time he snatched for himself after teaching the religious sciences during the day, so that in less than two years he came to a "complete understanding of the sciences of the philosophers." He then spent a third year reviewing and analyzing in depth what he had learned.

Although he studied all available philosophy, it is clear he valued most that of Aristotle—"who systemized logic and organized the sciences, securing a high degree of accuracy and bringing them to maturity"—and Al-Farabi and Avicenna, for "none of the Islamic philosophers has accomplished anything comparable to the achievements of these two men."[35] It is their philosophy—in particular, that of Avicenna—he presented in his encyclopedia of the sciences, *Maqasid al-falasifa* (Intentions of the Philosophers), and attempted to refute in his *Incoherence of the Philosophers*. Scholars have long held that Al-Ghazali compiled his *Intentions of the Philosophers*, a clear and orderly presentation of Avicennian logic, metaphysics, and physics, only to refute it in his *Incoherence of the Philosophers*. Indeed, Al-Ghazali himself writes in the introduction to the *Intentions* that one cannot refute the philosophers—as he was asked to do by an unnamed coreligionist—without first thoroughly understanding their teachings, and thus he needed to present them as coherently and accurately as possible, without distinguishing between truth and falsehood, before undertaking their rebuttal in the *Incoherence*. At the conclusion of the *Intentions*, Al-Ghazali writes that he will now begin the *Incoherence* to show the falsehood of those of the philosophers' opinions that are false. Yet recent scholars have pointed out that the *Incoherence* does not refer to the *Intentions*, is not based on its arguments, and uses a different terminology than it does. They accordingly suggest that *Intentions* was not written with the *Incoherence* in mind, and that the statements at the beginning and end of the *Intentions* that point to the connection between the two works may be a later addition.[36] While there is not yet a definitive solution to the puzzle of the relation between the *Intentions* and the *Incoherence*, it is undisputed that Al-Ghazali was very learned in Islamic Aristotelian philosophy by the time he wrote his devastating critique of it in the *Incoherence*. But what was his attitude toward Aristotelian philosophy and what did he wish to critique in the *Incoherence*? Al-Ghazali explains that most of its teachings in metaphysics are contrary to the truth, in logic it is mostly correct, and in the natural sciences the truth is mixed with error.[37] In other words, Al-Ghazali basically accepted the Aristotelian logic of the philosophers and many, if not most, of their teachings on natural science, but disagreed with them on most metaphysical issues; that is, he accepted most of the arguments and teachings he presented in the *Intentions*. One recent scholar has, in fact, argued that Al-Ghazali does not intend to prove the falsehood of all—or even most—of the philosophical teachings in the *Incoherence*, but only to show that their teachings are not proven by demonstration, their own standard for attaining certain truth.[38] What Al-Ghazali cannot accept are their three teachings for which he accuses them of unbelief (*kufr*), and which he attempts to refute in the *Incoherence*: (1) their belief in the pre-eternality of the world, and that it is thus not created in time; (2) their belief that God does not know the particulars, but only universals; and (3) their denial of the resurrection of the dead. The charge of unbelief in Islam meant that those who maintained the doctrines in question needed to be killed, and this threatened the future of the Farabian tradition of Aristotelian philosophy in Islam. Averroes understood this well and tried unsuccessfully to neutralize Al-Ghazali's charges first in his legal treatise *The Decisive Treatise, Determining What the Connection Is Between Religion and Philosophy* (*Fasl al-maqal*), and then in his far more serious *Tahafut al-tahafut* (*Incoherence of the Incoherence*). The aim of this latter work was not to prove any theologico-philosophical teachings, but rather to "show the different degrees of assent and conviction attained by the assertions in the *Incoherence of the Philosophers*, and that the greater part has not reached the degree of certainty and demonstration."[39] In the shorter work, he cleverly defined philosophy as "nothing more than study of existing beings and reflection on them as indications of the Artisan."[40] How could one condemn such a noble discipline? In the context of his defense of philosophy, he also turned to Al-Ghazali's three charges of unbelief against the philosophers, and tried to show that they are not true. For example, in discussing the claim that they deny God's knowledge of particulars, Averroes explains that the cause of confusion here is the failure of Al-Ghazali and the theologians to distinguish God's knowledge from ours. Our knowledge of particulars is an effect of the object known, whereas God's knowledge is the opposite of this, that is, the cause of the object known. The former is originated knowledge; the latter is eternal knowledge that does not change. This latter knowledge transcends the qualification as particular or universal. Averroes's claim is that not only do the philosophers believe that God knows all, but that their view is more suitable to Islam, for only they appreciate the exalted nature of God's knowledge.[41] Averroes's response to Al-Ghazali's charges is far more detailed in the *Incoherence of the Incoherence*, but what is particularly significant is his relatively short reply there to Al-Ghazali's claim that the Muslim Aristotelians deny bodily resurrection. Averroes denies the charge and writes that the philosophers "regard this doctrine [of resurrection] as most important and believe in it most, and the reason is that it is conducive to an order amongst men on which man's being, as man, depends and through which he can attain the greatest happiness proper to him." For Averroes, true "philosophers believe that religious laws are necessary political arts, the principles of which are taken from natural reason and inspiration, ... and one must not object ... to any of the general religious principles."[42] They thus believe in the doctrine of resurrection, not because it is proven demonstratively but because it is necessary for the political order of the religious community. Accordingly Averroes agrees with Al-Ghazali that the philosopher who publicly denies resurrection is an unbeliever and merits the harsh punishment dictated by Islam.

> *Halevi's presentation of the philosopher at the beginning of book 1 was patterned after Ibn Bajja.*

Some thirty years after Al-Ghazali's death, Halevi wrote his defense of Judaism, the *Kuzari*. A prime goal of the book was to defend Judaism against the teachings of the philosophers. Like Al-Ghazali, Halevi was most concerned with the Muslim Aristotelians. While they had not yet significantly influenced Jewish thinkers, Halevi seems to have known their teachings well. Shlomo Pines, who showed that Halevi's presentation of the philosopher at the beginning of book 1 was patterned after Ibn Bajja, while the presentation of philosophy in book 5 reflects the teachings of Avicenna, held that Halevi "was greatly impressed by the latter, and he may have tried, notwithstanding the critique of philosophy ... to adapt his own views or his own terminology ... to this newly discovered framework."[43] There seems little doubt that Halevi was emboldened in his critique of the philosophers by Al-Ghazali.[44] Both were learned students of philosophy who seem to have considered Aristotle, and in particular Avicenna's version of his teachings, to be the most reliable philosophy; and both were concerned that certain of his teachings were mistaken, went counter to religion, were heretical, and needed to be refuted. Despite his critique of the philosophers, Halevi believed that if something is demonstrated logically it must be true.[45] Like Al-Ghazali, he therefore expressed the fear that people who see the true demonstrations the philosophers bring in mathematics and logic will be led to assume falsely that all their arguments in natural science and metaphysics are proven demonstratively.[46] And like Al-Ghazali, he strove to show that this was not the case. Halevi's critique of the philosophers was no less damning than that of Al-Ghazali, although it engendered no response such as the *Incoherence* of Averroes. At the beginning of the book, the philosopher reveals to the king that philosophers deny, among other things, that God knows particulars, that he created the world, and that man will be resurrected. But, as Averroes explained, no true philosopher would publicly deny the fundamental principles of religion. Indeed, the story is told that when Ibn Tufayl arranged for the young Averroes to meet the Almohad prince, Abu Yaʿqub, and the prince asked him about the opinion of the philosophers regarding the creation or eternity of the heavens, Averroes was overcome with confusion and fear and could not answer.[47] The response of Halevi's philosopher to the king's request about his beliefs is very different from that of the young Averroes, and not at all what one should have expected of a wise philosopher. Avicenna had taught that it is not "proper for any man to reveal that he possesses knowledge he is hiding from the multitude. … Rather, he should let them know of God's majesty and greatness through symbols and similitudes."[48] In other words, Halevi's philosopher broke the cardinal rule of the philosophers by revealing truths concerning the principles of religion that must not be stated except through symbols and similitudes. For Maimonides these fundamental truths of religion are called the "secrets of the Torah" (*sitre torah*), and must be concealed from the multitude and only taught to the worthy through private master-student teaching. Maimonides never mentioned Halevi, whose *Kuzari* he certainly knew, and it may be that his silence was in part because he believed Halevi had betrayed philosophy.

Another learned critique of the Aristotelians is that by Hasdai Crescas, the great Jewish philosopher, rabbi, and leader of Aragon Jewry. Like Al-Ghazali, Crescas was the leading scholar and teacher of his religious community of his period, and used his profound knowledge of Aristotelian philosophy and science to defend his religion against the heterodox teachings of that philosophy. Crescas was determined to play by the rules and refute the teachings of the philosophers on the basis of Aristotelian logic. His assault began with a revolutionary critique of some of the fundamental concepts of Aristotelian science, such as the basic

Judah Halevi, *Kuzari*, frontispiece of the Venetian edition, J. di Gara, 1594. Bibliothèque Nationale de France, Rare Books Reserve, A 5207, t. 1, fol. 1.

Aristotelian theories of time and space, and the Aristotelian rejection of actual infinity and the void. The most striking similarity between Al-Ghazali and Crescas, apart from their common pious goal of refuting the Aristotelianism current in their day, is that Al-Ghazali was the only Muslim student of philosophy who recognized the importance of prefacing his critique of philosophy with a separate, clear, and even, at times, improved account of that philosophy, while Crescas was the only Jewish student of philosophy who prefaced his critique of philosophy with a separate, clear, and even, at times, improved account of that philosophy. Like Al-Ghazali, Crescas made clear that he intended to concern himself only with the arguments of the best philosophers of the day. At the time of Al-Ghazali, this meant the writings of Al-Farabi and Avicenna; at the time of Crescas, this meant the science of Aristotle, his followers, and commentators, such as Al-Farabi, Avicenna, Al-Ghazali (that is, in his *Intentions of the Philosophers*), Averroes, Ibn Daʾud, and Maimonides.[49] While Al-Ghazali was able to accept much of Aristotelian natural science as true, Crescas, living three centuries later, and whose science was related to the new physics based in Paris and Oxford, was not. Thus, in preparing the way for his defense of the principles of Judaism, Crescas "opened for us the vistas of a new conception of the universe."[50]

Significantly, in their assessments and critiques of the Muslim philosophers, just as in their overall approaches to philosophy and science, the medieval Jewish philosophers often benefited from and valued certain Muslim thinkers far more than certain

Jewish ones. Philosophical schools and affiliations were not defined by religious borders, but crossed them freely almost without notice.

Accomplishments of the Muslim and Jewish philosophers

The works of the Muslim and Jewish philosophers are of interest and importance from two broad perspectives: first, in their efforts to recover, preserve, clarify, interpret, correct, and improve the philosophy and science of the Greek philosophers and their contemporary followers; and second, in their efforts to employ their knowledge of logic, philosophy, and science to attain the truth concerning God and the fundamental teachings of their faith, such as those regarding creation, prophecy, Divine Law, God's attributes, his knowledge of particulars, his providence, free will, the nature of the soul, its immortality, human perfection, and ultimate reward and punishment.

The Muslim philosopher who most influenced the medieval Jewish and Christian philosophers was Averroes, but his impact on his coreligionists was minimal. As a philosopher, Averroes is most famous as the Commentator on Aristotle,[51] but is also well known for his defense of philosophy, the *Incoherence of the Incoherence*, against the accusations of Al-Ghazali. While there were Hebrew translations of all or virtually all of Averroes's thirty-six commentaries on Aristotle, and Latin translations of at least thirty-two of them, five major commentaries are no longer extant in the original Arabic: the *Middle Commentary on the Physics*, the *Long Commentary on the Physics*, the *Middle Commentary on the Metaphysics*, the *Commentary on De animalibus*, and the *Middle Commentary on the Nicomachean Ethics*. And while most of those Averroesian commentaries that survive in Arabic are extant in only a few manuscripts, many of the Hebrew and Latin translations survive in dozens of manuscripts. For Averroes, Aristotle originated the art of logic, natural science, and divine science, and he completed them. Averroes saw the task of philosophy in his day—his own task—to teach and explain the words of Aristotle. While Averroes repeatedly portrays himself as a mere explicator of Aristotle, there are also significant, creative aspects to his commentaries.[52] Maimonides immediately recognized the great importance of Averroes's commentaries for understanding Aristotle, and following his high recommendation of the commentaries, in Hebrew translation they became the medium through which Jews learned Aristotelian science, replacing even the works of Aristotle. A whole new genre of philosophical writing in Hebrew soon developed, that of the supercommentaries on Averroes's commentaries on Aristotle, and these commentaries, in particular, those of Gersonides, also became very popular. Gersonides explained that his goal in his supercommentaries on the short commentaries was to explain these texts concisely, "for even though most of what Averroes says is very clear, there remain some profound things that he does not sufficiently explain."[53]

751

His task in his supercommentaries on Averroes's middle commentaries was more ambitious, for there he sought not only to explain difficult passages, but also to refute Averroes and Aristotle when he did not agree with them.[54] In fact, however, many of his main arguments against Aristotle and Averroes are found in his court commentaries on the books of natural science.[55] In the Latin West, almost at once with the translation of his long commentaries, Averroes became known simply as the Commentator, the most reliable guide to understanding Aristotle. Yet significantly, with few exceptions, his commentaries were not appreciated in the medieval Muslim world, and we know of no important Arabic commentaries on them.[56] Perhaps the reason for this silence may be understood in light of a mid-thirteenth-century report that praised Averroes as "the imam of philosophy of our time," but added that philosophy is "a science that is detested in al-Andalus. One cannot study it in public, and for this reason writings on this subject are concealed."[57] One thirteenth-century author who did acknowledge that he studied Averroes's commentaries, directly or indirectly, was the provocative Sufi philosopher and unabashed critic of the philosophers, Ibn Sab'in of Murcia (1217–70). According to Ibn Sab'in, who had derogatory things to say about Averroes's intellect, Averroes worshipped Aristotle and followed him almost blindly, but he was a reliable interpreter of him.[58]

The Muslim philosopher who most influenced fellow Muslims was Avicenna. An explanation of Avicenna's lasting influence on generations of Muslim scholars, even after it became imprudent to study the works of Muslim philosophers, is that his writings were much more compatible with traditional Islamic beliefs than those of the other great *falāsifa*. For example, according to Avicenna, there is a soul-body dualism: the soul is not simply a physical being but a complete substance independent of any relation it has to the body. This teaching goes well with the religious belief in the immortality of the individual human soul. Avicenna's impact on Muslim philosophy in the West—in particular in the twelfth century, its golden period—is not as strong as one might have expected because he was seen as at times parting from the teachings of Aristotle. This is seen most clearly in Averroes's critical attitude toward him. Avicenna is best known for his psychological and metaphysical teachings, for example, his metaphysical proof for the existence of God, his understanding of essence and existence, his distinction between necessary and possible, his doctrine of God's knowledge of particulars, his theory of the soul and how man acquires knowledge, his notion of prophecy, his doctrine of immortality and the perfection of man. Among the Jews, Avicenna was not as important as Al-Farabi and Averroes, but he still had an impact, beginning with Ibn Da'ud and Maimonides, particularly in the area of theological teachings, such as God as Necessary Existent and the metaphysical proof for the existence of God, and religious concepts such as the intellectual love of God and intellectual worship

"All men naturally desire knowledge. An indication of this is our esteem for the senses," begins Aristotle's *Metaphysics*, book 1, seen here in its Latin translation. Above, an illumination by Girolamo da Cremona shows a philosophical *disputatio*; at left, Thomas Aquinas, Avicenna (crowned *senex rex*), and Averroes, in the Venetian edition (1483) of the Latin text of Aristotle with assorted commentary from Averroes. New York, Pierpont Morgan Library.

of God.[59] As already noted, his science was not so popular as he was seen as straying from the path of Aristotle. Among the Scholastics, Avicenna was, after Averroes, the most influential Muslim philosopher. His greatest influence was in the fields of psychology and metaphysics via Latin translations of the *Healing*, although the sections on logic and natural science from it were also translated into Latin and well known. Avicenna's influence on the Scholastics was early— already at the end of the twelfth century—and continued to be strong through most of the thirteenth century.[60] The Scholastics turned to Averroes for understanding Aristotle, but Avicenna appealed to them particularly because of his intellectual freedom. He often intentionally parted from Aristotle and presented his own philosophy—psychological, metaphysical, and theological teachings that could, with caution and wisdom, be integrated into the doctrines of the Christian faith.

Arabic and Hebraic science

Apart from the *falāsifa* and contemporaneous with them, numerous Muslim scientists made important contributions in diverse fields, such as natural science, astronomy, astrology, the various mathematical sciences, geometry, and medicine. With few notable exceptions, the same cannot be said of the pre-Maimonidean Jewish scholars. Thus, it has recently been said of one of the leading early Jewish scientists, Abraham ibn Ezra, that "even though in his scientific corpus occasional critical tones may be heard, we will hardly find in it any significant innovation, not to mention any scientific breakthrough."[61] The main contribution of the pre-Maimonidean Jewish philosophers—those who were influenced primarily by the Neoplatonists and the Muslim theologians—was in the area of providing a rational explication and defense of the principles of Judaism and a rational understanding of Divine Law and the commandments. Thus, for example, we see a new area of study, *ta'ame ha-misvot* (the reasons for the commandments), developed by Saadia, that would through the ages counter those rabbis who held that these reasons are hidden and cannot be known by us because of the "incapacity of our intellects or the deficiency of our knowledge."[62] In the century following Maimonides's death and the emergence of Hebrew in place of Arabic as the language of philosophy of the Jews, remarkably few of the Neoplatonic and *kalamic* texts that so influenced prior Jewish philosophy were translated into Hebrew. In their place, the Arabic-to-Hebrew translation movement focused on Averroes's commentaries, the works of the Muslim Aristotelians, and basic texts in mathematics, astronomy, and medicine.

▸ See article by Gad Freudenthal, pp. 796–815.

These texts of Greek and Arabic philosophy and science were studied carefully as part of a program of education to learn the sciences in a systematic and orderly fashion. Of special interest in this century is the popularization of Aristotelian science (relatively speaking)—or, at least, the making accessible of this science—through the composition of reader-friendly Hebrew encyclopedias of science and philosophy of various lengths, structures, and aims.[63] While the inspiration for these Hebrew encyclopedias no doubt came from the tenth- and eleventh-century Arabic encyclopedias and enumerations of sciences, in some cases the material for them came from Averroes's commentaries, often word for word. The goal of the systematic study of Aristotelian science, whether through translations or encyclopedias, was the acquisition of knowledge and understanding, necessary for human happiness and perfection. Yet this does not mean that these Jewish students were passive readers of the texts, who accepted blindly the principles and claims of Aristotelian natural science. The desire to understand and explicate inevitably gave rise to critique and innovation. While during this period there were few creative medieval Jewish scientists of the stature of Gersonides—who made original contributions in the fields of natural science, astronomy, and mathematics, and even invented observational instruments such as the Jacob Staff for observing, among other things, the distance between two stars[64]—centuries of Arabic scientific inquiry in new Hebrew garb made it possible for Jews to master the sciences of their day and, in some instances, to contribute to the progress of science. At the same time, these same Jewish thinkers used their philosophical and scientific learning to reexamine the age-old debates concerning the principles of their religion, at times offering new perspectives or solutions to the problems.

Epilogue

It has been nearly a century since Husik's famous concluding statement to his *History of Mediaeval Jewish Philosophy* that "there are Jews now, and there are philosophers, but there are no Jewish philosophers and there is no Jewish philosophy."[65] His view expressed a sentiment of his time that is, to some extent, still with us today, and it applies equally to Muslim philosophers and Muslim philosophy. The gap between Athens and Jerusalem or Athens and Mecca seems to some today hopelessly unbridgeable, and few seem to notice or care. While there are many renowned Jewish professors of philosophy throughout the world's universities, there are few who engage in the kind of rational defense and explication of the principles of their religion that was the hallmark of medieval religious philosophy, and there are even fewer Muslim philosophers who do so. Today's Jewish and Muslim philosophers are barely known to their coreligionists, and do not influence one another. It seems that many of those most interested in the rational explication of religious teachings are drawn to the history of philosophy and the interpretation of the great medieval thinkers. And just as the similarities between certain medieval Muslim and Jewish philosophers were far greater than those between certain philosophers of the same religion, so certain present-day Muslim and Jewish interpreters of those philosophers often are in far greater agreement with each other about the religious significance of these medievals than they are with some of their coreligionist colleagues.

---

1. Peter Adamson, *Al-Kindi* (Oxford: Oxford University Press, 2007), 7.
2. Ibid., 16; on Al-Kindi's views, see 23–25.
3. See, for example, Gerhard Endress, "The Circle of al-Kindi: The Early Arabic Translations from the Greek and the Rise of Islamic Philosophy," in *The Ancient Tradition in Christian and Islamic Hellenism*, ed. Gerhard Endress and Remke Kruk (Leiden: Research School CNWS, 1997), 43–76.
4. See below, "Medieval Assessments of the Muslim and Jewish Philosophers."
5. See the assessment of the foremost scholar of Al-Farabi, Muhsin Mahdi, *Alfarabi and the Foundation of Islamic Political Philosophy* (Chicago: University of Chicago Press, 2001), esp. 1–3. For a different picture, see Majid Fakhry, *Al-Farabi: Founder of Islamic Neoplatonism* (Oxford: Oneworld, 2002).
6. *Book of Definitions*, trans. in A. Altmann and S. M. Stern, *Isaac Israeli: A Neoplatonic Philosopher of the Early Tenth Century* (Oxford: Oxford University Press, 1958), 12.
7. Ibid., 25.
8. Ibid., 113.
9. Ibid., 117.
10. *Book of Definitions*, 25–26; for possible sources, see Altmann and Stern, *Isaac Israeli*, 185–95.

11. Saadia Gaon, *The Book of Beliefs and Opinions*, trans. Samuel Rosenblatt (New Haven, CT: Yale University Press, 1948), 6 and 27–28.

12. Ibid., 31.

13. Ibid., 2 and 9.

14. Ibid. On these sources of knowledge, see Israel Efros, "Saadia's Theory of Knowledge," in *Saadia Studies*, ed. Abraham B. Neuman and Solomon Zeitlin, Philadelphia, 1943 (*Jewish Quarterly Review* 33), 133–70.

15. Alfred L. Ivry, *Al-Kindi's Metaphysics* (Albany: State University of New York Press, 1974), 116.

16. I. R. Netton, *Muslim Neoplatonists: An Introduction to the Thought of the Brethren of Purity* (London: George Allen and Unwin, 1982), 78–79.

17. Adamson, *Al-Kindi*, 43–44.

18. Judah Halevi, *Kuzari*, ed. David H. Baneth and Haggai Ben-Shammai (Jerusalem: Magnes Press, 1977), 1.67, p. 18; cf. 1.89, p. 25.

19. I use the technical Arabic term *falāsifa* (lit., philosophers) to refer to those philosophers who followed in the tradition of Muslim philosophy inaugurated by Al-Farabi.

20. See Shlomo Pines, "Shiʿite Terms and Conceptions in Judah Halevi's *Kuzari*," *Jerusalem Studies in Arabic and Islam* 2 (1980): 210–19. See also Diana Lobel, *Between Mysticism and Philosophy: Sufi Language of Religious Experience in Judah ha-Levi's "Kuzari"* (Albany: State University of New York Press, 2000), 170–71.

21. See T.A.M. Fontaine, *In Defence of Judaism: Abraham Ibn Daud* (Assen/Maastricht: Van Gorcum, 1990) and Amira Eran, *Me-Emuna Tamma le-Emuna Rama* (Tel-Aviv: Hakibbutz Hameuchad, 1998). It seems increasingly likely that Ibn Daʾud may be identified with Avendauth, the cotranslator with Dominicus Gundissalinus of philosophical works by Al-Ghazali and Avicenna. See Fontaine, *In Defence of Judaism*, 262–63, and for new evidence, see Yossi Esudri, "R. Abraham Ibn Daʾud and His Philosophical Book *The Exalted Faith*: Miscellanea" (in Hebrew), in *Adam le-Adam: Studies Presented to Warren Zev Harvey*, ed. Ari Ackerman, Esti Eisenmann, Aviram Ravitsky, and Shmuel Wygoda (forthcoming).

22. Gersonides, *Wars of the Lord*, trans. Seymour Feldman, 3 vols. (Philadelphia: Jewish Publication Society of America, 1984–99), 1:93. On Gersonides's originality and his critique of Aristotle, see Ruth Glasner, *Gersonides: A Scientific Biography* (Oxford: Oxford University Press, forthcoming), esp. chaps. 2 and 4.

23. Gersonides, *Wars of the Lord*, 3.3, 2:107.

24. Hasdai Crescas, *Or Hashem* (Light of the Lord), introduction, trans. in Warren Harvey, "Hasdai Crescas's Critique of the Theory of the Acquired Intellect," Ph.D. diss., Columbia University, 1973, 363–66.

25. For an account of such Neoplatonic trends, see Dov Schwartz, *Yashan be-Qanqan Hadash* (Jerusalem: Bialik Institute, 1996).

26. See Max Meyerhof, "Von Alexandrien nach Baghdad," *Sitzungsberichte der Preussischen Akademie der Wissenschaften, phil.-hist. Klasse* 23 (1930): 389–429, esp. 394 and 405.

27. Muhsin Mahdi, *La Cité vertueuse d'Alfarabi, op. cit.*, 80.

28. Mahdi, *Alfarabi and the Foundation of Islamic Political Philosophy*, 52–56.

29. Ed. by Muhsin Mahdi in *Nusus falsafiyya*, ed. ʿUthman Amin (Cairo, 1976), 76–78.

30. Al-Ghazali, *The Incoherence of the Philosophers*, trans. Michael E. Marmura (Provo, UT: Brigham Young University Press, 1997), 4.

31. Cited in Y. Tzvi Langermann, "Another Andalusian Revolt? Ibn Rushd's Critique of al-Kindi's *Pharmacological Computus*," in *The Enterprise of Science in Islam: New Perspectives*, ed. Jan P. Hogendijk and Abdelhamid I. Sabra (Cambridge, MA: MIT Press, 2003), 359.

32. Ibn Khaldun, *The Muqaddimah: An Introduction to History*, trans. Franz Rosenthal (2nd ed.; Princeton, NJ: Princeton University Press, 1967), 3:116; cf. 250.

33. See Steven Harvey, "Did Maimonides' Letter to Samuel ibn Tibbon Determine Which Philosophers Would Be Studied by Later Jewish Thinkers?" *Jewish Quarterly Review* 83 (1992): 51–70.

34. Steven Harvey, "Why Did Fourteenth-century Jews Turn to Al-Ghazali's Account of Natural Science?" *Jewish Quarterly Review* 91 (2001): 359–76.

35. Al-Ghazali, *Deliverance from Error*, trans. by W. Montgomery Watt in *The Faith and Practice of Al-Ghazali* (London: Allen and Unwin, 1953), 29–32. Is it true that he did not know philosophy until he "began to study them in his thirties"? See Frank Griffel, *Al-Ghazali's Philosophical Theology* (Oxford: Oxford University Press, 2009), 29–31.

36. See, for example, Jules Janssens, *Ibn Sina and His Influence on the Arabic and Latin World* (Aldershot: Variorum, 2006), chaps. 10–11; and Griffel, *Al-Ghazali's Philosophical Theology*, chap. 3.

37. Al-Ghazali, *Intentions of the Philosophers*, intro., 3; cf. *Deliverance from Error*, 33–38.

38. Griffel, *Al-Ghazali's Philosophical Theology*, 98–101.

39. Averroes, *Incoherence of the Incoherence*, trans. Simon van den Bergh (London: Luzac & Co., 1954), 1:1.

40. Averroes, *Decisive Treatise*, trans. in George F. Hourani, *Averroes on the Harmony of Religion and Philosophy* (London: Luzac & Co., 1961), 44.

41. Ibid., 54–55.

42. Averroes, *Incoherence of the Incoherence*, natural sciences, fourth discussion, 1:359.

43. Pines, "Shi'ite Terms and Conceptions in Judah Halevi's *Kuzari*," 210–19. See note 20.

44. See Lobel, *Between Mysticism and Philosophy*, 6–7, 171–76.

45. Judah Halevi, *Kuzari*, 1.67. See note 18.

46. Ibid., 5.14; cf. Al-Ghazali, *Deliverance from Error*, 33–37. See note 35.

47. See the account translated in Hourani, *Averroes on the Harmony of Religion and Philosophy*, 12–13.

48. Avicenna, *The Metaphysics of "The Healing,"* trans. Michael E. Marmura (Provo, UT: Brigham Young University Press, 2005), book 10, chap. 2, 366.

49. Hasdai Crescas, *Light of the Lord*, book 1, intro., trans. in Harry A. Wolfson, *Crescas' Critique of Aristotle* (Cambridge, MA: Harvard University Press, 1929), 130.

50. Wolfson, *Crescas' Critique of Aristotle*, 37. See also, Warren Zev Harvey, *Physics and Metaphysics in Hasdai Crescas* (Amsterdam: J. C. Gieben, 1998).

51. On Averroes's reputation as the Commentator of Aristotle among the medieval Jews and Scholastics, see Steven Harvey, "Why Did Jews Begin to Consider Averroes the Commentator?" in *Florilegium medievale*, ed. José Meirinhos and Olga Weijers (Louvain-la-Neuve: Fédération Internationale des Instituts d'Études médiévales, 2009), 279–96.

52. See, for example, Ruth Glasner, *Averroes' Physics: A Turning Point in Medieval Natural Philosophy* (Oxford: Oxford University Press, 2009).

53. Gersonides, *Commentary on Averroes' Short Commentary on the Physics*, London, Jews College MS Bet Hamid. 43, fol. 126a.

54. Gersonides, *Commentary on Averroes' Middle Commentary on the Physics*, Paris MS Bibliothèque Nationale Hebr. 964, fol. 1b. For a clear illustration of Gersonides's disagreements in his commentaries, see Ruth Glasner, "Gersonides's Theory of Natural Motion," *Early Science and Medicine* 1 (1996): 151–203.

55. Ruth Glasner has made this point clearly in several studies. See, for example, her article "On the Writing of Gersonides's Philosophical Commentaries," in *Les Méthodes de travail de Gersonides et le maniement du savoir chez les scolastiques*, ed. C. Sirat, S. Klein-Braslavy, and O. Weijers (Paris: Vrin, 2003), particularly 93–103.

56. Ibn Khaldun apparently wrote many epitomes of the commentaries in the fourteenth century. See Muhsin Mahdi, *Ibn Khaldun's Philosophy of History* (Chicago: University of Chicago Press, 1964), 35–36, esp. note 5.

57. This account by Ibn Sa'id is cited in Al-Maqqari, *Nafh al-tib*, ed. R. Dozy et al., in *Analectes sur l'histoire et la littérature des arabes d'Espagne* (Leiden, 1855–61), 2:125.

58. See Anna A. Akasoy, "Ibn Sab'in's *Sicilian Questions*: The Text, Its Sources, and Their Historical Context," *al-Qantara* 29 (2008): 115–46, esp. 133–46.

59. See Steven Harvey, "Ibn Sina's Influence on Jewish Thought: Some Reflections," in *Avicenna and His Legacy: A Golden Age of Science and Philosophy*, ed. Y. Tzvi Langermann (Turnhout, Brepols, 2009).

60. See, for example, Dag Nikolaus Hasse, *Avicenna's "De Anima" in the Latin West: The Formation of a Peripatetic Philosophy of the Soul, 1160–1300* (London: Warburg Institute / Turin: Nino Aragno Editore, 2000), and Jules Janssens and Daniel De Smet, *Avicenna and His Heritage* (Leuven: Leuven University Press, 2002).

61. Shlomo Sela, *Abraham Ibn Ezra and the Rise of Medieval Hebrew Science* (Leiden: Brill, 2003), 324.

62. The quote is from Maimonides, *Guide for the Perplexed*, 3:26. See, in general, Isaac Heinemann, *La loi dans la pensée juive*, French adaptation by Charles Touati (Paris: Éditions Albin Michel, 1962).

63. See *The Medieval Hebrew Encyclopedias of Science and Philosophy*, ed. Steven Harvey (Dordrecht: Kluwer Academic, 2000).

64. See, for example, Bernard R. Goldstein, "Levi Ben Gerson's Contributions to Astronomy," in *Studies on Gersonides*, ed. Gad Freudenthal (Leiden: Brill, 1992), 3–19.

65. Husik, *History of Mediaeval Jewish Philosophy*, 432.

Saadia Gaon: The Adaptation of Traditional Jewish Culture to the New Arab Culture

Saadia ben Yosef Al-Fayyumi,[1] usually called Saadia Gaon, is one of the most important and influential figures in what is known as "medieval" Jewish culture. His uniqueness has as much to do with the number of fields to which he made fundamental contributions as with the innovativeness of his achievements.

His biography is probably the best-known text associated with Jewish history of the first millennium. Born in the region of Fayyum, Middle Egypt, in 882, Saadia lived in the land of Israel, probably in Tiberias, beginning in about 910. After spending time in Syria before 921, he settled in Baghdad, where he died in 942. He was famous from his early youth, having composed the *Sefer Egron*,[2] a major Hebrew-Arabic dictionary, at the age of twenty and a treatise against the Karaites shortly thereafter. In Baghdad, Saadia was involved in an important dispute between the religious authorities of the land of Israel and those of Babylonia (the traditional Jewish name for Iraq) on the methods for determining the Jewish calendar. Despite his Egyptian origins—at the time, the Egyptian Jewish communities were within the sphere of influence of the authorities of the land of Israel—he sided with the Babylonian masters. His intercession was decisive in shifting the balance in their favor; from then on, and until the first half of the eleventh century, the Babylonians were the undisputed authorities in religious matters for almost all the Jewish communities. In 928 Saadia was named *gaon* of the Talmudic academy (yeshiva) of Sura, the most prestigious office for religious and intellectual matters. His appointment was unprecedented,

since Saadia came from a relatively remote territory and therefore did not belong to the world of the Babylonian yeshivas. The originality of his work, in fact, probably reflects the eccentricity of his intellectual training, far from the traditional centers of rabbinical education. The principal task of the *geonim* was to serve as directors of the yeshivas and to compose the *teshuvot* (legal "responsas"), but Saadia was also a philosopher, poet, linguist, exegete, and polemicist.

Saadia's multifaceted body of work displays a number of central and recurrent characteristics. It is distinguished by its defense of Judaism, rabbinical Judaism in particular, against the criticisms of authors belonging to other religions— especially Islam—and against Jewish currents or attitudes opposing the rabbinical tradition as a whole or certain of its aspects. It takes issue with Karaism in the first place but also with movements that considered the rational exploration of religious matters illegitimate and—at the other extreme— those that pointed out contradictions and injustices in that tradition. Saadia is therefore constantly in search of a balance between revealed doctrine and rabbinical tradition on one hand, and free, rational investigation on the other. He also devotes particular attention to correct usage and the elegant aspects of the Hebrew language, which is apparent both in his theoretical studies (lexicons and grammars composed in Arabic) and in his poetic texts, whether polemical or religious (the *piyyutim*). Saadia wanted to provide the Jews with both the rules and examples of beautiful Hebraic writing. As a poet, he was also formally innovative, paving the way for the great Andalusian school in the following centuries. This approach went hand in hand with his constant references to the Arabic language and to Arab culture, usually implicit but sometimes clearly acknowledged. It is not only that Saadia composed most of his works in Judeo-Arabic (a literary Arabic with Egyptian dialectal influences, written in Hebrew characters), which was in itself a novelty for a rabbinical authority, but in addition, in his writings as a lexicographer, linguist, philosopher, and biblical exegete, he made countless and obvious references to the language, texts, and theoretical arguments of the Arabs. According to some researchers, it is even possible

Piyyut (liturgical poem) composed by Saadia Gaon for the holiday of Simchat Torah. Fragment from the Cairo Geniza. Cambridge University Library: Mosseri IA.41.

to consider Saadia's writings as a systematic effort to adapt traditional Jewish culture to the new Arab culture.

The most salient formal characteristic of his writings is their systematic nature. In nearly all his theoretical works, Saadia, inspired by certain Arab authors but sometimes going beyond them, took care to provide a table of contents and theoretical and methodological introductions to his detailed analyses. He also produced monographs on particular themes, especially on the *halakha* (religious law). These monographs collected, in orderly fashion, writings on a single subject, for example, contracts, which before that time had been dispersed in the treatises of the Talmud and in the *teshuvot* of earlier *geonim*.

The scope, novelty, and qualities of his oeuvre, as well as its overall tone, show that Saadia believed he was entrusted with a mission: to introduce a Judaism that conformed to tradition but that was also open to the many intellectual tensions pervading Arabo-Muslim culture at a time of great turmoil. He often described himself as the one to whom the task had fallen to provide answers for coreligionists who were suffering from doubt and bewilderment. Saadia always considered himself responsible for the Jewish community as a whole: his polemical *Sefer ha-Galuy*, directed against David ben Zakkai, the "exilarch" (lay leader of the Babylonian community) who had divested him of his role as *gaon*, only to reinstall him a few years later, deals as much with what Saadia views as the fundamental values of Jewish culture as it does with the dispute at hand.

Saadia Gaon's most enduring influence was surely in the field of philosophy. His magnum opus, the *Kitab al-Amanat wa-l-I'tiqadat* (*Book of Beliefs and Opinions*), was translated into Hebrew by Yehuda Ibn Tibbon under the title *Sefer emunot ve-de'ot* and has come down to us in its entirety, unlike a large portion of his works.[3] Although, from the standpoint of strict chronology, Saadia was not "the first Jewish philosopher," he was the first to produce a systematic body of work in which Jewish religious beliefs were analyzed rationally, so that they might become "opinions," which is to say, convictions based on reason. The believer would thereby become an autonomous subject and would not merely be dependent on a revelation imposed from the outside. Some theoretical arguments in this book display a remarkable originality, acuity, and even "modernity," so much so that they can be extracted from their religious context as valid elements of general philosophy. The frame of reference for this book is the *kalām*, rational Muslim philosophy in its Mu'tazilite version, but Saadia does not passively adopt the conclusions of that current of thought.

Another field in which Saadia exerted a significant influence was biblical translation. For a long time, the Jewish Arabophone world adopted as its standard version his Arabic translation of many parts of the Bible, known as the *Tafsir*, which was more akin to a targum, that is, a translation-interpretation, than a literal translation. Moreover, Saadia wrote Arabic commentary on several books of the Bible.

As for his Hebrew texts, especially his religious poems (*piyyutim*), even today they are included in the liturgies of many Jewish communities, after being part of a siddur, or prayer book, composed by Saadia himself. By contrast, the pioneering quality of his linguistic writings has only very recently been recognized, since the writings have come down to us in incomplete form and are marred by errors. It has only been in the last few decades, thanks to the discoveries in the Cairo Geniza and the study of neglected manuscripts, that specialists have established that Saadia was the first author to take on the task of systematically examining the Hebrew language,[4] taking his inspiration from Arabic, of course, but also rising to the level of general linguistics at certain points. ●

Professor in the Department of Hebrew and Jewish Languages and Civilizations at the Institut National des Langues et Civilisations Orientales (INALCO), Alessandro Guetta teaches the intellectual history of the European Jews in the modern period. He recently published Philosophy and Kabbalah: Elijah Benamozegh and the Reconciliation of Western Thought and Jewish Esotericism *(State University of New York Press, 2008).*

---

1. In Arabic: Sa'id ibn Yusuf al-Fayyumi.

2. *Sefer Egron*, ed. Nehemiah Allony (Jerusalem: Academy of the Hebrew Language, 1967).

3. *Sefer emunot ve-de'ot*, translated into modern Hebrew by Y. Qafah (Jerusalem, 1970); translated into English as *The Book of Beliefs and Opinions*, trans. Samuel Rosenblatt (New Haven, CT: Yale University Press, 1948).

4. *The Dawn of Hebrew Linguistics: The Book of Elegance of the Language of the Hebrews by Saadia Gaon*, ed. Aharon Dotan (Jerusalem: World Union of Jewish Studies, 1997), 2 vols. (in Hebrew).

Interfaith Intellectual Exchanges in Tenth-Century Baghdad: Rationality as Common Denominator

Tenth-century Baghdad was an intellectual center where the sciences, philosophy, and the arts thrived. No less important than these spectacular intellectual developments was a profound evolution in social attitudes. In fact, believers of different religions and proponents of various philosophical options met regularly to discuss controversial philosophical and theological subjects. These meetings were unusual: the participants agreed from the start that the arguments put forward would appeal solely to reason, to the exclusion of scriptural "proofs" taken from the sacred books of the different religions. In other words, the only arguments admitted were ideas and דקג, modes of reasoning shared by all participants, not assertions based on texts recognized by only some of them. The result of the rapid rise of philosophy and science in Islamic territories was the appearance of the *kalām*, the rational theology of Islam. Such meetings were in fact organized by its theologians, the *mutakallimūn*.

The historian al-Humaydi (1036–95) reports a valuable and eloquent eyewitness account from the time in his *Jadhwat al-muqtabis fi tarikh ʿulamaʾ al-Andalus* (*On the Andalusian Scholars*). It was discovered by the great scholar Reinhart Dozy (1820–83), who published a translation in 1853.[1] I provide the text without modernizing Dozy's spelling; I have modified the page layout and added two explanatory notes in brackets.

Gad Freudenthal

Al-Homaidī tells of a devout Spanish theologian named Abou-Omar Ahmed ibn-Mohammed ibn-Sadī, who visited Baghdad at the end of the tenth century. He later met the famous Malekite doctor of al-Kairawān, Abou-Mohammed ibn-abī-Zaīd, who asked him whether, during his stay in Baghdad, he had attended the sessions of the *motecallimīn* [*mutakallimūn*].

"I attended them twice," replied the Spaniard, "but I have been very careful not to return."

"Why is that?" asked Ibn-abī-Zaīd.

"You be the judge," responded Abou-Omar. "At the first session I attended, there were not only Muslims of every branch, orthodox and heterodox, but also infidels, Guebres, materialists, atheists, Jews, and Christians, in short, unbelievers of every kind. Every branch had its leader, charged with defending the opinions it professed, and each time one of these leaders entered the room, everyone stood as a sign of respect, and no one returned to his place before that leader had taken his seat. The room was soon packed, and when it was clear that it was full, one of the unbelievers took the floor. 'We have gathered together to reason,' he said. 'You know all the conditions: you Muslims will not put forward any objections to us drawn from your book [that is, the Qur'an] or founded on the authority of your prophet [that is, the Hadith]; for we believe in neither. Each of us will therefore limit himself to arguments drawn from human reason.' Everyone applauded at these words."

"You can imagine," Abou-Omar continued, "that, having heard such things, I did not return to that assembly. It was proposed, however, that I should visit another. I went, but the scandal was the same."

---

1. Reinhart Dozy, book review of *Averroès et l'averroïsme* by Ernest Renan, *Journal asiatique*, 5th series, 2 (1853): 90–96, quotation on 93.

The Andalusian Philosophical Milieu
Makram Abbès

The Andalusian philosophical milieu of the Middle Ages holds the key to understanding the dual transmission of knowledge between East and West at that time. First, the centers of cultural life under the Abassids communicated their knowledge to Andalusia (tenth to twelfth centuries). Shortly thereafter, philosophical works from Andalusia were dispersed to the major intellectual centers of Christian Europe. Because of this dual movement of cultural transfer, Arabic Spain was the site of one of the most significant historical moments in terms of scientific exchanges and the development of ideas. Through a study of the relations between Jewish and Muslim philosophers, we will get an overall sense of that milieu and will come to understand how the "Andalusian myth" continues to have a strong impact on philosophy. The embellishments attributable to that myth must be weighed against the historical realities and the exaggerated traits stripped away through a precise contextualization of the issues. It was primarily through Averroes and Maimonides, two major thinkers who belonged to the Andalusian milieu, that the discussions central to intellectual pursuits in the Middle Ages were undertaken. These discussions continue to mark our own time in different ways.

Makram Abbès

A graduate of the École Normale Supérieure in Fontenay-Saint-Cloud, Makram Abbès is a senior lecturer at the École Normale Supérieure in Lyons. His research concerns the moral and political philosophy of Islam, especially the themes of war and government. He is the author of *Islam et politique à l'âge classique* (PUF, 2009). In 2010 he was named a junior member of the Institut Universitaire de France.

The "Andalusian myth" in philosophy

For the eleventh-century poet Ibn Zaydun, Andalusia served as a metaphor for the land of milk and honey, where, as in Baudelaire's poem, everything was "luxe, calme et volupté" (luxury, calm, and voluptuousness).[1] For the nineteenth-century Romantics, that place exemplified the theme of ruins, the decline of civilization, paradise lost, and the impossibility of love between people of different faiths.[2] Not only in literature but also in philosophy, that region represented—still represents—a living myth that was put to multiple uses. Leo Strauss, for example, believed that the "medieval Enlightenment," as expressed in philosophies that took both faith and reason into account, had its most illustrious representative in the Andalusian philosopher Maimonides (1135–1204).[3] Maurice-Ruben Hayoun, analyzing the intellectual history of Judaism, follows a thread that leads from Maimonides in the twelfth century to Hermann Cohen in the twentieth, passing through the Averroeist readings in Maimonides's *Guide for the Perplexed* in the Middle Ages and through the Jewish Enlightenment that emerged with Moses Mendelssohn during the Aufklärung.[4] Alain de Libera, considering the different representations, primarily in the West, of the figure of Averroes (1126–98) and its various historiographical metamorphoses, argues that Averroes, "as he is presented," is truly "the emblematic figure of an essentially ambiguous 'model.' He now tends to be elevated to the pinnacle of a more or less idealized *convivencia*, the theoretical product of a form of society that, through him, would provide food for thought even as it provides hope."[5] Aware that the "Andalusian model" must not be taken as "a pious image offered up as nostalgia to illustrate the golden age of coexistence among the three communities stemming from the Book," de Libera, in spite of everything, uses that model as "a means to rescue from obscurity, and to point out the existence of, both an unthought debt and a forgotten legacy,"[6] namely, the role that Arab culture played in the intellectual formation of medieval Europe. It is therefore possible to say that, in philosophy and not only in literature or politics—for example, in the ideological conflicts rife throughout Spain in the nineteenth and twentieth centuries[7]—Andalusia has functioned as a myth, one that certainly contains exaggerated and much embellished traits but that nevertheless continues to be seductive and to command admiration. Indeed, how can we not see in that image of a society that recognized the religious Other, and where different religious groups intermingled and exchanged ideas, the embodiment of something extraordinary for its time?

That reference to the Andalusian model remains key for understanding one of the major aspects of the philosophy that developed in that region between the tenth and thirteenth centuries. But we should not go so far as to make Andalusia a society without conflicts, without crises, and without clashes among its different components: such a society cannot exist, unless it ceases to be *political.* In the East, it was usually Christian philosophers who emerged in the wake of al-Farabi (870–950), the Brethren of Purity (tenth century), and al-Tawhidi (930–1023). Yahya ibn ʿAdiyy, for example, was a student of al-Farabi, and Bishr ibn Matta ibn Yunis belonged to the intellectual circles of tenth-century Baghdad. But one of the characteristics of the Andalusian philosophical space was that it was also the birthplace for many Jewish philosophers. Hence Saʿid al-Andalusi (1029–70), in his *Book of the Categories of Nations*, an introduction to universal knowledge and the role that the different nations play in its elaboration, ends with a chapter devoted to the Jewish scholars, especially those of Andalusia. His contemporary Abu l-Fadl, notes Saʿid, "resides in Saragossa and belongs to an illustrious family of Andalusian Jews descending from the prophet Moses—may salvation come to him! That scholar has studied the sciences in rational order and has acquired great erudition in the various branches of knowledge, following the best methods. He has mastered the Arabic language and has a good knowledge of poetry and rhetoric. He is outstanding in arithmetic, geometry, and astronomy. He has understood music theory and is attempting to apply it. Finally, he has a perfect knowledge of logic and of the practice of research and observation. More recently, he has aspired to study the natural sciences. He first took on Aristotle's *On Generation and Corruption*, which he ultimately mastered. He then undertook the study of *On the Heavens* and *On the Cosmos*. When I left him, in 458/1065, he had already penetrated their mysteries. If he lives long enough, and if his zeal is sustained, Abu l-Fadl will soon know philosophy to perfection, and the various parts of that science will no longer hold any secrets for

> *There is a dimension of alterity that can be achieved only if we think of the Other as part of the 'We'.*

him. And yet he is still only a very young man. But God in the Highest, who is omnipotent, grants his blessings to whomever he pleases."[8] This portrayal of a Jewish philosopher by a Muslim scholar shows that the Andalusian model extended beyond religious tolerance, to which discussions have often confined it. For if the notion of tolerance, especially in its weaker sense, refers to an acceptance of the Other that occurs in spite of ourselves, Sa'id's text shows that there is a dimension of alterity that can be achieved only if we think of the Other as part of the "We." In other words, through his work, which in the mid-eleventh century established a space for acknowledging scientific recognition, Sa'id demonstrates respect for those who possess knowledge, whatever their religion, and attests to the existence of a comprehensive protocol of recognition, which is the foundation for all protocols of coexistence among religious faiths. This space allows for an appreciation of merit and talent but also for real friendship:[9] Abu Ja'far ibn Hasdai, the grandson of Abu l-Fadl, who left Zaragoza to settle in Egypt, maintained a friendly and scientific correspondence with the first Andalusian philosopher, Ibn Bajja, or Avempace (1085–1138), as he is known in the Latin world.[10] Furthermore, this space made it possible for religious minorities to reach the highest echelons of the political world, even while retaining their differences. For example, despite his virulent attacks on Islam, Samuel ha-Nagid, known as Ibn al-Naghrila (993–1056), was sought out for the post of secretary within the administration, thanks to his perfect mastery of the Arabic language. He then became aide to Vizier Ibn al-'Arif and, upon the latter's death, vizier to the Zirid king of Granada.[11] Finally, this space allowed for discursive exchanges, through sometimes violent polemics, between, for example, Ibn Naghrila and Ibn Hazm (994–1064). It is often forgotten that polemics, which are generally viewed in a negative light, are also the means to grasp the arguments of a theological, political, or philosophical adversary. They oblige participants to reestablish knowledge on the foundation of shared assumptions and thus imply a certain consensus, at least about the possibility of debating and engaging in dialogue. Polemicists are forced to take into account other people's opinions, even if the final objective is still to refute them.

See article by Mercedes García-Arenal, pp. 111–129.

See articles by Steven Harvey, pp. 737–757, and Yoram Erder, pp. 778–787.

That is why, though the defense of the faith remained the objective of the polemicist Ibn Hazm, he did not refrain from socializing with Jewish friends, as we read, for example, in his *Ring of the Dove*.[12] Polemics were, in fact, practiced much more within each religious community than across communities, as shown by Ibn al-Naghrila's attacks on the Karaites, and by the Andalusian Jews' adoption of the Muslim tradition of *kalām* (dialectical theology), which can be defined as an art of polemics.

Such observations should not lead us to idealize Andalusian society to such an extent that we reduce the notions of "tolerance," "freedom of conscience," and "pluralism" to the horizons that define our modernity. Medieval societies remained in large part determined by religious frameworks, even for minorities, who embraced their traditions and their place within a community space that safeguarded their identities. But apart from the religious allegiances that rooted them in particular traditions

The sovereignty of the Andalusian Muslims is represented here by a Spanish-Muslim prince in royal costume. Detail from an ivory box, art from the Caliphate of Cordoba, 1004–5, Museo de Navarra, Comunidad Foral de Navarra, Pamplona.

or situations, for Andalusians of the Jewish or Christian religion, or of some other faith, philosophical knowledge was a gateway to the universal. At the time, this knowledge was expressed in Arabic and belonged to the overall context of Islamic culture. The innovations that allowed Arab culture to blossom in the East and in Andalusia were integrated by Jewish scholars and thinkers, whether in the area of grammar, poetry, mysticism, or philosophy: "Until 1200," notes Colette Sirat, "almost all the great works of Jewish thought and all the scientific texts were written in Arabic."[13] The example of Maimonides illustrates this point: although the Talmudic writings were composed in Hebrew, his philosophical magnum opus, *Guide for the Perplexed*, and other scientific works, such as the *Treatise on Logic*, were written in Arabic. In addition to the Greek masters, Maimonides refers to the Eastern *falāsifa*, as well as to those of Andalusia, which attests to his place as a philosopher within a cultural space dominated by the names of al-Farabi (870–950),

767

Ibn Bajja, and Ibn Rushd (1126–98). Given the importance of that linguistic accul-turation, which brought the Jewish and Muslim spheres into close proximity, it is not surprising that authors who wrote in Latin, such as Albertus Magnus and Saint Thomas Aquinas, mention *The Source of Life*, written by Ibn Gabirol, or Avicebron (1020–58), as the work of an "Arab philosopher." Avicebron's Jewish faith did not become common knowledge until the thirteenth century, with Falquéra's translation into Hebrew of excerpts from that book.[14]

In recalling the general cultural context in which these philosophers lived, we should not forget the persecution of minorities and the marks of inferiority inflicted on the religious Other, especially during times of political ferment. There are records of massacres of Jews in Granada in the mid-tenth century during struggles between the kings of the *taifa*s, and the Almohads (r. 1147–1269) persecuted the Andalusian Jews and Christians, who were accused of supporting the advance of the Reconquista. The Almohad regime, driven to maintain the forceful ideology that had brought it to power, was rather unstable, precisely because of the vague-ness of the doctrine of its spiritual founder, al-Mahdi ibn Tumart (1078?–1130), and of his opportunism. It is therefore not odd that the persecution of minorities, especially during times of political crises, was used as a lever activated by its rulers to win the favor of the masses and of the religious authorities. That lever—used as a kind of scapegoating—operated both against religious minorities and against doc-trines judged dangerous or disciplines considered suspect, such as philosophy. For example, when a sovereign saw his power weakening and found that he needed the approval of the masses, sites of difference (religious, ideological, or scientific) were the first targets of repression. The initial reaction of Andalusian society to the inte-gration of the philosophical sciences supports that argument. Al-Hakam II (961–76) had only just introduced the books of the ancients into his library when his son, Hisham al-Mu'ayyad bil-Lah (976–1009), anxious to secure legitimacy from the doctors of law—intermediaries between the circles of power and the masses—ordered the philosophy books burned. This gesture immediately preceded the politi-cal breakup of the caliphate of Cordova and the formation of the *taifa* kingdoms: it was the expression of an existing political crisis and of a need for the legitimation of power, which often entailed the marginalization of a group, discipline, or cur-rent of thought. The same phenomenon occurred in the late twelfth century, when the Almohad dynasty subjected Averroes to torture at the end of his life (1195–97) and condemned him as a philosopher, as a result of plots hatched by his adversaries within the political apparatus.

The emergence of the Andalusian philosophical milieu

Now that we have a general idea of the Andalusian philosophical context, we can turn to the question of its formation. According to Sa'id al-Andalusi, the first intellectual historian of Andalusia, philosophy was introduced into that region of the Muslim world at the initiative of Caliph al-Hakam II, who collected in his library many texts on science and philosophy brought back from the great intellectual centers in the East. From the late tenth century on, therefore, the names of a few scholars began to be mentioned. They did not have the same intellectual scope as the great masters who achieved fame in the East, however, such as al-Kindi (801–73) or al-Farabi. It is therefore clear that in philosophy, literature, and the religious sciences, the East played the role of pioneer and served as a model for innovation and creativity. For that reason, there is a gap of nearly a century between the blossoming of the philosophical disciplines in Baghdad (ninth century) and their reception in Cordova (tenth century). Furthermore, though certain aspects of cultural and literary life spread rather quickly—genres of poetry and artistic currents, for example—developments in the field of science occurred more slowly, because they required preparation on the part of scholars, a shift in their methodological approach, and familiarity with the epistemological foundations of the new disciplines.

Ibn Tumlus (1150?–1223), who left behind a few invaluable pages on this transfer of knowledge between the East and Andalusia, explains at the beginning of his *Introduction to the Art of Logic* that it took a long time for some disciplines in the religious and philosophical sciences to become established in Andalusia. In addition, they often encountered a certain resistance from Andalusian conservatism. Because of their normativity, these fields had pretensions of governing the operation of society; as a result, changes within them always elicited mistrust among Andalusian scholars, who were extremely attached to Malikism and wary of the legal innovations and theological doctrines coming from the East. In fact, whereas the Muslim East had a rich diversity of legal currents, Malikism was almost the only legal doctrine widespread in the Maghreb and Andalusia. For that reason, as Ibn Tumlus notes, the Andalusians' first reaction to the sciences imported from the East was rejection. Over time, however, they came to accept and integrate these currents.[15] Such was the case, for example, for the discipline of the prophetic traditions (Hadith), which had a limited place in Malekite law, but which, in the East, underwent significant expansion and systematization in the ninth and tenth centuries. The attempt to introduce this discipline into Andalusia at first elicited a negative reaction from the doctors of law. A little later, however, they accepted the changes they had previously called impiety and heresy.[16] The same reaction occurred in the field of theology in the early eleventh century, then in the philosophy of al-Ghazali (1058–1111) in the early twelfth century, and finally, in the philosophical sciences, especially logic. Ibn Tumlus, in particular, wanted to legitimate the teaching and acquisition of logic. It is clear from his introduction that he sought to highlight his role as the originator of a "new science" that might meet with rejection from scholars and plunge society into confusion, before society eventually accepted it and appreciated it for its real value. In this respect, his thesis is overstated, since logic had existed from the mid-eleventh century on, as Saʿid al-Andalusi notes, and definitively took root with Avempace's commentaries on al-Farabi's works of logic and Averroes's writings on Aristotle's logic. But what matters in Ibn Tumlus's introduction is that it accurately describes the Andalusians' attitude toward the new disciplines and indicates their conservatism, which, however, did not prevent the Andalusians from afterward surpassing their Eastern predecessors.

One of the aspects that Saʿid al-Andalusi brings to light in his history of the philosophical formation of Andalusians is the omnipresence of what is known as the "quadrivium" (ʿulūm al-ta-ʿālim), which comprises arithmetic, geometry, music, and astronomy. *The Book of the Categories of Nations* mentions many mathematicians, geometers, astronomers, and logicians who emerged in the second half of the ninth century.[17] This information is key since it shows the importance of the mathematical sciences in the curriculum of the Andalusian scholars of the tenth and especially the eleventh century. The observation would be confirmed by Ibn Tufayl (1110–85) in the introduction to his philosophical novel *Hayy ibn Yaqzan*.[18] By

⟩ See Nota bene on *Hayy ibn Yaqzan*, pp. 854–855.

contrast, noetics and metaphysics, traditionally the capstone of scientific curricula were only weakly represented in this generation of founders of Andalusian science. This aspect is an indication of the specific nature of the practice of the science of the ancients in Andalusia until the late eleventh century, when the first true Andalusian philosopher, Ibn Bajja, made his appearance.[19] As a musician interested primarily in physics (the theory of motion) and secondarily in the other sciences (astronomy, geometry), he was heir to this Andalusian scientific tradition. At the same time, he personified the openness of the Andalusian scientific school to two important Eastern philosophical domains: political science and metaphysics. His knowledge of these two disciplines led him to ponder, first, the significance that philosophy ought to have in public life, and, second, the question of the supreme purpose of existence. It is for this reason that Ibn Tufayl is placed in the forefront of a new generation of philosophers, who took a greater interest in speculation. With Ibn Bajja, philosophy acquired a purpose, since, as Ibn Tufayl suggests, it is supposed to lead to true perfection, which the practice of the "exact" sciences alone cannot achieve.[20] It is therefore necessary to complement the practice of science with the study of the soul, the intellect, happiness, the philosopher's social status, and so on. Al-Farabi's subjects are the core of Ibn Bajja's philosophy, whereas the first phase of his scientific course of study is dominated by the sciences of the quadrivium, as he mentions with reference to his philosophical curriculum in a letter to his friend Ibn Hasdai.[21]

In his conclusion to the *Guide*, Maimonides repeated this idea but in an allegorical mode. Using the parable of the sovereign and the people who surround him to represent the idea of a knowledge that can lead to man's ultimate perfection (in his parable, proximity to the sovereign signifies knowledge of the divine), he explains to his disciple Joseph ibn Yehuda, to whom he dedicated the *Guide*, that knowledge of logic and mathematics, two fields in which Joseph excelled, did not by itself allow entry into the palace. At this stage, Maimonides tells him, you resemble "those who go round about the palace in search of the gate. . . . When you understand Physics, you have entered the hall; and when, after completing the study of Natural Philosophy, you master Metaphysics, you have entered the innermost court, and are with the king in the same palace. You have attained the degree of the wise men, who include men of different grades of perfection."[22]

In grasping the principal aspects of the path of Andalusian philosophy, we understand something fundamental about its identity. Some have maintained that, unlike the philosophy of the Arab East, that of Andalusia was more attached to rationalism and less vulnerable to the appeal of mysticism, flights of the imagination, and mental gymnastics. This view, held by the Moroccan thinker Mohamed Abed al-Jabri, in particular, relies on two arguments borrowed from Averroes's thinking: in the first place, Averroes defends *apodeixis*, the demonstrative method, and returns to Aristotle's own mode of thought, dismissing the Neoplatonic commentaries; second, in posing the problem of the juncture between philosophy and religion, Averroes is intent on distinguishing clearly between the two realms, not reconciling or diluting them in a synthesis that would be harmful to both.[23] This characterization of Averroes is accurate, but it is wrong to consider it typical of Andalusian philosophers as a whole and to contrast those philosophers with the Eastern philosophers on the basis of their adherence to demonstrative rationality.

Averroes and Maimonides

The Andalusian intellectual milieu, in fact, saw the emergence of a category of Neoplatonic philosophers, including Ibn Gabirol (Avicebron), who would have to be placed within the lineage of al-Kindi and his Eastern or Andalusian-Maghrebi successors, such as Ibn Ishaq al-Isra'ili (850–932?). A second category comprises thinkers who attempted to move beyond Aristotelianism and who set out to criticize philosophy by turning its own weapons against it: these were primarily authors influenced by al-Ghazali, such as Yehuda Halevi, who, in his famous *Kuzari*, did battle both with the philosophers, destroyers of faith in his view, and the Karaites, who represented a real theological danger for rabbinism in Spain.[24] Ibn Tufayl, who held al-Ghazali in high esteem—he considered him a saint who had reached the shores of the divine—can also be placed in this category, since he displays his own rather pronounced Avicennian penchant for "Eastern philosophy," *hikma al-mashriqiyya*. With the Iranian philosopher Suhrawardi, that tendency would soon be transformed into *hikma ishrāqiyya*, the "philosophy of illumination."[25]

▶ See Counterpoint on the *Kuzari*, pp. 130–131.

▶ See Nota bene on *Hayy ibn Yaqzan*, pp. 853–855.

The third category, and the one that occupies the largest place in the history of human thought, is composed of two men, Averroes and Maimonides. They never met, though their respective biographies and the intellectual complicity that united them have provided the ingredients for an imagined and imaginative encounter.[26]

This complicity was able to take root partly because Maimonides consulted a few of Averroes's writings while composing *The Guide for the Perplexed*. It is obvious, however, that the similarities stem more from the Andalusian intellectual climate to which both men belonged and to which Maimonides remained faithful even several years after his exile to Egypt. "The philosophical background of Maimonides and Averroes," notes Shlomo Pines, "was identical, since it was shared by all Aristotelians of the Spanish school. They had the same kind of naturalistic temperament . . . and the same suspicions about Avicenna's neo-Platonic penchants and probably also about his tendency to look at mystical experience as revelatory of the supreme level of being."[27]

Real convergences between the two authors can be traced along three axes, all meriting consideration of each thinker's particular intellectual nuances: first, the positions they adopted toward Islamic theology and its theologians (the *mutakallimūn*); second, their view of the role of physics within the philosophy curriculum; and third, their political thought.

For Averroes and for Maimonides, the *kalām* is a negation of the possibility of establishing a science that would lead to certainty. One of the purposes of the *Guide*, as announced by Maimonides himself, is to test the demonstrative validity of the arguments the theologians present to prove the existence of God. He thematizes the fundamental principles of their doctrine in twelve points, seeking to uncover the flaws in their reasoning. Assimilating the Karaites and the *geonim* (the heads of certain Talmudic academies in Iraq who were strongly influenced by the Mu'tazilite current) to the Muslim theologians, he shows how the reasoning of these theologians is marred by sophisms and aporias that it is impossible to defend without scandalizing the scientific world or cultivating a certain taste for the absurd. These lines of reasoning do not lead to certainty in the divine sciences because their premises and the elements on which they are based (atomism, the negation of causality) leave believers trained in the scientific method, and who do not wish to find any opposition between the teachings of scripture and those of philosophy, in a state of perplexity. Averroes makes the same argument in his works (*The Incoherence of the Incoherence*, *The Decisive Treatise*, and *The Unveiling of the Methods*), which are directed primarily against the Asharite theological current. But apart from the doctrinal aspects on which he and Maimonides agree, Averroes discerns a factor in theology and sectarianism, and in the fanaticism that fuel them, that necessarily leads to division within public life and a rift in the body politic. He concludes that it is indispensable to neutralize beliefs that may be harmful to civic harmony and to limit the political use of religion.[28]

The second aspect that Maimonides and Averroes share is their attachment to Aristotle's empiricism and their fidelity to the naturalist curriculum. This is a continuation of their critique of the *kalām*, since the theologians' aim was to emphasize the omnipotence of divine will by denying natural causality. Averroes, capital-

Hebrew translation, by the Provençal Kalonymus ben Kalonymus, of Averroes's "Commentary on Aristotle's *Treatise on Meteorology*." Paris, Bibliothèque Nationale de France, ms. Hebrew 951, folios 77 (verso) and 78.

izing on the theologians' critique, cannot refrain from directing his reproaches at Avicenna, who separated metaphysics from physics by arguing that physics, and especially the science of motion, is not indispensable for proving the existence of God. That existence, Avicenna claimed, can be demonstrated on the basis of contingent being, which needs a necessary Being, two purely metaphysical notions. Averroes remains faithful to Aristotle, whereas Maimonides tends rather to distinguish two aspects in the matter. He takes advantage of the state of crisis in Ptolemy's astronomical system: at the time, the Andalusian astronomers had formulated many criticisms of the theory of epicycles and eccentrics, which does not correspond to an accurate representation of the heavens. Maimonides says that if we can still have doubts about the superlunary world, it is better to affirm the limits of human reason on that subject and claim accurate knowledge only about the sublunary world (the world here below). According to him, though Aristotle remains an obligatory reference point for knowledge of the system of nature, persistent doubts about celestial physics prevent us from settling questions about the movements of the spheres and everything concerning the universe (created or eternal) and God. Without denying secondary causes, which are intrinsic to the things of nature and provide all explanations of physics with an intelligible and knowable end, Maimonides ultimately agrees with the theologians in their central assertion about the world's creation.

But that decision stems from the religious creed and is not a scientific position, since the ship of science cannot in this case take us to the shores of certainty. Thus, Maimonides says that he accepts the doctrine of creation for personal reasons, linking the justification of God's existence not to physical proofs but to the advent of the prophets and to divine intervention in history. For him, the religious tradition provides a solution that can save men from doubt, something that cannot be achieved by an astronomy against which many objections can be formulated.[29]

The third and final similarity has to do with political philosophy. The Andalusian philosophers (Avempace, Averroes, and Maimonides), heirs to al-Farabi, were the worthy successors of that founder of Islamic political philosophy. They actively contributed to a reflection on religious law that is undeniably the source of the secularization of knowledge and of a scientific understanding of the place of religion in society. All the elements that Averroes and Maimonides consider—the role of the prophet as founder of a political community that possesses laws assuring its perpetuation, the philosopher's place within public life, the conditions of possibility for the practice of philosophy, the interpretation of the truths of the sacred texts, and the communication of these truths to the masses—demonstrate that they had a real political philosophy that, despite its Platonic origins, developed from their course of study, steeped in the Aristotelian tradition. There is no doubt that Maimonides's participation in these debates allowed Judaism to capitalize on a politicization of religious questions, omnipresent within the philosophical and theological traditions of Islam.[30] Leo Strauss's writings make this clear, since his approach to the works of Averroes and Maimonides centers on the definition of the art of writing that enabled these authors to escape the danger of persecution while articulating their views on political issues. This makes it possible for Strauss to understand these works in their entirety within the sphere of political questions.

A unique moment?

The preceding remarks on Averroes and Maimonides will prove helpful in responding to two fundamental questions. First, what is the link between the Jewish and Muslim philosophers in Andalusia? And second, what is the specificity of the Andalusian intellectual milieu when compared to the Muslim East? Regarding the first question, let us recall, as the medievalist Raymond Scheindlin has noted, that in the intellectual history of Judaism, no community achieved the same level of cultural richness that the community of Andalusian Jews experienced between the ninth and twelfth centuries. That blossoming, which was a reflection of the real impact of an intellectual life shared with the non-Jews,[31] must not obscure the fact that this symbiosis was not confined to Andalusia, and that it is possible to find examples of much more intense encounters, exchanges, and reciprocal influences in the East. The comparison between Maimonides and Averroes reveals the degree to which their similarities are attributable to the school and intellectual atmosphere to which they both belonged. It is that atmosphere that led Maimonides, who spent most of his life in Egypt, to sign his texts "the Andalusian" and to take pride in having been educated by scholars who were the disciples of other illustrious Andalusian philosophers, such as Avempace. The second question is linked to an overall interpretation of the nature of the philosophical activity that emerged in Andalusia. Some

> " *The comparison between Maimonides and Averroes reveals the degree to which their similarities are attributable to the intellectual atmosphere to which they both belonged.* "

researchers have wanted to see that activity as the avatar of a certain rationalism, in opposition to the mysticism that supposedly dominated in the East. This thesis is part of the "Andalusian myth" and has many uses, often of an ideological nature.[32] In addition, it obscures certain aspects specific to the Andalusian intellectual milieu. In fact, that milieu saw the emergence, among both Jews and Muslims, of Neoplatonic philosophers (Avicebron); of thinkers steeped in the *kalām*, who took al-Ghazali as their model (Yehuda Halevi, Ibn Tumlus); of thinkers who benefited from the integration of Aristotelianism and then from its transcendence by Avicennism (as illustrated by Ibn Tufayl); and finally, of personalities who, relying on a solid scientific curriculum, were able to courageously take on the theological-political problem. It would therefore be necessary to take into account the richness and diversity of the Andalusian philosophical milieu in order not to posit an opposition between the East and Andalusia based on dubious arguments. The subsequent intellectual history of Andalusia confirms that interpretation: viewed from the standpoint of Andalusia, which converted to the views of al-Ghazali when he was rehabilitated upon the Almohads' accession to power in the mid-twelfth century, Averroes's project was more or less isolated. For example, Ibn Tufayl, who composed *Hayy ibn Yaqzan* at the end of his life, when Averroes was intellectually productive, does not mention the man for whom he served as mentor vis-à-vis the Almohad sovereigns. Nor does he acknowledge Averroes as an accomplished philosopher. In my view, that provides sufficient evidence of the difference in the two men's projects: Ibn Tufayl favored "Ghazalism," while Averroes fiercely opposed it.[33] That philosophical orientation was reinforced in Andalusia in the thirteenth century by Ibn Sabʿin (1217–70), who conducted a famous philosophical correspondence—now known under the title *The Sicilian Questions*—with Frederick II of Hohenstaufen. That work attests to a shift in philosophical themes toward questions that philosophy shared with mysticism, and which were fostered by the traditions of spiritual philosophy stemming from Neoplatonism. The same orientation appeared a century later among Jewish authors very critical of Maimonides and of the Averroeists in general, as the example of Rabbi Hasdai Crescas (1340–1410) demonstrates. His *Light of the Lord*, written in Castilian, in some sense repeats the gesture of al-Ghazali, whose aim was to refute the system of Aristotelian physics. It thus prepares the way for the emergence of the modern scientific revolutions. According to Harry Austryn Wolfson, Crescas provided the impetus for the genesis of Spinoza's thinking,[34] just as Ibn Tufayl, who was eclipsed for nearly five centuries by the success of Averroes, exerted a decisive influence on the Enlightenment authors, especially regarding the autonomy of the individual and the theme of natural religion.[35]

---

1. Charles Baudelaire, *Les fleurs du mal*, in *Oeuvres complètes* (Paris: Gallimard, 1975), 53.

2. For example, Théophile Gautier's *Émaux et camée*, W. Irving's *Tales of the Alhambra*, and Chateaubriand's *Les aventures du dernier Abencérage*.

3. Kenneth Hart Green, ed., *Leo Strauss on Maimonides: The Complete Writings* (Chicago: University of Chicago Press, 2013); see also G. Sfez, *Leo Strauss, foi et raison* (Paris: Beauchesne, 2007), 84–85.

4. Maurice-Ruben Hayoun, "La tradition philosophique juive: Des Lumières de Cordoue aux Lumières de Berlin," in *L'héritage andalou*, ed. T. Fabre (Paris: Éditions de l'aube, 1995), 29–38.

5. Alain de Libera, "Une figure emblématique de l'héritage oublié," in *L'héritage andalou*, ed. Fabre, 17.

6. Ibid., 19.

7. On this point, see M. de Epalza, "Le modèle andalou: Une tolérance intolérable," in *L'héritage andalou*, ed. Fabre, 117–22. See also *Histoire de l'Andalousie: Mémoire et enjeux*, ed. J.-A. Alcantud and F. Zabbal (Montpellier: L'Archange Minotaure, 2003), 211–74.

8. Saʿid al-Andalusi, *Tabaqat al-umam*, trans. Régis Blachère as *Livre des catégories des nations* (Paris: Larose éditeurs, 1935), 159–60, translation slightly modified.

9. Ibn Bassam, an eleventh-century Andalusian scholar, devotes a chapter to Ibn Hasdai in his literary encyclopedia, providing selections from his poetry and prose. See *Al-Dhakhira* (Beirut: Dar al-kutub al-ʿilmiyya, 1998), 290–311.

10. Ibn Abi Usaybiʿa, *Tabaqat al-atibba* (*Classes of Physicians*) (Beirut: Dar al-kutub al-ʿilmiyya, 1998), 458. See the text of one of these exchanges in J.-E. Alaoui, *Rasaʾil falsafiyya li-Abi Bakr ibn Bajja* (Beirut: Dar al-Thaqafa / Casablanca: Dar al-nashr al-maghribiyya, 1983), 77–81.

11. Roger Arnaldez, *À la croisée des trois monothéismes: Une communauté de pensée au Moyen-Âge* (Paris: Albin Michel, 1993), 158–59.

12. See ʿAli ibn Ahmad Ibn Hazm, *The Ring of the Dove: A Treatise on the Art and Practice of Arab Love*, trans. A. J. Arberry (London: Luzac, 1953).

13. Colette Sirat, *La philosophie juive médiévale en terre d'Islam* (Paris: Presses du CNRS, 1988), 26. See also Roger Arnaldez's arguments in the chapter entitled "La civilisation de Cordue," in *À la croisée des trois monothéismes*, 153–275, and in the articles in *The Cambridge Companion to Medieval Jewish Philosophy*, ed. Daniel H. Frank and Oliver Leaman (Cambridge: Cambridge University Press, 2003).

14. Sirat, *La philosophie juive médiévale*, 19 and 89.

15. Ibn Tumlus, *Al-Madkhal li-sinaʿat al-mantiq* [*Introduction to the Art of Logic*], ed. A. Palaçios (Madrid, 1916), 9–14.

16. Ibid., 11.

17. Saʿid al-Andalusi, *Tabaqat al-umam*, 122.

18. Ibn Thofail [Ibn Tufayl], *Hayy ben Yaqdhan*, trans. L. Gauthier (Beirut: Imprimerie catholique, 1936), 10.

19. Other philosophers, such as Ibn Gabirol and al-Kirmani (who introduced the writings of the Brethren of Purity into Andalusia), did not write a great deal, or indeed at all. And Malik ibn Wuhaby al-Ishbili, a contemporary of Ibn Bajja who was lauded for his mastery of the speculative sciences, abandoned philosophy, succumbing to the pressures placed on him by the religious milieus.

20. Ibn Thofail, *Hayy ben Yaqdhan*, 10–11.

21. See Alaoui, *Rasaʾil falsafiyya li-Abi Bakr ibn Bajja*, 77–81.

22. Moses Maimonides, *The Guide for the Perplexed*, trans. Michael Friedländer (London: Routledge & Kegan Paul, 1904), part 3, chap. 51, http://en.wikisource.org/wiki/The_Guide_for_the_Perplexed_(Friedlander).

23. See Mohamed Abed al-Jabri, *Introduction à la critique de la raison arabe*, trans. A. Mafoud and M. Geoffroy (Paris: La Découverte et l'Institut du monde arabe, 1994), 95–157. Oliver Leaman makes the same argument about the difference between the philosophical spirit of the Andalusians and that of Easterners in "Is There a Distinctly Andalusi Philosophy?" *MARS (Le Monde Arabe dans la Recherche Scientifique)* 9 (1998): 75–85.

24. See M.-C. Hernandez, *Histoire de la pensée en terre d'Islam*, trans. R. Béhar (Paris: Editions Desjonquères, 2005), chap. 12, "Le développement de la pensée sépharade (XIᵉ–XIIᵉ siècles)," 426–28.

25. The philosophy of illumination, inspired by the writings of Avicenna, was founded by Suhrawardi in the twelfth century. See, in particular, his *Kitab Hikmat al-Ishraq* [*Book of Oriental Wisdom*], translated into French by Henry Corbin as *Le livre de sagesse orientale* (Paris: Gallimard, 2003). For the reception of that Avicennian theme in Andalusia, see D. Gutas, "Tufayl on Ibn Sina's Eastern Philosophy," *Oriens* 34 (1994): 222–41.

26. Jacques Attali, *La confrérie des éveillés* (Paris: Le Livre de Poche, 2006); and Ili Gorlizki, *Maïmonide—Averroès: Une correspondance rêvée*, trans. Philippe Bobichon, preface by Colette Sirat (Paris: Maisonneuve et Larose, 2004).

27. Shlomo Pines, *La liberté de philosopher: De Maïmonide à Spinoza*, trans. Rémi Brague (Paris: Desclée de Brouwer, 1997), 182. For the links between Maimonides and other philosophers from the East and Andalusia, see the entire chapter titled "Les sources philosophiques du *Guide des perplexes*," 89–233; and *Maïmonide philosophe et savant*, ed. Tony Lévy and Roshdi Rahed (Leuven: Peeters, 2004).

28. I take the liberty of referring to my *Islam et politique à l'âge classique* (Paris: PUF, 2009), 249–53, in which I develop these points.

29. On this subject, see Herbert Davidson, "Maimonides' Secret Position on Creation," in *Studies in Medieval Jewish History and Literature*, ed. I. Twersky (Cambridge, MA: Harvard University Press, 1979), 16–40.

30. See Pines, *La liberté de philosopher*, 145; and S. Harvey, "Islamic Philosophy and Jewish Philosophy," in *The Cambridge Companion to Arabic Philosophy*, ed. Peter Adamson and Richard Taylor (Cambridge: Cambridge University Press, 2005), esp. 355–61.

31. Raymond Scheindlin, "The Jews in Muslim Spain," in *The Legacy of Muslim Spain*, ed. S. Khadra-Jayyusi (Leiden: Brill, 1994), 188. See also Haïm Zafrani, "Les territoires de la rencontre judéo-musulmanes," in *L'héritage andalou*, ed. Fabre, 105–15.

32. For the ideological use of that thesis, see the sources listed above, note 7.

33. There is a vague mention in Ibn Tufayl of people who practice philosophy but who are not yet worthy of the name "philosopher." See Ibn Thofaïl, *Hayy ben Yaqdhan*, 11–12.

34. Harry Austryn Wolfson, *Crescas' Critique of Aristotle* (Cambridge, MA: Harvard University Press, 1929).

35. Samar Attar, *The Vital Roots of European Enlightenment: Ibn Tufayl's Influence on Modern Western Thought* (Lanham, MD: Lexington Books, 2010).

The Karaites and Mu'tazilism
Yoram Erder

In the time of the *geonim* (directors of the Talmudic academies), Karaism was greatly influenced by the Muslim Mu'tazilite theological movement. The Karaites, though largely divided on many questions, adopted all the doctrinal fundaments of Mu'tazilism, both in the area of scriptural exegesis and in discussions of the essential theological themes for which the Mu'tazilites were the standard-bearers within Islam. Beginning in the eleventh century, the Karaites, who belonged to the group known as the Avelei Tsion (Mourners of Zion), having settled in Jerusalem, set out to compose theological texts constituting a genre in their own right. As a result, they found themselves caught up in the polemics pervading the Mu'tazilite movement of the time. They also contributed toward the spread of the Mu'tazilite doctrine within the Fatimid caliphate, which, however, showed no affinity for that current of thought. When the center of gravity of Karaism shifted to Byzantium in the twelfth century, some Karaite Mu'tazilite literary works were translated from Judeo-Arabic into Hebrew, even as new Karaite works of Mu'tazilite inspiration continued to be composed there. In the thirteenth century, a breach opened between the Karaites and Mu'tazilism, under the influence of the philosophy spread by the Rabbanite writings.

Yoram Erder

A professor of history at Tel Aviv University, Yoram Erder is a specialist on relations between Jews and Muslims and on Palestine at the time of Islam's emergence, as well as on the first Karaite movement. His publications include *The Karaite Mourners of Zion and the Dead Sea Scrolls: Toward an Alternative History of Rabbinical Judaism* (Hakibbutz Hameuchad, 2004; in Hebrew).

The determining influence of Mu'tazilism on the Karaites

There is no doubt that the Karaite movement, which originated in Iraq and Persia in the second half of the ninth century, was a result of the cultural exchange between Judaism and Islam during the time of the *geonim* in the Middle East. Mu'tazilism constituted one of the elements of Islam that had a determining influence on Karaism during its formative phase, between the tenth and eleventh centuries, in the field of biblical exegesis and in the formation of its theology. Because the majority of Karaite texts at the time were composed in Judeo-Arabic, it was easy for the principles of Mu'tazilism in particular, and of Islam in general, to make inroads in Karaite literature. In the twelfth century, the Byzantine Karaites preserved the

Mu'tazilite-Karaite tradition that had developed in the Islamic countries, translating into Hebrew Karaite works of a Mu'tazilite character. Subsequently, the Karaites of Byzantium and Turkey took their distance from Mu'tazilism and moved closer to Rabbanite philosophy.

The influence of Mu'tazilism exerted itself not only on the Karaites but also on the Rabbanites during the time of the *geonim*, as attested in the works of Saadia Gaon and Samuel ben Hofni Gaon. Medieval theologians were not unaware that the Karaites' debt toward Mu'tazilism was much greater than that of the Rabbanites, however. The Muslim Al-Mas'udi, for example, said that the Karaites represented a minority among the Jews and were the people of *al-'adl wa-l-tawhīd*, the school of divine justice and unity.[1] He therefore defined the Karaites as Mu'tazilites of the Jewish community. In the Muslim literature, in fact, the Mu'tazilites were called the disciples of *al-'adl wa-l-tawhīd* because of two doctrinal principles: *tawhīd*, the belief in the oneness of God, and *'adl*, divine justice, which rewards the righteous and punishes the unrighteous in the afterlife. The Mu'tazilite theologians believed that men would be judged by God because, having the freedom to choose between good and evil, they were responsible for their actions. In *Guide for the Perplexed* (1.71), Maimonides points out the influence of Mu'tazilism on certain *geonim* and Karaite theologians. The fourteenth-century Karaite Aaron ben Eliya also reports Mu'tazilism's influence on the first Karaites: "When Israel split apart into two sects, the Karaites and the Rabbanites, the Karaite sages and a small number of Rabbanites embraced the Mu'tazilite doctrine."[2]

Given the preponderant place of Mu'tazilism in Karaite ideology, the presence or absence of a Mu'tazilite component in the various Jewish groups during the time of the *geonim* can serve as a criterion for determining who was truly Karaite. The first Karaites, who emerged in the tenth century, intently studied the Halakhic writings of Anan ben David (second half of the eighth century), who came from a family of exilarchs and is considered the founder of the Ananite current. From the twelfth century on, the Karaites came to consider Anan ben David the founder of their movement, even though he was not actually born in the second half of the ninth century and, having lived before the appearance of Mu'tazilism, could not have been influenced by it. The early Karaites also studied the writings of Benjamin al-Nahawandi (first half of the ninth century), who called his followers Ba'alei Mikra, "masters of Scripture." Some scholars consider him a Karaite, but in my view, he was not: for one thing, Mu'tazilite elements are absent from his doctrine. Like the Mu'tazilite theologians, al-Nahawandi was also confronted with the problem of interpreting the anthropomorphic descriptions of the divine in the Bible. Unlike Mu'tazilism, however, which posited a single God, al-Nahawandi argued that the God of the Bible, endowed with bodily attributes, was actually the angel who had created the world. As for the higher God who sits above the angel, he is detached from our world, lacking material attributes.

Daniel al-Qumisi, the first Karaite whose name has come down to us, was already a Mu'tazilite. Originally from Persia, he immigrated to the land of Israel in about 880 and was one of the founders of the Avelei Tsion (Mourners of Zion), the Karaite community of Jerusalem. That city became the largest center of Karaism in the tenth and eleventh centuries. An appeal in Hebrew for 'alya, immigration to the land of Israel, is attributed to al-Qumisi. It sets out the foundations of his doctrine, which were very clearly influenced by Mu'tazilism.[3] Ya'qub al-Qirqisani, a Babylonian Karaite theologian from the first half of the tenth century, believed that the reason al-Qumisi denied the existence of angels was precisely to mark himself off from the angelogical doctrine of al-Nahawandi.[4] Al-Qirqisani himself composed a *Book of Lights and Beacons*, which he defined as a *sefer ha-mitsvot*, that is, an enumeration of the biblical commandments, though a perusal of that book reveals that this definition is too limited. The volume bears the mark of a strong Mu'tazilite influence and quotes several specific Mu'tazilite texts.[5] The obvious influence of Mu'tazilism on Karaism invalidates one of the foundations of Rabbanite polemics, which claimed that the Karaites were the direct heirs of the Sadducees from the era of the Second Temple. No Sadducean texts have come down to us, and this is not the place to pursue the nature of that sect. For our purposes, it is important to recall that, according to the theological literature, the Sadducees did not believe in divine reward and punishment or in the afterlife. Such views are diametrically opposed to Mu'tazilite doctrine. Yet Maimonides, who underscores Mu'tazilism's influence on the Karaites in his *Guide for the Perplexed*, does not hesitate to argue, in his commentary on the Mishnah, that the Karaites are the Sadducees of his generation.[6] The parallel between Karaites and Sadducees was in fact very common in the Middle Ages. Some rabbis, however, such as Ibn Kammuna (thirteenth century), held a different view: "The Karaites cannot be Sadducees . . . because they believe in the resurrection of the dead, reward, punishment, and the afterlife."[7] Before Ibn Kammuna, Yehuda Halevi also distinguished the Karaites from the Sadducees: chapter 3 of his *Kuzari* is devoted entirely to the polemic with the Karaites.

> *The Karaites emancipated themselves from the Rabbanite tradition. They set about interpreting the Bible using new methods, often influenced by Islam.*

See article by Geneviève Gobillot, pp. 788–795.

The Mu'tazilite influence on the Karaite interpretation of the Bible

In rejecting oral law, the Karaites emancipated themselves from the Rabbanite tradition. They set about interpreting the Bible using new methods, often influenced by Islam. This was their most notable undertaking. But even as the Karaites were developing their system for interpreting the Bible, the Muslims had not yet worked out their definitive exegesis of the Qur'an. One bone of contention that led to bitter disputes between the various tendencies of Islam was the place of Muslim oral law, the Hadith, in relation to the Qurʾan, the book of divine revelation. Researchers have emphasized the influence on the Karaites of the Kharijites, some of whom completely repudiated the Hadith.[8] The founder of the Hanafite *madhhab*, the Sunni Abu Hanifa—who, according to some sources, met Anan in prison—refused

Opening page of a Karaite Bible, Palestine, tenth century. London, British Library, ms. or. 2540, fol. 3.

⟩ See article
by Phillip
Ackerman-
Lieberman,
pp. 683–693.

to take the Hadith as the sole reference for Muslim law, appealing to the magistrate's personal and reasoned assessment and to analogical deduction (*qiyās*) during the trial. The *qiyās* method is easily recognizable in the interpretation the Karaites were giving of the *halakha*, so much so that Saadia Gaon, the greatest polemicist against the Karaites, railed against the use of *qiyās* in interpreting commandments whose justification was not made explicit in the biblical text itself (*mitsvot sham ʿiyyot*).

It is clear that Muʾtazilism constituted one of the most notable influences on the Karaites' biblical exegesis, leading them in particular to grant preeminence to the rational approach (*ʿaql*). To study the sacred texts on the basis of reason, it was necessary to know the rules of syntax and grammar; in the time of the *geonim*, in fact, the Karaites were leaders in the development of Hebrew grammar. One consequence of interpreting the biblical texts with the aid of rational and linguistic tools was that the Karaites' commentaries conflicted with those of the Rabbanite theologians, who based themselves on the *derash*, a method that took its distance from the literal interpretation of the words (*peshaṭ*). The Karaites criticized the Rabbanite theologians' *midrash aggadah* with weapons employed by Muʾtazilism, entering into disputes with their Muslim adversaries, that is, with those who wanted to establish jurisprudence solely on the Hadith.[9] The rational approach led the Karaites to posit that the biblical commandments had been given in a literal sense (*zāhir*)—not in an esoteric one (*bāṭin*)—so that everyone could understand and respect them. This was also the position of the Muʾtazilites. The Karaites, like the Rabbanites, learned from Muʾtazilism to distinguish the rational commandments (*ʿaqliyyat*) from the received commandments (*sam ʾiyyat*), revealed by God through the prophets. The meaning of the rational commandments is clear and easily comprehensible by human reason and would therefore stand even in the absence of revelation. By contrast, the meaning of the *sam ʾiyyat* is not always obvious for the people obliged to observe them. The Qurʾan (3:7) establishes a distinction between verses that are clear and accessible to all (*muhkamat*) and obscure verses (*mutashabihat*), which must not be interpreted literally but instead require an "ascendant" interpretation, or *ta ʾwil*. Human wisdom and the context in which the word appears (*qarina*) tell the exegete whether he must understand it in literal terms or rather strive to find its hidden meaning. For the Muʾtazilite theologians, it was clear that the material attributes of the divine had to be interpreted in an allegorical rather than a literal manner. The Karaites scrupulously applied that method to the Bible.

The Mourners of Zion and Muʾtazilism

The Mourners of Zion (Avelei Tsion) represented the largest Karaite community in Jerusalem during the time of the *geonim*. Medieval theologians had noted the connection between the Karaites and Muʾtazilism, but the interpretive methods of the Karaites of Jerusalem did not stem solely from Muʾtazilite rationalism. The

Mourners of Zion movement was essentially messianic: its doctrine was strongly influenced by the Qumran texts, now known as the Dead Sea Scrolls. A portion of these scrolls was already circulating in the land of Israel in the ninth century, as the presence of a copy of the Damascus Document in the Cairo Geniza indicates.[10] To hasten redemption, the Mourners of Zion devoted their time to reciting supplications and, as a sign of mourning, did not eat meat or drink wine. Under the influence of Mu'tazilism, they studied the commandments using a rational approach. The Mourners would no doubt have preferred a different method, since their approach gave no univocal responses and left many questions open, but they were forced by the circumstances to accept it. They were, in fact, awaiting the arrival of a Teacher of Righteousness (Moreh Tsedek), whom they equated with the prophet Elijah. The mission of the Teacher of Righteousness, who was supposed to manifest himself on the eve of the Messiah's coming, was to teach the commandments to the people while at the same time dissipating doubts and controversies. The Mourners believed that in the books of the Prophets, and in other biblical books that they believed contained prophetic themes—such as the book of Daniel, the Song of Songs, and the Psalms—predictions about their own time lay concealed. It was possible to uncover them, they thought, by revealing the hidden levels of the text (*bātin*) rather than confining themselves to the external and literal level (*zāhir*). According to the Karaites, uncovering the hidden, prophetic level was the only means to hasten redemption. It would seem that, apart from the influence of the Qumran writings, the Karaites' interpretive method owed a great deal to a familiarity with the Imamite or Ismaili Shi'ite movements existing in the land of Israel under Fatimid domination. The biblical commentaries of the Mourners of Zion contain a mix of rational commentaries influenced by Mu'tazilism and messianic allegorical commentaries inspired by Shi'ism. It is interesting to note that the Imamite Shi'ites were also influenced by Mu'tazilite theology, especially after they lost the source of their legal authority in 941, with the Major Occultation of the twelfth imam, whose return as al-Mahdi (the Guided One) they await.[11]

The allegorical commentaries by the Mourners of Zion on the prophecies clarify their relationship to Islam in general and to Mu'tazilism in particular. That relationship was ambivalent. The Mourners were perfectly well aware that their communities in the Middle East had come into being under the aegis of Islam. Their proximity to that religion made obvious the gap between Islam and the Rabbanites on certain Halakhic subjects. The Jews, including the Karaites, believed that their lives were better under the Islamic yoke than under Christian domination, and that the tension between Christianity and Judaism was greater than that between Islam and Judaism. That said, the Karaites considered Islam less a revealed religion than a false dogma inspired by earlier sects, and they fought hard against that dogma. They hoped for the destruction of Islam, which would also mean the redemption of Israel. In his commentary on Psalm 22:1, Yefet ben 'Eli declares that "just as the light of dawn arises in the East and shines until the sun illuminates the entire earth, so the destruction of Mecca and of the sons of Qedar [i.e., the Muslims] represents the first sign of redemption."

In his commentary on Psalm 42:10, 'Eli evokes the economic oppression of the Jews under Islamic rule. It seems he considered religious repression the worst blot. The Jews were often forced to participate in interfaith debates (*majlis*), at which they had to defend their religion under arduous conditions. The statement of the Andalusian Muslim theologian Ibn 'Arabi (1148), who lived in Jerusalem between 1092 and 1095, has come down to us: he describes the victory of the Muslim theologians in a dispute of this type in Jerusalem, in which the Karaite Yashar ben Hesed (Sahl b. al-Fadl al-Tustari) probably participated. (I shall return later to Sahl's contribution to the Karaite-Mu'tazilite corpus.)[12] It often happened that a Mu'tazilite Muslim theologian attacked the Jews. Similarly, despite the widely known influence on the Karaites of Mu'tazilism, it is not rare to find virulent Karaite criticisms of that doctrine. And, before the eleventh century, when the Karaites undertook to compose theological treatises clearly influenced by Mu'tazilism, they had a tendency to conceal that inspiration in their writings.

Nevertheless, a thorough examination of Yefet ben 'Eli's commentaries shows that he was able to distinguish between the Mu'tazilite Muslims and other non-Jews, and he seems to have nurtured the hope that the Mu'tazilites would not be destroyed on the day of the Last Judgment but would convert to Judaism. The Mourners of Zion maintained that, after the Last Judgment, only those who believed in divine unity and who called God by his name would be saved, as it is written: "Whosoever shall call on the name of the Lord" (Joel 2:32; KJV). Yefet ben 'Eli was not unaware that, among the Muslims, the Mu'tazilite theologians believed in the unity of God and in human free will, and opposed the materialist interpretation of the attributes of divinity. Their faith may be authentic, he argued, but it is nonetheless negative, because it is based on the Qur'an, which is not a revealed book. According to him, all Christians will be destroyed on Judgment Day, because they believe in the Trinity, which is in total contradiction with divine unity. "The remnant of Ishmael," that is, the Muslims who survive Judgment Day, will convert to Judaism of their own volition. There is no doubt that he is alluding here to the Mu'tazilites.[13]

> " *The Mu'tazilite contribution to Islam is perceptible primarily in the realm of theology.* "

The influence of Mu'tazilism on the Karaite theological literature

The Mu'tazilite contribution to Islam is perceptible primarily in the realm of theology. Islam's major conquests in the Middle East placed the Muslims in contact with ancient Greek literature in fields as varied as philosophy, science, and medicine. After these works were translated into Arabic, the Muslims created a literature in their own language in these specific fields. Mu'tazilite sages were the first Muslim theologians to take on the problem of God's essence and the proofs of his existence. They were interested in the relationship between God and human beings and in other existential questions that humanity had confronted since the earliest times: the essence of man; the importance of reason and speech, which, according to them, marked the difference between humanity and the animal kingdom; the source of good and evil in a world governed by a single God; free will, which allows men to choose between good and evil; the role of the sacred books and their interpretation; and the importance of the prophet, the intermediary between God and men.

For the Mu'tazilite theologians, the answer to these questions was difficult to discover because of the gap between the rationalist method they favored and their religious faith. They argued that the physical world was made up of an aggregation of atoms. Substances became differentiated by accidents that conferred distinctive characteristics on them, such as color or taste. Unlike atoms, these characteristics were immaterial and did not possess volume. Among the Jews, it was the Karaites who adhered most closely to Mu'tazilite atomism.

It was not until the eleventh century that the Mourners of Zion undertook to compose theological works of their own. The Karaites proved sufficiently versed in Mu'tazilite discourse to take an active role in the internal debates among the Muslim Mu'tazilites. They were thus led to study the Muslim Mu'tazilite texts more deeply and to copy them out faithfully in order to preserve them in their libraries. Some unknown manuscripts of the Muslim Mu'tazilite literature were even discovered thanks to Karaite copies and quotations the Karaites used as illustrations in their writings.[14] The Mourners of Zion played an important role in introducing the Muslim Mu'tazilite debates of Iraq and Persia into the land of Israel and Egypt. The first Mourners who settled in Jerusalem were from those regions, and their descendants maintained close ties to their places of origin. Mu'tazilism associated itself with Imamite Shi'ism in Iraq from the beginning, but the Ismaili Fatimids who governed Egypt and the land of Israel from 969 on expressed reservations about the movement. As a result, the Mourners of Zion were the true propagators of Mu'tazilism in the territories the Fatimids controlled.

It would seem that the first theological summa of a Mu'tazilite nature, published by the Karaites of Jerusalem under the title *Kitab al-ni'ma*,[15] was the work of Levi ben Yafet, son of Yafet ben 'Eli, one of the greatest Karaite theologians of the tenth century, who lived in Jerusalem. Levi, like a number of Karaites after him, was influenced by the Mu'tazilites of Basra and not those of Baghdad. This book is unique of its kind: biblical quotations abound, and it does not speak openly of the Muslim Mu'tazilites. It appears that it was not widely distributed in Karaite circles. The most important contribution to the theological literature influenced by Mu'tazilism was made by Yusuf al-Basir (d. 1040), whose works were widely dispersed. His most famous books are *Kitab al-Muhtawi* (*The Universal Book*), translated into Hebrew under the title *Sefer Ne'imot*, and *Kitab al-Tamyiz* (*The Book of Discernment*), also translated into Hebrew. Yusuf al-Basir was an expert on the polemics internal to Muslim Mu'tazilism. He considered himself the disciple of 'Abd al-Jabbar (d. 1024), the great Mu'tazilite theologian of Basra. For that reason, he felt justified in entering into a polemic with Abu l-Husayn al-Basri (d. 1045), who had attacked al-Basir's master. Al-Basir's texts constituted the first serious criticisms of Abu l-Husayn. As a result, al-Basir found himself on the front lines of the polemic between Muslim Mu'tazilites. The dispute between the two Muslim masters had to do, among other things, with the Mu'tazilite doctrine of atoms used to demonstrate the existence of God, creator of the world.[16] The Mu'tazilite literature forged a very strong connection between theology and the sources of Muslim law (*usūl al-fiqh*). Yusuf al-Basir had himself linked the two fields, as we discover in his *Kitab al-istibsar fi al-fra'id*. In this book, he argues that it is meaningless for the believer to respect the commandments if he is incapable of reasoning and grasping their significance. Once the obligation to understand the commandments and the reality of divine justice is taken into account, it is impossible to believe that God does not recompense (*'iwad*) eight-day-old males for the suffering produced by circumcision, or animals subjected to ritual slaughter. Al-Basir also treats the question of the received commandments, whose meaning is not always apparent to those who must respect them.[17] Yeshu'a b. Yehuda, a disciple of Yusuf al-Basir, also contributed to the Karaite Mu'tazilite literature.

Whereas Yusuf al-Basir supported the Mu'tazilite theologian 'Abd al-Jabbar at the expense of Abu l-Husayn al-Basri in 1044, Sahl ibn Fadl, who lived in Jerusalem in the second half of the eleventh century, defended Abu l-Husayn. In his book *Maqdisiyyat* and in other writings, he cites texts by Abu l-Husayn that have come down to us through Sahl.[18] In the introduction to his *Kitab al-ima'* (*The Book Collecting All the Theoretical and Practical Components of the Obligation Imposed by God*), Sahl explains that he was asked to write a book on the model of the *Kitab al-Jumal*, by the Imamite Shi'ite theologian al-Sharif al-Murtada (d. 1044). This volume constitutes a transitional phase in the synthesis of Mu'tazilite theology and the Imamite Shi'ite doctrine. In addition, in his book Sahl links principles of jurisprudence to Mu'tazilite theology.

Karaism, which originated in the territories of Islam, was strongly marked by this religion. The influence of Mu'tazilism is proof of that. With the destruction of the Karaite community of Jerusalem in 1099, following the First Crusade, and the decline of the Jews' condition in Muslim Mediterranean countries, the Karaites' center of activity shifted to Byzantium. Their literary heritage, composed in Judeo-Arabic, was translated into Hebrew, including the texts influenced by Mu'tazilism. In the twelfth century, the impact of Mu'tazilism on the Byzantine Karaites was tangible, as illustrated by Yehuda Hadassi's *Eshkol ha-kofer*, written in Hebrew. Subsequently, as a result of the rapprochement between the Karaites and the

Rabbanites of Byzantium, and also later, under the Ottoman Empire, the Karaites gradually abandoned the Muʾtazilite doctrine in favor of the philosophy influenced by the Rabbanite literature.

---

1. ʿAli b. al-Husayn al-Masʿudi, *Kitab al-Tanbih wa-l-ishraf* (Leiden: Brill, 1894), 11–112.

2. Aaron ben Eliya, *ʾEtz Hayim* [*Tree of Life*], ed. F. Delitzsch (Leipzig, 1841), chap. 1, p. 4.

3. H. Ben-Shammai, "Major Trends in Karaite Biblical Exegesis in the Tenth and Eleventh Centuries," in *Karaite Judaism: A Guide to Its History and Literary Sources*, ed. M. Polliack (Leiden: Brill, 2003), 341–44. It is possible that al-Qumisi published a theological book in Judeo-Arabic called *Kitab al-tawhid* [*The Book of Divine Unity*].

4. Yaʾqub al-Qirqisani, *Kitab al-anwar wa-l-maraqib*, ed. L. Nemoy (New York: Alexander Kohut Memorial Foundation, 1939–43), 330.

5. G. Maqdisi, "Dialectic and Disputation: The Relation between the Texts of Qirqisani and Ibn ʿAqil," in *Mélanges d'islamologie: Volume dédié à la mémoire d'Armand Abel*, ed. P. Salmon (Leiden: Brill, 1974), 201–6.

6. Maimonides, *The Commentary to Mishnah Aboth*, Aboth 1:3.

7. L. Nemoy, "Ibn Kammunah's Treatise on the Differences between the Rabbanites and the Karaites," *Proceedings of the American Academy for Jewish Research (PAAJR)* 36 (1968): 146.

8. M. Cook, "ʿAnan and Islam: Origins of Karaite Scripturalism," *Jerusalem Studies in Arabic and Islam (JSAI)* 9 (1987): 161–82.

9. Wael B. Hallaq, *A History of Islamic Legal Theories* (Cambridge: Cambridge University Press, 1997), 18.

10. N. Wieder, *The Judean Scrolls and Karaism*, 2nd ed. (Jerusalem: Ben-Zvi Institute, 2005).

11. W. Madelung, "Imamism and Muʾtazilite Theology," in *Shiʿism imamite*, ed. T. Fahd (Paris: Presses Universitaires de France, 1970), 13–29.

12. See also G. Schwarb, "Sahl b. al-Fadl al-Tustari's *Kitab al-Ima*," *Ginzei Qedem* 2 (2006): 67–71.

13. Y. Erder, "The Attitude of the Karaite Yefet ben ʿEli toward Islam in the Light of His Interpretation of Psalms 14 and 53," *Michael* 14 (1997): 29–49 (in Hebrew).

14. H. Ben Shammai, "A Note on Some Karaite Copies of Muʾtazilite Writings," *Bulletin of the School of Oriental and African Studies (BSOAS)* 37 (1974): 295–304.

15. D. Sklare, "Levi ben Yefet and His *Kitab al-niʿma*: Selected Texts," in *A Common Rationality: Muʾtazilism in Islam and Judaism*, ed. C. Adang et al. (Wurzburg: Ergon, 2007), 157–216.

16. W. Madelung and S. Schmidtke, "Yusuf al-Basir's first Refutation (Naqd) of Abul l-Husayn al-Basri's Theology," in *A Common Rationality*, ed. Adang et al., 229–96.

17. D. E. Sklare, "Yusuf al-Basir: Theological Aspects of His Halakhic Works," in *The Jews of Medieval Islam: Community, Society, and Identity*, ed. D. Frank (Leiden: Brill, 1995), 249–70.

18. W. Madelung and S. Schmidtke, *Rational Theology in Interfaith Communication: Abu l-Husayn al-Basri's Muʾtazili Theology among the Karaites in the Fatimid Age* (Leiden: Brill, 2006), 61–100.

Judaism and Islam According to Ibn Kammuna

Geneviève Gobillot

When Ibn Kammuna, a Jewish philosopher from Iraq, completed his *Examination of the Three Faiths* on Judaism, Christianity, and Islam, he was certainly aware that he had participated in the advance of humanity toward the better world of peace and brotherhood to which religious and sages have always said they aspired. How much more painful must his astonishment have been four years later, when, at the doors of his besieged house, a mob of his fellow citizens clamored for his death and the destruction of his book. Perhaps he felt that his efforts had definitively gone up in smoke, or worse, that they had in the end contributed toward fanning the very flames of incomprehension and hatred that he had wanted to fight. Perhaps he held on to a glimmer of hope about the future of his humanistic and universalist ideas. No one can know, since history has nothing to say about it. By contrast, everyone who becomes acquainted with this text, miraculously preserved over the centuries, is in a position to know what to make of that legacy, intended for all without distinction as to origin or religion.

Geneviève Gobillot

A professor of history of Arabo-Muslim ideas at the Université de Lyon-III, Geneviève Gobillot currently devotes most of her research to the principles of Qur'anic theology in the light of the "hermeneutic thresholds" constituted by the major inspired commentaries of Judaism, Christianity, and Judeo-Christianity. She recently coauthored *Islam et coran: Idées reçues sur l'histoire, les textes et les pratiques d'un milliard et demi de musulmans* (Le Cavalier Bleu, 2011).

The tragic fate of a humanist philosopher

Sa'd Ibn Mansur Ibn Kammuna (d. 1284 or 1285), a Jewish physician, thinker, and writer in the Arabic language, was a native of Baghdad, where he lived and pursued his activities. Known and respected by his contemporaries as much for his scientific works as for his literary writings, he composed, among other things, a treatise on ophthalmology, which was judged remarkable by specialists.[1] But he devoted most of his writings, six of which have come down to us, to theology and philosophy. In them he treats such questions as wisdom, rationality, the problem of the possible, and the immortality of the soul, which he was proud to have been the first to demonstrate solely by means of logical proofs.[2] He also wrote commentaries on works by Avicenna and other philosophers, and on the Iranian mystic Shihab al-Din al-

Suhrawardi (1155–91).[3] His studies are strewn with references to the writings of the greatest thinkers of Islam, such as al-Ghazali and Fakhr al-Din al-Razi, and to those of famous Jewish authors, such as Maimonides and Yehuda Halevi, who, like Ibn Kammuna, wrote in Arabic. He also composed a treatise on the differences between Rabbanites and Karaites.[4] But it was his magnum opus that made a real mark on the history of ideas: *Tanqih al-abhath lil-milal al-thalath* (*Examination of the Three Faiths*).[5]

The extraordinary circumstances surrounding the composition and diffusion of this text are particularly worthy of note. Ibn Kammuna wrote it within a context unique in the history of Iraq: the period of domination of the Mongol princes of the Buddhist faith, vassals of the enormous empire founded by Genghis Khan. Its capital was none other than the mystic Kharakorum, which Marco Polo visited between 1271 and 1295 and described in his writings. By the second half of the thirteenth century, Baghdad was merely the capital of the Irano-Iraqi province of the Ilkhanate, nominally under the authority of Kublai Khan (r. 1259–94). For some forty years, the region was ruled by the Mongol princes. The first of them, Halaqu, conqueror of Baghdad, reigned from 1254 to 1265. His brother Abaqa, also a Buddhist, succeeded him, ruling from 1265 to 1282. Then another of his brothers, Nikudar, a convert to Islam, reigned for two years, from 1282 to 1284. Finally, Ibn Kammuna lived the last months of his life under the reign of Arghun (1284–91), son of Abaqa and a Buddhist like his father. That brief spell ended in 1295, when Ilkhan Ghazan (r. 1295–1304) converted to Islam, the majority religion in the territory he governed.

Backed by Jewish and Christian as well as Muslim administrators, the law of reference for these first Buddhist conquerors was the legal code known as "Yassa," which Genghis Khan and his successors imposed in the name of the "eternal blue sky." The chronicler al-Juwayni describes it as a law independent of all religions, a law that considered them "to be one, without distinguishing one from another."[6] Under these circumstances, for the first time in six centuries, Islamic law applied only to Muslims, who had in principle become citizens like everyone else, in an empire that extended beyond the borders of their former influence.

Ibn Kammuna must have had highly visible duties at court during that period: on one hand, he received the title of "glory of the state" (*'izz al-dawla*), and his son was awarded that of "star of the state" (*najm al-dawla*); on the other, he dedicated at least three of his works to high officials. It was no doubt for that reason, as well as for his vast learning, that he was entrusted with the task—unofficially, it appears—of composing a work that might incite the faithful of all religions in the empire to establish relations of conviviality and mutual respect.

The book was completed in 1280. For a few years, it circulated exclusively among the intellectual elite. Then, in 1284, it was released to the general public, under circumstances unknown to us. The sociopolitical situation had changed, however, since the province was now ruled by Nikudar, a prince who had converted to Islam and who had just restored the old prerogatives to his coreligionists. The populace of Baghdad raged against the author who had dared not only to present Muhammad's prophecy as being on a par with others but had also engaged in a critical reflection—in the philosophical sense of that expression—on Islam along with the other religions. They congregated to invade his house and put him to death. The military prefect managed to disperse the mob by assuring them that Ibn Kammuna would be burned at the stake the next day, outside the city. In reality, he was hidden and transported in a trunk to Hilla, a small town near the capital, where his son held the post of secretary. He died there a few months later from the shock and sadness caused by the brutal incomprehension with which his book had been met.

The scope of the concessions to Islam in the *Tanqih*

Nonetheless, what is characteristic of Ibn Kammuna's introductory declaration, even more than its objectivity and tolerance, is its impartiality and kindness: "I shall speak of each of the three religions (presented chronologically, in order of their appearance) from the standpoint of the fundamental principles of its belief. I shall proceed with an exposition of the arguments of its faithful, concerning the veracity of the message of its founding prophet. Finally, I shall add the objections made to these arguments on one hand, and the responses provided on the other, drawing attention to the most remarkable of these and distinguishing those that must be considered convincing from those that have no real impact. In all that, I shall display the most complete impartiality, seeking never to show a preference for one religion over another."[7]

> *What is characteristic of Ibn Kammuna's introductory declaration is objectivity and tolerance impartiality and kindness: 'I shall speak of each of the three religions from the standpoint of the fundamental principles of its belief.'*

This passage echoes in a remarkable way a declaration in Fakhr al-Din al-Razi's *Nihayat al-ʿuqul*. Responding to friends who reproached him for giving too large a place in his writings to the "heretics," al-Razi wrote: "My book differs from others in this field. . . . First, all the questions and arguments are fully proven and are treated in such a way that my work will be for each faith a better account of its doctrines than that which appears in its own books. I have simply cited the quintessence of all the doctrines. When I was unable to find an adequate expression of the arguments in favor of certain positions, I sought to the end to present them in the most favorable way. In spite of that, in the last instance, I refute and reject all doctrines, with the exception of those that are chosen by orthodox Islam, and I prove in conclusion that it is they one must believe in and obey."[8]

The Prophet Muhammad and Moses. Persian miniature taken from *Mi'raj nameh* (*The Miraculous Journey of Muhammad*) by 'Attar, Herat, 1436. Paris, Bibliothèque Nationale de France, ms. or. suppl. turc 190, fol. 38 (verso).

The similarity between the two methods is obvious, especially since it is known that the Jewish thinker Ibn Kammuna was greatly inspired by the Muslim al-Razi's *Nihayat al-'uqul* in the composition of his *Tanqih*. Nevertheless, though the two books develop around a common principle, namely, the objective presentation of the various religious branches under consideration, with the support of all the logical arguments existing in their favor, Ibn Kammuna's book is distinguished by two essential traits: his concern to consider them all equal and his decision to remain neutral to the end. That comparison with the thinking of Fakhr al-Din al-Razi, one of the most impartial Muslim thinkers in religious matters—and with whom Ibn Kammuna maintained a kind of posthumous dialogue in indirect speech in the part of the *Tanqih* reserved for Islam—allows us to highlight what is truly extraordinary about the consideration Ibn Kammuna's book grants to the "other."

In principle, such an attitude of sincerity and respect ought to have earned his book a minimal recognition from the interested parties. But exactly the opposite occurred. His coreligionists, it seems, totally ignored his effort;[9] the Christians on the whole criticized him very harshly.[10] As for the Muslims, in addition to the reaction on the street he had to endure during his lifetime, many refutations appeared after his death. If we look closely, however, his concessions to the two other religions, and especially to Islam, are as significant as the energy he devotes to defending the intangibility and imperishability of the prophecy of Moses.

In the first chapter, concerned with the general definition of prophecy, he endeavors to propose a totally consensual formulation of the three religions, but one, above all, that could please the Sunni Muslims. He proceeds to make several fundamental concessions to their doctrine, sometimes even at the expense of the positions of Judaism. For example, he renounces portraying Moses as the only prophet who achieved the highest degree of prophecy. In fact, according to Maimonides, from whom Ibn Kammuna borrowed his system of classification almost in its entirety, all the prophets experienced a convulsive trembling and an extreme agitation during their visions, except Moses, who was always in a state of perfect calm.[11] Ibn Kammuna makes absolutely no allusion to that exception and confines himself to a general definition of the question. Yet he undoubtedly knew that, according to the Muslim tradition, as reported in certain hadith, Muhammad was often subject to such agitation and heard frightening noises when receiving revelation.

Another essential concession is Ibn Kammuna's assertion that Adam was a prophet: "The divine order was addressed in the first place to Adam, father of humanity, may salvation come to him. He was a prophet, and Abel was his successor."[12] Such a belief, however, was never accepted by Judaism—except among some Kabbalists—or by Christianity. Maimonides, for his part, thought the belief was Sabaean in origin.[13] It is found in particular in the *Pseudo-Clementine Homilies*, a second-century Judeo-Christian text that claims that the True Prophet, who journeys across the ages changing name and shape, was originally Adam, who emerged from the hands of the Creator and had access to all knowledge.[14] Although a comparable doctrine appears only implicitly in the Qur'an, it was elaborated extensively in Islam on the basis of the prophetic traditions, in the form of the "Muhammadan light," one of the central themes of Neoplatonic mysticism.[15] It appears in slightly different form in texts such as the *Liber generationis Mahumeth*. That book was translated into Latin by Hermann of Dalmatia on the orders of Peter the Venerable to increase understanding of the Qur'an, whose doctrine he wanted to refute,[16] proof of the importance granted to that theme at the time. The text enumerates a succession of prophets, beginning with Adam and concluding with the crowning achievement of Muhammad's perfect prophecy. The concept of "Muhammadan light" is formulated in accordance with a Gnostic view: the coming forth of the light of Muhammad, borne by all the prophets since the beginning, marks the advent of salvation. God, in creating Adam and Eve, placed within them a light that they transmitted to their descendants and that thus traveled from prophet to prophet until it reached 'Abd al-Muttalib, grandfather of the Prophet, and 'Abdallah, his father. Through that light of knowledge, fully manifested in the Qur'an, the salvation of the universe will come about.

It should also be noted that the *Tanqih* describes Jesus solely as a prophet, which, though not an absolute contradiction of Christian belief, represents only a partial view of it, one that is altogether in line with Qurʾanic doctrine. Finally, as indicated by Moshe Perlmann, editor of that treatise by Ibn Kammuna, the author adopts the point of view of Muslim theology, where the difference between prophecy (*nubuwwa*) and mission (*risāla*) lies in the fact that prophecy does not produce a new faith, whereas that is precisely the function of a mission.[17] Finally, let us note Ibn Kammuna's adoption of specific expressions and laudatory epithets, such as "the noble Qurʾan" (*al-Qurʾān al-karīm*), which led some specialists to assume wrongly that he had converted to Islam.

From the acknowledgment of alterity to the consciousness of universality

As Claude Gilliot has pointed out, it had to be a Jew who first took that kind of approach.[18] The chronological position of Judaism with respect to the two other religions that embrace Abraham's teachings emancipates that faith from any theological-dogmatic necessity to acknowledge the claims to authenticity of the other religions. By contrast, Islam and Christianity are compelled not to overlook Judaism and to concede at least a certain basis of truth to its texts, since their own often refer to them. Within that context, Ibn Kammuna thus stands as a pioneer who did not hesitate to embark on an extremely complex intellectual, human, and spiritual exploration. He had to update the mechanisms that, in all three religions, governed the processes of excluding the "other" from access to the Truth. His reflections indicate that there are two such processes: abrogation and the closure of revelation. Abrogation consists of the claim, on the part of each religion, to replace completely and categorically the Law of the previous faith, which is declared null and void. In fact, many Christians in the East and West called for the abolition of Mosaic Law, as the Jacobite Ibn Mahruma confirms in his fourteenth-century refutation of the *Tanqih*.[19] As for Islam, its *dhimma* system, whatever its modalities of application, demonstrated on a daily basis the inferiority of citizens attached to laws that the Qurʾan considered abrogated by God. As for the closure of revelation—at issue in Judaism as much as in the other religions—it consists of the conviction that the divine message was definitively complete after the revelation of the founding prophet of each faith.

▶ See article by Mark R. Cohen, pp. 58–71.

Ibn Kammuna tackled the first of these two concepts by demonstrating that, as soon as one acknowledges the authenticity of Moses's prophecy, as the Christians do, since they accept the Old Testament, it is impossible to believe that the Law Moses gave must be abolished. Similarly, if one accepts the prophecy of Jesus as well as that of Moses, as the Qurʾan does, it is unthinkable to proclaim the abrogation of their respective laws. As for the closure of revelation, in taking the initiative to move beyond it, at least by accepting intellectually that others may arrive at an authentic relationship with God by a different path, Ibn Kammuna courageously turned age-old and apparently immutable prejudices on their head. He invited the faithful of the three Abrahamic religions to agree to take risks in the subtle, dialectical game of "self" and "nonself," and to finally accede to the impartial and benevolent point of view of God himself, who made prophecy a blessing for all. Ibn Kammuna seeks to incite his readers to admit that God, through the universality of prophecy, calls people to a supreme Wisdom that transcends the partial expression of certain truths taking the form of Revelation. That first Wisdom, without abolishing the secondary wisdom that governs the mechanisms of self-differentiation for each religious branch, invites believers to move beyond that second wisdom when the problem arises of what attitude to adopt toward the "other."

From that standpoint, it is clear that the relativization of the concept of closure at the beginning of the *Tanqih* implies that believers must break out of the confined circle of the "three rings," to which Friedrich Niewöhner has linked Ibn Kammuna's thinking.[20] Ibn Kammuna thus recalls that "the Magi claimed that Zarathustra was a prophet and reported many miracles attributed to him, that the Sabaeans embraced the prophetic powers of Hermes Trismegistus and Agathodaimon and others, and that the Indians and Turks, as well as other peoples, had individuals who claimed to be prophets and to attain very high spiritual levels." Ibn Kammuna concludes that he has chosen to speak of Judaism, Christianity, and Islam simply because "it is not possible to mention all the people who have claimed to make prophecies or everything that has been transmitted concerning the proofs provided by their prophets."[21] Finally, he goes so far as to intimate, with great subtlety, that on these questions a great difference might exist between the positions of the Qur'an and those of his Muslim contemporaries.[22]

Nevertheless, a context favorable to such an initiative had to present itself, since approaches leading to a true "exchange" can occur only between individuals who are free and equal. This is undoubtedly why the initiative was undertaken in the Baghdad of the Buddhist princes. At almost exactly the same moment, another representative of the thinking of the "three rings," Ramon Llull, set out in his *Book of the Gentile and the Three Wise Men* to conceptualize structures for a multiethnic and multifaith society allowing everyone to live in knowledge and respect for all differences.

---

1. *Al-Kafi al-Kabir fi al-Khul* (*Treatise on Medications of the Eye*). See Baron V. Rosen, *Les manuscrits arabes de l'Institut des langues orientales* (Saint Petersburg: Academie Imperiale de Sciences, 1877), no. 175, 101.

2. Codex Landberg 510 (unicom), folios 58–70, Yale University Library, facsimile reproduction edited by L. Nemoy under the title *The Arabic Treatise on the Immortality of the Soul* (New Haven, CT: Yale University Library, 1944) (see first and last page), translated into English by L. Nemoy, in *Ignaz Goldziher Memorial Volume* (Jerusalem: Rubin Mass, 1958), 2:85–99.

3. In *Al-Tanqihat fi sharh al-Talwihat* (*Examination of the Commentary on "Observations on Logic and Wisdom"*); see Moritz Steinschneider, *Die Arabische Literatur der Juden* (Frankfurt am Main: J. Kauffmann, 1902), no. 5, 240; Hajji Khalifa, 2:240, no. 3581.

4. See H. Hirschfeld, *Arabic Chrestomathy in Hebrew Characters* (London, 1892), 69–103.

5. The Arabic text was edited by M. Perlmann under the title *Saʿd b. Mansur Ibn Kammuna's Examination of the Inquiries into the Three Faiths: A Thirteenth-Century Essay in Comparative Religion* (Berkeley: University of California Press, 1967). Perlmann then published his own English translation, accompanied by a commentary, under the title *Ibn Kammuna's Examination of the Three Faiths: A Thirteenth-Century Essay in Comparative Religion* (Berkeley: University of California Press, 1971).

6. Al-Juwayni, *The History of the World-Conqueror*, trans. Andrew Boyle (Manchester, UK: Manchester University Press, 1958), 26.

7. Perlmann, ed., *Saʿd b. Mansur Ibn Kammuna's Examination of the Inquiries into the Three Faiths* (Arabic text), 1.

8. *Nihayat al-ʿuqul fi-dirayat al-usul* (*The Extreme Limit of Intelligence in the Comprehension of the Principles*), quoted in F. Kholeif, *A Study on Fakhr al-Din al-Razi and His Controversies in Transoxiana* (Beirut: Dar al-Machreq, 1966), 41, quoted in Roger Arnaldez, *Fakhr al-Din al-Razi, commentateur du Coran et philosophe* (Paris: Vrin, 2002), 21.

9. See Dominique Urvoy, *Les penseurs libres dans l'Islam classique* (Paris: Albin Michel, 1996), 209–10.

10. For example, the famous response of Ibn Mahruma, translated into French with commentary by Monsignor Habib Bacha, *Hawashi (Notes) d'Ibn al-Mahruma sur le "Tanqih" d'Ibn Kammuna* (Rome: Pontificio Istituto Orientale, 1984).

11. Maimonides, *Guide for the Perplexed*, part 2, chap. 35; Maimonides, *Commentarius in Mischnam: E codicibus Hunt. 117 et Pococke 295 in Bibliotheca Bodleiana Oxoniensi servatis et 72–73 Bibliothecae Sassooniensis Letchworth*, ed. David S. Sassoon and Samuel Miklos Stern (Copenhagen, 1956), introduction to chap. 10 (11) of the *Sanhedrin Treatise*, seventh article of faith, 169–73; Maimonides, *Book of Mishnah Torah Yod Ha-Hazakah, Yesodei Ha Torah Treatise*, chap. 7, paragraph 6. That state of serenity corresponds to a Greek conception of "inhabitation by a higher spirit," as Origen, for example, describes it.

12. Perlmann, ed., *Saʿd b. Mansur Ibn Kammuna's Examination of the Inquiries into the Three Faiths* (Arabic text), 22.

13. Maimonides, *Guide for the Perplexed*, part 3, chap. 29.

14. *Pseudo-Clementine Literature: The Clementine Homilies*, trans. Thomas Smith, vol. 8 of *The Ante-Nicene Fathers: The Writings of the Fathers down to A.D. 325*, edited by A. Cleveland Coxe (New York: Christian Literature Company, 1885–96), n.p., available online at http://en.wikisource.org/wiki/Ante-Nicene_Fathers/Volume_VIII/Pseudo-Clementine_Literature/The_Clementine_Homilies.

15. See Tustari, *Tafsir*, in G. Bowering, *The Mystical Vision of Existence in Classical Islam: The Qurʾanic Hermeneutics of the Sufi Sahl al-Tustari (d. 283/896)* (Berlin: Walter de Gruyter, 1980), 156.

16. This text bears the Arabic title *Kitab Nasab Rasul Allah*. In the manuscript of the Bibliothèque de l'Arsenal, it occupies folios 11 recto to 18 recto (Corpus Toledanum), Paris, Bibliothèque de l'Arsenal, 1162. It is attributed to Saʿid Ibn ʿUmar.

17. See Perlmann, ed., *Ibn Kammuna's Examination of the Three Faiths: A Thirteenth-Century Essay in Comparative Religion*, 15n5.

18. Claude Gilliot, book review of Freidrich Niewöhner, *Veritas sive varietas*, *Arabica* 38 (1991): 382–89.

19. Habib Bacha, *Hawashi*, introduction, lxxiii.

20. See M. Niewöhner, *Veritas sive varietas: Lessings Toleranzparabel und das Buch von den drei Betrügern* (Heidelberg: Verlag Lambert Schneider, 1988); Abdelwahab Meddeb, *Sortir de la malédiction: L'islam entre civilisation et barbarie* (Paris: Seuil, 2008), 231–38; Georges Minois, *Le traité des trois imposteurs: Histoire d'un livre blasphématoire qui n'existait pas* (Paris: Albin Michel, 2009); Geneviève Gobillot, "Ibn Kammuna: Les trois anneaux de la prophétie?" *Tsafon* 50 (Autumn 2005–Winter 2006): 23–48, special issue in honor of Jean-Marie Delmaire.

21. Perlmann, ed., *Saʿd b. Mansur Ibn Kammuna's Examination of the Inquiries into the Three Faiths* (Arabic text), 21.

22. See Geneviève Gobillot, "Le Coran rêvé d'Ibn Kammuna," *Publication of the Proceedings of the Colloquium of April 16–18, 2009*, ed. Tawfiq Bin Amer (in Arabic), Department of Philosophy, University of Tunis.

From Arabic to Hebrew: The Reception of the Greco-Arab Sciences in Hebrew (Twelfth–Fifteenth Centuries)
Gad Freudenthal

Science and philosophy did not develop spontaneously within Judaism. The intellectual activities of traditional Jewish cultures generally focused on the canonical texts of the tradition: the Bible, the Mishnah, the Talmud. Any other type of knowledge, that is, any knowledge not vested with the authority of the canonical texts and of revelation, was considered "foreign." This point, fundamental for understanding Jewish intellectual history, was forcefully stated in 1933 by the great historian Julius Guttmann: "The history of Jewish philosophy is a history of the successive absorption of foreign ideas."[1]

I will consider here the reception of science in the Hebrew-speaking world, for the most part from the early twelfth century on. This cultural transfer took place in Southern Europe, where the language of Jewish culture was Hebrew, in contrast to the Islamic world, where the Jews spoke and wrote in Arabic. By "science" I mean primarily the body of knowledge that originated in Greek rationalist science, which was later elaborated in Arab culture and transmitted to Hebrew-speaking Jews through translations from Arabic or, more rarely, from Latin.

Precisely because the Jews traditionally studied the canonical texts, the introduction of secular knowledge—knowledge external to the Jewish cultural sphere—would prove problematic. Since in that field science and philosophy were perceived as foreign bodies from the start, before they could be accepted, their legitimacy had to be recognized. Often, in fact, the study of the secular sciences was fiercely combated.[2]

Since the "foreign" sciences were not part of the traditional corpus, Jewish scholars who wished to study them had to turn to non-Jewish sources. The

Gad Freudenthal

Director emeritus of research at the Centre National de la Recherche Scientifique and a professor at the University of Geneva, Gad Freudenthal is the author, notably, of *Aristotle's Theory of Material Substance* (Oxford University Press, 1999) and *Sciences in the Medieval Hebrew and Arabic Traditions* (Ashgate, 2005). He has also edited several volumes, including *Studies on Gersonides: A Fourteenth-Century Jewish Philosopher-Scientist* (Brill, 1992); *Studies on Steinschneider*, with Reimund Leicht (Brill, 2011); and *Science in Medieval Jewish Cultures* (Cambridge University Press, 2012). He is the director of the review *Aleph: Historical Studies in Science and Judaism*, created in 2001.

historian of science Abdelhamid I. Sabra has distinguished two phases in the process of cultural transmission: first, a culture *imports* and *appropriates* a body of knowledge of foreign origin; second, it assimilates or *naturalizes* it. Cultural historians speak, in this case, of "acculturation."[3]

A Jewish-Muslim "symbiosis"?

The process by which medieval Judaism appropriated rationalist Greco-Arab thought—including scientific developments—began in the Eastern Arab Muslim Empire in the late ninth century. Over the next two centuries, this knowledge became an integral part of Judeo-Arab culture. Some historians have called the cultural relations established between that culture and Arab cultures a form of *symbiosis*.[4] In most Arabophone Jewish intellectual circles—with the exception of the most traditionalist—elementary scientific and philosophical knowledge was part of the intellectual tool kit of any educated person. This "naturalization" of Greco-Arab culture by Arabophone Jewish scholars is reflected in books of the period in every realm of intellectual activity: not only in works of religious philosophy but also in writings devoted to specifically Jewish disciplines such as the halakha (law), biblical exegesis, Hebrew grammar, and poetry. Science, or rather some elements of scientific knowledge, were thus integrated into Jewish culture. It is important to remember that Arabic-speaking Jewish scholars had mastered Classical Arabic: an Arabophone Jewish man of letters therefore had access, in principle, to all the works of Arab science, a central aspect of the Jewish-Muslim "symbiosis."

Things were very different in the Christian world. In that context, historians, far from referring to a symbiosis between Judaism and the dominant culture, use the terms "seclusion" and "isolation." This holds to varying degrees for all the Jewish cultures in Christian Europe, be it in the South, where rationalist philosophy was favorably received (Christian Spain, Central and Southern Italy, and the French Midi), or in the North (Ashkenaz, Tsarfat, England), where it was rejected. With a few exceptions, Jewish scholars in the medieval West did not know Latin and therefore did not have direct access to the accumulated knowledge of the majority cultures.[5] As a result, any transmission of knowledge to the Jewish cultural environment in Christian Europe came about, and could only come about, via translations into Hebrew (or through books, encyclopedias in particular, compiled in Hebrew by Arabophone scholars). This was the condition sine qua non of their reception by Jews in the medieval West. The gate by which scientific knowledge could be introduced into Hebrew Jewish culture was therefore narrow.

Medieval science in Hebrew: The predilection for Arabic

Beginning in the second half of the twelfth century and continuing uninterrupted for some two centuries, Jewish encyclopedists and translators made a significant share of the Greco-Arab philosophical and scientific corpus available to their coreligionists who did not know Arabic—or, in fact, Latin—in Southern France,

Italy, and Northern Spain. A large number of philosophical and scientific works by Greek and Arab authors (meticulously described in Moritz Steinschneider's monumental *Die hebraïschen Übersetzungen des Mittelalters und die Juden als Dolmetscher,* 1893) were thus translated from Arabic into Hebrew. This massive naturalization of science and philosophy by Jewish cultures, which had previously dedicated themselves exclusively to the study of the texts of the tradition, occurred when Arabic-speaking men of letters from al-Andalus, having been immersed in Judeo-Arab and Arab Muslim cultures, sought refuge in the Midi after fleeing the Almohad persecutions. It was in Southern France, therefore, that they undertook a vast project of translating philosophical and scientific works into Hebrew.[6] This project took a decisive leap forward with the translation from Arabic into Hebrew of Maimonides's *Guide for the Perplexed* in 1204. The publication in Hebrew of that prestigious book conferred legitimacy on the study of philosophy and science, at least for some Jews. Philosophy and science would now benefit from an interest as keen as it was long-lasting.

> " *Beginning in the second half of the twelfth century Jewish encyclopedists and translators made a significant share of the Greco-Arab philosophical and scientific corpus available to their coreligionists.* "

Modalities for the reception of science by Jewish communities

Although the Jews of Northern France and of Ashkenaz still opposed the study of science and philosophy,[7] the communities of the Midi were the site of the reception and transmission of science in Christian Europe. The question therefore arises: To what extent did the Jewish communities really appropriate received scientific knowledge? A second question follows from the first: What were the limits of that process or, more specifically, which scientific disciplines were neither transmitted nor naturalized? Also, did Jewish scholars make their own contributions to received scientific knowledge, or were they content to appropriate it as it had come to them?[8] The translation of scientific and philosophical works from Arabic into Hebrew was a large-scale process. When it ended in the mid-fourteenth century, the scholars of Hebrew culture had at their disposal a large corpus of scientific works providing access to a significant share of the Arab scholars' knowledge. Let me cite merely a few of the most important authors: al-Farabi and Ibn Rushd in logic; Euclid and Archimedes in mathematics; Ptolemy, Jabir Ibn Aflah, al-Battani, al-Bitruji, and Ibn al-Haytham in astronomy; and finally, nearly all of Ibn Rushd's commentaries on Aristotle, in physics and metaphysics. This remarkably steady transmission process attests to a sustained demand on the part of medieval Jewish scholars for scientific and philosophical works.

One key aspect takes on particular importance within the context of this book: the appropriation of the "foreign sciences" by Jewish speakers of Hebrew occurred primarily through Arabic and very seldom through Latin. It is noteworthy that the Jewish cultures of the Midi and, to a lesser degree, of Italy, preferred to use Arabic sources "imported" from the Iberian Peninsula rather than consult works in Latin that were available in their immediate vicinity. Medicine was the only exception: as of the fourteenth century, that field benefited greatly from contributions

> **It is noteworthy that the Jewish cultures of the Midi preferred to use Arabic sources 'imported' from the Iberian Peninsula rather than consult works in Latin that were available in their immediate vicinity.**

in Latin. The distrust of Latin culture would not ease until the late fourteenth century, and it was not until the fifteenth that what could be called a "Hebrew scholastics" emerged, in Northern Spain.[9] The scientific and philosophical tradition in Hebrew was therefore for the most part a continuation of the Greco-Arab tradition.

	Hebrew Translations from Arabic		Hebrew Translations from Latin	
	Science and Philosophy	Medicine	Science and Philosophy	Medicine
12th century	28	1	0	18
13th century	116	45	12	17
14th century	100	37	34	62

Source: Freudenthal, "Arabic and Latin Cultures as Resources for the Hebrew Translation Movement."

Distribution of Hebrew Translations by Discipline, Source Language, and Century

A few figures now available allow us to form a precise idea of the scope of that translation movement. Two phenomena are worthy of note. First, the preference granted to texts translated from Arabic is most clear in the thirteenth century, with 161 books translated from Arabic but only 29 translated from Latin. It is manifest, albeit to a lesser degree, in the fourteenth century as well, with 137 books translated from Arabic, 96 from the Latin. In analyzing these figures, we need to distinguish between science and philosophy on one hand and medicine on the other. In the thirteenth century, 116 works of science and philosophy were translated from Arabic but only 12 from Latin. In the fourteenth century, that ratio was 100 to 34. The proportion of works translated from Latin certainly increased, but the numbers were still modest. For works in medicine, by contrast, a spectacular change came about during this same period: in the thirteenth century, 45 works in medicine

Hebrew translation of Avicenna's major medical treatise of the Middle Ages, *Canon of Medicine*, by Zecharia ben Isaac ben Shealtien. Hen in Spain, late fourteenth century. Bologna, Biblioteca Universitaria.

were translated from Arabic and only 17 from Latin, but this ratio was reversed in the fourteenth century, with 35 works translated from Arabic and 72 translated from Latin. It follows that, from the twelfth to the fourteenth centuries, the Jewish Hebrew-speaking scholars and philosophers demonstrated a clear and consistent preference for works translated from Arabic. By contrast, Hebrew medicine turned more and more for its knowledge to works produced in the dominant Latin cultural environment.

It should be noted, however, that the distrust toward Latin culture was not equally shared by all parts of Jewish culture. In Italy, there was a tradition—modest to be sure—of scientific and philosophical translations from Latin parallel to translations from Arabic.[10] Most translations of philosophical and scientific works from Latin into Hebrew were done by Italian Jewish men of letters. In Italy, then, the appropriation of foreign knowledge came about through two channels: translations into Hebrew from Arabic and from Latin appeared simultaneously, most done by émigrés from al-Andalus. In the communities of the French Midi, the rarity of translations from Latin clearly indicates that Italy and Southern France were reacting differently to Latin culture. But in Italy as well, the philosophico-scientific tradition was primarily sustained by works translated from Arabic and, like its Provençal counterpart, was overall a continuation of the Judeo-Arab philosophical culture.

A complex picture of the cultural transfer to Hebrew therefore emerges: between the twelfth and fourteenth centuries, the Jewish cultures of Southern Europe naturalized a body of scientific and philosophical knowledge—its content sometimes outdated—from a remote cultural environment rather than from the rapidly growing Latin cultural milieu that was within their reach. Medical literature followed a different trajectory, however. In the fourteenth century, after a period of dependency on Arab culture, it ultimately came to privilege the medical knowledge developed in the Latin West.

The causes and limits of transmission

The preference given to the distant Arab culture over the nearby Latin culture can be explained in rough terms by the difference in attitude toward the Jews within the majority societies: the Muslim world was more tolerant and less aggressive than Christian societies.[11] Nevertheless, what is striking is the cultural transfer as such, that is, the causes behind the appropriation of "foreign" sciences by southern Jewish cultures. Indeed, the integration of rationalist knowledge into Jewish culture marked a significant break with the past, a true cultural revolution that merits analysis.

This cultural shift came about because some members of the Jewish intellectual elite accepted Maimonidean philosophy as an axiology. Indeed, Maimonides had elevated the study of science and philosophy to the dignity of a religious obligation.[12] He writes: "He who wishes to attain to human perfection, must therefore first study Logic, next the various branches of Mathematics in their proper order, then Physics, and lastly Metaphysics."[13] Science had thus become part of the intellectual tool kit for anyone aspiring to perfect the soul in keeping with Maimonidean philosophy. Since most Jewish men at the time could read and write, and since philosophy had acquired respectability in most southern Jewish communities, it follows that the study of science, far from being the monopoly of a small social group, was a fairly widespread phenomenon.

Two observations confirm this statement. First, the years 1303–6 witnessed the outbreak of a virulent controversy over the study of philosophy.[14] It was triggered by the attempt of opponents of philosophy to forbid the study of both philosophy and science, if not to everyone then at least to those under twenty-five. These subjects must have been commonly taught, therefore, since no one would launch a campaign to proscribe a nonexistent practice. Second, the sheer number of Hebrew manuscripts of scientific texts that have come down to us indicates the prevalence of scientific studies. Ibn Rushd's writings are a good example: there are about twenty extant manuscripts of the Hebrew translation of his Epitome of Aristotle's *Physics*; eighteen copies of his Epitome of *De caelo*; and thirty-six copies of his Middle Commentary on the same work. Finally, twenty-five manuscripts have come down to us of his Epitome of the *Parva naturalia*. It should also be added that almost all of Ibn Rushd's commentaries were the object of supercommentaries written in Hebrew by Jewish scholars. These fairly large numbers attest that his works were continually being studied and taught.

Despite the impressive numbers, the appropriation and naturalization of this knowledge had its limits. However surprising it might seem, the most advanced and most innovative scientific contributions made by the Arab Muslim (and also Latin)

Arabic translation of Euclid's *Elements*. Oxford, Bodleian Library, ms. Thurston 11, fol. 35a.

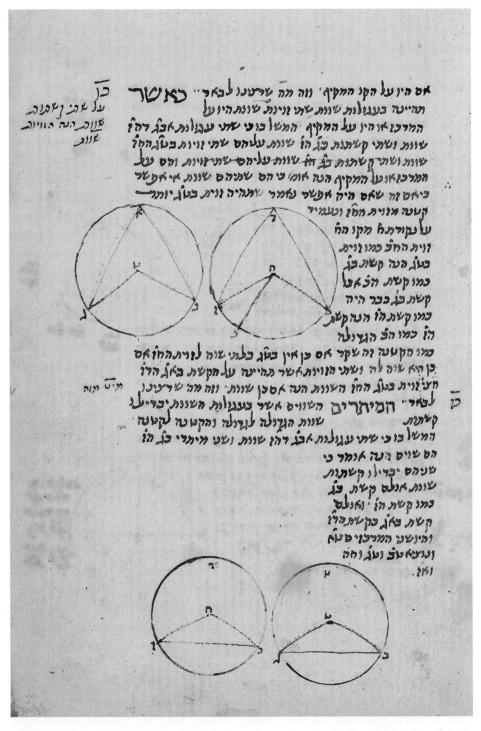

Hebrew translation of the Arabic edition of Euclid's *Elements*, copy from Abraham ben Judah of Crete. Oxford, Bodleian Library, ms. Hunt. 561, fol. 38b.

cultures remained unknown to Jewish scholars writing in Hebrew. Furthermore, Jewish men of letters contributed little to the general progress of science in the medieval world: there are few counterparts in the Jewish world to such Arab scientific geniuses as al-Biruni, Ibn al-Haytham, Thabit, or Ibn Qurra, or even to Robert Grosseteste and Roger Bacon in the Latin West. In what follows, I will provide support for these claims before attempting to give a sociological explanation for them.[15] There is no doubt that the science to which Jews devoted the most attention was astronomy. This interest did not wane over time: evidence of it has been gathered everywhere and in every era.[16] The causes are difficult to determine with certainty. The astronomers themselves advanced two explanations: first, the practical importance of astronomy for correctly determining the Hebrew calendar, a fundamental framework for religious practice; and second, the obvious pertinence of astronomy for the study of metaphysics. It is not certain, however, that astronomers were actually involved in determining the calendar. Similarly, though the study of metaphysics assumed a certain familiarity with the heavens, the knowledge required was elementary and did not necessarily involve an advanced practice of astronomy. As a result, it is hard to say whether the astronomers' claims about the lofty value of their science reflect a reality or are merely rhetorical, intended to justify their scientific practice. But whatever the source of their interest in astronomy, it was without a doubt the science practiced most diligently by Jews in the Middle Ages, at a level rivaling that of their Arab and Latin counterparts.

As for mathematics, a number of Greek treatises—in the first place, Euclid's *Elements*—were translated from Arabic into Hebrew. It is all the more significant, therefore, that some essential fields of mathematics remained totally unknown to the Jews. This was especially true for algebra. That branch of mathematics, to which the most prestigious Arab mathematicians dedicated themselves—and which, in fact, constituted one of the most spectacular innovations of medieval science—left few traces in the Hebrew literature of the Middle Ages. The first translations into Hebrew of works on algebra, done by Mordekhai Finzi, did not appear until the mid-fifteenth century.[17] How does one account for this obvious lack of interest in a major scientific discipline within the Jewish communities, where mathematicians of genius were certainly not lacking? I suggest the following explanation: when the Jews began to study mathematics, Euclid's works in particular, they did so for one of two reasons: either mathematics was for them a propaedeutic to metaphysics, in that it prepared the intellect to apprehend abstractions; or it was a prerequisite to the study of astronomy. Algebra, however, serves neither of these purposes. On one hand, medieval scholars saw algebra as a mere tool or "device,"[18] in other words, a mere technique for solving equations. They therefore considered it a discipline devoid of philosophical value, merely an early stage in the study of metaphysics. On the other hand, before the fifteenth century, algebra did not seem to have any practical use. From the standpoint of the medieval Jewish scholar, algebra was simply irrelevant. This is the categorical judgment of the famous twelfth-century Aristotelian philosopher Abraham Ibn Daud of Toledo. An Arabic speaker with a firsthand knowledge of Arab science and philosophy, he certainly knew what algebra was, but he considered it without value. Among the people he believed were wasting their time on vanities, thereby putting at risk their perfection and their soul's happiness, he includes someone "who consumes all of his time in what is more inferior" to medicine, for example,

> one who consumes his time with number and with [other] strange actions, such as the man who wants to boil fifteen quarters of new wine so that a third returns, which he boils until the quarter is lacking from it. He pours from what remains two-quarters, and next [the wine] is boiled until a quarter is lacking from it in the fire. [Then] he pours from what remains two quarters until a quantity of what remains is left in accordance with what he wanted. [There are men who do this and other] things like these vanities that maybe ought not ever to happen. They think that by [such experiments] they improve the science of number, and similarly [improve] particular matters in the science of geometry. But in truth only what is necessary in [number] is introduced into the science of geometry.[19]

The important thing, then, was to acquire the kind of knowledge that fulfilled a religious obligation: metaphysics and the propaedeutic sciences. The other disciplines had no spiritual value. We may assume that this attitude was widespread among medieval Jewish scholars and may consider it a reason that algebra did not hold their attention. Scientific matters were considered socially legitimate only if they proved relevant for a knowledge of God and served religious practice. Mathematical research as an end in itself was thus devoid of legitimacy from the start. This, it seems to me, also accounts for why Jewish scholars made very few original contributions to the progress of mathematics. The rare and brief mathematical writings in Hebrew that merit the term "original" are for the most part studies derived from research in astronomy. The lack of interest in the two other disciplines of the quadrivium, music and optics, can be explained along similar lines.

In the physical sciences, alchemy, one of the most flourishing disciplines in Arab culture and the Latin West, is remarkable for its absence in the Jewish world, despite its considerable influence on the Renaissance and on the birth of modern science. Moritz Steinschneider and Gershom Scholem have both pointed out the virtual nonexistence of medieval Hebrew texts on alchemy. Nothing or almost nothing about alchemy was translated into Hebrew, and Hebrew-speaking Jews did not know the names of even the most illustrious alchemists, such as Jabit ibn Hayyan al-Razi, or, among the Latins, Geber. Not a single work on alchemy was written in Hebrew during the Middle Ages. The notion of transmutation does occasionally appear as a *metaphor*, but no Jewish philosopher, it seems, ever dreamed of seriously coming to grips with this notion.[20]

The same is true for the famous medieval theory that claimed that metals are composed of sulfur and mercury. It makes almost no appearance in the Hebrew scientific literature. Yet this theory (which has nothing to do with the postulate of transmutation) played a crucial role in the philosophy of nature during the Middle Ages and Renaissance, both in the Arab world and in the Latin West.

This lack of interest in alchemy did not entail a rejection of the idea of transmutation in itself, which was perfectly well accepted by some Jewish authors, albeit rejected by others. How are we to account for this phenomenon? A plausible explanation is that the influential members of Jewish communities, being engaged in economic activities, were especially wary of the alchemists, who easily fell under suspicion of producing counterfeit coins. In addition, it could not have been easy to acquire manuscripts dealing with an esoteric (hence secret) science such as alchemy. The physical sciences proper, that is, the study of the subjects Aristotle discusses in his *Physics*, were the object of constant interest on the part of Jewish philosophers. The reason may be that physics laid out the premises for any discussion of the existence and incorporeality of God and the eternal nature of the world. This interest, based originally on religious grounds, led some to pursue these subjects and to become deeply involved in reflections within this discipline.[21] Nevertheless, Jewish scholars do not seem to have been familiar with the most innovative theories of Arab physics or with those of the Latin West, for example, the concept of impetus (the precursor, in some sense, to the notion of inertia). This may be because these theories, of Avicennian inspiration, were inaccessible to Hebrew-speaking scholars, since,

> *How are we to explain why the dialectical movement between translation and research, characteristic of the progress of science in the Arab environment, did not produce the same effects within medieval Hebrew culture?*

for historical reasons, there were virtually no Hebrew translations of Avicenna.[22] This brief account leads to a somewhat paradoxical conclusion. On one hand, the sciences were very widely practiced by the Jews; on the other, certain scientific disciplines were virtually neglected. Moreover, given the extent of appropriation into Hebrew of Arab science, we can only be astonished at the lack of new, original contributions on the part of medieval Jewish scholars, astronomy being the only exception.

How can we explain this state of affairs? Why did the interest in science stop at the threshold of certain disciplines? And how are we to interpret the fact that, of the many scholars who dedicated themselves to science, so few enriched their field with original contributions? In short, how are we to explain why the dialectical movement between translation and research, characteristic of the progress of science in the Arab environment,[23] did not produce the same effects within medieval Hebrew culture?

Two sources of interest in science

In response to this question, let me advance a hypothesis that may also serve as a summary of my preceding remarks. For the Jewish scientist who adopted Maimonides's positive attitude toward "foreign knowledge," the practice of science, in order to be legitimate, had to deal either with subjects connected to religious philosophy or with those that could provide a concrete and applicable skill.

The primary motivation of the Jewish scholar who devoted himself to philosophical studies was to elaborate a *religious* philosophy, that is, to interpret in philosophical terms the revealed religion of Moses. (Let us not forget, moreover, that most medieval Jewish scholars seldom pursued "secular" studies, preferring to dedicate themselves to the canonical texts.) Medieval Jewish philosophy was, therefore, to borrow the expression of the great historian Julius Guttmann, a *philosophy of Judaism*: "Whereas the Islamic Neoplatonists and Aristotelians dealt with the full range of philosophy, Jewish thinkers relied for the most part on the work of their Islamic predecessors in regard to general philosophic questions, and concentrated on more specifically religio-philosophic questions."[24] In the famous parable of the levels of human knowledge, Maimonides explicitly warns against the exclusive study of the sciences: "My son, so long as you are engaged in studying the Mathematical Sciences and Logic, you belong to those who go round about the palace in search of the gate." The physical sciences take the scholar further: someone who has completed his studies in physics is inside the palace and has "entered the hall." Nevertheless, the true aim of studying was to know God: "When, after completing the study of Natural Philosophy, you master Metaphysics, you have entered the innermost court, and are with the king in the same palace. You have attained the degree of the wise men."[25] For Maimonides, therefore, and for most philosophers who followed him, all sciences, from mathematics to physics, were only a propaedeutic to genuine science, which is the divine science of metaphysics. Fundamentally, then, men must "devote themselves entirely to God, [and] exclude from their thought every other thing."[26]

As a result of this attitude, Jewish philosophers privileged the scientific disciplines concerned with theology. Even when they considered topics of general philosophy, their purpose was to clarify the revealed truth of scripture. In addition, Jewish philosophers, following Maimonides's view, believed that "Aristotle is undoubtedly correct as far as the things are concerned which exist between the sphere of the moon and the centre of the earth. Only an ignorant person rejects it."[27] For the needs of religious philosophy, the Aristotelian description of the world was sufficient, and there was no point in calling any of it into question. The study of the mathematical sciences was valuable primarily as a propaedeutic to the study of metaphysics. But that motivation could not lead to the study of a discipline such as algebra or to an attempt to raise or solve new mathematical problems.

In other words, Jewish philosophy had always conceived of itself as a religious philosophy; it therefore did not consider the search for truth by means of reason a legitimate end in itself. For the medieval Jewish philosopher, reason was rarely autonomous, and knowledge of reality was not often an objective worth pursuing for its own sake.

The second motivation for the study of "foreign" sciences, particularly logic and mathematics, lay in their practical utility. Logic was considered indispensable for philosophical and religious discussions. The mathematical sciences, astronomy in the first place, were held to be particularly useful in daily life and in the practice of religion. This explains why Jewish scholars were deeply engaged with these disciplines.

Two exceptions prove the rule: Levi ben Gershom, also known as Gersonides (1288–1344), and Hasdai Crescas (ca. 1340–1410/1411). Hasdai Crescas, to whom we owe a penetrating criticism of Aristotle's physics, was driven by the ambition to *refute* the very foundations of the Greek philosopher's ideas.[28] Ironically, the most important critique of Aristotle's physics to be produced by a medieval Jewish philosopher did not come from a thinker seeking to study physical reality in more depth but from someone whose ambition was to dispose of Greek philosophy altogether.

▶ See article by Steven Harvey, pp. 737–757.

Levi ben Gershom, it seems to me, was the only medieval Jewish thinker who can be considered a true scientist. He was one of the great astronomers of the Middle Ages and among the few to have actually been involved in astronomical observations at that time. The author of specialized treatises in mathematics and logic, he openly promoted the idea of scientific progress.[29] We may therefore wonder what allowed Levi ben Gershom to break through the strictures described above. I have attempted elsewhere to show that the answer is to be sought in his *soteriology*, that is, his theory concerning the fate of the human soul after physical death.[30] For Levi ben Gershom, knowledge, particularly empirical knowledge, is the very condition for human happiness and for the immortality of the rational soul. The knowledge of intelligibles, he claims, gives rise to an *individual* intellect, which persists and survives in its individuality after death. Moreover, Levi ben Gershom claims that the truth of scripture and the truth obtained by reason are one and the same. He even goes so far as to postulate that science is indispensable for the correct apprehension of revealed truths, and vice versa. His theology implies that the soul's happiness is achieved through scientific research. He was thus the only Jewish thinker in the Middle Ages to uphold the legitimacy of the autonomous pursuit of knowledge. The case of Levi ben Gershom illustrates my general thesis, in that his approach to science deviated from the prevailing Maimonidean view, which was that any rational research should either bear on theology or be practically useful. It is important to emphasize that

Levi ben Gershom was no less profoundly "religious" than the other Jewish philosophers. In no way do I wish to suggest that there is an inherent, irreducible opposition between religion and science. On the contrary, Levi ben Gershom gives an original interpretation of the concept of the "religious" when he says that the path leading to a knowledge of God—and, as a result, of the afterlife—passes through scientific research. It is this personal theology that may have allowed him to main-

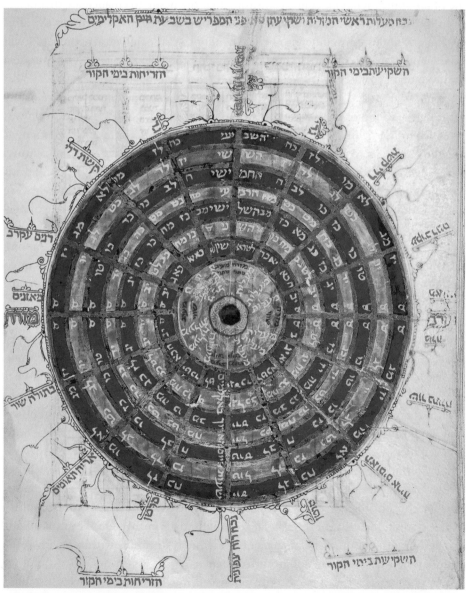

Diagram showing the sunrises and sunsets of the zodiac signs credited to Abraham bar Hiyya according to al-Battani, which in turn follows Ptolemy. Manuscript from the fifteenth century, French Midi or Spain. London, British Library, ms. or. 11796, fol. 57 (verso).

tain his dual commitment: to religion on one hand, since he wrote commentaries on almost the entire biblical corpus, and to scientific research on the other.

The limits of interest in science: A sociological perspective

Yet the Jewish scholars' limited interest in science cannot be imputed solely to their theological preoccupations. Two questions arise: What made their commitment to the philosophico-religious context so strong that the desire to emancipate themselves from it so rarely arose? And how did such a compelling consensus about the aims of religious philosophy come into being? In adopting a sociological approach, I will be able to hazard a response to these questions. In the following text, I will pursue a few avenues of research that I believe merit further investigation.

One important social factor that may provide an explanation was the absence of any organized teaching of philosophy. At a time when traditional Jewish education was provided in flourishing yeshivot, philosophy and science seem to have been taught only privately. There were occasional exceptions to this rule in the fifteenth century, especially in Christian Spain, but these change nothing in the overall picture. Jewish communities tolerated philosophical activity on an individual basis. Conversely, they did everything in their power to foil attempts to institutionalize the teaching of philosophy. To fully take stock of the consequences of this absence, we need only consider what was happening during the same period in European universities. Among Jewish philosophers and scientists, there were no lines of descent from master to student, like those naturally produced in the universities and also in the yeshivot. As a result, the transmission of knowledge and of research was not at all continuous. Even more important, the European university had established official standards for discussion to which both masters and disciples adhered and which, by their very structure, fostered a new kind of knowledge. For example, debates around the *potentia Dei absoluta et ordinata* (absolute and ordered power of God) or around what is or is not possible *secundum imaginationem* (in accordance with the imagination) opened the way to a type of research freed from the bonds of theological and philosophical postulates.[31] And it was precisely this detachment, the "emancipation" from received ideas—both philosophical and theological—that was missing from Jewish scholars' thinking. None of the medieval Jewish philosophers, with the exception of Levi ben Gershom, considered his role that of a scholar devoted to autonomous pursuits. In sociological terms, the university, by its very social structure, gave rise to a new social role, that of the scholar, a "professional" engaged in the autonomous search for truth.[32] But in the absence of academic institutions within Jewish communities, no such phenomenon occurred there.

Let us go even further. The absence of institutionalized structures for teaching philosophy was itself merely the consequence of the Jews' living conditions in the Middle Ages. Medieval Jewish society was traditional in the sense that it was "a society which regards its existence as based upon a common body of knowledge and values handed down from the past."[33] But in the absence of territorial concentration and state authority, and with no organized religious hierarchy disposing of centralized means of coercion, the knowledge and values—the *symbols*—shared by all members of Jewish society were the only bonds that guaranteed social cohesion. This is why controversies about the legitimacy of philosophy were so virulent: at stake was nothing less than Jewish society's collective identity and, as a result, its social unity. At the dawn of the fourteenth century, Kalonymus ben Kalonymus, a major poet and the translator of scientific works, described this situation with rare perspicacity. He wrote in his *Eben Bohan* (*The Touchstone*) that, as a result of the introduction of philosophy among the Jews, "a confusion of opinions has come about . . . Each district upholds its own persuasion . . . each condemning the other saying: 'I am afraid there is some heresy [in its opinion]. My God is not like its God.'" And Kalonymus concludes: "Our Gods are as numerous as our towns."[34]

In such a traditional society, the intellectual's social role is to transmit symbols that cement social relations. The role of the Jewish scholar consisted of teaching and interpreting the Law, and he sometimes turned to philosophy to do so. The purpose of Jewish philosophy was to contribute toward the interpretation of scripture, if only in philosophical terms. Here again, a comparison to Christian society is enlightening: Christian scholars of the time belonged to religious orders, which meant they did not have to pursue economic activities within society at large. As a result, their reference group consisted of other scholars who shared the same values. They could therefore dispense with referring constantly to religious texts to legitimate their views. By contrast, the Jewish scholar's only reference group was the community as a whole, which expected every discourse to be legitimated through reference to scripture. Social bonds kept the Jewish

> **"The role of the Jewish scholar consisted of teaching and interpreting the Law, and he turned to philosophy to do so. "**

scholar securely fastened to the texts of the tradition, and he could not emancipate himself without risking exclusion from his social group. This, I believe, is the fundamental explanation for why the Jewish philosopher remained within the confines of the philosophy of Judaism.

The well-known fourteenth-century convert Alfonso de Valladolid, formerly Abner of Burgos, illustrates this point: "Since my youth and until my old age," he writes in his philosophico-mathematical work *Meyasher 'Aqob* (*Straightening the Curved*), "I begged God . . . for one single thing, namely, to know whether it is possible to find a rectilinear surface equal to the surface of the circle, according to the truth and not approximately, as previous scholars have done."[35] This is exactly the sort of preoccupation that we seek in vain in medieval Jewish writings. Whatever might have been Abner's motivation for converting, it was probably not by chance that this scholar, driven by the desire for a purely theoretical knowledge, a knowledge without import for specifically Jewish matters, pursued a path strewn with philosophico-theological doubts, and one that took him outside the Jewish community.

A concluding remark: Soteriology and scientific progress; a comparative view (Islam, Judaism, Christianity)

The circumstances that conditioned the naturalization of science in the Hebrew-speaking medieval Jewish communities can usefully be compared to those that determined the development and then (relative) decline of Arab science, followed by the scientific revolution in the seventeenth century. A brief remark will suffice to illustrate this point. According to A. I. Sabra, the rapid expansion of Arab science was the work of such scholars as al-Farabi, Ibn Sina, Ibn al-Haytham, al-Biruni, and Ibn Rushd, who, though attentive to religious problems, embraced a philosophy that granted a soteriological value to the autonomous pursuit of truth.[36] These scholars conformed to a sociological type that A. I. Sabra calls the "philosopher-scientist." Arab science began its (relative) decline when that ideology gradually gave way to a notion, propagated especially by al-Ghazali, that the research on which human happiness depends is essentially theological in nature. This notion rejects all sciences except those with an instrumental value: astronomy, for determining the weather, the visibility of the moon, and the *qibla*; and medicine, for keeping one's body in good health. The social role of the man of science changed: the "philosopher-scientist" was replaced by the "jurist-scientist," who devoted himself primarily to jurisprudence and no longer to the search for the scientific and philosophical truth about the world.[37]

From a sociological standpoint, the conditions that led to the relative decline of Arab science resemble those that prevailed in a *permanent* manner in the Jewish communities, where the scholar's social role remained closely linked to the study of the tradition. It is not immaterial that, like Levi ben Gershom—the only Jewish scholar writing in Hebrew who shared the ideal of autonomous research as an end in itself—Muslim philosopher-scientists based their own epistemological position on soteriology, considering philosophical and scientific research the only means for achieving eternal happiness.

> " *Like Levi ben Gershom Muslim philosopher-scientists based their own epistemological position on soteriology.* "

This parallel acquires further historical significance in light of the famous "Merton thesis," which concerns the social conditions underlying the scientific revolution of the mid-seventeenth century. The sociologist Robert K. Merton has shown that the reason the nascent scientific community rallied behind the idea of autonomous scientific research—a determining factor in the emergence of the New Science—can be found in Protestant theology, which taught that salvation can come only through knowledge of the physical world.[38] In the three cases mentioned, the factors that gave rise to a scientific boom are strikingly similar. Levi ben Gershom, the three great Arab Muslim scholars, and the seventeenth-century Puritan scientists all embraced theological systems that recognized the legitimacy of autonomous research, thus providing a strong motivation to engage in such research. It was precisely this sort of legitimation and motivation that Maimonidean theology, hegemonic among medieval Jewish rationalists, foreclosed.

The place granted to science and philosophy in Hebrew-speaking medieval Jewish communities meant that, in the course of the thirteenth century, Greco-Arab philosophy and science became an integral part of the worldview of a large portion of the Jews of Spain and of the French Midi. They constituted an essential element of the Maimonidean definition of Jewish identity. This social function, however, did not lead to a desire to acquire specialized scientific knowledge that lacked metaphysical or immediately practical import. Nor did it provide a motivation for autonomous scientific research, except in astronomy. In other words, a delimited body of knowledge and a solid description of the world adequately fulfilled the needs of Jewish society. But this function of science precluded the emergence of scientific research activities like those that arose and developed in Arab Muslim medieval societies and in the Latin West. Jewish scholars in the Christian world, having appropriated science and integrated it into their religious philosophy, did not seek to modify it and—with a few exceptions—did not make any original contributions to it. They were content to be "consumers" of scientific knowledge, without seeking to become its "producers." The originality and creativity of the Hebrew-speaking Jews of the French Midi and of Spain appeared in realms other than science, namely, in the Halakha (Law) or in mysticism. Ultimately, Jews did not enter the world of science until centuries later, during the Enlightenment especially.

---

1. This article incorporates elements taken from previous studies I have published, some of them fairly old: "The Place of Science in Medieval Hebrew-Writing Jewish Communities: A Sociological Perspective," in *Rashi, 1040–1990: Hommage à Aphraïm E. Urbach: Congrès européen d'études juives*, ed. Gabrielle Sed-Rajna (Paris: Les Éditions du Cerf, 1993), 599–613; "Les sciences dans les communautés juives médiévales de Provence: Leur appropriation, leur rôle," *Revue des études juives* 152 (1993): 29–136; and "Arabic and Latin Cultures as Resources for the Hebrew Translation Movement." On certain points, this article no longer reflects my current thinking. The French translation of texts originally written in English is by Charles Hutner. I would like to express my profound gratitude to Sylvie Anne Goldberg at the École des Hautes Études en Sciences Sociales, Paris, for her editorial work. [The English version of this article was translated from the French, with reference to the English-language sources listed above—JMT.]
Julius Guttmann, *Philosophies of Judaism: The History of Jewish Philosophy from Biblical Times to Franz Rosenzweig*, trans. David W. Silverman (New York: Doubleday, 1964), 3.

2. A similar phenomenon occurred within Islamic culture and for the same reasons. See, for example, Muhsin Mahdi, "Language and Logic in Classical Islam," in *Logic in Classical Islamic Culture*, ed. G. E. van Grunebaum (Wiesbaden: Otto Harrassowitz, 1970), 51–83.

3. A. I. Sabra, "The Appropriation and Subsequent Naturalization of Greek Science in Medieval Islam: A Preliminary Statement," *History of Science* 25 (1987): 223–43. For a relativization of this distinction, see Roshdi

Rashed, "Problems of the Transmission of Greek Scientific Thought into Arabic: Examples from Mathematics and Optics," *History of Science* 27 (1989): 199–209.

4. The term "symbiosis" was introduced in this context by S. D. Goitein. See his *Jews and Arabs: Their Contacts through the Ages* (New York: Schocken, 1964), 11, 127. See also S. M. Wasserstrom, *Between Muslim and Jew: The Problem of Symbiosis under Early Islam* (Princeton, NJ: Princeton University Press, 1995), 3–12.

5. See Gad Freudenthal, "Arabic and Latin Cultures as Resources for the Hebrew Translation Movement: Comparative Considerations, Both Quantitative and Qualitative," in *Science in Medieval Jewish Cultures*, ed. G. Freudenthal (New York: Cambridge University Press, 2011), 74–105.

6. See the classic article by I. Twersky, "Aspects of the Social and Cultural History of Provençal Jewry," *Journal of World History* 11, nos. 1–2 (1968): 185–207; and also Gad Freudenthal, "Transfert culturel à Lunel au milieu du douzième siècle: Qu'est-ce qui a motivé les premières traductions provençales de l'arabe en hébreu?," in *Des Tibbonides à Maïmonide: Rayonnement des Juifs andalous en Pays d'Oc médiéval*, ed. Danielle Iancou-Agou and Élie Nicolas (Paris: Cerf, 2009), 95–108.

7. See the articles collected in Gad Freudenthal, ed., *Science and Philosophy in Ashkenazi Culture: Rejection, Toleration and Accommodation*, in the *Jahrbuch des Simon-Dubnow-Instituts / Simon Dubnow Institute Yearbook*, vol. 8 (Lepizig: Vandenhoeck & Ruprecht, 2009), 13–315.

8. I cannot consider medicine here, though it had a fairly significant influence on the processes described. For an overall view, see Carmen Caballero-Navas, "Medicine among Medieval Jews: The Science, the Art, and the Practice," in Freudenthal, ed., *Science in Medieval Jewish Cultures*, 320–42.

9. Mauro Zonta, *Hebrew Scholasticism in the Fifteenth Century: A History and Source Book* (Dordrecht: Springer, 2006).

10. For a survey of medieval translations from Latin into Hebrew, see Alexander Fidora, Resianne Fontaine, Gad Freudenthal, and Yossef Schwartz, eds., *Latin-into-Hebrew: Studies and Texts*, 2 vols. (Leiden: Brill, 2013).

11. For a comprehensive view, see Mark R. Cohen, *Under Crescent and Cross: The Jews in the Middle Ages* (Princeton, NJ: Princeton University Press, 1994). See also Freudenthal, "Arabic and Latin Cultures as Resources for the Hebrew Translation Movement."

12. Herbert A. Davidson, "The Study of Philosophy as a Religious Obligation," in *Religion in a Religious Age*, ed. S. D. Goitein (Cambridge, MA: Association for Jewish Studies, 1974), 53–68; revised version in his *Maimonides the Rationalist* (Oxford: Littman Library, 2011), 1–14.

13. Maimonides, *Guide for the Perplexed*, trans. Michael Friedländer (New York: Dutton, 1904), part 1, chap. 34.

14. Charles Touati, "La controverse de 1303–1306 autour des études philosophiques et scientifiques," *Revue des études juives* 128 (1968): 21–37, repr. in his *Prophètes, Talmudistes, Philosophes* (Paris: Cerf, 1990), 201–17.

15. A comprehensive view of the sciences as they were practiced by Jews in the Middle Ages can be found in Freudenthal, ed., *Science in Medieval Jewish Cultures*. A chronological list of works translated into Hebrew is provided in that volume in Mauro Zonta's "Medieval Hebrew Translations of Philosophical and Scientific Texts: A Chronological Table," 17–73.

16. Bernard R. Goldstein, "Astronomy among Jews in the Middle Ages," in Freudenthal, ed., *Science in Medieval Jewish Cultures*, 136–46.

17. But see Tony Lévy, "L'algèbre arabe dans les textes hébraïques (1): Un ouvrage inédit d'Isaac ben Salomon al-Ahdab (XIVᵉ siècle)," *Arabic Sciences and Philosophy* 13 (2003): 269–301; and, more generally, "The Hebrew Mathematics Culture (Twelfth–Sixteenth Centuries)," in Freudenthal, ed., *Science in Medieval Jewish Cultures*, 155–71.

18. As in al-Farabi's *Ihsa al-ulum* (*ilm 'l-hiyal, hokhmat ha tahbulot, ingenium*).

19. Abraham ben David Ibn Daud, *The Exalted Faith*, trans. Norbert M. Samuelson (Cranbury, NJ: Associated University Presses, 1986), 132 (section 123a), brackets in the original English edition. Maimonides adopts precisely the same attitude in his famous *Treatise of Eight Chapters* (chap. 5).

20. Moritz Steinschneider, *Die Hebräischen Übersetzungen des Mittelalters und die Juden als Dolmetscher* (Berlin, 1893; repr., Graz: Akademische Druch und Verlaganstalt, 1956), 273; G. Scholem, "Alchemie und Kabbala," *Eranos Jahrbuch* 46 (1977): 1–96, French translation in *De la création du monde jusqu'à Varsovie*, by Maurice-Ruben Hayoun (Paris: Cerf, 1990). For an overview, see Gad Freudenthal, "Medieval Alchemy in Hebrew: A Noted Absence," in Freudenthal, ed., *Science in Medieval Jewish Cultures*, 343–58. Raphael Patai's *The Jewish Alchemists: A History and Source Book* (Princeton, NJ: Princeton University Press, 1994) is rich but contains errors.

21. For a comprehensive view, see Ruth Glasner, "The Evolution of the Genre of the Philosophical-Scientific Commentary: Hebrew Supercommentaries on Aristotle's Physics," in Freudenthal, ed., *Science in Medieval Jewish Cultures*, 182–206. A real scientific controversy about physics took place in the fourteenth century. It has been studied by Ruth Glasner in *A Fourteenth-Century Scientific Philosophic Controversy: Jedaiah Ha-Penini's Treatise on Opposite Motions and Book of Confutation* (Jerusalem: World Union of Jewish Studies, 1998) (in Hebrew).

22. For a survey, see Gad Freudenthal and Mauro Zonta, "Avicenna amongst Medieval Jews: The Reception of Avicenna's Philosophical, Scientific and Medical Writings in Jewish Cultures, East and West," *Arabic Sciences and Philosophy* 22 (2012): 217–87.

23. Rashed, "Problems of the Transmission of Greek Scientific Thought in Arabic."

24. Guttmann, *Philosophies of Judaism*, 55.

25. Maimonides, *Guide for the Perplexed*, part 3, chap. 51.

26. Ibid.

27. Ibid., part 2, chap. 22; cf. part 2, chap. 24.

28. Harry Austryn Wolfson, *Crescas' Critique of Aristotle* (Cambridge, MA: Harvard University Press, 1929); Warren Zev Harvey, *Physics and Metaphysics in Hasdai Crescas* (Amsterdam: J. C. Gieben, 1998).

29. The scientific works of Gersonides are the main subject in Gad Freudenthal, ed., *Studies on Gersonides: A Fourteenth-Century Philosopher-Scientist* (Leiden: Brill, 1992).

30. Gad Freudenthal, "Sauver son âme ou sauver les phénomènes: Sotériologie, épistémologie et astronomie chez Gersonide," in Freudenthal, ed., *Studies on Gersonides*, 317–52.

31. Cf. the concise and illuminating notes in Jacques Verger, "Condition de l'intellectuel aux XIIIᵉ et XIVᵉ siècles," in *Philosophes médiévaux: Anthologie de textes philosophiques (XIIIᵉ–XIVᵉ siècles)*, ed. Ruedi Imbach and Maryse-Hélène Méléard (Paris: UGE, 1986), 11–49. The key importance, for the emergence of modern science, of discussions about the *potentia Dei absoluta et ordinata* and the notion of what is possible *secundum imaginationem* is laid out in Amos Funkenstein, *Theology and the Scientific Imagination: From the Middle Ages to the Seventeenth Century* (Princeton, NJ: Princeton University Press, 1986).

32. Cf. Joseph Ben-David, *Scientific Growth: Essays on the Social Organization and Ethos of Science*, ed. G. Freudenthal (Berkeley: University of California Press, 1991); and *The Scientist's Role in Society: A Comparative Study*, 2nd ed. (Chicago: University of Chicago Press, 1984).

33. Jacob Katz, *Tradition and Crisis: Jewish Society at the End of the Middle Ages* (New York: Schocken, 1971), 3.

34. Kalonymus b. Kalonymus, *Even Bohan*, ed. A. M. Habermann (Tel Aviv: Mahbarot le-sifrut, 1956), 44.

35. Alfonso, *Meyashsher Aqov*, ed. and trans. into Russian by G. M. Gluskina (Moscow, 1983), 139 (fol. 94a, lines 4–8 of the manuscript, reproduced in the book).

36. Sabra, "The Appropriation and Subsequent Naturalization of Greek Science."

37. Al-Ghazali was not, of course, the *cause* of that change of conception, merely the one who formulated it most eloquently and perhaps most influentially. Thus, the beginning of that (relative) decline does not necessarily coincide with his lifetime.

38. The classic formulation of that thesis is in R. K. Merton, *Science, Technology and Society in Seventeenth-Century England* (1938; New York: Harper, 1970). J. Ben-David gives a penetrating analysis of Merton's thesis in "Puritanism and Modern Science: A Study in the Continuity and Coherence of Sociological Research," in his *Scientific Growth*, 343–60.

Shi'ism and Judaism: A Relation Marked by Paradox

Mohammad Ali Amir-Moezzi

Both Shi'ism and Judaism are diverse faiths, and it is always tricky, not to say problematic, to speak of their relationship as if they were monolithic entities. Orientalists and specialists in both Islamic studies and Judaic studies differ greatly in their assessment of the Shi'ites' position in relation to the Jews during the classical period of Islam. To cite only two major scholars, Ignaz Goldziher in *Vorlesungen über den Islam* (1910), and Shlomo D. Goitein in *Jews and Arabs* (1955), both believe that the attitude of Shi'ism, unlike that of Sunnism, is strongly imbued with fanaticism and intolerance, which makes any reconciliation with the faithful of Judaism almost impossible. At the other end of the spectrum, Julius Wellhausen (in many articles and especially in his *Prolegomena to the History of Israel*, 1878), Joel Kraemer (in

Mohammad Ali Amir-Moezzi

Mohammad Ali Amir-Moezzi is director of studies at the École Pratique des Hautes Études (EPHE-Sorbonne) and a specialist in the history of Qur'anic exegesis and in classical Islamic theology. He is the author of *Le guide divin dans le shi'isme originel* (Verdier, 1997; new ed. 2007); *La religion discrète: Croyances et pratiques spirituelles dans l'islam shi'ite* (Vrin, 2006); and *Le Coran silencieux et le Coran parlant: Sources scriptuaires de l'islam entre histoire et ferveur* (CNRS Éditions, 2011). He is also the editor of the *Dictionnaire du Coran* (Robert Laffont, 2006).

Humanism in the Renaissance of Islam, 1986), and Steven Wasserstrom (in *Between Muslim and Jew*, 1995) emphasize the spirit of openness of the different forms of Shi'ism—in contrast to a certain sort of Sunnism—to other religions and cultures, especially Judaism. Meir Bar-Asher maps out a middle position in his article (written in Hebrew) on the place of the Jews and Judaism in ancient Shi'ism.[1] He highlights the multivalence of its attitude, which vacillated between rejection at the juridical level and a form of identification fully embraced at the doctrinal level. I shall adopt that balanced and subtly nuanced position while trying to provide further evidence in support of this view.

The Jews and the Children of Israel: A fundamental dichotomy

The ambiguity of Shi'ism on this question (and, in a different way, of Sunnism as well) may well have originated in the Qur'an, which clearly recognizes two sorts of Jews. In the first place, there are "the good and true Jews," those of the Old Testament, the chosen people of God and of the biblical prophets—Abraham, Jacob, Moses, and others—who are designated more than forty times by the expression Banu Isra'il, the Children or Descendants of Israel. Second, there are "the bad Jews," those of the postbiblical period and especially those living in Arabia at the time of the advent of Islam, which the Qur'an designates about ten times as *al-yahūd* (the Jews). Although consid-

> " *The ambiguity of Shi'ism on this question may well have originated in the Qur'an.* "

ered among "the People of the Book," these Jews are accused of having falsified their scriptures, betraying their prophets and wise men, and, implicitly, of having wrongly rejected the message of Muhammad, who, however, is presented as the continuator and successor of the great patriarchs and prophets of Israel. That dichotomous perception seems to be reflected in two distinct religious issues within Shi'ism: the negative attitude toward "the Jews" in the juridical realm, and the hagiographic and apologetic position toward the Children of Israel at the doctrinal level.

The status of the Jews in Shi'ite law

As Bar-Asher rightly points out, the place of the Jews—always called *al-yahūd*—in the law of the Twelver Imamites (the main branch of Shi'ism) has as its center of gravity the notion of impurity (*najāsa*), which is understood primarily through different and sometimes contradictory interpretations of Qur'an 9:28, regarding the impurity of the associationists. Whereas Sunnism tends to take flexible positions depending on the circumstances, the majority of Shi'ite jurists adopt a categorical attitude of rejection. That attitude is summed up by Muhammad Baqir al-Majlisi (d. 1699 or 1700), author of the monumental *Bihar al-Anwar*, one of the largest encyclopedias of Shi'ite traditions, compiled from the most ancient sources. According to al-Majlisi, the physical impurity of the People of the Book and its legal consequences stem from "their internal impurity resulting from their fundamental wickedness and the corruption of their beliefs." The most noteworthy implications of the Muslim attitude toward the People of the Book—and hence toward the Jews—has to do with the consumption of their food and with marriage to their women. The two practices are linked in Qur'an 5:5, which, unlike the principal commentaries that will be given of it in both Sunnism and Shi'ism, seems rather permissive: "All good things have this day been made lawful to you. The food of those to whom the Book was given is lawful to you, and yours to them. Lawful to you are the believing women and the free women from among those who were given the Book before you, provided that you give them their dowries and live in honor with them, neither committing fornication nor taking them as mistresses."[2]

Muslim theologian-jurists, making use of the literature of the Hadith, Qur'anic exegesis, and *Al-Sira* (*The Life of the Prophet*), considerably limited the scope of that verse. Among the variety of attitudes, the majority of Sunnis would permit, under some conditions, the consumption of food, including the meat of slaughtered animals prepared in accordance with the rites of the People of the Book, as well as marriage to their women. Such marriages, however, are considered inferior in status to those with Muslim women. On the whole, the Shi'ites are stricter in their interpretation of the verse. In the case of food, it is permitted to consume "dry foodstuffs" such as cereals, vegetables, or fruit, but in no case meat. Even if the name of God was mentioned during the act of slaughter, the animal is not purified, given the falseness of the People of the Book's faith in God.

Similarly, for the majority of Shi'ite scholars, marriage to a woman belonging to the People of the Book can be concluded only temporarily, as a *mut'at al-nisa'* (the notorious "temporary marriage" of the Shi'ites), which is considered markedly inferior to the highly respected institution of permanent marriage.

It is necessary to add, however, that even in ancient times the Shi'ite attitude always had nuances, hesitations in fact, since the plurality of opinions and the consideration of situations that supposedly require a modification of one's position are already indicated in the tenth- and eleventh-century sources. Are the People of the Book among the "associationists" mentioned in Qur'an 9:28? What is the correct interpretation of sura 5:5? Must the faithful respect the prohibitions concerning the consumption of meat and permanent marriage if their life is placed in danger as a result of them? What is the weight of "intention" and sincerity in the practice of the prohibitions? Once again, al-Majlisi attempts—obviously with difficulty—to provide a synthesis of the question, which in the last instance turns on the notion of impurity: "Our jurists," he writes, "agree that all unbelievers, with the exception of the Jews and the Christians, are impure; and a majority maintain that even these two groups are impure."

The Shi'ites' almost obsessive preoccupation with purity and impurity, probably based on the sense that they belong to a religious elite, seems to stem from influences that originated elsewhere. On this issue, Goldziher points out the many similarities between Zoroastrianism and Shi'ism.[3] A. J. Wensinck, in his entry "Nadjis" in the *Encyclopaedia of Islam*, and M. Cook, in his now-classic study of Islamic dietary laws,[4] both emphasize the many influences of ancient Jewish law (though the Jewish categories of purity and impurity, *tahara* and *tum'a*, have no practical import in Judaism after the destruction of the Temple of Jerusalem). The late S. Soroudi, in her remarkable article on the notion of impurity in Judaism,[5] studies the close proximity between the Zoroastrian and Jewish laws and their joint influence on Shi'ite legal precepts, especially in Iran.

The doctrinal proximity of Judaism and Shi'ism

Let us now turn to the question of doctrine. In his *Istibsar*, Abu Ja'far al-Tusi (d. 1067), the great Shi'ite scholar of the Buyid era, in an attempt to explain the differences among Shiʿite jurists in their attitude toward the Jews, and especially to justify the moderation and flexibility of some of these jurists, puts forward as one of the reasons "the discipline of the arcana" or "the obligation to keep the secret [*taqiyya*]." Hence, these jurists, seeking to conceal their allegiance to Shiʿism in a hostile Sunni environment, dissimulated their characteristic rigor in favor of a moderation that was very close to Sunni positions. Bar-Asher, for his part, cites what he considers a contemporary example of that practice of *taqiyya*, namely, the case of Sheikh Fadlallah, one of the principal religious authorities of the Lebanese Shiʿites, who, Bar-Asher says, proclaimed "the purity" of the People of the Book in order to move closer to Sunni positions, while attenuating the specificity of his Shiʿism. Yet when we examine the writings concerning the Sunni controversy with the Shiʿites, we may legiti-

ʿAli, cousin and son-in-law of the Prophet, with his sons and successors, Hasan ibn Ali and Hussain ibn Ali. Popular Persian image, 1837.

mately doubt the effectiveness of this supposed tactic of dissimulation. For the Sunni polemicists, in fact, Shiʿism is not distinguished by its severity toward the Jews or its juridical resemblance to Sunnism but, on the contrary, by its proximity to, even culpable complicity with, Judaism. In his *Al-ʿIqd al-farid*, the Andalusian Ibn ʿAbd Rabbih (d. 939) lists nine articles of faith, as fundamental as they are reprehensible, shared by Judaism and Shiʿism. The same sort of accusation can be found in al-Isfaraʾini and in Abu Yaʿla ibn al-Farraʾ, eleventh-century theologians belonging to the Asharite movement. A few centuries later, the Hanbalite scholar and polemicist Ibn Taymiyyah (d. 1328), in his famous *Minhaj al-sunnah*, gives a list of twenty-nine articles of faith, beliefs, and practices common to the Jews and the Shiʿites. A few examples: the Jews claim that sovereignty belongs only to the descendants of David, just as the Shiʿites profess that it is restricted to the descendants of ʿAli; the Jews, like the Shiʿites, rock back and forth while praying; both the Jews and the Shiʿites put off their evening prayers until the stars come out; the Jews falsified the Torah, just as the Shiʿites falsified the Qurʾan; and so on. It hardly matters whether all these accusations have a historical basis or whether these lists are pertinent as a whole: what counts is the proximity between Judaism and Shiʿism as seen by their adversaries. This is why, early on, the phrase uttered by anti-Shiʿite polemicists assumed the aspect of an adage: "The Shiʿites are the Jews of the Muslim community."

In fact, if we turn to the Shiʿite sources themselves, they lay claim to something more than a proximity to Judaism but not necessarily in the way the Sunni polemicists perceive it. According to a worldview central to Shiʿism, every religious reality has two levels: an apparent, manifest, exoteric level (*zāhir* in Arabic) and a hidden, secret, esoteric level (*bātin*). In prophetology, the divine Word, revealed from time to time to humans and set in writing in the form of a Book, also possesses a manifest aspect and a hidden dimension, a "letter" and a "spirit," to borrow the Pauline expression. The prophet-lawmaker, though he obviously knows the hidden meaning of scripture, has the mission of bringing the letter of revelation to a majority of a particular community. But every prophet is accompanied in his mission by one or several imams, whose task is to initiate a minority of the faithful into the spirit, the esoteric sense of scripture. That minority of initiates are the "Shiʿites" of each religion. For example, Moses is considered the messenger of the letter of the Torah for the majority of Jews. His imam, Aaron (or Joshua, in other traditions), had the mission of initiating a minority of the community, "the Jewish Shiʿites," into the hidden meaning of the Torah. Similarly, Jesus brought the letter of the Gospel (always in the singular in Islam) to the Christians in general. His imams, the apostles (and more particularly, Simon Peter), initiated "the Christian Shiʿites" into the esoteric dimension of their Book. Finally, Muhammad offered the letter of the Qurʾan to the Muslims. His imams, namely, ʿAli and the imams descended from him, had the mission of initiating a minority, the historical Shiʿites, into the secret meaning of the Qurʾan. In the long chain of initiation of Friends or Allies of God (*walī*; pl. *awliyā*), composed of prophets, imams, saints, and faithful initiates during every era, from Adam and Abel to the prophet of Islam and his imams, the most holy figures of Shiʿism—Muhammad, ʿAli, and the imams descended from him—usually associated their persons, their teachings, and their faithful with the "Descendants of Israel," through the traditions attributed to that people. For example, according to a prophetic Hadith reported in a large number of Shiʿite sources, Muhammad declared: "I am the servant of God [*ʿabd allāh*], and my name is Ahmad; I am the servant of God, and my name is Israel [Israʾil, that is, Jacob]." In the same way, the twelve sons of Jacob, or the twelve tribes of Israel, are identified with the twelve imams of Twelver Shiʿism. In many traditions, one or another imam declares that in the Qur'an references to the Children of Israel designate, at the exoteric level, the biblical prophets and the Jewish faithful, while at the esoteric level they refer to the imams belonging to the family of the holy prophet and the Shi'ites. Similarly, the adversaries of 'Ali and his followers, in this case the first two caliphs, Abu Bakr and 'Umar, are often compared or quite simply called "Pharaoh" and "Haman," the enemies of the Children of Israel in the Qur'an.

The emblematic Hadith illustrating the notion that the Shi'ites perceive themselves as the continuation, even the replica, of the "people of the Covenant"—the Children of Israel—is the famous "Hadith of position" (*hadīth al-manzila*). The Prophet is said to have told 'Ali: "Your position in relation to me is identical to that of Aaron in relation to Moses." In fact, the Shi'ites often call themselves *ahl al-walāya*, which could easily be translated as "the people of the divine Covenant" (*walāya*, a central doctrinal term in Shi'ism, comes from the same root as the word *walī*, "friend" or "ally," mentioned above). The names of 'Ali's two sons, Hasan and Husayn, the Prophet's only male descendants, are said to be identical to those of the sons of Aaron, Shabar and Shubayr, and it is true that both triliteral roots, *h.s.n* in Arabic and *sh.p.r* in Hebrew-Aramaic, connote "grace" or "beauty." In the Shi'ite sources, 'Ali combines the prophetic qualities of Moses, the religious authority of Aaron, and the royal attributes of David. The Supreme Name of God, reminiscent of the unpronounceable Name of the God of Israel, has incommensurable supernatural powers: according to the Shi'ite texts, it is a magic formula in Hebrew known to the imams. It is thanks to this knowledge that 'Ali performed the miracle that the Old Testament attributes to Joshua: making the sun reverse its course. Thus, within Islam, the Shi'ites fully embrace their minority status, perceiving it as a sign of divine election, just as the Children of Israel did.

The question of messianism

Strong convergences are also perceptible in other major doctrinal matters. To begin with, the notion of messianism is central to both faiths, and certain events to which the historical sources allude seem to indicate a close proximity between Shi'ites and Jews in the early days of Islam. Many Jewish messianic movements had come into being in the two centuries preceding the advent of the Arab religion: in the late fifth century, "the Second Moses" emerged in Crete; and the armed revolts of the Samaritans against Byzantine power took place in Palestine in 484, 529, and 556. In Southern Arabia, the Jewish king Dhu Nuwas, in his struggles against the Abyssinian Christians in the first half of the sixth century, was considered the Messiah by his faithful. Such was also the case in the Hejaz for the poet-soothsayer Samaw'al ibn Adiya, just before Muhammad's birth. A good number of Jews at the time were therefore caught up in the fervor of awaiting the Messiah. It is likely that Muhammad was able to concentrate in his person the messianic hopes of some

Jews of Arabia. Many of them, who could be called Judeo-Muslims, believed in the veracity of the prophetic mission of Muhammad, who was considered to be sent by God, but only to guide the Arab people. It seems that, after the Prophet's

> *It seems that, after the Prophet's death, these Jews shifted their expectations to the person of ʿAli. This phenomenon is especially attested in Iran.*

death, these Jews shifted their expectations to the person of ʿAli. This phenomenon is especially attested in Iran. For example, it is reported that ʿAli's accession to the caliphate was welcomed by an enormous wave of joy by tens of thousands of Jews from the cities of Isfahan and Piruz-Shapur. Although he may have been a legendary figure, the Yemeni Jewish convert ʿAbdallah ibn Sabaʾ, the eponym for the Shiʿite sect of the Sabaʾiyya, later called the Mukhtariyya, is said to have been the first to declare ʿAli identical to Joshua and subsequently to the awaited Messiah. And a study of the chains of transmitters of the messianic Shiʿite tradition seems to show that they were especially well developed in the first centuries of Islam among the Shiʿites of Yemen originally living in the city of Kufa, almost all of whom converted from Judaism. In the same way, messianic aspects taken from Judaism are clearly identifiable in the claims attributed to the so-called extremist sects of the Harbiyya, the Mansuriyya, and the different groups of the Waqifa, where one imam or another descended from ʿAli, or one heresiarch or another, was identified with the eschatological Savior. Conversely, the Isawiyya, the messianic movement of the Jewish revolutionary Abu ʿIsa of Isfahan (d. about 750), whom a large number of historians consider the most important Jewish "prophet" between Shimon bar Kokhba in the second century and Sabbatai Zevi in the seventeenth, displays obvious sympathies and doctrinal similarities with Shiʿism and Shiʿite eschatological beliefs.

The centrality of hermeneutics

Other similarities are sometimes found even in the details of doctrinal arguments. For example, many parallels exist between the methods for naming an imam (*nass*) and those for ordaining a rabbi (*simikha*); and between the notion of the imam's occultation (*ghayba*) and its implications, on one hand, and the doctrine of exile (*galut*) and its consequences on the other. Finally, let us note the importance in both religions of the practice of hermeneutics, in the sense of a revelation of the hidden meaning of scripture. Shiʿism defines itself as the hermeneutic doctrine par excellence of Islam. The imam is an imam because he possesses the knowledge of the secret meanings of the Qurʾan, because he is the "master of hermeneutics" (*sāhib al-taʾwil*). The foundations and methods of the Shiʿite discipline of exegesis seem largely beholden to the Christian doctrine of the "four senses" of scripture (literal, allegorical, moral, and anagogic), which is itself close to the four interpretive methods of Judaism: literal exegesis (*peshat*), implied hidden meaning (*remez*), homiletic perception (*derash*), and mystical and symbolic interpretation (*sod*). The Jews from Islamic lands, in their study of the literal and esoteric layers of the Torah, may in turn have been inspired by Imamite and Ismaelite Shi'ite hermeneutics. This, at least, is what the great twelfth-century Muslim religious historian al-Shahrastani wrote in his description of the different medieval Jewish schools present on Islamic territories. Furthermore, it is well known that the Shi'ite philosophical doctrines, especially Ismaelite thought, exerted a large influence on major Jewish thinkers between the tenth and twelfth centuries, for example, on Isaac Israeli, Ibn Gabirol, Yehuda Halevi, and the Karaite Yefet ben 'Ali, in writings that Samuel Stern describes as the "Judeo-Ishmaelite *ta'wīl*."[6]

What are we to conclude from the paradoxical position of Shi'ism toward the Jews and Judaism? First, this ambiguous attitude is based on that of the Qur'an toward two categories of Israelites: on one hand, the real "Children of Israel," a chosen people and the true faithful of the biblical patriarchs and prophets; and on the other, the deviant "Jews," falsifiers of the Messengers' news and betrayers of their divine missions. Second, it is possible to say that the Shi'ites, basing themselves on the omnipresent pair *zāhir/bātin* (the two levels of any religious reality, apparent and hidden, exoteric and esoteric), used the Jews as paradigmatic models to illustrate their own history and their own doctrines. The negative attitude toward the "bad Jew" arises primarily in a juridical context, within the framework of the law, the exoteric discipline par excellence. Conversely, at the doctrinal level, where the esoteric finds fertile ground for expressing itself, the positive attitude toward the "true Jew" reaches its heights, since the Children of Israel, the chosen people, are identified with the Shi'ites, whereas the "bad Jews" are said to symbolize the enemies of Muhammad, 'Ali, and their descendants. Like their prototypes, these enemies were the falsifiers of the Qur'an, those who betrayed their prophet and his "true Islam." At the same time, the fate of the people of Israel, liberated from the yoke of their enemies (who are punished by God) and saved from exile, awaiting a savior to come, provided a bright horizon of hope to the Shi'ites, a persecuted and ostracized minority who were often the victims of bloody repressions.

---

1. M. Bar-Asher, "Al meqom ha-yahadut ve-ha-yehudim ba-sifrut ha-datit shel ha-shi'a ha-qeduma" [On the Place of Judaism and the Jews in Ancient Shi'ism], *Pe'amin* (*Studies in Oriental Jewry*) 61 (1994): 16–36.

2. [Verses from the Qur'an are taken from *The Koran*, trans. N. J. Dawood (New York: Penguin, 1995)—JMT].

3. I. Goldziher, "Islamisme et Parsisme," *Revue de l'Histoire des Religions* 43 (1901): 1–29, reprinted in his *Sur l'Islam: Origines de la théologie musulmane* (Paris: Desclée de Brouwer, 2003), chap. 5, 113–41.

4. M. Cook, "Early Islamic Dietary Law," *Jerusalem Studies in Arabic and Islam* 7 (1986): 217–77.

5. S. Soroudi, "The Concept of Jewish Impurity and Its Reflection in Persian and Judeo-Persian Traditions," *Irano-Judaica* 3 (1993): 1–29.

6. See A. Altmann and S. M. Stern, *Isaac Israeli: A Neoplatonic Philosopher of the Early Tenth Century* (Oxford: Oxford University Press, 1958) and S. Pines, "Shi'ite Terms and Conceptions in Judah Halevi's *Kuzari*," *Jerusalem Studies in Arabic and Islam* 2 (1980): 165–251.

Isma'ilism and Medieval Jewish Thought in Islamic Territories

From its beginnings in about the mid-ninth century, the Isma'ili branch of Shi'ite Islam was notable for its astonishing capacity to assimilate doctrines originating in ancient Christian, Jewish, and Manichaean Gnostic traditions, even while elaborating a philosophy profoundly marked by Neoplatonism, and especially by the Arabic paraphrases of Plotinus's *Enneads*, which had just been composed in Baghdad within the circle of the "first Arab philosopher," al-Kindi.

Esoteric in nature, Isma'ili thought proposes to clarify the "hidden meaning" (*bātin*) of Qur'anic revelation, as the Prophet Muhammad entrusted it to his successor, 'Ali, and which was then transmitted through the imams of his descent. Nevertheless, this exegetical method was not confined to the Qur'an but was also applied to the texts revealed by the earlier prophets, particularly the Torah of Moses and the Gospel of Jesus. As a result, it is not rare to find in Isma'ili writings passages taken from the Bible and the Gospels, sometimes quoted in Hebrew or Syriac. For the Isma'ilis, the three monotheistic religions may differ in their laws and precepts, but these are only the expression of a single hidden meaning.

In practice, this conception translated into a relative tolerance toward the Jewish and Christian minorities when the Isma'ilis exercised political power. Such was the case under the Fatimid Empire, founded in 909 in what is now Tunisia—and that quickly expanded into Libya, Egypt, and part of Syria. This was also true in Yemen, where dissident Isma'ilis (the Tayyibi) created a state, in about the mid-twelfth century, around the capital city of San'a. At the time, these regions had large Jewish communities, which, under the Isma'ili regime, experienced rapid economic and intellectual development. This is attested in the countless documents discovered in the Geniza of the Ben Ezra Synagogue in Old Cairo, a storehouse containing manuscripts of all sorts, which Jewish custom prohibited from destroying because of the sacred character of Hebrew writing.

In addition to that geographical proximity, a certain intellectual affinity seems to have existed between the Isma'ilis and the Jews. Even in the first Isma'ili texts that have come down to us, which date to the late ninth century, the idea emerges that God in his absolute transcendence created the world ex nihilo by his Will (*Irāda, Mashī'a*), his Word (*Kalima*), and his Imperative (*Amr*), *kun* (Let it be!). Isma'ili authors describe in detail the complicated processes by which God derived, from the letters that compose those words, the other letters of the Arabic alphabet. These twenty-eight letters then formed the substratum from which the universe was generated. Such speculations on the formation of the letters and their numeric value have many similarities to the Jewish Gnostic literature, especially the *Book of the Creation* (*Sefer Yetzirah*). This book not only influenced Isma'ili thought but also gave rise to several commentaries written by Jews under the Fatimid Empire.

In addition to Gnosis, Isma'ilism was profoundly marked by Neoplatonism, especially the philosophy of Plotinus. In the Arab Muslim world, Plotinian thought was known in a form adapted to monotheism, which was disseminated under Aristotle's name. The Arabic paraphrase of the last three *Enneads* was presented as a "theology," the capstone of Aristotle's *Metaphysics*. According to the *Pseudo-Theology of Aristotle*, the transcendent deity, identified with the Plotinian "One," created the universal Intellect, from which the universal Soul and Nature proceeded in a succession of emanations. That text had considerable influence on the development of philosophy in Islamic territories. Nevertheless, there is a fuller version (known as the "long version"), which is distinguished from the better-known version (called the Vulgate) by a number of additions and doctrinal modifications. For example, the long version introduces an intermediary hypostasis, the Verb or Word, between God the Creator and the Intellect.

All the known manuscripts of that version are in Judeo-Arabic (a form of Arabic written in Hebrew characters), and almost all the authors who cite it are Jews. Muslim philosophers usually refer to the Vulgate. There is a well-known exception, however: the Isma'ili thinkers. Like their Jewish colleagues, they used the long version of the *Theology of Aristotle*, as well as a few other Neoplatonic writings that rarely seem to have circulated outside Jewish and Isma'ili circles. This phenomenon, which remains unexplained, raises the delicate problem of the milieu in which these texts originated. Were they composed by Jews and adopted by the Isma'ilis, or vice versa? In any event, by virtue of these shared sources, Jewish Neoplatonism, which began with Isaac Israeli, a physician in the court of the first Fatimid caliph, bears many resemblances to Isma'ili Neoplatonism. Similar conceptions appear with respect to divine transcendence, the creating Verb, the Intellect, the process of emanation, the role played by the universal Soul in the generation of the physical world, the nature of the human soul, its connection to the body, and many other themes. Whereas the Jewish authors based their doctrines on the Torah and the rabbinical literature, the Isma'ilis took the Qur'an and the hadith as their scriptural foundation. But they did not hesitate to make use of the sacred texts of the other religious traditions as well.

Miniature from the manuscript of the *Rasa'il Ikhwan al-safa'* (*Encyclopedia of the Brethren of Purity*), written by a group close to Isma'ili philosophers, Baghdad, 1287. MS Istanbul, Süleymaniye Yazma Eser Kütüphanesi, Esad Efendi 3638, f. 4r.

An eloquent example appears in the *Book of the Quietude of Intellect* (*Kitab Rahat al- ʿAql*), by the Isma'ili philosopher Hamid al-Din al-Kirmani (d. about 1021). Al-Kirmani, though still Neoplatonic in his inspiration, abandoned the Plotinian cosmology of his Isma'ili predecessors, according to which the intelligible world is composed of three hypostases (the Intellect, the Soul, and Nature). Rather, he adopted the system of the Arab Muslim philosopher al-Farabi (also adopted by Avicenna), who introduced a series of ten Intellects between God and the sublunary world, each of which corresponds to a celestial sphere. These Intellects, separated from the transcendent God by an unbridgeable abyss, generate the sensible world and govern the cycles of generation and corruption, as well as the fate of souls here below. The number ten is at the very heart of al-Kirmani's thinking: each Intellect corresponds to a number between one and ten, which gives rise to specialized arithmological speculations on the decade.

As a Muslim, al-Kirmani invoked many Qurʾanic verses in support of his system, sometimes proposing audacious interpretations. But he also discovered his theories in a passage identified as the "Torah," which he quotes first in Hebrew, followed by an Arabic translation: "By ten imperatives He created the world; by ten words He established the world; God for you is the world's treasures." In fact, these verses are not from the Bible: they come from rabbinical literature. Al-Kirmani's exegesis is directly associated with the first chapter of the *Sefer Yetzirah*. According to that text, God created the world with the ten numbers of the decade (the ten *sefirōt*) and the twenty-two letters of the Hebrew alphabet. The ten *sefirōt*, which are among the principles of the universe's genesis, are linked to the divine Word: they are "inhabited" by the Word of God and act at his command. We thus discover in the writings of an Isma'ili Muslim author from the early eleventh century a set of considerations on the ten *sefirōt*, including their respective names (al-Kirmani designates, for example, the first

Intellect as "the crown of Intellects," *tāj al-ʿuqūl*, while the Kabbalists often name the first *sefirah* "the highest crown," (*kether ʿelyon*). As it happens, these considerations would be widely diffused within Judaism only at a later time. Al-Kirmani also identifies the ten *sefirōt* with the ten Intellects of Arab Muslim philosophy. The question, still largely unexplored, therefore arises: What influence did Shi'ite thought, and especially Isma'ili thought, have on the Jewish Kabbalah?

Just as Judaism influenced certain aspects of Isma'ili thought, Isma'ili conceptions related to the succession of prophetic cycles, the status of the prophet, the nature of the revealed texts, and their exegesis were taken up by Jewish authors, especially in the famous *Kuzari* by Yehuda Halevi (d. about 1140). But it was especially in Yemen, within the entourage of the Tayyibi Isma'ilis, that this influence was most pronounced. For example, Nethanael ben al-Fayyumi composed his *Garden of Intellects* (*Bustan al-ʿuqul*) in San'a in 1164. That work, in its very structure, closely resembles the esoteric writings of the Tayyibi. Like them, Nethanael borrows al-Kirmani's cosmology, which he interprets in the light of the *Epistles of the Brothers of Purity* (*Ikhwan al-Safa*), a vast encyclopedia compiled in the tenth century in a milieu close to Isma'ilism. He makes his own use of Isma'ili speculations on the numbers seven and twelve, even citing esoteric interpretations of the Qurʾanic verses. Indeed, for Nethanael, Muhammad was a prophet and the Qurʾan a revealed text, which, however, is addressed only to the Arabs and not to the Jews.

Also in Yemen, Jewish thought experienced a true renaissance in the fourteenth and fifteenth centuries. Its best-known representative, Hoter ben Shlomo, was also indebted to Tayyibi Isma'ili literature, having borrowed its technical vocabulary and principal themes. In the absence of studies, this phenomenon of osmosis—called "Jewish Isma'ilism" or "Isma'ili Judaism"—between two traditions that appear to be so different raises many unresolved questions.

How did these Jewish authors gain access to the Tayyibi literature, which in principle should not have circulated outside the limited circle of initiates, bound by an oath not to divulge the arcana of their religion? Generally speaking, that interaction between Isma'ilism and Judaism deserves to be better known, since it constitutes an important element in the complex issue of Judeo-Muslim relations in the Middle Ages.[1] ●

Director of research at the Centre National de la Recherche Scientifique in Paris, Daniel de Smet is a specialist in Isma'ilism and the author of *La quiétude de l'Intellect: Néoplatonisme et gnose ismaélienne dans l'oeuvre de Hamid ad-Din al-Kirmani* (Peeters, 1995); *Empedocles Arabus: Une lecture néoplatonicienne tardive* (Paleis der Academiën, 1998); *Les épîtres sacrées des Druzes: Rasa'il al-Hikma; Introduction, édition critique et traduction annotée des traités attribués à Hamza b. 'Ali et à Isma'il al-Tamimi* (Peeters, 2007); and *La philosophie ismaélienne: Un ésotérisme chiite entre néoplatonisme et gnose* (Le Cerf, 2012).

---

1. See Daniel de Smet, *La philosophie ismaélienne: Un ésotérisme chiite entre néoplatonisme et gnose* (Paris: Le Cerf, 2012); Colette Sirat, *La philosophie juive médiévale en terre d'Islam* (Paris: CNRS, 1988); and Alexander Altmann and Samuel Miklos Stern, *Isaac Israeli: A Neoplatonic Philosopher of the Early Tenth Century* (Chicago: University of Chicago Press, 2009).

European Judaism and Islam: The Contribution of Jewish Orientalists

Michael L. Miller

Jews played a central role in the development of Islamic studies in nineteenth-century Europe, particularly in Germany, France, and Hungary. In their youth, many of these scholars had received a traditional Jewish education, and their knowledge of Semitic languages (Hebrew and Aramaic) and rabbinic literature not only made Arabic and Islam more approachable but also enabled them to notice similarities between Judaism and Islam that were not as apparent to Christian orientalists like de Sacy, Umbreit, Fleischer, and Nöldeke. Jewish orientalists tended to be more favorably inclined toward Islam than their Christian counterparts, which often gave their research a less polemical—and more respectful—character. Nevertheless, they did not hesitate to examine Islamic texts with the same kind of scientific scrutiny to which they subjected their own biblical and rabbinic traditions. In particular, they focused their research on the historical development of the Qurʾan and on the life of Muhammad, quite often highlighting purported Jewish influences on the Prophet and his religion. Many Jewish orientalists also devoted their time to the discovery, translation, and analysis of medieval Jewish Arabic and Persian texts, sometimes glorifying the milieu in which they were composed. As Jewish scholars in nineteenth-century Europe, they were keenly aware that their religion was often an impediment to professional advancement. While some, like Vámbéry and Chwolson, became professors after converting to Christianity, others, like Munk and Goldziher, received the same honor only after their contributions to Islamic studies had long been recognized.

Michael L. Miller

An associate professor in the Nationalism Studies Program at Central European University in Budapest, Michael L. Miller specializes in the impact of nationalist conflicts on the religious, political, and cultural development of Jewish communities in Central Europe. His publications include *Rabbis and Revolution: The Jews of Moravia in the Age of Emancipation* (Stanford University Press, 2010).

Germany

Abraham Geiger (1810–74) was the first modern Jewish scholar to make a significant contribution to the study of Islam. Born to a traditional Jewish family in Frankfurt am Main and educated in Marburg, Heidelberg, and Bonn, Geiger published a Latin essay in 1832 that earned him a doctorate and served as the basis for his self-published German work *Was hat Mohammed aus dem Judenthume aufgenommen* (1833). Written at the behest of Georg Wilhelm Freytag, this essay sought to identify the Jewish influences on Islam, and as such, it served as a groundbreaking "attempt at modern comparative religion."[1] Unlike Protestant orientalists who viewed Christianity as the ultimate religion and dismissed Muhammad as an "imposter" or "fanatic," Geiger expressed great respect for the "pure monotheism of Islam" and its "free spirit of inquiry," extolling Muhammad as an "enthusiast."[2] He identified parallel practices in Judaism and Islam, and showed how the Qur'an had borrowed biblical and rab-binic accounts and then distorted or Islamicized them. Geiger, like many of his Jewish contempo-raries, viewed the Judeo-Islamic milieu, in par-ticular Muslim Spain, as a high point in Jewish history, a model for the kind of Judaism he tried to (re)form in nineteenth-century Germany; unlike medieval Christendom (or contemporary Orthodox Judaism), medieval Islam, in his view, was open to science and scholarly

❯ See article by Gordon D. Newby, pp. 46–47.

> ❝ *Geiger, like many of his Jewish contemporaries, viewed the Judeo-Islamic milieu, in particular Muslim Spain, as a high point in Jewish history.* ❞

inquiry. Geiger's scholarship also contained an implicit critique of German academia, which had marginalized Jews and Jewish history. Indeed, by demonstrating that Judaism was the mother of both Christianity and Islam, he strove to show that his own faith—and not Christianity—was the true basis of Western civilization.

Geiger devoted most of his subsequent career to the scholarly study of Judaism, but his focus on the Qur'an and the life of Muhammad paved the way for other Jewish orientalists. For example, Gustav Weil (1808–99), a student of Umbreit in Heidelberg and de Sacy in Paris, wrote a biography of Muhammad (1843) and a historical-critical introduction to the Qur'an (1844), as well as the first German translation of *Thousand and One Nights* (1837–41) and histories of the caliphate and the Islamic peoples. Weil taught Oriental languages at the University of Heidelberg, alongside Hermann Reckendorf (1825–75), who translated the Qur'an into Hebrew (Leipzig, 1857).

The philological and historicist approach to the Qur'an and the life of Muhammad continued to characterize the work of the next generation of Jewish orientalists, many of whom studied with Germany's leading Arabists[3]: Fleischer in Leipzig and Nöldeke in Göttingen, Kiel, and Strasbourg. In Leipzig, Fleischer cultivated a spirit of openness and respect that attracted many Jewish students, such as Moritz Steinschneider (1816–1907) and Adolf Jellinek (1821–93), both from Moravia; Daniel Chwolson (1819–1911) from Vilnius (then part of the Russian Empire); Jakob Barth (1851–1914) from Baden; Hartwig Derenbourg (1844–1908) from Paris; Samuel Landauer (1846–1937) from Bavaria; and Ignác Goldziher (1850–1921), Immanuel Löw (1854–1944), and Eduard

Baneth (1855–1930) from Hungary. In 1845, Fleischer founded the Deutsche Morgenländische Gesellschaft, Germany's first oriental society, which began publishing a scholarly journal, *Zeitschrift für die Deutsche Morgenländische Gesellschaft*, that provided many Jewish orientalists with a remarkably open and receptive scholarly forum.[4] Some of Fleischer's students, like Jakob Barth, later studied with Nöldeke, whose Jewish disciples also included Hartwig Hirschfeld (1854–1934) from Prussia and Hermann Solomon Reckendorf (1863–1923) of Heidelberg, whose father had translated the Qurʾan into Hebrew.

> *Many Jewish orientalists took great interest in Jewish encounters with Islam, paying special attention to Jewish writings in Arabic and Persian.*

Many Jewish orientalists took great interest in Jewish encounters with Islam, paying special attention to Jewish writings in Arabic and Persian. Steinschneider, the "father of Hebrew bibliography," wrote a treatise on Muslim circumcision and compiled extensive bibliographies of Judeo-Arabic literature, including one on polemical literature in Arabic. Barth wrote a groundbreaking study of comparative Semitic languages. Baneth, who taught at the Reform rabbinical seminary in Berlin, translated part of Maimonides's Arabic commentary on the Mishnah into Hebrew. Derenbourg, who taught in Paris, edited (together with his father, Joseph) a medieval Hebrew-Arabic grammar book as well as Maimonides's Mishnah commentary; father and son planned to publish the collected works of Saadia Gaon (d. 942), who wrote extensively in Judeo-Arabic. Hirschfeld, who taught at Jews' College in London, wrote on Jewish elements in the Koran and translated Judah Halevi's *Kuzari* into German from the original Judeo-Arabic. Samuel Landauer, a librarian in Strasbourg, published, inter alia, the Judeo-Arabic original of Saadia Gaon's *Beliefs and Opinions*.

France

German-Jewish orientalists left their mark on French academia, where already in 1864 the Prussian-born Salomon Munk (1803–67) was appointed professor of Hebrew, Chaldean, and Syriac languages at the Collège de France, after Ernst Renan was forced to resign. At the time, it would have been inconceivable for a professing Jew in Germany or Hungary to be appointed to such a position.[5] Munk, who had cataloged the oriental manuscripts at the Bibliothèque Nationale in Paris, researched medieval Judeo-Arabic literature, especially Maimonides's *Guide for the Perplexed*. Most famously, he identified the Spanish Jewish poet Solomon ibn Gabirol as the author of the Neoplatonic treatise *Fons Vitae*, originally written in Arabic. Hartwig Derenbourg, who taught Arabic at the Séminaire Israélite de France, was named professor of Arabic grammar at the École des Langues Orientales Vivantes in 1879, and at the École des Hautes Études in 1884.

Hungary

Hungary deserves a place of pride in the history of European orientalism, and no name is more closely associated with Hungarian orientalism than Ignác Goldziher (1850–1921), who has been called the "creator of Islamic studies," as well as the "shaykh" who transmitted his scholarly wisdom to a generation of disciples. Goldziher, a child prodigy who published his first scholarly work in 1862 at the age of twelve, studied under Arminius Vámbéry, a polyglot adventurer who trained a whole cohort of Hungarian Jewish orientalists, including Wilhelm Bacher, Bernát Munkácsi, and Ignác Kunos.

Arminius Vámbéry (1832–1913), one of the most colorful figures in Hungarian history, was born Hermann Vamberger, son of impoverished Jewish parents. A natural polyglot, he had already acquired several European languages as a teenager, and he went on to master Arabic, Turkish, and Persian as an adult. Vámbéry, like many of his Hungarian contemporaries, saw his linguistic pursuits as part of a larger project of discovering the Eastern origins of the highly peculiar Hungarian language. He also dreamed of finding the ancestral home of the Magyars, which he presumed to be in Central Asia. After spending six years in Constantinople, where he learned Turkish from Ahmet Effendi and served as secretary to Foreign Minister Fuat Pasha, Vámbéry published a German-Turkish dictionary (1858). Then, from 1861 to 1864, he traveled to Mecca, Iran, Bukhara, and elsewhere in Central Asia, disguised much of the time as a Sunni dervish. In 1865, he was appointed professor of oriental languages at the University of Budapest, a position he was able to hold because he had converted to Christianity. (He may have also converted to Islam.) Vámbéry published many travelogues of dubious reliability, but he also published important scholarly works on Turkic linguistics, Central Asian history, contemporary Islam, and on the origins of the Magyars. He firmly believed that Hungarian was more closely related to Turkish than to Finno-Ugric languages.

The Hungarian Islamicist Ignác Goldziher (1850–1921).

Among Vámbéry's students at the University of Budapest were Wilhelm (Vilmos) Bacher (1850–1913), Bernát Munkácsi (1860–1937), and Ignác Kunos (1862–1937). Bacher, who was Goldziher's brother-in-law, subsequently studied at universities in Breslau and Leipzig, as well as at the rabbinical seminary in Breslau. A leading Talmud scholar, he was appointed professor in 1877 at the newly established Budapest Rabbinical Seminary, where he later served as director. He made important contributions to the study of Judeo-Arabic and Judeo-Persian literature. Munkácsi and Kunos were cofounders of *Keleti Szemle: Revue orientale pour les études ouralo-altaïques* (Budapest, 1900–1932), which explored the once popular hypothesis that Uralic languages (e.g., Finno-Ugric) and Altic languages (e.g., Turkish) are related. Kunos specialized in Turkish linguistics and dialectology and was a pioneer in the study of folk poetry and folk customs in Anatolia.

Ignác Goldziher (1850–1921) holds the honor of being the first nonconverted Jew to be appointed full professor at the University of Budapest. Already in 1872, at the age of twenty-two, he was appointed lecturer, but he did not receive a chair until 1905, long after he had established himself as Hungary's most important orientalist. In fact, his primary job was as secretary of the Jewish community in Pest, a position that limited the time he could devote to scholarship. Considering Goldziher's prodigious contribution to the field of Islamic studies, it is tempting to contemplate how much greater his contribution might have been had his ancestral faith not been an obstacle to his academic advancement.

Goldziher approached the study of Islam with a critical, historicist sensibility. In his scholarship, he showed how Islam developed over the centuries under the influence of foreign ideas, mostly Christian and Jewish, but also Buddhist and pagan. As Islam came into contact with Persian, Syrian, and Hellenistic culture, Goldziher believed that it absorbed practices, concepts, and institutions that had been foreign to the Arabian Peninsula and its belligerent, concupiscent, and wine-loving inhabitants.

Goldziher can be seen as the pioneer of critical hadith studies. In the hadith, he saw evidence of contradictory statements and teachings, leading him to ascribe the Islamic oral tradition to opposing schools that had emerged after Muhammed's death, and not—as had been customary—to Muhammad and his companions.

Goldziher also penned groundbreaking works on the Zahirite school of Muslim jurisprudence, Qur'anic exegetical traditions, Islamic sects and sectarianism, pre-Islamic and Islamic culture, Arabic philology, Arab historiography and literature, and Islamic veneration of saints. He was also one of the founding editors of the *Enzyklopädie des Islam* (Leiden, 1913–36), to which he contributed many entries. Theodor Nöldeke, the great German orientalist, praised Goldziher posthumously as "a master of Arab theology and philosophy" with no rival. His reputation has endured to this day.

Goldziher's two most important disciples were Martin Schreiner (1863–1926) and Bernhard (Bernát) Heller (1871–1943), both of whom studied at the Budapest

Rabbinical Seminary and at the University of Budapest. Schreiner, who taught at the Reform rabbinical seminary in Berlin from 1894 to 1902, wrote important studies on Muslim-Jewish polemics, Islamic religious philosophy, Islamic heretics, and the impact of Islamic philosophy on medieval Jewish thought. Heller, who was director of the Jewish high school in Budapest and a professor at the Budapest Rabbinical Seminary, made groundbreaking contributions in the field of comparative folklore. In particular, he traced themes that were common to rabbinic literature, early Christianity, and early Islamic legends. He also examined the popular stories about ʿAntar, the noble Bedouin warrior.

Jewish orientalists as Jewish advocates

In some cases, Jewish orientalists—even those who had converted to Christianity—put their scholarly knowledge (or reputation) at the service of the Jewish community, often at times of rising anti-Jewish sentiment. Munk, for example, accompanied Sir Moses Montefiore, the British Jewish philanthropist, and Adolphe Crémieux, the French Jewish statesman, to Egypt during the Damascus affair (1840) to plea on behalf of the Jews accused of ritual murder. Chwolson, who taught in Saint Petersburg, Russia, published several works defending the Jews against ritual murder accusations from the 1860s onward. Famously, Vámbéry arranged a meeting in 1901 between Abdul Hamid, the Ottoman sultan, and Theodor Herzl, the father of political Zionism, who had hoped to secure the sultan's support for increased Jewish settlement in Ottoman Palestine. Goldziher defended Jews and Judaism within the scholarly community, refuting Ernst Renan's notorious claim that the Semitic mind lacked creativity and was prone to dogmatism. Like Geiger before him, Goldziher highlighted the universalistic nature of Judaism, arguing that it was not only the basis of Christianity and Islam, but also the cornerstone of Western civilization.

---

1. Jacob Lassner, "Abraham Geiger: A Nineteenth-Century Jewish Reformer on the Origins of Islam," in *Jewish Discovery of Islam: Studies in Honor of Bernard Lewis*, ed. Martin Kramer (Syracuse, NY: Syracuse University Press, 1999).

2. John M. Efon, "Orientalism and the Jewish Historical Gaze," in Martin Kramer (ed.), *Jewish Discovery of Islam. Study in Honor of Bernard Lewis* (Syracuse, 1999), 83.

3. Johann Fück, *Die arabischen Studien in Europa bis in den Anfang des 20. Jahrhunderts* (Leipzig, 1955).

4. Holger Preissler, "Heinrich Leberecht Fleischer: Ein Leipziger Orientalist, seine jüdischen Studenten, Promovenden und Kollegen," in *Bausteine einer jüdischen Geschichte der Universität Leipzig*, ed. Stephan Wenderhorst (Leipzig: Leipziger Universitätsverlag, 2006).

5. Moïse Schwab, *Salomon Munk: Sa vie et ses œuvres* (Paris: E. Leroux, 1900).

Present-Day Iran
and the Israeli Orientalists

Many authors writing about postrevolutionary Iran have described it as a country of paradoxes. One of these paradoxes concerns the place granted to Jewish and Israeli orientalists, especially Iranists and specialists in Islamic studies. This place marks a striking divergence from the official anti-Zionist and anti-Israeli (and, more rarely, anti-Semitic) discourse of the authorities.

In the Islamic Republic, at least two encyclopedias, the *Great Islamic Encyclopedia (Da'erat al-ma'aref-e bozorg-e eslami)* and the *Book of Knowledge of the Islamic World (Danesh-name-ye jahan-e eslam)* accord a large place to the Western orientalists and Islamic scholars in general, and to the major Jewish and Israeli scholars in particular. In the field of Iranology, Shaul Shaked's *From Zoroastrian Iran to Islam* received the national prize for the best Iranist work in the Islamic Republic in 2001.[1] Shaked, an Iranist scholar who teaches at the Hebrew University of Jerusalem, was officially asked to write a new preface for his prize-winning book, which has been admirably translated into Persian. The wealth of books is even greater in Islamology. Many of Ignaz Goldziher's writings in the fields of Islamic scholastic theology, the history of doctrine, and canon law have been translated into Persian. Two groups of contemporary scholars can be distinguished. In philosophy and theology, Shlomo Pines and his students hold a privileged place. Annotated translations of many of Pines's articles and of books on Ibn al-Rawandi by Sarah Stroumsa, one of his most notable students, have also appeared. In addition, studies devoted to the Qur'an, the Hadith, historiography, and the sources of law are widely represented in translation by the writings of Menahem Meir Kister, a famous philologist and historian from Hebrew University, and by the works

of his successors. These include a translation of Etan Kohlberg's book on Ibn Tawus and his library,[2] and of Meir Bar-Asher's works on Shi'ite Qur'anic exegesis and on the Nusayris. These translations have often been prepared by Shi'ite religious scholars and are taught in the theological institutions of the holy city of Qom. The book I wrote with Etan Kohlberg, *Revelation and Falsification*,[3] despite its Israeli coauthor and its sensitive subject matter (it is the first edition of the most ancient source concerning the falsification of the Qur'an), earned several laudatory reviews in scholarly journals. It has given rise to interesting intellectual debates. Its translation into Persian, accompanied by several discussions of controversies by theologians, will appear shortly, also in Qom.

In that city—the intellectual and spiritual center of Shi'ism for more than a millennium—and also in Tehran, entire institutions with dozens of researchers are devoted to translating into Persian Western Islamological works or even scholarly works on Judaism, its doctrine, and its history. These include official institutions, such as the University of Tehran, the Dar al-Hadith Institute, and even, in Qom, the Institute for Religion and Beliefs (*mo'assesse-ye adyan va madhaheb*). Kohlberg's book was translated by a Shi'ite theologian for the Grand Library of Ayatollah Mar'ashi'. And in Mashhad, another Shi'ite holy city since the ninth century, the Mausoleum to the Eighth Imam (Astan-e Qods-e Razavi), a major official institution, supervises other translations of Western Islamic scholars.

Finally, in addition to the private publishing houses, a number of scholarly journals have played a decisive role in translating or reviewing works by scholars, including Israelis: journals such as *Ma'arif* and *Nashr-e Danesh* (published by Iran University

Press); *Olum-e hadith*, *Haft asman*, and *Ayene-ye Pajuhesh* (published by the Islamic Propaganda Office in Qom); and *Ketab-e mah-e din* (published by the Ministry of Islamic Guidance). In recent years, many of Professor Kister's articles on the early days of Islam have appeared in Persian. So, too, have articles on the Qur'an by Uri Rubin and on Caliph 'Umar by Avraham Hakim. Both authors currently teach in Tel Aviv. •

Mohammad Ali Amir-Moezzi is director of studies at the École Pratique des Hautes Études (EPHE-Sorbonne) and a specialist in the history of Qur'anic exegesis and in classical Islamic theology. He is the author of Le guide divin dans le shi'isme originel *(Verdier, 1997; new ed., 2007);* La religion discrète: Croyances et pratiques spirituelles dans l'islam shi'ite *(Vrin, 2006); and* Le Coran silencieux et le Coran parlant: Sources scriptuaires de l'islam entre histoire et ferveur *(CNRS Éditions, 2011). He is also the editor of the* Dictionnaire du Coran *(Robert Laffont, 2006).*

---

1. Shaul Shaked, *From Zoroastrian Iran to Islam: Studies in Religious History and Intercultural Contacts* (Aldershot: Variorum, 1995).
2. Etan Kohlberg, *A Medieval Muslim Scholar at Work: Ibn Tawus and His Library* (Leiden: Brill, 1992).
3. Mohammad Ali Amir-Moezzi and Etan Kohlberg, eds., *Revelation and Falsification: The "Kitab al-Qira'at" of Ahmad ibn Muhammad al-Sayyari* (Leiden: Brill, 2009).

Chapter V

Mysticism

Embodied Letter: Sufi and Kabbalistic Hermeneutics
Elliot R. Wolfson

The complex and variegated, and at times conflictual and contentious, relationship of the three Abrahamic faiths, Judaism, Christianity, and Islam, can be profitably understood by the Heideggerian notion of *Zusammengehören*, a term that denotes the belonging-together or the drawing-near of what persists in the difference of being the same.[1] To grasp the subtlety of this point, we must attend to Heidegger's somewhat counterintuitive distinction between "the identical" (*das Gleiche*) and "the same" (*das Selbe*). In "Die Onto-Theo-Logische Verfassung der Metaphysik" (a lecture delivered on February 24, 1957, in Todtnauberg as part of a seminar on Hegel's *Wissenschaft der Logik*), he put it this way: "But the same [*das Selbe*] is not the merely identical [*das Gleiche*]. In the merely identical, the difference disappears. In the same the difference appears, and appears all the more pressingly, the more resolutely thinking is

Elliot R. Wolfson

Elliot R. Wolfson is Abraham Lieberman Professor of Hebrew and Judaic Studies at New York University. His specialties include Jewish mysticism and medieval and modern philosophy. Among his publications is *Language, Eros, Being: Kabbalistic Hermeneutics and Poetic Imagination* (Fordham University Press, 2005), which received the National Jewish Book Award for Excellence in Scholarship in 2006. His most recent book is *A Dream Interpreted within a Dream: Oneiropoiesis and the Prism of Imagination* (Zone Books, 2011), which won the American Academy of Religion Award in the category of "Constructive-Reflective Studies."

concerned with the same matter in the same way."[2] Heidegger sometimes expressed the difference between selfsameness (*Selbigkeit*) and identicalness (*Gleichheit*) by noting that the quality of the belonging-togetherness (*Zusammengehörigkeit*) applies to the former and not to the latter.[3] From Heidegger's perspective, we can say meaningfully that things belong together only if they are not identical; sameness, on this score, is discernible through difference, not in a Hegelian sense of a dialectical resolution of antinomies, which is what Heidegger labels "identicalness," but in a more profound coincidence of opposites according to which one thing is similar to the other by virtue of their dissimilarity.[4] I submit that the intricate relationship of the liturgical communities of Islam and Judaism is best envisioned by a conceptual model, whereby the proximity of one thing to another is determined by the distance that separates what is juxtaposed.

Esotericism and hermeneutics

In this essay, I will limit my analysis to the hermeneutical assumptions of the esoteric currents in Judaism and Islam, referred to, respectively, as Kabbalah and Sufism. In spite of the many discrepancies between these two traditions, and indeed, the wide diversity that characterizes each in its own right, in the domain of hermeneutics there are many interesting parallels. I would go so far as to say that Kabbalists and Sufis share in what Henry Corbin designated the "central postulate of esoterism and of esoteric hermeneutics (*ta'wīl*)," the "conviction that to everything that is apparent, literal, external, exoteric (*ẓāhir*) there corresponds something hidden, spiritual, internal, esoteric (*bāṭin*)."[5] Corbin was addressing the specific phenomenon of Shi'ism, but I do not think it inappropriate to expand the scope of his words to depict the nature of esotericism more generally, especially as it is expressed in the mystical traditions of both Islam and Judaism.[6] At the core of this hermeneutic is the archaic theory of correspondence articulated, perhaps most famously, in the beginning of the *Emerald Tablet*, a series of gnomic utterances attributed to the legendary Hermes Trismegistus:[7] "I speak not fictitious things, but that which is certain and true. What is below is like that which is above, and what is above is like that which is below, to accomplish the miracles of one thing."[8] The ontological belief that the material world is a replica of the spiritual world of ideal archetypes resonates with the hermeneutical claim that the sacred text has an external and an internal meaning, the former related to the visible, physical world and the latter to the invisible, metaphysical realm. The point is enunciated clearly in the following passage from *Sefer ha-Zohar*, the main anthology of Kabbalistic homilies that began to circulate in the last decades of the thirteenth century but that was not redacted into a discernible textual form until the sixteenth century: "All that the blessed holy One made in the earth was in the mystery of wisdom, and everything was to manifest the supernal wisdom to human beings, so that they may learn from that action the mysteries of wisdom. And all of them are appropriate, and all of the actions are the ways of the Torah, for the ways of the Torah are the ways of the blessed holy One, and there is not even a minuscule word that does not contain several ways, paths, and mysteries of the supernal wisdom."

To view corporeal matters as a sign of that which exceeds the corporeal is one of two dominant attitudes to the physical realm that one can discern in the writings of Kabbalists in the late Middle Ages. In consonance with contemporaneous patterns of Christian and Islamic piety, but especially the former, for the Kabbalists, the body was a site of tension, the locus of sensual and erotic pleasure, on one hand, and the earthly pattern of God's image, the representation of what lies beyond representation, the mirror that renders visible the invisible, on the other. It should come as no surprise, then, that in spite of the negative portrayal of the body and repeated demands of preachers and homilists to escape from the clasp of carnality, in great measure due to the lingering impact of Platonic psychology and metaphysics on the spiritual formation of medieval spirituality, the flesh continued to serve as the *prima materia* out of which ritual gestures, devotional symbols, and theological doctrines were fashioned. However, there is a critical difference that distinguishes Christianity from the various forms of mystical devotion that evolved historically in Judaism and Islam.

In the domain of the theological, which cannot be surgically extracted from other facets of medieval Christian societies, the dual role of body as "stigma of the fall" and "instrument of redemption" was mediated by the Eucharist, the central priestly rite that celebrated the mystery of transubstantiation instantiated in the miraculous consecration of bread and wine into body and blood, the sacrament believed to occasion liturgically the presence of Christ, a prolepsis of the Second Coming, fostering thereby the "paradoxical union of the body with the evanescence of the sacred."[9] As one might expect, Jews and Muslims provided alternative narratives to account for the commingling of the corporeal and transcendent, the visible and the invisible, the literal and the symbolic. Focusing on sources composed within rabbinic circles in places as diverse as Palestine, Provence, Catalonia, Castile, the Rhineland, Italy, northern France, and England, just to name some of the geographic spots wherein Jewish occultism can be detected in the twelfth and thirteenth centuries, we can identify a hermeneutic principle that explains the theomorphic representation of the human as divine and the anthropomorphic representation of the divine as human, the transfiguration of flesh into word, which I will pose alongside of—not in binary opposition to—the more readily known Christological incarnation

> " *Jews and Muslims provided alternative narratives to account for the commingling of the corporeal and transcendent, the visible and the invisible, the literal and the symbolic.* "

of the word into flesh.[10] To be sure, I think it artificial to distinguish these positions too sharply, for the hypothetical tenability of the word becoming flesh rests on the assumption that flesh is, in some sense, word, but flesh can be entertained as word only if and when word, in some sense, becomes flesh. As it happens, in the history of medieval Latin Christendom, there is evidence of scribal inscriptions placed on the hearts of male and female saints—a hyperliteral reading of the figurative "book of the heart"—a gesture that effected the transformation of the written word into flesh and, conversely, the transformation of flesh into the written word.[11] Notwithstanding the compelling logic of this reversal, and the empirical evidence to substantiate it, the distinction should still be upheld in an effort to account for the difference in the narratological framework of the two traditions, a difference that ensues from, though at the same time giving way to, an underlying sameness, sameness in the Heideggerian sense of belonging-together, as I noted in the opening paragraph. To translate my thinking into contemporary academic discourse: pitched in the heartland of Christian faith, one encounters the logocentric belief in the incarnation of the word in the flesh of the person Jesus, whereas in the textual panorama of medieval Kabbalah and Sufism, the site of the incarnational insight is the onto-graphic inscripting of flesh into word and the consequent conversion of the carnal body into the ethereal, luminous body—the body composed of the supernal light of the Primordial Adam in the Jewish tradition or of Muhammad in the Islamic tradition—finally transposed into the literal body, the body that is the letter, hyperliterally, the name that is, respectively, the Torah or the Qur'an.[12] The dominant discursive narrative of Christians, on the one hand, and that of the Jews and Muslims, on the other, both presume a correlation of body and book, but in an inverse manner: for the former, the literal body is embodied in the book

> *The landscape of medieval Kabbalistic and Sufic esotericism share the following assumption: the nature of material beings is constituted by the letters that make up their names.*

of the body; for the latter, the literal body is embodied in the body of the book.[13] Turning specifically to the landscape of medieval Kabbalistic and Sufic esotericism, we can speak of the following shared assumption: the nature of material beings is constituted by the letters that make up their names; Hebrew for the Jews and Arabic for the Muslims was viewed as the primal language, the *ursprache*, the single Adamic language that is purportedly the source to which all the other languages may be traced. Nothing, to the best of my knowledge, is comparable in medieval Western or Eastern Christianity. The legacy of the Johannine prologue regarding the word that was made flesh did not result in the logos being restricted to any one linguistic matrix, even if the original text was written in Greek.

Ontology and the Hebrew alphabet

Let me begin with the Kabbalistic perspective: the ontic character of the natural or essential language is not to be sought in its semantic morphemes, the particular cultural configurations of Hebrew, but in the phonemic and graphemic potentiality contained in this language, the matrix whence the sentient forms envisaged within the visual fields of our reality are constituted.[14] Jacob ben Sheshet, the thirteenth-century Catalan Kabbalist, offers a succinct formulation of this basic tenet of medieval Jewish esotericism: "The matter of the letters comprises the forms of all created beings, and you will not find a form that does not have an image in the letters or in the combination of two, three, or more of them. This is a principle alluded to in the order of the alphabet, and the matters are ancient, deep waters that have no limit."[15] Consider as well the following *Zoharic* passage elucidating the assertion that Israel is distinguished among the Gentile nations (*goyim*) for only they can lay claim to possessing language that preserves a veritable written and oral form (*ketav we-lashon*). "Through each letter they can envision the image [*diyoqna*)] and form [*ṣiyyura*] as is appropriate. In the idolatrous nations, however, this mystery is not considered for they do not have a script [*ketav*] or speech [*lashon*]."[16] Denying the two basic linguistic forms to other idolatrous nations—a cipher for Christendom—is a significant gesture of marginalization. Obviously, the anonymous Kabbalist responsible for this text does not mean to say that non-Jews are so illiterate that they cannot speak or write. The point is not literacy but ontological accessibility. To deny an ethnic group oral and written language is to deny it access to the world in its metaphysical sense since being and language are intertwined. Only the Jews, strictly speaking, are ethnoculturally endowed with the code through which the mysteries of being can be deciphered.

A close parallel to Jacob ben Sheshet's passage is found in the following remark of Abraham Abulafia, the thirteenth-century exponent of the ecstatic or prophetic Kabbalah, which has been set in sharp contrast to the trend of theosophic Kabbalah. Commenting on the statement in *Sefer Yesirah*, a treatise that first became influential in the ninth and tenth centuries, though some maintain that parts of it are much older in provenance,[17] that by means of the letters the Creator "forms the soul of every creature and of the soul of everything that will be formed,"[18] Abulafia writes: "Indeed, each and every body is a letter [*ot*] … and every letter is a sign [*ot*], signal [*siman*], and verification [*mofet*] to instruct about the divine overflow [*shefa ha-shem*] that causes the word [*ha-dibbur*] to emanate through its mediation. Thus, all of the world, all the years, and all the souls are replete with letters."[19] The influx that bestows vitality upon all beings of the world—classified by Abulafia in terms of the threefold division expounded in *Sefer Yesirah*, *olam*, *shanah*, and *nefesh*, literally "world," "year," and "soul," but denoting more broadly the temporal, spatial, and human planes of existence, each of which is constituted by the Hebrew letters—is here identified as the word (*dibbur*). For Abulafia, the older cosmological speculation is reinscripted within the standard medieval worldview, yielding the belief that the intellectual efflux, which informs the cosmos, is made up of the twenty-two Hebrew letters, and these collectively are the word of God, which is also identified as the tetragrammaton, and this, in turn, with the Torah in its mystical valence.[20] Viewing the body as a letter, and the letter as a sign that points to the intellectual overflow permeating reality, provides a theoretical ground to undergird an alternate conception of the flesh, or what may be called *linguistic embodiment*, a transposed materiality that is rooted in the belief that the body, at its most elemental, is constituted by semiotic inscrip-tion.[21] As Abulafia put it in *Hayyei ha-Olam ha-Ba*, "The letters are the force of the root of all wisdom and knowledge without doubt, and they themselves are the matter

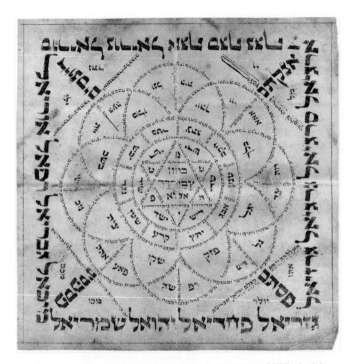

Graphic composition of amuletic type mixing divine names of biblical origin, divine names of Kabbalistic origin (in which the divine name is comprised of forty-two letters), and alphabetic combinations based on verses, all framed by the names of angels; late nineteenth century. Paris, Museum of European and Mediterranean Civilizations.

of prophecy [*homer ha-nevu'ah*], and they appear in the mirror of prophecy as if they were dense bodies that speak to a man mouth to mouth in accord with the abundance of the rational form that is contemplated in the heart that converses with them, and they appear as if they are pure, living angels that move them."[22] In *Sefer ha-Hesheq*, a relatively short treatise that proffers a Kabbalistic exposition of the Maimonidean ideal of *'ishq*, we are told that the mind (*maḥashavah*) of the adept at the peak of the ecstatic conjunction to the object of his yearning "imagines an image of the letters [*ṣiyyur ha-otiyyot*] that are imagined, contemplated, and thought, rational thoughts replete with letters, which are the true forms, imagined in the image and likeness of the ministering angels, for each letter is a vision from the prophetic visions, and each of them is pure splendor."[23]

We can elicit from the Kabbalistic sources—and with respect to this matter I do not detect a fundamental difference between the theosophic and the prophetic Kabbalah—a cosmic semiotics predicated on the confluence of the verbal and the visual: it is not only that the letters are the acoustic instruments of divine creativity, but it is through them that the image and form of all that exists is apprehended ocularly. The widely held belief on the part of Kabbalists that the name (*shem*) of an entity is its essence (*guf*)—when cast in the terminology of Western epistemology, the realist as opposed to the nominalist orientation—presupposes an intrinsic connection between language and being, which rests, in turn, on the assumed correlation of letter and matter, a correlation likely springing from the mythopoeic sensibility expressed in detail in the second part of *Sefer Yesirah*.

Saying the unsayable

What exists in the world, examined subphenomenally, are the manifold permutations of the twenty-two Hebrew letters, themselves enfolded in the four-letter name

YHWH, the name through the nameless—demarcated by the middle of the thirteenth century as Ein Sof—declaimed. On this score, there is no tension in the Kabbalistic teaching between the views that ultimate reality is ineffable and that reality is constituted by language, or specifically Hebrew. The apophatic tendency to submerge all forms of sentient imaging in the One beyond all form cannot be completely severed from the kataphatic insistence on the possibility of apprehending the forms by which the divine can be known and experienced. The juxtaposition of the kataphatic and apophatic in the history of Kabbalistic speculation has fostered the awareness on the part of the ones initiated in the secret gnosis that the mystical utterance is an unsaying, which is not the same as the silence of not-speaking, a speaking of the unspoken, a knowing of the unknown, a seeing of the unseen.[24] Language, accordingly, serves as the index of its own inability to be indexed, the computation of indeterminacy. If truth is truly beyond language, then silence alone is appropriate to truth, but this silence, as I have already said, is realized not in not-speaking but in unsaying, which is a saying nonetheless. If not-speaking were the only way to articulate truth, then nothing would be spoken, but if nothing would be spoken, then nothing would be unspoken. It is not only that every act of unsaying presupposes a previous saying or that any saying demands a corrective unsaying, but, more paradoxically, *every saying is an unsaying*, for what is said can never be what is spoken insofar as what is spoken can never be what is said. To express the point more prosaically, images of negation are not the same as the negation of images, for if the latter were faithfully heeded, the former would truly not be, as there would be nothing of which to (un)speak and hence there would be no data for either study, critical or devotional. Mystical claims of ineffability—to utter unutterable truths—utilize images that are negative but no less imagistic than the affirmative images they negate.[25]

Signs of Allah

A precise analogue to the perspective I have outlined is found in Islamic mysticism; indeed, with respect to this matter, the notional proximity between Islam and Judaism is far more conspicuous than between either of them and Christianity. As with so much of Islamic occultism, or, one might say, Islamic spiritualism more generally, the starting point is an expression in the Qur'an in a section that delineates various signs (*āyāt*) of the divine in the world, which serve as part of the liturgical glorification of Allah in evening and morning (30:17–27).[26] The signs consist of the creation of man from dust and the creation of his spouse, the helpmate, with whom man can settle down and live harmoniously (20–22), the creation of the heavens and earth, and the diversity of ethnic and racial identities (22), the creation of patterns of human behavior and natural phenomena (23–24), and, finally, the fact that all things in the heavens and earth arise by the command, or will, of Allah

(25). Everything that is in the cosmos, therefore, may be viewed as a sign marking the way to the One that is both within and outside the cosmos. These signs, we learn from another sura, should not be worshipped, for prayer is to be directed exclusively to Allah, the all-hearing and all-knowing (41:37–38). At the end of the sura, after a sustained chastisement of the "unbelievers," "Allah's enemies" (26–28), which, unquestionably, refers in this context to the Jews who rejected the claims of the prophet and the authority of the Qur'an, the new book of revelation, there appears the following remark, "We shall show them our signs in the distant regions and in their own souls, until it becomes clear to them that it is the Truth" (53). The Jews will be shown the signs in the "horizons," that is, the created universe, and in "human souls," until they finally discern the truth. The word "sign," *āya*, denotes the presence of the deity concealed in the manifestations of natural and psychological phenomena, *signa naturalia* and *signa data*, in Augustinian terms.[27] When read esoterically, the significance of the sign is that it points beyond itself to the reality for which there is no sign; the plurality of signs reveal the transcendent one by veiling it in the multiplicity of forms by which it is revealed. In a manner similar to the Kabbalistic approach to the Torah, for the Sufi, each letter of the Qur'an is a sign—at once aurally and visually manifest—that comprises an infinity of meaning, inasmuch as the scriptural text is the incarnation of the divine form; hermeneutically, this infinity is manifest in the potentially endless explications of the text elicited by countless readers, links in the cumulative chain of interpreters that stretches across the divide of time. Here it would be opportune to recall the contemporary notion of "infinite semiosis," as expressed in Robert Corrington's summation of Umberto Eco: "All semiosis is prospectively infinite, because any given sign will have its own plentitude of dimensions and its own movement outward into uncountable radii of involvement."[28] From the standpoint of medieval Sufis and Kabbalists, the innumerable transmutations of meaning stem from the fact that each

Calligraphic names of Muhammad and of 'Ali, Mohammad Fat'hiyab, Iran, early nineteenth century, National Museum of Natural History, Paris.

sign/letter is a component of the textual corpus that constitutes the name of the nameless, the veil that renders the invisible visible, and the visible invisible.

Moreover, the occult wisdom in both traditions proffered a view of the cosmos in similar terms: Everything is a sign, a discrete indivisible, that guides one to the in/significant beyond the universe, devoid of all forms and images, the oneness of being (*waḥdat al-wujūd*) present in all things by virtue of being absent from all things. The world, accordingly, may be viewed as the book in which one discerns (de)scripted forms that lead from the visible to the invisible or, better, from the visible invisibility to invisible visibility, from faces manifestly hidden to faces hiddenly manifest.[29]

The phenomenon of the sacred text

The full implication of the Islamic notion of nature as the book in which the divine will is exposed, and the paradoxes that pertain to the presumption that the natural and psychological phenomena are signs by which one discerns the unseen, are drawn by the esoteric interpreters of the Qurʾan, the inscribed text of revelation, the "rolled-out parchment," whose words are considered to be signs of divine intention, linked especially to the eschatological day of judgment, comparable to entities in nature, such as the mountain and the sea (Q 512:1–8). The esoteric reading elevates the book itself to a supreme position, embellishing the tradition that assigned the Qurʾanic expression *umm al-kitāb*, literally, "mother of the book" (Q 3:7, 13:39, 43:4), to the Qurʾan itself, *al-lawḥ al-maḥfūz*, the "well-preserved tablet" (Q 85:21–22), the *Urschrift*, fore/script, that comprises the forms of all that exists. Read esoterically, the Arabic letters—the bones, tissue, and sinews of the Qurʾanic body—are signs that point to the unseen and thereby reveal the light by concealing it. The attitude of Sufis articulated by Annemarie Schimmel presents a perfect analogue to the perspective affirmed by Kabbalists with respect to Hebrew: "Learning the Arabic letters is incumbent upon everybody who embraces Islam, for they are the vessels of revelation; the divine names and attributes can be expressed only by means of these letters—and yet, the letters constitute something different from God; they are a veil of otherness that the mystic must penetrate."[30] The metaphor of the veil is instructive, as the function of the veil is to disclose but at the same time to hide; indeed it discloses by hiding and hides by disclosing. In a similar vein, the letters of the matrix text—Torah for Kabbalist, Qurʾan for Sufi—reveal and conceal the divine essence, the *face* beyond all veils, the pre/face devoid of form, the pre/text devoid of letter. Just as Kabbalists were wont to speak of the Torah as the divine body (*guf elohi*), or as identical with the name YHWH, so a tradition reported in the name of the Prophet portrays the Qurʾan as proceeding from and returning to Allah. Kabbalist and Sufi would agree that if one remains bound to the letters of the scriptural text, then one is fettered by an idolatry of the book, mistaking the image for the imageless, the figurative for the prefigurative, but both would also insist that the way beyond the letters (scripted and/or voiced) is by way of the letters, visual-auditory signs, semiotic ciphers at once visible and audible—seen as heard, heard as seen—signs that communicate the incommunicable, not through an equational model of symbolic logic, but through an implicational model of poetic allusion. The affinity to the Kabbalistic orientation becomes even more pronounced when we consider the embellishment of these motifs in the theosophic gnosis of the Spanish Sufi Muhyiddin Ibn

> *Kabbalist and Sufi would agree that if one remains bound to the letters of the scriptural text, then one is fettered by an idolatry of the book, mistaking the image for the imageless.*

al-ʿArabi. Just as the Qurʾan is the book that manifests the invisible through verbal images, so the cosmos is a book that unveils the divine presence through veils of phenomenal existence. In Ibn ʿArabi's own words, "God dictates to the hearts through inspiration everything that the cosmos inscribes in *wujūd*, for the cosmos is a divine book inscribed."[31] Two Qurʾanic motifs are combined here, the identification of cosmic phenomena as signs pointing to the unicity of all being and the idea of the heavenly book, the primordial scripture, inscribed by the divine pen, *qalam* (Q 68:1). In another passage, the hypostatic dimension is foregrounded as Ibn ʿArabi offers the Muslim corrective to the Christological Trinity: "The Christians supposed that the Father was the Spirit (*al-Rúh*), the Mother Mary, and the Son Jesus; then they said 'God is the Third of Three,' not knowing that 'the Father' signifies the name Allah, and that 'the Mother' signifies the *Ummu 'l-Kitáb*, i.e., the ground of the Essence, and that 'the Son' signifies the Book, which is Absolute Being because it is a derivative and product of the aforesaid ground."[32] The common thread that ties together the triad of potencies is the belief in the ontological reality of the Arabic letters; the first manifestation, envisioned as the father, is the most sacred of names, Allah, the second manifestation, envisioned as the mother, corresponds to *umm al-kitāb*, the primordial text or the ground of the Essence, and, finally, the third manifestation, envisioned as the son, is the book, the absolute being that derives from the ground. There is much more to say about Ibn ʿArabi and the different layers of the Islamic esoteric tradition, but what is most critical for our purposes is to underscore the hypostatic personification of the Qurʾanic text as the tablet that contains all cosmic forms that serve as the veils through which God is manifest and the concomitant figural representation of the cosmos as the book that comprises all semiotic signs that point to the truth that cannot be signified.

▶ See article by Michael Barry, pp. 869–890.

Beyond the veil

As is well known, basic to Sufism is the belief that the objective for one who walks the path is to rend the veil, to behold truth in its naked form. However, and this is a point that I do not think is often appreciated by scholars, inasmuch as rending the veil reveals that which has no image, the unknowable essence that cannot be essentialized, the inaccessible presence that cannot be represented, it must be said that the veil conceals the face it reveals by revealing the face it conceals. Language is decidedly inadequate to mark the middle ground wherein concealing and revealing are identical in virtue of being different and different in virtue of being identical. Epistemologically, the matter may be expressed in the following terms utilized by Ibn ʿArabi: the veil conveys both the incomparability (*tanzīh*) of the face and the image seen through the veil, for the image that is seen is an image and not the face, and the similarity (*tashbīh*) of the face and the image, for in the absence of an image the face could not be perceived.[33] In *Fusus al-hikam*, Ibn ʿArabi notes that to become an imam and a master of spiritual sciences, one must maintain both the incomparability and similarity of the ultimate reality in relation to all other existents in the chain of being, for to insist exclusively on either transcendence or immanence is to restrict that reality inappropriately.[34] The mandate to lift the veils, therefore, does not result in discarding all possible veils; indeed, there can be no "final" veil to lift, as there must always be another veil through which the nonmanifest will be made manifest. In this respect, the Sufi sensibility remained faithful to the Qurʾanic declaration that it is not fitting for God to speak to a human "except by inspiration, from behind a veil, or by the sending of a messenger" (42:51); that is, by way of an intermediary that renders the unseen (*ghayb*) visible. What is unveiled in the unveiling, therefore, is not the face behind the veil, but the veil before the face; that is, unveiling is the metaphorical depiction of removing the shells of ignorance that blind one from seeing the truth of the veil in the veil of truth: God and world are identical in their difference.[35] The transcendence of God, the unity of the indiscriminate one (*ahadiyyat al-ahad*), renders all theological discourse at best analogical, since there is no way to speak directly about that which transcends all being, yet the divine is immanent in all things—indeed, mystically conceived, there is nothing but the single true reality that is all things, the unity of multiplicity (*ahadiyyat al-kathra*).[36]

The self-manifestation of God, therefore, must be through the multitude of veils that make up the cosmos. The paradoxical nature of the veil to disclose what is occluded by way of occluding what is disclosed is evident in the tradition concerning the response of the archangel Gabriel to Mohammed's query whether he had ever seen the Lord, "As it is, between me and Him there are seventy veils of light. If I ever came close to the one nearest to me I would get burnt."[37] If the highest of angels cannot approach the lowest of the veils separating him from the divine, how much more so must it apply to beings of the natural world? All that we consider real is veritably a veil; truth comes forth as unveiling the unveiling of the veil so that the unveiled is seen in the veil of the unveiled; disposing the veil would result, by contrast, in veiling the veil and the consequent effacing of the face.

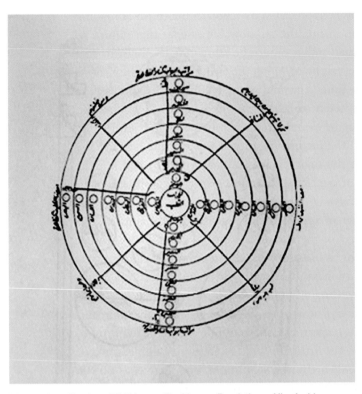

Diagram from *Futuhat al Makkiyya* or *The Meccan Revelations* of Ibn Arabi.

Ibn ʿArabi elaborated the paradoxical mystery of the veil and its unveiling in a somewhat more technical philosophic tone commensurate with his speculative gnosis. "There is nothing in existence but veils hung down. Acts of perception attach themselves only to veils, which leave traces in the owner of the eye that perceives them."[38] Ephemeral contingencies are but veils hiding the eternal being, the necessary of existence, but it is through the concealment of these veils that the invisible is rendered visible. "Thus the Real becomes manifest by being veiled, so He is the Manifest, the Veiled. He is the Nonmanifest because of the veil, not because of you, and He is the Manifest because of you and the veil."[39]

In another passage, Ibn ʿArabi expresses the matter as a commentary on the aforementioned hadith that God possesses seventy veils of light and darkness: "The dark and luminous veils through which the Real is veiled from the cosmos are only the light and the darkness by which the possible thing becomes qualified in its reality because it is a middle. . . . Were the veils to be lifted from the possible thing, possibility would be lifted, and the Necessary and the impossible would be lifted through the lifting of possibility. So the veils will remain forever hung down and nothing else is possible. . . . The veils will not be lifted when there is vision of God. Hence vision is through the veil, and inescapably so."[40]

The veil thus signifies the hermeneutic of secrecy basic to the esoteric gnosis of Sufism, envisioning the hidden secret revealed in the concealment of its revelation and concealed in the revelation of its concealment. Accordingly, the task is to discard the veils to reveal the truth, but if the veils were all discarded, there truly would be truth to see. This is the import of the statement that the "veils will not be lifted when there is vision of God." If the unseen, the hidden reality that is the face, is to be seen, the vision manifestly must be "through the veil."[41] The Sufi ideal of seeing without a veil is coming to see that there is nothing ultimately to see but the veil that there can be a seeing without any veil. This is an exact parallel, both philologically and conceptually, to the *Zoharic* passage in which it is emphasized that God places the secret, which is the light, in the words of the Torah, and the sage, who is full of eyes, sees it "through the garment" (*mi-go levusha*)[42]—the secret is beheld through the garment, and not by removing it. The polysemous and dissimulating nature of truth is such that when one removes the garment one does not uncover truth disrobed but yet another garment through which the invisible is arrayed.

Anthropomorphism reversed

We may conclude, therefore, that for Kabbalist and Sufi alike, the letter is the body, the verbal image by which the imageless is disclosed in the concealment of its disclosure. Such a perspective reverses the allegorical approach to scriptural anthropomorphisms promoted by medieval philosophic exegetes in the two traditions; that is, instead of explaining anthropomorphic characterizations of God as a figurative way to accommodate human understanding, the attribution of corporeal images to an incorporeal God indicates that the real body, the body in its most abstract tangibility, is the letter, a premise that I have called the principle of poetic incarnation. When examined from the esoteric perspective, anthropomorphism indicates that human and divine corporeality are entwined in a mesh of double imaging through the mirror of the text, which renders the divine body human and the human body divine. Phenomenologically speaking, the life-world of Kabbalists and Sufis revolves about the axis of the embodied text of textual embodiment.

Beyond providing a radically different hermeneutical key to interpret scripture, the understanding of textual embodiment had practical implications in the mystical approach to ritual. A hallmark of Kabbalism and Sufism was to view sacramental behavior as an instrument through which the physical body is conjoined to and transformed in light of the imaginal body of God manifest in the inscribed body of the text. The experience of being assimilated into the light as a consequence of fulfilling the ritual is predicated on the assumption that the action below stimulates the light

> *"The life-world of Kabbalists and Sufis revolves about the axis of the embodied text of textual embodiment."*

above; since the commandments are part of the scriptural text, and the latter is identical with or comes from God, ritualized gestures serve as the means by which the soul separates from the body and ascends to the light, augmenting the overflow of the divine efflux. In this matter, too, the mystical current in medieval Islam and Judaism is to be distinguished from Christianity: ritual performance is the means by which the corporeal body is textualized and the textual body corporealized. Compliance with ceremonial practice facilitates the transformation of the carnal body into the textual body, a state of psychosomatic equilibrium wherein the body becomes the perfect vehicle to execute the will of the soul, and the soul the perfect guide in directing the will of the body. The soul thus mirrors the embodiment of God's glory in the Torah or in the Qur'an by donning the name that is envisioned in the form of an *anthropos*. As the incorporeal assumes the bodily contours of the scriptural text, the body of one who observes the law is transformed into a ritualized body composed of the very same letters. Just as the way beyond language is through language, so the way beyond body is through body. This holds a key to understanding the role of asceticism in the formation of the mystical pietism affirmed in Kabbalistic and Sufi teaching: separation from sensual matters is not seen as a way to obliterate the body—commitment to *shari'a* or to *halakha* respectively precluded such an unmitigated renunciation of the natural world, even under the weight of a Neoplatonized Aristotelian metaphysics that looked derisively at the material body—but as a means for the metamorphosis of the mortal body into an angelic or astral body, a body whose limbs are constituted by the letters of the name, the anthropomorphic configuration of the scriptural corpus. Adorned in the apparel of this luminous body, the soul is conjoined to and incorporated within the divine name.

---

1. Martin Heidegger, *Identity and Difference*, trans. and intro. Joan Stambaugh (New York: Harper & Row, 1969), 29; German text, 92.

2. Ibid., 45; German text, 111.

3. Martin Heidegger, *Country Path Conversations*, trans. Bret W. Davis (Bloomington: Indiana University Press, 2010), 25; German text, Martin Heidegger, *Feldweg-Gespräche* (*GA*, 77) (Frankfurt am Main: Vittorio Klostermann, 1995), 39.

4. Heidegger, *Identity and Difference*, 29; German text, 92.

5. Henry Corbin, *Creative Imagination in the Sufism of Ibn 'Arabi*, trans. Ralph Manheim (Princeton, NJ: Princeton University Press, 1969), 78.

6. See Paul B. Fenton, "Henry Corbin et la mystique juive," in *Henry Corbin: Philosophies et sagesses des religions du livre; Actes du Colloque "Henry Corbin," Sorbonne, les 6-8 Novembre 2003*, ed. Mohammad Ali Amir-Moezzi, Christian Jambet, and Pierre Lory (Turnhout: Brepols Publishers, 2005), 153.

7. Titus Burckhardt, *Alchemy: Science of the Cosmos, Science of the Soul*, trans. William Stoddart (London: Stuart & Watkins, 1967), 196–97; Allison Coudert, *Alchemy: The Philosopher's Stone* (London: Wildwood House, 1980), 27–28; Gareth Roberts, *The Mirror of Alchemy: Alchemical Idea and Images in Manuscripts and Books from Antiquity to the Seventeenth Century* (Toronto: University of Toronto Press, 1994), 68–70.

8. John Read, *Prelude to Chemistry: An Outline of Alchemy, Its Literature and Relationships* (Cambridge, MA: MIT Press, 1966), 54.

9. Françoise Jaouën and Benjamin Semple, "Editors' Preface: The Body into Text," *Yale French Studies* 86 (1994): 1–4. On the Eucharist, the glorified flesh of Christ, and the indwelling of the divine presence in the saintly body, see Henri De Lubac, *Corpus Mysticum, L'Eucharistie et l'église au moyen age*, 2nd rev. ed. (Paris: Aubier, 1949); Ernst H. Kantorowicz, *The King's Two Bodies: A Study in Medieval Political Theology* (Princeton, NJ: Princeton University Press, 1957), 193–272; Rowan Williams, "Troubled Breasts: The Holy Body in Hagiography," in *Portraits of Spiritual Authority: Religious Power in Early Christianity, Byzantium and the Christian Orient*, ed. Jan Willem Drijvers and John W. Watt (Leiden: Brill, 1999), 63–78, esp. 67–72.

10. For earlier roots to the Kabbalistic conception, see Elliot R. Wolfson, "Judaism and Incarnation: The Imaginal Body of God," in *Christianity in Jewish Terms*, ed. Tikva Frymer-Kensky, David Novak, Peter Ochs, David Fox Sandmel, and Michael A. Signer (Boulder, CO: Westview Press, 2000), 239–54.

11. Eric Jager, *The Book of the Heart* (Chicago: University of Chicago Press, 2000).

12. The identification of the name and the Torah has been explored by a number of scholars of whom I will here mention a few representative examples. See Gershom Scholem, "Der Sinn der Tora in der jüdischen Mystik," in *Zur*

Kabbala und ihrer Symbolik (Zürich: Rhein-Verlag, 1960), 55–64 (French translation in *Le Nom et les symboles de Dieu*, 105–11); Moshe Idel, "The Concept of Torah in Hekhalot Literature and Its Metamorphosis in Kabbalah," *Jerusalem Studies in Jewish Thought* 1 (1981): 23–84, esp. 49–58 (Hebrew); Isaiah Tishby, *The Wisdom of the Zohar*, trans. David Goldstein (Oxford: Oxford University Press, 1989), 1079–82.

13. For a similar account in a different cultural context, see John Lagerwey, "Écriture et corps divin en Chine," in *Corps des dieux*, ed. Charles Malamoud and Jean-Pierre Vernant (Paris: Éditions Gallimard, 1986), 383–98. It is of interest to note that the author begins his essay with an epigram from Jeremiah 7:23–24.

14. Still instructive on this topic is the much-commented-upon essay by Gershom Scholem, "Der Name Gottes und die Sprachtheorie der Kabbala," *Eranos Jahrbuch* 39 (1970): 243–99, reprinted in Gershom Scholem, *Judaica 3: Studien zur jüdischen Mystik* (Frankfurt am Main: Surhkamp Verlag, 1973), 7–70. The French version of this essay appears in Gershom Scholem, *Le Nom et les symboles de Dieu dans la mystique juive*, trans. Maurice R. Hayoun and Georges Vajda (Paris: Cerf, 2010), 55–99.

15. Jacob ben Sheshet, *Sefer Meshiv Devarim Nekhohim*, ed. Georges Vajda, intro. Georges Vajda and Efraim Gottlieb (Jerusalem: Israel Academy of Sciences and Humanities, 1968), 154, and *Sefer Ha-Emunah we-ha-Bittahon*, in *Kitvei Ramban*, ed. Hayyim D. Chavel (Jerusalem: Mosad ha-Rav Kook, 1964), 2:392–93: "There is no letter in the *alef-beit* that does not allude to the holy One, blessed be he."

16. *Zohar* 3:204a.

17. For a scholarly review on the origin and dating of this composition, see Klaus Herrmann, *Sefer Jezira: Buch der Schöpfung* (Frankfurt am Main: Verlag der Weltreligionen, 2008), 184–204.

18. *Sefer Yesirah* (Jerusalem, 1990), 2:2. According to the textual reconstruction of A. Peter Hayman, *Sefer Yesirah: Edition, Translation and Text-Critical Commentary* (Tübingen: Mohr Siebeck, 2004), 53, 100–102 (§19), these words are a later interpolation.

19. Abraham Abulafia, *Osar Eden Ganuz* (Jerusalem, 2000), 66. The role of language in Abulafia's Kabbalah has been noted by various scholars and especially by Idel, who has discussed this theme in many studies. For a representative list of the relevant sources, see Moshe Idel, *Language, Torah, and Hermeneutics in Abraham Abulafia* (Albany: State University of New York Press, 1989), 12–14, 16–27, 143–45n55, 146n71; Elliot R. Wolfson, *Abraham Abulafia— Kabbalist and Prophet: Hermeneutics, Theosophy, and Theurgy* (Los Angeles: Cherub Press, 2000), 58–59, 62–64.

20. Idel, *Language, Torah, and Hermeneutics*, 29–38, 46–55, 79–81, 101–9, 163n33, 171n88, 193–94n78; and *Absorbing Perfections: Kabbalah and Interpretation* (New Haven, CT: Yale University Press, 2002), 319–51.

21. For a more elaborate analysis of this theme, see Elliot R. Wolfson, "Textual Flesh, Incarnation, and the Imaginal Body: Abraham Abulafia's Polemic with Christianity," in *Studies in Medieval Jewish Intellectual and Social History: Festschrift in Honor of Robert Chazan*, ed. D. Engel and L. H. Schiffman (Leiden: Brill, 2012), 189–226.

22. Abraham Abulafia, *Hayyei ha-Olam ha-Ba* (Jerusalem, 1999), 159.

23. Abraham Abulafia, *Sefer ha-Hesheq* (Jerusalem, 2002), 10.

24. I am here reiterating the argument in Elliot R. Wolfson, *Language, Eros, Being: Kabbalistic Hermeneutics and Poetic Imagination* (New York: Fordham University Press, 2005), 215.

25. See Denys Turner, *The Darkness of God: Negativity in Christian Mysticism* (Cambridge: Cambridge University Press, 1995), 35; Steven T. Katz, "Mystical Speech and Mystical Meaning," in *Mysticism and Language*, ed. Steven T. Katz (New York: Oxford University Press, 1992), 3–41; and "Utterance and Ineffability in Jewish Neoplatonism," in *Neoplatonism and Jewish Thought*, ed. Lenn E. Goodman (Albany: State University of New York Press, 1992), 279–98; Elliot R. Wolfson, "Negative Theology and Positive Assertion in the Early Kabbalah," *Da'at* 32–33 (1994): v–xxii.

26. *Le Coran, L'Appel*, trans. and ed. André Chouraqui (Paris: Robert Laffont, 1990).

27. Giovanni Manetti, *Theories of the Sign on Classical Antiquity*, trans. Christine Richardson (Bloomington: Indiana University Press, 1993), 166–67.

28. Robert S. Corrington, *Ecstatic Naturalism: Signs of the World* (Bloomington: Indiana University Press, 1994), 67.

29. Annemarie Schimmel, *Deciphering the Signs of God: A Phenomenological Approach to Islam* (Albany: State University of New York Press, 1994), xii–xiii. On the nexus of body and writing in Islamic sources, see also Malek Chebel, *Le Corps en Islam* (Paris: Presses Universitaires de France, 1984), 175–90.

30. Annemarie Schimmel, *Mystical Dimensions in Islam* (Chapel Hill: University of North Carolina Press, 1975), 411. For the introduction of gender, and specifically the feminine character, to depict the nature of the sign and the spirit, see *Approaching the Qur'an: The Early Revelations*, intro. and trans. Michael Sells (Ashland, OR: White Cloud Press, 1999), 201–4.

31. Cited in Chittick, *The Self-Disclosure of God: Principles of Ibn al-'Arabi's Cosmology* (Albany: State University of New York Press, 1998), 5.

32. Cited in Reynold A. Nicholson, *Studies in Islamic Mysticism* (Cambridge: Cambridge University Press, 1921), 140n1.

33. Chittick, *Self-Disclosure*, xxi–xxii; *The Sufi Path of Knowledge: Ibn al-Arabi's Metaphysics of Imagination* (Albany: State University of New York Press, 1989), 68–76; and *Imaginal Worlds: Ibn al-'Arabi and the Problem of Religious Diversity* (Albany: State University of New York Press, 1994), 23–29. See also Nicholson, *Studies in Islamic Mysticism*, 140; Ronald L. Nettler, *Sufi Metaphysics and Qur'anic Prophets: Ibn 'Arabi's Thought and Method in "Fusus al-Hikam"* (Cambridge, UK: Islamic Texts Society, 2003), 7–11, 18–22, 80–88, 116–22.

34. Ibn al-'Arabi, *The Bezels of Wisdom*, trans. and intro. Ralph W. J. Austin, preface by Titus Burckhardt (New York: Paulist Press, 1980), 74–75.

35. Schimmel, *Mystical Dimensions*, 268. On the narrowing of the ontic gap between God, world, and soul in Sufi mysticism, see the wealth of material translated and analyzed by Helmut Ritter, *The Ocean of the Soul: Men, the World and God in the Stories of Farid al-Din 'Attar*, trans. John O'Kane with editorial assistance of Bernd Radtke (Leiden: Brill, 2003), 615–36.

36. Chittick, *Sufi Path of Knowledge*, 364. For a more detailed discussion of this theme, see the elaborate treatment of Fritz Meier, "The Problem of Nature in the Esoteric Monism of Islam," in *Spirit and Nature: Papers from the Eranos Yearbooks* (New York: Pantheon Books, 1954), 149–203.

37. Anton M. Heinen, *Islamic Cosmology: A Study of as-Suyuti's Al-Hay'a as-Saniya Fi L-Hay'a as-Sunniya, with Critical Edition, Translation, and Commentary* (Wiesbaden: Franz Steiner Verlag, 1982), 133.

38. Chittick, *Self-Disclosure*, 110; and "The Paradox of the Veil in Sufism," in *Rending the Veil: Concealment and Secrecy in the History of Religions*, ed. Elliot R. Wolfson (New York: Seven Bridges Press, 1999), 74.

39. Chittick, *Self-Disclosure*, 129; and "Paradox of the Veil," 81–82.

40. Chittick, *Self-Disclosure*, 156; and "Paradox of the Veil," 74–75.

41. Chittick, *Self-Disclosure*, 105, 107–8, 113, 115, 156.

42. *Zohar* 2:98b. For a fuller discussion of this passage, see Elliot R. Wolfson, *Luminal Darkness: Imaginal Gleanings from Zoharic Literature* (Oxford: Oneworld Publications, 2007), 73–74.

Parallelism between Avicenna's *Hayy ibn Yaqzan* and Ibn Ezra's *Hay ben Meqitz*

Ibn Ezra (1089–1164) wrote his Hebrew-language *Hay ben Meqitz* with the primary intention of competing with Avicenna's (980–1037) more famous Arabic *Hayy ibn Yaqzan*. Since Islamicate Jews spoke and wrote Arabic, it is important to understand that what Ibn Ezra effectively offered his audience was the exact same allegorical account of ascent and vision found in Avicenna's text, but one that was now firmly embedded within the familiar language and categories of the Bible and later Jewish texts from late antiquity. Both texts are predicated on a celestial ascent, the recounting of divine topographies, and an ultimate cosmic initiation, all of which were the mythic bedrock from which both Judaism and Islam were formed. Both Avicenna and Ibn Ezra do this, however, by framing it in the language and categories of Neoplatonism. Avicenna, for example, used the familiar Islamic trope of Muhammad's Night Journey (*mi'raj*) to introduce non-Islamic philosophical ideas in Islam. Ibn Ezra, by contrast, used Avicenna's narrative to create what he considered to be a better Hebrew version.

Avicenna's *Hayy ibn Yaqzan* recounts the soul's journey through a structured and hierarchical cosmos with the help of a celestial guide called Hayy ibn Yaqzan (lit., "Living, son of Awake"). As the two begin their ascent, they encounter a number of individuals whom Hayy describes as pernicious to the journey that will follow. These "individuals" are actually allegorical personifications of the various faculties (e.g., the irascible faculty, the imaginative faculty) that get in the way of philosophical speculation. As the two proceed on their journey, they reach a threshold at which the unnamed protagonist must undergo a ritual initiation that will enable him to progress into the next level. This occurs as Hayy and the initiate approach "a flowing spring near the tranquil spring of life." After the initiate immerses himself in the spring, drinking its healing waters, he is ritually purified and able to continue on his journey. The successful initiation, as Hayy tells him, enables him to cross vast deserts, walk on water, and ascend sacred mountains.

Following these ordeals, the unnamed protagonist enters into two regions. The first is referred to as the "West," and is associated with matter. Following an understanding of this matter, which is essentially tantamount to Aristotelian physics, Hayy introduces the initiate into each of the eight celestial spheres that occupy the rest of the Western part of the universe on a vertical hierarchy. Following this, Hayy ibn Yaqzan turns toward the so-called Eastern part of the cosmos, the region associated with form. Hayy leads the initiate toward the region that occupies the space above both East and West. Finally, the unnamed protagonist reaches the end of his ascension, whereupon he encounters the king, an allegorical figure for the Necessary Existent, that is, that whose existence is necessary for the sustenance of the universe and all that it encompasses.

Abraham ibn Ezra translated many Arabic texts into Hebrew, thus functioning as an important conduit between the two traditions. His *Hay ben Meqitz* is a text that works on multiple levels. On one level it is a pastiche of biblical phrases that enabled twelfth-century Jews to embrace and legitimate the intellectual and aesthetic ideals of Neoplatonism, in much the same manner that Avicenna did before him. On another level, *Hay ben Meqitz* "Judaizes" the basic narrative found in Avicenna's *Hayy* and, in so doing, tries to lay claim to it.

Although Ibn Ezra borrows the basic plot, structure, and characters from Avicenna's text, he does so in such a manner that the new creation derives its

Persian miniature from *Miʿraj nameh* (*The Miraculous Journey of Muhammad*) by Mir Haydar, Herat, around 1436. Paris, Bibliothèque Nationale de France, ms. or. turc. 190, folio 49 (verso).

grounded within the semantic field of Muhammad's Night Journey. In this regard, Ibn Ezra incorporates the motifs and images that are associated with earlier Jewish mystical sources and, much like Avicenna before him, manipulates them in the light of the categories provided by Neoplatonism.

Although the narrative accounts that we encounter in *Hayy ibn Yaqzan* and *Hay ben Meqitz* are virtually identical, Ibn Ezra's text attempts to demonstrate that Jewish sources also deal directly and dramatically with notions of ascent. Like Avicenna before him, he is interested in legitimating the potentially dangerous teachings of philosophy by grounding them within the familiar categories of his own religious and literary tradition. However, he also had to show his Jewish audience that the twin themes of ascent and vision, although central to Neoplatonism, did not resonate solely within the Islamic ascent narrative associated with the *miʿraj*.

Whereas Avicenna had tried to show his audience that philosophical ascent was qualitatively similar to Muhammad's Night Journey, Ibn Ezra here goes a step further: not only is the concept of philosophical ascent religious and something that religious texts endorse, it is a phenomenon that is as Jewish, if not more so, as it is Islamic. This permits him to show his audience, who undoubtedly would have been familiar with Islamic claims to monotheistic legitimation through the *miʿraj* narrative, that the themes of ascent, vision, and gnosis existed in Jewish sources, ones that predated the advent of Islam. Ibn Ezra seems to have written his *Hay ben Meqitz* to demonstrate to his readers that all of the themes encountered in the phenomenon of philosophical ascent, themes that Avicenna had framed in terms of Muhammad's Night Journey, are biblical and thus Jewish.[1] ●

vocabulary, terms of reference, and, ultimately, its potency from the biblical narrative. By doing this, ibn Ezra attempted to show his Jewish audience, on a religious level, that his own version was better than that of Avicenna, and, on a philosophical level, that latent in the biblical narrative reside the truths of philosophy. Explicit in his "Judaization" of this work, then, is the notion that Jews no longer needed to read the original Arabic version of the narrative.

Ibn Ezra, like Avicenna before him, is interested in grounding the concept of philosophical awakening in the familiar categories provided by his religious tradition. In addition, however, he also seeks to show how the motif of ascent is something that is not solely Islamic and, as Avicenna had implied,

Aaron W. Hughes is the Gordon and Gretchen Gross Professor of Jewish Studies at the State University of New York. In addition to numerous books and articles, he is the

author of The Art of Dialogue in Jewish Philosophy *(2008) and* The Invention of Jewish Identity: Bible, Philosophy, and the Art of Translation *(2010), both published by Indiana University Press.*

---

1. For further reading, see Henry Corbin, *Avicenna and the Visionary Recital*, trans. Willard Trask (Princeton, NJ: Princeton University Press, 1960); Peter Heath, *Allegory and Philosophy in Avicenna* (Philadelphia: University of Pennsylvania Press, 1992); Aaron W. Hughes, "A Case of 12th-Century Plagiarism? Abraham ibn Ezra's *Hay ben Meqitz* and Avicenna's *Hayy ibn Yaqzan*," *Journal of Jewish Studies* 55, no. 2 (2004): 306–31; and Aaron W. Hughes, *The Texture of the Divine: Imagination in Medieval Islamic and Jewish Thought* (Bloomington: Indiana University Press, 2004), which includes a full English translation of Ibn Ezra's *Hay ben Meqitz* in the appendix.

Respectful Rival: Abraham Maimonides on Islam
Elisha Russ-Fishbane

Islam occupies a unique position in the medieval Jewish imagination. From the tenth through the thirteenth centuries, Islamic society was for many Jews the bastion of civilization and culture, in which Jews played a vital and transformative role.[1] Yet as members of a proud religious minority, many Jews regarded the religion of Islam with deep ambivalence. Jews at once repudiated Islam as a legitimate faith while singling it out from all others as an exponent of pure monotheism on par with its Jewish precursor. As such, Islam occupied a middle position in Jewish law, outside the divine covenant yet the subject of special treatment in contrast to Christianity and other religious traditions.[2] On the rare occasions when it was contested, Islamic monotheism was upheld by no less an authority than Moses Maimonides as a matter beyond dispute.[3] Yet Maimonides elsewhere denounced Islam as a prophetic forgery and crude distortion of its Jewish forebear.[4] This deep-seated ambivalence toward Islam, a leitmotif of medieval Jewish literature, is nowhere more evident than in the works of Maimonides's only son, Abraham, much of whose legacy is defined by his profound engagement with the spiritual heritage of Islam.[5]

Elisha Russ-Fishbane

Elisha Russ-Fishbane is a historian specializing in the history and culture of Jews in the medieval Islamic world. He completed his PhD dissertation, "Between Piety and Politics: The Life and Leadership of Abraham Maimonides," in 2009. He teaches at Wesleyan University.

Revitalizing Judaism through Sufism

The career of Abraham Maimonides (1186–1237) is replete with paradox. In his capacity as head of Egyptian Jewry, known as *ra'īs al-yahūd* in Arabic and *nagīd* in Hebrew, Abraham represented his community before the Muslim authorities and regulated its internal bureaucracy. What is more, as the primary rabbinic authority of his generation, Abraham supervised all matters of synagogue life and communal jurisprudence. In these capacities, Abraham served as the guardian of tradition in its various forms. Yet alongside his official role, Abraham simultaneously spearheaded a movement of Jewish pietism, whose adherents (*ḥasidim*) derived much of their inspiration from contemporary Islamic mysticism. By the thirteenth century, Sufism had developed into a spiritual network of orders and brotherhoods, each of which operated under the guidance of a recognized master (*shaykh*). Rites of initiation and regimented spiritual exercises proliferated and would prove a powerful social force throughout Egypt, North Africa, and the Near East in the centuries that followed.

Against this background, Abraham and his circle looked to the Sufi movement as a living model for spiritual renewal in their own communities. It was not the first time that Sufism had been used as a blueprint for Jewish piety in the Islamic world, but the Egyptian pietists proved both more explicit and more extensive than their predecessors in their invocation of Sufi models. The first Jewish author to reflect Sufi influence was Bahya ibn Paquda in the second half of the eleventh century.[6] Abraham in particular did not shy from explicit appropriations or adaptations of Sufi ritual. He actively incorporated both the outer trappings of the movement (including spiritual fellowship, guidance under a *shaykh*, discrete rituals of meditation and fasting, and the wearing of distinctive garments), and much of its religious vocabulary and devotional ideals. But remarkable as this was, Abraham's embrace of Islamic rites did not end there. He favored a modification of synagogue ritual to include well-known symbols of Islamic prayer, most notably prostration, kneeling, and the arrangement of worshippers in orderly rows. Rather than limit these changes to

Young man visiting a dervish, Herat, around 1595–1600, Paris, Louvre Museum.

pietist circles, Abraham directed his appeal to the entire community in an effort to stimulate a spiritual revival among his coreligionists. It is little surprise that Abraham's efforts generated a storm of controversy within the Jewish community.[7] Pietists were subjected to religious scrutiny both in the public eye, within rabbinical courts, and in the privacy of their own families.[8]

The head of the Jews, in spite of his high position, was hardly immune to criticism. Charges were leveled that the proposed changes constituted religious innovation and brazen imitation of Islamic worship. To these accusations, Abraham offered a powerful rebuttal. His changes to synagogue ritual, he argued, were mere restorations of ancient Jewish practice that were lost over the course of the exile and later adopted within the Muslim community. The religious innovation, he countered, lay with those who persisted in their errors and spurned what he maintained were originally Jewish rites. As for prostration, Abraham cautioned: "Be careful not to confuse a new [rite] with an ancient one that has been neglected . . . Prostration is an obligation of the law and ancient custom of the people yet neglected over many years in exile. And when one is made aware that it is an obligation and adopts it in practice, the deluded and ignorant consider it a religious innovation."[9] What was true of prostration and other synagogue reforms was even more so of Sufi rites. Abraham identified a range of practices prevalent among the Sufis that preserved, in his view, the path of piety cultivated by the ancient prophets. Prophecy, in this conception, was a state of inner illumination that was the culmination of rigorous spiritual training and moral refinement.[10] Abraham and his circle argued that Sufism drew inspiration for its ascetic regimen and discipleship from the biblical prophets, asserting that these were originally an integral part of the Jewish tradition that must now be reappropriated by the community. A host of biblical passages were adduced to assert that Sufi rites, from austere poverty to ragged or woolly garments, were "among the many things transmitted (*intaqala*) to the Sufis of Islam."[11] Abraham assured his readers that comparisons with Sufi practice were warranted in that "the Sufis imitated the prophets and followed their example," rather than the reverse.[12]

> **Abraham Maimonides identified a range of practices prevalent among the Sufis that preserved, in his view, the path of piety cultivated by the ancient prophets.**

Muslim heirs of the Jewish prophets

Interestingly, Abraham viewed the transfer of Jewish wisdom to the Gentiles as the fulfilment of a biblical prophecy that foresaw the saints of the world drawing from Israel's spiritual heritage.[13] This then provided the opening for Abraham to acknowledge that, "as for us, we have adopted the tradition from them and follow their example in the wearing of the ragged cloak and other things."[14] It is striking that in passages such as these, the polemical argument was directed not at Muslims or Sufis but at his own coreligionists, who were said to have abandoned their heritage to a rival religion. At one point, Abraham even appealed to his community's sense of pride, insisting that the pietists were merely reappropriating what was rightfully theirs: "Consider these marvelous traditions and grieve at how they were transferred from us to another religion and [all but] disappeared from among us! [I]n their interpretation of the verse, 'If you do not heed [God's word], my soul shall weep on account of pride,'[15] [our sages] remarked: 'What is the meaning of "on account of pride"'? [Namely] on account of the pride of Israel that has been taken from them and given to the nations of the world."[16] To Israel's shame, Abraham implied it is within the Muslim community that one may now find traces of prophetic worship. It is among the Sufis, the spiritual heirs of the prophets, that one may discover the path leading to prophecy, rather than among the latter's direct descendants. If there is a polemic implicitly addressed toward Islam, it is the suggestion that Sufis are mere repositories of prophetic wisdom rather than its originators. But what is troublesome for Abraham is not Islamic piety per se but the very presence of such piety in Islam. His rhetoric functions paradoxically as a kind of polemic of praise, while the true target of his critique is the internal audience to whom the book is addressed. Abraham adopted a similar approach to the religion of Islam elsewhere in his writings. What he took with one hand, he gave with the other. Following his father, Abraham contended that the Islamic religion is a poor imitation of its Jewish exemplar, while affirming that Islamic monotheism has remained pure and faithful to its model.[17]

Praise of Islamic monotheism

With regard to specific laws, although we have no evidence that he engaged in open debates with Muslim scholars,[18] Abraham did not hesitate to identify what he considered defects due to ignorance and error: the prohibition of wine in Islamic law, the Islamic custom to pray within the precincts of a bathhouse, and the elaborate adornment of mosques (lamenting its influence on local synagogue decoration).[19] Abraham also maintained that the Torah calls for a greater level of sanctity than Islamic law,[20] and further commented on the prevalence in Arab/Muslim society to swear false or vain oaths,[21] again lamenting that Jews had been influenced by the reprehensible standards of society at large.

Yet what Islam lacked in individual laws, Abraham implied, it made up for in the fundamentals of its faith. At times, his tribute to Islam was couched in a thinly veiled critique of his own coreligionists. This was evident enough in his polemical epistle against the rabbinic scholars of Montpellier, who consigned his father's philosophical writings to the flames over matters of theology. Before chastising the French community for its own errors, he painted a rather flattering portrait of Islamic faith and, equally significant, Jewish faith in the realm of Islam. In the process, Abraham described Islamic worship as nothing less than a sanctification of the divine name and the fulfillment of a biblical promise.

> [The rejection of anthropomorphism] is not doubted by any single Jew from east to west who dwells in the realm of Islam. The Muslims themselves adopted this belief from the Jews and established their religion upon it. They rejected the foolishness and ignorance of their ancestors' idol worship . . . , as it is written: "Nations shall come to You from the corners of the earth and declare, 'Our ancestors have inherited lies, vanity that is of no avail'" [Jer. 16:19]. It was further said by another prophet: "From the rising of the sun to its setting, My name is great among the nations" [Mal. 1:11]. And because their worship is pure monotheism, scripture likened it to the sacrificial rite offered for His name, as it is written: "And in every place incense and a pure offering are brought for My name" [Mal. 1:11]. Whoever differs and asserts that the Creator, may He be magnified and exalted, has a physical form . . . is a heretic and has no place in the world to come.[22]

On the surface, Jews are portrayed as the original bearers of prophetic religion, whose monotheistic faith served as direct inspiration for the rise of Islam and its renunciation of idolatry. But despite Islam's subsidiary role as a beneficiary and imitation of its predecessor, its unadulterated worship of the one God has glorified the divine name "from the rising of the sun to its setting," an allusion to the global spread of Islam. Jews, too, are commended for their unquestioning monotheism, but the juxtaposition with Islam reveals the subtext of Abraham's critique. No Jew "in the land of Iraq and the [countries] to the east,[23] in Syria and the holy land, in Egypt and the land of the Maghreb" espouses anything but the strictest monotheism. Anyone who lives under Islam and ascribes a physical form to the deity "would be the object of ridicule, scorn, and derision, even in the presence of an ignoramus."[24] But Jewish belief outside of Islam is a different story entirely. Abraham minced no words when describing the "counterfeit faith" of the Jews of Montpellier, who burned his father's books. "It stands to reason," he observed, "that they would receive the support of the Christians, whose belief is not far removed from their own."[25] The contrast with Christendom underscores Abraham's allegation that Islam, with its unwavering monotheism, has exerted a salutary influence on its Jewish minority.[26]

Islam, a milestone in the universal mission of Judaism

Abraham Maimonides's approach to Islam is therefore dialectical and ambivalent. His considerable praise of Islamic faith, worship, and piety is the most explicit of any Judeo-Arabic author before or after his time. To declare Islamic belief and prayer a glorification of the divine name and Islamic piety the direct continuation of the prophetic tradition is nothing short of extraordinary. Yet what freed him to make such pronouncements was his parallel claim that what is commendable in Islam was merely of Jewish origin. We have seen how Abraham used this claim to censure his own people for its neglect of its ancestral traditions. But, as the following passage suggests, Abraham likewise believed it to be the universal mission of the Jewish people to enlighten other nations and serve as a spiritual model of the religious life.

> The aim of the Law is for other nations to imitate us and follow [our] example, just as the members of a nation follow the example of its spiritual leaders, [as scripture says,] "You shall be unto me a nation of priests" [Exod. 19:6]. This purpose is either for the Law [to be adopted by other nations] in full, as will be the case in the end of days and as occurs in the case of individual converts, or else for it [to be adopted] in part. This has occurred in the case of one of the religions that arose after the giving of the Torah, which [affirms] the foundations of the Law, such as God's unity and incorporeality . . . For this reason, the Torah says, "Israel is my firstborn,"[27] for the firstborn takes priority over the other children, if one can even refer to the others as children at all. In reference to this, scripture said, "[Be faithful in its observance, for it is a sign of your wisdom and discernment in the eyes of the nations,] who will learn of these statutes and declare, 'Surely this great nation is a wise and discerning people . . . , for what nation has such upright statutes and laws . . . ?'" [Ex. 19, 6]. This is precisely what has transpired. So have the nations declared and so have they done, while our own wisdom and distinction have all but disappeared from among us and are now to be found in another religion on account of our sins. This is comparable to an heir who has neglected and relinquished his inheritance until it is acquired by another who takes it over and claims it as his right.[28]

Judaism and Islam, in Abraham's imagination, serve as mirror images of each other. One's strength constitutes the other's deficiency, such that the two rivals remain locked in a tight embrace of mutual dependence and negation. Islam, in this view, is but a shadow of its Jewish forebear and yet the latter must turn to its imitator time and again for inspiration. The restoration of Israel's privileged status among the nations will come at the expense of its monotheistic rival, while the very renewal of its spiritual mission requires an ongoing engagement with Islam.

> **"Judaism and Islam, in Abraham's imagination, serve as mirror images of each other."**

Much like its parallel struggle with Christianity, the ascendency of one entails the diminishment of the other, both religiously and politically.[29] Ironically, despite the unequal status and occasional harassment experienced by Jews under Islam, Abraham believed in the possibility of spiritual renewal precisely because of the extensive religious freedoms granted to the Jewish community under Islamic law.[30] For Abraham Maimonides, the temporal and spiritual ascent of Islam and its eventual demise are inextricably bound up in the fate of Israel.

In his interpretation of the prophetic verses in Genesis regarding Abraham's progeny, he accounted for the rise of a rival monotheistic religion as the fulfillment of the divine blessing to Ishmael, the beginning of which corresponded with Judaism's diminished state in exile, "during a period of [Israel's] weakness on account of its sins."[31] By the same token, Israel's redemption will ensue when "the descendants of Ishmael" and Esau will in turn subdue themselves to their former subjects: "'[A]nd you shall be master over your brothers'—when you become the sole beneficiary of the Abrahamic blessing, to the exclusion of the others."[32] The new order envisioned by Abraham was as much a political reversal as a spiritual one, in which widespread conversion and submission to the religion of Israel would follow.[33] In the meantime, before the unfolding of the anticipated redemption, Judaism remained firmly within the embrace of Islam. In Abraham's paradoxical vision, the only hope for the ultimate restoration and renewal of Israel lay in its ability to draw strength from that very embrace, by modeling its spiritual transformation on the living example of Islam.

---

1. For a good overview of Jewish intellectual and literary culture in this formative period, see Raymond Scheindlin, "Merchants and Intellectuals, Rabbis and Poets: Judeo-Arabic Culture in the Golden Age of Islam," in *Cultures of the Jews*, ed. David Biale (New York: Schocken Books, 2002), 2:11–84.

2. For an overview of Jewish attitudes in medieval Islam, see Stroumsa, "Jewish Polemics against Islam and Christianity in the Light of Judaeo-Arabic Texts," in *Judaeo-Arabic Studies*, ed. N. Golb (Amsterdam: Harwood Academic Publishers, 1997): 241–50.

3. See *Teshuvot ha-Rambam*, ed. Y. Blau (Jerusalem: Rubin Mass, Ltd., 1986), 3:725–28.

4. A number of studies have been devoted to Maimonides's complex attitude toward Islam. See D. Novak, "The Treatment of Islam and Muslims in the Legal Writings of Maimonides," in *Studies in Islamic and Judaic Traditions*, ed. W. Brinner and S. Ricks (Atlanta: Scholars Press, 1986), 233–50; E. Schlossberg, "The Attitude of Maimonides toward Islam," *Pe'amim* 42 (1990): 38–60 (in Hebrew); G. Blidstein, "The Stance of Islam in Maimonidean Halakhah," in *Multiculturalism in a Democratic and Jewish State*, ed. M. Mautner et al. (Tel Aviv: Tel Aviv University Press, 1998), 465–76. For a comparative treatment, see H. Kreisel, "Maimonides on Christianity and Islam," in *Jewish Civilization: Essays and Studies*, ed. R. Braunder (Philadelphia: Reconstructionist Rabbinical College, 1985), 3:153–62; D. Lasker, "Tradition and Innovation in Maimonides' Attitude toward Other Religions," in *Maimonides after 800 Years*, ed. J. Harris (Cambridge, MA: Harvard University Press, 2007), 167–82.

5. For a general introduction to Abraham Maimonides, see P. Fenton, "Abraham Maimonides (1186–1237): Founding a Mystical Dynasty," in *Jewish Mystical Leaders and Leadership in the 13th Century*, ed. M. Idel and M. Ostow (Lanham, MD: Jason Aronson, 1998), 127–54, and the present author's dissertation, "Between Politics and Piety: Abraham Maimonides and his Times," Harvard University, 2009.

6. On Bahya and his Sufi background, see D. Lobel, *A Sufi-Jewish Dialogue: Philosophy and Mysticism in Bahya Ibn Paquda's "Duties of the Heart"* (Philadelphia: University of Pennsylvania Press, 2007).

7. On this controversy and Abraham's extensive response, see "Between Politics and Piety," 191–201, 282–306.

8. For Abraham's defense of the pietist in light of communal objections, see Bodl. MS Heb. c. 28, fol. 45–46, published by S. D. Goitein in "A Treatise in Defence of the Pietists by Abraham Maimonides," *Journal of Jewish Studies* 16

(1965): 113–14. For a reflection of domestic disputes, see the composite text published by P. Fenton in "A Mystical Treatise on Prayer and the Spiritual Quest from the Pietist Circle," *Jerusalem Studies in Arabic and Islam* 16 (1993): 145.

9. *Sefer ha-Maspik le-ʿOvdey Hashem*, ed. N. Dana (Ramat Gan: Bar-Ilan University, 1989), 161 (hereafter *Sefer ha-Maspik*). For a different but related reply to his critics, see also *Teshuvot Rabbenu Avraham ben ha-Rambam*, ed. A. Freimann and S. D. Goitein (Jerusalem: Meqitze Nirdamim, 1937), 62–65, no. 62 (hereafter *Teshuvot*).

10. On prophecy in medieval Jewish thought, see H. Kreisel, *Prophecy: The History of an Idea in Medieval Jewish Philosophy* (Dordrecht: Kluwer Academic Publishers, 2001). On the prophetic views and aspirations of the Egyptian pietists, see P. Fenton, *Deux traités de mystique juive* (Paris: Verdier, 1987), 70–80.

11. *The High Ways to Perfection of Abraham Maimonides*, trans. and ed. S. Rosenblatt (Baltimore: Johns Hopkins University Press, 1927–38), 2:222, ll. 15–17 (hereafter *High Ways*).

12. See ibid., 2:320, ll. 7–9, on the wearing of distinctive clothing. See also ibid., ll. 1–3, and 2:348, ll. 13–16.

13. The enigmatic prophecy is taken from Deut. 33:3, of which Abraham cited the final expression, "he shall take from your words." See *High Ways*, 2:266, ll. 4–10, and 2:422, ll. 14–16. Read in this light, the entire verse becomes a prophetic reference to the saints of the world. The verse could then read as follows: "Indeed He is a lover of the nations, all of His saints are in your hand; they followed in your footsteps and take from your words." All other traditional commentators read this verse as a reference to Israel rather than the nations, making Abraham's interpretation all the more significant.

14. See *High Ways*, 2:266, ll. 4–10, esp. ll. 9–10. The key words translated above are *wa-naḥnu nanqul ʿanhum wanuttabiʿ min aṯārihim*.

15. Jer. 13:17.

16. *High Ways*, 2:322, ll. 15–20, paraphrasing from BT *Hagigah* 5b.

17. As in other legal writings on Islam, Abraham's ruling on the subject affirms its place as a monotheistic religion. See *Teshuvot*, 56, no. 56.

18. Abraham referred to polemical arguments of Muslim theologians on Mosaic prophecy and offered a rebuttal in his biblical commentary, but there is no hint of an open debate with these theologians. See *Perush*, 309–11 (Exod. 19:19). By contrast, Abraham does describe a personal debate with Christian theologians, ibid., 203–5 (Exod. 49:10). He devoted a chapter of his *Kifāyah* to refuting the Islamic assertion that the Torah has been abrogated. See Bodl. MS Heb. d 23, beginning on fol. 1, verso, and cf. *Sefer ha-Maspik*, 151, 153–54. On this topic, see H. Lazarus-Yafeh, *Intertwined Worlds: Medieval Islam and Bible Criticism* (Princeton, NJ: Princeton University Press, 1992), 19–49, and further examples in M. Friedman, *Maimonides, the Yemenite Messiah, and Apostasy* (Jerusalem: Ben-Zvi Institute, 2002), 110n111.

19. See these examples, respectively: *Sefer ha-Maspik*, 307–8; 2 Firk. 1.2924.1, verso, translated into Hebrew by P. Fenton, "Communion with God in the Thought of Abraham Maimonides: Fragments from the Lost Section of *The Sufficient Guide for the Servants of God*," *Daʿat* 50 (2003), 116 (in Hebrew); *Sefer ha-Maspik*, 107–8.

20. See *Perush Rabbenu Avraham ben ha-Rambam*, trans. and ed. E. Wiesenberg (London: Sassoon, 1959), 357–59 (ex. 22:30; hereafter *Perush*).

21. See *Sefer ha Maspik*, 296, 305, as well as 309–10.

22. *Milhamot ha-Shem*, ed. R. Margaliot (Jerusalem: Mossad Harav Kook, 1953), 51–52.

23. Ibid., 24.

24. Ibid., 54.

25. Ibid., 55, alluding to the allegation that the papal inquisition was enlisted to help with the burning of Maimonides's works.

26. Like his father, Abraham designated Christianity as idolatrous. See *Sefer ha-Maspik*, 150 and 251, and *Perush*, 315–17 (Exod. 20:3). Abraham maintained that Christians derived their belief in a son of God from a literal interpretation of the prophetic books, in contrast to the usual charge that Christians interpret verses allegorically. See *Milḥamot ha-Shem*, 74.

27. Ibid., 4:22.

28. *Sefer ha-Maspik*, 152–53.

29. See *Perush*, 63–65 (Gen. 25:23).

30. See *Sefer ha-Maspik*, 112, on religious freedom under Islam. On inequality and Jewish vulnerability in Islamic society, see ibid., 105 and 253.

31. Ibid., 43–45 (Gen. 21:13; wrongly listed by Wiesenberg as 21:17). In his interpretation of this verse, Abraham went beyond his father's view of the divine promise to Ishmael as a blessing on the latter's physical descendants rather than the religion of Islam per se. See Maimonides's "Epistle to Yemen," in *Iggeret Teman*, ed. A. S. Halkin (New York: American Academy for Jewish Research, 1952), 40–42. See esp. the comments of M. Friedman, "A Note on the

Biblical Commentary of Abraham Maimonides," *Sinai* 114 (1994): 103, and his additional remarks in *Maimonides, the Yemenite Messiah, and Apostasy*, 99–100. It is interesting to note that, in this interpretation, Abraham also diverged from his earlier approach to Ishmael's blessing in the *Kifayah*, which corresponded with that of his father in the "Epistle to Yemen." See *Sefer ha-Maspik*, 209–10.

32. *Perush*, 79 (Gen. 27:29).

33. See *Sefer ha-Maspik*, 152, and *Perush*, 303 (Exod. 19:6).

The Temple According to Jalal al-Din Rumi

What the Qur'an calls *al-Masjid al-Aqsa* (the farther mosque, or oratory) is nothing other than the Temple that David was unable to build and that Solomon did build (see the commentary of al-Tabari on that occurrence in the Qur'an, sura 17:1). With that expression, Islam reappropriated the Temple of the Jews. And the mosque that was built in the early eighth century on the Temple Esplanade is a sign of that reappropriation. But Rumi, as an Islamic mystic, sought to resolve the paradox about the Temple that he had inherited from the two previous monotheistic and scriptural traditions: for the Jews, the Temple is here and nowhere else; for the Christians, it is everywhere and nowhere. Rumi seems to take both views into account. The Temple is truly here, it is the *Masjid al-Aqsa* that was built and maintained by Solomon; and it is everywhere and nowhere, because the Temple that is identifiable in space and time is a metaphor for the inner temple.

Abdelwahab Meddeb

388–94
Because David encountered serious difficulties[1]
in building the Farther Mosque of stone,[2]
God gave him a revelation: "Abandon that plan,
You will not succeed in completing that structure.
It is not in Our Order that you should erect
that Farther Mosque, O chosen one."
"You who know secrets, what is my
crime? Why do you forbid me that act?"
"Though committing no crime, you are responsible
for several deaths; for many have suffered
injustice: they were the victims of your voice,
they breathed their last while listening to it.
Much blood was spilled because
of your voice, your beautiful song that delights the soul."
. . . .
406–7
"The Mosque will not be built by your toil
and strength: it is your son who will build it; his act
is your act; man of wisdom, know that the
faithful are bound in union everlasting."
. . . .

467–85

When Solomon began the construction
– holy as the Kaaba, august as Mina[3] —
splendor and magnificence emanated therefrom;
this great building was not sad as others are.
From the start each stone, extracted
from the mountain, said clearly: "Take me!"
Like the water and earth from which the house
of Adam was made, light shone from the pieces of mortar.
The stones moved without being carried
and these doors and walls came brightly to life.
God says the wall of Paradise is not marred
and inanimate like some other wall;
like the wall of the body, it is endowed with intelligence:
the house is alive, for it is the King of Kings's.
The tree, the fruit, the clear water, all speak
and converse with the resident of Paradise,
for Paradise was not made of materiality,
it was made of acts and intentions.
Every structure is built of water and dead earth
but this edifice arose from living piety.
Another one mirrors the flaw in its foundation,
and this one reflects knowledge and action.
Throne, palace, crowns, and robes question
the resident of Paradise, and give him their reply.
The carpet folds without the servant's aid;
the house is swept without the use of a broom.
Look at the house of the heart: troubled by care,
without a servant, it was swept by repentance.
The throne moved forward without a porter; the knocker
and door were the musician and singer.
The life of the eternal Dwelling lies in the heart:
my language cannot describe it, what use is there in trying?
When Solomon went each morning
to the Mosque to guide his servants,
he exhorted them either by sermon and song,
or by acts, prostrations or prayers.
Exhortation by acts has a greater effect
since it reaches everyone, whether deaf or hearing.

. . . .

1288–92

Each morning when Solomon came to pray
at the Farther Mosque, he saw that a
new plant had grown, and he spoke to it:
"Tell me your name and what you are used for.
What are you? Are you a remedy? What is your name?
For whom are you harmful? For whom of use?"
Each plant revealed its effects and its name:
"I give life to this one, death to that,
I am poison for one, sweet for another: so is
my name inscribed on the Tablet of Decrees."

. . . .

1313–16

At every moment, from your own thoughts,
a new plant grows in your Farther Mosque.
Like Solomon, give it its due,
learn to know it, do not kick it away,
for the various plants grow up
to tell you the story of terra firma.
Sugar cane or simple reed,
the plant is interpreter of the earth.

. . . .

1355–57

As was his habit, worthy Solomon
went to the Mosque at first glimmer.
Doing as he would every day
he saw the new plants in the Mosque.
The pure-eyed heart sees the secret, a bud
invisible to the common man.

. . . .

1373–81

Solomon saw that a new plant
had grown in a corner like a sprout.
He saw a rare plant, green
and fresh, its color dazzled the eye.
The plant greeted him straightaway, and he
in amazement returned its greeting.
He said: "What is your name? Speak, O mouthless."
It replied: "I am the carob tree, king of the world."
"What, then, is special about you?"
"Wherever I grow, the place turns desolate.

I, carob tree, am the corrupter of dwellings.[4]
I destroy what was built by water and clay."
Then Solomon knew that his end
had come and that he would have to depart.
He said: "So long as I'm there, not one of the scourges
of earth will touch this Mosque.
So long as I'm here and I exist
the Mosque will never know harm."

Masnavi, Book 4

Translated from the Persian into French by Jenia Jianfar and Abdelwahab Meddeb.

---

1. Each verse of the original poem (composed of two hemistichs) corresponds to two lines in our translation.
2. The Temple of Jerusalem, so named in the Qur'an (17:1).
3. Reference to another station of the pilgrimage, on the outskirts of Mecca.
4. Alliteration between *kharrrūb* (carob) and *kharāb* (corrupter, ruin).

Jews, Islamic Mysticism, and the Devil

Michael Barry

Texts by Islam's greatest mystics dealing with Jews, directly or through allusion, generally dismay—at least at first glance. Contrary to usual perceptions of medieval Sufism as somehow more "tolerant," Jewish figures in actual Classical Sufi texts appear no less devilishly caricatural as any in medieval Christian literature or art. In fact, prevailing views of Jews in either dominant medieval culture—Christian or Islamic—appear luridly similar, with Jews depicted as spiritually blind creatures who rejected Divine Truth's light as revealed through Jesus or Muhammad. Scorn and sarcasm characterize allegorical depictions of Jews by medieval Muslim poets and also manuscript painters who closely reflected these poets' ideas. Only far deeper exploration of Sufi meditation concerning the very Devil himself restores a nobler, even tragically grander image of the stiff-necked Jew within a God-willed cosmic order: as a creature heroically damned, like his model Satan the Archangel, for daring too much to defend the monotheistic principle against God himself—by maintaining God's own absolute Transcendence, against God's own command to bow down and humbly venerate God's own Immanence in Man.

_____
Michael Barry

Michael Barry teaches medieval and modern Islamic culture at Princeton University. His books include *Colour and Symbolism in Islamic Architecture* (Thames and Hudson 1996), *Figurative Art in Medieval Islam and the Riddle of Bihzad of Herat* (1465–1535) (Rizzoli 2005), *Kabul's Long Shadows* (LISD, Princeton 2011), and the forthcoming *'Attar's Canticle of the Birds* (with Leili Anvar and Dick Davis, Éditions Diane de Selliers, 2014).

Dramas

"*Shem'u shamayim*! Hear, O heavens, and give ear, O earth: for the Lord hath spoken, I have nourished and brought up children, and they have rebelled against me. The ox knoweth his owner, and the ass his master's crib: but Israel doth not know, my people doth not consider. Ah, sinful nation, a people laden with iniquity, a seed of evildoers, children that are corrupters: they have forsaken the Lord, they have provoked the Holy One of Israel unto anger, they are gone away backward." So Isaiah the Prophet (1:2–4) inveighed against his own people some seven hundred years before the Common Era in words resounding in Christian ears for another twenty centuries with ringing hatred for Jews: "*vae genti peccatrici*, ah sinful people," or rather, in the Vulgate's harsher Latin quoted here, "woe unto the sinful people," for John (12:39–40) in turn thunderingly echoed Isaiah's wrath: "therefore they could not believe, because that Esaias [Isaiah] said again, he hath blinded their eyes, and hardened their hearts; that they should not see with their eyes, nor understand with their heart, and be converted, and I should heal them."

Nor less scathingly did the Qur'an (2:40–42) upbraid God's chosen people for blindly rejecting his later messengers: "O Children of Israel! call to mind the (special) favor which I bestowed upon you, and fulfill your Covenant with Me as I fulfill My Covenant with you, and fear none but Me. / And believe in what I reveal, confirming the revelation which is with you, and be not the first to reject faith therein, nor sell My Signs for a small price; and fear Me, and Me alone. / And cover not Truth with falsehood, nor conceal the Truth when ye know (what it is)" (Yusuf 'Ali trans.). One may grin wanly at the tragic irony suffered by a major spiritual community portrayed by its twin successor faiths as first chosen then rejected by their common God for turning away from him—or weep: at the record of riots, and ovens lit in the words of Judaism's own prophets. No equivalent exists in the world's other spiritual families to the harshness with which the two latter-born Abrahamic religions exalted then crushed their historic matrix, not only through cruel or humiliating subjugation but also through repeated formulaic utterances and depictions in liturgy and art—even atop the dizziest heights of mystical speculation.

In historical practice, again as well known, medieval Islamic kingdoms in observance of Qur'anic Law normally (although not always) did extend broader tolerance than most contemporary Christian polities to tributary Jewish communities administered by their own rabbis in exchange for payment of the *jizya* tax demanded of all non-Muslim subjects. Moreover, neither in the past nor today might devout Muslims withhold deep reverence, also enjoined by the Qur'an, toward great ancient Hebrew figures like Noah and Abraham, Joseph and Moses, David and Solomon: a cliché of modern interfaith debates. But today's ecumenical debates are not at issue here. Disquieting fact remains that towering medieval Muslim authors poured upon the Jews of their own day a disdain as degrading as any drenching traditional Christian letters. Verses by Firdawsi, Nizami, 'Attar, or Rumi appear steeped in sectarian contempt recalling some of the worst in *The Merchant of Venice* or canto 23 of Dante's *Inferno*. A modern reader's sense of unease only dissipates through dispassionate historical approach.

To be sure, Jews depicted in medieval Islamic, as in traditional Christian literature, represent not so much distinct human beings as allegorical types, emblematic of satanic blindness. Yet the stylistic art of the greater Persian and Arabic poets nevertheless sometimes does confer upon several of these Jewish figures a human-seeming vividness and traits of agonizing realism as to render them, as it were, tragic objects of what has often been termed the "austere pity" of Dante's poetry: like Shakespeare's Shylock or Dante's own damned souls.

The Jew "of evil thought" in Firdawsi and Nizami

Firdawsi's eleventh-century *Shahnameh* or "Book of Kings" founded Iranian epic memory, notably lauding the feats of the ancient (fifth century CE) Persian Sasanian monarch Bahram as legendary lion-hunter, dragon-slayer, and slaughterer of Iran's invaders. But the poet further stresses, in ironic assonance, this heroic king's ferocious jest one day at the expense of a lowly Jewish shopkeeper, one Baraham. This stingy and cowardly Jew rushes out to retrieve from a ditch a silken kerchief absent-mindedly dropped, or so it seems, by the passing mounted king—in fact, the king has wrapped therein his own horse's dung. The Jewish miser Baraham, as victim of his own greed, crawls for dung in the mire, in contrast to the splendid and generous Shah Bahram, riding his magnificent stallion before whom the Jew is dragged: "They rushed to bring before him Baraham the Jew of evil thought and evil name."[1] Subtler as a stylist, but no less harsh toward Jews, Nizami, the master Persian-language poet of late twelfth-century Azerbaijan, and certainly the most celebrated, admired, and widely imitated narrative writer in traditional Eastern Islamic civilization, eschews Firdawsi's folkloric farce for spiritual allegory—only to further reinforce the image of the "Jew of evil thought" (*Jahūd-i bad-andēsh*). In his *Tale of the Green Pavilion*,[2] Nizami sketches without a doubt the vilest Jew in all Persian literature, the arrogant free-thinking philosopher Malikha, whose very name is derived by the poet from an Arabic root signifying "corruption": with an added *a* at the end, to make it sound Aramaic. Nizami's Malikha the Jew represents absolute "evil thought." He is a babbling rationalist blindly incapable of perceiving the Divine Immanence coursing through all creation: "In his thought, this Jew was kneaded all of evil, a serpent in his sorcery and the Synagogue's own dragon."[3]

In Nizami's tale, two travelers, Malikha, this evil Jew, and his companion, Bishr, the true believer (whose Arabic name signifies "good tidings" like the Evangel) become lost together in a desert. Close to perishing, Bishr and Malikha miraculously discover an oasis, marked by a soaring tree with luxuriant foliage sheltering a source of water. Bishr drinks of this fount. But Malikha, after drinking also, wishes to bathe therein and cleanse himself of the travel's filth, despite the protests of his pious companion, aghast that such a blasphemous wretch should want to soil this limpid water and so forbid it to all other travelers in the desert: a transparent image of Judaism seeking to prevent other peoples from learning of the true God in this arid lower world. But when he plunges into the fount, Malikha drowns in its depths. Bishr gathers the dead man's belongings, reaches the city, and searches for the dwelling of Malikha's widow, to return her husband's clothes and purse. A lovely young woman, now, opens her door to him. Bishr immediately recognizes a face that he had once glimpsed in the street, when a gust of wind had suddenly torn off the veil from the countenance of a beautiful passing woman. This lady had been none other than the spouse of the said Jew. Bishr had fallen in love, at a glance, with this Jewish lady, and had forthwith run off into the desert to escape illicit temptation. But now, thanks to the ignoble Malikha's death, the virtuous Bishr legitimately weds his ravishing widow, a female symbol of the soul henceforth delivered from Judaism to embrace the faith of her new spouse, like Shylock the Jew's daughter Jessica eloping with the good Christian youth Lorenzo in Shakespeare's bitterest of comedies.

As soon as the Jewish lady weds Bishr, moreover, this lovely convert in Nizami's tale at once doffs her yellow-tinted robe, and dons a green-tinted robe, the color of Islam. Such a changing of robes in Nizami's allegory limpidly alludes to the strip of yellow cloth known as the *ghiyār*, which Jews in Islamic lands were legally compelled to wear in the form of a scarf or sash, to distinguish them from their Muslim neighbors (this discrimination in dress was imitated by medieval Western Christians from Spanish Islamic usage when the Papal Lateran Council of 1215 in turn imposed a yellow cloth patch, or star, to be worn on their costume by all Jews under Christian rule): "Bishr pursued his heart's desire with this fairy-faced one, upon her he chanted magic spells for to ward off evil's eye, and out of Jewishness led forth his queen, far away did he cast off the darkness that eclipsed her moon, and so he purified her silken robe of the *ghiyār*—the Jewish strip—and she became like to a lily, white, to spring out of a tawny patch of fenugreek. Now that he saw that she no longer dwelt far off from Heaven's folk, he had her sewn a robe of green like to a Houri, Heaven's maid. Better to be robed in green than wear the yellow mark, befitting far to be cloaked thus from head to toe in green. The color green denotes all healthy crops, and green adorns the angels of the sky. If toward the color green, beyond all other tints, do yearn our souls, upon things green as well our eyes sparkle with joy."[4]

Bishr the Pious fishes out the body of the diabolic Malikha from the bottom of the magic well that is the source of life; illustration attributed to Bihzad. The Tree of Life leans to the left above the saint; a devil-rock writhes in pain at left. From "Tale of the Princess in the Green Pavilion," in the *Khamseh* of Nezami, Herat, 1494. London, British Library, ms. or. 6810, folio 175.

Bihzad's mystical anti-Jewish illustration

The famous Eastern Islamic manuscript painter Bihzad explored important symbolic aspects of Nizami's tale in one of several illustrations for a luxurious copy of the poet's collected works presented to Herat's sultan Husayn Mirza Bayqara in 1494 CE.[5] Bihzad's illumination depicts the moment when Malikha the Jew drowns in the desert well, which symbolizes the Fount of Life. The good companion Bishr tries in vain with his staff to fish up the miscreant's corpse, sunk far into the fount's depths. The Jew's garments appear neatly folded near the well's margin, shown here, however, tinted in blue and black, not yellow, but no less denoting colors of mourning and sorrow in medieval Islamic tradition. In Bihzad's painting, Bishr for his part wears a joyous green tunic, befitting his saintly rank.

A huge rock formation springs up to the upper left of Bihzad's desert landscape, twisting backward as if turning violently away from the painting's Holy Fount. Such indeed is the case. Closer inspection reveals that Bihzad's rock is made up of a grotesque, diabolic creature, masking its sight with its own stone paw, while a cavern yawns in the middle of its rock-face like a maw screaming in pain. This rock, in fact, signifies the Jew. The figure of a seemingly grimacing and screaming rock is a recurrent visual motif in traditional Eastern Islamic painting. Such a twisted rock with lurking diabolic features symbolizes the Devil, one of whose Arabic names, precisely, is Sakhr, "the rock": because heavy, blind, and minerally dense "like unto a rock," according to Qur'anic commentators.[6] In Bihzad's painting, the Devil-Rock, deprived of sight, fails to perceive the Divine Reality welling up from the fount, just as Malikha the Jew, who drowned in the fount in Nizami's tale, had always closed his eyes to the mystery of Holy Manifestation.

By contrast, Bihzad's miraculous tree, flourishing in the midst of this desert, is rendered by the artist as a flourishing plane-tree, adorned with motley autumnal foliage. The painter's tree leans lovingly over both the Holy Fount and the saintly Bishr who sounds its depths. Bihzad's visual conceit of such an autumnal tree reflects here not only the letter of Nizami's poem, but also a visionary text by the immensely influential thirteenth-century Spanish Sufi Ibn 'Arabi, whose writings were studied as far east as Central Asia and, notably, in the fifteenth-century kingdom of Herat, where they were carefully translated by the leading theologian Jami, spiritual adviser to the sultan who was Bihzad's own patron. Ibn 'Arabi notably wrote: "Indeed, I looked toward Universal Being and how it came to be created, and toward what therein lies concealed, and how it has been cosmically ordered, and I beheld all the Universe like unto a single Tree."[7] As one late thirteenth-century Persian-language Central Asian commentator translated, "This Tree is All, and All is this Tree."[8]

The inclination of Bihzad's tree over both fount and saint, in accordance with common pictorial allegory in fifteenth- to seventeenth-century Eastern Islamic manuscript art, signifies the Love felt by the Universe both for the Fount of Life and for the countenance of the saint, as twin Manifestations of the Divine, or *tajalli*. The *tajalli*, or Divine Manifestation (the Epiphany or Theophany of Christian Greek writings), is precisely what Malikha the Jew failed to recognize, drowning instead in his bewilderment within the depths of the Fount of Being. Through his inclining tree, the fifteenth-century painter renders one of Ibn 'Arabi's major symbolic visual images:

"When the Muhammadan branch appeared . . . the Qur'an descended for to confirm it, and the Tree of All Beings shivered with joy and its colors and twigs all trembled. Yet from the branches of this Tree, there arose one, [the Devil], who moved forth toward the Left side, and inclined toward delusion. Now, when the winds were sent forth to deliver the prophetic message, 'We sent Thee not, but as a Mercy for all creatures' [Qur'an 21:107, Yusuf 'Ali trans.], those beforehand prepared for the Divine Beauties to whiff such scents did incline thereto with yearning, but those whose sense of scent was stopped, and whose capacity to receive had been wrenched away from them, were debarred therefrom, and so the storms of the Divine Power raged against them, and these who once flourished now withered, their countenance of joy turned into a frown, and their hope to thrive was blasted to despair."[9]

According to Ibn 'Arabi's visual symbolism, branches detached from the Tree of Life become withered because deprived of sap; such branches signify the dead and despairing souls fated to become the Devil's prey (similar to the dry trunks destined to fall beneath John the Baptist's ax in the imagery of the Gospels, as in Matthew 3:10, or to the thorny twigs in Dante's forest of the suicidal damned in *Inferno*, canto 13). Rumi in turn devotes a whole tale (*Mathnawi* , book 2, verses 2604–2792) to the Devil as God's chief wood-cutter, charged by God to roam this earth and ruthlessly to fell all its withered trunks—signifying damned souls—and so to consign them to the fire. Members of Bihzad's royal workshop were well aware of such allegories of dead wood in the writings of Ibn 'Arabi, Nizami, Rumi, and Jami. Bihzad appropriately scatters his desert landscape with hooked, thorny stumps crossing their branches in blind agony, further to signify Malikha's damnation, pictorially associated by the artist with the Devil's tortured and screaming rock: for the Jew's damnation, and the Devil's, are fundamentally one and the same.

'Attar's mystical subtleties

Nizami's contemporary, the great Persian mystical poet 'Attar, in his *Ilahi-Nameh* or "Godly Book" brings further yet more subtle nuances to bear upon the sadness of such traditional Islamic perception of Jews by twisting the blade in deeper.

According to 'Attar, once upon a time a Muslim emir grew rich through legal tribute or *jizya* owed him by his many Jewish subjects. But then a certain Sufi devotee wished to humble himself publicly both before this emir and before all the kingdom, and, most especially, in the eyes of God, by proclaiming himself so abject that he did not deserve to pay even one hundred times over the *jizya* tribute to one hundred of the kingdom's most abject Jews—and this, despite the fact that such Jews constituted absolute abjection: "I answered the king: thus do I know, that I am so steeped in shame, that I know that I should render unto one hundred abject Jews the *jizya* that they, from me, might rightly demand."[10] The word "abject" is borrowed here from Fuad Rouhani's authoritative French translation, but 'Attar's original Persian *parēshān* could also signify "troubled," "perplexed," or "distracted"—and in 'Attar's view, the Jews were "distracted" for failing to acknowledge Muhammad and, before him, Jesus, even though Jesus, in his immense mercy, forgave them: "Jesus the most pure passed one day through a street where the shameless Jews cast insults upon him; but he, of purity born, with clear brow answered them with prayers; said one to him: 'Are you not troubled, that they should so insult you, and you with prayers answer them?' Christ answered him: 'Only what every soul holds in store may such a soul disburse.'"[11]

In 'Attar's understanding, Judaism, Christianity, and Islam represent three successive spiritual stages in humanity's perception of the divine reality: Jews, according to the Sufi view, upheld God's transcendence without recognizing his immanence; Christians became too absorbed in the contemplation of God's immanence and so forgot to maintain God's equally important transcendence; only accomplished Muslims, correctly guided by Muhammad, might perceive at once the single and transcendent God—and also God manifest, and immanent, throughout all creation.

In 'Attar's meditation, however, no mere ritual or external practice, however diligent, suffices to denote the true or spiritual inner Muslim. Only assiduous humility and an unrelenting and deep-probing meditation help spiritually to resolve within the devotee's mind the paradoxical riddle of Sufism's God: exalted over all earthly things, yet also present and visible in all earthly things. 'Attar thus tells the story of a certain Muslim sage who humbly refused, upon his deathbed, to be buried among other Muslims—because he did not believe himself worthy. Nor, however, did this Sufi wish to be buried among the Jews—for whom he had only the harshest words. This sage's humility derived, instead, from his own self-perceived failure to have pierced and reconciled, throughout his lifelong meditation, the twin transcendent and immanent aspects of the Divine. Or rather, the sage acknowledged his lifelong failure to pass beyond the mere Judaic phase of upholding God's transcendence, to reach the higher and far more difficult mystical perception of Divine Transcendence and Immanence fully united, which is the boon of true Islamic spirituality; instead, the unhappy sage had lingered in between: "The Light of Muslims I have not; how should I then be buried in the

A Sufi poet points down at Iblis (the devil, his face darkened, with a yoke around his neck) as God's woodcutter, charged, with the help of his followers, to cut dead wood (signifying damned souls). Illustration by Bihzad for 'Attar's history of the fool drowned by the weight of his beard, with added visual reference to the tale of the caliph Mu'awiya and the devil in Rumi's *Mathnavi*. In 'Attar, *Mantiq at-Tayr*, Herat, 1487. New York, Metropolitan Museum of Art.

true believers' plot? But nor with the Jews do I wish to be buried, these Jews who for the Prophet never showed concern. Between both yards should lie my burial ground; to such ground carry me, for I belong neither to one, nor to the other group. A Muslim's way I have followed not, nor have I trod the path of Jews. Between the first and second lies my place, until whatever fate of mine befalls."[12]

'Attar cultivated a decidedly Sufi taste for the spiritual paradox: the sudden "overflow" or *shath* of apparently absurd or saucy statements designed to jolt conventional believers out of their ordinary mental grooves and provoke a lively awakening of their mystical perception. The poet here appears even to overturn his previous condemnation of Judaism, indeed, instead to praise Jews.

'Attar thus relates how the Prophet Muhammad one day surprised the future caliph 'Umar leisurely perusing a copy of the Torah, and scolded him for it: not for so peering into the Holy Book of the Jews, but for not then truly implicating himself fully in the Jewish faith, for not becoming completely involved in either Judaism or Islam.

> *Better the sincere Jew, 'Attar affirms, and also the zealous Christian, devout Zoroastrian, or truly pious Hindu, than a lukewarm Muslim, observant in words but not in heart.*

'Attar's sectarian stand seems here to fissure: indeed, better the sincere Jew, 'Attar affirms, and also the zealous Christian, devout Zoroastrian, or truly pious Hindu, than a lukewarm Muslim, observant in words but not in heart: "'Umar one day took up a passage of the Torah; the Prophet, when he saw him, thus spoke: one must not so toy with the Torah unless you intend to become a true Jew; truly must you become a true Jew, for better a Jew, than any lukewarm folk. You remain neither this, nor yet that; half-measures are forbidden; here [in the spiritual path] behoove no half-measures; you show yourself neither a wholehearted infidel, nor yet, in your faith, are you wholehearted. Tell me then, in what stage do you find yourself?"[13] 'Attar here embraces Sufism's twin extreme attitudes: scorn for the Jews, considered to have fallen from God's grace for having rejected first Jesus then Muhammad, but admiration nevertheless for those Jews truly sincere and learned in their faith (reminding one, for that matter, of Islamic civilization's historic debt to brilliant converted Jews like Ka'b al-Ahbar and Wahb ibn Munabbih, among the very earliest elucidators of the Qur'an).

Even the great Rumi . . .

Mawlana or *Mevlana* ("our lord") Jalaluddin Rumi (1207–73), the Central Asian–born poet who taught under the protection of the Seljuk sultans of Konya in Turkey, ranks among Sufi sages as one of the most tolerant and humane toward Jews, or at any rate, and far more important, was so considered by his spiritual tradition, whether in his adopted home in Anatolia or throughout the Islamic world, in the many centuries following his death. Rumi's fourteenth-century Persian-language hagiography written by Aflaki thus tells how members of all the tributary religions present in Konya in 1273 during Rumi's funeral vied with the Muslims in carrying the master's bier: "all wept, each group marched forth holding up their sacred text according to their respective custom, reciting verses from the Psalter, Torah, and Gospels, and wailing cries of mourning; the Muslims could hardly keep them back with sticks and the flats of their swords."[14] If Aflaki is to be believed, Rumi's generous teachings led Konya's Jews to glimpse the underlying and abiding "Muhammadan Reality" (*Ḥaqīqa Muḥammadiya*) in their own Moses, just as their Christian neighbors were similarly led to see this same Muhammadan Reality in their own Christ—or to quote the exact words: "If you Muslims see the Reverend Mevlana as the 'Muhammad' of his own age, we know him as our own 'Moses,' as our own 'Jesus.'"[15]

Rumi's personal tolerance and kindness are not in question here, but certainly his own theology's strict allegorical demands—compelling depiction of Jews as souls spiritually afflicted with diabolic blindness—remain as harsh in his verses as any in Dante's poetry in much the same period in the Christian West. As with Dante again, every verse in Rumi's own great poem mirrors the poet's entire cosmology encompassing both the exalted and the atrocious—like the universe itself. Rumi's own divine comedy, the *Mathnawi-i Maʿnawi* or "Spiritual Couplets," draws, like Dante's spiritual epic, upon multiple literary sources. Again, like the Florentine poet, Rumi sets an exceedingly somber tone almost at the very outset of his poem by telling the story of a cruel Jewish king—a shadow of the historical Herod Antipas the Tetrarch—as persecutor of Jesus and of the early Christians.

Now, according to Rumi, spiritual opacity is an allegorical trait associated not only with Jews—"and cover not Truth with falsehood, nor conceal the Truth when ye know (what it is)," according to the Qurʾan's explicit words in 2:42—but with the Devil himself, described in sundry classical Islamic texts as symbolically bleary-eyed, squint-eyed, cross-eyed, one-eyed, nearsighted, or blind, with all his bewildered disciples. One outward sign of Antichrist, in Islamic tradition, is that he is one-eyed, like one aspect of the Devil, to which the Antichrist character closely corresponds. This figure of Antichrist from John's book of Revelation haunted Near Eastern imaginations into Islamic times under the Arabic name of Dajjal "the Deceiver." According to Islamic eschatology, Dajjal the Antichrist will appear among men at the end of time to spread corruption on the earth, before the triumphal return of a Qurʾanic Jesus. Christ will then overthrow Dajjal from the highest minaret in Damascus to proclaim Judgment Day and full accomplishment of the Muhammadan cycle of prophetic revelation. Yet despite his many disguises, Dajjal remains recognizable because one-eyed or otherwise afflicted and disfigured with diseased sight. In the popular Sufi lore pervading *The Thousand and One Nights* (as collected in fifteenth-century Egypt), one demon imprisoned by Solomon in a pillar of stone, in the midst of the desert, thus cries out to passing travelers both his despair and his name: Dahish ibn al-Aʿmash, "The Amazed, son of the Bleary-Eyed" (in "The Tale of the City of Brass"); in another story, three princes each blinded by the Devil in one eye tell a caliph how each committed grave spiritual sin but now repented for following the Devil by all three becoming wandering mendicant dervishes (in "The Tale of the Three Ladies of Baghdad").

According to the *Gulshan-i Raz* or "Rose-Bower of Mystery," a standard Persian reference book in richly textured verses of allegorical Sufi images composed for his disciples in 1317 by Mahmud Shabistari, "blind is the view that assimilates God to all earthly things in His visible Immanence or *Tashbīh* (Christians and idolaters); but it is to be one-eyed to perceive only God's invisible transcendence or *Tanzīh* (like the Jews)."[16] This same grim idea—assimilating those who suffer as "one-eyed" to the spiritual opacity of the Jews, and in turn to the Devil's own "one-eyed" or "squint-eyed" spiritual state—is further dramatically allegorized by Rumi in one of the great opening tales of his *Mathnawi*.

The Jewish king portrayed in Rumi's tale as persecuting the world's first Christians is explicitly compared by the poet with Dajjal the Antichrist himself. For this tyrant too harasses the followers of Christ. His eyesight is squinting or befogged. His very name is King Ahwal, that is, "the Cross-Eyed," "Squint-Eyed," or "Bleary-Eyed One." He puts thousands of Christian martyrs to death. But when this cruel Hebrew monarch realizes that he will never, ever be able to uproot the new sect by force, he listens to the cruel advice of his fanatical minister, a Jewish devotee who proclaims himself ready to endure every sacrifice in order to defend ancient Judaism by suffocating Christianity at birth (Rumi's Ottoman commentators, well aware of Christian dogma, tended to identify this character in the poem, simply called "the Jewish minister" by the poet, with Saint Paul himself).

> *According to Sufi perception, a single abiding Holy Spirit breathed through the entire succession of prophets since Adam.*

This perfidious Jewish vizier suggests to the king to ruin the Christians, instead, by means of a trick. The king should publicly accuse the vizier as a Christian and sentence him to a scaffold before all the people, there to have his nose, ears, and hands cut off by the executioner. Thus mutilated and hideous, the vizier will then be able to credibly introduce himself among the Christians as one of their own, and delude them separately, unbeknownst to one another, with lying and mutually contradictory doctrines, whence, according to the poet, the subsequent breakup of Christianity among warring sects: "Among the Jews there was a king who wrought oppression, an enemy of Jesus and a destroyer of Christians. / 'Twas the epoch of Jesus and the turn was his [i.e., it was his turn to appear as a prophet]: he was the soul of Moses, and Moses the soul of him; / But the squint-eyed [double-seeing] king separated in the way of God those two Divine [prophets] who were [really] in accord [with each other]."[17]

Now, what Rumi's King Ahwal "the Bleary-Eyed" Jew fails to perceive, from the very beginning of the fable, is the underlying mystery of prophecy. According to Sufi perception, a single abiding Holy Spirit breathed through the entire succession of prophets from Adam through Abraham and Moses and Jesus, until Muhammad. This Spirit was also a single radiant Light, which was one and the same Muhammadan Light (*Nūr Muḥammadī*) or eternal Muhammadan Reality (*Ḥaqīqa Muḥammadiyya*), shining through and upon the countenances of all these prophets. According to deeper levels of Sufi understanding, the Light of Prophecy first became manifest in the person of Adam as the Perfect Man or Prototypical Human Being (*Insān Kāmil* = the *anthropos teleios* of Byzantine theology and Adam Kadmon of the thirteenth-century Castilian Jewish Kabbalists): that is, Adam before the Fall. Upon the countenance of this primordial Adam therefore first glimmered the eternal Muhammadan Light, before the bedazzled angels. But Adam succumbed to the Devil's wiles in this lower world, and his countenance darkened. To save humanity and lead it back to the straight path of correct perception of the Divine, a succession of prophets from Enoch to Jesus has been needed—each of whom, however, manifested the same Muhammadan Light upon his respective countenance, although with nuances in the

Adam, the Perfect Man, and the prostration of the angels, except for the Devil, according to a Persian rendition of Tha'labi's *Tales of the Prophets*, around 1595 (?). Paris, Bibliothèque Nationale de France, ms. or. suppl. Persian 1313, fol. 6v.

Light suitable to the specific message of each of these holy envoys who were, nevertheless, every single one of them, the Perfect Man of each's own time. Thus, the Muhammadan Light has been fundamentally the same to shine through Enoch and Noah, Abraham and Joseph, Moses and David, Solomon and Christ. This is the central mystery that Rumi's King Ahwal fails to grasp.

The Light blazed forth again in purest brightness through Muhammad, when the Prophet of Islam in mystical ecstasy attained supreme revelation in his visionary, heavenly ascent as high as the Throne of God: as the New Adam free of sin, or Perfect Man, sent to complete humanity's cycle of fall and redemption. But the spiritually one-eyed or squint-eyed Jews, then Christians, misled by the blinding masks and disguises of the Devil, have failed to distinguish the Muhammadan Light's abiding glow, which yet shone so clearly through their own prophets Moses and Jesus. Rumi ends his tale in deliberate echo to Qur'an 61:6, which reads: "And remember, Jesus, the son of Mary, said: 'O Children of Israel! I am the apostle of Allah (sent) to you confirming the Law [*Tawrāt,* "Torah"] (which came) before me, and giving Glad Tidings [Evangels] of an Apostle to come after me, whose name shall be Ahmad" (Yusuf ʿAli trans.). Since according to Muslim readings, Jesus foretold that after him would come an elect one or *Muṣṭafā,* that is *Aḥmad,* "the most lauded one," a transparent variant of the name Muhammad, Rumi writes: "The name of Mustafā was in the Gospel—(Mustafā) the chief of the prophets, the sea of purity" (book 1, verse 727, Nicholson trans.).[18]

Rumi himself, of course, never expresses anything but veneration for Moses and Jesus—as holy prophets illuminated each in their own day by the Muhammadan Reality. But the squint-eyed king of his fable symbolizes rigid Judaism, incapable of recognizing Jesus and even less Muhammad announced by Jesus. The Hebrew tyrant of the tale fails to decipher the deeper sense of Moses's message, in his stubborn insistence to contemplate only the letter's most opaque surface of an immutable Law. Rumi's Jewish king thus persecutes Jesus's disciples, but cannot see that Jesus himself, who appeared in his own age, pursued Moses's prophetic cycle—just as the Jews of Medina, many centuries later, would reject Muhammad also: "covering the Truth with falsehood" and "concealing the Truth when they knew it" to borrow the Qurʾanic phrasing. Aflaki, Rumi's early Ottoman Muslim chronicler, sympathetically understood that the Jewish and Christian crowds in Konya who so loudly mourned Rumi at his funeral had respectively recognized in the sublime poet the true "Moses" or "Jesus" of their own time—and so does Aflaki actually praise them. But in the much deeper view of Rumi himself, followed by his chronicler Aflaki, Judaism and Christianity *as such* nevertheless symbolize two abiding, fundamental errors of spiritual perception, that is, two permanent bodies of incomplete and forever mistaken dogma, indeed, two categories of mental deficiency for all time to come—and this would remain the case even if all the *individual* Jews and Christians of Konya in 1273 had happily happened to convert to Islam while the poet lay dying. The medieval attitude (among all three Abrahamic creeds) toward alleged religious error, or heresy, might be likened here to that of the modern mathematician regarding a mistake; a mathematical error remains a permanent error, even if the given *individual* mathematician happens, fortunately, to correct himself. Such a mathematically rigid intellectual approach, regarding disapproved spiritual attitudes, likewise structures the entire symbolic hierarchy of the damned in Dante's *Inferno,* where all those souls who either remained unaware of Christ, or rejected him, are doomed to linger forever, as permanent symbols or emblems of their own specific spiritual state: whether good pagans like Virgil, estimable Muslims like Averroes, or evil Jews like Caiaphas the high priest.

The "squint-eyed" Jew who failed to see the Oneness of Muhammadan Light

The Jewish King in Rumi's fable, therefore, unfortunately expresses the Sufi poet's intimate conviction regarding Judaism itself. The evil Hebrew monarch in the poet's story is fated to remain an allegorical "squint-eyed one" or Ahwal: because forever deficient in clear spiritual sight, and so permanently incapable of perceiving the central Sufi mystery of prophecy, as a pathetic ruler who blinks his symbolically weak eyes and turns them away from the same and eternal Muhammadan Light that shone through the true Moses and the true Jesus as successive manifestations of the Perfect Man.

The name Ahwal, given by Rumi to his Jewish king, requires some further comment here, since the word used by the poet normally signifies "seeing double"—one more characteristic trait attributed to the Devil (along with one-eyed affliction) in Islamic lore. According to Rumi, the holy persons of Moses and Jesus, despite historical appearances, corresponded not to *two*, but only to *one single* Prophetic Reality. The unfortunate Jewish king, however, "saw them double," as if they were altogether distinct individuals. Here the Sufi poet resorts to mordant irony with a pinch of comedy similar to Dante's fierce little jokes in the depths of Hell. Rumi's bewildered Jewish ruler believes that he defends the intransigent monotheism of Mosaic Law against the early Christians. In fact, this king's mental attitude splits the universe *in twain*. Jesting at the Jewish king's expense, Rumi introduces a funny little anecdote about a master glassblower's cross-eyed apprentice: "The master said to a (squint-eyed) pupil, 'Come on; go, fetch that bottle out of the room.' / Said the squint-eyed one: 'Which of the two bottles shall I bring to you? Explain fully.' / 'There are not two bottles,' replied the master; 'go, leave off squinting and do not be seeing more (than one).' 'O master,' said he, 'don't chide me.' Said the master, 'Smash one of those two.' / The bottle was one, though in his eyes it seemed two; when he broke the bottle, there was no other. / When one was broken, both vanished from sight: a man is made squint-eyed by (evil) propensity and anger. / Anger and lust make a man squint-eyed, they change the spirit (so that it departs) from rectitude. / When self-interest appears, virtue becomes hidden: a hundred veils rise from the heart to the eye. / When the cadi lets bribery gain hold of his heart, how should he know the wronger from the wretched victim of wrong? / The king, from Jewish rancor, became so squint-eyed that (we cry), 'Mercy, O Lord, mercy (save us from such affliction)!' / He slew hundreds of thousands of wronged (innocent) believers, saying, 'I am the protection and support of the religion of Moses.'"[19]

Even thus briefly touched upon by the poet with a shaft of comic light, Rumi's Jewish king, who "sees double," nevertheless does correspond to the Devil, as all the poem's Ottoman commentators have stressed.[20] Indeed, the poet multiplies explicit allusions to Satan, warning his readers from unknowingly sealing the Devil's pact by quoting a proverb that directly echoes Nizami's diabolic *Tale of the Turquoise Pavilion*—where a demon disguised offered to help an unwary traveler by extending his hand to grasp: only to lure his victim into further perils. Rumi in turn admonishes, "Since there is many a devil who hath the face of Adam, it is not well to give your hand to every hand."[21]

Because they ignored this proverb's force, the unsuspecting Christians in Rumi's tale placed their misguided trust in the rascally, mutilated Jewish vizier whose mission

While the Tree of Life bows before her *Tajalli* (theophany), the crested hoopoe as Solomon's messenger addresses the world's bird-souls, turning her back upon the puzzled hunter with musket who signifies the Devil; in the rocks, multiple iterations of Sakhr, the devil figure trapped in stone by Solomon. Illustration by Habib Allah of Mashhad to the *Mantiq al-Tayr* by ʾAttar, "The Hoopoe Addresses the Assembled Birds," Isfahan, 1609. New York, Metropolitan Museum of Art.

not only foreshadowed the Dajjal's, whose name means literally "to deceive," but whose actions literally reflected yet another Arabic name for the Devil himself, Iblis. Rumi, in accordance with all Islamic tradition in his day, closely associated this name Iblis with the Arabic word *talbīs*, which conveys such notions as "disguise," "camouflage," "ambiguity," or again, "deceit." R. A. Nicholson renders the title to the subsection of Rumi's tale that begins with verse 1, 348, *Talbis-i Vazir ba Nusara*, as, "How the vizier brought the Christians into doubt and perplexity"; one might more literally suggest, "The deceitful diabolization of the Christians by the vizier."

At any rate, Rumi's own words make clear, and beyond all doubt, that his Jewish vizier fully plays the role of Antichrist the One-Eyed Dajjal, the diabolic false prophet of the end of days, to blear the spiritual eyes of unwary souls and lead them all astray: "The Christians all gave their hearts to him: what (how great), indeed, is the blind conformity of the vulgar! / They planted love of him within their breasts, they were regarding him as the vicar of Jesus. / He inwardly (in reality) was the accursed one-eyed Antichrist [Dajjal]. O God, do Thou (hear and) answer the cry (of those in trouble)—what a good helper art Thou!"[22]

The "Devil's use" according to al-Hallaj

Mystical Islam's farthest-reaching meditations on the Devil's necessary "veiling," then punishment, go back to outrageous utterances for which the wandering dervish al-Hallaj became notorious, before he was crucified for heresy by Baghdad's aghast caliphal authorities in 922 CE. Unanimous Sufi posterity, however, came to revere al-Hallaj as a spiritual master and saint. Al-Hallaj's extraordinary speculations regarding Satan's damnation mainly revolve around those verses in the Qurʾan's second sura (2:42)—quoted at the beginning of this essay—which so closely echo Isaiah in bitterly inveighing against the children of Israel: "cover not Truth with falsehood, nor conceal the Truth when ye know (what it is)" (Yusuf ʿAli trans.). The first words in the Arabic now read: *Lā talbisū l-Ḥaqq*, with the noun *al-Ḥaqq* or "Truth," as it happens, also representing one of the very names of God revealed unto Muhammad, and the verb *talbisū* or "ye conceal" conjugating the three consonants that form the Arabic root-stem *l-b-s*, generally implying such notions as "revetment," "veiling," "cloaking," or "masking."

According to traditional glosses of Qurʾanic verse 2:42 (Suyuti's fifteenth-century Egyptian commentary may serve here to summarize them all) when the Jews of Medina refused to recognize Muhammad as God's new envoy, thereby "masking" the Truth announced in their own Scriptures: "Cover not [mingle not] the Truth [that was revealed unto you] with falsehood [the Truth which you diminish], nor conceal the Truth [which Muhammad described] when ye know [that it is the Truth]."[23] This Qurʾanic passage, now, immediately follows the dramatic narrative of Satan's damnation, and the headlong fall of that proud archangel whom the second sura, in verses 30–36, calls Iblis.

Satan, in Arabic *Shayṭān*, in Hebrew signified the "adversary," the angel of contradiction who first appears in the book of Job before turning, in the last few centuries before Christ, under the influence of Persian dualism into the very personification of the principle of Evil. Then Iblis, the other usual name for the Devil in Islam, derives, of course, from Christian Greek διάβολος, the "Divider" or "Slanderer" of Matthew 4:1, whence also comes the Latin *diabolus*. Nevertheless, Islamic tradition, by inverting consonants, determinedly sought to link this Qurʾanic name Iblis (2:34) to the Arabic root-stem *l-b-s*, in the Qurʾanic verb used only a few verses later (2:42) to convey the diabolic "dissimulation" of the Truth by the Jews in Medina: "conceal not the Truth." Such diabolic etymology, now, by closely linking, in effect, the story of the archangel who fell for refusing to worship Adam, with the case of the wretched Jews expelled from Medina for rejecting Muhammad's prophecy, to signify in both cases a "dissimulation" or "veiling" of the Truth or the Divine Message, might not agree with strict linguistic history, yet nevertheless appeared charged with profound spiritual truths to Sufi readers of the Qurʾan.

In one of his famously difficult mystical texts, *Ta-Sin al-Azal wa-l-Iltibas* or "Book of the Mysterious Letters Regarding Pre-Eternity and the Veil of Ambiguity", al-Hallaj first stressed the link which he discerned between the Fallen Archangel, on the one hand, and such notions as "veiling," "revetment," "mask," "entanglement," on the other, as expressed by two Arabic nouns derived from the same Arabic root-stem *l-b-s*: *talbīs* and *iltibās*, both in Arabic usage taken to mean either "dissimulation" or "ambiguity" (whence also more ordinary Arabic words like *libsa*, "costume," and *libās*, "dress").[24]

The highly complex Sufi notion conveyed by the twin, deliberately contrasted terms of *Tajalli*, the Divine Manifestation or Theophany (as in Christ's Transfiguration atop Mount Tabor in Matthew 17:1–9 or Mark 2:2–9), and *Iltibās*, or diabolic "veiling," might be sketched as follows, in accordance with Ibn ʿArabi's early thirteenth-century summation: God, invisible and transcendent, created this visible universe. This visible universe, now, thus became God's mirror. But this universe was only a diffuse and clouded mirror: in modern terminology, a cosmos largely devoid of self-awareness. But when God created the Human Being, God brought forth into the universe a particular consciousness that was finally capable of conceiving, or thinking, God. This Human consciousness, pure and sharp in the case of Prophets and Saints, serves as God's own pure, sharp, and polished mirror: as it were, serving to reflect God made Visible unto God Invisible. The Perfect Man—who was first Adam, then each of the prophets until Muhammad, and since Muhammad the line of saints—thus looms as the visible mirror of an invisible God. In this mirror that is Man, God looks upon God. Man is thus the Theophany: or God Manifest in Man. But the falling Archangel, doomed to become the Devil, failed to recognize this mirrored God in Man. Thereby, the human figure turned into a "veil" before the Devil's deficient spiritual eyesight. Moreover, God, by his very own Creation, "veils" the Godhead unto the spiritually clouded eyes of those incapable of recognizing him within either of his two mirrors: the diffuse mirror that is the cosmos, and the sharp mirror that is Man. The Devil thereby comes to symbolize the very "Veil" of God. God masks the Godhead unto the Devil's weak eyes, but in fact the Devil himself, without realizing it, acts as a mask of God, chosen by God, willfully brought forth by God, in order to debar from the vision of God those spiritually unworthy to behold their God. In Islamic mystical thought, the Devil is thus, first and foremost, himself the very "Veil" that serves to "cloak" or "mask" the Truth.

Even where the Devil does affirm his belief in God, it is primarily to maintain the dogma of an eternally transcendent and so invisible God. But the Devil errs here, and damns himself, for refusing to look into the cosmic and also the human mirror of a God who is Immanent as well—and therefore visible. This is how the Devil, as conceived in Sufi thought, does come to resemble the Jews as perceived, at any rate, by their Christian and then by their Muslim foes, portrayed by both later creeds as members of an earlier creed who stubbornly maintained throughout the centuries the invisible transcendence (*tanzīh*) of their God, but forever refused to see the visible immanence (*tashbīh*) of God mirrored in Jesus, then in Muhammad, whom the Jews did historically reject in turn.

The Devil thus becomes the first victim of his own entanglements, because his own spiritual mask permanently veils his eyesight, since he fails to see through his own mask to recognize the Theophany or *Tajallī* appearing before him in the mirroring countenance of the Perfect Man (be he Adam, Jesus, or Muhammad), that is, the mirror of their perfect prophetic consciousness spotlessly reflecting the Divine. The twelfth-century Iraqi theologian Ibn al-Jawzi violently criticized al-Hallaj's apparent admiration for a heroic-seeming Satan, but did pay al-Hallaj the ultimate compliment of borrowing from the master's own "diabolic" etymology to castigate al-Hallaj himself, referring to the earlier master's thought as a *Talbīs Iblīs*, or "Devil's Camouflage," by which Ibn al-Jawzi meant the "revetment" of ambiguous illusions, woven throughout this lower world, and within our own minds, through the dizziness of our senses, by Satan himself, constantly seeking to make us err, just as he errs himself, as he stubbornly tries to turn away our spiritual eyes from the Divine Truth. As master of cosmic illusion in this lower world, Sufism's Devil resembles in many respects the demon Mara who attempts through his web of visual sorceries to distract the meditating Buddha from perceiving the underlying reality of the Universe. Iranian Manichaeism in the third century CE retained this aspect of Buddhist thought in its portrayal of Satan as an evil god locked in perpetual combat against the God of Good, and as demonic lord over this lower world of the senses that is visible to our eyes but illusory. Medieval schools of thought in both Christendom and Islam absorbed many Manichaean ideas (far more than they knew), dedicating enormous spiritual energy to imagining (and dreading) an earthly existence largely dominated by this Satan the Tempter under his many names: Shaytan the Adversary, Dajjal the Deceiver, Iblis the Veiler: one who deceives so many souls because he is deceived himself.

Nevertheless, despite his own diabolic etymology for Iblis as the Veiler, al-Hallaj, certainly the boldest of all Sufis in shocking crowds in his own day with spiritual paradoxes that seemed utterly to turn the normal sense of words inside out (or *bi-'aks al-ma'ānī*, "in reversal of the meanings," referring to the trap of perception into which the Devil falls because he sees all significances in reverse),[25] nevertheless appeared impertinently to rehabilitate the insolent Devil himself, and even to glorify him. First, al-Hallaj seemed to justify Satan's apparently heroic refusal to recognize the Divine Manifestation in Adam. When God created Adam, the Devil indeed refused to bow down before a creature wrought by God, hence, other than God. When threatened with eternal damnation by God, the Devil accepted perpetual martyrdom both in the proper sense of "bearing witness" and in the derived sense of "victim": as one chastised with exile, devoured by flames, yet proclaiming himself a "humble lover," *muḥib dhalīl*, like a Sufi, in the very name of the intransigently defended principle to worship no other god but God, even were he forever to register, in his own tormented person, the primordial principle ordained by the Divinity Itself. Al-Hallaj consequently makes his Devil cry out these verses: "*Juḥūdī laka taqdīs-un*: To reject (Thy command) is to affirm Thee holy! My wit in Thee is all bewildered! For there is no Adam without Thee! And what in between is Iblis!"[26] Al-Hallaj further stupefied audiences in Baghdad with affirmations like these: "Among heaven's folk there was not a monotheist (*muwaḥḥid*) like unto Iblis: for the Essence shifted before him, he forbade himself any glance in his journey, and he worshipped the Worshipped One in ascetic isolation."[27] Al-Hallaj even dared to affirm: "I compete with the Devil and Pharaoh in spiritual chivalry (*futuwwa*). For the Devil said: 'If I had prostrated myself, the very name of chivalry would have fallen away from me.' And Pharaoh said: 'If I had believed in His Envoy (Moses), I myself should have fallen from the rank of chivalry.'"[28] This double rejection of Adam by the Devil, who consequently fell into the flames, and of Moses by Pharaoh, who perished in the waves, or twin successive refusals of the Perfect Man of their own respective day by the blasted archangel and the drowned ruler of Egypt, thus appear exalted as twin examples of heroic knighthood by al-Hallaj's mystical impertinence.

The greatness and wretchedness of the Devil

In the view of mature Sufi thought as crystallized in the works of the Spanish-born mystic Ibn ʿArabi, God and Man constitute twin poles. An Invisible God is mirrored in Visible Man. Satan is damned between both poles for failing to recognize God mirrored in Man.

According to Ibn ʿArabi's chapter dealing with Adam, in his seminal *Gemstones of Wisdom* (or *Bezels of Wisdom*, *Fusus al-Hikam*) completed in Damascus in about 1220.

Satan's damnation is the tragedy of an archangelic soul fated forever to mirror the darker side of God before God's Manifestation. When God becomes Manifest in Man, and Immanent through Man, then God shows unto the world the Divinity's aspect of Love and Grace (*Lutf*). But because Satan rejected such Immanence, and maintained only the Divine's invisible Transcendence, then Satan came to reflect the Divinity's Wrath (*Qahr*). Since, according to Ibn ʿArabi, every Name signifies a reflection of a given aspect of the Divine, then Satan, too, remains a mirror—albeit a cracked, partial piece of the mirror of the Divine, since "the Devil is but a fraction of the Cosmos":[29] and the mirroring Cosmos, itself, is none other but God Manifest. What the fallen archangel reflects is the Cosmic Wrath, which overwhelms and damns him.

In pre-Eternity, according to al-Hallaj, whose symbolic etymologies Ibn ʿArabi for his own part took care to sound in immense depth, the archangel's mirroring name had been ʿAzazil (literally "the Might of God," but with a further, disquieting symbolic implication suggested by the originally unrelated Arabic root-stem *ʿ-z-l*, "to become separate," that is, from God). Once damned, the archangel Iblis "the Veiler" turns into the Terrible Name of the Divinity that knowingly hides Itself from the eyesight of all unworthy souls. The Divinity of Wrath thus speaks unto the Divinity Itself, but through the Devil's voice—only the Devil, with tragic irony, does not know this. The Devil is only an angel, and worse, a rebel angel, and the angels who fell with him are mere specks of the cosmic mirror that only correspond to diverse impulses and faculties within the consciousness of sovereign Man himself; in the case of the fallen angels, these specks represent such negative mental faculties in Man as lust and wrath: "All this was merely sedition, and such sedition [i.e., the sedition or mischief, which the recalcitrant angels accusingly said that Adam and his seed would one day spread throughout the world] is precisely what befell unto them."[30] Even when proclaiming himself God's "humble lover," the Devil is fated to love only the Wrathful Aspect of the Divine: "Each faculty thereof is veiled by its own self, and sees not beyond its own essence . . . Each and every one individual knows of the Divine Truth only what each one individual's own essence bestows . . . The Divine Names are, in their essence, the Named One Itself [the Divinity]; they are none other than It [the Divinity]."[31]

According to Ibn ʿArabiʾ, one name of God is the Truth, *al-Ḥaqq*. By definition, non-Truth does not exist, hence, everything that is Truth exists, and all that exists is God, since God is the Truth: this is Ibn ʿArabiʾs absolute pantheism or monism. In Ibn ʿArabiʾs conception of existence, moreover, each Name designates a mental category, just as a given numeral in mathematics designates a specific given quantity, and may in no way go beyond or "conceive" a number superior to itself. Satan, as the Evil "who veils," is thus certainly a part of the Truth. Yet the Devil, by his very name Iblis, designates his own essential delimitation as the Veiler. The Devil thus represents that part of the Cosmos—or God—that signifies the terrifying aspect of God veiling Himself to the unworthy, the God of Wrath.

This logical, even rigidly, and, as it were, mathematically cruel grid in the great medieval perception of the universe tended to slice accepted perceptions of human (or angelic) psychology into distinct fractions. In Ibn ʿArabiʾs view, for example, only in the consciousness of the Perfect Man did all the Names of the Cosmos, however contradictory in themselves, become reconciled. But Satan was not the Perfect Man, hence, his limited awareness mirrored contradictory Cosmic Names that, within his own defective meditation, clashed and crushed him. Like Dante questioning his damned heroes in Hell with a touch of both admiration and austere pity for their irreversible doom, al-Hallaj proclaims his esteem for the "monotheistic" Devil's heroic "spiritual chivalry," paired with Pharaoh's "chivalry," for thus intransigently championing God's Transcendence and Lordship—two of the Names of the Divine, after all—against the very God who crushes them both.

Just as Iblis is consigned to perpetual damnation in Sufi thought, so each of Dante's damned souls manifests his or her own particular deficient mental category, or name of a sin, which with implacable logic, both defines and condemns the victim to everlasting Hell: like Caiaphas the Jewish high priest "so vilely crucified, but prone, in eternal exile," in canto 23 of the *Inferno* (verses 125–26), for having, in his spiritual blindness, called for the crucifixion of Christ. But recognition of a given damned soul's tragic delimitation prevents neither Dante, nor al-Hallaj, nor Ibn ʿArabi, from expressing admiration for this or that estimable quality—Ulysses's wanderlust, Pharaoh's or the Devil's spiritual heroism in stubbornly championing God's transcendence—within the soul of this or that damned victim consigned to everlasting pain. The early twelfth-century Persian mystic Ahmad al-Ghazali (brother of the celebrated orthodox theologian Abu-Hamid al-Ghazali) thus dared even proclaim: "Whoever fails to learn his monotheism (*tawḥīd*) from the Devil himself, is himself a heretic (*zindīq*)!"[32]

But in so depicting, after al-Hallaj, a rather magnificently damned Satan, was Ibn ʿArabi also thinking of the heroic aspect of the *Jews* themselves (as perceived, of course, by Christians and Muslims) in so consenting to endure, in this lower world but in the face of God, perpetual martyrdom for obstinately denying God's immanence, in order to affirm God's invisible transcendence?

He may have. The Spanish Sufi master's *Gemstones of Wisdom* depicts the biblical prophet Noah as preaching an intransigent monotheism to the idolaters of his own day, calling upon them to renounce the cult of carved and graven images, in order to worship only a single, invisible, and transcendent God. Now, such was the prevalence of idolatry among Noah's contemporaries, Ibn ʿArabi allows, that the patriarch was indeed compelled to insist upon the Divinity's absolute transcendence, *tanzīh*. Nevertheless, Ibn ʿArabi stresses that Noah, too, fell into opposite excess, because Noah refused to recognize the Divinity's immanence—*tashbīh*—shining forth through multiple aspects in the visible manifestations of the Universe, including through the idols of the pagans themselves.[33]

Ibn ʿArabi's sardonic words, used to qualify Noah's preaching here, closely echo the vocabulary of al-Hallaj himself, where the Baghdad master ironically designated the Devil, too, as a "monotheist" or *muwaḥḥid* who fell into "separated solitude" or *ifrād*, for obstinately championing Transcendence alone. Ibn ʿArabi writes, "Know then, and may God help you here by bestowing unto you something of His Spirit / Intelligence, that to maintain Transcendence alone, in the eyes of those versed in spiritual truths regarding the Divine Aspect, is essentially a limitation and a restriction. Whoever maintains Transcendence alone is either ignorant, or a knave. And if either this same ignorant one, or this same knave, champions this absolute creed, and proclaims it, and affirms his belief in the Law [*sharīʿa*], but still maintains Transcendence alone, and stops short at the stage of Transcendence, and sees nothing beyond, then such a one is indeed a knave, one who belies the Divine Truth and the Prophets blessed by God, even if such a one does not even know it himself. He imagines that he grasps the truth, but he only belongs to the transitory past."[34]

Ibn ʿArabi, in a brief poem, summarizes the essential mystery of Sufism, which neither Noah nor the Devil could fathom. God is, at once, invisible and transcendent, and visible and immanent. Those who, like Noah and the Devil, defend only God's invisible transcendence, in their veiled vision, fail to encompass the mystery of the perfect circle of existence uniting the twin bows, transcendence and immanence, vouchsafed only to the vision of the Perfect Man. According to the opening verses of the poem:[35]

> If you affirm Transcendence alone,
> You limit Him,
> And if you affirm Immanence alone,
> You restrict Him;
> But if you affirm them both at once
> Will you be strengthened
> As an Imam, Prince in Gnosis.

Yet one medieval Sufi who seems like al-Hallaj to have rehabilitated the Devil himself—and by implication the Jews—to high heroic rank, in eternal guardianship of

God's jealous transcendence, upon God's own left side of Wrath, is the early twelfth-century Persian mystic 'Ayn-ul-Quzat of Hamadan, who writes:

"The path into this mystery is not vouchsafed to each and every one. The Devil preaches on this path, but his preaching calls *away* from Him, while Mustafā (Muhammad) preaches *toward* Him. God has placed the Devil as warden at the Gate of His Holy Majesty, saying unto him: 'Thou art our lover; defend thou, then, this Palace of our Jealous Otherness, ward off strangers therefrom, and sing thou this thy call:

> The Beloved said unto me: 'sit thou before my Gate,
>
> And suffer none to enter who embraces not
>
> My Godhead's Ultimate.'"[36]

---

1. Jules Mohl, Persian text, new ed. (Paris, 1978), 5:570–71.

2. This is the tale told to King Bahram by the Princess of Monday in the *Haft Paykar* or "Seven Icons".

3. Nizami, *Haft Paykar: Hikayat-i Gunbad-i Sabz*, Persian text ed. T. A. Magerramov (Baku/Moscow, 1987), 390, verse 205.

4. Ibid., 394, verses 238–44.

5. British Library, *Khamseh* of Nizami, Herat (in modern-day Afghanistan), 1494, Or. 6810, folio 175 verso.

6. 'Abd-ur-Razzaq al-Qashani (Pseudo-Ibn 'Arabi), *Tafsir al-Qur'an al-Karim* (mystical gloss to the Qur'an, four-teenth century [Beirut 1968] 2:356, commentary to verse 38:34: "This [demon] is called "Sakhr" [the rock] on account of his inclination to whatever is lowest, his adhesion like unto a rock toward heaviness"). On corresponding depictions of the Jews as rocks—heavy and blind—in traditional Western Christian literature and art, see Augusto Gentili, *Le storie di Carpaccio: Venezia, i Turchi, gli Ebrei* (Venice: Marsilio, 1996), 147.

7. Ibn 'Arabi, *Shajarat al-Kawn* [The Tree of Being], Cairo ed. (1941), 2; the thought of Ibn 'Arabi pervades writings by Bihzad's spiritual master, Jami of Herat, notably his *Naqd al-Nusus fi Sharh Naqsh al-Fusus* [Text Regarding Precise Points concerning the Stamping of the Gemstones], ed. W. Chittick (Tehran, 1977).

8. 'Azizuddin-i Nasafi (Bukhara, late thirteenth century), *Kitab-i Insan-i Kamil* [The Book of the Perfect Man], Persian text ed. by M. Molé (Tehran/Paris, 1962), *Dar Bayan-i an-kih tamam-i mawjudat yak Dirakht ast* [Discourse Relating as to How the Totality of Beings Are a Single Tree], 240–43.

9. Ibn 'Arabi, *Shajarat al-Kawn*, 7.

10. 'Attar, *Ilahi-Nameh*, new ed. of the Persian text by M. R. Shafi'i Kadkani (Tehran, 1388 AH/2000), 287, book 14, verses 3911–12; French trans. by Fuad Rouhani (intro. L. Massignon) (Paris, 1961), 273.

11. Ibid., Persian text, 297, book 14, verses 4146–49.

12. Ibid., Persian text, 332, book 17, verses 4870–74.

13. Ibid., Persian text, 184, book 5, verses 1686–90.

14. Aflaki (fourteenth century), *Manaqib-ol-'Arifin* [Stages of the Saints], Persian text ed. Tahsin Yazici (Ankara, 1959), 2:592.

15. Ibid.

16. Verses 102–11, Persian text, ed. Whinfield (London, 1880), 8–9, 10–11; H. Roshandil, ed. (Tehran, 1969), 62.

17. *Mathnawi*, book 1, verses 324–26, Persian text, ed. R. A. Nicholson (London 1925), 1:21; English trans. R. A. Nicholson, 1:21; for R. A. Nicholson's commentaries with the Saint Paul reference and suggested sources of the tale, ibid., 4:34–65; one might here add the ancient folkloric motif (found in Herodotus, *Histories*, 3:152–60) of the Persian king Darius the Great's loyal minister Zopyrus, who allowed himself to be so mutilated, the better to intro-duce himself as a fugitive from the king into besieged Babylon, lull and deceive the enemy defenders, and so secretly to open the gates to Darius.

18. See Nicholson's comments, 4:65, regarding the attractive hypothesis (but which he criticizes) that early Muslim scholars interpreted the Greek word Paraclete (*paraklētos*, the "Comforter") in John 14:26 to read *periklytos*, "the most lauded" (*Aḥmad* or *Muḥammad* in Arabic), contending that Christians knowingly altered the original. In Sufi understanding, while the prophetic function proper closed with Muhammad's mission, there abides in every age a Perfect Man whose mystical meditation reflects the cosmos; Seljuk and Ottoman hagiographies considered Rumi to have been such a saintly Perfect Man. Sufism distinguishes between legislating prophecy (*nubuwwa*) and sainthood proper (*walāya*), qualities certainly perceived as conjoined in the Perfect Men who were also prophets from Adam to

Muhammad; sainthood as such, however, abides in every age since Muhammad in the persons of the imams according to Shi'ite thinkers, or among great Sufi masters like Rumi, according to Sunni thinkers; as saints, the imams and/or the great Sufi masters have also been regarded as Perfect Men.

19. *Mathnawi*, book 1, verses 327–37 (R. A. Nicholson trans.).

20. Nicholson, commentary to verse 1, 365, p. 38.

21. Mathnawi, book 1, verse 316 (R. A. Nicholson trans.).

22. *Mathnawi*, book 1, verses 371–73 (R. A. Nicholson trans.).

23. *Tafsir al-Imamayn al-Jalalayn*, the Qur'an with marginal commentaries by Jalaluddin al-Muhalla and Jalaluddin as-Suyuti (Cairo, 1948), 8.

24. In al-Hallaj, *Kitab at-Tawasin* (tenth century CE), Arabic text ed. with the Persian commentary of Rozbihan-i Baqli of Shiraz (1128–1209) by Louis Massignon (Paris, 1913); Islamic tradition's set purpose to derive every foreign word, whether Greek, Latin, Persian, or Aramaic, to be found in the Qur'an, from purely Arabic roots, reflects a perception of the Holy Book as a manifestation of the Divine Word *revealed in and through the Arabic language*; hence, every word in the Scripture was taken to reflect a given aspect of the Creator's thought, which it behooved Muslim commentators to uncover through the *Arabic* idiom alone, the better to perceive and in depth to meditate on all its implied symbolic meanings. (The contention, however, by some literalist Muslim commentators, that Iblis was a jinni, not a fallen angel, is of very little pertinence to the high mystical tradition discussed here.)

25. Al-Hallaj in Massignon (1913), 41.

26. Arabic text in Massignon (1913), 43, and Qasim Mir Akhuri, *Majmu'eh-yi Athar-i Hallaj* (Tehran, 2001), no. 43, p. 285; French trans. in Massignon, *La Passion de Hallaj, martyr mystique de l'Islam*, new ed. (Paris: Gallimard, 1975), 3:327; Persian trans. in Akhuri, *Majmu'eh-yi Athar-i Hallaj*, 393–94.

27. Massignon (1913), 42, French trans. Massignon (1975), 3:327.

28. Massignon (1913), 50.

29. Ibn 'Arabi, *Fusus al-Hikam*, ed. 'Afifi (Cairo, 1946), 55.

30. Ibid., 51.

31. Ibid., 49, 50, and 119.

32. Quoted in the *Talbis Iblis* or "Camouflage of the Devil" by the orthodox theologian Ibn al-Jawzi; Arabic text in Massignon, *Recueil de textes inédits concernant l'histoire de la mystique en pays d'Islam* (Paris: Geuthner, 1929), 96.

33. See here T. Izutsu's study, *Sufism and Taoism* (Berkeley: University of California Press, 1984, chap. 4.

34. *Fusus*, ed. cit. p. 68.

35. Ibid., 70.

36. 'Ayn-ol-Qozat ('Ayn al-Qudat) Hamadhani, *Tamhidat*, ed. 'A. Osayran (Teheran, 1962), par. 296, p. 228.

Chapter VI
Art and Literature

Biblical Prophets and Their Illustration in Islamic Art
Rachel Milstein

The Muslims' interest in the Bible is based on the Qur'anic message that presents Muhammad as the "seal of the prophets," that is to say, a natural continuation of the Jewish and Christian monotheism. In accord with this idea, the Qur'an adopts the biblical historiography with certain of its theological and mythological aspects. Various biblical episodes appear in the Qur'anic text, either as short references or as detailed stories, serving as archetypes for Muhammad himself.

In the following centuries, when the growing population of Iranian converts to Islam introduced its own nonbiblical traditions, the Qur'anic text was interpreted and enriched by historians and theologians, often in a highly syncretistic way. The immense variety of literary details that were thus collected in the first centuries of Islam was a fertile ground for later authors and poets who composed new versions of the stories according to their ideologies and styles. In the issuing literature, the list of the biblical figures who transmitted and propagated the message of monotheism includes Adam and two of his sons, Noah, the Patriarchs, Moses and Jethro, the kings and biblical prophets, Jesus, John the Baptist, and his alleged father Zacharias.

Rachel Milstein

Rachel Milstein is a professor of Islamic art in the department of Islamic and Middle Eastern Studies at the Hebrew University of Jerusalem. Her recent publications include *La Bible et la Miniature Islamique* (Presses Universitaires de France, 2005).

Images of the prophets did not appear in Islamic art until the twelfth or thirteenth century. The absence of religious iconography during the earlier centuries can be explained by the absolutely secular character of the figurative arts, which were reserved in the palaces of the ruling classes. But then, as a result of political and demographic changes in Mesopotamia, Muslim and Christian artists exchanged ideas and techniques. In the thirteenth century, Muslim metalworkers in

Mesopotamia engraved and inlaid vessels of Christian worship, such as gourds for holy water with scenes from the New Testament. Muslim manuscript painters had a close knowledge of illuminated Coptic, Byzantine, and Jacobite Bibles from which they occasionally borrowed motifs for their own paintings.

Yet the only known image of a biblical figure at that time, from Syria or Iraq, is a small drawing of the prophet-king Solomon, perhaps a paper amulet, to be introduced into a silver box and carried on the body. The magic aspect of the drawing is enhanced by the presence of a demon next to the wise king, and the hexagram that Solomon holds in front of his chest. This hexagram, known in the middle Ages as "King Solomon's seal," was considered a strong magical device. Other paper amulets from that period depict Moses's magical rod in the shape of two intertwined snakes or dragons, which was considered a beneficial motif in the entire Middle East. Moses himself does not appear.

Hence, narrative illustrations of the prophets were not painted before the turn of the fourteenth century, in manuscripts of historical texts. This genre was introduced by the Mongol conquerors of the eastern Muslim world, who at that time adopted Islam as a state religion. The biblical stories were used by the new converts as models for their own political decisions. The earliest manuscript known to us seems to be *The Book of History* (*Tarikhnama*) by Bal'ami, a Persian adaptation of the *History* of Tabari. Next comes the *Book of Ancient Remnants* or *Chronologies* (*Kitab al-athar al-Baqiya min al-Qurun al-Khaliya*) by al-Biruni, this being an

> **"*Narrative illustrations of the prophets were not painted before the turn of the fourteenth century, in manuscripts of historical texts. This genre was introduced by the Mongol conquerors of the eastern Muslim world. "***

account of calendars and holy days in various religions. Contemporary with the latter is the *Compendium of Chronicles* (*Jami' al-Tawarikh*) by Rashid al-Din. As befitting the genre and purpose of these texts, their visual interpretation focuses on the historical role of the prophets as leaders and founders of religious communities and dynastic lineage. The iconography of the illustrations thus conveys messages of political nature or social morale, in particular, the concept of justice, which was the basis of legitimization of the Mongol rulers. Therefore, in these manuscripts, even miracles are depicted in the context of either political struggles of power or that of conversion to monotheism. In Rashid al-Din's *Jami' al-Tawarikh*, the lavish pictorial cycles of the lives of Moses and Muhammad stand apart in the otherwise concise presentation of the other prophets. Jesus, the second messenger who received a written law from the Lord, is not depicted in this manuscript. His existence is only referred to by the illustration of the Annunciation. This partiality may be explained by the fact that the learned author, himself the patron of the manuscript, was a converted Jew. In his historical compilation, therefore, the biblical (Old Testament) period is written and illustrated twice, the first time being an integral part of world history, according to the traditional Muslim point of view. The second recount, on the other hand, is dedicated to the history of the children of Israel alone, and reflects the national attitude of the Bible.

The rise of illustrated biographies

Illustrated volumes of pious nature came into vogue in the fifteenth century, when Tamerlane's dynasty reigned in Eastern Iran and Central Asia. The new artistic genre comprised anthologies of spiritual poesy, as well as the first illustrated copy of a group of texts entitled *Stories of the Prophets* (*Qisas al-Anbiya*). The literary style of these compilations reflects an oral tradition of moral tales and discourses, which were recounted, and probably acted, by a professional storyteller (*qas*; pl., *qusas*) in the vicinity of mosques. The biographies of the prophets in these texts, summarized into their most meaningful quests and confrontations, encompass the main lines of the Muslim historiography and dogmas. With one to three paintings accompanying every biography the pictorial cycle of this fifteenth-century volume, serves as a prototype of many more illustrated manuscripts of *Stories of the Prophets* in the following century.

The illustrations of the prophets are no less syncretistic than

The prostration of the angels before Adam and the refusal of Iblis, the facing figure at right. Paris, Shiraz or Baghdad, late sixteenth century. Paris, Louvre Museum, MAO 375.

‖ See article
by Michael
Barry,
pp. 869–890.

their texts. Thus, Adam in paradise is depicted as a king, with angels prostrating themselves before him according to God's order. Only Satan refused the order and therefore was banished from paradise and found revenge by leading astray Adam and his progeny. In a few sixteenth-century illustrations, probably from an extremist Sufi context, Satan is portrayed as a pious Muslim who would not prostrate himself before anyone but God. Since then Satan has appeared in every generation of mankind, and therefore the prophets were sent to lead humanity in the right way to God.

In order to fulfill the heavy mission of combat against paganism and heresy, the individual designated to be a prophet has to attain the rank of a "Perfect Man" (*insan kamil*), the highest degree of spiritual purity among human beings. Therefore, the prophets must go through a spiritual test in water, fire, or another symbolic form of death and rebirth before they can start their religious mission. Hence, many prophetic biographies recount episodes of fire ordeals (such as Abraham in the fire of the Chaldeans and Moses in the oven, where he was concealed by his mother) or trials in a cave (Abraham in his infancy, Joseph in the pit and later on in the Egyptian prison, or Muhammad on his way to Medina), in water (Jonah in the belly of the fish), and even inside a tree (Zacharias). In the iconography of these stories, the archangel Gabriel is often depicted as bringing a dress from paradise for the prophet who, having accomplished the ordeal successfully, is compared to a newborn baby in need of a dress of honor to denote his new and elevated status.

The place of biblical prophets in Sufi legends

Many occurrences of the prophetic mission, in either historical texts or didactic poesy, strongly reflect the influence of Sufi orders upon the ruling classes, who were the patrons of literature and art. According to the ideology of Sufi circles, the prophets as Perfect Men embody the ideal of the Sufi quest; hence, the illustrations of their stories may enhance the concepts of beauty and love. The most popular expression of mystical love among the biblical repertory is therefore the story of Joseph and the Egyptian lady. A touching episode presents the Egyptian, Zulaykha, as subject to the scorn of other aristocratic ladies, because she was in love with a slave. She therefore invited the ladies to a party, and there, when they were peeling fruits with knives, she summoned Joseph to their presence. In front of his beauty, the ladies fainted or lost their minds and cut their hands instead of the fruits.

A notable example of this trend is the great success of the poem *Yusuf o Zuleikha*, by the Sufi sheikh ʿAbd al-Rahman Jami. Based on the Koranic account of Joseph's story, Jami's romance turns the biblical hero into a symbol of the utmost beauty in the created world. Mad with love for him, the Egyptian lady Zuleikha eventually seeks the Creator of beauty and thus becomes a metaphor of the Muslim mystic. This fable of the Sufi quest for unification with God was rewritten by later poets, and interpreted by many painters. The most famous among them was the Sufi devotee Behzad, who,

Illustration by Bihzad in the *Bustan* (Garden) of Saadi, depicting an episode in the history of Yusuf and Zulaykha, Herat, 1488–89. Cairo, National Library of Egypt, Adab Farsi 908, fol. 52 (verso).

in the late fifteenth century, painted a fabulous labyrinth of rooms and doors through which Zuleikha, a symbol of the lover, led Joseph toward an expected union.

King Solomon as symbol

During the same period, although among different circles, the representation of King Solomon became popular in the Turkoman capitals of Western Iran. In a double-page composition, the king is seen in court, usually accompanied by Balqis, the queen of Sheba, and always surrounded by angels, demons, and representatives of all living beings, real and imaginary. This composition served as a frontispiece in manuscripts of the Iranian *Book of Kings* (*Shahnama*), which were profusely copied and illustrated by the fifteenth- and sixteenth-century workshops of Shiraz. From there it spread to other schools and to a larger variety of texts. In a literary genre known as Wonders of the Created World (*'Aja'ib al-Makhluqat*), for example, the king is depicted as a master of the occult, due to his knowledge of the languages of all the animals, and his seal ring of a divine origin. However, it is mainly as an archetype of the religious and just ruler, a poet, sage, scientist, and builder of the Temple, that the prophet-king Solomon became the most prominent biblical figure in the art of Islam. Seated on his artful throne, among his fabulous court, the image of Solomon reappears in the court paintings of Iran, India, and the Ottoman Empire from the sixteenth through the nineteenth centuries. His image served as a visual reference to the royal patrons of these works, who often alluded to, or even entitled themselves as, the second Solomon, or Solomon of his time. In the Mogul Empire, hints of the Solomonic legend may appear in the decorations of the royal palaces.

Along with King Solomon, the complete list of prophets became a useful tool of propaganda when, during the sixteenth century, new political entities divided the lands of Islam along ethnic and religious lines. Questions of legitimacy were raised as a part of the fervent struggles, especially between the Sunni monarchs of the Ottoman Empire and the Shi'ite Safavid dynasty in Iran. Both sides, looking for spiritual roots to support their claims, anchored their rule in the family tree of world monarchs and prophets. For the Ottomans, who conquered the lands of the Bible, including Jerusalem with the holy site of the Temple, the events and heroes of the two testaments became all the more relevant. As a result, manuscripts of *Stories of the Prophets* reappeared in Persian-speaking centers of the two empires. Illustrated genealogical books (*silsilanama*) and historical albums, *The Best of Histories* (*Zubdat al-Tawarik*), were prepared in the Ottoman-speaking centers, while in didactic poetry

> *It is mainly as an archetype of the religious and just ruler, a poet, sage, scientist, and builder of the Temple, that the prophet-king Solomon became the most prominent biblical figure in the art of Islam.*

with Shiʿite flavor, the stories of certain biblical figures served as prototypes of the tragic fate of early victims from Ali's family.

Evolution and diversification of images

A new type of album with images of the prophets was probably inaugurated in the sixteenth century. The now dispersed prototype of these large-sized albums, entitled *Book of Divination* (*Falnama*), was designed by some of the famous painters of the Iranian monarch Shah Tahmasp. Copied several times in the Ottoman Empire, and at least in one Indian sultanate, this genre seems to have been popular among practitioners of magic and divinations. These magicians made their clients open the volumes randomly in one of the full-page images of the prophets, which were faced by pages of divination. The big size of these volumes suggests that they were also presented, and perhaps consulted, in public.

From the seventeenth to the nineteenth centuries, when the patronage of book illustration in Iran and the Ottoman Empire dwindled, complete cycles of biblical paintings were hardly produced. The most popular biblical subjects, such as the confrontation between Moses and Pharaoh, the Exodus of the Children of Israel from Egypt, and Joseph's beauty striking the ladies of Egypt, were still separately painted, on pen boxes, mirrors, and book bindings rather than as a part of a text. Only the saga of Joseph in Egypt, in the words of the poet Jami, was illustrated without interruption during this period.

With the advent of printing, the stories of the prophets found a new life, at first in Iran at the turn of the twentieth century, as a part of a popular, if limited, industry of lithographed books. Then, during the entire century, color prints in a postcard-sized spread in the markets of many Muslim countries, mainly in Iran and Egypt. The style of these pictures reflects the modern Western mode of book illustration, and quite often the large posters of American films, but the content of the episodes remained traditional. Along with the small cards, larger printed cardboards with the complete series of prophets within squares still circulate in marketplaces. There storytellers, the modern metamorphoses of the medieval *qusas*, point to the relevant pictures on the poster as they tell the stories of the prophets to a circle of passersby. In the modern media of cinema and television, realizations of biblical narratives are rare, but Youssef Chahine's interpretation of Joseph's story, in his film *The Immigrant*, is an important contribution to the corpus of biblical representations in the lands of Islam.

▶ The following Nota bene, which constitutes a short survey of the iconography of Moses, demonstrates how the life of a prophet was variously interpreted by Islamic painting.

Moses in Islamic Painting

The most complex biblical figure in Islamic literature is without a doubt Moses, the first messenger of God, who received a written Law and founded a religious community. All the episodes of his dramatic biography testify to his sanctity: both his birth and his death are clad in mystery; he was elevated from humble origins to the rank of a prince; an immense light emanated from him; he made more miracles than the Prophet Muhammad; he spoke with God without an intermediary; and all throughout his life, he struggled against various manifestations of paganism, heresy, and the powers of darkness. His role as a vanquisher of satanic powers is seen in a fifteenth-century Persian miniature of an iconic nature, which depicts the three messengers of God—Moses, Jesus, and Muhammad—in superimposed planes.

Muhammad, accompanied by his close friends, is seen enthroned in the foreground; Jesus on his mother's lap, surrounded by disciples, is located in the back; while Moses, at the center, is seen striking the ankle of a giant with his rod. This huge, half-naked figure, which dominates the upper part of the composition and even protrudes into the upper margins, is ʿUj ibn ʿAnaq, a mythical Islamic manifestation of Satan. He planned to kill the Israelites, as they were marching in the desert, by throwing a heavy rock upon their entire camp. But then Moses hit ʿUj's ankle with his rod, the giant fell down, and the rock smashed his head. In this painting, ʿUj embodies the concepts of heresy and evil, which are active in this world and will be vanquished on doomsday. The three messengers, Moses, Jesus, and Muhammad, together with all the

The infant Moses (Musa) is found by the servants of the Pharaoh's wife. Miniature from the *Jami al-Tawarikh or Compendium of Chronicles* by Rashid al-Din, Iran, fourteenth century. Edinburgh, University of Edinburgh Library, ms. or. 20, fol. 7 (verso).

Moses (Musa), his face encircled by a halo of light, accompanied by seventy elders, hears the divine revelation from the cloud. Miniature from the *Jami al-Tawarikh or Compendium of Chronicles* by Rashid al-Din, Iran, fourteenth century. Edinburgh, University of Edinburgh Library, ms. or. 20, fol. 8 (recto).

other prophets, were sent by God to warn humanity from being tempted and going astray under the influence of these satanic powers.

A narrative depiction of Moses bringing about the death of ʿUj appears in the two earliest illustrated manuscripts of world history texts, by Balʿami and by Rashid al-Din. However, the historical narratives in these two manuscripts provide the reader with different interpretations of the motivating powers. Rashid al-Din, a rationalistic historian working for the Mongol rulers of Iran, who personally surveyed the production of his *Universal History*, was interested mainly in great heroes, community leaders, and ruling dynasties. No wonder, then, that the first painting of Moses's life cycle in this manuscript shows the box in which his mother sent him floating down the Nile, where he was found by the female slaves of Pharaoh's wife.

This depiction, unique in the history of Islamic painting, is followed by a few rare episodes, such as Moses's ascension to receive the Law on Mount Sinai and his death in an unknown place after having recited his testament to the elders of the Israelites. In Balʿami's manuscript, on the other hand, Moses's life is represented mainly by miracles committed by him: the turning of his rod into a serpent in the presence of Pharaoh and his combat with the giant ʿUj. An episode that appears in the two manuscripts, namely, the punishment of the idolaters of the golden calf, demonstrates their different perspectives. The painter of this episode in Rashid al-Din's *Universal History* depicted Moses, in his role of leader, backing the members of his tribe, who are killing the idolaters, while the artist in Balʿami's manuscript represented Moses as an intercessor between men and God, raising his hands and entreating heaven.

Moses, in Rashid al-Din's manuscript, is the only prophet whose head is encircled by a halo of light. In fact, rays of light emanate from his head when he and the Israelites watch the Egyptian army drowning in the Red Sea during the events of Exodus. This light, an attribute of Moses since his birth, is said to have become so intense after his first revelation that his own wife was blinded every time she looked at him, and he was eventually obliged to cover his face with a *hijāb*. This light connects the image of Moses with ancient solar gods, as well as with Jesus in Christian iconography, which most probably served as a model for this painting.

At the same time, light is the very essence in mystical interpretations of Exodus, which integrated the Gnostic belief that a fragment of Light has been exiled to the material world, which is the domain of Evil. In a process of syncretism between Gnostic and monotheistic concepts and myths, Egypt became a symbol of paganism and Pharaoh is believed to be punished not because he refused to let the Israelites go, but because he considered himself a god and ordered his people to worship him. In view of this attitude, the Muslim mystics often used the image of Pharaoh as an archetype for those who do not free themselves from their individual ego and therefore cannot be saved.

Thus, Moses's confrontation with Pharaoh, and even more so with the magicians of Egypt and their crafts, are often seen as a focal point in the prophet's career as a vanquisher of heresy. These two episodes assume such an importance that in Islamic painting after Rashid al-Din, that is to say from the fifteenth century on, they took over almost all other iconographic representations of Moses's story. The miracle of Moses's rod, which swallowed the creatures produced by the magicians of Egypt, attained such popularity that in the later part of the sixteenth century it became a tour de force of the best Iranian painters. In illustrated manuscripts of the *Stories of the Prophets*, the depiction of this combat was reserved for the most famous artists, sometimes guest masters. In these paintings, the magicians and their crafts are represented as wild or demonic creatures, Moses's rod being transformed into a huge dragon in the Chinese style. In most of the illustrations Moses is represented as holding a full-faced sun. The light of the sun serving as a symbol of the prophetic light, Moses is thus depicted as an archetype of Perfect Man, whose heart is so purified from all attachments to the material world that like a polished mirror, it can reflect the light of the Absolute.

This highly appreciated iconography disappeared in the following centuries, and only two episodes have remained popular even until our own days: Moses threatening Pharaoh with his rod and the Egyptians drowning in the Red Sea. It is not impossible that these two stories were widespread even between the fourteenth and seventeenth centuries, the heyday of Islamic painting, especially among the public at large rather than the royal courts. In this case, it was not only due to their miraculous nature but also because of their humoristic aspect and the way they make fun of the king. And yet, another episode of a miraculous nature and humoristic possibilities, the story of Korah, who refuted Moses's authority and was swallowed by the earth with all his properties, has rarely been illustrated, perhaps because it deals with a nonroyal opponent of Moses. However, in at least one case, the iconography of this struggle was updated so as to reflect the political tension between the sixteenth-century Ottoman Empire and the neighboring dynasty in Iran—the Safavids (.5, *Qisas al-anbiya*ʿ, Naysaburi, the Ottoman Empire, ca. 1570–80, Istanbul, Topkapı Museum, H. 1226, fol. 126r). In this sixteenth-century illustration to an Ottoman manuscript of *Stories of the Prophets*, one of Korah's partisans, in the lower plane, is seen wearing the emblematic Safavid headdress, shaped as a red round cap with a long upright spoke. Thus he identifies Moses's enemies as the Shiʿite Safavids, and the prophet himself, the legitimate leader of the monotheistic community, as Sunnite, like the Ottoman dynasty.

In later days in Iran, Moses's confrontation with Pharaoh became so popular that from the confined realm of manuscript illustration, it spread into the public art sphere of printed books, rugs, and metalwork. In all these manifestations of popular religious art, the magical rod that turned into a dragon is depicted so big and frightening that, in a few cases, even Moses himself is seen as struck by fear from this miraculous phenomenon. ●

Rachel Milstein is a professor of Islamic art in the department of Islamic and Middle Eastern Studies at the Hebrew University of Jerusalem. Her recent publications include La Bible et la Miniature Islamique *(Presses Universitaires de France, 2005).*

Images of Jews in Ottoman Court Manuscripts

Lâle Uluç

Illustrated Ottoman manuscripts produced at the court workshop (*nakkaşhane*) in Istanbul do not customarily include identifiable images of Jews. A notable exception, however, is an illustrated copy of the *Kitab-i Siyer-i Nebi* (*The Book of the Life of the Prophet*) of Mustafa ibn Yusuf ibn Omar al-Maulavi al-Erzerumi, known as Darir the Blindman, produced at the Ottoman court studio and dated 1003 (1594–95).[1] Although the text had been written in Turkish some two hundred years earlier in Cairo at the behest of the Mamluk sultan,[2] the Ottoman court copy of 1594–95 is its earliest illustrated version. An Ottoman palace expense register specifies that it was produced at the order of Sultan Murad III (1574–95) at the palace atelier in six volumes. It was begun during the reign of Murad III, but its illustrations, which numbered more than eight hundred,

Lale Uluç

Lale Uluç holds a PhD from the Institute of Fine Arts at New York University and teaches at Boğaziçi University in Istanbul. She is the author of *Turkman Governors, Shiraz Artisans, and Ottoman Collectors: Sixteenth Century Shiraz Manuscripts* (Turkiye Is Bankasi, 2006) and, with Nurhan Atasoy, *Impressions of Ottoman Culture in Europe: 1453–1699* (Armaggan Publications, 2012).

were completed after his death, and it was presented to the next sultan, Mehmed III (1595–1603).[3] Five of its volumes survive: volumes 1, 2, and 6 at the Topkapı Palace Museum Library in Istanbul,[4] volume 3 as part of the Spencer Collection of the New York Public Library,[5] volume 4 at the Chester Beatty Library in Dublin,[6] and a copy of volume 4 at the Turkish and Islamic Arts Museum in Istanbul,[7] while volume 5 is considered to be lost.[8]

Dress codes

Although only a few visual records of sixteenth-century Ottoman Jews exist,[9] it is commonly believed that more Jews lived under Ottoman rule than in any other state in the world for much of the sixteenth and seventeenth centuries.[10] Ottoman society had a distinct dress code, with clothing laws that targeted everyone living within the empire, including the ruling classes. Garments of certain materials and colors reflected a person's religion and position in society, making immediately visible the status of each, and enabling all others to treat him accordingly.[11]

See article by Gilles Veinstein, pp. 164-170.

Written sources (sultans' decrees, Jewish writings, and travel accounts) provide some insights into the dress codes that had to be followed by various groups within the society, including the Jews. Extant images of sixteenth-century Ottoman Jews also help clarify how they were dressed. Comments by sixteenth-century travelers show that they wore yellow turbans, while the physicians among them wore high red hats. Imperial decrees appear to have been issued mostly to prohibit the use of clothing that was reserved for the sultan's Muslim subjects by non-Muslims.[12] Yellow turbans worn by Ottoman Jews appear to have only been mentioned in travelers' accounts. For the red hats, however, a sultan's decree exists from about 1580 ordering Jews to wear red hats like their forebears.[13]

An early source that includes images of Ottoman Jews is the travelogue of the French geographer Nicolas de Nicolay. It has two woodcut images of Jewish male figures; one identified as a physician, and the second as a draper from Constantinople.[14] Although the images are black and white, the accompanying text clearly states that the physician wears a tall red hat, which was a trademark of Jewish doctors, and the draper wears a yellow turban, which, as is also remarked in the text, was a typical Jewish headdress.[15] Both the French scientist and diplomat Pierre Belon du Mans, who traveled through the Ottoman lands between 1547 and 1549, and the German traveler Hans Dernschwam (1494–1568), who visited Istanbul between the years 1553 and 1555 in the train of the Hapsburg envoy Ogier Ghiselin de Busbecq, remark on the headgear of Ottoman Jews. Belon writes, "Jewish travelers wear the yellow turban,"[16] and Dernschwam, in addition to mentioning that Ottoman Jews wore yellow turbans, also specifies that "some, who pretend to be physicians or surgeons" wore red pointed, elongated hats.[17] A second sixteenth-century visual source that matches these descriptions is a watercolor painting dated 1574 from the Gennadius Library in Athens. It depicts two Ottoman Jews, one wearing a yellow turban and the other a red hat.[18]

The illustrated copy of Darir's *Siyer-i Nebi* of 1594–95, which is the third sixteenth-century source with visual references to identifiable Jews, is, to my knowledge, the earliest Ottoman court manuscript that includes representations of Jews.[19] Three types of distinctive clothing were used in the illustrations that represent a Jew or the members of a Jewish tribe. The first is the same as that of the Christian monks from the same manuscript.[20] Although in one image all Jews are in monks' outfits (ill. 1),[21] other illustrations appear to use it only for representing a learned Jew (or a rabbi?).[22] This becomes clear in several illustrations in which only the learned Jew wears the black monk outfit, while the rest of the Jews are represented wearing red hats (ill. 2).[23]

Jews in monklike habits are found only in the first volume of the manuscript. In the other volumes, they are at times distinguished by two types of headgear: yellow turbans and red hats, which are precisely the two types of headgear that Ottoman Jews are reported to have worn in Istanbul during the sixteenth century.[24] Stanford Shaw comments that "during much of the 16th century Romaniote Jewish men usually wore yellow turbans, while the newly arrived

اولسون قدم رنجه قيلوب يول زحمتن جكوب كلمكدن
مراد وكوز نذردردى انلرايتديلرايدين اولوسى واى ملت

Satan, disguised as a learned Jew, invites Jews to create trouble for the Muslims. Darir, *Siyer-i Nebi*, 1594–95, vol. 1, TSMK H.1221, fol. 59 (recto).

The Jews of Damascus discuss the coming of the last prophet, Muhammad, with a learned Jew. Darir, *Siyer-i Nebi*, 1594–95, vol. 1, TSMK H.1221, fol. 122 (recto).

Sephardic Jews, who abandoned their Spanish costumes, wore officially assigned red hats shaped like sugar loaves."

In some illustrations, such as the cycle showing the various stages in the life of Salman, a Zoroastrian youth who hears of the coming of Muhammad and at the end of a life of two hundred years eventually manages to meet him to become Muslim, the only figure represented with a yellow turban is the Jew, who buys Salman as his slave, in a single image of the cycle, while all other protagonists wear white turbans.[25] Another cycle that consistently represents Jews in yellow turbans is that of the meeting of a group of Jews in the house of a prominent member of their tribe, Nufayl bin Ghawth, with the pagan Abu Hisham spying on them, disguised as a woman.[26]

This was far from a methodical approach, however, since at times the protagonists in a specific scene, Jews, pagans, and Muslims, were all shown wearing white turbans.[27] In other compositions, members of the pagan tribes were shown wearing yellow turbans.[28] Some of the Quraysh leaders, such as Abu Hisham, Abu Jahl, and Abu Sufyan, are all represented with yellow turbans in some of the illustrations and in white turbans in others.[29]

Diverse representations

The various uses of the yellow turban suggest that the choices were made by the diverse artists illustrating the manuscript and not dictated by an individual supervising the overall project. The production of such a huge undertaking, with more than eight hundred illustrations, clearly involved the participation of many artisans.[30] The disparate choices that they made confirm the modern assumption that personal experience and previous knowledge of individual artists affected their work. Thus, some may have used white turbans for Jew or pagan, not making a distinction throughout; others may have used the yellow turban as a conscious choice to represent the members of Jewish tribes, while yet others may have simply repeated a model, unaware that it was a particular turban color representing a religious group. There are also several illustrations that show a group of people with diverse-colored turbans;[31] this may also be a conscious way of showing that the non-Muslims were a mixture of people with various beliefs, or conversely it may be just a convention. Another possibility is suggested by the armor of the Quraysh soldiers in some of the illustrations that depict them confronting Muhammad's Muslim army. The pagan Quraysh soldiers are often depicted wearing the typical European/Christian helmets

Muslim armies face the Quraysh in the Battle of Badr. Darir, *Siyer-i Nebi*, seventeenth century (?), vol. 4, TIEM 1974, fol. 248 (recto) (corresponds to CBL T. 419, fol. 221 [verso]).

Kahin Satih, the soothsayer, tells Nushirvan that the idols are fallen, the fire on the sacred altar has gone out, and places have been destroyed by earthquakes, because the last prophet of God was born. Darir, *Siyer-i Nebi*, 1594–95, vol. 1, TSMK H.1221, fol. 231 (recto).

Detail that shows a Jewish subject wearing a red hat, in an illumination representing Murad III attending Friday services. Nadiri, *Divan*, ca. 1600, TSMK H.889, fol. 42 (recto).

with an upturned visor, as a device to distinguish the enemy army, while the Muslim troops wear the Eastern helmets similar to those used by contemporary Ottoman soldiers (ill. 3).[32]

Frankish (European) bonnets are also put to the same use in the manuscript. They are mostly employed to identify Christians, but were also employed to indicate the members of Nushirvan's Persian court (ill. 4).[33] Thus, in both these instances, non-Muslims are represented in Christian headgear, suggesting that perhaps yellow turbans were also employed as a similar device to pick out the non-Muslims by some of the illustrators of the *Siyer-i Nebi*.

The red hats, on the other hand, are used with more precision throughout the manuscript to always indicate Jews. This may be due to the fact that they were the customary headgear of Jewish doctors who belonged to the imperial palace corps of physicians and were thus in contact with members of the royal household. The artists of the Ottoman court copy of the *Siyer-i Nebi*, who belonged to the *ehl-i hiref* (corps of court artisans),[34] must therefore have personally witnessed their red hats. Uzunçarşılı cites Ottoman archival documents that mention the palace corps of physicians (*etıbba-i hassa*). One dated 1604 shows that Jewish physicians were so numerous that they were grouped under a separate body called the corps of Jewish physicians (*cemaat-i etıbba-i yahudiyan*).[35] Their prominence caused the German traveler Salomon Schweigger to think that all the doctors who attended to the sultan were Jewish.[36] Two physicians had to always be present at the Ottoman court,[37] and had special quarters within the inner palace (Enderun),[38] which must have made some of the household artists of the sultan identify their red hats with Jews in general.

The only image of an identifiable Jew from an Ottoman court manuscript other than the *Siyer-i Nebi* that I have noticed is found in the representation of "Murad III Going to Friday Services," from the *Divan* of Nadiri, illustrated by the artist Naksi in the beginning of the seventeenth century (ill. 5).[39] The person with a tall red hat on the lower left corner of the image must be a Jew among the crowd of people who are striving to hand their petitions to the rarely sighted sultan.

Jewish influence in the Ottoman Court

Modern scholarship unanimously agrees that "the rise and splendor of Ottoman Jewry" was at its highest during the sixteenth century,[40] which is considered its golden age, as well as that of the Ottomans in general. In the second half of the century important Jewish families settled in Istanbul and gained prominence in the financial sphere.[41] Some Jews became indispensable to the sultans and members of the ruling elite as physicians, especially Solomon ben Nathan Ashkenazi (1520–1602), who was physician and adviser to sultans Selim II and Murad III.[42] Furthermore, the predominance of Jewish doctors within the inner court of the palace, in a position that gave them access to the sultan at a personal level, indicates a general trust and respect for their qualifications.[43]

Besides their professional services as physicians, the role played by the sultan's Jewish subjects in public life as advisers to the government, tax farmers, financial agents, and scribes is revealed by Ottoman archival documents to be far beyond the size of their community.[44] In both international and interregional trade, as well as diplomacy, Jewish participation also peaked in the sixteenth century, especially since Jews

The Prophet's father, Abdullah, his brothers, and his uncle in battle with the Jews. Darir, *Siyer-i Nebi*, vol. 1, 1594–95, TSMK H.1221, fol. 131 (recto).

An Arab woman shopping at the bazaar of the Jewish tribe, Qaynuqa, near Medina. Darir, *Siyer-i Nebi*, seventeenth century (?), vol. 4, TIEM 1974, fol. 357r (corresponds to CBL T. 419, fol. 310 [recto]).

could be trusted to develop the necessary connections with the Christian powers of Europe without engaging in traitorous activities.[45]

This generally positive attitude of the court toward Jews is reflected in the illustrations of the *Siyer-i Nebi* as well. Although the Jewish tribes, together with all non-Muslims, are at times represented in battle with the Prophet's troops (ill. 6),[46] these were among the battles ordinarily conducted by the Muslim army against all non-Muslims—pagan, Christian, or Jewish. On the other hand, even when Darir's text is especially damning for a Jewish tribe, this is not reflected in the accompanying illustration. An example is an image representing an Arab woman who was at the bazaar of the Jewish tribe Qaynuqâ near Medina. According to the story that ultimately relates the breaking of a peace pact between the Muslims and the Jews, a veiled Arab woman comes to the Qaynuqa bazaar to sell a piece of jewelry. One of the Jewish merchants wishes to see her face, and when she refuses, he pulls up her skirts to reveal her private parts. She starts to wail, and when a passing Muslim kills the Jewish merchant, the Jews attack and kill the Muslim, as a result of which the pact is broken.[47] The image shows no details from this rather juicy tale; it just represents the Arab woman, modestly covered from head to toe, shopping at the Jewish bazaar (ill. 7).[48]

Although such restraint may be considered commonplace in an Ottoman court manuscript, contrary examples exist. One is the *Nusretname* of the Ottoman historian Mustafa Ali (d. 1600), which was also produced at the Ottoman court studio approximately a decade earlier than the *Siyer-i Nebi* in 992 (1584) and for Murad III, the same sultan who had ordered the production of the *Siyer-i Nebi*. It is the chronicle of the Ottoman-Safavid conflict of 1578–79, and the negative Ottoman attitude against the Shi'ite Safavids is not only expressed in the text but can also be felt through some of its images.[49]

In conclusion, the illustrations of the Ottoman court copy of Darir's *Siyer-i Nebi* can be perceived as visual sources bearing witness to their times and providing some insights into the various groups of people living within the Ottoman borders, the Jews being among them.

---

1. A considerable amount of literature exists on this manuscript: Vladimir Minorsky, *Chester Beatty Library: A Catalogue of the Turkish Manuscripts and Miniatures* (Dublin: Hodges, Figgis and Co., 1958), 30–40; Ernst Grube, "The Siyar-i Nabi of the Spencer Collection in the New York Public Library," in *Atti del secondo congresso internazionale di arte turca, Venezia 1963* (Naples: Istituto Universitario Orientale Seminario di Turcologia, 1965), 149–76; Carol Fisher, "The Pictorial Cycle of the Siyer-i Nebi: A Late Sixteenth-Century Manuscript of the Life of Muhammad," PhD diss., Michigan State University, 1981; and "A Reconstruction of the Pictorial Cycle of the Siyar-i Nabi of Murad III," *Ars Orientalis* 14 (1984): 75–96; Zeren Tanındı, *Siyer-i Nebi: Islam Tasvir Sanatında Hz. Muhammed'in Hayatı* (Istanbul: Hürriyet Vakfı Yayınları, 1984); Barbara Schmitz, *Islamic Manuscripts in the New York Public Library* (New York: Oxford University Press, 1992), 238–54; Elaine Wright, *Islam: Faith, Art, Culture; Manuscripts of the Chester Beatty Library* (Dublin: Scala, 2009), 33.

2. Grube, "The Siyar-i Nabi," 152n10; Tanındı, *Siyer-i Nebi*, 26–27; Fisher, "A Reconstruction," 76.

3. Topkapı Palace Museum Archive D.12292. Rıfkı Melül Meriç, *Türk Nakış San'atı Araştırmaları* (Ankara: Ankara Üniversitesi İlâhiyât Fakültesi, 1953), 58, 70–71; Grube, "The Siyar-i Nabi," 168n21; Tanındı, *Siyer-i Nebi*, 31–32; Fisher, "The Pictorial Cycle," 8 and 13n1.

4. Topkapı Palace Museum Library (hereafter TSMK), H.1221, H.1222, H.1223. Fehmi Edhem Karatay, *Topkapı Sarayı Kütüphanesi Türkçe Yazmalar Kataloğu* (Istanbul: Topkapı Sarayı Müzesi, 1961), nos. 483, 484, 485. I would like to thank Zeynep Çelik Atbaş for providing me with the digital images of all three volumes.

5. Spencer Collection of the New York Public Library (hereafter Spencer Turk ms. 3). Grube, "The Siyar-i Nabi"; Schmitz, *Islamic Manuscripts*, 238–54. Digital images of the illustrations of the manuscript can be accessed by searching for "siyar" on the library's Internet site, http://digitalgallery.nypl.org/nypldigital/index.cfm.

6. Chester Beatty Library (hereafter CBL), T. 419; Minorsky, *Chester Beatty Library*, 30–40; Wright, *Islam: Faith, Art, Culture*, 33.

7. Turkish and Islamic Arts Museum (hereafter TIEM), ms. 1974; Kemal Çığ, "Türk ve İslam Eserleri Müzesi'ndeki Minyatürlü Kitapların Kataloğu," *Şarkiyat Mecmuası* 3 (1959): 61; Filiz Çağman and Zeren Tanındı, *Topkapı Palace Museum: Islamic Miniature Painting* (Istanbul: Tercüman Kültür ve Sanat Yayınları, 1979), 66. I would like to thank Sevgi Kutluay for providing me with the color photographs of the illustrations of the manuscript.

8. The subjects of all the illustrations in the surviving volumes are given by Fisher, "The Pictorial Cycle," 332–69, and Tanındı, *Siyer-i Nebi*, unnumbered pages after page 144. The subjects were determined by Tanındı for volumes 1, 2, and 6, TSMK H.1221, H.1222, and H.1223; Grube, for volume 3, Spencer Turk ms. 3; and Minorsky, for volume 4 CBL T 419. The subjects of the illustrations of Spencer Turk ms. 3 are also recorded by Barbara Schmitz.

9. Minna Rozen, *A History of the Jewish Community in Istanbul: The Formative Years, 1453–1566* (Leiden: Brill, 2002), 285.

10. Avigdor Levy, ed., *The Jews of the Ottoman Empire* (Princeton, NJ: Darwin Press, 1994), xiii.

11. Jennifer Scarce, "Principles of Ottoman Turkish Costume," *Costume* 22 (1988): 13–31; Esther Juhasz, "Costume," in *Sephardi Jews in the Ottoman Empire: Aspects of Material Culture*, ed. Esther Juhasz (Jerusalem: Israel Museum, 1990), 121; Stanford Shaw, *The Jews of the Ottoman Empire and the Turkish Republic* (London: Macmillan, 1991), 78–79; Madeline J. Zilfi, "Whose laws? Gendering the Ottoman Sumptuary Regime," in *Ottoman Costumes, from Textile to Identity*, ed. Suraiya Faroghi and Christoph K. Neumann (Istanbul: Eren, 2004), 132.

12. Ahmet Refik Altınay, *Onuncu Asr-ı Hicrîde İstanbul Hayatı: 1495–1591* (Istanbul: Enderun Kitabevi, 1988), 47 and 51, doc. nos. 6 and 13; and *Onbirinci Asr-ı Hicrîde İstanbul Hayatı: 1592–1688* (Istanbul: Enderun Kitabevi, 1988), 20 and 52, doc. nos. 41 and 98; and, *Onikinci Asr-ı Hicrîde İstanbul Hayatı: 1689–1785* (Istanbul: Enderun Kitabevi, 1988), 182, doc. no. 222. Muslims were also forbidden from imitating the dress of the non-Muslims; see Matthew Elliot, "Dress Codes in the Ottoman Empire: The Case of the Franks," in *Ottoman Costumes, from Textile to Identity*, ed. Suraiya Faroghi and Christoph K. Neumann (Istanbul: Eren Yayınevi, 2004), 108–10.

13. Altınay, *Onuncu Asr-ı Hicrîde İstanbul Hayatı*, 51, document 14; Abraham Galanté, *Documents officiels concernant les Juifs de Turquie* (Istanbul: Haim Rozio, 1931), 116, document 6, cited by Juhasz, "Costume," 124 and 167n39.

14. Nicolas de Nicolay, *Les quatres premiers livres des navigations et pérégrinations orientales* (Lyon: Guillaume Raville, 1568), 106 and 150.

15. Ibid., 105 and 150.

16. Pierre Belon du Mans, *Les Observations de Plusieurs Singularités et Choses Memorables, trouvées en Grece, Asie, Judée, Egypte, Arabie, et autre pays étranges* (Paris: Hiérosme de Marnef et Vve Guillaume Cavellat, 1588), book 3, chapter 13, p. 400, cited by Elliot, "Dress Codes in the Ottoman Empire," 105n10.

17. Hans Dernschwam, *İstanbul ve Anadolu'ya Seyahat Günlüğü*, trans. Yaşar Önen (Ankara: Kültür ve Turizm Bakanlığı 1987), 147.

18. Sylvyo Ovadya and Amalia S. Levy, *Jewish Costumes in the Ottoman Empire* (Istanbul: Gözlem Gazetecilik Basın ve Yayın A.Ş, 2001), pl. 7; Rozen, *A History of the Jewish Community in Istanbul*, fig. 9, p. 296, reproduces another image from the same source and identifies it as a manuscript from the Gennadius Library, Athens, AB986.

19. My comments pertain to the first, second, and sixth volumes, TSMK H.1221, H.1222, and H.1223; the third volume, Spencer Turk ms. 3; and the copy of the fourth volume, TIEM 1974. I have not had the chance to see volume 4 of the manuscript, CBL T 419, but TIEM 1974 appears to be a faithful copy of the compositions.

20. The first volume of the work, TSMK H.1221, fol. 88v, includes an image of a Christian monk dressed in an identical outfit.

21. TSMK H.1221, fol. 59r.

22. TSMK H.1221, fols. 61v, 65v, 122a.

23. TSMK H.1221, fols. 65v, 122a.

24. Besides European travelers (see notes 16–19), see his book, *The Jews of the Ottoman Empire*, 80.

25. Spencer Turk ms. 3, fol. 405v; see Mehmet Faruk Gürtunca, *Kitab-ı Siyer-i Nebi* (Istanbul: Sağlam Kitabevi, 1977), 2:522.

26. Spencer Turk ms. 3, fols. 211v–222r; see Gürtunca, *Kitab-ı Siyer-i Nebi*, 2:362–66. Tanındı, *Siyer-i Nebi*, pl. 41.

27. Spencer Turk ms. 3, fol. 359r.

28. Spencer Turk ms. 3, fol. 236v.

29. Spencer Turk ms. 3, fols. 227v, 230r, and 234r, show Abu Hisham with a yellow turban; Spencer Turk ms. 3, fol. 209r, shows Abu Jahl with a yellow turban, and the cycle of Abu Sufyan from TIEM 1974 shows him with a yellow turban, fols. 529v, 533r, 539r, 540r, 541r, and 543r.

30. For various amounts of styles or hands that each scholar has detected in the *Siyer-i Nebi* volumes they studied, please see Grube, "The Siyar-i Nabi," 168–76; Fisher, "The Pictorial Cycle," 74–105; Tanındı, *Siyer-i Nebi*, 38–43; Schmitz, *Islamic Manuscripts*, 239–43.

31. Spencer Turk ms. 3, fols. 75r and 136r.

32. TIEM 1974, fol. 248r, representing the two armies opposite each other before the battle of Badr. Inscriptions specify the Muslim (*Islam çerisi*) and Quraysh troops (*Kureyş çerisi*). CBL T 419, fol. 217r, and its copy, TIEM 1974, fol. 244r, both have the Quraysh army wearing European helmets; see Wright, *Islam: Faith, Art, Culture*, 20–21, fig. 5. TIEM 1974, fol. 244r, has an inscription above the army with European helmets identifying it as the Quraysh troops (*asker-i Kureyş*). Also see Tanındı, *Siyer-i Nebi*, pls. 37, 55, 56, 57, and 58. Muslim troops are represented in CBL T 419, fol. 342r, and its copy, TIEM 1974, fol. 390r; see Wright, *Islam: Faith, Art, Culture*, 88–89, fig. 29.

33. TSMK H.1221, fol. 231r. This image shows Kahin Satih, the soothsayer from Damascus, before Nushirvan. Kahin (soothsayer) Satih is a legendary character who looks like a sack since he does not have any bones in his body. The Ottoman artists have represented him to indicate these mythical attributes.

34. Esin Atıl, *Süleymanname: The Illustrated History of Süleyman the Magnificient* (New York / Washington, DC: H. Abrams / National Gallery of Art, 1986), 35–44; Filiz Çağman, "Mimar Sinan Döneminde Saray'ın Ehl-i Hiref Teşkilatı," in *Mimar Sinan Dönemi Türk Mimarlığı ve Sanatı* (İstanbul: Türkiye İş Bankası Kültür Yayınları, 1988), 73–79; Lale Uluç, "The Common Timurid Heritage of the Three Capitals of Islamic Arts," in *Istanbul, Isfahan, Delhi, Three Capitals of Islamic Art: Masterpieces from the Louvre Collection* (Istanbul: Sabancı University Sakıp Sabancı Museum, 2008), 39–53, and "Onaltıncı Yüzyılda Osmanlı-Safevi Kültürel İlişkileri Çerçevesinde Nakkaşhanenin Önemi" [Ottoman-Safavid Relations in the Sixteenth Century and the Importance of the *Nakkaşhane*], *Osmanlılar IV, Doğu-Batı* 54 (2010): 23–61 (in Turkish).

35. İsmail Hakkı Uzunçarşılı, *Osmanlı Devletinin Saray Teşkilatı* (Ankara: Türk Tarih Kurumu Basımevi, 1988), 365, note 2 (a *ruznamçe* register dated 1013 AH, Kamil Tasnifi, no. 1), note 3 (*Ayn-ı Ali risalesi*, 94), and note 4 (Eyyubi Efendi Kanunnamesi, 26).

36. Salomon Schweigger, *Sultanlar Kentine Yolculuk, 1578–1581*, trans. Türkis Noyan (Istanbul: Kitap Yayınevi, 2004), 169.

37. Uzunçarşılı, *Osmanlı Devletinin Saray Teşkilatı*, 364, citing Mouradgea d'Ohsson, *Tableau général de l'empire Othoman* (Paris, 1787–1824), 7:10; Schweigger, *Sultanlar Kentine Yolculuk*, 169.

38. Kumbaracızade, *Hekim-Başı Odası*, 5–6, fig. 1.

39. Esin Atıl, *Turkish Art* (Washington, DC / New York: Smithsonian Institution Press / Harry N. Abrams, 1980), pl. 31.

40. Baron, *A Social and Religious History of the Jews*, 120–21, cited by Halil İnalcık, *An Economic and Social History of the Ottoman Empire, Vol. 1: 1300–1600* (Cambridge: Cambridge University Press, 1994), 214.

41. Rhoads Murphey, "Jewish Contributions to Ottoman Medicine, 1450–1800," in *Jews, Turks, Ottomans: A Shared History; Fifteenth through the Twentieth Century*, ed. Avigdor Levy (Syracuse, NY: Syracuse University Press, 2003).

42. See Shaw, *The Jews of the Ottoman Empire*, 83 and 89–90.

43. Murphey, "Jewish Contributions," 64.

44. According to Halil İnalcık, "One can see the Jewish presence in all kinds of Ottoman archival documentation: in the *Mühimme*, or proceedings of the imperial council, in the registers and papers of the finance department, and in the court records of the *kadi*, or judge, which deal with legal and commercial transactions and administrative matters"; see his "Foundations of Ottoman-Jewish Cooperation," in *Jews, Turks, Ottomans: A Shared History; Fifteenth through the Twentieth Century*, ed. Avigdor Levy (Syracuse: Syracuse University Press, 2002), 3.

45. Shaw, *The Jews of the Ottoman Empire*, 93.

46. TSMK H.1221, fol. 131r.

47. Gürtunca, *Kitab-ı Siyer-i Nebi*, 2:849–50.

48. TIEM 1974, fol. 357r. The same image from the Dublin copy, CBL T. 419, fol. 310r, is reproduced in Tanındı, *Siyer-i Nebi*, pl. 59.

49. An example is TSMK 1365, fol. 229r; see Lale Uluç, "The Representation of the Execution of the Safavid Begum from the *Nusretname* of Mustafa Ali," presented under the title "A Sixteenth-Century Ottoman Representation of Misogyny?" on September 20, 2011, at the 14th International Congress of Turkish Arts at the Collège de France in Paris (to be published among the papers of the conference).

Synagogues in the Islamic World
Dominique Jarrassé

A specific Jewish culture developed as a result of integration into the Islamic countries, and its originality, as well as its proximity to Islamic civilization, found expression in the architecture of the synagogue. When the Europeans arrived, however, they tended to impel the Jews, not without resistance, to build synagogues on stylistic and monumental models borrowed from European architecture. Thus, a strictly internal and hidden place of worship, in keeping with the tradition of an Israelite temple, was transformed into a symbol of emancipation and integration into modern society. It would be insufficient, in studying the synagogues of a territory stretching from the Atlantic Ocean to the borders of India and China, and dating from the seventh century to the present, simply to divide them up by nation or century. I will therefore strive to focus on certain areas and moments that may have led to the construction of fairly well-identified types of synagogues.

Dominique Jarrassé

Dominique Jarrassé is a professor of contemporary art history at the Université de Bordeaux and at the École du Louvre. His research focuses especially on synagogues: *L'âge d'or des synagogues* (Herscher, 1991); *Une histoire de synagogues françaises: Entre Occident et Orient* (Actes Sud, 1997); *Synagogues: Une architecture de l'identité juive* (Adam Biro, 2001); and *Synagogues de Tunisie* (Esthétiques du Divers, 2010). He also studies the ethnicization of art history.

Increasingly rare sources

The difficulty in studying synagogues in the Islamic world lies not only in the scope of the object of study but also in the absence of sources and studies in this field. Although there are countless books on European synagogues, an enormous lacuna exists in the historiography of the Islamic world. We do have the overviews of Shlomo Dov Goitein, Norman A. Stillman, Harvey E. Goldberg, and Bernard Lewis to provide context. But there are almost no studies of the synagogues from the standpoint of architecture, apart from a few monographs in Hebrew—including the pioneering work of Jacob Pinkerfeld on a part of the Maghreb in 1953—and a few journeys illustrated with photos.[1] The author of *L'art juif en terre de l'Islam* (*Jewish Art in the Islamic World*; 1959) had the audacity to write, "This brief study ought to have granted the foremost place to Jewish architecture, but it is remarkable that it has never really thrived in Islamic countries." Synagogues, he believed, were not part of his field, "either because of their architectural poverty or because of the recent time of their construction."[2] Fifty years later, the lacunae remain, and many synagogues have vanished.

Specialists in Islamic civilization view such religious buildings merely as institutions, rarely in terms of the details of their construction and history, even though these provide a revealing glimpse of the Jews' status. In many countries, moreover, most of the archives were lost when the Jews departed. Only fieldwork could make up for the absence of sources. But how many buildings, sometimes dating back millennia, have been destroyed, defaced, or left in ruins! Of others, only postcards remain.

What is a synagogue?

The first characteristic of the synagogue is not to be an architectural type, having architecture-specific forms imposed by tradition, but to be a functional space devoted to an assembly (*bet haknesset*) and prayer (*bet tfila*), hence the Judeo-Arabic designation *sla* (the prayer). Apart from the furnishings necessary to the faith—a cupboard in which to place the Torah scrolls and a platform—nothing is obligatory. As for the separation between the sexes required by tradition, though it gave rise to architectural solutions, such as the women's gallery, the question did not arise in Islamic countries before the contemporary period, since women did not participate in worship.

It is therefore logical that the synagogue should be built in accordance with vernacular modes of construction, in local forms. Two factors contributed toward this absence of a specific architecture. First, the *dhimma* and the famous Pact of ʿUmar prohibited on principle the construction of new places of worship and called for discretion, even invisibility, thereby coinciding with one of the tendencies of domestic architecture in the Mediterranean world. Second, the synagogue could not perform the same symbolic role that the cupola or minaret played in the forms and landscape of the Islamic city, and that the cathedral tower or church steeple played in the Christian city. Until the nineteenth century, when historicism imposed a new approach to the question by assigning to architecture a role in the affirmation of national and religious identities, the synagogue in the Islamic world generally belonged to the domestic space. It was not a monument, and any lavishness was internal, hidden. It is possible to see this as an Islamic "influence," but in reality, it was a parallel and then intersecting development that began in antiquity. The *dhimma* would explain why certain synagogues were built underground, since this made available an imposing space without allowing the building to rise much higher than the surrounding houses: to enter the Great Synagogue of the Hara in Tunis, you

> " *The synagogue in the Islamic world generally belonged to the domestic space. It was not a monument, and any lavishness was internal, hidden.* "

had to descend ten steps. European influence and colonization disrupted this vision by introducing the quest for a synagogal style, which resulted in differentiation and assimilation; the synagogue now resembled the mosque less than it did the church, thus bearing witness to what the West considered an "emancipatory" process.

Mosques and synagogues

There are relatively few examples remaining of the original simplicity that characterized the synagogue in the Islamic world, when, that is, it did not preexist Islam, since the ancient and Byzantine-style monuments—the same ones that contributed toward the development of the mosque—must have persisted in the early centuries of the conquest. Let us note the functional proximity between the synagogue and the mosque: the absence of a "priest" and the identical basis of the ritual (prayer, reading, sermon). It was even said that, as late as the eighteenth century, Ottoman rabbis opposed the practice among the Jews of Alexandria of removing their shoes and sitting on the ground in the synagogue, a tradition they shared with the Karaites. The simplicity of the space of the mosque, stemming from the House of the Prophet, coincided with that of the synagogue, which was no longer the destroyed Temple of Jerusalem but rather an oratory.

Perhaps it was in Yemen, whose synagogues we know through a few photos from the years 1900–1930, that people became aware of that original simplicity: a room in a house, carpets on the floor on which the faithful sat, a cupboard in the wall for the *sefarim*, a few shelves, a few textiles on the wall, and hanging lamps.

A few vernacular buildings still attest to this sobriety: in particular, the Tripolitan synagogues that Mordechai Hakohen (1856–1929) mentions in his *Highid Mordekhai*.[3] They are also known through the work of a Berlin painter, Ismaël Gentz (1862–1914), who became interested in them in 1889–90. At present, there is little more than the small Tripolitan synagogue of Hara Sghira in Djerba to bear witness to this type: a courtyard behind a high blank wall, a simple door under a somewhat Moorish arch, and a room with a masonry *dukana* (banquette) around its perimeter, lit by only a few small, windowless openings.[4]

Monumentality was introduced under the influence of the European architects who came to work in the Ottoman Empire or in Egypt, then with the advent of colonization, which promoted Europeanization. This influence is symbolized by cathedral-style synagogues such as the one in Oran (1880–1918), the largest in North Africa, or the Sha'ar Hashamayim on Adly Street in Cairo (by the architects Maurice Cattaui and Eduard Matasek, 1905).

See article by Mercedes Volait, pp. 928–933.

Multiple territories

The synagogues of Moorish Spain were large. Although some of them, such as the one in Córdoba (1315), were built under Muslim rulers, the two most famous, in Toledo—now called Santa María la Blanca and El Tránsito, after the names of the churches that occupied them—were constructed under Christian sovereigns. They are in the Mudejar style; that is, they are adorned with structures and decorations produced by Muslim artisans, with stucco arabesques dominating. Santa María la Blanca, from about 1200, is so similar to the Almohad mosque of Kutubiyya in Marrakesh, by virtue of its hypostyle plan,

The ancient synagogue Santa María la Blanca in Toledo, Spain, constructed in the thirteenth century.

its galleries of Moorish arches, and its arabesque decoration, that we may wonder whether it was actually built to resemble it.

El Tránsito, built in 1357 by Pierre de Castille's treasurer Samuel Halevi Abulafia as an annex to his palace, displays more lavish stucco decorations, similar to those of Córdoba. We ought not to overlook such buildings, which would influence the synagogues of Morocco after the Jews were expelled from Spain but also all of nineteenth-century Europe, which fell under the spell of the Hispano-Moorish style. We would also have to study the synagogues of Sicily, where the Jews, even after the island fell into Norman hands in the eleventh century, remained Arab in culture, and those in the Balkans from the fifteenth to the nineteenth centuries. But very few traces remain of the synagogues built in European countries under Islamic domination: Bulgaria, Greece, and Bosnia. Salonika, the second-largest community in the empire, welcomed Sephardim in the sixteenth century, and they built synagogues reflecting their origins, next to those of the Romaniot Jews. Seven large and twenty-five small synagogues may have disappeared in the Salonika fire of September 1890. By contrast, present-day Turkey still has synagogues that may have been founded in the sixteenth century, such as La Sinyora (perhaps named after the famous Doña Gracia Nasi) or Bikur Holim (rebuilt in 1800 but burned down many times), both in Izmir.

At the eastern edge of the Islamic world, in the cities of Samarkand and Bukhara in Turkestan (Uzbekistan), almost nothing is known about the synagogues dating to before the Russian conquest, which ushered in an era of economic prosperity in these communities. It was therefore between 1867 and 1917 (in 1916, Samarkand had thirty-two of them) that the synagogues still surviving today were built, usually within the opulent dwellings of large-scale merchants. Although these synagogues came into being under the Russian administration, their architecture is typical of Islamic Central Asia, and they are located in neighborhoods that preserve the configuration of the traditional *mahalla*. They are usually large, high-ceilinged rooms running lengthwise and occupying a wing of the house, covered with stucco, ceramic, stalactite cornices, panels, and bays closed off with chiseled plaster, even ceilings with painted coffers, all brightly colored. This was the case for the Abramov (1903), Kusayev (1914), and Kalantarov (1905–16) synagogues in Samarkand.

The Koutoubia Mosque in Marrakesh.
Photograph by Roland Sabrina Michaud, 1975.

In Palestine, the magnificent synagogues of Safed in Galilee belong to the Ottoman period. Most were rebuilt after the 1837 earthquake in all the traditions of the Diaspora, combined with local modes of construction: the Abuab, decorated with naïve paintings; the Ashkenazi Ari Synagogue, adorned with a holy ark in sculpted wood, as in Galicia, and with a raised Oriental-style *teba* (platform); the Sephardic Ari Synagogue; and the Alsheich, among others. In the nineteenth century, even Jerusalem had synagogues with large domes typical of construction during the Ottoman period, for example, the famous Hurva Synagogue. Thanks to the aid of Baron James de Rothschild, the Hurva was rebuilt in 1854–64 by the architect Assad Bey, who was also given the task of restoring the mosques of the Temple Mount. The dome of Tiferet Israel (1856–72) was also visible in the urban landscape. It was obviously crucial to indicate the presence of synagogues in the Jerusalem sky, alongside the Holy Sepulchre and the Dome of the Rock. Witness the astonishing decision in 2010 to rebuild an identical Hurva Synagogue, which had been reduced to ruins during the Jordanian occupation in 1948 and, between 1968 and 1973, was the object of a fascinating project by Louis I. Kahn (1901–74).

A few ancient types

The status of the Jews evolved very little in the Islamic world during the medieval and modern periods, except in a small number of countries, for example,

Turkey. Some of the trends marking the architecture of synagogues at that time obviously resulted from the social situation of the Jewish minority but also from the vernacular systems of construction, which favored integration, even invisibility. Nevertheless, a few synagogues from the Middle Ages, on sites already occupied before Islamization, were more massive. The combination of a courtyard and galleries seems to have been the most stable model, consistent with an organization of space similar to that of the mosque. The courtyard could even hold a *teba* covered with a four-columned edicule, often attached to the laver. The Great Synagogue of Aleppo,[5] no doubt using the foundations of a Byzantine basilica with three galleries (part of it bears the date 834, but it seems to have been rebuilt in 1418, after Tamerlane's invasion), was ultimately composed of several spaces for worship, each with a *teba* and a *hekhal* (an ark holding the Torah scrolls) of its own. It was frequently expanded, but its originality still lies in its external *teba* and a stand for the *tekiah* (the rite of blowing into the shofar).

> **The combination of a courtyard and galleries seems to have been the most stable model, consistent with an organization of space similar to that of the mosque. The courtyard could even hold a teba *covered with a four-columned edicule, often attached to the laver.***

In Fustat (Old Cairo), the oldest synagogue, the Ben Ezra, vied with a Coptic church on the same piece of land.[6] In the twelfth century, it replicated the church's structures, which date to the ninth century. It therefore has a basilical plan, a central nave marked off by two lateral naves surmounted with galleries. In fact, there is a striking contrast between the colonnades on the ground floor, reminiscent of ancient basilicas, and the upper floor, made up of Roman arches with bicolored keystones. The marble *teba* occupies the center, directly in line with a holy ark, which is itself raised. Every element, from the floor to the wood ceiling, is abundantly decorated with stucco and with paintings that display the traditional motifs of Islamic art.

In Baghdad, the Abbasid capital that inherited the legacy of Babylon and that of the Sura and Pumbedita academies, the Great Synagogue was also distinguished by its columns, described by the traveler Benjamin of Tudela in about 1170: "The Great Synagogue of the Exilarch is built of marble columns in every imaginable color, covered with gold and silver. Written on these columns in gold letters are various passages from the Psalms. At the front of the ark are about ten marble steps, with the Exilarch seated on the top one."

It is difficult to find medieval synagogues in the Maghreb, and the oldest ones do not seem to date back to before the fifteenth century. That is said to be the age of the Tunis synagogue in Hara, the neighborhood of the medina that seems to have been allotted to the Jews by the city's patron saint, Sidi Mahrez (951–1022), reputed to be their protector. The date attributed to the synagogue is based on the presence of Hafsid capitals (named after the dynasty that ruled Ifriqiya from 1228 to 1574), but it is known that such chalice capitals continued to be used for a long time. The

Interior of the Hara Sghira Synagogue in Tunisia, Alliance Israélite Universelle Library.

synagogue was remodeled several times, in particular in the late seventeenth century, as suggested by certain Muradite capitals, and in about 1914, when it was given a facade and new ceramics. The entire structure was razed in November 1961.

Similar capitals, no doubt Muradite, adorn the arches of a part of the Moknin synagogue, hidden behind the souk of jewelers: these same arches decorate the Sidi Saheb Mosque in Kairouan, built in the seventeenth century. The beautiful Moknin synagogue, possessing two skylights and a wall of large *hekhalot*, can be dated to ❯ See Nota bene on El Ghriba Synagogue, pp. 926–927. the second half of the seventeenth century. Another synagogue in Tunisia, the Great Synagogue in Hara Kebira, Djerba, also belongs at least partly to the seventeenth century. Its plan, close to that of the mosques, with a small integrated courtyard and two rows of arches running lengthwise, argues for an early date. Long the only synagogue no doubt, it is imposing, with seven *hekhalot*, and was the object of frequent repairs. One beam bears the date of 1735, one *hekhal* that of 1836. It appears to be of an older architectural type than the Ghriba, the most famous synagogue on the island, which, according to legend, dates back to the destruction of the Temple of Jerusalem. The Testur synagogue, now merely rubble, might attest to the Moriscos' arrival in 1610. Far removed from Andalusian lavishness, it is built of coated brick with massive columns. It therefore belonged more to the vernacular architecture: constructed on a square plan, it is similar to a type of synagogue identified in Morocco. Morocco still has synagogues associated with the arrival of the Jews expelled from Spain (the Megorashim): the Andalusian influence is perceptible there. In the *mellah* of Fes, two synagogues date back to the seventeenth century: the El Fassiyine, rebuilt by families faithful to the rite of the Musta'rabim (that is, of the Arabs); and the Rabbi Shlomo Ibn Daban, recently restored, which still has its carved wood *teba*. As always, these synagogues have no facade; built on a rectangular plan, they are notable for the presence of large central columns. The Saba Synagogue, perhaps more recent (seventeenth to eighteenth centuries), is also in Fes. Located on the upper floor, it has a square plan occupied in the center by four columns supporting a skylight, all covered with chiseled and painted stucco. In Tétouan, the Yitzhak Ben Gualid Synagogue, dating to about 1790, also illustrates the integration of a space of worship into a building. It has a complex plan with mezzanines and annexes, and zenithal lighting. The building also had a rabbinical tribunal and a yeshiva on the second floor. The chief rabbi's apartment was on the third.

During the Ottoman Empire in the eighteenth century, many synagogues evolved into wooden structures, but most were rebuilt or greatly modified in the following centuries in keeping with European tastes. The magnificent Ahrida Synagogue in Istanbul (named after the natives of Ohrid, Macedonia) still has a *hekhal* that represents that intersection of different aesthetics: the furnishings are decorated with traditional mother-of-pearl encrustations, while the coping displays the Tablets of the Law marked off by volutes worthy of Baroque churches.

Vernacular architecture

It is often impossible to date synagogues that follow trends of vernacular construction. Evidence of them is preserved in the Maghreb, especially in Berber territories. We thereby ascertain that Jews lived among the Matmata, tribes known for their cave dwellings. It is difficult to say whether their synagogue, built partly underground (the *hekhal* gallery) and partly in drystone (the entrance), was original or whether it was a residence that had been dug out previously. One of the most beautiful community complexes preserved in Tunisia is in Tamezret, where there is still a synagogue with arcades, two baths carved into the rock, the rabbi's house, and outbuildings, all in whitewashed stone completely integrated into the local environment. Such synagogues also existed in Nefzaoua, a mountain massif in Libya, but we do not know whether there are any vestiges remaining of them. The Moroccan mountains, by contrast, do have original synagogues made of local materials—stone, cob, and palmwood frames—characterized by four large central columns, such as the one in Ifran on the Anti-Atlas Mountain, which might date to 1626, and those in Tillin, Assaka, and Taroudant. Jacob Pinkerfeld identified this type in his 1954 survey.[7]

Extrapolations have been made regarding the ancestry of these four pillars, in the middle of which stands the *teba* of a type widespread in Poland in the seventeenth and eighteenth centuries. But the materials and elevations are totally different, and that superficial comparison rests only on the ground-level plan. Similarly, the fine wood columns that support the omnipresent skylights in Southern Tunisia are irrelevant:

these technical solutions were long determined by the use of palmwood. When the Djerbians acquired T-irons imported by settlers, they enlarged their skylights, increasing the volume of what was defined as a "Djerbian" (and Gabesian) type, that is, a square plan with twelve arcades supporting a large skylight, usually with twelve windows illuminating the central *teba*, while the *hekhalot* remained in the shadows. That type spread throughout Southern Tunisia by means of colonization. The most beautiful example extant is the synagogue in Tataouine. In these regions, the skylight played the role of a Muslim cupola, a true landmark in the urban landscape.

Europeanization and colonization

The major rupture introduced by the colonizing and emancipatory West came with the tradition arising from a symbiosis with the Islamic milieu. It initiated a process of extroversion and monumentality. Nevertheless, there was resistance to the European model, and the oratory tradition persisted. When families built a synagogue, it sometimes remained hidden: hence, even in modern Casablanca in 1934, the Dahan family synagogue, a small jewel in the Andalusian style, was installed in the back of a building. Nevertheless, under the European influence, synagogues, which tended to become official community buildings, were given facades facing the street, sometimes with domes. Some displayed Jewish symbols on the outside. Questions even arose about the style to give them. The synagogue, under the sway of Western modernity, could be treated in the Orientalist or neo-Roman style,

> *"Under the European influence, synagogues, which tended to become official community buildings, were given facades facing the street, sometimes with domes. Some displayed Jewish symbols on the outside."*

or it could adopt the geometric forms of concrete public buildings from the 1930s. Several factors explain the proliferation of synagogues: the end of the restrictions imposed by the Pact of 'Umar; the influence of Europe, which increased its penetration into Islamic countries, conquering some of them; and the use of new materials that facilitated a monumentality unusual in this context. This process ran parallel to a social and cultural, even linguistic, evolution (think of the Gallicization of the Jews, from Tétouan to Iran, brought about by the Alliance Israélite Universelle). And these hopes for integration entailed the construction of large European-style synagogues. In the nineteenth century, that monumental style was a symbol of emancipation but also of the Christianization of places of worship, through the adoption of historicist architectural styles.

The colonizers understood that the introduction of a monumental, communitarian, and centralized synagogue model was an instrument for transforming the faithful, even the "native" rabbis (as opposed to the rabbis trained in France). In the 1850s, the administration of Algiers commissioned a synagogue from Viala du Sorbier: he

The Grand Synagogue of Oran, constructed in 1880, Alliance Israélite Universelle Library.

gave it a central plan, a dome, and Moorish cornice elements. It is an astonishing sight when compared to the large number of synagogues built in Algeria on models from Alsace or from the French subprefectures. As in European countries, the Algerian synagogue took on the status of a public building. Sétif is an exemplary case: in 1853 the architect Montbabut boasted that he had constructed, in his own words, the "first Israelite religious building" "in the European style" (to that end, he imported timber from France). In actuality, it was an Alsatian model, and the leader of the community hailed it as follows: "In adopting the style of modern architecture for this synagogue and in making it accessible to the fairer sex, you have provided proof of the influence exerted over you by your contact with the French population, which is destined to bring about such an auspicious change in the mores of this country."

Monumentality reached its peak with the synagogue of Oran (1880–1918), which also combined domes and turret-minarets, Orientalist in their inspiration—though borrowed from the Tempelgasse Synagogue in Vienna

▶ See Nota bene on Alexandria, pp. 280–283.

(Ludwig Förster, 1858)—with a church plan and furnishings. Most of the venerable synagogues were rebuilt at this time. Rich families constructed "temples," such as the Baron Jacob Menashe Temple (1863) and Temple Green (1900) in Alexandria, and Temple Sasson in Glymenopoulo (1910). Actual models seem to have circulated throughout the Mediterranean world: usually classical or Renaissance in style, they had a three-nave basilical plan, a raised porch (often with three portals), a row of bays, and a high pointed or curvilinear gable topped with the Tablets of the Law, as in France or Germany. Most of the synagogues of Algeria and the Middle East are close to that model. The best example in Egypt is the Eliyahu Hanavi in Alexandria; in Beirut, it is the Magen Abraham . Others exist in Salonika, Istanbul, and elsewhere.

Beginning in the 1930s, modernist synagogues were erected in the large communities, for example, the Temple Eliahu Hazan in Sporting, a neighborhood of

Alexandria (1937), or, in connection with the Reconstruction, the synagogues of Bizerte (1954) and Sfax (1955).

Vanishing buildings or patrimonialization?

The Jews' departure from the Arab countries, for the most part within a single decade (1948–62), led to the abandonment of thousands of synagogues and oratories. How many such buildings still remain? More than one might think. In my systematic survey in Tunisia, I found sixty-five of the eighty-five synagogues built over the last two centuries, only about fifteen of which are in current use (including twelve in Djerba).[8] In the big cities, in Algeria, for example, many were turned into mosques (Algiers, Oran), *kuttab*, or community centers. Some synagogues were sold to individuals; many were left in ruins (Tripoli). A few remaining communities or families are attempting to preserve them in Casablanca, Tangiers, Tunis, Djerba, Sousse, Alexandria, Cairo, Beirut, Istanbul, and Tehran.

❱ See Nota bene on Ben Ezra Synagogue, pp. 922–923.

A new valorization is beginning to surface, however. These synagogues are an integral part of the cultural heritage of each country, even its jewels. Their restoration as historical or tourist monuments has taken shape in conjunction with the construction of a national culture that does not deny its multifaith past. Restoration initiatives have thus taken place in the last twenty years. Cairo saw the restoration first of the Ben Ezra Synagogue in 1992, then of the Maimonides yeshiva in 2010 (supposedly built shortly after the physician's death in 1204). In Morocco, the Foundation for Moroccan Jewish Heritage, which already has a museum in Casablanca, has safeguarded synagogues in Ifran and Tétouan;[9] and the Ibn Danan Synagogue was restored in 1999. In Tunisia, the Great Synagogue dating to 1937 had its colors and symbolic decorations restored in 1997; the refurbished synagogue of El-Kef became a museum in 1994. In August 2010, the renovation of the Magen Abraham Synagogue in Beirut was completed, one of the four or five synagogues surviving there.

❱ See article by Kirsten Schulze, pp. 436–443.

---

1. Jacob Pinkerfeld, *Batei haKnesset veAfrika haTsefonit* [*The Synagogues of North Africa*] (Tel Aviv: Bialik, 1974).

2. Leo Aryeh Mayer, *L'art juif en terre d'Islam* (Geneva: Kundig, 1959), 38. [Unless an English-language source is provided in the notes, quoted passages are my translation from the French—JMT.]

3. Highid Mordekhai, *The Book of Mordechai: A Study of the Jews of Libya*, ed. H. E. Goldberg (Philadelphia: Institute for the Study of Human Issues, 1980).

4. Jacob Pinkerfeld, "Un témoignage du passé en voie de disparition: Les synagogues de la région de Djerba," *Cahiers de Byrsa* 7 (1957): 127–37 and plates.

5. "Treasures of the Aleppo Community," exhibition, Israel Museum, Jerusalem, 1988.

6. Phyllis Lambert, ed., *Fortifications and the Synagogue: The Fortress of Babylon and the Ben Ezra Synagogue, Cairo* (London: Weidenfeld and Nicolson, 1994).

7. Pinkerfeld, *Batei haKnesset veAfrika haTsefonit*.

8. Colette Bismuth-Jarrassé and Dominique Jarrassé, *Synagogues de Tunisie: Monuments d'une histoire et d'une identité* (Kremlin-Bicêtre: Editions Esthétiques du Divers, 2010).

9. Joel Zack, *The Synagogues of Morocco: An Architectural and Preservation Survey* (New York: World Monuments Fund, 1993).

The Ben Ezra Synagogue in Old Cairo

Interior of Ben Ezra Synagogue in Cairo. Photograph by Erich Lessing in 2000.

A study of the Ben Ezra Synagogue, located in "Old Cairo," reveals the close relationship that existed between Jewish culture and the culture of the ancient Near East, especially at the level of popular traditions and folklore. This relationship is visible in the mural decoration of the synagogue—stucco and paint—in the stained-glass windows and hangings, and in the religious objects and their symbolism, closely linked to the Torah. This proximity is revealed as well in the timing of the various Jewish celebrations and in the popular beliefs and practices associated with this building.

"Old Cairo"—the former Fustat—covers an area of about ten square kilometers (four square miles).

Many archaeological monuments are located there, such as the Babylon Fortress, the Hanging Church, the Mosque of Amr ibn al-As, and finally, the Ben Ezra Synagogue. Jewish families used to inhabit that neighborhood, but in 1948 there were only 142 left, and now there are none at all.

The synagogue known by the name "Ben Ezra" is next to the fortress. It is generally thought that it was built after the Romans' destruction of the Second Temple in 70 CE.[1] The documents, however, show that in reality it dates to the time of Ibn Tulun (835–84), founder of a dynasty that ruled only briefly. The synagogue was restored, if not rebuilt, by a Sephardic Jewish merchant by the name of Abraham ben Ezra, who had purchased it from the sultan. At the time, it was a church dedicated to the archangel Michael. But the Christians were no longer in a position to pay the taxes associated with that structure, according to the description the historian al-Maqrizi (1374–1442) gives of the neighborhoods of Cairo.[2] The current monument is located over the vestiges of an ancient Egyptian temple, which the Egyptian Antiquities Organization undertook to restore in 1978, in cooperation with the Royal Architectural Institute of Canada. Work was completed in 1994, and at that date the monument as a whole, placed on the national registry, ceased to belong to the Jewish community.

The edifice, which bears the traces of each successive period of its use, has a basilical floor plan: three rows of columns with a broader central bay. The decorations, in carved wood and colored glass, have a notable Islamic character, except that the Star of David motif has been introduced into them, as well as decorative motifs specific to the panels of the *hekhal*, the cupboard in which the Torah is stored. The synagogue faces toward

Jerusalem. Inside stands a pulpit, as in churches and mosques, where the preacher ascends after the prayer. The laver, placed in the middle of the courtyard in mosques, is generally against the south wall of a synagogue, as is the case here. The upstairs gallery was reserved for women, and above the ceiling of that room was the site of the Geniza, where the documents collected each year were deposited and "buried," since the sacredness attached to Hebrew letters prohibited their being destroyed. Later, these documents were taken from the Geniza and transferred to a sort of cellar, accessible by narrow steps opening onto the courtyard. This Geniza constitutes an important basis for recent research on medieval Jewish history and, more broadly, provides invaluable evidence about life in the Islamic world at that time.

Next to the synagogue is a small room that was used as a school, a *kuttāb* of sorts, where students learned the Torah while seated on carpets around their teacher. Another room, down seven steps, holds the basins of the *mikveh*, the ritual bath. These are stone basins fed with running water directly from the Nile. Al-Maqrizi reports that it was there that Moses came to meditate during his confrontation with Pharaoh. An olive tree is said to have sprung up from his rod, and the gigantic tree was still green in the time of King al-Ashraf Sha'ban. Because the king wanted to build a school with the wood of that tree, workers took an ax to it. The mutilated tree remained as it was, until a Jew engaging in fornication caused its decay.[3] It is believed that the site of the sanctuary on the back wall is where Moses beseeched the Lord to have Pharaoh allow his people to leave Egypt. It is in this synagogue that the most ancient manuscripts of the Hebrew Bible were found, written on gazelle-skin parchment—in particular, an exemplar of the book of Esther, the Megillah.

All the woodwork is decorated and encrusted with ivory. Cylindrical cupboards, decorated with arabesque motifs, protect the Torah scrolls, which have a silver-plated casing. The magnificent main door displays motifs in relief. The windows are adorned with colored glass. The women's gallery is made of marble and is surrounded by a metal balustrade. The menorah is in cast iron, its central column divided into three branches. Carved wood, encrustations, arabesques, stained-glass windows, and cast iron are all examples of crafts practiced by the Jews, especially during the Mamluk period.[4] The painted decorations on the walls consist solely of the Star of David, the goblet, and vegetal and geometric motifs. As in Islamic art, the vegetal and geometric motifs are used not only for decorative purposes but also as symbols. Circles and triangles belong to the mental universe of Jewish and Muslim mystics, and parallel lines evoke the two different worlds, material and spiritual. Arabic and Hebrew letters are also found on fabrics embroidered in gold. Palm tree and lion motifs are specific to medieval Jewish art, as is the use of colored fabrics, all of which no doubt stem from the Canaanite and Babylonian influences. ●

Suzan Youssef is a researcher in Egypt. She has worked in particular on cults of saints common to the Jews and Muslims in Egypt.

1. André Raymond, *Le Caire: Histoire d'une ville* (Paris: Fayard, 1933).
2. Al-Maqrizi, *Al-Khitat*, vol. 2 (Cairo, 1973) (in Arabic).
3. Ibid., 464–65.
4. Soad Maher, *The Islamic Arts* (Cairo, 1986) (in Arabic).

The Synagogue Known as El Tránsito in Toledo

Synagogue of El Tránsito in Toledo; the Hebrew and Arabic letters are sculpted in the wood at the base of the different balconies. Photograph by René Mattes.

Under the Umayyad dynasty, Spain was the site of a brilliant Jewish culture, which reached its apogee in the tenth century. But there is no synagogue attesting to that sometimes mythified "golden age." The synagogues that remain belong to a period of symbiosis following the Catholic kings' Reconquista of Toledo in 1085 and of Córdoba in 1236. Four surviving synagogues all undeniably belong to the Mudejar style of Islamic architecture, which continued to develop under the Christian kings.

The Toledo synagogue called Santa María la Blanca, dating to about 1200, displays many similarities with Almohad architecture. Some sources attribute it to Joseph ben Shoshan, adviser to Alfonso VIII, since his epitaph (he died in 1205) notes that he had a synagogue built around that date. A magnificent space organized into four rows of eight Moorish arches, surmounted by a frieze of blind polylobed arcatures and traceries—also found on the capitals bearing crossettes and pinecones—the synagogue is similar to mosques constructed during the same period, such as the Almohad mosque of Kutubiyya in Marrakesh. The Church of Corpus Christi in Segovia, also a former synagogue, has the same arcades across three naves but has lost its decoration. Two others, one in Cordova dating to 1315, the other in Toledo, called El Tránsito, built in 1357, display very similar decorations. They were the last salvo of a culture increasingly persecuted by fanatical ecclesiastics or Christian converts, who brought about the destruction of the synagogues. Sometimes, however, the synagogues were converted into churches, which paradoxically "preserved" them. In *Sinagogas españolas* (1955), F. Cantera Burgos identifies more than 120 synagogues within the borders of present-day Spain. The most astonishing of these is still the one that became El Tránsito de Nuestra Señora, which is now the Museo Sefardi in Toledo, a masterpiece in the Mudejar, or Hispano-Moorish, style.

Like many medieval synagogues, the one in Toledo is lavish on the interior but displays an austere exterior that blends into the urban context: the walls and facade, constructed out of brick, made it indistinguishable from the surrounding buildings. Only the high roof visible from the outside hints at an imposing internal space worthy of a palace. The man who commissioned this synagogue was none other than Samuel Halevi, treasurer to Peter I of Castile, who had it built as an annex to the royal residence in 1357, in the same Mudejar style that the king had chosen for the Alcázar of Seville.

The worship hall measures 23 × 9 meters (about 75½ × 29½ feet), with a 12-meter (nearly 40-foot) ceiling. Lateral galleries serve as annexes and allow access to the women's balcony. This is, in fact, a major trait of this building: the presence of a gallery for the women, an arrangement that would also be found in most of the synagogues of Western Europe with the advent of the modern age. This system may have been favored by the synagogue's location adjacent to the palace, where access to it could be restricted. A Hebrew inscription from the Song of Miriam, about the crossing of the Red Sea, seems to attest to the function of the women's gallery.

A magnificent larch wood frame, polychrome, is decorated with carved motifs, encrustations of ivory, and a frieze that seems to have been inspired by Kufic script: here again, a mark typical of the techniques used by Muslim artisans on that structure. Under the cornice runs a long line of Hebrew writing composed of biblical quotations from the Psalms and the Prophets. The inscriptions extend onto the walls, framing the panels and friezes. There is also an allusion to Bezalel, the artist inspired by God to build the Tabernacle in the desert. Farther down, a level of arcatures, made up of paired colonnettes and polylobed arches, alternates with openwork bays and blind arcatures. The entire interior is trimmed with lace stucco decorated with arabesques, roses, and traceries. This type of decoration is also found on the bands of molding along the lateral walls and the east wall, which is crowned with a stalactite cornice, its lower part taken up by a niche formed by three polylobed arches into which the Torah scrolls were to be placed. That east wall, the most ornate, is organized into panels of tracery inside lozenges, surrounded by lintels that bear Hebrew inscriptions, the square letters well integrated into the decoration. Cartouches hold inscriptions, including a dedication honoring the king and his minister (somewhat reminiscent of the dedications placed in the *mihrab* in mosques) and medallions with the coat of arms of Castile and León. Grapevine motifs also appear on the lateral friezes. Down to its smallest details—tracery, floral motifs, palmettes, pinecones, and so on—the ornamentation is common to Muslim buildings, Christian palaces, and synagogues of that time. It is still attested today, in more modest fashion, by the Córdoba synagogue. In fact, in the women's gallery, Arabic inscriptions have found their way into the decoration. The edifice was thus unusually lavish.

Samuel Halevi enjoyed the benefits of this synagogue for only a short time, since he rapidly fell into disgrace with the king, who wanted to seize his wealth. In 1391 Toledo was the scene of violent persecutions. As for the synagogue, in the wake of the expulsion of the Jews and the Moors, it was turned into a church dedicated to Saint Benedict, for the use of the Order of Calatrava (1494). It took the name "El Tránsito," "the passage," because of an image of the Assumption of the Virgin. Transformed, but with the decorations and inscriptions left in place, it was equipped with altars and stalls. It even accommodated tombs, including one with its own niche. "Rediscovered" in the nineteenth century, the synagogue, an essential witness to the life shared by the three monotheistic cultures and to medieval Spanish art, was declared a national historic monument in 1887. ●

Dominique Jarrassé is a professor of contemporary art history at the Université de Bordeaux and at the École du Louvre. His research focuses especially on synagogues: L'âge d'or des synagogues *(Herscher, 1991);* Une histoire de synagogues françaises: Entre Occident et Orient *(Actes Sud, 1997);* Synagogues: Une architecture de l'identité juive *(Adam Biro, 2001); and* Synagogues de Tunisie *(Esthétiques du Divers, 2010).*

El Ghriba Synagogue in Djerba, Pilgrimage Site

A series of legends surrounds the birth of El Ghriba synagogue on the island of Djerba in Tunisia. Priests fleeing Jerusalem at the time of the destruction of the Temple—the First Temple in 586 BCE or the Second in 70 CE—are said to have arrived there with a stone or a door from the Temple (hence the original name of the community of Hara Sghira: Dighet, the door). This was a common way of establishing a relationship between the Diaspora and the sole sanctuary of Judaism. The second legend, modeled on a saint's cult typical of Maghrebi Islam, tells of a girl who lived apart from the village, hence her name, *ghriba*, "the isolated one." Living in a remote cabin, "isolated"—just like the

synagogue—she died all alone. But when the Jews of the neighboring village approached, they discovered her body still intact, attesting to her holiness. She was then buried in a cave and became the object of an annual pilgrimage associated with the feast of Lag BaOmer. Popular practices, which consist of placing eggs in the cave and of following the procession of the *menara* (a cart decorated with scarves that evoke the menorah and the Torah), or of making libations and offerings of dried fruit, are in fact disapproved of by the rabbis. Other North African cities also have synagogues called El Ghriba: El Kef, Ariana, Annaba, and so on.

Tradition and the texts bear witness to the fact that the synagogue has been there for a long time. So, too, does the existence of original rites, which give the island of Djerba a status close to that of the Holy Land. The building was regularly rebuilt and embellished: its current state dates for the most part to the nineteenth century, and major modifications were made in the 1920s–30s. The building has two halls. At the heart of the synagogue is a sort of hypostyle sanctuary, with the grotto in the back surmounted by the holy arks. It is the custom to remove one's shoes upon entering. An imposing *teba* (platform) is arranged under a skylight, at the junction between the two parts. The main hall is an enormous space under a skylight, highly decorated with gleaming ceramics (most of them recent). Bordered by galleries of arcades, it welcomes the *batlanim* (scholars), who study there throughout the day. Jacob Pinkerfeld, the first to have studied the architecture of that building (in 1954), hypothesized that there were originally seven *hekhalot*, now reduced to five, and also a large uncovered courtyard. An examination of the positioning of the arks substantiates the view

Interior of the synagogue of El Ghriba, the oldest synagogue in Tunisia. Photograph by Dominique Jarrassé.

that there were once two additional *hekhalot* to the north. By contrast, the photographic documentation of the 1910s–30s shows that, rather than a courtyard, the main hall was a series of three square spaces bordered by arcades, no doubt open to the air, as in the Great Synagogue of Hara Kebira.

Despite its fame, El Ghriba synagogue remains a rather unusual pilgrimage site and does not serve as an architectural model. It is also an active synagogue for worship and study. So that the faithful will be obliged to go there, the other synagogues of Hara Sghira are not allowed to possess scrolls. El Ghriba was complemented by an *ukala*, a large caravansary for lodging pilgrims from all over, and especially from Libya. This festive pilgrimage, still practiced, has such great value as an identity marker that it, like the synagogue itself, was resuscitated by the Tunisian Jews in Israel. ●

Dominique Jarrassé is a professor of contemporary art history at the Université de Bordeaux and at the École du Louvre. His research focuses especially on synagogues: L'âge d'or des synagogues *(Herscher, 1991);* Une histoire de synagogues françaises: Entre Occident et Orient *(Actes Sud, 1997);* Synagogues: Une architecture de l'identité juive *(Adam Biro, 2001); and* Synagogues de Tunisie *(Esthétiques du Divers, 2010). He also studies the ethnicization of art history.*

The Contribution of Jewish Architects to Egypt's Architectural Modernity

Mercedes Volait

Many architects of the Jewish faith, whether from families long settled on the banks of the Nile or part of the waves of immigrants who contributed to the formation of modern Egypt, have distinguished themselves in the field of architecture and in the protection of the heritage of Cairo and Alexandria. One of the most engaging figures was the Hungarian Max Herz (1856–1919), who, as chief architect on the Committee for the Conservation of Monuments of Arab Art, oversaw the fate of the historic monuments of Cairo for more than a quarter of a century. He also completed one of the most monumental mosques in the Egyptian capital. Although the idea of a "Jewish architecture" is meaningless, given the heterogeneity of career paths and sensibilities, the proximity that many of these architects maintained with Egyptian society and culture is likely attributable in great part to the Jewish community's deep roots in the country.

Mercedes Volait

Research director at the Centre National de la Recherche Scientifique, Mercedes Volait is a specialist in the history of the architecture and national heritage of modern Egypt. She is the author of *Figures de l'orientalisme en architecture* (Edisud, 1996); *L'Égypte d'un architecte: Ambroise Baudry (1838–1906)* (Somogy, 1998); *Le Caire–Alexandrie: Architectures européennes, 1850–1950* (Institut Français d'Archéologie Orientale, 2001); *Architectes et architectures de l'Égypte moderne (1830–1950)* (Maisonneuve et Larose, 2005); *L'orientalisme architectural entre imaginaires et savoirs* (Picard, 2009); and *Fous du Caire: Excentriques, architectes et amateurs d'art en Égypte (1867–1914)* (L'archange minotaure, 2009).

The Jewish architects' attachment to Egypt

From the late nineteenth century onward, many architects of the Jewish faith distinguished themselves in Egypt in the field of architecture, in the conservation of the country's historic monuments, or in both areas. Some came from families who had lived in Egypt "since time immemorial," as is sometimes still said. Most arrived with the successive waves of political and economic immigration that, beginning with Muhammad Ali's reign, swelled the ranks of the Egyptian professional classes. Maurice Joseph Cattaoui belonged to that first category: he identified himself as an "Ottoman subject" when he entered the École des Beaux-Arts in Paris in 1893, before returning to practice his profession in Egypt. His patronym does, in fact, belong to a lineage whose presence in Cairo may date back to the Fatimid period (tenth century) and is, in any case, attested by the late eighteenth century. Partner to the Austrian architect Edward Matasek (1867–1912)—a Latin Catholic—Cattaoui bequeathed to the center of Cairo one of its most curious buildings, the Great Synagogue of Shaar Hashomayim (Heaven's Gate; 1902–4). That massive edifice combines subtle references to the architecture of the ancient Egyptians and elements borrowed from the decorative repertoire of the Temple of Jerusalem (the large palm leaves that form a regular pattern on the facade), as Charles Chipiez and Georges Perrot, historians of the ancient world, reconstituted it in 1887. These are delivered in a package that is clearly art nouveau, down to the details of their workmanship. More exactly, the synagogue is Secessionist, the Austrian version of that style. In its way, the structure embraces multiple identities and temporalities—"here" and "now" but also "elsewhere" and "long ago." It aspires to be at once modern, primitivist, and Egyptian.[1] Cattaoui and Matasek were also the architects of the enormous covered market at Bab al-Louq, the central market of Cairo (1912), which from the time of its construction was said to be the most hygienic and most modern in existence. They also designed many residences for prominent personalities in the Jewish community of Cairo. Their colleague Gaston Rahim Aghion (b. 1886), like Cattaoui trained at the Beaux-Arts in Paris, also came from a family—Alexandrian in his case—with extensive roots in Egypt. He, however, declared himself a subject of the Netherlands. The acquisition of consular protections was very sought-after in the cosmopolitan Egypt of the Khedival period, given the tax exemptions and the near impunity before the law attached to the status of protected persons. That status was a legacy of the notorious "Capitulations," the treaties the European powers had signed with the Sublime Porte from 1535 on, to shield their subjects from local laws.

The great majority of the Jewish architects who made their careers in Egypt, however, were part of the waves of immigration that flooded the country from the early decades of the nineteenth century, hoping to participate in the modernization policy instigated by the ruling dynasty, and later, when Egypt came under British protection, in the country's economic prosperity. Many of these architects belonged to the second or even third generation of Egyptian immigrants. Giacomo Alessandro Loria (1879–1937), to whom we are beholden for a number of Alexandrian structures in the neo-Venetian style of the 1920s, was born to Italian parents in the city of Mansoura. Max Edrei (1889–1972), who designed countless buildings in Cairo (including the imposing art deco palace for the Mixed Tribunals, which today houses the Supreme Court; and, in 1937, Cairo's first skyscraper, the Immobilia), was born in El Senbellawein, a town on the Nile Delta. His family worked a farm there after a migratory journey that had begun in Aleppo, with an intermediate stop in Algeria, where they became French by virtue of the Crémieux decree, before settling in Egypt. Giuseppe Mazza (b. 1891), an Italian who—to the great displeasure of his community of origin—chose in 1938 to become Egyptian, taking the name Youssef Mazza Mehdi, was a native of Alexandria. A prolific builder, he produced several art deco buildings in Heliopolis and in the central area of Cairo, including the Seif al-Din buildings in the Garden City neighborhood.[2] Belonging to this same group and age cohort was Gaston Rossi (1887–1972), grandson of Dr. Eliahu Rossi, a native of Ferrara, who arrived in 1838 to serve as physician to the pasha and then set down roots in Egypt.[3]

Others were not so solidly attached. The Hungarian Max (Miksa) Herz (1865–1919), one of the most engaging figures involved in conserving Egypt's national heritage, was among them. His acquaintance with the country was the result of sheer chance. After studying architecture in Budapest, then in Vienna, young Max was invited to join an Austro-Hungarian family that had undertaken a grand tour, which included Italy and Egypt, as a private tutor to their child. For a young architect from a modest background, this was an unhoped-for opportunity to see in situ the masterpieces he had studied in books. Having arrived in Cairo in October 1880 for a stay of a few weeks, Herz was offered a position as a draftsman within the technical bureau of the *waqf* administration (the equivalent of the administration of religion), which oversaw a good portion of the charitable foundations. One thing led to another, and in 1890 Herz was named chief architect on the Committee for the Conservation of Monuments of Arab Art, a group created in 1881 at the initiative of French art lovers, to inventory and assure the preservation of Cairo's historic monuments. This mission was extended to the other cities of Egypt in 1895. Tackling his task head-on, Herz exerted tremendous efforts to learn about, consolidate, and restore Cairo's historic monuments, until circumstances forced him to leave Egypt in 1914, when all enemy aliens of the Allies were expelled. He went into exile in Switzerland, where he died shortly thereafter. For a quarter of a century, he had worked to produce the most complete study possible of the buildings for which he was responsible, relying on sources both European and Arab, as well as on a careful examination of the structures in situ. He thus promoted a form of scholarly restoration respectful of the condition of the buildings, a relatively original practice for the time in both Egypt and Europe. Overseeing a very large patrimony (in 1883, nearly seven hundred monuments deserving of protection were identified in Cairo), he chose to direct his efforts toward the large sanctuaries, but without overlooking more modest structures, even civic architecture. The monumental Sultan Hassan Mosque (fourteenth century) was restored at his initiative between 1902 and 1915. So too was the fortress mosque of Ibn Tulun, one of the most ancient, which would finally be returned to the Muslim faith in 1918, after about a century of interruption in its original function, with its magnificent chiseled stuccos meticulously reconstituted. Herz also restored several *sabil-kuttab* (the two-story structures composed of a fountain below and a school above that are so characteristic of Cairo). He brought back to life two caravansaries that were nearly in ruins; the two main gates in the Fatimid wall, Bab al-Nasr and Bab al-Futuh, and the House of Gamal al-din al-Dhahabi (1634), a rare vestige of Cairo domestic architecture from the Ottoman period. In 1896, his mission was broadened to include the Coptic buildings of Cairo

> *Tackling his task head-on, Max Herz exerted tremendous efforts to learn about, consolidate, and restore Cairo's historic monuments.*

Al-Rifaʿi Mosque in Cairo, which was constructed by the Jewish Hungarian architect Max Herz. Photograph by Arnaud du Boistesselin.

and the rest of Egypt. It was also he who ensured that the minutes of the sessions of the Committee for the Conservation of Monuments of Arab Art were written up and published. Today these minutes constitute a gold mine for anyone interested in the history of Egypt's historic monuments. As of 1901, Herz also held the position of curator at the Museum of Arab Art and worked to enlarge its collections and to catalog them. In the end, he left behind a not insignificant number of buildings he had designed in Cairo, inspired by his knowledge of historic monuments. These include the Zogheb villa (1898, demolished in 1963), a residence with facades brightened by beautiful *mashrabiyas* and interior decorations fashioned with the greatest care in the Mamluk style (coffered ceilings, niches adorned with stalactites, inlaid doors, openwork balusters). Herz's crowning achievement was the completion in 1912 of the colossal al-Rifaʿi Mosque, a structure begun under the reign of Khedive Ismaʿil, on which construction had been suspended in 1885 as a result of technical problems, when it was only half built.[4]

The public works projects launched in the liberal Egypt of the post–World War I period, when the experiment of a constitutional monarchy—gradually emancipating itself from the British presence—was under way, once again attracted their share of architects of the Jewish faith. They were among the cohorts of professionals who came to try their luck on the banks of the Nile. Antoine Backh in 1916, and Serafino Seifallah di Jeva and Max Mourad Balassiano in the following decades, actively participated in the development of the new city of Heliopolis. Each created dozens of buildings and villas in the most diverse genres, in keeping with the tastes of their (usually local) clientele. Some of these architects in search of a career in Egypt chose to practice their profession under a pseudonym, such as Vittorio del Burgo (1910–98). He arrived in 1933 and continued to work there well after 1956, even though the exodus to Europe, the United States, Brazil, or Australia—begun by the Jews of Egypt in 1948—accelerated at that time. Among del Burgo's final accomplishments, one in particular holds our attention by virtue of its architectonic audacity. A prayer hall for the workers in a textile factory in Musturud, on the outskirts of Cairo, the building has a very modernist hexagonal plan, which is at odds with the historicist style conventionally adopted by the European architects who built mosques in Egypt.[5]

A heterogeneous community with diverse architectural styles

Such was the diversity of career paths and identities of the members of the Jewish community, whose faith sometimes stood in for nationality in official documents but who were nevertheless known for their social and cultural heterogeneity.[6] These men, a minority in the Islamic world, had the Jewish religion in common, but they did not all necessarily make the same use of it. For every Maurice Cattaoui, who seems to have worked primarily within the Jewish community, how many others maintained only the loosest of ties with their community of origin and religious faith, or even changed religions? Herz, devoted to the Hapsburgs and an ardent Hungarian nationalist, does not appear to have granted a large place in his life to Judaism. This diversity of religious positions had its counterpart in the multiplicity of architectural styles. Gaston Aghion displayed in his residential buildings a respectable modernity, hardly distinguishable from the tempered modernism in vogue in the major Egyptian cities during the interwar period. By contrast, Gaston Rossi, a lover of painting (Matisse, in particular) and very much in touch with the French artistic scene, was resolutely oriented toward a certain avant-garde and in that respect represents a relative exception. In 1981 he became project architect to Auguste Perret, a French architect of great renown, who had received the commission for a luxurious modernist mansion for Elias Awad Bey in Cairo but could not pursue the project to its completion. Rossi was also the Cairo representative for the New York architect Thomas Lamb. In that capacity, he supervised construction of the spectacular art deco cinema that Metro-Goldwyn-Mayer had decided to build in Cairo, and that it inaugurated in the first days of 1940 with a showing of *Gone With the Wind*. Having begun his apprenticeship as a very young man in the offices of the Committee for the Conservation of Monuments of Arab Art under Herz Bey, Rossi retained throughout his life a keen taste for the Mamluk and Ottoman architecture of Cairo, which was called "Arab architecture" at the time. One of his designs bears the imprint of this style: the Bayt al-Azraq (Blue House), built near the pyramids for Alfred Chester Beatty, a rich collector of Oriental manuscripts. This house, with a very modern exterior, is constructed around an open-air courtyard covered with marble mosaic paving stones, with a fountain at its center, as could be found in the grand halls of the great historic residences of Cairo. Through this repurposing of materials, no doubt salvaged from some demolition, Rossi made free but very real use of classical Arab Muslim architecture.

The broad palette of tastes and aesthetic sensibilities of the Jewish architects active in cosmopolitan Egypt in the past century makes it absurd from the outset to characterize what a Jewish architecture in Egypt may be or may have been. Let us simply note that, when compared to other groups, nearby or far away, the relationship between these men and their host country was different, often

> **"The broad palette of tastes and aesthetic sensibilities of the Jewish architects makes it absurd from the outset to characterize what a Jewish architecture in Egypt may be or may have been. "**

closer, because of the Jews' historic roots in Egypt. That proximity to, even identification with, Egyptian culture no doubt explains as well why some of the best connoisseurs and collectors of Islamic art in Egypt were of the Jewish faith, such as the appraiser Maurice Nahman (descended from a *raya*[7] of Macedonia who opened the first textile factories in Al-Mahalla al-Kubra during Muhammad Ali's reign) or the art lover Ralph Harari. It may seem surprising, within the current context of the Israeli-Palestinian conflict and the religious hatred it has fed, that a Jewish architect designed Muslim places of worship or worked for many long years to learn about and protect the historic mosques of Cairo. Such astonishment, however, would be remarkably anachronistic. Even before the age of empires, the participation of Jewish artisans in the construction of mosques was not unknown. A room preserved at the Museum of Islamic Art in Cairo offers tangible proof. Composed of door leaves covered with silverwork, the object dates to the late eighteenth century and comes from the Sayyida Zaynab Mosque. Its latch bears the signature of an artisan by the name of Yahuda Aslan, a name typical of Jewish onomastics in Egypt.[8] This is a reminder that goldsmithery was among the trades practiced by the Jewish artisans throughout the Ottoman period. For Jewish professionals, architecture and heritage conservation were key sectors of activity during the Khedival period, and then during the monarchical period, before the unrest caused by decolonization once more led the Jews on the path of exodus.

---

1. Sergey R. Kravstov, "Reconstruction of the Temple by Charles Chipiez and Its Applications in Architecture," *Ars Judaica* (2008): 25–42.

2. Ezio Godoli and Milva Giacomelli, *Architetti e ingegneri italiani dal Levante al Magreb (1848–1945)* (Florence: Maschietto, 2005).

3. Mercedes Volait, *Architectes et architectures de l'Égypte moderne (1830–1950): Genèse et essor d'une expertise locale* (Paris: Maisonneuve et Larose, 2005).

4. Istvan Omos, *Max Herz Pasha (1856–1919): His Life and Career* (Cairo: Institut français d'archéologie orientale, 2009).

5. Doris Abouseif, "An Italian Architect in Cairo: A Portrait of Vittorio del Burgo," in *Le Caire–Alexandrie: Architectures européennes, 1850–1950*, ed. Mercedes Volait (Cairo: Institut français d'archéologie orientale, 2001), 193–99.

6. Gudrun Krämer, *The Jews in Modern Egypt, 1914–1952* (Seattle: University of Washington Press, 1989).

7. *Raya*: a non-Muslim subject required to pay the capitation tax in the Ottoman Empire.

8. Bernard O'Kane, ed., *The Treasures of Islamic Art in the Museums of Cairo* (Cairo: American University of Cairo Press, 2006), 221.

James Sanua's Ideological Contribution to Pan-Islamism
Eliane Ursula Ettmueller

Born in Cairo in 1839, James Sanua was a playwright, teacher, satirical journalist, and one of the most active Freemasons in his native city until 1878, the year he added yet another occupation, that of publishing caricatures in magazines. He lived at a time generally considered the golden age of the Jewish community in Egypt. The Muslim, Christian, and Jewish residents of that semiautonomous Ottoman province of the Nile Valley, not content to convey their ideas and promote their political convictions in secret societies such as the Masonic lodges, also published reviews that favored equality and mutual respect. Here I shall focus on the interconnections among the Muslim and Jewish intellectuals to show how James Sanua was able to make remarkable use of and further develop "pan-Islamic" or (perhaps a preferable term) "Islamic nationalist" propaganda.

Eliane Ursula Ettmueller

Eliane Ursula Ettmueller holds a doctorate in Islamic Studies from the University of Heidelberg, where she was part of a research team on Asian satire (in the Asia and Europe Group). She devotes her research to the modern political thought of Islam and has published *The Construct of Egypt's National-Self in James Sanua's Early Satire and Caricature* (Klaus Schwarz Verlag, 2012).

A Jew devoted to Islam

Ya'qub Sannu' (1839–1912), who used the pen name James Sanua from the beginning of his literary career (although, on the pretext of "retransliterating" his name into Arabic, he also adopted the spelling "James Sanuwa"), openly sympathized with Islam throughout his life. He attributed that orientation to the "miracle of his birth": his mother, after losing several children, had discreetly consulted a sheikh, who assured her that she would give birth to a healthy son if she dedicated him to Islam. Sanua transcribes that promise in these lines from his poetic autobiography:

> Hope to have a son, my daughter,
> An old imam told my mother;
> But if you wish to be proud of him
> He must be consecrated to Islam.

From the Qur'an let him study
The very pure and righteous law.
And may he then vow his love
To our religion, to our faith.[1]

From a binational education to Young Egypt

After growing up in a polyglot and binational environment among members of
the upper-middle classes, Sanua left to study the arts and literature in Livorno, a
free port in Tuscany where minorities from throughout Europe had settled. This
was particularly true of the Jewish community, to which his father was attached
by nationality. When the young James arrived in that city in 1853, several theaters were open every night, and various political magazines disseminated the new
ideas—the satirical review *The Inferno*, for example, reproduced splendid caricatures.
Many Masonic lodges also succeeded in finding a place within the urban landscape
of Livorno. Everything suggests, therefore, that Sanua was not content to study
Goldoni and then return to his native country,[2] where he created the first Arab
Egyptian theatrical company (its members, to gauge by their names, were Jewish
and Christian as well as Muslim).[3] In the end, he was most certainly familiar as well
with the revolutionary and nationalist ideas propagated by the leading figures in the
Giovine Italia (Young Italy) movement, such as Mazzini and Garibaldi.

Sanua in fact makes fun of the "old Arab" in the earliest pamphlet of his to have survived. In his *Arabo Anziano*, written in Italian, he does not neglect to ridicule that
conservative who regrets having sent his son to Paris, where the boy lost his faith. At
the same time, however, the lamentations in verse of that outrageously decrepit and
ignorant old man criticize the satanic cult of the Freemasons for aspiring above all to
"abolish the religions of the sheikhs, the priests, and the rabbis."[4] This is a particularly ambiguous remark, given that the old Arab ultimately proposes that his teacher
(that is, Sanua) accompany him to the stall where, he announces prophetically, he
will buy the red shirts made by "Garibaldi, tailor to the French."[5]

Once Sanua returned to his native city in 1868—the year he began to teach at
the Polytechnic Institute in Cairo—he was admitted to La Concordia, the 1,226th
lodge of the Ancient Free and Accepted Masons of England. Ten years later, he was
among the members of the Kakwkab al-Sharq.[6] From the start, the Egyptian lodges
had welcomed Muslims as well as Christians and Jews. In 1867, the Muslim ʿAbd
al-Halim Pasha, son of Muhammad Ali, was elected grand master not only of the
Grand Orient of Egypt, a French obedience, but also of the Grand Lodge in the
English district.[7] Another important Muslim Masonic master, who dispensed his
teachings without discrimination to members of all three of the largest religious
communities of the Nile, was Jamal al-Din al-Afghani, who lived in Egypt for eight
years, beginning in 1871.[8] He urged his disciples to get involved in politics, to speak

The first published modern Egyptian caricature. It shows Abou Naddara dressed as a *khawaja* while defending an Egyptian peasant against the Khedive Ismai'l. The latter implores Abou Naddara to stop publication of his subversive newspaper. *Rihlat Abu Nazzara Zarqa*, no. 1, August 7, 1878, page 1.

out publicly, and to publish newspapers. The Christian Adib Ishaq, the Muslim 'Abd Allah Nadim, and the Jewish James Sanua followed his advice. Each of them created various daily newspapers on his personal initiative, and all three were contributors to the review *Misr al-fatat* (*Young Egypt*). According to Tarrazi's *History of Arab Journalism*,[9] the first of its kind, this review was founded in 1877 and appeared in both Arabic and French. Adib Ishaq assumed the task of revising the French articles before translating them into Arabic, while James Sanua, Salim al-Naqqash, 'Abd Allah Nadim, and Ibrahim al-Laqqani supplied occasional contributions. The review *Misr al-fatat* was most likely founded before the secret society of the same name, for which it became the mouthpiece in 1879 (both disappeared shortly thereafter, however).[10] The historian Juan Cole explains that the dissolution of Young Egypt may have resulted from a disagreement between the Syrian Christians and the Egyptian Muslims.[11] According to him, the Syrian Christians—who felt more or less protected by their foreign passports—wanted to continue to publish the review underground, whereas the Egyptian Muslims preferred not to irritate the authorities. The reaction of Jewish members in the group to this dispute has not been recorded, but Cole's hypothesis would suggest that they joined with the Christians, since most Jews also had a second nationality. This particularity assuredly made them less vulnerable to the arbitrariness of the khedive (viceroy) but did not spare them from being exiled.

The birth of the Islamic nationalist sheikh James Sanua Abu Naddara

After his first daily newspaper was banned in May 1878, Sanua was forced to leave the country. Henceforth he resided at the Lodge du Centre, a hotel located at 6 rue Geoffroy-Marie in Paris, in a mostly Jewish neighborhood. On August 7 of that same year, he began a career as a satirical journalist and publisher, which he would pursue without interruption for the next three decades. His first Parisian newspaper took the form of a travel narrative written by his fictive alter ego, Abu Naddara ("the man in glasses"). To judge by his physical appearance, this character is indisputably a *khawājā* (in other words, a rich non-Muslim Egyptian resident, influenced by Europe).[12] He encourages his compatriots to modernize Egypt by following the French example and by applying the sociopolitical programs of the secret societies that had admitted him into their ranks. In the "portrait" Sanua uses to illustrate that position, he dresses his alter ego in European clothes.[13] This caricature, the first in modern Egyptian history, would not prevent its author from later disguising the man in glasses as a flutist,[14] then as a clarinetist,[15] and finally as a snake charmer,[16] as each successive magazine was banned. In these multiple guises, Sanua many times

> **"In these multiple guises, Sanua many times encouraged the religious communities to unite, even going so far as to maintain that progress, civilization, and the liberation of his country depended on the goodwill of the Jews, Christians, and Muslims. "**

encouraged the religious communities to unite, even going so far as to maintain that progress, civilization, and the liberation of his country depended on the goodwill of the Jews, Christians, and Muslims. He invited them all to sit down together, as brothers, in a *bīrriyya* (pub or beer garden).[17] By about 1881, however, the political situation seemed so precarious to Sanua that the character Abu Naddara, once such a "charmer," was transformed into a very serious sheikh, who attempted instead to unite his "nation" under the banner of Islam to ward off the threat of British occupation.

From July to September 1881, Sheikh Abu Naddara launched three appeals (*sayha*), each a warning to his people. These apocalyptic prophecies are written in Classical Arabic, in contrast to Sanua's usual language, which is more colloquial. Verses from the Qurʾan are sometimes quoted word for word, sometimes adapted and combined to serve his purpose. Consider the introduction: "The Judgement of God will surely come to pass: do not seek to hurry it on [Qurʾan 16:1]. O people of Egypt, he now warns you [Qur'an 53:56]. Like others before it [Qur'an 3:144], it is transmitted [clearly] to you, this is eloquent Arabic speech [Qur'an 16:103]. It comes from the depths of an honest heart. He does not speak out of his own fancy [Qur'an 53:2], he is not in error, nor is he deceived [Qur'an 53:1]. He pleads blindly for the rights of the nation. You shall before long come to know [Qur'an 102:3] the meaning of my words. That which is coming is near at hand [Qur'an 53:57] . . . Obvious disasters are occurring. You have become spendthrifts and gamblers, and your hearts leapt up to your throats [Qur'an 33:10]. Evil has seized hold of you, debasing you. Hoisted above your heads, the British flag has been the undoing of careless souls!"[18]

After this formal introduction and the menacing address that follows—with the recurrent "O people of Egypt"—the prophet-sheikh enumerates the most appalling attributes of the local tyrants in matters of religion and sets out to lambaste their heresy. Not afraid to use anti-Semitic stereotypes, he calls Prime Minister Riyad the "son of a Jewish weigher" (*ibn al-wazzān al-yahūdī*),[19] who cannot be trusted because "his voice is English and his origins are Jewish, though he expresses himself in Egyptian Arabic."[20]

Sanua, like Muhammad Rashid Rida forty years later,[21] emphasized that only by maintaining its ties to Ottoman Turkey would Egypt be able to fight the unbelievers. He concluded: "However different the Egyptians and the Ottoman Turks may be, they belong to a single entity, by virtue of their religion [*milla*] and their faith [*dīn*]."[22] While reminding the religious scholars (*'ulamā*) that obedience to the caliph is a divine obligation, he further recommended that his compatriots build "*al-'urwat al wuthqā* [the indissoluble alliance of believers] to better protect the nation and promote general progress."[23] Three years later, Jamal al-Din al-Afghani and Muhammad 'Abduh would name their famous periodical favorable to pan-Islamic ideology after the same concept. However, in the wake of his third appeal, Sheikh Abu Naddara ultimately exhorted the *'ulamā* to preach the unity of all Arabs, ideologically contained within an *'umma*.

Sanua had addressed himself to intellectuals who belonged to the three monotheistic religions existing in Cairo. His political propaganda initially encouraged all Egyptians, in keeping with the Enlightenment ideals of the Masons, to recognize their fraternity despite their differences, in such a way that the deliberate construction of a "nation" (*watan*) could come about. But during his exile in Paris, once he understood that he was not being heeded on the other bank of the Mediterranean, the previously conciliatory *khawājā* turned into a sinister prophet of the last days. The prospect of British occupation seemed increasingly menacing to him, and Sheikh Abu Naddara therefore shouted Qur'anic suras whose overall eschatological tone, reworked to a greater or lesser extent, was intended to incite the Egyptian people to take up the defense of their religious community (*'umma*). In this way, Sanua contributed toward forging an *Islamic nationalist* propaganda, urging the Egyptian population to fight for its nation in the name of Islam. In Sanua's prophetic appeals, the "nation" was suddenly identified with the Muslim *'umma*, while religious differences were by and large ignored, though he did not refrain from using one-sided, anti-Semitic allusions, with the sole aim of accusing, humiliating, and caricaturing public figures who might thwart his nationalist plans. Ultimately, Sheikh Abu Naddara (a designation Sanua did not hesitate to use until his death) went a step further: what he ardently desired, namely, the union of all Arabs under the leadership of the *'ulamā'*, the local representative of the caliph of Istanbul, clearly amounted to a conservative form of pan-Islamism overseen by the Ottoman Empire.

---

1. Cheikh James Sanua Abou Naddara Chaër-el-Molk, *Ma vie en vers et mon théâtre en prose*, new modified and abridged edition (Paris: Imprimerie Montgeronnaise, 1912), 2.
2. Jacques Chelley, "Le Molière égyptien," *Abou-Naddara*, no. 6, August 1, 1906.
3. Al-Shaykh Ya'qub Sannu', *Muliyir misr wa-ma yuqasi* [*The Modern Egyptian and What He Endures*] (Beirut: Al-Matba'a al-adabiyya, 1912).
4. James Sanua, *L'Arabo Anziano* (Cairo: Nuova Tipografia di P. Cumbo, 1869), 40.
5. Ibid., 30.
6. Juan R. I. Cole, *Colonialism and Revolution in the Middle East: Social and Cultural Origins of Egypt's 'Urabi Movement* (Cairo: American University in Cairo Press, 1999), 138.
7. Karim Wissa, "Freemasonry in Egypt 1798–1912: A Study in Cultural and Political Encounters," *Bulletin of the British Society for Middle Eastern Studies* 16, no. 2 (1989): 147–48.
8. Nikki R. Keddie, *Sayyid Jamal ad-Din "al-Afghani": A Political Biography* (Berkeley: University of California Press, 1972).
9. Filib di Tarrazi, *Tarikh al-sihafa al-'arabiyya* [*History of Arab Journalism*], vol. 2 (Beirut: Al-matba'a al-adabiyya, 1913), 162–65 and 214–17.
10. Ibid. (1914), 3:57.
11. Cole, *Colonialism and Revolution in the Middle East*, 155–57.
12. Jean-Luc Arnaud, "Des *khawaga* au Caire à la fin du XIXᵉ siècle: Éléments pour une définition," *Égypte / Monde arabe* 11 (1992): 39–46.
13. *Rihlat Abi Nazzara Zarqa*, no. 1 (August 7, 1878): 1.
14. *Abu Suffara*, June 4–20, 1880.
15. *Abu Zammara*, July 17–August 27, 1880.
16. *Al-Hawi / Le Charmeur*, September 22, 1880–March 25, 1881.
17. *Abu Suffara*, no. 1 (June 4, 1880): 163.
18. *Abu-Naddara*, no. 6 (July 8, 1881): 160; Eliane Ursula Ettmueller, *The Construct of Egypt's National-Self in James Sanua's Early Satire and Caricature* (Berlin: Klaus Schwarz Verlag, 2012), 258. [Passages from the Qur'an are quoted and adapted from *The Koran*, trans. N. J. Dawood (New York: Penguin, 1995)—JMT.]
19. *Abu-Naddara*, no. 6 (July 8, 1881): 160, 161; Ettmueller, *The Construct of Egypt's National-Self*, 259.
20. Ibid.
21. Henri Laoust, *Le califat dans la doctrine de Rashid Rida*, annotated translation of *Al-Khilafa au al-Imama al-'uzma* [*The Caliphate or the Supreme Imamate*] (Paris: Librairie d'Amérique et d'Orient, 1986).
22. *Abu-Naddara*, no. 7 (August 1, 1881): 168–72; Ettmueller, *The Construct of Egypt's National-Self*, 260.
23. *Abu-Naddara*, no. 8 (September 9, 1881): 178; Ettmueller, *The Construct of Egypt's National-Self*, 260.

Al-Samawʾal ibn ʿAdiya,
a Pre-Islamic Jewish Poet

In his *Tabaqat fuhul al-shuʿaraʾ* (*Categories of the Excellent Poets*),[1] considered one of the founding texts of poetry criticism among the Arabs, the Abbasid critic Muhammad ibn Sallam al-Jumahi (767–846) devotes an entire chapter to Arab Jewish poets, placing al-Samawʾal at the top. The few lines attributed to each of these Arab Jewish poets do not allow us to grasp their respective poetic personalities, and for the most part they merely offer variations on themes habitually treated in classical Arabic poetry: generosity toward the friend and visitor, ferocity toward the enemy, praise of wine, tears shed over the vestiges of desert encampments, descriptions of man as a creature destined to die, and quest for a glory that only an intrepid nature and an enterprising spirit allow one to attain. Of these poets, only al-Samawʾal remained in the Arab collective memory, thanks to a few excerpts of poems attributed to him, and especially thanks to a legend or history telling of a glorious episode in his life, of which his poetry in some sense constitutes the celebration or illustration. The few poems attributed to al-Samawʾal were gathered by Niftawayhi (858–935) into a small collection (*diwān*), which Father Louis Shaykhu published in 1909. Although the attribution of these poems to al-Samawʾal is in dispute, two or three of them may be considered authentic. They are quoted in authoritative works, including Jumahi's *Tabaqat*, but also in the *Hamasa*, an anthology composed by the illustrious Abbasid poet Abu Tammam (804–46). As for the story about al-Samawʾal, in addition to being mentioned by all the anthologists of classical Arabic poetry as a prelude to his verses, it is told with a great many details by Abu I-Faraj al-Isfahani (897–967), who devotes a brief chapter to the Jewish poet in volume 22 of his famous *Kitab al-Aghani* (*Book of Songs*).[2]

Father Louis Shaykhu refers to al-Isfahani's work and to other ancient sources in his introduction to al-Samawʾal in the first volume of *Al-Majani* (*The Harvests*),[3] his anthology of classical Arabic poetry. He reconstitutes the poet's genealogy, a genealogy that contributed in great part to the construction of his legend and bestowed a particular resonance on it. According to the Lebanese anthologist, al-Samawʾal (the Arabic equivalent of "Samuel") ibn ʿAdiya' was a native of Yathrib (the future Medina). His father or grandfather, who stemmed from an Israelite family, had settled in Tayma, on the caravan trade route between the Hejaz and Syria (Al-Sham). There he cultivated a farm paddock, built a large stone house with a massive enclosing wall that made it look like a true fortress, and dug a well inside. In a region acquainted only with leather tents and pavilions, the house quickly became famous. Because of its black stones studded with a few white ones, the fort was called "Al-Ablaq" ("The Dappled," a term usually used to describe horses and other animals that have a white coat with touches of black or gray, or the reverse). Travelers and caravanners found refuge there, to rest or to protect themselves from the raids of Bedouins and bandits.

It was in that house that al-Samawʾal, after inheriting it, is said to have lodged the poet Imruʾ al-Qays, author of the most famous of the Arabic *Muʿallaqat* (*Great Odes*) of the pre-Islamic period. Disappointed by the Arab tribes from whom he had solicited help to battle the assassins of his father, the king, and to regain his throne, Imruʾ al-Qays decided to go plead with the Byzantine emperor Justinian for his aid. According to the legend or heroic history of al-Samawʾal, as Imruʾ al-Qays was leaving, he entrusted to his host a precious array of weapons that had been passed on from father to son. The Ghassanid Al-Harith ibn Abi Shamir, upon hearing this news, came to demand the arms from al-Samawʾal, who refused to hand them over. As one of al-Samawʾal's sons, returning from the hunt, passed in front of the wall surrounding the house, Al-Harith took the opportunity to seize him and threatened to kill him if Imruʾ al-Qays's weapons were refused him. Al-Harith was then told to kill the son of al-Samawʾal, since al-Samawʾal for his part could not go back on his word. Al-Harith carried out his threat. Since then, the Arabs call anyone displaying an indefectible loyalty "more loyal than al-Samawʾal" (awfā min al-Samawʾal).

In his boast poems, which are among the poetic excerpts attributed to him, al-Samawʾal evokes the house in question:

> [My grandfather] ʿAdiyaʾ exhorted me one day
> not to destroy the work of his hands.
> ʿAdiyaʾ had built an impregnable fortress
> and a well, from which I draw water as I please.

Confirmation and a new version of the exploit are provided in a different story, centered on another of al-Samawʾal's sons and on al-Aʿsha al-Akbar, also a pre-Islamic poet and the author of a great ode (muʿallaqa). ʿAmr ibn Thaʿlaba al-Quzaʿi is said to have captured a few men, including al-Aʿsha. With his captives, he stayed for a time at Al-Ablaq, enjoying the hospitality of Shurayh, al-Samawʾal's son and heir. The captive poet al-Aʿsha, who was blind, then sent verses he had written to Shurayh, in which the poet reminded him of his father's loyalty toward Imruʾ al-Qays and implored Shurayh to grant the poet his freedom. Shurayh asked ʿAmr to let him have a few of his captives. The other proposed that Shurayh choose among them. Shurayh replied that he wanted only "that blind man" and thereby obtained al-Aʿsha's release.

Among the few poems by al-Samawʾal that are judged to be authentic, the poem in the lām form remains the most famous, since it is the longest and best constructed. The simplicity of the vocabulary, even for a present-day reader somewhat removed from Classical Arabic, and the poem's pleasant musicality are among the factors contributing to its celebrity. In addition, the words resonate with and echo one another, in a sort of perpetual oscillation. It is a boast poem, and the paean to al-Samawʾal's people can be understood as being addressed to his tribe, a procedure used by all the Arab poets, but also to his Hebrew community, which is not mentioned by name. Al-Samawʾal begins by pointing out the great virtue of humility and the evil of ostentation, recalling that a man's true garb is his morals: "He who protects his honor from all stain / every garment will be beautiful on him." Al-Samawʾal uses that word of wisdom to reply to a fictive female interlocutor, who reminds him—pitying him and his family—of their small number. His reply is that "the noble are always few in number," a maxim that would find a perfect translation in Charles de Gaulle's famous line: "Sur les sommets, il n'y a pas foule!" (No crowds on the mountaintop!). Besides, what does the modesty of their number matter when their neighbors are protected and ennobled, while those of others are debased and degraded?

Arriving at the evocation of Al-Ablaq, the fortified home inherited from his family, al-Samawʾal magnifies it into a "mountain." He gives a description that conforms in every detail to a poetic code in force among the ancient Arab poets, dominated by hyperbole and superlatives:

> We possess a mountain that protects those given refuge,
> indomitable, which the eye cannot scale,
> its foundations are rooted deep in the earth,
> and its inapproachable peak reaches toward the stars,
> it is Ablaq the Unique, of vast renown,
> which withstands all those who would try to take it.

In keeping with the main theme, boasting, he declares that his people do not die in bed; comparable in generosity to water from the sky, they pass the torch of glory from lord to lord; their word is always deed; their fire never goes out and is always ready to feed visitors; and finally, for the members of their community, they are like the shaft around which millstones turn.

Through this implacable defense of a small group that grows larger by means of initiative and feats, this poem ultimately provided Arab poetic and cultural history with many quotations: many of its lines have the value of proverbs. A great deal of the poem's effectiveness comes from the auspicious duplicity of its register. Read as a paean to the Jews of Arabia, it guarantees them the status of a real collectivity within the Arab collectivity. Understood as a paean to the tribe in the usual sense of the word, it partakes of the hymn that the ancient Arab poets endlessly raised up to the institution of the tribe. If literature, if we are to believe Jacques Derrida, is metonymic in its essence, and a text, to be a text, must always leave me as a reader the possibility of "slipping" into it, of finding myself in it, then this poem would be a vast metonym in which plural readings meet and cross-fertilize one another, continually flowing back and forth. ●

A professor in the Department of Arabic Studies at the Institut National des Langues et Civilisations Orientales (INALCO) in Paris, Kadhim Jihad Hassan is also a poet, essayist, and translator. His publications include La part de l'étranger: La traduction de la poésie dans la culture arabe *(Sindbad/Actes Sud, 2007) and* Le labyrinthe et le géomètre, essais sur la littérature arabe classique et moderne, suivi de Sept figures proches *(Aden, 2008).*

---

1. Available in the critical edition by Mahmud Shakir, 2 vols. (Cairo: Dar Al-maʾarif, 1952).

2. Several editions are available, including one in twenty-five volumes (Beirut: Dar al-thaqafa, 1983).

3. Published in 1882, it was revised and reissued by a committee of faculty members from the Lebanese University under the supervision of Ifram al-Bustani (Beirut: Dar al-Mashriq, 1946) and has often been reissued since. On al-Samawʾal, see 1: 343ff. of the fourth edition (1993).

Arabic Ars Poetica in Biblical Hebrew: Hebrew Poetry in Spain

Masha Itzhaki

Hebrew poetry in Spain, which took root in Córdoba in the tenth century under the caliphate of ʿAbd al-Rahman III, stemmed from two extremely strong cultural influences: Classical Arabic poetry and the language of the Bible. Biblical Hebrew is the raw material for the Jewish poets of Andalusia, from which they deliberately draw the linguistic tools needed for their poems. From its first appearance, Andalusian Hebrew poetry used the full variety of themes and prosody of Arabic poetry, those of the pre-Islamic period, those of the Abbasid period, and those typical of al-Andalus.

By virtue of its prosody, the development of its themes, and the ornamentation of its language (*al-badī*), this poetry therefore belongs to a well-established normative framework borrowed directly from the Arabic ars poetica of its time. The Hebrew poets in Muslim Spain consciously adopted the elements of Arabic poetry already in place, while deploying the genius and secrets of biblical language. Within that cultural context, the poetic text was conceived as a work of art whose beauty resides in language. Each line was judged in isolation, and literary criticism focused on formal perfection.

Masha Itzhaki

Masha Itzhaki is a professor at the Institut National des Langues et Civilisations Orientales. She is the director of the Centre de Recherches Moyen-Orient Méditérranée and of *Yod*, a review of Hebrew and Jewish Studies. Her works include *Jardin d'Éden, jardins d'Espagne: Anthologie bilingue de la poésie hébraïque en Espagne et en Provence*, in collaboration with Michel Garel (Seuil/BNF, 1993); *D'Espagne à Jérusalem: Juda Hallévi (1075–1141)* (Albin Michel, 1997); *Poésie hébraïque amoureuse, de l'Andalousie à la mer rouge*, a bilingual anthology (up to the eighteenth century) in collaboration with Michel Garel (Somogy, 2000); *The Works of Yehuda Al-Harizi*, part of a series on the Hebrew poets of medieval Spain (Tel Aviv University Press, 2008) (in Hebrew); and *A Message upon the Garden: Studies in Medieval Jewish Poetry* (in collaboration with A. Guetta) (Brill, 2008).

Poetic sources

Both for profane medieval Hebrew poetry (what is known as "courtly poetry") and for sacred poetry (poetry accompanying rites at the synagogue), the Bible was the sole linguistic source, considered at the time comparable in its beauty and grandeur to the Qurʾan. It was within this innovative perspective that the Bible also became an aesthetic object: the scriptural verse was considered equivalent to a line of poetry, and it was on the basis of this altogether modern notion that the poets writing in Hebrew embarked on a competition of sorts with their Arab colleagues. Using to best advantage the antiquity of the Bible when compared to that of the Qurʾan, the Jewish poets sought to demonstrate that all the beauty of Arabic rhetoric could already be found in the Torah. Moshe Ibn Ezra (born in Granada in about 1055, he died in Northern Spain after 1135), a poet and philosopher, and a great admirer of Arabic poetry, devotes a long chapter of his *Kitab al-muhadara wa-l-mudhakara* (*Treatise of Studies and Debates*),[1] a theoretical work in Arabic on the art of poetry, to an exposition of Hebrew rhetoric drawn from the Bible, comparing it to Arabic rhetoric taken from the Qurʾan. Furthermore, he acknowledges that Arabic gave rise to poetic genius; that it was "to languages what spring is to the seasons."

▶ See Counterpoint on this text, pp. 636-637

To illustrate the poetic openness of the Jewish poets, I have chosen to focus on the three genres typical of that flourishing culture: the *qasīda*, the *muwashshah*, and the *maqāma*.

The *qasīda*, or the pre-Islamic inheritance

The *qasīda*, a long monorhymed and monometric poem, is considered the purest and most perfect form of Arabic poetry. It seems to have originated with a magnificent collection of pre-Islamic poetry called the *Muʿallaqat* (*Great Odes*),[2] which brings together the works of three great Arab poets: al-Asha, ʿAmr ibn Kulthum, and Imru al-Qays (d. ca. 530). This landmark genre of Arabic poetry found a place among the Andalusian poets writing in Hebrew. Some long poems in Biblical Hebrew respect to the letter the unity of meter and rhyme of Classical Arabic poetry, and include erotic introductions in the spirit of the Bedouin *nasīb*, in which the narrative concerns the quest for the beloved. The aim of these introductions is to "win hearts, turn heads to look at [the poet], and gain the attention of listeners," as Ibn Qutayba (828–889), a literary critic of the classical period, writes in his *Kitab al-shiʿr wa-l-shuʿaraʾ* (*On Poetry and the Poets*). When the poet is assured that he has the attention and the ear of his audience, he continues with a short poetic transition (one or two lines only), which leads to the main part of the poem, in most cases a panegyric (*madīh*) of the sheikh, king, or patron.

Samuel Ibn Naghrila (993–1056), the vizier of Granada, was the object of such a paean, written by Joseph Ibn Hasdai. Titled *Shira Yetomah* (*A Unique Poem*), it is one of the first Hebrew *qasīdas*. In another *qasīda* dedicated to Ibn Naghrila, Solomon Ibn Gabirol (1020–57) composed an amorous introduction in the style of the Song of Songs. Here are its first lines:[3] "Dawn arising / . . . But then who is she? / Spilling forth the pure and lovely brightness of the sun, / Glorious beauty of a fine princess / Fragrant with myrrh, sparkling incense." A "Mistress of every charm" is at the heart of a panegyric by Yehuda Halevi (1075?–1141), dedicated to Solomon Ibn Prutziel.[4] And Moshe Ibn Ezra describes in detail the desert landscape and remnants of the past (*al-wuqūf ʿalā l-atlāl*) as the introductory backdrop to his personal poems about wandering through Northern Spain.[5]

The Hebrew *qasīda* does not have the mimetic character of the ancient Arabic poems, which transport us back in time. Desert nights, the wandering beloved, and ruins, though present in the Andalusian texts written in Hebrew, were no longer part of everyday life and clearly belonged to a traditional poetic fiction that had to be respected. This phenomenon raises several questions that still call for extensive research: How is it that these long, carefully crafted poems about the desert nomads of the pre-Islamic period, with a single rhyme and meter and with images and tales drawn from that remote landscape, appeared in the courts of the Jewish aristocracy of the Andalusian *taifas* in the eleventh and twelfth centuries, written in Biblical Hebrew? And what significant modifications resulted from that shift to a different culture? Would that transfer to the Hebrew poetry of Northern Spain and Provence later be repeated, this time under Christian domination in the twelfth and thirteenth centuries?

The *muwashshah*, from the profane to the sacred

The *muwashshah*—*Shir Ezor* in Hebrew—known in the West as "strophic poetry," constitutes an original aspect of literary production in the medieval Muslim West. Having appeared in Muslim Spain in the tenth century, it introduced a metrical and linguistic break, despite the characteristics it shared with the ancient poetic form of the *qasīda*. Moving beyond the former structures of composition (the unity of meter and rhyme), innovating at the thematic level, and introducing vernacular Arabic as well as Common Romance into their poems, the representatives of this art put their own mark on the literary heritage of Classical Arabic. Long ignored by specialists in Arabic poetry, the *muwashshah* was rediscovered by the Orientalists, thanks to the final refrain, called *kharja*, generally taken from spoken language, which constitutes the oldest written trace of the medieval Iberian dialect. Andalusian strophic poetry, transmitted orally by successive generations of musicians and singers in the Maghreb and in the East, was in fact saved from oblivion, despite the anonymity of a large portion of its creators.

In principle, it is a poem composed of four to seven strophes, each divided into two parts. For the first, longer part, the rhyme changes from one strophe to the next; for the second part, which is only one or two lines, the rhyme and meter are fixed throughout the entire poem. In most cases, these two lines appear as an "opening" or "guide" (*matla* in Arabic, *madrikh* in Hebrew) that frames the entire poem. The rhyme scheme is therefore as follows: (aa)bbb/aa. ccc/aa. ddd/aa. eee/aa, and so on. This structure allows for much richer musical variety than in the classical *qasīda*.

Ritual of Rosh Hashanah and Yom Kippur, followed by the *Keter Malkhut* of Solomon ibn Gabirol, Catalonia, around 1460–70. Paris, Bibliothèque Nationale de France, ms. or. Hebrew 593, fol. 101 (verso) and 102.

In medieval Andalusian poetry, whether in Arabic or Hebrew, this form was used especially for drinking songs and love poems, which were set to music and sung at banquets given by the notables. The first Jewish poet to compose a *muwashshah* was Samuel Ibn Naghrila (in any event, three examples of his poems have come down to us). But it was Moshe Ibn Ezra and Yehuda Halevi who perfected this structure in its Hebrew version and even further improved the system of versification. These strophic poems generally end with *kharjas* in Arabic or, later, in Castilian, but always in Hebrew characters and respecting the rhyme and meter already imposed at the start of the poem.

The development of the Hebrew *muwashshah* was particularly rapid in the realm of synagogal poetry. It became one of the most widespread forms of Spanish liturgical poetry. These poems multiplied because of their strophic structure and musical character, which allowed the officiant and the community of the faithful to divide up the parts. Biblical verses could also be inserted, and the poem with its refrain could be set to music. This particularity of Spanish Jewish *piyyutim* (sacred poems) demonstrates a convergence, unique of its kind, between Arabic and Hebrew, and between the profane and the sacred.

▶ See article by Mohamed Hawary, pp. 713-719.

The *maqāma*: The first steps toward narration

In this particular context of an unequivocal cultural openness, another Arabic literary genre, having originated in the East, made its way to the West as a unique form of Hebrew expression: this was the *maqāma*, or "session." It appeared in Arabic in the tenth century, invented by the Iranian poet Ahmed Ibn Hossein al-Hamadhani in his *Maqamat*, which consists of four hundred "sessions." It was he who developed the well-defined structure of the *maqāma*, which marked a shift from pure classical poetry to poetic narration. The work is composed in rhymed prose broken up by rhymed poems. It tells of an encounter between two imaginary characters: a narrator, who as a general rule represents the author, and a colorful hero who assumes different aspects in each tale—wise man or bandit, ascetic or bon vivant—and who meets with all sorts of adventures. Each encounter constitutes a narrative unit, a *maqāma* (*mahberet* in Hebrew), or "session" in English. Whether a wanderer or a poor Bedouin, the hero always extricates himself from the most difficult situations by the virtuosity of his repartee and the vastness of his culture. His discourse, always edifying, is embellished with wordplay and humorous considerations on the mores of his time.

This literary genre reached its apogee in Arabic with Al-Qasim al-Hariri, who lived in Basra between 1054 and 1122. Al-Hariri was a virtuoso of language, and his writings conformed to the tastes of the elites of his time, who liked to gather and engage in verbal sparring matches, vying with one another in displays of erudition. Al-Hariri was a philologist and used a very ornate language. His hero Abu Zayd was known to everyone, and the texts of his *maqāmat*, magnificently illustrated—in particular, by Yahya ibn Mahmud al-Wasiti in Baghdad in 1237—were copied and distributed in almost the same manner as the Qur'an.[6]

It was Yehuda al-Harizi who proved himself master of this literary genre in Hebrew.[7] Born in Spain in about 1165, he was a typical example of the roving poet dependent on patrons. In the late twelfth century, he spent time in various cities of Provence. Then he returned to Toledo and, in about 1215, definitively departed for the East—first Egypt, then the Holy Land, and finally Mesopotamia. He died in Aleppo in 1225.[8]

Between 1194 and 1197, al-Harizi, a translator, first embarked on the exegesis of Maimonides's *Mishneh Torah*, written in Arabic but with Hebrew characters. In his introduction to the treatise *Zera'im*, al-Harizi inserted his translator's credo: "I copy one word for another, but my primary objective is a clear presentation of the content." Within that perspective, he translated Maimonides's *Guide for the Perplexed*, after receiving a commission from Provençal Jewish patrons. His fluent and comprehensible style drew criticism from his rival, Samuel Ibn Tibbon, who produced a more scholarly but less literary version of that famous work. Jewish scholars deemed Ibn Tibbon's Hebrew version superior, but it was al-Harizi's more flowing and readable version that would be used as the basis for the first translation of that fundamental work into Latin.

We now know that not only did al-Harizi freely adapt a few texts by al-Hamadhani but that he also translated them.[9] His masterpiece as a translator, however, is without a doubt the Hebrew version of Ahmed al-Qasim al-Hariri's *Maqamat*, under the Hebrew title *Mahbarot Ittiel* (*The Notebooks of Ittiel*). He completed this work after receiving a commission from generous patrons in Toledo. Al-Harizi's version, a free adaptation in fluent Hebrew, was hailed as a success of the first order by lovers of language, or rather, of two languages, Hebrew and Arabic, in Spain and beyond the peninsula. Unfortunately, only a single manuscript of this work remains (Oxford, 1976), and it contains only twenty-five *maqāmāt* (the second session, then the last twenty-four).[10] A modern version based on this sole source appeared in Israel in 1951.[11]

Al-Harizi, a true bilingual, managed to translate into Biblical Hebrew most of the linguistic improvisations of his Arab predecessor al-Hariri. For example, he succeeded in rendering into Hebrew an epistle that can be read two ways, from beginning to end and vice versa, and a poem that remains coherent even when the second hemistich of each line is omitted. The allusions to the Qur'an find equivalents in quotations from biblical verses, and the names of persons, as well as places, are also transformed into biblical names. By this means, al-Harizi made accessible to the Western Jewish audience a typically Eastern Arab literary model.

Al-Harizi wrote poetry in both Hebrew and Arabic. Among his works is a book of *tajnis*, *Sefer ha-Anaq* in Hebrew (*Book of the Necklace* in English). But the largest part of his literary opus consists of the book of Hebrew *maqāmāt* that he himself composed, entitled *Tahkemoni*. He wrote this book during his various travels in the East, with the declared aim of increasing the renown of Hebrew in regions where knowledge of the language was already beginning to decline. He says so explicitly in one of the introductions to the work, written in Arabic, in which he speaks of the Oriental Jews, who barely know Hebrew, and of his obligation to revive this sacred language through an original and purely poetic writing. The structure of the book, which is dedicated to several patrons from different cities, follows al-Hariri's classical model: fifty notebooks, forty-nine of them in rhymed prose, embellished with rhymed poems. Each notebook contains an independent narrative: an adventure; a social satire; an evocation of travels; a polemic between the pen and the sword, wine and water, generosity and stinginess, or soul and body; and even studies on Hebrew poetry and literary criticism. The heroes, as required, are two in number: the narrator Heyman the City Dweller (*Heyman Ha-Ezrahi*) and his friend, Heber the Wanderer (*Hever Ha-Keini*), the main protagonist of the book. The language is astonishingly rich and supple, the vocabulary essentially biblical, and the author often makes a surprising and parodic use of it. In short, al-Harizi imported to Western Jews, generally speakers of Hebrew, the Eastern model of the Arabic *maqāma*; and, during his many journeys, he exported that same model, but in its Hebrew version, to Jews in the East, generally Arabic speakers.

Of the Spanish Jewish poets writing in Hebrew, al-Harizi was the only one to compose a work on the model of the Eastern *maqāma*, that is, as a collection of sessions in which each chapter, while depicting the same protagonists, constitutes a tale in itself. The other writers in Hebrew preferred a more Western version, in which a single thread runs through the entire work. Such is the case, for example, in Joseph Ibn Zabara's *Sefer ha-sha'ashu'im*, which appeared in Barcelona during the same period. Nevertheless, al-Hariri's model—in its Hebrew version by al-Harizi—reappeared in thirteenth-century Italy, in the famous *Notebooks of Immanuel*, by Immanuel ben Solomon (Immanuel of Rome), a unique work that would require a separate study.

Revisited themes

These three key examples clearly demonstrate the importance of the contribution of Arab culture, which played a vital role in the growth of Jewish culture in medieval Spain. They allow us to understand the role of that culture in the manifestation of the originality of Hebrew poetry. It is clear that the themes of Hebrew poetry also reflect subjects and images characteristic of the Arab universe. In love poetry, these include, for example, the yearning for a beloved woman who is off wandering; the suitor, prisoner to her love; the cruel beloved, who coats her lips with her lovers'

عَلَى شَاطِئِ النَّهرِ وَصُورَةُ الْبَغِيِّ فَرِيبَ الْعَجُوزِ فَوَقَفَتْ عَلَيْهَا زَمِنَهُ وَتَبِرِيَّهُ

وَمِمَّا بِإِزَاءِ بُسْتَانٌ مِـــــــــنْ بَسَاتِينِ نَهْرِ الثَّرْثَارِ

"Bayad, paralyzed with terror, at the banks of a river," Andalusian miniature in *Hadith Bayad wa Riyad* (History of Bayad and Riyad), thirteenth century, Vatican Apostolic Library, ms. ar. 368 fol. 19 (recto).

blood and whose eyes launch arrows that pierce the heart of any man who desires her; lovesickness; the fire of love; the beauty of young ladies, which surpasses the brilliance of the sun and moon; and many other themes. Hebrew love poems are called *shirei hesheq*, a term that immediately evokes the Arabic *'ishq*. These poems are so closely linked to Arabic poetry that some—by Samuel Ibn Naghrila and Moshe Ibn Ezra, for example—even evoke love between men. Another genre with a special place in medieval Andalusia was undoubtedly the poetry of the garden and of flowers.[12] It is associated with the evocation of springtime, of rains at the end of winter, and especially of the feasts of notables surrounded by the fragrances and colors of their gardens. In that sense, this poetry constitutes an important chapter in courtly poetry. Through it, the poet, within the context of a contractual dependency, praises his patron with the perfect image of his palace. The poetic text expresses what the visual arts, because of religious prohibitions, could not: it illustrates a reality captured with the senses, as a painting constructed of words. This verbal drawing, in which the sensual holds an essential place, follows the very precise style of *al-Wassf* (description) in Arabic ars poetica, and borrows much of its metaphorical system.[13] What is delightful is not only the reiteration of the same themes but also the Jewish poets' ability to adopt original images from the treasuries of Arabic poetry and to use them in a way that diverges from their original context.

1. Critical edition and translation into Spanish by Montserrat Abumalhan Mas (Madrid: Institute of Philology, 1985), translated into Hebrew under the title *Shirat Israel* [*Hebrew Poetry*] by Ben-Tzion Halper (Leipzig: Shtibel, 1924). A bilingual edition by Abraham Halkin, in Hebrew characters, has also appeared (New York, 1975).

2. See *Les Mu'allaqat ou Les sept poèmes préislamiques*, translated from the Arabic by Pierre Larcher with introduction and notes; preface by André Miquel (Saint-Clément-de-Rivière: Éditions "Fata Morgana," 2000), 136.

3. See Masha Itzhaki and Michel Garel, *La poésie hébraïque amoureuse* (Paris: Somogy, 2000), 62–63.

4. Ibid., 92–93.

5. For a detailed analysis of the Hebrew *qasida*, see Israël Levine, *M'eil Tashbetz* [*An Embroidered Tunic*] (Tel Aviv, 1995), 15–39.

6. See Sylvestre de Sacy, J. Reinaud, and H. Derenbourg, *Les séances de Hariri* (Paris: Imprimerie impériale, 1847–1853); and J. N. Mattock, "The Early History of the *Maqama*," *Journal of Arabic Literature* 15 (1984): 1–18.

7. See the detailed study by H. Schirmann and E. Fleischer, "Yehuda Al-Harizi," in *Hebrew Poetry in Christian Spain and in Provence* (Jerusalem: Magnes Press and the Ben-Zvi Institute, 1997), 145–220 (in Hebrew); and Masha Itzhaki, *Yehuda al-Harizi: Selected Texts, with Introduction* (Tel Aviv: Tel Aviv University Press, 2008) (in Hebrew).

8. These travels are the subject of several *maqāmāt* in his *Tahkemoni* (chaps. 28, 42, and others); see, for example, S. M. Stern, "An Unpublished Maqama by al-Harizi," in *Papers of the Institute of Jewish Studies, London, I* (Jerusalem, 1964), 186. Regarding his last years in the East, see Joseph Sadan, "Un intellectuel juif au confluent de deux cultures: Yehuda al-Harizi et sa biographie arabe," in *Judios y musulmanes en al-Andalus y el Magreb: Contactos intelectuales*, ed. Maribel Fierro (Madrid: Casa de Velázquez, 2002), 105–51.

9. On this subject, see J. Schirmann, "On the Question of the Origins of the *Tahkemoni*," in *History of Hebrew Poetry*, 1:371, as well as Y. Dishon, "The Poets in Spain, the Third *Maqāma* of the *Tahkemoni*," in *A Tribute to Israël Levin* (Tel Aviv, 1994), 79–94 (in Hebrew).

10. See E. Fleischer, "An Overlooked Fragment of the Translation by Yehudah Al-Harizi of the Maqam[a]s of Al-Hariri," *Journal of Jewish Studies* 24 (1973).

11. Y. Peretz, ed., *Mahbarot Itel* (Tel Aviv, 1951).

12. I discuss this genre in *Elei ginat arougot* [*Toward the Garden Beds*] (Tel Aviv, 1988). For this study, I used the Andalusian anthology *Kitab al badi fi-l-sasf al-rabi'* [*The Book of the Descriptions of Springtime*] as a model.

13. Israël Levine studies this question thoroughly in his three-volume *Me'il Tachbetz* [*Secular Hebrew Poetry in Spain*] (Tel Aviv, 1980–1996). A large number of chapters in that book analyze how certain poetic genres and various themes function in Arabic literature.

Ibn Sahl of Seville, a Jewish Poet Who Converted to Islam

In his voluminous *Nafh al-tib min ghusn al-Andalus al-ratib* (*The Scents Exuding from the Moist Branch of al-Andalus*),[1] Abu al- ʿAbbas al-Maqarri (d. 1631) mentions several Jewish poets who wrote in Hebrew and occasionally in Arabic. The only one who stands out is Ibn Sahl, who left a *diwān* in that language that takes up nearly a hundred pages. We possess one ancient and three recent Arabic editions, plus a supplement that collects a few unpublished fragments.[2]

Abu Ishaq Ibrahim Ibn Sahl, known as al-Ishbili ("from Seville") but also as al-Israʾili ("the Israelite"), was one of the distinguished poets of al-Andalus (Muslim Andalusia) in the thirteenth century. He was born to a Jewish family in Seville in 1212 or 1213. He spent the greater part of his life in his native city and left only in his final years. Ibn Sahl devoted himself completely to poetry; he did not go to work as a *kātib* (secretary to the chancellery) until a short time before his death. The city of Seville, subject to the reign of the Almohads and threatened by the advance of the Christian rulers of Spain, was at the time pervaded by a dull, gray atmosphere. Ibn Sahl found his only means of escape in poetry and in platonic love, which he ardently celebrates in his poems.

His poetic talent apparently manifested itself when he was sixteen, and it was at that same age that he is believed to have converted to Islam. He abandoned Seville at the time of its reconquest by Ferdinand III in 1248 and went to live in Ceuta, where he was hired as a secretary for the governor (*wālī*) Abu Ali Ibn Khalas. The *wālī*, sending his son as an emissary to Abu ʿAbdullah al-Mustanir I, the Hafsid ruler of Ifriqiya, charged the poet with accompanying his son. But a turbulent storm sank the ship transporting them, sealing the fate of all its passengers. Upon learning of the poet's death by drowning at the age of forty, one of the grandees of the time purportedly said, "The pearl has returned to its element!"[3]

Some of his contemporaries doubted the sincerity of his conversion to Islam, but Ibn Sahl responded to such suspicions with a patient and understanding silence. In any event, as Hussain Monés reminds us in his entry on the poet in the *Encyclopaedia of Islam*,[4] no material advantage could be anticipated from such a conversion in the Muslim Seville of the time. Moreover, forced conversion was not practiced under the Almohads, as it would be under the Catholic kings after the Reconquista. And in one of his poems, Ibn Sahl himself explains his conversion:

> *The love of Muhammad turned me from the love of Moses;*
> *without his divine largesse, I should not have found the right path.*
> *It was not out of loathing [for my former faith], but because*
> *the law of Moses was abrogated by Muhammad's law.*

Further complicating the situation, in most of his poems Ibn Sahl celebrates his platonic love for a Jewish youth named Moses, before turning away from him for another youth by the name of Muhammad. This has encouraged critics, even in our own time, to consider poems in the first vein as allusions to Ibn Sahl's original religion and as the expression of his regret for having abandoned it. Poems in the second vein are viewed as confirmation of his loyalty toward his new faith. Such conjectures, however, do not withstand even a superficial examination of the poems, which, in both phases, are packed with erotic images and steeped in an obsessiveness altogether typical of love. In one of his poems, the poet, who had a keen interest in wordplay, even places the prophet Moses side by side with—contrasts him with—the Moses who is the object of his adulation: "By Moses in times past was the magic broken / By Moses does now the magic arrive."

As moderns, we cannot consider the sincerity of the Sevillian poet's conversion a pertinent question. Indeed, it would be surprising if a convert never recalled his former faith. Furthermore, the proximity between the two monotheistic religions would likely have encouraged bouts of nostalgia, reminiscences, and a desire for a synthesis between the two cultures. Ibn Sahl accomplishes that synthesis so well that it alone suffices to dispel any suspicion of hypocrisy or duplicity on his part.

Apart from a few poems by Ibn Zaydun (1003–70), Ibn Khafaja (1058–1137), and a few others, the literary genius of al-Andalus undoubtedly lay not so much in poetry as in the works of its great prose writers such as Ibn Shuhayd, who was a poet as well (992–1034), Ibn Hazm (994–1064), Ibn Tufayl (1105–85), and Ibn Arabi (1164–1240). All the same, a lovely landscape poetry and the invention of the poetic form known as the *muwashshah* remain the two most decisive poetic contributions of the Arabs of Spain. In a style inspired by music and song, the *muwashshahs* replaced the famous Arabic *qasida*. Whereas the *qasida* has a single meter and a single rhyme throughout the poem, the *muwashshah* consists of stanzas with various line lengths and several rhymes. Its style in itself constituted a revolution in the aesthetic of classical Arabic poetry and would serve as an example for the inventors of Arabic free verse in the modern age.

In addition to his mastery of the art of the *muwashshah*, Ibn Sahl bestowed on al-Andalus the gift of a sensuous, often sensual poetry, marked by frequent wordplay and homophony, practices that undoubtedly constituted a means of diversion for his melancholic nature. His poetry is filled with astonishing, often audacious, comparisons and evocations not lacking in originality:

Beauty took up residence in him,
having granted to others only furtive favors.
Jewels draw their brilliance from him, who never wears them.
Do the stars need to imitate gems?

His poems also have a real psychological acuity. They are studies, as it were, of what it means to be in love. They also provide variations on the theme of the sickly gauntness of lovers:

It is not that I am drowned in my tears,
it's that my heart, worn out, grew so light that it floated,
the tears in my eyes have in your absence
flooded over the specter of sleep, finally blotting it out.

But Ibn Sahl's poetic virtuosity is most obvious in his *muwashshahs*. That is especially true of the poem that, a century later, would inspire a famous *muwashshah*, still widely read and sung in our own time, by the Granadan vizier and poet Lisan al-Din ibn al-Khatib (1313–74). In it Ibn Sahl displays great perspicacity in his analysis of feelings and accomplishes lofty musical feats. It is no doubt his own condition as one devoted to platonic love that he describes when he writes:

O full moons appearing on the day of separation,
sparkling, guiding me from peril to peril,
in love I have no sin but this:
from you comes beauty, from me eyes that look.
Mortally wounded, I delight in my beloved and aspire to be near him only in thought.

As in most of his poems, nature, by virtue of the enormity of its spectacle, serves as a reservoir

"A messenger speaks to Bayad near the river and gives him a letter from Riyad," Andalusian miniature in Hadith Bayad wa Riyad (History of Bayad and Riyad), thirteenth century, Vatican Apostolic Library, ms. ar. 368 fol. 17 (recto).

In me tears spark flames
that flare up as they please,
on his cheeks they are coolness and peace;
in my innermost depths, they are conflagration.
In keeping with love's law I shield myself
from the lion in him, and in him love the gazelle. ●

A professor in the Department of Arabic Studies at the Institut National des Langues et Civilisations Orientales (INALCO) in Paris, Kadhim Jihad Hassan is also a poet, essayist, and translator. His writings include La part de l'étranger: La traduction de la poésie dans la culture arabe (Sindbad/Actes Sud, 2007) and Le labyrinthe et le géomètre, essais sur la littérature arabe classique et moderne, suivi de Sept figures proches (Aden, 2008).

of similes and metaphors. In their vividness and contrasts, they help him to grasp the bewildering nature of the ever-fleeing object of his desire:

Each time I complain of my passion for him, he smiles
like the hills abounding in clouds,
Rain spills down like the atmosphere at a funeral,
but they in their joy celebrate a wedding.

Often as well, the cleavage produced in the poet by the perpetual nonpossession of the love object feeds a predilection for an oppositional rhetoric:

1. See the critical edition by Ihsan ʿAbbas, 8 vols. (Beirut: Dar Cadir, 1988).
2. On the basis of an old edition by Hasan ibn Muhammad al-Attar in 1862, one edition of Ibn Sahl's Diwan was brought out by Ihsan ʿAbbas (Beirut: Dar Cadir, 1967); another by Muhammad Qabʿa (Tunis: Kulliyyat al-adab wa-l-ʿulum al-insaniyya, 1985); and a third by Yusra ʿAbd al-Ghaniyy ʿAbd Allah (Beirut: Dar al-kutub al-ʿilmiyya, 2002). M. Qabʿa also published Ashʿar li-Ibn Sahl al-Israʾili lam tun-shar [Unpublished Poetry of Ibn Sahl the Israelite] (Tunis: Kulliyat al-adab wa-l-ʿulum al-insaniyya, 1980).
3. Quoted, but without naming the person who uttered it, in different entries on Ibn Sahl, including Father Louis Shaykhu's entry in his anthology of classical Arabic poetry, Al-Majani [The Harvests, 1882], revised and reissued by a committee of faculty members from the Lebanese University under the supervision of Ifram al-Bustani, 4th ed. (Beirut: Dar al-Mashriq, 1993), 5:91.
4. Encyclopaedia of Islam, 2nd ed. (Leiden: Brill, 1954), s.v. "Ibn Sahl" (H. Monés).

The Figure of the Jew in
A Thousand and One Nights
Dominique Jullien

The world of the *Arabian Nights*, also known as *A Thousand and One Nights*, presents us with a rich mosaic of peoples. To the geographical variety of the tales, which take the reader on voyages from India to Italy, Africa to Iraq, and Persia to the Sunda Islands, must be added the cultural diversity of the medieval Muslim world, a fundamentally multiethnic world, as reflected in the tales. Contrary to the situation in Christian lands, in which the Jews represented the only religious minority in uniformly Christianized regions, the Jews of Islam were one religious minority among others. The Jews were tolerated in the Islamic world—which did not exclude discriminatory measures, applied differently according to countries and periods. But by and large the chance the Muslim world offered its Jewish minorities to survive, and even to prosper, was unquestionably superior to that offered by Christian countries. The Jewish figures in the *Arabian Nights* reflect that cultural, social, and religious complexity.

Dominique Jullien

Dominique Jullien is a professor of comparative literature at the University of California, Santa Barbara. Her publications include *Les Amoureux de Schéhérazade: Variations modernes sur les Mille et une nuits* (Droz, 2009); *Récits du Nouveau Monde: Les voyageurs français en Amérique de Chateaubriand à nos jours* (Nathan, 1992); and *Proust et ses modèles: Les Mille et une nuits et les Mémoires de Saint-Simon* (José Corti, 1989).

The role of the Jews in the composition and dissemination of the work

Given that the *Arabian Nights* were the product of a long process of amalgamation unfolding over several centuries and countries, it is natural to pose the question of a Jewish contribution, alongside other sources: Indian, Persian, Arabian, Egyptian, and so on. This is especially the case given the density of the cultural exchanges between the Jewish and Muslim communities during the medieval period. Some European orientalists of the nineteenth century liked to imagine a Jewish origin for the *Arabian Nights*, being particularly attentive to the mythological motif of the heroine who saves her people. That hypothesis of the biblical origin of the

> " *Victor Cousin, reflecting on the similarities between the frame prologue of* Nights *and the biblical story of Esther goes so far as to consider the possibility of a Jewish origin of the frame prologue.* "

Aladdin and the genie of the magic lamp echoes the Jewish legend in which Solomon holds power over the genies. Ottoman miniature from the nineteenth century, Istanbul, Library of the University of Istanbul.

Nights immediately became the object of a spirited debate in scholarly circles. Victor Cousin, reflecting on the similarities between the frame prologue of *Nights* (Scheherazade's ruse of telling one tale each night to King Shahryar, thereby succeeding in saving the young women from certain death) and the biblical story of Esther (who succeeds in saving the Jewish people from the massacre to which the Persian king Assuerus, advised by his minister Aman, consented), goes so far as to consider the possibility of a Jewish origin of the frame prologue.[1] This hypothesis was adopted by a number of critics, and even found its way into the *Encyclopedia Britannica*, but it was refuted by another eminent scholar, the folklorist Emmanuel Cosquin, who countered with an Indian origin of the frame tale.[2]

Besides the frame tale, several short narratives seem to come from the Talmudic tradition, as we will see below. They stage Jewish characters of admirable piety and are part of the repertoire of professional storytellers; naturally, they have become acclimatized to both the structure of the *Nights*, the flexibility of which is open to the most variegated narratives, and the spirit of a collection, for which the *adab* or exemplary narrative intended for edification is a major source.

The collection also contains legendary motifs of Jewish origin, which were blended into the Persian, Indian, or Arabian stories, as in the legend about Solomon's power over rebellious genies. The oldest source of that legend is the biblical Book of Wisdom [Wisdom of Solomon] or yet again the *Antiquities of the Jews* by Flavius Josephus; the legend passed into Qur'anic folklore and turns up in some of the most famous tales in the *Nights*, such as "The Merchant and the Genie," "The Fisherman," and "The Brass City," in which the genies are imprisoned in vases as punishment for disobeying Solomon; an echo of this belief is recognizable in "Aladdin," in which the genie is imprisoned in a lamp.

From the beginning, the book seems to have been well known in the Jewish milieu. The earliest known mention of the book by its present title of "A Thousand and One Nights" goes back to the eleventh century: "The Thousand and One Nights" is listed in the catalog of a Jewish library in Cairo around 1150; the manuscript is presently kept in the Bodleian Library of Oxford. There are two manuscript fragments of Judeo-Arabic versions of *A Thousand and One Nights* dating back to the seventeenth century, one in the Firkovitch collection of Saint Petersburg and the other in the Taylor-Schechter collection of Cambridge. The only complete Judeo-Arabic manuscript of the *Nights* that we have dates from 1866 and was written in Calcutta, a city that had a strong Iraqi-Jewish immigration in the 1930s; today, this manuscript is kept in Jerusalem.

The representation of Jewish characters

The Jews, an integral part of the society of the *Nights*, are also very much in evidence, though generally in a marginal way, in the tales. The Burton translation is the richest in Jewish characters. It is also the longest, with ten volumes, followed two years later by six supplementary ones. The stories that depict Jews are often unfavorable toward them, but not always, as we shall see. The Jews are rarely main characters in the *Nights*, with the exception of a few heroines, such as Zayn al-Mawassif, the wife of the Jewish merchant (see below). Their representation in the tales is stereotyped (this should not surprise us in these narratives, in which all the characters, including the heroes, are one-dimensional actors rather than characters endowed with psychological depth) and, by and large, rather negative. Moreover, this is just as true of the other ethnic minorities (Bedouins, blacks) or religious ones (Christians). The Bedouins are dirty and brutal; the blacks are lubricious. The Christians, too, are caricatured, often as drunks, since the Qurʾanic ban on alcohol does not apply to them. Thus, in "The Hunchback's Tale," a drunken Christian beats the Hunchback, whom he takes for a thief, and is about to be executed for the murder of a Muslim.[3] By and large, Christians play the role of the villain. An old Christian woman, disguised as a dervish, assassinates two kings.[4] The hero, Grain-de-Beauté, kidnapped by a Christian pirate ship, is enslaved in Genoa for fifteen years.[5] The beautiful slave Zumurrud is drugged and kidnapped from her master by a Christian.[6]

As for their place in society, the Jews are represented in a realistic manner. In the tales, as in the historical reality, they practice various trades, always urban: merchants, money changers, pawnbrokers, goldsmiths, physicians. It is a Jewish physician who tries to treat the Hunchback. A tenacious prejudice depicts them as grasping, motivated solely by profit, dishonest. The Jewish physician in the story of the Hunchback falls down the stairs as a result of his greed: he is in such a hurry to open the door of a patient he believes to be rich that he rushes down the stairway without waiting for the light. Another dishonest Jew is the merchant who takes advantage of Aladdin's ignorance to buy treasures from him for a ridiculously low price.[7] The stereotype would also have it that they are rich: in the caliph's story of the fisherman, we see a poor fisherman trade his monkey (which, without his knowing it, symbolizes his fate) for the Jewish lender's monkey; thanks to this exchange, the fisherman gets rich at the expense of the Jew.[8]

A more hostile image is that of the Jewish magician. A sinister Jewish sorcerer inflicts three animal metamorphoses on his Muslim prisoner, and requires him to perform degrading and dangerous tasks. In a just turn of events, he is punished by the successive loss of his daughter and of his own life.[9] Several stories contain a motif that would later be adopted by Shakespeare in *The Merchant of Venice*: in contrast to the Jewish father, who is afflicted with all the defects, a daughter (or sometimes a wife), who is endowed with all the perfections, falls in love with the hero and converts to Islam. This religious motif also has a practical narrative value in that it permits a polygamous denouement, as in the story of Ali, in which the hero ends up marrying both the young Muslim girl and the converted Jewess. As for the Jewish fathers and husbands, they usually don't measure up to the Muslim hero, and are killed if they attempt to resist or refuse to convert (see again the story of Ali). The husband of Zayn al-Mawassif is a brute who beats his wife and ends up buried alive (or imprisoned for life, in Mardrus, who for once attenuates the original), while the lovers, exonerated by their adherence to the true faith (or their conversion to it, in some versions), abandon themselves with impunity to the pleasures of love.[10]

Sometimes the Jewish characters are treated in a cavalier fashion by the justice of the country. Zayn al-Mawassif's husband (though he is in the right) is forced to confess under torture that he is not legally married to her. There are some scenes in which the Jewish protagonists are summarily executed without further ado. Having succeeded in escaping from prison in Baghdad with the help of the head guard, Grain-de-Beauté is surprised by two Jews, very wealthy money changers, and well known to the caliph. The two troublesome witnesses are stripped and their throats cut forthwith, without the least scruple.[11] In general, the negative image of the Jew is integrated into the economy of the tale in that, poetic justice having most often been done in the end, the reader is invited to rejoice at the defeat of the Jewish protagonist, and to look on it not as a misfortune that strikes the victim of religious persecution but as the deserved punishment of an obstinate guilty party. The inferiority of the unbeliever, in contrast to that of the woman or the slave, is entirely voluntary in the view of medieval Islam, since all he has to do to end discrimination is embrace the one true faith.

A positive image?

Some rarer tales, on the other hand, offer a positive image of Jews. These tales are not found in Galland or Mardrus, but several, which highlight the piety of a Jewish character, appear in the editions from Bulaq and Calcutta, and have been collected by Burton and subsequently by Bencheikh and Miquel. Thus, in "The Devout Israelite," the generosity of the Jewish weaver, who gives all his day's earnings to the beggar, is rewarded when he finds a pearl in the rotten fish that was all he had left for his meal. He exchanges the pearl for a large sum of money, and tries to give half of it to the beggar, but then the latter reveals his angelic nature and leaves him in possession of all the money.[12] In "The Island King and the Pious Israelite," a pious Jew, having lost his entire fortune, sets sail with his wife and his sons. They are shipwrecked and each lands on a different island. The man discovers treasures on his island, of which he becomes king. In the end, his reputation for piety grows, and he finds his family.[13] "The Jewish Qadi and his Pious Wife" is reminiscent of the biblical story of Susanna: the woman falsely accused of adultery becomes a recluse whose reputation for miraculous holiness draws crowds; she ultimately confounds her accusers.[14]

Caught up in the rich labyrinth of the *Nights*, these stories, which come from the Jewish tradition, passed into the Muslim tradition of edifying tales intended for the populace; they have become narratives of universal wisdom. Beyond the religious allegiance of the heroes, what counts in these stories is their moral dimension. They celebrate the human virtues—generosity, piety, uprightness, patience—common to all religions. Their presence in the *Nights* is living proof of the cultural commonality, the rapid circulation of the stories through time and space, and the shared traditions that characterize this gigantic narrative amalgamation.

Jewish readers and translators of the *Nights*

The same complex linguistic and cultural symbiosis may be seen in the reception of the *Nights* by the Jewish culture. In the Middle Ages, the Jews played an important role as intermediaries in the transmission of the stories between the East and the West, particularly the Jews from Spain and Italy who knew Arabic. This could explain the resemblance between certain tales from the *Nights* and certain stories by Chaucer and Boccaccio of the fourteenth century. Later, the *Thousand and One Nights* regained its popularity in the Jewish culture thanks to Antoine Galland's translation. The Ashkenazi world was the first to welcome the work. By 1718, there was a Yiddish version—a sort of adaptation of the German translation of Galland, dating from 1712. Hence, that version was incomplete, since we know that the full Galland translation was not published in its entirety until 1717. Its title is not recognizable and the name Scheherazade does not even appear. It was not until 1796 that a true Yiddish translation was published in Frankfurt.

In the Sephardic culture—despite the proximity of the Arabian sources—the book was also filtered through the Galland version. The first Judeo-Arabic translation based on the Galland version (in Arabic, written with Hebrew letters) appeared in Oran in 1882. Just before the First World War, in 1913, a partial translation in Ladino or Judeo-Spanish was published in Izmir, Turkey; it is another retranslation by Galland.

An emblematic figure: Rafael Cansinos Asséns

Rafael Cansinos Asséns, the first translator of the *Nights* into Spanish (from Arabic, that is, since an anonymous version based on Galland had been circulating in Spain since the eighteenth century, subsequently followed by a translation of Weil's German version, and the Mardrus version had been translated by the novelist Vicente Blasco Ibáñez by 1916), published his translation after the Second World War.[15] Cansinos, in his preface, wonders about the paradoxical absence, in the Spain of the three cultures, of a translation of the *Nights* into Judeo-Spanish, the language of medieval Spain of the three cultures, a language still maintained by the Sephardic populations originating in Spain. Why, when everything in multicultural Spain seemed destined to give the *Nights* a privileged place, was there no translation of this book? After all, medieval Spain had translated other Arabic works, such as the *Book of Kalila and Dimna* and the *Forty Vizirs*; and King Alfonso X, known as "the Wise," welcomed scholars of all three cultures at his court. Furthermore, all medieval Spanish literature, *romancero* first and foremost, is steeped in Moorish influence. This dream of a Judeo-Spanish version of the *Thousand and One Nights* that would be the incarnation of the religious and cultural symbiosis of the Spain of Al-Andalus was lived, in a sense, by the Sevillian Cansinos in his very flesh. Cansinos converted to Judaism, translated the *Talmud*, the *Nights*, and the Qur'an, and was one of the first to highlight in his writings the contribution of Jewish and Muslim cultures to the historical legacy of Spain. His translation claims to bear witness to a bygone era of harmony, a late substitute for a text (lost or nonexistent) produced by the confluence of the three cultures. We find this same idealized vision in Renan, who, in his famous *Averroès et l'averroïsme* (1861), nostalgically evokes the brief and blessed days of the *convivencia*, when Christians, Jews, and Muslims lived in peace, when languages, texts, and ideas circulated freely, and when "all worked harmoniously together to produce the oeuvre of a common civilization." Jorge Luis Borges, a reader of Renan and a disciple of Cansinos, a great aficionado of the *Nights*, pays homage to this most multicultural of works, this wayfaring work par excellence:[16] if the *Nights* symbolized the Orient for Borges, it was not in the vague and vaguely pejorative sense that the word carried in the time of Proust, for example—in whose work the qualifier "Oriental" is applied indistinctly, in virtue of a constant slippage between two exoticisms, the Jewish and the Arabian, so that a painter who wanted to represent Ali Baba, for example, would give him the traits "of the heaviest 'punter' at the Balbec tables"[17]—but in a deeper and more universal sense. If the *Nights* embody the Orient, it is because they give us a glimpse of the crossroads of cultures that, beyond the division that has been made during the modern era between the Jewish and the Muslim worlds gives all of us "Those beloved marvels / That were Islam's and that are yours / And mine today" ("Metaphors of One Thousand and One Nights"). Setting out from the humble shop of a Jewish bookseller in Cairo, this cosmopolitan book pursues its path from Argentina to Japan—its stories belonging to everyone and no one, effortlessly passing through borders, languages, and religions.

---

1. Victor Chauvin, *La Recension égyptienne des "Mille et une nuits"* (Brussels: Office de Publicité, 1899).

2. Emmanuel Cosquin, "Le Prologue-cadre des *Mille et une nuits*," *Revue biblique* 6 (1909): 7–49; included in *Études folkloriques* (Paris: Champion, 1922), 265–347.

3. Sir Richard Francis Burton, trans., "The Hunchback's Tale," in *A Plain and Literal Translation of the Arabian Nights' Entertainments*, 10 vols. (Benares: Kama-Shastra Society, 1885), 1:255–325; Antoine Galland, trans., "Histoire du petit bossu," in *Les mille et une nuits*, 3 vols. (Paris: Garnier-Flammarion, 2004), 1:357, 2:72; Joseph-Charles Mardrus, trans., "Histoire du Bossu avec le Tailleur," in *Les mille et une nuits*, 2 vols. (Paris: Laffont, coll. Bouquins, 1980), 1:146–223; Jamel Eddine Bencheikh and André Miquel, trans., "Conte du tailleur, du bossu, du juif, de l'intendant et du chrétien," in *Les mille et une nuits* (Paris: Gallimard, Bibliothèque de la Pléiade, 2005), 1:209–85.

4. Burton, trans., "Tale of the King Omar Bin al-Nu'uman and His Sons Sharrkan and Zau al-Makan," in *A Plain and Literal Translation*, 2:77–333, 3:1–114; Mardrus, "Histoire du roi Omar Al-Neman et de ses deux fils merveilleux Scharkan et Daoul-Makan," in *Les mille et une nuits*, 2:292–492; Bencheikh and Miquel, trans., "Conte du roi Umar an-Nu'man et de ses deux fils Sharr-Kan et Daw al-Makan," in *Les mille et une nuits*, 1:366–548.

5. Burton, trans., "Ala al-Din Abu'l-Shamat," in *A Plain and Literal Translation*, 4:29–94; Mardrus, trans., "Histoire de Grain-de-Beauté," in *Les mille et une nuits*, 1:625–66; Bencheikh and Miquel, trans., "Conte de Ala ad-Din Abu sh-Shamat," in *Les mille et une nuits*, 1:963–1025.

6. Burton, trans., "Ali Shar and Zumurrud," in *A Plain and Literal Translation*, 4:187–228; Mardrus, trans., "Histoire de la belle Zoumourroud avec Alischar fils de gloire," in *Les mille et une nuits*, 1:744–70; Bencheikh and Miquel, trans., "Conte de Ali Shar et de sa servante Zumurrud," in *Les mille et une nuits*, 1:1125–64.

7. Burton, trans., "Ala al-Din," in *A Plain and Literal Translation*, 3:51–265; Galland, trans., "Histoire d'Aladin," in *Les mille et une nuits*, 3:7–119; Mardrus, trans., "Histoire d'Aladdin et de la lampe magique," in *Les mille et une nuits*, 2:324–92.

8. Burton, trans., "Khalifa the Fisherman of Baghdad," in *A Plain and Literal Translation*, 8:145–204; Mardrus, trans., "Histoire de Khalife et du Khalifat," in *Les mille et une nuits*, 2:101–33; Bencheikh and Miquel, trans., "Conte de Khalîfa le pêcheur," in *Les mille et une nuits*, 2: 302–34.

9. Burton, trans., "Mercury Ali of Cairo," in *A Plain and Literal Translation*, 7:172–209; Mardrus, trans., "Histoire d'Ali Vif-Argent," in "Histoire des artifices de Dalila-la-Rouée," in *Les mille et une nuits*, 1:962–89; Bencheikh and Miquel, trans., "Histoire de Ali Vif-Argent," *Les mille et une nuits*, 2:899–931.

10. Burton, trans., "Masrur and Zayn al-Mawasif," *A Plain and Literal Translation*, 8:205–63; Mardrus, trans., "Les amours de Zein al-Mawassif," in *Les mille et une nuits*, 2:237–52; Bencheikh and Miquel, trans., "Conte de Masrur et Zayn al-Mawasif," in *Les mille et une nuits*, 2:335–83.

11. Mardrus, trans., "Histoire de Grain-de-Beauté," in *Les mille et une nuits*, 1:656; Bencheikh and Miquel, trans., "Conte de Ala ad-Din Abu sh-Shamat," in *Les mille et une nuits*, 1:1008.

12. Burton, trans., *A Plain and Literal Translation*, 4:283–85; Bencheikh and Miquel, "Conte du juif charitable," in *Les mille et une nuits*, 2:60–62.

13. Burton, trans., *A Plain and Literal Translation*, 5:290–94; Bencheikh and Miquel, trans., "Conte du pieux Israélite devenu roi," in *Les mille et une nuits*, 2:370–75.

14. Burton, trans., "The Jewish Qadi and His Pious Wife," in *A Plain and Literal Translation*, 5:256–59.

15. Rafael Cansinos Asséns, trans. and preface, *Libro de las Mil y una noches*, 3 vols. (Mexico: Aguilar, 1966 [1st ed., 1955]).

16. Jorge Luis Borges, "Metáforas de Las Mil y Una Noches," in *Historia de la noche* (1977), trans. as "Metaphors of One Thousand and One Nights," by Jack Ross [first published in *Magazine* 1 (2003): 36–38]. See also two essays, "Les Traducteurs des *Mille et une nuits*," in *Histoire de l'Eternité*, in *Œuvres complètes* (Paris: Gallimard, Bibliothèque de la Pléiade, 1993), 1:416–36, and "Les Mille et une nuits," in *Sept nuits*, in *Œuvres complètes* (Paris: Gallimard, Bibliothèque de la Pléiade, 1999), 2:668–80.

17. Marcel Proust, *Remembrance of Things Past*, trans. Moncrieff and Kilmartin (London: Vintage Books, 1982), 794; *A l'ombre des jeunes filles en fleurs*, 2:98 (Paris: Bibliothèque de la Pléiade, 1954 edition, 2:739).

Judeo-Persian Literature
Vera Basch Moreen

Jews have lived in Iran for almost three millennia and became profoundly acculturated to many aspects of Iranian life. This phenomenon is particularly manifest in the literary sphere, defined here broadly to include belles lettres, as well as nonbelletristic (i.e., historical, philosophical, and polemical) writings. Although Iranian Jews spoke many local dialects and some peculiar Jewish dialects, such as the hybrid lo-Torah[i] (Heb. + Pers. suffix of abstraction), meaning "non-Torahic" (a dialect that combines both Semitic [Hebrew and Aramaic] and Persian elements), their written, literary language was Judeo-Persian (Farsi in Hebrew script), which was close to the *dari* (Pers., court, house) language of classical Persian literature, despite the fact that it retained some Middle Persian (Pahlavi) features in its early phases and some colloquial features throughout its development.[1]

Vera Basch Moreen

Vera Basch Moreen is an independent scholar and a specialist in Judeo-Persian studies, she coedited *The Encyclopedia of Jews in the Islamic World* (Brill, 2011). Her publications include *In Queen Esther's Garden: An Anthology of Judeo-Persian Literature* (Yale University Press, 2000).

Earliest literary traces

Fifty-four tomb inscriptions from Afghanistan dating between the eighth and thirteenth centuries represent not only the first traces of written Judeo-Persian but of New Persian as well.[2] Because many of the Jews of Iran and the broader Persianate world (including Afghanistan and Bukhara) had been literate since biblical times, they maintained the Hebrew alphabet for written communication in the vernacular as Jews had done in all parts of the world. The earliest available documents are two commercial letters from Dandan-Uiliq (East Turkestan) from the eighth century,[3] two letters in the Cairo Geniza from the tenth and eleventh centuries, and a law report from Ahvaz (Khuzistan) dated 1020–21.[4] They demonstrate that Judeo-Persian orthography was fully developed well before actual "literary" texts appeared. Clearly, Iranian Jews remained close to the Torah, as fragments of biblical books in Hebrew dating from the ninth century were discovered in Iran. These, in turn, led to the rise of Judeo-Persian commentaries intended to explicate the Torah in the peoples' vernacular. Among these (most only in fragments) are commentaries on the books of Ezekiel, Daniel, Isaiah, Proverbs, Ruth, and the Song of Songs. In addition to preserving important linguistic Middle Persian (Pahlavi) features, several of these commentaries display the Karaite leanings of their anonymous authors.[5] The oldest-known Judeo-Persian manuscript of the Pentateuch dates from 1319, while the oldest Judeo-Persian translation, that of Jacob b. Joseph Taus, dates from 1556.[6] Many fragments of Bibles and Apocrypha were collected by Giambattista Vecchietti in the seventeenth century from Iran's major Jewish towns. Two important lexicographical works connected with the Bible, Talmud, and Midrashic literature have come to light thus far: Solomon b. Samuel of Urganj's (Khwarizm) *Sefer ha-Melitsa*, composed in 1339, and Moses b. Aaron b. She'erit Shirvani's *Agron*, composed in 1459.[7] Judeo-Persian literature as belles lettres appeared only at the beginning of the fourteenth century, although the lack of earlier texts does not necessarily prove their complete absence. Western Judeo-Persian manuscript collections (more such manuscripts no doubt still exist in Iran) include a great variety of genres, such as translations of the Bible, secular and religious poetry, chronicles, rabbinical works, lexicography, translations of medieval Hebrew poetry, transcriptions of classical Persian poetry, and original epics; belles lettres, especially poetry, appears to dominate every collection, thus confirming that Iranian Jewry shared the love of this genre with their Muslim compatriots.[8]

Epics

Judeo-Persian manuscript collections include a fairly large number of popular Persian mystical epic romances transcribed into the Hebrew alphabet, such as Nizami's (d. 1209) *Khosrow va Shirin* (Pers., Khosrow and Shirin) and Jami's (d. 1492) *Yusuf va Zulaykha* (Pers., Joseph and Zulaykha). Although no Judeo-Persian copy of *Shah-nama* (Pers., The Book of Kings), Iran's great national epic by Firdawsi (completed in 1010), has surfaced thus far, it is, along with the romances, the major literary model that inspired the writing of original Judeo-Persian epics. Mowlana (Pers., "our master") Shahin-i Shirazi (fl. 14th century) was the first—and undoubtedly the best—Iranian Jewish poet. He wrote several *masnavi*s (romance epics in rhymed couplets) based on various episodes from Genesis, Exodus, Ruth, Job, Esther, Ezra, and Nehemiah. By recounting sacred Jewish narratives through exclusively Persian rhetorical and literary motifs, he endeavored to create a Jewish "national epic" in the

> **" By recounting sacred Jewish narratives through exclusively Persian rhetorical and literary motifs, the Jewish poet Shahin endeavored to create a Jewish 'national epic' in the spirit of Firdawsi's masterpiece. "**

spirit of Firdawsi's masterpiece. Shahin's Pentateuchal epics, the so-called *Bereshit-nama* (Pers., The Book of Genesis), composed in 1327, *The Tale of Job* (based on the book of Job), and *Musa-nama* (Pers., The Book of Moses [based on Exodus]), composed in 1358, describe and endow biblical heroes with many characteristics emblematic of Persian epic heroes. Similarly, in *Ardashir-nama* (Pers., The Book of

Ardashir [Ahasuerus]) and *Ezra-nama* (Pers., The Book of Ezra), composed in 1333 and based on the biblical books of Esther, Ezra, and Nehemiah, respectively, Shahin reimagined Queen Esther's marriage to Ardashir (Ahasuerus) as a loving union that came to be divinely rewarded by their engendering Cyrus the Great, the future savior of Babylonian/Iranian Jewry. Despite his acculturated approach, Shahin's poetry possesses a clear Jewish ethos.[9]

'Imrani (1454, after 1536) was Shahin's best imitator and perhaps more versatile than his model. He set to verse much of the books of Joshua, Ruth, 1 Samuel, and parts of 2 Samuel in *Fath-nama* (Pers., The Book of Conquest), his most important epic. Among his other works were *Ganj-nama* (Pers., The Book of Treasure), which versified part of the Mishnaic tractate Avot, *Hanukkah-nama* (Pers., The Book of Hanukkah), and *Asara haruge ha-malkut* (Heb., The Ten Martyrs of the Kingdom) and *Qisse-yi haft baradarn* (Pers., The Story of the Seven Brothers), also

known as *Musibat-nama* (Pers., The Book of Calamity), all based on well-known rabbinic narratives. His *Vajibat va arkan-i sizdahgani-yi iman-i Isra'el* (Pers., The Thirteen Principles of Israel's Faith) is based on Maimonides's (d. 1204) foundational study of the same. Additional minor didactic poems display 'Imrani's thorough familiarity with a wide range of Jewish learning, colored, however, by Sufi expressions and concepts that he appears to have identified with Jewish parallels.[10]

Poets such as Khwajah Bukhara'i, who set to verse the book of Daniel in 1606, and Aaron b. Mashiah, who versified the book of Judges in 1692, continued the tradition of setting biblical books into Persian verse.[11]

Religious and lyrical poetry

Iranian Jewish poets also wrote numerous religious and lyrical verses, mostly in Judeo-Persian, but quite a few are Hebrew or bilingual (Hebrew-Judeo-Persian, Aramaic-Judeo-Persian) poems with highly diverse themes, such as *Purim-nama* (Pers., The Book of Purim), the poem written expressly for the beloved Iranian Jewish holiday

The ground swallows Korach and his rebellious companions (Numbers 16:32). Judeo-Persian miniature in the *Musa-Nama (Book of Moses)* from the poet Shahin, fourteenth century. Jerusalem, Israel Museum, ms. 180/54, fol. 138 (verso).

of Purim Mullah Gershom's (seventeenth century?), and Benjamin b. Misha'el's (whose pen name was "Amina"; 1672/73, after 1732/33) various poems on the 'Akeda (Heb., The Sacrifice of Isaac), the Twelve Tribes of Israel, and a bilingual (Judeo-Persian-Hebrew) reworking of Solomon Ibn Gabirol's (d. ca. 1058) Azharot (Heb., Warnings). Some Judeo-Persian poets also wrote panegyrics in honor of God (Shihab Yazdi, eighteenth century?), the Messiah (Siman Tov Melammed [whose pen name was Tuvya]; d. 1823 or 1828), and a number in honor of Moses (Benjamin b. Misha'el, Yusuf Yahudi [eighteenth century]) and the prophets Ezekiel (Yehezqel Khwansari; eighteenth century?), Ezra (anonymous), and Elijah (Babai b. Lutf; seventeenth century).

Numerous *ghazals* (short lyrical poems) and *ruba'iyat* (quatrains) by the greatest Iranian poets, such as Sa'di (d. 1292) and Hafiz (d. 1389), were transcribed into Judeo-Persian. Although Judeo-Persian imitations and original creations are difficult to distinguish because they are often anonymous, use pen-names not necessarily identifiable as belonging to Jewish poets, and focus on traditional Persian lyrical themes, such as the beauty of the beloved, his/her absence or presence, and his/her fickle nature, some that are identifiable, such as the lyrical verses of Benjamin b. Misha'el, are remarkable.[12]

Historical writings

Iranian Jews produced few historical documents as far as it is known. Two Judeo-Persian chronicles of vital importance for their history and for Iranian history as a whole in the seventeenth and eighteenth centuries, especially given the scarcity of historical documents produced by Iranian minorities, are *Kitab-i Anusi* (The Book of a Forced Convert) of Babai b. Lutf and *Kitab-i Sar-Guzasht-i Kashan dar bab-i 'ibri va goyimi-yi sani* (The Book of Events in Kashan concerning the Jews; Their Second Conversion) by Babai b. Farhad (Babai b. Lutf's grandson). Both of these works are sound historical documents that recount a number of internal Jewish communal events, and also several external events that affected the Jews. The first chronicle covers selected events between 1617 and 1662, and the second between 1721 and 1731. They tend to emphasize persecutions, at times detailing their causes, extent, and duration, as these were experienced by the chroniclers themselves, particularly in Kashan, their hometown. Both chronicles are written in the popular Persian *masnavi* form, and the later one shows a marked deterioration in language and literary style.[13]

A short narrative poem from Bukhara, known as *Khodaidad* (Pers. for the Hebrew name Natan'el, "God gave"), is of unclear authorship. It was probably written at the end of the eighteenth or the beginning of the nineteenth century and recounts movingly the martyrdom of an ordinary cloth merchant persecuted by local Muslims.[14]

Philosophy, polemics, and mysticism

Only one major Jewish Iranian text with philosophical-polemical content is known thus far, Rabbi Judah b. El'azar's *Hobot Yehudah* (Heb., The Duties of Judah), written in 1686. The author was a physician from Kashan, and he displays considerable learning in medieval Islamic and Jewish philosophy, as well as traditional religious sources. He discusses the principles of the Jewish faith as propounded by Maimonides (d. 1204) in a Judeo-Persian prose style full of Hebrew words and quotations. Polemical arguments against various Muslim charges defending, in particular, the eternity of the heavenly Torah and the superiority of Moses's prophecy form an interesting dimension of this work.[15]

Although traces of "practical Kabbalah," in the form of amulets, spells, and prognostications, appear frequently in Judeo-Persian manuscripts, it is not yet possible to know the extent of the spread of Kabbalah in Iran. Some involvement is to be presumed from the name of Rabbi Joseph of Hamadan, who was active in Castile at the beginning of the fourteenth century. What is more certain is that many Iranian Jews were strongly attracted to and influenced by Islamic mysticism (Sufism). A mystical-philosophical treatise by Siman Tov Melammed known as *Hayat al-ruh* (Ar., The Life of the Soul) is based on the works of Maimonides and on Bahya b. Paquda's (ca. 1050–1156) *Hobot ha-levavot* (Heb., The Duties of the Heart). A grand amalgam of Jewish and Muslim mystical and philosophical concepts, it is written in both Judeo-Persian and Hebrew, and in both prose and verse.[16]

Writing in Judeo-Persian has meant that Iranian Jews severed themselves perhaps deliberately, but probably more on account of their tradition to preserve the script of the Torah, from the mainstream of Iranian literature, which is hardly aware of this body of work to this day. This "graphic barrier" was not, however, entirely unbridgeable, as the great variety of Judeo-Persian literary works attests to the distinctly one-way influence of their non-Jewish literary environment. The Judeo-Persian literary heritage remains largely unexplored. Much work needs to be done in the field in order to assess its merits for both the Persian and Jewish literary canons.

1. Gilbert Lazard, "La judéo persan, entre le pehlevi et le persan," *Studia Iranica* 6 (1987): 167–76.

2. Benzion D. Yehoshua-Raz, *From the Lost Tribes in Afghanistan to the Mashhad Jewish Converts of Iran* (in Hebrew) (Jerusalem: Bialik Institute, 1992), figs. 53–67.

3. Only one such letter had been known until now, but now see Zhang Zhan, "Jews in Khotan in Light of the Newly Discovered Judaeo-Persian Letter," in *Irano-Judaica* 7 (Jerusalem: Ben-Zvi Institute, forthcoming).

4. Thamar Gindin, "Judeo-Persian Literature. 1. Early Period," in *Encyclopedia of Jews in the Islamic World* (Leiden: Brill, 2010), 3:64–65.

5. Shaul Shaked, "Two Judaeo-Iranian Contributions: 1. Iranian Functions in the Book of Esther; 2. Fragments of Two Karaite Commentaries on Daniel in Judaeo-Persian," in *Irano-Judaica: Studies Relating to Jewish Contacts with Persian Culture throughout the Ages*, ed. Shaul Shaked (Jerusalem: Ben-Zvi Institute, 1982), 292–322.

6. Walter J. Fischel, "Judaeo-Persian. 1. Literature," in *Encyclopaedia Islamica*, 4:308a.

7. Vera Basch Moreen, "Judeo-Persian Literature. 2. Medieval Period," in *Encyclopedia of Jews in the Islamic World*, 3:66.

8. See, for example, Amnon Netzer, *Manuscripts of the Jews of Persia in the Ben-Zvi Institute* (in Hebrew) (Jerusalem: Ben-Zvi Institute, 1985), and Vera Basch Moreen, *Catalogue of Judeo-Persian Manuscripts in the Library of the Jewish Theological Seminary of America* (New York: Jewish Theological Seminary, forthcoming).

9. Vera Basch Moreen, *In Queen Esther's Garden: An Anthology of Judeo-Persian Literature* (New Haven, CT: Yale University Press, 2000), 26–119.

10. Ibid., 119–43.

11. Ibid., 143–58.

12. Ibid.; see chapters 11 and 12.

13. Vera Basch Moreen, *Iranian Jewry's Hour of Peril and Heroism: A Study of Babai Ibn Lutf's Chronicle (1617–1662)* (New York: American Academy for Jewish Research, 1986), and *Iranian Jewry during the Afghan Invasion: The Kitab-i Sar Guzasht-i Kashan of Babai Ibn Farhad (1721–1731)* (Stuttgart: Franz Steiner Verlag, 1990).

14. Carl Salemann, "Chudaidat: Ein judisch-bucharisches Gedicht," *Memoires de l'Académie Impériale des Sciences de St. Pétersbourg* 42 (1897): 1–30.

15. Amnon Netzer, *Duties of Judah by Rabbi Yehudah Ben El'azar* (in Hebrew) (Jerusalem: Ben-Zvi Institute, 1995).

16. Moreen, *In Queen Esther's Garden*, 260–67.

Illuminated Judeo-Persian Manuscripts

Just as they emulated the language and rhetoric of classical Persian literature, Iranian Jews imitated the book arts of the Iranian tradition of illuminated manuscripts, which flourished especially in the Timurid and Safavid eras (ca. 1400–1700). Only thirteen Judeo-Persian illuminated manuscripts have come to light thus far; the earliest dates from the second half of the seventeenth century.

By content, illuminated Judeo-Persian manuscripts fall into three categories: (1) Hebrew transliterations of popular Persian *masnavi*s (epic romances; narrative poems in rhymed couplets), such as Jami's (d. 1492) *Yusuf va Zulaykha* (Joseph and Zulaykha), Nizami's (d. 1209) *Haft Paykar* (Seven Portraits), and *Khosrow va Shirin* (Khosrow and Shirin); (2) individual album leaves of verse with various portraits; and (3) original Judeo-Persian epics based on biblical themes that also include much Jewish and Muslim legendary lore. The third category is the most interesting by far. Judeo-Persian miniature paintings imitate the miniature paintings that adorn manuscripts of the *Shahnameh* of Firdawsi (the most famous epic of Persian literature, completed in 1010) and Persian epic romances. The most notable Judeo-Persian miniature paintings illustrate the biblical epics of Mowlana Shahin (fl. fourteenth century), especially his *Musa-nama* (The Book of Moses) and *Ardashir-nama* (The Book of Ardashir),[1] and 'Imrani's (1454, d. after 1536) *Fath-nama* (The Book of Conquest).[2] Judeo-Persian miniature paintings cannot be compared with their Persian counterparts produced by royal workshops; they resemble more closely provincial and bazaar imitations of the royal workshops. The similarity of figures, backdrops, decorative elements, and the use of inferior pigments suggests that illuminated Judeo-Persian manuscripts emerged from a more impoverished material environment. They also tend to be the work of one painter per manuscript rather than the collective effort of a workshop. The identity of the painters cannot be determined, as all Judeo-Persian miniature paintings are unsigned. The painters may have been Jews or they may have been Muslims especially commissioned, as some of the discrepancies between a number of inscriptions within the paintings and the paintings themselves, as well as the widespread use of painterly clichés of Judeo-Persian, suggest. On the other hand, it is also likely

In this triptych miniature, Zulaykha (top right), on the roof with her nurse, longs for the imprisoned Yusuf (Joseph); Yusuf (left, largest panel) meditates in his cell; Ya'qub (Jacob, bottom right) mourns his son Yusuf. From Yusuf va Zulaykha by Jami, New York, Jewish Theological Seminary of America, ms. 1496, fol. 8 (recto).

that Jewish painters, like their Muslim colleagues, simply took significant liberties with the texts they illustrated. If the painters were Muslims, illuminated Judeo-Persian manuscripts may represent striking examples of Jewish-Muslim cooperation.

Most Judeo-Persian manuscripts, including illuminated ones, were copied by owners for their private use, as colophons indicate. Calligraphers who worked for patrons are also generally anonymous. At least two manuscripts were copied in the excellent hand of Nehemiah ben Amshal of Tabriz, of whom we have no further information.[3]

Just like the identity of the painters and most calligraphers, the identity of the patrons of illuminated Judeo-Persian manuscripts remains unknown. It would stand to reason that these manuscripts were made for important members of larger, more prosperous Jewish communities, such as Isfahan and Kashan, and that they were treasured heirlooms. While the originality of Judeo-Persian illuminated manuscripts, both in terms of style and content, is less obvious in the Iranian artistic context that they imitate, it is particularly arresting when the miniature paintings are compared with illuminated Jewish manuscripts from medieval and Renaissance Europe. ●

Vera Basch Moreen works at the Center for Advanced Judaic Studies at the University of Pennsylvania. A specialist in Judeo-Persian studies, she coedited The Encyclopedia of Jews in the Islamic World *(Brill, 2011). Her publications include* In Queen Esther's Garden: An Anthology of Judeo-Persian Literature *(Yale University Press, 2000).*

1. Israel Museum (IM) 180/54; Hebrew Union College (HUC) 2102; Stiftung Preussischer Kulturbesitz (SPK) Or. Oct. 2885 and SPK Or. Qu. 1680 Jewish Theological Seminary of America (JTSA) 40919, respectively, and 'Imrani's (1454, d. after 1536) *Fath-nama* (The Book of Conquest), BL Or. 13704; BZI 4602.
2. BL Or. 13704; BZI 4602.
3. IM 180/54 and SPK Or. Oct. 2885.

The Music of al-Andalus: Meeting Place of Three Cultures

Dwight Reynolds

Among the many intellectual and artistic contributions with roots in medieval Islamic Spain, Andalusian music is probably the most widely known in the Arab world and the least well known in the West.[1] Andalusian music certainly merits attention in its own right as a rich tradition that has been transmitted orally for more than a thousand years and that continues to be performed in many regions of the Middle East, but it also merits special attention as the primary vehicle for the collective memory of, and nostalgia for, medieval Islamic Spain, which constitutes such powerful aspects of Arab and Sephardic Jewish cultures.[2] Although in modern times we may "remember" al-Andalus through images of monumental architecture, such as the Alhambra and the Great Mosque of Córdoba, these images did not circulate among Middle Eastern Arabs or Jews during the centuries after the expulsions. The writings of even the most famous Andalusian authors, such as Ibn Rushd (Averroes), Ibn ʿArabi, Ibn Hazm, Judah Halevi, Samuel Hanagid, and Maimonides, were only studied by a small intellectual elite. It is rather Andalusian poetry—specifically poetry conveyed in song— that has spoken powerfully to Arab and Sephardic communities over the centuries through performances in diverse contexts such as weddings, festivals, cafés, Sufi lodges, synagogues, wealthy private households, and royal courts. In the daily lived experience of Arabs and Sephardic Jews, songs of al-Andalus (or in the Andalusian style) have remained the single-most potent catalyst for the deep emotional ties felt even now toward a society that disappeared half a millennium ago.

Dwight Reynolds

Dwight Reynolds is associate professor in the Department of Religious Studies at the University of Southern California. He is the author of *Heroic Poets, Poetic Heroes: The Ethnography of Performance in Arabic Oral Epic Tradition* (Cornell University Press, 1995), editor of the volume *Interpreting the Self: Autobiography in the Arabic Literary Tradition* (University of California Press, 2001), and writer of the article "Music" in the *Cambridge History of Arabic Literature: The Literature of Al-Andalus* (Cambridge University Press, 2000).

The branches

Andalusian music has its most ancient origins in the indigenous music of the Iberian Peninsula on the one hand and the music of the Arabian Peninsula on the other. These cultures from opposite ends of the Mediterranean first came into direct contact in the eighth century, and out of that contact emerged a series of new musical traditions with distinctive characteristics. The overall history may be imagined as a tree with roots in both the Western and Eastern Mediterranean, with its trunk in Islamic Spain (eighth to fifteenth centuries), and with four main branches stretching out in different directions. To the north stretched a branch that reached the music of the Christian kingdoms of Northern Spain, impacted to a greater or lesser degree the sudden appearance of the troubadours in Southern France, and contributed, to all of medieval Europe, musical instruments such as the lute and the rebec (Ar., *rabab*). Another branch reached southward and eastward along the southern Mediterranean littoral, as far as Iraq and Yemen, a region throughout which there remain vibrant Andalusian musical traditions even today. A third branch followed the Sephardic diaspora, particularly the path of those communities who resided in Arab-speaking countries after leaving the Iberian Peninsula and who from there immigrated to modern Israel, France, and elsewhere. The final branch has continued through time in Southern Spain via the music of the Moriscos, intermingling with the folk musical traditions of Andalusia, including flamenco, and reemerging most recently in the revival of Andalusian music by Spanish artists such as Eduardo, Gregorio, and Carlos Paniagua, Luis Delgado, Begoña Olavide, Rosa Zaragoza, and others.

Contacts

This essay traces the history of the Andalusian musical tradition in the Iberian Peninsula, with a focus on moments of musical contact and influence among Muslims, Jews, and Christians. Of these two terms, *contact* is the easier to define and to document, while *influence* is a far more elusive process to capture, both theoretically and historically. First of all, influence does not necessarily follow naturally upon contact, though many often assume that it does; for every case of musical influence, there are also documented cases of musical traditions existing side by side for long periods without influencing each other to any great extent precisely because they define themselves by the difference that separates them. These neighboring but distinct traditions are often bound closely to issues of social identity: in short, we are who we are, and you are who you are, in part because we listen to our music and you listen to yours.

> " *In music, as in architecture and other arts, elements and structures cross linguistic and social borders.* "

In addition, influence takes place on a broad and subtle spectrum of possibilities that ranges from the borrowing of simple and discrete elements (such as an instrument, a bowing technique, a method of breathing, or a musical phrase), to transformative interactions that lead to hybrid genres and styles, to imitation or outright adoption. Far too often the term *influence* is perceived only in pejorative terms and is rejected out of hand, particularly by purists, because there is an assumption that to admit influence somehow implies a negation of the unique creativeness or innovativeness of the recipient (or acquiring) tradition, whereas in reality nothing could be further from the truth. In music, as in architecture and other arts, elements and structures cross linguistic and social borders as part of the very process of creativity, which results in distinctive new traditions over time.

The development of Arab music

The spread of Islam in the seventh century was accompanied by the rapid diffusion of the Arabic language and writing system. The writing of biographical notices, histories of various sorts, and collections of poems soon emerged as principal genres of Arabic literary output. Although a number of works about music and musicians were written in the eighth and ninth centuries, these were almost entirely assimilated into and supplanted by the *Great Book of Songs* (*Kitab al-aghani al-kabir* by Abu al-Faraj al-Isbahani [d. 967]). This remarkable work offers us hundreds of song lyrics, descriptions of performances, biographies of poets, composers, and singers, but sadly no actual melodies.

▶ See
Counterpoint
from the *Kitab
al-Aghani*,
pp. 52–53.

From the twenty-odd volumes of the *Great Book of Songs*, we know that Arab music at the time of the conquest of Iberia in 711 had already developed into a rich and sophisticated tradition, though it had perhaps not yet attained the levels of opulence that were to be reached in ninth- and tenth-century Baghdad.[3] During the Umayyad period (661–750), the city of Medina in particular was known as the musical center of the new Islamic Empire, and it was here that singers and musicians came to be trained before they sought careers either as free citizens or as owned performers ("slaves") in urban centers such as Damascus, Basra, Kufa, Jerusalem, Mecca, and elsewhere. In general, songs were created in a three-part process: (1) poets composed monorhymed odes, sometimes reaching up to a hundred verses in length; (2) composers, or sometimes composer-singers, selected a very small number of verses from larger poems, usually no more than four or five, and set them to music; and (3) the resulting song was then taught to a professional singer and accompanying musicians to be performed publicly. Quite often later singers and/or composers took up earlier songs and either added to them or improved them, creating a new version that competed with the older version in the performance repertory.[4] Composers and singers drew from several centuries of poetic composition, preserved primarily in oral tradition. One interesting aspect of this repertory is that it included the work of pagan, Muslim, Christian, and Jewish poets, all of whom were native speakers of Arabic. In the golden age of Arab medieval music (eighth to eleventh centuries), song lyrics were as likely to be from pagan as from Muslim poets, and the repertory also featured a smaller number of Christian and Jewish poets. The Christian poet al-Akhtal (ca. 640–ca. 710), for example, was the primary court poet of the caliph ʿAbd al-Malik (r. 685–710), the builder of the Dome of the Rock, while others, such as Abu Zubayd al-Taʾi (d. ca. 680) and the pre-Islamic Christian poet ʿAdi ibn Zayd (d. ca. 600), were only slightly less famous. The Christian singer Hunayn b. Baluʿ al-Hiri (fl. early eighth century) also came to prominence in this period. The Jewish poet al-Samawʾal ibn ʿAdiya (sixth century) remained proverbial for centuries for keeping to his oath even at the threatened cost of his son's life. Also noteworthy is that the rapidly expanding Islamic Empire soon incorporated many different ethnicities, such as Greeks, Egyptians, Nubians, Kurds, Iranians, Berbers, and so forth, and this ethnic and linguistic mixture rapidly came to be reflected among composers and singers, a substantial percentage of whom were not ethnically Arab.

⟩ See Nota bene on Samawʾal ibn ʿAdiya, pp. 940–942.

In 711 when the Muslim armies first crossed the Strait of Gibraltar to pursue the conquest of the Iberian Peninsula, both Arabs and Iberians possessed rich musical traditions, and both societies were profoundly multiethnic, as well as multilingual. Iberia was a crucible of many peoples, including Tartessians, Turdetans, Celts, Basques, Phoenicians, Greeks, Romans, Jews, Suevi, Alans, Vandals, and Visigoths, while the Islamic conquest brought with it elements of Arab, Greco-Byzantine, Jewish, Persian, Kurdish, Egyptian, and Berber cultures. In Iberia, a Visigothic elite, which constituted only a small percentage of the overall population, held power (shared in part with the "Hispano-Roman" nobility) over numerous regions, each with its distinct cultural and linguistic heritage, while Jews represented the lowest class and were subjected to a series of increasingly harsh laws restricting their right to own land, practice trades, and marry. Only slaves were of lower social rank. On the other hand, the nascent Islamic Empire consisted of a similarly small Arab elite, followed in power by non-Arab converts to Islam, the "protected minorities" (*alil al-dhimma*: Christians and Jews), slaves, and non-monotheists. In 711, Spaniard did not meet Arab; rather, two complex conglomerate civilizations came into contact.

The formative period: Eighth to twelfth centuries

It is not clear if the early Muslim governors of al-Andalus were patrons of the arts or not. Iberia was, both literally and figuratively, the "Wild West" of the Islamic Empire. The year 822, however, provides the symbolic starting point for Andalusian music as a tradition distinct from the music of the Arab East, the year in which the single-most famous figure in the history of Arab music, Abu l-Hasan ʿAli ibn Nafiʿ, commonly known by his stage name, Ziryab (blackbird, or lark), arrived in al-Andalus. Three accounts of Ziryab's life have come down to us that differ in a number of crucial details, so it is difficult to be certain of all of the facts. However, when he landed in al-Andalus after crossing the Strait of Gibraltar, he was met by a messenger who brought him the sad tidings that al-Hakam II, who had invited Ziryab to Córdoba, had recently died, but the messenger was able to add that the new ruler, ʿAbd al-Rahman II, was eager to welcome Ziryab to the Cordoban court. That messenger was named Abu Nasr Mansur Abu al-Buhlul. He was the head musician of the court—and he was Jewish. For anyone familiar with the extremely harsh laws against Jews that had been promulgated by the Visigoths before the Islamic conquest, it is striking that the lead musician of the Muslim court, and the personal envoy of the emir, was a Jew.

According to most histories of Arab music, including oral testimony given by many modern Andalusian musicians in North Africa, Ziryab was the genius who formulated the Andalusian musical tradition that has come down to us today. This, however, is historically very improbable, for the Andalusian repertory known today is composed almost entirely of two types of poetry—*muwash-shah* and *zajal*—which were not invented until after Ziryab's era. In fact, a thirteenth-century text that was discovered only in the last century tells us as much. In the two chapters on music that have survived from a much larger work by Ahmad al-Tifashi (d. 1253), the author tells us that Ziryab did indeed develop a new style, which became so popular that, at least in al-Andalus, all others were abandoned. But he adds that Ziryab's style only held sway until the early twelfth century, when the famous composer Ibn Bajja (d. 1139) combined "the songs of the Christians with those of the East, thereby inventing a style found only in al-Andalus, toward which the temperament of its people inclined, so that they rejected all others."[5] This simple phrase constitutes one of the most remarkable, and yet one of the most impenetrable, statements in the history of Andalusian music. Did Ibn Bajja meld the two styles in both lyrics and melody? Did he put Arabic poetry to Christian tunes? Did he perhaps apply Arab musical modes to Christian music or vice versa? Or is this possibly a reference to the new poetic form of the *muwashshah*, even though other sources say it was invented nearly two centuries earlier? We simply cannot say for certain at this point, but it is remarkable that an Arab writer in North Africa should characterize the Andalusian music of his day as a mixture of Christian and Arab song, and even more noteworthy that he attributes this innovation to a single musical genius.

❱ See article by Masha Itzhaki, pp. 943–951.

Whether al-Tifashi's statement refers to the new poetry or not, the *muwashshah* genre in and of itself embodied a type of cultural mixing, at least in its earliest stages. In a number of the oldest examples that have come down to us, the final two or three verses of the poems, known as the *kharja*, are bilingual, that is, composed of words of both Romance (the spoken popular form of Latin) and of colloquial Andalusian Arabic. These few dozen bilingual verses have been the subject of more academic debate than the entire corpus of tens of thousands of *muwashshahs* written in subsequent centuries. The new poetic forms were revolutionary: they were stanzaic, every verse ended in a rhyme but many different rhymes were used throughout the poem, and they possessed a type of semi-refrain in which the central rhyme recurred but each time with different words. This combination

"Bayad playing the lute in a garden for his lady and her court," *Andalusian miniature in Hadith Bayad wa Riyad (History of Bayad and Riyad)*, thirteenth century, Vatican Apostolic Library, ms. ar. 368 fol. 10 (recto).

had never been found in Arabic before; nor had it existed in Latin. Romance, the spoken colloquial Latin of everyday life, had not yet become a written language, so it is difficult to determine what the contribution from oral Iberian poetic traditions may have been, though this has been a matter for intense speculation on the part of scholars.

The new poetry was also quite popular among the Jewish communities of al-Andalus who first composed Arabic poems in the new forms, but then also adapted them to Hebrew. Hebrew *muwashshahat* became one of the signature genres of the florescence of secular Hebrew poetry in medieval Islamic Spain. The Andalusian *muwashshah* also spread throughout North Africa and in the eastern Mediterranean, and already by the twelfth century, Egyptians and Syrians were composing *muwashshahs* of their own, and continued doing so until the early twentieth century.

The historian Ibn Khaldun (d. 1406) wrote that in al-Andalus muwashshah songs were popular at all levels of society: "[they] were appreciated by all of the people, both elite and masses, due to the ease of understanding them and the familiarity oftheir style."[6] The Cordoban jurist Ibn al-Hajj provides the following disapproving description of a Cordoban wedding in one of his fatwas: "It is the custom of the common people to celebrate until dawn on the night of a wedding; men, women, and youths sing and dance around the family's home."[7] This is complemented by another description of a wedding celebrated in the streets of Cordoba penned by the biographer Ibn Humaydi: "Al-Nakuri, the woodwind-player sat in the middle of the gathering wearing a brocade cap on his head and a suit of raw silk in the 'ubaydi style. His horse was richly decorated and was held by a youth while he played the alboque [Ar.al-buq; a reed instrument] and sang amorous verses of Ahmad ibn Kulayb complementing his beloved, Aslam: 'Aslam, that young gazelle, delivered [aslama] me to passion. An antelope with an eye that obtains whatever he desires.'"[8]

The question arises of whether or not there is evidence of Andalusian music actually being performed in the north of the Iberian Peninsula. The answer, quite simply, is yes. Ten years after the death of Alfonso X in 1284, we find thirteen Arab and one Jewish musician among the twenty-seven musicians in the household of his son, Sancho IV of Castile (r. 1284–95); thus more than half of the court's professional musicians were Andalusians, presumably paid to perform Andalusian music. But this is only the tip of the iceberg, for Moorish and Jewish musicians were also found in the thirteenth-century royal household of Pedro III of Aragon (r. 1276–85), as well as in the fourteenth century in the courts of Jaume II of Aragon (r. 1291–1327), Juan I of Aragon (r. 1387–96),

> *In 1322 the Council of Valladolid severely condemned the custom of employing Muslim and Jewish musicians to perform inside churches, particularly during nightlong vigils.*

Juan II of Castile (r. 1406–54), Alfonso IV of Aragon (r. 1327–36), and Pedro IV of Aragon (r. 1336–87).[9]

Although it may at first be surprising to find Moorish and Jewish musicians in so many of the Christian courts of the north, there is further evidence that indicates an even deeper level of musical contact. In 1322 the Council of Valladolid severely condemned the custom of employing Muslim and Jewish musicians to perform inside churches, particularly during nightlong vigils where the singing of songs and the playing of musical instruments were "completely contrary to that for which the vigils had been instituted."[10] We also find evidence of participation by Muslims and Jews in the civil ceremonies of the Christian kingdoms. During the reign of Juan II of Castilla (1406–54), Prince Enrique was to be wed to Princess Blanca, daughter of King Juan of Navarra. In 1440, as she and her mother the queen traveled south for the marriage ceremony, they arrived in the small town of Briviesca, north of Madrid: "where they were solemnly received by all of the inhabitants of the city, each official waving his banner as best he could, with great dances and much enjoyment and delight; and after them came the Jews with their Torah and the Muslims with their Qur'an, in the manner that is usually done for Kings who have recently come to the throne in other parts; and there came many trumpets, players of wind instruments, tambourines, and drums (*atabales*), which made much noise as if a great host were approaching."[11] This practice appears to have been widespread from the number of mentions found in various sources.[12]

Influences

We have thus seen documentary evidence of music in the ninth-century court of Córdoba performed by Christian, Jewish, and Arab musicians and similar groups of professional Christian, Muslim, and Jewish musicians performing in the Christian courts of Northern Spain during the twelfth to fifteenth centuries. The dominant style of Andalusian music in the twelfth and thirteenth centuries is portrayed by at least one Arab commentator as a mixture of Arab and Christian song, and the most famous song genre of al-Andalus, the *muwashshah*, first emerged with a bilingual coda in Romance and Arabic, and was then quickly adapted into Hebrew as well. Middle Eastern musical instruments moved north in the early centuries, while new instruments developed in Christian realms moved south in later centuries. Christians hired Muslim musicians to perform in their churches, and Christians, Muslims, and Jews performed together in state- and church-sponsored celebrations under Christian rule. In the fifteenth century, Christian royalty and nobles in the north danced Moorish *zambras* from the south at their festivities. In the early sixteenth century, Queen Isabel of Portugal personally intervened to protect the musical traditions of the Moriscos from Christian hard-liners led by Cisnero, though later rulers eventually prohibited the use of the Arabic language, the wearing of Morisco dress, and the performance of Morisco music and dance. Together, these examples constitute a rather impressive portrait of musical contacts and influences, particularly when we consider that these are but the bits and pieces that have survived by chance for centuries in the documentary record. Without a doubt, the real process of musical contacts and influences took place among the common people, popular musicians who traveled from one festival to another, the hack musicians who performed at weddings and in taverns, at private gatherings and in the marketplaces. This is the level of cultural contact where he who pays the piper calls the tune, regardless of his religion, tongue, or dress, and the musician is always ready to please. As is often the case, these popular musicians almost certainly maintained a diverse repertory in order to be able to please any paying patron.

> *The realm of music must be characterized, at the very least, as a meeting place of the three cultures.*

I would like to close, however, with a word of caution: these musical contacts in and of themselves do not necessarily imply social or religious tolerance, a theme that is often raised in discussions of al-Andalus. Music is but one part of a much larger and more complex organization of social and cultural interactions. What I believe the evidence examined here does demonstrate is that in medieval Iberia, musical cultures were in constant contact and influenced each other in many ways over many centuries. With that in mind, any attempt to portray Andalusian music or medieval Spanish music as entirely independent and uninfluenced by the other would simply be historically inaccurate. Cultural mixings, influences, and hybridization are messy processes and difficult to analyze, but they are also, almost irrefutably, the way of the world and of all human culture. Whether or not this evidence of musical contact and influences tells us anything about religious or social tolerance must await a much broader analysis, the realm of music must be characterized, at the very least, as a meeting place of the three cultures.

*A longer version of this article appeared under the title "La Música Andalusí como Patrimonio Cultural Circum-Mediterráneo," in Gunther Dietz and Gema Carrera, eds., *El patrimonio cultural, multiculturalidad y gestión de la diversidad* (Seville: Instituto Andaluz del Patrimonio Histórico, 2005), 128-141.

1. Andalusian music is meant here, unless otherwise specified, not as the music of the modern southern Spanish region of Andalusia (Sp., *musica andaluza*), but rather those musical traditions that originated in medieval Islamic Spain or al-Andalus (Sp., *musica andalusí*). Unlike Spanish, English unfortunately uses a single adjective for these two distinct ideas.

2. Dwight F. Reynolds, "Musical Membrances of Medieval Muslim Spain," in *Charting Memory: Recalling Medieval Spain*, ed. Stacy N. Beckwith (New York: Garland, 2000), 229–62.

3. George D. Sawa, *Music Performance Practice in the Early Abbasid Era, 132–320 A.H./750–932 A.D.* (Toronto: Pontifical Institute of Medieval Studies, 1989).

4. For a more detailed description of these processes, see Hilary Kilpatrick, *Making the Great Book of Songs: Compilation and the Author's Craft in Abu l-Faraj al-Isbahani's "Kitab al-Aghani"* (London: Routledge Curzon, 2003), chapter 3, "On Songs and Singers."

5. Benjamin Liu and James Monroe, *Ten Hispano-Arabic Strophic Songs in Modern Oral Tradition* (Berkeley: University of California Press, 1989), 42.

6. 'Abd al-Rahman Ibn Khaldun, al-Muqaddima (Tunis: al-Dar al-tunisiyya li-1-nashr, 1989), 2:767.

7. Ahmed Tahiri, Las clases popular es en al-Andalus (Malaga: Editorial Sarria, 2003), 91.

8. Muhammad ai-Humaydi, Jadhwat al-muqtabis (Beirut: Dar ai-Kitab al-Lubnani, 1983), 223. This passage is quoted in Tahiri, Las clases popular es, p. 92, however, the phrase "el canto de la muwashsha . . . celebre entre la 'amma de Cordoba" (the singing of the muwashshaha ... famous among the masses of Cordoba) does not occur in the Arabic text and is apparently an interpolation by the author.

9. See the detailed discussion of Moorish and Jewish *juglares* [minstrels] in the courts of Northern Spain in Ramon Menendez Pidal, *Poesia Juglaresca y juglares* (Madrid: Editorial Espasa-Calpe, 1991) and the numerous original documents reproduced in Maria del Carmen Gomez Muntane, *La musica en la casa real catalano-aragonesa durante los anos 1336–1432* (Barcelona: Bosch, 1979).

10. Ibid., 110 and 139.

11. Cayetano Rossell, *Crâniens de los Reyes de Castilla* (Madrid, 1953), 2:565. My thanks to Teofilo Ruiz (UCLA) for directing me to this example.

12. Pidal, *Poesia Juglaresca*, 141.

The Iranian Jewish Musician Morteza Neydavoud

Morteza Neydavoud (1900–1990) playing his tār, a stringed Iranian instrument.

The Jews of Iran, who have never represented more than a tiny portion of the population, constituted for centuries, and even in the twentieth century, the majority of Iranian musicians. Many grand masters of traditional music were in fact of Jewish ancestry or religion, even when, for the sake of convenience, they bore Muslim names. It should be noted that the status of musician, *motreb*, an artist whose services are very much in demand but who at the same time is somewhat looked down upon, was particularly well suited to the situation of a minority. Some Jewish musicians became true celebrities, greatly contributing to the preservation of the richness

of traditional Persian music in the twentieth century. Morteza Neydavoud, for example, was born in Tehran in 1900 to a family of musicians. His grandfather Yahya Khan, and then his father, Bala Khan, were specialists in the *zarb* (goblet drum). Neydavoud attended the schools of the Alliance Israélite Universelle. He himself learned to play the *tār*, a stringed instrument, becoming the disciple of the great musician Darwish Khan.

One of the things that distinguished Neydavoud's music was his style of playing. He was an extraordinary *tār* player. Alone or accompanied on the violin by his brother Musa Khan, he composed and played melodies that have remained famous. His genius allowed him to invent new forms in a type of music whose traditional constraints remained very strong. He thus produced truly popular songs, without violating classical norms. In particular, his *Morq-e sahar*, based on a poem by the famous poet Malek osh-Sho'ara Bahar, is still sung at the end of major popular celebrations. The poem was written as a response to the dashed hopes surrounding the Constitutional Revolution of 1906, crushed by the despotism of Muhammad Ali Shah in 1908. Its evocation of freedom, which Neydavoud set to music in about 1920, continued to have a pressing urgency throughout the twentieth century. In fact, during the events that shook Iran in 1978 upon the fall of the Pahlavi monarchy, demonstrators would sing refrains from *Morq-e sahar*, which became the rallying sign of freedom and justice.

In addition to being a teacher, Neydavoud hosted a radio program for some ten years. In the early 1970s, he was invited by the Ministry of Information and Communication to tape-record the corpus of traditional Iranian music. He recorded nearly three hundred pieces in the various classical modes (*dastgāh*, *gushe*, *radif*). When the manager of the radio station offered to compensate him for this work, which had taken him more than a year and a half to complete, Neydavoud refused to accept any payment. According to the historian Nasiri-Far, he declared, "My beloved homeland and my people have offered me the pleasure of this art of music. In return, I give back to this same people and to this land what I drew from them. It is not necessary to compensate me. Thanks to music, the people of my country have demonstrated all their kindness toward me, and that is enough."

Morteza Neydavoud died in San Francisco at his son's home in 1990. ●

After receiving a master's degree in sociology—his studies focused on the Basif of Iran—from the Écoles des Hautes Études en Sciences Sociales in 1995, Alain Chaouli defended his thesis entitled "Les musiciens juifs en Iran aux xixe et xxe siècle et leur contribution à la sauvegarde du patrimoine musical iranien" (The Jewish Musicians in Iran in the Nineteenth and Twentieth Centuries and Their Contribution to the Preservation of the Iranian Musical Heritage), at the Sorbonne in 2002.

Cheikh Raymond, the "Hseïni" (1912–1961)

Raymond Raoul Leyris (1912–61), called Cheikh Raymond, Jewish Algerian oudist and singer.

On January 16, 2012, in the Moufdi Zakaria Palace of Culture that overlooks the city of Algiers, the Algerian minister of culture officially inaugurated the "Nawba" exhibition, devoted to the figures of urban music in Algeria. That exhibition was the prestigious centerpiece of the event "Tlemcen, Capital of Islamic Culture." Raymond Leyris, belatedly acknowledged in France under the name "Cheikh Raymond," was one of the nineteen personalities considered representative of the Constantine medina. The Algerian press did not fail to cover this completely unprecedented event: for the initiated, this was truly a public confirmation of the return of the eminent Algerian artist to his own people.[1]

Born out of wedlock, the son of Céline Leyris and a Jewish merchant from Batna who died in the war, Raymond was fundamentally a child of Constantine.[2] He was entrusted at a very young age to the care of a poor but generous Jewish foster family and received an upbringing rooted as much in the Jewish faith as in the medina shared by Arabs and Jews. He had the good fortune to learn from the great musicians of the city, particularly from Cheikh Si Tahar Benkartoussa. His extraordinary talent, already recognized in the 1930s, does not in itself explain the aura of Céline's son. Humble, respectful of knowledge, hardworking, and good with people, Raymond found the basic framework for his art in the legacy of the medina. Singing in Arabic, performing at both Muslim and Jewish family celebrations, he became one of the key figures in the urban musical heritage of Algeria, thanks especially to his many radio and television broadcasts, and his recordings.

On June 22, 1961, Raymond Leyris was assassinated by a bullet to the back of the neck, at the entrance to the popular street market of Souk El Assar. This assassination continues to elicit questions and speculations. As the regional daily *La Dépêche de Constantine et de l'Est Algérien* reported, it also left people deeply aggrieved, especially within the Muslim community of Constantine.

Objectively, the tragic conditions of his death served to legitimate the mass departure of the Constantine Jewish community, which—as Raymond's intimate circle has attested—was more resistant than has usually been admitted to an artist adulated by Muslim music lovers and, in fact, persuaded of the righteousness of the cause of Algerian self-determination. According to Raymond, as reported by one of his friends, the Algerian people could thereby "rediscover our roots."

As the informed observer knows, Raymond's official return to the national space owed a great deal to the attachment that Algerian music lovers felt for him. The internal exile imposed for so long on Si Tahar Benkartoussa's pupil resulted in part from the tumult caused by the unending conflict in Palestine. But

Cheikh Raymond's name was also freely bandied about in the Algerian press and at specialized colloquia. And attentive listeners to the high-quality broadcasts "Carnets de famille" (Family Notebooks) and "Carnets d'Algérie (Algerian Notebooks) on Algerian Radio 3 (a Francophone station) also had the pleasure of (once again) hearing his voice. These are obviously significant markers, especially since, for years, a number of those who had agreed to erase Raymond from collective memory—on no acknowledged historical grounds—also boasted in private that they were in possession of his precious recordings.

Some recordings of Raymond Leyris are now available on the Algerian market, though not necessarily those—reputed to be early artifacts—that, during the years when he was given the cold shoulder or subjected to inquisition, circulated within a discreet but efficient circle of initiates. This group kept alive the memory of his voice and his lute, but also of his life, his loved ones, and his aesthetic choices.

Historical and ethnomusicological research—albeit too timid in Constantine and throughout Algeria—will resituate Raymond within his lineage. They will express, more rigorously than the ideological fog that hovers too closely around his fate, the extraordinary place he occupied within the Algerian musical field. Often summoned against his will to testify in favor of the improbable mingling of communities in Algeria, Céline's son remained, above all, a child of the urban soil of Constantine, sustained by profound religious convictions and physically inscribed in the Arab poetic tradition.

The death of his violinist Sylvain Ghrenassia in 2004 marked the official end to the adventure of the Cheikh Raymond orchestra,[3] but even more to the long historical cycle of Constantine Jewish musicians who illustrated and defended the heritage of the medina.

Beyond the much-remarked-upon tribute that the French popular singer Enrico Macias paid to his father-in-law (Macias, the son of Sylvain Ghrenassia, married the grand master's daughter), it is in the stubborn filiation of the *malouf* singers El Hadi Rahmani and Mourad Laib that Raymond has remained alive. He still incites Constantine to dream, and the last word ought to come from that city: the Rhumel River, which irrigates Constantine, has permanently inscribed in its memory the fact that Raymond was a *Hseïni*, an "excellent." ●

Abdelmadjid Merdaci holds a doctorate in sociology and is a teaching researcher at the Mentouri University of Constantine. His publications include Dictionnaire des musiques citadines de Constantine *(Champ Libre, 2008).*

1. Abdelmadjid Merdaci, "Raymond Leyris, une survie algérienne," in *El Watan* (1993).

2. Bertrand Dicalé, *Cheikh Raymond: Une histoire algérienne* (Paris: First Ed., 2011).

3. Abdelmadjid Merdaci, "Les sanglots longs du violon," in *El Watan* (2004).

Chapter VII
Memory and History

The Jews of the Maghreb: Between Memory and History
Abdelkrim Allagui

Studies by Maghrebi academics on the Jews of the Maghreb during the modern and contemporary period belong to a relatively new field of research. An assessment of the state of scholarship on the Jewish minority reveals significant differences among the three countries of the Maghreb. Morocco and Tunisia are clearly a step ahead of Algeria. Since the 1980s, special interest in Judeo-Muslim relations has been apparent in Morocco, as illustrated, for example, by Mohamed Kenbib's remarkable graduate thesis.[1] Several themes of research, such

Abdelkrim Allagui

A professor in the Faculty of Human and Social Sciences at the University of Tunis, author of a thesis and several articles on the Jewish minority in Tunisia, Abdelkrim Allagui has published, notably, "L'école de l'Alliance israélite universelle en Tunisie pendant le protectorat: L'exemple de l'école de Sousse," *Revue d'Histoire Maghrébine* 37, no. 137 (February 2010).

as Zionism, the Jewish press, local monographs, and the relations between the Moroccan nationalist parties and the Jews have been addressed in various theses and dissertations, and are the object of debate in various seminars. In Algeria and Libya, research began a few years ago but remains timid. I would like to consider the example of Tunisia, which, I believe, is emblematic of a tendency taking shape in the Maghreb as a whole.

Is the history of minorities formulated in accordance with the same "canons" as that of "normal" societies, those of the majority groups? Thanks to the studies of A. M. Thiesse and B. Anderson, among others, we have learned the importance of a "national narrative" or "national romance" in constituting a national imaginary, a narrative identity. The question becomes more complicated when we turn to what is conventionally called a "national minority." Is this a micronation within the nation, whose construction would obey the same impulses? Obviously not. A "middling" definition of the notion of minority takes into account their smaller number but also and especially their subordination, more or less accepted, to the majority group (the society or nation).

"If I Forget Thee, O Tunis": From nostalgia to history

For the Jews of Tunisia, caught as they were between the colonizers and the colonized, matters are much more complex. Perceived at times as auxiliary troops in support of the colonial power, at others as one indigenous people among others, their status straddled different milieus. They constituted both a community apart and a national minority. That, in any case, was the experience of the vast majority of Jews of Tunisia. Subsequently, the history, or rather histories, of the Jews of Tunisia would be understood in terms of what could be called the "Albert Memmi syndrome," summed up in a line from that author's *Pillar of Salt:* "My life keeps coming back to me as a lump in the throat: I am not reducible."

▶ See article by Michael Laskier, pp. 415–433.

The memory of the Tunisian Jews began to take shape, to be traced out little by little, like the pieces of an improbable puzzle: in "exile," or rather, in the host or adopted countries, Israel and France. Individual recollections, from Cohen-Hadri and Charles Haddad to Gérard Haddad, and autofiction, from Memmi to Serge Moati,[2] redolent of jasmine and unleavened bread, are generally remembrances of an adolescence that, if not happy, was at least bathed in the womblike warmth of the native land. The memory of this community is echoed in another memory, less loquacious but also steeped in nostalgia, namely, official or state memory, which, since the departure of the Jews of Tunisia, has tended to idealize the recollection of a *convivencia* characteristic of Tunisian society. The case of the Jews of Tunisia, however, serves to invalidate pet theses of Paul Ricoeur and other philosophers or specialists in the human sciences, for whom memory and identity are so close as to be indistinguishable. It was only when there were almost no Jews left in Tunisia that an infatuation with the memory of the Jews of Tunisia, and later with their history, first appeared. It was more a matter of putting a past into words, recording a collective slice of life, in order to save it from oblivion. It was Jews who were already Gallicized, or who had become Israelis, who undertook that historiographical salvage operation, to borrow an expression from Michel de Certeau (the first to have pointed out the importance of the institutional context in determining the object of history). It is therefore striking that Lucette Valensi was the first to make the transition to the history of the Jews of Tunisia.

A historian of great renown and a major figure in the Annales School, Lucette Valensi began to study minorities after publishing her magnum opus, *Tunisian Peasants in the Eighteenth and Nineteenth Centuries.* She asks questions that from the start take their distance from the memorial posture, either plaintive or distraught or simply astonished. Instead of wondering, "How can one be a Tunisian Jew, then be one no longer?" she asks: "How did they endure so long? What upheavals shattered the modus vivendi that had bound the different elements of society to one another?"[3] Then, postulating that the impact of human beings in history is not always indexed to their numbers, she posits the legitimacy of a Tunisian Jewish history. At the same time, the former director of the *Annales* review produces a history of Jewish "history": "My ancestors," she writes, "did not write history. If they did not feel the need for it, it was because only one history made sense, sacred history. . . . : the Jews, a people of history par excellence, have a history book as their holy book. The injunction to remember—*zakhor*—is repeated ad nauseum in the Bible and reinforced by the injunction not to forget." In seeking to compensate for the omissions of her forbears, the historian invites us to partake instead in a profane history of the Jews of Tunisia. Doubly profane, we might say: emancipated from sacred history but also from sanctified memory.

After that inaugural effort, Paul Sebag took up more or less where Valensi left off. Sebag's case is extremely significant. He defines himself paradoxically as "a Frenchman in my soul and in my heart" and as a "Tunisian patriot." A strange identity, whose authenticity can be assessed once one knows the life story of that sociologist-turned-historian from Tunis, who ended up a historian of the Jews of Tunisia. Paul Sebag's founding work is,[4] in its very form, emblematic of its author's method: the style, sober to the point of austerity, leaves no room for nostalgia or for any other kind of effusiveness. The sociologist became a historian to fill a void that no historian (by profession) had the notion to fill before him: to write a comprehensive history of the Jews of Tunisia, from their origins to the present day.

Sebag's task is to respond to an identity in disarray. He does not seek to understand Tunisian society. Paradoxically, there is something religious about the attempt to preserve a Judeo-Tunisian identity by means of a book. Of Sebag's historical overview, Valensi notes: "A fully secular project, remote from any theological preoccupation, studying Tunisian Judaism as a sociological fact, it nonetheless harks back to a religious model. For indeed, what allowed the dispersed Jews . . . to endure as Jews? A book, the Old Testament . . . Some have said that history is the religion of those who have lost faith."[5] That judgment may appear harsh. For in the end it has been established—and the great historian Valensi knows this better than anyone—that "Jewish identity," an ambiguous syntagma if ever there was one, appeals, of course, to the Book, that "portable territory," as she says so well, but also involves other parameters. One of the most enduring is the gaze of the other, that demiurge-gaze that produces Jewishness through hatred, exclusion, folklorization, even mere astonishment (*how can one be Jewish?* to paraphrase Montesquieu).

"The irony might be that it will be the Muslim Tunisians who, attached to the historical heritage of their country, will therefore take up the study of, pursue knowledge about, Tunisian Judaism," observes Valensi.[6] This problematic is less surprising than it seems, since the word "irony" must be understood in the philosophical sense. All in all, the author of *Tunisian Peasants* was only anticipating what had already happened. My own investigations and those of others have continued, or have proceeded hand in hand with, a movement that began in Tunisia in the 1970s and that has proceeded at a steady pace since the 1980s. The Jewish community of Tunisia has been the object of study in scattered, isolated articles and in works devoted to the history of Tunisia as a

Cover of the work *Mémoires Juives* (Jewish Memories) by Lucette Valensi and Nathan Wachtel, published by Éditions Gallimard in 1986, in the "Archives" collection.

whole. The apprehension of the fate of that community has wavered between evasive allusions and succinct chapters. Mohamed Habib Belkhoja did devote a book to the Jews of the Maghreb but, despite its merits, that trailblazing text belongs to a prehistoriographical approach to matters of history. In his thesis written in the 1970s, M. Aziz Ben Achour speaks of the rise of the Jewish elite in the nineteenth century.[7] Earlier, in 1973, Fayçal El Ghoul had submitted a dissertation on the Palestinian question, as seen through the Tunisian press.[8] The Tunisian Jews are at issue, of course, but in this pioneering Tunisian research, concern with the Palestinian question takes precedence over interest in the Jewish community.[9] The book Ali Mahjoubi devoted to the origins of Zionism confirms that tendency. Later, Hedi Timoumi, in his "L'activité sioniste en Tunisie: 1897–1948" (Zionist Activity in Tunisia: 1897–1948), analyzes the historical conditions governing the birth of the Zionist movement in Tunisia. This text constitutes a first nod toward research on the Jewish community of Tunisia.

▶ See article by Michel Abitbol, pp. 297–311. Following the events in Palestine of 1929, the Palestinian question became the bone of contention and a marker of identity between Muslim nationalists and Tunisian Zionists. Until a very late date, however, it would remain primarily a political marker, one that has little affected, and even less structured, Judeo-Muslim relations. What must be kept in mind above all about this first body of research on the Jews of Tunisia—focused on Zionism, its currents, and its actions—is therefore the gap between the interest and importance of studies on Zionism in Tunisia and the relative weakness of that movement, at least until World War II. There is, as it were, an inversion in the proportions between research and the facts themselves.

Toward a historiography of the Jews of Tunisia

Interest in the history of the Jews of Tunisia has increased and grown stronger thanks to the convergence of two dynamics. The institutionalization of Tunisian research on the question (the formation of academic departments specializing in memory and heritage) and the broadening of research in France have been reinforced by a para-academic movement specializing in the history of the Jews of Tunisia, especially around the Société d'Histoire des Juifs de Tunisie, headed by Claude Nataf. The synergy of these two processes will give a significant boost to research through the organization of meetings and conferences held in France and Tunisia. This will surely not fail to encourage young researchers to take an interest in that new field of research.

The history of the Jews of Tunisia is now inseparable from national history. It is not a "negligible quantity," an obsolete, dead, or worse, amputated part of the national "body." Total history, that great ambition of the Annales School in its glory days, has now been relativized, of course: the great holistic designs have given way to the protean fragmentation of history.

The history of the Jewish minority is also inseparable from social history. Long absent from official history, they became an object of academic research only belatedly. In addition, the studies devoted to that minority long focused on the political activities of the urban elites. The blossoming of social history has had the ultimate effect of integrating minorities, and the number of historians taking an interest in them continues to grow. Perhaps we should add that the drive for social history owes a great deal to the convergence of Tunisian academic work with the coming of age of Judeo-Tunisian research in France. The memorial moment celebrating a more or less embellished past has had its day, and research now places itself on the terrain of history. And since every history feeds in one way or another on memory, whether recorded in the archives or peddled as life stories, a dual peril often lies in wait: the abuses of memory and the abuses of forgetting. Everyone knows that to be interested in the contemporary history of the Jews is to expose oneself to mistrust from two quarters: from the major specialists, who look down their noses somewhat at raiders who trample their exclusive preserve; and from a certain "anti-Zionism," which is ultimately suspicious of any research on the Jews. I dispelled that suspicion in my introduction.

The most formidable historiographical question underlying that great suspicion is the following: Is there a transnational history of the Jewish people that would account for a common fate of Jews throughout the entire world, irrespective of borders? It is a more difficult question than one might think. "The collision between a historiography that insists absolutely on the specific and one that endeavors to reintegrate the great massacre into the currents of universal history, which is not always a matter of course, can only be violent," wrote Pierre Vidal-Naquet. He went on to say: "Among the perverse effects of that instrumentalization of genocide is the constant and skillfully maintained confusion between hatred of the Nazis and hatred of the Arabs."[10] In reality, the history of the Jews of Tunisia has escaped the two tropisms of historiography described by that great historian of the ancient world.

I do not wish to disqualify memory. Rather, I leave it to the memorialists and to evenings of fraternization, reserving history for the historians alone, while preserving it from victimist passions and nationalist arrogance. Only history will be able to account for a fate that is not "reducible," as Albert Memmi admirably said.

---

1. Mohamed Kenbib, "Juifs et Musulmans au Maroc, 1859–1948," published by the Faculty of Letters, Mohammed V University in Rabat, 1994.

2. Serge Moati, *Villa Jasmin* (Paris: Fayard, 2003).

3. Lucette Valensi, "Une histoire des juifs de Tunisie est-elle nécessaire? Est-elle possible?," in *Histoire communautaire, Histoire plurielle, la communauté juive de Tunisie* (Tunis: Centre de publication universitaire, 1999), 51–63.

4. Paul Sebag, *Histoire des juifs de Tunisie des origines à nos jours* (Paris: L'Harmattan, 1991).

5. Valensi, "Une histoire des juifs de Tunisie est-elle nécessaire?" 59.

6. Ibid.

7. Ben Achour and Mohamed Aziz, *Catégories de la société tunisoise dans la deuxième moitié du XIXᵉ siècle* (Tunis: Institut national d'archéologie et d'art, 1989).

8. Fayçal El Ghoul, "La question palestinienne à travers la presse tunisienne: 1917–1936," thesis in history, University of Nice, 1973–74.

9. Ali Mahjoubi, *The Origins of Zionist Colonization in Palestine* (Tunis: Cérès Productions, 1990) (in Arabic).

10. Pierre Vidal-Naquet, *Les assassins de la mémoire* (Paris: Seuil, 1995), 130.

Memory and Interconnected Identities

How is it possible to reinvent origins for oneself on the basis of fragmentary memories? The link between Islam and Judaism may be approached through this question. I shall compare not two religions but two similar attitudes that have continually intersected, especially in the Maghreb. The origin of these attitudes—if there is an origin—lies in a narrative both fragmentary and incomplete, something retained since childhood and transmitted from generation to generation.

Take the city of Fes, Morocco, where I was born. The city of Bhalil is ten kilometers away, Sefrou twenty. Moroccans of the Jewish faith have been in that region since the Ottoman period, well before the arrival of the Muslim conquerors. It is said that in Fes, since time immemorial—a time that is indeterminate and hazy, like memory—the dressmakers were Jews. Until the 1960s, the most skilled were the Fassis, who do in fact belong to the Jewish faith. It is said that in Fes, many Muslim families are of Jewish ancestry. It is sometimes said that Fes itself is Jewish.

At a time when Morocco was beginning its struggle for independence against the French occupier, the people with the greatest freedom to move around Morocco, without raising suspicions that they were resistance fighters, were Moroccans of the Jewish faith. The French authorities tolerated commerce and travel within the territory, so long as those responsible were not Muslims but Jews. Why? Recall that the Moroccans who fought against colonialism—particularly members of Al Istiqlal, the Independence Party, which is still active—embraced their association with Islam. As a result, the Jews came to embody shifting borderlines and belonged to no territory. The French considered them neutral in the battle taking shape, even though many Jews participated in the struggle against the occupier. In 1946–48, any Fes merchant traveling through the cities of southern Morocco could, in fact, be considered Jewish by virtue of his mobility. When, in Montaigne's words, you are "brought up in the same laws and customs and the same atmosphere,"[1] why seek out difference?

Among the Moroccan families of the Jewish faith, some had been in Morocco since the Roman period, while others had fled the Spanish Inquisition in the sixteenth century and taken up residence in North Africa. At a time when Spain was laying waste the continent of Latin America by imposing its religion and its law, it was also driving both the Jews and the Muslims from its territory. These two peoples were united in a single destiny: diaspora. Montaigne, who lived during the time of that cruelty, tells of it in his *Essays* (book 1, chap. 14). The king of Castile expelled the Jews; the king of Portugal welcomed them, only to then dispossess them. He chartered vessels "to transport them to Africa," but the crew subjected them to a thousand humiliations. Montaigne writes: "The sailors, . . . besides many other indignities, kept them at sea, sailing back and forth, until they had used up their victuals and were constrained to buy some from their captors at such high prices and over so long a period that they were set ashore with nothing left but their shirts. When this inhumanity was reported to those who had remained on land, most of them resolved to slavery; some made a show of changing religion."[2]

But the cruelty did not end there. On land, children were separated from their parents and instructed in the Christian religion. It is therefore not surprising that many Jews imitated the custom of the Isle of Cea, killing themselves or "through love and compassion throwing their children into wells to escape the law."[3] All of Andalusian culture, as it was known, was a witness to that common fate, and it is difficult to say which portion fell to the Jews and which to the Muslims. What is characteristic of a culture is the interconnectedness of its modes of life.

Colette Guedj's novel *Le journal de Myriam Bloch (The Journal of Myriam Bloch)* also points to this Arab culture common to the Jews and Muslims, and emphasizes the inscrutable position of the North African Jews. Referring to her character Myriam Bloch, the author notes: "In fact, where is her place? Between the Sephardic Jews, for whom she is a renegade, and the Ashkenazi Jews, for whom she is only a Sephardim; between the religious Jews, who consider her a 'bad Jew' (in not respecting the rules), and the nonreligious Jews, with whom she does not necessarily, which is to say, systematically, feel in harmony . . . between all these contradictory identities that are and are not hers, between all these betweens, the space is very confined."[4]

The body is the sentinel for that space of the "between": the tasted and savored dish, the sensuous, highly corporeal accent. Because of the heterogeneous fragments of this life of the body, this hybrid identity, about which it is difficult to say whether it is more Jewish than Muslim, can never coincide with itself.

During World War II, the lives of the North African Jews were spared. But this did not prevent them from having "negative prehensions,"[5] to borrow a concept from the American philosopher A. N. Whitehead. That expression allows us to understand the elements left out of alternatives. A choice is explained not only in terms of what action was taken but also in terms of

A street in Fes, not far from the neighborhood of Moulay Idriss. Photograph by Bruno Barbey, 1984.

what was dismissed, excluded. There are a whole host of events that did not take place, even though they *might have* taken place. Here is an example of a negative prehension: King Mohammed V refused to hand over Moroccans of the Jewish faith to the Vichy government, being duty-bound, he said, to protect all his subjects without distinction of religion. The protection of the Jews that resulted from that royal refusal is crucial.

In functioning as hypothetical alternatives, these events that did not take place are part of the general fate of Judeo-Arab culture. Colette Guedj writes of her character: "She had not lost her life, her parents had not died in the concentration camps. She knows now that, if she had not been lucky enough to find herself 'overseas' at that moment, she, like so many other French and foreign Jews, might have been rounded up, deported, even exterminated in the concentration camps."[6]

Those who saw these hypothetical alternatives turn into categorical realities lost their sensory means of expression: the body slipped into a nonplace, an "unplace," an unacknowledgment. So reports Stefan Zweig, a Jew who found himself in Europe, not North Africa, during World War II: "For all that I had been training my heart for almost half a century to beat as that of a *citoyen du monde* [world citizen] it was useless. On the day I lost my passport I discovered, at the age of fifty-eight, that losing one's native land implies more than parting with a circumscribed area of soil."[7]

The loss of your passport is the equivalent of the loss of your body: you are stripped naked, vulnerable, in an unbearable immediacy. You lose yourself as corporeal boundary in a public nonspace of exclusion, withdrawal, even suicide.

Hypothetical alternatives also serve to show us the way out of solipsism. No man is an island. There are others around us, and there are also all those who might have been around us and who are somewhere else, in the realm of the living or the dead. They occupy a place. There is no solipsism, therefore, no logic of identity. That logic, like the will, is always being foiled: you can aspire to be tragic and ignore the fact that, in reality, you are made for comedy. You can also play with that knowledge, pretend not to know. That is the art of Charlie Chaplin, "the poor 'little Yid' who does not recognize the class order of the world because he sees in it neither order nor justice for himself."[8] So let us laugh with Chaplin, let us reopen the shutters,[9] and let the laughter of children cover our own, since our own laughter is more like a smile as breathless as fear.[10]

If the waking dream of the novel is free-floating, as its imaginary or imagined aspect would have it, the dream-work, in the absence of providing roots, provides an itinerary. Why speak of Stefan Zweig and Chaplin rather than confine ourselves to the Sephardic Jews who lived in the Arab Muslim countries? First, because it is always good to compare without equating; and second, because the risk of too much specificity always entails a large number of aberrations. How, in fact, are we to characterize a "Jewish culture"?

Shlomo Pines raises the issue: "It can be argued that, at a certain time, the Jews found themselves within the space of Greco-Roman culture; then, at another time, within that of Arab culture; and then within that of Christian European culture. If we pay attention to these facts, the concept of 'Jewish culture' becomes problematic at the very least."[11] Because it is problematic, it invites us to bear witness to its traces, its origins, its fragments, to make it into a concept that speaks to us because it is interconnected with non-Jews, because the Muslims in particular live within the intimacy of "Jewish culture." ●

A professor of philosophy at the Université de Paris Est-Créteil Val-de-Marne, Ali Benmakhlouf has published books on Arab philosophers and on logicians. He is the author of Averroès (Belles Lettres, 2000; Vrin, 2000; Ellipses, 2007); Al-Farabi (Seuil, 2007); Gottlob Frege (PUF, 1997; Vrin,

2002; Ellipses, 2002); Russell (PUF, 1996; Ellipses, 2001; Belles Lettres, 2008); Montaigne (Belles Lettres, 2008); and L'identité, une fable philosophique *(PUF, 2011).*

---

1. *The Complete Essays of Montaigne*, trans. Donald Frame (Stanford, CA: Stanford University Press, 1958), book 2, chap. 5, 264.

2. Ibid., book 1, chap. 14, 35.

3. Ibid., 36.

4. Colette Guedj, *Le journal de Myriam Bloch* (Paris: J.-C. Lattès, 2004), 84–85.

5. See A. N. Whitehead, *Process and Reality* (New York: Free Press, 1929; new ed., 1978), 41–42.

6. Guedj, *Le journal de Myriam Bloch*, 116.

7. S. Zweig, *The World of Yesterday: An Autobiography* (Lincoln: University of Nebraska Press, 1964).

8. Hannah Arendt, "The Jew as Pariah: A Hidden Tradition," in *The Jew as Pariah: Jewish Identity and Politics in the Modern Age*, trans. Ron H. Feldman (New York: Grove Press, 1978), 81.

9. The last sentence of Guedj's novel: "Then we will reopen the shutters."

10. Think of Albert Cohen's *O vous, frères humains* (Paris: Gallimard Education, 1972).

11. Shlomo Pines, *La liberté de philosopher: De Maïmonide à Spinoza*, trans. Rémi Brague (Paris: Desclée de Brouwer, 1997).

The Kahina: Jewish Symbol, Islamic Narrative

Kahena, by Jean Atlan (1913–60), a French painter born in Constantine. Paris, National Modern Art Museum, Centre Georges Pompidou.

In modern Jewish literature, whether written in Hebrew, French, or English, the Kahina is depicted as a Jewish queen who tenaciously and heroically opposed Islam at the time of the Muslim expansion.[1] Because of this, the Kahina functioned as a symbol for North African Judaism from the colonial period on, and her status was not called into doubt. The Moroccan writer Georges Memmi writes, for example: "My mother, twelve years old at least, remembers Queen Kahina. She remembers converted Jews, who became too faithful and were a wound to her, and numerous others who resisted and of whom she was so proud."[2] His brother Albert Memmi adds: "The first reliable mention of our presence here is in the historian El-Milli's Arab-Berber chronicles, which cite, among the companions of the notorious Judeo-Berber woman the Kahina, a certain El-Mammi."[3] Others have made the Kahina into a symbol for the confrontation between Islam and Judaism, referring to the moment when the Arabs emerged as a conquering nation. As André Chouraqui writes: "The last battles of the Jewish people before the modern age thus date not to the struggle against Rome in the first century CE in Palestine, as is often said, but to the seventh century, against the Arabs, on African soil."[4]

Nevertheless, that queen, indisputably Jewish for the Jews, is not so for the Arabs. Nor is she Jewish for the Berbers, who consider her a Berber from the Shawiya territories. Her name, "Kahina," which may mean "seer," was supposedly given to her by the Arabs, either because of her presumed supernatural powers or to discredit her among her own people, who later became Muslims. Among the Berbers, she is a pagan, and as such the national symbol for the heroic resistance against the Arab invasion. The Algerian writer Kateb Yacine evokes her in that capacity in *L'oeuvre en fragments* (*Work in Fragments*).[5] Here the queen in revolt is Dihya, who, addressing peasants threatened by Muslim horsemen, forbids them to continue referring to her by the pejorative term "Kahina," or "witch":

First Peasant: What if the Arabs were right?
Second Peasant: Are they not men of God?

First Peasant: The Jews and Christians,

    Do they not also believe

    In the one and only God?

Dihya: These religions, which are all the same,

Serve foreign kings.

They want to take our country from us,

The best land is not enough for them.

They want the soul and spirit of our people as well. . . .

The only God we know

Can be seen and touched:

I kiss him before you,

He is the living land,

The land that makes us live,

The free land of Amazigh!"[6]

Despite the Berbers' rejection of the notion of a Jewish Kahina, and then—in Kateb Yacine's text, for example—the queen's refusal to be called "Kahina" (witch) by the Arabs, the character is often designated by that term. And in Algeria, especially among the Kabyles, "Kahina" is a common Berber given name. For the Arabs, the Kahina is primarily a Berber queen who at first opposed Islam but later accepted it. The proof is that she asked her two sons to join with her enemies. Not only did they wage battle against their mother's army, but they also contributed decisively to the Islamization of North Africa and even Spain. The Arab historians of the modern period, taking up a supposedly classical Arab historiographical tradition, argue that the Berbers are of Yemeni or even Palestinian origin. If that were the case, they would be part of the Arab world, which would explain the Kahina's final gesture: her adoption of Islam for her sons and, as a result, for her people. In the Arab narrative, then, the Kahina becomes the symbol for the "brotherhood" between the Arabs and the Berbers, and her story explains the origin of the Arab and Muslim Maghreb.[7]

The question that therefore arises is: Where did the idea that the Kahina was Jewish come from? Apart from her name, whose resemblance has been noted to the well-known Jewish name "Cohen," or "Cahen," one passage—the only one in fact—that may explain this Jewish origin can be found in the famous *Histoire des Berbères (History of the Berbers)*, a French translation of Ibn Khaldun by Baron de Slane, published in 1852: "A portion of the Berbers professed Judaism, a religion they had received from their powerful neighbors, the Israelites of Syria. Among the Jewish Berbers were the Djeraoua, a tribe that lived in the Auras and of which the Kahina, a woman who was killed by the Arabs during the first invasions, was a member."[8] But that translation by a famous nineteenth-century orientalist, done during the colonial period, is not accurate.[9] A more literal translation of the same paragraph would be: "Hence, perhaps (*rubbamā*) some (*ba'd*) Berbers professed Judaism, which they took (*akhadhūh*) from the Children of Israel when their might had increased, because of the proximity of Syria and its power, as was the case for the inhabitants of the Aurès Mountains, the tribe of the Kahina, who was killed by the Arabs at the beginning of the conquest, and as was the case for Nafusa, the Berbers of Ifriqiyya, Qandalawa, Madyuna, Bahlula, Ghiyata, Banu Fazzan, Berbers of the far west."[10]

Often cited to prove the Jewishness of the Kahina, that passage, from volume 6 of the *Kitab al 'Ibar (Book of Examples, or Book of Considerations of the History of the Arabs, the Persians, and the Berbers)* needs to be read in context. Ibn Khaldun begins his analysis of the status of the Berbers by arguing that they were pagans (*mājūs*), but with a few exceptions. According to him, these exceptions can be attributed to the fact that the Berbers adopted the religion of the peoples who ruled them: they adopted the religion of the kings of Yemen, and then, when they were conquered by the Romans, they became Christian. In the passage quoted above, Ibn Khaldun is speaking of the tribe of the Jrawa, and he begins his sentence cautiously, indicating that "perhaps" or "probably" (*rubbamā*) the Jrawa adopted the religion of the Jews and professed

Judaism. Another important detail, often neglected in the debate on the Kahina, is that in Ibn Khaldun's text, the chapter mentioning the Berbers' religions before the advent of Islam is separated from the account of the Kahina's gesture, which does not appear until volume 7 (10–11), the "account of the Kahina and her people the Jrawa, etc." In de Slane's text, that separation does not exist: the comment that the Jrawa are Jewish is an integral part of the account of the Kahina opposing the Arabs. Thus, she appears to be Jewish, a trait that would be decisive for the structure of the colonial narrative. In the Arabic text, however, that detail is not part of a narrative centered on a racial conflict between Arabs and Berbers but rather part of a medieval narrative structure in which the author seems to have tossed in events at random, the goal being merely to mention the Berbers' heroic deeds in any order whatever.[11] No analyses have yet dealt with that major difference between the narrative structure of the medieval historical account, as Ibn Khaldun presents it, and the modern structure within which de Slane renders the Arabic text into French.

After a first victory, the Kahina, despite her resistance, was killed in battle by the Arabs. Ibn Khaldun interprets that episode as a struggle between Berbers and Muslims over the spread of Islam, a struggle also waged during the Prophet's lifetime against the non-Muslims in Egypt, Syria, Persia, and even Arabia. In de Slane's telling, the Arabs (and not the Muslims) find themselves facing a Jewish woman and her people (since the translator incorporates as a certainty the passage from book 6 that expresses the possibility that the tribe is Jewish).

The episode of the Kahina, which supposedly took place in the seventh century, appeared in Muslim historiography only two hundred years later, in the ninth. These first accounts, prior to those of Ibn Khaldun, were terse in the extreme. The first text, by the historian ʿUsfuri (d. 854), consists of a single sentence, which notes that General Hassan went to Ifriqiyya and killed the Kahina of the Berbers.[12] Gradually,

however, that minimal account was augmented by various narrative elements and acquired a fuller form in Ibn Khaldun's work four centuries later. That author reproduced all the elements of Muslim historiography and added details, probably drawn from the Berber genealogists, such as the Kahina's name, age (she supposedly lived to be 127), and the fate of the Jrawa, who, he says, vanished from the region. Some of them, he adds, ended up in Melila (7:11).

Nevertheless, Ibn Khaldun's accounts, unlike those of his Eastern predecessors (from Baghdad, Damascus, and Medina), belong not to the historiographical tradition of the futūhāt, "conquests," but rather to a regional tradition of the fadāʾil, paeans, in this case, paeans demonstrating the Berbers' great historical merit. The Arab chronicles of the conquests were originally a discursive practice vital for the Islamic state in establishing the facts about the conversion of the various peoples, especially for tax purposes. The tradition of the fadāʾil, by contrast, grew out of a concern to do justice to the Berbers, who were often denigrated in the narratives of conquest. Ibn Khaldun therefore classifies the Berbers as one of the great nations, alongside the Romans, the Greeks, and the Persians. In that respect, the story of the Kahina is part of an account of the Berbers' heroic feats.[13] The author mentions the tribe of the Jrawa, which was part of the large Znata group. He notes that they were numerous and that they pledged their allegiance to the Franks (the "Latins" in de Slane's translation). Ruled by the Franks, the Jrawa professed Christianity (7:10). Ibn Khaldun also relates that the Jrawa lived in the Aurès Mountains, and he provides information that might explain the name "Kahina": "she had kahāna" (7:11), that is, the ability to read the future and to predict events. He also says that this power came to her from her "devil." In addition, Ibn Khaldun notes her genealogy and her real name: "Dihya daughter of Tabna son of Niqan, son of Bawra, son of Msksari son of Afrad son of Wasila son of Jraw" (ibid.). To whom do these names refer?[14] Did they have a historical existence? Where did all this information on her genealogy come from? Is it credible? These are important questions, to which we cannot give even an approximate answer. It is clear that, in the narrative of the Kahina, no reference is made to her religion. Especially from the colonial period onward, her name was taken as an indication, if not proof, of her Judaism. But Ibn Khaldun explains it in a completely different manner: her name refers to her capacity to know the invisible things of her people (11). Therein lies a phenomenon altogether unique in the history of texts: Baron de Slane's translation, which affirms that the Jrawa were Jews, was recognized as authoritative (or at least was considered a reliable source) in relation to the original Arabic text,[15] and had great success among Jewish writers.

But how did we get from Ibn Khaldun's caution to modern certainty?[16] The solution does not lie only in the avidity for symbols that existed at a time when the Jews of the region represented a political phenomenon of colonization. According to nineteenth-century colonial ethnography, for the populations in the region of the Aurès Mountains, the Kahina had the vague character of an antiheroine without religion, an unbeliever who opposed the "companions of the Prophet."[17] She appears in a poem from the same period as "a cruel woman" who caused suffering among the Jews.[18] But these accounts did not enjoy the same fortune as Ibn Khaldun's text translated by Baron de Slane. In addition to having the status of a historical narrative "corrected" by an orientalist scholar, that text came from a great Arab historian and thus provided the clarity missing from the oral tradition (and hence from memory).

With the Crémieux decree (1871), which automatically granted the Jews full French citizenship—unlike their Muslim neighbors, who retained their status as a native people subject to the Code de l'Indigénat— the story of the Kahina acquired a new significance, which would take on added strength. The Kahina reappeared as a Jew among Jewish writers and

historians.[19] The story was changed to give an interpretation that repositioned the Jews within the history of the region and conferred a special status on them. In that region, they were considered distinct from the so-called indigenous population, not in terms of their religion but in terms of their race.

Whether the Kahina was actually Jewish, Judaized, Christian, or pagan, we cannot know—and that is not the important thing. From the standpoint of anthropology, what matters is that the Kahina became an obligatory symbol for North African Judaism. As a symbol, she had the function, precisely, of giving a group a sense of identity that predated and lay outside of a supposedly historical truth. What makes the Kahina extraordinary is that she is a symbol shared with other groups. Embraced by the Jews of North Africa and even those of the Diaspora, she is also an important symbol for both the Berbers and the Arabs. ●

Associate professor of African and African American studies and anthropology at the University of Kansas, Abdelmajid Hannoum is the author of Colonial Histories, Postcolonial Memories *(Heinemann, 2001) and* Violent Modernity *(Harvard University Press, 2010).*

1. See Abdelmajid Hannoum, *Colonial Histories, Postcolonial Memories* (Portsmouth, NH: Heinemann, 2001), esp. 49–51 and 55–61.

2. Georges Memmi, *Qui se souvient du café Rubens?* (Paris: J. C. Lattes, 1984), 28.

3. Albert Memmi, *Le scorpion* (Paris: Gallimard, 1969), 25.

4. André Chouraqui, *Histoire des Juifs en Afrique du Nord* (Paris: Hachette, 1987), 86.

5. According to field research conducted in the region in June 2005. See also Kateb Yacine, "La Kahina," *Dérives* 31–32 (1982) and *L'oeuvre en fragments* (Paris: Sindbad, 1986); Nabil Farès, *La mémoire de l'absent* (Paris: Seuil, 1974); Mohamed Kayr-Eddine, *Agadir* (Paris: Seuil, 1967).

6. Yacine, *L'oeuvre en fragments*, 429.

7. For more details, see Hannoum, *Colonial Histories, Postcolonial Memories.*

8. William de Slane, trans., *Histoire des Berbères* by Ibn Khalhun (Paris: Geuthner, 1925), 1:208.

9. For the problems related to de Slane's translation of Ibn Khaldun, see Hannoum, "Translation and the Colonial Imaginary: Ibn Khaldun, Orientalist," *History and Theory* 42 (2003): 61–81.

10. Ibn Khaldun, *Kitab al ʿIbar* (Beirut: Dar al Kutub, 1992), 6:126, my translation from the Arabic.

11. See Hannoum, "Translation and the Colonial Imaginary."

12. Abu ʿAmr al-ʿUsfuri ibn Khayyat, *Tarikh* (Najf, 1967), 2:267.

13. See Maya Shatzmiller, *L'histoire Mérinide, Ibn Khaldun et ses contemporarins* (Leiden: Brill, 1982), esp. 132.

14. Other names mentioned in the Arabic text: "Duhya [*sic*] daughter of Matiya son of Tifan, queen of the Aurès" (Ibn Khaldun, *Kitab al ʿIbar*, 6:28), and "Liwahiyya" (ibid., 121). Both de Slane's and Abdesselam Cheddadi's translations mention Dihya in the same place that the Arabic text mentions Liwahiyya. See Cheddadi's translation *Peuples et nations du monde* (Paris: Sindbad, 1986), 2:482. Is this an error in the Lebanese edition or another name that no one has ever discussed?

15. For more details on that important textual event, see Abdelmajid Hannoum, "Translation and the Colonial Imaginary"; and "The Historiographic State," *History and Anthropology* 19 (2008): 91–114.

16. That certainty has given rise to various claims. For example, Mohamed Talbi, followed recently by Yves Modéran, strips the Kahina of her Jewish status and makes her a Christian. Mohamed Talbi, "Un nouveau fragment de l'histoire de l'Occident musulman, 62–196/682–812): L'épopée d'al Kahina," *Cahiers de Tunisie* 19 (1971): 19–52. See also Yves Modéran, "Dihya," in *Encyclopédie Berbère*, ed. Gabriel Camps (Aix-en-Provence: Edisud, 2005), 27:4102–4111.

17. See Émile Masqueray, "Traditions de l'Aurès," *Bulletin de la Correspondance Africaine*, year 4 (1885): 72–110.

18. See David Gazès, *Essai sur l'histoire des Israélites de Tunisie* (Paris: Armand Durlacher, 1888).

19. By way of examples, see Nahum Slouschz, "La race de la Kahina," *Revue indigène* 44 (1909): 573–83; Jacques Vehel, Raphaël Levy, and Vitalis Danon, *La Hara conte* (Paris: Ivrit, 1929); and more recently, Charles-André Julien, revisited by Roger Le Tourneau, *Histoire de l'Afrique du Nord* (Paris: Payot, 1952).

The Jews of India

The Jewish communities of India consist of three main groups—the Jews of Cochin, the Bene Israel, and the Baghdadi Jews.[1] The Jews of Cochin, resident in the Indian state of Kerala, represent the oldest Indian Jewish community, whose documented history dates back to the Middle Ages. The Bene Israel could be described as one of the so-called newly discovered Jewish groups, as they became known to Western audiences in the nineteenth century. According to a Bene Israel legend, their ancestors arrived on the Konkan coast of Western India in 175 BCE after they fled ancient Palestine to escape the persecutions of Antiochus Epiphanes. The Baghdadi Jews comprise the descendants of Arabic-speaking Jews who came to India in the eighteenth and nineteenth centuries and settled mainly in the cities of Mumbai and Kolkata. After the establishment of the State of Israel, the majority of Indian Jews made an aliyah. At the moment there are about four thousand Jewish people left in India, most of whom belong to the Bene Israel community living in and near Mumbai.

The second half of the twentieth century witnessed the development of two Judaizing movements on the subcontinent[2]—that of the Bnei Menashe (also known as Shinlung), who emerged in the early 1950s from the Christianized tribes of Chin, Kuki, and Mizo settled in the Indian states of Mizoram, Manipur, Assam, and

At the Cochin Synagogue, a leader of the local Jewish community presents a fragment of a Torah scroll dating from before the eighteenth century. Photograph by Jean-Baptiste Rabouan.

the plains of Burma, and that of the Bene Ephraim of Andhra Pradesh, who came from the community of Madiga Dalits and established their first synagogue in 1991.[3]

The community that has had the closest contact with Indian Muslims is probably that of the Bene Israel. Indeed, Bene Israel sources of the later British period suggest that the relations between the two groups had always been very good and involved instances of cooperation. For instance, Muslims would allow the Bene Israel to use their cemeteries in towns where there were no separate Bene Israel cemeteries, and generally perceived the Bene Israel as a community that was religiously close to that of their own.[4]

In the first half of the twentieth century, Indian Muslim attitudes toward the Jews were to some degree affected by the Palestine issue. Educated Muslims by and large adopted a negative attitude toward Zionism from the outset. After the First World War, M. A. Ansari and the Ali brothers launched the Khilafat movement, which argued that Palestine must remain under Muslim rule.[5] The movement disintegrated in 1924, but the tradition of anti-Zionist sentiments among Indian Muslims survived. It has been suggested that the Palestine issue may have also generated anti-Jewish feelings among some Indian Muslims.[6]

Before the partition, a sizable Bene Israel community existed in Karachi (now Pakistan). No tensions existed between the Bene Israel and local Muslims at the time. However, shortly after India and Pakistan gained independence and the State of Israel came into existence, large numbers of Bene Israel left Pakistan for India, the United Kingdom, the United States, and other parts of the world, fearing anti-Zionist backlash from the local population.[7]

In independent India the relations between Jews and Muslims remained peaceful; however, in recent years anti-Israeli feelings of militant Islamic organizations based in South Asia appeared to present a security issue. In 2004 Indian press reported that the police of Hyderabad (the capital of Andhra Pradesh) uncovered a plot by alleged agents of an Islamic militarist organization based in Pakistan, Lashkar-e-Tayyiba (Army of the Righteous or Army of the Pure), to attack local Jewish families. After this incident, and subsequently after the Mumbai attacks of 2008, when the Chabad Lubavitch Jewish Center was taken over by terrorists and an Israeli rabbi and his wife were murdered together with other hostages, the Bene Ephraim community based in Andhra Pradesh applied to the police to protect their synagogue.[8] The possibility of terrorist attacks organized from Pakistan remains an area of concern for the Bene Ephraim, who at the same time report that their relations with local Muslims are exceptionally good. ●

Yulia Egorova is a senior lecturer in anthropology at Durham University. Her publications include Jews and India: Perceptions and Image *(Routledge, 2006).*

1. For research on the Bene Israel, Cochini, and Baghdadi Jews of India, see Shirley Berry Isenberg, *India's Bene Israel* (Berkeley, CA: J. L. Magnes Museum, 1988); Nathan Katz, *Who Are the Jews of India?* (Berkeley: University of California Press, 1999); *Indo-Judaic Studies in the Twenty-First Century*, Nathan Katz et al. (New York: Palgrave Macmillan, 2007); Joan G. Roland, *Jewish Communities of India* (Piscataway, NJ: Transaction, 1998); Shalva Weil, *India's Jewish Heritage* (Mumbai: Marg Publications, 2002, 2005).
2. For a wider context of Judaizing movements, see Tudor Parfitt and Emanuela Trevisan Semi, *Judaising Movements* (London: Routledge, 2002).
3. For more information on the Bnei Menashe, see M. Samra, "Buallawn Israel: The Emergence of a Judaising Movement in Mizoram, Northeast India," in *Religious Change, Conversion and Culture*, ed. L. Olson, Sydney Studies in Society and Culture (1996), 105–31; Shalva Weil, "Dual Conversion among the Shinlung in North-East India," *Studies in Tribes and Tribals* 1, no. 1 (2003): 43–57. For the Bene Ephraim, see Y. Egorova and S. Perwez, "The Children of Ephraim: Being Jewish in Andhra Pradesh," *Anthropology Today* 26, no. 6 (2010): 14–19.

4. Yulia Egrova, *Jews and India: Perceptions and Image* (London: Routledge, 2006), 87.

5. Cf. Joan Roland, *Jewish Communities of India*, 84.

6. T. R. Sareen, "Indian Response to the Holocaust," in Anil Bhatti and Johannes H. Voigt (eds.), *Jewish Exile in India* (New Delhi: Manohar, in association with Max Mueller Bhavan, 1999), 61.

7. Yoel M Reuben, *The Jews of Pakistan: A Forgotten Heritage* (Mumbai: Bene Israel Heritage Museum and Genealogical Research Center, 2012), 75–80.

8. Yulia Egorova and Shahid Perwez, *The Jews of Andhra Pradesh: Contesting Caste and Religion in South India* (New York: Oxford University Press, 2013).

Jewish Communities in Sub-Saharan Africa

In the nineteenth century, encounters with Protestant and Catholic missionaries led a few African groups to a dawning awareness of their "Jewish identity." Since the Middle Ages, travel narratives, such as those of Eldad ha-Dani in the ninth century or of Benjamin of Tudela in the twelfth, had fed imaginations about the existence of a "Jewish kingdom" in Africa. So too had Christian legends about the kingdom of Prester John, also in the twelfth century, and the imaginary travels of Sir John Mandeville in the fourteenth. In Jewish but also in Christian minds, those fantastic tales, which revealed the presence of Jews beyond the mythic Sambatyon River, reinforced the myth of the Lost Tribes of Israel living in a utopian land. A consensus among missionaries and other colonial observers established the Judeo-Semitic origin of the Africans, while the myth of the Lost Tribes introduced narrative structures that made sense on all sides.[1] The missionaries, by bringing the New Testament and by identifying as Hebrew the African groups they encountered, provided them with points of entry into a history of origins, the elements of a new discourse, and new narratives of identity that linked them to the Jewish world. The spread of the missionaries' own prophetic vision of Judaism would contribute toward transforming the history of some of these groups.

In recent decades, various groups in Sub-Saharan Africa, with no geographical connections to one another, have undertaken to affiliate themselves with Judaism or to convert. These include: the members of the Zakhor movement in Timbuktu, Mali; the Abayudaya in Uganda; the community of the House of Israel in Ghana; the Ibo-Benei-Yisrael in Nigeria; the Tutsi Hebrews of Havila in Rwanda and Burundi; the Lemba in South Africa; and the Jews of Rusape in Zimbabwe. These new communities have adopted practices that are often remote from normative Judaism; taken as a whole, such practices constitute a new kind of Judaism.[2] Within most of these groups, the process of reshaping identity, an undercurrent since the colonial period, has gained in force and speed by virtue of the existence of the Falashas (Beta Israel) of Ethiopia and their fate. In reconciling a Jewish identity with an African identity, the recognition of the Falashas, which established their kinship with the Jewish world, led to the creation of the concept of "black Jew." The Falashas' displacement from Ethiopia to Israel in 1980 and 1990, when they were fleeing the persecutions of the Ethiopian political regime, and the international interest elicited by these spectacular events, served as a spark among groups for whom Jewishness was already an issue. They saw that modern exodus with biblical connotations as confirmation of the existence of a mythic Jewish African community, possessing mysterious roots, that had returned to the Promised Land.

Most of the African groups that assert their Jewish identity initially practiced Christianity, having been converted by missionaries—with the exception of the members of the Zakhor community in Timbuktu, whose members practice the Muslim religion, while working for recognition of their Jewish identity.

The association Zakhor ("Memory" in Hebrew) was formed in Timbuktu in 1993 and has about a thousand members. In a manifesto published in 1996, the members of that group acknowledged that they were Jews and proclaimed: "The time has come to remember, and this time is one of the most difficult in our history. . . . It is up to us to turn back the years, across the generations, to recall our Israelite origins, about which our fathers' fathers kept silent, and to take on that origin. Zakhor was created with that aim in view."[3] United around the Malian historian Ismaël Daidé

Haidara, the members of the Zakhor community—Muslims therefore—declare themselves the direct descendants of the Jews of Tuat, a region on the edge of the Sahara Desert in Western Algeria. We know that the Jews of Tuat, traders and caravanners for the most part, were persecuted by Sheikh Abdelkirm el Meghili in 1492. The explorer Leo Africanus, who traveled to Gourara in about 1506, observed at the time that "many Jews [had] lived there" and that "they [had been] the victim of a strange persecution in the year of the fall of Granada."[4] He added that Sheikh el Meghili "offered 7 gold *mithcals*" to anyone who would kill a Jew and ordered the destruction of the synagogues of Tuat. We may hypothesize that some of these Jews fled to the northeast or west, while others might have reached the kingdom of Gao, farther south of the Sahara, by following the caravan routes.

If a few survivors of Tuat found refuge among other Jews settled along the Niger, the peace they enjoyed was brief. Shortly thereafter, under the influence of el Meghili, Askia Muhammad I (Askia the Great), who ruled that region, promulgated an edict evicting the Jews from the Songhai Empire. Leo Africanus's writings indicate that "the king was a mortal enemy of the Jews, and none could live in the city."[5] Five centuries later, Haidara commented: "The Jews, having come to the Great Nile of the Arabs [the Niger], could go no farther, and stopped. Given the choice between the Qurʾan and the sword, they converted."[6] And so, he concluded, "they became Muslims." The patriarchs who founded Zakhor now claim that the three families comprising their community are "the Kehath Levites, now called 'Kati,' the Cohens, and the Abanas."[7] According to Haidara, the first Jewish converts to Islam appear in the written sources as members of the court of the Askia, the dynasty in power at the time. He mentions the Kati family, and especially Alfa Mahmud Kati, who was reputed for his learning and who, alongside his administrative career, undertook in 1519 to compose the *Tarikh el-Fettash*, the first historical work of the Niger bend.

At this point, we do not know of any written document coming directly from the populations of Tuat. If Jewish annals did exist, they were buried under centuries-old layers of Arab chronicles. Nevertheless, the research conducted in the Saharan oases by Émile-Félix Gautier and Alfred Georges Paul Martin in the early twentieth century yielded information on the possible Jewish origins of the first inhabitants of Tuat and Gourara.[8] Their activities, commerce or goldsmithery, put them in contact with the West African populations, who supplied gold powder, Muslims being forbidden to do gold work or anything else closely or remotely related to usury. Tadeusz Lewicki's research also speaks of a transformation in the late eighth century of obscure oases into renowned caravan centers and important Jewish settlement sites.[9] Michel Abitbol's study on trans-Saharan commerce reveals that the Jews on the edges of the Sahara participated in that activity from the eighth century on, sometimes settling near centers of production.[10]

The historical sources on a Jewish presence in Tuat and the involvement of Jews in trans-Saharan commerce provide only indirect and secondary evidence, general outlines of the history to which the Jews of Timbuktu lay claim.[11] Nevertheless, under the auspices of UNESCO, the progressive discovery in that city of ancient manuscripts dating to the thirteenth century constitutes a scientific windfall, as yet unpublished, that could shed new light on the Jews' settlement in that region.[12]

In our own time, the members of Zakhor, living in a country that is 90 percent Muslim, want to be recognized by Israel and by Mali as both Jewish and Malian. Since the right to religious freedom is totally protected by the 1992 constitution, the form of Islam practiced in Mali has heretofore been moderate, tolerant, and adapted to local relations between Muslims and minority groups. The recent religious tensions and the takeover of Northern Mali in 2012 by the Islamists in the Movement for Unity and Jihad in West Africa, a group linked to al-Qaʿida, cannot be inconsequential for that community, which is calling for its sociocultural heritage and its identity as Banu Israel to be safeguarded. ●

Edith Bruder is a research associate in the Department of the Languages and Cultures of the Near and Middle East in the School of Oriental and African Studies (SOAS) at the University of London. She is the author of The Black Jews of Africa: History, Religion, Identity *(Oxford University Press, 2008).*

1. See Edith Bruder, *The Black Jews of Africa: History, Identity, Religion* (New York: Oxford University Press, 2008); Tudor Parfitt, *The Lost Tribes of Israel: The History of a Myth* (London: Weidenfeld and Nicolson, 2002), chap. 1.

2. Bruder, *Black Jews of Africa*, chaps. 9 and 10.

3. I. Maïga, "L'éveil de la communauté noire de Tombouctou," *Le Républicain*, March 27, 1996.

4. Leo Africanus, *Description de l'Afrique*, trans. A. Epaulard, with notes by T. Monod, H. Lhote, and R. Mauny (Paris: A. Maisonneuve, 1980), 1:89–93, 2:423, 429.

5. Ibid., 2:468.

6. Quoted in Sennen Andriamirado, "Juifs, noirs et maliens," *Jeune Afrique*, no. 1879, January 8–14, 1997.

7. Ibid.

8. Alfred Georges Paul Martin, *À la frontière marocaine, les oasis sahariennes: Gourara, Touat, Tidikelt* (Paris: Challamel, 1908), 37; Émile-Félix Gautier, *Le Sahara* (Paris: Payot, 1928), 104.

9. Tadeusz Lewicki, "L'État nord-africain du Tahert et ses relations avec le Soudan occidental de la fin du VIIIᵉ siècle au IXᵉ siècle," *Cahiers et Études Africaines* 2 (1962): 513–35.

10. Michel Abitbol, "Juifs Maghrébins et commerce transsaharien du VIIIᵉ au XVᵉ siècle" (*Sol, la parole et l'écrit: 2 000 ans d'histoire africaine; Mélanges à Raymond Mauny*, vol. 2 (1981), 561–77); Joseph Cuoq, *Recueil de sources arabes* (Paris: CNRS, 1975), 46. Joseph Cuoq believes that the settlement of the Jews in these regions was one of the reasons for the prosperity of Tuat.

11. Martin, *À la frontière marocaine*; Raymond Mauny, *Tableau géographique de l'Afrique de l'ouest au Moyen Âge* (Dakar: IFAN [Institut français d'Afrique noire], 1961).

12. Jean-Michel Dijan, *Les Manuscrits de Tombouctou*, Paris, J.-C. Lattès, 2012.

Jewish Pilgrimages in Egypt
Suzan Youssef

Cults of saints are a fundamental phenomenon in Egyptian popular culture. They attest to the preservation of a large share of archaic beliefs associated with magical and totemic practices and with agrarian mythologies. The cult of "saints" (*awliya'* for Muslims, *qaddissin* for Christians, *siddiqin* or *tsaddiqim* for Jews) manifests that continuity in everyday practices, most often orally but sometimes in written form. What is being played out is the relation between human beings and their environment but also the relation to their humanity itself, to the mental and symbolic universe reflected in language, religion, and art, all within an extreme diversity of cultures, modes of behavior, practices, and symbolic expressions. The differences that distinguish the various communities from one another make that phenomenon all the richer and contribute to its historical continuity.

Suzan Youssef

Suzan Youssef is a researcher in Egypt. She has worked in particular on cults of saints common to Jews and Muslims in Egypt.

These ancient roots are constantly sending forth new growth. The presence of holy men and their mausoleums in cantons and villages allows people to redefine the relationship between self and other. Also, and perhaps especially, it allows them to affirm an identity of their own through a local saint, who is considered the natural leader of the community and its representative.

A variety of practices

The celebrations that take place around the saint's tomb allow for a great variety of practices. Participants find an opportunity to liberate themselves from all constraints and to give free rein to all the positive energies of their imagination. It is a moment of collective joy, a festival of color and music, where the idea of a victory over death is forcefully expressed. The saint, though dead, remains alive in the hearts of those who gather to celebrate his "anniversary" (*mawlid*). Both Muslims and Christians respect these traditional cults and, moreover, have integrated them into their own religious practices.

A vast body of literature has considered the phenomenon of Muslim and Christian saints. By contrast, practices similar in every particular, but associated with Jewish mausoleums in Egypt, have been little studied. This can easily be explained by the scarcity of studies in Arabic dealing with the Jews' popular arts and traditions. Specialists in this field are few. In addition, the Jewish mausoleums in Egypt can be counted on the fingers of one hand—there are, in fact, only three. In any event, after 1948 the celebrations associated with them occasioned only indifference in official circles. At the level of popular consciousness, however, interest has persisted, especially among individuals who were born into the Jewish religion and later converted to Islam.

The first of these mausoleums is located in the Musky, the old Jewish quarter of Cairo. This is the tomb of Maimonides, which is housed within the outer walls of the synagogue that bears his name. The second is the mausoleum of Sidi al-Amshati, located in El-Mahalla El-Kubra, in the Gharbia Governorate. Celebrations no longer take place there. The third, finally, is in the Beheira Governorate, on what is known as the Demtiwa farm, next to the city of Damanhur. This mausoleum is currently the object of great interest both in the popular consciousness and among the political authorities.

It should also be noted that these beliefs, which have to do with the righteous (*tsaddiqim*), hold an important place in traditional Jewish culture. They were reinforced by the historical vicissitudes that have marked the collective fate of the Jews. In addition, Deuteronomy mentions the obligation to make the pilgrimage to the Temple of Jerusalem (16:16) three times a year, for the three major holidays: Pessah, Shavuot, and Sukkot. Philo of Alexandria left behind a picturesque account of these pilgrimages to Jerusalem, which were accompanied by songs and dances in which the women participated. The destruction of the Second Temple in 70 CE all but put an end to them. In the later (Byzantine and Islamic) periods, pilgrimages by a small number of Egyptian Jews continued, but in a vastly different atmosphere, sadness and mourning having replaced jubilation.

The Kabbalah says that when the saints—or rather, the "righteous"—die, their spirits are united with the Lord. As a result, their death became the object of celebrations and prayers, which gradually turned into actual pilgrimages to their tombs, with the faithful coming in great numbers to ask for the intercession of the righteous one.

A different phenomenon appeared after the creation of the State of Israel. A number of mausoleums were built in outlying areas of the country, intended for new immigrants, poor Jews from the East, who saw them as an opportunity to become better integrated into Israeli society. Indeed, participation at the banquet, organized near the saint's tomb, aroused a feeling of spiritual union among the faithful and with the saint as well.

I shall first consider Jewish saints in Dakahlia Governorate who became Muslims. Then, following the methods of fieldwork associated with folklore studies, I shall turn to the mausoleum of Rabbi Yaakov Abu Hasira in Damanhur.

Jewish holy men who converted to Islam

The mausoleum of Saint Abdullah ibn Salam is located on el-Rob'a Hill—where vestiges from the Pharaonic era have been discovered—in the village of Emir Abdullah ibn Salam, in the district of Senbellawein, in Dakahlia Governorate. He was a holy man who, after many conversations with the Prophet Muhammad, became a Muslim and took the name by which he is now known. It is said that he waged war alongside the Prophet, and that, when he died on the battlefield, his body took flight. His head was buried in the village named after him, another part of his body was buried under a stela in the middle of Lake Manzala, and the third part in another village by the name of Barq el-Ezz. Also on el-Rob'a Hill, where the saint's mausoleum was built, stands a tall structure that the residents of the village call the "castle of the Jewess." It is said that contact with these stones can cure infertility in women. Next to the saint's mausoleum is a second one, that of Sett Helwa, wife of Abdullah ibn Salam. This monument is also called the "dome of the apparition," because it is said that one has only to spend the night under that cupola and ask to see a saint, any one whatsoever, for the image of that saint to appear on the wall. The two monuments were combined into a single one in 2004. In the cemetery zone west of the mausoleums is a sort of grotto, named after the saint, where infertile women throw themselves on the ground and plead for a cure. The saint appears at night in the form of a protective warrior, dressed in white and mounted on a horse. This image combines Jewish and Islamic beliefs with the traditional representation of Mari Guirguis (Saint George).

The mausoleum of Saint Abu Samra Zaydan is located in the village of Mit Fares, in the district of Beni Ubayd Talkha, in Dakahlia Governorate. Popular tradition portrays the saint as a Jewish notable who embraced Islam and died on the battlefield alongside the Muslims. His mausoleum is adjacent to the principal mosque of the village. Powers of healing are attributed to this saint.

Yaakov Abu Hasira, a local saint for Muslims

The pilgrimage to the tomb of the Moroccan righteous man Rabbi Yaakov Abu Hasira (or Abuhatzeira, 1805–80) has assumed considerable importance in the North African Jewish tradition, second only to the cult of Shimon bar Yochai, the second-century sage to whom the *Zohar*, a major Kabbalistic work, is attributed (his tomb is in Meron, in Galilee). Members of the Abuhatzeira family, originally from Tafilalet in southern Morocco, had been renowned as saints, Kabbalist scholars, and miracle workers for several generations. Rabbi Yaakov is buried in Egypt because that is where he died, on his way to the land of Israel. His grandson, Rabbi Israël Abu Hasira (1889–1984), known as "Baba Sali," was also a major holy and ascetic figure. He left Morocco to settle in Palestine in 1922. He is buried in Netivot, a city in southern Israel between Beersheba and Gaza, and his tomb is also the object of intense devotion.

> **"*The Egyptian people do not distinguish among Muslim, Coptic, and Jewish 'saints.'*"**

The Egyptian people do not distinguish among Muslim, Coptic, and Jewish "saints." They simply establish rankings among them, a hierarchy of sorts. First, there are the *awliya'*, who belong to the family of the Prophet, then the Companions, the martyrs, and the holy men. Last come the local saints, who are not known beyond the limits of a particular village or region and who are the object of a cult only for its residents. Abu Hasira once belonged to that category. His name is closely associated with the hamlet of Demtiwa and surrounding villages, and, until 1978, his renown among non-Jews did not extend beyond the borders of Beheira. The Egyptians learned of him only through the stir set off in the press around that local pilgrimage, within the context of tense relations with Israel.

The caretaker of the tomb is a Muslim Egyptian woman who makes sure that the site is clean and who welcomes pilgrims. Until 1977, a single family, by the name al-Farrash, passed on these duties from one member to another. They were paid by the Israelite Association of Alexandria. The monument was open every Sunday until 1956. In 1967, it was closed down. From time to time, an employee of the association would come with the key to clean it. Celebrations around the mausoleum of Rabbi Yaakov resumed and took an official turn after Egyptian-Israeli relations were normalized in 1978. In any event, the personality of Abu Hasira himself, and the rituals observed near his tomb, have continued to pique the curiosity of researchers.

The residents of Demtiwa, a kilometer from the city of Damanhur, are primarily small-scale farmers living from the sale of their products. The population does not exceed two thousand. A few residents work in Damanhur. The buildings in the village are modest, most of them only one story. Two roads lead there from Damanhur: one passes north of the Mahmoudieh Canal and over the Abu Rish Bridge, while the other goes by the east port and the Saad Farm. At the time of the annual celebrations, the latter road is reserved for the exclusive use of pilgrims.

The mausoleum is at the top of a hill. In Egyptian popular beliefs, all tombs located on hills assume great importance, since they protect the surrounding villages from being submerged by floodwaters. As for Abu Hasira himself, the residents have long believed that he was a Muslim saint, to whom, in fact, many miracles were attributed. Most of the people queried, especially those who are young or middle-aged, said they did not know exactly to what religion Abu Hasira belonged. They only knew he was a holy man and that he performed miracles. His name is said to come from the mat or carpet (*hassira*) he lay on, as el-Ikhbara notes: "He knew in advance the time of his death; he had said he would die on a Sunday, and in fact he died on that day. He was a holy man, who possessed nothing but a mat; he slept on half the carpet and covered himself with the other half. He was found lying dead on that carpet. When they made the road that goes from the Mahmoudieh Canal to the village, the mausoleum was erected there." In reality, that nickname, "father of the mat" (*abu hassira*), comes from Rabbi Yaakov's grandfather Rabbi Shmuel, who, in the eighteenth century, miraculously traveled over water with the aid of his carpet. The residents of the place are not really interested in whether the saint they venerate was Jewish or Muslim. Some even believe that the story of Abu Hasira is associated with the period of Christianization in Egypt, which began in Alexandria.

The residents of the place often make casual visits to the mausoleum. They climb the hill and walk around the monument, or simply around the hill, without climbing to the top. For locals, a visit to the holy site is generally motivated by medical concerns—infertility, skin diseases—or is an effort to keep the evil eye away from their herds. Before Friday prayer, women stand behind the monument and sprinkle holy water on themselves, pronouncing the words: "Abu Hasira, give us your secret!" During the prayer, they leap from one grave to another, invoking the saint aloud.

The monument of Rabbi Ya'akov Abuhatzeira. Photograph: Diarna.

After 1978, the pilgrimage to Abu Hasira's mausoleum took on much greater importance among the Jews. During these annual celebrations, no Egyptian is allowed to approach the monument, which is placed under increased surveillance by security forces.

The Jewish pilgrimage to Damanhur

The Jewish presence in Damanhur dates to the early nineteenth century. It was followed by successive waves of immigration, undertaken for political reasons, in 1871, 1877, 1883, and 1892. At the turn of the twentieth century, however, a large number of Jews left Damanhur and went to settle in Alexandria, where opportunities for earning a living were plentiful at the time. When they died, they were often buried near the mausoleum of Saint Abu Hasira, which is why there are no fewer than eighty-nine Jewish graves in its immediate vicinity. Paradoxically, the importance conferred on that mausoleum has to do with the Jewish belief that everyone must be buried in the land of Israel: the fact that the holy man died in a foreign country while on his way to Jerusalem shows that his mission was not completed, and that another will come after him to bring salvation to the children of Israel.

From an administrative standpoint, the mausoleum belongs to the Israelite Association of Alexandria, which oversees the religious affairs of the Rabbanite Jews of Alexandria and of the Beheira Governorate. The organization has its headquarters in the Eliyahu Synagogue, located on Dr. Hassan Fadali Street, not far from El Nabi Daniel Street. The monument was restored in 1945. A restoration commission was constituted, with the particular aim of receiving contributions from the faithful. It was decided that all those who contributed

Annual Jewish pilgrimage to El Ghriba, the ancient synagogue in Djerba, Tunisia. Photograph by Patrick Zachmann, 2008.

between fifty and a hundred pounds would have their names inscribed in gold letters on a stela affixed to the entrance of the mausoleum. Contributors of twenty-five pounds would have their names inscribed on a stone plaque attached to the outside of the enclosing wall. Another restoration took place when Egyptian-Israeli relations were normalized. Today the monument is surrounded by village houses on three sides, with only the entrance remaining completely clear. A few stairs lead up to it. The mausoleum itself consists simply of a vast rectangular room measuring four by three meters, with a three-meter-high ceiling and a terraced roof.

The inscription on the tomb is composed in Hebrew letters vocalized above the line, like Arabic letters, and not below, as is the case in Modern Hebrew. In reality, the language used is that of the Talmud of Babylon, a mix of Hebrew and Aramaic. Oddly, the year of the holy man's death is not indicated, only the month. The tomb itself is in the northeast corner and measures about two meters by thirty centimeters. The stone is whitewashed and has decorative black lines; a marble slab on top bears the inscription. Along the south wall stands a marble table, about a meter and a half long, used for candles, which are planted in sand.

The annual celebrations (hillula)

In popular Jewish tradition, the most important time to make a pilgrimage to a tomb is on the anniversary of the saint's death, known as *hillula*. The word literally means "celebration, feast": it evokes the joy of marriages and popular festivals and refers to the Kabbalistic notion that the soul of the righteous one is united with God in death, as a mystic betrothal. The term originally applied to celebrations on the thirty-third day after Pessah in Meron, at the tomb of Rabbi Shimon bar Yochai, whose ecstatic disappearance is described at the end of the *Zohar*.

After 1978, Jewish pilgrims began to come in great numbers between January 1 and January 25, which corresponds to the Hebrew month of Tevet, since the saint's *hillula* falls on the nineteenth day of Tevet. During the week before the start of celebrations, they arrive from every part of the world, especially Morocco and France. The road from Alexandria to Damanhur is jammed with tour buses, which, for reasons of security, are prohibited from stopping along the way. The

> **"After 1978, Jewish pilgrims began to come in great numbers from every part of the world, especially Morocco and France."**

city of Damanhur is placed under high surveillance, and the road leading to the village of Demtiwa along the Mahmoudieh Canal is closed to normal traffic. The majority of the pilgrims are elderly or middle-aged, with only a few young people. A large pavilion is set up, with tables arranged into a horseshoe shape and covered with white cloths. Leather goods, dishes, mineral water, beer, and paper plates are on offer under makeshift awnings. Vendors also place *kippot* [skullcaps] and prayer shawls (*tallit*) on their tables, along with jewelry, talismans, and candlesticks. Pictures of the saint are displayed as well. Various privileges are auctioned off: that of being the first to enter the mausoleum, to hold its key, or to light a candle for the saint. As soon as the doors are opened, the crowd surges forward, singing hymns, while the rabbi and the members of the brotherhood line up on the right side of the entrance to make way for the faithful. The pilgrims start walking around the tomb, soon joined by the rabbi and members of the brotherhood. Then the crowd splits into two groups, with members of the brotherhood lining up in front of the northeast wall. Some of the faithful gather in front of the tomb and place bottles of water, clothing, and candles on the gravestone, so that the saint will bestow his blessing on these objects. The pilgrims wash their faces, and some rub their knees against the stone. Women lean forward and burst into sobs, while the men stand back, engaged in silent prayer. Still others read prayers aloud. All the men have *kippot* on their heads and wear prayer shawls.

In the middle of the group formed by the brotherhood stands the saint's descendant, a man with a full face and clear complexion, wearing a white Moroccan-style *abaya* [loose, robelike garment] over his European clothes and a white *kippah* embroidered with gold thread. When he begins a hymn, he opens out his prayer shawl to form a canopy over the heads of those in attendance. The women take hold of the fringe of the shawl and kiss it, while young people take photographs or make videos, seemingly indifferent to the atmosphere of religious fervor.

Then women bring in pastries on metal or cardboard trays, or on upside-down tambourines: round or square cookies, little cakes, apricots, almonds, sometimes peanuts, and caramels. They circulate among the pilgrims, holding out their trays, and no one can refuse what they offer.

During that time, some of the faithful go off to sit near the tombs located behind the monument. They set down cookies nearby, before making an offering of them, or place money on the gravestones before making a gift to the rabbi. Since there is no longer an Egyptian rabbi, a Moroccan rabbi officiates. He has come from France, where he lives, and is dressed in a black morning coat and a stiff black felt hat, in the manner of European rabbis. He stands near the mausoleum, loudly calling on the faithful in Hebrew to give money for the poor. People throng around him to make their offerings, often in dollars, and from time to time someone turns the box over and empties out its contents. Part of that money is used to relieve the suffering of impoverished Jews; the rest goes to maintain the monument.

After about an hour and a half, everyone leaves the mausoleum. Members of the brotherhood line up on the right side of the door, along with the leader of the Jewish community of Alexandria. From time to time, a man or woman breaks away from the crowd and approaches Abu Hasira's descendant to ask his advice. He replies, grants his blessing in exchange for cash, and reassures the person before him, saying that the problem will be solved and everything will turn out for the best.

On the other side of the monument, near the west wall, a group of some ten men gathers to pray, silently or out loud. Then everyone congregates around the buffet, laden with all sorts of prepared dishes brought there by Maghrebi faithful. They rush about, setting out pistachios, pumpkin seeds, couscous, cold cuts, boiled potatoes, rice, bread rolls, bottles of mineral water, wine, and arrack. Young people put meat kebabs on to roast. They have brought the meat with them, since no butchers in Egypt practice kosher slaughter. The caretaker does her best to help out in serving the food.

The rabbi and the members of the brotherhood sing in unison with the pilgrims. The women ululate and beat their hands, wave handkerchiefs, and sway to the rhythm of the song, accompanied by tambourines. The music has a marked oriental character, resembling the *mawwāl*. One singer begins the verse, then the others reply. This type of four-line poem, sung or chanted, is called a *piyyutim*:

> *Yaakov was made perfect by the Lord:*
> *Now he remains silent.*
> *He looks at the deep water,*
> *For he is full of understanding.*
> *In the wisdom of the Kabbalah,*
> *I shall acquire glory and renown,*
> *Profundity of learning, attention in listening,*
> *For he is the great Yaakov.*

A profusion of symbols

All these rituals are rich in the symbolism of Jewish culture. The act of erecting a tent, for example, is a reference to the Tabernacle, where the Lord spoke with Moses. It was a customary practice that at the funeral of a religious or important man, gold coins were thrown into each corner of the grave to appease the evil spirits by giving them a share of the inheritance.[1] The act of lighting candles evokes the saint's presence; the more candles there are, the more likely the saint's spirit will be summoned to the site. The prayer at the west wall of the monument refers to the Temple of Jerusalem and to the Western Wall. The northeast side is associated with the Jewish custom of burying the dead so that they face east. That way, they will be able to take the road to Israel when they are resurrected. Pilgrims take away a little soil from the mausoleum, so as to enjoy its blessing during the following year: it is said to have the power to heal.

Recently, Yaakov Abu Hasira's *hillula* has become a political and cultural issue in Egypt. As it happens, the Egyptian public knows next to nothing about traditional Jewish culture. Although a few specialists defend the legitimacy of studying the Diaspora Jews' popular culture, the press has been extremely polemical in dealing with the question, associating these traditional rites with Zionist designs. As a result, the debate has ended up in the courts. But the various manifestations of popular culture ought rather to be considered texts, cultural objects that can be translated into many diverse languages, in accordance with differences in time and place, and depending on the religious, political, and economic context. The folklorist presents these documents from the point of view of those who belong to the culture studied. It is then up to observers to extract the multiple meanings and interpretations, both new and traditional. The folkloric material has both a local and a universal character. Nothing is ever univocal.

---

1. Haïm Zafrani, *Deux mille ans de vie juive au Maroc: Histoire, culture, religion* (Paris: Maisonneuve et Larose, 1983), 108.

The Tomb of Esther in Iran

The story of Esther takes place in Iran in the fifth century BCE, under Xerxes (or Ahasuerus; r. 486–465), the Achaemenid king "whose empire stretched from India to Ethiopia and comprised one hundred and twenty-seven provinces" (Esther 1:1; New Jerusalem Bible). He lived amid "white and violet hangings fastened with cords of fine linen and purple thread to silver rings on marble columns, couches of gold and silver on a pavement of porphyry, marble, mother-of-pearl and precious stones" (Esther 1:6–7). Esther, perfumed with aromatics, massaged with "oil of myrrh," and dressed by seven virgins, became the favorite of the gynaeceum and was crowned to replace Queen Vashti. But before she crossed the threshold of the harem, her cousin and guardian Mordecai—Esther was an orphan—advised her to be discreet "about her race or parentage" (Esther 2:10). In other words, not a word about being Jewish. She did not have to seduce the sovereign with her words. Her "good figure" and "beautiful face" (Esther 2:7) spoke in her favor.

In the palace, she was a queen sheltered from every worry. She would not remain so for long. One day, Mordecai appeared at the royal gates in rent

The tomb of Esther and Mordecai in Hamadan, Iran. Photograph by Z. Radovan.

garments, in sackcloth and ashes. The message he wanted to transmit to his adopted daughter had to do with the threat looming over the Jewish community. The second-most important person in the state, the mighty Haman, had just sent out a decree ordering "the destruction, slaughter and annihilation of all Jews, young and old, including women and children" (Esther 3:12–13). Esther, caught off guard, sent Mordecai a change of clothing. He refused it, had a copy of the extermination order delivered to her, and implored her to reveal her identity, so as to win the king over to their cause and save them from death (Esther 4:8). Esther hesitated. She could not cross the threshold to her own master's inner court. If she saw him without having been summoned, she would pay with her life. But her people were in dire straits. She had to acknowledge her roots, whatever the price: "Do not suppose that, because you are in the king's palace, you are going to be the one Jew to escape. . . If you persist in remaining silent at such a time, . . . both you and your father's whole family will perish" (Esther 4:12–14). "If I perish, I perish," was Esther's reply. From that moment on, she was no longer Hadassah, whose name means "the hidden, the secret" in Hebrew. She was the one who unveiled herself, a Jew exposed to extermination. She took off her sumptuous garments, put on mourning clothes, covered her head with ashes and filth, and prayed to the Lord: "Come to my aid, for I am alone . . . I will stake my life. . . . O Lord . . . heed the voice of the despairing . . . and free me from my fear!" (Esther 4:17, I and z).[1] After fasting and prayer, she dressed in her splendor once again and, at the risk of her life—despite being forbidden—she crossed all the thresholds to the king. When their eyes met, she fainted away. But when she came to, the king's voice, far from condemning her for her sacrilege, was protective of her. "'What is the matter, Queen Esther?' the king said. 'Tell me what you want; even if it is half my kingdom, I grant it you'" (Esther 5:3). As her only reply, she invited the king and Haman to a banquet. There, after hearing for

the second time the king's assurances that he would grant her all her wishes, she issued an invitation to a second banquet. The next day, for the third time, the king repeated his offer: "Tell me what you ask . . . it is granted in advance!" (Esther 7:2). Esther the "hidden," the "secret," finally revealed her identity: "For we have been handed over, my people and I, to destruction" (Esther 7:4). Then she continued: "The persecutor, the enemy? Why, this wretch Haman!" (Esther 7:6).

The king immediately ordered the conspirator hanged. Haman was executed on a gallows that he had erected for Mordecai (Esther 7:10). Nevertheless, Esther's mission was unfinished: she still had to save her people. Again she violated the law and went to the inner court to ask the king to rescind the condemnation decree. The king agreed and then ordered Mordecai to inform in writing the Jews, the satraps, and the governors "of the provinces stretching from India to Ethiopia, a hundred and twenty-seven provinces" (Esther 8:9). In these letters, Xerxes granted the Jews "the right to assemble in self-defense, with permission to destroy, slaughter, and annihilate any armed force of any people or province that might attack them, together with their women and children, and to plunder their possessions" (Esther 8:11). That decree bore the date of the thirteenth day of the twelfth month, Adar. That is the origin of the feast of Purim: the reversal of fortune, the shift in the scales from extermination to freedom of worship, from mourning to celebration—the opposite of the Shoah. These biblical scenes took place in Susa, in Southern Iran. But the mausoleum of Esther and Mordecai is in Hamadan (the former Ecbatana, summer capital of the Achaemenids), in Northern Iran, 330 kilometers from Tehran. The mausoleum, which has a brick cupola, is reminiscent of Islamic architecture. The various sources agree that the current monument, dating to between the thirteenth and seventeenth centuries, was built on the site of ancient tombs, which, according to the Jews, are the burial place of the two biblical figures. A long path leads to a very low entrance. In one of the rooms, two cenotaphs are covered with embroidered silks. Two gilded plaques indicate their names in three writing systems—Hebrew, Persian, and Latin: רתסא אסתר, "Ester," and اخدرم مردخای , יכדרמ , "Mordekhay." The walls are decorated with Hebrew characters, with a tablet containing the Ten Commandments in Persian, and with a text in Hebrew tracing Mordecai's genealogy back to Moses. Above them is a Star of David. The mausoleum also has a Torah scroll dating to the seventeenth century. Sir Robert Ker Porter, who visited Hamadan in the early nineteenth century, reports that the leader of the Jews of Hamadan held the key to the mausoleum and had likely done so since the sacred couple's burial.[2] In our own time, the caretaker in charge of maintaining the mausoleum says that "Esther" is derived from the Persian *Setareh*, which means "star."

In 2009 the Islamic Republic added this mausoleum to the list of national treasures of Iran. The tomb is a pilgrimage site for the Jews, who celebrate the feast of Purim there, in particular, but it is also a holy site for the Muslims and Christians, who visit all year long. •

A specialist in the religions of Iran (Buddhism, Christianity, and Muslim mysticism), Nahal Tajadod is the author of many works: Mani, le Bouddha de lumière: Catéchisme manichéen chinois *(Le Cerf, 1990);* Les porteurs de lumière: L'épopée de l'Église de Perse *(Albin Michel, 2008);* À l'est du Christ: Vie et mort des chrétiens dans la Chine des Tang: VIIᵉ–IXᵉ siècle *(Plon, 2000); and* Sur les pas de Rûmi *(Albin Michel, 2006; new ed., 2012).*

---

1. [My translation is from the French Bible de Jérusalem (1998)—JMT.]
2. Sir Robert Ker Porter, *Travels in Georgia, Persia, Armenia, Ancient Babylonia,* 2 vols. (London, 1821–22).

Aspects of Family Life among Jews in Muslim Societies

Harvey E. Goldberg,
Wasfi Kailani

Family life, among Jews and Muslims, carried forward many cultural features that were widespread in the Middle East since antiquity. The specifics of each society also reflected the impact of the two religions as these evolved over time. The norms and practice of family life entailed ongoing adjustment among taken-for-granted lifestyles, explicit values, and canonized written sources. A systematic comparison between biblical and Qur'anic prescriptions, or between *fiqh* and *halakha*, would far exceed the boundaries of this article. We will thus limit ourselves to an anthropological outlook on the shared cultural values between Jews and Muslims concerning family life, as well as their differences. Historically, Judaism antedated Islam, but the extensive reach of Islam and its cultural and religious creativity later had an impact on Jewish society and culture. Frequently the matter of influence is unclear. Trying to determine what is "Muslim" and what is "Jewish" often is unproductive in the realm of family life, where deep cultural assumptions and taken-for-granted norms typically remain unarticulated.

Harvey E. Goldberg

Harvey E. Goldberg is the Sarah Allen Shaine professor emeritus of sociology and anthropology at the Hebrew University of Jerusalem. His work, which includes a translation from Hebrew of an indigenous account of the Jews of Libya, *The Book of Mordechai*, by Mordecai HaCohen (1980, 1983), has sought to combine anthropology and Jewish studies. He is the author of *Cave Dwellers and Citrus Growers* (Cambridge University Press, 1972), *Jewish Life in Muslim Libya* (University of Chicago Press, 1990), and edited *Sephardi and Middle Eastern Jewries* (Indiana University Press, 1996).

Wasfi Kailani

A Jordanian specialist on Jerusalem, Wasfi Kailani received his doctorate in sociology and anthropology in 2007 from the Hebrew University of Jerusalem (dir. Harvey Goldberg and Yitzhak Reiter). His research concerns identity, religion and boundaries among different socieities in Jordan, Israel, and Palestine.

Medieval family institutions and customs

Regarding the early centuries of Islam, the question of mutual reciprocal influences entails guesswork, while from the high Middle Ages, evidence is available that allows some systematic comparison of historic institutions. A central source of data from this period are documents in both Hebrew and Arabic (mostly written in Hebrew script) that were preserved in a synagogue in Fustat (Old Cairo) in Egypt, and came to the attention of scholars late in the nineteenth century. A leading researcher of these materials, Shlomo Dov Goitein, has discussed social history, including matters of family life, and examined a range of documents that included wedding contracts, trousseau lists, personal letters, and rabbinic decisions. His research illuminates many aspects of Jewish family life within a wider Muslim context. It illustrates the ongoing dynamic in which daily life and the ever-present inputs of communal traditions are meshed.[1]

By the tenth century, Arabic had become the "mother tongue" of Jews throughout the Arab realm, while Hebrew, along with some Aramaic, continued to be central in worship and in studying the Torah. Jewish wedding contracts (*ketubot*) continued to be written in Aramaic, reflecting their earlier formulations in Roman Palestine and in Babylonia (Iraq), while Muslim wedding contracts were in Arabic. At the same time, there were points of overlap that enable interesting comparisons and contrasts indicating how everyday assumptions and practices were punctuated by the impact of explicit communal norms, written religious traditions, or state intervention. These social processes highlight both similarities and distinctions between the family lives of Jews and Muslims in values, terminology, and the institutions that shaped them.

General attitudes toward the "place of women" are one realm that exhibits the two sides of this shared cultural coinage. Both Muslims and Jews took it for granted that women mostly should be "at home." This applied to girls approaching marriageable age, whose reputation was at stake, along with concern over premature sexual contact they might have with men, as well as to married women whose actual or imagined behavior could reflect upon the honor of husbands or of patrilineal relatives. But the extent of exclusion of unmarried girls from wider social occasions and contact appears to have been stronger among Muslims than among Jews or Christians in Egypt; the latter might attend synagogue or church, which provided an opportunity for men to see them or chat with them.

With regard to married women, the prevailing norm was that their proper place was within the confines of the house. Here, too, we find Jews not following this principle to the extent expected in Islam. In the writings of Moses Maimonides (1135/38–1204) there appears to be push and pull in opposite directions. In one place, possibly resisting Muslim conceptions, Maimonides insists that women should not be seen as prisoners in their homes, while elsewhere he praises the principle expressed in the book of Psalms (14:45): "the honored place of a princess is on the inside."[2] It appears that Jews came to incorporate the norms of the wider society, but internally sought to reformulate outside influences in terms of their own traditions and cultural experience. At a much later period in North Africa, a woman described her own limited mobility while unmarried to being "closed up like a scroll of the Torah in the cabinet in the synagogue."

How a marriage is contracted

These sets of norms resonate with the differing legal principles regarding the right of women to make decisions concerning their own marriage. When young, the guardian of a Muslim woman is normally her father, while at an older age some male guardian must assent to any marriage. Jewish legal tradition, which predates Islam, inserts an age factor into the matter. A father is entitled to decide on a husband for his minor daughter, but once she reaches a state of maturity, called *bogeret* (twelve and one half years of age), she can decide on her own and must be consulted by parents wishing to choose a husband for her. The common custom that appears in documents from medieval Cairo, nevertheless, is that even mature women chose a male representative to receive the first obligatory marriage payment from a future husband. This representative, called *paqid* in Hebrew or *wakil* in Arabic, is not required by law, but brings Jewish practice and ambience in line with the conventional forms in wider Muslim society. Perhaps the existence of two distinct linguistic expressions reflects the optional, rather than mandatory, status of this practice.

It is also useful to disentangle the levels of terminology, institutions, and historical development in regard to the central transactions that constitute marriage among Muslims and Jews. The act of marrying a woman in Islam entails a man transferring a monetary sum to a woman, which is called *mahr* in Arabic. In many cases the actual payment may be divided into an immediate initial payment that makes the marriage valid, and a later promised payment (or payments) written into a marriage contract

Establishment of a marriage contract in the Grand Atlas Mountains, Imilchil, Morocco. Photograph by Bruno Barbey, 1972.

and due at a later date. The technical Arabic terms for initial and delayed payment also appear with reference to Jewish marriages but carry different formal meetings.

In the Hebrew Bible, marrying a woman entailed the transfer of money by the man, and the Hebrew word *mohar* appears in that context. No mention of a written marriage document appears in the Bible itself, but a written contract called a *ketuba* later evolved as a central feature of marriage in early rabbinic literature. By this time, the transfer of money that legally creates a marriage had become minimal due to inflation, and the central concern of the *ketuba* was a written promissory debt defining what a woman would receive from her husband or his family in the event that she is divorced or widowed. One rabbinic source even suggests that the *mohar* has become the future amount promised in the *ketuba*. A Jewish groom would still have to make a small transfer of monetary value to bring about the marriage, and could also add to that a significant gift, which together constituted an "immediate payment" parallel to the prevailing Arabic terminology. Correspondingly, the amount written in the *ketuba* regarding divorce or widowhood might be referred to as the "delayed" payment, which echoed the Arabic formulation, but the legal content of the institutions behind this terminology within Jewish family life was not equivalent to what they entailed among Muslims. It is thus not surprising that a few cases are documented in which Jewish individuals involved in a dispute over marriage turn to a Muslim court, and it is also understandable that a common response of the Muslim state court was to return the matter to a Jewish tribunal.

> " *Contact between Muslims and Jews becomes even more complex as European influences begin to play a role in family life.* "

Another example of the cross-currents of influence concerns a dramatic feature of marriage celebrations. An important aspect of marriage, from the ancient through the contemporary Middle East, has been the virginity of a bride. A widespread practice has been to publicly display a bloodstained sheet or garment after the first conjugal act of the new couple following their formal marriage. One of the oldest examples of this practice is alluded to in the book of Deuteronomy (22:17). It continued to be common in Middle Eastern communities, and in the Middle Ages there were attempts among Jews to institutionalize a formal blessing appropriate to the occasion. Some rabbinic authorities, in particular Maimonides, disapproved of it; the practice eventually disappeared both in the Middle East and in the European milieus.

European influences and ethnographic examples

Regarding more recent times, unraveling contact between Muslims and Jews becomes even more complex as European influences begin to play a role in family life and its ceremonial expression. This is evident from the early modern period, when Jews from the Iberian Peninsula (Sephardim) began to reach many regions of the Muslim world, even before the dramatic European expansion in the nineteenth century. In addition, ethnographic descriptions that now are available enable us to view patterns of family life in preceding centuries with enhanced subtlety and insight.

Jews from Spain and Portugal began reaching parts of the Muslim Mediterranean from the fourteenth century onward, carrying with them cultural imprints from both Muslim and Christian civilizations. Christian influences were the most recent, and were reflected in differences between the Iberian Sephardim and the local Jewish communities that always had resided within the Islamic realm, as well as between Jews and Muslims. Each group valued family privacy and female modesty, but there were palpable differences between the norms of North African culture shaped by the Maliki school of Islamic law and the comparative openness of relations between genders characterizing the Sephardi newcomers. This is evident, even today, in the (former) Jewish quarter (*mellah*) of Fes in Morocco. There, regular, parallel, and open streets, lined by visible balconies from which women might look out and be seen, contrast with the "irregularity" of streets and many cul-de-sacs in Muslim neighborhoods that served to bolster the private life of families.

Moroccan society, viewed as a whole, incorporated such differences and variation, which also continued to exist among the Jews themselves. In various ways, the status of women was higher among the Megorashim (lit., Jews that had been "expelled" from Spain) than among the local Jews (Toshavim). Sephardi rules of inheritance gave more rights to women than did the older local principles. Polygamy existed as an option within both groups, and although clearly not preferred, was easier to arrange in the indigenous Maghribi Jewish communities. Awareness of these differences existed on both shores of the Mediterranean. Jewish men in Italy knew that taking a second wife was possible in Tripoli if a first wife did not bear children, and might travel there to marry a second woman with rabbinical approval. Over the course of the nineteenth century, such an option lost its relevance as Jews in Europe came to see themselves as part and parcel of European states and civilization, and consequently distanced themselves from "Oriental" practices.

Signing the marriage contract of an Orthodox Jewish couple at Groningen, the Netherlands. Photograph by Robert Mulder.

The introduction of European influences was thus gradual. In some regions the linkage and overlap between Muslim and Jewish norms and practices continued to be as strong as it had been in the Middle Ages, and perhaps grew even stronger. In medieval *ketubot* from the Cairo Geniza (unlike Muslim marriage contracts), the name of God does not appear in the highlighted superinscription because that document might be torn up in the event of a divorce and a final payment to the woman. Other Jewish documents, however, often would invoke an appellation of God as headings. The medieval stricture against placing God's name on a *ketuba* was not maintained in all instances, however, and some marriage contracts from nineteenth-century Tripoli begin by citing God the "Merciful," a designation that has roots in Jewish tradition but also strongly resonates with Islamic forms. This convention is especially notable as an aspect of culture that directly engages rabbinic tradition.

Marriage customs

It makes little sense to label practices and customs as categorically Jewish or Muslim when they formed part of a broad and long-standing regional tradition. If this is true regarding aspects of marriages that are linked to expressed religious norms, it certainly applies to anonymous lifestyles known through ethnographic description. Recent ethnographic accounts direct attention to the contexts and social patterns that might underline Jewish-Muslim differences on the one hand, or affirm—if only through silence—their commonalities on the other. Following are examples related to wedding practices, as they have been documented in an area running from Southern Tunisia through Eastern Libya.[3]

Some of the material components of wedding agreements and celebrations were supplied to Muslims by Jewish merchants, craftsmen, and peddlers. Among them are henna leaves used in cosmetic decoration, spices for cooking, textiles, and jewelry. It is thus not surprising that they are prominent in the celebrations of both communities. While Jews for the most part were not directly engaged in farming, Jewish weddings in rural regions could reflect the centrality of the agricultural regime. In a Jebel Nefusa wedding, a Jewish bride sat down upon a millstone and a plow, after which her hands and feet were decorated with henna, while in a neighboring region, Muslim wedding songs would emphasize the importance of hard work for men at the planting and harvesting season.

A widespread feature of wedding rituals throughout the Mediterranean and beyond are gestures of tearing or breaking. In Jewish life, breaking a glass within a wedding ceremony has been given the canonical meaning of mourning for the destroyed Temple in Jerusalem. But other gestures of breaking existed in North Africa, such as the mother of the groom tearing a sleeve from the garment of the bride-to-be during a preparatory celebration, the groom smashing a jug of water on the way to the nuptial home, or the bride throwing and smashing a raw egg against the doorpost or wall of the groom's house that she is to enter for the first time. In some cases, a Temple-mourning explanation was attached to these acts by Jews, but it is clear that parallel practices existed among Muslims in the same regions. It remains a challenge to unravel what circumstances give rise to interpretations of customs that mark the specificity of a given community when it clearly shares much in common with neighbors of a different religion.

This very sharing itself may stimulate religious specialists to seek ways of underscoring the distinctiveness of their own community and traditions. One might also assume that the motivation for self-differentiation is stronger within a minority group that is concerned about cultural assimilation than within the majority population. A push toward delineation and symbolic separation from the other, however, existed in both directions. A Muslim in Tripoli describing the local practice of circumcision, which is deeply ingrained in Muslim life but not mandated in the Qur'an, indicated that aspects of the custom are followed so as to be "distinguished from the Jews." Awareness of similarity may thus create a potential dilemma of religion and of identity in wider circles than that of ritual experts. In Jewish weddings in Jerba, Muslim guests might be present during some

> *In Jewish weddings in Jerba, Muslim guests might be present during some of the preparatory days of celebration, but were absent during the culminating wedding evening in which a rabbi guides the steps of the ceremony.*

of the preparatory days of celebration, but were absent during the culminating wedding evening in which a rabbi guides the steps of the ceremony and musicians play traditional hymns.

The ability to attach interpretations highlighting a specific religious tradition to widespread practices held in common with others yields a dynamic process that takes diverse forms in different historical circumstances. That process may still be seen in contemporary Israel, where immigrants from Muslim countries now form part of a Jewish majority, while some feel that aspects of their customs are looked down upon because they reflect the Middle Eastern milieu from which they originated. This is a new context for "Judaizing" popular practices that in the past did not elicit attempts at interpretation or justification. The cosmetic use of henna in wedding celebrations has become the object of such an interpretive thrust. The three consonantal letters of its spelling in Hebrew are now presented as an acronym pointing to a text in the Mishnah (*Shabat* 2:6) that indicates the special religious obligations of women: *halah* (a ritual dough offering taken from the Sabbath bread), *niddah* (abstention from sexual congress during the menstrual period), and *hadlakat haner* (lighting Sabbath candles). An ancient Middle Eastern custom thus continues to spread throughout Jewish Israeli society as families originating from the Middle East and from Europe intermarry, even as interpretive efforts are made that loosen it from its historic moorings. This process, emerging from within circles of the religiously devout, seeks to assert the relevance of religion in realms that previously were part of everyday life, and still characterize Muslims in the region.

---

1. S. D. Goitein, *A Mediterranean Society: The Jewish Communities of the Arab World as Portrayed in the Documents of the Cairo Geniza*, vol. 1, *Economic Foundations* (Berkeley: University of California Press, 1978).

2. *Mishneh Torah, Sefer Nashim, Hilkhot Ishut* 13, 13–14.

3. Lucette Valensi, "Religious Orthodoxy or Local Tradition: Marriage Celebration in Southern Tunisia," in *Jews Among Arabs: Contacts and Boundaries*, ed. M. R. Cohen and A. L. Udovitch (Princeton, NJ: Darwin Press, 1989); and Harvey E. Goldberg, *Jewish Life in Muslim Libya: Rivals and Relatives* (Chicago: University of Chicago Press, 1990).

Citizenship, Gender, and Feminism in the Contemporary Arab Muslim and Jewish Worlds

Stéphanie Latte Abdallah, Valérie Pouzol

The question of gender and women's roles in the Arab Muslim and Jewish worlds is linked primarily to the multiplicity of social, economic, political, and geographical situations in which they have lived and continue to live in the contemporary period. Given the extreme diversity of groups and situations, we have chosen to focus our comparison on the collective and political formulations of religion inherent in gender issues and, in turn, in women's activism. Women's roles and the particular way they have been defined by religious affiliation, whether Muslim or Jewish, are bound to contexts that have dictated specific possibilities for action, distinct national interpretations of texts and of religious law, as well as very different religious currents. From the early twentieth century to the 1990s, moreover, the contemporary period was characterized by the birth and growth in the public sphere of secular feminist movements. In the last decade of that century, the pioneering feminists were joined by emerging religious feminist currents, both Islamic and Orthodox Jewish. These currents were historically continuous with previous movements and contributed toward the diversification of repertoires for action and of the resources women have mobilized to assert their rights and roles in all realms.

Stéphanie Latte Abdallah

Director of Research at CNRS (Institute of Study and Research on the Arab and Muslim World, Aix-en-Provence), she is the author of *Femmes réfugiées palestiniennes* (Presses Universitaires de France, 2006) and *À l'ombre du Mur: Israéliens et Palestiniens entre occupation et séparation* (Actes Sud, 2011), and has written for, most notably, *Féminismes islamiques, Revue des mondes musulmans et de la Méditerranée* (vol. 128, no. 2, December 2010).

Valérie Pouzol

Director of Studies at the University of Paris VIII, she is the author of *Clandestines de la paix: Israéliennes et Palestiniennes contre la guerre* (Éditions Complexe, IHTP, CNRS, 2008).

At first, a fragmented and conservative Jewish world

In the contemporary period, the Jewish world has been plural, resulting in distinct social, political, and cultural situations in the Diaspora and then, after 1948, within the context of the State of Israel. It is astonishing to note the diversity among coreligionists in the early twentieth century between, for example, a Moroccan Jewish woman living in the *mellah*, an assimilated German Jewish woman, and a Russian Jewish woman fleeing the pogroms. The various host countries did not all grant the same rights to the Jewish communities: although the Jews of Western Europe were emancipated in the early 1870s,[1] those of Eastern Europe and in the Russian Empire were greatly discriminated against and persecuted. In the Muslim world, and especially in the Ottoman Empire, the Jews' personal status is difficult to fathom: the *dhimma* pact was gradually called into question (over time, the Jews were no longer required to pay the *jizya*), but the legal framework (*millet*) applied to the non-Muslim communities remained the frame of reference, with each community managing the personal status of its members, women in particular.[2] Upon emancipation, Jewish women of the Diaspora would enjoy civil rights in their host countries, especially in matters of divorce and inheritance, and would thus circumvent discrimination. By contrast, in countries that still granted a great deal of autonomy to the Jewish communities, religious laws (especially on inheritance) would continue to be applied.

In these different sociocultural and political contexts, the relation to religion, to tradition, and more generally to Jewish culture has varied as a function of the collective trajectory of the population (persecution, immigration, integration), one's individual trajectory, and, above all, one's social class. Beyond the differences, however, Jewish feminist inquiry and action developed in the contemporary period not by abandoning tradition but, on the contrary, by making a larger place within it for at least some women. From the nineteenth century on, that feminist movement has been favored by complex sociohistorical factors: access to education for Jewish girls of the Diaspora, the Jewish debate on modernity, and the various reforms of Judaism. In mostly scattered communities, traditional Orthodox Judaism—characterized by a continued acceptance of the Law and by a rigorous orthopraxy—took care to assign women the roles of wives and mothers dedicated to sanctifying and exercising influence in the home.[3] In the history of a geographically dispersed people, who before 1948 did not possess autonomous national structures, the family was designated as the place of cohesiveness, fertility, and the transmission of religious and cultural values. Hebrew jurisprudence proved very conservative in matters of family law, particularly divorce law. The *get* (religious writ of divorce) has always been at the heart of the polemic and has occupied a central place in rabbinical literature since the time of the Talmud. The prerogative to dissolve a marriage, by means of a written document, falls exclusively, unilaterally, to the husband (Deuteronomy 24: 1–4). A man who denies his wife a *get* renders her *aguna* (chained) and prevents her from remarrying under Jewish Law. Any future cohabitation will be considered adulterous and any subsequent children born to her illegitimate. Traditional Judaism also established a gendered division of roles within religious practice: only men are obliged to study the Law and to reflect on its theoretical foundations; women, exempted from study, are guardians of the rites and sanctity of the home. Jewish Law thus seeks to protect the purity of the family and to promote men's progress in their studies. It therefore codified all aspects of daily life, and, in particular, the couple's sexual life (*niddah* laws).

The beginning of Jewish women's access to education

The traditional figure of the Jewish mother, occupied with sanctifying her home, has been called into question, especially within contemporary national contexts in which Jewish women have found different possibilities for education and new models of integration. Everywhere, schools have played a role in the secularization of education and have acted as a powerful factor of acculturation, even when they remain in the hands of Jewish institutions. Nation-states in Europe and the United States but also in the Russian Empire, in their quest for modernity and their desire to promote assimilation, understood what was at stake. They opened schools and assigned them the task of integrating Jewish communities into the European states or of Americanizing or Russifying them. The opportunities for study that certain host countries offered Jewish girls played an important role in their progress but also in their ability to take their distance from traditional religious roles.[4] During the waves of migration between the late nineteenth and early twentieth centuries, the United States offered Jewish emigrants from Germany, and especially from Russia, a free and compulsory education that relegated religious instruction to an elective taught outside school. That access to education was also momentarily possible in the Russian Empire, when in 1844 official elementary schools were created to convert the Jews. Although the vast majority of Russian women were still illiterate in the late nineteenth century, women of the Jewish middle class attended high school and university. That process slowed in 1887 with the establishment of a *numerus clausus*. Girls' education was the subject of intense debates in Jewish societies at the time and met with strong resistance from parents motivated by the fear of educated but unmarried daughters. The issue of education was also alive in Islamic territories, particularly during the last days of the Ottoman Empire, when Western Jews undertook to "regenerate" their brothers and sisters from the East by promoting hygiene and education, especially through the schools of the Alliance Israélite Universelle.

An evolution in the Haskalah movement

In addition to these new exogenous opportunities, contemporary developments and inquiries within Judaism itself offered women the possibility of emancipation from the traditional model. Reform Judaism arose in Germany during the Enlightenment as part of the Haskalah movement. From the late eighteenth century on, in the face of the question of the Jews' emancipation and their access to modernity, this current believed it had to adapt to the sociohistorical context. It rethought the role of women, granting greater equality between the sexes, gradually abolishing the strict separation between men and women at the synagogue, and allowing women to study and exercise religious responsibilities as rabbis and cantors. Masorti Judaism, of a more conservative cast, appeared in Germany during the period following emancipation and spread to the United States in 1886. It also advocated an evolution of Judaism in accordance with the interpretation of the texts and of the tradition. From the start, these two non-Orthodox movements recommended a minimal religious education for girls as well as boys. In the United States, the first bat mitzvah (coming-of-age religious ceremony for twelve-year-old girls) took place in 1922.[5] In the late nineteenth century, these two Jewish movements raised the question of women's access to the rabbinate, especially in the United States, at a time when some Protestant currents were ordaining the first women ministers. In 1973, the liberal Jewish movement in America (Reform) ordained the first female rabbi and, in the Masorti community, women have been counted in the prayer quorum (*minyan*) since 1974. They were admitted for rabbinical studies in 1983 and began to be ordained as rabbis in 1985.

> *In the United States, the first bat mitzvah (coming-of-age religious ceremony for twelve-year-old girls) took place in 1922.*

In the late nineteenth century, the national Jewish question and the rise of political Zionism also raised the issue of women's rights. Those involved in the project of nation building were committed to creating a new Jewish man, the antithesis of the man of the Diaspora, who was judged weak and degenerate, and was persecuted as a result. But Zionist ideologues had trouble imagining what a new Jewish woman might be, and, especially, what rights ought to be granted her within the new state framework. Theodor Herzl, the father of political Zionism, believed that women ought to obtain political rights, but that they were not to meddle too much in public affairs. Zionism, which exalted virility and masculinity, made life difficult for militant and pioneering Zionist women. Many of these women had studied at university and had been politically active before joining the first Zionist communities in Palestine. They fought on a daily basis to obtain full integration into the Zionist project,[6] militating for the right to work but also for the right to vote in the institutions of the Yishuv.

With the State of Israel's declaration of independence on May 14, 1948, the principle of sexual equality was clearly articulated, and Israeli women immediately obtained civil and political citizenship.[7] But, in the aim of maintaining the new state's unity, Ben-Gurion made a significant concession to the religious parties: for the Jews of Israel, rights relating to personal status (marriage and divorce) have, since 1953, been under the exclusive jurisdiction of the Orthodox rabbinical tribunals. This is particularly restrictive, since there is as a result no civil marriage.[8] Nevertheless, religious institutions can be circumvented in part, because they remain subject to civil laws. Hence, by the terms of the 1951 law on equal rights for women passed in the Knesset, a woman's right to property remains unchanged and inalienable after marriage. That law must be applied by every tribunal called on to adjudicate a conflict on the question. Similarly, on the matter of alimony, civil and religious authorities have concurrent jurisdiction and hear different cases, but only the religious tribunals can dissolve a marriage. On matters of inheritance, civil estate law grants full equality between men and women, but only if the case does not come before a rabbinical court. The principles of equality laid out in the declaration of independence, having no constitutional standing, have been evaded. Nevertheless, since the 1950s several laws have been passed to fight against discrimination in the workplace and the army, and against sexual harassment.

Legal discrimination in the independent states of the Arab and Muslim worlds

In the early twentieth century, the situations of women in the Arab Muslim world were extremely diverse. They varied depending on the milieu, the class, and the social group to which the women belonged. The powers and laws that applied to them also differed as a function of the particular political authority, whose influence, moreover, vacillated a great deal, depending on which region of the Ottoman Empire the women lived in or to which colonial laws—French, British, or Italian—they were subject. And some countries, such as Iran, escaped both Ottoman imperial domination and the colonial yoke. Imperial or colonial laws were also combined with the local and customary legal provisions of the various communities—peasants, Bedouins, city dwellers—and of the many faiths present in that vast geographical space.

The project of nation building raised the woman question in public debates in most Arab countries and in those of the Middle East. This preoccupation was sustained by nationalist currents of thought and by the first feminist writings and demands, which emerged in Egypt in the late nineteenth and early twentieth centuries, and in other places later on. These modes of inquiry were sometimes taken up by men: the Egyptian Qasim Amin was a notable figure within that current. The first concern of these men and women was to transform traditional women, who would otherwise hold back society as a whole and who had to be able, through their roles as mothers, to raise in a modern and enlightened manner the new citizens of the nation under construction. Feminism and the women's movements gained in strength during the struggles waged against the colonizer in various regions. In Palestine, these movements took root in the fight for the acknowledgment of the existence and identity of a nation and in the Pan-Arabism of the 1950s and 1960s. Initially, the women involved, supported by men who belonged to the same movements, incorporated their feminist demands into the nationalist ideologies, giving priority to the national question and considering the woman question a secondary matter that would be resolved after national liberation. On the whole, their expectations were dashed: during the period following independence, the nascent states often did not grant equal rights to women, despite their involvement in anticolonial struggles.

Most of the states that achieved independence adopted laws that were clearly discriminatory toward women, particularly laws on personal status and nationality and a number of provisions in the penal codes. Although all the laws of the Arab countries (with the exception of certain Gulf monarchies) had their source in positive law, the personal status codes (family codes) were based on Islam or on other religions of the region (the different faiths in some countries of the Mashriq, such as Lebanon and Jordan). These codes, reformed and amended in various ways since the early twentieth century in response to feminist activism, therefore attest to "national" religious interpretations by states and regimes, which have arbitrated within Muslim law (*fiqh*) as a function of what are essentially political choices. The discrimination contained in all these codes concerns the minimum age at which girls may marry, the need for a guardian to contract a marriage, unilateral divorce by men, male authority within the couple, parental authority granted to the father, polygamy, and unequal access to legitimate inheritance by virtue of the man's economic responsibility within the household. Furthermore, women were unable to transmit their nationality to their children and husbands, though that provision was partly amended in all countries where the codes were reformed in the 1990s or 2000s.

State feminism and women's citizenship

A few nation-states developed a strong state feminism early in the twentieth century, which translated into the adoption of personal status codes that marked clear advances in equality between men and women. Turkey did so in 1926 by secularizing its code, which was directly inspired by the Swiss civil code; Tunisia followed in 1957, then the shah's Iran, and also the People's Democratic Republic of Yemen, until its reunification with North Yemen in 1990.

The Tunisian code, the most egalitarian in the Arab world, was introduced as part of an effort to adapt legislation from within the confines of Islam and Muslim law (*ijtihad*). It replaced guardianship overseeing the marriage of women (*wilaya*) with consent by both spouses, set the minimum age for marriage at eighteen, and substituted judicial divorce for unilateral repudiation by the husband. The personal status code continued to be amended under the presidency of Ben Ali, particularly in 1993 (shared parental authority, an end to the wife's obedience to the husband). Other rights were obtained at the same time, such as the capacity for a woman to transmit her nationality to her children and husband, but only if he is Muslim or converts to Islam. By contrast, discrimination concerning inheritance has persisted. Abortion rights were recognized in Tunisia in 1973 (within the Arab countries and the Middle East, only Turkey has legalized abortion), and a far-reaching family planning policy was set in place. In Tunisia, as in Turkey, state feminism sought to remove women's veils: the ban on wearing the veil in public schools, established in the first years of Bourguiba's presidency, was gradually extended to public universities, then to the entire education system, to the administration, and to all public and private institutions.

In Morocco, the important and much-remarked-upon reform of the family code (*mudawana*) in 2004, which made the code nearly egalitarian, came about through that same principle of *ijtihad* and through the religious authority conferred on the king by virtue of his status as commander of believers. It promoted a moderate Islam and was accompanied by a reform of the religious sphere that made it inclusive of women: the training and appointment of woman clergy (*murshidat*), who are public employees, and of theologians (*alemat*). But some discriminatory provisions remain in the code: those concerning inheritance; laws regulating polygamy, which was restricted but not abolished; and the prohibition on marriage between a Moroccan woman and a non-Muslim.

Feminist demonstration in Cairo in 1956.

Much more limited amendments were introduced into the Egyptian, Algerian, and Jordanian codes in the 2000s. In Egypt in 2000, then in Jordan and Algeria, divorce reform gave women the means to ask for a divorce in exchange for giving up financial claims and returning the dowry given her by her husband at the time of the marriage (this is known as *khul* divorce). In Egypt, the mother's right to custody of her children was extended to the age of fifteen, though parental authority still falls to the father. Conversely, the reform of the Algerian code overturned the father's exclusive parental authority, but only in the case of divorce. At the same time, it called into question the automatic granting of custody to the mother (until the child reaches a certain age) or, in her absence, to the female branch (the maternal grandmother), as practiced in most of the countries that have reformed their codes only a little or not at all.

Tunisia is among a handful of countries, along with Turkey, Algeria (2005), Egypt (2004), Morocco (2004), and Libya, where women can now transmit their nationality to their children and, more rarely, to their husbands.

Most of the governments of the twenty-two Arab and Middle Eastern countries were not (and still are not) democratic. The women's rights they have defended are quite limited, since they have not granted full citizenship to all. They have also barred democratic freedom of expression and the independent feminist movements that already existed. Usually, these regimes have established or further developed forms of state feminism: first, by replacing the banned organizations with others affiliated with the state; and second, by co-opting woman technocrats to implement state policies. Although a few countries have distinguished themselves by a strong state feminism, others have merely granted citizenship rights to women and promoted education. During the 1970s and 1980s, women of all social classes, and not just those belonging to the elite, collectively gained access to secondary and higher education, in all countries except Yemen. Since the 2000s, women have graduated in larger proportions than young men in many countries. For example, in Iran, Tunisia, and even Saudi Arabia and Bahrain, they represent about 60 percent of students. Young women have thus entered the university in force, even in the conservative countries of the Gulf, which enforce strict separation between the sexes. In Arabia, women's campuses have, since the early 2000s, made it easier for young women to continue their schooling.

As for political rights, women were generally granted the right to vote and to run for office long ago, often when their country achieved independence—at the same time as the men, therefore—or with a delay of a few years or a decade. In Algeria they obtained these rights in 1962, in Lebanon in 1952, in Egypt under Nasser in 1956, in Tunisia in 1959, and in Turkey in 1934. On the whole, however, there are few women in national assemblies and few female state ministers. Although political representation has remained predominantly male, discrimination in this area has been less prominent when a lack of democracy and of representation, even a lack of access to the vote, has been an issue for both men and women. For a long time, authoritarianism has also made the established political sphere irrelevant, while being generally unfavorable toward women. Women have often been discouraged from becoming involved in politics when repression of the opposition made activism personally costly or even dangerous. Conversely, quotas adopted for various elections in some countries have often gone hand in hand with the political promotion of women likely to support the regimes. Such was the case in Egypt for the sixty-four seats in Parliament set aside for women, a quota set in place by Suzanne Mubarak that primarily benefited the president's party, and for the quota established in Jordan in 2003. With the revolutions and political activism of the Arab Spring, these quotas are being rethought from a democratic standpoint in some countries: Tunisia, Morocco, and Jordan.

Secular feminism and religious feminism in the Jewish world

Although history has recorded a few learned women who taught and spread their knowledge, women have tended to make their mark in the areas of philanthropy and charity. It was not until the contemporary period that Jewish women collectively organized and expressed their will to promote their rights. Before the birth of the feminist movements, Jewish women had an important role in Jewish and non-Jewish societies, as journalists, writers, and intellectuals.[9] In the late eighteenth century, Berlin *salonnières* were a special but emblematic example of such assimilated Jewish intellectual women of the Enlightenment, at the juncture between the Jewish and non-Jewish worlds. For some women, political and revolutionary action was a means of escaping community norms. Revolutionary Jewish women such as Rosa Luxemburg and Emma Goldman participated in radical movements and strikes, becoming a model of women's emancipation by reversing traditional sex roles in their pursuit of equality.

In the late nineteenth century, more and more Jewish women came to play a role in public life, whether in the Jewish worker's movement (they represented a third of the members of the Bund when it was founded in 1897) or in Zionism.

It was in Germany, the land of assimilation and of Reform Judaism, that the first Jewish feminist movement as such originated. In 1904 a woman from an Orthodox family, Bertha Pappenheim, wishing to combine German Jewish culture with the transmission to girls of their Jewish cultural and religious heritage, founded the Jüdischer Frauenbund (League of Jewish Women).[10] That organization, whose membership comprised as much as 20 percent of the Jewish women of the country, promoted both feminist objectives and a Jewish identity, by building shelters for single women, day care centers, and group homes for working girls, while denouncing the conservative attitude of traditional Judaism toward women's education and legal status. The Jüdischer Frauenbund played a fundamental role within the Jewish community until its dissolution by the Nazis in 1938. But it was in the United States during the 1970s that an autonomous Jewish feminist movement developed, first within non-Orthodox (majority) Judaism and then within the Orthodox world itself. Reform Judaism, then the Conservative (Masorti) movement, thrived within the context of "Americanization," promoting, from the late nineteenth century on, a debate on women's place in religion. Indisputably, it created a favorable ideological climate for challenging received ideas, asking questions, and making changes. The Jewish feminist movement was rooted in the legacy of the 1960s: the civil rights movement, the rise of second-wave feminism (the pursuit of social and professional equality for American women), and the protests on American college campuses. Jewish women had already participated in the first wave of feminism by supporting the suffragist movement,[11] and they recommitted themselves to the second wave. Betty Friedan, author of *The Feminine Mystique* (1963), played an important role. In 1973, during the first National Jewish Women's Conference in New York, which brought together women from all currents of Judaism, the idea of a Jewish women's movement arose. It took concrete form three years later with the publication of *Lilith*, the first Jewish feminist review. This movement, which took an interest in the presence of women within the tradition of Judaism, and in women's connections to that tradition, benefited at the time from the rise of women's studies in American universities. Since then, non-Orthodox forms of Judaism, which are in the majority in North America, have granted women a status close or equal to that of men: celebration of the bat mitzvah, women's participation in the *minyan*, the ordination of woman rabbis. As of 1997, a feminist movement also began to develop in the Orthodox world around the organization founded by Blu Greenberg, the Jewish Orthodox Feminist Alliance. In addition to equal access to the synagogue and to prayer, and, especially, the right to be called up to read the Torah, Orthodox feminists wanted the right to study and to become better integrated professionally. Gradually allowed to read the same texts as the men in some institutes, they wished to be able to teach in their turn, to become experts in religious law, and to exercise a quasi-rabbinical authority.

This multiform North American Jewish feminism profoundly influenced the movement that, with a slight delay, began to develop in Israel in 1973, under the influence of young North American graduates who had recently immigrated to the country. They brought with them feminist literature and their militant experiences. Israeli society, they discovered, could be traditional, male chauvinistic, and nationalistic.[12] Feminism in Israel, which developed in a very private and dispersed manner, made use of the legacy of its American Jewish counterpart but formulated its own message. Feminists railed against the Israeli "egalitarian sham," questioned the handling of women's marital status, and denounced domestic violence, the militarization of society, and discrimination in employment and in access to political responsibilities. This movement was deeply divided between secular feminism, often radical and politicized, and more consensual, institutional feminism. In 1998, a third current, Orthodox feminism, entered the fray. The feminist movement in Israel also became profoundly ethnicized: historically dominated by educated Ashkenazi women, since the mid-1990s it has been flooded with Sephardic women who demand acknowledgment of the discrimination against them within Israeli society and who are creating their own militant spaces (*Ahoti*). These women have also further developed an argument that links gender oppression to that of race and class. In Israeli society, in the face of war and the military occupation of the Palestinian territories, feminism is for many militants inextricably linked to the fight for peace and to opposition to the occupation. In that sense, the golden age of the women's peace movements during the First Intifada gave a second wind to an Israeli feminism in stagnation, combining the two struggles based on the principle of the interconnectedness among different forms of oppression.[13] The feminist struggle and women's fight for peace have made it possible to raise sensitive questions associated with oppression in the broader sense. Women have come out of the closet about domestic violence, sexual harassment (especially in the army), and homophobia, in a country where the heterosexual family is a pillar of national security as well as the heart of Jewish identity. In the mid-1980s, Orthodox Israeli women began to fight for a presence in ritual spaces, demanding the right to pray publicly but also to exercise religious responsibility within community institutions. In particular, they exerted pressure to integrate study centers.[14] That first

Cover of the magazine *Lilith*, the "magazine for Jewish women," third issue, spring/summer 1977.

silent revolution allowed some women to attain positions within the community as attorneys of family law (*to᾽enot rabaniot*) or as rabbinical advisers (*yo᾽etsot rabaniot*). These women have ensured a professional female presence in religious courts that had previously been the exclusive preserve of men. In Jerusalem in 1998, a forum of Orthodox Zionist women called "Kolech" (Thy Voice) was held to advance the public and private status of women within the context of the halakha. In Israel, however, that Orthodox feminist revolution has remained largely cut off from the Israeli feminist movement, which

> **"*Feminism is for many militants inextricably linked to the fight for peace and to opposition to the occupation.*"**

on the whole remains secular. Although Orthodox women such as Alice Shalvi have integrated and become the heads of major Israeli feminist institutions (in Shalvi's case, the Women's Network, or Schdulat-ha-nashim), relations have often been strained in a country where tensions between secularists and the religiously observant are growing. Some secular and radical feminist militants, in fact, criticize their religious counterparts for living in Israeli settlements in the Palestinian territories.

The three waves of feminism in the Arab and Muslim worlds

Between 1920 and 1940, nationalist and anticolonialist struggles gave birth to the first wave of Arab women's and feminist movements. Egyptian feminism appeared in the early twentieth century, at the same time as its European and American counterparts—in dialogue with them, not as an echo of them.[15] Egypt introduced that first feminist activism to the Arab world around famous figures such as Huda Shaarawi. From the early days, these feminists wanted to take on religious arguments, since various "national" and sexist interpretations of Muslim law (*fiqh*) were the basis of the personal status codes and of some penal provisions.

After the period of struggle against colonization, the priorities of the second wave of feminism (that of the 1960s–80s) continued to be very political, with forceful activism in favor of democratizing the regimes and demands for the social and political participation of groups in the independent states that, especially since the 1980s, were no longer the elites. Within that context, feminists demanded full citizenship for women: the right to vote but also to education, access to skilled professions to give them valuable economic roles, rights within the family, and so on.

During these early periods, the feminist movements were for the most part secular (they included women belonging to the different faiths and denominations of Islam and Christianity) and steeped in Marxist, Socialist, and/or pan-Arab currents of thought, though rare religious voices were also heard in Lebanon and Egypt.

The women's and feminist movements of the third wave, which began in the early 1990s, diversified concerns, turning much more clearly toward equality within the family but also taking on legal issues, family relationships and problems, difficulties encountered by couples in everyday life (including dysfunction and violence), the female employment sector, and the place of women in the religious sphere. That wave incorporated some of the early secular movements, which were revived, democratized, and emancipated from the opposition parties (often leftist and pan-Arab) to which they had been linked.[16] But, to an equal degree, the third wave was marked by the appearance of Islamic feminism and young feminist groups created in the early 2000s.

The emergence of Islamic feminism in the early 1990s, first in Iran, then in various places around the globe (the United States, Malaysia, Morocco, and Europe, then, over time, in many Arab or Muslim countries) within the context of globalization, came in response to the successful re-Islamization of societies beginning in the 1970s–80s and, in that context, to the presence en masse of women in religion. It arose as a globalized intellectual movement of hermeneutics and religious exegesis intended to promote equality between the sexes in all areas: rereading and interpretive studies of the Qur'an, of the traditions and sayings of the Prophet (hadith), and of Muslim law (*fiqh*). Although these woman thinkers work on various texts, they rely in the last instance on the authority of the Qur'an, which has allowed them more easily to criticize texts composed by jurists or reported by a human chain. From the very first, therefore, the necessary distinction between the shari'a, the path of God revealed to the Prophet in the Qur'an, and the *fiqh*, the human efforts to translate that path into legal provisions, was reestablished.[17]

A first hermeneutics focused on historicizing the founding texts and traditions. Since the 2000s, it has been replaced by a more radical contextualization centered on the spirit of the Qur'anic text, the current condition of social relations (*ma'amalat*), and contemporary understandings of justice and equality, which places Islam within a universal perspective. It considers the Qur'an not a fixed text but an open one, within which certain points need to be categorically refuted.

In addition, feminist theologians have engaged in an intellectual competition to create new religious centralities, to spread their alternative egalitarian thinking about women in Islam, and to gain recognition or find a place within existing institutions. In Morocco in 2008, the Islamic feminist Asma Lamrabet, head of the International Group of Studies and Reflection on Women and Islam, formed a partnership between that group and an influential religious institution, the League of Ulema of Morocco (Rabita Mohammadia). The league, which brings together liberal thinkers, is headed by Ahmed Abbadi, an internationally renowned Muslim theologian. The Rabita Mohammadia shares the desire to promote a new Muslim reformism, which rereads the sacred texts from the perspective of gender equality. In Turkey, the task of rereading the hadith, in line with the interpretations of Fatima Mernissi,[18] has been undertaken by a Turkish female theologian, Hidayet Tuksal. A short time ago, this project was integrated into the vast government program to remove misogynous hadith, whose veracity or interpretation has proved problematic, from all the publications and broadcasts of the Ministry of Religious Affairs, which oversees the country's mosques. In the largest Muslim country, Indonesia, woman theologians, usually from families of ulema or of activists in the country's two major Islamic organizations (Muhammadiyah and Nahdlatul Ulama), have received solid religious training. Since the 1990s they have been engaged in rereading religious texts from a feminist perspective. This reform movement is supported by the network of Islamic state universities where these theologians teach, and where modernist and more traditional clerics, both men and women, have come together to produce new exegeses. Knowledge of these new interpretations has grown since the 2000s, through the establishment of centers for the study of gender and through the participation of certain centers of Islamic studies that distribute their reformist works on the *fiqh* to conservative ulema. These centers, in fact, invented the term *fiqh al-nissa* (women's *fiqh*).[19]

This intellectual reform of Islam has been expressed in demands to increase the religious authority of women and to give them access to other positions. Women have attained a few of these: they are theologians (*alemat*), clergywomen (*murshidat*), and preachers (*da'iyat*), who give classes in their homes, in clubs, in mosques, or in Qur'an memorization centers. In addition, the mixed-sex prayer conducted by the Islamic feminist and imam Amina Wadud in New York in 2005, heavily covered by the media, has produced imitators and has led to the institutionalization of that practice in South Africa, North America, and Europe. In England, for example, the Muslim Educational Center of Oxford regularly holds mixed prayers, where the sermon (*khutbah*) is delivered by a woman. There are also calls, but only by some of the Islamic feminists, for women to have access to the imamate. A subject of

Amina Wadud (right) conducts the Friday Muslim services at Synod House, Cathedral of Saint John the Divine, New York, March 18, 2005. Photograph by Gregory Bull.

less religious controversy is the desire of women in various places of the Arab and Muslim worlds to become mufti (*muftiat*). In Indonesia, they already have access to these posts. In Egypt, Suad Saleh, a professor of Islamic jurisprudence at Al-Azhar University (the central institute of Sunnism) and the daughter of an *alim*, is waging a campaign to allow women to become *muftiat*, based on religious arguments.[20]

More generally, the resources conferred by these new Islamic theologies support women's social and political trajectories.[21] Islamic feminism has gradually been organized into networks at a global scale and has influenced movements or groups in the various countries. As of the early 2000s, Islamic feminism, in becoming diversified, has come to have greater influence over the religious sphere in women's activism and in Islamic political movements, which have seized on this new militant resource.[22] Although it is therefore necessary to speak of Islamic "feminisms" (in the plural), let us note that a growing number of participants in Islamic feminism, not all of whom embrace the label "feminist," have in the last decade or so come from the ranks of political Islam. The general designation "Islamic feminism" has gradually become apposite, even essential, in such contexts. By contrast, the specific concept of gender (designated by the English term in some places, translated as naw *ijtima'i* in others) from which the Islamic feminists are working has recently given rise to controversies and heated criticism within most of the political Islamist movements, since it supposedly blurs the familial roles of men and women and sexual identities, which is to say, the heterosexual norm.

These third-wave movements have imagined different ways to engage in politics. They inaugurated an alternative militancy centered on short-term coalitions of groups, sometimes with radically different political and ideological views but united around common causes. These causes in common have attenuated the old antagonism between secular and religious movements in favor of more pragmatic avenues by which women are asserting their rights and aspirations. The reformation of Islam and of feminism brought about by Islamic feminism has also made it possible to debate more effectively subjects relating to the family. On the one hand, feminist exegesis and its influence within Islam have strengthened the religious argument, decisive in matters of family law. On the other hand, its congruence with secular activism has increased pressure on governments. The reform of the Moroccan *mudawana* in 2004, long promoted by secular women, then taken up by religious women and by the king's mobilization of Islam as a frame of reference, is an excellent example of the snowball effect achieved by shared demands. More generally, in the interest of promoting juridical equality within the family, the global Islamic feminist network Musawah is reflecting on the religious concept of *qawama*, which, having made the man head of the household, is the source of inequalities within the family, including matters of inheritance. Since the 1990s, then, some more radically feminist demands have been reformulated. They have crystallized precisely through the involvement of both secular and Islamic women and through the bonds they have gradually established with one another. In Bahrain and Kuwait, women's movements have challenged the social boundaries of the community and the nationalist and Islamist parties, and have built alliances beyond the supposed opposition between secular and religious women, by virtue of the priority given to the "feminist" paradigm. Through these actions, women earned the right to vote and to run for elected office, in 2002 and 2005 respectively. In Kuwait, other political causes are now the object of joint demands, for example, the right of women to transmit their nationality to their children, especially when they have married aliens, and a larger presence of women representatives in Parliament.[23] These alliances have regularly been at work in various countries, especially Jordan, advocating for the transmission of women's nationality to their children and husbands, for female quotas (reconceived in democratic terms) in elections, and, more recently, for a whole set of family issues that had previously been the object of controversy between secular and religious women, for example, family planning and the raising of the legal age for marriage. It is not surprising, therefore, that in the 1990s an unambiguous term for feminism, *nisawiyya*, appeared in the Arab world for the first time, replacing *nisa'iyya*, which means both "feminist" and "feminine" (or "relating to women").[24]

These have all been pioneering forms of activism. Early on, they spurred militant modes of action that were pragmatic, postideological, nonpartisan, and beyond identity politics. These modes would also be adopted in the protests and revolutionary uprisings of the Arab Spring, especially in youth movements. The revival of militantism by these third-wave movements is also illustrated in the emergence of less institutionalized groups—without historical ties to political parties and organizations such as Marwa Mehaiza (Union of Women)—intended to promote more flexible networks. New feminist groups were created in the early 2000s, such as Ishtar in Syria and Nasawiyya and Kafa in Lebanon. They are loosely structured (relying on the Internet and social networks), so as to be as free, participatory, and democratic as possible. These nonpartisan groups form short-term alliances with other movements, based on the cause to be defended. They are, however, very political, linking sexual equality, violence, sexism, and even the right to choose one's own mode of sexual expression, including homosexuality (Helem, Meem), to issues of citizen rights, the political system, and—in Lebanon—democratization through "de-confessionalization." In Lebanon, these young organizations have introduced into public debate demands and issues previously suppressed by Arab feminist movements. In that country, heretofore little affected by feminist activism, the insights introduced by the concept of gender have clearly been taken into account, and individual liberties associated with the body have been raised. These include not only violence (domestic violence, so-called honor crimes, and rape, themes that have also been debated elsewhere since the mid-1990s) and abortion (legal in Tunisia and Turkey and under debate elsewhere, particularly in Morocco) but also questions of sexual freedom, including homosexuality. The silence of Arab feminisms on body issues and sexuality has only just begun to be broken, despite the pioneering and, at the time, very subversive writings on sexuality and women's bodies by the Egyptian feminist and physician Nawal al-Saadawi. Although these writings, dating to the 1960s, inspired the second generation of feminists, such subjects were not previously among the public causes defended by the women's organizations.

These issues have come to light in various places, linked to the individual freedom over one's own body and one's sexuality (sex outside of marriage, homosexuality, abortion, and so on). At the same time, since the late 2000s certain currents of Islamic feminism have addressed questions associated with gender and sexuality (including homosexuality), even though Muslim homosexual movements were generally founded in the Muslim communities of Europe and the United States—though also in South Africa, Palestine, Lebanon, and Morocco. Some have linked such activism to the defense of the idea of an inclusive Islam.

In the twentieth century, most regions of the Arab Muslim world succeeded in creating independent states, whereas the Jewish world, with the exception of the State of Israel, still remains in diaspora. Despite these different political situations, a comparison of women's contributions to collective nationalist struggles and nation-building projects reveals major similarities. Not only have women taken part in the different movements of collective emancipation; their rights and status have also been debated, often polemically. During these periods, access to education, and to the experience of political struggle, have been powerful factors in emancipating women from both religious norms and from conservative social models. The advent of political independence in the Arab Muslim world has often been disappointing for women, even though on the whole they have achieved political rights. In the absence of real democracy, discriminatory personal status codes have generally been promulgated. Women have not had the right to transmit their nationality, and penal provisions have often been very unfavorable toward them. In Israel, ultimately in a rather similar manner, women's participation in Zionism was given its due, but the immediate acquisition of political rights did not eclipse the persistent influence of the religious tribunals in the management of certain fundamental aspects of personal status, namely, marriage and divorce.

These sites of tension and these struggles for access to citizenship led to the emergence early on of a strong feminist challenge, culminating in movements of collective mobilization. These currents have questioned national laws, practices, religious interpretations, and the different forms of discrimination thereby generated. The movements have favored new norms and modes of life, in keeping with the idea of gender equality and access to full citizenship. In the different Arab Muslim and Jewish spaces, we are gradually witnessing an expansion of militant repertoires, in which secular and religious forms of feminism coexist. Their joint presence in the fields of action has involved new ways of fighting together, despite differences, in a great number of countries of the Arab Muslim world and in the Jewish diaspora. In Israel, by contrast, ideological antagonism has increased. Recently, some but not all of these currents have taken into account the impact of the concept of gender and have inaugurated new forms of activism that more openly defend women's personal rights, for example, those associated with the body, sexuality, and sexual orientation.

---

1. Emancipation placed the Jews under the jurisdiction of common law. See Evelyne Odiel-Grausz, "Les Juifs d'Europe occidentale au XIXᵉ siècle," in *Les Juifs dans l'histoire*, op.cit, 411–438.

2. Frédéric Abécassis and Jean-François Faü, "Les Juifs dans le monde musulman à l'âge des nations (1840–1945)," in Part 6 of *Les Juifs dans l'histoire: De la naissance du judaïsme au monde contemporain*, ed. Germa, Lellouch, and Patlagean, 545–70.

3. See the different entries on the family, women, and feminism in Jean-Christophe Attias and Esther Benbassa, *Dictionnaire des mondes juifs* (Paris: Larousse, 2008).

4. Nancy Green, "La femme juive: Formation et transformations," in *Histoire des femmes: Le XIXᵉ siècle*, ed. Michelle Perrot and Geneviève Fraisse (Paris: Plon, 1991), 215–29.

5. Béatrice de Gasquet, "Savantes, militantes, pratiquantes: Panorama des féminismes juifs américains depuis les années 70," in *Quand les femmes lisent la Bible*, ed. Janine Elkouby and Sonia Sarah Lipsyc (Paris: Éditions In Press, 2007), 257–68.

6. Vincent Vilmain, "Myriam Schach (1867–1956): Féministe et nationaliste juive," *Diasporas* 11 (2008): 135–48.

7. Karine Shebabo, "Vers une nécessaire sécularisation du droit personnel israélien," *Les Cahiers de CREMOC* [Centre de recherche sur l'Europe et le monde contemporain] 30 (2004): 67.

8. That principle of legal impossibility can be attenuated by a civil judge who recognizes as internal law a civil marriage granted abroad, in conformity with the laws of that country.

9. Nancy Green, "La femme juive: Formation et transformations," 218.

10. See Vincent Vilmain, "Féministes et nationalistes? Les femmes dans le sionisme publique, 1868–1928," graduate thesis directed by Denis Pelletier, École Pratique des Hautes Études, 2011.

11. Elinor Lerner, "American Feminism and the Jewish Question, 1890–1940," in *Antisemitism in American History*, ed. David A. Gerber (Urbana: University of Illinois Press, 1986).

12. Marcia Freedman, *Exile in the Promised Land* (Ithaca, NY: Firebrand, 1990).

13. Valérie Pouzol, *Clandestines de la paix: Israéliennes et Palestiniennes contre la guerre* (Paris: Éditions Complexe-IHTP, 2008).

14. Valérie Pouzol, "Entre silence et fracas: Émergence et affirmation des luttes féministes dans les communautés juives orthodoxes en Israël (1970–2009)," in *Des engagements féminins au Moyen-Orient (XXᵉ et XXIᵉ siècles)*, ed. Leyla Dakhli and Stéphanie Latte Abdallah, issue of *Le Mouvement Social* (April–June 2010): 29–43.

15. Margot Badran, *Feminists, Islam, and Nation: Gender and the Making of Modern Egypt* (Princeton, NJ: Princeton University Press, 1994).

16. Stéphanie Latte Abdallah, "Genre et politique," in *La politique dans le monde arabe*, ed. Élizabeth Picard (Paris: Armand Colin, 2006), 127–47, and "Vers un féminisme politique hors frontières au Proche-Orient: Regard sur les mobilisations en Jordanie (années 1950–années 2000)," *Vingtième siècle: Revue d'histoire*, special issue on *Proche-Orient: Foyers, frontières et fractures* 103 (July–September 2009): 177–95.

17. Ziba Mir-Hosseini, *Islam and Gender: The Religious Debate in Contemporary Iran* (Princeton, NJ: Princeton University Press, 2000), and "Islam and Feminism: Whose Islam? Whose Feminism?" *Contestations . . . Dialogues on Women's Empowerment, Islam and Feminism* 1 (2010), http://www.contestations.net/issues/issue-1/.

18. Fatima Mernissi, *Le harem politique* (Paris: Albin Michel, 1987), translated as *Women and Islam: An Historical and Theological Inquiry* (Oxford, UK: Basil Blackwell, 1991).

19. Andrée Feillard and Nelly Van-Doorn, "Une nouvelle génération féministe au sein de l'islam traditionnaliste: Une exception indonésienne?" *Revue des Mondes Musulmans et de la Méditerranée* 128 (2010): 113–33.

20. Margot Badran, *Feminism in Islam: Secular and Religious Convergences* (Oxford, UK: Oneworld Publications, 2009).

21. See Stéphanie Latte Abdallah, "Les féminismes islamiques au tournant du XXIᵉ siècle," *Revue des Mondes Musulmans et de la Méditerrannée* 128 (2010): 13–31.

22. See Stéphanie Latte Abdallah, "Les féminismes islamiques contemporains: Influences sur le féminisme, la sphère religieuse et l'islam politique," *Islamochristiana* 37 (2011): 17–34.

23. May Seikaly, "Bahreïni Women in Formal and Informal Groups: The Politics of Identification," in Dawn Chatty, Annika Rabo (ed.), *Organizing Women: Formal and Informal Women's Groups in the Middle East* (Oxford, New York: Berg, 1997), 125–146; Haya Al-Mughni, "The Rise of Islamic Feminism in Kuwait," REMMM, n 128, 2010, *op. cit.*, 167–182.

24. Margot Badran, "Between Secular and Islamic Feminism/s: Reflections on the Middle East and Beyond," *Journal of Middle East Women's Studies* 1, no. 1 (Winter 2005): 6–28.

"Muslim Body" versus "Jewish Body": The Invention of a Division

Samir Ben-Layashi

Two pioneering books, now considered classics of "body literature" in the field of Muslim or Jewish culture, opened the way for two generations of scholars. The first was Abdelwahab Bouhdiba's *La sexualité en Islam* (Sexuality in Islam),[1] the second,

Samir Ben-Layashi

A researcher at the Moshe Dayan Center of Tel Aviv University, Samir Ben-Layashi has published, notably, "Myth, History, and Realpolitick: Morocco and Its Jewish Community," *Journal of Modern Jewish Studies* (March 2010).

Daniel Boyarin's *Carnal Israel: Reading Sex in Talmudic Culture*.[2] Bouhdiba's and Boyarin's originality lay in breaking away from traditions that came close to constituting models for thinking and writing and rewriting "Muslim" or "Jewish" bodies.

Bouhdiba and Boyarin, two precursors

In what I may venture to call the Islamic "human sciences," it was almost impossible to write the "Muslim" body apart from commentary on the canonical religious texts, the Qur'an and the hadith.[3] Jewish studies, by contrast, placed the emphasis on Western anti-Semitism, especially in Germany, and avoided going back to the origins to ascertain whether the Judeo-Christian scriptures carried a "bad seed" within themselves. Scholars saw European anti-Semitism in the twentieth century as a modern phenomenon, linked to the technological revolutions and the emancipatory, progressive, positivist ideologies, even the economic systems, of the nineteenth century and beyond.[4] Their aim was to find a secular, rational, and modern explanation, if possible, without turning to religion. Their studies used medical and psychoanalytical tools of analysis and drew on psychology: Freud had become the Moses of modern times.[5] Scholars combed through the scientific discourse of the Nazis and of nineteenth-century European physicians, especially Germans, who had "examined" the Jews and found them different physiologically.[6] This dark cultural-biological phenomenon consisted of wanting to "correct" the Jew. This physical correction, they believed, might bring about an ethical correction, allowing the project of emancipation (of the European Jew), begun in the Enlightenment, to reach its completion.[7]

In general, this scholarly literature conceded that anti-Semitism had remote origins but insisted that it had undergone a transformation. As Sander Gilman explained, the term "anti-Semitism" was coined "as part of the scientific discourse of race in the nineteenth century." It is "half of the dichotomy of 'Aryan' and 'Semite.'... The terms were taken from nineteenth-century linguistics." He adds that "language has played a vital role as a marker of Jewish difference. Thus the complaint, voiced again recently in the 'letters to the editor' of the *Times Literary Supplement*, that 'Arabic, like Hebrew, is a Semitic race; and in so far as it is possible to talk of an Arab race, that race is Semitic. It is therefore nonsense to talk about Muslim anti-Semitism,' quite misses the point."[8] Gilman is one of the few scholars in Jewish studies who mentions the "Arab race" as a basis for comparison with the "Jewish race," though he does so only in a short interpolated clause, without going into details. Most of the studies that deal with the Jewish body establish comparisons to the "Christian," "Western," and "white" body, measuring it by that yardstick. Comparisons to the "Muslim body" or "Arab body" are almost never made, even though that body displays enormous similarities to the Jewish body at both the theoretical and practical levels. When comparisons exist, they are often between religious laws and texts,[9] rarely between the cultural, social, or corporeal practices of the Muslims and Jews. An anthropological study on the Jewish community of Casablanca, dating to the 1990s, constitutes an exception,[10] as does Patricia Hidirigou's field study, a remarkable comparison between the Maghrebi hammam and the *mikveh* (Jewish ritual bath) in Paris.[11] Before Bouhdiba's and Boyarin's books, we found ourselves in a historiographically interesting situation: the literature of the "Muslim body" did not manage to rid itself of the religious text; by contrast, its counterpart, concerned with the "Jewish body," did everything it could to avoid an interpretation based on scripture, whether Jewish or Christian. Bouhdiba and Boyarin showed that it was possible to change the analytical tools in order to think the same thing differently and to arrive at new conclusions.

> **The literature of the 'Muslim body' did not manage to rid itself of the religious text; by contrast, its Jewish counterpart did everything it could to avoid an interpretation based on scripture.**

It seems to me that, in *La sexualité en Islam*, Bouhdiba was trying to achieve two aims. First, he sought to focus on the reciprocal connections between the sexual and the sacred in Islam through the sexual practices of Muslims as they were recounted, inscribed, and even prescribed in the different sources. These sources could be canonical, like the Qur'an, the hadith, and the *fiqh* (Islamic law or jurisprudence); or they could be profane, like the medieval erotic literature written in Arabic (for example, *The Thousand and One Nights* or Muhammad ibn Muhammad al-Nafzawi's *Perfumed Garden*), which Bouhdiba placed alongside popular magazines and modern novels. His second aim was implicit: to begin an intellectual dialogue by issuing an invitation of sorts to the Christian West to join the Muslim East on a universal platform, that of the body and sexuality. According to Bouhdiba, a gap needed to be filled. In the West, the relation to the body, to the flesh, and to sexuality is conceived and experienced through the notions of sin, remorse, regret, guilt, chastity, and celibacy. Easterners (that is, the Muslims, to the exclusion of Eastern Christians and Jews) celebrate the body, glory in sexuality, and delight in the flesh.

In contrast to *La sexualité en Islam*, which appeared in France within a historico-philosophical tradition straddling the history of ideas and the history of private life, *Carnal Israel* belongs to American Jewish studies, within the framework of cultural studies, queer studies, and gender studies related to Judaism.[12] Boyarin opens the Jewish "library" to reconnect with Talmudic culture and literature. First, he calls into question Augustine's thesis that "what divides Christians from rabbinic Jews is the discourse of the body."[13] Even in the twentieth and twenty-first centuries, people have continued to ruminate on this thesis in Christian religious seminars. Boyarin attempts to dispute Augustine's view by showing that it has nothing to do with the Talmudic tradition of Palestinian Judaism. Rather, it belongs wholly to Hellenized Judaism, that of Paul, from which Christianity emerged. Hellenized Judaism carried with it both a Stoic notion of the body and a rabbinical misogyny, which consisted of forbidding women from studying the Torah.[14] According to Boyarin, rabbinical Judaism became misogynous as a result of its Hellenization (it responded in kind to the Christian West). And if the body became the fundamental point of difference between Judaism and Christianity, it was only because Augustine did not look further than first-century Hellenic Palestinian Judaism, and ignored the later Talmudic tradition.

Like Bouhdiba, who tried to break the monopoly of the Qur'an, the hadith, and the *fiqh* on the phenomenology of Muslim sexuality and Muslims' bodies, Boyarin tried to put an end to the double monopoly of the Torah and the New Testament on the bodies and sexuality of the Jews. Although Bouhdiba's and Boyarin's strategies are different, their aim remains the same: to bring about a rapprochement with the "Christian body."

Escaping the relation to religious norms

In the mid-1970s, Fatima Mernissi, a Moroccan sociologist who received her training in the feminist environment of American universities, introduced into Middle Eastern and North African studies a new form of writing about women: an "emancipatory" writing very much in tune with a feminist orientation that places the emphasis on woman and her ridiculed sexual desires, on the physical segregation between girls and boys, and on the sexual and sex-based domination of the male. Segregation by sex, for example, accounts for the distorted notion of gender in the Moroccan *moudawana* (family code), as it applies to women.[15] And yet, in *Beyond the Veil*, as in almost all her writings, Mernissi did not focus fetishistically on the female body or grant a conspicuous place to sexuality, even though that is ultimately what interested her. She chose rather to show how the secular tradition of Islamic thought and the "sacred" nature of the texts on which it is founded do not allow a critical and free reading, especially of the texts dealing with women's sexuality and bodies.

Malek Chebel, an Algerian anthropologist and psychoanalyst trained in the French academic tradition, is situated midway between the Tunisian Bouhdiba and the Moroccan

❱ See article by Stéphanie Latte Abdallah and Valérie Pouzol, 1025–1041.

Mernissi. Chebel borrows Bouhdiba's method of reading and interpreting scriptures, as well as the canonical and semicanonical texts of medieval literature. But, in terms of his intellectual commitment to an emancipation of the male and female body in Muslim culture (not to be confused with the Muslim *faith*), Chebel is closer to Mernissi, that is, to a certain "Islamic feminism."[16] For example, he rejects all cultural relativism, arguing that "barbarous acts," such as female genital excision, have nothing to do with Islam and must be battled without complacency. As for male circumcision, though he minimizes its symbolic function in Islam and reduces it to a functional role associated with hygiene, he does not condemn it as he condemns female excision and other genital mutilations. We may wonder however, whether he would not be in favor of the eradication of *Muslim* circumcision, though he has never said so explicitly. As for *Jewish* circumcision, he recognizes it as an essential symbolic value. Circumcision, he writes, "has its importance for Jewish identity and plays only a minor role in the Islamic tradition."[17]

Photograph by the Moroccan artist Majida Khattari in the collection "Luxe, désordre, et volupté" (Luxury, Chaos, and Will), an exploration of Eastern themes and the representation of women in Islam; exhibited in Casablanca, March 2013, at Atelier 21.

Like Gilman, who furtively touches on Islam, Chebel flirts timidly with Judaism, not daring to move toward a more extensive comparison. In my opinion, both scholars are a little too preoccupied with the Westerner's gaze directed at the bodies of the Muslims and Jews. They might have taken an interest in the gaze that Muslims and Jews focus on one another's bodies.

Bouhdiba, Boyarin, Mernissi, Chebel, Gilman, and Hidiroglou all have one desire in common: to "kill" the Text and espouse the practice. They have moved on from the Text—which debases the body of the Muslim and the Jew—but without ridding themselves of it entirely. Theirs is a twofold mission, and a great deal still remains to be done. Gilman and Hidiroglou represent exceptions in the sense that, from the outset, they choose to base their analyses on different foundations: Gilman opts for psychoanalysis,

Hidiroglou for societal practices she observed as an anthropologist, showing how they contradict religious discourse. The specificity of these two authors lies in the fact that they sacrifice the Text on the altar of practice.

An Israeli body literature?

In the 1980s and 1990s, an academic literature, known as "body literature," came into being, first in American universities, then in England, and later in Europe, becoming such a presence that some wondered: Why all the academic fuss about the body?[18] It was clear that the body was going to persist for a long time as an inexhaustible field of study, a weapon of resistance against dominant ideologies and cultures. Hence, a series of studies on the body have appeared recently in several Arab countries and in Israel, each of them considering the notion in accordance with the cultural, societal, and political needs of the country in which the research was carried out. In Israel, for example, the body is becoming a favorite subject of the post-Zionist historians, supporters of the Sephardi Jewish intellectual movement Keshet Mizrahit, which is fighting against Ashkenazi cultural dominance in that country. In the Arab world, it is feminists, gay men and lesbians, and avant-garde writers and artists who have seized on the body to make their voices heard—voices that were believed to be nonexistent. The body has turned out to be a very political subject-object. In three novels published in the 1980s, Dror Mishani showed that modern Israeli literature had discovered the Sephardi question, *mizrahiyyut*, and

> *A series of studies on the body have appeared recently in several Arab countries and in Israel, each of them considering the notion in accordance with the cultural, societal, and political needs.*

with it the body of the *mizrahi* Jew. This "discovery" was not insignificant, nor was it the result of a search for an Ashkenazi alter ego. It came in the wake of the 1977 elections, which marked the victory of the Likud Party over the Ashkenazi labor establishment. The Sephardi Jewish vote contributed toward Israeli literature's discovery of the voice of the "Sephardi body," the "Oriental body" (the "Arab-Jewish" body,[19] Keshet Mizrahit militants would say). Until then, Israeli literature had been a little too preoccupied with the "regeneration," even the "correction," of the Jewish body in exile, *guf galuti* in Hebrew, a model that Ashkenazi literary discourse had inherited from anti-Semitic European discourse, and that it attempted to apply to the body of the Sephardi Jew.[20]

In *Le corps sioniste* (The Zionist Body), Michael Gluzman proposes a new historiographical model, rereading the classic texts of twentieth-century Hebrew literature as a discourse that molded and is still molding the "Jewish body" and Jewish masculinity. Gluzman concludes that, between the Zionist texts written prior to the advent of the State of Israel in 1948 and post-1948 Israeli literature, a sharp and clear break occurred, "almost in the space of a single day,"[21] in the way the body was rendered into discourse. All of a sudden, Hebrew literature ceased to be about the *abstract body* (the stunted, pale, sickly, and effeminate body of the diaspora and exile) and began to focus on the *concrete body*, the body of flesh and blood, healthy, strong, immune, and virile, a body worthy of political sovereignty.[22] The idyllic model of this personification, this shift from the metaphysical to the physical, from text to flesh, remains above all the body of the (male) Ashkenazi Israeli soldier: handsome, strong, sensual, white but tanned (a body well-adapted to the burning sun of the East). Ironically, this idyllic prototype of the body of the *Sabra* (the Jew, whether male or female, who was born in Israel) would later become the ultimate model for the antihero of "classic" Israeli literature in the post-1948 period (Amos Oz, David Grossman, A. B. Yehoshua). Let me add to Gluzman's remarks that this model would end up "contaminating" even the antihero of Israeli artistic creations aspiring to be antimilitarist, postmodernist, and post-Zionist, such as the films *Waltz with Bashir* (2008) and *Lebanon* (2009).

Because the army—military service—is still the social machine that manufactures the Jewish, Israeli, Ashkenazi, and Zionist body, the body of the Other is no longer the Muslim body or the Arab body or even the Palestinian body: it is the body of the "Oriental" Jew or "Arab Jew," who is caught in a contradictory situation. He is a Jew spiritually and culturally, but physically he is the fraternal twin of the Arab "Enemy." And though he does not altogether resemble him, he was his "cotenant" in a previous life. Hence his original sin: that of being an Arab Jew. The soldier Rahamim Ben Hamou (his family name suggests he is Moroccan), one of the protagonists in a novel Gluzman analyzes, embodies that situation. Everyone makes fun of him, ridicules him; he is nicknamed "double zeros," an icon for public toilets in Israel. He is so convinced of his inferiority and the weakness of his body, to the point of internalizing it, that he sees his deliverance as if in a hallucination: "The body trembles. The body is afraid, the body weeps. The body dreams of its perfection, of its freedom."[23]

Almog Behar, a young Israeli writer whose parents were born in Israel but whose grandfather was Iraqi, perfectly incarnates—through his body and through the writing on his body—what Mishani and Gluzman are trying to historicize. In his *Ana Min al-Yahud* (*Yid*, an Arabic title for a book in Hebrew), Behar evokes that close and delicate bond of body-language-identity. *Ana Min al-Yahud* announces the emergence of that Eastern/Sephardi, half-Jewish, half-Arab (neither Jewish nor Arab) body, a new form of the "*Sabra* body." It stands in opposition to the Jewish body of exile, the Ashkenazi body, but at the same time represents the joining of the two bodies, which (according to the expectations of Zionist discourse) is supposed to be not merely a crossbreed but the (re)birth of a new body, this time corrected and without mental reservations, hence perfect.

Behar is bearded, his beard thick and unkempt, and he has a scar on his face. It is the face of the *Sabra*, which modern Zionism brought into the world and watched grow up. Even worse, of late Behar has suddenly "caught" an accent, not just any accent but an Arab accent. Israeli police officers in the streets of (West) Jerusalem often stop him and ask for his papers because of his "Arab mug." (The French have invented an ingenious expression for this infraction: *le délit de sale gueule*, "the crime of I-don't-like-your-face"). At one of these "routine" stops, Behar cannot find his identity card, which he may have lost. And with that, he loses his *sabra* accent (that is, his non-accent) and acquires in its place the accent of his Iraqi grandfather, Anwar, whom he has never seen, since Anwar died before Almog was born. "And then [the police] started to frisk me, to search my clothes, passing the metal detector over my body stripping me by their silence of my words and ideas. . . . One of the two said to the other: 'Look, he's circumcised, he really is a Jew, that Arab.' And the other replied: 'An Arab is circumcised too, and explosive belts have nothing to do with circumcision.' They continued their search. In reality, just as I handed my body over to them, explosive belts started to constrict my heart. They began to swell, refusing to be neutralized, making a noise that gradually grew louder. But since they were not made of metal or gunpowder, these belts were able to escape the detector."[24]

The "Sephardi question" in Israel is hardly new.[25] It is a migratory phenomenon that has its roots in the immigrants' countries of origin, as in the case of the Moroccan Jews, the largest Sephardi community in Israel.[26] One of the solutions proposed for this "problem" is "mixed" marriages between Ashkenazi and Sephardi Jews. A few Israeli scholars find that "puericulturist" (or eugenic) solution racist, since it proposes a biological solution to a cultural problem and suggests that the Jews can solve their sociocultural problems only by marrying among themselves.[27]

Matters between *askhenazim* and *sefardim* do not end there, however. In Israel, the voices of other bodies rise up, the voices of those the Israelis call "Israeli Arabs," though they are Palestinians by origin and Israeli in their civic identity (but not only in that). The writer Sayed Qashu is the spokesman for these Palestinian Israeli young people who rub shoulders on a daily basis with young (Jewish) Israelis, or with the "new Israelis" who emerged from the most recent social protests, known as the "tent protests" (sum-

See articles by Laurence Louër, pp. 452–457, and Kadhim Jihad Hassan, pp. 573-579.

mer 2011).[28] Qashu is Palestinian by origin, Israeli by identity (abstract, philosophical identity or concrete, political, practical identity; identity of daily life or even first-level identity in the ordinary sense of the term—the blue identity card he carries in his pocket). The important thing is that he is fundamentally an Arab writer who writes in Hebrew: "I come off as more Israeli than your average Israeli. I'm always delighted to hear that from Jews. 'You don't look at all Arab,' they tell me. There are even some who tell me that's racism, but I've always taken it as a compliment. As an achievement. In fact, that's what I always wanted to be, a Jew. I worked hard at it, and finally, I succeeded."[29]

More and more, Qashu, like his elders, physically resembles the (Jewish) Israelis, the "new Israelis." His daily life is exactly the same as theirs. He thinks like them on most matters in life: no one is obliged to think like everyone else. Nevertheless, he is puzzled and asks the (Jewish) Israelis: "Why do you treat us differently when we are the same?" The answer to this question will decide the future reality between Palestinians and Israelis on one hand and between Jewish and Arab Israelis on the other.

Freedom of expression in the Arab Muslim world

Body "fever" also left traces in the Arab countries. Let me mention the magnificent novel by Ahlem al-Mosteghanemi, *Dhakirat al-Jasad* (1994), translated into seventeen languages, in French under the title *Mémoires de la chair* (*Memories of the Flesh*).[30] This novel is a true celebration of carnal love, love of country (Algeria), and the desire for language (Arabic). A celebration of love, period. It is a text in a new language and an innovative idiom that vacillates between an elemental eroticism and the sublimation of the female Arab body: "I want to love you here, in a house built like your body, a house designed like an Andalusian house... to lodge your love in a house that resembles you, following the curves of Arab femininity."[31] In my view, *Memories of the Flesh* opened up body literature—in Arabic, in the Arab world, and by Arab women—to the writers' community and to the general public. This literature is no longer confined to academics, as had previously been the case.

In some Arab countries, such as Lebanon, Egypt, Tunisia, Algeria, and Morocco, the wave of new press freedoms in the 1990s contributed toward the appearance of relatively independent newspapers and magazines, including tabloids, which introduced a new discourse on the body into the public space and popular discourse. Readers of both sexes, who could not share their intimate questions within their families or even among friends (out of bashfulness and/or social hypocrisy), could now express themselves in the name of medicine, psychoanalysis, psychology, gynecology—in the name of science—while remaining anonymous. The phenomenal success of the supplement *Mina al-Qalb ila al-Qalb* (Heart to Heart), which appears on Tuesdays and Thursdays in the Moroccan weekly *Al-Ahdath al-Maghribiyya*, attests to the efficacy of this trend. In addition, the intellectual review *Alam al-Fikr* (*The World of Thought*), widely read and distributed throughout the Arab world, devoted an entire issue to the body seen from several angles: religious, philosophical, literary, aesthetic, theatrical. It adopted a universal point of view but still insisted on the specificity of the Arab Muslim context.[32]

The key event in this area at the start of the new century was no doubt the appearance in Beirut of the first erotic magazine in the Arab world, *Jasad* ("body" in Arabic). Joumana Haddad, its founder and editor in chief, who is also a poet, novelist, and essayist, decided in 2007 to bring out this *magazine of the body in all its states*, violating every taboo—homosexuality, fetishism, masturbation, and other forms of bodily pleasures. The entire magazine is in Arabic. One of the advantages of this magazine, then, is that it rescues Arab men and women from their linguistic alienation. Let us remember that, in the Arab world, everything obscene or scatological—and even obstetric gynecology—is expressed, whether in spoken or written form, in a foreign language: English in the Middle East, French in North Africa.

This freedom of expression on sexual questions, and on the body in general, is certainly a major issue for the Arab Muslim world, even for the liberals, who in 2011 launched political "springs" or "revolutions." A real revolution necessarily affects men and women in the practices of their everyday lives, their relations to the body, the skin, the flesh.

---

1. Abdelwahab Bouhdiba, *La sexualité en islam* (Paris: Presses universitaires de France, 1975).

2. Daniel Boyarin, *Carnal Israel: Reading Sex in Talmudic Culture* (Berkeley: University of California Press, 1993).

3. Georges-Henri Bousquet, *L'éthique sexuelle de l'Islam* (Paris: Maisonneuve et Larose, 1966).

4. Verner Sombart, *The Jews and Modern Capitalism*, trans. M. Epstein (Glencoe, IL: Free Press, 1951).

5. Steven Beller, *Vienna and the Jews, 1867–1939: A Cultural History* (New York: Cambridge University Press, 1989), 14–32.

6. Robert Jay Lifton, *The Nazi Doctors: Medical Killing and the Psychology of Genocide* (New York: Basic Books, 1986).

7. Adam Sutcliffe, *Judaism and Enlightenment* (New York: Cambridge University Press, 2003); see also Allan Arkush, *Moses Mendelssohn and the Enlightenment* (Albany State University of New York Press, 1994).

8. Sander Gilman, *The Jew's Body* (New York: Routledge, 1991), 5.

9. Benjamin H. Hary, John L. Hayes, and Fred Astren, eds., *Judaism and Islam: Boundaries, Communication, and Interaction: Essays in Honor of William M. Brinner* (Leiden: Brill, 2000).

10. André Levy, "Controlling Space, Essentializing Identities: Jews in Contemporary Casablanca," *City & Society* 9, no. 1 (1997): 175–99.

11. Patricia Hidiroglou, "Du hammam maghrébin au *miqveh* parisien," *Journal of Mediterranean Studies* 4, no. 2 (1994): 242–63.

12. On this literature, see *Gender and Jewish History*, ed. Marion A. Kaplan and Deborah Dash Moore (Bloomington: Indiana University Press, 2011).

13. Boyarin, *Carnal Israel*, 2. See also his introduction, 1–30.

14. Ibid., 31–60.

15. Fatima Mernissi, *Beyond the Veil: Male-Female Dynamics in Muslim Society* (London: Al-Saqi Books, 1975; rev. ed., 1985), 148–49.

16. Raja Rhouni, *Secular and Islamic Feminist Critique in the Work of Fatima Mernissi* (Leiden: Brill, 2010); see the introduction, 1–40.

17. Malek Chebel, *Manifeste pour un islam des Lumières* (Paris: Hachette Littérature, 2011), 57; *Histoire de la circoncision des origines à nos jours* (Paris: Presses universitaires de France, 1999); and *Le corps en Islam* (Paris: Presses universitaires de France, 1999).

18. Caroline Walker Bynum, "Why All the Fuss about the Body? A Medievalist's Perspective," *Critical Inquiry* 22 (1995): 1–33.

19. Yehouda Shenhav, *The Arab Jews: A Postcolonial Reading of Nationalism, Religion, and Ethnicity* (Stanford, CA: Stanford University Press, 2006), 19–48.

20. Dror Mishani, *Bekol ha-Inyan ha-mizrahi yish eze absurd* [literally, In Every *Mizrahi* Subject There Is an Absurd). Published in English as *The Ethnic Unconscious: The Emergence of "Mizrahiut" in the Hebrew Literature of the Eighties* (Tel Aviv: Am Oved, 2006), 54–55.

21. Michael Gluzman, *Ha-Guf ha-Tziuni* [The Zionist Body: Nationalism, Gender, and Sexuality in Hebrew Literature], 209.

22. Ibid., 209–13.

23. Ibid., 222.

24. Almog Behar, *Ana Min al-Yahud* (Tel Aviv: Bavel, 2008), 56–57 (my translation into French from the original Hebrew).

25. For a recent historical study from the point of view of the Mizrahi Jews, dealing in particular with the sociocultural movements in Israel and the tensions between Ashkenazi and Sephardim—based on race and skin color among other things—from the 1950s to the present, see Sami Shalom Chetrit, *Intra-Jewish Conflict in Israel: White Jews, Black Jews* (New York: Routledge, 2010).

26. Yaron Tsur, *Kilhila Qru'a* [A Divided Community: The Jews of Morocco and Nationalism, 1943–1954] (Tel Aviv: Am Oved, 2001).

27. Dafna Hirsch, "'Infusion of New Blood Can Only Heal and Strengthen': Zionist Physicians and Mixed Marriages," in *Racism in Israel*, ed. Yahouda Shenhav and Yossi Yona (Jerusalem: Van Leer Institute, 2008), 160–85 (in Hebrew).

28. In summer 2011, Israel had the largest social protest in its history; the expression "new Israelis" was launched by the general secretary of the National Union of Israeli Students on the evening of Saturday, September 3, on the vast State Plaza, before a crowd of about 300,000 people demanding social justice.

29. Sayed Qashu, *'Arabim Rokdim* [Dancing Arabs] (Tel Aviv: Modan Publishing House, 2002), 67.

30. Ahlem Mosteghenimi, *Mémoires de la chair* (Paris: Albin Michel, 2002).

31. Ibid.

32. *Alam al-Fikr* 37, no. 4 (April–June 2009).

Flavors and Memories of Shared Culinary Spaces in the Maghreb

Joëlle Bahloul

Over the some twelve centuries that the Jews and the Muslims lived together in the Mediterranean world and the Near East, relations between the two communities were nowhere so dense and reciprocal as in the leisurely routines of everyday life. This rich relationship between two religious communities with a turbulent history has not been documented as meticulously as their hostile relations and their segregation. The colonial period in the Maghreb, which lasted until the 1950s, was emblematic of these everyday exchanges. In analyzing Judeo-Muslim cultural and social relationships as they were expressed in the Jewish diet and Jewish cuisine in particular,[1] I shall focus on a privileged realm of exchanges between communities. The private space, the flavors, the smells, and the gestures of everyday life can break down divisions that exist in the public space. Women who care for and cook for their families are at the heart of that powerful dialogue between communities, as they were during the turbulent decades of the colonial period in the Maghreb.

Joëlle Bahloul

An ethnologist and a professor in anthropology and Jewish studies at Indiana University, Joëlle Bahloul is the author, notably, of *Le culte de la table dressée, rites et traditions de la table algérienne* (A.M. Metailié, 1983).

A different history, that of everyday life

In the tradition of social and cultural history, the study of everyday life in the private space has for several decades constituted a fruitful field of research and of intellectual exchange with neighboring disciplines. In resituating the repetitive practices of domesticity within their social and political context, historians frequently adopt some of the approaches familiar to ethnologists and, more generally, to social and cultural anthropologists, occupying the terrain traced out by Michel de Certeau and by the Annales school.[2] Daily life is therefore no longer an exotic field of exploration: it is history in private acts. So, too, the history of the relationship between the Jews and Muslims was shaped by the intimate practices of everyday life.

It would suffice to decipher the cookbooks and various historical documents related to diet in the two religious communities to highlight the density of their cultural exchanges in private life.[3] In the Mediterranean world, several aspects of Judeo-

Muslim culinary traditions have attested to that phenomenon since the premodern period. The terminology and culinary particularities surrounding certain foods point to the intensity of trans-Mediterranean migrations and exchanges between the Jews and Muslims of that region. Thus, for example, we find puff pastry stuffed with meat (beef/veal, lamb/mutton, pigeon, chicken, or even fish), under the name *pastilla*, *b'stilla*, or *bestel*, from the major cities of Andalusia to those of the eastern Maghreb, and in both Jewish and Muslim cuisines. This dish traveled across the centuries and across communities, where families put it on the menu for the major holidays of their religious calendars. The anthropologist Claudia Roden indicates that, among the Jews of Morocco, this recipe was believed to have been brought from Andalusia in the sixteenth century by ancestors fleeing the Spain of the Inquisition.[4] This expert in North African and Middle Eastern cuisine describes a similar belief among the Muslims of Morocco concerning a variant of the recipe: puff pastry stuffed with pigeon meat, which is said to have originated in medieval Muslim Spain.[5]

The period between the end of the nineteenth century and the second half of the twentieth century is particularly pertinent for analyzing the relations between the two communities in private and domestic life. Over the course of nearly a century, the Jews of the predominantly Muslim North African and Middle Eastern countries gradually obtained their social and political emancipation. In many localities, however, Jews continued to reside in the *mellah* or *hara* (the Jewish neighborhoods of Muslim cities) or nearby, because of the density of their intercommunity social relations. These had been in place for decades, and Jews remained attached to them even in the colonial period.[6] Paradoxically, colonialism often had the effect of bringing Jews closer to the Muslims, in neighborhoods where families of modest means often lived side by side, sometimes even in large building complexes whose residents belonged to various faiths.[7] By contrast, colonialism contributed toward a greater separation between well-off Jews and their former Muslim neighbors, who did not have the same opportunities for upward mobility. But in the places where Jews lived close to Muslims, they shared their everyday lives in cramped and overpopulated domestic worlds, even while respecting religious differences. Often they exchanged recipes or borrowed a few ingredients they had forgotten to buy at the market. Very rarely did they share meals, however, primarily because of the great difference in women's status in the two communities. These complex exchanges unfolded during the preparation of everyday and holiday meals and concerned the choice of ingredients as well as culinary techniques.

▶ See article by Emily Gottreich, pp. 223-230.

Women in the foreground

The women of each community played the predominant role in these everyday exchanges, because of their presence—more or less constant, depending on the historical conditions—in the domestic space, and by virtue of the sexual division of domestic and culinary labor in most Mediterranean societies.[8] It was the women who prepared the menus, sometimes together in the interior courtyards of multifamily houses. Shopping practices, however, distinguished the Jewish from the Muslim women, especially in the twentieth century. Jewish women could more often be found at the market, whereas Muslim women tended to be confined to the domestic space. It was their husbands and sons who did the errands.

The rhythm of daily activities brought Jewish and Muslim women together for the preparation of certain foods. That process is depicted in works of literature and in the arts, particularly in a recent film by the French director Philippe Faucon. *Dans la vie* (*In Life*) is the story of the close relationship between two women from Algeria,[9] one Jewish, the other Muslim, who now live in Toulon. Both are in exile in France, and recent events in the streets threaten to come between them. But the Muslim, hired to care for the sick and elderly Jewish woman, decides to resist the pressures from young people in her neighborhood and to maintain a close relationship with her Jewish companion, through the necessary tasks of private life. The film is a meticulous dramatization of everyday domesticity, which becomes the arena for a Judeo-Muslim friendship reestablished through the women's memories of their

A Jewish woman and a Muslim woman (played by the actresses Ariane Jacquot and Zohra Mouffock) show their solidarity in the film *Dans la Vie* (*In the Life*), directed by Philippe Faucon, 2008.

native Algeria, memories that the repetitive acts revive at every moment. In France, as clashes in the street divide Jews and Muslims, these women restore the ancient connections between their respective communities through conversations around the stove and the table.

Similar ingredients, different cuisines

In the colonial markets of the Maghreb and the Middle East, Jews and Muslims exchanged foods, ideas on how to prepare them, and, in some ritual circumstances, advice on how to consume them. In the colonial society of the first half of the twentieth century, especially in small towns, the Jewish-Muslim relations centered on food were generally more extensive than those the Jews maintained with their Christian neighbors.

The Maghrebi Judeo-Muslim diet included the full range of vegetables, legumes, grains, and fruits of the Mediterranean world. Spices and aromatic herbs, such as cumin, coriander (fresh leaves or dried seeds), caraway seeds, saffron, red or black pepper, cinnamon, nutmeg, cloves, parsley, mint, and anise were used in the Jewish and Muslim cuisines of the Arab Muslim Mediterranean world. For the most part, the two communities also used the same cooking fats, with the exception of butter, which was more often used in Muslim cuisines. Since Jewish dietary prescriptions prohibit cooking meat products in any dairy product and serving these two types of products on the same menu,[10] Jewish cooks did not have the habit of using butter in savory dishes. Jewish pastries also rarely included dairy products (except in certain ritual dishes where they are required). In general, pastries were the favorite dessert at meals on the religious calendar. But since these meals usually included meat products, dairy products were not allowed in the sweets consumed.

Olive oil and peanut oil were widely used in both cuisines, as was honey (in pastries) and vinegar (in vinaigrettes and canned vegetables), garlic, and onion. Vegetables and legumes often had a similar place in Jewish and Muslim cuisines of the Maghreb and the Middle East. The only differences lay in the culinary calendar governing the use of these ingredients.

Maghrebi couscous, with its panoply of squash, carrots, cardoons, turnips, fava beans (fresh in their pods), and chick-peas, was the indispensable dish for Friday night dinner among the Jews as they began the Shabbat, and this dish was also found at almost all the major holidays on the Muslim religious calendar. Couscous was so emblematic of the multiethnic culinary art

> **Couscous**
>
> Couscous, an African culinary invention (from Northern Africa, in particular), is a symbol of *baraka*, "luck or good fortune," in Muslim communities. It is also found on the table at Jewish feasts in the Maghreb. It is called *moghrabieh* (the Maghrebi dish) in the Middle East, which invented its own version of it, with a base of large semolina grains, now commonly called "Israeli couscous."

of the region that some North African Jews had a special version of it for Passover, despite the prohibition on consuming boiled or fermented grains of wheat and rice. Couscous appeared on the Passover menu, but the grains were replaced by rounds of unleavened bread, crushed and thrown into the stock just before serving. Beef was the meat most often used in Jewish couscous, since it constituted *the* meat par excellence in the culinary traditions of these North African communities.[11]

Two vegetables are of particular interest, since they appeared in Maghrebi cuisines without distinction for religion: cardoons and Swiss chard. The cardoon is an ancient plant food that was part of the cuisine of ancient Rome.[12] The Maghrebi Jews consumed it in a stew, by preference in the usual Shabbat dish: *t'fina*, or *dafina*, a stew cooked overnight on Friday and composed of a great variety of vegetables, meats, grains, fats, and other ingredients. *Daf* may include various vegetables, depending on the season, but for the Jews of the Eastern Maghreb it was frequently composed of cardoons combined with turnips and white beans. Cardoons are in season in the spring and were therefore often found in meals during Passover week, like their botanical cousin the artichoke. Swiss chard was also considered a superior vegetable, appearing in dishes on Jewish holidays, especially in *t'fina* in eastern Algeria. Generally seasoned with garlic, it was combined with chickpeas and fat pieces of beef to celebrate the supreme rites of the Jewish calendar.

In their use of foods from the plant kingdom, Jewish and Muslim cuisines thus imitated each other, incorporating these vegetables into their respective religious celebrations. Meat-based foods, on the contrary, were a major factor of distinction between the Jews and the Muslims, despite the prohibition by both Judaism and Islam on the consumption of pork. During the colonial period, and especially after World War I, the Jews of the western Mediterranean saw a gradual improvement in their standard of living. In dietary terms, this translated into an increase in the consumption of meat. This process, which began in the urban middle class, spread to the lower social strata after World War II. In the 1950s, Maghrebi Jews ate meat not only for their holiday and Shabbat meals but also at a few regular meals during the week. For the most part, the Muslim populations did not experience a similar increase in their standard of living. Over the course of the twentieth century, then, meat gradually came to distinguish the two groups, as socioeconomic differences came to be added to those of a religious order.

The religious differences are regulated by the fundamental sacred texts of the two religions. Both prohibit the consumption of pork. Muslim families, especially in the upper social strata, thus tended to buy their meat from local kosher butchers. Until decolonization, and especially in the years following World War II, the diet of the majority of the Jews of the Maghreb conformed to the alimentary prescrip-

Kosher and Halal

Kosher means "valid, certified," while *halal* means "licit, legitimate." The meaning of the two words is therefore similar. As commonly used, they designate the status of foods permitted the Jews and Muslims, respectively. The Torah forbids the consumption of mammals that do not chew their cud and that do not have cloven hooves, as well as reptiles, shellfish, insects, fish without scales, and birds of prey. It also forbids blood, certain fats, and the combination of meat and milk. Finally, the Oral Torah strictly regulates slaughter and requires the verification of the integrity of the internal organs. Similarly, the rules of halal are defined in the Qur'an and the sunna. The Qur'an explicitly forbids pork, blood, animals whose throats have not been slit, and alcohol, and also requires that the Name of God be pronounced at the moment of slaughter. It recognizes the halal character of meats slaughtered by the Jews and Christians (with certain restrictions). As a result, in accordance with religious policy in Islamic countries during the Middle Ages, and for economic reasons today, the validity of kosher slaughter, combined with Muslim practices, came to be widely recognized.

tions and prohibitions laid out in the biblical, Talmudic, and rabbinical texts. These do not allow the consumption of the meat of nonruminant mammals (rabbits, horses, and pigs, for example, were all domesticated in the Mediterranean world), or of crustaceans and other shellfish, or of game animals. It was only in the 1950s that the Jews, as part of the process of emancipation and Westernization, gradually abandoned the religious precepts relating to diet and began to make use of ingredients belonging to the cuisines of Western Europe, including foods forbidden by the Jewish tradition.

Ritualization of exchanges

In the twentieth century, the respective religious systems of the two communities drew often-impermeable borders that separated the daily lives of Jews and Muslims of the Maghreb and the Middle East. Nonetheless, religious rituals also often contributed toward establishing regular and lasting exchanges. The celebration of Passover in the early spring is a pertinent example of these processes of dietary exchanges between Jews and Muslims. In the month preceding the first Passover meal, tradition requires a spring cleaning of every room in the dwelling, and especially of the kitchen cupboards that contain foodstuffs. The principle behind this cleaning is religious in nature: the home must be cleared of any trace of fermented food and of any food old enough that it might contain a form of fermentation. These foodstuffs, united under the generic Hebrew term *hametz*, are impure (nonkosher) for the eight days of the Passover celebration and are strictly banned from the week's menus. All grains (primarily wheat and rice), semolina, flour, fresh pastries and baked goods, and dried beans dating to before the beginning of Passover must leave the house. This tradition, which is respected even in our own time, often took the form in the Maghreb of the symbolic and "temporary" gift of these foods by Jewish families to their Muslim neighbors.

The last day of Passover week was marked by the ritual breaking of the dietary prohibitions, often called "Mimuna" among the Jews of the Maghreb.[13] This very festive dinner, when many Jewish family members gathered with their neighbors, friends, and relations, was composed of various dishes whose ingredients are forbidden during Passover week: pastries, blintzes, leavened flat bread, and, obviously, the famous couscous, which, in this joyous atmosphere, was served sweet, with sugar, honey, raisins, and candy. During this holiday, which marked the symbolic reinsertion of the Jewish community into its local dual-community environment, the Muslims were invited to the Jewish celebration. In many cases, when they had kept the forbidden foods for their Jewish neighbors, they returned these foodstuffs after the feast, in the form of pastries made by Muslim cooks. In the Maghreb, before the mass Jewish migrations of the 1960s, Mimuna constituted the interfaith and intercommunity event par excellence, the annual celebration of Judeo-Muslim cohabitation in the domestic, familial, and ritual culture.

Collective memory by the plateful

Since decolonization in the late 1950s to mid-1960s, and the mass migrations that resulted from it, a good number of changes have been introduced into the traditional dietary codes: in tastes and flavors, in the selection of ingredients, and in the techniques for preparing and cooking the traditional dishes. Particularly for Maghrebi Jews who settled in France, these changes have translated into a reduction in the quantity of cooking fats and in the variety of spices and aromatics, a simplification of culinary techniques, and a reduction in preparation time. Even more significant, however, a number of families who have experienced various forms of upward mobility have gradually abandoned some of the dietary prohibitions and have begun to consume forbidden meats, under specific social and temporal circumstances. These phenomena resulted from a change in the role of Jewish women within the organization of familial, domestic, and ritual life, and also in the evolution of tastes as a function of dietary ideologies that developed in European society in the second half of the twentieth century. With exile, the Judeo-Arab dietary habits and the traditions that sustained them have come to be restricted to times of religious and familial rituals. On ordinary days, by contrast, the Jews' diets now include certain (meat-based) ingredients prohibited by their religion.

As a result, Judeo-Muslim relations centered on food have come to occupy a profound place in the collective memories of the Jews who migrated from the predominantly Muslim Mediterranean world, and also in the memories of the Muslims who have remained there. The family stews and the flavors of Jewish religious holidays have been transformed into memories of the native countries and cultures of the émigrés.

The *pied-noir* ritual of couscous, prepared by an Algerian woman, in the film *Coup de Sirocco*, with Marthe Villalonga, directed by Alexandre Arcady, 1979.

It is noteworthy that, for some Muslims who have remained in their native countries and who knew Jews as neighbors, their recollection of the now-vanished Jewish cultures often consists of food memories. I would like to give an example of this phenomenon of alimentary memorialization, which I have observed in my ethnographic research over the last four decades. During an ethnographic trip I took to Constantine in 1979 to observe a Jewish pilgrimage on the occasion of the Lag BaOmer holiday,[14] I had the opportunity to visit the house where the maternal branch of my family had lived in Sétif (eastern Algeria) until 1962, at which time they departed for France. I was working at the time on the processes associated with the remembrance of shared residences by the Sétifian Jews in France and by the Muslims who had remained in Algeria.[15] Upon my arrival in the inner courtyard of this house, with its Andalusian architecture, I was welcomed by a small group of girls and women who lived there. They asked me who I was and whom I wished to see. Some of the former neighbors of my aunts and cousins still lived in the house, seventeen years after all the Jewish families—that is, nearly half the residents at the time—had left. The excitement of the introductions was followed by a flood of memories from my hostesses.[16] Before taking my leave of this hospitable gathering, I received two "souvenir gifts" from the house: a woman's housecoat and "Jewish bread," made by one of the women. This loaf was in fact challah, the Shabbat bread regularly made by Jewish cooks on Friday before the start of the weekly day of rest. A brioche-style bread baked in the oven and made from a leavened dough that is then braided, it stood apart from the bread the Muslims of that city made, which was usually grilled on a three-legged portable stove called a *kanun*.

The women asked me to share these gifts with their former Jewish neighbors when I returned to Paris. The Muslim residents' collective memory of these neighbors thus took material—if not objectified—form in objects with alimentary and domestic functions, those that had formerly been performed in common by the two religious communities. The housecoat held the memory of a life in common within the domestic world, despite religious differences and, in the recent colonial period, despite social and political distinctions. Almost twenty years after the Jews' departure, the Muslims had not forgotten. They even seemed to be perpetuating the memory of these Jews through their most frequently repeated religious rituals, that of Shabbat in particular. The challah was in fact offered to me as a *superior*, festive bread; or rather, it had been transformed into that by domestic memory. The Jews left, but their bread stayed in the memories of gestures and tastes held by their former neighbors.

Judeo-Muslim relations: Between cuisine and virtual communication

In the first decade of the twenty-first century, these memories found particularly favorable networks of reproduction in virtual modes of communication. The food memories of the Jews in the Muslim world find their densest and most interactive expression on the Internet. On ethnic Web sites such as Dafina.net,[17] Zlabia.com,[18] and Harissa.com,[19] in the Nebi Daniel Association,[20] and on Iraqijews.org[21] and Dafouineuse (Facebook), gustatory memories are exchanged between Jews and Muslims: local recipes, specific ingredients, unforgettable flavors of their shared native countries. What is remarkable about these Web sites is the possibility they offer for free access, for the participation of users in exchanges and conversations. The Facebook page Dafouineuse contains many photos of the famous Shabbat dish *daf*, which has acquired the amazing capacity to create global links between Jews and Muslims. The photos, whose aim is clearly memorial, encourage Web users to post their family recipes and to engage in debates about the authenticity of the recipes posted, but above all, to create a climate of communication where memories of a time when the Jews and Muslims lived together in these countries of origin can be expressed. That global communica-

> *The food memories of the Jews in the Muslim world find their densest and most interactive expression on the Internet.*

tion system is proof, half a century after the great Jewish migrations, that the original cultures have not disappeared. They now use sophisticated technological media for their reproduction and transmission beyond religious, geographical, and political borders. The *daf* has not ended its peregrinations.

1. This chapter is based on a more complete study of these social and cultural phenomena; see J. Bahloul, *Le culte de la table dressée* (Paris: Editions Métailié, 1983).

2. Michel de Certeau, *L'invention du quotidien* (Paris: Gallimard, 1979). On the Annales school, see Philippe Ariès and Georges Duby, eds., *Histoire de la vie privée*, 5 vols. (Paris: Seuil, 1985–87); published in English as *A History of Private Life*, trans. A. Goldhammer (Cambridge, MA: Harvard University Press, 1992–98).

3. The most recent research on dietary practices in the premodern Muslim world can be found in the British historian David Waines's *Food Culture and Health in Pre-Modern Islamic Societies* (Leiden: Brill, 2011).

4. C. Roden, *The Book of Jewish Food: An Odyssey from Samarkand to New York* (New York: Alfred A. Knopf, 1996), 374.

5. C. Roden, *A Book of Middle Eastern Food* (London: Penguin Books, 1968), 114.

6. S. Miller, ed., *The Architecture and Memory of the Minority Quarter in the Muslim Mediterranean City* (Cambridge, MA: Harvard Graduate School of Design, 2010).

7. For a study of these residences, see J. Bahloul, *La maison de mémoire: Ethnologie d'une demeure judéo-arabe en Algérie (1937–1961)* (Paris: Editions Métailié, 1992).

8. D. Donath, *L'évolution de la femme israélite à Fès* (Aix-en-Provence: La Pensée Universitaire, 1962).

9. Philippe Faucon, *Dans la vie*, Istiqlal Films, 2007.

10. By virtue of a religious and not merely literal reading of Exodus 23:19.

11. See Bahloul, *Le culte de la table dressée*.

12. G. Gibault, *Le cardon et l'artichaut* (Paris: Gibault, 1907); I. Gozzini Giacosa, *A Taste of Ancient Rome* (Chicago: University of Chicago Press, 1994).

13. Harvey E. Goldberg, "The *Mimuna* and the Minority Status of Moroccan Jews," *Ethnology* 17, no. 1 (1978): 75–87.

14. See the resulting article: J. Bahloul, "Retour à Constantine: Une expérience collective de juifs maghrébins établis en France," in *Lucette Valensi à l'oeuvre*, ed. F. Pouillon (Paris: Editions Bouchène, 2002), 61–71.

15. This research is the basis for my book *La maison de mémoire*.

16. No men were in the house in the middle of the day.

17. Web site for Jews originally from or still living in Morocco (in French).

18. Web site for Algerian Jews (in French).

19. Web site for Tunisian Jews (in French).

20. Or http://www.nebidaniel.org: Web site for Egyptian Jews (in French).

21. Web site for Iraqi Jews (in English). This site is managed by an Iraqi Jewish congregation in New York.

General Bibliography

Primary sources are not included in this bibliography: they are mentioned in the articles and the references can be found in the notes at the end of the corresponding articles.

General works

Amir Moezzi, Mohammad Ali, eds. *Dictionnaire du Coran.* Paris: Robert Laffont, coll. "Bouquins," 2007.

Angeles Gallego, Maria, Bleaney, Heather, and Garcia Suarez, Pablo, eds. *Bibliography of Jews in the Islamic World.* Leiden: Brill, 2010.

Bibliographie, *Les Juifs du Maghreb et d'al-Andalus.* Essaouira: Bibliographie publiée à l'occasion de la tenue du colloque international «Migrations, identités et modernité au Maghreb», 17–20 March 2010.

Brill, Alan. *Judaism and World Religions. Encountering Christianity, Islam, and Eastern Traditions.* New York: Palgrave Macmillan, 2012.

Courbage, Youssef, and Fargues, Philippe. *Christians and Jews under Islam.* Trans. Mabro, Judy. [*Chrétiens et juifs dans l'Islam arabe et turc.* Paris: Fayard, 1992]. London and New York: I.B.Tauris, 1996.

Dammen McAuliffe, Jane. et al., eds. *Encyclopaedia of Qur'an.* Leiden: Brill, 2001–2006.

Encyclopedia Judaica. 16 vols. + 8 vols. + 2 vols. Jerusalem and New York: Keter Publishing House and MacMillan Company, 1971–1972.

Ettinger, Shmuel, ed. *History of the Jews of Islamic Countries (in Hebrew).* Jerusalem: Merkaz Zalman Shazar, 1981.

Fleet, Kate, Krämer, Gudrun, and Matringe, Denis, et al., eds. *Encyclopædia of Islam.* Leiden: Brill, 2007–.

Friedmann, Yohanan. *Tolerance and Coercion in Islam. Interfaith Relations in the Muslim Tradition.* Cambridge and New York: Cambridge University Press, 2003.

Gall, Lothar, and Willoweit, Dietmar, eds. *Judaism, Christianity, and Islam in the Course of History. Exchange and Conflicts.* Munich: R. Oldenbourg Verlag, 2011.

Germa, Antoine, Lellouch, Benjamin, and Patlagean, Evelyne, eds. *Les Juifs dans l'histoire.* Seyssel: Champ Vallon, 2011.

Goitein, Shlomo Dov. *Jews and Arabs. A Concise History of Their Social and Cultural Relations.* [New York: Schocken. 1974]. Mineola, NY: Dover Publications, 2005.

Golb, Norman, ed. *Judaeo-Arabic Studies.* Chur (Suisse): Harwood Academic Publishers, coll. "Studies in Muslim-Jewish Relations," 1997, 3.

Goodman, Martin, ed. *The Oxford Handbook of Jewish Studies.* Oxford: Oxford University Press, 2002.

Hary, Benjamin H. Hayes, John L., and Astren, Fred, eds. *Judaism and Islam. Boundaries, Communication, and Interaction: Essays in Honor of William M. Brinner.* Leiden, Boston and Cologne: Brill, 2000.

Hunt, Stephen, ed. *Judaism and Islam.* Farnham: Ashgate, 2010.

Laato, Antii, and Lindqvist, Pekka, eds. *Encounters of the Children of Abraham from Ancient to Modern Times.* Leiden: Brill, 2012.

Landau, Jacob M. *Jews, Arabs, Turks. Selected Essays.* Jerusalem: Magnes University Press, 1993.

Laskier, Michael M., and Lev, Yaacov, eds. *The Convergence of Judaism and Islam. Religious, Scientific, and Cultural Dimensions.* Gainesville: University Press of Florida, 2011.

Laskier, Michael M., and Lev, Yaacov, eds. *The Divergence of Judaism and Islam. Interdependence, Modernity, and Political Turmoil.* Gainesville: University Press of Florida, 2011.

Lewis, Bernard. *The Jews of Islam.* Princeton: Princeton University Press, 1984.

Nettler, Ronald L., ed. *Studies in Muslim-Jewish Relations.* Chur: Harwood Academic Publishers, coll. "Studies in Muslim-Jewish Relations," 1993, 1.

Nettler, Ronald L., ed. *Medieval and Modern Perspectives on Muslim-Jewish Relations.* Chur: Harwood Academic Publishers, coll. "Studies in Muslim-Jewish Relations," 1995, 2.

Nettler, Ronald L., and Taji-Farouki, Suha, eds. *Muslim-Jewish Encounters. Intellectual Traditions and Modern Politics.* Chur: Harwood Academic Publishers, coll. "Studies in Muslim-Jewish Relations," 1998, 4.

Parfitt, Tudor, ed. *Israel and Ishmael: Studies in Muslim-Jewish Relations.* Basingstoke: Palgrave Macmillan, 2000.

Stillman, Norman. *The Jews of Arab Lands. A History and Source Book.* Philadelphia: Jewish Publication Society, 1979.

Stillman, Norman A., et al., eds. *Encyclopedia of Jews in the Islamic World.* Leiden: Brill, 2010.

Trigano, Shmuel, ed. *Le Monde séfarade. Vol. 1: Histoire, Vol. 2: Civilisation.* Paris: Le Seuil, 2006.

Part I: The Middle Ages

Adang, Camilla. *Islam frente a Judaismo. La polémica de Ibn Hazm de Córdoba.* Madrid: Aben Ezra Ediciones, 1994.

Adang, Camilla. *Muslim Writers on Judaism and the Hebrew Bible: From Ibn Rabban to Ibn Hazm.* Leiden: Brill, 1996.

Alfonso, Esperanza. *Islamic Culture through Jewish Eyes. Al-Andalus from the Tenth to Twelfth Century.* London and New York: Routledge, 2008.

Ali, M. Athar. "Muslims' Perception of Judaism and Christianity in Medieval India." In *Modern Asian Studies,* 1, 1999, 33, 243–255.

Arié, Rachel. *L'Espagne musulmane aux temps des Nasrides (1232–1492).* Paris: Editions de Boccard, 1973.

Ashtor, Eliyahu. *History of the Jews in Egypt and Syria during the Reign of the Mamluks* (in Hebrew). Jerusalem: Mossad ha-Rav Kook, 1944–1970, 3 vols.

Ashtor, Eliyahu. *A Social and Economic History of the Near East in the Middle Ages.* Berkeley: University of California Press, coll. "Near Eastern Center Series," vol. 13, 1976.

Ashtor, Eliyahu. *The Jews of Moslem Spain.* Trans. Klein, Aaron, and Machlowitz Klein, Jenny. Philadelphia: The Jewish Publication Society, 1973–1984, 3 vols.

Barakat, Ahmad. *Muhammad and the Jews. A Re-examination.* New Delhi: Vikas Publishing House, 1979.

Bareket, Elinoar. *Fustat on the Nile. The Jewish Elite in Medieval Egypt.* Leiden: Brill, 1999.

Ben-Ezer, Ehud. "Arab Images in Hebrew Literature, 1900–1930." *New Outlook,* 1986, 3.

Berend, Nora. *At the Gate of Christendom. Jews, Muslims, and "Pagans" in Medieval Hungary, c. 1000-c. 1300.* Cambridge: Cambridge University Press, 2001.

Brann, Ross. *The Compunctious Poet. Cultural Ambiguity and Hebrew Poetry in Muslim Spain.* Baltimore: The Johns Hopkins University Press, 1991.

Brann, Ross. *Power in the Portrayal. Representations of Jews and Muslims in Eleventh and Twelfth Century Islamic Spain.* Princeton: Princeton University Press, 2002.

Brann, Ross. "The Arabized Jews." In *The Cambridge History of Arabic Literature. The Literature of al-Andalus.* Menocal, María R., Scheindlin, Raymond P., and Sells, Michael A., eds. Cambridge: Cambridge University Press, 2006, 435–454.

Bresc, Henri. *Arabes de langue, juifs de religion. L'évolution du judaïsme sicilien dans l'environ-nement latin, XIIᵉ–XVᵉ siècles.* Paris: Bouchène, 2001.

Bresc, Henri. "La Sicile médiévale, terre de refuge pour les juifs: migration et exil." *Al-Masaq,* 1, 2005, 17, 31–46.

Bresc, Henri. "La schiavitù in casa degli ebrei siciliani del Tre e Quattrocento." *Quaderni storici,* 42, 3, 2007, 126, 679–698.

Brett, Michael. "The Islamisation of Egypt and North Africa." In *The First Annual Levtzion Lecture, delivered 12 January 2005,* Jerusalem: The Nehemia Levtzion Center for Islamic Studies, 2006.

Brody, Robert. *The Geonim of Babylonia and the Shaping of Medieval Jewish Culture.* New Haven: Yale University Press, 1998.

Caballero Navas, Carmen, and Alfonso, Esperanza, eds. *Late Medieval Jewish Identities. Iberia and Beyond.* New York: Palgrave-Macmillan, 2010.

Cahen, Claude. *Orient et Occident au temps des Croisades.* Paris: Aubier-Montaigne, 1983, chap.13.

Chazan, Robert, and Rustow, Marina, eds. *The Cambridge History of Judaism. Jews in the Medieval Islamic World.* Cambridge: Cambridge University Press, forthcoming, vol. V: the medieval Period, VIIe–XVe.

Chouraqui, André. *Jerusalem, ville sanctuaire.* Paris: Hachette, 1996.

Cohen, Hillel. *The Rise and Fall of Arab Jerusalem. Palestinian Politics and the City since 1967.* London: Routledge, 2011.

Cohen, Mark R. *Jewish Self-Government in Medieval Egypt. The Origins of the Office of Head of the Jews, ca. 1065–1126.* Princeton: Princeton University Press, 1980.

Cohen, Mark R. "Islam and the Jews: Myth, Counter-Myth, History." *Jerusalem Quarterly,* 1986, 38, 125–137.

Cohen, Mark R. "The Neo-Lachrymose Conception of Jewish-Arab History." *Tikkun,* 1991, 55–60.

Cohen, Mark R. *Under Crescent and Cross. The Jews in the Middle Ages.* Princeton: Princeton University Press, 1994.

Cohen, Mark R. "The Jews under Islam: From the Rise of Islam to Sabbatai Zevi." In *Sephardic Studies in the University,* Gerber, Jane S., and Abitbol, Michel, eds. Madison, NJ: Fairleigh Dickinson University Press, 1995, 43–119.

Cohen, Mark R. "What Was the Pact of 'Umar? A Literary-Historical Study." *Jerusalem Studies in Arabic and Islam,* 1999, 23, 100–157.

Cohen, Mark R. *Poverty and Charity in the Jewish Community of Medieval Egypt.* Princeton: Princeton University Press, 2005.

Cohen, Mark R. "The 'Convivencia' of Jews and Muslims in the High Middle Ages." In *The Meeting of Civilizations. Muslim, Christian and Jewish.* Ma'oz, Moshe, ed. Brighton and Portland: Sussex Academic Press, 2009, 54–65.

Cole, Peter. *Selected Poems of Shmuel HaNagid Translated from the Hebrew.* Princeton: Princeton University Press, 1996.

Constable, Olivia R., ed. *Medieval Iberia: Readings from Christian, Muslim and Jewish Sources.* Philadelphia: University of Pennsylvania Press, 1997.

Cressier, Patrice, Fierro, Maribel, and Molina, Luis, eds. *Los Almohades: problemas y perspectivas.* Madrid: CSIC, 2005, 2 vols.

Donner, Fred M. *Muhammad and the Believers. At the Origins of Islam.* Cambridge, MA: Belknap Press, 2010.

Dunlop, Douglas M. *The History of the Jewish Khazars.* Princeton: Schocken Books, 1954.

Fattal, Antoine. *Le Statut légal des non-musulmans en pays d'Islam.* Beirut: Imprimerie Catholique, 1958.

Faü, Jean-François. *Les Juifs dans la Péninsule arabique. V^e–XVIe siècles.* Paris: Paul Geuthner, 2008.

Fierro, Maribel, ed. *Judíos y musulmanes en al-Andalus y el Magreb. Contactos intelectuales.* Madrid: Casa de Velásquez, 2002.

Fierro, Maribel. "Conversion, Ancestry and Universal Religion: The Case of the Almohads in the Islamic West (6th/12th–7th/13th Centuries)." *Journal of Medieval Iberian Studies,* 2010, 2, 155–173.

Firestone, Reuven. "The Failure of a Jewish Program of Public Satire in the Squares of Medina." *Judaism,* 1997, 438–452.

Firestone, Reuven. "Jewish Culture in the Formative Period of Islam." In *Cultures of the Jews. A New History.* Biale, David, ed. New York: Schocken Books, 2002, 261–294.

Fishel, Walter J. "Jews in the Economic and political Life of Medieval Islam." *Royal Asiatic Society Monographs,* 1937, 22.

Frank, Daniel, ed. *The Jews of Medieval Islam. Community, Society and Identity. Proceedings of an International Conference Held by the Institute of Jewish Studies, University College London, 1992.* Leiden: Brill, 1995.

Frank, Daniel H, and Leaman, Oliver, eds. *The Cambridge Companion to Medieval Jewish Philosophy.* Cambridge: Cambridge University Press, 2003.

Franklin, Arnold. *This Noble House. Jewish Descendants of King David in the Medieval Islamic East.* Philadelphia: University of Pennsylvania Press, 2013.

Freidenreich, David M. *Foreigners and Their Food. Constructing Otherness in Jewish, Christian, and Islamic Law.* Berkeley, Los Angeles, London: University of California Press, 2011.

Freidenreich, David M., and Goldstein, Miriam, eds. *Beyond Religious Borders. Interaction and Intellectual Exchange in the Medieval Islamic World.* Philadelphia: University of Pennsylvania Press, 2012.

Frenkel, Miriam. *Lover and Generous: The Ruling Elite of Alexandrian Judaism in the Middle Ages* (Hebrew). Jerusalem: Institut Ben Zvi, 2006.

Gallego, Maria A., ed. *Reason and Faith in Medieval Judaism and Islam.* Leiden: Brill, forthcoming.

García-Arenal, Mercedes. "Les Bildiyyn de Fès, un groupe de néo-Musulmans d'origine juive." *Studia Islamica,* 1987, 66, 115–143.

García-Arenal, Mercedes. "Rapport entre les groupes dans la péninsule ibérique: La conversion des juifs à l'islam (xiie–xiie siècles)." *Revue du Monde Musulman et de la Méditerranée,* 1992, 63–64, 91–102.

García-Arenal, Mercedes. "Jewish Converts to Islam in the Muslim West." *Israel Oriental Studies,* 1997, XVII.

García-Arenal, Mercedes, ed. *Islamic Conversions. Religious Identities in Mediterranean Islam.* Strasbourg: European Science Foundation, 2001.

García-Arenal, Mercedes. "Al-Andalus et l'Espagne. La trajectoire d'un débat." In *Construire un monde? Mondialisation, pluralisme et universalisme.* Baduel, Pierre R., ed. Paris: IRMC - Maisonneuve et Larose, 2007, 32–53.

Gil, Moshe. "The Constitution of Medina: A Reconsideration." *Israel Oriental Studies,* 1974, 4.

Gil, Moshe. "The Origins of the Jews of Yathrib." *Jerusalem Studies in Arabic and Islam,* 1984, 4, 206.

Gil, Moshe. *A History of Palestine, 634–1099.* Trans. Broido, Ethel. Cambridge: Cambridge University Press, 1992.

Gil, Moshe. *Palestine during the First Muslim Period (634–1099). Part II: Cairo Geniza Documents.* Trans. Broido, Ethel. [*(Erets Yisra'el ba-tekufa ha-muslemit ha-rishona).* Tel Aviv: 1983]. Cambridge: Cambridge University Press, 1997.

Gil, Moshe, and Fleischer, Ezra. *Yehuda Halevi and His Circle. 55 Geniza Documents* (in Hebrew). Jerusalem: World Union of Jewish Studies and Rabbi David Moshe and Amalia Rosen Foundation, 2001.

Gil, Moshe. *Jews in Islamic Countries in the Middle Ages.* Trans. Strassler, David. Leiden and Boston: Brill, 2004.

Goitein, Shlomo Dov. "Contemporary Letters on the Capture of Jerusalem by the Crusaders." *Journal of Jewish Studies,* 1952, 3, 162–177.

Goitein, Shlomo Dov. "Obadyah, a Norman Proselyte (Apropos the Discovery of a New Fragment of his 'Scroll')." *Journal of Jewish Studies,* 1953, 4, 74–84.

Goitein, Shlomo Dov. *A Mediterranean Society. The Jewish Communities of the Arab World as Portrayed in the Documents of the Cairo Geniza.* Berkeley: University of California Press, 1967–1993, 6 vols.

Goitein, Shlomo Dov. "An Eleventh-Century Letter from Tyre in the John Rylands Library." *Bulletin of the John Rylands Library,* 1971–1972, 54, 94–102.

Goitein, Shlomo Dov. "Tyre-Tripoli-'Arqa: Geniza Documents from the Beginning of the Crusader Period." *The Jewish Quarterly Review,* 2, 1975, New Series 66, 69–88.

Goitein, Shlomo Dov. *A Mediterranean Society. An Abridgment in one Volume.* [Jacob Lassner]. Berkeley: University of California Press, 1999.

Goitein, Shlomo Dov, and Friedman, Mordechai A. *India Traders of the Middle Ages. Documents from the Cairo Geniza ("India Book").* Leiden: Brill, 2008.

Goitein, Shlomo Dov, and Friedman, Mordechai A. *Joseph Lebdî, Prominent Indian Trader. Cairo Geniza Documents* (in Hebrew). Jerusalem: Ben Zvi Institute and Rabbi David Moses and Amalia Rosen Foundation, 2009.

Goitein, Shlomo Dov, and Friedman, Mordechai A. *Abrahama ben Yiju, Merchant and Craftsman in India. Cairo Geniza Documents* (in Hebrew). Jerusalem: Ben Zvi Institute and Rabbi David Moses and Amalia Rosen Foundation, 2010.

Goitein, Shlomo Dov, and Friedman, Mordechai A. *Madmun Nagid of Temen and the India Trade. Cairo Geniza Documents* (in Hebrew). Jerusalem: Ben Zvi Institute and Rabbi David Moses and Amalia Rosen Foundation, 2010.

Goldberg, Jessica L. *Trade and Institutions in the Medieval Mediterranean. The Geniza Merchants and Their Business World.* Cambridge: Cambridge University Press, 2012.

Grévin, Benoît. *Le Coran de Mithridate.* Rome: Mémoire inédit de l'École française de Rome, 2005–2006.

Hames, Harvey J., ed. *Jews, Muslims and Christians in and around the Crown of Aragon.* Leiden: Brill, 2003.

Hartman, David. *Crisis and Leadership. Epistles of Maimonides.* Philadelphia: Jewish Publication Society, 1985.

Hirschberg, Haim Zeev. *A History of the Jews in North Africa.* Leiden: Brill, 1974–1981, 2 vols.

Hoffman, Adina, and Cole, Peter. *Sacred Trash. The Lost and Found World of the Cairo Geniza.* New York: Schocken Books, 2011.

Hoyland, Robert, ed. *Muslims and Others in Early Islamic Society.* Farnham: Ashgate, 2004.

Kedar, Benjamin Z. *Crusade and Mission. European Approaches toward the Muslims.* Princeton: Princeton University Press, 1984.

Kedar, Benjamin Z. "The Subjected Muslims of the Frankish Levant." In *Muslims under Latin Rule 1100–1300,* Powell, James M., ed. Princeton: Princeton University Press, 1990, 135–174.

Kedar, Benjamin Z. *The Franks in the Levant, 11th to 14th Centuries.* Aldershot: Ashgate Variorum, 1993.

Kedar, Benjamin Z. "Multidirectional Conversion in the Frankish Levant." In *Varieties of Religious Conversion in the Middle Ages,* Muldoon, James, ed. Gainesville: University Press of Florida, 1997, 190–199.

Kedar, Benjamin Z. "On the Origins of the Earliest Laws of Frankish Jerusalem: The Canons of the Council of Nablus, 1120." *Speculum,* 2, 1999, 74, 310–335.

Kedar, Benjamin Z. *Franks, Muslims and Oriental Christians in the Latin Levant. Studies in Frontier Acculturation.* Aldershot: Ashgate Variorum, 2006.

Kister, Meir J. "Do Not Assimilate Yourselves…" *Jerusalem Studies in Arabic and Islam,* 1989, 12, 321–371.

Klorman, Bat-Zion Eraqi. "Jewish and Muslim Messianism in Yemen." *International Journal of Middle East Studies,* 2, 1990, 22, 201–228.

Klorman, Bat-Zion Eraqi. "Muslim Supporters of the Jewish Messiahs in Yemen." *Middle Eastern Studies,* 4, 1993, 29, 714–725.

Kraemer, Joel L., ed. *Perspectives on Maimonides. Philosophical and Historical Studies.* Oxford: Oxford University Press, 1991.

Lane Poole, Stanley. *A History of Egypt in the Middle Ages.* London: Routledge, 1968.

Lassner, Jacob. *Jews, Christians, and the Abode of Islam. Modern Scholarship, Medieval Realities.* Chicago: University of Chicago Press, 2012.

Lecker, Michael. *Muslims, Jews and Pagans. Studies on Early Islamic Medina.* Leiden: Brill, 1995.

Lecker, Michael. "Wâqîdî's account on the status of the Jews of Medina: A Study of a Combined Report." *Journal of Near Eastern Studies,* 1, 1995, 54, 15–32.

Lecker, Michael. "Zayd b. Thabit, a Jew with Two Sidelocks: Judaism and Literacy in Pre-Islamic Medina." *Journal of Near Eastern Studies,* 4, 1997, 56, 259-273.

Lecker, Michael. *The "Constitution of Medina." Muhhammad's First Legal Document.* Princeton: Darwin Press, 2004.

Lev, Yaacov. *State and Society in Fatimid Egypt.* Leiden: Brill, 1991.

Levy-Rubin, Milka. *Non-Muslims in the Early Islamic Empire. From Conquest to Coexistence.* Cambridge: Cambridge University Press, 2011.

Libson, Gideon. "Islamic Influence on Medieval Jewish Law? Sepher ha-'Arevut [Book of Surety'] of Rav Shmuel ben Hofni Gaon and its Relationship to Islamic Law." *Studia Islamica,* 1990, 73, 5–23.

Luzzatto, Philoxène. *Notice sur Abou-Iousouf Hasdai Ibn-Schaprout, médecin juif du dixième siècle, ministre des khalifes omeyyades d'Espagne Abd-al-Rahman III et el-Hakem et promoteur de la littérature juive en Europe.* Paris: Impr. de Mme Vve Dondey-Dupré, 1852.

Mandalà, Giuseppe. "La migrazione degli Ebrei del Garbum in Sicilia (1239)." *Materia giudaica,* 1–2, 2006, 11, 179–199.

Mann, Jacob. *The Jews in Egypt and in Palestine under the Fatimid Caliphs.* [Oxford: Oxford University Press, 1922]. New York: Ktav Publishing, 1970 (repr.).

Mann, Jacob. *Texts and Studies in Jewish History and Literature.* [New York: Hebrew Union College Press, 1931]. New York: Ktav Publishing, 1972 (repr. 2 vols.).

Mann, Vivan, et al., eds. *Convivencia. Jews, Muslims, and Christians in Medieval Spain.* New York: George Braziller, 1992.

Manzano Moreno, Eduardo. *Conquistadores, emires y califas. Los Omeyas y la formación de al-Andalus.* Madrid: Crítica, 2006.

Margariti, Roxani Eleni. *Aden & the Indian Ocean Trade. 150 Years in the Life of a Medieval Arabian Port.* Chapel Hill: University of North Carolina Press, 2007.

Marín, Manuela. *Individuo y sociedad en al-Andalus.* Madrid: Mapfre, 1992.

Marín, Manuela. *Al-Andalus y los andalusíes.* Barcelona: Icaria, 2000.

Mayer, Hans. "Latins, Muslims, and Greeks in the Latin Kingdom of Jerusalem." *History,* 1978, 63.

Meri, Joseph W. *The Cult of Saints among Muslims and Jews in Medieval Syria.* New York: Oxford University Press, 2002.

Molénat, Jean-Pierre. "Sur le rôle des Almohades dans la fin du christianisme local au Maghreb et en al-Andalus." *Al-Qantara,* 2, 1997, 18, 389–413.

Newby, Gordon D. *The Making of the Last Prophet.* Columbia: University of South Carolina Press, 1989.

Newby, Gordon D. *A History of the Jews of Arabia.* Columbia: University of South Carolina Press, 2009.

Nirenberg, David. *Communities of Violence. Persecution of Minorities in the Middle Ages.* Princeton: Princeton University Press, 1996.

Pahlitzsch, Johannes, and Korn, Lorenz, eds. *Governing the Holy City. The Interaction of Social Groups in Jerusalem between the Fatimid and the Ottoman Periods.* Wiesbaden: Reichert, 2004.

Prawer, Joshua. *The Latin Kingdom of Jerusalem. European Colonialism in the Middle Ages.* London: Weidenfeld and Nicolson, 1972.

Prawer, Joshua. *The History of the Jews in the Latin Kingdom of Jerusalem.* Oxford: Clarendon Press, 1988.

Reif, Stefan C. *A Jewish Archive from Old Cairo. The History of Cambridge University's Genizah Collection.* Richmond: Curzon, 2000.

Riley-Smith, Jonathan. "Some Lesser Officials in Latin Syria." *English Historical Review,* 1972, 87, 1–15.

Rubin, Uri. "The 'Constitution of Medina': Some Notes." *Studia Islamica,* 1985, 62.

Rubin, Uri. *Between Bible and Quran. The Children of Israel and the Islamic Self-Images.* Princeton: Darwin Press, 1999.

Rustow, Marina. *Heresy and the Politics of Community: The Jews of the Fatimid Caliphate.* Ithaca: Cornell University Press, 2008.

Saenz-Badillos, Ángel. "Les recherches sur les juifs d'al-Andalus dans les vingt-cinq dernières années." *Revue du Monde Musulman et de la Méditerranée,* 1992, 63–64, 63–79.

Samsó, Julio. *Las ciencias de los antiguos en al-Andalus.* Madrid: Mapfre, 1992, 80–82.

Scheindlin, Raymond P. "The Jews in Muslim Spain." In *The Legacy of Muslim Spain,* Jayyusi, Salma Khadra, ed. Leiden: Brill, 1992, 188–200.

Scheindlin, Raymond P. "Merchants and Intellectuals, Rabbis and Poets: Judeo-Arabic Culture in the Golden Age of Islam." In *Cultures of the Jews. A New History,* Biale, David, ed. New York: Schocken Books, 2002, 301–368.

Scheindlin, Raymond P. *The Song of the Distant Dove. Judah Halevi's Pilgrimage.* Oxford: Oxford University Press, 2008.

Schildgen, Brenda Deen. *Pagans, Tartars, Moslems, and Jews in Chaucer's Canterbury Tales.* Gainesville: University Press of Florida, 2001.

Schirmann, Hayim. *History of Hebrew Poetry in Muslim Spain* (in Hebrew). Jerusalem: Magnes Press, 1996.

Schirmann, Hayim. *Hebrew Poetry in Spain and Provence* (in Hebrew). Tel Aviv: Mossad Bialik, 1959–70, 2 vols.

Serjeant, R. B. "The Sunnah Jâmi'ah, Pacts with the Yathrib Jews, and the Tahrîm of Yathrib: Analysis and Translation of the Documents Comprises in the So-Called 'Constitution of Medina'" *Bulletin of the School of Oriental and African Studies,* 1978, 41, 1–42.

Simonsohn, Uriel I. *A Common Justice. The Legal Allegiance of Christians and Jews under Early Islam.* Philadelphia: University of Pennsylvania Press, 2011.

Torres Balbás, Leopoldo. "Mozarabías y juderías de las ciudades hispanomusulmanes." *Al-Andalus,* 1954, 19, 172–197.

Tritton, A. S. *The Caliphs and Their Non-Muslim Subjects. A Critical Study of the Covenant of Umar.* London: F. Cass, 1970 [1930].

Udovitch, Abraham L. "The Jews and Islam in the High Middle Ages: A Case of Muslim Views of Differences." In *Gli Ebrei nell'Alto Medioevo.* Spoletto: Centro italiano di studi sull'alto medioevo, 1980, 655–683.

Udovitch, Abraham L. *Partnership and Profit in Medieval Islam.* Princeton: Princeton University Press, 1981.

Wasserstein, David J. *The Rise and Fall of the Party-Kings. Politics and Society in Islamic Spain 1002–1086.* Princeton: Princeton University Press, 1985.

Wasserstein, David J. "The Muslim and the Golden Age of the Jews in al-Andalus." *Israel Oriental Studies,* 1997, 17, 179–196.

Wasserstein, David J. "Islamisation and the Conversion of the Jews." In *Islamic Conversions. Religious Identities in Mediterranean Islam,* García-Arenal, Mercedes, ed. Strasbourg: European Science Foundation, 2001.

Watt, W. Montgomery. *Muhammad at Medina.* Oxford: Clarendon Press, 1956.

Weinberger, Leon. *Jewish Prince in Moslem Spain. Selected Poems of Samuel Ibn Nagrela.* Tuscaloosa: University of Alabama Press, 1973.

Wensinck, Arent Jan. *Muhammad and the Jews of Medina.* Berlin: KS Verlag, 1982.

Yahalom, Joseph. *Yehuda Halevi. Poetry and Pilgrimage.* Jerusalem: Magnes Press, 2009.

Part II: The Modern World

Abitbol, Michel. *Les commerçants du Roi: Tujjār al-sultan. Une élite économique judéo-marocaine au XIXᵉ siècle: lettres du Makhzen, traduites et annotées.* Paris: Maisonneuve et Larose, 1998.

Adang, Camilla, and Schmidtke, Sabine, eds. *Contacts and Controversies between Muslims, Jews and Christians in the Ottoman Empire and Pre-modern Iran.* Würzburg: Ergon-Verlag, 2010.

al-Maghari, Mina. *Madinat Mogador-Essaouira. Dirasa tarikhiyya wa-athariyya.* Rabat: Dar Abi Ragrag li'l-Tibaʻa l'il-Nashr, 2006.

Alonso Acero, Beatriz. "Judíos y musulmanes en la España de Felipe II: Los presidios norteafricanos, paradigma de la sociedad de frontera." In *Felipe II (1527–1598). Europa y la monarquía católica,* Martínez Millán, José, ed. Madrid: Editorial Parteluz, 1998, vol. 2, 11–28.

Avitsur, Shmuel. "History of the Woolen Industry of Salonica (in Hebrew)." *Sefunot,* 1971–1978, 12.

Babinger, Franz. "Jaʻqûb Pascha, ein Leibarzt Mehmed's II." In *Rivista degli Studi Orientali,* 1951, 26, 87–113.

Bali, Rifat N. *Model Citizens of the State. The Jews of Turkey during the Multi-party Period.* Madison, NJ: Fairleigh Dickinson University Press, 2012.

Baron, Salo W. "The Jews and the Syrian Massacres of 1860." *Proceedings of the American Academy for Jewish Research (PAAJR),* 1932–1933, 4.

Baron, Salo W. "Late Middle Ages and Era of European Expansion (1200–1650)." In *A social and religious history of the Jews,* New York: Columbia University Press, 1983, 18, 163.

Beldiceanu, Nicoara. *Les actes des premiers sultans conservés dans les manuscrits turcs de la Bibliothèque Nationale à Paris. Actes de Mehmed II et de Bayezid II du ms. Fonds turc anc. 39.* Paris and The Hague: Mouton, 1960.

Berger, Haim. *Crossing Borders. Jews and Muslims in Ottoman Law, Economy and Society.* Istanbul: Isis Press, 2008.

Binswanger, Karl. *Untersuchungen zum Status der Nichtmuslime im Osmanischen Reich des 16. Jahrhunderts mit einer Neudefinition des Begriffes « Dhimma ».* Munich: Trofenik, 1977.

Capsali, Eliyahu. *Seder Elihahu Zuta.* Jerusalem: The Ben Zvi Institute of Yad Ben Zvi and the Hebrew University, 1975.

Cohen, Amnon, and Lewis, Bernard. *Population and Revenue in the Towns of Palestine in the Sixteenth Century.* Cohen, Amnon, and Lewis Bernard, eds. Princeton: Princeton University Press, 1978.

Cohen, Amnon. *Jewish Life under Islam. Jerusalem in the Sixteenth Century.* Cambridge, MA: Harvard University Press, 1984.

Cohen, Amnon. "Ritual Murder Accusations against the Jews during the Days of Suleiman the Magnificent." *Journal of Turkish Studies,* 1986, 10, 73–78.

Cohen, Amnon. *Economic Life in Ottoman Jerusalem.* Cambridge: Cambridge University Press, 1989.

Corcos, David. *Studies in the History of the Jews of Morocco.* Jerusalem: R. Mass, 1976.

Dankoff, Robert. *An Ottoman Mentality. The World of Evliya Celebi.* Leiden and Boston: Brill, 2004.

de Bunes Ibarra, Miguel Angel. "La vida en los presidios del Norte de África." In *Relaciones de la Península Ibérica con el Magreb. siglos XIII–XVI,* García-Arenal, Mercedes, and Viguera, María Jesús, eds. Madrid: Consejo Superior de Investigaciones Científicas, 1988, 561–590.

Emecen, Feridun M. *Unutulmuş bir cemaat. Manisa yahudileri.* Istanbul: Eren, 1997, 35–37.

Epstein, Mark Alan. *The Ottoman Jewish Communities and Their Role in the Fifteenth and Sixteenth Centuries.* Fribourg: Klaus Schwarz Verlag, 1980, 178–180.

Fischel, Walter J. *Jews in the Economic and Political Life of Mediaeval Islam.* London: Royal Asiatic Society Monographs, 1937, no. 22.

Frankel, Jonathan. *The Damascus Affair. "Ritual Murder," Politics, and the Jews in 1840.* Cambridge: Cambridge University Press, 1997.

Galanté, Avram. *Histoire des juifs de Turquie.* Istanbul: Isis, 1985–1986.

García-Arenal, Mercedes, and de Bunes Ibarra, Miguel Angel. *Los españoles y el norte de África. siglos XV–XVIII.* Madrid: Mapfre, 1992.

García-Arenal, Mercedes, and Wiegers, Gerard. *Entre Islam e Occidente. Vida de Samuel Pallache, judío de Fez.* Madrid: Siglo 21, 1999.

Georgeon, François, and Dumont, Paul, eds. *Vivre dans l'Empire ottoman. Sociabilités et relations intercommunautaires (XVIII*ᵉ*–XX*ᵉ* siècle).* Paris: L'Harmattan, 1997.

Goldberg, Harvey E. *Jewish Life in Muslim Libya. Rivals and Relatives.* Chicago: University of Chicago Press, 1990.

Goldberg, Harvey E., ed. *Sephardi and Middle Eastern Jewries. History and Culture in the Modern Era.* Bloomington: Indiana University Press, 1996.

Gottreich, Emily. *The Mellah of Marrakesh. Jewish and Muslim Space in Morocco's Red City.* Bloomington: Indiana University Press, 2007.

Grunebaum-Ballin, Paul. *Joseph Naci, duc de Naxos.* Paris and The Hague: Mouton, 1968.

Hacker, Joseph. "Ottoman Policy towards the Jews and Jewish Attitudes towards the Ottomans during the Fifteenth Century." In *Christians and Jews in the Ottoman Empire. The Central Lands,* Braude, Benjamin, and Lewis, Bernard, eds. New York: Holmes and Meier, vol.1, 1982, 117–125.

Hathaway, Jane. "The Grand Vizier and the False Messiah: The Sabbatai Sevi Controversy and the Ottoman Reform in Egypt." *Journal of the American Oriental Society,* 4, 1997, 117, 665–671.

Hathaway, Jane. "The Sabbatai Sevi Movement and the Expulsion of Yemen's Jews in 1679." *Ciépo,* 2004, 16, 285–303.

Haykel, Bernard A. *Revival and Reform in Islam. The Legacy of Muhammad al-Shawkânî.* Cambridge: Cambridge University Press, 2003.

Heyd, Uriel. "Moses Hamon, Chief Jewish Physician to Süleyman the Magnificent." *Oriens,* 1963, 16, 152–170.

Ḥibshî, ʿAbd Allah al-. "Wathîqa taʾrîkhiyya ʿann yahûd al-yaman." *Al-Bayân,* 1974, 98, 52–58.

Hirschberg, Haïm Zeev. *A History of the Jews in North Africa, from Ottoman Conquests to Present Times.* 2 vols. Leiden: Brill, 1974.

Ilbert, Robert. *Alexandria 1860–1960. The Brief Life of a Cosmopolitan Community.* Alexandria: Harpocrates Publishing, 1997.

Israel, Jonathan. "The Jews of Spanish Oran and Their Expulsion in 1669." *Mediterranean Historical Review,* 1994, 9–2, 235–255.

Jacobs, Martin. *Islamische Geschichte in jüdischen Chroniken. Hebräische Historiographie des 16. und 17. Jahrhunderts.* Tübingen: Mohr Siebeck, 2004.

Jacobs, Martin. "Exposed to all the Currents of the Mediterranean – A Sixteenth-Century Venetian Rabbi on Muslim History." *Association for Jewish Studies Review,* 2005, 29, 33–60.

Klein-Franke, Aviva. "The First Scholarly Missionary to South-Arabia as a Source for the History of the Jews of Yemen." *Peʿamim,* 1984, 18, 80–101.

Kobler, Franz. *A Treasury of Jewish Letters. From the Famous and the Humble.* Philadelphia: Jewish Publication Society, vol.1, 1953.

Kriegel, Maurice. "La prise d'une décision: L'expulsion des juifs d'Espagne en 1492." *Revue Historique,* 1978, 260, 49–90.

Kritovoulos, Michael. *History of Mehmed the Conqueror.* Trans. Riggs, Charles T. Westport, CT: Greenwood Publishing Group, 1954.

Kushner, David, ed. *Palestine in the Late Ottoman Period: Politics, Social and Economic Transformation.* Jerusalem, Iad Yzhak Ben-Zvi and Leiden: Brill, 1986.

Ladero Quesada, Miguel Angel. *España en 1492.* Madrid: Hernando, 1978.

Landau, Jacob. *Jews in Nineteenth-Century Egypt.* New York: New York University Press, 1969.

Laurens, Henry. *La Question de Palestine. L'invention de la Terre sainte (1799–1922).* Paris: Fayard, vol. 1, 1999.

Lellouch, Benjamin. "Les juifs dans le monde musulman du xvᵉ au milieu du xixᵉ siècle." In *Les Juifs dans l'histoire,* Germa, Antoine, Lellouch, Benjamin, Patlagean, Evelyne, eds. Seyssel: Champ Vallon, 2011, 289.

Leroy, Béatrice. *L'Expulsion des juifs d'Espagne.* Paris: Berg International, 1990.

Les Relations entre juifs et musulmans en Afrique du Nord. xixᵉ–xxᵉ siècles. Paris: CNRS Editions, coll. "Colloques internationaux du CNRS," 1980.

Levy, Avigdor. *The Sephardim in the Ottoman Empire.* Princeton: Darwin Press, 1992.

Levy, Avigdor. *The Jews of the Ottoman Empire.* Princeton: Darwin Press, 1994.

Levy, Avigdor. *Jews, Turks, Ottomans. A Shared History, Fifteenth Through the Twentieth Century.* Syracuse, NY: Syracuse University Press, 2002.

Lewis, Bernard. "The Privilege Granted by Mehmed II to His Physician." *Bulletin of the School of Oriental and African Studies,* 1952, 14/3, 550–563.

Lewis, Bernard. "The Pro-Islamic Jews." In *Islam in History. Ideas, Men and Events in the Middle East.* London: Alcove Press, 1973, 137.

Loeb, Laurence D. "Jewish-Muslim Socio-Political Relations in Twentieth Century South Yemen." In *Proceedings of the Second International Congress of Judeo-Yemenite Studies.* Princeton and Haifa: Institute of Semitic Studies, 1999, 71–99.

Malka, Eli S. *Jacob's Children in the Land of the Mahdi. Jews of Sudan.* Syracuse, NY: Syracuse University Press, 1997.

Mazower, Mark. *Salonica, City of Ghosts. Christians, Muslims, and Jews, 1430–1950.* New York: Alfred A. Knopf, 2005.

Meissner, Renate. *Die südjemenitischen Juden. Versuch einer Rekonstruktion ihrer traditio-nellen Kultur vor dem Exodus.* Frankfort-sur-le-Main: Peter Lang GmbH, 1999.

Meyuhas Ginio, Alisa, ed. *Jews, Christians, and Muslims in the Mediterranean World after 1492.* London: Frank Cass, 1992.

Moreen, Vera Basch. *Iranian Jewry's Hour of Peril and Heroism. A Study of Babai Ibn Lutf's Chronicle (1617–1662).* New York: Columbia University Press, 1987.

Moreen, Vera Basch. "The Kitab-i Anusi of Babai ibn Lutf (Seventeenth Century) and the Kitab-i Sar Guzasht of Babai ibn Farhad (Eighteenth Century): A Comparison of Two Judaeo-Persian Chronicles." In *Intellectual Studies on Islam. Essays Written in Honor of Martin B. Dickson.* Mazzaoui, Michel M., and Moreen, Vera Basch, eds. Salt Lake City: University of Utah Press, 1990.

Moreen, Vera Basch. *Iranian Jewry during the Afghan Invasion. The Kitab-i Sar-Guzasht-i Kashan of Babai b. Farhad.* Stuttgart: Steiner-Verlag. Wiesbaden, 1990.

Nahon, Gérard. *La Terre sainte au temps des kabbalistes. 1492–1592.* Paris: Albin Michel, 1997.

Nehama, Joseph. *Histoire des Israélites de Salonique.* Thessaloniki: Mohlo, vol.1, 1935.

Netzer, Amnon. "Redifot u-shemadot be-toldoth yehude Iran ba-me'ah ha-17." *Pe'amim,* 1980, 6, 33–56.

Newman, Andrew J. *Safavid Iran. Rebirth of a Persian Empire.* London: I. B. Tauris, 2006.

Patai, Raphael. *Jadid al-Islam. The Jewish "New Muslims" of Meshhed.* Detroit: Wayne State University Press, 1997.

Paudice, Aleida. *Between Several Worlds, the Life and Writings of Elia Capsali. The Historical Works of a 16th-Century Cretan Rabbi.* Munich: Meidenbauer, 2009.

Pires, Tomé. *The Suma Oriental of Tomé Pires. An Account of the East, from the Red Sea to Japan, Written in Malacca and India 1512–1515.* Trans. Cortes, Armando. London: The Hakluyt Society, 1944.

Pourjavady, Reza. "Muslim Polemics against Judaism and Christianity in 18th Century Iran: The Literary Sources of Aqa Muhammad 'Ali Bihbahani's (1144/1732–1216/1801) 'Radd-i shubuhat al-kuffar.'" *Studia Iranica,* 1, 2006, 35, 69–94.

Ratzaby, Yehuda. "Documents about the History of the Jews of Yemen." *Sefunot,* 1958, 2, 287–320.

Rodionov, Mikhail. "Silversmiths in Modern Ḥaḍramawt." *Erythræum,* 1997, 1.

Rodrigues da Silva Tavim, José Alberto. *Os judeus na expansão portuguesa em Marrocos durant o século XVI. Origens e actividades duma comunidade.* Braga: APPACDM Distrital de Braga, 1997.

Roth, Cecil. *The Sassoon Dynasty.* London: Robert Hale Publishing, 1941.

Roth, Cecil. *Dona Gracia of the House of Nasi.* Philadelphia: Jewish Publication Society, 1948.

Roth, Cecil. *The House of Nasi. The Duke of Naxos.* Philadelphia: Jewish Publication Society, 1948.

Roth, Cecil. *A History of the Marranos.* New York: Meridian Books, 1959.

Rozen, Minna. *A History of the Jewish Community in Istanbul. The Formative Years, 1453–1566.* Leiden and Boston: Brill, 2002, 12.

Sahillioğlu, Halil. "Yeniçeri çuhası ve II. Bayezid'in son yıllarında yeniçeri çuha muhasebesi." In Istanbul: *Güney-Doğu Avrupa Araştırmaları Dergisi,* 1974, 2–3, 415–467.

Savory, Roger. *Iran under the Safavids.* Cambridge: Cambridge University Press, 1980.

Schaub, Jean-Frédéric. *Les Juifs du roi d'Espagne. Oran 1509–1669.* Paris: Hachette Littératures, 1999.

Schiltberger, Johannes. *Captif des Tatars.* Trans. Rollet, Jacques. Toulouse: Anacharssis, 2008, 99.

Schmuelevitz, Aryeh. *The Jews of the Ottoman Empire in the Late Fifteenth and the Sixteenth Centuries. Administrative, Economic, Legal and Social Relations as Reflected in the Responsa.* Leiden: Brill, 1984, 31.

Scholem, Gershom. *Sabbatai Sevi. The Mystical Messiah, 1626–1676.* Princeton: Princeton University Press, 1976.

Schroeter, Daniel J. *Merchants of Essaouira. Urban Society and Imperialism in Southwestern Morocco, 1844–1886.* Cambridge: Cambridge University Press, 1988.

Schroeter, Daniel J. *The Sultan's Jew. Morocco and the Sephardi World.* Stanford: Stanford University Press, 2002.

Serjeant, R.B. "Materials for South Arabian History." *BSOAS,* 1950, 13.

Serjeant, R.B. "A Judeo-Arab House-Deed from Ḥabbān (with Notes on the Former Jewish Communities of the Wāḥidī Sultanate)." *JRAS,* 1953, 117–131.

Sharf, Andrew. *Jews and Other Minorities in Byzantium.* Bar-Ilan University Press, 1995.

Shaw, Stanford J. *The Jews of the Ottoman Empire and the Turkish Republic.* London: MacMillan, 1991.

Shûmân, Mohammed 'Alî. *Al-Yahûd fî Misr al-'Uthmaniyya hatâ al-Qarn al-tâsi' 'achir.* [*Les Juifs en Egypte de l'époque ottomane au XIXᵉ siècle*]. Cairo: Al-Hay'a al-Masriyya, 2000.

Starr, Josuah. *Jews in the Byzantine Empire, 641–1204.* Athens: 1939.

Taïeb, Jacques. *Être juif au Maghreb à la veille de la colonisation.* Paris: Albin Michel, coll. "Présences du judaïsme," 1998.

Taïeb, Jacques. *Sociétés juives au Maghreb moderne (1500–1900). Un monde en mouvement.* Paris: Maisonneuve et Larose, 2000.

Tobi, Yosef. "The Appeal of the Officers of Constantinople to R. Shalom 'Irāqī, the President of the Jews of Yemen in 1742." *Shalem,* 1974, 1.

Tobi, Yosef. "Reports on the Jews of Yemen in Arabic Writings of Yemen." *Pe'amim,* 1995, 64, 18–56.

Tobi, Yosef. *The Jews of Yemen. Studies in Their History and Culture.* Leiden: Brill, 1999.

Tsadik, Daniel. "Religious Disputations of Imami Shi'is against Judaism in the Late Eighteenth and Nineteenth Centuries." *Studia Iranica,* 1, 2005, 34, 95–134.

Tsur, Yaron. "Entre Tunis et Alger. Les élites juives vers 1800." In *De Tunis à Paris. Mélanges à la mémoire de Paul Sebag,* Nataf, Claude, ed. Paris: Editions de l'éclat, 2008.

Umarî, Ḥusayn ibn Abd Allâh. *The Yemen in the 18th and 19th Centuries. A Political and Intellectual History.* London: Ithaca Press, 1985.

Valensi, Lucette. *Fables de la Mémoire. La glorieuse bataille des Trois Rois (1578): Souvenirs d'une grande tuerie chez les chrétiens, les juifs & les musulmans.* Paris: Éditions Chandeigne, 2009.

Vatin, Nicolas, and Veinstein, Gilles. *Le Sérail ébranlé. Essai sur les morts, dépositions et avène-ments des sultans ottomans, XIVᵉ–XIXᵉ siècle.* Paris: Fayard, 2003.

Veinstein, Gilles. "Une communauté ottomane: Les juifs d'Avlonya (Valona) dans la deuxième moitié du xvıᵉ siècle." In *Gli Ebrei e Venezia, secoli XIV–XVIII,* Cozzi, Gaetano, ed. Milan: 1987, 781–828.

Veinstein, Gilles. "La draperie juive de Salonique. Une relecture critique de Joseph Nehama." In *The Jewish communities of Southeastern Europe from the Fifteenth Century to the End of World War II,* Hassiotis, Ioannes K., ed. Thessaloniki: Institute for Balkan Studies, 1997, 579–589.

Veinstein, Gilles. "L'administration ottomane et le problème des interprètes." In *Études sur les villes du Proche-Orient, XVIᵉ–XIXᵉ siècles. Hommage à André Raymond,* Marino, Brigitte, ed. Damas: Institut français d'études arabes de Damas, 2001, 65–79.

Veinstein, Gilles. "La prise de Constantinople et le destin des zimmî ottomans." *Archivum Ottomanicum,* 2005–2006, 23, 343–346.

Veinstein, Gilles. "The Ottoman Jews: Between Distorted Realities and Legal Fictions." *Mediterranean Historical Review,* 1, June 2010, 25, 54–57.

Wahid Qazvini, Muhammad Tahir. *'Abbasnama.* Arak: Chapkhana-yi Farvardi, 1951.

Wittmayer Baron, Salo. *A Social and Religious History of the Jews. Late Middle Ages and Era of European Expansion (1200–1650).* New York: Columbia University Press, 1983.

Yerasimos, Stéphane. "La communauté juive d'Istanbul à la fin du xvıᵉ siècle." *Turcica,* 1995, 27, 101–130.

Yeroushalmi, David. *The Jews of Iran in the Nineteenth Century.* Leiden, Boston: Brill, 2009.

Yerushalmi, Yosef Haim. *From Spanish Court to Italian Ghetto. Isaac Cardoso: A Study in Seventeenth-Century Marranism and Jewish Apologetics.* Seattle: University of Washington Press, 1982.

Zand, Michael. "Conversion of Jews to Islam in Central Asia in 18–19 Centuries and the Formation of the Chala (Central Asian Crypto Jews Group)." In *14th International Congress of International Association for the History of Religions, Abstracts.* Winnipeg: University of Manitoba, 1980, 94.

Part III: The Present

Abel, Félix-Marie. *Géographie de la Palestine.* Paris: Gabalda, 2 vols., 1967.

Abitbol, Michel, ed. *Judaïsme d'Afrique du nord aux XIXᵉ-XXᵉ siècles. Histoire, société et culture.* Jerusalem: Institut Ben-Zvi, 1980.

Abitbol, Michel. *The Jews of North Africa during the Second World War.* Trans. Tihanyi Zentelis, Catherine. [*Les Juifs d'Afrique du Nord sous Vichy.* Paris: Maisonneuve et Larose, 1981]. Detroit: Wayne State University Press, 1989.

Abû Hnaysh, Amal Ahmad 'Abd al-Latîf. "Mirrors of Self and the Other" (in Arabic). On the website www.Diwanalarab.com.

Abu-Lughod, Ibrahim. *The Transformation of Palestine. Essays on the Origin and Development of the Arab-Israeli Conflict.* Evanston, IL: Northwestern University Press, 1972.

Achcar, Gilbert. *The Arabs and the Holocaust. The Arab-Israeli War of Narratives.* [*Les Arabes et la Shoah. La guerre israélo-arabe des récits.* Paris: Sindbad, 2010]. New York: Metropolitan Books, 2010.

Adwan, Sami, and Bar-On, Dan, et al., eds. *Side by Side. Parallel Histories of Israel-Palestine.* Beit Jallah: Peace Research Institute in the Middle East, 2003.

Ageron, Charles-Robert. "Une émeute antijuive à Constantine, août 1934." *Revue de l'Occident musulman et de la Méditerranée,* 1973, 13–14, 23–40.

Ageron, Charles-Robert. "Les populations du Maghreb face à la propagande allemande." *Revue d'Histoire de la Deuxième Guerre mondiale,* 1979, 114, 1–39.

Allagui, Abdelkarim. "L'État colonial et les juifs de Tunisie de 1881 à 1914." *Archives juives,* 1, 1999, 32, 32–39.

Andrews, Fannie Fern. *The Holy Land under Mandate.* Boston: Mifflin, 1931.

Ansky, Michel. *Les Juifs d'Algérie du Décret Crémieux à la Libération.* Paris: Éditions du Centre, 1950.

Arendt, Hannah. "Zionism Revisited." *The Menorah Journal,* 1945, 33.

Ayoun, Richard. "Les Juifs d'Algérie pendant la guerre d'indépendance (1954–1962)." *Archives juives,* 1, 1996, 29, 15–29.

Baer, Gabriel. *Fellah and Townsman in the Middle East. Studies in Social History.* London: Frank Cass, 1982.

Baer, Marc David. *The Dönme. Jewish Converts, Muslim Revolutionaries, and Secular Turks.* Stanford: Stanford University Press, 2010.

Baldensperger, Philip J. "Religion of the Fellahin of Palestine: Answers to Questions." *Palestine Exploration Fund,* 1893, 25, 307–320.

Baldensperger, Philip J. "Birth, Mariage and Death among the Fellahin of Palestine." *Palestine Exploration Fund,* 1894, 26, 127–144.

Baldensperger, Philip J. "Orders of Holy Men in Palestine." *Palestine Exploration Fund,* 1894, 26, 22–38.

Baldensperger, Philip J. *The Immovable East. Studies of the People and Customs of Palestine.* London: Sir Isaac Pitman and Sons, 1913.

Bali, Rifat N. "The Image of the Jew in the Rhetoric of Political Islam in Turkey." *Cahiers d'études sur la Méditerranée orientale et le monde turco-iranien (CEMOTI),* 1999, 28, 95–108.

Bauml, Yair. *A Blue and White Shadow. The Israeli Establishment's Policy and Actions among Its Arab Citizens. The Formative Years 1958–1968.* Tel Aviv: Pardès, 2007.

Beinin, Joel. *The Dispersion of Egyptian Jewry. Culture, Politics and the Formation of a Modern Diaspora.* Berkeley: University of California Press, 1998.

Beit-Hallahmi, Benjamin. *Original Sins. Reflections on the History of Zionism and Israel.* London: Pluto Press, 1992.

Ben Yehouda, Eliezer. *Le Rêve traversé.* Paris: Éditions du scribe, 1988.

Ben-Rafael, Eliezer, and Peres, Yochanan. *Is Israel One? Religion, Nationalism and Multiculturalism Confounded.* Boston and Leiden: Brill, 2005.

Benvenisti, Meron. *Sacred Landscape. The Buried History of the Holy Land since 1948.* Berkeley: University of California Press, 2002.

Berdugo, Arlette. *Juives et juifs dans le Maroc contemporain. Images d'un devenir.* Paris: Geuthner, 2002.

Bessis, Juliette. *La Méditerranée fasciste. L'Italie mussolinienne et la Tunisie.* Paris: Karthala, 1981.

Bishara, Azmi. "The Arabs and the Holocaust: An Analysis of the Problematics of a Conjunction" (in Hebrew). *Zmanim,* summer 1995, 53, 54–71.

Boustany, Wadih F. *The Palestine Mandate, Invalid and Impracticable.* Beirut: Beirut American Press, 1936.

Brand, Laurie A. *Palestinians in the Arab World.* New York: Columbia University Press, 1988.

Breger, Marshall J. Reiter, Yitzhak, and Hammer, Leonard, eds. *Sacred Space in Israel and Palestine. Religion and Politics.* London: Routledge, 2012.

Brugger, Winfried, and Karayanni, Michael, eds. *Religion in the Public Sphere. A Comparative Analysis of German, Israeli, American and International Law.* Heidelberg: Springer and Max Planck Institute for Comparative Public Law and International Law, 2007.

Buber, Martin. *A Land of Two Peoples. Martin Buber on Jews and Arabs.* New York: Oxford University Press, 1983.

Budeiri, Musa. *The Palestine Communist Party.* London: Ithaca Press, 1979.

Bunzl, John, ed. *Islam, Judaism, and the Political Role of Religions in the Middle East.* Gainesville: University Press of Florida, 2004.

Calvert, John. "Radical Islamism and the Jews: The View of Sayyid Qutb." *Studies in Jewish Civilization,* 1996, 8, 213–229.

Campos, Michelle Ursula. *Ottoman Brothers. Muslims, Christians, and Jews in Early Twentieth-Century Palestine.* Stanford: Stanford University Press, 2011.

Canaan, Tawfiq. "Modern Palestinian Beliefs and Practices relating to God." *Journal of the Palestine Oriental Society,* 1, 1934, 14, 59–91.

Caplan, Neil. *Palestine Jewry and the Arab Question 1917–1925.* London: Frank Cass, 1978.

Caplan, Neil. *Futile Diplomacy. Arab-Zionist Negotiations and the End of the Mandate.* London: Frank Cass, vol. 2, 1986.

Carpi, Daniel. "The Mufti of Jerusalem, Amin el-Husseini, and His Diplomatic Activity during World War II (October 1941–July 1943)." *Studies on Zionism,* spring 1983, 7.

Charbit, Denis. *Le Sionisme. Textes fondamentaux.* Paris: Albin Michel, 1998.

Chérif, Mustapha. *Islam and the West. A Conversation with Jacques Derrida.* [*Islam et Occident. Conversation avec Jacques Derrida.* Paris and Algiers: Odile Jacob/Barzakh, 2006]. Chicago: University of Chicago Press, 2008.

Chikhi, Beïda. *Maghreb en textes. Écriture, histoire, savoirs et symbolique.* Paris: L'Harmattan, 1996.

Cohen, Hayyim J. *The Jews of the Middle East, 1860–1972.* Jerusalem: Israel University Press, 1973.

Cohen-Hadria, Elie. *Du Protectorat français à l'indépendance tunisienne. Souvenirs d'un témoin socialiste.* Nice: Centre de la Méditerranée moderne et contemporaine, 1976.

Cole, Joshua. "Antisémitisme et situation coloniale pendant l'entre-deux guerres en Algérie." *Vingtième siècle,* 2010, 108, 3–23.

Darwich, Mahmoud. *La terre nous est étroite et autres poèmes.* Trans. Sanbar, Elias. Paris: Poésie-Gallimard, 2000.

Darwish, Mahmoud. *La Palestine comme métaphore.* Arles: Sindbad/Actes Sud, 1997.

De Bar, Luc Henri. *Les Communautés Confessionnelles du Liban.* Paris: Editions Recherche sur les Civilisations, 1983.

Debono, Emmanuel. "Le rapprochement judéo-musulman en Afrique du Nord sous le Front populaire: Succès et limites." *Archives juives,* 2, 2012, 45, 89–106.

Debrauwere-Miller, Nathalie, eds. *The Israeli-Palestinian Conflict in the Francophone World.* New York: Routledge, 2009.

Derrida, Jacques. *Le monolinguisme de l'autre, ou la prothèse d'origine.* Paris: Galilée, 1996.

Dieckhoff, Alain. *Les espaces d'Israël.* Paris: Fondation pour les études de Défense nationale, 1987.

Dieckhoff, Alain. *Israéliens et Palestiniens. L'épreuve de la paix.* Paris: Aubier, 1993.

Doumani, Beshara. *Rediscovering Palestine: Merchants and Peasants in Jabal Nablus 1700–1900.* Berkeley: University of California Press, 1995.

Dugas, Guy. *La littérature judéo-maghrébine d'expression française. entre Djéha et Cagayous.* [Paris: L'Harmattan, 1988]. Philadelphia: Celfan Edition Monographs, 1990.

Dugas, Guy. *Bibliographie critique de la littérature judéo-maghrébine d'expression française, 1896–1990.* Paris: L'Harmattan, 1992.

Dugas, Guy. "Ni paradis perdu, ni terre promise. Le juif dans le regard du musulman, le musulman dans le regard du juif à travers leurs littératures de langue française." In *Juifs et musulmans en Tunisie, fraternité et déchirements. Actes du colloque international de Paris, Sorbonne, 22–25 mars 1999,* Fellous, Sonia, ed. Paris: Somogy, 2003.

Dumper, Michael. *Islam and Israel. Muslim Religious Endowments and the Jewish State.* Washington, DC: Institute for Palestine Studies, 1994.

Eisen, Robert. "Muslims and Jews: Common Ground." *The Washington Post,* 9 May 2006.

Eisenman, Robert H. *Islamic Law in Palestine and Israel. A History of the Survival of Tanzimat and Shari'a in the British Mandate and the Jewish State.* Leiden: Brill, 1978.

El Maleh, Edmond. "Juifs marocains et Marocains juifs." *Les Temps Modernes,* October 1977, 375ff.

El Maleh, Edmond. "Au seuil de l'interdit: Interrogations." *Revue d'Études Palestiniennes,* winter 1982, 2.

El Maleh, Edmond. "Le visage d'une négation." *Revue d'Études Palestiniennes,* autumn 1983, 5.

El Maleh, Edmond. *Mille ans, un jour.* Paris: La Pensée Sauvage, 1986.

Eldridge, Claire. "Remembering the Other: Postcolonial Perspectives on Relationships between Jews and Muslims in French Algeria." *Journal of Modern Jewish Studies,* 3, 2012, 11, 299–317.

Elmaleh, Abraham, ed. *In Memoriam. Hommage à Joseph David Farhi.* Jerusalem: La Famille Farhi, 1948.

El-Taji, Maha T. *Arab Local Authorities in Israel. Hamulas, Nationalism and Dilemmas of Social Change.* Seattle: University of Washington, PhD dissertation, 2008.

Fellous, Sonia, ed. *Juifs et musulmans en Tunisie. Fraternité et déchirements.* Paris: Somogy, 2003.

Ferre, André. "Protégés ou citoyens?" *Islamochristiana,* 1996, 22, 79–117.

Filiu, Jean-Pierre. *Apocalypse in Islam.* [*L'Apocalypse dans l'Islam.* Paris: Fayard, 2008]. Berkeley: University of California Press, 2012.

Fischbach, Michael R. *Records of Dispossession. Palestinian Refugees' Property and the Arab-Israeli Conflict.* New York: Columbia University Press, 2003.

Flapan, Simha. *The Birth of Israel. Myths and Realities.* New York: Pantheon Books, 1987.

Gershman, Norman H. *Besa. Muslims Who Saved Jews in World War II.* Syracuse, NY: Syracuse University Press, 2008.

Ghandour, Zeina. "Religious Law in a Secular State: The Jurisdiction of the Shari'a Courts of Palestine and Israel." *Arab Law Quarterly,* 1990, 25, 30–31.

Gilbert, Martin. *Jerusalem in the Twentieth Century.* London: Pimlico, 1996.

Gordon, Daniel. "Juifs et musulmans à Belleville (Paris 20e) entre tolérance et conflit." In *Cahiers de la Méditerranée,* 2003, 67.

Goren, Tamir. "Pourquoi les habitants arabes ont-il quitté Haïfa? Retour sur une controverse." *Cathedra,* 1996, 80, 175–208.

Govers, Andrew, and Walker, Tony. *Behind the Myth. Yasser Arafat and the Palestinian Revolution.* London: W. H. Allen, 1990.

Graham-Brown, Sarah. *Palestinians and Their Society, 1880–1946. A Photographic Essay.* London: Quartet Books, 1980.

Granott, Abraham. *The Land System in Palestine. History and Structure.* London: Eyre and Spottiswoode, 1952.

Habîb, Najma Khalîl. *Al-numûdhaj al-insânî fî adab Ghassân Kanafânî.* Beirut: Bisân/Mu'assasat Ghassân Kanafânî al-thaqâfiyya, 1999.

Habibi, Emile. *Al-Waqâ'i' al-gharîba fi-ikhtifâ' Sa'îd abî l-Nahs al-Mutasha'il.* Beirut: dâr Ibn Haldûn, 1974.

Hadawi, Sami. *Palestinian Rights and Losses in 1948.* London: Saqi Books, 1988.

Haddad, Heskel. *Jews of Arab and Islamic Countries. History, Problems, Solutions.* New York: Shengold Publishers, 1984.

Halbreich-Euvrard, Janine, ed. *Israéliens-Palestiniens. Que peut le Cinéma?* Paris: Editions Michalon, 2005.

Halevi, Ilan. *Question juive. La tribu, la loi, l'espace.* Paris: Éditions de Minuit, 1981.

Halperin-Kaddari, Ruth. "Women, Religion and Multiculturalism in Israel." *UCLA Journal of International Law and Foreign Affairs,* 2000, 5, 339–343.

Halpern, Ben. *The Idea of the Jewish State.* Cambridge, MA: Harvard University Press, 1969.

Hamli, Mohsen. "The 1948 Controversy over the Accession of Jews to the Caïdal Corps in Tunisia." *Journal of North African Studies,* 4, 2006, 11, 435–445.

Harkabi, Yehoshafat. *The Arabs' Position in Their Conflict with Israel.* New York: Hart Publishing Company, 1972.

Hassan, Kadhim Jihad. *Le Roman arabe (1834–2004). Bilan critique.* Arles: Sindbad/Actes Sud, 2006.

Hasson, Shlomo, and Karayanni, Michael, eds. *Barriers on the Road to Equality.* Jerusalem: The Floersheimer Institute for Policy Studies, 2006.

Heacock, Roger, ed. *Temps et espaces en Palestine.* Beirut: Institut français du Proche-Orient, 2008.

Herf, Jeffrey. *Nazi Propaganda for the Arab World.* New Haven and London: Yale University Press, 2009.

Hertzberg, Arthur, ed. *The Zionist Idea. A Historical Analysis and Reader.* New York: Atheneum, 1969.

Hirszowicz, Lukasz. *The Third Reich and the Arab East.* Toronto: Toronto University Press, 1966.

Hollander, Isaac. *Jews and Muslims in Lower Yemen. A Study in Protection and Restraint, 1918–1949.* Leiden: Brill, 2005.

Hourani, Albert. *The Emergence of the Modern Middle East.* New York: Macmillan, 1981.

Huneidi, Sahar. *A Broken Trust: Herbert Samuel, Zionism and the Palestinians 1920–1925.* London and New York: I.B. Tauris, 2001.

Ingrams, Doreen. *Palestine Papers 1917–1922. Seeds of Conflict.* London: John Murray, 1972.

Iyad, Abou. *Palestinien sans patrie. Entretiens avec Eric Rouleau.* Paris: Fayolle, 1978.

Jacobson, Abigail. *From Empire to Empire. Jerusalem between Ottoman and British Rule.* Syracuse, NY: Syracuse University Press, 2011.

Kanafani, Ghassan. *Des hommes dans le soleil.* Trans. Seurat, Michel. [*Rijâl taht al-shams*]. Paris: Sindbad, 1977.

Kanafani, Ghassan. "Returning to Haifa." In *Palestine's Children. Returning to Haifa and Other Stories.* Trans. Harlow, Barbara, and Riley, Karen E. Boulder, CO: Lynne Rienner Publishers, 2000.

Karayanni, Michael. "Living in a Group of One's Own: Normative Implications Related to the Private Nature of the Religious Accommodations for the Palestinian-Arab Minority in Israel." *UCLA Journal of International Law and Foreign Affairs,* 2007, 12.

Kassir, Samir, and Mardam-Bey, Farouk. *Itinéraires de Paris à Jerusalem, la France et le conflit israélo-arabe.* Washington, Lyon: Institut des études palestiniennes, 2 vols., 1992.

Kattan, Naïm. *Farewell, Babylon. Coming of Age in Jewish Baghdad.* Trans. Fischman, Sheila. [*Adieu Babylone. Mémoires d'un juif d'Irak.* Paris: Albin Michel, 2003]. Vancouver: Raincoast Books, 2005.

Katz, Ethan. "Did the Paris Mosque Save Jews? A Mystery and Its Memory." *Jewish Quarterly Review,* 2, 2012, 102, 256–287.

Kazdaghli, Habib. "L'engagement des juifs tunisiens dans l'anticolonialisme 1919–1956." In *Histoire communautaire, histoire plurielle. La communauté juive de Tunisie.* Tunis: Centre de publication universitaire, 1999, 217–237.

Kazdaghli, Habib. "Bourguiba et la communauté juive de Tunisie au lendemain de l'indé-pendance." In *Bourguiba, les Bourguibiens et la construction de l'État national,* Temimi, Abdeljalil, ed. Zaghouan: Publications de la Fondation Temimi pour la Recherche scientifique et l'information, 2001, 55.

Kazzaz, Nissim. *The Jews of Iraq in the Twentieth Century* (in Hebrew). Jerusalem: Ben-Zvi Institut, 1991.

Kenbib, Mohammed. *Juifs et musulmans au Maroc, 1859–1948. Contribution à l'étude des relations intercommunautaires en terre d'Islam.* Rabat: Université Mohammed-V, 1994.

Kenbib, Mohammed. "Le régime de Vichy, la France Libre et les nationalistes marocains." Rabat: *Majallat Kuliyat al-Adab,* 1995, 133–148.

Kenbib, Mohammed. "Le Roi Mohammed V dans la mémoire collective des Juifs marocains." Rabat: *Al Manahil,* 2005, special issue.

Kepel, Gilles, ed. *Al Qaeda in Its Own Words.* Trans. Ghazaleh, Pascale. [*Al-Qaida dans le texte.* Paris: PUF, 2008]. Cambridge, MA: The Belknap Press, 2008.

Khadra Jayyusi, Salmâ. "Andalusi Poetry: the Golden Period." In *The Legacy of Muslim Spain,* Khadra Jayyusi, Salmâ, ed. Leiden: Brill, 1992.

Khalidi, Walid. "The Fall of Haifa." *Middle East Forum,* 10, December 1959, 34.

Khalidi, Walid. "Why Did the Palestinians Leave?" *Middle East Forum,* 6, July 1959, 34.

Khalidi, Walid. "Plan Dalet: The Zionist Blueprint for the Conquest of Palestine." *Middle East Forum,* 9, November 1961, 37, 22–28.

Khalidi, Walid. *From Haven to Conquest.* Beriut: Institut des études palestiniennes, 1971.

Khalidi, Walid. *All That Remains. The Palestinian Villages Occupied and Depopulated by Israel in 1948.* Washington, DC: Institut des études palestiniennes, 1992.

Khatibi, Abdelkebir. *Vomito blanco. Le sionisme et la conscience malheureuse.* Paris: 10/18, 1974.

Khatibi, Abdelkebir. *Le même livre. Correspondance avec Jacques Hassoun.* Paris: Éditions de l'Éclat, 1985.

Kimmerling, Baruch. *Zionism and Territory. The Socio-territorial Dimensions of Zionist Politics.* Berkeley: Institute of International Studies, University of California, 1983.

Klieman, Aaron S. *Foundations of British Policy in the Arab World. The Cairo Conference of 1921.* Baltimore: The Johns Hopkins University Press, 1970.

Kramer, Gudrun. *The Jews in Modern Egypt, 1914–1952.* Seattle: University of Washington Press, 1989, 167–221.

Kretzmer, David. *The Legal Status of the Arabs in Israel.* Boulder, CO: Westview Press, 1990.

Kupferschmidt, Uri M. *The Supreme Muslim Council. Islam under the British Mandate for Palestine.* Leiden: Brill, 1987.

Laâb, Abdellatif i, ed. *La Poésie palestinienne contemporaine (anthologie). Choix et traduction.* Paris: Éditions Messidor, 1990.

Lafon, Jacques. *Jerusalem.* Paris: Editions Monchrestien, 1998.

Landau, Philippe E. "Les Juifs de Tunisie et la grande guerre." *Archives juives,* 1, first quarter 1999, 32, 40–52.

Laskier, Michael M. *The Jews of Egypt, 1920–1970. In the Midst of Zionism, Anti-Semitism and the Middle East Conflict.* New York: New York University Press, 1992, 73–297.

Laskier, Michael M. *North African Jewry in the Twentieth Century. The Jews of Morocco, Tunisia, and Algeria.* New York and London: New York University Press, 1994, 84–253.

Laskier, Michael M. *Israel and the Maghreb. From Statehood to Oslo.* Gainesville: University Press of Florida, 2004.

Laurens, Henry. *La Question de Palestine. vol. 2: Une mission sacrée de civilisation (1922–1947).* Paris: Fayard, 2002.

Layish, Aharon. *Women and Islamic Law in a Non-Muslim State. A Study Based on Decisions of the Shari'a Courts in Israel.* New York: John Wiley and Sons, 1975.

Lesch, Ann Mosely. *Arab Politics in Palestine, 1917–1939. The Frustration of a Nationalist Movement.* Ithaca and London: Cornell University Press, 1979.

Levallois, Agnès, and Pommier, Sophie. *Jerusalem, de la division au partage?* Paris: Éditions Michalon, 1995.

Leveau, Rémy, and Schnapper, Dominique. *Religion et Politique. Juifs et Musulmans Maghrebins en France.* Paris: Association française de science politique, Centre d'études et de recherches internationales, 1987.

Lewis, Bernard. *Semites and Anti-Semites. An Inquiry into Conflict and Prejudice.* New York: W. W. Norton and Company, 1999.

Liebman, Charles S. *Religious and Secular. Conflict and Accommodation between Jews in Israel.* New York: Avi Chai, 1990.

Litvak, Meir, and Webman, Esther. *From Empathy to Denial. Arab Responses to the Holocaust.* London and New York: Hurst Publishing Co. and Columbia University Press, 2009.

Livingstone, John W. "Ali Bey al-Kabir and the Jews." *Middle Western Studies,* 2, 1971, 7.

Lockman, Zachary. *Comrades and Enemies. Arab and Jewish Workers in Palestine, 1906–1948.* Berkeley: University of California Press, 1979.

Louër, Laurence. "L'intifada d'Al-Aqsa: Quelle place pour les citoyens arabes dans l'état juif ?" *Cultures et Conflits,* 2001, 41, 101–119.

Louër, Laurence. *To Be an Arab in Israel.* New York: Columbia University Press, 2003.

Louër, Laurence. "Les Arabes israéliens: un enjeu pour Israël et le futur État palestinien." *Moyen Orient,* 2010, 5.

Lustick, Ian. *Arabs in the Jewish State. Israel's Control of a National Minority.* Austin: University of Texas Press, 1980.

Ma'oz, Moshe. *Ottoman Reform in Syria and Palestine, 1840–1861. The Impact of the Tanzimat on Politics and Society.* Oxford: Clarendon Press, 1968.

Ma'oz, Moshe, ed. *Studies on Palestine during the Ottoman Period.* Jerusalem: Magnes Press, 1975.

Ma'oz, Moshe. "Muslims, Jews and the Israeli–Palestinian Conflict in Israel." *Journal of Foreign Affairs,* 3, 2009, 3.

Ma'oz, Moshe, ed. *Muslim Attitudes to Jews and Israel. The Ambivalence of Rejection, Antagonism, Tolerance and Cooperation.* Brighton and Portland: Sussex Academic Press, 2010.

Mandel, Maud S. *Muslims and Jews in France. A Genealogy of Conflict.* Princeton: Princeton University Press, forthcoming.

Mandel, Neville J. *The Arabs and Zionism before World War I.* Berkeley: University of California Press, 1976.

Mardam-Bey, Farouk, and Sanbar, Elias. *Jerusalem, le sacré et le politique.* Arles: Sindbad/Actes Sud, 2000.

Mardam-Bey, Farouk, and Sanbar, Elias. *Le Droit au retour. Le problème des réfugiés palestiniens.* Arles: Sindbad/Actes Sud, 2002.

Mazie, Steven V. *Israel's Higher Law. Religion and Liberal Democracy in the Jewish State.* Lanham, MD: Lexington Books, 2006.

Méïr, Esther. "The Bagdad Pogrom–June 1–2, 1941." *Pé'amim,* 1981, 8, 21–37.

Melka, Robert Lewis. *The Axis and the Arab Middle East, 1930–1945.* Ann Arbor: University of Michigan, PhD dissertation, 1966.

Memmi, Albert. *The Liberation of the Jew.* Trans. Hyun, Judy. [*La libération du Juif.* Paris: Payot, 1966]. New York: Orion Press, 1966.

Memmi, Albert. *Juifs et Arabes.* Paris: Gallimard, 1974.

Memmi, Albert. *The Colonizer and the Colonized.* [*Portrait du colonisé précédé du Portrait du colonisateur.* Paris: Buchet-Chastel, 1957]. London: Souvenir Press, 1974.

Memmi, Albert. *The Pillar of Salt.* [*La Statue de sel.* Paris: Gallimard, 1966]. Boston: Beacon Press, 1992.

Memmi, Albert. *Le Juif et l'autre.* Étrépilly: Christian de Bartillat, 1995.

Memmi, Albert. *Portrait of a Jew.* Charleston: Forgotten Books, 2012.

Menahem, Nahum. *Syrian and Lebanese Jewry at the Crossfire of Arab Nationalism and the Zionist Movement.* Jerusalem: Hebrew University Press, 1990.

Menashri, David. "The Jews of Iran: Between the Shah and Khomeini." In *Anti-Semitism in Times of Crisis,* Gilman, Sander, and Katz, Steven, eds. New York: New York University Press, 1991.

Montefiore, Simon Sebag. *Jerusalem. The Biography.* New York: Alfred A. Knopf, 2011.

Morris, Benny. *The Birth of the Palestinian Refugee Problem, 1947–1949.* Cambridge: Cambridge University Press, 1987.

Morris, Benny. *Israel's Border Wars 1949–1956. Arab Infiltration, Israeli Retaliation, and the Countdown to the Suez War.* Oxford: Clarendon Press, 1993.

Morris, Benny. *Righteous Victims. A History of the Zionist-Arab Conflict, 1881–2001.* New York: Vintage Books, 2001.

Moubarac, Youakim. "La question de Jerusalem." *Revue d'études palestiniennes,* 1982, 4, 3–55.

Müller, Dietmar. "Orientalism and Nation: Jews and Muslims as Alterity in Southeastern Europe in the Age of Nation-States, 1878–1941." *East Central Europe,* 1, 2009, 36, 63–99.

Nafi, Basheer M. *Arabism, Islamism and the Palestine Question 1908–1941. A Political History.* London: Ithaca Press, 1998.

Nataf, Claude. "La communauté juive de Tunisie sous le protectorat français." *Archives juives,* 1, first quarter 1999, 32, 4–19.

Neher-Bernheim, Renée. *La Déclaration Balfour.* Paris: Julliard, coll. "Archives," 1969.

Nicault, Catherine. *Une Histoire de Jerusalem (1850–1967).* Paris: CNRS Éditions, 2008.

Parfitt, Tudor, and Egorova, Yulia, eds. *Jews, Muslims, and Mass Media. Mediating the 'Other.'* New York: RoutledgeCruzon, 2004.

Patai, Raphael. *The Vanished Worlds of Jewry.* London: Weidenfeld and Nicolson, 1981.

Picaudou, Nadine. *La décennie qui ébranla le Moyen-Orient 1914–1923.* Brussels: Complexe, 1992.

Porath, Yehoshua. *The Emergence of the Palestinian Arab National Movement 1918–1929.* London: Frank Cass, 1977.

Reiter, Yitzhak. *Islamic Institutions in Jerusalem. Palestinian Muslim Organizations under Jordanian and Israeli Rule.* The Hague: Kluwer Law International, 1997.

Rodinson, Maxime. *Israël et le refus arabe. 75 ans d'histoire.* Paris: Editions du Seuil, 1968.

Rose, Norman Anthony. *The Gentile Zionists. Anglo-Zionist Diplomacy, 1929–1939.* London: Frank Cass, 1973.

Roumani, Judith. "Responses to North African Independence in the novels of Dib, Memmi and Koskas: The End of Muslim-Jewish Symbiosis?" *Middle East Review,* 2, 1987, 20, 33–40.

Rubin Peled, Alisa. *Debating Islam in the Jewish State. The Development of Policy toward Islamic Institutions in Israel.* Albany: State University of New York Press, 2001.

Saadoun, Haïm, ed. *Ouvertement et en secret. Les grandes vagues d'immigration des Juifs issus des pays musulmans 1948–1967.* Jerusalem: Institut Ben-Zvi, 1999.

Said, Edward W., and Hitchens, Christopher. *Blaming the Victims. Spurious Scholarship and the Palestinian Question.* London: Verso, 1988.

Said, Edward W. *The Question of Palestine.* London: Vintage, 1988.

Sanbar, Elias. *Figures du Palestinien. Identité des origines, identité de devenir.* Paris: Gallimard, 2004.

Saquer-Sabin, Françoise. *Le Personnage de l'Arabe palestinien dans la littérature hébraïque du XXᵉ siècle.* Paris: CNRS Éditions, 2002.

Satloff, Robert. *Among the Righteous. Lost Stories from the Holocaust's Long Reach into Arab Lands.* New York: PublicAffairs, 2006.

Scham, Paul, Salem, Walid, and Pogrund, Benjamin, eds. *Shared Histories. A Palestinian-Israeli Dialogue.* Jerusalem: Left Coast Press, 2006.

Schechtman, Joseph. *On Wings of Eagles. The Plight, Exodus, and Homecoming of Oriental Jewry.* New York: Thomas Joseloff, 1961.

Schulze, Kirsten E. *The Jews of Lebanon. Between Coexistence and Conflict.* Brighton: Sussex Academic Press, 2009.

Schulze, Kirsten E. "Point of Depature: The 1967 War and the Jews of Lebanon." *Israel Affairs,* 4, 2009, 15, 335–354.

Sebag, Paul. "Les juifs de Tunisie au xixe siècle d'après J.J. Benjamin II." *Les Cahiers de Tunisie,* 1959, 28, 489–510.

Sebag, Paul. *Histoire de juifs de Tunisie des origines à nos jours.* Paris: l'Harmattan, 1991.

Segev, Tom. *1949, The First Israelis.* London and New York: The Free Press, 1986.

Shepperd, Naomi. *The Zealous Intruders. The Western Rediscovery of Palestine.* San Francisco: Harper and Row, 1987.

Signoles, Aude. *Le Hamas au pouvoir. Et après?* Paris: Milan, 2006.

Simon, Patrick, and Tapia, Claude. *Le Belleville des Juifs tunisiens.* Paris: Éditions Autrement, 1998.

Sivan, Emmanuel. "Islamic Fundamentalism, Antisemitism, and Anti-Zionism." In *Anti-Zionism and Antisemitism in the Contemporary World.* Wistrich, Robert S., ed. Houndsmill and Basingstoke: Macmillan in association with the Institute of Jewish Affairs, 1990, 74–84.

Smooha, Sammy. "Arab-Jewish Relations in Israel: Alienation and Rapprochement." *Peaceworks,* 2010, 67.

Sprinzak, Ehud. *The Ascendance of Israel's Radical Right.* New York: Oxford University Press, 1991.

Stillman, Norman A. *Jews of Arab Lands in Modern Times.* Philadelphia: Jewish Publication Society, 1994.

Stora, Benjamin. *Nationalistes algériens et révolutionnaires français au temps du front populaire.* Paris: L'Harmattan, 1987.

Stora, Benjamin. *Ils venaient d'Algérie. L'immigration algérienne en France (1912–1992).* Paris: Fayard, 1992.

Stora, Benjamin. *Les Trois Exils. Juifs d'Algérie.* Paris: Stock, 2006.

Taggar, Yehuda. "The Farhud in the Arabic of Iraqi Writers and Statesmen." *Pé'amim,* 1981, 8, 38–45.

Taieb, Jacques. "L'échec de l'intégration des juifs de Tunisie." In *La fin du judaïsme en terres d'islam,* Trigano, Shmuel, ed. Paris: Denoël, 2009, 359–378.

Taieb, Jacques. "1881, année zéro." *Archives juives,* 1, first quarter 1999, 32, 20–31.

Tessler, Mark. *A History of the Israeli-Palestinian Conflict.* Bloomington: Indiana University Press, 2009.

Udovitch, Abraham L., and Valensi, Lucette. "Être juif à Djerba." *Communauté juives des marges sahariennes du Maghreb,* 1982, 199–225.

Udovitch, Abraham L., and Valensi, Lucette. *The Last Arab Jews. The Communities of Jerba, Tunisia.* London: Harwood Academic, 1984.

Vidal-Naquet, Pierre. *The Jews. History, Memory, and the Present.* Trans. Curtis, Daniel Ames. [*Les Juifs, la mémoire et le présent.* Paris: La Découverte. 1995]. New York: Columbia University Press, 1996.

Wasserstein, Bernard. *The British in Palestine. The Mandatory Government and the Arab-Jewish Conflict 1917–1929.* Oxford: Blackwell, 1991.

Waxman, Dov, and Peleg, Ilan. *Israel's Palestinians. The Conflict Within.* New York: Cambridge University Press, 2011.

Weinstock, Nathan. *Une si longue présence. Comment le monde arabe a perdu ses juifs, 1947–1967.* Paris: Plon, 2008.

Yasîn, Râʾida. "The Image of the Jew in Palestinian Literature in the Occupied Territories (in Arabic). Article published on www.diwanalarab.com.

Zytnicki, Colette. "Les juifs et la Tunisie: Le temps de la séparation (1945–1967)." *Archives juives,* 1, first quarter 1999, 32, 77–89.

Part IV: Transversalities

Abitbol, Michel. *Juifs maghrébins et commerce transsaharien du VIIIᵉ au XVᵉ siècle. 2000 ans d'histoire africaine, le sol, la parole et l'écrit, mélanges en hommage à Raymond Mauny.* Paris: Société française d'Histoire d'outre-mer, 1981.

Abitbol, Michel, ed. *Communautés juives des marges sahariennes du Maghreb.* Jerusalem: Institut Ben Zvi, 1982.

Abitbol, Michel, ed. *Relations judéo-musulmanes au Maroc. Perceptions et réalités.* Paris: Stavit Editions, 1999.

Abu Khadra, Zayn al-ʾAbidin. *Egypt in Contemporary Hebrew Literature* (in Arabic). Cairo: Dâr al-thaqâfah al-nashr, 1988.

Abu Khadra, Zayn alʾAbidin. "The Influence of Arabic Rhetoric on Hebrew Literature" (in Arabic). *Journal de l'Université du Roi-Saoud,* 1993.

Abu Khadra, Zayn alʾAbidin. *A Generation in Quest of Identity: A Study of Being Israeli* (in Arabic). Oriental Studies Center, 1997.

Adamson, Peter. *Al-Kindi.* Oxford: Oxford University Press, 2007.

Adang, Camilla. "A Jewish Reply to Ibn Hazm: Solomon b. Adret's Polemic against Islam." In *Judíos y musulmanes en al-Andalus y el Magreb,* Madrid: Casa de Velázquez, 2002.

Adang, Camilla, ed. *A Common Rationality: Mutazilism in Islam and Judaism.* Wurzburg: Ergon Verlag in Kommission, 2007.

Adang, Camille, Fiero Belo, Maria Isabel, and Schmidtke, Sabine, eds. *Ibn Hazm of Cordoba. The Life and Works of a Controversial Thinker.* Leiden: Brill, 2013.

Adelman, Howard Ernest Tzvi. "A Rabbi Reads the Qur'an in the Venetian Ghetto." *Jewish History,* 2012, 26, 125–137.

Albera, Diogini, and Couroucli, Maria, ed. *Sharing Sacred Spaces in the Mediterranean. Christians, Muslims, and Jews at Shrines and Sanctuaries.* Bloomington: Indiana University Press, 2012.

al-Humaydi, Muhammad. *Gadwat al-muqtabas fî dikr wulât al-Andalus.* Beirut: Dar al-Kitab al-Lubnani, 1983.

al-Jabri, Mohamed Abed. *Introduction à la critique de la raison arabe.* Trans. Mahfoud, Ahmed, and Geoffroy, Marc. Paris: La Découverte-Institut du monde arabe, 1994.

Al-Rifaʾi, Jamal Ahmad. *The Influence of Hebrew culture on Contemporary Palestinian Poetry (study on Darwish poetry)* (in Arabic). Cairo: Dâr al-thaqâfah al-jadîdah, 1994.

Al-Rifaʾi, Jamal Ahmad. "The Influence of the Arab-Islamic Philosophy on the Logic of Maimonides" (in Arabic). *Risâlat al-Mashreq,* 2000.

Al-Rifaʾi, Jamal Ahmad. "The Translation of the Arabic Legacy by the Jews in the Middle Ages: A Study on the Problems of Translation of Al-Ghazali in Hebrew" (in Arabic). *Risâlat al-Mashreq,* 2001.

Altmann, Alexander, and Stern, Samuel M. *Isaac Israeli. A Neoplatonic Philosopher of the Early Tenth Century.* Oxford: Oxford University Press, 1958.

Amanat, Mehrdad. *Jewish Identities in Iran. Resistance and Conversion to Islam and the Baha'i Faith.* London: I.B. Tauris, 2011.

Amir-Moezzi, Mohammad Ali. *The Divine Guide in Early Shi'ism. The Sources of Esotericism in Islam.* [*Le Guide divin dans le shîisme originel. Aux sources de l'ésotérisme en islam.* Paris: Verdier, 1992]. Albany: State University of New York Press, 1994.

Ammara, Muhammad Hasan. "Ivrit loanwords." In *Encyclopedia of Arabic Language and Linguistics,* Versteegh, Kees, ed. Leiden: Brill, vol. 2, 2007, 464–467.

Anderson, J.N.D. *Law Reform in the Muslim World.* London: Athlone Press, 1976.

Andres, Ramon. *Diccionario de Instrumentas Musicales.* Barcelona: Peninsula, 2001.

Andriamirado, Sennen. "Juifs, noirs et maliens." *Jeune Afrique,* January 1997.

Arnaldez, Roger. *À la croisée des trois monothéismes. Une communauté de pensée au Moyen Âge.* Paris: Albin Michel, 1993.

Arnold, Sir Thomas W. *The Old and the New Testaments in Muslim Religious Art.* London: Published for the British Academy by H. Milford, Oxford University Press, 1932.

Arnold, Sir Thomas W. *Painting in Islam. A Study of the Place of Pictorial Art in Muslim Culture.* New York: Dover Publications, 1965.

Astren, Fred. *Karaite Judaism and Historical Understanding.* Columbia: University of South Carolina Press, 2004.

Attar, Samar. *The Vital Roots of European Enlightenment. Ibn Tufayl's Influence on Modern Western Thought.* Lanham, MD: Lexington Books, 2010.

Auroux, Sylvain. *Histoire des idées linguistiques.* Liège and Brussels: Mardaga Éditeur, 1989–2000.

Avishur, Yitzhak. *A Dictionary of the New Judeo-Arabic Written and Spoken in Iraq (1600–2000).* Tel Aviv: Archeological Center Publications, 2008–2010, 3 vols.

Ayoun, Richard, and Cohen, Bernard. *Les Juifs d'Algérie. 2000 ans d'histoire.* Paris: J.-C. Lattès, 1982.

Bahloul, Joëlle. *Le Culte de la table dressée.* Paris: Éditions A. M. Métailié, 1983.

Bahloul, Joëlle. *The Architecture of Memory. A Jewish-Muslim Household in Colonial Algeria, 1937–1962.* [*La Maison de mémoire. Ethnologie d'une demeure judéo-arabe en Algérie (1937–1961).* Paris: Éditions A. M. Métailié, 1992]. Cambridge: Cambridge University Press, 1996.

Bahloul, Joëlle. "Retour à Constantine. Une expérience collective de juifs maghrébins établis en France." In *Lucette Valensi à l'œuvre,* Pouillon, François, ed. Paris: Éditions Bouchène, 2002, 61–71.

Baker, Colin F. "Judaeo-Arabic Material in the Cambridge Genizah Collections." *Bulletin of the School of Oriental and African Studies,* 3, 1995, 58, 445–454.

Bar Asher, Meïr. "The Place of Jews and Judaism in the Religious Literature of Early Shi'ism" (in Hebrew). *Pe'amim,* 1994, 61, 16–36.

Bearman, Peri, Peters, Rudolph, and Vogel, Frank E., eds. *The Islamic School of Law: Evolution, Devolution, and Progress.* Cambridge, MA: Islamic Legal Studies Program of Harvard Law School, 2005.

Beckwith, Stacy N., ed. *Charting Memory. Recalling Medieval Spain.* New York: Garland, 2000.

Beeri, Tova. "Shlomo Mazal-Tov and the Beginning of the Influence of the Turkish Song on Hebrew Poetry" (in Hebrew). *Pe'amim,* 1994, 59, 65–76.

Ben-Ari, Eyal, and Bilu, Yoram. "Saints' Sanctuaries in Israeli Development Towns: On a Mechanism of Urban Transformation." *Urban Anthropology and Studies of Cultural Systems and World Economic Development,* 2, 1987, 16, 243–272.

Ben Shammai, Haggai. "The Attittude of Some Early Karaites towards Islam." In *Studies in Medieval Jewish History and Literature,* Twersky, Isadore, ed. Cambridge, MA: Harvard University Press, vol. 2, 1984, 3–40.

Ben Shammai, Haggai. "Studies in Karaite Atomism." *JSAI,* 1985, 6, 243–298.

Ben Shammai, Haggai. "The Scholarly Study of Karaism in the Nineteenth and Twentieth Centuries." In *Karaite Judaism,* Polliack, Meira, ed. Leiden and Boston: Brill, 2003.

Ben Shammai, Haggai. "Major Trends in Karaite Biblical Exegesis in the Tenth and Eleventh Centuries." In *Karaite Judaism,* Polliack, Meira, ed. Leiden and Boston: Brill, 2003.

Ben Shammai, Haggai. "Sa'adya Gaon." In *Encyclopedia of Jews in the Islamic World,* Stillman, Norman, ed. Leiden and Boston: Brill, vol. 4, 2010, 197–204.

Bensoussan-Bursztein, Daniel. "Entre sémite et indo-européen: instrumentalisation d'un concept linguistique." *Cahiers Bernard Lazare,* 2011, 326, 10–14.

Bergounioux, Gabriel. "«Aryen», «indo-européen», «sémite» dans l'université française." *Histoire Epistémologie Langage,* 1, 1996, 18, 109–126.

Bergounioux, Gabriel. "L'orientalisme et la linguistique. Entre géographie, littérature et histoire." *Histoire Epistémologie Langage,* 2, 2001, 23, 39–57.

Bergsträsser, Gotthelf. *Introduction to the Semitic Languages. Text Specimens and Grammatical Sketches. Translated with Notes and Bibliography and an Appendix on the Scripts by Peter D. Daniels.* Winona Lake, IN: Eisenbrauns, 1983.

Berthier, Annie, and Zali, Anne, eds. *Torah, Bible, Coran. Livres de parole.* Paris: Bibliothèque Nationale de France, 2005.

Bismuth-Jarrassé, Colette, and Jarrassé, Dominique. *Synagogues de Tunisie. Monuments d'une histoire et d'une identité.* Kremlin-Bicêtre: Éditions Esthétiques du Divers, 2010.

Blanc, Haim. *Communal Dialects in Baghdad.* Cambridge, MA: Harvard University Press, 1964.

Bland, Kalman. "An Islamic Theory of Jewish History: The Case of Ibn Khaldun." *Journal of Asian and African Studies,* 3–4, 1983, 18, 189–197.

Blau, Joshua. *A Grammar of Mediaeval Judaeo-Arabic.* Second enlarged edition. Jerusalem: The Magnes Press, 1980.

Blau, Joshua. *Judeo-Arabic Literature. Selection of Articles* (in Hebrew). Jerusalem: The Magnes Press, 1980.

Blau, Joshua. *The Emergence and Linguistic Background of Judaeo-Arabic. A Study of the Origins of Neo-Arabic and Middle-Arabic.* [Oxford: Oxford University Press, 1965]. Jerusalem: Institut Ben-Zvi, 1981.

Blau, Joshua, and Reif, Stefan C. *Genizah Research after Ninety Years. The Case of Judaeo-Arabic.* Cambridge: Cambridge University Press, 1987.

Blau, Joshua. *Studies in Middle Arabic and Its Judaeo-Arabic Variety.* Jerusalem: The Magnes Press, 1988.

Blau, Joshua. "The Linguistic Character of Saadia Gaon's Translation of the Pentateuch." *Oriens,* 2001, 36, 1–9.

Blau, Joshua. *A Dictionary of Medieval Judaeo-Arabic Texts.* Jerusalem: The Academy of the Hebrew Language and the Israel Academy of Sciences and Humanities, 2006.

Blau, Joshua. "Saadia Gaon a-t-il également composé sa traduction biblique à l'intention des musulmans?" (in Hebrew). *Masora le-Yosef,* 2012, 7, 475–487.

Blidstein, Gerald. "The Stance of Islam in Maimonidean Halakhah." In *Multiculturalism in a Democratic and Jewish State,* Mautner, Menachem, et al., eds. Tel Aviv: Tel Aviv University Press, 1998, 465–476.

Bobzin, Harmut. "Translations of the Qur'an." In *The Encyclopaedia of the Qur'an.* Leiden and Boston: Brill, vol. 5, 2006, 340–358.

Bochman, Victor. "The Jews and The Arabian Nights." *Ariel: The Israel Review of Arts and Letters,* 1996, 103, 39–47.

Borrmans, Maurice. "Pluralism and Its Limits in the Qur'an and the Bible." *Islamochristiana,* 1991, 17, 1–14.

Borrmans, Maurice. "Le livre et ses lectures." In Trans. Pouthier, J.-L. *Le Monde de la Bible,* 1998, 115, 12–13.

Bourget, Carine. *The Star, the Cross, and the Crescent. Religions and Conflicts in Francophone Literature from the Arab World.* Lanham, MD: Lexington Books, 2010.

Brenet, Jean-Baptiste, ed. *Averroès et les averroïsmes juif et latin. Actes du colloque international (Paris, 16–18 June 2005).* Turnhout: Brepols, 2007.

Brinner, William, and Ricks, Stephen D., eds. *Studies in Islamic and Judaic Traditions.* Atlanta: Scholar's Press, 1986, 233–250.

Brosh, Na'ama. *Biblical Stories in Islamic Painting.* Jerusalem: The Israel Museum, 1991.

Bruder, Edith. *The Black Jews of Africa. History, Identity, Religion.* New York: Oxford University Press, 2008.

Cabasso, Gilbert. *Juifs d'Égypte. Images et textes.* Paris: Editions du Scribe, 1984.

Campanini, Saverio. "Pici Mirandulensis bibliotheca cabbalistica latina. Sulle traduzioni latine di opere cabbalistiche di Flavio Mitridate per Pico della Mirandola." *Materia Giudaica,* 1, 2002, 7, 90–96.

Catalogue d'exposition, *Treasures of the Aleppo Community.* Jerusalem: Musée d'Israël, 1988.

Chetrit, Joseph. "Ambivalence et hybridation culturelle: Interférences entre la culture musulmane et la culture juive au Maroc." Magnes, *Perspectives,* 2002, 9.

Chetrit, Joseph. *Diglossie, Hybridation et Diversité intralinguistique. Études socio-pragmatiques sur les langues juives, le judéo-arabe et le judéo-berbère.* Paris: Louvain, 2007.

Chetrit, Joseph. *Trésors et textures d'une langue. Études socio-pragmatiques sur le judéo-arabe d'Afrique du Nord et son composant hébraïque: articles, poèmes, récits et proverbes.* Jerusalem: Bialik Institute, 2009.

Clark, Harry. "The Publication of the Koran in Latin: A Reformation Dilemma." *Sixteenth Century Journal,* 1984, 15, 3–12.

Cohen, David. *Le parler arabe des Juifs de Tunis. Textes et documents linguistiques et ethnographiques.* Paris: Mouton, vol. 1, 1964.

Cohen, David. *Le parler arabe des Juifs de Tunis. Étude linguistique.* Paris: Mouton, vol. 2, 1975.

Cohen, Marcel. *Le parler arabe des Juifs d'Alger.* Paris: H. Champion, 1912.

Cohen, Mark R., and Udovitch, Abraham Labe. *Jews Among Arabs. Contacts and Boundaries.* Princeton: Darwin Press, 1989.

Cohen, Mark R. "Islam and the Jews: Myths, Tales-Myths, History" (in Hebrew). *Zmanim,* 1990, 36, 53–61.

Cohen, Mark R. "On the Interplay of Arabic and Hebrew in the Cairo Geniza Letters." In *Studies in Arabic and Hebrew Letters in Honor of Raymond P. Scheindlin.* Decter, Jonathan P., and Rand, Michael, eds. Piscataway, NJ: Gorgias Press, 2007, 17–35.

Cohen-Tannoudji, Denis. *Entre Orient et Occident, juifs et musulmans en Tunisie.* Paris: Editions de l'Eclat, 2007.

Cook, Michael. "Early Islamic Dietary Law." *Jerusalem Studies in Arabic and Islam,* 1986, 7, 217–277.

Cook, Michael. "'Anan and Islam. Origins of Karaite Scripturalism." *Jerusalem Studies in Arabic and Islam,* 1987, 9, 161–182.

Dannenfelt, Karl H. "The Renaissance Humanists and the Knowledge of Arabic." *Studies in the Renaissance,* 1995, 2, 96–117.

De Frede, Carlo. *La prima traduzione italiana del Corano sullo sfondo dei rapporti tra Cristianità e Islam nel Cinquecento.* Naples: Istituto Universitario Orientale, 1967.

De Zayas, Rodrigo. *La musica en el Vocabidista granadino de Fray Pedro de Alcala 1492–1505.* Séville: El Monte, 1955.

Decter, Jonathan P. "The Rendering of Qur'anic Quotations in Hebrew Translations of Islamic Texts." *Jewish Quarterly Review,* 3, 2006, 96, 336.

Derenbourg, Joseph. *Version arabe du Pentateuque de r. Saadia ben Iosef al-Fayyoúmi, revue, corrigée et accompagnée de notes hébraïques, avec quelques fragments de traduction française d'après l'arabe par J. Derenbourg.* Paris: E. Leroux, 1893.

Diem, Werner, and Edzard, Lutz. "Ein unhöflicher Brief und liebliche Verse. Ein Genizadokument des 11.–12. Jahrhunderts n. Chr." *Zeitschrift der Deutschen Morgenländischen Gesellschaft,* 2, 2011, 161, 265–304.

Djian, Jean-Michel. "Les manuscrits trouvés à Tombouctou." *Le Monde Diplomatique,* August 2004.

Dorn Sezgin, Pamela. "Hakhamim, Dervishes, and Court Singers: The relationship of Ottoman Jewish Music to Classical Turkish Music." In *The Jews of the Ottoman Empire,* Levy, A., ed. Princeton: Princeton University Press, 1994, 585–632.

Droixhe, Daniel. *La Linguistique et l'appel de l'histoire.* Geneva and Paris: Droz, 1978.

Edzard, Lutz. "Linguistic Features of a Judeo-Arabic Text of the qiṣaṣ al-'anbiyā' Genre." In *Middle Arabic and Mixed Arabic: Diachrony and Synchrony,* Zack, Liesbeth, and Schippers, Arie, eds. Leiden: Brill, 2012, 83–94.

Egorova, Yulia. *Jews and India. Perceptions and Image.* London: Routledge, 2006.

Egorova, Yulia. "From Dalits to Bene Ephraim: Judaism in Andhra Pradesh." *Religions of South Asia,* 1, 2010, 4, 105–124.

Egorova, Yulia, and Perwez, Shahid. "The Children of Ephraim: Being Jewish in Andhra Pradesh." *Anthropology Today,* 6, 2010, 26, 14–19.

Elon, Menachem. *Jewish Law. History, Sources, Principles.* Philadelphia: Jewish Publication Society, 1994.

Endress, Gerhard. "The Circle of Al-Kindî. The Early Arabic Translations from the Greek and the Rise of Islamic Philosophy." In *The Ancient Tradition in Christian and Islamic Hellenism,* Endress, Gerhard, and Kruk, Remke, eds. Leiden: Research School CNWS, 1997, 43–76.

Erder, Yoram. "The Attitude of the Karaite Yefet ben 'Eli to Islam in Light of His Interpretation of Psalm 14:53" (in Hebrew). *Michael,* 1999, 14, 29–49.

Faber, Alice. "Genetic Subgrouping of the Semitic Languages." In *The Semitic Languages,* Hetzron, ed. Robert, London: Routledge, 1997, 3–15.

Fabre, Thierry, ed. *L'Héritage andalou.* Paris: Éditions de l'aube, 1995.

Faroghi, Suraiya, and Neumann, Christoph K., eds. "Dress Codes in the Ottoman Empire: The Case of the Franks." In *Ottoman Costumes, from Textile to Identity.* Istanbul: Eren Yayınevi, 2004, 108–110.

Fenton, Paul B. *Deux traités de mystique juive.* Paris: Éditions Verdier, 1987.

Fenton, Paul B. "Judaeo-Arabic Literature." In *Religion, Learning and Science in the 'Abbasid Period,* Young, M. J. L., Latham, John D., and Serjeant, Robert B., eds. Cambridge: Cambridge University Press, 1990, 464.

Fenton, Paul B. "Abraham Maimonides (1186–1237): Founding a Mystical Dynasty." In *Jewish Mystical Leaders and Leadership in the 13th Century,* Idel, Moché, and Ostow, Mortimer, eds. Lanham, MD: Jason Aronson, 1998.

Fenton, Paul B. "Jewish-Muslim Relations in the Medieval Mediterranean Area." In *The Cambridge Genizah Collections. Their Contents and Significance,* Reif, Stefan C., ed. Cambridge: Cambridge University Press, 2002, 152–159.

Fenton, Paul B. "Henry Corbin et la mystique juive." In *Henry Corbin. Philosophies et sagesses des religions du livre. Actes du Colloque "Henry Corbin."* Amir-Moezzi, Mohammed Ali, Jambet, Christian, and Lory, Pierre, eds. Turnhout: Brepols, 2005, 153.

Fenton, Paul B. *Philosophie et exégèse dans le jardin de la métaphore de Moïse ibn 'Ezra, philosophe et poète andalou du XIIe siècle.* Leiden: Brill, 1997.

Fernandez de la Cuesta, Ismael. *Historia de la musica espanola. Desde los origenes hasta el «ars nova».* Madrid: Alianza Editorial, 1983.

Fernandez Manzano, Reynaldo. *De las melodias del reino Nazari de Granada a las estructuras musicales cristianas.* Granada: Diputacion Provincial de Granada, 1985.

Firestone, Reuven. *Journeys in Holy Lands. the Evolution of the Abraham-Ishmael Legends in Islamic Exegesis.* Albany: State University of New York Press, 1990.

Fischel, Walter J. "Judaeo-Persian Literature." In *Encyclopaedia Islamica.* Leiden: Brill, vol. 4, 1978, 308–312.

Fontaine, T. A. M. *In Defence of Judaism. Abraham Ibn Daud: Sources and Structures of ha-Emunah ha-Ramah.* Assen and Maastricht: Van Gorcum, 1990.

Frank, Daniel H., and Leaman, Olivier. *The Cambridge Companion to Medieval Jewish Philosophy.* New York: Cambridge University Press, 2003.

Frenkel, Miriam, and Lev, Yaacov, eds. *Charity and Giving in Monotheistic Religions.* Berlin: De Gruyter, 2009.

Freudenthal, Gad, ed. *Studies on Gersonides, a Fourteenth-Century Philosopher-Scientist.* Leiden: Brill, 1992.

Freudenthal, Gad. "Transfert culturel à Lunel au milieu du XIIe siècle. Qu'est-ce qui a motivé les premières traductions provençales de l'arabe en hébreu?" In *Des Tibbonides à Maïmonide. Rayonnement des juifs andalous en pays d'Oc médiéval,* Iancou-Agou, Danielle, and Nicolas, Elie, eds. Paris: Cerf, 2009, 95–108.

Freudenthal, Gad. "Arabic and Latin Cultures as Resources for the Hebrew Translation Movement. Comparative Considerations, Both Quantitative and Qualitative." In *Science in Medieval Jewish Cultures,* Freudenthal, Gad, ed. New York: Cambridge University Press, 2011, 74–105.

Freudenthal, Gad, and Zonta, Mauro. "Avicenna amongst Medieval Jews. The Reception of Avicenna's Philosophical, Scientific and Medical Writings in Jewish Cultures, East and West." *Arabic Sciences and Philosophy,* 2012, 22, 217–287.

Fück, Johann. *Die Arabischen Studien in Europa bis in den Anfang des 20. Jahrhunderts.* Leipzig: Harrassowitz, 1955.

Funkenstein, Amos. *Theology and the Scientific Imagination. From the Middle Ages to the Seventeenth Century.* Princeton: Princeton University Press, 1986.

Geva-Kleinberger, Aharon. "Ivrit." In *Encyclopedia of Arabic Language and Linguistics,* Versteegh, Kees, ed. Leiden: Brill, vol. 2, 2007, 461–464.

Gindin, Thamar. "Judeo-Persian Literature. 1. Early Period." In *Encyclopedia of Jews in the Islamic World,* Stillman, Norman A., ed. Leiden and Boston: Brill, 2010, 64–65.

Gindin, Thamar E. *The Early Judaeo-Persian Tafsirs of Ezekiel. Text, Translation and Commentary.* Vienna: Académie des sciences, forthcoming, 3 vols.

Gobillot, Geneviève. "Le Coran, commentaire des Écritures." *Le Monde de la Bible,* May–June 2006, 171, 24–29.

Gobillot, Geneviève. "Apocryphes de l'Ancien et du Nouveau Testament." In *Dictionnaire du Coran,* Amir Moezzi, Mohammad Ali, ed. Paris: Robert Laffont, coll. "Bouquins," 2007, 57–63.

Gobillot, Geneviève. "L'abrogation (nâsihk et mansûhk) dans le Coran à la lumière d'une lecture interculturelle et intertextuelle." *Al-Mawâqif,* 2008, special issue, actes du premier colloque international sur Le phénomène religieux, nouvelles lectures des sciences sociales et humaines, 6–19.

Gobillot, Geneviève. "Le Coran rêvé d'Ibn Kammûna." In *Actes du colloque du 16 au 18 avril 2009,* Ben Amer, Tawfiq, ed. Tunis: Université de Tunis, faculté de philosophie, 2009.

Goitein, Shlomo Dov. *Jews and Arabs. Their Contacts through the Ages.* New York: Schocken Books, 1955.

Goitein, Shlomo Dov. "The Origin and Nature of the Muslim Friday Worship." In *Studies in Islamic History and Institutions.* Leiden: Brill, 1966, 111–125.

Goldberg, Harvey E., ed. *Highid Mordekhai. The Book of Mordechai. A Study of the Jews of Libya.* London: Darf Publishers, 1980.

Goldberg, Sylvie Anne. *La Clepsydre. t. I: Essai sur la pluralité des temps dans le judaïsme.* Paris: Albin Michel, vol. 1, 2000.

Goldberg, Sylvie Anne. *La Clepsydre. t. II: Temps de Jerusalem, temps de Babylone.* Paris: Albin Michel, vol. 2, 2004.

Goldenberg, E. S. "Hebrew Language: The Components of Arabic-Influenced Hebrew." *Encyclopedia Judaica,* 16, 1971, 1625–1635.

Goldziher, Ignác. "Islamisme et Parsisme." *Revue de l'Histoire des Religions,* 1901, 43, 1–29.

Goldziher, Ignác. *Vorlesungen über den Islam.* Heidelberg: Carl Winter's Universitätsbuchhandlung, 1910.

Gollaher, David. *Circumcision. A History of the World's Most Controversial Surgery.* New York: Basic Books, 2000.

Gomez Muntane, Maria del Carmen. *La musica en la casa real catalano-aragonesa durante los anos 1336–1432.* Barcelona: Bosch, 1979.

Grévin, Benoît. "Un témoin majeur du rôle des communautés juives de Sicile dans la préservation et la diffusion en Italie d'un savoir sur l'arabe et l'Islam au XVe siècle: Les notes interlinéaires et marginales du «Coran de Mithridate» (ms. Vat. Ebr. 357)." In *Chrétiens, juifs et musulmans dans la méditerranée médiévale. Etudes en hommage à Henri Bresc.* Grévin, Benoît, Nef, Annliese, and Tixier, Emmanuelle, eds. Paris: De Boccard, 2008, 45–56.

Grévin, Benoît. "Le Coran de Mithridate (ms. Vat. Ebr. 357) à la croisée des savoirs arabes dans l'Italie du xvᵉ siècle." *Al-Qantara,* 2, 2010, 31, 513–548.

Griffel, Franck. *Al-Ghazâli's Philosophical Theology.* Oxford: Oxford University Press, 2009.

Hacker, Joseph. "Patterns of the Intellectual activity of Ottoman Jewry in the 16th and 17th Centuries." *Tarbiz,* 4, 1984, 53, 569–603.

Hallaq, Wael B. *A History of Islamic Legal Theories.* Cambridge: Cambridge University Press, 1997.

Hallaq, Wael B. *The Origins and Evolution of Islamic Law.* Cambridge: Cambridge University Press, 2005.

Hames, Harvey J. "A Jew amongst Christians and Muslims: Introspection in Solomon Ibn Adret's Response to Ibn Hazm." *Mediterranean Historical Review,* 2, 2010, 25, 203–219.

Harry, Benjamin. *Multiglossia in Judeo-Arabic. With an Edition, Translation, and Grammatical Study of the Cairene Purim Scroll.* Leiden: Brill, 1992.

Harry, Benjamin, and Ben Shammai, Haggai, eds. *Esoteric and Exoteric Aspects in Judeo-Arabic Culture.* Leiden: Brill, 2006.

Harvey, Steven, ed. *The Medieval Hebrew Encyclopedias of Science and Philosophy.* Dordrecht: Kluwer Academic Publishers, 2000.

Harvey, Steven. "Why Did Fourteenth-Century Jews Turn to Al-Ghazâli's Account of Natural Science?" *Jewish Quarterly Review,* 2001, 91, 359–376.

Harvey, Steven. "Ibn Sīnā's Influence on Jewish Thought: Some Reflections." In *Avicenna and His Legacy. A Golden Age of Science and Philosophy,* Langermann, Y. Tzvi, ed. Turnhout: Brepols, 2009.

Heath, Jeffrey. *Jewish and Muslim Dialects of Moroccan Arabic.* London: Routledge, 2002.

Hernandez, Miguel Cruz. *Historia del pensamiento en el mundo islámico.* Madrid: Alianza, 2000.

Hidiroglou, Patricia. "Du hammam maghrébin au miqveh parisien." *Journal de Méditerranéen Studies,* 2, 1994, 4, 242–263.

Hirschberg, Haïm Zeev. *Israel in Arabia* (in Hebrew). Jerusalem: Mossad Bialik, 1946.

Hughes, Aaron W. *The Texture of the Divine: Imagination in Medieval Islamic and Jewish Thought.* Bloomington: Indiana University Press, 2004.

Hughes, Aaron W. "A Case of 12th Century Plagiarism? Abraham ibn Ezra's Hay ben Meqitz and Avicenna's Hayy ibn Yaqzan." *Journal of Jewish Studies,* 2, 2004, 55, 306–331.

Huglo, Michel. "Gerbert." In *The New Grove's Dictionary of Music and Musicians,* Sadie, Stanley, ed. London: Macmillan Reference, 250, 1980, 7.

Husik, Isaac. *A History of Medieval Jewish Philosophy.* [New York: Macmillan. 1918]. Philadelphia: Jewish Publication Society of America, 1941.

Ibrahim Abu al-Majd, Layla. "L'influence arabo-islamique sur le contenu de la prière juive." In *Proceedings of the Seminar on Arab Influences on the Hebrew Language, Religious Thought and Jewish Literature through the Ages* (in Arabic). Cairo: Université Al-Shams, 1992, 26–27.

Ibrahim Abu al-Majd, Layla. *Poetic Rhythm: A Comparative Study between Arabic and Hebrew Prosody* (in Arabic). Le Caire: Université du Caire, 2002.

Ibrahim Abu al-Majd, Layla. *Woman between Judaism and Islam* (in Arabic). Cairo: Dâr al-thaqâfah al-nashr, 2007.

Inalcik, Halil. *The Ottoman Empire. The Classical Age 1300–1600.* London: Phoenix, 1973.

Isaac, Ephraim, and Tobi, Yosef, eds. *Judaeo-Yemenite Studies. Proceedings of the Second International Congress.* Princeton: Princeton University Press, 1999.

Isenberg, Shirley Berry. *India's Bene Israel, a Comprehensive Inquiry and Source Book.* Bombay: Popular Prakashan, 1988.

Israeli, Raphael. "Islam and Judaism in China." *Asian Profile,* 1, 1977, 5, 31–42.

Itzhaki, Masha. *Juda Halévi. D'Espagne à Jerusalem (1075?–1141).* Trans. Abergel, Flore. Paris: Albin Michel, 1997.

Ivry, Alfred. "Philosophical Translation from the Arabic in Hebrew during the Middle Ages." In *Rencontres de cultures dans la philosophie médiévale. Traducteurs et traductions de l'Antiquité tardive au XIVᵉ siècle.* Hemesse, J., and Fattori, M., eds. Louvain: Peeters, 1990, 167–186.

Jeffery, Arthur. *The Foreign Vocabulary of the Qur'ān.* [Baroda: Oriental Institute, 1938]. Leiden: Brill, 2007.

Juhasz, Esther, ed. *Sephardi Jews in the Ottoman Empire. Aspects of Material Culture.* Jerusalem: The Israel Museum, 1990.

Katsh, Abraham I. *Judaism and the Koran.* New York: A.S. Barnes and Co., 1962.

Katz, Nathan. *Who Are the Jews of India?.* Berkeley, Los Angeles, and London: University of California Press, 2000.

Katz, Nathan, Chakrabarty, Ranabir, and Sinha, Braj M., eds. *Indo-Judaic Studies in the Twenty-First Century. A View from the Margin.* New York: Palgrave Macmillan, 2007.

Khalil, Mohammad Hassan. *Between Heaven and Hell. Islam, Salvation, and the Fate of Others.* New York: Oxford University Press, 2013.

Khan, Geoffrey. *Arabic Legal and Administrative Documents in the Cambridge Genizah Collections.* Cambridge: Cambridge University Press, 1993.

Khan, Geoffrey. "Tiberian Hebrew Phonology." In *Phonologies of Asia and Africa,* Kaye, Alan, ed. Winona Lake, IN: Eisenbrauns, 1997, 85–102.

Kilpatrick, Hilary. *Making the Great Book of Songs. Compilation and the Author's Craft in Abu l-Faraj al-Isbahani's Kitab al-Aghani.* London: Routledge, 2003.

Kraemer, Joel L. *Humanism in the Renaissance of Islam. The Cultural Revival during the Buyid Age.* Leiden: Brill, 1986.

Kraemer, Joel L. *Maimonides. The Life and World of One of Civilization's Greatest Minds.* New York: Doubleday, 2008.

Kramer, Martin, ed. *Jewish Discovery of Islam. Studies in Honor of Bernard Lewis.* Syracuse, NY: Syracuse University Press, 1999.

Lambert, Phyllis, ed. *Fortifications and the Synagogue. The Fortress of Babylon and the Ben Ezra Synagogue, Cairo.* London: Weidenfeld & Nicholson, 1994.

Langermann, Y. Tzvi. *Monotheism and Ethics. Historical and Contemporary intersections among Judaism, Christianity, and Islam.* Leiden: Brill, 2012.

Lapidus, Ira M. *A History of Islamic Societies.* Cambridge: Cambridge University Press, 2002.

Lasker, Daniel J. *From Judah Hadassi to Elijah Bashyatchi: Studies in Late Medieval Karaite Philosophy.* Leiden: Brill, 2008.

Lazard, Gilbert. "La judéo persan, entre le pehlevi et le persan." *Studia Iranica,* 1987, 6, 167–176.

Lazarus Yafeh, Hava. "Jewish Knowledge of the Qur'ân." *Sefunot,* 1991, 5, 6.

Lazarus Yafeh, Hava. *Intertwined Worlds. Medieval Islam and Bible Criticism.* Jerusalem: Mossad Bialik, 1998.

Leaman, Olivier. "Is There Distinctly Andalusi Philosophy?" *M.a.r.s. (Le Monde arabe dans la recherche scientifique),* 1998, 9, 75–85.

Levi Della Vida, Giorgio. *Ricerche sulla formazione del piu' antico fondo dei manoscritti orientali della biblioteca Vaticana.* Vatican City: Biblioteca Apostolica Vaticana, 1939.

Lévy, Tony. "Arabic Algebra in Hebrew Texts (1). An Unpublished Work by Isaac ben Salomon al-Adab (14th Century)." *Arabic Sciences and Philosophy,* 2, 2003, 13, 269–301.

Lévy, Tony, and Rashed, Roshdi. *Maïmonide philosophe et savant.* Louvain: Peeters, 2004.

Lévy, Tony. "The Hebrew Mathematics Culture (Twelfth–Sixteenth Centuries)." In *Science in Medieval Jewish Cultures,* Freudenthal, Gad, ed. New York: Cambridge University Press, 2011, 155–171.

Libson, Gideon. *Jewish and Islamic Law. A Comparative Study of Custom during the Geonic Period.* Cambridge, MA: Islamic Legal Studies Program of Harvard Law School, 2003.

Liu, Benjamin, and Monroe, James. *Ten Hispano-Arabic Strophic Songs in the Modern Oral Tradition.* Berkeley and Los Angeles: University of California Press, 1989.

Lobel, Diana. *Between Mysticism and Philosophy. Sufi Language of Religious Experience in Judah ha-Levi's Kuzari.* Albany: State University of New York Press, 2000, 170–171.

Lobel, Diana. *A Sufi-Jewish Dialogue: Philosophy and Mysticism in Bahya Ibn Paqkdas Duties of the Heart.* Philadelphia: University of Pennsylvania Press, 2007.

Madelung, Wilferd. "Imamism and Mu'tazilite Theology." In *Le Shi'isme imamite,* Fahd, Toufic, ed. Paris: PUF, 1970, 13–29.

Madelung, Wilferd, and Schmidtke, Sabine. *Rational Theology in Interfaith Communication. Abu l-Husayn al-Basri's Mu'tazili Theology among the Karaites in the Fatimid Age.* Leiden: Brill, 2006.

Mahdi, Muhsin. *Alfarabi and the Foundation of Islamic Political Philosophy.* Chicago: University of Chicago Press, 2000.

Mainz, Ernst. "Koranverse in hebräischer Schrift." *Der Islam,* 1933, 21, 229.

Maman, Aharon. *Comparative Semitic Philology in the Middle Ages. From Sa'adiah Gaon to Ibn Barūn (10th–12th C.).* Translated into English by David Lyons (Studies in Semitic Languages and Linguistics, vol. 40). Leiden: Brill, 2004.

Mansour, Joseph. "Baghdad Arabic Jewish." In *Encyclopedia of Arabic Language and Linguistics,* Versteegh, Kees, ed. Leiden: Brill, vol. 1, 2007, 231–241.

Marmol Carvajal, Luis del. *Historia del rebelion y castigo de los moriscos del reyno de Granada.* Granada: Delegaciòn Provincial de la Consejeria de Cultura, 1996–1998.

Martin Moreno, Antonio. *Historia de la Musica Andaluza.* Séville: Editoriales Andaluces Unidas, 1985.

Marzolf, Ulrich. *Narrative Illustrations in Persian Lithographed Books.* Leiden: Brill, 2001.

Meddeb, Abdelwahab. *Sortir de la malédiction. L'islam entre civilisation et barbarie.* Paris: Le Seuil, 2008.

Meddeb, Abdelwahab, ed. *La Venue de l'étranger. Dédale,* autumn 1999, 9 and 10.

Meddeb, Abdelwahab, ed. *Multiple Jerusalem. Dédale,* spring 1996, 3 and 4.

Menendez Pidal, Ramon. *Poesia Juglaresca yjuglares. Origenes de las literaturas romanicas.* Madrid: Editorial Espasa-Calpe, 1991.

Miller, Susan Gilson, ed. *The Architecture and Memory of the Minority Quarter in the Muslim Mediterranean City.* Cambridge, MA: The Harvard Graduate School of Design, 2010.

Milstein, Rachel. *La Bible dans l'art islamique.* Paris: PUF, 2005.

Minguez, José Maria. *Alfonso VI.* Guipuscoa: Nerea, 2000.

Minorsky, Vladimir. *Chester Beatty Library. A Catalogue of the Turkish Manuscripts and Miniatures.* Dublin: Hodges, Figgis and Co. Ltd., 1958.

Mithridates, Flavius. *Sermo de Passione Domini. Edition avec introduction and commentaires de Haim Wirszbuski.* Jerusalem: The Israel Academy of Sciences and Humanities, 1963.

Monnot, Guy. "Le Panorama religieux de Fahr al-Din al-Razi." *Revue de l'histoire des religions,* 3, 1986, 203, 263–280.

Moreen, Vera Basch. *Miniature Paintings in Judeo-Persian Manuscripts.* Cincinnati: Hebrew Union College Press, 1985.

Moreen, Vera Basch. *In Queen Esther's Garden. An Anthology of Judeo-Persian Literature.* New Haven, CT, and London: Yale University Press, 2000.

Moreen, Vera Basch. *Catalogue of Judeo-Persian Manuscripts in the Library of the Jewish Theological Seminary of America.* New York: Jewish Theological Seminary, forthcoming.

Navarro Garcia, José Luis. *Cantes y Bailes de Granada.* Malaga: Arguval, 1993.

Nemoy, Leon. "Ibn Kammunah's Treatise on the Differences between the Rabbanites and the Karaites." In *PAAJR,* 1968, 36, 146.

Netzer, Amnon. *An Anthology of Persian Poetry of the Jews in Iran.* Tehran: Farhang-i Iran Zamin, 1973.

Netzer, Amnon. *Manuscripts of the Jews of Persia in the Ben Zvi Institute.* Jerusalem: Ben Zvi Institute, 1985.

Netzer, Amnon. *Duties of Judah by Rabbi Yehudah Ben El'azar.* Jerusalem: Ben Zvi Institute, 1995.

Netzer, Amnon, ed. *Padyavand: Judeo-Iranian and Jewish Studies Series.* Los Angeles: Mazda Publishing, 1996–1999, 3 vols.

Neumann, Abraham B., and Zeitlin, Solomon, eds. *Saadia Studies, Jewish Quarterly Review.* Philadelphia: The Dropsie College for Hebrew and Cognate Learning, 1943.

Nuovo, Angela. "Il Corano arabo ritrovato (Venezia, P. e A. Paganini, tra l'agosto 1537 e l'agosto 1538)." *La Bibliofilia,* 1987, 83, 237–271.

Nykl, Alois R. *Hispano-Arabic Poetry and Its Relation with the Old Provencal Troubadours.* Baltimore: J.H. Furst Company, 1946.

Olender, Maurice. *The Languages of Paradise. Race, Religion, and Philology in the Nineteenth Century.* [*Les langues du paradis.* Paris: Gallimard-Le Seuil, 1989]. Cambridge, MA: Harvard University Press, 1992.

Ovadya, Sylvyo, and Levy, Amalia S. *Jewish Costumes in the Ottoman Empire.* Istanbul: Gözlem Gazetecilik Basın ve Yayın A.Ş, 2001.

Paper, Herbert. *A Judeo-Persian Pentateuch.* Jerusalem: Institut Ben Zvi, 1972.

Parfitt, Tudor. *The Lost Tribes of Israel. The History of a Myth.* London: Weidenfeld and Nicolson, 2002.

Parfitt, Tudor, and Trevisan Semi, Emanuela. *Judaising Movements. Studies in the Margins of Judaism.* London: Routledge, 2002.

Patai, Raphael. "The Seminary and Oriental Studies." In *The Rabbinical Seminary of Budapest 1877–1977,* Carmilly-Weinberger, Moshe, ed. New York: Sepher Hermon, 1986.

Paul, Ludwig, ed. *Persian Origins. Early Judaeo-Persian and the Emergence of New Persian.* Wiesbaden: Harrassowitz Verlag, 2003.

Perlmann, Moshe. *Ibn Kammûna's Examination of the Three Faiths. A Thirteenth-Century Essay in Comparative Religion.* Berkeley, Los Angeles, London: University of California Press, 1971.

Piemontese, Angelo Michele. "Islamic Manuscripts in the West." In *The Significance of Islamic Manuscripts,* Cooper, John, ed. London: al-Furqān Islamic Heritage Foundation, 1992, 45–54.

Piemontese, Angelo Michele. "Il Corano latino di Ficino ed i Corani arabi di Pico e Monchates." *Rinascimento,* 1996, 36, 227–273.

Piemontese, Angelo Michele. "Le iscrizioni arabe nella Poliphili Hypnerotomachia." In *Islam and the Italian Renaissance.* Burnett, Charles, and Contadini, Anna, eds. London: The Warburg Institute, University of London, 1999, 199–220.

Pines, Shlomo. "Shī'ite Terms and Conceptions in Judah Halevi's Kuzari." *Jerusalem Studies in Arabic and Islam,* 1980, 2, 210–219.

Pinkerfeld, Jacob. "Un témoignage du passé en voie de disparition: les synagogues de la région de Djerba." *Cahiers de Byrsa,* 1957, 7, 127–137.

Polliack, Meira. *The Karaite Tradition of Arabic Bible Translation.* Leiden: Brill, 1997.

Pourjavady, Reza, and Schmidtke, Sabine. *A Jewish Philosopher of Baghdad. 'Izz al-Dawla Ibn Kammūna, d. 683/1284, and His Writings.* Leiden: Brill, 2006.

Powers, David S. *Law, Society, and Culture in the Maghrib, 1300–1500.* Cambridge: Cambridge University Press, coll. "Cambridge Studies in Islamic Civilization," 2002.

Rashed, Roshdi. *Encyclopedia of the History of Arabic Science.* London-New York: Routledge, 1996, 3 vols.

Ratzhaby, Yehuda. *Patterns Borrowed from Jewish Literature* (in Hebrew). Ramat-Gan: Editions de l'Université Bar-Ilan, 2006.

Reif, Stefan C. *Hebrew Manuscripts at Cambridge University Library. A Description and Introduction.* Cambridge: Cambridge University Press, 1997.

Retsahvi, Yehuda. *Dictionnaire de la langue arabe du Tafsir de Rav Sa'adya Gaon. (Dictionary of Rav Sa'adya Gaon's Tafsir Arabic)* (Hebrew). Ramat Gan: Edition de l'université Bar-Ilan, 1985, 151–155.

Retsahvi, Yehuda, and Schwartz, Michael. "Dictionary of Rav Sa'adya Gaon's Tafsir Arabic" (in Hebrew). *Leshonenu,* 1988, 52, 200–206.

Reuben, Yoel Moses. *The Jews of Pakistan. A Forgotten Heritage.* Mumbai: Bene Israel Heritage Museum and Genealogical Research Centre, 2012.

Ribera y Tarrago, Julian. *La musica de las Cantigas de Santa Maria.* Madrid: Tip. de la Revista de Archivos, 1922.

Ribera y Tarrago, Julian. *La musica arabe y su injluencia en al Espanola.* Valencia: Pre-Textos, 2000.

Riche, Pierre. *Gerbert d'Aurillac le pape de l'an mil.* Paris: Fayard, 1987.

Riveline, Yossef Yoel. "Biblical Exegesis of Rav Saadia Gaon after Its Translation (in Hebrew)." *Tarbiz,* 1938, 20, 133–166.

Rödiger, Emil. "Mitteilungen zur Handschriftenkunde; Über ein Koranfragment in Hebräischer Schrift." *ZDMG,* 1860, 14, 485–489.

Roland, Joan G. *The Jewish Communities of India.* New Brunswick, NJ: Transaction Publishers, 1999.

Rosell, Cayetano, ed. *Cronicas de los Reyes de Castilla. Volume II. Biblioteca de Autores Espanoles.* Madrid: Ediciones Atlas, 1953, 68.

Roth, Ernst. *Verzeichnis der Orientalischen Handschriften in Deutschland.* Wiesbaden: F. Steiner, 1965.

Sadan, Joseph. "The Arabian Nights and the Jews." In *The Arabian Nights Encyclopedia,* Marzolph, Ulrich, ed. Santa Barbara, CA: ABC Clio, vol. 1, 2004, 42–46.

Saïd, Susan. *Popular Beliefs about Jewish Shrines, A Study on the Mausoleum of Rabbi Jacob Abihserra* (in Arabic). Cairo: Dâr al-'ayin, 1997.

Salemann, Carl. "Chudaidat: Ein jüdisch-bucharisches Gedicht." *Mémoires de l'Académie Impériale des Sciences de St. Pétersbourg,* 1897, 42, 1–30.

Samra, Myer. "Buallawn Israel: The Emergence of a Judaising Movement in Mizoram, Northeast India." In *Religious Change, Conversion and Culture,* Olson, Lynette, ed. Sydney: Association for Studies in Society and Culture, 1996.

Sareen, Tilak Raj. "Indian Response to the Holocaust." In *Jewish Exile in India, 1933–1945,* Bhatti, Anil, and Voigt, Johannes H., eds. New Delhi: Manohar, in association with Max Mueller Bhavan, 1999, 61.

Sarshar, Homa, ed. *Esther's Children. A Portrait of Iranian Jewry.* Beverly Hills and Philadelphia: Center for Iranian Jewish Oral History and Jewish Publication Society of America, 2002.

Sarwat, Okasha. *The Muslim Painter and the Divine. The Persian Impact on Islamic Religious Painting.* London: London Park Lane, 1981.

Sawa, George. *Music Performance Practice in the Early Abbasid Era. 132–320 A.H./750–932 A.D.* Toronto: Pontifical Institute of Medieval Studies, 1989.

Schacht, Joseph. *An Introduction to Islamic Law.* Oxford: Clarendon Press, 1964.

Schlossberg, Eliezer. "The Attitude of Maimonides toward Islam." *Pe'amim,* 1990, 42, 38–60.

Schorsch, Ismar. "Converging Cognates: The Intersection of Jewish and Islamic Studies in Nineteenth Century Germany." *Leo Baeck Institute Yearbook,* 2010, 55, 3–36.

Schwab, Moïse. *Salomon Munk. Sa vie et ses œuvres.* Paris: E. Leroux, 1900.

Sela, Shlomo. *Abraham Ibn Ezra and the Rise of Medieval Hebrew Science.* Leiden: Brill, 2003.

Shahlan, Ahmad. *Ibn Rushd and Medieval Jewish Thought* (in Arabic). Marrakech, 1999.

Shahlan, Ahmad. *Manshûrât Wizârat al-Awqâf wa l-Shu'ûn al-Islâmîyyah.* Rabat: Manshûrât Wizârat al-Awqâf wa l-Shu'ûn al-Islâmîyyah, 2006.

Shaked, Shaul, and Netzer, Amnon, eds. *Irano-Judaica. Studies Relating to Jewish Contacts with Persian Culture Throughout the Ages.* Jerusalem: Institut Ben Zvi, 1992–2003, 5 vols.

Shami, Rashad. *Les forces religieuses en Israël, entre la pensée de l'État et le jeu de la politique.* Cairo: Oriental Studies Center, 1994.

Shapira, Dan. "The Turkic languages and Literatures." In *Karaite Judaism,* Polliack, Meira, ed. Leiden and Boston: Brill, 2003, 657–707.

Shenhav, Yehuda. *The Arab Jews. A Postcolonial Reading of Nationalism, Religion, and Ethnicity.* Stanford: Stanford University Press, 2006, 19–48.

Simon-Nahum, Perrine. *La cité investie. La science du judaïsme français et la République.* Paris: Éditions du Cerf, 1992.

Sirat, Colette. *La Philosophie juive médiévale en terre d'Islam.* Paris: Presses du CNRS, 1988.

Sirat, Colette, Klein-Braslavy, Sara, and Weijers, Olga, eds. *Les Méthodes de travail de Gersonide et le maniement du savoir chez les scolastiques.* Paris: Vrin, 2003.

Soroudi, Sarah Sorour. "The Concept of Jewish Impurity and Its Reflection in Persian and Judeo-Persian Traditions." *Irano-Judaica,* 1994, 3, 142–170.

Soykut, Mustafa. *Image of the Turk in Italy.* Berlin: Klaus Schwarz, 2001.

Steiner, Richard C. *A Biblical Translation in the Making. The Evaluations and Impact of Saadia Gaon's Tafsir.* Cambridge and London: Harvard University Center for Jewish Studies, 2010.

Steinschneider, Moritz. *Hebräische Bibliographie.* Berlin: Benzian, 1860.

Steinschneider, Moritz. *Polemische und apologetische Literatur in arabischer Sprache zwischen Muslimen. Christen und Juden.* [1877]. Hildesheim: Olms, 1966.

Stern, Samuel M. *Studies in Early Ismâ'ilism.* Leiden and Jerusalem: Brill, 1983.

Stevenson, Robert. *Spanish Music in the Age of Columbus.* The Hague: Martinus Nijhof, 1960.

Stillman, Norman. "Yahūd." In *The Encyclopaedia of Islam, New Edition.* Leiden: Brill, 2002, 11, 239–242.

Stroumsa, Sarah. "Jewish Polemics against Islam and Christianity in the Light of Judaeo-Arabic Texts." In *Judaeo-Arabic Studies,* Golb, Norman, ed. Amsterdam: Harwood Academic Publishers, 1997, 241–250.

Stroumsa, Sarah. *Maimonides in His World. Portrait of a Mediterranean Thinker.* Princeton: Princeton University Press, 2009.

Szpiech, Ryan. "Citas árabes en caracteres hebreos en el Pugio fidei del dominico Ramón Martí: Entre la autenticidad y la autoridad." *Al-Qantara: Revista de Estudios Árabes,* 2011, 32, 71–107.

Tahiri, Ahmed. *Las clases populares en al-Andalus.* Malaga: Editorial Sarria, 2003.

Thiesse, Anne-Marie. *La Création des identités nationales.* Paris: Le Seuil, 1999.

Tobi, Yosef. "Challenges to Tradition: Jewish Cultures in Yemen, Iraq, Iran, Afghanistan, and Bukhara." In *Cultures of the Jews. A New History,* Biale, David, ed. New York: Schocken Books, 2002, 821–856.

Tobi, Yosef. *Proximity and Distance. Medieval Hebrew and Arabic Poetry.* Trans. Rovosky, Murray. Leiden: Brill, 2004.

Trautmann-Waller, Céline, ed. *Quand Berlin pensait les peuples.* Paris: CNRS Editions, 2004.

Trevisan Semi, Emanuela. "De Lodz à Addis- Abeba, Faitlovitch et les Juifs d'Ethiopie." *Les Cahiers du Judaïsme,* 2001, 10, 60–71.

Vajda, Georges. *Juda ben Nissim ibn Malka. Philosophe juif marocain.* Paris: Larose, 1954.

Vajda, Georges. *Isaac Albalag. Averroïste juif, traducteur et annotateur d'Al-Ghazâlî.* Paris: Vrin, 1960.

Vajda, Georges. "Autour de la théorie de la connaissance chez Saadia." *Revue des études juives,* 1967, 126, 135–189; 375–397.

Vajda, Georges. *Al-Kitab al-muhtawi de Yusuf al-Basir. Texte, traduction et commentaire.* Leiden: D. R. Blumenthal, 1985.

Valensi, Lucette. "Une histoire des juifs de Tunisie est-elle nécessaire? Est-elle possible?" In *Histoire communautaire, Histoire plurielle, la communauté juive de Tunisie.* Tunis: CPU, 1999, 51–63.

Valensi, Lucette. "Multicultural Visions: The Cultural Tapestry of the Jews of North Africa." In *Cultures of the Jews. A New History,* Biale, David, ed. New York: Schocken Books, 2002, 781–820.

Verger, Jacques. "Condition de l'intellectuel aux XIIIe et XIVe siècles." In *Philosophes médiévaux. Anthologie de textes philosophiques (XIIIe–XIVe siècles).* Imbach, Ruedi, and Méléard, Maryse-Hélène, eds. Paris: UGE [10/18], 1986, 11–49.

Waardenburg, Jacques, ed. *Muslim Perceptions of Other Religions.* New York: Oxford University Press, 1999.

Wasserstrom, Steven M. *Between Muslim and Jew. The Problem of Symbiosis under Early Islam.* Princeton: Princeton University Press, 1995.

Wehr, Hans. *Verzeichnis der Arabischen Handschriften in der Bibliothek der Deutschen Morgenländischen Gesellschaft.* Leipzig: Kommissionsverlag F.A. Brockhaus, 1940.

Weiditz, Christoph. *Das Trachtenbuch des Christoph Weiditz von seinen Reisen nach Spanien (1529) undden Niederlanden (1531/32).* Valencia: Ediciones Grial, 2001.

Weil, Shalva. *India's Jewish Heritage: Ritual, Art and Life Cycle.* Mumbai: Marg, 2002.

Weil, Shalva. "Dual Conversion among the Shinlung in North-East India." *Studies in Tribes and Tribals,* 1, 2003, 1, 43–57.

Weil, Shalva. "Motherland and Fatherland as Dichotomous Diasporas: The Case of the Bene Israel." In *Les Diasporas. 2000 ans d'Histoire,* Anteby, Lisa, Berthomière, William, and Sheffer, Gabriel, eds. Rennes: Presses Universitaires de Rennes, 2005.

Weingrod, Alex. *The Saint of Beersheba.* New York: State University of New York Press, 1990.

Weinstein, Myron M. "A Hebrew Qur'an Manuscript." *Studies in Bibliography and Booklore,* 1971, 10, 19–52.

Wieder, Naphtali. *Islamic Influences on the Jewish Worship.* Oxford: East and West Library, 1947.

Wolfson, Elliot R., ed. *Rending the Veil: Concealment and Secrecy in the History of Religions.* New York and London: Seven Bridges Press, 1999.

Yadin, Azzan. *Scripture as Logos: Rabbi Ishmael and the Origins of Midrash.* Philadelphia: University of Pennsylvania Press, 2004.

Yehoshua-Raz, Benzion D. *From the Lost Tribes in Afghanistan to the Mashhad Jewish Converts of Iran.* Jerusalem: Bialik Institute, 1992, 53–67.

Youssef, Suzanne el-Saïd. *Yearbook of the Sociology of Islam. Dimensions of Locality: Muslim Saints, Their Place and Space.* Stauth, Georg, and Schielke, Samuli, eds. New Brunswick, NJ, and London: Transcript Verlag, 2009, 169–181.

Zack, Joel. *The Synagogues of Morocco. An Architectural and Preservation Survey.* New York: World Monuments Fund, 1993.

Zafrani, Haïm. *Littératures dialectales et populaires juives en Occident musulman: L'écrit et l'oral.* Paris: Geuthner, 1982.

Zafrani, Haïm. *La Version arabe de la Bible de Sa'adya Gaon. L'Ecclésiaste et son commentaire, le «Livre de l'ascèse».* Paris: Maisonneuve et Larose, 1989.

Zafrani, Haïm. *Juifs d'Andalousie et du Maghreb.* Paris: Maisonneuve et Larose, 1996.

Zafrani, Haïm. *Two Thousand Years of Jewish Life in Morocco.* [*Deux Mille Ans de vie juive au Maroc.* Paris: Maisonneuve et Larose, 1999]. Jersey City, NJ: Ktav Publishing, 2005.

Zafrani, Haïm. *Le judaïsme maghrébin. Le Maroc, terre des rencontres des cultures et des civilisations.* Rabat: Marsam, 2003.

Zafrani, Haïm. *Etudes et recherches sur la vie juive intellectuelle au Maroc. De la fin du XVᵉ au début du XXᵉ siècle.* Paris: Paul Geuthner, 2003 (2nd ed.), 3 vols.

Zhan, Zhang. "Jews in Khotan in Light of the Newly-Discovered Judeo-Persian Letter." *Irano-Judaica,* forthcoming.

Index of Names

Nasser, Gamal Abdel: 361, 392, 401, 405, 416, 420, 421, 424, 435, 1032
Nataf, Claude: 988
Natan'el: 965
Nathan of Gaza: 198, 228
Nebuchadnezzar: 239, 694
Nehama, Joseph: 180, 181
Nehemiah: 963, 964
Nesry, Carlos de: 303, 305
New Adam: 879
Newman, Dana: 569
Neydavoud, Morteza: 980, 981
Nicholas II: 322
Nicholas of Cusa: 154
Nicholson, R. A.: 882
Nicolay, Nicolas de: 903
Niebuhr, Carsten: 255
Niewöhner, Friedrich: 794
Niftawayhi: 940
Nikudar: 789, 790
Nirenberg, David: 113
Nissim Abu'l-Faraj: 153
Nizami: 870–874, 881, 963, 968
Noah: 200, 619, 678, 870, 879, 888, 891
Noguès, Charles: 362, 517
Nöldeke, Theodor: 828–830, 832
Noth, Albrecht: 68
Nushirvan: 906

Obama, Barack: 522, 547, 558
Ochildiev, David: 267
Ohayon family: 231
Olavide, Begoña: 971
Ollivier, Émile: 289
Oppert: 678
Orpaz, Yitzhak: 394
Otto I (Holy Roman emperor): 134
'Ovadya: 95
Ourguiba, Habib: 424
Ovadyah (Obadiah): 158
Oz, Amos: 394, 396, 1047

Pahlavi, Mohammad Reza: 495
Pallache, Samuel: 225, 229
Paniagua, Carlos: 971
Pappenheim, Bertha: 1033
Pariente, Juda: 234
Pasha, 'Abd al-Halim: 935
Pasha, Fazli: 251
Pasha, Fuat: 831
Pasha, Ismail: 282
Pasha, Yakub: 168
Passi, David: 184
Paul VI (pope): 411
Pedro III of Aragon: 976
Pedro IV of Aragon: 977
Peel, Lord: 330
Peres, Shimon: 528, 532
Perlmann, Moshe: 793, 795
Perret, Auguste: 932
Perrot, Georges: 929
Perviriz, Gabriel: 177
Pessoa, Fernando: 570
Petahiah of Regensburg: 96
Pétain, Philippe: 350, 352, 363, 366
Peter I of Castile: 925
Peter the Venerable: 642, 792
Philip IV: 235
Philo of Alexandria: 1006
Pico Della Mirandola, Giovanni: 153, 647
Picot, Georges: 326
Pictet, Adolphe: 679
Pines, Shlomo: 748, 772, 834, 992
Pinkerfeld, Jacob: 911, 918, 926
Pinsker, Simhah: 644
Pinto family: 231
Pires, Tomé: 239
Pivert, Marceau: 365
Plato: 739
Plotinus: 739, 824
Polo, Marco: 789
Pope Sixtus IV: 173
Pope Urban V: 634
Porte, the Sublime: 180, 181, 184, 214, 274, 275

Index of Places

Illustration Credits

Opening pages: Part I (pp. 26–27), El Transito Synagogue in Toledo, Spain; Hebrew and Arabic inscriptions are carved into the wood at the base of various balconies. Photograph by René Mattes. Part II (pp. 162–163), *A Jewish Wedding in Morocco*, Eugène Delacroix, 1839?, Paris, Louvre Museum. Part III (pp. 284–285), the Dome of the Rock and the Western Wall in Jerusalem. Photograph by Benjamin Rodel. Part IV (pp. 605–606), The prophets Muhammad and Moses, Bibliothèque Nationale de France.

AFP: 500, 511 (© Pierre Andrieu); 406, 450 and back of jacket (© David Silverman); 1054 (© Philippe Faucon)

Aga Khan Museum, Toronto: 172, 623

Agence Opale: 575 (© Hannah Assouline); 543 (© Philippe Matsas)

AKG: 237, 327, 335, 721, 1014 and back of jacket (© Bible Land Pictures); 914 (© Bildarchiv Monheim); 854 (© BNF); 147, 634 (© British Library); 162, 209, 895, 922 (© Erich Lessing); 706 (© Gérard Degeorge); 29 and front of jacket, 119, 121, 767 (© Oronoz); 723 (© RIA Nowosti); 213, 619, 717, 728, 735, 819, 825, 915 (© Roland and Sabrina Michaud); 746 (© Royal Library/Copenhagen); 360 (© Ullstein bild)

Archives of the Ministry of Foreign Affairs, France: 325

Archives of the UNRWA: 379, 382

Arnaud du Boistesselin: 931

Associated Press Images: 1031; 541 (© Eitan Hess-Ashkenazi); 1037 (© Gregory Bull); 531 (© Kamran Jebreili); 446, 484 (© Lefteris Pitarakis); 475 (© Miguel Villagran); 487 (© Oded Balilty); 523 (© Peter Hillebrecht); 453 (© Tara Todras-Whitehill); 455 (© Sebastian Schneider)

Atelier 21: 1045 (© Majida Khattari/L'Atelier 21)

Augustus Film: 601 (© Augustus Film/Seamus Murphy)

Bibliothèque Nationale de France: 35 and back of jacket, 63, 87, 167, 169 and back of jacket, 180, 204, 691, 750, 773, 791, 879, 946

Bodleian Libraries: 607, 608, 743, 802, 803

The Bridgeman Art Library: 191, 204 (© Bibliothèque Nationale de France, Paris/ Archives Charmet); 61, 898, 899 (© University of Edinburgh Library); 108 (© De Agostini Picture Library); 698 (© Jerusalem, National Library/Giraudon); 677 (© Ken Welsh); 255 (© The Israel Museum); 219 (© The Israel Museum/Gift of Boris Schatz); 216 (© The Israel Museum/Bequest of Suzanne and Henri Chayett, France)

British Library: 219, 781, 809, 872

Micha Bar Am); 432 (Robert Capa © International Center of Photography); 497 (© Paolo Pellegrin); 1010 (© Patrick Zachmann)

Max Mandel: 618 (© Collection of the Grand Rabbi Eliahu Khodabash Karmili, Milan); 687 (© Dominican Institute for Oriental Studies, Tashkent)

The Metropolitan Museum of Art: 875, 882

Musée d'Art et d'Histoire du Judaïsme: 276 (© Félix Bonfils); 227 and back of jacket (© Christophe Fouin); 197 (© Niels Forg); 313 (© Photo Mario Goldman)

Museum of Turkish and Islamic Arts, Istanbul: 905, 907

al-Nahar News: 441

National Museum of Natural History, Paris: 844

The New York Public Library: 45, 141 (© The Spencer Collection)

Pierpont Morgan Library, New York: 753

REA: 473 (© Rina Castelnuovo for *The New York Times*)

Rihlat Abu Nazzara Zarqa: 936

RMN: 842 (© Picture Library MNATP); 231 (© Louvre Museum, Jean-Gilles Berizzi); 893 (© Louvre Museum/ Raphaël Chipault); 655 (© Louvre Museum, Christian Larrieu); 857 (© Hervé Lewandowski); 221 (© Musée de Cluny, Jean-Gilles Berizzi)

Roger-Viollet: 517

Rue des Archives: 355, 367, 389 (© Archives of *Süddeutsche Zeitung*); 1059 (© Etienne George); 341 (© Mary Evans); 363, 385 (© Tallandier); 287 (© The Granger Collection, New York); 599 (© BCA); 310 (© Varma)

Special collections: 290 and back, 314 (Benjamin Stora); 293, 295 (Elias Sanbar); 296 (Collection Raad, Institute for Palestinian Studies); 549 (© Boukhari); 504 (© Le Droit de Vivre); DR: 306, 332, 423, 460, 462, 493, 587, 831, 848, 980, 982

Tel Aviv University: 643

Theater J: 567 (© Stan Barouh)

Théâtre Les Ateliers de Lyon: 584 (© Christian Gannet)

University of Bologna Library: 800 and back of jacket

University of Manchester Library: 656

Vatican Apostolic Library: 152, 950, 954, 975

Maps:

La Documentation Française: 175;

Magnard: 76 (*Histoire-Géographie* 5ᵉ, 2005); 95 (*Histoire* 2ᵈᵉ, 2001); 115 (*Histoire* 5ᵉ, 2005); 387, 395 (H*istoire Terminale S*, 2004), 481 (*Histoire Terminale*, 1998); DR: 48, 224.

The editors thank Jean-François Barrielle and Hazan Publishers, Max Mandel and Mondadori Publishers, the Cambridge University Library and the Diarna Project (Geo-Museum of North African and Middle Eastern Jewish Life) for their assistance.

Contents

Part II: The Modern World

Part IV: Transversalities

Prologue

Chapter I: Founding Books, Mirror Images

Chapter II: Mirrored Languages

Chapter III: Two Religions of the Law

Editors
Jean Mouttapa with Anne-Sophie Jouanneau

Editorial consulting: Hélène Monsacré

Designer: Cécile Vagne
Compositor: Nord Compo
Jacket designer: Cécile Vagne (French edition), Carmina Alvarez (English edition)
Illustration research: Anne-Sophie Jouanneau
with Mei Duong, Solenne Leclerc and Céline Trescases
Maps: Éditions Magnard and Nord Compo
Production: Alix Willaert and Agathe Herlin
Coordination with Princeton University Press:
Solène Chabanais and Aurélie Lapautre

Translations: Luc Barbulesco, Christian Cler, Sylvie Cohen et Marta Teitelbaum,
Sylvie Courtine-Denamy, Maayane Dalsace, Julien Darmon, Cécile Déniard,
Bernard Frumer, Nelly Hansson, Charles Hutner, Dominique Lepreux, Daphné Rabeuf,
Jean-François Sené and Sylvie Taussig (French edition); Jane Marie Todd
and Michael B. Smith (English edition).

The editors warmly thank

Nelly Hansson and Corinne Evens,

as well as Catherine Mac Millan, Jessica Marglin, Charlotte Raimond,
Danaé Tourrand-Viciana and Yannis Tavé.

They wish to pay tribute to the memory of
Gilles Veinstein (1945–2013), professor at the Collège de France and
member of the editorial committee to whom this book owes so much.